International Jurisdiction and Commercial Litigation

Uniform Rules for Contract Disputes

A Elisabeth et Dick

International Jurisdiction and Commercial Litigation

Uniform Rules for Contract Disputes

by

Hélène van Lith

T·M·C·Asser Press

Published by T·M·C·ASSER PRESS
P.O. Box 16163, 2500 BD The Hague, The Netherlands
<www.asserpress.nl>

T·M·C·ASSER PRESS' English language books are distributed exclusively by:

Cambridge University Press, The Edinburgh Building, Shaftesbury Road,
Cambridge CB2 2RU, UK,
or
for customers in the USA, Canada and Mexico:
Cambridge University Press, 100 Brook Hill Drive, West Nyack, NY 10994-2133, USA
<www.cambridge.org>

Cover design: Camille Chartiot

ISBN 978-90-6704-303-8

FOREWORD

Rules and practices on international jurisdiction of domestic courts differ significantly between various countries as to their underlying assumptions, structure, formulation and outcome. The divide is particularly noticeable between common law jurisdictions with open-ended *ex post* determinations and exceptions and the civil law tradition of closed rules determining international jurisdiction *ex ante* with scant exceptions. But also in civil law countries, there are substantial differences as diverging criteria such as nationality and presence of assets are being used. A very limited number of bilateral conventions have addressed issues of international jurisdiction and have sometimes even complicated the resolution of jurisdictional problems.

In Europe, the Brussels 1968 Convention and the 2001 Brussels Regulation as well as the Lugano Convention have revolutionalised the law on international jurisdiction with a regional model for uniform rules. This model has been followed in Latin America with similar MERCOSUR rules. A world-wide effort to come with a comprehensive framework under the auspices of the Hague Conference on Private International Law, however, failed.

Globalisation of business transactions does not stop at the borders of regional organisations and seems to require more than national rules on jurisdiction, a patch-work of bilateral treaties or uniform regional rules. At present, there seems to be a mismatch between international jurisdiction and globalisation and a fresh and in-depth analysis is required to better reflect on ways of aligning jurisdiction with the needs of a globalising world in order to reduce transaction costs and provide a common platform for resolution of jurisdictional problems. This challenge is vast and has already been met in relation to forum selection clauses with the adoption of the 2005 Hague Convention on Choice of Court Agreements. But any analysis starts with the foundations of the law on international jurisdiction and the book I have the privilege to introduce, intends precisely to contribute to an analysis and reflection upon the root issues of and possible solutions to international jurisdictional problems.

On the basis of an extensive description and analysis of the major models regarding contractual disputes (American, English and European), Ms. Van Lith develops a conceptual framework distinguishing between general grounds for jurisdiction (which are always available) and special grounds (which are available only where there is a sufficient connection with the forum state). This basic distinction is then applied to claimants, defendants, the contractual claims that are the subject of the dispute and the presence of assets in the forum state.

As to general grounds for jurisdiction, Ms. Van Lith advocates a pragmatic approach where, in a world-wide model, a general ground should not be the starting point of the analysis but be reduced to a subsidiary and alternative function to avoid jurisdictional gaps and to enable a claimant to avoid uncertainties and costs when contemplating to sue a defendant at a place where it has substantial business activities in relation to the contract. Jurisdiction at the defendant's home court should, thus, in her opinion no longer be the central paradigm of international jurisdiction but be limited to its role of avoiding gaps and provide a claimant with limited forum shopping possibilities. In that same vein, the paradigm proposed by Ms. Van Lith ought to shift to special grounds of jurisdiction based on sufficient connection between the defendant and the forum state. In that respect, she proposes jurisdiction at the place where the defendant has a fixed place of business from which he carries out business activities directly related to the claimant's contractual claim. Absent such a place of business, jurisdiction is to be vested in the courts of the country where the defendant is engaged in substantial business activities in relation to the contract with a limited forum shopping for a claimant in favour of the court of the defendant's home country. Other general or special grounds for jurisdiction (such as claimant-related connections or property-based connections) are rejected because they do not meet the proposed paradigm of sufficient connection.

As to exceptions to international jurisdiction rules as proposed, Ms. Van Lith comes to the conclusion that a general escape provision is to be avoided except for the 'transacting business' rule where – in accordance with the paradigm proposed – international jurisdiction can be avoided in favour of the defendant's home court when the dispute is insufficiently connected with the forum making it unfair under the circumstances to expect the defendant to be subjected to the jurisdiction of that court. In this respect, a balanced approach to predictability and flexibility is being proposed.

A brief summary of the conclusions of this book indicates that the author has made an important and foundational study of the law of international jurisdiction in making inroads into traditional assumptions regarding state sovereignty and defendant's private interests. Moreover, she has been looking beyond accepted knowledge in a quest for a new equilibrium between state and private interests and the values of different legal traditions meeting the requirements of a globalising society while staying within accepted boundaries of private international law searching for sufficient connections between the contractual dispute and the domestic court most apt to adjudicate any such dispute. The quality of the analysis and the reflection undoubtedly will contribute to a better understanding of the law on international jurisdiction and, thus, to its application in adjudicatory decisions and to policy making at national, regional and world-wide levels.

Professor Filip De Ly
Erasmus University School of Law

ACKNOWLEDGEMENTS

While doing research and writing this book I received immense support and valuable comments from a number of people and was privileged that several Institutions opened their doors and resources to me.

First and foremost I wish to thank and express my respect for Professor Filip De Ly, who offered guidance and wrote the Foreword. I am indebted to Associate Professor Xandra Kramer. Her unmistakable, continuous support and constructive comments helped elicit the final text. I am grateful to Hans van Loon, Secretary General of the Hague Conference on Private International Law, for the opportunity to assist the HCCH's valuable work during the diplomatic negotiations for the Worldwide Jurisdiction Project.

The Swiss Institute for Comparative Law in Lausanne and the Max Planck *Institut für Ausländisches und Internationales Privatrecht*, Hamburg, gave me access to countless valuable sources which greatly contributed to the book. Thanks to Professor Richard Garnett and the Melbourne University Law School I had the opportunity to gain valuable insights on the common law during my stay as visiting scholar. Je tiens à remercier les membres du Groupe de Travail Contrats Internationaux qui me rappellent à chaque réunion qu'il existera toujours une différence entre la théorie et la pratique.

From the Department of Private International Law and Comparative Law of Erasmus School of Law I want to thank Walthera Hudig-van Lennep with whom I had the privilege of sharing intensive lecturing duties and Laura van Bockhove, Abiola Makinwa, Andrada Tiru and Jasna Arsić-Dapo.

Special thanks to Camille Chartiot for the cover-design and to Hilmara Requena for her conscientious editing work.

I got by with a little (big) help from my friends: Teun Struycken jr., Jeremy Kingsley, Thomas Keijser, Tanya Greeves, Simon Ponten, Marie Sophie van Muyden, Miklós Redner, Gabry Vanderveen and last but not least, my precious Cathalijne van der Plas, Sander Uitdenbogaard, and my brother Nils van Lith.

My father's advice made me consider starting this project in the first place, my mother's endless energy gave me the necessary basic tools to complete it. I dedicate this book to both of them. As for Simon, he told me he did nothing, but he kept encouraging me to finish with those final words: the end.

I have tried to state the law as on 1 November 2008.

Jouy and Paris, Easter 2009 Hélène VAN LITH

TABLE OF CONTENTS

ABBREVIATIONS

A	
AC	Law Reports: Appeal Cases
ATF	Arrêts du Tribunal Fédéral
All ER	All England Law Reports
B	
BCLC	Butterworths Company Law Cases
BGB	Bundesgesetzbuch (German Civil Code)
BGH	Bundesgerichtshof
BGHZ	Entscheidungen des Bundesgerichtshofes in Zivilsachen
Bull.	Bulletin
BverFG	Bundesverfassungsgericht
BverFGE	Entscheidungen des Bundesverfassungsgericht
C	
Cal.	California Reports
Cal.Rptr.	California Reporter
Cal. App.	Carlifornia Appelate Report
CC	Code Civil
Ch. D.	Law Reports: Chancery Division
CPC	Codice de Procedura Civile (Italian Code of Civil Procedure)
Cour de cass. ch. civ.	Cour de cassation chambre civil
Cour de cass. ch. com.	Cour de cassation chambre commercial
D	
DCC	Dutch Civil Code – or Burgerlijk Wetboek (BW)
ECJ	European Court of Justice
ECR	European Court Reports
EHRR	European Human Rights Reports
EWCA	Court of Appeal, Civil Division
EWHC	High Court, Administrative Court
F	
F.	Federal Reporter
F. Supp.	Federal Supplement
H	
HL	House of Lords
HR	Hoge Raad der Nederlanden (Dutch Supreme Court)
I	
Ill.	Illinois Reports
I.L.Pr.	International Litigation Procedure
IPRax	Praxis des internationalen Privat- und Verfahrensrechts
J	
JCP	La semaine juridique: édition générale/Juris-classeur Périodique

K

KB	Law Reports: King's Bench Division

L

L.Ed.2d	United States Supreme Court Reports, Lawyers' Edition
Ll. L. Rep./Lloyd's Rep.	Lloyd's Law Reports
LR	Law Reports
LOPJ	*Ley Orgánica del Poder Judicial* (Spanish Law on Judicial Organization)

M

Mich.	Michigan Reports

N

NCPC	Nouveau Code de Procédure Civile (French Code of Civil Procedure)
N.E.	North Eastern Reporter
NIPR	Nederlands Internationaal Privaatrecht
NJ	Nederlandse Jurisprudentie
NJW	Neue Juristische Wochenschrift
N.Y.S.	New York Supplement
N.W.	North Western Reporter

O

OJ	Official Journal of the European Communities/Union

P

P.	Pacific Supplement
PIL	Private International Law

Q

QB	Queen's Bench

R

RabelsZ	Zeitschrift für Ausländisches und Internationales Recht
Recueil des cours	*Recueil des cours de l'Académie de Droit International de la Haye*
RIW	Recht der Internationalen Wirtschaft
Rv.	Wetboek van Burgerlijke Rechtsvordering (Dutch Code of Civil Procedure)

S

S.Ct.	Supreme Court Reporter
SDIA	Swiss Debts and Insolvency Act
So.2d	Southern Reporter
S.W.	South Western Reporter

U

U.S.	United States/United States Reports

W

WLR	Weekly Law Reports
WPNR	Weekblad voor privaatrecht, notariaat en registratie

Z

ZPO	Zivilprozeßordnung (German Code of Civil Procedure)
ZZP	Zeitschrift für Zivilprozess

'Come, let us go down and confuse their language, so that they will not understand one another's speech' [1]

'A certain degree of international unification of law is necessary to put an end to the chaotic situation in which international legal relations are found today. ... Lawyers must be awakened to the conscience of the new world and must be instilled with an international spirit which has lain dormant during a century of retreat of national law. In this lies a task of comparative law. The road will sometimes be hard.' [2]

---

[1] Genesis 11:7

[2] R. David, 'The Methods of Unification', *American Journal of Comparative Law* (1968), 13-27, at 27.

Chapter 1

INTRODUCTION

This book deals with judicial jurisdiction of state courts in international disputes, in particular those arising out of transnational commercial contracts entered into between private entities, individuals, and corporations.[1] The present study examines whether any common grounds in jurisdiction rules exist and, as the case may be, whether a uniform global jurisdictional system for international contractual disputes is achievable. The question of jurisdiction of state courts to adjudicate transnational commercial disputes becomes relevant when a contract or dispute has an international dimension, for example because the parties are located in different countries, such as a sales contract with an Australian seller and a Dutch buyer, or because the contract calls for performance outside the states of the parties' seats. For a proper understanding of the relevance of jurisdiction in international court litigation, the following introductory remarks will put this study into the context of international commercial litigation.

1.1 International Jurisdiction in Commercial Litigation

Cultural, social, and commercial exchanges between private individuals or corporations from different corners of the globe are intensifying. As businesses continue to carry out activities across international borders, the number of international commercial relationships is growing. Inevitably, this also leads to international legal disputes in civil and commercial matters. The traditional method to settle international disputes is by litigating in national courts. One of the first questions raised in international court litigation is: which court has jurisdiction to adjudicate the dispute? Although this jurisdictional question appears logical and simple, the answer is far from simple. In times of the so-called 'globalization of the law',[2] the regulation of international jurisdiction of state courts has, remarkably, not kept up

[1] Jurisdiction to adjudicate should be distinguished from jurisdiction to prescribe (legislative power) and jurisdiction to enforce (executive power).

[2] See Hatzimihail and Nuyts, talking about 'legal globalization', N. Hatzimihail and A. Nuyts, 'Judicial Cooperation between the United States and Europe in Civil and Commercial Matters: An Overview of Issues', in *International Civil Litigation in Europe and Relations with Third States* (2005), 1-25, at 7. See on the issue in general, E. Loquin and C. Kessedjian, eds., *La mondialisation du droit* (2000); P. Berman, 'The Globalization of Jurisdiction', 151 *University of Pennsylvania Law Review* (2002), 311-545; A. Johnston and E. Powles, 'The Kings of the World and Their Dukes' Dilemma: Globalisation, Jurisdiction and the Rule of Law', in *Globalisation and Jurisdiction* (2004), 13-54, at 14-20; H. van Loon, 'Globalisation and The Hague Conference on Private International Law', 2 *International Law FORUM du droit international* (2000), 230-234; and see on the Americanisation of the law, H. Muir Watt, 'La fonction subversive du droit comparé', *Revue internationale de droit comparé* (2000), 503-527, referring to B. Audit, *L'americanisation du droit* (2001), and P. Wautelet, 'What Has International Private Law Achieved in Meeting the Challenges Posed by Globalisation?', in *Globalisation and Jurisdiction* (2004), 55-77, at 56.

with the legal consequences of the increasing number of international disputes. The regulation of 'traditional' adjudication by state courts over international disputes is still national law-based.[3] Apart from the few successful regional uniform regulations of international jurisdiction,[4] individual states determine the scope of their judicial powers according to their own rules of jurisdiction. States have different approaches in regulating international jurisdiction. Many of these differences are usually explained by the more general differences between the legal traditions of *common law* versus *civil law*. One of the principal differences is that courts of Anglo-American tradition have considerable discretion in determining their competence over an international dispute, whereas Continental European countries have limited or closed sets of jurisdiction rules leaving the courts with little discretion.

As a result, the identification of the competent court – or courts – in international litigation becomes quite a complex and difficult task for the parties involved. An international litigator searching for judicial relief through state courts will often find himself stuck in a web of national jurisdiction rules or in a 'jurisdictional jungle'.[5] For the parties involved, this may lead to jurisdictional uncertainty in international legal relationships and disputes.

1.1.1 The Relevance of International Jurisdiction

The complexity of determining the competent court in such a 'jurisdictional web' is all the more striking in view of the importance of the jurisdictional question. First and foremost, the competent court will, according to its own conflict of law rules, determine the law applicable to the case, or apply the *lex fori*.[6] The outcome of a dispute is therefore strongly dependent on which court has jurisdiction over the case. Differences in procedural law, varying from one forum to another, also influence the course and outcome of international court litigation.[7] Finally, once

---

[3] In most legal orders, the question of international jurisdiction traditionally belongs to the discipline of private international law or conflict of laws. Contrary to what its name suggests, the discipline of private international law originates from national law: according to Juenger 'neither its rules nor the rules to which they refer, are of an international or supranational nature', F. Juenger, 'The Problem with Private International Law', in *Private Law in the International Arena: From National Conflict Rules towards Harmonization and Unification: Liber Amicorum Kurt Siehr* (2000), 289-309, at 290. However, the more unified the rules of private international law, the more 'international' or 'supranational' the discipline will become. See P. de Vareilles-Sommières, *La compétence internationale de l'état en matière de droit privé: Droit international public et droit international privé* (1997), at 224. See A. Lowenfeld, *International Litigation and the Quest for Reasonableness: Essays in Private International Law* (1996), at 2-3. The jurisdictional question is considered by Brand to be the 'jurisdictional subpart of private international law', see R. Brand, 'Balancing Sovereignty and Party Autonomy in Private International Law', 25 *University of Pittsburg School of Law Working Paper Series* (2005), at 4.

[4] See below, Sect. 1.3.1.

[5] By analogy to M. Reimann, *Conflicts of Law in Western Europe: A Guide through the Jungle* (1995).

[6] Except in cases where the parties have agreed upon the applicable law by way of a choice of law agreement.

[7] These procedural divergences include, among others, the existence of trial jury, procedural delays, the possibility of judicial review, judicial costs, and the existence of contingency fees. See below under Sect. 1.1.2 on forum shopping.

the court has rendered judgement, the underlying jurisdictional foundation of the court's judgement plays a significant role when its recognition and enforcement is sought in another country by one of the parties. If the court of origin based its jurisdiction on excessive grounds – in the sense that jurisdiction is founded on a (very) weak link between the dispute and the forum – the recognition and enforcement of the judgement by another state may be problematic.

Apart from these legal consequences illustrating the relevance of the jurisdictional question, there are other more practical aspects to the question of international jurisdiction. Litigating in a foreign court often involves language barriers, paying additional travel expenses and finding local legal counsel. The importance of jurisdiction in international litigation and its effect on the merits of a case make it worthwhile 'litigating on where to litigate'.[8] The competence of national courts is therefore often fiercely argued. Such 'judicial battles' involve a lot of energy, time and procedural costs, sometimes at the expense of the merits of the case, if resources are exhausted by the jurisdictional battle.

1.1.2 Forum Selection and Forum Shopping

International court litigation is characterized by the fact that, as a rule and apart from situations where parties validly agreed on a dispute settlement clause, it is the plaintiff who chooses one forum over another by simply instituting proceedings. Several courts can be available to the plaintiff to commence proceedings, either because more than one jurisdictional regime asserts jurisdiction over the same case,[9] or because a unified jurisdictional regime provides for alternative jurisdiction rules.[10] A well-advised claimant will logically institute proceedings at the most favourable forum, thus improving its chances of success.[11] The result is a race to the court, since the party who institutes proceedings first, gets to select its preferred forum.[12] Forum selection by the claimant for the most favourable forum is called forum shopping.[13] Traditionally the lack of unification – or 'decisional

[8] See also W. O'Brian Jr., 'The Hague Convention on Jurisdiction and Judgments: The Way Forward', 66 *The Modern Law Review* (2003), 491-509, at 597; A. von Mehren, 'Theory and Practice of Adjudicatory Authority in Private International Law: A Comparative Study of the Doctrine, Policies and Practices of Common- and Civil-Law Systems: General Course on Private International Law (1996)', 295 *Recueil des cours* (2003), 9-431, at 195-196; L. Silberman, 'Developments in Jurisdiction and Forum Non Conveniens in International Litigation: Thoughts on Reform and a Proposal for a Uniform Standard', 28 *Texas International Law Journal* (1993), 501-529, at 502; and A. Bell, *Forum Shopping and Venue in Transnational Litigation* (2003), § 1.32 *et seq*., at 15.

[9] Also known as positive jurisdiction conflicts see below Sect. 1.2.1.

[10] This will be demonstrated in Chapter 2 which covers unification in Europe. See also A. Briggs, *Civil Jurisdiction and Judgments* (2005), § 2.10, at 34, on the need to be the first to commence proceedings.

[11] See R. Geimer, *Internationales Zivilprozeßrecht* (2005), § 1096, at 373, stating that it is a lawyer's duty to advise his client on the most favourable forum with the best chances of success.

[12] In the words of Geimer '*Entscheidend wäre die Parteirolle*', Geimer, *Internationales Zivilprozeßrecht*, § 1101, at 375.

[13] See for other definitions 'Forum Shopping Reconsidered', 103 *Harvard Law Review* (1990), 1677-1696, at 1677 *et seq.* (editorial article). See also the House of Lords in *The Atlantic Star*, [1974] AC 436, at 442.

harmony'[14] – in conflict of law rules is considered to be the main incentive for forum shopping. A plaintiff will carefully weigh the differences in conflict of law rules determining the applicable law and will choose a forum applying the most favourable substantive law.[15] It has rightfully been argued that unification of conflict of law rules, or of substantive law for that matter, would not prevent forum shopping.[16] By selecting the forum, the claimant will also consider the availability of high damages awarded by the available forums, the level of procedural costs and cost liabilities, the existence of a jury trial and pre-trial discovery, potential delays for rendering judgements and the availability of contingency fees.[17] For example, U.S. courts are often considered to be attractive to foreign tort victims, as U.S. courts are said to award higher (punitive) damages and include generous trial juries.[18] Along with the language, cultural differences and other practical considerations mentioned above, alleged differences in the quality and independence of the judiciary among world courts also influence parties to choose for or avoid a particular forum.[19]

The legitimacy of forum shopping in itself has been debated, as well as whether forum shopping should be encouraged by allowing claimants to shop. This debate is not only concerned with parties' interests but also with the effects of forum shopping on the workload of some more popular forums, leading to overcrowded docks.[20] Nonetheless, the fact remains that forum shopping is a natural conse-

---

[14] This refers to the words 'decisional harmony' found in the title of Juenger's article, F. Juenger, 'Jurisdiction, Choice of Law and the Elusive Goal of Decisional Harmony', in *Law and Reality: Essays on National and International Procedural Law in Honour of Cornelis Carel Albert Voskuil* (1992), 137-147.

[15] See P. Hay, 'Flexibility versus Predictability and Uniformity in Choice of Law. Reflections on Current European and United States Conflicts Law', 226 *Recueil des cours* (1991), 281-412, at 308-309, explaining and condemning the phenomenon of 'law shopping' by means of jurisdiction rules. See also A. Nuyts, 'Forum Shopping et Abus du Forum Shopping dans l'Espace Judiciaire Européen', 3 *Global Jurist Advances* (2003), at 6; available at: http://www.bepress.com/gj/advances/vol3/iss1/art2.

[16] See in general the article by F. Ferrari, '"Forum Shopping" Despite International Contract Law Conventions', 51 *The International and Comparative Law Quarterly* (2002), 689-708; and H. Schulze, 'Declining and Referring Jurisdiction in International Litigation: The Leuven/London Principles', 25 *South African Yearbook of International Law* (2000), 161-180, at 164.

[17] According to M. Whincop, *Policy and Pragmatism in the Conflict of Laws* (2001), at 188, a plaintiff looks for 'minimising litigation costs and award-maximising forum'.

[18] See the famous statement by Lord Denning, often cited in the forum shopping debate: 'As a moth is drawn to the light, so is a litigant drawn to the United States', in *Smith Kline & French Laboratories Ltd. and Others v. Bloch*, [1983] 1 WLR 730 (CA), at 733-734.

[19] According to Park, the fear of biased courts also strongly influences the plaintiff's choice for a particular forum, see W. Park, 'The Relative Reliability of Arbitration Agreements and Court Selection Clauses', in *International Dispute Regulation* (1997), at 6.

[20] Participating in this debate are, among many others, K. Siehr, '"Forum shopping" im internationalen Rechtsverkehr', 25 *Zeitschrift für Rechtsvergleichung* (1984), 124-144, at 133; K. Clermont and T. Eisenberg, 'Exorcising the Evil of Forum Shopping', 80 *Cornell Law Review* (1995), 1507-1535; F. Juenger, 'Forum Shopping Domestic and International', 63 *Tulane Law Review* (1989), 553-574; F. Juenger, 'What's Wrong with Forum Shopping?', 16 *Sydney Law Review* (1994), 5-13; B. Opeskin, 'The Price of Forum Shopping: A Reply to Professor Juenger', 16 *Sydney Law Review* (1994), 14-27; J. Kropholler, 'Das Unbehagen am Forum Shopping', in *Festschrift für Karl Firsching zum 70. Geburtstag* (1985), 165-173.

quence of differences among available fora.[21] A more interesting question is asked by Juenger, namely, 'if the forum shoppers are free from blame what about the shops?'[22] While forum shopping is only possible when more than one court is available to the plaintiff, it is more interesting to identify the bases upon which courts accept jurisdiction and whether these bases are excessive, or in another term 'exorbitant'. Eliminating exorbitant jurisdiction rules and restricting the plaintiff's choice of fora by unifying jurisdiction rules will reduce forum shopping.[23]

Despite a plaintiff's natural procedural advantage due to his privilege to select the forum, defendants are however not always defenceless. 'Reversed forum shopping' occurs when a proactive defendant seeks an anti-suit injunction or declaratory judgement in another court.[24] Alternatively, 'anti-shopping' devices are available in common law jurisdictions. In those jurisdictions a defendant can request the court to stay proceedings on the basis of the *forum (non) conveniens* doctrine, which in practice results in evaluating the claimant's choice of forum.[25]

1.2 International Litigation and the Principle of Party Autonomy

A growing need for efficient international dispute resolution on the one hand and the complexity of international litigation by state courts on the other, led the international trade community to turn to alternative dispute settlement methods, such as arbitration, to settle their international disputes.[26] The principle of party autonomy implies that parties are not only free to agree on which law will govern their contract, but also on how their disputes will be settled and by whom.[27] Today, party autonomy plays a fundamental role in international dispute resolution. In fact, the question of unification of jurisdiction rules only becomes relevant if the parties have not – or have not *validly* – agreed how and where their disputes will be resolved.

---

[21] See the famous statement made in *The Atlantic Star*, [1974] AC 436, at 471: '"Forum-shopping" is a dirty word; but it is only a pejorative way of saying that, if you offer a plaintiff a choice of jurisdictions, he will naturally choose the one in which he thinks his case can be most favourably presented: this should be a matter neither for surprise nor for indignation.'

[22] F. Juenger, 'Forum Non Conveniens – Who Needs It?', in *Wege zur Globalisierung des Rechts: Festschrift für Rolf A. Schütze zum 65. Geburtstag* (1999), 317-336, at 319. According to Juenger 'Instead of casting aspersions on forum shoppers, we should applaud them for putting this important question into stark relief', see Juenger, 'What's Wrong?', at 13.

[23] See Bell, *Forum Shopping and Venue*, § 1.19 *et seq.*, at 9.

[24] Ibid., § 4.04, at 135 *et seq.*; Geimer distinguishes '*Steuerungsmoglichkeiten en Abwehrstrategien des Beklagten*', see Geimer, *Internationales Zivilprozeßrecht*, § 1108-1124, at 376-381.

[25] See Chapter 4 on 'England'. See also J. Fawcett, *Declining Jurisdiction in Private International Law* (1995), at 22.

[26] See in this sense S. Greenberg, 'Resolving International Business Disputes', in *Guide to Export-Import Basics: Vital Knowledge for Trading Internationally* (2008), 59-76 and Park, 'The Relative Reliability', at 4.

[27] *Black's Law Dictionary*, 8th edn. (2004) and see Lowenfeld, *The Quest for Reasonableness*, at 199 *et seq.*

1.2.1 Choice of Forum and Forum Fixing

Parties to international court litigation are free to designate a particular court or forum, by way of a jurisdiction clause – or choice of forum clause – to hear their case either exclusively or non-exclusively.[28] By *fixing* the competent forum in advance, parties avoid having to litigate in an unknown or distant forum. Such *forum fixing* avoids uncertainty and the 'jurisdictional battle' described above.[29] However, the validity of the jurisdiction clause still depends on the requirements arising out of the national law of the chosen court. In addition, especially courts from the common law tradition are allowed to refuse jurisdiction if they consider the chosen forum inappropriate for the dispute lying before them.[30] Finally, although scarce, some national jurisdictional regimes will not give effect at all to an express choice of a particular forum.

Judgements rendered by agreed courts are more likely to be recognised and enforced in other countries, because they result from the parties' consent. At present, successful international instruments regulating the validity and effect of a choice of forum are lacking in transatlantic business relations.[31] The Hague Convention on Choice of Court Agreements of 30 June 2005, which was drafted by The Hague Conference for Private International Law is still in the process of ratification and has not yet entered into force. [32] However, this important Convention should, if successful, contribute to more certainty around choice of forum clauses and resulting judgements.[33]

1.2.2 The Alternative: The Success of International Arbitration

The current lack of clarity on the jurisdictional question creates uncertainty. This is one reason for the success of the alternative dispute resolution mechanism: international commercial arbitration.[34] International commercial arbitration has taken the lead in international litigation as the principal way to settle international disputes.[35] Available only where the parties have entered into an arbitration agree-

---

[28] See for an exhaustive overview A. Briggs, *Agreements on Jurisdiction and Choice of Law* (2008) and see also Park, 'The Relative Reliability', at 7, referring to jurisdiction clauses as 'prorogation agreements'.

[29] See Geimer, *Internationales Zivilprozeßrecht*, § 1125, at 382, and see for other *pros* and *cons* of *forum fixing*, P. Kuypers, *Forumkeuze in het Nederlandse internationaal privaatrecht* (2008), at 35-42.

[30] According to the *forum non conveniens* doctrine, see Chapters 3, 4, 5 and 8.

[31] See Sect. 1.3.2, below.

[32] See http://www.hcch.net/index_en.php?act=conventions.text&cid=98. On 19 January 2009, the outgoing State Department Legal Advisor, John Bellinger, signed the Hague Convention on Choice of Court Agreements on behalf of the U.S.A. Mexico is the first party to the Convention through accession on 26 September 2007. Regarding the EU, on 5 September 2008 a Proposal for a Council Decision on the signing by the European Community of the Convention on Choice-of-Court Agreements of 2005 was presented, see COM(2008) 538 final.

[33] As also discussed by K. Kramer, 'De forumkeuze als betrouwbaar alternatief voor het arbitraal beding in de internationale handelspraktijk? Het nieuwe Haags Forumkeuzeverdrag', *Nederlands Tijdschrift voor Handelsrecht (*2006), 165-172.

[34] P. Sanders, *Quo Vadis Arbitration? Sixty Years of Arbitration Practice: A Comparative Study* (1999), at 2.

[35] See P. Schlosser, 'The 1968 Brussels Convention and Arbitration', 7 *Arbitration International* (1991), 227-242, at 228; P. Schlosser, 'The Competence of Arbitrators and of Courts', 8 *Arbitration*

ment, this alternative way to settle disputes gives one or more arbitrators – 'private judges' – the power to resolve the dispute by rendering a binding decision.[36] Since arbitration is – but for a few exceptions – voluntary and is founded on the parties' consent, the parties waive their traditional right of access to judicial adjudication by national courts and entrust the settlement of their disputes to arbitrators to the exclusion of court proceedings.[37]

Apart from the other alleged advantages of arbitration in comparison with court litigation, such as speed, confidentiality, efficiency and expertise,[38] the increasing use of international arbitration is unmistakably due to the success of the *New York Convention* of 1958.[39] This Convention facilitates the recognition of foreign arbitral awards and most importantly for present purposes, stipulates validity requirements for international arbitration agreements.[40] The above-mentioned Hague Convention on the Choice of Court Agreements could equally increase the use of *choice of forum* clauses and complement the New York Convention.

Another significant advantage of international arbitration over court proceedings is that by its very nature the latter is 'coloured' by cultural or political aspects of a national legal order, whereas in international arbitration parties agree on the procedural rules, including the language of the proceedings and the composition of the arbitral tribunal.[41] Parties generally do not want to risk court proceedings in an unknown or distant court, or even in a suspected biased court.[42] Moreover, one of the parties will have an advantage over the other or even a 'home court advantage'.[43] Only dispute settlement mechanisms, which are based on the con-

---

International (1992), 189-204, at 190. Another alternative dispute resolution mechanism worth mentioning in the present context is 'expert determination'. See for a more detailed overview of alternative dispute resolution (ADR) mechanisms in international disputes, F. De Ly, 'Applicable Law and Dispute Resolution Clauses: A Premilinary Report', in *Les grandes clauses des contrats internationaux, Brussels Conference, March 11-12, 2005* (2005), 167-234.

[36] The arbitration agreement or arbitration clause – a private agreement based on consent of the parties to arbitrate – constitutes the very basis for the arbitration process and its arbitral award.

[37] International arbitration, however, still needs the support of the courts, especially for the enforcement of arbitral awards. See Sanders, *Quo Vadis?*, at 19; see also Schlosser, 'The 1968 Brussels Convention and Arbitration', at 228.

[38] Critics challenge the so-called advantages, especially in light of a recent trend of juridicalisation of international arbitration proceedings. See in general F. Lowenfeld, 'Book Review: Quo Vadis Arbitration? Sixty Years of Arbitration Practice', 95 *American Journal of International Law* (2001), 728-731, and L. Silberman, 'International Arbitration: Comments from a Critic', *American Review of International Arbitration* (2002), 9-18.

[39] Convention on the Recognition and Enforcement of Foreign Arbitral Awards, signed in New York on 10 June 1958. See also Sanders, *Quo Vadis?*, at 9.

[40] Art. 2 of the New York Convention requires such an agreement to be in writing and obliges the courts of Contracting States to give effect to such an agreement. See also http://www.uncitral.org/uncitral/en/uncitral_texts/arbitration/NYConvention.html.

[41] Schlosser claims that '[l]acking any transnational judiciary, arbitration is an absolute necessity in international trade', see Schlosser, 'The Competence of Arbitrators and of Courts', at 189.

[42] 'Arbitration justifies itself in a cross-border business context principally as a tool to minimize the real or imagined dangers of litigation abroad: a mechanism to reduce the risk of ending up before a biased foreign judge who will apply unfamiliar procedures in a strange language', Park, 'The Relative Reliability', at 4 *et seq.*

[43] See Lowenfeld, *The Quest for Reasonableness*, at 198.

sent of parties, have the ability to 'delocalize' or 'denationalize' transnational disputes.[44]

International arbitration is however not best suited for every international dispute, especially those arising out of small and medium sized contracts, but the complexity of international jurisdiction for court litigation leaves parties with arbitration as the sole option to settle their dispute.[45] Parties should be given a real choice between state courts and arbitration; a choice that will not exist as long as a jurisdictional framework for international court litigation is lacking.

1.3 Unification of International Jurisdiction Rules

Unification efforts in the field of private international law[46] have mainly been focused on conflict of law rules, rather than on international jurisdiction rules.[47] In the field of international commercial matters in general, and contractual disputes in particular, little unification of international jurisdiction has been achieved at a world-wide level.[48] International conventions are considered the principal source of the unification of private international law.[49] As a rule, they are negotiated and drafted by state delegates and based on a political consensus among the participating states. The principal objection to this method of unification is the lack of flexibility to adapt to changes in a dynamic legal world.[50]

---

[44] See in general, L. De Lima Pinheiro, 'The "Denationalization" of Transnational Relationships: Regulation of Transnational Relationships by Public International Law, European Community Law and Transnational Law', in *Aufbruch nach Europa: 75 Jahre Max-Planck-Institut für Privatrecht* (2001), 429-446, at 429.

[45] See in general, R. David, 'The Methods of Unification', 16 *American Journal of Comparative Law* (1968), 13-27, at 24.

[46] In the international arena, unification also takes place in other fields of law, such as in procedural law and substantive law. The United Nations Convention on Contracts for the International Sale of Goods, Vienna 1980 (CISG) is often used to illustrate a successful instrument of uniform substantive law, as it has been ratified by many states and elaborated within the *United Nations Commission for International Trade Law (UNCITRAL)* whose 'business is the modernization and harmonization of rules on international business', see http://www.uncitral.org/uncitral/en/index.html. Some consider different forms of unification to 'go hand in hand', see P. Glenn, 'Unification of Law, Harmonization of Law and Private International Law', in *Liber memorialis François Laurent, 1810-1887* (1989), 783-793, at 783; others see them as each other's opposite, see R. David, 'Unification du droit et arbitrage', in *Verhagen Lectures: Erasmus University Faculty of Law, 20 September 1976* (1977), at 6.

[47] A. Miaja de la Muela, 'Les principes directeurs des règles de compétence territoriale des tribunaux internes en matière de litiges comportant un élément international', 135 *Recueil des cours* (1973), 1-96, at 41-42.

[48] Most bilateral agreements in this field aim at recognition and enforcement of each other's judgements, but are less concerned with international jurisdiction. In this context it is worth mentioning that an attempt to elaborate a U.K./U.S. bilateral agreement failed after long negotiations. See in general the articles of H. Smit, 'The Proposed United States-United Kingdom Convention on Recognition and Enforcement of Judgements: A Prototype for the Future', 17 *Virginia Journal of International Law* (1977), 443-468; and P. Hay and R. Walker, 'The Proposed U.S.-U.K. Recognition-of-Judgements Convention: Another Perspective', 18 *Virginia Journal of International Law* (1978), 753-768.

[49] See also Bell, *Forum Shopping and Venue*, § 3.03 *et seq.*, at 50.

[50] See K. Zweigert and H. Kötz, *Introduction to Comparative Law* (1998), translated by Tony Weir from the German, *Einführung in die Rechtsvergleichung auf dem Gebiete des Privatrechts*, at

1.3.1 Regional Unification

a) *Europe*

Regional unification of jurisdiction rules has proved most successful in Europe. The 1968 Brussels Convention on Jurisdiction and Enforcement of Judgements[51] turned out to be a successful regional unification instrument of jurisdiction rules in the field of civil and commercial matters.[52] Its successor, Council Regulation 44/2001, is currently in force in all the EU Member States.[53] Its provisions have been extended to Switzerland, Norway and Iceland by virtue of a 'parallel' Lugano Convention.[54] As a result, judicial powers in the EU and the remaining EFTA states are allocated by uniform jurisdiction rules, and judgements are automatically recognized and enforced according to the same 'Brussels Model'. As Stephen Cromie roughly summarises, 'The courts of the world are now divided into two categories: those whose jurisdiction is decided wholly by their own rules of Private International Law, and those of countries which are parties of the Brussels and/or Lugano Conventions.'[55]

The particularity of this Brussels Model is that it is a 'double convention':[56] not only does the instrument eliminate barriers to the free movement of judgements by regulating recognition and enforcement of judgements within the EU and EFTA borders, it also contains direct uniform jurisdiction rules allocating judicial powers among the participating states. The jurisdictional question is therefore directly linked to the question of recognition and enforcement of foreign judgements.[57]

25: 'Multilateral treaties are very difficult to achieve and rather clumsy in operation.' See also S. Baumgartner, *The Proposed Hague Convention on Jurisdiction and Foreign Judgements: Trans-Atlantic Law Making for Transnational Litigation* (2003), at 68, arguing that transatlantic law-making has become a laborious task, especially considering the attitude of some countries towards international treaties.

[51] The Brussels Convention on Jurisdiction and Enforcement of Judgements in Civil and Commercial Matters of 27 September 1968 was first published in French in OJ 1972 L 299/32 and in English in OJ 1978 L 304/36 [hereafter 'Brussels Convention']. See Chapter 2, Sect. 2.1.

[52] The Convention entered into force in 1971 between the original six Member States.

[53] Council Regulation on Jurisdiction and the Enforcement of Judgements of Civil and Commercial Matters (EC) No. 44/2001 of 22 December 2000, OJ 2001 L 12. Denmark's exceptional position will be explained in the following chapter.

[54] The Lugano Convention on Jurisdiction and the Recognition and Enforcement of Judgments in Civil and Commercial Matters enacted for the States of the European Free Trade Association (EFTA) was signed on 16 September 1988, published in OJ 1988 L 319/9. A new Lugano Convention has recently been approved to replace the 1988 Lugano Convention in order to align it with the modifications of the Brussels Regulation. The official text of the revised Lugano Convention is published in OJ of 21 December 2007 L 339 at 3, which also includes the Council Decision of 15 October 2007 on its signing, on behalf of the Community (2007/712/EC), L 339, at 1. See also the Proposal for a Council Decision of 29 February 2008 concerning the conclusion of the new Lugano Convention, COM (2008) 116 final 2008/0048.

[55] S. Cromie and W. Park, *International Commercial Litigation* (1990), at 3.

[56] See Baumgartner, *The Proposed Hague Convention*, fn. 269, at 55, stating that very few *double* bilateral conventions have been elaborated prior to the Brussels Convention of 1968.

[57] See among others R. Michaels, 'Some Fundamental Jurisdictional Conceptions as Applied in Judgment Conventions', 123 *Duke Law School Legal Studies* (2006), at 11-12.

The Brussels Model consists of a 'closed' set of uniform jurisdiction rules which replaces national jurisdiction rules.

b) *Latin America*

Apart from this 'pan-European' unification, other regional unification efforts are to be found in Latin America.[58] The Latin American States are pioneers of the regional unification of private international law. Latin American unification is twofold: the first private international law treaties, known under the Montevideo Treaties and revised in 1939-1940, were adopted in 1889[59] and in 1928 a comprehensive code for private international law, the Bustamante Code, was approved in Havana at the Sixth Conference of American States.[60] Both instruments already included provisions dealing with international jurisdiction, even though the main body of the Treaties and Code consists of conflict of law rules.[61]

After the OAS was established, its Inter-American Juridical Committee[62] resumed efforts to unify private international law and attempted to merge the Bustamante Code and the Montevideo Treaties in light of the U.S. Restatements of Conflict of Laws, but without much success.[63] Currently unification of private in-

---

[58] Association of Southeast Asian Nations (ASEAN) whose purpose is to promote regional peace and stability in Southeast Asia through abiding respect for justice and the rule of law, is limited to legal cooperation. See also Van Loon, 'Globalisation and The Hague Conference', at 233; R. Graveson, 'Private International Law: A Century of Unification', in *Liber memorialis François Laurent, 1810-1887* (1989), 795-804, at 797; and http://www.aseansec.org.

[59] These treaties were the result of several South American Governments working on unification and codification of private international law by holding the first Congress of Private International Law in Montevideo. See A. Garro, *Armonización y unificación del derecho privado en América Latina: Esfuerzos, tendencias y realidades* (1992), at 10-13; A. Villela, 'L'unification du droit international privé en Amérique latine', 73 *Revue critique de droit international privé* (1984), 233-265, at 245.

[60] The first International Conference of American States began in 1889, long after Simón Bolívar expressed his idea of unification of law within the region in 1826. In 1948, the Organisation of American States (OAS) was created. See J. Siqueiros, 'La Conferencia de La Haya y las Convenciones Interamericanas de Derecho Internacional Privado', in *Liber Amicorum Homenaje a la Obra Científica y Académica de la Profesora Tatiana B. de Maekelt* (2001), at 84; and Villela, 'L'unification en Amérique latine', at 235-239. The Bustamante Code was the result of the work of an International Commission of American Jurists in 1912. See OAS General Secretariat, 'Comparative Study of the Bustamante Code, The Montevideo Treaties and the Restatement of the Law of Conflict of Laws' (Washington D.C.: Inter-American Juridical Commitee OAS, 1964), at 6; Garro, *Armonización y unificación en América Latina*, at 13. See for an extensive historical overview of the Bustamente Code, J. Samtleben, *Internationales Privatrecht in Lateinamerika: Der Código Bustamante in Theorie und Praxis* (1979). The Code was ratified by many Latin American States. According to Caffrey, the U.S. never ratified the Code, claiming that they were unable to grant its approval 'due to constitutional grounds', see B. Caffrey, *International Jurisdiction and the Recognition and Enforcement of Foreign Judgments in the LAWASIA Region* (1985), at 14.

[61] For international jurisdiction provisions, see Arts. 314-339 of the Bustamante Code and Arts. 72-73 and 77-93 of the Montevideo Treaties.

[62] The permanent committee of the Inter-American Council of Jurists created at the Third International Conference in 1906, http://www.oas.org/speeches/speech.asp?sCodigo=06-0067. See General Secretariat, 'Comparative Study', at 3; Siqueiros, 'Convenciones Interamericanas', at 86.

[63] See General Secretariat, 'Comparative Study', at 3; and K. Nadelmann, 'The Need for Revision of the Bustamante Code on Private International Law', 65 *American Journal of International Law* (1971), 782-793, at 783. See http://www.oas.org/dil/PrivateIntLaw-HistDevPriLaw-Eng.htm. The

ternational law is in the hands of the Specialized Conferences on Private International Law (CIDIP),[64] whose works have been 'modest and realistic'[65] and limited to rules of applicable law and international judicial cooperation in very specific areas.[66] International jurisdiction has scarcely been touched.[67]

When the Southern Common Market – or *Mercado Común del Sur* (MERCOSUR) – was founded in 1991 by the Treaty of Asunción to promote economic integration by means of free trade and free movement of goods, peoples, and currency, the MERCOSUR Countries[68] also committed themselves to reconcile their legislations in pertinent areas in order to reinforce the integration process.[69] It is in this context that unification efforts made by MERCOSUR are sometimes referred to as the 'subregional' unification of private international law.[70] Three years after it was founded, one of the decisions of the Council of the Common Market involved the regulation of international jurisdiction in contractual matters in the Buenos Aires Protocol, underlining 'the importance of adopting common rules on international jurisdiction in contractual matters, for the purpose of promoting the development of economic relations among the State Parties' private sectors' and stating that in the area of international business 'contracting is the legal format of the commerce that takes place in connection with the integration process'.[71] The 1992 Protocol of

---

Inter-American Council of Jurists ceased to exist in 1970, see Siqueiros, 'Convenciones Interamericanas', at 87.

[64] According to the OAS's Charter, Specialized Conferences 'deal with special technical matters or … develop specific aspects of inter-American cooperation', available at http://www.oas.org/dil/PrivateIntLaw-HistDevPriLaw-Eng.htm.

[65] Garro, *Armonización y unificación en América Latina*, at 6.

[66] Villela, 'L'unification en Amérique latine', at 247-256; G. Lucas Sosa, *El Derecho Internacional Privado Interamericano y Derecho de Integración (CIDIP V Mexico 1994)* (1996), at 26-29; Siqueiros, 'Convenciones Interamericanas', at 88-91.

[67] In 1984, CIDIP-III adopted international instruments on international civil law and international procedural law and these include the Inter-American Convention on Jurisdiction in the International Sphere for the Extraterritorial Validity of Foreign Judgments. The text is to be found in 56 *RabelZ* (1992), at 149-152. The Convention is not yet in force and focuses primarily on international recognition. Issues of international jurisdiction are programmed for the CIDIP VII (resolution AG/RES 2065 (XXXV-0/05), at http://www.oas.org/dil/CIDIP-VII_res.2065.htm).

[68] MERCOSUR is a regional trade agreement between Argentina, Brazil, Paraguay, Uruguay and recently Venezuela. The Treaty of Asunción was later amended and updated by the 1994 Treaty of Ouro Preto. Bolivia, Chile, Colombia, Ecuador and Peru currently have an associate member status.

[69] Art. 1 of the Treaty of Asunción.

[70] D. Fernández Arroyo, *Derecho Internacional Privado Interamericano: Evolución y Perspectivas* (2000), at 72.

[71] See the Preamble of MERCOSUR/CMC/DEC. Nº 01/94; Buenos Aires Protocol on International Jurisdiction in Contractual Matters available at http://www.sice.oas.org/trade/mrcsrs/decisions/AN0194_e.asp. Such protocols are similar to international conventions, which require ratification by each state individually. See on its legal effects, J. Samtleben, 'Der MERCOSUR als Rechtssystem', in *Wirtschaftsrecht des MERCOSUR – Horizont 2000: Tagung im Max-Planck-Institut für ausländisches und internationales Privatrecht am 21.-22. Januar 2000* (2001), 52-94, at 53 and fn. 10, who indicates that Uruguay has not yet ratified this jurisdiction protocol. See also J. Vervaele, 'Mercosur and Regional Integration in South America', 54 *The International and Comparative Law Quarterly* (2005), 387-410, at 392 *et seq.*

Las Leñas deals with mutual recognition of judgements and appears to be clearly inspired by the 1968 Brussels Convention.[72]

1.3.2 Failed Efforts of Universal Unification: The Hague Project

By far the most important institution for the unification of private international law at a global level is the intergovernmental organization of The Hague Conference on Private International Law (HCCH).[73] Its purpose is to work for the progressive unification of the rules of private international law[74] and to 'work for a world in which persons – as well as companies – can enjoy a high degree of legal security'.[75] Apart from conventions in family matters, the HCCH adopted three conventions directly and indirectly dealing with international jurisdiction in commercial disputes.[76] These conventions are 'simple' conventions, meaning that they principally deal with international recognition and enforcement of judgements and that the jurisdictional question is only dealt with indirectly by way of a jurisdictional requirement.[77] These conventions, however, are of very little practical relevance as one entered into force for three countries only.[78] The most recently concluded convention is the Convention of 30 June 2005 on Choice of Court Agreements, whose potential importance has been explained above. This Choice of Court Convention is the abridged result of a much wider project covering many specific issues of international jurisdiction and which started in 1993 as the 'Hague Project on International Jurisdiction and Enforcement in Civil and Commercial Matters'. In 1992, the U.S. Department of State proposed to Georges Droz, Secre-

---

[72] According to Vervaele, 'Mercosur and Regional Integration', at 401. See MERCOSUR/CMC/DEC. N° 05/92; see also MERCOSUR/CMC/DEC. N° 10/96 on International jurisdiction in matters relating to consumers.

[73] As suggested by T.M.C. Asser and at the initiative of the Dutch Government, the HCCH began to organize *ad hoc* 'conferences'. The first was held in 1893. At its seventh conference in 1955, the HCCH became a permanent international organization. See H. van Loon, 'Quelques réflexions sur l'unification progressive du droit international privé dans le cadre de la Conférence de La Haye', in *Liber memorialis François Laurent, 1810-1887* (1989), 1133-1150, at 1133.

[74] Statute of the HCCH of 15 July 1955 (including amendments adopted, approved and entered into force on 1 January 2007). See Van Loon, 'Quelques réflexions', at 1142 and Graveson, 'A Century of Unification', at 798.

[75] At http://www.hcch.net/index_en.php?act=text.display&tid=26.

[76] The Convention of 15 April 1958 on the Jurisdiction of the Selected Forum in the Case of International Sales of Goods, not in force, but signed by Austria, Belgium, Germany and Greece. The Convention of 25 November 1965 on the Choice of Court, not yet in force, only signed by Israel; and the Convention of 1 February 1971 on the Recognition and Enforcement of Foreign Judgments in Civil and Commercial Matters with its Supplementary Protocol, both entered into force on 20 August 1979, but are only ratified by Cyprus, The Netherlands and Portugal.

[77] The additional Protocol to the 1971 Hague Convention includes, however, a list of exorbitant jurisdiction grounds allowing Contracting States to not recognize a judgement if it is based on one of these jurisdiction grounds. See for more definitions Michaels, 'Some Fundamental Jurisdictional Conceptions', at 11.

[78] As noted by the HCCH 'even if the Conventions have not been ratified, they have an influence upon legal systems, in both Member and non-Member States. They also form a source of inspiration for efforts to unify private international law at the regional level.' At http://www.hcch.net/index_en.php?act=text.display&tid=26.

tary General of the HCCH, to prepare a convention on the recognition and enforcement of judgements.[79] From the U.S.'s perspective, the regional unification of the Brussels Model was disfavouring U.S. domiciled defendants: although the use of national exorbitant jurisdiction rules against defendants domiciled in Europe was prohibited, they could still be used against defendants domiciled outside the territory. Furthermore, judgements based upon these exorbitant jurisdiction grounds could be recognized and enforced in every other participating Member State.[80] In contrast, foreign judgements seem to be easily recognized in the U.S. on the basis of the Foreign Money Act.

At the Seventeenth Session of the HCCH in May 1993, it was decided to include on the agenda the work in the field of 'recognition and enforcement of foreign judgements in commercial and civil matters'. While considering the nature of a possible world-wide convention, the Working Group compared the double convention of the Brussels Model and the simple convention of the 1971 Hague Convention. The Working Group proposed a convention of a mixed type, as suggested by the American scholar Arthur von Mehren.[81] Such a 'mixed convention' would, like a double convention, include uniform rules for direct jurisdiction *and* rules for recognition and enforcement of judgements. However, as opposed to a double convention the jurisdiction rules would be divided in three groups:[82]

- *Permitted* jurisdiction rules on a *white list*: judgements obtained on the basis of such a white jurisdiction ground are required to be recognized and enforced by other states.
- *Prohibited* jurisdiction rules on a *black list*: judgements based on these jurisdiction grounds are to be refused recognition and enforcement by other states.
- All other national, not uniform, jurisdiction rules belonged to a *grey list*: enforcement and recognition of these judgements would be left to the law of the enforcing state.

---

[79] According to Adler a letter was sent on 5 May 1992 by the former Legal Advisor of the U.S. Department of State, Edwin D. Williamson, to Georges Droz, see M. Adler, 'If We Build It, Will They Come? – The Need for a Multilateral Convention on the Recognition and Enforcement of Civil Monetary Judgements', *Law & Policy in International Business* (1994), 79-111, fn. 5, referring to a U.S. Department of State, Fact Sheet of February 1993.

[80] See Chapter 2, Sect. 2.2, for the mechanism and structure of this Brussels Model. On this point see the famous and critical articles by K. Nadelmann, 'Jurisdictional Improper Fora in the Treaties of Recognition and Enforcement of Judgements: The Common Market Draft', 67 *Columbia Law Review* (1967), 995-998, answered by L. de Winter, 'Excessives Jurisdiction in Private International Law', *The International and Comparative Law Quarterly* (1968), 706-720; F. Juenger, 'La Convention de Bruxelles du 27 septembre 1968 et la courtoisie internationale: Réflexions d'un américain', *Revue critique de droit international privé* (1983), 37-51, and K. Russell, 'Exorbitant Jurisdiction and Enforcement of Judgements: The Brussels System as an Impetus for United States Action', 19 *Syracuse Journal of International Law & Commerce* (1993), 57-92.

[81] Adler, 'The Need for a Multilateral Convention', fn. 99, refers to the suggestion of Arthur von Mehren for a mixed convention in a Final Report to the U.S. Department of State, 'Recognition Convention Study' (1992).

[82] See Prel. Doc. No. 1 of May 1994 – Annotated checklist of issues to be discussed at the meeting of the Special Commission of June 1994 (Permanent Bureau of the Hague Conference on Private International Law, 1994), at 6-8.

On 30 October 1999, the Special Commission, consisting of experts, adopted a preliminary draft Convention on Jurisdiction and Foreign Judgements in Civil and Commercial Matters. An extensive and clear Report drawn up by Peter Nygh and Fausto Pocar accompanied the draft and explained the compromises made. However, what was supposed to be a closing diplomatic conference in June 2001, with the adoption of the draft transforming it into an approved convention, turned into a 'complete disaster'.[83] The 1999 draft, which was based on consensus, turned into a 'bracketed' text in which any compromise reached was questioned and therefore withdrawn. After having established that consensus was lacking for a wide range convention, state delegations discussed the possibility of a 'bottom-up' approach rather than the 'top-down' approach previously taken by the HCCH. In April 2002, the Commission I of General Affairs and Policy of the HCCH identified a list of *hard-core issues* upon which negotiations should be continued, covering choice of court clauses, defendant's domicile, submissions, branches, trusts, physical torts and counter-claims.[84] Nonetheless, the drafts became dead letters. Finally it was decided to downscale the project to cover only choice of court agreements. This approach proved more successful. The fact that this ambitious world-wide project resulted in failure, illustrates the complexity of international unification of jurisdiction law. Yet, time, energy, costs and above all the efforts made by state delegates and experts to achieve a mutual understanding of one another's systems should not be thrown away; and 'throwing the baby *and* its bathwater' should be avoided.[85] The failure of The Hague negotiations should not be a permanent disappointment.

1.3.3 Other Instruments of Unification

Another important legislative method of unification[86] is the elaboration of instruments principally drafted by experts in the field rather than by state delegates.[87] In contrast to international conventions, these instruments are not legally binding, but should be considered as 'recommendations' for national legislators.[88] The follow-

---

[83] D. Bennet, 'The Hague Convention on Recognition and Enforcement of Foreign Judgments – A Failure of Characterisation', in *Intercontinental Cooperation through Private International Law: Essays in Memory of Peter E. Nygh* (2004), 19-25, at 20.

[84] Result of the meetings of 24th of April 2002, Minutes No. 5 (morning session).

[85] Brand, *The Hague Preliminary Draft Convention on Jurisdiction and Judgments: Proceedings of the Round Table* (2005), at 77; P. Nygh, 'Declining Jurisdiction under the Brussels I Regulation 2001 and the Preliminary Draft Hague Judgments Convention: A Comparison', in *Reform and Development of Private International Law – Essays in Honour of Sir Peter North* (2002), 303-334, at 308.

[86] Not to be confused with non-legislative means of, or 'spontaneous' unification of, law at the international level, which occurs through unification in practice, see B. Trompenaars, *Pluriforme Unificatie en Uniforme Interpretatie* (1989), at 13; J. Sauveplanne, 'Eenvormig Privaatrecht', *Themis* (1961), 225-280, at 240-241; F. De Ly, *Europese Gemeenschap en privaatrecht: Uitwerking van inaugurele rede Erasmus Universiteit Rotterdam* (1993), at 30.

[87] See in general, K. Nadelmann, 'The International Unification of Law: Uniform Legislation versus International Conventions Revisited', 16 *American Journal of Comparative Law* (1968), 28-50, David, 'The Methods of Unification', at 19-21; and J. Sauveplanne's contribution, in D. Kokkini-Iatridou, *Een inleiding tot het rechtsvergelijkende onderzoek* (1988), at 52; and G. Parra Aranguren, *Curso General de Derecho Internacional Privado: Problemas Selectos y Otros Estudios* (1998), at 71.

[88] According to Zweigert the method of a model law is less heavy-handed and is rather a matter of recommendation than of obligation, see Zweigert and Kötz, *Comparative Law*, at 25.

ing international non-governmental organizations drafted recommendations and general principles dealing with international jurisdiction. The International Law Association (ILA), founded in 1873 in Brussels, is (the most) widespread non-governmental organization with numerous branches world-wide, consisting of academics and practicing professionals whose main objective is 'the study, clarification and development' of public and private international law.[89] With respect to international jurisdiction in commercial matters, the most significant committee is the now defunct 'Committee on International Civil and Commercial Litigation'. Its work resulted in Resolution No. 1/2000, also known as the *Leuven/London Principles on declining and referring jurisdiction in civil and commercial matters* and in Resolution 4/2002 regarding the *Paris/New Delhi Principles on Jurisdiction over Corporations*.

Also in 1873, in Ghent, a group of eleven international lawyers, among whom P. Mancini and T.M.C. Asser, created the Institute of International Law or '*Institut de Droit International*' (IDI) to contribute to and to promote the development of international law.[90] In 2003 its 'Second Commission' adopted the 'Bruges Resolution' on 'the principles for determining when the use of the doctrine of forum non conveniens and anti-suit injunctions is appropriate'.

Although the Rome-based organization UNIDROIT[91] principally focuses on the unification of substantive law, in 2004 it adopted, together with the American Law Institute (ALI),[92] the Principles of Transnational Civil Procedure. These rules are meant to serve as 'guidelines for code projects in countries without long procedural traditions' and 'initiate law reforms even in countries with long and high quality procedural traditions'. They are to be applied 'by analogy in international commercial arbitration'.[93] Principle 2 of the ALI/UNIDROIT Principles of Transnational Civil Procedure deals with 'Jurisdiction over Parties'.

---

[89] See http://www.ila-hq.org. The ILA has a consultative status with a number of the United Nations' Specialized Agencies.

[90] See Art. 1(2) of its Statute, at http://www.idi-iil.org. The IDI received the Nobel Peace Prize in 1904 in recognition of its action in favour of arbitration among states as a peaceful means of settling disputes.

[91] The International Institute for Unification of Private Law, at http://www.unidroit.org.

[92] The ALI, founded in 1923, addresses the uncertainty of law in the U.S. by developing Restatements of the Law. In the light of The Hague negotiations on a Worldwide Jurisdiction Convention and encouraged by State Department officials present at The Hague, the ALI started a project that would meet the needs of U.S. law on jurisdiction issues even if The Hague Negotiations would not result in an international convention. See A. Lowenfeld and L. Silberman, *International Jurisdiction and Judgements Project* (2000), at 18-30; on the jurisdiction aspects, see A. Lowenfeld and L. Silberman, eds., *The Hague Convention on Jurisdiction and Judgments: Records of the Conference Held at New York University School of Law on the Proposed Convention* (2001), at B-1-2 and see B-4.

[93] See Jr. Hazard, M. Taruffo *et al.*, *ALI/Unidroit Principles and Rules of Transnational Civil Procedure* (2003). Multiple references are to be found in 6(4) *Uniform Law Review* (2001), 739-925, which is dedicated to this particular project of the American Law Institute and UNIDROIT, with contributions from among others, H. Kronke, M. Storme, Ph. Fouchard, J. Walker, A. Gidi, and Th. Pfeiffer.

1.3.4 Desirability of Unification at an International Level

The 'driving force' behind the success of regional unification in Europe, and to a lesser extent in Latin America, clearly originates from a desire for economic and political integration. Although the opening of the First Preliminary Document of The Hague Judgment Project refers to a general process of liberalisation of the world economy, reasons for unification of jurisdiction rules at an international level differ and should therefore be placed in a different context.[94] The desirability for unification of jurisdiction rules at a world-wide level should be understood as a need for an international legal framework regulating cross-border commercial activities and its disputes in a 'globalizing world', rather than a process that forms part of an economic and a political integration.[95] Several scholars have argued that such a legal framework does not necessarily involve the unification of international jurisdiction. Instead they favour the approach of a simple convention whose primary aim is to guarantee international recognition and enforcement of judgements world-wide and which merely includes indirect jurisdiction grounds as jurisdictional requirements.[96] In their view, when economic and political reasons for unification are lacking, there is no need for unified jurisdiction rules, a framework for world-wide recognition and enforcement of judgements would suffice.[97] A more general malaise in the unification movement strengthens this view.[98] The ideology, or as Pierre Mayer calls it, 'the metaphysical interest' behind international unification of the law of the beginning of the 20th century has become unpopular.[99]

---

[94] Prel. Doc. No. 1 of May 1994: Checklist Special Commission, at 4, places international jurisdiction in the context of present times in which 'the various economic regions in the world are becoming more interdependent every day – a process that will be further enforced by the creation of the World Trade Organization'. See also M. Reimann, 'Parochialism in American Conflicts Law', 49 *American Journal of Comparative Law* (2001), 369-389, at 387.

[95] See the statement of M. Kovar (U.S. Delegation) at the meeting of Monday, 22 April 2002, Morning Session: (United States) Commission I, General Affairs and Policy The Hague Conference. Kovar noted in Minutes (No. 1), at 7, that the 'original attempt to draft a double convention was perhaps a mistake as not all nations viewed the process from the point of view of economic and political integration. Rather, it should be seen as an international method for creating a civil law framework to enhance international trade and commerce.' See also his answer to Professor Beaumont in J. Kovar, 'The United States as an Actor in Private International Law', in *Private Law, Private International Law, & Judicial Cooperation in the EU-US Relationship* (2005), 153-159, at 154.

[96] See in particular comments by Pierre Mayer in *Proceedings of a Round Table*, at 93 and 98.

[97] Kovar, 'The United States as an Actor', at 158, refers to unification projects in the field of maintenance.

[98] The unification movement appears to be 'in crisis', see B. Fauvarque-Cosson, 'Comparative Law and Conflict of Laws: Allies or Enemies? New Perspectives on an Old Couple', 49 *American Journal of Comparative Law* (2001), 407-427, at 415; see also Zweigert and Kötz, *Comparative Law*, at 27.

[99] According to Pierre Mayer this metaphysical interest or this romantic idea behind unification of international jurisdiction rules 'which is associated with the spectacle of uniformity: in this globalised world, let us harmonise our rules, let us have uniform grounds of jurisdiction' is misplaced. He does not understand this desire outside a political union and does not think that 'uniformity is, in itself desirable, or that it serves any useful purpose; on the contrary, trying to achieve uniformity brings with it serious drawbacks', in *Proceedings of a Round Table*, at 95.

Why then is the unification of international jurisdiction rules desirable? As a general rule, unification of law is still considered to be desirable if it meets the 'specific needs of international legal business'.[100] In that respect it is undeniable that the desirability of unification of jurisdiction lies in the fact that the international community would benefit from jurisdictional certainty and predictability in cross-border activities and transnational commercial contracts.

This has been underlined in a 2003 survey presented by the International Chamber of Commerce (ICC) to government officials drafting the proposed Hague Convention on Jurisdiction. The survey revealed that businesses are faced with jurisdictional uncertainty in international contractual relations, which has in some cases even affected significant business decisions.[101] The regulation of jurisdiction in transnational commercial disputes between private entities carrying out activities across national borders requires a uniform and international approach, transcending national rules (and interests), if one wants to promote certainty, predictability and justice for international trade.[102] In view of these objectives of unification of international jurisdiction rules, a *simple* convention guaranteeing mutual recognition and enforcement on a world-wide scale will not eradicate the 'jurisdictional web' of rules in international litigation, and the 'anarchy'[103] of national jurisdiction rules will persist.[104]

The uncertainty, as a result of the lack of a set of unified national jurisdiction rules, also results in either positive or negative jurisdiction conflicts. Positive jurisdiction conflicts occur when several courts claim jurisdiction over the dispute by virtue of their national jurisdiction rules, resulting in multiple competent forums and consequently leading to forum shopping. The number of available courts increases especially when jurisdiction is asserted over a dispute on the basis of an exceedingly weak connection with the forum. Negative conflicts of jurisdiction arise when no forum, according to its national jurisdiction rules, confers jurisdiction over a dispute, leaving parties empty handed and with no available court to

[100] Only then would 'the vast amount of energy which is required to carry through any project for the unification of law' be justified according to Zweigert and Kötz, *Comparative Law*, at 27. But see in contrast Mayer in *Proceedings of a Round Table*, at 94, disagreeing with promoting international trade as the 'official aim' for unification.

[101] See the news archives of the ICC at http://www.iccwbo.org/policy/law/iccef/index.html, Paris, 2 April 2003, 'Jurisdictional certainty is essential in international contracts'; and Paris, 29 August 2003, 'Business hails Hague jurisdictional treaty draft', available at http://www.iccwbo.org/policy/law/icced/index.html.

[102] The following statement also applies to unification of jurisdiction rules: 'the advantage of unified law is that it makes international legal business easier' and 'reduces the legal risks … and hereby gives relief both to the businessman who plans the venture and to the judge who has to resolve the disputes to which it gives rise. Thus unified law promotes greater legal predictably and security.' Zweigert and Kötz, *Comparative Law*, at 25.

[103] C. McLachlan, 'Interim Report Declining & Referring Jurisdiction in International Litigation', presented at the International Law Association, London Conference, 2000, at 4.

[104] However it should be noted that indirect jurisdiction rules as a requirement for international recognition and enforcement of foreign judgements, like those embodied in the first Protocol of The Hague Convention on Recognition of 1971, have a potential harmonising effect on direct jurisdiction rules, as they exclude recognition when the judgement is founded on exorbitant jurisdiction rules.

resort to. Such a 'jurisdictional vacuum'[105] often results in a '*déni de justice*'.[106] Regulating jurisdiction conflicts by mechanisms of *lis pendens* on the one hand, and the *forum necessitatis* rule on the other, will however not be sufficient to deal with jurisdictional uncertainty when it comes to the question of 'where to litigate' in the first place.[107]

Jurisdictional certainty through unification of international jurisdiction can be achieved by finding uniform jurisdiction rules suitable for international (contractual) disputes. This entails eliminating exorbitant jurisdiction rules, avoiding multiple forums and finding acceptable and feasible connecting factors for a uniform jurisdictional system.

1.3.5 The Next Step: Progressive Unification

It is generally believed that the more difficult the unification is, the more valuable it gets, and the more ambitious the unification project, the harder it becomes to reach consensus. In the field of conflict of law rules, unification proceeded area-by-area: each convention carefully delimited its scope of application to specific *rationae materiae*; from the applicable law to specific contracts for the international sale of goods,[108] to the law applicable to specific torts such as traffic accidents.[109] The same path should be followed for the unification of international jurisdiction. This calls for rigorously delimiting the material scope and defining the subject matter autonomously in order to avoid problems of qualification.[110] Despite the HCCH's statutory mission of 'progressive unification',[111] the Jurisdiction Project followed the Brussels Model, and aimed at unifying a wide range of jurisdiction rules in the field of civil and commercial matters.[112] It proved to be too ambitious and too difficult. If one wants to achieve successful unification, it is necessary to restore the progressive unification approach.[113] Future work of the HCCH in the field of international jurisdiction should be carried out area-by-area, beginning with disputes arising out of contractual relationships.[114]

---

[105] Schulze, 'The Leuven/London Principles', at 161.

[106] Either the court lacks jurisdiction because it does not have the legal basis to take jurisdiction, or the court has the competence but will not take the case because it has a discretionary power to refuse to do so. In those cases several systems apply the *forum necessitatis* rule. See in general F. Ibili, *Gewogen rechtsmacht in het IPR: Over forum (non) conveniens en forum necessitatis* (2007).

[107] These mechanisms harmonise jurisdiction rules but do not provide for uniform jurisdiction rules, which is needed for jurisdictional certainty. But the 'primary objective of harmonization is not uniformity', see Glenn, 'Unification of Law', at 783.

[108] Hague Convention of 22 December 1986 on the Law Applicable to Contracts for the International Sale of Goods.

[109] Hague Convention of 4 May 1971 on the Law Applicable to Traffic Accidents.

[110] Van Loon, 'Quelques réflexions', at 1142.

[111] See above Sect. 1.3.2.

[112] See Pocar, *Proceedings of a Round Table*, at 75; and see Van Loon, 'Globalisation and The Hague Conference', at 231.

[113] See the Minutes No. 1 Commission I General Affairs and Policy of the Conference, at 4, where Kovar states 'that the [U.S.] Delegation believed the widely desired trade-off with "general doing business" jurisdiction on the black list was more concrete and easier to sell in the area of product liability than when it applied to all civil and commercial litigation.' See Chapter 7.

[114] See also Brand, *Proceedings of a Round Table*, at 91: '[B]egin with the status quo in the multilateral system (where the world stands now) and try to move step-by-step forward to a more coopera-

1.4 Some Difficulties Due to the Nature of Civil Jurisdiction

1.4.1 International Law and State Sovereignty

International law does not impose restrictions on the reach of national jurisdiction rules.[115] In 1927, the Permanent Court of International Justice (PCIJ), the predecessor of the International Court of Justice (ICJ), ruled in its sole decision on jurisdiction that states can regulate jurisdiction as long as they do not interfere with the sovereignty of other states.[116] Based on the principle of territorial sovereignty, the Court argued that there is no 'general prohibition to states to extend the application of their laws and the jurisdiction of their courts to persons, property and acts outside their territory.'[117] However, the PCIJ continued 'jurisdiction is strictly territorial' in the sense that jurisdiction 'cannot be exercised by a State outside its territory'.[118] In other words, State A cannot impose on the courts of State B to take jurisdiction in an international dispute. Yet, both states are free to regulate the reach of the judicial powers of their judiciary with 'a wide measure of discretion' and 'every state remains free to adopt the principles which it regards as best and most suitable'.[119] This explains why judicial powers of some states have a wider reach than others. Only international conventions can limit this freedom. Allocation of international jurisdiction by the unification of the rules means in practice that a state loses the freedom to decide in which cases it will take jurisdiction. By international agreement, the state will instead allow another state to have jurisdiction over the dispute. Judicial adjudication and state sovereignty are closely linked. Therefore, the unification of international jurisdiction rules is sometimes felt as an interference with state sovereignty and for that reason it remains a sensitive and political issue.

tive, comprehensive approach. This approach would attempt to move private international law forward from where it is now, without necessarily saying "we have to go all the way"'.

[115] Johnston and Powles, 'The Kings of the World', at 21 *et seq.*; Wautelet, 'What Has International Private Law Achieved?', at 59; H. Schack, *Internationales Zivilverfahrensrecht* (2006), § 330, at 121; J. Bertele, *Souveränität und Verfahrensrecht: Ein untersuchung der aus dem Völkerrecht ableitbaren Grenzen staatlicher extraterritoriale Jurisdiktion im Verfahrensrecht* (1998), at 51-54; A. Neale and M. Stephens, *International Business and National Jurisdiction* (1998), at 18-19; F. Mann, 'The Doctrine of International Jurisdiction', 111 *Recueil des cours* (1964), 1-162, at 9; and see in general A. Strauss, 'Beyond National Law: The Neglected Role of the International Law of Personal Jurisdiction in Domestic Courts', 36 *Harvard International Law Review* (1995), 373-424; C. McLachlan, 'The Influence of International Law on Civil Jurisdiction', in *Hague Yearbook of International Law* (1993), 125-144, J. Verheul, 'The "*forum actoris*" and International Law', in *Essays on International & Comparative Law in Honour of Judge Erades* (1983), 197-206; Miaja de la Muela, 'Les principes directeurs', at 27 *et seq.*; M. Akehurst, 'Jurisdiction in International Law', 46 *British Yearbook of International Law* (1974), 145-257; and J. Stevenson, 'The Relationship of Private International Law to Public International Law', 52 *Columbia Law Review* (1952), 561-588.

[116] Please note however that the case dealt with criminal proceedings.

[117] *S.S. Lotus* case, 7 September 1927, 1927 PCIJ Series A, No. 10, at 19.

[118] Ibid., at 18-19.

[119] Ibid., at 19. See also F. Marchadier, *Les objectifs généraux du droit international privé à l'épreuve de la Convention Européenne des droits de l'homme* (2007), at 226-227.

1.4.2 Jurisdiction Rules, Connecting Factors and Territoriality

Although international law does not impose any particular restriction on the regulation of jurisdiction,[120] traditionally international jurisdiction is based on a particular *connection* with the forum.[121] Apart from jurisdiction based on consent, most *connecting factors* are found in jurisdiction on the basis of a specific connection with the territory of the state[122] and therefore the allocation of jurisdiction has long been indisputably linked with the principle of territoriality.[123] Territoriality in the narrow sense of the word requires a 'physical connection' with the territory.[124] For the purpose of the present study, territoriality will be considered in its broadest sense: i.e. any connection between the territories of the forum can be jurisdiction-creating, as long as it can be 'localized' or is 'situated' in that forum.

Today, the effects of globalisation, the world-wide web and e-commerce on transnational relationships challenge the foundation of jurisdiction based on traditional principles of territoriality which require a physical connection with the forum. Several scholars demand a different approach to jurisdiction, for instance abandoning the territoriality principle in its narrow sense.[125]

1.4.3 Interaction with the Applicable Law

Ideally the competent court should be determined independently from the applicable law. The civil law tradition generally applies a strict separation between the jurisdictional question and the question of applicable law.[126] Contrastingly, other

---

[120] Except with respect to state immunity.

[121] Some countries use internal or territorial jurisdiction rules – allocating jurisdiction for national disputes within their territory – to determine whether their courts have international jurisdiction. This is also known as the 'transposition' of internal jurisdiction rules to international cases. See also Fawcett, *Declining Jurisdiction*, at 2. Other countries however have developed jurisdiction rules specifically designed for international disputes.

[122] In some cases jurisdiction has been based on the ground of 'personal connections' with the forum. Nationality-based jurisdiction is the best illustration of this.

[123] '*Rien n'est plus territorial que de rendre la justice. C'est là que chaque Etat est le plus chatouilleux de son indépendance. La justice ne peut être rendue que sur le territoire même de l'Etat auquel appartient l'autorité judiciaire instituée*', J.-P. Niboyet, *Cours de Droit International Privé Français* (1949), at 436. See also A. Huet, 'Compétence des Tribunaux français à l'égard des litiges internationaux', Fascicule 581-10-51 *Juris-Classeur Droit International* (2002), at 13; and R. Michaels, 'Territorial Jurisdiction after Territoriality', in *Globalisation and Jurisdiction* (2004), 106-130, at 128; Glenn, 'Unification of Law', at 162.

[124] Such as the U.S. territorialist theory of the *Pennoyer* Regime. See for more details, Chapter 5 which is dedicated to the situation in the U.S.

[125] See in general M. Berliri, 'Jurisdiction and the Internet, and European Regulation 44 of 2001', in *E-commerce: law and jurisdiction* (2003), 1-13 and R. Freer, 'American and European Approaches to Personal Jurisdiction Based upon Internet Activity', http://papers.ssrn.com/sol3/papers.cfm?abstract_id=1004887 (2007); but see Michaels, 'Territorial Jurisdiction', at 121 and 127 on 're-territorialization' of jurisdiction law; and Johnston and Powles, 'The Kings of the World', at 13 *et seq.*

[126] This is the classic concept of separation of the two questions or '*Eigenständigkeit der Zuständigkeitsregelung*' and contrasts with the *Gleichlauf* principle. H. Batiffol, 'Observations sur les liens entre la compétence judiciaire et la compétence législative', in *De conflictu legum* (1962), 55-66; Miaja de la Muela, 'Les principes directeurs', at 24-25 and 60; Von Mehren, 'Theory and Practice', at 36 and 157; and for general works, A. Heldrich, *Internationale Zuständigkeit und anwendbares Recht*

legal systems favour the *lex fori* rule, in which case the jurisdictional question is inseparably mingled with the applicable law question, and asserting jurisdiction to a particular forum automatically means applying the law of the court to the dispute. Several examples show that questions of applicable law sometimes interfere with the jurisdictional question and that in order to determine the competent court the applicable law to the dispute becomes relevant. Under English common law, for instance, the English courts are, under specific circumstances, competent when English law governs the contract.[127] In Europe, the court of the place of performance is competent to hear disputes related to contractual matters, but courts often need to turn to the applicable law to the contract (*lex causae*) in order to determine the place of performance.[128]

Some of the same connecting factors for jurisdiction are also to be found in conflict rules. However, two fundamental differences between the nature of conflict of law rules and jurisdiction rules should be underlined. First, with respect to international jurisdiction it is possible to have multiple competent forums to rule over an international dispute, but only one substantive (national) law can apply to it.[129] Moreover, and setting aside uniform rules of allocation of jurisdiction, national jurisdiction rules are unilateral, as they are unable to allocate jurisdiction to a foreign court, as opposed to conflicts of laws rules which are generally multilateral and can determine the application of foreign law.[130]

In this context, it is worth mentioning that the civil law tradition generally applies the principle of *jura novit curia*; the court is supposed to know the law, including foreign law. As a consequence, the court seized is expected to examine, investigate and apply foreign law when raised by a party and sometimes at its own motion.[131] This stands in contrast to the common law tradition where courts have a more passive role towards the application of foreign substantive law. The status of foreign law is considered a fact to be raised, pleaded and proved by the parties during proceedings.[132] In a world-wide context, the relevance of international jurisdiction varies as to the different attitudes towards the application of conflict of law rules.[133]

(1969) and P. Mayer, 'Droit international privé et le droit international public sous l'angle de la notion de la compétence', 68 *Revue critique de droit international privé* (1979), 1 *et seq.*, at 349 *et seq.*, at 537 *et seq.*

127 Rule 6.20(5)(c) CPR. This is also called *forum legis*. See Chapter 4 of this book.

128 See Art. 5(1) of the Brussels Regulation.

129 P. Lagarde, 'Le principe de proximité dans le droit internationale privé contemporain. Cours général de droit international privé', 196 *Recueil des cours* (1986), 9-238, at 129-130; and Lowenfeld, *The Quest for Reasonableness*, at 3.

130 See also Lagarde, 'Le principe de proximité', at 130.

131 According to J. Mance, 'The Future of Private International Law', 1 *Journal of Private International Law* (2005), 185-195, at 191: 'Common law courts expect parties to plead and by expert evidence prove foreign law. German courts tend to look to academics and institutes, such as the Max Planck Institute for opinions on the relevant foreign law.'

132 See C. Pejovic, 'Civil Law and Common Law: Two Different Paths Leading to the Same Goal', 32(3) *Victoria University of Wellington Law Review* (2001), 817-841, at 831, when foreign law is not proven, then the *lex fori* is the default applicable law.

133 Some scholars have identified a general 'homeward trend' in the determination of the applicable law, arguing that the *lex fori* is more often applied. The result is that 'the designation of the

1.5 Problem Statement and Objective

At present, the road to international court litigation remains a very uncertain one. Apart from regional unification and unification in specific areas, the current state of affairs of jurisdiction rules in international court litigation is characterized by its complexity and does not provide legal certainty, predictability and justice which are needed by the international community in this dynamic world. Although parties can either choose a specific court or an arbitral tribunal to settle their dispute, there are still many cases where litigators will be left in the hands of ordinary jurisdiction rules.[134] There is an evident necessity for uniform rules governing issues of international jurisdiction in international disputes in general and in cross-border commercial contract disputes in particular.

The objective of this study is to contribute to a better understanding of the different approaches to international jurisdiction and its aim is to explore the possibilities of reconciling these differences in order to come to common grounds of jurisdiction in international commercial litigation. More specifically, by building a bridge of mutual understanding between common law and civil law traditions by way of analysing existing jurisdiction rules emanating from these traditions, this study will examine to what extent acceptable uniform jurisdiction rules can be found for disputes arising out of cross-border commercial contracts.

1.6 Scope

This study will focus on all jurisdiction rules to which parties, individuals and corporate entities, involved in disputes arising out of regular commercial contractual relationships can be subjected, for which purpose each jurisdictional provision asserting jurisdiction over disputes arising out of a contract will be studied. Furthermore, it involves examining rules of *general jurisdiction* designed to establish jurisdiction regardless of the nature of the claim; rules of *special jurisdiction* primarily designed for jurisdiction over contractual matters, as well as provisions establishing jurisdiction on the basis of commercial activities carried out by individual and corporate defendants. The complexity of corporate entities and large economic operators requires detailed study of international jurisdiction over corporations. However, this study is not limited to business-to-business (B2B) contracts and will include claims involving natural persons carrying out business activities and concluding commercial contracts, as long as they are not consumers.[135]

The scope of this study is limited to 'regular' or 'general' commercial contracts. Specific or 'protected' contracts, such as consumer, employment and insurance

applicable law is now coming to depend on jurisdictional standards'. See for example, Th. de Boer, 'Forum Preferences in Contemporary European Conflicts Law: The Myth of a "Neutral Choice"', in *Festschrift für Erik Jayme* (2004), 39-55, at 47 and 51.

134 Either because the parties have not agreed on a dispute resolution clause, or when one of the parties successfully invokes the invalidity of a dispute resolution clause. Many arbitral and court proceedings involve the preliminary question on the validity of the dispute settlement clause.

135 See below. Jurisdiction rules in consumer contracts fall outside the scope of the present study, but see for an exhaustive overview J. Hill, *Cross-border consumer contracts* (2008).

contracts will not be covered and given the specific legal problems and jurisdictional implications arising out of e-commerce, international jurisdiction over disputes arising out of e-contracts will also not be discussed in the present study. Excluded are also (contractual) claims concerning infringements of intellectual property rights,[136] admiralty or maritime matters, insolvency and related matters, (contractual) rights *in rem* in immoveable property and tenancies of immoveable property, the carriage of passengers and goods[137] and family matters.[138]

Since this study is limited to claims originating out of a contractual relationship between the parties, it excludes any dispute arising out of tortuous acts, whether they involve product liability, personal injury tort or environmental torts or claims based on human rights violation.[139] For the same reason, (anti-) trust claims and claims for damages based on an act giving rise to criminal proceedings will be excluded.

Any jurisdiction based on consent or prorogation of jurisdiction by way of a choice of court agreement included in international contracts is left outside the scope of this study since this is covered by The Hague Convention on Choice of Court Agreements. Finally, and, notwithstanding their practical importance, the same goes for provisional and protective measures. Although jurisdiction rules of a more procedural nature such as jurisdiction over third parties, multiple defendants – or class actions, related actions, counter-claims and *lis pendens* also affect the exercise of jurisdiction over contractual claims, they will not be considered as such. Nor will jurisdiction arising out of necessity, the *forum necessitatis*, be dealt with either.

The question of recognition and enforcement of foreign judgements around the world is indisputably linked to the jurisdictional question, but is not the main concern of this study. As this book is principally limited to examining direct jurisdiction rules, it excludes issues of recognition and enforcement and indirect jurisdiction rules as requirements for the recognition of judgements.[140]

---

[136] This includes the validity of intellectual property rights other than copyright and related rights.

[137] This study will exclude any specialized conventions dealing with areas relating to international carriage, transport and maritime matters, such as the Rhine Navigation Convention of 17 October 1868; the Warsaw Convention 1929 for the Unification of Certain Rules Relating to International Carriage by Air and protocols; the Brussels Convention 1952 on Certain Rules concerning Civil Jurisdiction in Matters of Collision; the Brussels Convention 1952 on Certain Rules relating to the Arrest of Sea-going Ships; the Geneva 1956 Convention on the Contract for the International Carriage of Goods by Road (CMR Convention); the International Convention 1969 on Civil Liability for Oil Pollution Damage and protocols; the Bern Convention 1980 Concerning International Transport by Rail and protocols; the Montreal 1999 Convention for the Unification of Certain Rules for International Carriage by Air; the Geneva 1999 International Convention on Arrest of Ships; the Hamburg Rules 1978 and the Rotterdam Rules 2009.

[138] By analogy of the scope of the Hague Convention on the Choice of Court Agreement and the Brussels Regulation, this includes the status and legal capacity of natural persons; maintenance obligations; other family law matters, including matrimonial property regimes and other rights or obligations arising out of marriage or similar relationships; and wills and succession.

[139] See in this respect the ECJ's *Lechouritou* decision of 15 February 2007, C-292/05 ECR I-1519.

[140] Also discussed above in Sect. 1.3.4.

Narrowing down the present study to conflicts arising out of contractual disputes is first of all justified by the fact that there are an extensive number of cases dealing with jurisdiction over claims relating to contractual matters. This not only indicates the need for uniform jurisdiction rules in contractual disputes, but also the lack of legal certainty and predictability in international commercial disputes.[141] Second, as explained above, the work of the HCCH should be continued with a step-by-step approach. Progressive unification starting with claims arising out of contracts will have more chances of success, as contractual disputes are closest to the freedom of contract and the self-determination of parties' contractual rights. Contractual parties are 'linked by a voluntary bond'.[142]

1.7 The Comparative Approach

> 'Unification of law cannot be achieved by simply conjuring up an ideal law on any topic and hoping to have it adopted. One must first find what is common to the jurisdictions concerned and incorporate that in the uniform law. Where there are areas of difference, one must reconcile them either by adopting the best existing variant or by finding, through comparative methods, a new solution which is better and more easily applied than any of the existing ones.'[143]

The chosen approach for the present study is the comparative approach.[144] Traditionally, the 'universal legal science'[145] of comparative law is a valuable instrument in private international law.[146] On numerous occasions, the negotiators at The Hague Conference have expressed the need for a comparative study to

[141] See Sect. 1.3.4 and see M. Keyes, *Jurisdiction in International Litigation* (2005), at 159.

[142] See also U. Magnus and P. Mankowski, eds., *Brussels I Regulation* (2007), § 23, at 100, and § 27, at 101: 'Consensual transactions are contracts. Obligations voluntarily assumed by agreements are contractual by their nature.'

[143] Zweigert and Kötz, *Comparative Law*, at 24.

[144] Ibid., at 2: 'Comparative law is the comparison of different legal systems of the world' with an extra dimension of internationalism. This study will therefore not take the approach of legal theory analyzing the role of the Sovereign State with respect to international jurisdiction. For an extensive study in this field see the works of Bertele, *Souveränität und Verfahrensrecht*, specifically at 112-193; T. Pfeiffer, *Internationale Zuständigkeit und prozessuale Gerechtigkeit: Die internationale Zuständigkeit im Zivilprozess zwischen effektivem Rechtsschutz und nationaler Zuständigkeitspolitik* (1995); J. Schröder, *Internationale Zuständigkeit: Entwurf eines Systems von Zuständigkeitsinteressen im zwischenstaatlichen Privatverfahrensrecht, aufgrund rechtshistorischer, rechtsvergleichender und rechtspolitischer Betrachtungen* (1971); J. Hudault, 'Sens et Portée de la compétence du juge naturel dans l'ancien droit français', 61 *Revue critique de droit international privé* (1972), 27-54 and 249-268; P. Neuhaus, *Grundbegriffe des Internationalen Privatrecht* (1976), in particular at 418; Ph. Thery, *Pouvoir juridictionnel et compétence* (1981); De Vareilles-Sommières, *La compétence internationale de l'état*; E. Pataut, *Principe de souveraineté et conflit de juridictions* (1999); and R. Michaels, 'Globalizing Savigny? The State in Savigny's Private International Law and the Challenge of Europeanization and Globalization', 74 *Duke Law School Legal Studies Paper* (2005), available at SSRN: http://ssrn.com/abstract=796228. See also the observations of Von Mehren, 'Theory and Practice', at 150-154.

[145] Zweigert and Kötz, *Comparative Law*, at 46.

[146] Ibid., at 6; Fauvarque-Cosson, 'Comparative Law and Conflict of Laws: Allies or Enemies?', at 409; and Miaja de la Muela, 'Les principes directeurs', at 12.

come to a better understanding of each other's jurisdictional systems.[147] Such a comparative 'education' is needed in order to overcome 'impatience', scepticism, legal pessimism or the so-called 'realism'.[148] Comparative law contributes to the (systematic) unification of law.[149] Although, it has been argued that comparative law and conflict of laws have different objectives, since comparative law seeks international unification and conflict of law rules seeks to 'coordinate' different substantive laws,[150] the opposite is true with respect to the 'jurisdictional pillar' of private international law. Especially because the objective is to find common grounds, comparative law is certainly not an 'enemy', but an ally in the unification process.[151] The ability of comparatists to '[free] legal thought from inhibiting conceptual constraints by paving the way to new ways of reading the law'[152] is crucial in such a process.[153]

Due to the complexity of sources of jurisdiction rules, a rule-based comparison will be carried out at three levels, namely at the national, regional and international level. At the national level, jurisdiction rules of the following individual countries will be analysed. France has been chosen not only because it is generally considered to be the 'parent system' of the Romanistic Systems in Continental Europe, but also because it uses the highly controversial nationality-based jurisdiction rules.[154] The German jurisdictional regime is indispensable, not only as the 'parent system' of the Germanic legal family, but also for its particular 'property-based' jurisdiction. The particularities and originality of the Swiss jurisdictional system justify a brief examination of this so-called 'affiliated' legal system of the Germanic family.[155] Although, the 2001 reform of the Dutch Code of Civil Procedure also partially followed the jurisdictional scheme of the Brussels Model, the Dutch system has retained some features typical of the assertion of jurisdiction to courts in The Netherlands.[156]

The common law tradition will be represented by England and the U.S.[157] The selection of these national systems is justified by the fact that they represent the

[147] Baumgartner, *The Proposed Hague Convention*, at 70, referring to a mutual comparative education for the successful conclusion of the proposed Convention.

[148] Reimann, 'Parochialism', fn. 66, at 385.

[149] Zweigert and Kötz, *Comparative Law*, at 16.

[150] Fauvarque-Cosson, 'Comparative Law and Conflict of Laws: Allies or Enemies?', at 407. See also A. von Mehren, 'The Role of Comparative Law in Practice of International Law', in *Festchrift für Karl Neumayer zum 65. Geburtstag* (1985), 479-486, at 483.

[151] The title of the article by Fauvarque-Cosson, 'Comparative Law and Conflict of Laws: Allies or Enemies?', makes a reference to this.

[152] Muir Watt, 'La fonction subversive', at 504 (English summary).

[153] See also Von Mehren, 'The Role of Comparative Law', at 486; Zweigert and Kötz, *Comparative Law*, at 16.

[154] Other systems traditionally belonging to the 'Romanistic' legal system, such as those of Italy and Spain, will be examined to illustrate the impact of the Brussels Model on national jurisdiction systems.

[155] Zweigert and Kötz, *Comparative Law*, at 41.

[156] The Dutch jurisdictional system is both of Germanic and Romanistic origin.

[157] Australian jurisdiction law will be, where relevant, considered as a variation on the traditional English common law system.

two main legal traditions, the common law and the civil law tradition.[158] These two legal traditions are at the origin of many other jurisdictional regimes around the world.[159]

The regional unification in Europe will be discussed in an exhaustive study of the Brussels Regulation. As far as relevant, the uniform jurisdiction derived from the regional organizations in Latin America will also be taken into account, but will not be dealt with separately.[160] Finally, at the international level the efforts of unification within the HCCH, the ILA and the IDI will also be examined.

1.8 Outline

This book could be divided in two parts: namely, the first part provides a successive, rather than a 'simultaneous', description of the selected jurisdictional regimes,[161] the second part deals with the comparison, analysis, explanation and assessment of the jurisdictional regimes.

In Chapter 2 the uniform jurisdiction rules as found in the Brussels Regulation No. 44/2001 representing the regional unification in Europe are outlined and this is followed by a description of national jurisdiction rules. Chapter 3 sets out with national reports describing the civil law tradition in France, Germany, Switzerland, and The Netherlands. The traditional English common law rules on jurisdiction are explained in Chapter 4, followed by the regulation of international jurisdiction in the United States of America in Chapter 5. In order to get a proper understanding of the diversity of U.S. jurisdiction law, the states of California, Florida, Michigan and New York have been selected as illustrations.[162]

The analysis commences in the second part with Chapter 6, in which the fundamental differences and contrasting approaches to international jurisdiction are analysed and explained. This chapter also develops parameters and assessment criteria that uniform rules should meet. Chapter 7 provides a detailed comparison of individual jurisdiction rules and connecting factors as encountered in the jurisdictional systems surveyed in the first part. Chapter 8 compares the discretionary powers and correction devices found in some legal systems. The comparison carried out in Chapters 7 and 8 will also consider, where relevant, the provisions of the Drafts of The Hague Convention on Judgements and the recommendations of the ILA and the IDI. Additionally, on the basis of the parameters and assessment criteria developed in Chapter 6, jurisdiction rules and correction devices are evaluated in order to find common grounds for uniform rules. The final chapter, Chapter 9, draws conclusions and suggests uniform jurisdiction rules for international commercial disputes.

---

[158] Zweigert and Kötz, *Comparative Law*, at 41; and Kokkini-Iatridou, *Inleiding tot het rechtsvergelijkende onderzoek*, at 137.

[159] This includes the mixed regimes of Quebec, Japan, China and Israel.

[160] Any uniform jurisdiction rules elaborated within MERCOSUR will be dealt with in Chapter 7, see the outline in Sect. 1.8.

[161] See Zweigert and Kötz, *Comparative Law*, at 43.

[162] See Chapter 5 for the selection criteria.

Chapter 2

UNIFORM JURISDICTION RULES IN EUROPE: THE BRUSSELS REGULATION

This chapter deals with the Brussels Regulation 44/2001 on Jurisdiction and the Recognition and Enforcement of Judgements in Civil and Commercial Matters.[1] Along with its predecessors, the 1968 Brussels Convention and the 1988 Lugano Convention,[2] the Regulation represents the Brussels jurisdictional regime or 'Brussels Model' on uniform jurisdiction rules. This model unifies rules of jurisdiction in civil and commercial matters and gaurantees the reciprocal recognition and enforcement of judgements between Member States and the free movement of judgements on EU territory.[3] The fact that the Regulation replaces national jurisdiction rules of both civil and common law tradition is of particular interest for the present study.

2.1 From the Convention to the Regulation

The Brussels jurisdictional regime finds its origins in the 1968 Brussels Convention,[4] and is considered the pioneer of further European unification in international jurisdiction. European economic integration was thought to benefit from the free movement of judgements within the territory of the European Community,[5] and this was considered easier to achieve by incorporating concrete direct jurisdiction rules in the Brussels Convention.[6]

[1] Council Regulation (EC) No. 44/2001 of 22 December 2000, OJ 2001 L 12; corrected by 301R0044R(01)/(0), amended by 302R1496 of 29 August 2002 [hereafter 'Brussels Regulation'].

[2] The Lugano Convention is currently applicable in Iceland, Norway and Switzerland.

[3] See also C-398/92 *Mund & Fester v. Hatrex*, [1994] ECR I-467, para. 11; Opinion AG Léger in C-281/02 *Owusu v. Jackson*, [2005] ECR I-1383; Opinion AG Tesauro in C-398/92 *Mund & Fester v. Hatrex*, [1994] ECR I-467, para. 190; see also P. Schlosser, 'A New Dimension of Human Rights' Consideration in Civil Procedure', *Rivista di diritto internazionale privato e internazionale* (1995), 31-40, at 32-33 and E. Peel, '*Forum Non Conveniens* and European Ideals', *Lloyd's Maritime and Commercial Law Quarterly* (2005), 363-377, at 367, emphasizing that the Brussels Model is primarily a 'judgements convention' guaranteeing the recognition of judgements.

[4] See Chapter 1, Sect. 1.3.1, fn. 50.

[5] See the official Expert Report of P. Jenard, 'Report on the Convention on Jurisdiction and the Enforcement of Judgments in Civil and Commercial Matters of 27 September 1968', OJ 1979 C 59 (1979) [hereafter Jenard Report], 1-65, at 3, and the current Recital 2 of the Regulation's Preamble. See also the ECJ's statements in C-260/97 *Unibank v. Christensen*, [1999] ECR I-3715, para. 14, referring to Case 148/84 *Brasserie du Pêcheur*, [1985] ECR 1981, para. 16; C-414/92 *Solo Kleinmotoren v. Boch*, [1994] ECR I-2237, para. 20; C-420/97 *Leathertex v. Bodetex*, [1999] ECR I-6747, para. 43; C-365/88 *Hagen v. Zeehage*, [1990] ECR I-1845, para. 17; and C-68/93 *Shevill and Others*, [1995] ECR I-415, para. 35. See also J. Pontier and E. Burg, *EU Principles on Jurisdiction and Recognition and Enforcement of Judgments in Civil and Commercial Matters* (2004), at 27.

[6] The original Art. 220 of the Rome Convention establishing the European Economic Community was the initial legal basis for the inter-governmental negotiations for the Brussels Convention. See H.

The Convention went into force on 1 February 1973 in the six founding Member States[7] and was accompanied by the official Expert Report of Jenard.[8] A uniform and autonomous interpretation of the Convention was guaranteed by a protocol enabling the ECJ to interpret its provisions.[9] New Member States to the European Community were required to accept the Brussels Convention as part of the Community's legal order and necessary adjustments or modifications were made by way of special 'accession' conventions.[10] Three Accession Conventions followed and brought some important modifications to the original text.[11] In 1988, a 'paral-

---

Duintjer Tebbens, 'The English Court of Appeal in *Re Harrods*: An Unwelcome Interpretation of the Brussels Convention', in *Law and Reality: Essays on National and International Procedural Law in Honour of Cornelis Carel Albert Voskuil* (1992), 47-61, at 47, referring to A. Struycken, *Naar eenheid van rechtsbedeling in Europa* (1971).

[7] These were France, Germany, Italy and the Benelux.

[8] Jenard Report; and see Briggs, *Civil Jurisdiction*, § 1.14, at 10-11. See also for important and early commentaries on the Convention, among others, L. Bartlett, 'Full Faith and Credit Comes to the Common Market: An Analysis of the Provisions of the Convention on Jurisdiction and the Enforcement of Judgements in Civil and Commercial Matters', 24 *The International and Comparative Law Quarterly* (1975), 44-60; G. Droz, *Compétence judiciaire et effets des jugements dans le Marché Commun: Etude de la Convention de Bruxelles du 27 septembre 1968* (1972); G. Droz, 'Entrée en vigueur de la Convention de Bruxelles concernant la compétence judiciaire et l'exécution des décisions en matière et commerciale', 62 *Revue critique de droit international privé* (1973), 21-41; H. Gothot and D. Holleaux, *La Convention de Bruxelles du 27 septembre 1968* (1985); K. Nadelmann, 'The Outer World and the Common Market Expert's Draft on Recognition of Judgements', *Common Market Law Review* (1967), 409-420; Struycken, *Naar eenheid van rechtsbedeling in Europa*; A. Struycken and J. Krings, 'The Rules of Jurisdiction in the EEC Convention on Jurisdiction and the Enforcement of Judgements in Civil and Commercial Matters', 25 *Netherlands International Law Review* (1978), 254-363; M. Weser, *La convention communautaire sur la compétence judiciaire et l'exécution des décisions: Etude des droits internes et des traités bilatéraux des Etats contractants* (1975); M. Weser, 'La libre circulation des jugements dans le Marché Commun', 1966-1969 *Travaux du Comité Français de Droit International Privé* (1969), 353-377; M. Weser, 'Les conflits de juridictions dans le cadre du Marché Commun. Difficultés et remèdes (suite et fin)', *Revue critique de droit international privé* (1961), 105-129.

[9] Protocol signed on 3 June 1971 and entered into force on 1 September 1975, published in OJ 1972 L 299. See on the importance of the ECJ's interpretation, Pontier and Burg, *EU Principles on Jurisdiction*, at 5. See also C-125/92 *Mulox v. Geels*, [1993] ECR 4075, para. 11, in which the ECJ states that an 'autonomous interpretation alone is capable of ensuring uniform application of the Convention'.

[10] Art. 63 Brussels Convention. The modifications were especially significant for the accession of the U.K., Ireland and Denmark. See T. Kruger, *Civil Jurisdiction Rules of the EU and Their Impact on Third States* (2008), § 1.21-24, at 19-21; P. Stone, *EU Private International Law Harmonization of Laws* (2006), at 15; and Briggs, *Civil Jurisdiction*, § 1.06, at 7. On the question of whether the Brussels Convention was considered *acquis communautaire*, see in general A. Struycken, 'Les conséquences de l'intégration européenne sur le développement du droit international privé', 232 *Recueil des cours* (1992), 256-383.

[11] On 9 October 1978 the first Accession Convention with the U.K., Ireland and Denmark was signed and published in OJ 1978 L 304/77, accompanied by the official expert report of P. Schlosser, 'Report on the Convention on the Accession of the United Kingdom of Denmark, Ireland and the United Kingdom of Great Britain and Northern Ireland to the Convention on Jurisdiction and the Enforcement of Judgments in Civil and Commercial Matters and to the Protocol on Its Interpretation by the Court of Justice', OJ 1979 C 59. As a result of Greece's accession to the EC in 1981, a second Accession Convention was signed on 25 October 1982, and entered into force on 1 April 1989. It is published in OJ 1982 L 388/1 and is accompanied by the Explanatory Report of M. Kerameus and M. Evrigenis, which is published in OJ 1986 C 298/1. The Convention of San Sebastian of 26 May 1989

lel' convention, with provisions almost identical to those of the Brussels Convention was drafted for countries of the EFTA in Lugano.[12] When in 1995, Austria, Finland and Sweden joined the European Union a fourth Accession Convention was signed. As a result 15 Member States adhered to the Brussels Convention in 1996.[13] At the end of 1997, an *ad hoc* working group, composed of representatives of all the EU Member States and of the three remaining EFTA States,[14] started revising both the Brussels and the Lugano Conventions and it completed its work in April 1999.

When Article 65 of the EC Treaty, as introduced by the Treaty of Amsterdam, went into force on 1 May 1999, the Area of Home and Justice Affairs was transferred under the Community's legislative control.[15] As a consequence, the European Community now has at its disposal community instruments that enable it to take further measures in the field of judicial cooperation in civil matters and in the development of a European Judicial Area (EJA).[16] The Brussels Regulation was the first of a series of Regulations leading to the 'europeanisation' or 'communitarization' of Private International Law.[17] The Brussels Regulation 44/2001 was formally adopted on 30 November 2000 and went into force on 1 March 2002.[18] It contains some significant changes in comparison to the original 1968 text, especially with respect to contract jurisdiction, and currently it is applied in all 27

refers to the accession of Spain and Portugal, published in OJ 1989 L 285/1, with the Explanatory Report of Cruz/Real in OJ 1990 C 189/35.

[12] The Lugano Convention on Jurisdiction and the Recognition and Enforcement of Judgments in Civil and Commercial Matters, published in OJ 1988 L 319/9. See P. Jenard and G. Möller, 'Report on the Lugano Convention on Jurisdiction and the Enforcement of Judgments in Civil and Commercial Matters', OJ 1990 C 189/57 [hereafter Jenard-Möller Report].

[13] Published in OJ 1997 C15/01; an explanatory report was not published. Several modifications brought on by the subsequent Accession Conventions, led to the publication of a consolidated version of the Brussels Convention, published in OJ 1998 C 027/28, corrected by OJ 2000 C 160/1.

[14] These are Iceland, Norway and Switzerland.

[15] Art. 65 in conjunction with 61(c) states: '... in order to establish progressively an area of freedom, security and justice the Council shall adopt measures in the field of judicial cooperation in civil matters as provided for in Article 65'; and under (b) it states that this includes 'promoting the compatibility of the rules applicable in the Member States concerning the conflict of laws and of jurisdiction', EC Treaty (consolidated text), OJ 2002 C 325. See on the competence of the EU, Magnus and Mankowski, eds., *Brussels I Regulation*, § 35, at 21.

[16] This was the result of the Tampere Summit in October 1999, see W. Kennett, 'Current Developments: Private International Law – The Brussels I Regulation', 50 *The International and Comparative Law Quarterly* (2001), 725-737. It was in line with the European Commission's Communication '*Towards a greater efficiency in obtaining and enforcing judgements in the European Union*' of 26 November 1997; COM(97)609 final – OJ 1998 C 33.

[17] See Baumgartner, *The Proposed Hague Convention*, at 62-66; and on the 'communitarization' of the Brussels Convention see G. Droz and H. Gaudemet-Tallon, 'La transformation de la Convention de Bruxelles du 27 septembre 1968 en Règlement du Conseil concernant la compétence judiciaire, la reconnaissance et l'exécution des décisions en matière civile et commerciale', *Revue critique de droit international privé* (2001), 601-652, at 606.

[18] By virtue of Art. 66 of the Regulation, it applies to all proceedings instituted after 1 March 2002 in the original 14 Member States; the Brussels Convention applies to proceedings instituted before that date. Proceedings instituted under the Convention but rendered after 1 March 2002, will be recognized under the Regulation's provisions on recognition and enforcement. This is called the restricted retroactivity of the Regulation.

EU Member States,[19] including Denmark, which has a special position.[20] The *ad hoc* working group revised the text of the Lugano Convention in order to align the 1988 Convention with the Regulation's modifications.[21] The European Council requested the ECJ to give an opinion on the question whether the conclusion of a new Lugano Convention by EU Member States would fall within the exclusive competence of the European Community or whether such competence was to be shared with the Member States. In February 2006, the ECJ gave its opinion affirming that the conclusion of a new Lugano Convention concerns the exclusive competence of the European Community and opens the door to the entry into force of a new Lugano Convention, quite similar to the Brussels Regulation.[22] As a consequence of the ECJ's opinion, the regulation of international jurisdiction in its widest sense now falls under the exclusive competence of the European Community, which accentuates the function of the Brussels Regulation as a community instrument.

The Brussels Regulation supersedes bilateral agreements between Member States,[23] i.e. the various versions of the Brussels Conventions and the Lugano Con-

---

[19] Like any other Regulation, the Brussels Regulation, by virtue of Art. 65 EC Treaty (consolidated version) has become part of the *acquis communautaire* and is therefore automatically applicable to the new Member States of Cyprus, the Czech Republic, Estonia, Hungary, Latvia, Lithuania, Malta, Poland, Slovakia and Slovenia (Accession Treaty published in OJ 2003 L 236). The Regulation entered into force on 1 May 2004. Bulgaria and Romania acceded to the EU and the Brussels Regulation entered into force for these countries on 1 January 2007 (Accession Treaty published in OJ 2005 L 157). On the temporal scope of the Brussels Regulation see also Stone, *EU Private International Law*, at 41-43.

[20] Denmark opted out of Title IV of the EC Treaty, including Art. 65, as stated in Arts. 1 and 2 of the Fifth Protocol to the EC Treaty (consolidated) concerning the position of Denmark. As a result, community instruments adopted in the field of judicial cooperation in civil matters do not apply to Denmark. This same right was reserved for the U.K. and Ireland under Art. 3 of that same Protocol, but in contrast to Denmark, these countries 'opted in' by expressing 'their wish to take part in the adoption and application of measures in this Area'. See A. Dicey, J. Morris *et al.*, *The Conflict of Laws* (2006), Vol. 1, § 11-015, at 310; and see the Regulation's Preamble (paras. 20-21). A parallel international agreement between the EC and Denmark was concluded, and as of 1 July 2007, the Council Decision 2006/325/EC of 27 April 2006 concerning the conclusion of the Agreement between the European Community and the Kingdom of Denmark on Jurisdiction and the Recognition and Enforcement of Judgments in Civil and Commercial Matters extends the provisions of the Brussels Regulation to Denmark (OJ 2006 L 120/22). The uniformity between community instruments is now restored and Denmark is expected to accept future amendments by the Council. See http://ec.europa.eu/civiljustice/news/archive/agreement_danemark_en.htm#en.

[21] The new text is to be found at http://ec.europa.eu/civiljustice/news/docs/draft_lugano_convention_en.pdf, or http://register.consilium.europa.eu/pdf/en/07/st12/st12247.en07.pdf. See Council Decision on the signing on behalf of the Community of 10 September 2007, 12247/07, JUSTCIV 218.

[22] See Opinion 1/03 of 7 February 2006. See also Mance, 'The Future', at 195.

[23] Art. 69 Regulation, including rectification with respect to bilateral agreements with the U.K., published in OJ 2001 L 307. Under Art. 59 of the Brussels Convention, Member States were allowed, even encouraged, to conclude bilateral agreements with third states, agreeing not to recognize judgements rendered on the basis of an exorbitant jurisdiction rule of another Member State against a domiciliary of that third state. See Jenard Report, at 61-62. Art. 72 Regulation states that it shall not affect these bilateral agreements concluded prior to the Regulation's entry into force, but does however not allow any new ones! This implies that the bilateral convention between the U.K. and Australia will remain in force, but a new agreement with New Zealand cannot be realized. See also Droz and Gaudemet-Tallon, 'La transformation', at 621-622 and H. Gaudemet-Tallon, *Compétence et exécution des jugements en Europe; Règlement n. 44/2001 Conventions de Bruxelles et de Lugano* (2002), at 20.

vention for those EFTA countries who acceded to the EU.[24] With respect to the uniform interpretation of the Regulation, a protocol is no longer needed to enable the ECJ to give preliminary rulings,[25] as it now derives its competence directly from Article 68(1) of the Treaty establishing the European Community (TEC).[26] Under this Article, and in contrast to the Protocol, only courts or tribunals of a Member State against whose decision no judicial remedy is available under national law are entitled to request a preliminary ruling from the ECJ.[27] The importance of such a supranational institution interpreting the Regulation is crucial in order to come to a uniform application and the ECJ indeed plays a very important and active role in the unification process.[28]

Although the structure and the majority of the jurisdiction rules of the Brussels Regulation are for the greater part identical to the Brussels and Lugano Conventions, some jurisdiction rules, especially those related to contractual matters, have been considerably modified.[29] However, decisions of the ECJ and the Convention's Explanatory Reports preceding the Regulation remain of great importance for the interpretation of the Brussels Model: the ECJ's interpretation of the unmodified provisions of the Brussels Convention are still of great relevance and the continuity between the instruments is ensured by paragraph 19 of the Regulation's Preamble. With respect to the modified provisions, until now few preliminary questions on the interpretation of the Regulation's new provisions have been addressed to the ECJ.[30] It is however to be expected that the ECJ will play the same important role

---

[24] In Art. 68(1) Regulation it states that an exception is made for 'the territories of the Member States which fall within the territorial scope of the [Brussels] Convention and which are excluded from this Regulation pursuant to Article 299 of the Treaty'.

[25] As described under ex Art. 234 TEC (ex Art. 177).

[26] See Dicey, Morris *et al.*, *Conflict of Laws*, § 2.03-2.04, at 26-27.

[27] Art. 68(1) TEC. See also Gaudemet-Tallon, *Compétence en Europe*, at 22.

[28] See in general H. Duintjer Tebbens, 'Judicial Interpretation of the 1988 Lugano Convention on Jurisdiction and Judgements in the Light of its Brussels Matrix: The Convergence Confirmed', in *Yearbook of Private International Law* (2001), 1-25; K. Vandekerckhove, 'De interpretatie van europees bevoegdheids- en executierecht', in *Het nieuwe Europese Internationale Privaatrecht: Van verdrag naar verordening* (2001), 11-29.

[29] See for the principal differences, A. Stadler, 'From the Brussels Convention to Regulation 44/2001: Cornerstones of a European Law of Civil Procedure', 42 *Common Market Law Review* (2005), 1637-1661, at 1639-1643; Magnus and Mankowski, eds., *Brussels I Regulation*, § 25, at 16-17; Dicey, Morris *et al.*, *Conflict of Laws*, § 11-019, at 311, for the interpretation of the Lugano Convention see § 11-063-065.

[30] Few questions have been addressed to the ECJ concerning the Regulation: C-386/05 *Color Drack*, [2007] ECR 0, dealing with Art. 5(1); C-103/05 *Reisch v. Kiesel*, [2006] ECR I-6827, dealing with Art. 6(1); C-283/05 *ASML v. SEMIS*, [2006] ECR I-12041, dealing with Art. 34(2); C-463/06 *FBTO Schadeverzekeringen v. Jack Odenbreit*, [2007] ECR I-11321, dealing with Art. 9(1)(b) and 11(2); *Glaxosmithkline et Laboratoires Glaxosmithkline v. Jean-Pierre Rouard* (C-462/06), OJ 2008 C 171, at 7, judgement of 22 May 2008, dealing with Art. 6(1). Several pending Cases C-533/07 *Falco Privatstiftung and Rabitsch v. Gisela Weller-Lindhorst*, OJ 2008 C 37, at 15, lodged on 29 November 2007 by *Oberster Gerichtshof* (Austria) on whether the right to use a right arising out of a licence agreement regards 'the provision of services' under Art. 5(1)(b). See the Advocate General Trstenjak's opinion of 27 January 2007. On the territorial scope see C-185/07 *Riunione Adriatica Di Sicurta SpA (RAS)/West Tankers Inc.*, OJ 2007 C 155, preliminary ruling from the House of Lords U.K. of 2 April 2007, decision rendered on10 February 2009; C-111/08 *SCT Industri Aktiebolag i likvidation v.*

in the interpretation of the Regulation. Unfortunately, an explanatory report concerning the Regulation is not available.[31]

2.2 Scope and Structure

2.2.1 International Element

The Regulation determines jurisdiction 'within the international legal order'[32] over disputes arising out of 'international relationships'.[33] The 'existence of an international element' is required, but the scope is not only limited to 'intra-community relations'.[34] According to the ECJ, 'the international nature of the legal relationship at issue need not necessarily derive' from mere connections with a number of Member States, either because of 'the subject-matter of the proceedings or the respective domiciles of the parties',[35] but the international nature also exists when the dispute involves a Member State and a non-Member State.[36] For example when the claimant and the defendant are domiciled in the same Member State, but the events at issue occurred in a non-Member State.[37]

Alpenblume Aktiebolag, OJ 2008 C 116, at 16, preliminary ruling from Sweden of 12 March 2008; C-347/08 *Vorarlberger Gebietskrankenkasse v. WGV-Schwäbische Allgemeine Versicherungs AG*, OJ 2008 C 272, at 11, preliminary ruling from the *Landesgericht Feldkirch* (Austria), lodged on 28 July 2008 dealing with Art. 9 (insurance contracts); C-167/08 *Draka NK Cables and others v. Omnipol Ltd*, OJ 2008 C 183, at 12, preliminary ruling from the *Hof van Cassatie* Belgium, lodged on 21 April 2008 dealing with Art. 43(1); C-189/08 *Zuid-Chemie B.V. v. Philippo's Mineralenfabriek N.V./S.A.*, OJ 2008 C 183, at 13, preliminary ruling from the *Hoge Raad* The Netherlands, lodged on 8 May 2008 concerning the interpretation of Art. 5(3).

[31] An explanatory report was however written by Fausto Pocar as rapporteur for the Working Party on the Revision of the Brussels I Convention but will probably remain unpublished due to the conversion of the draft revised convention into the Brussels Regulation. See on this point Droz and Gaudemet-Tallon, 'La transformation', at 607, arguing that explanatory reports are not common practice for community regulations.

[32] C-89/91 *Shearson Lehmann Hutton Inc. v. TVB*, [1993] ECR I-139, para. 10; see also A. Nuyts, *L'exception de forum non conveniens: Etude de droit international privé* (2003), at 238.

[33] See C-365/88 *Hagen v. Zeehage*, [1990] ECR I-1845; see also Jenard Report, at 8.

[34] C-281/02 *Owusu*, [2005] ECR I-1383, para. 25 and Jenard Report, at 8; C. Chalas, 'Note: *Owusu* C-281/02', 94 *Revue critique de droit international privé* (2005), 708-722, at 703-704; C. Hare, '*Forum Non Conveniens* in Europe: Game Over or Time for Reflexion?', *Journal of Business Law* (2006), 157-179, at 161; F. Ibili, 'Civil Jurisdiction and Enforcement of Judgements in Europe: At Last the EC Court of Justice on *Forum Non Conveniens*', 53 *Netherlands International Law Review* (2006), 127-139, at 132.

[35] C-281/02 *Owusu v. Jackson*, [2005] ECR I-1383, para. 26.

[36] Ibid., para. 26 *et seq.*; and see Opinion AG Léger in C-281/02 *Owusu v. Jackson*, [2005] ECR I-1383, para. 151. See below, Sect. 2.2.3.

[37] An example can be found in C-281/02 *Owusu v. Jackson*, [2005] ECR I-1383; see Opinion AG Léger in C-281/02 *Owusu v. Jackson*, [2005] ECR I-1383, para. 162; and Nuyts, *L'exception*, § 171, at 246. In contrast see Peel, 'European Ideals', at 365.

2.2.2 The Substantive Scope

The Brussels Regulation determines jurisdiction[38] concerning 'civil and commercial matters'.[39] The concept 'civil and commercial' is to be interpreted autonomously in order to avoid confusion as to the divergent national significations.[40] The ECJ ruled that in order to determine whether an action involves a civil and commercial matter, 'it is necessary to identify the legal relationship between the parties to the dispute and to examine the basis and the detailed rules governing the bringing of the action'.[41] In sum, the Regulation covers all actions based on relationships between parties governed by private law as opposed to actions in the public law domain between an individual and a public authority exercising its powers.[42]

---

[38] It should be stressed that the Regulation does not cover (other) procedural measures. See C-365/88 *Hagen v. Zeehage*, [1990] ECR I-1845, paras. 17 and 20; and C-159/02 *Turner v. Grovit*, [2004] ECR I-3565, para. 29; Opinion AG Ruiz-Jarabo Colomer in C-159/02 *Turner v. Grovit*, [2004] ECR I-3565, para. 37; Opinion AG Léger in C-281/02 *Owusu v. Jackson*, [2005] ECR I-1383, para. 260. See Nuyts, *L'exception*, § 173, at 250 and Stone, *EU Private International Law*, at 35-36.

[39] Art. 1: 'the Regulation shall not extend to revenue, customs or administrative matters. Furthermore, the Regulation does not apply to: (a) the status or legal capacity of natural persons, rights in property arising out of a matrimonial relationship, wills and succession; (b) bankruptcy, proceedings relating to the winding-up of insolvent companies or other legal persons, judicial arrangements, compositions and analogous proceedings; (c) social security; (d) arbitration.' See for more details on the exceptions under Art. 1's substantive scope, Stone, *EU Private International Law*, at 24-31 and Briggs, *Civil Jurisdiction*, § 2.26-2.30, at 51-55. See for the exception concerning arbitration, C-190/89 *Rich v. Società Italiana Impianti*, [1991] ECR I-3855. The reference for a preliminary ruling on the scope of the Brussels Regulation regarding anti-suit injunctions and international arbitration procedures is of even greater importance in international litigation. The ECJ ruled in its decision *Riunione Adriatica Di Sicurta SpA (RAS)/West Tankers Inc* C-185/07 rendered on 10 February 2007 that it is incompatible with the Regulation to restrain a person from commencing or continuing proceedings before the national courts of another Member State on the ground that such proceedings would be contrary to an arbitration agreement. See also the Opinion of A.G. Kokott of 4 September 2008. See further Stone, *EU Private International Law*, at 31-35; Briggs, *Civil Jurisdiction*, § 2.30, at 55-58; Gaudemet-Tallon, *Compétence en Europe*, at 28-38; and in general the articles by P. Jenard, 'Opinion', 7 *Arbitration International* (1991), 243-250; Schlosser, 'The 1968 Brussels Convention and Arbitration', and P. Kaye, 'The Judgements Convention and Arbitration: Mutual Spheres of Influence', 7 *Arbitration International* (1991), 289-298. See for unresolved questions related to the exception of arbitration, J. Beraudo, 'The Arbitration Exception of the Brussels and Lugano Conventions: Jurisdiction, Recognition and Enforcement of Judgments', 18 *Journal of International Arbitration* (2001), 13-26, and J. van Haersolte-van Hof, 'The Arbitration Exception in the Brussels Convention: Further Comments', 18 *Journal of International Arbitration* (2001), 27-38.

[40] See Case 29/76 *LTU v. Eurocontrol*, [1976] ECR 1541, para. 5. See Briggs, *Civil Jurisdiction*, § 2.24, at 46; C. van der Plas, *De Taak van de rechter in het IPR: Een verkenning van de grenzen van de taak van de Nederlandse rechter bij de toepassing van vreemd Privaat- en Publiekrecht* (2005), 327-329; Schlosser, 'Schlosser Report', § 24, at 82-83; A. Gardella and L. Radicati di Brozolo, 'Civil Law, Common Law and Market Integration: The EC Approach to Conflicts of Jurisdiction', 51 *American Journal of Comparative Law* (2003), 611-637, at 616-617.

[41] C-265/02 *Frahuil v. Assitalia*, [2004] ECR I-1543, para. 20.

[42] See for instance Case 29/76 *LTU v. Eurocontrol*, [1976] ECR 1541, para. 5. See also Case 814/79 *Netherlands v. Rüffer*, [1980] ECR 3807; C-172/91 *Sonntag v. Waidmann*, [1993] ECR I-1963; C-271/00 *Gemeente Steenbergen v. Baten*, [2002] ECR I-10489, para. 31; C-266/01 *TIARD v. Netherlands*, [2003] ECR I-4867, paras. 23 and 36; and C265/02 *Frahuil v. Assitalia*, [2004] ECR I-1543, para. 21. For further details, see Briggs, *Civil Jurisdiction*, § 2.24, at 46-50 and Stone, *EU Private International Law*, at 22-24.

By virtue of Article 71 of the Regulation, specialized conventions regulating jurisdiction and enforcement of particular matters such as those relating to the international carriage of goods, transport or nuclear incidents[43] will prevail over the Regulation's provisions.[44]

2.2.3 The Territorial Scope

The 'pivotal'[45] criterion for the applicability of the uniform Brussels jurisdictional regime is that the defendant should be domiciled in one of the EU Member States whose territory should be regarded 'as a single entity'.[46] According to Recital 8 of the Regulation's Preamble '[t]here must be a link between proceedings to which this regulation applies and the territory of the Member States bound by this regulation'.[47] The Regulation's applicability should not be based on *any* connecting factor with the Regulation's territory but on the 'main connecting factor', namely the defendant's domicile, as specified in Article 2(1).[48] In that respect the plaintiff's domicile is irrelevant and can also be located outside the Brussels territory, i.e. in a non-Member State.[49] As a consequence, the set of uniform jurisdiction rules also apply to disputes between a defendant domiciled in a Member State and a plaintiff domiciled in a non-Member State.[50]

The drafters of the Brussels Model cared to avoid discrimination between nationals and applied the defendant's domicile criterion, *irrespective* of the nationality of either of the parties.[51] In line with the anti-discriminatory principle of Article 12 TEC,[52] Article 2(2) establishes the principle of equality of treatment by assimilating nationals from different Member States with nationals of third countries. Conversely, difference of treatment between residents and non-residents is allowed. According to Article 3(1) all persons, whether EU nationals or not, domiciled in the EU are subject to the same set of jurisdiction rules, as they may be sued in the

[43] See Stone, *EU Private International Law*, at 37-40.

[44] See C-406/92 *Tatry*, [1994] ECR I-5439, para. 27. The Lugano Convention makes it clear that agreeing upon new specialized conventions, such as The Hague Choice of Court Agreement now falls under the exclusive competence of the EC. For this Convention, see Chapter 1, Sect. 1.2.1.

[45] Duintjer Tebbens, '*Re Harrods*: An Unwelcome Interpretation', at 55.

[46] Jenard Report, at 13. According to Art. 68 of the Regulation, by virtue of Art. 299 TEC this does not apply for overseas territories. See for those territories for which the Brussels Convention will remain applicable, Kruger, *Impact on Third States*, § 1.26, at 21 *et seq.*; Droz and Gaudemet-Tallon, 'La transformation', at 612-614.

[47] See also Opinion AG Léger in C-281/02 *Owusu v. Jackson*, [2005] ECR I-1383, para. 211.

[48] C-412/98 *Group Josi v. UGIC*, [2000] ECR I-5925, para. 28.

[49] Ibid., para. 56; and see Opinion AG Léger in C-281/02 *Owusu v. Jackson*, [2005] ECR I-1383, paras. 98, 109-112 and 137; and see Droz, *Compétence judiciaire*, at 23-25.

[50] C-412/98 *Group Josi v. UGIC*, [2000] ECR I-5925, paras. 59 and 61 and Opinion AG Fennelly in C-412/98 *Group Josi v. UGIC*, [2000] ECR I-5925, paras. 16 and 22. Confirmed in C-281/02 *Owusu v. Jackson*, [2005] ECR I-1383, para. 27; see Kruger, *Impact on Third States*, § 2.67-2.70, at 86-87; P. Muchlinski, 'Corporations in International Litigation: Problems of Jurisdiction and the United Kingdom Asbestos Case', 50 *The International and Comparative Law Quarterly* (2001), 1-25, at 12-13; Nuyts, *L'exception*, § 184, at 265.

[51] See Art. 2(2), see C-412/98 *Group Josi v. UGIC*, [2000] ECR I-5925, para. 34.

[52] Ex Art. 6. See F. van der Velden, 'Nationaliteit als Europese jurisdictiegrond', in *Op recht* (1996), 357-365, at 358-359; Vlas in Magnus and Mankowski, eds., *Brussels I Regulation*, § 12, at 74.

courts of other Member States only by virtue of those rules.[53] National jurisdiction rules, especially the exorbitant jurisdiction rules stipulated in Annex I of the Regulation, are not applicable to residents of Member States.[54] Thus, the Brussels Model intends to give persons domiciled on Brussels territory 'privileges of jurisdiction'[55] by prohibiting the use of national jurisdiction rules, especially exorbitant jurisdiction rules as set out in Annex I, and imposes direct jurisdiction rules on all defendants domiciled on its territory.[56] Conversely, third states' residents[57] are not given this 'jurisdictional protection'. By virtue of Article 4(1) national jurisdiction rules, including the exorbitant jurisdiction rules, will still apply to residents of third states.[58] In this respect, Article 4(2) also assimilates Member State's nationals with claimants residing in that Member State, by stating that a claimant – irrespective of its nationality, provided it is domiciled in a Member State – may avail itself of the State's jurisdiction rules in the same way as the nationals of that State.[59] As a consequence, jurisdiction founded on claimant's nationality, such as Article 14 of the French Civil Code, will be avaible to all claimants residing in that forum.[60]

There are four exceptions to the general territorial scope rule under Article 2, two of these exceptions are explicitly provided in Article 4. Rules of exclusive jurisdiction provided for under Article 22, such as disputes involving immoveable property, are applicable without taking the parties' domicile into consideration. Exclusive jurisdiction is based on the 'existence of a particularly close connection' between the dispute and a Member State, such as for instance the location of property in the forum, and justifies the applicability of exclusive jurisdiction 'ir-

---

[53] See Jenard Report, at 14.

[54] Art. 3(2); see below Sect. 2.2.7.

[55] Jenard Report, at 21. See Droz who indicates that Art. 2(2) constitutes a '*prime d'intégration*' for EU residents, Droz, *Compétence judiciaire*, at 41. See for a critical analysis on this privilege Kruger, *Impact on Third States*, § 2.60, at 83 and see especially in relation to the protection of residents of third states § 8.08, at 397, where Kruger recommends to delete the words 'persons domiciled in a Member State' in Art. 3(1) and to delete Art. 4 entirely.

[56] Art. 3(1) and (2).

[57] Even if those residents are nationals of one of the Brussels or Lugano States. According to Jenard it is unclear why the drafters have not extended the reach of the Brussels regime to EU nationals residing outside the territory, thus further limiting the application of exorbitant jurisdiction rules, see Jenard Report, at 21. *Contra* B. Audit and G. Bermann, 'The Application of Private International Norms to "Third Countries": The Jurisdiction and Judgements Example', in *International Civil Litigation in Europe and Relations with Third States* (2005), at 60.

[58] See C-412/98 *Group Josi v. UGIC*, [2000] ECR I-5925, para. 52, where the ECJ states that the provision of Art. 4 'constitutes a confirmation of the fundamental principle set out in the first paragraph of Article 2'.

[59] See Vlas in Magnus and Mankowski, eds., *Brussels I Regulation*, § 5, at 77.

[60] P. Mayer and V. Heuzé, *Droit international privé* (2007), § 299, at 218: '*Le but est de faire disparaître une égalité entre les Français et les étrangers domiciliés en France.*' R. Geimer, 'The Brussels Convention – Successful Model and Oldtimer', 4 *European Journal of Law Reform* (2002), 19-35, at 21; Gaudemet-Tallon, *Compétence en Europe*, § 95, at 67. Vlas in Magnus and Mankowski, eds., *Brussels I Regulation*, § 5, at 77. See for particular problems related to the *forum non conveniens*, A. Briggs, 'The Death of Harrods: *Forum Non Conveniens* and the European Court', *Law Quarterly Review* (2005), 535-540, at 538; and A. Briggs, 'The Impact of Recent Judgements of the European Court on English Procedural Law and Practice', *University of Oxford Faculty of Law Research Paper Series* (2006), at 15-16.

respective of the domicile both of the defendant and of the plaintiff'.[61] Secondly, for the application of the prorogation of jurisdiction provision under Article 23 of the Brussels Regulation, Article 4(1) merely requires that only one of the parties, either the plaintiff or the defendant, be domiciled in a Member State.[62]

Although Article 4 does not make any reference to the applicability of jurisdiction rules concerning protected contracts, Articles 9(2), 15(2) and 18(2) establish a 'legal fiction' in the event the insurer, the non-consumer party or the employer, respectively, are not domiciled in one of the Member States. They are nevertheless deemed 'for the purposes of applying the protective jurisdictional rules in that sphere' to be domiciled in one of the Member States if they have a branch, agency or other establishment in a Member State and the dispute arises out of its operations.[63] The last exception to the applicability criterion of Article 2 was established by the ECJ in *Overseas Union Insurance Ltd v. New Hampshire Insurance Company* and deals with Articles 27-30 whose objective is to coordinate the jurisdiction of different courts over similar or related claims. The ECJ decided that the *lis pendens* rule established by Article 27[64] applies 'irrespective of the domicile of the parties to the two sets of proceedings'.[65]

2.2.4 Types of Jurisdiction Rules

The ***general jurisdiction rule*** of Article 2 establishes general jurisdiction at the defendant's domicile, regardless of any specific connection between the claim and the forum. Recital 11 of the Regulation's Preamble explicitly states that the principle is that 'jurisdiction is generally based on the defendant's domicile and jurisdiction must always be available on this ground save in a few well-defined situations in which the subject-matter of the litigation or the autonomy of the parties warrants a different linking factor'. These well-defined situations, in which the defendant may or must be sued in the courts of another Member State, are exhaustively listed.[66] The following categories of jurisdiction rules derogate from the Regulation's main rule of defendant's domicile:[67]

---

[61] C-412/98 *Group Josi v. UGIC*, [2000] ECR I-5925, paras. 46 and 51. See also Opinion AG Léger in C-281/02 *Owusu v. Jackson*, [2005] ECR I-1383, paras. 136-137.

[62] C-412/98 *Group Josi v. UGIC*, [2000] ECR I-5925, para. 41, in which the ECJ established that the same applies for *voluntary appearance* under Art. 24.

[63] Opinion AG Léger in C-281/02 *Owusu v. Jackson*, [2005] ECR I-1383, paras. 133-134. See with respect to this consumer protection provision C-318/93 *Brenner v. Reynolds*, [1994] ECR I-4275, para. 18.

[64] Art. 21 Brussels Convention.

[65] C-351/89 *Overseas Union v. New Hampshire Ins.*, [1991] ECR I-3317, para. 18. See also Stone, *EU Private International Law*, at 58; J. Beraudo, 'Le Règlement (CE) du Conseil du 22 décembre 2000 concernant la compétence judiciaire, la reconnaissance et l'exécution des décisions en matière civile et commerciale', *Journal du droit international (Clunet)* (2001), 1033-1084, at 1035.

[66] See C-269/95 *Benincasa v. Dentalkit*, [1997] ECR I-3767, point 13, confirming C-89/91 *Shearson Lehmann Hutton Inc. v. TVB*, [1993] ECR I-139, points 14-16; C-26/91 *Handte v. Traitements*, [1992] ECR I-3967, para. 13; C-412/98 *Group Josi v. UGIC*, [2000] ECR I-5925, para. 36.

[67] See Droz, *Compétence judiciaire*, at 41, and Gaudemet-Tallon, *Compétence en Europe*, at 55.

Special or ***alternative*** jurisdiction rules under Articles 5-7 derogate 'only by way of exception' from the defendant's domicile rule.[68] They are called 'alternative jurisdiction rules' because they provide the plaintiff with an alternative or additional competent forum, besides the defendant's domicile.[69] Special jurisdiction asserts jurisdiction limited to the specific nature of the claim, i.e. claims involving contractual matters and claims arising out of the operation of a branch.[70] The drafters considered this 'special connection' between the forum and the claim to be substantial enough to provide the claimant with an additional forum.[71]

Jenard justified the adoption of such alternative forums 'by the fact that there must be a close connecting factor between the dispute and the court with jurisdiction to resolve it'.[72] Secondly, special jurisdiction rules are justified for reasons relating to 'the sound administration of justice and the efficacious conduct of proceedings'.[73] According to the Jenard Report, 'claimant may, at his option, bring the proceedings either in that [alternatively competent] court or in the competent courts of the State in which the defendant is domiciled.'[74] This second justification aims at bringing procedural balance between parties by giving the plaintiff a choice among competent forums at his convenience and compensating for the advantage given to the defendant by Article 2.[75] The fact that the Brussels Model provides the plaintiff with the option to choose from among competent forums allows a certain degree of *legitimate forum shopping.*[76] However, the ECJ repeatedly warned that it is also in the interest of legal certainty and thus of the parties to avoid too many courts having jurisdiction, especially those without a close connection between the dispute and the forum.[77]

The ECJ repeatedly confirmed both justifications by stating that:

---

[68] For the non-exclusivity of those rules, see Magnus and Mankowski, eds., *Brussels I Regulation*, § 9-10, at 93.

[69] C-256/00 *Besix v. WABAG*, [2002] ECR I-1699, para. 53; C-412/98 *Group Josi v. UGIC*, [2000] ECR I-5925, para. 40.

[70] Other forms of special jurisdiction is attributed in maintenance claims (Art. 5(2)), claims relating to tort (Art. 5(3)), and civil claims for damages based on acts giving rise to criminal proceedings (Art. 5(4)). Art. 6 attributes special jurisdiction in relation to multiple defendants, third parties and counter-claims. Art. 7 concerns actions relating to liability from the use or operation of a ship. The alternative jurisdiction rules under Art. 5 connect the claim with the forum on the basis of territorial connections, whereas those under Arts. 6 and 7 are founded on a more procedural connection with the forum. See Ch. Kohler, A. Huet *et al.*, 'Special Jurisdiction under the Article 5 – Part 1: General Remarks and Jurisdiction in Matters Relating to Contract', in *Civil Jurisdiction and Judgments in Europe* (1992), 47-83, at 47.

[71] This special connection is however not substantial enough to substitute the main jurisdiction rule as is the case with exclusive jurisdiction (Art. 22) and to a lesser extent with protective jurisdiction under Arts. 8 to 21.

[72] Jenard Report, at 22. See also Kohler, Huet *et al.*, 'Special Jurisdiction Art. 5', at 47.

[73] C-220/88 *Dumez v. Helaba*, [1990] ECR I-49, para. 17.

[74] Jenard Report, at 22.

[75] Magnus and Mankowski, eds., *Brussels I Regulation*, § 1, at 90.

[76] Geimer, *Internationales Zivilprozeßrecht,* § 1100, at 374.

[77] Case 38/81 *Effer v. Kantner*, [1982] ECR 852, para. 3; C-14/76 *De Bloos v. Bouyer*, [1976] ECR 1497, paras. 7 and 9; and C-159/02 *Turner v. Grovit*, [2004] ECR I-3565, para. 30.

> '[A]lthough article 5 makes provision in a number of cases for a special jurisdiction, which the plaintiff may choose, this is because of the existence, in clearly defined situations of a particularly close connecting factor between a dispute and the court, which may be called upon to hear it, with a view to the efficacious conduct of the proceedings.'[78]

The fact that special jurisdiction provides the plaintiff with an additional competent court has led the ECJ to impose a restrictive interpretation with respect to special jurisdiction, as it must

> 'not give rise to an interpretation going beyond the cases expressly envisaged by the Brussels [Regulation], for otherwise the general principle laid down in the first paragraph of Article 2 would be undermined and a claimant might be able to affect the choice of a court unforeseeable for a defendant domiciled in the territory of a Contracting State'.[79]

Special jurisdiction rules have been interpreted restrictively in order not to extend their reach and completely undermine the defendant's domicile rule by providing the defendant with too many alternative forums.[80]

Special jurisdiction rules determine both international and local jurisdiction by directly designating the court that is locally competent without reference to the domestic rules of the Member States.[81] In other words, special jurisdiction rules also assert jurisdiction as an internal territorial jurisdiction rule.[82] This stands in contrast to Article 2 which provides for general jurisdiction to the courts of the Member State in which the defendant is domiciled, but leaves it to the internal rules of that Member State to determine which of its national courts has jurisdiction to hear the dispute. This is justifiable by the fact that special jurisdiction rules are based on a specific connection between the claim and a specific place and therefore a specific court.[83]

---

[78] First stated by the ECJ in its decision concerning tort jurisdiction under Art. 5(3) in Case 21/76 *Bier v. Mines de potasse d'Alsace*, [1976] ECR 1735. See also C-220/88 *Dumez v. Helaba*, [1990] ECR I-49, para. 17; repeated with respect to Art. 5(5) in Case 33/78 *Somafer v. Saar-Ferngas*, [1978] ECR 2183, para. 7; and with respect to Art. 5(1) in Case 34/82 *Peters v. ZNAV*, [1983] ECR 987, para. 11.

[79] C-256/00 *Besix v. WABAG*, [2002] ECR I-1699, para. 54; Case 189/87 *Kalfelis v. Schröder*, [1988] ECR 5565, para. 19; C-26/91 *Handte v. Traitements*, [1992] ECR I-3967, para. 14; C-89/91 *Shearson Lehmann Hutton Inc. v. TVB*, [1993] ECR I-139, paras. 15-16; C-269/95 *Benincasa v. Dentalkit*, [1997] ECR I-3767, para. 13; C-51/97 *Réunion Européenne and Others*, [1998] ECR I-6511, para. 16; and C-412/98 *Group Josi v. UGIC*, [2000] ECR I-5925, paras. 49-50.

[80] See the valuable contribution by Kohler, Huet *et al.*, 'Special Jurisdiction Art. 5', at 47; and see also Gaudemet-Tallon, *Compétence en Europe*, at 127; Pontier and Burg, *EU Principles on Jurisdiction*, at 122-123; Magnus and Mankowski, eds., *Brussels I Regulation*, § 13, at 95.

[81] See also C-386/05 *Color Drack*, [2007] ECR 0, para. 30.

[82] See Jenard Report, at 19 and 22; and Opinion AG Jacobs in C-96/00 *Gabriel*, [2002] ECR I-6367, para. 21.

[83] See Schlosser, 'Schlosser Report', at 98. See also Gaudemet-Tallon, *Compétence en Europe*, at 126 and J. Fawcett, P. North *et al.*, *Cheshire, North & Fawcett: Private International Law* (2008), at 228.

Finally, special jurisdiction rules only indicate an alternative court if it is located in one of the Member States. If the rule indicates a court outside the territorial scope of the Regulation, special jurisdiction is not available, and accordingly, the only forum available to the plaintiff is the defendant's domicile as stipulated in Article 2.[84]

Protective jurisdiction replaces the main rule of Article 2 and serves the purpose of protecting the weaker party.[85] Article 2 does not play any role in matters relating to insurance claims, consumer contracts and employment contracts. Rather jurisdiction is regulated by Articles 8-21.

Exclusive jurisdiction under Article 22 is attributed to a court when the nature of the action itself is so narrowly connected with the forum that it is justified to simply set aside the main jurisdiction rule of Article 2.[86] Exclusive jurisdiction under Article 22 applies for example to proceedings concerning immoveable property in which case the court where the property is located has this exclusive jurisdiction.[87] This court will be exclusively competent and parties are not allowed to agree upon a different court.

Prorogation of jurisdiction whether expressly by agreement in accordance with Article 23, or tacitly by a voluntary appearance of the defendant according to Article 24,[88] equally derogates from the main rule of defendant's domicile and is based on the parties' consent.

Jurisdiction over claims concerning provisional and protective measures is regulated by Article 31. The procedural jurisdiction rules of Articles 27 to 30, which deal with *lis* pendens, play an important role in avoiding conflict of jurisdiction.

---

[84] Case 32/88 *Six Constructions v. Humbert*, [1989] ECR 341.

[85] Under the Convention, the jurisdiction rule concerning employment contracts was regarded as a special alternative jurisdiction rule. See F. Pocar, 'La protection de la partie faible en droit international privé', 188 *Recueil des cours* (1984), 339-418, at 397-399; P. Mayer, 'La partie faible en droit international privé', in *La protection de la partie faible dans les rapports contractuels: Comparaison Franco-Belges* (1996), at 543-546; Pontier and Burg, *EU Principles on Jurisdiction*, at 124-138. See also C-412/98 *Group Josi v. UGIC*, [2000] ECR I-5925, para. 39; C-96/00 *Gabriel*, [2002] ECR I-6367, para. 39; and C-89/91 *Shearson Lehmann Hutton Inc. v. TVB*, [1993] ECR I-139, paras. 19, 20, 22 and 24. Opinion AG Léger in C-281/02 *Owusu v. Jackson*, [2005] ECR I-1383, para. 128.

[86] See Jenard Report, at 35; affirmed by the ECJ in C-115/88 *Reichert*, [1990] ECR I-27, para. 10; Case 73/77 *Sanders v. Van der Putte*, [1977] ECR 2383, paras. 12-14; see also Opinion AG Geelhoed in C-73/04 *Klein v. Rhodos Management*, [2005] ECR I-8667, para. 5.

[87] According to Art. 22 of the Regulation exclusive competence is also given in matters relating to the 'validity of the constitution, the nullity or the dissolution of companies or other legal persons or associations of natural or legal persons' (Art. 22(2)); 'the validity of entries in public registers' (Art. 22(3)); 'the validity of patents, trade marks, designs, or other similar rights required to be deposited or registered' (Art. 22(4)); and 'in proceedings concerned with the enforcement of judgments' (Art. 22(5)).

[88] Art. 24 covers situations in which, the court seized by the plaintiff is in principle not competent under the set of jurisdiction rules of the Regulation, but the defendant nevertheless appears at the proceedings without contesting the court's jurisdiction.

2.2.5 Hierarchical Structure

These jurisdiction rules have a particular hierarchical structure, which are determined by the following criteria:[89]

1) Does the matter relate to an exclusive jurisdiction ground?
2) Has there been a tacit prorogation of the court according to Article 24?
3) Does the claim concern a protective jurisdiction rule?
4) Did the parties agree upon a court in particular as stipulated in Article 23?
5) Does the claim arise out of an action for which alternative jurisdiction rules provide a forum that is different from the forum indicated in Article 2?
6) If the claim concerns a provisional protective matter, a court competent by virtue of one of the above-mentioned provisions also has jurisdiction to order provisional or protective measures; other courts might grant provisional or protective measures on the basis of Article 31.[90]

A court seized is only required to declare itself incompetent on its own motion in two cases: in matters establishing exclusive jurisdiction,[91] and when a defendant does not enter in appearance, however the jurisdiction of the court seized would not normally be derived from the regulation.[92] It is therefore important for the defendant to contest jurisdiction directly. It is defendant's responsibility to argue the incompetence of the adjudicating court. Droz's statement arguing that the claimant '*n'a qu'à choisir un avocat qui connait la convention*'[93] also applies to the defendant.

2.2.6 A 'Convention Double'

The Brussels Model is a 'convention double', which means that apart from allocating jurisdiction among EU courts, the Brussels Model guarantees free movement of judgements by automatically recognizing each judgement given by a court of a Member State.[94] As a rule, the recognizing court may not examine the jurisdiction of the state of origin, even if the judgement is based on exorbitant national juris-

[89] See also the hierarchy as explained by Briggs, *Civil Jurisdiction,* § 2.08, at 30; and see N. Hatzimihail, 'General Report: Transnational Civil Litigation between European Integration and Global Aspirations', in *International Civil Litigation in Europe and Relations with Third States* (2005), 595-675, at 643.

[90] Provided that a real connecting link exists between the subject matter of the measures sought and the territorial jurisdiction of the Member State of the court before which those measures are sought. See Case C-391/95 *Van Uden Maritime BV v. Firma Deco-Line*, [1998] ECR I-07091.

[91] Art. 25; see also C-116/02 *Gasser v. Misat*, [2003] ECR I-14693, para. 52.

[92] Art. 26(1).

[93] Droz, *Compétence judiciaire*, at 52.

[94] See Arts. 32-34 and see the substantial scope of Art. 1. In order to meet the initial goal of Art. 220, which aims for the 'free movement of judgements' between the Member States, a *traité simple* that merely comprises rules for recognition – and eventually incorporating indirect jurisdiction rules as a requirement for recognition – would have sufficed. However it was considered necessary to also determine the international jurisdiction of their courts. Droz, *Compétence judiciaire*, at 9 and 50; Weser, *La convention communautaire*, at 208.

diction rules.[95] Hence, a jurisdictional test is prohibited at the recognition stage,[96] except when the judgement has been rendered in violation with protective jurisdiction rules concerning insurance and consumer contracts and exclusive jurisdiction.[97] An appeal on one of the grounds for non-recognition specified in Articles 34 and 35 can only be lodged at the enforcement stage.[98] One such ground states that a judgement shall not be recognized if the recognition is manifestly contrary to public policy in the Member State in which recognition is sought.[99] The consequence of automatic recognition in combination with the prohibition of jurisdictional review is crucial to understand the Brussels Model and the critique against it, coming especially from residents of third countries.[100] Primarily the Regulation's prohibition of exorbitant jurisdiction rules as set out in Annex I does not extend to residents of third states. Moreover, judgements rendered against them by a court of a Member State based on these exorbitant rules, will automatically be recognized by other EU courts. Scholars have marked this aspect of the Brussels Model as 'xenophobian'.[101]

2.2.7 'Exorbitant' Jurisdiction Rules

Once the Regulation applies, national jurisdiction rules are set aside by Article 3(1) and superseded by a set of uniform jurisdiction rules stipulated in Sections

[95] Art. 35(2).

[96] Arts. 35(3) and 45(1) Regulation.

[97] Art. 35(1) referring to Sects. 3, 4 or 6 of Chapter 2.

[98] See Art. 43(1).

[99] Art. 34(1); see L. Strikwerda, 'De invloed van het EVRM op het Europse IPR: Aantekeningen bij de Krombach-uitspraak van het Hof van Justitie EG', in *Europeanisering van het Nederlands recht: Opstellen aangeboden aan Mr. W.E. Haak* (2004), 252-260, at 254.

[100] As explained by Kruger, *Impact on Third States*, § 2.58 at 81.

[101] See F. Juenger, 'A Shoe Unfit for Globetrotting? Symposium Fifty Years of International Shoe, The Past and the Future of Personal Jurisdiction', 28 *The University of California Davis Law Review* (1995), 1027-1045, at 1044; P. Borchers, 'Comparing Personal Jurisdiction in the United States and the European Community: Lessons for American Reform', 40 *American Journal of Comparative Law* (1992), 121-157, at 132, argues that 'The Brussels Convention overtly discriminates against outsiders'. N. Fragistas, 'La compétence internationale en droit international privé', 104 *Recueil des cours* (1961), 159-271, at 176; see in general on exorbitant jurisdiction De Winter, 'Excessives Jurisdiction'; Juenger, 'la courtoisie internationale'; G. Dannemann, 'Jurisdiction Based on the Presence of Assets in Germany', 41 *The International and Comparative Law Quarterly* (1992), 632-637; R. Gassmann, *Arrest im Internationalen Rechtsverkehr: Zum Einfluss des Lugano-Ubereinkommens auf das schweizerische Arrestrecht* (1998); H. Grothe, '"Exorbitante" Gerichtszuständigkeiten im Rechtsverkehr zwischen Deutschland und den USA', 58 *RabelsZ* (1994), 687-726; J. Krafft, *'Exorbitante' Gerichtsstände im internationalen Zivilprozessrecht der Schweiz: Insbesondere nach dem Lugano-Übereinkommen* (1999); Nadelmann, 'Jurisdictional Improper Fora'; Russell, 'Exorbitant Jurisdiction'; H. Schack, 'Vermögensbelegenheit als Zuständigkeitsgrund: Exorbitant oder Sinnvoll?', *Zeitschrift für Zivilprozess* (1984), 46-68; O. Struyven, 'Exorbitant Jurisdiction in the Brussels Convention', *Jura Falconis: Juridisch Wetenschappelijk studenten tijdschrift KU Leuven* (1999); M. Moura Ramos, 'The New EC Rules on Jurisdiction and the Recognition and Enforcement of Judgments', in *Law and Justice in a Multistate World: Essays in Honor of Arthur T. von Mehren* (2002), 199-217, at 210; see also Audit and Bermann, 'The Application of Private International Norms to "Third Countries"', at 64.

2 to 7 of the Regulation.[102] The drafters felt the need to identify some jurisdiction grounds that should particularly be prohibited. These '*exorbitant*' jurisdiction rules – as they are also called – are listed in Annex I. This enumeration is not exhaustive;[103] in fact all national jurisdiction rules should be considered 'exorbitant' for the simple reason that they are set aside by a set of uniform jurisdiction rules.[104] Nonetheless, the purpose of Article 3(2) is to identify some rules that are more 'exorbitant' than others, even though it may seem redundant.[105] The purpose of Annex I according to Jenard is to prohibit 'the application of the most important and best known of the rules of exorbitant jurisdiction'.[106] In a more general sense, the 'exorbitant' character of a rule lies in the fact that jurisdiction is based on a very weak connection between the forum and the dispute.[107] The *Kerameus* and *Jenard-Möller* Reports made an attempt to categorize jurisdiction rules as follows.[108]

2.2.7.1 *Nationality*

General jurisdiction based on the nationality of either party is banned from the Brussels jurisdictional regime.[109] Nationality-based jurisdiction as applied in France and Luxembourg asserts general jurisdiction and is not limited to the nature of the claim.[110] Jurisdiction founded on the sole basis of nationality is marked exorbitant under the Brussels jurisdictional regime,[111] because its connection with the forum is regarded as insufficient and it violates the anti-discrimination principle

[102] Jenard Report, at 19. See also Weser, *La convention communautaire*, at 110-112, on the necessity for the abrogation of exorbitant jurisdiction rules.

[103] See for example Jenard-Möller Report, at 71, who refer to a Swedish rule conferring jurisdiction over persons domiciled in a Contracting State on the basis that the contract was entered into force in Sweden. This ground was not listed as exorbitant by Art. 3(2) of the Lugano Convention, but was nevertheless marked as such by its explanatory report.

[104] Jenard Report, at 19. For example, Annex I of the Brussels Regulation marks the whole set of Italian national jurisdiction rules as exorbitant, even though, since the Italian Reform, these rules are almost identical to the uniform jurisdiction rules of the Brussels Model and are therefore by their very nature not 'particularly' exorbitant. According to Art. 74(1) of the Regulation, Member States are required to give notice of amendments of national jurisdiction law if any are marked as exorbitant under Annex I. Each Accession Convention to the Brussels Convention resulted in the exclusion of some national jurisdiction rules.

[105] See P. Schlosser, 'Jurisdiction in International Litigation: The Issue of Human Rights in Relation to National Law and the Brussels Convention', *Rivista di diritto internazionale* (1991), 5-34, at 5; Nygh, 'Declining Jurisdiction', at 308.

[106] Jenard Report, at 19.

[107] Vlas in Magnus and Mankowski, eds., *Brussels I Regulation*, § 2, at 74-75.

[108] K. Kerameus and I. Evriginis, 'Evrigenis and Kerameus Report on the Accession of the Hellenic Republic to the Community Convention on Jurisdiction and the Enforcement of Judgments in Civil and Commercial Matters', OJ 1986 C 298 (1986), 1 *et seq.*, at 12 and Jenard-Möller Report, at 71.

[109] See also C-412/98 *Group Josi v. UGIC*, [2000] ECR I-5925, para. 54, and the observations made by Geimer, 'Successful Model', at 32.

[110] Arts. 14 and 15 of the French and Luxembourg Civil Codes, see for France Chapter 3, Sect. 3.4.3. Nationality-based jurisdiction was formerly known in Belgium, Portugal and Italy. See also F. Mann, 'The Doctrine of International Jurisdiction Revisited after Twenty Years', 186 *Recueil des cours* (1984), 9-116, § 2, at 70.

[111] See Jenard Report, at 19.

under EC Law which makes it inconsistent with European integration.[112] Nationality-based jurisdiction has always been controversial and it is hardly surprising that it is termed exorbitant and is prohibited in the Brussels Model.[113]

2.2.7.2 Forum Actoris

The Brussels Model is particularly hostile towards establishing *general* jurisdiction on the basis of claimant's connecting factors to the forum.[114] Any form of ascertainment of general jurisdiction on the basis of a claimant's domicile, habitual or temporary residence is considered exorbitant. Not only does Article 3(2) condemn the '*forum actoris*', as (previously) used in some national systems,[115] but it is a logical consequence of the general and fundamental defendant's domicile rule under the Brussels Regulation.[116] Only on 'exceptional grounds' and under very special circumstances, does the Brussels Regulation assert *special* jurisdiction merely on the basis of the domicile of the claimant and allows derogation from the general jurisdiction rule.[117] But setting these circumstances aside, 'it must be concluded that the system of rules on conferment of jurisdiction established by the Convention is not usually based on the criterion of the plaintiff's domicile or seat'.[118]

2.2.7.3 *Property*

Several Member States can exercise jurisdiction over a defendant on the basis that property belonging to the defendant is situated on its territory. Whether defend-

---

[112] See also P. Kaye, 'Nationality and the European Convention on the Jurisdiction and Enforcement of Judgments', 37 *The International and Comparative Law Quarterly* (1988), 268-282, at 268, and Van der Velden, 'Nationaliteit als Europese jurisdictiegrond', at 358-359 and 361-364.

[113] M. Weser, 'Bases of Judicial Jurisdiction in the Common Market Countries', 10 *American Journal of Comparative Law* (1961), 323-344, at 324-325; Nadelmann, 'Jurisdictional Improper Fora', at 999; De Winter, 'Excessives Jurisdiction', at 706-707.

[114] C-220/88 *Dumez v. Helaba*, [1990] ECR I-49, paras. 16 and 19; C-412/98 *Group Josi v. UGIC*, [2000] ECR I-5925, para. 50; and Opinion AG Léger in C-420/97 *Leathertex v. Bodetex*, [1999] ECR I-6747, para. 95.

[115] The *forum actoris* was formerly known in The Netherlands (under the ancient regime of Art. 126(3) of the Dutch Code of Civil Procedure) and Belgium (Art. 638 of the Belgian Judicial Code). Both countries have however reformed their international jurisdiction rules. See for The Netherlands Chapter 3, Sect. 3.2.

[116] See C-412/98 *Group Josi v. UGIC*, [2000] ECR I-5925, para. 50; C-220/88 *Dumez v. Helaba*, [1990] ECR I-49, para. 16; C-89/91 *Shearson Lehmann Hutton Inc. v. TVB*, [1993] ECR I-139, para. 17; Case 32/88 *Six Constructions v. Humbert*, [1989] ECR 341, para. 13; and see Opinion AG Léger in C-168/02 *Kronhofer v. Maier*, [2004] ECR I-6009, paras. 23-24. See for reasons in favour of the *forum actoris*, J. Verheul, 'The "*forum actoris*" and International Law', in *Essays on International & Comparative Law in Honour of Judge Erades* (1983), 197-206. See Chapter 7, Sect. 7.4, for the comparative analysis of the *forum actoris*.

[117] See Arts. 5(2), 9 and 16. See among others C-412/98 *Group Josi v. UGIC*, [2000] ECR I-5925, paras. 37 and 47; and see Opinion AG Léger in C-168/02 *Kronhofer v. Maier*, [2004] ECR I-6009, para. 25.

[118] C-412/98 *Group Josi v. UGIC*, [2000] ECR I-5925, para. 53; and see Opinion AG Fennelly in C-412/98 *Group Josi v. UGIC*, [2000] ECR I-5925, para. 14.

ant's property is located, seized,[119] or subjected to sequestration[120] in the forum[121] does not constitute a sufficient connection between the forum and the defendant for jurisdiction under the Brussels Model and is therefore marked 'exorbitant'.[122] Moreover, the Jenard Report points out that Article 23 of the German *Zivilprozess-ordnung* often turns into a *forum actoris* for German nationals.[123]

2.2.7.4 *Presence*

Some jurisdictional systems establish jurisdiction based on defendant's (physical) presence in the territory of the court's state, where he was properly served with a writ. This jurisdiction ground is rejected under the Brussels uniform jurisdictional scheme.[124] The exorbitant nature of presence-based jurisdiction lies in the fact that mere presence does not constitute a sufficiently substantial connection with the forum to establish and accept jurisdiction under a uniform jurisdictional regime, 'especially because of the possibility of free movement of judgments resulting from the 1968 Convention, there is no longer any justification for founding jurisdiction on the mere temporary presence of a person in a state of the court concerned'.[125]

2.2.7.5 *The Place of Signature*

With respect to special jurisdiction grounds, the Brussels Model rejects jurisdiction over contractual disputes founded on the mere fact that a contract was signed or concluded in the forum.[126] The fact that the contract was signed in a particular country is not considered to establish a sufficient connection with the forum, even if the claim arises out of that contract.[127]

---

[119] For the *forum arresti*, see 'Schlosser Report', at 100, dealing with Scotland but see in contrast Weser, *La convention communautaire,* at 110. See also Art. 10 Dutch Code of Civil Procedure discussed in Chapter 3, Sect. 3.2.4.

[120] See the Swiss *forum sequestri*, Art. 40 of the Federal Law of Private International Law of 1987 explained in Chapter 3, Sect. 3.3.3, and see Art. 3(2) Lugano Convention.

[121] The *forum patrimonii* is known in Germany (Art. 23 German Code of Civil Procedure, see Chapter 3, Sect. 3.5.5), Austria (Art. 99 of the *Jurisdiktionsnorm*), Sweden (Art. 32 Swedish Code of Civil Procedure), Denmark (Art. 246(3) Danish Law of Civil Procedure), Greece (Art. 40 Greek Code of Civil Procedure), Finland (Chap. 10, 1st section, 1st paragraph, 4th litter of the Code of Judicial Procedure). Under Art. 3(2) of the Lugano Convention property-based jurisdiction as known in Iceland (Art. 77 Icelandic Civil Proceedings Act) and Norway (Art. 23 Norwegian Civil Proceedings Act, Sect. 3, 1st litter) is marked as exorbitant.

[122] See 'Kerameus/Evriginis Report', at 12; Mann, 'Doctrine of International Jurisdiction Revisited', § 1, at 69.

[123] Jenard Report, at 19.

[124] U.K., Ireland and Finland. See Annex I, 5th and last litter. For Finland Chap. 10, 1st section, 1st paragraph, 4th sentence of the Finish Code of Judicial Procedure.

[125] 'Schlosser Report', § 86, at 100. See also Mann, 'Doctrine of International Jurisdiction Revisited', § 1, at 70.

[126] Jenard Report, at 20.

[127] See also Mann, 'Doctrine of International Jurisdiction Revisited', § 4 and 5, at 70.

2.3 The Closed System of the Brussels Model

The Brussels Model provides a complete set of jurisdiction rules, setting national jurisdiction rules aside and outlawing national 'exorbitant' jurisdiction rules. The rules are designed to grant jurisdiction to the court that is 'best qualified to determine a dispute'[128] and they consist of closed norms wherein 'no room is left for the exercise of any discretionary latitude'.[129] The set of jurisdiction rules under the Brussels Regulation is mandatory.[130] Declining jurisdiction in favour of another 'more appropriate' forum within or outside the EU territory is not allowed.[131] Practical and factual considerations, which are generally taken into account by the *forum non conveniens* doctrine,[132] with respect to, among others, the expense of the proceedings, the possibility of recovering their costs, the logistical difficulties resulting from the geographical distance and the impossibility of enforcing cross-claims against the other defendants, 'are not such as to call into question the mandatory nature of the fundamental rule of jurisdiction contained in Article 2 of the Brussels Convention'.[133]

2.3.1 The Exclusion of the *Forum Non Conveniens* Doctrine

The *forum non conveniens* doctrine should not be understood as a connecting factor or jurisdiction rule as such and is for that reason not explicitly marked as 'exorbitant' under the Regulation's Annex I. The doctrine involves jurisdictional discretion on the basis of which the court may decline to exercise jurisdiction. Among the European Member States, the doctrine forms an essential part of the jurisdictional systems of the U.K. and Ireland.[134] Under English law, a court has discretionary powers to decline the exercise of its jurisdiction on the ground that 'a court in another State, which also has jurisdiction, would objectively be a more appropriate forum, in which the case may be tried more suitably for the interests of all the parties and the ends of justice'.[135] The doctrine functions as a 'correction mechanism' to the outcome of statutory jurisdiction rules: once the court seized 'assumes' jurisdiction on the basis of the jurisdiction rules it still has discretionary

---

[128] E. Peel, 'Introduction', in *Forum Shopping in the European Judicial Area* (2007), 1-23, at 17; L. Collins and G. Droz, 'La recours à la doctrine du forum non conveniens et aux "anti-suit injunctions": Principes directeurs. 2ème Commission', 70 *Annuaire de l'Institut de droit international* (2003), 13-94, at 22, referring to Case 38/81 *Effer v. Kantner*, [1982] ECR 852.

[129] 'Schlosser Report', § 76, at 97.

[130] Peel, 'European Ideals', at 366.

[131] See above C-281/02 *Owusu v. Jackson*, [2005] ECR I-1383; and see C. Chalas, *L'exercise discrétionnaire de la compétence juridictionnelle en droit international privé* (2000), § 594, at 535.

[132] See for the English application of the doctrine Chapter 4, Sect. 4.3.

[133] C-281/02 *Owusu v. Jackson*, [2005] ECR I-1383, paras. 44-45.

[134] See Chapter 4, Sect. 4.3, for the English application of the *forum non conveniens* provision. See for a general overview of the Irish variant of the *forum non conveniens* rule, P. Huber, 'Forum Non Conveniens – The Other Way Round', *IPRax* (1996), 48-52.

[135] According to Lord Goff in *Spiliada Maritime Corp. v. Cansulex Ltd.*, [1987] AC 460, at 476, also cited by the ECJ in C-281/02 *Owusu v. Jackson*, [2005] ECR I-1383, para. 8. See Chapter 4, Sect. 4.3, for the specific factors considered to take or decline jurisdiction pursuant to the English version of the *forum non conveniens* doctrine.

powers to decline jurisdiction.[136] Not the convenience of the courts is appreciated, but the *appropriateness* of conferring jurisdiction on it.[137] The application of the *forum non conveniens* doctrine, which declines jurisdiction in favour of a Member State as well as in favour of a court of a non-Member State, is now rigorously excluded from the Brussels jurisdictional system.[138]

2.3.1.1 *The Accession of Common Law Systems*

Although the issue of the *forum non conveniens* was discussed by the drafters of the 1968 Convention, neither the Convention nor the Regulation contains any provision related to the *forum non conveniens* doctrine.[139] Unknown to the six initial Contracting States,[140] Jenard made no reference to the *forum non conveniens* doctrine in his Report on the first Brussels Convention.[141] Conversely, Droz's explanatory oeuvre to the Convention was rather explicit with respect to his view on the (in)compatibility of the *forum non conveniens* with the Brussels Model: '*il faut tuer dans l'œuf cette source de chicane*'.[142] By the time the U.K. and Ireland adhered to the 1968 Brussels Convention, the six initial Continental Member States were operating under the assumption that the Brussels Model was a closed system. Schlosser explicitly states in his Report on the Accession Convention of those countries that 'according to the views of the delegations from the Continental Member States of the Community such possibilities [of discretion] are not open to the courts of those States when, under the 1968 Convention, they have jurisdiction and are asked to adjudicate'.[143]

---

[136] See for an extensive comparison of correction mechanisms Chapter 8 and see Duintjer Tebbens, '*Re Harrods*: An Unwelcome Interpretation', at 59.

[137] See W. Kennett, '*Forum non Conveniens* in Europe', 43 *Cambridge Law Journal* (1995), 552-577, at 555; and see Opinion AG Léger in C-281/02 *Owusu v. Jackson*, [2005] ECR I-1383, para. 26.

[138] This is the case since C-281/02 *Owusu v. Jackson*, [2005] ECR I-1383. See F. Ibili, 'Book review: A. Nuyts, "*L'Exception de* forum non conveniens"', *Netherlands International Law Review* (2005), 299-302, at 299.

[139] See C-281/02 *Owusu v. Jackson*, [2005] ECR I-1383, para. 37; and J. Fawcett, 'Common law Practices and the Brussels Convention', *www.ipr.be* (2005), 103-110, at 105.

[140] 'Schlosser Report', § 76, at 97.

[141] Also observed by Droz, *Compétence judiciaire*, at 128; A. Mennie, 'The Brussels Convention and the Scottish Courts' Discretion to Decline Jurisdiction', *The Juridical Review* (1989), 150-172, at 159; G. Hogan, 'The Brussels Convention, Forum non Conveniens and the Connecting Factors Problem', 20 *European Law Review* (1995), 471-494, at 474. Nuyts takes the view that the fact that the 1968 text does not mention the *forum non conveniens* doctrine should be considered as ignorance of the doctrine rather than a firm condemnation, see Nuyts, *L'exception*, § 150, at 214; and he is joined in this opinion by Peel, see Peel, 'European Ideals', at 370.

[142] Droz, *Compétence judiciaire*, § 206, at 129, as translated by AG Léger in Opinion AG Léger in C-281/02 *Owusu v. Jackson*, [2005] ECR I-1383, in fn. 113: 'Mr Droz stated forcefully that the doctrine had no place in the Brussels Convention, taking the view that "it would be better to throttle this source of chicanery at birth"'.

[143] 'Schlosser Report', § 78, at 97; see also for some comments on the Schlosser Report from writers from common law systems, Hogan, 'Connecting Factors Problem', at 474-475; Mennie, 'Brussels Convention and the Scottish Courts' Discretion', at 160; and Peel, 'European Ideals', at 369. See also Opinion AG Léger in C-281/02 *Owusu v. Jackson*, [2005] ECR I-1383, paras. 222-224; and Nuyts, *L'exception*, § 151, at 215.

Interestingly, the doctrine was already applied in Scotland before it was officially and fully introduced in England in 1987 by the *Spiliada Maritime Corp. v. Cansulex Limited* case,[144] hence, considerably some time after the publication of the Jenard and Schlosser Reports in 1979 and more or less at the same time the Brussels Convention entered into force in the U.K.[145] But the Schlosser Report, particularly concerned with the Scottish and Irish practice, already indicated that the U.K. and Irish delegations did not press for a formal adjustment of the 1968 Convention.[146] To the desolation of some, the two common law countries had not seen fit to introduce a *forum non conveniens* type of reasoning into the negotiations.[147]

Since Article 3(2) identified the typical common law principle, founding jurisdiction on the mere presence of the defendant in the territory, as exorbitant, Schlosser argued that correcting those jurisdiction rules by means of the *forum non conveniens* doctrine was 'largely unnecessary'.[148] It was generally accepted that the six original Contracting States and the new adhering states firmly condemned the doctrine to decline jurisdiction in favour of another Contracting State.[149] In contrast, Nuyts takes the view that the Schlosser Report simply expresses the unfavourable attitude of the six original Contracting States towards the doctrine and that the adhering common law countries refrained from insisting on the inclusion of the doctrine and instead the *status quo* was maintained.[150] Surprisingly, the Civil Jurisdiction and Judgement Act of 1982 implementing the Brussels Convention states that '[n]othing in the Act shall prevent a court in the United Kingdom from staying … or dismissing any proceedings on the ground of forum non conveniens or otherwise, where to do so is not inconsistent with the 1968 Convention'.[151]

Nonetheless, even though consecutive accession conventions and the Regulation have not felt the need to explicitly reject the doctrine,[152] the exclusion of the

144 [1987] AC (460). Mention can also be made of the *Abidin Daver* Case, [1984] AC 398; All ER 470.

145 1 January 1987, see Duintjer Tebbens, '*Re Harrods*: An Unwelcome Interpretation', at 59; Nuyts, *L'exception*, § 151, at 216.

146 'Schlosser Report', § 78, at 98; but see in contrast W. O'Brian Jr., 'The Hague Convention on Jurisdiction and Judgments: The Way Forward', 66 *The Modern Law Review* (2003), 491-509, at 494.

147 F. Juenger, 'Forum Non Conveniens – Who Needs It?', in *Wege zur Globalisierung des Rechts: Festschrift für Rolf A. Schütze zum 65. Geburtstag* (1999), 317-336, at 334.

148 'Schlosser Report', § 78, at 98; see also Schlosser in A. Lowenfeld, *The Hague Convention on Jurisdiction and Judgments: Records of the Conference Held at New York University School of Law on the Proposed Convention* (2001), at 16; 'They [the English] said at that time that it is not English; it is Scottish rather than English'; see in contrast Peel, 'European Ideals', at 372, deploring that 'a valuable tool against the worst excesses of forum shopping is no longer available'.

149 See also Geimer, 'Successful Model', at 26, admiring the 'British flexibility and pragmatism'.

150 Nuyts, *L'exception*, § 151, at 216.

151 Act of 13 July 1982, in Art. 49. However, as Chalas rightfully reminds us, the CJJA is the first text explicitly mentioning the *forum non conveniens* doctrine in the pre-*Spiliada* period, see Chalas, *L'exercise discrétionnaire*, § 610, fn. 523, at 554 and see Chapter 4, Sect. 4.1, for the CJJA.

152 G. Cuniberti, '*Forum Non Conveniens* and the Brussels Convention', *The International and Comparative Law Quarterly* (2005), 973-981, at 974.

forum non conveniens doctrine among courts of Contracting States was generally accepted[153] and affirmed by the ECJ in *Owusu*.[154]

2.3.1.2 *The Relation between Non-Member States' Courts*

The *Owusu* decision indisputably precludes a court of a Member State from declining jurisdiction in favour of a non-Member State under the Brussels jurisdictional scheme.[155] Both claimant, Mr Owusu, and the principal defendant, Mr Jackson, were domiciled in England where the action was brought on the basis of the defendant's domicile criteria under Article 2.[156] The dispute had no connection with any other Member State, but the events at issue occurred in a non-Member State. Jackson had let a holiday villa to Owusu in Jamaica, where the latter suffered a very serious accident.[157] Owusu brought an action for breach of contract against Mr Jackson in England. Defendant Jackson claimed that the English court should not exercise its jurisdiction in relation to the claim against him and requested a stay of proceedings on the basis of the *forum non conveniens* doctrine by arguing that the case had closer links with Jamaica. 'For the interest of all the parties and the ends of justice', he argued, the case might be more suitably tried when the Jamaican courts have jurisdiction.[158] Although the decision also deals with the applicability of the Brussels Model,[159] the principal question concerned the possibility for a court to exercise its discretionary powers, available under its national law, to decline to hear proceedings brought on the basis of Article 2 in favour of a non-Member State.[160] The affirmative answer of the ECJ is assumed to equally preclude the application of the *forum non conveniens* when claimant seizes a court on a jurisdictional basis other than Article 2, such as Article 5(1).[161] Nor should

---

[153] See for more references Chalas, *L'exercise discrétionnaire*, § 596, at 536; Nuyts, *L'exception*, § 152, at 217 and § 161, at 233.

[154] C-281/02 *Owusu v. Jackson*, [2005] ECR I-1383, para. 37.

[155] Ibid., para. 46. The decision as well as the reasoning of the courts are heavily criticized, mainly by common laywers, but also by a few Continental lawyers see in general the articles of Cuniberti, '*FNC* and the Brussels Convention'; Chalas, 'Note; *Owusu*'; H. Duintjer Tebbens, 'From Jamaica with Pain', in *Crossing Borders: Essays in European and Private International Law, Nationality Law and Islamic Law in Honour of Frans van der Velden* (2006), 95-103; Ibili, 'Civil Jurisdiction'. See for the critical articles from common lawyers, among others, Hare, '*FNC* in Europe: Game Over?', Ch. Knight, 'Owusu and Turner: The Shark in the Water?', 66 *Cambridge Law Journal* (2007), 288-301; T. Hartley, 'The European Union and the Systematic Dismantling of the Common Law of Conflict of Laws', 54 *The International and Comparative Law Quarterly* (2005), 813-828 and Peel, 'European Ideals'.

[156] Mr Owusu also brought an action in tort in the U.K. against several other defendants, i.e. Jamaican companies. In order to simplify the facts the action against Mr Jackson will be considered as the main action and Jackson as the man defendant. See C-281/02 *Owusu v. Jackson*, [2005] ECR I-1383, para. 12.

[157] C-281/02 *Owusu v. Jackson*, [2005] ECR I-1383, para. 10.

[158] Ibid., para. 15. See similar terms used in the English *Spiliada* rule in Chapter 4, Sect. 4.3.1.

[159] See C-281/02 *Owusu v. Jackson*, [2005] ECR I-1383, para. 23 *et seq.*; and also in this sense Nuyts, *L'exception*, § 183, at 263.

[160] C-281/02 *Owusu v. Jackson*, [2005] ECR I-1383, para. 22.

[161] See Fawcett, 'Common Law Practices', at 106; and G. Cuniberti and M. Winkler, 'Note: Owusu C-281/02', *Journal du droit international* (2005), 1185-1991, at 1191; but see also Opinion AG

it make any difference if parties are not domiciled in the same state – as was the case in *Owusu* –, or when claimant is domiciled in a non-Member State, for this Brussels regime excluding the doctrine to be applicable.[162] The mandatory nature of Article 2 and of the set of jurisdictional rules in general,[163] the uniform application of those rules[164] and the principle of legal certainty,[165] led the ECJ to exclude the *forum non conveniens* doctrine in favour of a non-Contracting State under the scope of the Brussels Model.[166] According to the ECJ, applying the doctrine would undermine the predictability of the set of jurisdiction rules and the principle of legal certainty requires that a normally well-informed defendant be reasonably able to foresee before which courts, other than those of the State in which he is domiciled, he may be sued. [167]

The ruling of the *Owusu* decision was awaited for a long time[168] and the application of the *forum non conveniens* doctrine in favour of a non-Member State within the Brussels framework was the subject of an animated debate illustrating the controversy between 'strict legal frameworks' and legal traditions allowing a wide range of discretionary powers.[169] The debate went beyond the question of the doctrine's consistency with the Brussels Model and still reflects the resistance of common law systems to the traditional Continental approach of rigid rules and vice versa.[170]

Léger in C-281/02 *Owusu v. Jackson*, [2005] ECR I-1383, para. 93; and Briggs, 'The Impact of Recent Judgements', at 15.

[162] This will be applicable within the substantial and territorial scope of the Brussels regime as explained above in Sect. 2.2; C-281/02 *Owusu v. Jackson*, [2005] ECR I-1383, para. 27; and see Fawcett, 'Common Law Practices', at 106.

[163] C-281/02 *Owusu v. Jackson*, [2005] ECR I-1383, para. 37; see especially on the relation between the exclusion of the *forum non conveniens* and the mandatory nature of Art. 2 the contribution of P. De Vareilles-Sommières, 'The Mandatory Nature of Article 2 of the Brussels Convention and Derogation from the Rule It Lays Down', in *Forum Shopping in the European Judicial Area* (2007), 101-115; see also Vlas in Magnus and Mankowski, eds., *Brussels I Regulation*, § 6-7, at 72; Chalas, 'Note; *Owusu*', at 705; see also Cuniberti, '*FNC* and the Brussels Convention', at 974-975 and Cuniberti and Winkler, 'Note: Owusu', at 1188, who are not convinced by the ECJ's arguments. The defendant's domicile rule of Art. 2 is explained in Sect. 2.5.

[164] C-281/02 *Owusu v. Jackson*, [2005] ECR I-1383, para. 43. According to the ECJ the uniform application of the Brussels jurisdiction rules is likely to be affected 'in so far as that [the *forum non conveniens*] doctrine is recognised only in a limited number of Contracting States, whereas the objective of the Brussels Convention is precisely to lay down common rules to the exclusion of derogating national rules.' See Ibili, 'Civil Jurisdiction', at 134; and Hartley, 'Systematic Dismantling', at 827 stating 'uniformity for the sake of uniformity'.

[165] C-281/02 *Owusu v. Jackson*, [2005] ECR I-1383, paras. 40-43; and see Cuniberti, '*FNC* and the Brussels Convention', at 977 *et seq.*

[166] C-281/02 *Owusu v. Jackson*, [2005] ECR I-1383, para. 46.

[167] Ibid., paras. 40-41; Peel, 'Introduction Forum Shopping', at18; Ibili, 'Civil Jurisdiction', at 133; and Cuniberti, '*FNC* and the Brussels Convention', at 977, who is surprised that the ECJ takes the defendant's interest into account instead of the claimant's interest to have his case heard by the court of his choice. See also Cuniberti and Winkler, 'Note: Owusu', at 1189-1190 or Briggs, 'The Impact of Recent Judgements', at 11, considering this statement as manifesting an 'egregious error'.

[168] Cuniberti and Winkler, 'Note: Owusu', at 1186.

[169] One of many and more recent debates on this issue can be found in Briggs, 'The Impact of Recent Judgements', at 3 *et seq.*

[170] Duintjer Tebbens, '*Re Harrods*: An Unwelcome Interpretation', at 52; R. Fentiman, 'Jurisdiction, Discretion and the Brussels Convention', 26 *Cornell International Law Journal* (1993), 59-99,

All interesting views advanced by scholars concerning the (in)compatibility of the *forum non conveniens* with the Brussels regime have now, since the Court's clear exclusion of the doctrine, become outdated.[171] One of the views, followed by mainly English common law authors and the English Court of Appeal, was based on the territorial scope of the Brussels Model and argued that the primary purpose of the Brussels Model, i.e. the allocation of jurisdiction among Member States' courts and the free movement of judgements, justifies a restricted scope of application dealing with intra-communitarian relationships only.[172] Consequently, when a court has jurisdiction by virtue of the set of jurisdiction rules of the Brussels regime, it should be allowed to decline jurisdiction in favour of a non-Member State court, since it does not fall within the scope of the Brussels regime and does not affect the jurisdiction of another Contracting State.[173]

This approach was followed by the English Court of Appeal in the notorious and controversial case of *Re Harrods (Buenos Aires) Ltd*, in which it was allowed to decline jurisdiction in favour of courts of non-Contracting States in the event no other Contracting state's court was connected with the case.[174] In *Re Harrods*, the corporate defendant was considered domiciled in England, based merely on the fact that he was incorporated in England, but he was in fact mainly operating in Argentina. The Swiss domiciled claimant brought action in England.[175] The Court of Appeal acknowledged the fact that the *forum non conveniens* exception could not

---

at 62, see in general for the debate Chalas, *L'exercise discrétionnaire*; Briggs, 'The Impact of Recent Judgements', Hartley, 'Systematic Dismantling', Duintjer Tebbens, 'From Jamaica with Pain', at 102-103; A. Clarke, 'The Differing Approach to Commercial Litigation in the European Court of Justice and the Courts of England and Wales', 18 *European Business Law Review* (2007), 101-129; Peel, 'European Ideals', Ibili, 'Civil Jurisdiction', at 139 and A. Briggs, '*Forum Non Conveniens* and Ideal Europeans', *Lloyd's Maritime and Commercial Law Quarterly* (2005), 378-382.

[171] H. Gaudemet-Tallon, 'Le "forum non conveniens", une menace pour la Convention de Bruxelles?; à propos de trois arrêts anglais récents', *Revue critique de droit international privé* (1991), 491-524, at 514-519; Fentiman, 'Jurisdiction, Discretion', at 95; Kennett, '*FNC* in Europe', at 568 *et seq.*; enumerated by Chalas, *L'exercise discrétionnaire,* § 613-619, at 558-567; and S. Beernaert and A. Coibon, 'La doctrine du *forum (non) conveniens* réconciliation avec le texte de la Convention de Bruxelles', 119 *Journal des tribunaux* (2000), 409-419, at 417-418. Nuyts distinguishes three principal theses in the doctrine, the third of which is a kind of compromising approach allowing the application of the *forum non conveniens* doctrine only under certain circumstances. Nuyts, *L'exception,* § 183, at 261-263; see for other suggestions Gaudemet-Tallon, 'Le "forum non conveniens", une menace?', at 510 and 521-522; Kennett, '*FNC* in Europe', at 563.

[172] See in that sense also the arguments of defendant (Mr Jackson) and the U.K. Government in C-281/02 *Owusu v. Jackson*, [2005] ECR I-1383, para. 32.

[173] See Fentiman, 'Jurisdiction, Discretion', at 96; L. Collins, 'Forum Non Conveniens and the Brussels Convention', 106 *Law Quarterly Review* (1990), 535-539, at 535-539; Nuyts, *L'exception*, § 175, at 253; but see in contrast Duintjer Tebbens, '*Re Harrods*: An Unwelcome Interpretation', at 49. See also Chalas calling this a 'restrictive notion' of the (territorial) scope, Chalas, *L'exercise discrétionnaire,* § 606-607, at 550-552; and A. Bell, *Forum Shopping and Venue in Transnational Litigation* (2003), § 4.65, at 163 who uses the term 'mono-dimensial' scope as it is mainly concerned with the allocation between contracting parties.

[174] *Harrods (Buenos Aires) Ltd (No. 2), Re*, [1992] Ch. 72; [1991] 3 WLR 397.

[175] The facts of the case illustrate the difficulties arising out of the 'domicile' concept for jurisdictional purposes. See also the comments made by Kennett, '*FNC* in Europe', at 566-568, arguing in favour of controlling the definition of domicile; and Hare, '*FNC* in Europe: Game Over?', at 171.

be applied in favour of another Contracting State, but allowed the doctrine in favour of Argentina, a non-Contracting State.[176] The Court argued that the territorial scope of Article 2 should not be interpreted in such a way as to exclude the *forum non conveniens* in favour of non-Contracting States as this would be beyond the objectives of the Brussels Convention.[177] The Court of Appeal's judges did not feel the need to request a preliminary ruling from the ECJ,[178] but the House of Lords addressed the case to the ECJ under the name *Ladenimor S.A. v. Intercomfinanz S.A.*[179] Unfortunately for the legal community, the parties settled their dispute[180] and the Court of Appeal consistently followed this *Re Harrods* approach in *Haji-Ioannou and Others v. Frangos and Others*[181] and *Ace Insurance SA-NV v. Zurich Insurance.*[182] In the latter case, the Court of Appeal even extended the reach of the doctrine to courts of non-Contracting States and it no longer required that proceedings should not be connected with other Contracting States.[183] The Court declined jurisdiction in favour of courts of non-Contracting States even if the defendant was domiciled in a Member State.[184]

The *Re Harrods* approach was heavily criticized.[185] Even the High Court of England was not convinced. In two similar cases *S&W Bersiford plc v. New Hampshire Insurance*[186] and *Arkwright Mutual Insurance Co. v. Bryanston Insurance Co. Ltd*[187] the High Court emphasized the mandatory nature of Article 2 and established that the Convention does not allow the *forum non conveniens* in favour of non-Contracting States.[188]

---

[176] Court of Appeal, [1992] Ch. 72; [1991] 3 WLR 397, at 413. See P. Kaye, 'The EEC Judgements Convention and the Outer World: Goodbye to Forum non Conveniens?', *The Journal of Business Law* (1992), 47-76, at 70-74; Chalas, *L'exercise discrétionnaire*, § 605, at 548-550.

[177] Court of Appeal, [1992] Ch. 72; [1991] 3 WLR 397, at 415; see Kaye, 'The EEC Judgements Convention and the Outer World', at 72; and Hogan, 'Connecting Factors Problem', at 477-479.

[178] In Tebbens' view, the Court of Appeal should have requested a preliminary ruling from the ECJ see Duintjer Tebbens, '*Re Harrods*: An Unwelcome Interpretation', at 52.

[179] The *Ladenimor* case was numbered C-314/92 and removed from the Register on 21 February 1994. See Fentiman, 'Jurisdiction, Discretion', at 61; Chalas, *L'exercise discrétionnaire*, § 612, at 558 and see § 624, at 572; Nuyts, *L'exception,* § 179, at 257.

[180] Kennett, '*FNC* in Europe', at 554; Nuyts, *L'exception,* § 179, at 257; Bell, *Forum Shopping and Venue,* § 4.63, at 163; Fawcett, 'Common Law Practices', at 10; Peel, 'European Ideals', at 363.

[181] [1999] 2 Lloyd's Rep. 337 (CA).

[182] [2000] 2 Lloyd's Rep. 423 and [2001] 1 Lloyd's Rep. 618 (CA); [2001] EWCA Civ 173. See also *Eli Lilly and Co v. Novo Nordisk*, [2000] I.L.Pr. 73 (CA).

[183] See Peel, 'European Ideals', at 366.

[184] See Nuyts, *L'exception,* § 180, at 257-258.

[185] Among others by Droz in Collins and Droz, 'The Principles', at 65.

[186] [1990] 2 All ER 321; [1990] 2 QB 631.

[187] [1990] 2 All ER 333; [1990] 2 QB 649.

[188] *Berisford*, [1990] 2 QB 643-645; and *Arkwright*, at 659. See for critical comments on the position of the High Court, A. Briggs, 'Spiliada and the Brussels Convention', *Lloyd's Maritime and Commercial Law Quarterly* (1991), 10-15; Collins, '*FNC* and the Brussels Convention', Kaye, 'The EEC Judgements Convention and the Outer World', at 58 *et seq.*; Hogan, 'Connecting Factors Problem', at 476; Fentiman, 'Jurisdiction, Discretion', at 67-68; Bell, *Forum Shopping and Venue,* § 4.62-4.66, at 161-164. See in contrast on the High Court's decision, Duintjer Tebbens, '*Re Harrods*: An Unwelcome Interpretation', at 51; see also Kruger, *Impact on Third States,* § 5.75-5.77 at 287-287; Nuyts, *L'exception*, § 177, at 254.

In *Lubbe v. Cape Plc*, the House of Lords refused to decline jurisdiction and cleverly avoided the *forum non conveniens* question, but Lord Bingham states that

> '[T]he correctness of the Court of Appeal decision in In re Harrods … was in issue. … Had it been necessary to resolve that question, I would have thought it necessary to seek a ruling on the applicability on article 2 from the European Court of Justice, since I do not consider the answer to that question to be clear.'[189]

In this case, the question was again not referred to the ECJ, yet, doubts concerning the Court of Appeal's approach were expressed, leaning in favour of the non-applicability of the *forum non conveniens* doctrine in relation to non-Contracting States.[190]

In the *Owusu* case, the Deputy High Court Judge in Sheffield argued, prior to the referring order of the Court of Appeal, that the set of uniform jurisdiction rules are applicable when the defendant's domicile is located in a Brussels State, even if the claimant is not. The Court stated that the *Re Harrods* approach of the Court of Appeal 'was bad law'.[191] The ECJ confirmed the High Court's position and incontestably excluded the use of discretionary powers to decline jurisdiction in favour of Member and non-Member States under the Brussels regime.

2.3.2 The Exclusion of Anti-suit Injunctions

In the *Turner* case,[192] the ECJ prohibited courts under the Brussels Model to grant restraining orders – or *anti-suit injunctions*.[193] This typical common law instrument[194] enables a court to issue an injunction to restrain a party to proceedings pending before it from commencing or continuing legal proceedings before a court of another State, when it appears that the party in question is acting in bad faith in order to impede proceedings already pending.[195] The ECJ followed the observations of the German and Italian Governments stating that granting such a restraining order is incompatible with the Brussels Model providing a 'complete set of

---

[189] *Lubbe and Others v. Cape Plc. and related appeals*, House of Lords HL, [2000] 1 WLR 1545, Lord Bingham of Cornhill, at 1561-1562. See also Chapter 4, Sect. 4.3.

[190] According to Nuyts, *L'exception*, § 181, at 258-260.

[191] See C-281/02 *Owusu v. Jackson*, [2005] ECR I-1383, para. 16.

[192] C-159/02 *Turner v. Grovit*, [2004] ECR I-3565; notes from T. Kruger, 'The Anti-Suit Injunction in the European Judicial Space: *Turner v. Grovit*', *The International and Comparative Law Quarterly* (2004), 1030-1040, J. van Haersolte-van Hof, 'Arrest Turner/Changepoint Weg met de anti-suit injunction', *Nederlands tijdschrift voor Europees recht* (2004), 228-230; X. Kramer, 'De harmoniserende werking van het Europees procesrecht: De diskwalificatie van de *anti-suit injunction*', *NIPR* (2005), 130-137; Knight, 'Owusu and Turner', and P. Vlas, 'Note: *Turner*', *NJ* (2007), 1559-1560.

[193] See for the appeal of anti-suit injunctions, Opinion AG Ruiz-Jarabo Colomer in C-159/02 *Turner v. Grovit*, [2004] ECR I-3565, para. 26.

[194] See Opinion AG Ruiz-Jarabo Colomer in C-159/02 *Turner v. Grovit*, [2004] ECR I-3565, para. 33; and Kramer, 'De harmoniserende werking', at 131.

[195] U.K. law limits the injunctions to cases where it is appropriate to do so, provided that the addressee of the injunction has engaged in wrongful conduct and that the applicant has a legitimate interest in seeking to prevent it, such as for instance in the case of an 'abuse of process'. See Opinion AG Ruiz-Jarabo Colomer in C-159/02 *Turner v. Grovit*, [2004] ECR I-3565, paras. 11-13. See also the definition provided by AG Léger in C-281/02 *Owusu v. Jackson*, [2005] ECR I-1383, para. 5.

rules on jurisdiction' and that '[e]ach court is entitled to rule only as to its own jurisdiction under those rules but not as to the jurisdiction of a court in another Contracting State'.[196] Contrary to the reference order submitted by the Court of Appeal,[197] the ECJ stated that an anti-suit injunction prohibiting a claimant from bringing an action in a court available to him in accordance with the Brussels provisions constitutes an 'interference with the jurisdiction of the foreign court which, as such, is incompatible with the system'.[198] Furthermore, the ECJ argued that such a restraining order involves an 'assessment of the appropriateness of bringing proceedings before a court of another [Member] State',[199] which involves a certain degree of appreciation by the courts and is contrary to the closed and mandatory nature of the Brussels Model.[200] Whether an anti-suit injunction to prevent proceedings in non-Member States is compatible with the Brussels Model, has not been addressed by the ECJ, and remains an unanswered question.[201]

2.3.3 Forms of Discretion

Under very specific situations, prescribed by the Brussels Model, a court seized must or *may* decline jurisdiction:[202] A court *must* decline jurisdiction on its own motion when another court has exclusive jurisdiction.[203] Furthermore, 'unless its jurisdiction is derived from the provisions of this Regulation',[204] the court seized *must* declare that it has no jurisdiction when the defendant domiciled in one Member State does not enter an appearance.

The *lis pendens* principle of Article 27 establishes that a court last seized *must* decline jurisdiction when another court was first seized.[205] The ECJ decided in

---

[196] C-159/02 *Turner v. Grovit*, [2004] ECR I-3565, paras. 20, 24 and 31.

[197] Stating that such an injunction does 'not involve a decision upon the jurisdiction of the foreign court but rather an assessment of the conduct of the person seeking to avail himself of that jurisdiction'. C-159/02 *Turner v. Grovit*, [2004] ECR I-3565, paras. 15-16.

[198] C-159/02 *Turner v. Grovit*, [2004] ECR I-3565, para. 27.

[199] Ibid., para. 28. According to the Opinion by AG Ruiz-Jarabo Colomer in C-159/02 *Turner v. Grovit*, [2004] ECR I-3565, para. 35, it is in this assessment that similarities are to be found as to the application of anti-suit injunctions and the *forum non conveniens* doctrine in the Brussels Model, even if these instruments 'differ considerably'. See also Opinion AG Léger in C-281/02 *Owusu v. Jackson*, [2005] ECR I-1383, para. 6; and Kruger, 'The Anti-Suit Injunction', at 1036.

[200] C-281/02 *Owusu v. Jackson*, [2005] ECR I-1383, para. 37; Cuniberti, '*FNC* and the Brussels Convention', at 974-975. De Vareilles-Sommières identifies three difficulties in the Brussels unified regime imposing on Member States to assume jurisdiction at defendant's domicile, see De Vareilles-Sommières, 'The Mandatory Nature of Article 2', at 105.

[201] Kruger, 'The Anti-Suit Injunction', at 1038-1039; Duintjer Tebbens, 'From Jamaica with Pain', at 101; Knight, 'Owusu and Turner', at 289 and 294; Vlas, 'Note: *Turner*', at 1560.

[202] Fentiman, 'Jurisdiction, Discretion', at 65.

[203] Art. 25 Brussels Regulation.

[204] See Art. 26(1); see also L. Collins, 'The Jurisdiction and Judgements Convention – Some Practical Aspects of United Kingdom Accession with Particular Reference to Jurisdiction', in *Harmonization of Private International Law by the E.E.C.* (1978), 91-102, at 95; and Fawcett, 'Common law Practices', at 107.

[205] '[Article 27] does not draw any distinction between the various heads of jurisdiction provided for in the Brussels [Regulation].' C-116/02 *Gasser v. MISAT*, [2003] ECR I-14693, para. 43; referring to C-351/89 *Overseas Union v. New Hampshire Ins.*, [1991] ECR I-3317, para. 13. This applies

Gasser that even when parties have validly agreed upon a court in accordance with the choice of court provision of Article 23, but another court was first seized by the claimant, then the chosen court, secondly seized, *must* nonetheless stay proceedings until the court first seized has declared that it has no jurisdiction.[206] This obligation to decline jurisdiction does not 'leave room for any discretion as to whether one of the courts seised is better placed than the other to deal with the substance of the case'[207] and should therefore not be considered as a 'variation' of the *forum non conveniens* rule.[208]

However, only if the jurisdiction of the first court seized is contested[209] and if it does not decline jurisdiction, the court secondly seized *may*, at its own discretion, choose to stay proceedings until the jurisdiction of the court first seized is established.[210] This court secondly seized may merely stay proceedings, but may not examine the jurisdiction of the first court 'as the second court is not in a better position than the court first seised to determine whether the latter has jurisdiction'.[211]

Another example where courts are allowed to have a certain degree of discretion involves cases where 'related actions are pending in the courts of different Member States' and in that case 'any court other than the court first seised *may* stay its proceedings'.[212]

According to Léger this limited degree of discretion will depend on the question 'whether the court first seised is better placed to deal with the case which the court second seised is called on to examine. In that connection, that mechanism

---

except in the case where the court secondly seized has exclusive jurisdiction, as the ECJ stated that the *lis pendens* rule applies 'without prejudice to the case where the court second seized has exclusive jurisdiction … and in particular under Article 16 [Article 22 Brussels Regulation] thereof'. The words 'in particular' in Art. 22 of the Regulation should however not be interpreted as a possible derogation of the *lis pendens* rule in favour of a chosen court secondly seized as was decided in C-116/02 *Gasser v. MISAT*, [2003] ECR I-14693, para. 54. In contrast see Opinion AG Léger in C-116/02 *Gasser v. MISAT*, [2003] ECR I-14693, para. 83.

[206] See C-116/02 *Gasser v. MISAT*, [2003] ECR I-14693, para. 54.

[207] Opinion AG Léger in C-281/02 *Owusu v. Jackson,* [2005] ECR I-1383, para. 250.

[208] Ibid. See for comparisons made to the common law *forum non conveniens* doctrine, Fentiman, 'Jurisdiction, Discretion', at 65; 'Schlosser Report', § 181, at 125; H. Gaudemet-Tallon, 'Les régimes relatifs au refus d'exercer la compétence juridictionelle en matière civile et commerciale', *Revue internationale de droit comparé* (1994), 423-435, at 423; Kaye, 'The EEC Judgements Convention and the Outer World', at 51-61; Hogan, 'Connecting Factors Problem', at 480; Kennett, '*FNC* in Europe', at 553-554.

[209] See C-351/89 *Overseas Union v. New Hampshire Ins.*, [1991] ECR I-3317, paras. 21 and 25. Confirmed by C-116/02 *Gasser v. MISAT*, [2003] ECR I-14693, para. 44.

[210] C-351/89 *Overseas Union v. New Hampshire Ins.*, [1991] ECR I-3317, para. 26. See A. Huet, 'Note: *Gasser*', *Journal du droit international* (2004), 641-645, at 644; R. Fentiman, 'Note: *Gasser* C-116/02', *Common Market Law Review* (2005), 241-259, at 244-245; P. Vlas, 'Note: *Gasser*', *NJ* (2007), at 1551.

[211] C-351/89 *Overseas Union v. New Hampshire Ins.*, [1991] ECR I-3317, para. 23. See Jenard Report, at 41; see also Opinion AG Léger in C-281/02 *Owusu v. Jackson*, [2005] ECR I-1383, para. 248.

[212] Art. 28(1) Brussels Regulation. See also Kaye, 'The EEC Judgements Convention and the Outer World', at 47-49 and Kennett, '*FNC* in Europe', at 553; Opinion AG Léger in C-281/02 *Owusu v. Jackson*, [2005] ECR I-1383, paras. 251-252.

might be compared (but only to that extent) to that of the doctrine of *forum non conveniens*'.[213]

It is, nevertheless, generally accepted that the limited discretion given to courts under the Brussels regime as a consequence of Articles 27 and 28 is not comparable to the wider discretionary powers given to courts in common law systems. One of the most obvious reasons is that any 'discretion' left to the court under Articles 27 and 28 is conditional to the existence of parallel proceedings in another Contracting State and is therefore different from applying a general *forum non conveniens* doctrine.[214]

2.3.4 The Doctrine of the Reflex Effect

From an early stage on George Droz pointed out that under specific circumstances, some jurisdiction rules could have a *reflex effect*.[215] Considered by some to be the civil law version of the *forum non conveniens* doctrine,[216] the *reflex effect* doctrine could result in declining jurisdiction in favour of a court located in a non-Member State, despite the fact that the defendant is domiciled in a Member State and that the Regulation applies.[217] The *reflex effect of* the Regulation could occur in three situations. First, when immoveable property is located in a non-Member State, second, in the case of prorogation of jurisdiction in which parties have chosen a court located outside the Brussels territory, or third, when a non-Member State's court was seized of a similar or related action before a court of a Member State. In each of these cases, concerning respectively exclusive jurisdiction of Article 22, prorogation of jurisdiction under Article 23, and the *lis pendens* rule under Articles 27-30,[218] the seized Member State's court would decline jurisdiction in favour of the non-Member State court and respect the spirit of the jurisdiction rule by analogously applying it in favour of a non-Member State court.[219]

In *Coreck Maritime*, the ECJ ruled that in case of a choice of forum clause in which parties agreed in favour of a court located in a non-Member State, Article 23 of the Regulation would not apply and therefore, the court seized should 'asses the

---

213 Ibid., para. 252. In contrast to the *forum non conveniens* doctrine, the court is not allowed to compare the 'appropriateness' of the other court, but is limited to examining the 'proximity' of the dispute with that court. See Kennett, '*FNC* in Europe', at 553; Cuniberti, '*FNC* and the Brussels Convention', at 975; Fentiman in Magnus and Mankowski, eds., *Brussels I Regulation*, § 25, at 486.

214 Opinion AG Léger in C-281/02 *Owusu v. Jackson*, [2005] ECR I-1383, para. 255.

215 Droz, *Compétence judiciaire,* § 164, at 108.

216 Ibid. See also Chalas, *L'exercise discrétionnaire*, § 620-624, at 567-572; Nuyts, *L'exception*, § 188, at 268; see Réponse Droz in Collins and Droz, 'The Principles', at 64; Beernaert and Coibon, 'La doctrine du *forum (non) conveniens* réconciliation', at 418.

217 Peel, 'European Ideals', at 375; Briggs, 'Ideal Europeans', at 379 and Hare, '*FNC* in Europe: Game Over?', at 175.

218 Nuyts, *L'exception,* at 248.

219 Knight also calls the doctrine the 'strict reflective effect' when courts stay proceedings in favour of a non-Member State court on the basis of the exact equivalent of a rule, see Knight, 'Owusu and Turner', at 292.

validity of the clause according to the applicable law'.[220] This has been understood as an acceptance of the *reflex effect* with respect to choice of forum clauses.[221]

In *Owusu* the Court was asked whether there are circumstances to decline jurisdiction in favour of a non-Member State. According to the U.K. Government, the referring English Court of Appeal specifically asked this question regarding the *reflex effect doctrine* in relation to Article 22, Article 23 or the *lis pendens* rule under Articles 27-30.[222] This question remained unanswered by the ECJ and therefore remains open.[223]

2.3.5 The Importance of Predictability and Legal Certainty

One of the principal objectives of the Brussels jurisdictional regime is to strengthen the legal protection of persons established in the European Community by laying down common rules for jurisdiction.[224] The Regulation's Preamble gives considerable weight to the principle of legal certainty by stating that 'the rules of jurisdiction must be *highly predictable*'.[225] Predictability is ensured by the closed system of the Brussels Model which reflects a 'genuine legal systematisation, which will ensure the greatest degree of legal certainty'.[226] Considerations of legal certainty and predictability are used by the ECJ in *Owusu* to exclude the use of discretionary powers.[227] The *forum non conveniens* doctrine or any other exception 'correcting' the outcome of jurisdictional rules by giving courts discretionary powers is considered unnecessary.[228] According to the ECJ, discretionary powers are 'liable to undermine the predictability of the jurisdictional scheme of the [Regulation] and consequently undermine the principle of the legal certainty'.[229] Similar considera-

---

220 C-387/98 *Coreck v. Handelsveen*, [2000] ECR I-9337, para. 19.

221 Stone, *EU Private International Law,* at 54; Knight, 'Owusu and Turner', at 291; Peel, 'European Ideals', at 376; Briggs, 'Ideal Europeans', at 382; and for some critical comments see Briggs, 'The Death of Harrods', at 537; Briggs, 'The Impact of Recent Judgements', at 14.

222 C-281/02 *Owusu v. Jackson*, [2005] ECR I-1383, para. 48.

223 See the Opinion of Léger on this point in paras. 70, 140 and 217. The ECJ considered there was no need to reply to that question as it involved advisory opinions on general or hypothetical questions that do not justify a reference for a preliminary ruling. C-281/02 *Owusu v. Jackson*, [2005] ECR I-1383, para. 50.

224 See the Convention's Preamble. This principle of legal certainty has been consistently repeated by the ECJ in among others C-26/91 *Handte v. Traitements*, [1992] ECR I-3967, paras. 18-19; C-288/92 *Custom Made v. Stawa*, [1994] ECR I-2913, para. 15; C-440/97 *GIE Groupe Concorde*, [1999] ECR I-6307, para. 23; C-256/00 *Besix v. WABAG*, [2002] ECR I-1699, paras. 24-25; and C-281/02 *Owusu v. Jackson*, [2005] ECR I-1383, para. 39.

225 Recital 11; repeated by Opinion AG Léger in C-281/02 *Owusu v. Jackson*, [2005] ECR I-1383, para. 278. Regarding the Recital's meaning see Nuyts who claims that it would be excessive to interpret the incorporation of the principle of predictability in the Regulation's Preamble as an exclusion of the *forum non conveniens* doctrine. Nuyts, *L'exception,* § 152, at 218-220.

226 Jenard Report, at 15.

227 C-281/02 *Owusu v. Jackson*, [2005] ECR I-1383, para. 38.

228 See Chalas, *L'exercise discrétionnaire,* § 595, at 536.

229 C-281/02 *Owusu v. Jackson*, [2005] ECR I-1383, para. 41. In line with Opinion AG Léger in C-281/02 *Owusu v. Jackson*, [2005] ECR I-1383, paras. 172-175 and 263. See also Clarke, 'The Differing Approach', at 116-119.

tions are to be found in *Gasser*[230] and *Turner*.[231] The principle of legal certainty and predictability precludes the allocation of jurisdiction on 'pure principles of appropriateness'.[232] Instead, the Brussels Model uses closed norms and connecting factors. Individuals should be able 'to foresee with sufficient certainty which court will have jurisdiction'.[233] The ECJ repeatedly stated that strengthening the legal protection of both claimant and defendant implies 'at the same time, allowing the plaintiff easily to identify the court before which he may bring an action and the defendant reasonably to foresee the court before which he may be sued'.[234] With respect to the claimant, the Schlosser Report observed that a 'plaintiff must be sure which court has jurisdiction. He should not have to waste his time and money risking that the court concerned may consider itself less competent than another, *and that the plaintiff's "right of choice"* should not be weakened by application of the doctrine of *forum non conveniens*.'[235] Conversely, a 'normally well-informed' defendant should be able to reasonably foresee before which courts he may be sued and the application of the *forum non conveniens* doctrine would make this impossible.[236]

2.4 Fundamental Rights

2.4.1 Non-discrimination on the Basis of Nationality

Since the Amsterdam Treaty brought judicial cooperation in civil matters into the Community framework,[237] the anti-discrimination provision embodied in Article 12 of the EC Treaty[238] also affects issues of international jurisdiction.[239] However,

[230] C-116/02 *Gasser v. MISAT*, [2003] ECR I-14693, para. 72; see A. Dickinson, 'Legal Certainty and the Brussels Convention: Too Much of a Good Thing?', in *Forum Shopping in the European Judicial Area* (2007), 115-136, at 121-123.

[231] C-159/02 *Turner v. Grovit*, [2004] ECR I-3565; see in general G.-P. Romano, 'Principe de sécurité juridique, système de Bruxelles I/Lugano et quelques arrêts récents de la CJCE', in *La Convention de Lugano. Passé, présent et devenir. Actes de la 19e Journée de droit international privé du 16 mars 2007 à Lausanne* (2007), 165-209 and see Clarke, 'The Differing Approach', at 116.

[232] M. De Cristofaro, 'Critical remarks on the Vienna Sales Convention's impact on jurisdiction', *Uniform Law Review* (2000), 43-68, at 58-59; and Gaudemet-Tallon, 'Le "*forum non conveniens*", une menace?', at 499.

[233] See ECJ in C-116/02 *Gasser v. MISAT*, [2003] ECR I-14693, para. 72.

[234] C-125/92 *Mulox v. Geels*, [1993] ECR 4075, para. 11; C-269/95 *Benincasa v. Dentalkit*, [1997] ECR I-3767, para. 26; C-334/00 *Tacconi*, [2002] I-7357, para. 20; C-295/95 *Farrell v. Long*, [1997] ECR I-168, para. 13; and C-256/00 *Besix v. WABAG*, [2002] ECR I-1699, para. 26. Opinion AG Léger in C-281/02 *Owusu v. Jackson*, [2005] ECR I-1383, para. 160. With respect to the position of the defendant see C-440/97 *GIE Groupe Concorde*, [1999] ECR I-6307, para. 24; and C-281/02 *Owusu v. Jackson*, [2005] ECR I-1383, para. 40.

[235] 'Schlosser Report', § 78, at 97. See also the observations of Opinion AG Léger in C-281/02 *Owusu v. Jackson*, [2005] ECR I-1383, para. 225.

[236] C-281/02 *Owusu v. Jackson*, [2005] ECR I-1383, para. 42.

[237] As explained above in Sect. 2.1.

[238] Art. 12 EC Treaty (former Art. 6) states that 'any discrimination on grounds of nationality shall be prohibited'.

[239] See for the influence of Art. 12 in other fields of European civil procedure, Briggs, *Civil Jurisdiction*, § 1.18, at 14-15. See in particular C-398/92 *Mund & Fester v. Hatrex*, [1994] ECR I-467, deal-

as explained above, the authors of the 1968 Convention already prevented any 'jurisdictional discrimination' on the basis of nationality'.[240]

2.4.2 The Relationship between Article 6(1) ECHR and the Brussels Model

The impact of the European Convention on Human Rights (ECHR) in general and of the *fair trial* principle under Article 6(1) in particular, on the Brussels Model is subject of a recent discussion. The ECHR applies to 'everyone *within* their jurisdiction' and has a particularly wide scope of application not limited to nationals or residents of Contracting States.[241] With respect to the determination of civil rights and obligations, Article 6(1) of the ECHR guarantees a '*fair and public hearing within a reasonable time by an independent and impartial tribunal established by law*' for everyone. The European Court of Human Rights in Strasbourg rejected a restrictive interpretation of the fundamental right of a *fair trial*[242] and included elements of the right to have *access to court* and the *equality of arms* inherent to the right protected under Article 6(1).[243] However, despite numerous decisions of the Strasbourg Court having extensively interpreted the meaning of a fair trial in criminal, civil and commercial cases, very few cases addressed the inter-relationship between Article 6(1) ECHR and international jurisdiction rules.[244] Unfortunately, none of those cases eventually reached the Strasbourg Court, as they were dismissed on procedural grounds and declared inadmissible.

The ECJ repeatedly refused to examine any relationship between the *fair trial* doctrine of Article 6(1) of the ECHR and the Brussels Model.[245] As a rule, the ECJ persisted in arguing that it can only rule upon one of the four fundamental freedoms and not on human rights standards in transnational civil procedure.[246]

---

ing with the enforcement of a judgement in another Contracting State party to the Brussels Convention and the prohibition of discrimination.

240 As explained in Sect. 2.2.3. See *contra* the observations made by Briggs, *Civil Jurisdiction*, § 1.20, at 21.

241 Art. 1 ECHR; see Hatzimihail, 'General Report', at 622; P. van Dijk and Y. Arai, *Theory and Practice of the European Convention on Human Rights* (2006), at 13.

242 Van Dijk and Arai, *Theory and Practice ECHR*, at 514.

243 Ibid., at 557 *et seq.* and 580 *et seq.*

244 See also F. Blobel and P. Spath, 'The Tale of Multilateral Trust and the European Law of Civil Procedure', 30 *European Law Review* (2005), 528-547, at 543.

245 P. Grolimund, 'Human Rights and Jurisdiction: General Observation and Impact on the Doctrines of *Forum Non Conveniens* and *Forum Conveniens*', 4 *European Journal of Law Reform* (2002), 87-118, at 90; see Chalas, *L'exercise discrétionnaire*, at 429, who argues that the ECJ does not have the authority to rule over the ECHR.

246 Schlosser, 'Human Rights' Consideration', at 34; J. Mance, 'Exclusive Jurisdiction Agreements and European Ideals', *The Law Quarterly Review* (2004), 357-365, at 360; Briggs, 'The Impact of Recent Judgements', at 7; J. Fawcett, 'The Impact of Article 6(1) of the ECHR on Private International Law', 56 *The International and Comparative Law Quarterly* (2007), 1-48, at 25, claims that the ECJ did not suggest any indirect effect of the ECHR in C-7/98 *Krombach v. Bamberski*, [2000] ECR I-1935. See below.

As a consequence the impact of Article 6(1) on international jurisdiction has been limited so far.[247]

In the *Debaecker v. Bouwman* case, the right of a fair trial was affirmed with respect to Article 27(2) of the Convention – Article 34(2) of the Regulation – and when the defendant was not served within sufficient time it constituted a ground for refusal of enforcement.[248] The ECJ stated that although the Convention's purpose was to 'secure simplification and enforcement of governing the reciprocal recognition of judgments',[249] this should not in any way undermine the right of a fair hearing.[250]

In the *Krombach* case,[251] the ECJ was requested to explore the relationship between Article 6(1) ECHR and the public policy exception as a ground for refusal of recognition of foreign judgements under the Brussels regime.[252] This decision deserves extra attention and is frequently used to illustrate the relation between the Brussels Model and Article 6(1) ECHR.[253] Although the ECJ's decision mainly focuses on the meaning of Article 6(1) ECHR as an exception for recognition under Article 27,[254] the other question addressed to the Court concerned the situation in which the court of origin based its jurisdiction solely on the nationality of the injured party and whether this should be considered as a public policy ground to refuse recognition of the judgements following Article 27(1).[255] The French court of origin based its jurisdiction on Article 5(4) of the Brussels regime which allows jurisdiction of a court seized in criminal proceedings to also rule over civil claims for damages, based on an act giving rise to those criminal proceedings, provided that it has jurisdiction under its own law to entertain civil proceedings.[256]

---

[247] Fawcett, 'Impact of Article 6(1)', at 2; Fentiman in Magnus and Mankowski, eds., *Brussels I Regulation*, § 39, at 491; Grolimund, 'Human Rights and Jurisdiction', at 88; Strikwerda, 'De invloed van het EVRM', at 260. See for the impact of Art. 6(1) on public policy exceptions, D. Bureau and H. Muir Watt, *Droit international privé* (2007), Vol. I, at 272-273.

[248] Like Art. 34(2) Regulation, that provision states that 'a judgment shall not be recognized, where it was given in default of appearance, if the defendant was not served with the document which instituted the proceedings or with an equivalent document in sufficient time and in such a way as to enable him to arrange for his defence, unless the defendant failed to commence proceedings to challenge the judgment when it was possible for him to do so.'

[249] See the Convention's Preamble.

[250] Case 49/84 *Debaecker v. Bouwman*, [1985] ECR 1779, para. 10; see also Stadler, 'Cornerstones', at 1659.

[251] C-7/98 *Krombach v. Bamberski*, [2000] ECR I-1935.

[252] See among others P. Vlas, 'The Principle of Fair Trial in International Litigation', in *Law and Reality: Essays on National and International Procedural Law in Honour of Cornelis Carel Albert Voskuil* (1992), 391-406, at 401-404; and G. Walter and S. Baumgartner, *Recognition and Enforcement Outside the Scope of the Brussels Convention and Lugano Conventions: Civil Procedure in Europe* (2000), at 27; see for other implications of Art. 6 in relation to the *ordre public*, P. Mayer, 'La Convention européenne des droits de l'homme et l'application des normes étrangères', 98 *Revue critique de droit international privé* (1991), 651-665, at 662-665; Hatzimihail, 'General Report', at 625-628.

[253] Grolimund, 'Human Rights and Jurisdiction', at 88-89; Geimer, 'Successful Model', at 34; Fawcett, 'Impact of Article 6(1)', at 25 *et seq.*

[254] Art. 34 Regulation in conjunction with Art. 26 Brussels Convention and Art. 33 Brussels Regulation. See C-7/98 *Krombach v. Bamberski*, [2000] ECR I-1935.

[255] See C-7/98 *Krombach v. Bamberski*, [2000] ECR I-1935, para. 17.

[256] Art. 5(4) Brussels Convention and Regulation.

The French court based its jurisdiction in the criminal proceedings on rules of the Code of Criminal Procedure that are similar to Articles 14 and 15 of the Civil Code and based its jurisdiction solely on the victim's nationality.[257] The ECJ was asked whether the court of a state in which enforcement was sought may take into account that the jurisdiction of the state of origin based its jurisdiction solely on grounds of nationality as a public policy exception within the meaning of Article 27(1) of the Brussels Convention.[258] In its preliminary observations the Court first confirmed that although the contracting parties are free to determine according to their own conceptions what public policy requires,[259] the ECHR and the right to a fair legal process has particular significance,[260] which should also be respected according to Article 6(2) of the Treaty on European Union.[261] But the ECJ refused to cover this nationality-based jurisdiction under the public policy exception of Article 27(1) as an immediate consequence of what is stated in Article 28(3) of the Brussels Convention: 'the test of public policy referred to in point 1 of Article 27 may not be applied to the rules relating to jurisdiction'.[262] One of the principal objectives of the Brussels Model was to facilitate free movement of judgements and any 'review of the rules of jurisdiction of the court that gave the judgment is prohibited', except in the event of a possible breach of the jurisdictional provisions concerning insurance, consumer contracts or exclusive jurisdictions.[263] According to Fawcett, the objectives of the Brussels system ensuring the free movement of judgements overrides the values guaranteed under Article 6(1) of the ECHR.[264]

This was even more flagrant in the *Gasser* case, in which the ECJ was directly confronted with the ECHR and was requested to deal with the question whether Article 6(1) could interfere with the *lis pendens* rule.[265] In *Gasser*, the (Italian) court first seized took an unjustifiably long time to establish whether it had jurisdiction, which obliged another court secondly seized, and initially chosen by the parties, to stay its proceedings. The referring court asked the ECJ to ascertain whether excessive length of proceedings, exceeding a three-year period, is contrary to the requirements of Article 6(1) ECHR and should justify derogation to the

---

[257] See Opinion of AG Saggio, delivered on 23 September 1999, in C-7/98 *Krombach v. Bamberski*, [2000] ECR I-1935, para. 10.

[258] Art. 34(1) Brussels Regulation, C-7/98 *Krombach v. Bamberski*, [2000] ECR I-1935, para. 17.

[259] See C-7/98 *Krombach v. Bamberski*, [2000] ECR I-1935, para. 22.

[260] Ibid., paras. 25-26 and Case 222/84 *Johnston v. Chief Constable of the Royal Ulster Constabulary*, [1986] ECR 1651, para. 18.

[261] C-7/98 *Krombach v. Bamberski*, [2000] ECR I-1935, para. 27; see Strikwerda, 'De invloed van het EVRM', at 256.

[262] C-7/98 *Krombach v. Bamberski*, [2000] ECR I-1935, para. 34; see also H. Muir Watt, 'Evidence of an Emergent European Legal Culture: Public Policy Requirements of Procedural Fairness under the Brussels and Lugano Conventions', 36 *Texas International Law Journal* (2001), 539-554, at 552; Stadler, 'Cornerstones', at 1659. Recourse to public policy is only available in exceptional cases.

[263] Art. 35(1), see also Opinion AG Saggio in C-7/98 *Krombach v. Bamberski*, [2000] ECR I-1935, paras. 14 and 16.

[264] Fawcett, 'Impact of Article 6(1)', at 32; Mance, 'European Ideals', at 363.

[265] Art. 21 Brussels Convention and Art. 27 Brussels Regulation.

lis pendens rule.[266] It was argued by *Gasser* and by the U.K. Government that such automatic application of the *lis pendens* rule could encourage delaying tactics.[267] A claimant could choose, even contrary to a jurisdiction agreement, a court known to take a particularly long time to establish jurisdiction in order to delay a judgement against him for several years to the disadvantage of the other party who also seeks to enforce its rights.[268] In order to render the *lis pendens* rule in conformity with Article 6(1) ECHR, it was suggested to allow the recognition of an exception in the event the claimant was acting in bad faith and the court first seized did not render a judgement within a reasonable time. On the contrary, the Italian Government and the Commission argued that such an exception would create legal uncertainty and that the Brussels Model is 'based on mutual trust and on the equivalence of the courts of the Contracting States and establishes a binding system of jurisdiction which all the courts within the purview of the Convention are required to observe'.[269] Furthermore, the Commission argued that any incompatibility with Article 6(1) should not be settled by the ECJ in the context of the Brussels Model, but should instead be examined by the European Court of Human Rights.[270] In its findings, the ECJ makes no reference to the ECHR or to the Strasbourg Court.[271] The ECJ's reasoning is based on the letter, spirit and aims of the Brussels jurisdiction regime and states that any derogation to the *lis pendens* rule on the ground that the court first seized deals with cases with excessive delays would be manifestly contrary to those aims.[272] According to the ECJ the mutual trust in each other's legal systems and judicial institutions must prevail, as well as the principle of legal certainty for individuals to foresee which court should have jurisdiction.[273] Apparently, the Brussels Model's goals of mutual trust and legal certainty override the defendant's procedural rights under Article 6(1) ECHR.[274]

The discussion concerning the *fair trial* doctrine of Article 6 ECHR as ultimate test for procedural fairness in jurisdictional allocation by the Brussels Regulation

---

[266] It would also entail restrictions on freedom of movement as guaranteed by Arts. 28, 39, 48 and 49 EC; C-116/02 *Gasser v. MISAT*, [2003] ECR I-14693, paras. 55 and 59. See also Opinion AG Léger in C-116/02 *Gasser v. MISAT*, [2003] ECR I-14693, para. 85.

[267] There could also be the risk of manipulation according to Muir Watt, see H. Muir Watt, 'Note: *Gasser*', *Revue critique de droit international privé* (2004), 459-464, at 461-462; see Blobel and Spath, 'Tale of Multilateral Trust', at 544.

[268] C-116/02 *Gasser v. MISAT*, [2003] ECR I-14693, paras. 61-62; see Opinion AG Léger in C-116/02 *Gasser v. MISAT*, [2003] ECR I-14693, paras. 67-69; Mance, 'European Ideals', at 359.

[269] C-116/02 *Gasser v. MISAT*, [2003] ECR I-14693, para. 67.

[270] Ibid., para. 69.

[271] Underlined by Vlas, 'Note: *Gasser*', at 1551 and regretted by Mance, 'European Ideals', at 364-365.

[272] C-116/02 *Gasser v. MISAT*, [2003] ECR I-14693, para. 70, followed by Opinion AG Léger in C-116/02 *Gasser v. MISAT*, [2003] ECR I-14693, paras. 89-90.

[273] C-116/02 *Gasser v. MISAT*, [2003] ECR I-14693, para. 72.

[274] See in this sense also Dickinson, 'Legal Certainty: Too Much of a Good Thing?', at 122-123; R. Fentiman, 'Access to Justice and Parallel Proceedings in Europe', 63 *The Cambridge Law Journal* (2004), 312-313, at 313; Mance, 'European Ideals', at 365; Fentiman, 'Note: *Gasser*', at 258; Fentiman in Magnus and Mankowski, eds., *Brussels I Regulation*, § 33, at 490; Blobel and Spath, 'Tale of Multilateral Trust', at 543, but see *contra* M.-L. Niboyet, 'Le principe de confiance mutuelle et les injonctions "Anti-suit"', in *Forum Shopping in the European Judicial Area* (2007), 77-89, at 85.

is directly linked to the question whether the ECHR is part of community law.[275] Institutional developments in European integration identify a general trend or desire to incorporate fundamental rights as an integral part of community law that would equally have its effect on the Brussels jurisdictional scheme.[276] In December 2000, the European Commission, together with the Council and Parliament, proclaimed the Charter of Fundamental Rights of the European Union. Besides Article 21(2) of that Charter affirming non-discrimination on the basis of nationality as a fundamental right,[277] Article 47 ensures the right to an effective remedy and to a fair trial.[278] Since the rejection of the European Constitution[279] by France and The Netherlands in 2005, the Inter-governmental Conference 2007 in Lisbon undertook the work of drafting a Reform Treaty in which the EU Charter would be an integrated part of community law.[280]

Apart from an integrated Charter of Fundamental Rights as part of community law, a recently accepted proposal envisages a significant role for the ECHR within the European Union and these are already called the European 'Bill of Rights' by some.[281] The Amsterdam Treaty explicitly mentions the ECHR as embodying 'general principles of community law', which shall be 'respected' by the Union.[282] The Reform Treaty proposes that the Union shall *accede* to the ECHR and its provisions shall then *constitute* general principles of the Union's law.[283] Community legislation will then have to be compatible with the ECHR and Article 6(1) in particular will have a direct impact on Community legislation.[284] An emerging *fair*

---

[275] Schlosser, 'The Issue of Human Rights', at 19-23; Chalas, *L'exercise discrétionnaire,* at 429; Strikwerda, 'De invloed van het EVRM', 257-258; Vlas, 'Note: *Gasser*', at 1551; and Magnus and Mankowski, eds., *Brussels I Regulation*, § 29, at 488.

[276] See in this sense J. Bomhoff, *Judicial Discretion in European Law on Conflicts of Jurisdiction: Looking for National Perspectives on European Rules for Jurisdiction over Multiple Defendants* (2005), at 81.

[277] At http://ec.europa.eu/justice_home/unit/charte/index_en.html; http://ec.europa.eu/justice_home/unit/charte/en/charter-equality.html.

[278] At http://europa.eu.int/comm/justice_home/unit/charte/en/charter-justice.html.

[279] The official name of this text is 'Treaty establishing a Constitution for Europe'.

[280] Art. 6(1) of the Treaty of Lisbon amending the Treaty on European Union and the Treaty establishing the European Community. (Draft Reform Treaty) Text to be found at http://www.consilium.europa.eu/showPage.asp?id=1317&lang=en&mode=g.

[281] Schlosser, 'The Issue of Human Rights', at 13 and 21; Muir Watt, 'Emergent European Legal Culture', at 543.

[282] Art. 6(2) Treaty of the European Union (Consolidated version OJ 2006 C 321E).

[283] Art. 6(2) and (3) of the Consolidated versions of the Treaty on European Union and the Treaty on the functioning of the European Union (OJ 2008 C115) following the Lisbon Treaty signed 13 December 2007 (OJ 2007 C306). The Treaty was meant to enter into force on 1 January 2009, provided that all Member States ratified the text in accordance with their respective constitutional requirements. The negative outcome of Ireland's referendum of 13 June 2008 presently hinders the entry into force of the Lisbon Treaty.

[284] Art. 14 of the ECHR provides for a similar anti-discrimination provision to that in the abovementioned Art. 12 EC Treaty. It is not unthinkable that in combination with Art. 6 ECHR, any nationality-based jurisdiction would be considered incompatible with community law, as was the case in C-7/98 *Krombach v. Bamberski*, [2000] ECR I-1935. See also Schlosser, 'Human Rights' Consideration', at 31; and F. Matscher, 'Quarante ans d'activités de la Cour européenne des droits de l'homme', 270 *Recueil des cours* (1997), 237-398, at 370-371.

trial doctrine as a 'blind alley' to correct the unfair exercise of state jurisdiction would then be foreseeable, but is at the moment not 'official'.[285] When that time comes, it will be necessary to re-schedule the relationship between mutual trust and fundamental rights.[286]

2.5 Defendant's Domicile – The General Jurisdiction Rule

Apart from containing the key criterion for the Regulation's territorial scope, Article 2 lays down the fundamental rule for jurisdiction of courts and 'constitutes one of the foundations on which the Convention largely stands'.[287] The rule states that 'persons domiciled in a Member State shall, whatever their nationality, be sued in the courts of that Member State'.[288]

Based on a connection between the forum and the defendant through his domicile, the rule provides for *general* jurisdiction and is therefore not limited to the nature of the claim.[289] The drafters' choice for the defendant's domicile is consistent with the practice of the national jurisdiction regimes of the six initial Contracting States,[290] and has often been used in several bilateral conventions preceding the Brussels Convention.[291] Jenard emphasized that the rule is common practice to judges and lawyers.[292]

The general rule emanates from the Roman maxim of the *actor sequitur forum rei* based on the idea that the claimant should follow – and sue – the defendant in his home state, as it is 'more difficult, generally speaking, to defend oneself in the courts of a foreign country'[293] and 'it makes it easier, in principle, for a defendant to defend himself' in his domicile.[294] This 'home court advantage' is justified by

---

[285] J. Hill, 'The Exercise of Jurisdiction in Private International Law', in *Asserting Jurisdiction: International and European Legal Perspectives* (2003), 39-62, at 40; and Grolimund, 'Human Rights and Jurisdiction', at 91 *et seq.*

[286] See also Stadler, 'Cornerstones', at 1660.

[287] Opinion AG Léger in C-281/02 *Owusu v. Jackson*, [2005] ECR I-1383, para. 170. Vlas in Magnus and Mankowski, eds., *Brussels I Regulation*, § 3, at 71.

[288] C-412/98 *Group Josi v. UGIC*, [2000] ECR I-5925, para. 55; C-116/02 *Gasser v. Misat*, [2003] ECR I-14693, para. 4; and Opinion AG Léger in C-420/97 *Leathertex v. Bodetex*, [1999] ECR I-6747, para. 95. As noted by Briggs, Art. 2 does not explicitly refer to 'defendant' but to the 'person' being sued, see Briggs, *Civil Jurisdiction,* § 2.111, at 136. Art. 2 identifies the State as competent, but internal territorial rules will have to determine which court will have jurisdiction, Gaudemet-Tallon, *Compétence en Europe,* § 84, at 60.

[289] See Vlas in Magnus and Mankowski, eds., *Brussels I Regulation*, § 5, at 71.

[290] See also Opinion AG Ruiz-Jarabo Colomer in C-440/97 *GIE Groupe Concorde*, [1999] ECR I-6307, para. 25.

[291] See the study done by Weser, *La convention communautaire,* at 146 *et seq.*

[292] See Jenard Report, at 19, and see also P. Byrne and J. Blayney, *The EEC Convention on Jurisdiction and the Enforcement of Judgements* (1990), at 25.

[293] Jenard Report, at 18.

[294] See in particular C-26/91 *Handte v. Traitements*, [1992] ECR I-3967, para. 14; C-256/00 *Besix v. WABAG*, [2002] ECR I-1699, para. 52; C-412/98 *Group Josi v. UGIC*, [2000] ECR I-5925, paras. 34-35; Opinion AG Léger in C-281/02 *Owusu v. Jackson* [2005] ECR I-1383, para. 170.

the fact that the person being sued is 'generally in a weaker position'[295] and should therefore be favoured in order to compensate the fact that he has to defend himself against the claimant's action.[296] This is especially of importance because the consequences under the Brussels Model are far-reaching: if a judgement is pronounced against the defendant, the Regulation's regime guarantees its recognition and enforcement throughout EU territory. Hence, the rule 'serves as a counterpoise to the facilities provided by the convention with regard to the recognition and enforcement of foreign judgements'.[297] It should be noted that recognition and enforcement of judgements is more likely to take place where the defendant is domiciled, since this is generally speaking also the place where his assets are located.

2.5.1 Determination of 'Domicile' for Natural Persons

Considering its importance under the Brussels jurisdictional scheme, it was necessary to indicate how to determine the defendant's domicile. The Regulation determines the domicile of a natural person differently than the corporate domicile. The domicile of a natural person is regulated by Article 59 which states that the court seized shall apply its internal law to determine whether a party is domiciled in the Member State.[298]

In order to determine a natural person's domicile, the Regulation thus refrains from providing an autonomous concept.[299] The domicile concept diverges among the legal systems of the Member States, especially under the common law of the U.K. and Ireland, where the concept is 'in substance a nationality in disguise'.[300] Continental European systems use the domicile criterion more as a factual concept rather than as representing a legal connection between the person and a particular

---

[295] C-295/95 *Farrell v. Long*, [1997] I-1683; see also Pontier and Burg, *EU Principles on Jurisdiction*, at 118. See in contrast Verheul, 'The "*forum actoris*"', at 201, arguing whether this favour is justified.

[296] See Jenard Report, at 18; Pontier and Burg, *EU Principles on Jurisdiction*, at 54, see some critical remarks by Kruger, *Impact on Third States*, § 2.66, at 85.

[297] Case 220/84 *AS-Autoteile v. Malhé*, [1985] ECR 2267, para. 15; see also Pontier and Burg, *EU Principles on Jurisdiction*, at 56 and 120.

[298] See also Art. 59(2). See Jenard Report, at 15; and Droz, *Compétence judiciaire*, at 54.

[299] See Gaudemet-Tallon, *Compétence en Europe*, § 85, at 60.

[300] Ibid., at 60-61. In the light of these divergences the U.K. also opted for a special definition of 'domicile' for the purpose of the Brussels Model, see P. Kaye, 'The Meaning of Domicile Under United Kindom Law for the Purpose of the 1968 Brussels Convention on Jurisdiction and the Enforcement of Judgments in Civil and Commercial Matters', *Netherlands International Law Review* (1988), 181-195; P. North, *Private International Law Problems in Common Law Jurisdictions* (1993), at 6-7; A. Briggs, *The Conflict of Laws* (2008), at 64; Briggs, *Civil Jurisdiction*, § 2.113, at 138-139; J. Hill, *International Commercial Disputes in English Courts* (2005), § 4.1.2, at 72 *et seq.*; Stone, *EU Private International Law*, at 60-61; Dicey, Morris *et al.*, *Conflict of Laws*, § 11-076, at 336; and 'Schlosser Report', at 95. See also 'The Report on the Application of the Brussels I Regulation in the Member States' carried out by the Institute for Private International Law at the University of Heidelberg under the direction of Prof. Dr. Burkhard Hess, Prof. Dr. Thomas Pfeiffer and Prof. Dr. Peter Schlosser, *September 2007* [hereafter 'Application Report], § 181-183, at 85-86. Available at http://ec.europa.eu/civiljustice/publications/publications_en.htm#5.

place. This could result in a defendant having more than one domicile.[301] Such multiplication of forums has apparently been accepted for this general jurisdiction rule. The Regulation's proposal suggested changing 'domicile' to 'habitual residence',[302] as the latter was thought easier to establish on the basis of facts. The Regulation's final version nevertheless maintained 'domicile', without giving any further explanations for natural persons.[303]

2.5.2 The Corporate Domicile

The domicile of a company or other corporate entity[304] is assimilated with the corporate seat and is defined autonomously in order 'to make the common rules more transparent and avoid conflicts of jurisdiction'.[305] Instead of referring back to the seized court's rules of private international law as was the case under the Brussels Convention, the new Article 60 attempts to combine the different approaches for determining a corporation's seat or domicile in one autonomous concept.[306] It provides three alternative connecting factors – a) the statutory seat,[307] b) the central administration, or c) the principal place of business.[308] In contrast to the statutory seat, both the central administration and the principal place of business are factual concepts that can be determined on a case-by-case basis.[309] As a result, Article 60[310] leads to multiplication of forums with general jurisdiction over the corporate

[301] Briggs, *Civil Jurisdiction*, § 2:112, at 138; Dicey, Morris *et al.*, *Conflict of Laws*, § 11-081, at 338. See also for other consequences, Kruger, *Impact on Third States*, § 2.21 at 67.

[302] 'Proposal for a Council Act establishing the Convention on Jurisdiction and the Recognition and Enforcement of Judgments in Civil and Commercial Matters in the Member States of the European Union' (Proposal), OJ 1998 C 33/20, COM(97) 609 final – 97/0339(CNS); see also P. Herzog, 'Rules on the International Recognition of Judgments (and on International Jurisdiction) by Enactments of an International Organization: European Community Regulations 1347/2000 and 44/2001', in *Law and Justice in a Multistate World: Essays in Honor of Arthur T. von Mehren* (2002), 83-105, at 92-94; P. Vlas, 'Herziening EEX: Van verdrag naar verordening', 6421 *WPNR* (2000), 745-753, at 748.

[303] See Mourre, stating that the habitual residence was considered to be an uncertain concept, incapable of bringing enough legal certainty, A. Mourre, *Droit judiciaire privé européen des affaires: Droit communautaire – droit comparé* (2003), § 87, at 64.

[304] I.e. the domicile of a company or other legal person or an association of natural or legal persons.

[305] Subpara. 11 of the Preamble.

[306] Under Art. 53 of the Brussels Convention the 'domicile' of a company or other legal person or association of natural or legal persons shall be determined by a court's national rules of private international law. See Gaudemet-Tallon, *Compétence en Europe*, § 88, at 62; P. Vlas, *Rechtspersonen* (2002), § 181, at 88-89; and Briggs, *Civil Jurisdiction*, § 2.116, at 141.

[307] Art. 60(2) explains that 'for the purposes of the United Kingdom and Ireland "statutory seat" means the registered office or, where there is no such office anywhere, the place of incorporation or, where there is no such place anywhere, the place under the law of which the formation took place.'

[308] This corresponds to the three criteria of the right of establishing a company within the Community under Art. 48 (ex-58) of the EC Treaty, but it also corresponds to the criteria used in the rules of private international law of the Member States. See Vlas, *Rechtspersonen*, § 178, at 87.

[309] Ibid.

[310] It might be worthwhile mentioning that the Regulation's proposal suggested a different definition of corporate domicile by proposing a 'habitual residence' which would be determined by the place of the central management, or failing that, its registered office. See Art. 2(2) Proposal as explained in Sect. 2.5.1.

defendant.[311] In the event a corporate defendant has its statutory seat in Member State A and its principal place of business in Member State B, both forums will be available to the claimant. In practice, it is the plaintiff who benefits from this way of determining the corporate domicile and the three criteria are at risk when the defendant's statutory seat does not coincide with his real seat.[312]

The strong connection between the forum and the defendant represented by one of the three connecting factors, justifies not only general jurisdiction over the corporate defendant, but also the multiplication of competent forums. However, the precise meaning of any of these connecting factors was regrettably not given and might still be subject to further autonomous interpretation by the ECJ.[313]

2.6 Special Branch Jurisdiction under Article 5(5)

Under Article 5(5) a person domiciled in another Member State, may be sued in the courts of another Member State where a branch, agency or other establishment [hereafter 'branch-establishment'] is situated, as a result of a dispute arising out of its operations.[314] A Belgian resident who has a 'branch-establishment' in Hungary is also amenable for suit in Hungarian courts over claims arising out of its operations.

As a special jurisdiction rule, Article 5(5) is justified by a particularly close connecting factor between the dispute and the court with jurisdiction to resolve it.[315] The branch-establishment could be considered as an extension of the defendant's domicile in another forum, or a '*quasi* domicile'.[316] According to the ECJ in *Somafer*, this special link 'comprises in the first place the material signs enabling the existence of the branch, … to be easily recognized, and in the second place the connexion that there is between the local entity and the claim directed against the parent body established in another state'.[317] With respect to the latter, the Court stated that the relation between the parent body – or defendant – and the branch-establishment on the one hand and the relation between the establishment and the third party – the claimant – on the other reflect a *special link*.[318]

The idea behind 'branch jurisdiction' is that a person who voluntarily founds an establishment in a forum to 'enhance the local reach of his own activities' and economically benefits from this kind of presence in a state should equally accept to

---

[311] Briggs, *Civil Jurisdiction,* § 2.114, at 139; Hill, *International Commercial Disputes*, § 4.1.11, at 75.

[312] Stadler, 'Cornerstones', at 1646.

[313] As also indicated by Briggs, *Civil Jurisdiction*, § 2.115, at 141, and as shown by the Application Report in § 188-189, at 89.

[314] See for the territorial scope Sect. 2.2.3; see Jenard Report, at 26; and see some interesting observations from Kruger, *Impact on Third States*, § 2.238-2.239, at 151-152; Mourre, *Droit judiciaire privé européen*, § 216, at 138.

[315] Jenard Report, at 22; repeated by ECJ in C-439/93 *Lloyd's v. Campenon Bernard*, [1995] ECR I-961, para. 21.

[316] Magnus and Mankowski, eds., *Brussels I Regulation*, § 270, at 219.

[317] Case 33/78 *Somafer v. Saar-Ferngas*, [1978] ECR 2183, para. 11.

[318] Ibid., para. 8.

be emanable for suit in that state.[319] Conversly, a party carrying out business with another party, through that party's branch-establishment, should be able to bring action in the forum where this branch is established and from which the dispute arose, instead of at his domicile. This does not necessarily have to lead to a *forum actoris*, but in practice a claimant would prefer to deal with a person's establishment in his home forum, if he has one, which leads to jurisdiction for the courts of the plaintiff's domicile.[320] Branch jurisdiction therefore facilitates a claimant's access to justice when his counter-party carried out business through a permanent branch-establishment in his home forum.[321]

According to Briggs, branch jurisdiction is justified by the fact that the 'defendant has set up a sufficient and permanent-looking establishment in another member state', and has therefore 'laid himself open to being sued there in just the same way as if he was domiciled there'.[322]

Branch jurisdiction consists of two fundamental aspects: first, a branch-establishment is to be determined on an independent and autonomous basis and has to satisfy the requirements as stipulated by the ECJ. Second, the claim has to arise out of the operations of that establishment, which implies that 'branch jurisdiction' confers special jurisdiction and is limited to claims arising out of this branch-establishment.

2.6.1 The Autonomous Meaning of Branch-establishment

In the *Somafer v. Saar Ferngas AG* case, the ECJ ruled that considerations of 'legal certainty and equality of rights and obligations for the parties' require an autonomous and independent interpretation of the concept of 'branch, agency or other establishment'.[323] The Court refused to define each concept and to interpret them separately; instead it defined a single concept by way of enumerating specific characteristics and requirements for 'branch-establishment'.[324] The 'establishment' concept of Article 5(5) is based on the same essential characteristics and requirements as the concepts 'branch' and 'agency'.[325] Those requirements are however not linked to any formalities required by national registers or national company laws.[326]

---

[319] Magnus and Mankowski, eds., *Brussels I Regulation*, § 270, at 219.

[320] See also Gaudemet-Tallon, *Compétence en Europe*, § 234, at 190; P. Volken, 'Note: *Lloyd's Register of Shipping*', *Schweizerische Zeitschrift für internationales und europäisches Recht* (1995), 138-141, at 141; and in contrast J.-M. Bischoff, 'Note: *Blanckeart* C 139/80', *Journal du droit international* (1982), 479-482, at 482; Magnus and Mankowski, eds., *Brussels I Regulation*, § 271, at 220.

[321] See J.-M. Bischoff, 'Note: *Lloyd's Register of Shipping* C-439/93', *Journal du droit international* (1996), 564-567, at 566; referring to Gaudemet-Tallon, *Compétence en Europe,* § 230, at 187. See also Hill, *International Commercial Disputes*, § 5.6.80, at 158.

[322] Briggs, *Civil Jurisdiction*, § 2.166, at 198.

[323] Case 33/78 *Somafer v. Saar-Ferngas*, [1978] ECR 2183, para. 8; and see Vlas, *Rechtspersonen,* § 202, at 99.

[324] Case 33/78 *Somafer v. Saar-Ferngas*, [1978] ECR 2183, paras. 4-8.

[325] Case 14/76 *De Bloos v. Bouyer*, [1976] ECR 1497, para. 21. See Gaudemet-Tallon, *Compétence en Europe,* § 228, at 185 and Magnus and Mankowski, eds., *Brussels I Regulation*, § 291, at 226.

[326] Magnus and Mankowski, eds., *Brussels I Regulation*, § 277, at 222 and § 281 *et seq*., at 223.

First of all, it is important to emphasize that the branch concept should be understood as being an effective and fixed[327] place of business.[328] The ECJ also stated that such a place of business should have

> 'the appearance of permanency, such as the extension of a parent body, has a management and is materially equipped to negotiate business with third parties so that the latter, although knowing that there will if necessary be a legal link with the parent body, the head office of which is abroad, do not have to deal directly with such parent body but may transact business at the place of business constituting the extension.'[329]

In *De Bloos* the ECJ emphasized that being subject to the direction and control of the parent body is one of the essential characteristics of the branch concept.[330] But the ECJ ruled that a corporate defendant 'domiciled' in France had not established itself in Belgium in the sense of Article 5(5) by having a grantee of an exclusive sales concession which was neither subjected to defendant's control nor to its direction and was not empowered either to negotiate in his name or to bind him.[331]

Likewise, in *Blanckeart*[332] where defendant had appointed an independent commercial agent, the ECJ refused to accept the 'dependency of the direction and control of that parent body' as required by Article 5(5).[333] The defendant, a furniture manufacturer Blanckeart with its seat in Belgium, could therefore not be sued on the basis of Article 5(5) in German courts where the agent was established. By way of a negative formulation the Court gave a set of three factors precluding the agent from having 'the appearance of permanency as an extension of the parent body'[334] and not being subjected to the direction of the defendant, as the agent is *a)* 'basically free to organize his own work without being subject to instructions from the parent body in that regard'; *b)* 'free to represent at the same time several rival firms producing or marketing identical or similar products'; and lastly *c)* 'does not effectively participate in the completion and execution of transactions but is restricted in principle to transmitting orders to the undertaking he represents.'[335] Without such element of control, being a commercial agent is not automatically sufficient for jurisdiction under Article 5(5).[336] Hartley points to a very important consequence of this decision: when a party wants to enter a foreign market he will have to choose between establishing a branch and merely appointing an agent. If he decides to appoint a commercial agent over whom he has no control he will not be

---

[327] Briggs, *Civil Jurisdiction*, § 2.167, at 199.

[328] Case 33/78 *Somafer v. Saar-Ferngas*, [1978] ECR 2183, para. 13. See also H. Duintjer Tebbens, *Civil Jurisdiction and Judgments in Europe* (1992), at 95.

[329] Case 33/78 *Somafer v. Saar-Ferngas*, [1978] ECR 2183, para. 12.

[330] Case 14/76 *De Bloos v. Bouyer*, [1976] ECR 1497, paras. 20 and 23; and see T. Hartley, 'Note: *Tessili*', *European Law Review* (1977), 57-63, at 61.

[331] Case 14/76 *De Bloos v. Bouyer*, [1976] ECR 1497, paras. 18-23; see T. Hartley, 'Note: *De Bloos v Bouyer*', *European Law Review* (1977), 57-63, at 61.

[332] Case 139/80 *Blanckaert & Willems v. Trost*, [1981] ECR 819; see the critical note by Bischoff, 'Note: *Blanckeart*', at 480-482.

[333] Case 139/80 *Blanckaert & Willems v. Trost*, [1981] ECR 819, para. 12.

[334] Ibid., para. 12.

[335] Ibid., para. 13.

[336] See Magnus and Mankowski, eds., *Brussels I Regulation*, § 292-295, at 226-227.

amenable for suit under Article 5(5). If however he decides to set up an establishment to carry out his business, he is bound to accept the fact that he is emanable for suit in that forum.[337]

In *Somafer*, the ECJ required an appearance of permanency of an 'easily discernible extension of the parent body' – i.e. the defendant.[338] This reflects that there is a link between the defendant and the branch-establishment, which is required in order for a third party to know that he does not necessarily have to deal with the parent body directly in order to be bound by the parent through this establishment. In this respect the branch-establishment should have a certain degree of autonomy to operate in the name and on behalf of the parent body.[339]

A branch-establishment should have the management and be materially equipped to negotiate business with third parties.[340] In this context, the ECJ was asked with respect to consumer contracts whether a defendant's registered office in the state of the consumer's, i.e. claimant's, domicile – which was effectively owned by it and had staff links with it but no authority to contract on defendant's behalf, acting only as intermediary and advising the consumer – was to be considered as a branch-establishment?[341] The authority to contract on the defendant's or the parental body's behalf is part of a certain degree of independence which seemed to be required in order to fulfill the requirements of Article 5(5). Although the Court did not need to answer this question, it is to be expected that when an establishment has no authority to contract on the defendant's behalf it should not be considered as a 'branch-establishment' in the sense of the *Somafer* definition of Article 5(5).[342]

However in the *Schotte* case the criterion of *appearance* received a somewhat different meaning.[343] The ECJ ruled that the conditions enumerated by *Somafer* in order to satisfy the branch concept of Article 5(5) might also be satisfied in a case where the establishment, which acted as an extension of a corporate defendant established in another Member State, is not a subsidiary of that corporation but is an independent company or even its parent company.[344] Schotte, a German domiciled claimant, brought actions in German courts against Parfums Rotschild SarL, a company with its seat in France. The dispute arose out of negotiations that

---

[337] T. Hartley, 'Note: *Blanckeart*', *European Law Review* (1981), 481-483, at 483.

[338] Case 33/78 *Somafer v. Saar-Ferngas*, [1978] ECR 2183, para. 12; and Case 139/80 *Blanckaert & Willems v. Trost*, [1981] ECR 819, para. 12. See also Magnus and Mankowski, eds., *Brussels I Regulation*, § 286-290, at 224-225.

[339] Gaudemet-Tallon, *Compétence en Europe,* § 230, at 186.

[340] See also Magnus and Mankowski, eds., *Brussels I Regulation*, § 274, at 221.

[341] C-89/91 *Shearson Lehmann Hutton Inc. v. TVB*, [1993] ECR I-139, Question 3, para. 7, not answered.

[342] See Briggs, *Civil Jurisdiction*, § 2.167, at 200; P. Vlas, 'Note: *Shearson Lehmann Hutton*', *TVVS Maandblad voor Ondernemingsrecht en rechtspersonen* (1993), 275-277, § 4, at 276; H. Gaudemet-Tallon, 'Note: *Shearson Lehmann Hutton*', *Revue critique de droit international privé* (1993), 325-332, at 330.

[343] See for critical comments Fawcett, North *et al.*, *Private International Law,* at 260; Gaudemet-Tallon, *Compétence en Europe*, § 228, at 185 and § 232, at 189; P. Vlas, 'Note: *Schotte v Parfums Rothschild*', *Netherlands International Law Review* (1992), 395-398, at 105; see the following contributions in Duintjer Tebbens, *Civil Jurisdiction*; by Schultsz, at 105; Pocar, at 115; and Droz, at 261.

[344] See Vlas, *Rechtspersonen,* § 205, at 100 *et seq.*

were conducted with Rotschild GmbH. The peculiarity of this case was that the defendant Rotshild SarL was in fact a subsidiary of Rotschild GmbH, an independent parent company, but the latter acted as an extension of its subsidiary's business relations and should for those reasons be considered as an establishment under Article 5(5).[345] The ECJ based its ruling on the argument of the appearance created by the establishment. The Court stated that

> 'third parties [claimant] doing business with the establishment acting as an extension of another company must be able to rely on the appearance thus created and regard that establishment as an establishment of the other company even if, from the point of view of company law, the two companies are independent of each other.'[346]

According to the Court, the close connection required for special branch jurisdiction is not only reflected in the relationship between the branch-establishment and the defendant, but also it refers to the way these two behave 'in their business relations and present themselves vis-à-vis third parties in their commercial dealings'.[347] Some others have viewed in *Schotte* some kind of 'jurisdictional piercing of the corporate veil': the legal personality of the parent company was neglected, instead the given appearance to third parties weighed heavier.[348]

In sum, a branch-establishment in the sense of Article 5(5) should have the appearance of permanence of the extension of the defendant, or create the appearance of being such an extension towards third parties on the one hand, and on the other hand it should be under the direction and control of the defendant, yet with a certain degree of independence to act by itself and bind third parties.[349]

2.6.2 Delimiting 'Disputes Arising out of the Operations'

Branch jurisdiction is special jurisdiction that is limited to disputes arising out of the branch's operations.[350] This means that the forum in which defendant's branch is located has no jurisdiction over other claims against the defendant. In *Somafer*, the Court distinguished three types of actions arising out of a branch's operations: a) actions relating to rights and contractual or non-contractual obligations concerning the management of the branch itself such as those concerning the location of the building where such entity is established or the local engagement of staff to work there; b) actions relating to undertakings which have been entered into at the place of business in the name of the parent body and which must be performed in the Contracting State where the place of business is established; c) and finally actions concerning non-contractual obligations arising from the activities the branch

---

[345] Case 218/86 *SAR Schotte v. Parfums Rothschild*, [1987] ECR 4905, para. 13. See in contrast Vlas, 'Note: *Schotte*', arguing that this unusual case should not be interpreted as establishing a general rule. See also Dicey, Morris *et al.*, *Conflict of Laws*, § 11-311, at 422.

[346] Case 218/86 *SAR Schotte v. Parfums Rothschild*, [1987] ECR 4905, para. 17.

[347] Ibid., para. 16.

[348] See Duintjer Tebbens, *Civil Jurisdiction*, at 96, and see the contribution by Schultsz, at 107, even if he claims that this doctrine of piercing the corporate veil 'has nothing to do with jurisdiction'.

[349] Magnus and Mankowski, eds., *Brussels I Regulation*, § 273, at 220.

[350] See also Duintjer Tebbens, *Civil Jurisdiction*, at 93.

has engaged in on behalf of the parent body in the place where it is established.[351] This categorization of actions arising out of the branch's operations seems to impose a 'geographical restriction' on the reach of branch jurisdiction by requiring that the actions arising out of the branch's operation had to take place in the forum where the branch is established. [352]

In *Lloyd's Register of Shipping v. Société Campenon Bernard* the ECJ rejected this restriction of the scope claiming it is undesirable to restrict such a valuable jurisdiction rule.[353] The Court emphasized the importance of providing the claimant with an additional forum on the bases of the establishment of a branch, which should not be rendered redundant by the fact that it would overlap with 'the place of performance of [the] obligation in question' and which provides for jurisdiction to the *forum contractus* under Article 5(1).[354]

In this case the defendant Lloyd's Register, a company established in England, was sued in French courts for operations of its French branch that were carried out in Spain by Lloyd's Spanish branch. The claimant, Campenon Bernard, had negotiated and concluded the contract and subsequently demanded payment solely from the French branch and therefore sued the defendant, on the basis of Article 5(5), in France. The question raised was whether branch jurisdiction under Article 5(5) requires that the undertakings entered into were to be performed in the Member State where the place of business was established.[355] In contrast to what was held in *Somafer*, the court did not accept the argument that the range of activity of a branch-establishment should naturally be 'confined to the territory of the forum wherein it is established'.[356] One of the court's arguments was based on the criterion of the branch having the *appearance of permanency* to third parties of being an extension of the parent body. It stated that a branch-establishment within the meaning of Article 5(5) is an entity capable of being the 'principal, or even exclusive, interlocutor for third parties in the negotiation of contracts'.[357] The fact that the Spanish branch performed the operations did not preclude the French branch from being the extension of the defendant. Since the claimant dealt with the French branch, it was irrelevant by whom the activities would be performed in the end.

---

[351] Case 33/78 *Somafer v. Saar-Ferngas*, [1978] ECR 2183, para. 13.

[352] W. Hudig-van Lennep, 'Note: *Lloyd's Register of Shipping*', *TVVS Maandblad voor Ondernemingsrecht en rechtspersonen* (1997), 221-222, at 222.

[353] C-439/93 *Lloyd's v. Campenon Bernard*, [1995] ECR I-961, para. 17; see also N. Enonchong, 'Service of Process in England on Overseas Companies and Article 5(5) of the Brussels Convention', 48 *The International and Comparative Law Quarterly* (1999), 921-936, at 930-933. This was welcomed by among others P. Vlas, 'Note: *Lloyd's Register of Shipping*', *Netherlands International Law Review* (1995), 425-428, at 428; G. Droz, 'Note: *Lloyd's Register of Shipping* C-439/93', *Revue critique de droit international privé* (1995), 774-776, at 776; T. Hartley, 'Note; *Lloyd's Register of Shipping*', *European Law Review* (1996), 162-164, at 164; Gaudemet-Tallon, *Compétence en Europe*, § 235, at 191; Magnus and Mankowski, eds., *Brussels I Regulation*, § 300, at 229.

[354] C-439/93 *Lloyd's v. Campenon Bernard*, [1995] ECR I-961, para. 17; and see Duintjer Tebbens, *Civil Jurisdiction*, at 93; Droz, 'Note: *Lloyd's*', at 776; Bischoff, 'Note: *Lloyd's*', at 565-566.

[355] C-439/93 *Lloyd's v. Campenon Bernard*, [1995] ECR I-961, para. 11.

[356] Ibid., paras. 14-15.

[357] Ibid., para. 19.

Moreover, the court argued that the special link justification for Article 5(5) does not require a close link between the branch-establishment with whom the claimant conducts negotiations and places an order and the place where the order will be performed.[358]

In sum, special branch jurisdiction under Article 5(5) is limited to disputes arising out of a branch's activities, but does not impose any restriction as to where the activities are to be performed, nor by whom they should be performed and lastly, the actions can arise either out of contractual relationships or non-contractual obligations.[359] The role of the branch-establishment is more important: did it conduct the negotiations, conclude the contract or operate on behalf of the defendant?

2.7 The *Forum Contractus* under Article 5(1)

Under the Brussels Convention, Article 5(1) gave rise to a great amount of preliminary questions addressed to the ECJ.[360] They principally dealt with the correct application of its connecting factor: the place of performance. The following statement by AG Ruiz-Jarabo Colomer is quite straightforward and reflects the general feeling of this complex rule:

> 'it seems to me paradoxical that a matter which fundamentally requires simple, practical answers enabling European courts – preferably at first instance – to establish quickly whether they have international jurisdiction or not, has been characterised, in both case-law and legal theory, by a high degree of theoretical thinking which has lost sight of the problems which have to be faced by the regular practitioners of judicial business.'[361]

Some authors even questioned the usefulness and justification of a special contract rule.[362] These interpretation problems were one of the reasons for revising the Brussels Convention.[363] The Regulation's proposal suggested reducing the contract jurisdiction rule to sales contracts only, but the Regulation maintained contract jurisdiction in relation to claims arising out of all types of contracts.[364]

---

[358] Ibid., para. 20.

[359] Ibid., para. 22. See for disputes arising out of non-contractual obligations, Stone, *EU Private International Law*, at 101 and Magnus and Mankowski, eds., *Brussels I Regulation*, § 298, at 228.

[360] More than 20 preliminary rulings were given by the ECJ only in the exercise of its power to interpret Art. 5(1) of the Brussels Convention. See the explanation below concerning contracts under Art. 5(1)(c).

[361] Opinion AG Ruiz-Jarabo Colomer in C-440/97 *GIE Groupe Concorde*, [1999] ECR I-6307, para. 3.

[362] Critical comments on the *forum contractus* and its connecting factor are to be found in G. Droz, 'Note: Shenevai', *Revue critique de droit international privé* (1987), 798-804, at 803; J. Hill, 'Jurisdiction in Matters Relating to a Contract under the Brussels Convention', 44 *The International and Comparative Law Quarterly* (1995), 591-619, at 616-619; Fawcett, North *et al.*, *Private International Law*, at 237; J. Newton, *The Uniform Interpretation of the Brussels and Lugano Conventions* (2002), at 44-46.

[363] See Droz and Gaudemet-Tallon, 'La transformation', at 605.

[364] See Art. 5(1) of the 'Proposal'.

The *forum contractus* will be discussed in its present form under the Brussels Regulation. First, some preliminary comments are necessary with respect to the justification of contract jurisdiction and will be followed by some preliminary questions concerning its scope. The uniform interpretation provided by the ECJ is of particular importance and deserves some special attention. Finally, the connecting factors under Article 5(1) will be discussed.

2.7.1 **Initial Justifications**

The Brussels *forum contractus* is of considerable practical importance and has been frequently used in court litigation in Europe.[365] According to Newton 'one could have imagined that the contract, if not already so, would become the most widely used device for intra-Community trade'.[366] Like other alternative jurisdiction rules this special rule foresees in an additional forum for claims related to contractual matters.[367] The Jenard Report initially justified alternative jurisdiction such as the *forum contractus* on two grounds.[368] First, the *forum contractus* was justified by the objective of proximity or close connection between the forum and the claim.[369] Second, the *forum contractus* aims at procedural balance between parties, by giving the plaintiff a choice to bring proceedings to a forum of his convenience, rather than to the *forum rei*.[370]

With respect to the justification of the close connection criterion, AG Leger considered[371] that the 'principle stems from the idea that it will be easier for a court which is geographically proximate to the contractual relationship at issue, through the knowledge it has of the facts of the case, to rule on the matter before it'.[372] One of the advantages of this presumed 'physical proximity' is that it facilitates the sound administration of justice, such as the administration of evidence and the

[365] P. Rogerson, 'Plus ça change? Article 5(1) of the Regulation on Jurisdiction and Enforcement of Judgments', *The Cambridge Yearbook of European Legal Studies* (2001), 382-406, at 383; Magnus and Mankowski, eds., *Brussels I Regulation*, § 23, at 100.

[366] Newton, *Uniform Interpretation*, at 43.

[367] L. Strikwerda, *De Overeenkomst in het IPR* (2004), fn. 62, at 31.

[368] Opinion AG Ruiz-Jarabo Colomer in C-440/97 *GIE Groupe Concorde*, [1999] ECR I-6307, para. 64. See for more grounds, Rogerson, 'Plus ça change?', at 385. See Sect. 2.2.4 for different types of jurisdiction rules.

[369] Jenard Report, at 22 and see Opinion AG Léger in C-420/97 *Leathertex v. Bodetex*, [1999] ECR I-6747, para. 102; Rogerson, 'Plus ça change?', at 384.

[370] Jenard Report, at 22; see in contrast R. Michaels, 'Re-Placements. Jurisdiction for Contracts and Torts under the Brussels I Regulation When Arts. 5(1) and 5(3) Do Not Designate a Place in a Member State.' in *International Civil Litigation in Europe and Relations with Third States* (2005), 129-156, at 149, stating that the Regulation has not a 'general desire' to provide the claimant with a choice between different forums.

[371] Opinion AG Léger in C-420/97 *Leathertex v. Bodetex*, [1999] ECR I-6747.

[372] Para. 103 of the Opinion, delivered on 16 March 1999. See also Case 56/79 *Zelger v. Salinitri*, [1980] ECR 89, para. 3; Case 266/85 *Shenavai v. Kreischer*, [1987] ECR 239, para. 6; C-288/92 *Custom Made v. Stawa*, [1994] ECR I-2913, para. 13. See also Opinion AG Ruiz-Jarabo Colomer in C-440/97 *GIE Groupe Concorde*, [1999] ECR I-6307, para. 64; and Opinion AG Lenz in C-288/92 *Custom Made v. Stawa*, [1994] ECR I-2913, para. 16; see also Vlas, 'Fair Trial in International Litigation', at 399.

efficacious conduct of proceedings.[373] But the drafters refused to introduce an open jurisdiction criterion establishing jurisdiction on the basis of a close connection:

> 'Article 5 does not establish that connecting factor [of the close connection] itself as the criterion for the choice of the competent forum. It is not possible for an applicant to sue a defendant before any court having a connection with the dispute since article 5 lists exhaustively the criteria for linking a dispute to a specific court.'[374]

Instead, close connecting factors such as the 'place of performance of the obligation in question' that does not, as will be shown, automatically lead to a forum closely or closest connected to the dispute were introduced.

In *Custom Made Commercial Ltd v. Stawa Metallbau GmbH* the Court acknowledges that 'a defendant may be sued in the courts for the place of performance of the obligation in question, even where the court thus designated is not that which has the closest connection with the dispute'.[375] The initial presumption of a close connection between the forum and the claim justifying the *forum contractus* appears to have lost considerable ground and seems to have been replaced by a, with respect to Article 5(1), newly introduced but well-known principle among the general objectives of the Brussels Model: the principle of legal certainty and foreseeability.[376] As a result, the presumed close connection or direct link between the contractual claim and the court is considered by some authors to be a false justification for making an additional forum available to the plaintiff.[377]

The second justification for the *forum contractus* follows from a desire to establish procedural balance in the Brussels jurisdictional structure.[378] According to the Jenard Report, a 'claimant may, at his option, bring the proceedings either in that court [*forum contractus*] or in the competent courts of the State in which the defendant is domiciled'.[379] The *forum contractus* constitutes an alternative forum,[380]

---

373 See Case 12/76 *Tessili v. Dunlop*, [1976] ECR 1473, para. 13; Case 266/85 *Shenavai v. Kreischer*, [1987] ECR 239, para. 6; C-125/92 *Mulox v. Geels*, [1993] ECR 4075, para. 17; and C-256/00 *Besix v. WABAG*, [2002] ECR I-1699, para. 31.

374 C-288/92 *Custom Made v. Stawa*, [1994] ECR I-2913, para. 12.

375 Ibid., para. 21.

376 See C-26/91 *Handte v. Traitements*, [1992] ECR I-3967. Affirmed by Case C-288/92 *Custom Made v. Stawa*, [1994] ECR I-2913, paras. 18 and 21; and see Newton, *Uniform Interpretation*, at 50; Rogerson, 'Plus ça change?', at 393.

377 Hill, 'Jurisdiction in Matters Relating to a Contract', at 616-619; Newton, *Uniform Interpretation*, at 44-46; V. Heuzé, 'De quelques infirmités congénitales du droit uniforme: L' example de l'article 5.1 de la Convention de Bruxelles du 27 septembre 1968', 89 *Revue critique de droit international privé* (2000), 589-639, at 631; Rogerson, 'Plus ça change?' at 393; J. Kropholler, *Europaïsches Zivilprozessrecht: Kommentar zu EuGVO und Lugano-Ubereinkommen* (2005), § 3, at 116.

378 Opinion AG Ruiz-Jarabo Colomer in C-440/97 *GIE Groupe Concorde*, [1999] ECR I-6307, para. 64; and see Newton, *Uniform Interpretation*, at 44.

379 Jenard Report, at 22.

380 Some others, such as Jayme, have rightfully stressed the competing nature of the *forum contractus* in relation to the defendant's forum of Art. 2 and identify Art. 5(1) as concurrent jurisdiction, see E. Jayme, 'Special Jurisdiction under Article 5 Part 1: The Role of Article 5 in the Scheme of the Convention, Jurisdiction in Matters Relating to Contract', in *Civil Jurisdiction and Judgements in Europe* (1992), 73-80, at 73.

or optional forum,[381] which gives the plaintiff a choice between the 'main forum' and the alternative *forum contractus* provided that the latter points to another Member State, which is not the defendant's domicile.[382] According to Gothot, the drafters of the Brussels Convention saw in the *forum contractus* a neutral forum, even if in practice the chosen connecting factor sometimes points to the plaintiff's forum.[383] The defendant's privilege to defend himself in his home forum is set aside in favour of giving the plaintiff the convenience to choose between two competent forums.[384] The Court explained this second justification by stating that this claimant's 'freedom of choice was introduced in view of the existence in certain well-defined cases of a particularly close relationship between a dispute and the court which may most conveniently be called upon to take cognizance of the matter'.[385]

According to AG Lenz contract jurisdiction acts as a counterweight to the general forum of the defendant's domicile and is 'regarded as part of a system in which the advantages and risks with regard to jurisdiction are allocated fairly between the plaintiff and the defendant. Proponents of this view seek in this way – with very different results – to turn Article 5(1) into a counterweight to the rule set out in Article 2'.[386]

One of the consequences of the alternative nature of special jurisdiction is the multiplication of competent forums, expressly allowed by the drafters of the *forum contractus*.[387] It stands in contrast to one of the main objectives of the Brussels Regulation: to reduce the number of competent forums and to avoid multiplication of forums.[388] For that reason, alternative jurisdiction rules are interpreted restrictively.[389] In its interpretation the Court has therefore often recalled the need to

---

[381] Facultative forum, see Droz, *Compétence judiciaire*, at 56-57.

[382] See Jayme, 'Special Jurisdiction under Art. 5', at 74; Hill, 'Jurisdiction in Matters Relating to a Contract', at 591; G. Bayraktaroglu, 'Note: Forum contractus and Article 5(1) of the Brussels I Regulation', 2 *Journal of International Commercial Law* (2004), 401-409, at 401; and see Opinion AG Ruiz-Jarabo Colomer in C-440/97 *GIE Groupe Concorde*, [1999] ECR I-6307, para. 25.

[383] H. Gothot and D. Holleaux, 'Note: *De Bloos and Tessili*', *Revue critique de droit international privé* (1977), 761-772, at 765. See Sect. 2.7.4.

[384] Strikwerda, *De Overeenkomst in het IPR*, fn. 60, at 30; Mourre, *Droit judiciaire privé européen*, § 101-103, at 71-72; and see also the Court's statement in C-26/91 *Handte v. Traitements*, [1992] ECR I-3967, para. 14. This has been emphasized in Opinion AG Léger in C-420/97 *Leathertex v. Bodetex*, [1999] ECR I-6747, para. 4; and see Opinion AG Ruiz-Jarabo Colomer in C-440/97 *GIE Groupe Concorde*, [1999] ECR I-6307, paras. 69-70.

[385] Case 12/76 *Tessili v. Dunlop*, [1976] ECR 1473, para. 13; confirmed among others by Case 56/79 *Zelger v. Salinitri*, [1980] ECR 89, para. 1, Case 266/85 *Shenavai v. Kreischer*, [1987] ECR 239, para. 6 and C-288/92 *Custom Made v. Stawa*, [1994] ECR I-2913, para. 12; and see Opinion AG Lenz in C-288/92 *Custom Made v. Stawa*, [1994] ECR I-2913, para. 15; Opinion AG Léger in C-420/97 *Leathertex v. Bodetex*, [1999] ECR I-6747, para. 74.

[386] Opinion AG Lenz in C-288/92 *Custom Made v. Stawa*, [1994] ECR I-2913, para. 18; agreed by Opinion AG Ruiz-Jarabo Colomer in C-440/97 *GIE Groupe Concorde*, [1999] ECR I-6307, para. 68.

[387] But see also the side effect of Art. 60, in conjunction with Art. 2 of the Brussels Regulation which also may lead to multiple forums due to the threefold definition of corporate domicile as explained above in Sect. 2.5.2.

[388] See C-125/92 *Mulox v. Geels*, [1993] ECR 4075, para. 11.

[389] As described in Sect. 2.2.4. See Case 189/87 *Kalfelis v. Schröder*, [1988] ECR 5565, para. 19; and Mourre, *Droit judiciaire privé européen*, § 102, at 71; Kohler, Huet *et al.*, 'Special Jurisdiction

avoid, as far as possible, 'a situation in which a number of courts have jurisdiction in respect of one and the same contract'.[390] But, in view of the freedom of choice of the claimant some authors have argued against the restrictive interpretation. The vivid opponent of this restrictive interpretation is Huet,[391] whose observations were recently supported by AG Ruiz-Jarabo Colomer in his Opinion to the *Concorde* case:

> 'They [the opponents of restrictive interpretation] contend that Article 5 ..., read in conjunction with Article 2, is based on the idea that, in certain particular cases, the plaintiff's interest must take precedence over the protection of the defendant and therefore that he should be given an option with regard to jurisdiction. To be effective, this right of option must not be construed restrictively; otherwise Article 5, point (1), and Article 2 could be fused into one and the same provision, the former being left with no effect at all.'[392]

2.7.2 The Scope of the *Forum Contractus*

The reach and importance of the *forum contractus* depends on the scope of the concept 'matters relating to contracts'[393] which 'serves as a criterion to define the scope of one of the rules of special jurisdiction available to the plaintiff'.[394] The defendant only escapes from this additional jurisdiction rule when the claim cannot be qualified as a matter related to contracts under Article 5(1).

2.7.2.1 *Autonomous Concept*

The ECJ repeatedly stated that for jurisdictional purposes 'matters relating to contracts' is to be interpreted independently from national concepts and is therefore an autonomous concept.[395] The first time the ECJ opted for an autonomous interpreta-

---

Art. 5', at 47; A. Huet, 'Special Jurisdiction under Article 5 Part 1: The Role of Article 5 in the Scheme of the Convention, Jurisdiction in Matters Relating to Contract', in *Civil Jurisdiction and Judgements in Europe* (1992), 63-71, at 63-64; and Gaudemet-Tallon, *Compétence en Europe*, at 127.

[390] C-256/00 *Besix v. WABAG*, [2002] ECR I-1699, para. 27; but see primarily Case 14/76 *De Bloos v. Bouyer*, [1976] ECR 1497, paras. 8-9; affirmed in Case 266/85 *Shenavai v. Kreischer*, [1987] ECR 239, para. 8; and C-420/97 *Leathertex v. Bodetex*, [1999] ECR I-6747.

[391] Huet claims that Art. 5(1) gives a choice to the plaintiff as part of the Brussels structure and should therefore not be interpreted restrictively, Huet, 'Special Jurisdiction under Art. 5', at 65.

[392] Opinion AG Ruiz-Jarabo Colomer in C-440/97 *GIE Groupe Concorde*, [1999] ECR I-6307.

[393] See Art. 63 Regulation for the special position with respect to Art. 5(1) of persons domiciled in Luxembourg; Gaudemet-Tallon, *Compétence en Europe*, at 129; Mourre, *Droit judiciaire privé européen*, § 106, at 73; and under the Convention see Weser, *La convention communautaire*, § 223-223*bis*, at 253-255 and G. Droz, *Le nouveau régime de la compétence judiciaire et des effets des jugements dans l'Europe des six: Pratique de la convention de Bruxelles du 27 septembre 1968* (1973), § 26, at 3.

[394] Case 9/87 *Arcado v. Haviland*, [1988] ECR 1539, para. 9.

[395] See Kohler, Huet *et al.*, 'Special Jurisdiction Art. 5', at 50; K. Hertz, *Jurisdiction in Contract and Tort under the Brussels Convention* (1998), at 68-71; and see T. Hartley, 'Unnecessary Europeanisation under the Brussels Jurisdiction and Judgements Convention: The Case of the Dissatisfied Sub-Purchaser. (Note: Handte)', *European Law Review* (1993), 506-516, at 506, who claims this to be 'europeanisation' under the Brussels Model resulting from extensive and unnecessary interpretation powers of the Court of Justice.

tion was in the *Peters* decision, in which it argued that it was necessary 'in order to ensure as far as possible the equality and uniformity of the rights and obligations' arising out of the Regulation.[396] It was irrevocably affirmed in the case *SPRL Arcado v. SA Haviland*.[397] Not only are autonomous common concepts justified to ensure the uniform application of the Brussels jurisdictional scheme, but more importantly, they ensure a greater objective of the Brussels Model 'to strengthen the legal protection of persons established in the Community by enabling the claimant to identify easily the court in which he may sue and the defendant reasonably to foresee in which court he may be sued'.[398]

The Court refused to determine the concept of 'matters relating to contracts' by the *lex causae*[399] or by the *lex fori*.[400] Conversely, it also refused to provide clear guidelines concerning the interpretation of the concept, let alone to provide a general and clear uniform definition.[401] Instead, the Court preferred a more pragmatic approach and defined 'matters relating to contracts' on a case-by-case basis. According to Gaudemet-Tallon such a general uniform definition could be dangerous, (risky) and unrealistic, even if the current situation is one of legal uncertainty.[402]

2.7.2.2 *Defining 'Contractual Matters'*

In order to determine the scope under Article 5(1), for further guidance it is necessary to to turn to a few ECJ cases interpreting the concept 'contractual matters'. In the *Peters* case the Court was confronted for the first time with the interpretation of 'matters related to contracts'.[403] The Court extended the concept by arguing that

---

[396] Case 34/82 *Peters v. ZNAV*, [1983] ECR 987, para. 9. See also Newton, *Uniform Interpretation,* at 47-48; Briggs, *Civil Jurisdiction*, § 2.125, at 148.

[397] Case 9/87 *Arcado v. Haviland*, [1988] ECR 1539, paras. 10-13. See note A. Huet, 'Note: *Arcado*', *Journal du droit international* (1989), 453-454, at 453; P. Vlas, 'Note: *Arcado*', *Netherlands International Law Review* (1992), 390-391; B. Audit, 'Note: *Arcado* Judgement of 8 March 1987, C 9/87', 35ième cahier *Recueil Dalloz Sirey* (1988), at 344 and see Hartley, 'Unnecessary Europeanisation', at 510-516. Confirmed in C-214/89 *Powell Duffryn v. Petereit*, [1992] ECR I-1745; *Handte v. Traitements*, [1992] ECR I-3967, para. 10; C-51/97 *Réunion Européenne v. Spliethoff's*, [1998] ECR I-6511, para. 15; C-334/00 *Tacconi v. HWS*, [2002] ECR I-7357, para. 19; and C-167/00 *Verein für Konsumenteninformation v. Henkel*, [2002] ECR I-8111, para. 35.

[398] C-334/00 *Tacconi v. HWS*, [2002] ECR I-7357, para. 20; and see C-256/00 *Besix v. WABAG*, [2002] ECR I-1699, paras. 25-26. See also Hertz, *Jurisdiction in Contract,* at 66-67.

[399] H. Gaudemet-Tallon, 'Note: *Peters*', *Revue critique de droit international privé* (1983), 667-670, at 668; see Gaudemet-Tallon, *Compétence en Europe,* at 131-132; and see H. Gaudemet-Tallon, 'Note: *Handte*', *Revue critique de droit international privé* (1992), 471-472, claiming that the underlying reason for refusing the *lex causae* could lie in the reticence of first examining the applicable law in order to determine the jurisdiction question.

[400] See also Newton, *Uniform Interpretation,* at 47-48; Mourre, *Droit judiciaire privé européen*, § 109-112, at 74-75; and Strikwerda, *De Overeenkomst in het IPR*, fns. 66-67, at 32-34.

[401] Newton, *Uniform Interpretation,* at 47; Strikwerda, *De Overeenkomst in het IPR*, fn. 67, at 33; Kohler, Huet *et al.*, 'Special Jurisdiction Art. 5', at 50; Gaudemet-Tallon, *Compétence en Europe*, § 178, at 131.

[402] See Gaudemet-Tallon, *Compétence en Europe*, at 133.

[403] Case 34/82 *Peters v. ZNAV*, [1983] ECR 987. See notes by T. Hartley, 'Note: *Peters*', *European Law Review* (1983), 262-264; Gaudemet-Tallon, 'Note: *Peters*'; A. Huet, 'Note: *Peters*', *Journal du droit international* (1983), 834-843; Kohler, Huet *et al.*, 'Special Jurisdiction Art. 5', at 51.

'obligations in regard to the payment of a sum of money, which have their basis in the relationship between an association and its members by virtue of membership, must be regarded as "matters relating to a contract"'.[404]

The Court held a similar reasoning in the *Arcado* case:[405] it looked at the source of the claim and indicated that whether or not the claim falls under Article 5(1) depends on the underlying (contractual) obligation. According to the Court it is beyond any doubt that 'a claim for payment of commission due under an independent commercial agency agreement finds its very basis in that agreement' and should therefore be 'a matter relating to a contract'.[406] Equivalently, the Court argued that 'the same view must be taken of a claim for compensation for the wrongful repudiation of such an agreement as the basis for such compensation is the failure to comply with a contractual obligation'.[407] Another interesting aspect of the *Arcado* decision was that for the first time, the Court referred to provisions of other European instruments, which defined 'contractual matters' more precisely. Not only was the contractual nature of the claim in *Arcado* supported/underlined by reference to Articles 15 and 17 of the Council Directive 86/653 of 18 December 1986,[408] the Court also confirmed the contractual nature of the claim by referring to Article 10 of the Convention on the Law Applicable to Contractual Obligations of 19 June 1980 [hereafter 'Rome Convention'].[409]

The most valuable guidelines concerning the interpretation of 'contractual matters' are to be found in the case *Jakob Handte & Co. GmbH v. Traitements Mécano-chimiques des Surfaces SA*.[410] The case involved a chain of contracts and the Court held that Article 5(1) 'is not to be understood as covering a situation in which there is no obligation freely assumed by one party towards another'.[411] This condition

---

[404] Case 34/82 *Peters v. ZNAV*, [1983] ECR 987, para. 15. This *link criterion* was also used in the C-214/89 *Powell Duffryn v. Petereit*, [1992] ECR I-1745, para. 16.

[405] Case 9/87 *Arcado v. Haviland*, [1988] ECR 1539, para. 9.

[406] Ibid., para. 12; see also Newton, *Uniform Interpretation*, at 48. The French and German version of the judgement is even clearer. In French '*toute demande qui a pour fondement même un contrat*', see Huet, 'Note: *Arcado*', and Gaudemet-Tallon, *Compétence en Europe*, § 178, at 133. In German: '*dass eine Klage auf eine vertragliche Anspruchsgrundlage gestützt ist*', see P. Schlosser, 'Zuständigkeit bei mehreren Beklagten an verschiedenen Wohnsizten Note: *Arcado*', *Recht der Internationalen Wirtschaft* (1988), 987-989, at 987. [Emphasis added]

[407] Case 9/87 *Arcado v. Haviland*, [1988] ECR 1539, para. 13.

[408] Council Directive on the coordination of the Laws of the Member States relating to self-employed commercial agents OJ 1986 L 382/17, referred to in para. 14 of Case 9/87 *Arcado v. Haviland*, [1988] ECR 1539.

[409] The consolidated version is to be found in OJ 1998 C 027, at 34-46. See below Sect. 2.7.3.2.e. See Case 9/87 *Arcado v. Haviland*, [1988] ECR 1539, para. 15. See Dicey, Morris *et al.*, *Conflict of Laws*, § 11-284, at 407; Huet, 'Note: *Arcado*', at 454; and Pontier and Burg, *EU Principles on Jurisdiction*, at 171. Schultz called this a vertical conceptual unification (*verticale begrippenunificatie*), J. Schultsz, 'Note: *Arcado*', *NJ* (1990), 1626-1627, at 1627, left column; Strikwerda, *De Overeenkomst in het IPR*, fn. 67, at 33; and Magnus and Mankowski, eds., *Brussels I Regulation*, § 30-33, at 104-105. Earlier attempts made by one of the parties in Case 34/82 *Peters v. ZNAV*, [1983] ECR 987 to refer to the Rome Convention on the law applicable to contractual obligations failed. See Gaudemet-Tallon, 'Note: *Peters*', at 668; Huet, 'Note: *Peters*', at 839.

[410] C-26/91 *Handte v. Traitements*, [1992] ECR I-3967; see Newton, *Uniform Interpretation*, at 49.

[411] C-26/91 *Handte v. Traitements*, [1992] ECR I-3967, para. 15; confirmed by C-51/97 *Réunion Européenne v. Spliethoff's*, [1998] ECR I-6511, para. 17 and C-334/00 *Tacconi v. HWS*, [2002] ECR

of entering freely into a 'contractual' obligation was emphasized in the case *Réunion Européenne.*[412] The case dealt with a claim against a sea carrier transporting pears from Melbourne via France to Rotterdam in which claimant, now being the insurer, sought redress for damage suffered to the fruit. The insurer relied on the bill of lading to establish the contractual relationship. The Court followed the line introduced in the *Handte* case by stating that there was no contractual relationship, since the bill of lading in question did not disclose any contractual relationship freely entered into between the consignee and the defendant.[413]

The Court imposes that parties must have entered into an agreement freely *inter partes* or at least must have authorized the conclusion of the contract. The latter condition was introduced in the *Frahuil* case, in which claimant started proceedings under Article 5(1) with respect to a claim arising out of a contract of guarantee.[414] Claimant sought recourse against the owner of the goods, who was not a party to the contract nor did he authorize the conclusion of that contract. Under these circumstances, the ECJ held that the claim was not a question of 'contractual matters' under Article 5(1) and as a consequence no *forum contractus* was available to the claimant.[415]

The Court generally applies a restrictive interpretation to the concept 'contractual matters'. In *Handte*, it used the principle of legal certainty to emphasize the restrictive interpretation with regard to the scope of the *forum contractus* under Article 5(1).[416] In other words, the principle of legal certainty precludes an interpretation by the ECJ leading to a wider reach of the *forum contractus* and going beyond the situations envisaged by the Convention.[417]

In *Handte*, the claim was brought by the sub-buyer of goods against the manufacturer, who was not the seller, and was related to defects in those goods or to their unsuitability for their intended purpose.[418] The Court reasoned that the majority of the Contracting States do not regard the liability of a manufacturer towards a sub-buyer for defects in sold goods to be of a contractual nature. It argued that

---

I-7357, para. 23; and C-265/02 *Frahuil v. Assitalia*, [2004] ECR I-1543, para. 24; see also Newton, *Uniform Interpretation,* at 49. According to Strikwerda this condition indicates the outer limits (*buitengrens*) of 'matters relating to contracts', L. Strikwerda, 'Note: HR 21 September 2001 C99/245HR', *NIPR* (2001), 467-470, at 469, middle column; see also Mance, 'The Future', at 190 and Magnus and Mankowski, eds., *Brussels I Regulation*, § 29, at 103.

412 C-51/97 *Réunion Européenne v. Spliethoff's*, [1998] ECR I-6511; Rogerson, 'Plus ça change?', at 386.

413 C-51/97 *Réunion Européenne v. Spliethoff's*, [1998] ECR I-6511, para. 19; see also Newton, *Uniform Interpretation,* at 50-51; J. van Haersolte-van Hof, 'Zeevervoer en artikel 5(3) EEX', *NIPR* (2000), 385-390, at 388; A. Briggs, 'Claims against Sea Carriers and the Brussels Convention', *Lloyd's Maritime and Commercial Law Quarterly* (1999), 333-337, at 334; H. Gaudemet-Tallon, 'Note: Réunion Européenne', *Revue critique de droit international privé* (1999), 333-340, at 334.

414 C-265/02 *Frahuil v. Assitalia*, [2004] ECR I-1543.

415 Ibid., para. 26.

416 C-26/91 *Handte v. Traitements*, [1992] ECR I-3967, para. 14. See also Newton, *Uniform Interpretation,* at 50; Gaudemet-Tallon, 'Note: *Peters*', at 667; Gaudemet-Tallon, 'Note: *Handte*', at 733; Pontier and Burg, *EU Principles on Jurisdiction*, at 170-171.

417 C-26/91 *Handte v. Traitements*, [1992] ECR I-3967, para. 18.

418 See Gaudemet-Tallon, *Compétence en Europe*, § 182, at 137-138; and Mourre, *Droit judiciaire privé européen*, § 118-120, at 79-82.

since there was no contractual relationship between them, it was not foreseeable for the defendant that an action would be brought against him and was therefore incompatible with the principle of legal certainty. This implies that 'not only must the nature of the dispute be analysed, but the identity of the potential *dramatis personae* must be reasonably predictable *inter se*', for a matter to be considered as 'contractual' according to Newton.[419]

Apart from the cases discussed above, the Court merely delimited the concept 'matters related to contracts' under Article 5(1) by elaborating the concept in relation to other matters, in particular to matters relating to tort under Article 5(3). Similarly, the Court and the Brussels Instruments distinguish '*general*' or '*regular*' contracts from *specific* contracts, like consumer contracts and employment contracts, which are covered by separate protective jurisdiction rules.[420]

2.7.2.3 *Contractual Matters versus Torts*

On several occasions the ECJ was asked to draw the line between matters relating to tort, delict or quasi-delict on the one hand, and matters relating to contracts on the other. This occurred in the *Kalfelis v. Bank Schröder* case.[421] In this case, the Court stated that matters relating to tort under Article 5(3) are fixed by deduction as it includes 'all actions which seek to establish the liability of a defendant and which are not related to a contract within the meaning of Article 5(1)'.[422]

In the *Reunion Européenne* case the Court explicitly classified the action as a tort claim and rejected the action as a contractual matter.[423] In *Handte*, the outer limits of 'contractual matters' in relation to matters related to tort under Article 5(3) could have been raised all the same as it concerned the liability of a manufacturer to a sub-buyer with respect to a defective product. As indicated by the referring French court, while under other national laws the action would have been classified as tortuous, notably under French law, it is qualified in some national laws as contractual.[424] As a result, both Article 5(1) and (3) could serve as jurisdictional bases.[425] But the ECJ refused to qualify this claim as 'contractual' under the autonomous interpretation of Article 5(1).

---

[419] Newton, *Uniform Interpretation,* at 50.

[420] See Sect. 2.2.4 for protective jurisdiction.

[421] Case 189/87 *Kalfelis v. Schröder*, [1988] ECR 5565; see also Gaudemet-Tallon, *Compétence en Europe*, § 181, at 136-137; and Kohler, Huet *et al.*, 'Special Jurisdiction Art. 5', at 49.

[422] Case 189/87 *Kalfelis v. Schröder*, [1988] ECR 5565, para. 18. This is now settled case law, see, inter alia, Case C-261/90 *Reichert v. Dresdner Bank*, [1992] ECR I-2149, para. 16; C-51/97 *Réunion Européenne v. Spliethoff's*, [1998] ECR I-6511, para. 22; C-167/00 *Verein für Konsumenteninformation v. Henkel*, [2002] ECR I-8111, para. 36; C-334/00 *Tacconi v. HWS*, [2002] ECR I-7357, para. 21; C-27/02 *Engler v. Janus Versand*, [2005] ECR I-481, para. 29.

[423] C-51/97 *Réunion Européenne v. Spliethoff's*, [1998] ECR I-6511, para. 26. See Pontier and Burg, *EU Principles on Jurisdiction*, at 172.

[424] Disappointingly the Court did not mention Art. 5(3), which undoubtedly would have served as a valid jurisdictional ground, see Gaudemet-Tallon, 'Note: *Handte*', at 736-737.

[425] See in this sense see P. Vlas, 'Article 5(1): *Forum Solutionis Contractus.* Note: *Handte*', *Netherlands International Law Review* (1993), 497-499, at 498.

In the *Tacconi* case,[426] the Court was faced with the question of pre-contractual liability following the failure to conclude the contract.[427] It ruled that pre-contractual liability of one party, characterized by the absence of obligations freely assumed between the parties, is not of a contractual nature, but should instead be considered as a matter related to tort.[428] According to the Court 'the obligation to make good the damage allegedly caused by the unjustified breaking off of negotiations could derive only from breach of rules of law, in particular the rule which requires the parties to act in good faith in negotiations with a view to the formation of a contract'.[429]

2.7.2.4 *Sub-classification of Contracts*

The structure of the Regulation recognizes that the nature of some contracts diverges and that a sub-classification of types of contracts is justified for jurisdictional purposes.[430] Among these sub-classifications are protective jurisdiction rules for consumer contracts regulated by Articles 15 to 17 and employment contracts governed by Articles 18 to 21. They are to be considered as a *lex specialis* to the general contract jurisdiction rule of Article 5(1).[431] For the delimitation of 'contractual matters' under Article 5(1), it is therefore necessary to determine whether an action has characteristics of one of these two sub-classifications of contracts,[432] since different connecting factors are used to establish jurisdiction for these types of contracts.[433] With respect to employment contracts, it should be observed that under the Brussels Convention this jurisdiction rule was incorporated under the

---

[426] C-334/00 *Tacconi v. HWS*, [2002] ECR I-7357.

[427] In German law pre-contractual liability, or '*culpa in contrahendo*', is considered a contractual matter. See on this issue P. Mankowski, 'Entscheidungsrezensionen – Die Qualifikation der culpa in contrahendo – Nagelprobe für den Vertrags-begriff des europäischen IZPR und IPR', 23 *IPRax* (2003), 127-134. However, it is uncertain whether pre-contractual obligations would fall under Art. 5(1). See for different meanings, Strikwerda, *De Overeenkomst in het IPR*, fn. 79-80, at 39-40; Strikwerda, 'Note *HR 21 Sept. 2001*', at 469; Mourre, *Droit judiciaire privé européen*, § 117, at 78-79; Gaudemet-Tallon, *Compétence en Europe*, fn. 177, at 130; Kohler, Huet *et al.*, 'Special Jurisdiction Art. 5', at 52 and in general Magnus and Mankowski, eds., *Brussels I Regulation*, § 53-58, at 116-119.

[428] See on this point some critical comments and observations by Strikwerda, *De Overeenkomst in het IPR,* fn. 77-78, at 38.

[429] C-334/00 *Tacconi v. HWS*, [2002] ECR I-7357, paras. 25-27. This contrasts with the Opinion of the AG Geelhoed who proposed to leave this qualification question to national law, see Mankowski, 'Die Qualifikation', at 132-133 and A. Huet, 'Note: *Tacconi*', *Journal du droit international* (2003), 668-671, at 671.

[430] See Huet, 'Note: *Tacconi*', at 671; see also the following statement by Briggs: 'The law has therefore embarked on the task of sub-classifying contracts, as opposed to having an omnibus special jurisdiction rule for all of them.' Briggs, *Conflict of Laws*, at 78.

[431] For consumer contracts see C-96/00 *Gabriel*, [2002] ECR I-6367, para. 13.

[432] Besides contracts involving agreed maintenance obligations (Art. 5(2)), insurance contracts (Arts. 8-14) and contracts concerning exclusive jurisdiction (Art. 22). See also Strikwerda, *De Overeenkomst in het IPR,* fn. 68-69, at 34-35.

[433] For consumer contracts see Art. 16 and C-89/91 *Shearson Lehmann Hutton Inc. v. TVB*, [1993] ECR I-139, paras. 20-22; C-269/95 *Benincasa v. Dentalkit*, [1997] ECR I-3767, para. 15; C-464/01 *Gruber v. Bay Wa*, [2005] ECR I-439, paras. 33, 35-36; and see A. Briggs, 'Note; Shearson Lehmann Hutton Inc. *v* TVB Treuhandgesellschaft', *Yearbook of European Law* (1993), 511-517, at 512; and Th. Rausher, 'Prozessualer Verbraucherschutz im EuGVÜ', *IPRax* (1995), 289-294, at 290-291.

general contract rule of Article 5(1), so that any new decision of the Court requesting the interpretation of the new provision of Article 18 of the Regulation could be subjected to a slightly different approach. Nevertheless, according to settled case law the scope of employment contracts is also to be determined autonomously.[434]

The modifications of the Regulation brought another sub-classification within the scope of the general *forum contractus* under Article 5(1). Sales contracts and service contracts are separately mentioned and their scope of application will most likely be determined independently from national law as well. However, no guidance as to their interpretation has been given at the time the Regulation entered into force. Problems with respect to their definition are to be expected in determining concepts such as 'sales of goods' and 'provision of services'. Kropholler suggests referring back to the first article of the CISG[435] to define the concept 'sale of goods'.[436] As for the provision of services, he claims that this is already a European concept defined by Article 50 TEC.[437] Other authors however do foresee problems in the scope of application of this provision, as the nature of contracts can take multiple forms.[438] Especially, a distributorship contract seems to be problematic to classify as either a service or sales contract or as being neither of them.[439]

2.7.2.5 *Validity and Existence of the Contract*

Equally relevant for the scope of the *forum contractus* is the question of the very existence or validity of the contract.[440] This aspect was addressed in the *Effer v. Kanter* case[441] and the Court was asked to determine whether Article 5(1) still forms a jurisdictional basis when the existence of the contract is disputed. The ECJ stated that the jurisdiction of the court seized under Article 5(1) 'includes the power to consider the existence of the constituent parts of the contract itself, since that is indispensable in order to enable the national court in which proceedings are

---

[434] See C-125/92 *Mulox v. Geels*, [1993] ECR 4075, paras. 10-11 and 16; C-383/95 *Rutten v. Cross Medical*, [1997] ECR I-57, paras. 12-13; C-37/00 *Weber v. Universal*, [2002] ECR I-2013, paras. 27-28 and 38; and C-437/00 *Pugliese v. Finmeccanica*, [2003] ECR I-3573, para. 16. Equally, according to settled case law the autonomous connecting factor for employment contracts is the obligation which characterizes such contracts, namely the employee's obligation to carry out the work. Case 133/81 *Ivenel v. Schwab*, [1982] ECR 1891, para. 20; Case 266/85 *Shenavai v. Kreischer*, [1987] ECR 239, para. 11; Case 32/88 *Six Constructions v. Humbert*, [1989] ECR 341, para. 10; and see Bayraktaroglu, 'Note: Forum contractus', at 406-407.

[435] At http://www.uncitral.org/english/texts/sales/CISG.htm.

[436] Kropholler, *Europaïsches Zivilprozessrecht*, § 38, at 131, notes that the German version of the concept '*verkauf beweglicher Sachen*' is an unusual term in German and derives from the French '*vente de marchandises*'. However, he does not expect serious consequences because of the different wording used under the CISG for '*Kaufvertrag*'. See also U. Magnus, 'Das UN-Kaufrecht und die Erfüllungsortzuständigkeit in der neuen EuGVO', *Internationales Handelsrecht* (2002), 45-52, at 47.

[437] Kropholler, *Europaïsches Zivilprozessrecht*, § 43, at 132.

[438] Beraudo, 'Le Règlement', at 1046; Briggs, *Civil Jurisdiction*, § 2.130, at 159; see for an exhaustive overview of the meaning of 'goods' and 'services', Magnus and Mankowski, eds., *Brussels I Regulation*, § 69-95, at 123-134.

[439] See Briggs, *Civil Jurisdiction*, § 2.131, at 160; Gaudemet-Tallon, *Compétence en Europe*, at 147 and Droz and Gaudemet-Tallon, 'La transformation', at 635.

[440] Strikwerda, *De Overeenkomst in het IPR*, fn. 72, at 36.

[441] Case 38/81 *Effer v. Kantner*, [1982] ECR 825.

brought to examine whether it has jurisdiction'.[442] By stating this, the Court intends to prevent that a claim of non-existence of the contract would deprive claimant of this alternative *forum contractus* and endanger Article 5(1) of being deprived of its legal effect.[443] As a result, the court first seized will have to examine 'at its own motion even, the essential preconditions for its jurisdiction, having regard to conclusive and relevant evidence adduced by the party concerned, establishing the existence or the inexistence of the contract'.[444] The court seized will therefore have to turn to substantial issues to be able to declare itself competent or not.[445] However, it should be noted that the principal claim in the *Effer* case did not concern the validity of the contract.[446] The argument of the contract's non-existence was merely used to challenge the competence of the court seized. It is uncertain what the court would have decided if the court seized was asked to declare the contract void or invalid: would it equally have to declare itself incompetent or would it have to reject the claim?[447]

2.7.3 The Connecting Factors

The *forum contractus* rule under Article 5(1) of the Regulation introduces a sub-classification of contracts with different connecting factors and reads as follows:

> 'A person domiciled in a Member State may, in another Member State, be sued:
> (a) in matters relating to a contract, in the courts for the place of performance of the obligation in question;
> (b) for the purpose of this provision and unless otherwise agreed, the place of performance of the obligation in question shall be:
> – in the case of the sale of goods, the place in a Member State where, under the contract, the goods were delivered or should have been delivered,
> – in the case of the provision of services, the place in a Member State where, under the contract, the services were provided or should have been provided,
> (c) if subparagraph (b) does not apply then subparagraph (a) applies;...'

The rule comprehends a *general* contract jurisdiction rule under Article 5(1)(a) establishing a connecting factor for all types of contracts and contains a *lex specialis* under Article 5(1)(b) for two specific types of contracts: contracts for the sale of goods and contracts for the supply of services. The *lex generalis* under Article 5(1)

[442] Ibid., para. 7; see also Huet, 'Note: *Tacconi*', at 670 in relation to C-334/00 *Tacconi v. HWS*, [2002] ECR I-7357; and see Rogerson, 'Plus ça change?', at 385.

[443] Case 38/81 *Effer v. Kantner*, [1982] ECR 825, para. 7.

[444] Ibid.

[445] Gaudemet-Tallon, *Compétence en Europe,* § 180, at 134; Briggs, *Civil Jurisdiction,* § 2.140, at 175; Kohler, Huet *et al.*, 'Special Jurisdiction Art. 5', at 53.

[446] Huet, 'Special Jurisdiction under Art. 5', at 68; Briggs, *Civil Jurisdiction,* § 2.140, at 175.

[447] Some authors have questioned what a court should do when it concludes that there was no contract: should it not have to conclude retrospectively that it had no jurisdiction; should the court merely decline jurisdiction under Art. 5(1); or should the court dismiss the claim as a whole? See Gaudemet-Tallon, *Compétence en Europe*; Strikwerda, *De Overeenkomst in het IPR,* fn. 47, at 37; Huet, 'Special Jurisdiction under Art. 5', at 68; Mourre, *Droit judiciaire privé européen,* § 114-115, at 77; Kohler, Huet *et al.*, 'Special Jurisdiction Art. 5', at 53; Newton, *Uniform Interpretation*, at 65-67; Magnus and Mankowski, eds., *Brussels I Regulation*, § 42-45, at 110-111.

(a) derives from the Brussels Convention and confers jurisdiction on 'the place of performance of the obligation in question', also called the *forum solutionis*.[448] When the *lex specialis* under Article 5(1)(b) does not apply and 'unless otherwise agreed', the *lex generalis* under Article 5(1)(a) will determine jurisdiction from among the courts of the Member States, as stated in Article 5(1)(c).

As will be demonstrated, the practical application of the connecting factor of Article 5(1) has been, and still is, quite problematic. The interpretation given of the 'place of performance of the obligation in question' by numerous decisions of the ECJ is still highly relevant for the interpretation of Article 5(1)(a). As will be explained below, the provision confers jurisdiction on the place of performance of the obligation 'upon which claimant's action is based'.[449]

For sale of goods contracts and contracts for the provision of services, and 'unless otherwise agreed', the Community legislator fixed the obligation in question by stating that the place of performance shall be respectively the place of delivery, and the place where the services are provided.[450]

The search for an adequate connecting factor is the subject of a continuous debate between the specific obligation theory, the characteristic performance theory, and the autonomous determination of the place of performance.[451] The *lex specialis* rule of Article 5(1)(b) was primarily enacted to deal with problems arising from the *forum solutionis* approach under Article 5(1) of the Brussels Convention.[452] The Regulation's approach appears at least to take away some of the problems for sales contracts and contracts for the provision of services. But legal scholars have raised quite a number of new questions regarding the application of the new provisions. In sum, in the attempt to simplify the jurisdiction rule of the European *forum contractus*, the Regulation only partially improved the application of Article 5(1). At the same time, the new provision brought up a number of new complex issues, which cannot yet be clarified. Most authors are therefore disappointed about the modifications that were brought by this Regulation.[453]

2.7.3.1 *An Autonomous Connecting Factor under Article 5(1)(b)*

For reasons of legal certainty, the Regulation abandoned the 'place of performance of the obligation in question' approach for claims arising out of sales and service

[448] See Jenard Report, at 23.

[449] According to ECJ settled case law, which is mainly based on Case 14/76 *De Bloos v. Bouyer*, [1976] ECR 1497 and Case 12/76 *Tessili v. Dunlop*, [1976] ECR 1473. As explained below in Sect. 2.7.3.2.

[450] This results in 'a tripartite identification of the obligation in question', Briggs, *Civil Jurisdiction*, § 2.131, at 159.

[451] See also Kohler, Huet *et al.*, 'Special Jurisdiction Art. 5', at 55.

[452] See also B. Gsell, 'Autonom bestimmter Gerichtsstand am Erfüllungsort nach der Brüssel I Verordnung', *IPRax* (2002), 484-491, at 483; J. Kropholler and M. von Hinden, 'Die Reform des europäischen Gerichtsstands am Erfüllungsort (Art. 5 Nr. 1 EuGVÜ)', in *Gedächtnisschrift für Alexander Lüderitz* (2000), 401-414, at 411.

[453] Among these are Magnus, 'Das UN-Kaufrecht und die Erfüllungsortzuständigkeit', at 46; Gaudemet-Tallon, *Compétence en Europe*, § 174, at 128; Gsell, 'Autonom bestimmter Gerichtsstand', at 486.

contracts,[454] and replaced it with an autonomous place of performance approach presumed to be closely connected with the contract.[455] In sales contracts, it is often the seller who requests payment of the price, whereas the buyer will often rely on the (non-)delivery of the goods or at least the non-conformity of the other contractual obligation, but in reality, it is often the non-performance or non-conformity which is the actual disputed obligation under the contract.[456]

The approach of Article 5(1)(b) avoids the complex determination of the 'obligation in question', as will be demonstrated in the following section.[457] The Regulation provides for a pragmatic determination of the place of performance of the 'obligation in question'[458] which originates from the characteristic performance theory.[459] The new autonomous approach is based on a more factual criterion instead of a normative concept such as the place of performance of the obligation in question.[460] At first sight, the advantages of this autonomous place of performance seem to be numerous; the *forum contractus* will be concentrated in one single forum, avoiding thereby the multiplication of forums and the fragmentation of the claim.

2.7.3.1.a *The place of delivery in sale of goods contracts*

Article 5(1)(b) states for sale of goods contracts that, unless otherwise agreed, the place of performance of the obligation in question is the place where, under the contract, the goods were delivered or should have been delivered. [461]

The place where, under the contract, the goods were delivered or should have been delivered is the connecting factor and is equally based on the close connection justification.[462] The obligation to deliver, which is generally considered as

---

[454] According to the Explanatory Memorandum to the proposal for a Council Regulation (EC) on jurisdiction and the recognition and enforcement of judgments in civil and commercial matters (presented by the Commission) COM/99/0348 final OJ 1999 C 376 E (at 14) [hereafter Explanatory Memorandum].

[455] C-386/05 *Color Drack*, [2007] ECR 0, para. 23 *et seq.*

[456] See G. Cordero Moss, 'Performance of Obligations as the Basis of Jurisdiction and Choice of Law (Lugano and Brussels Conventions Article 5(1) and Rome Convention Article 4)', 68 *Nordic Journal of International Law* (1999), 379-396, at 390 and P. Punt, 'Naar een meer karakteristieke jurisdictie?', in *Aan Wil besteed* (2003), 425-448, at 440.

[457] Magnus, 'Das UN-Kaufrecht und die Erfüllungsortzuständigkeit', at 46.

[458] According to Gaudemet-Tallon the wording 'the obligation in question' does not have a function, as the only obligation 'in question' is the delivery obligation, any other obligation no longer constitutes a jurisdiction ground and is therefore superfluous, see Gaudemet-Tallon, *Compétence en Europe*, § 187, at 146.

[459] Punt, 'Karakteristieke jurisdictie', at 444.

[460] Magnus and Mankowski, eds., *Brussels I Regulation*, § 96, at 134, observing that this factual concept is based on a general 'anti-*Tessili*' or 'anything but *Tessili*'-feeling determining the place of performance under rule a.

[461] The choice of the place of delivery and the place of provision of services is a logical one and is consistent with the proposals made since Case 12/76 *Tessili v. Dunlop*, [1976] ECR 1473, in which the Italian defendant proposed the place where the defective goods had been delivered as connecting factor; see Hartley, 'Note: *Tessili*', at 59; Gothot and Holleaux, 'Note: *De Bloos and Tessili*', at 766; Opinion AG Lenz in C-288/92 *Custom Made v. Stawa*, [1994] ECR I-2913, para. 82.

[462] Kropholler, *Europaïsches Zivilprozessrecht*, § 46, at 134.

the characteristic obligation of a sales contract, is the determinative obligation for contract jurisdiction under this *lex specialis*.[463]

The connecting factor consists in an objective localization of the place of performance for sales contracts, i.e. the place of delivery, regardless of the obligation that forms the basis of the legal proceedings.[464] According to the Explanatory Memorandum of the Regulation's proposal, the place of delivery applies 'regardless of the obligation in question, even where this obligation is the payment of the financial consideration for the contract. It also applies where the claim relates to several obligations.'[465]

Although this connecting factor was generally welcomed, it raises new problems. Some problems concerning the scope of this specific contract rule have been discussed previously.[466] The determination of the place of delivery is more problematic than it was initially thought to be and will need further clarification or interpretation by the ECJ.[467]

The place of delivery 'under the contract'

The meaning of the words 'under the contract' is ambiguous and confusing. When delivery is made at the place determined under the contract, no particular problems arise,[468] but the utility of these words have been questioned.[469] According to Briggs, the words 'under the contract' refer to the obligation under the contract 'as if to exclude reference to those arising out of it'.[470] As a result, problems arise when the contract does not mention any factual place of delivery. Should one return to normative concepts deriving from substantive law to determine the place of delivery?[471] Does 'under the contract' mean that when no place of delivery has been agreed, Article 5(1)(b) does not apply and one should refer back to the *forum solutionis* under Article 5(1)(a)?[472] Such an interpretation would be contrary to the legislator's desire to provide for an objective place of performance and would limit the scope of Article 5(1)(b) considerably. Conversely, the words 'under the contract' could also mean the place of delivery according to the law applicable to the contract[473] or as stated by some '*l'économie générale du contrat*'.[474] If the ECJ decides that the *lex causae* will determine the place of delivery when the contract

---

463 Gaudemet-Tallon, *Compétence en Europe*, § 198, at 158.

464 Ibid. Magnus and Mankowski, eds., *Brussels I Regulation*, § 100, at 136.

465 See Explanatory Memorandum, at 14.

466 See Sect 2.7.2.4.

467 See Gsell, 'Autonom bestimmter Gerichtsstand', at 486; see also Magnus and Mankowski, eds., *Brussels I Regulation*, § 115-127, at 145-151, for particular problems.

468 Kropholler, *Europaïsches Zivilprozessrecht*, § 4.

469 Gaudemet-Tallon, *Compétence en Europe*, § 202, at 162.

470 Briggs, *Conflict of Laws,* fn. 153, at 77.

471 Gsell, 'Autonom bestimmter Gerichtsstand', at 486-487.

472 A. Huet, 'La Convention de Vienne du 11 avril 1980 sur les contrats de vente internationale de marchandises et compétence des tribunaux en droit judiciaire Européen', in *Le droit international privé: Esprit et méthodes. Mélanges en l'honneur de Paul Lagarde* (2005), 417-430, at 428.

473 Gaudemet-Tallon, *Compétence en Europe*, § 202, at 162; Magnus and Mankowski, eds., *Brussels I Regulation*, § 104, at 139.

474 Huet, 'Convention de Vienne et compétence', at 428.

does not explicitly mention a place of delivery, similar problems will arise for the application of the *lex generalis*.

Factual delivery without a contractual place of delivery

Likewise, what should be decided when no place of delivery was specified under the contract, but delivery was made? Should one refer to Article 5(1)(a), or should one refer to the *lex causae* to examine whether that delivery was made 'under the contract' according to its applicable law, or should one accept the factual place of delivery instead?[475] Kropholler opts for the last option favouring a more factual and objective connecting factor establishing jurisdiction at the place of factual delivery, provided that the receiver accepted the goods.[476]

Non-delivery and no specified place of delivery

If no delivery has taken place or the place is factually difficult to localize and there has not been a place of delivery specified under the contract, different solutions have been proposed.[477] Either the law governing the contract, the *lex causae*, will determine the place of delivery,[478] or the *lex fori* will determine the place of delivery,[479] or Article 5(1)(a) through (c) will resolve the matter by applying the *forum solutionis*.

Wrongful delivery: Factual delivery versus contractual delivery

Equally uncertain is the question whether the factual delivery or the delivery 'under the contract' is conclusive. Obviously, when no delivery has been made, the rule establishes jurisdiction to the place where the goods 'should have been delivered' under the contract. But what if the goods have been delivered at another place than contractually agreed? Does that give jurisdiction to the place where the wrongful delivery took place, in which case the factual delivery becomes the decisive element?[480] Or contrarily, should the place where the goods 'should have been delivered' remain the competent forum, especially if the counter-party does not accept the goods delivered at this wrong place?[481] Or, should the *forum contractus* be

---

[475] See above and see Huet, 'Convention de Vienne et compétence', at 428; Magnus and Mankowski, eds., *Brussels I Regulation*, § 112, at 144.

[476] Kropholler, *Europaïsches Zivilprozessrecht*, § 47, at 135; followed by Magnus, 'Das UN-Kaufrecht und die Erfüllungsortzuständigkeit', at 47; and see Magnus and Mankowski, eds., *Brussels I Regulation*, § 108, at 142.

[477] Droz and Gaudemet-Tallon, 'La transformation', at 160 and Gaudemet-Tallon, *Compétence en Europe*, § 200, at 160. An original solution was recommended by Magnus, namely the UNIDROIT Principles of International Commercial Contracts (at http://www.unidroit.org), and to some extent the *lex mercatoria* could provide a place of delivery, see Magnus, 'Das UN-Kaufrecht und die Erfüllungsortzuständigkeit', at 48; Magnus and Mankowski, eds., *Brussels I Regulation*, § 106-107, at 141.

[478] Huet, 'Convention de Vienne et compétence', at 429 and Gaudemet-Tallon, *Compétence en Europe*, § 202, at 162.

[479] See Beraudo, 'Le Règlement', at 1044.

[480] As cautiously suggested by Gaudemet-Tallon, see Gaudemet-Tallon, *Compétence en Europe*, § 202, at 162; Droz and Gaudemet-Tallon, 'La transformation', at 635; Magnus, 'Das UN-Kaufrecht und die Erfüllungsortzuständigkeit', at 47; and Magnus and Mankowski, eds., *Brussels I Regulation*, § 101, at 137-138.

[481] Kropholler, *Europaïsches Zivilprozessrecht*, § 47, at 136; see also Magnus, 'Das UN-Kaufrecht und die Erfüllungsortzuständigkeit', at 47.

found at both the contractual place of delivery *and* the place of factual delivery?[482] Or finally, does a wrongful delivery impede the application of Article 5(1)(b), as delivery was not made under the contract and should Article 5(1)(a) therefore apply via the application of Article 5(1)(c)?[483]

Delivery in a third state

According to the Explanatory Memorandum, the general rule under Article 5(1)(a) applies when Article 5(1)(b) designates a court in a non-Member State, i.e. the place of delivery is not in a Member State.[484] Most authors agree that if the sales contract points to a place of delivery in a non-Brussels Regulation State, the *lex specialis* under Article 5(1)(b) will not apply and the general rule Article 5(1)(a) will designate the competent forum, i.e. the place of performance of the obligation in question.[485] Although the Explanatory Report is quite clear on this point, it is theoretically still possible that the court rules otherwise. Why should there be a second chance for a contract forum under Article 5(1)(a) when the *lex specialis* already clearly established that the *forum contractus* lies in a non-Member State?[486] Should the conclusion then not simply be that there is no *forum contractus* instead of finding another on the basis of the *forum solutionis* which is so heavily criticized for its lack of uniformity and the fact that it does not warrant a close connection? In that respect, Magnus proposes that in the event that a place of delivery is located in a third state, the place of performance of the characteristic obligation should be determinative, since the *De Bloos* approach was overruled by the Brussels Regulation for contracts of sale of goods and the provision of services.[487]

Multiple places of delivery

The new Article 5(1) fails to indicate the place of performance in the event that, under the contract, goods have been or should have been delivered in several places.[488] Several options have been put forward.[489] Should the claimant have a choice from among each place of delivery with respect to a claim relating to all those deliveries or should jurisdiction for a particular place be limited to the delivery or performance made in that place? Or, conversely, should there be only one place of delivery competent to hear the claim, for instance the place closest connected[490] or

[482] Gaudemet-Tallon, *Compétence en Europe*, § 199, at 159.

[483] Huet, 'Convention de Vienne et compétence', at 428.

[484] Explanatory Memorandum, at 14.

[485] See Beraudo, 'Le Règlement', at 1046; Kropholler, *Europaïsches Zivilprozessrecht*, § 53, at 138; Gaudemet-Tallon, *Compétence en Europe*, § 198, at 159; Huet, 'Convention de Vienne et compétence', at 430; Magnus, 'Das UN-Kaufrecht und die Erfüllungsortzuständigkeit', at 49; Michaels, 'Re-Placements', at 133-134.

[486] See the critical observation of Kruger, *Impact on Third States*, § 2.200, at 135-136.

[487] Magnus, 'Das UN-Kaufrecht und die Erfüllungsortzuständigkeit', at 49.

[488] As acknowledged by the ECJ in C-386/05 *Color Drack*, [2007] ECR 0, para. 17.

[489] For these options see Gaudemet-Tallon, *Compétence en Europe*, § 199, at 159; Kropholler, *Europaïsches Zivilprozessrecht*, § 50, at 136-137; Michaels, 'Re-Placements', at 142; Magnus and Mankowski, eds., *Brussels I Regulation*, § 120, at 148.

[490] See Michaels, 'Re-Placements', at 142; or follow the example of Art. 4(2) Rome I Convention.

the place of the principal delivery?[491] Should one find recourse to the 'place of performance of the obligation in question' under Article 5(1)(a).[492] Or finally, should one decide that there is no contract jurisdiction, as the place of performance could not be determined? The latter was already proposed in the Regulation's Proposal but not retained in its final version.[493] The suggested options apply in the event the deliveries are located in different Member States or in one single Member State.

The *Color Drack* case is the first case dealing with Article 5(1)(b) of the Regulation and the ECJ was asked to determine the place of performance in relation to a contract for the sale of goods in which case the goods were delivered in different places but in *a single* Member State.[494] The claimant, Color Drack GmbH a company registered in Austria, purchased sunglasses from Lexx International Vertriebs GmbH registered in Germany. Color Drack paid the price and parties agreed that Lexx should deliver the glasses directly to the customers in different places in Austria. The dispute concerned Lexx's refusal to take back unsold goods and to reimburse the price to Color Drack as was contractually agreed.[495] The referring Austrian Court asked the ECJ whether 'Article 5(1)(b) of Regulation No 44/2001 applies in the case of a sale of goods involving several places of delivery within a single Member State and, if so, whether, where the claim relates to all those deliveries, the plaintiff may sue the defendant in the court for the place of delivery of its choice'.[496] The ECJ, first confirmed that the *lex specialis* rule applies whether there is one place of delivery or several,[497] as the Regulation does not intend to 'exclude cases where a number of courts may have jurisdiction';[498] second, that conferring jurisdiction on several places of delivery is not incompatible with the Regulation's objective of predictability;[499] and finally, the objective of proximity is met since the provision will in any event grant jurisdiction to the courts of that Member State.[500] The Court then stressed the importance of *one* court having jurisdiction to hear all claims arising out of the contract, and explained the Community legislator's choice for the autonomous place of performance as the place of delivery due

[491] As suggested by Kropholler, *Europaïsches Zivilprozessrecht,* § 50, at 137; Gaudemet-Tallon, *Compétence en Europe*, § 199, at 159, referring to M. Ancel, *La prestation caractéristique du contrat* (2002), § 450.

[492] See Gaudemet-Tallon, *Compétence en Europe*, § 199, at 159, again referring to Ancel.

[493] Art. 5(1) of the Commission's Proposal Act reads that a party to a contract can be sued: 'in matters relating to a contract for sale of goods, in the courts of the place where the delivery was or should have been carried out, except in cases where the goods were delivered, or deliverable, to more than one place.' See also Kropholler, *Europaïsches Zivilprozessrecht*, § 50, at 137; Michaels, 'Re-Placements', at 142.

[494] See for notes on this case S. Leible and Ch. Reinert, 'Note: *Color Drack* C-386/05', *Europäische Zeitschrift für Wirtschaftsrecht* (2007), 370-373, and J. Harris, 'Sale of Goods and the Relentless March of the Brussels I Regulation', 123 *Law Quarterly Review* (2007), 522-528.

[495] C-386/05 *Color Drack*, [2007] ECR 0, para. 9.

[496] Ibid., para. 15.

[497] Ibid., paras. 28 and 36, AG Bot concurring in Opinion AG Bot, para. 115.

[498] C-386/05 *Color Drack*, [2007] ECR 0, para. 29.

[499] Ibid., para. 32.

[500] Ibid., para. 35.

to the need to centralize all disputes concerning contractual obligations.[501] In that respect the Court determined that where there are several places of delivery the place with the closest connecting factor between the contract and the court should have jurisdiction and that the principal delivery should be determined 'on the basis of economic criteria'.[502] The court seized has to consider what the prinicipal delivery is.[503] In the absence of such economic criteria, the claimant may choose from among the places of delivery where he wants to sue the defendant, provided that each of the places of delivery has a sufficiently close link to the 'material elements of the dispute'.[504] According to the ECJ this is not contrary to defendant's right to foresee in which courts he may be sued; claimant is sufficiently protected while all potential courts are located in the same Member State.[505]

The question remains unsolved in relation to several places of delivery in a number of Member States. It is not unthinkable that the solution would be different from the *Color Drack* solution: the Court explicitly pointed out that its considerations are not without prejudice to future answers concerning the deliveries in multiple Member States.[506] In *Color Drack* the ECJ relied heavily on the fact that the foreseeability of the defendant was not infringed as all potential places pointed to the courts of the same Member State. Although, as argued in *Color Drack*, the Regulation does not exclude multiple competent courts, one of its main objectives is to avoid multiplication of competent forums, especially when these are located in different Member States,[507] and to avoid irreconciliable judgements.[508] The Court would more likely opt for limiting jurisdiction to the place of delivery with respect to claims related to that specific delivery only,[509] or, especially if the claim is related to all deliveries, simply refuse contract jurisdiction in contracts for the sale of goods with multiple deliveries in several Member States and avoid *forum shopping*.[510]

---

[501] Ibid., para. 39.

[502] Ibid., para. 40. This is in contrast with the Opinion given by AG Bot, who stated that it is for national law to determine whether the plaintiff may sue the defendant in the court of any place of delivery or whether he must bring his action in the court of one of those places in particular, para. 130.

[503] See Harris, 'Sale of Goods and the Relentless March', at 524.

[504] C-386/05 *Color Drack*, [2007] ECR 0, para. 42.

[505] Ibid., para. 44. See also Opinion AG Bot in C-386/05 *Color Drack*, [2007] ECR 0, para. 107.

[506] C-386/05 *Color Drack*, [2007] ECR 0, para. 16.

[507] See C-125/92 *Mulox v. Geels*, [1993] ECR 4075, para. 11.

[508] This was not a problem in C-386/05 *Color Drack*, [2007] ECR 0; see Opinion AG Bot in C-386/05 *Color Drack*, [2007] ECR 0, para. 101. It could be a problem for multiple deliveries in several Member States, Harris, 'Sale of Goods and the Relentless March', at 524.

[509] This is an analogous application of C-68/93 *Shevill v. Presse Alliance*, [1995] ECR I-415, which dealt with tortuous matters under Art. 5(3) and where jurisdiction was limited to the harm caused in the State of the court seized. See Kropholler, *Europaïsches Zivilprozessrecht*, § 50, at 137.

[510] This would be in line with the decision taken in C-256/00 *Besix v. WABAG*, [2002] ECR I-1699 (as explained in Sect. 2.7.3.2.a regarding the obligation not to do) especially if the delivery has 'no geographical limit'. See also Magnus, 'Das UN-Kaufrecht und die Erfüllungsortzuständigkeit', at 49, and see Opinion AG Bot in C-386/05 *Color Drack*, [2007] ECR 0, para. 31, referring to the German Government's position equally based on C-256/00 *Besix v. WABAG*, [2002] ECR I-1699.

2.7.3.1.b *Contract for the provision of services*

For a service contract, the determinative obligation in question is the provision of services; and the connecting factor is the place where, still under the contract, the services were or should have been provided.[511] As identified above, similar problems as to the place of delivery may arise in relation to the determination of the place of the provision of services.[512]

2.7.3.1.c *'Unless otherwise agreed'*

It is assumed that the words 'unless otherwise agreed' under Article 5(1)(b) give parties the opportunity to deviate from this determinative place of performance of the obligation in question fixed for sales and service contracts, yet, the exact meaning is unclear.[513] One of the interpretations is that parties are allowed to reject the *lex specialis* under Article 5(1)(b) and agree to refer back to the *lex generalis* under Article 5(1)(a) by using the *forum solutionis* as connecting factor to determine the competent contract forum.[514]

Another interpretation is that the 'unless otherwise agreed' formula allows parties to agree upon another place of performance, different from the place of delivery or the place of provision of services as stipulated under Article 5(1)(b). For example, parties could agree that the place of performance for the sale of goods is not the place of delivery, but the obligation of payment or any other place of performance. If such an agreement on another objective place of performance were to be allowed by the ECJ, it is most likely that parties would have to comply with the same requirements applicable to the agreed place of performance under the *lex generalis* of Article 5(1)(a) as established by the settled case law of the ECJ.[515] One of these requirements imposes that the elected place of performance should not be 'fictive', with the sole purpose of avoiding the requirements for a valid forum selection clause and thereby constituting a wholly artificial place of performance, in which case such an agreement will have to comply with Article 23.

In that respect it should be assumed that a simple contractual clause fixing the place of payment is not explicit enough to 'otherwise agree' to derogate to the place of delivery or the place of provision of service under Article 5(1)(b).[516] An example of such an explicit derogation would be: 'for the purpose of this contract the place of performance of the obligation in question shall be considered to be the place of payment'. As rightfully argued by Briggs, if such a provision should be

---

[511] Art. 5(1)(b), 2nd litter of the Regulation.

[512] See Magnus and Mankowski, eds., *Brussels I Regulation*, § 113-114, at 144-145.

[513] Huet, 'Convention de Vienne et compétence', at 429; Gaudemet-Tallon, *Compétence en Europe*, § 201, at 160.

[514] Huet, 'Convention de Vienne et compétence', at 429; Gaudemet-Tallon, *Compétence en Europe*, § 201, at 161.

[515] As explained above in Sect. 2.7.3.2.f on the agreed place of performance and Case 56/79 *Zelger v. Salinitri*, [1980] ECR 89, para. 5 and C-106/95 *MSG v. Gravières Rhénanes*, [1997] ECR I-911, paras. 30-31.

[516] According to Gaudemet-Tallon, *Compétence en Europe*, § 201, at 161.

incorporated for jurisdictional purposes in a sales contract it would be the oddest term to find in a contract.[517]

2.7.3.2 *The Place of Performance of the Obligation in Question under Article 5(1)(a)*

When Article 5(1)(b) does not apply, the Regulation holds on to the *forum solutionis* or the place of performance of the obligation in question on which the claim is based.[518] This means that the *forum solutionis* determines the competent forum for all other contracts, except for sales contracts or service contracts.[519] Additionally, Article 5(1)(a) applies when the place of delivery or of the provision of services is located outside the Regulation's territory and, as identified above, may apply in circumstances where difficulties to determine those places arise.[520]

The Jenard Report explains why this connecting factor is the appropriate one:

> 'The court for the place of performance of the obligation will be useful in proceedings for the recovery of fees: the creditor will have a choice between the courts of the State where the defendant is domiciled and the courts of another State within whose jurisdiction the services were provided, particularly where, according to the appropriate law, the obligation to pay must be performed where the services were provided. This forum can also be used where expert evidence or inquiries are required.'[521]

Shortly after the Brussels Convention entered into force, the Court was asked to clarify what was meant with 'the place of performance of the obligation in question'. Two cases are crucial for the determination of the *forum solutionis* and it entailed a two-step process:[522] the *Tessili* case[523] and the *De Bloos* case[524] which were both rendered on the same day by the ECJ.[525] *De Bloos* identified the obligation to be performed, or the 'identification of the obligation in question',[526] and *Tessili* localized the place of performance by virtue of the *lex causae*, or the applicable law to the contract.[527]

---

[517] Briggs, *Civil Jurisdiction*, § 2.131, at 160; and Gaudemet-Tallon, *Compétence en Europe*, § 201, at 161.

[518] See Jenard Report, at 23; in contrast Weser, *La convention communautaire*, at 248, identifying Art. 5(1) as the *forum executionis*.

[519] Magnus and Mankowski, eds., *Brussels I Regulation*, § 128, at 151.

[520] As explained above in Sect. 2.7.3.1.a.

[521] Jenard Report, at 23-24, repeated in Case 133/81 *Ivenel v. Schwab*, [1982] ECR 1891, para. 11.

[522] Borchers, 'Comparing Jurisdiction', at 141.

[523] Case 12/76 *Tessili v. Dunlop*, [1976] ECR 1473.

[524] Case 14/76 *De Bloos v. Bouyer*, [1976] ECR 1497.

[525] Case 12/76 *Tessili v. Dunlop*, [1976] and Case 14/76 *De Bloos v. Bouyer*, [1976] published in the same ECR respectively at 1473 and at 1497.

[526] Case 14/76 *De Bloos v. Bouyer*, [1976] ECR 1497, paras. 11 and 13; see also C-288/92 *Custom Made v. Stawa*, [1994] ECR I-2913, para. 22.

[527] Case 12/76 *Tessili v. Dunlop*, [1976] ECR 1473, para. 13. See the threefold (painstaking) tasks imposed on the seized court described in Opinion AG Ruiz-Jarabo Colomer in C-440/97 *GIE Groupe Concorde*, [1999] ECR I-6307, paras. 28-30 and 45. See A. Huet, 'Note: *Tessili*', *Journal du droit international* (1977), 714-719, at 719.

2.7.3.2.a *The obligation in question*

The Court concluded in *De Bloos v. Bouyer*[528] that the 'obligation in question' cannot refer to any obligation arising under the contract[529] but only refers to the contractual obligation forming the basis of the legal proceedings,[530] in other words the obligation, which corresponds to the contractual right upon which the plaintiff's action is based.[531] This means that the *forum contractus* depends on the action brought by the plaintiff and that any place of performance of a contractual obligation is a potential *forum contractus*.[532] The idea behind this approach is based on the weight given to the independence of each contractual obligation.[533]

The Court repeatedly justified the 'obligation in question' approach by the fact that that place 'usually constitutes the closest connecting factor between the dispute and the court having jurisdiction over it, and it is this connecting factor which explains why, in contractual matters, it is the court of the place of performance of the obligation which has jurisdiction.'[534] This 'physical proximity' enables the court to determine 'the nature of that relationship in the fullest possible knowledge of the facts of the case'.[535]

By choosing for the obligation in question on which the claim is based, the Court refused the interpretation of 'any obligation arising out of the contract'. Such an interpretation would create a situation in which a number of courts have jurisdiction in respect of one and the same contract and would result in a multiplication of competent forums, which is contrary to the objectives of the Brussels Model.[536] Nonetheless, the '*De Bloos*' approach gives rise to particular difficulties in a number of circumstances where it is difficult to identify the obligation in question.

---

528 Case 14/76 *De Bloos v. Bouyer*, [1976] ECR 1497.

529 Ibid., para. 10; repeated, among others, in Case 266/85 *Shenavai v. Kreischer*, [1987] ECR 239, para. 8; and C-420/97 *Leathertex v. Bodetex*, [1999] ECR I-6747, para. 31. The original text of Art. 5(1) of the 1968 Convention differed in the different translations. The French and Dutch versions of the Brussels Convention did not specify which obligation was meant under Art. 5(1), while the German and Italian versions mentioned the obligation in question. See Kohler, Huet *et al.*, 'Special Jurisdiction Art. 5', at 53; Punt, 'Karakteristieke jurisdictie', at 438; and J.-M. Bischoff and A. Huet, 'Note: *Shenevai*', *Journal du droit international* (1987), 465-472, at 466, stating that the decision taken in Case 14/76 *De Bloos v. Bouyer*, [1976] ECR 1497, is the solution closest to the proposed original text of the provision, which follows the text as it is provided in these other languages.

530 Case 14/76 *De Bloos v. Bouyer*, [1976] ECR 1497, para. 11.

531 Ibid., para. 13.

532 In contrast Kohler, Huet *et al.*, 'Special Jurisdiction Art. 5', at 54.

533 For that reason it is also referred to as the 'isolation principle'. See also Opinion AG Lenz in C-288/92 *Custom Made v. Stawa*, [1994] ECR I-2913, para. 77.

534 Case 266/85 *Shenavai v. Kreischer*, [1987] ECR 239, para. 18; affirmed in C-288/92 *Custom Made v. Stawa*, [1994] ECR I-2913, paras. 12-13 and C-440/97 *GIE Groupe Concorde*, [1999] ECR I-6307, para. 29. Emphasized by Bischoff and Huet, 'Note: *Shenevai*', at 466, and Gothot and Holleaux, 'Note: *De Bloos and Tessili*', at 768; see in contrast Huet, 'Note: *Peters*', at 838.

535 See Opinion AG Lenz in C-288/92 *Custom Made v. Stawa*, [1994] ECR I-2913, para. 16, referring to AG Mancini.

536 Case 14/76 *De Bloos v. Bouyer*, [1976] ECR 1497, para. 9.

The original obligation
In *De Bloos*, the Court was asked to determine what the 'obligation in question' entailed when damages were sought after a failure of delivery. Should the *original* or *independent* contractual obligation be considered or should the obligation to pay damages, as a consequence of the breach of the original obligation, be considered as the obligation in question?[537] The ECJ decided that the *original* obligation was conclusive, rather than choosing to replace the original or independent obligation under the contract with the place of performance.[538] As the 'obligation in question' approach allows different contractual obligations to provide for a *forum contractus*, the Court had to limit these obligations to the *original* obligations. Another reason, according to *Gothot*, for focusing on the original obligation rather than on the obligation replacing the unperformed contractual obligation lies in the principle of a sound administration of justice. The court of the place of performance of the obligation in question that replaces the original obligation has no link or close connection with the forum.[539]

In French terminology this 'obligation in question' is not only referred to as '*l'obligation litigieuse*' but is also called '*obligation contractuelle autonome*', hereby emphasizing that only the 'original' or 'independent' contractual obligation is conclusive for the 'place of performance of the obligation in question'.[540]

Multiple obligations
Another difficulty with the *forum solutionis* approach occurrs when the plaintiff commences proceedings on the basis of a number of obligations arising under the same contract. Which obligation should then be identified as the obligation in question? The maxim of '*accessorium sequitur principale*' established in *Shenavai* implies that when various obligations are at issue, the *principal obligation* determines the place of performance for jurisdiction.[541] Although the preliminary question was not concerned with this issue, the finding of the Court was generally wel-

[537] The Court distinguished two types of actions: first, when the plaintiff demands damages or seeks dissolution of the contract on grounds of wrongful conduct of its counter-party, the obligation in question is the (non-performance) of the obligation arising out of the contract and upon which the claim is based, see Case 14/76 *De Bloos v. Bouyer*, [1976] ECR 1497, paras. 14-16. In those actions the obligation in question is not the obligation to pay damages itself, but the non-performance of the *original* contractual obligation gives rise to claims of payment of damages or the dissolution of the contract. The second type involves actions of compensation. The Court ruled that it is for the national court to ascertain whether, under the law applicable to the contract, the claim involves an independent contractual obligation or an obligation replacing the unperformed contractual obligation, see Case 14/76 *De Bloos v. Bouyer*, [1976] ECR 1497, para. 17; repeated in Case 266/85 *Shenavai v. Kreischer*, [1987] ECR 239, para. 9; see also Gothot and Holleaux, 'Note: *De Bloos and Tessili*', at 769-772.

[538] Briggs, *Civil Jurisdiction*, § 2.135, at 167.

[539] Gothot and Holleaux, 'Note: *De Bloos and Tessili*', at 768-769.

[540] Ibid., at 761.

[541] Case 266/85 *Shenavai v. Kreischer*, [1987] ECR 239, para. 19; confirmed by C-420/97 *Leathertex v. Bodetex*, [1999] ECR I-6747, para. 15; see also Opinion AG Léger in C-420/97 *Leathertex v. Bodetex*, [1999] ECR I-6747, para. 30; Magnus and Mankowski, eds., *Brussels I Regulation*, § 132, at 153.

comed,[542] even if the Court did not give further guidance as to how to determine the principal obligation from among several obligations.[543] Only several years later did the Court hint at referring back to the applicable law to determine the principal obligation: 'Some of the questions which might arise in this context, such as … the principal obligation where there are several obligations, could hardly be resolved without reference to the applicable law.'[544]

But how should the court seized act when it is unable to identify the principal obligation because none of the obligations are subordinated to one in particular? How can the court seized determine whether it has jurisdiction over a composite claim based on two obligations of equal rank arising from the same contract, in the event that one of those obligations is to be performed in the state where the court is situated and the other in another Contracting State? Moreover, assuming the court seized accepts jurisdiction, should the same court hear the whole case, or is its competence limited to the claim based on the obligation that is to be performed in the state where it is situated? These questions were submitted to the ECJ in the *Leathertex* case.[545] In the first place, the Court stated that it is for the national court to assess the relative importance of the contractual obligations at issue.[546] The Court followed the submissions of the German and British Governments arguing that not only two obligations which form the basis of an action should be regarded as equal in rank by the court seized, but also that the jurisdiction to deal with each of them should lie with the court of the place where the obligations are to be performed. The same court should not have jurisdiction to hear the whole case.[547] The consequences of the *Leathertex* decision are therefore, that a court might have special jurisdiction with respect to only a fraction of the claim, namely the claim based on the obligation that has to be performed in the state where the court is situated. Any fragmentation of jurisdiction resulting therefrom should therefore be accepted.[548] According to the Opinion of AG Leger, the possibility that the case will be 'split between several fora'[549] is however not favouring the Convention's aim to strengthen the legal protection of persons which implies the need to avoid, wherever possible, a situation in which a number of courts have jurisdiction over one and the same contract.[550] The Court acknowledges the disadvantages of having different courts ruling on different aspects of the same dispute, but observes that the plaintiff always has the option, under Article 2 of the Convention, to bring his

---

[542] Some authors would have preferred to refer back to the characteristic obligation approach, see Droz, 'Note: Shenevai', at 798; Bischoff and Huet, 'Note: *Shenevai*', at 465 and Rogerson, 'Plus ça change?', at 387.

[543] Gaudemet-Tallon, *Compétence en Europe*, § 186, at 144; Hertz, *Jurisdiction in Contract*, at 95 *et seq.*

[544] C-440/97 *GIE Groupe Concorde*, [1999] ECR I-6307, para. 26.

[545] C-420/97 *Leathertex v. Bodetex*, [1999] ECR I-6747.

[546] Ibid., paras. 21 and 23.

[547] Ibid., paras. 40-42.

[548] Ibid., para. 25.

[549] Opinion AG Léger in C-420/97 *Leathertex v. Bodetex*, [1999] ECR I-6747, para. 23.

[550] Ibid., paras. 62-63.

entire claim before the courts of the place where the defendant is domiciled.[551] But unlike in the *Besix* case where an obligation in question involving an obligation not to do resulted in the annulment of the *forum contractus*,[552] in this case the Court preferred to keep the special jurisdiction rule for the sake of the freedom of choice of the plaintiff, even if it leads to the fragmentation of the case.

Obligation not to do

The limits of the 'place of performance of the obligation in question' approach were identified in the above-mentioned *Besix* case. The Court was asked how to locate the place of performance of an obligation *not* to do. Such an obligation is applicable without geographical limits and its place of performance

> 'is not capable of being identified with a specific place or linked to a court which would be particularly suited to hear and determine the dispute relating to that obligation. By definition, such an undertaking to refrain from doing something in any place whatsoever is not linked to any particular court....'[553]

The Court concluded by stating that an obligation not to do, with no geographical limits, makes it impossible to determine a *forum contractus*, and the main jurisdiction rule of Article 2 is left as the sole jurisdiction ground 'which provides a certain and reliable criterion'.[554]

2.7.3.2.b *The systematic refusal of the characteristic obligation*

This 'obligation in question' approach also called the *specific performance theory*[555] or '*prestation litigieuse*'[556] contrasts with the characteristic performance theory.[557] This *characteristic performance theory* localizes the place of performance of all obligations arising under the contract at the 'focal point'of the contractual relationship: the place of performance of the obligation characterizing the contract.[558] The drafters' choice for the *forum solutionis* was explained by Jenard in his report and confirmed by the ECJ in the *De Bloos* case, and it was followed by a consistent refusal to take into account the characteristic obligation of a contract.[559]

The Ivenel *exception*

The ECJ made one exception to this consistent refusal for employment contracts: it formulated a specific connecting factor for employment contracts based on their characteristic obligation. Under the Brussels Regulation, employment contracts are

---

551 C-420/97 *Leathertex v. Bodetex*, [1999] ECR I-6747, para. 41 and see also Opinion AG Léger in C-420/97 *Leathertex v. Bodetex*, [1999] ECR I-6747, paras. 20-21 and 76.

552 See next section.

553 C-256/00 *Besix v. WABAG*, [2002] ECR I-1699, para. 49.

554 Ibid., para. 50.

555 Hill, 'Jurisdiction in Matters Relating to a Contract', at 592.

556 Huet, 'Note: *Peters*', at 838.

557 Magnus and Mankowski, eds., *Brussels I Regulation*, § 131, at 153.

558 Case 266/85 *Shenavai v. Kreischer*, [1987] ECR 239, para. 4; see H. Gaudemet-Tallon, 'Note: *Ivenel*', *Revue critique de droit international privé* (1983), 120-126, at 121.

559 Gothot and Holleaux, 'Note: *De Bloos and Tessili*', at 767; Weser, *La convention communautaire*, at 221-248; Kohler, Huet *et al.*, 'Special Jurisdiction Art. 5', at 53.

part of the protective jurisdiction rules, but the initial Convention did not provide for such a specific regime for employment contracts. They fell under the general *forum contractus* of Article 5(1) of the Brussels Convention.[560] Although employment contracts fall outside the scope of the present study[561] the debate in the *Ivenel* case which leads to a specific connecting factor emanating from the characteristic performance theory, is relevant for the current discussion of Article 5(1)(b).

In *Ivenel*, policy considerations led the Court to decide to protect the weaker party – the employee – who required special protection.[562] The Court decided that for employment contracts only, thus by way of exception,[563] the obligation that had to be taken into account 'is the obligation which characterizes the contract'.[564] The Court designated the characteristic obligation as the obligation in question under Article 5(1) and deviated from the *De Bloos* decision but only with regard to employment contracts.[565] But the Court also justifies the characteristic obligation approach for employment contracts on the basis of the *close connection* justification.[566] In the cases following the *Ivenel* case, the Court however refused to use this close connection justification to establish a characteristic performance approach for the general contract rule. This refusal is explained by the fact that such an approach would lead to one connecting factor that is not necessarily closely connected to each specific claim, for all claims arising out of the contract.[567]

After the limited 'turnover' of the general rule established in *De Bloos* by the *Ivenel* case, the 'obligation in question' approach was challenged several times. In the *Shenevai* case the Court was asked in a very explicit way which approach should be taken as a general rule for contract jurisdiction. In a dispute concerning proceedings for the recovery of fees, commenced by an architect commissioned to draw up plans for the building of houses, the Court was asked to determine whether this contractual relation would be covered under the exception made for employ-

---

[560] Case 133/81 *Ivenel v. Schwab*, [1982] ECR 1891. See for the position of employment contracts in the Lugano Convention, Cordero Moss, 'Performance of Obligations', at 383.

[561] See on the scope of this book Chapter 1, Sect. 1.6.

[562] Case 133/81 *Ivenel v. Schwab*, [1982] ECR 1891, paras. 16-20; confirmed by Case 266/85 *Shenavai v. Kreischer*, [1987] ECR 239, para. 10; see T. Hartley, 'Note: *Ivenel*', *European Law Review* (1982), 328-331, at 329; J. Verheul, 'Note: Ivenel', *Netherlands International Law Review* (1983), 248-251, at 248; questioned by Bischoff and Huet, 'Note: *Shenevai*', at 467.

[563] See Gaudemet-Tallon, 'Note: *Ivenel*', at 122; see also the ECJ's statement in C-288/92 *Custom Made v. Stawa*, [1994] ECR I-2913, para. 24.

[564] Case 133/81 *Ivenel v. Schwab*, [1982] ECR 1891, para. 20; confirmed in Case 266/85 *Shenavai v. Kreischer*, [1987] ECR 239, para. 11. See Verheul, 'Note: Ivenel', at 249.

[565] See Gaudemet-Tallon, 'Note: *Ivenel*', at 123, calling this a '*revirement*' of the rule established in Case 14/76 *De Bloos v. Bouyer*, [1976] ECR 1497; and see J. Verheul, 'Note: *Shenevai*', *Netherlands International Law Review* (1987), 100-102, at 100.

[566] Case 133/81 *Ivenel v. Schwab*, [1982] ECR 1891 para. 15, see also Gaudemet-Tallon, 'Note: *Ivenel*', at 122 and G. Droz, 'Delendum est forum contractus? Vingt ans après les arrêts *De Bloos* et *Tessili* interprétant l'article 5.1 de la Convention de Bruxelles du 27 septembre 1968', 41 *Recueil Dalloz: Cahier Chronique* (1997), 351-356, at 352.

[567] Schack considered such a characteristic performance approach not suitable for a general rule, see H. Schack, 'Note: Custom Made', *Zeitschrift für Europäisches Privatrecht* (1995), 659-668, at 662; and see Geimer '*Konnexitätserwagungen*', R. Geimer, 'Note: *Shenevai*', *NJW* (1987), 1132-1133, at 1133.

ment contracts in the *Ivenel* decision.[568] In other words, the Court had to decide whether this dispute displayed 'special features' or 'particularities' analogous to those which gave rise to the characteristic obligation approach in the *Ivenel* case. The Court decided it did not and affirmed the 'obligation in question' factor for contracts in general, hereby refusing a case-by-case approach determining whether 'particularities' would justify adhering to the characteristic obligation approach.[569] The Court continued by stating that the characteristic obligation would not be a suitable approach in terms of the variety and multiplicity of contracts. According to the Court a characteristic obligation approach would create uncertainty as to how the characteristic obligation of all these various types of contracts should be determined.[570] This argument, based on the existence of 'too many' types of contracts to identify the characteristic obligations by law, is often put forward.[571] Yet some authors have argued that in most contracts the identification of the characteristic obligation is quite straightforward: in a sale of goods contract it is the seller's performance, in a lease-contract it is the lessor's performance, in a carriage-contract, it is the carrier's, and so on.[572] Nonetheless, the characteristic performance is not always clearly identifiable.[573] Some contracts are complex and lay down several obligations for both parties.[574] Others do not have *one* characteristic obligation since the obligations are each other's equal. This is the case in swap-agreements.[575]

Other arguments against the application of the characteristic obligation approach relate to the balance between the interests of the parties. With the characteristic obligation approach the contract forum will always be the same forum, and will, in most cases, be in the advantage of one party, usually the party who has to perform the characteristic obligation.[576] Therefore, some authors find it understandable that the connecting factor for contract jurisdiction varies according to whom the plaintiff is, and his claim.[577]

Nonetheless, the characteristic performance approach consists in allocating jurisdiction to one court only, considering the contracts as *a whole*.[578] It has the advantage of concentrating all claims in one forum, by providing for one single *forum contractus* and of contributing to more legal certainty for the parties, since they can identify the *forum contractus* in advanced regardless of the obligation in question.

It has often been observed that the 'obligation in question' approach results in the multiplication of forums with respect to one contract that are not necessarily closely connected to the contract itself and this approach does not respect the unity

---

[568] Case 266/85 *Shenavai v. Kreischer*, [1987] ECR 239, para. 5.

[569] Para. 17; affirmed by C-420/97 *Leathertex v. Bodetex*, [1999] ECR I-6747, paras. 36-37.

[570] Para. 17; underlined by Bischoff and Huet, 'Note: *Shenevai*', at 466.

[571] See on this issue the position of Punt, 'Karakteristieke jurisdictie', at 444.

[572] Hartley, 'Note: *Ivenel*', at 330. In para. 18 of the Ruiz Opinion it is said that 'As there are many different types of contracts, the place of performance should be determined by reference to each type.'

[573] Hill, 'Jurisdiction in Matters Relating to a Contract', at 612.

[574] Ibid.; Punt, 'Karakteristieke jurisdictie', at 444.

[575] Punt, 'Karakteristieke jurisdictie', at 444; Hartley, 'Note: *Ivenel*', at 330.

[576] According to De Cristofaro, 'Critical Remarks', at 60.

[577] Cordero Moss, 'Performance of Obligations', at 390.

[578] Geimer, 'Note: *Shenevai*', at 1133.

of the contract.[579] With the characteristic performance approach, parties will know beforehand where the potential *forum contractus* is located, as this does not depend on the contractual obligation upon which the claimant will found his action, which facilitates the sound administration of justice.[580] Even if some authors recognize that it will not always lead to the forum most closely connected to the claim.[581]

The perseverance of the obligation in question

The Court repeatedly affirmed the *De Bloos* rule of the obligation in question in the cases *Custom Made*,[582] the *Groupe Concorde*,[583] the *Leathertex* case,[584] and the *Besix* case.[585] Not only did it refuse to determine the place of performance by reference to the obligation characterizing the contract, but it also systematically rejected the identification of the place of performance 'on the basis of factual considerations, that is, on the basis of the specific circumstances of the case evidencing a particularly close connection between the case and a Contracting State'.[586] The Court's perseverance in holding on to the 'obligation in question' approach established by *De Bloos* to determine the *forum contractus* has been subject to much criticism.[587] Most of this critique focussed on the complex identification and the legal uncertainty deriving from its application of the *forum solutionis*. One of the fiercest statements was made by AG Ruiz in his Opinion to the *Concorde* case:

> 'It is all the fault of De Bloos! From the very beginning, the answer should have been to take account only of the characteristic obligation of the contract for the purpose of Article 5, point (1). Then it would have been possible, in the overwhelming majority of cases, to designate a place of performance for procedural purposes close to the essential elements of the contract.'[588]

2.7.3.2.c *The* Tessili *approach*

The '*other*' landmark decision in the *Tessili* case addressed the question on whether the place of performance should be interpreted autonomously, or if one should refer to national law to determine the place of performance.[589] The Court ruled that it is up to the court seized to 'determine in accordance with its own rules of conflict of laws what is the law applicable to the legal relationship in question and define

[579] Case 266/85 *Shenavai v. Kreischer*, [1987] ECR 239, para. 14; Huet, 'Note: *Peters*', at 838.

[580] Droz, 'Delendum', at 352; Huet, 'Note: *Tessili*', at 717.

[581] Gothot and Holleaux, 'Note: *De Bloos and Tessili*', at 768.

[582] C-288/92 *Custom Made v. Stawa*, [1994] ECR I-2913, para. 26. In Opinion AG Lenz in C-288/92 *Custom Made v. Stawa*, [1994] ECR I-2913, paras. 50-58 and 63, the court was faced with a 'frontal attack' on Case 12/76 *Tessili v. Dunlop*, [1976] ECR 1473. See for an exhaustive overview, Hertz, *Jurisdiction in Contract*, at 104-110.

[583] C-440/97 *GIE Groupe Concorde*, [1999] ECR I-6307, paras. 25 and 32.

[584] C-420/97 *Leathertex v. Bodetex*, [1999] ECR I-6747, paras. 33 and 36-37.

[585] C-256/00 *Besix v. WABAG*, [2002] ECR I-1699, paras. 36-40.

[586] Ibid., para. 37.

[587] Gothot and Holleaux, 'Note: *De Bloos and Tessili*', at 766.

[588] Opinion AG Ruiz-Jarabo Colomer in C-440/97 *GIE Groupe Concorde*, [1999] ECR I-6307, para. 103.

[589] See Huet, 'Note: *Tessili*', at 714, who seems to be relieved that this first decision on the question was followed by others.

in accordance with that law the place of performance of the contractual obligation in question'.[590] In short, the *lex causae* determines the place of performance under Article 5(1)(a) Regulation.

This *Tessili* approach received a lot of critique. According to Cristofaro, the *lex causae* approach is not only difficult to apply 'because it presupposes, at a very preliminary stage of the litigation, the solution to very complex questions of private international law' it also 'involves an examination of the merits of the case, at a time when the judge still has to solve the jurisdictional issue'.[591] Another major objection is that this approach will often lead to a *forum actoris*. According to AG Ruiz-Jarabo Colomer 'the fact that the courts of the plaintiff's domicile are more and more often imposed as a general forum for matters relating to contracts must be mentioned as one of these undesirable effects'.[592]

Various attempts to urge the Court to revise this *Tessili* approach were unsuccessful.[593] Instead, the *lex causae* approach was repeatedly affirmed by consecutive decisions of the ECJ.[594] One of the latest tentative attempts to reverse *Tessili* took place more than 20 years later; in the *Concorde* case, the ECJ addressed the same question under similar circumstances as the *Tessili* case. The referring court, the French *Cour de cassation*, more or less asked the ECJ to abandon its settled case law and to give an autonomous interpretation of the 'place of performance of the obligation'.[595] Yet, the ECJ vigorously maintained its position.[596]

The Court also refused the application of the *lex fori*.[597] The *lex fori* approach is often used by national courts for national contract jurisdiction and implies that

---

[590] Case 12/76 *Tessili v. Dunlop*, [1976] ECR 1473, para. 13; confirmed, among others, by C-288/92 *Custom Made v. Stawa*, [1994] ECR I-2913, para. 26; C-440/97 *GIE Groupe Concorde*, [1999] ECR I-6307.

[591] De Cristofaro, 'Critical Remarks', at 49; see in that sense also Opinion AG Ruiz-Jarabo Colomer in C-440/97 *GIE Groupe Concorde*, [1999] ECR I-6307, para. 44.

[592] Opinion AG Ruiz-Jarabo Colomer in C-440/97 *GIE Groupe Concorde*, [1999] ECR I-6307, para. 44.

[593] See also De Cristofaro, 'Critical Remarks', at 46, stating that the German Federal Supreme Court twice requested a change of approach by asking for another preliminary ruling in Case 266/85 *Shenavai v. Kreischer*, [1987] ECR 239 and C-288/92 *Custom Made v. Stawa*, [1994] ECR I-2913. The French Government did the same in C-440/97 *GIE Groupe Concorde*, [1999] ECR I-6307 and the Belgian Government in C-420/97 *Leathertex v. Bodetex*, [1999] ECR I-6747. See Gaudemet-Tallon, *Compétence en Europe*, § 194, at 153-154, and D. Leipold, 'Internationale Zuständigkeit am Erfüllungsort – das Neueste aus Luxemburg und Brüssel', in *Gedächtnisschrift für Alexander Lüderitz* (2000), 431-453, 431-444.

[594] Case 133/81 *Ivenel v. Schwab*, [1982] ECR 1891, para. 7; Case 266/85 *Shenavai v. Kreischer*, [1987] ECR 239, para. 7 and further in paras. 16-20; C-125/92 *Mulox v. Geels*, [1993] ECR 4075, paras. 12-13; C-288/92 *Custom Made v. Stawa*, [1994] ECR I-2913, para. 26; C-440/97 *GIE Groupe Concorde*, [1999] ECR I-630, para. 32; C-420/97 *Leathertex v. Bodetex*, [1999] ECR I-6747, para. 33 and C-256/00 *Besix v. WABAG*, [2002] ECR I-1699, para. 33.

[595] C-440/97 *GIE Groupe Concorde*, [1999] ECR I-6307, para. 8. See Opinion AG Ruiz-Jarabo Colomer in C-440/97 *GIE Groupe Concorde*, [1999] ECR I-6307, para. 16.

[596] C-440/97 *GIE Groupe Concorde*, [1999] ECR I-6307, para. 10.

[597] Gothot listed reasons why the *lex causae* should be preferred above the *lex fori*, see Gothot and Holleaux, 'Note: *De Bloos and Tessili*', at 763-765. See also Gaudemet-Tallon, *Compétence en Europe*, § 191, at 149.

the national substantive contract law of the forum determines the place of performance, regardless of the law applicable to the contract.[598]

Again, the use of the *lex causae* to determine the place of performance was thought to guarantee a close connection between the dispute and the court, which is particularly appropriate for reasons of efficient organisation of the procedure and the ease of taking evidence.[599] Again several authors and especially AG Ruiz in the *Concorde* case questioned whether the *Tessili* approach would guarantee a close connection.[600]

2.7.3.2.d *The rejection of an autonomous determination*

The fact that the ECJ refused to give an autonomous definition of the 'place of performance', breaks with a general trend of establishing autonomous concepts in which the Court vigorously advocated the importance of a uniform interpretation.[601] An autonomous place of performance could aim at uniform interpretation by using independent concepts prevailing over national interpretations of the substantive laws of Member States. It has even been argued that determining an autonomous place of performance by means of comparative law might reinforce the harmonizing effect of Article 5(1).[602] Instead, the ECJ adhered to the conflictualist method to determine the place of performance and argued that it does not appear possible to provide for substantial guidance as to its interpretation due to the 'differences obtaining between national laws of contract and to the absence at this stage of legal development of any unification in the substantive law applicable'.[603] For the time being the *Tessili* solution was considered an interim solution.[604] Furthermore, as argued by the British Government, an autonomous interpretation would involve a decision on substantive law, which would go beyond the purpose of the Convention, even if the ECJ rightfully stressed 'that the interpretation of the said words and concepts ... does not prejudge the question of the substantive rule applicable to the particular case'.[605] Paradoxically, the solution chosen by the Court does not

---

598 See De Cristofaro, 'Critical Remarks', at 44.

599 Case 266/85 *Shenavai v. Kreischer*, [1987] ECR 239, para. 18; C-288/92 *Custom Made v. Stawa*, [1994] ECR I-2913, paras. 12-13; C-440/97 *GIE Groupe Concorde*, [1999] ECR I-6307, para. 29, and most recently reaffirmed by C-256/00 *Besix v. WABAG*, [2002] ECR I-1699, para. 31; see also the Opinion AG Lenz in C-288/92 *Custom Made v. Stawa*, [1994] ECR I-2913 and H. Gaudemet-Tallon, 'Note: Custom Made', 83 *Revue critique de droit international privé* (1994), 698-707, at 700.

600 Opinion AG Ruiz-Jarabo Colomer in C-440/97 *GIE Groupe Concorde*, [1999] ECR I-6307, para. 55; Magnus and Mankowski, eds., *Brussels I Regulation*, § 140, at 159.

601 Gothot and Holleaux, 'Note: *De Bloos and Tessili*', at 762; E. Jayme, 'Note: Custom Made – Einklägergerichtstand für den Verkäufer – Der EuGH verfehlt den Sinn des EuGVÜ', *IPRax* (1995), 13-14, at 13; Pontier and Burg, *EU Principles on Jurisdiction*, at 75; see also C-440/97 *GIE Groupe Concorde*, [1999] ECR I-6307, para. 11.

602 Opinion AG Lenz in C-288/92 *Custom Made v. Stawa*, [1994] ECR I-2913, para. 63.

603 Case 12/76 *Tessili v. Dunlop*, [1976] ECR 1473, para. 14; repeated in C-440/97 *GIE Groupe Concorde*, [1999] ECR I-6307, para. 18. Opinion AG Lenz in C-288/92 *Custom Made v. Stawa*, [1994] ECR I-2913, para. 46; Huet, 'Note: *Tessili*', at 716.

604 See the Commission's point of view as indicated in Opinion AG Ruiz-Jarabo Colomer in C-440/97 *GIE Groupe Concorde*, [1999] ECR I-6307, para. 22.

605 Case 12/76 *Tessili v. Dunlop*, [1976] ECR 1473, para. 11; see Hartley, 'Note: *Tessili*', at 59; Huet, 'Note: *Tessili*', at 717.

remove any differences between national laws. On the contrary, by applying the *lex causae*, these differences come back through the back door.[606]

The variety of contracts was again put forward by the ECJ as another reason not to give an autonomous definition to the place of performance of an obligation.[607]

Apart from introducing uniform concepts to determine an autonomous place of performance, several other ways have been stipulated to achieve an autonomous interpretation.

It has often been suggested to designate a place of performance by reference to the particular circumstances of the case and the nature of the relationship that created the obligation in question.[608] This solution was advanced by the French *Cour de cassation* in the *Groupe Concorde* case but was rejected by the Court on the basis that that would 'be insufficient to resolve all questions linked to application of that provision'.[609] Droz has also suggested a similar approach based on a 'simple localisation of facts'.[610] Such a case-by-case approach in order to provide an independent definition for the place of performance was also advocated by the U.K. Government in the *Groupe Concorde* case.[611] However, according to AG Ruiz a case-by-case approach was categorically rejected, on the basis that this would not be in favour of legal certainty. He stated that

> 'it would compel the court to examine the substance of the case in detail and, because of the uncertainty as to the result of the assessment of the facts which the court would have to make, would open the door to diverging judgments and, ultimately, to the multiplication of bases of jurisdiction.'[612]

Another possibility advanced by AG Lenz in the *Custom Made* case was an autonomous determination based on the concepts of physical proximity or close connection with the forum. When the *lex causae* rule leads to a *forum contractus* which is not physically proximate to the dispute, its outcome should be set aside in favour of a different court, such as for instance in the case involving a sale of goods contract, the place of delivery.[613] According to AG Lenz, the *lex causae* approach is not the

---

[606] Huet, 'Note: *Tessili*', at 716-717.

[607] Case 12/76 *Tessili v. Dunlop*, [1976] ECR 1473, para. 14; see Huet, 'Note: *Tessili*', at 717; and see on the complication of mixed contracts and Art. 5(1)(b) Regulation, U. Schroeter, 'Vienna Sales Convention: Applicability to "Mixed Contracts" and Interaction with the 1968 Brussels Convention', 5 *The Vindobona Journal of International Commercial Law and Arbitration* (2001), 74-86, at 85.

[608] See Opinion AG Ruiz-Jarabo Colomer in C-440/97 *GIE Groupe Concorde*, [1999] ECR I-6307, paras. 48 and 73; see also P. Vlas, 'Note: GIE Groupe Concorde', 595 *NJ* (2001).

[609] C-440/97 *GIE Groupe Concorde*, [1999] ECR I-6307, para. 25.

[610] Droz, 'Delendum', at 353.

[611] See Opinion AG Ruiz-Jarabo Colomer in C-440/97 *GIE Groupe Concorde*, [1999] ECR I-6307, para. 19. According to the U.K. Government, an independent concept would not only promote legal certainty and ensure the equality and uniformity of the rights and obligations of the parties, but it would also reduce the potential for forum shopping.

[612] Opinion AG Ruiz-Jarabo Colomer in C-440/97 *GIE Groupe Concorde*, [1999] ECR I-6307, para. 83.

[613] Opinion AG Lenz in C-288/92 *Custom Made v. Stawa*, [1994] ECR I-2913, paras. 72-75 and 80; see in contrast Hertz, *Jurisdiction in Contract,* at 107; but see De Cristofaro, 'Critical Remarks', at 56.

appropriate rule to designate a court closely connected with the facts of the case, since originating from substantive law it is merely concerned with the allocation of risks and advantages between the plaintiff and the defendant.[614] But Lenz also warns that an open 'physical proximate' rule in which the court seized determines whether it is closely connected with the dispute, might undermine the concept of place of performance and turn Article 5(1) into a vague *forum conveniens* rule.[615]

The ECJ's refusal to seek for an autonomous determination for the place of performance disappointed several authors.[616] The solution of the *lex causae* is thought to be incompatible with the Brussels regime's aim to strengthen the legal protection of persons established in the Community.[617] It has been observed that the choice for the *lex causae* rather than the *lex fori* is in itself an autonomous interpretation, since it prevents courts from applying their national substantive law and obliges them to turn to the law governing the legal relationship in question.[618] Nonetheless, even if the *lex causae* is preferable to the *lex fori*,[619] it was generally considered incomplete and unsatisfactory.[620]

It should be mentioned that AG Lenz and AG Ruiz along with other authors rightfully observed that the concept of place of performance originates from substantive law, which has a different purpose than rules that allocate jurisdiction.[621] A substantive place of performance constitutes 'an act by which the obligation due is fulfilled vis-à-vis the creditor, thus extinguishing his claim and fulfills the contract.'[622] AG Lenz observes that

---

[614] See Opinion AG Lenz in C-288/92 *Custom Made v. Stawa*, [1994] ECR I-2913, para. 18; repeated by Ruiz in Opinion AG Ruiz-Jarabo Colomer in C-440/97 *GIE Groupe Concorde*, [1999] ECR I-6307, para. 56.

[615] Paras. 63 and 71 of Opinion AG Lenz in C-288/92 *Custom Made v. Stawa*, [1994] ECR I-2913; see De Cristofaro, 'Critical Remarks', at 57 and A. Huet, 'Note: Custom Made', *Journal du droit international* (1995), 461-465, at 464; see also the opinion of AG Leger in C-420/97 *Leathertex v. Bodetex*, [1999] ECR I-6747, paras. 119 and 129.

[616] Huet, 'Note: *Tessili*', at 715; M. Fallon, 'Le principe de proximité dans le droit de l'Union Européenne', in *Le droit international privé: Esprit et méthodes mélanges en l'honneur de Paul Lagarde* (2005), 241-262, at 243; Schack, 'Note: Custom Made', at 662 and 666.

[617] Huet, 'Note: *Tessili*', at 715; and see Opinion AG Ruiz-Jarabo Colomer in C-440/97 *GIE Groupe Concorde*, [1999] ECR I-6307, para. 84.

[618] Huet, 'Note: *Tessili*', at 716. See also Opinion AG Lenz in C-288/92 *Custom Made v. Stawa*, [1994] ECR I-2913, para. 64 *et seq.*

[619] *Contra* Huet, 'Note: *Tessili*', at 718-719.

[620] See Jayme, 'Note: Custom Made', at 13; Schack, 'Note: Custom Made', at 663; De Cristofaro, 'Critical Remarks', at 48; see C-440/97 *GIE Groupe Concorde*, [1999] ECR I-6307, para. 16; and Opinion AG Ruiz-Jarabo Colomer in C-440/97 *GIE Groupe Concorde*, [1999] ECR I-6307, para. 2.

[621] Opinion AG Lenz in C-288/92 *Custom Made v. Stawa*, [1994] ECR I-2913, paras. 23, 26 and 63; confirmed by Opinion AG Ruiz-Jarabo Colomer in C-440/97 *GIE Groupe Concorde*, [1999] ECR I-6307, paras. 50, 55 and 87; G. Steenhoff, 'Pleidooi voor een crediteursforum bij (internationale) geldschulden', in *Het NIPR geannoteerd: annotaties opgedragen aan Dr Mathilde Sumampouw*, (1996), 194-202 at 198; Schack, 'Note: Custom Made', at 660; Schroeter, 'Vienna Sales Convention', at 81.

[622] Opinion AG Lenz in C-288/92 *Custom Made v. Stawa*, [1994] ECR I-2913, para. 24; see also Opinion AG Ruiz-Jarabo Colomer in C-440/97 *GIE Groupe Concorde*, [1999] ECR I-6307, para. 58.

> 'substantive law generally determines merely the allocation of the risks and burdens connected with the transfer of money, the availability of which does not depend on the place of performance of the obligation in question. I cannot understand what that purely economic allocation of risks has to do with the question whether the debtor has to accept the creditor's suing him at a particular place.'[623]

Ruiz argues that such substantive criteria have their *raison d'être* in substantive law, but should not be transposed into the field of jurisdictional competence.[624] The *lex causae* approach determines a 'substantive place of performance' rather than a 'procedural place of performance' which would be more appropriate for jurisdictional purposes, and is therefore considered 'inconsistent and arbitrary'.[625]

2.7.3.2.e *The role of uniform substantive law and conflicts rules*

The *lex causae* approach results in a national interpretation of the place of performance as a connecting factor for contract jurisdiction. Instruments of unified law, either uniform substantive law or uniform conflict of rules, reduce those divergences.[626] The *lex causae* approach of *Tessili*[627] leads in some cases to the application of uniform substantive rules, as has occurred in *Custom Made*,[628] where the *Uniform Law on the International Sale of Goods* annexed to The Hague Convention of 1 July 1964 (ULIS) was applied to determine the place of performance.[629] The ECJ stated that the interpretation of *Tessili* must also be accepted in the event that the conflicts rules of the court seized result in the application of a 'uniform law'.[630]

With the enactment of the Brussels Regulation and the *lex specialis* of Article 5(1)(b), some uniform laws will lose considerable ground, but the decision of *Custom Made* will remain relevant with respect to other uniform laws.[631]

In the *Custom Made* case, the conflict rule of the court seized resulted in the application of Article 59(1) of the ULIS stating that the buyer must pay the price to the seller at the seller's place of business or, if he does not have a place of business, at his habitual residence. The place of performance of the obligation to pay

---

[623] Opinion AG Lenz in C-288/92 *Custom Made v. Stawa*, [1994] ECR I-2913, para. 21; followed by De Cristofaro, 'Critical Remarks', at 48.

[624] Opinion AG Ruiz-Jarabo Colomer in C-440/97 *GIE Groupe Concorde*, [1999] ECR I-6307, para. 50; see also Punt, 'Karakteristieke jurisdictie', at 441 and 445.

[625] Hill, 'Jurisdiction in Matters Relating to a Contract', at 602.

[626] See Gaudemet-Tallon, *Compétence en Europe*, § 192, at 150; Jayme, 'Special Jurisdiction under Art. 5', at 77; De Cristofaro, 'Critical Remarks', at 46. See for critical observations on Art. 5(1) in relation to uniformity, the article by Heuzé, 'Quelques infirmités congénitales'.

[627] See Huet, 'Note: Custom Made', at 462, referring to the consistent application of Case 12/76 *Tessili v. Dunlop*, [1976] ECR 1473 as '*modicus*'.

[628] C-288/92 *Custom Made v. Stawa*, [1994] ECR I-2913.

[629] Convention relating to a Uniform Law on the International Sale of Goods, 1964 Annex Uniform Law on the International Sale of Goods, 834 United Nations Treaty Series (1972), at 107 *et seq*. See also http://www.cisg.law.pace.edu/cisg/text/ulis.html for the current status and see for the German position, Schack, 'Note: Custom Made', fn. 4, at 659.

[630] C-288/92 *Custom Made v. Stawa*, [1994] ECR I-2913, paras. 27 and 29.

[631] For other instruments of unified substantive law mentioned by Gaudemet-Tallon, such as the UNIDROIT Convention on International Financial Leasing, Ottawa, 28 May 1988, which might be relevant under Art. 5(1)(a), see Gaudemet-Tallon, *Compétence en Europe*, § 193, at 153.

the price in a sales contract, as the obligation in question, was the place of establishment of the plaintiff supplier; in this case the seller's establishment. Several authors expressed their concern that the *forum contractus* will turn into a seller's forum, *ein Verkäufergerichtsstand*, often resulting in a *forum actoris* in the event the seller is the plaintiff.[632] Article 59 of the ULIS corresponds essentially to its successor[633] Article 57 of the CISG.[634] The decision of the ECJ would therefore be the same if the applicable law had been the CISG.[635] Consequently, when the CISG is the applicable law to an international sales contract and the obligation in question concerns the payment of the purchase price, the *Custom Made* approach automatically leads to the place of business or habitual residence of the seller.[636] When the seller is the plaintiff this will lead to the *forum actoris*;[637] when the seller is the defendant this would lead to the 'defendant's domicile' and the *forum contractus* would not be an alternative competent forum, leaving the plaintiff with no choice among competent forums and Article 5(1) would become a *lettre morte*.[638]

In the event claimant does not request payment but delivery and the CISG is still the applicable law, the place of performance of the delivery will be determined by Article 31 of the CISG.[639] Article 31 of the CISG stipulates that when parties have not specified any particular place of delivery, the obligation to deliver consists in

[632] Jayme, 'Note: Custom Made', at 14; Gaudemet-Tallon, *Compétence en Europe*, § 192, at 151; Schack, 'Note: Custom Made', at 661; De Cristofaro, 'Critical Remarks', at 48; but see in contrast Huet, 'Note: Custom Made', at 463; and Huet, 'Convention de Vienne et compétence', at 425.

[633] De Cristofaro, 'Critical Remarks', at 46. See also Hager, who considers the ULIS as the predecessor of the CISG, in P. Schlechtriem and I. Schwenzer, *Kommentar zum Einhetlichen UN-Kaufrecht* (2004), at 594; P. Schlechtriem and I. Schwenzer, *Commentary on the UN Convention on the International Sale of Goods (CISG)* (2005), § 1, at 630.

[634] Art. 57 of the CISG reads: '(1) If the buyer is not bound to pay the price at any other particular place, he must pay it to the seller: (a) at the seller's place of business; or (b) if the payment is to be made against the handing over of the goods or of documents, at the place where the handing over takes place.' See J. Lookofsky, *Understanding the CISG* (2008), § 4.12, at 94-95; and Hager, in Schlechtriem and Schwenzer, *Kommentar zum Einhetlichen UN-Kaufrecht*, at 597-598.

[635] See Gaudemet-Tallon, 'Note: Custom Made', at 702; P. Vlas, 'Article 5(1) Forum solutionis contractus – Note: Custom Made', *Netherlands International Law Review* (1994), 339-344, at 344; Huet, 'Note: Custom Made', at 462; De Cristofaro, 'Critical Remarks', at 47; see also Huet, 'Convention de Vienne et compétence', at 424; and see J. Lookofsky and K. Hertz, *Transnational Litigation and Commercial Arbitration: An Analysis of American, European and International Law* (2004), Chap. 2.2.2(A); Schlechtriem and Schwenzer, *Commentary CISG*, § 10, at 633.

[636] Art. 1(1)(a) and (b) determines the territorial scope of the CISG. See also De Cristofaro, 'Critical Remarks', at 47 and M. Fogt, 'Blick in das Ausland – Gerichtsstand des Erfüllungsortes bei streitiger Existenz des Vertrages, Anwendbarkeit des CISG und alternative Vertragsschlussformen (Østre Landsret 23. 4. 1998)', 21 *IPRax* (2001), 358-364, at 360-362.

[637] See Huet, 'Convention de Vienne et compétence', at 425; and see also Jayme, 'Special Jurisdiction under Art. 5', at 78, referring to the plaintiff's forum as the *forum actoris et venditoris*.

[638] Huet, 'Note: *Tessili*', at 716; Magnus, 'Das UN-Kaufrecht und die Erfüllungsortzuständigkeit', at 46; C. Forsyth and Ph. Moser, 'The Impact of the Applicable Law of Contract on the Law of Jurisdiction under the European Conventions', 45 *The International and Comparative Law Quarterly* (1996), 190-197, at 195-196. See Opinion AG Lenz in C-288/92 *Custom Made v. Stawa*, [1994] ECR I-2913, para. 32.

[639] See also Huet, 'Convention de Vienne et compétence', at 424; Magnus, 'Das UN-Kaufrecht und die Erfüllungsortzuständigkeit', at 46 and Gaudemet-Tallon, 'Note: Custom Made', at 703.

placing the goods at the buyer's disposal at the place where the seller had his place of business at the time of the conclusion of the contract.[640]

The role of the CISG under the Brussels Regulation

Under the Brussels Convention the application of the *forum solutionis* in combination with the ULIS or the CISG often resulted in a creditor's forum when payment was requested.[641] Under the new *forum contractus* rule of the Brussels Regulation, the place of payment is irrelevant when the claim arises out of a sales or service contract, since the *lex specialis* rule of Article 5(1)(b) determines the place of delivery as the *forum contractus* over all claims arising out of the sales or service contract, regardless of the underlying contractual obligation. As a result, Article 57 of the CISG, which determines the place of payment in international sales contracts, will be irrelevant for determining the competent contract forum under Article 5(1)(b) with respect to sales contracts.[642] However, under some very specific circumstances, the interaction between Article 5(1) of the Brussels Convention and the CISG, as explained above, will still occur under the Brussels Regulation.[643]

First of all, under the *lex specialis* of Article 5(1)(b), Article 31 CISG is likely to play a significant role in the event the contract does not stipulate an agreed place of delivery and delivery was not made:[644] if one refers to the *lex causae* to determine the place where the goods should have been delivered and provided that the CISG is the applicable law to the contract, Article 31 will determine the place where the goods should have been delivered. The other option to this problem was to refer back to the *lex generalis* under Article 5(1)(a), which results in the application of the *lex causae* to determine the place of delivery and hence in applying the CISG in some cases.[645]

As identified above, the *forum solutionis* approach remains the connecting factor for sales contracts where the place of delivery is located in a non-Member State. Since Article 5(1)(b) does not apply, Article 5(1)(a) will by virtue of Article 5(1)(c) determine the competent forum and apply the CISG if this is the applicable law to the contract.[646]

---

[640] Unless the contract involves the carriage of goods, then the delivery consists of handing the goods over to the first carrier for transmission to the buyer (Art. 31(a) CISG). If the delivery relates to specific or unidentified goods to be drawn from a specific stock or to be manufactured or produced and at the time of the conclusion of the contract the parties knew that the goods were, or were to be manufactured or produced at, a particular place, the delivery consists of placing the goods at the buyer's disposal at that place (Art. 31(b) CISG). Schroeter, 'Vienna Sales Convention', at 81 *et seq.*

[641] See also Steenhoff, 'Pleidooi voor een crediteursforum', at 200.

[642] See also Magnus, 'Das UN-Kaufrecht und die Erfüllungsortzuständigkeit', at 49 and 51; Gaudemet-Tallon, *Compétence en Europe*, § 193, at 152; Huet, 'Convention de Vienne et compétence', at 429; Schroeter, 'Vienna Sales Convention', at 84.

[643] See on the role of the CISG in the Brussels Regulation, in general Magnus, 'Das UN-Kaufrecht und die Erfüllungsortzuständigkeit', and Huet, 'Convention de Vienne et compétence'.

[644] See Huet, 'Convention de Vienne et compétence', at 429; and Magnus, 'Das UN-Kaufrecht und die Erfüllungsortzuständigkeit', at 49.

[645] See Sect. 2.7.3.2.c for the *Tessili* approach and see Huet, 'Convention de Vienne et compétence', at 428.

[646] Huet, 'Convention de Vienne et compétence', at 430; Magnus, 'Das UN-Kaufrecht und die Erfüllungsortzuständigkeit', at 45.

Lastly, the words 'unless otherwise agreed' could give parties the opportunity to agree to deviate from the *lex specialis* under Article 5(1)(b) and to prefer the *lex generalis* under Article 5(1)(a).

In those situations, the *forum solutionis* will still apply to contracts concerning the sales of goods and the provision of services and if the CISG is applicable, Article 57 for the place of payment or Article 31 for the place of delivery of the CISG will still play a significant role depending on which obligation is requested.

Uniform rules on conflict of laws

Although the *Custom Made* case concerned the application of uniform substantial law, the outcome is the same when the *lex causae* is determined by unified conflict rules such as the Rome Convention or its successor the Rome I Regulation.[647] In that case the applicable law to the contract will be determined by those uniform conflict rules, which will in turn determine the place of performance. The unification process of conflict rules has moved forward considerably since the *Tessili* judgement in 1976. At that time the ECJ argued against an autonomous concept of place of performance because of the absence of the 'legal development of any unification of the *substantive* law applicable'.[648] Later, the Court gratefully referred to the Rome Convention thanks to which there 'is no risk that the law applicable to the determination of the place of performance will vary depending on the court seised'.[649]

Although such uniform instruments do not reduce the differences between national substantive contract laws, it ideally results in the application of the same conflict rule to determine the place of performance.[650] However, the Rome Convention gives quite some discretion to the courts to determine the *lex causae.*[651] Apart from the situation where the parties have made a valid choice of law under Article 5 of the Rome Convention, the court seized has a significant amount of discretion in ascertaining the *lex causae* under Article 4.[652] Under Article 4(2) the Rome Convention determines that the applicable law to the contract is the law of the 'country where the party who is to effect the performance which is characteristic of the contract has, at the time of conclusion of the contract, his habitual residence', because this place is presumed to be the law with the closest connection

[647] See for general comments on the impact of the Rome Convention on jurisdictional issues, Forsyth and Moser, 'The Impact of Applicable Law', and see Gaudemet in Gaudemet-Tallon, *Compétence en Europe*, § 192, at 150-151. The Rome I Regulation stands for The Regulation (EC) No 593/2008 of the European Parliament and the Council on the law applicable to contractual obligations, OJ 2008 L 177 at 6-16; see for the final proposal COM/2005/0650 final – COD 2005/0261.

[648] Case 12/76 *Tessili v. Dunlop*, [1976] ECR 1473, para. 14; see also Opinion AG Léger in C-420/97 *Leathertex v. Bodetex*, [1999] ECR I-6747, para. 91.

[649] C-440/97 *GIE Groupe Concorde*, [1999] ECR I-6307, para. 30.

[650] See Gaudemet-Tallon, *Compétence en Europe,* at 151; Jayme, 'Note: Custom Made', at 13; Cordero Moss, 'Performance of Obligations', at 387. See in general M. Whincop, *Policy and Pragmatism in the Conflict of Laws* (2001), at 46.

[651] See De Cristofaro, 'Critical Remarks', at 52; and Huet, 'Note: Custom Made', at 463.

[652] See P. Lagarde and M. Guiliano, 'Report on the Convention on the Law Applicable to Contractual Obligations', OJ 1980 C 282/1-50 and see Cordero Moss, 'Performance of Obligations', at 384; Forsyth and Moser, 'The Impact of Applicable Law', at 193.

to the contract as required under Article 4(1).[653] Primarily, this article implies that one has to find the characteristic performance in order to identify whose habitual residence will be conclusive for the place of performance. But secondly, the court is allowed to deviate from the characteristic performance when it is of the opinion that another performance has a closer connection to the obligation.[654] Under the new Rome I Regulation the margin of appreciation to determine the *lex causae* is considerably reduced: Parties still have the freedom of choice of law under Article 3, but in absence of a choice, the new Rome I provision under Article 4(1) explicitly determines the characteristic performer of a range of type of contracts; for instance for a sale of goods contract the characteristic performer is the seller and thus, the applicable law shall be governed by the law of the country where the seller has his habitual residence.[655] If the contract in question does not fall into one of the categories of Article 4(1), the court will have to determine which party is required to effect the characteristic performance of the contract pursuant to Article 4(2). This presumption of the characteristic performer is harder to be rebutted than it was under the Rome Convention, as Article 4(5) determines that only when a contract is *manifestly more closely connected* with another country.

The interaction between uniform conflict of laws instruments and jurisdictional instruments is not to be underestimated. Especially with respect to the interpretation of jurisdictional concepts, the ECJ has turned to other European instruments.[656]

But the European legislator has not chosen for an analogous approach to the same connecting factor for jurisdictional purposes as for the applicable law to contracts. Although both instruments search for a close connection, the Rome Convention presumes the law closest connected with the contract to be the law of the state where the party who is to effect the performance which is characteristic of the contract has his habitual residence or central administration.[657] Conversely, Article 5(1)(a) stipulates that the place of performance of the obligation in question is chosen and the characteristic performance rejected. The autonomous place of performance under Article 5(1)(b) confers jurisdiction on the place of performance of the characteristic obligation, i.e. delivery or provision of service, but does *not* refer

[653] As a rule, the characteristic performance is usually considered to be the non-pecuniary obligation. See De Cristofaro, 'Critical Remarks', at 48, and Forsyth and Moser, 'The Impact of Applicable Law', at 194.

[654] Art. 4(5) Rome Convention provides that Art. 4(2) 'shall not apply if the characteristic performance cannot be determined, and the presumptions in paragraphs 2, 3 and 4 shall be disregarded if it appears from the circumstances as a whole that the contract is more closely connected with another country.'

[655] Art. 4(1)(a) Rome I; see also sub (b) a contract for the provision of services shall be governed by the law of the country where the service provider has his habitual residence; and see sub (e) a franchise contract shall be governed by the law of the country where the franchisee has his habitual residence; sub (f) a distribution contract shall be governed by the law of the country where the distributor has his habitual residence; and sub (g) a contract for the sale of goods by auction shall be governed by the law of the country where the auction takes place, if such a place can be determined.

[656] On the scope of the *forum contractus*, see Sect. 2.7.2 above.

[657] Art. 4(2).

to the habitual residence or seat of the party who has to perform this characteristic obligation as is required under Article 4 of the Rome Convention.[658]

2.7.3.2.f *Agreed place of performance*
Under Article 5(1)(a), parties are allowed to specify the place of performance. If the clause is valid according to the applicable law of the contract, subject to the conditions it lays down, the court of that elected place of performance has jurisdiction.[659] Such an agreement on the place of performance of the obligation is sufficient to establish a *forum contractus* and it does not have to comply with any special requirements of form, such as the requirements for a valid choice of forum clause under Article 23. However, there must be a real connection between the agreed place of performance and the true substance of the contract.[660] If the designation of the place of performance had the mere purpose to agree on a competent court without having to comply with the requirements of a choice of forum clause, this agreed place of performance will be considered as 'fictive' and therefore void.[661]

2.7.4 **Justifications Reviewed**

The idea behind the *forum contractus* was to provide for a neutral forum, based on the connection between the claim and the forum instead of on a connection between the defendant and the forum. Parties who agreed to perform a contractual obligation at a particular place should also accept to be sued in its courts.[662] In practice, the connecting factor rarely leads to a third neutral forum.[663] Instead it will point to the defendant's domicile, in which case Article 5(1) is rendered obsolete, as it does not provide for an alternative forum additional to that specified in Article 2, or to claimant's forum.[664]

The *lex specialis* rule under Article 5(1)(b) could easily, although not necessarily, coincide with the place of business of either parties. If the place of delivery is at the buyer's place of business, which is common in sale of goods contracts, a *forum*

[658] Cordero Moss, 'Performance of Obligations', at 386.

[659] Case 56/79 *Zelger v. Salinitri*, [1980] ECR 89, para. 5.

[660] C-106/95 *MSG v. Gravières Rhénanes*, [1997] ECR I-911, paras. 30-31; confirmed among others by C-440/97 *GIE Groupe Concorde*, [1999] ECR I-6307, para. 28.

[661] C-106/95 *MSG v. Gravières Rhénanes*, [1997] ECR I-911, para. 31; see also Gaudemet-Tallon, *Compétence en Europe*, § 196, at 157. For more details on 'fraudulent' designations of the place of performance, see S. Vrellis, 'Some Remarks on "Fraudulent" Designation of the Place of Performance of the Obligation', in *Civil Jurisdiction and Judgments in Europe* (1992), 81-83, at 81.

[662] Steenhoff, 'Pleidooi voor een crediteursforum', at 197; L. Strikwerda, 'Drie fora: *forum actoris, forum necessitatis* en *forum non conveniens*', paper presented at T.M.C Asser Instituut 'De internationale bevoegdheid van de Nederlandse Rechter volgens de nieuwe bepalingen van het Wetboek van Burgerlijke Rechtsvordering', The Hague, 1996, at 98; Verheul, 'The "*forum actoris*"', at 201; Punt, 'Karakteristieke jurisdictie', at 448; and the Opinion AG Lenz in C-288/92 *Custom Made v. Stawa*, [1994] ECR I-2913, para. 21.

[663] See Droz, 'Delendum', at 355, with respect to Art. 5(1) of the Brussels Convention.

[664] Briggs, *Civil Jurisdiction*, § 2.123, at 146; Cordero Moss, 'Performance of Obligations', at 391; Bayraktaroglu, 'Note: Forum contractus', at 408; Hill, 'Jurisdiction in Matters Relating to a Contract', at 613; Droz, 'Note: Shenevai', at 800 and 803; Bischoff and Huet, 'Note: *Shenevai*', at 472.

actoris could emerge when the buyer is unsatisfied with the delivery, or conversely, when the buyer refuses payment, the seller will have to go to the seller's forum.[665]

Under the general rule under Article 5(1)(a) this especially happens when the obligation in question is the payment.[666] As indicated above, some national laws consider pecuniary obligations as *querable* to be performed at the place of the creditor's domicile and thus results in a *forum actoris*. Other substantive laws consider the obligation to pay as portable to be performed at the debtor's domicile thus leading to the defendant's forum.[667]

Hence, the original proximity justification for contract jurisdiction, searching for a close connection between the claim and the forum, is not attained in practice. The practical outcome of a *forum actoris* is particularly problematic, as it contradicts most European procedural traditions and is clearly marked exorbitant under Article 3 of the Brussels regime. With respect to the other principal justification for contract jurisdiction, the establishment of procedural balance, a *forum actoris* has been considered by some to over-compensate the favour given to the defendant by the *forum rei* rule.[668] Others have however welcomed the outcome of a *forum actoris*, since it provides for an available forum at the place of residence of creditors and considers plaintiff's forum to be often closely connected with the claim.[669] They argue that especially when the claim concerns money payments and pecuniary obligations, creditors often merit the same privilege given to defendant by virtue of Article 2 and should therefore be protected.[670]

Legal certainty

The original contract rule under Article 5(1) of the Convention was surrounded by uncertainty and is still considered by many to be unacceptable and arbitrary.[671] The determination of the *forum contractus* depends on the obligation in question, the action brought by claimant, which makes it impossible for the defendant to foresee where he could potentially be sued. Moreover, the localization of the place of performance which is to be determined by the *lex causae* makes it difficult for both defendant and claimant to predict which court will have contract jurisdiction.

---

665 See Magnus and Mankowski, eds., *Brussels I Regulation*, § 100, at 137.

666 See Opinion AG Ruiz-Jarabo Colomer in C-440/97 *GIE Groupe Concorde*, [1999] ECR I-6307, para. 49; Punt, 'Karakteristieke jurisdictie', at 439; Gaudemet-Tallon, 'Note: Custom Made', at 703; De Cristofaro, 'Critical Remarks', at 55; Hill, 'Jurisdiction in Matters Relating to a Contract', at 601.

667 See Opinion AG Ruiz-Jarabo Colomer in C-440/97 *GIE Groupe Concorde*, [1999] ECR I-6307, para. 52; and B. Ancel, 'Note: Gie Groupe Concorde', 89 *Revue critique de droit international privé* (2000), 260-264, at 262-263; Briggs, *Civil Jurisdiction*, § 2.138, at 172-173.

668 Newton, *Uniform Interpretation*, at 44. See Opinion AG Geelhoed in C-334/00 *Tacconi v. HWS*, [2002] ECR I-7357, para. 70; and Opinion AG Ruiz-Jarabo Colomer in C-440/97 *GIE Groupe Concorde*, [1999] ECR I-6307, para. 70.

669 See on this concept Gaudemet-Tallon, *Compétence en Europe*, § 193, at 153.

670 See in that respect Newton, *Uniform Interpretation*, at 45, Strikwerda, *De Overeenkomst in het IPR*, at 31; Jayme, 'Special Jurisdiction under Art. 5', at 73-74; and Steenhoff, 'Pleidooi voor een crediteursforum', at 197; Strikwerda, 'Drie fora: *forum actoris*', at 98; Verheul, 'The "*forum actoris*"', at 201.

671 De Cristofaro, 'Critical Remarks', at 48; Jayme, 'Note: Custom Made', at 14; Schack, 'Note: Custom Made', at 663; Steenhoff, 'Pleidooi voor een crediteursforum', at 198; Briggs, *Civil Jurisdiction*, § 2.138, at 173.

This laborious way of determining the competent forum in contractual matters is extremely unpredictable.

In an attempt to bring more legal certainty to Article 5(1), the new *lex specialis* under Article 5(1)(b) introduced an autonomous place of performance for contracts of sale of goods and the provision of services. The approach chosen is one of a more 'factual place of performance' instead of a complex determination of a 'substantive' or 'legal' place of performance.[672] The new provision under Article 5(1)(b) does not pretend to indicate the forum most closely connected to the claim but is thought to bring a certain degree of foreseeability and legal certainty which is clearly lacking under Article 5(1)(a). Although the ECJ held on to the *specific obligation* approach under Article 5(1)(a) and refused to provide an autonomous interpretation of the place of performance, the European legislator took the step towards an autonomous interpretation, by focussing on the characteristic obligation of the contract.[673] After accepting an established autonomous place of performance for employment and consumer contracts, jurisdiction over matters concerning contracts for the sale of goods and provision of services are now also determined by an autonomous connecting factor.[674]

It is not unthinkable, as pointed out by Punt, that the door is now open for the ECJ to provide for other autonomous places of performances for other types of contracts. For instance it could formulate a rule of thumb to determine the characteristic obligation for mutual agreements based on the idea that the obligation in question is the obligation of the most characteristic performance.[675]

But the new provision raises new problems and also creates uncertainty. First, it leads to the categorization of contracts under the Article 5(1)(b) category or the Article 5(1)(a) category, for which no guidelines were provided. Second, as explained above, in a number of situations, it is unclear how to determine the place of delivery or the provision of services. This makes it difficult for parties to predict where the *forum contractus* will be located. The search for an adequate connecting factor for contract jurisdiction is not over.

2.8 Conclusion

The Brussels Model derives from the civil law tradition and regulates jurisdiction over contractual disputes by means of a closed and limited set of jurisdiction rules of mandatory nature. Other (exorbitant) jurisdiction rules are banned and there is no room left for judicial discretion. The connecting factors of the rules are formulated by closed norms, as opposed to open norms that are left to the court's appreciation on a case-by-case basis.

Although one of its objectives was to restrict the number of competent courts available to the plaintiff, the Brussels Model contains a variety of rules that could

---

[672] Droz, 'Delendum', at 356; Michaels, 'Re-Placements', at 147; Rogerson, 'Plus ça change?', at 404.

[673] Cordero Moss, 'Performance of Obligations', at 392.

[674] Gsell, 'Autonom bestimmter Gerichtsstand', at 491.

[675] Punt, 'Karakteristieke jurisdictie', at 444.

lead to several competent fora and thus allowing *forum shopping*.[676] In contractual disputes, the claimant has at his disposal, defendant's domicile under Article 2, special branch jurisdiction under Article 5(5) and special contract jurisdiction under Article 5(1). When the corporate defendant's statutory seat does not coincide with his principal place of business or his place of central administration, Article 2 leads to multiple competent forums. When the defendant carries out business activities through a branch-establishment, the court of the state in which the branch is established is competent over claims arising out of its activities. Those jurisdiction rules are based on a connection between the parties and the forum, and differ from the special contract jurisdiction rule under Article 5(1) which is based on a close connection between the claim and the forum. Especially the connecting factor for contract jurisdiction has proved to be problematic in its practical application. It fails to guarantee a competent court closely connected with the dispute and its complexity does not warrant for legal certainty. Considerations of legal certainty, mutual trust and uniform application prevail over the initial justifications of proximity and protection of the parties which were at the origin of the many fixed connecting factors used in Articles 2, 5(1) and 5(5).

The driving force behind the European unification under the Brussels Model has been and still is the European (economic) integration. The principle of mutual trust in one another's legal systems and judicial institutions plays a crucial role.[677] The ECJ's decisions in *Turner*,[678] *Gasser*[679] and *Owusu*[680] illustrated that mutual trust underlines the allocation system of the Brussels Model.[681] Based on the idea of 'parity between courts',[682] differences between courts are not taken into account.[683] Instead the allocation system of the Brussels Model is based on neutrality

---

[676] This is the case when no choice of court agreement has been made between parties.

[677] See Recitals 16 and 17 Regulation, with respect to recognition of judgements. See the doubts raised by Blobel and Spath, 'Tale of Multilateral Trust', at 533-534 and 540; Clarke, 'The Differing Approach', at 121-122.

[678] C-159/02 *Turner v. Grovit*, [2004] ECR I-3565, para. 24; see Niboyet, 'Le principe de confiance mutuelle', at 78 *et seq.*

[679] C-116/02 *Gasser v. MISAT*, [2003] ECR I-14693, para. 72; see also Muir Watt, 'Note: *Gasser*', at 464.

[680] C-281/02 *Owusu v. Jackson*, [2005] ECR I-1383, para. 37.

[681] Magnus and Mankowski, eds., *Brussels I Regulation*, § 2, at 7; Clarke, 'The Differing Approach', at 119-121. Its success is sometimes explained by this trust. See Hartley, 'The European Court, the Brussels Convention/Regulation and the Establishment of an Efficient System for International Litigation in Europe', at 396, proposing legislative reform regarding the outcome of these three cases. See Blobel and Spath, 'Tale of Multilateral Trust', at 529-530 on whether trust can be imposed by judicial decree, and see Kramer, 'De harmoniserende werking', at 137, for some critical observations and examples on mutual trust in practice.

[682] Fentiman in Magnus and Mankowski, eds., *Brussels I Regulation*, § 26, at 486.

[683] A court judgement establishing jurisdiction on exorbitant jurisdiction rules will still be recognized as if it established jurisdiction in conformity with the Brussels Model. See Blobel and Spath, 'Tale of Multilateral Trust', at 530; F. Buonaiuti, 'Forum Non Conveniens Facing the Prospective Hague Convention and E.C. Regulation on Jurisdiction and the Enforcement of Judgments in Civil and Commercial Matters', 39 *Rivista di diritto europeo* (1999), 3-48, at 34.

of the rules and on 'jurisdictional blindness'[684] courts are not allowed to consider the appropriateness of another court.

[684] See Magnus and Mankowski, eds., *Brussels I Regulation*, § 26, at 486; Kruger, 'The Anti-Suit Injunction', at 1035-1036; Kramer, 'De harmoniserende werking', at 131-132.

Chapter 3

NATIONAL JURISDICTION RULES IN CONTINENTAL EUROPE

This chapter deals with some of the jurisdictional systems of civil law tradition in Continental Europe. As Chapter 2 explained, the Brussels Regulation is primarily based on the civil law tradition and was the result of a compromise between the jurisdictional systems of the six initial European Member States in order to come to uniform jurisdiction rules. The fact that the Brussels Model is a unified system makes the nature of uniform jurisdiction rules different from national jurisdiction rules that unilaterally determine the reach of their judiciary powers. It is this unilateral character of national jurisdiction rules that makes the following chapter crucial for the present study. The purpose of this chapter is twofold: primarily, it intends to give an overview of the jurisdictional system of the civil law tradition; and subsidiarily, it examines the influence of a uniform jurisdictional system on the existing national jurisdictional systems.

With respect to the latter, this chapter will first discuss the situation in Italy, Spain, The Netherlands and Switzerland, whose jurisdictional systems were reformed and modelled on the provisions of the Brussels Model.[1] The Spanish and Italian reforms are illustrations of national systems closely following the Brussels Model. Although, the new set of jurisdiction rules of the Dutch reform is also strongly inspired by the Brussels Model, it has kept a unilateral approach to international jurisdiction. The Swiss reform is particularly interesting for its original structure. Moreover, the Swiss version of property-based jurisdiction constitutes another interesting feature of the Swiss jurisdictional scheme.

The French and German systems are examples of original national jurisdictional systems. They have not recently reformed their jurisdictional regime and have kept their exorbitant jurisdiction rules, such as nationality-based and property-based jurisdiction. Moreover, the French jurisdictional system is considered to be the 'parent system' of the Romanist legal family and the German jurisdictional system the 'parent system' of the Germanic legal family.

It is important to note that, by virtue of Article 4 of the Brussels Model, national jurisdictional regimes only apply outside the scope of the Brussels Regulation and the Brussels and Lugano Conventions.[2] This implies that each national jurisdiction

[1] In this context it is worth mentioning that although according to some scholars it was considered desirable to give the ECJ jurisdiction over the interpretation of national jurisdiction rules directly modelled on the Brussels Model, the ECJ clearly lacks this jurisdiction since it considered that this is a matter of national law and not of community law. The ECJ refused jurisdiction in a decision following a British request for preliminary ruling on the Civil Jurisdiction and Judgements Act of 1982, modelled on the Brussels Convention, see C-346/93 *Kleinwort Benson v. City of Glasgow*, [1995] ECR I-615. This most likely still applies now that the Brussels Regulation replaced the Brussels Convention.

[2] See for the scope of the Brussels Model, Chapter 2, Sect. 2.2.

rule based on the defendant's domicile has lost its practical importance, as according to Article 2 of the Brussels Model in conjunction with Articles 59 and 60 of the Brussels Regulation or Articles 52 and 53 of the Brussels and Lugano Conventions, the Brussels Model applies in the event that the defendant is domiciled in a Brussels or Lugano State.

3.1 Italy and Spain: The Influence of the Brussels Model

The Italian and Spanish jurisdictional regimes are interesting because both systems narrowly follow the Brussels Convention.[3] The Italian reform ('*Riforma*') explicitly refers to Sections 3, 4 and 5 of the second title of the Brussels Convention, whereas the Spanish reform ('*Reforma*') literally copies the Convention's provisions. What is even more remarkable is that Spain did not adhere to the Brussels Convention until 26 May 1989,[4] but its jurisdictional reform, which was already completed in 1985, was entirely modelled on the Brussels Convention.[5]

In both countries, critics have however objected to the direct reference or copying of conventional rules in national statutes whose purpose is to unilaterally assert jurisdiction for its courts. The critics stated that such reference ignores the multilateral character of the uniform jurisdiction rules of the Brussels Model.[6]

3.1.1 The Italian *Riforma*

The reform of 31 May 1995 enacted a new Italian Statute on Private International Law[7] including rules for international jurisdiction under Articles 2 to 11.[8]

Prior to the reform, international jurisdiction of Italian courts was regulated by Article 4(1) and 4(2) of the Italian Code of Civil Procedure.[9] These provisions did

---

[3] The Belgian PIL Statute of 16 July 2004, *Loi du Portant le Code de Droit International Privé: Wet houdende het Wetboek van Internationaal Privaatrecht*, also narrowly follows the Brussels Model but its structure is modelled on the Swiss PIL Statute. See Sect. 3.3 below. Text can be found at http://www.ipr.be.

[4] Entered into force on 1 February 1991.

[5] J. Fernández-Flores de Funes, *Manual de derecho internacional privado* (1980), at 319-320; J. Alonso-Cuevillas Sayrol, *La competencia jurisdiccional internacional de los tribunales españoles del orden civil* (2006), at 67.

[6] Alonso-Cuevillas Sayrol, *La competencia jurisdiccional internacional*, at 68; A.-L. Calvo Caravaca and J. Carrascosa Gonzalez, *Derecho Internacional Privado* (2006), Vol. 1, § 24, at 149; F. Pocar, 'Le rôle des critères de compétence judiciaire de la Convention de Bruxelles dans le nouveau droit international privé italien', in *E pluribus unum, Liber amicorium, G Droz: On the Progressive Unification of Private International Law* (1996), 357-367, at 363.

[7] '*Riforma del sistema Italiano di diritto internazionale*', *La Gazetta Ufficiale, Supplemento Ordinario*, N. 128 of 3 June 1995, entered into force on 2 September 1995 (with the exception of Title IV which entered into force on 1 June 1996). See for the English translation, A. Montanari and V. Narcisi, *Conflict of Laws in Italy* (1997) and A. Giardina, 'Note; Italy, Law Reforming the Italian System of Private International Law', 35 *International Legal Materials* (1996), 760-782.

[8] Internal territorial jurisdiction – *la competenza per territorio* – is still regulated by Arts. 18 to 20 of the Italian Code of Civil Procedure, see A. Migliazza, 'Rilievi sulla Giurisdizione, sulla Competenza territoriale e sulla competenza internazionale', in *La Riforma del Diritto Internazionale Privato e Processuale, Raccolta in Ricordo di Eduardo Vitta* (1994), 363-368.

[9] *Codice de Procedura Civile* (CPC). The famous PIL Statute of 1865 embodied in the Italian Civil Code (CC) realized by the well-known expert Prof. Stanislao did not include international jurisdiction

not explicitly regulate jurisdiction over an Italian defendant and as a result, Italian courts assumed jurisdiction over international disputes involving an Italian defendant, even if the dispute itself was not connected with Italy.[10] This jurisdictional system was strongly nationality-based and presupposed the exclusivity of the Italian judge over Italian citizens as a means of protection.[11] It included a far-reaching jurisdiction rule in matters relating to contracts. If the contract was concluded in Italy, Italian courts would assume jurisdiction without requiring any other connection with the Italian forum. Not surprisingly, Article 3(2) of the Brussels Convention marked the nationality criteria and the *forum celebrationis* previously embodied in Article 4 CPC as exorbitant. A general desire to modernize the jurisdictional regime in line with conventional rules called for a reform and the abolishment of nationality-based jurisdiction in particular.[12]

The reform radically changed the Italian approach to jurisdiction. Following the example of the Brussels Convention, the principle of the *actor sequitur forum rei* is the main jurisdiction rule and nationality-based jurisdiction has been abandoned.[13] Article 3(1) states that 'Italian courts shall have jurisdiction if the defendant is domiciled or resides in Italy or has a representative in this country who is enabled to appear in court pursuant to Article 77 of the Code of Civil Procedure, as well as in the other cases provided for by law'.[14] This paragraph refers to specific matters regulated elsewhere by statute[15] and indicates that the Italian jurisdictional system

rules. Its provisions were integrated as preliminary general provisions to the Italian Civil Code and survived the reform of the Italian CC in 1942 with minor modifications. A. Bonomi, 'The Italian Statute on Private International Law', *International Journal of Legal Materials* (1999), 246-267, at 247.

[10] Art. 4(1) CPC reads: 'a foreigner may be sued in an Italian court if he is resident or domiciled in Italy, or if he has an address for service there or has a representative who is authorized to bring legal proceedings in his name, or if he has accepted Italian jurisdiction, unless the proceedings concern immovable property situated abroad'. Art. 4(2) CPC reads: 'a foreigner may be sued in the courts of the Italian Republic if the proceedings concern property situated in Italy, or succession to the estate of an Italian national, or an application for probate made in Italy, or obligation which arose in Italy or which must be performed there'. See A. Bonomi, 'Die Übereinkommen von Brüssel und Lugano und die Novellierung des italianischen internationalen Zivilprozessrechts', in *Die Übereinkommen von Brüssel und Lugano* (1997), 118-137, at 122; V. Starace, 'Le champ de la juridiction selon la loi de réforme du système italien de droit international privé', 85 *Revue critique de droit internationale privé* (1996), 67-82, at 69.

[11] See in general A. Giardina, 'Les caractères généraux de la réforme?', 85 *Revue critique de droit internationale privé* (1996), 1-19. and M. Weser, 'Bases of Judicial Jurisdiction in the Common Market Countries', 10 *American Journal of Comparative Law* (1961), 323-344, at 325.

[12] F. Pocar and C. Honorati, eds., *Il nuovo diritto internazionale privato italiano* (1997), at 20; Giardina, 'Les caractères généraux', at 7. The preparations for a reform were officially started in 1982 by Prof. Vitta, see Giardina, 'Les caractères généraux', at 3; G. Gaja, ed., *La Riforma del Diritto Internazionale Privato e Processuale, Raccolta in Ricordo di Eduardo Vitta* (1994).

[13] Broggini in Bariati, ed., *Legge 31 Maggio 1995, N. 218: Riforma del sistema Italiano di diritto internazionale privato* (1996), under Art. 3, at 906-907; Bonomi, 'Novellierung', at 123-124.

[14] '*La giurisdizione italiana sussiste quando il convenuto è domiciliato o residente in Italia o vi ha un rappresentante che sia autorizzato a stare in giudizio a norma dell'art. 77 del codice di procedura civile e negli altri casi in cui è prevista dalla legge.*' Translation by Montanari, see Montanari and Narcisi, *Conflict of Laws in Italy*.

[15] For example in the Code of Navigation.

is an open one; international jurisdiction rules are not exclusively enacted in the PIL Statute.[16]

At the same time, the rule exposes the particularity of the Italian version of the *forum rei* rule.[17] After primarily establishing jurisdiction on defendant's '*domicilio*'[18] or '*residenza*',[19] Italian courts are subsidairily competent over a foreign defendant who has a legal representative authorized to appear in his name in legal proceedings in Italy. This ground was already known under Article 4 of the CPC, which might explain the fact that it was re-introduced.[20] Accordingly, Article 3(1) considers that having a legal representative in Italy constitutes a sufficient connection with the forum to establish general jurisdiction over a defendant residing outside Italy, provided that 1) the claim involves particular (business) matters in which the legal representative is entitled to represent the defendant in court; 2) that this has been stated in writing; and 3) that the defendant himself cannot appear in court, for example because he is not domiciled or resident in Italy.[21] Although, the statute's definition of 'legal representative' is somewhat unclear, and some translations define 'representative' as 'agent',[22] it should not be confused with a 'branch office'.[23] Not all 'legal representatives' are branch offices and vice versa.[24] A legal representative is able to act on the defendant's behalf in front of Italian courts by virtue of an explicit statement of the defendant. The simple fact of having a branch office in Italy is not sufficient according to Italian case law.[25]

Apart from Article 3(1) regulating general jurisdiction, the second subparagraph provides for special jurisdiction in specific matters by directly referring to the Brussels Convention. Article 3(2) provides that[26]

---

[16] See for more details Broggini in Bariati, ed., *Riforma*, at 907.

[17] Pocar, 'Le nouveau droit international privé italien', at 359; Bonomi, 'Novellierung', at 124.

[18] A defendant's *domicilio* is determined by Art. 43 of the Italian CC, which focuses on the place where defendant has his principal centre of activities and interests. Neither the Italian CC nor the PIL Statute differentiates between natural and corporate persons, but the corporate *domicilio* is determined by its principal seat. See Broginni in Bariati, ed., *Riforma*, under Art. 3, at 907. G. Campeis and A. De Pauli, *La procedura civile internazionale* (1991), Vol. 5, at 116.

[19] 'Residence' should be understood as 'habitual residence' and is determined by Art. 43 CC, second paragraph.

[20] Pocar and Honorati, eds., *Il nuovo diritto internazionale privato italiano*, fn. 3, at 155. This criterion was added in 1993, at a later stage in the drafting process.

[21] Art. 77 states: '*Il procuratore generale e quello preposto a determinati affari non possono stare in giudizio per il preponente, quando questo potere non è stato loro conferito espressamente, per iscritto, tranne che per gli atti urgenti e per le misure cautelari. Tale potere si presume conferito al procuratore generale di chi non ha residenza o domicilio nella Repubblica e all'institore.*' Campeis, *La procedura civile internazionale*, at 116.

[22] Montanari translates '*rappresentate*' as 'agent', see Montanari and Narcisi, *Conflict of Laws in Italy*.

[23] Pocar, 'Le rôle des critères de compétence judiciaire de la Convention de Bruxelles dans le nouveau droit international privé italien', at 359.

[24] F. Pocar, 'Das Neue italienische Internationale Privatrecht', 17 *IPRax* (1997), 145-161, at 147.

[25] This 'legal representative' could only in some cases coincide with branch jurisdiction under Art. 5(5) Brussels Model, see Bonomi, 'Novellierung', fn. 15, at 124.

[26] Art. 3(2): '*La giurisdizione sussiste inoltre in base ai criteri stabiliti dalle sezioni 2, 3 e 4 del titolo II della Convenzione concernente la competenza giurisdizionale e l'esecuzione delle decisioni in materia civile e commerciale e protocollo, firmati a Bruxelles il 27 settembre 1968, resi esecutivi con*

> 'Italian courts shall further have jurisdiction according to the criteria set out in Sections 2, 3, and 4 of Title II of the Convention on Jurisdiction and Enforcement of judgements in civil and commercial matters and protocol, signed at Brussels ... rendered effective in Italy by the law of June 21, 1971, No. 804, and successive modifications in force in Italy, even if the defendant is not domiciled in the territory of a contracting State....'[27]

As a consequence of this direct reference to the Brussels Convention, international jurisdiction of Italian courts is regulated in accordance with Article 5(1), establishing contract jurisdiction, and Article 5(5), providing for branch jurisdiction.[28] Aside from settled case law stemming from the ECJ, national case law originating from other Member States interpreting the Brussels Convention should also be taken into account for the interpretation of the PIL Statute where it refers to the Brussels Convention.[29] The Italian PIL Statute was not adjusted in accordance with the modifications brought by the Brussels Regulation.[30]

3.1.2 The Spanish *Reforma*

After a period of '*imperialismo jurisdiccional*',[31] in which unpredictable case law determined international jurisdiction for Spanish courts, the 1985 Spanish '*Reforma*' established clear rules in Articles 21 and 22 of the Law on Judicial Organization – *Ley Orgánica del Poder Judicial* (LOPJ).[32] Its principal objective is to satisfy Article 24 of the Spanish Constitution by not only guaranteeing access to justice but also requiring that the exercise of jurisdiction be founded on a legal basis.[33]

---

la legge 21 giugno 1971, n. 804 e successive modificazioni in vigore per l'Italia, anche allorchè il convenuto non sia domiciliato nel territorio di uno Stato contraente, quando si tratti di una delle materie comprese nel campo di applicazione della Convenzione. Rispetto alle altre materie la giurisdizione sussiste anche in base ai criteri stabiliti per la competenza per territorio.'

As translated by Montanari and Narcisi, *Conflict of Laws in Italy*.

[27] For matters not covered by the Brussels Convention, the last sentence of Art. 3(2) refers back to the internal venue rules. This is remarkable as transposition of territorial jurisdiction rules to international cases was unknown to the former jurisdictional system.

[28] See for branch jurisdiction under the Brussels Model, Chapter 2, Sect. 2.6.

[29] See Art. 2(2) PIL Statute. Pocar and Honorati, eds., *Il nuovo diritto internazionale privato italiano*, at 154, *testi e documenti*; Giardina, 'Les caractères généraux', at 8; Bonomi, 'Novellierung', at 120.

[30] It should be noted that Annex I of the Brussels Regulation, enlisting the exorbitant jurisdiction rules of Art. 3(2), considers Arts. 3 and 4 as 'exorbitant' even if these rules directly refer to the Brussels Model. Art. 74 of the Brussels Regulation states 'that the Member States shall notify the Commission of the texts amending the lists set out in Annexes I'. One possible explanation for this is that the Italian Government interprets any national jurisdiction rule as 'exorbitant' once the Regulation applies. See Chapter 2, Sect. 2.2.7.

[31] Miaja de la Muela used this concept to indicate that the former Spanish system was characterized by judge made law and controversial sentences that resulted in total legal uncertainty. A. Miaja de la Muela, 'El "imperialismo jurisdiccional" español y el derecho internacional privado', in *Miscellany in Honor of Charalambos N. Fragistas on the Occassion of His 35th Anniversary as Professor of the University* (1968), 89-128. See Alonso-Cuevillas Sayrol, *La competencia jurisdiccional internacional*, at 66.

[32] Law No. 6/1985.

[33] Calvo Caravaca and Carrascosa Gonzalez, *Derecho Internacional Privado*, § 6, at 142-143. According to Fernández-Flores de Funes, *Manual*, at 318-319, the reform breaks with the '*imperialismo jurisdiccional*' which leads to the constitutionalization of Spanish jurisdiction law.

The majority of the provisions embodied in Article 22 LOPJ, including its hierarchical structure, are literally copied from the Brussels Convention.[34] Article 22(1) regulates exclusive jurisdiction and prorogation of jurisdiction is regulated in Article 22(2) which also ensures the *forum rei* rule.[35] Article 22(3), (4) and (5) regulate special jurisdiction. Branch jurisdiction is regulated in Article 22(4) and the provisions are identical to Article 5(5) of the Brussels Convention.[36]

One significant difference with the Brussels Convention is however to be found in Article 22(3) LOPJ which regulates special jurisdiction in contractual matters. Not only does this provision give jurisdiction to Spanish courts if 'contractual obligations' are to be performed in Spain,[37] but also when the contract was concluded there.[38] The latter, also known as the *forum celebrationis*,[39] is marked as exorbitant under the Brussels Model.[40]

3.2 The Netherlands

3.2.1 **Introduction**

Despite a long tradition in the legal science of private international law, the codification process in The Netherlands with respect to international jurisdiction only commenced at the end of the last century.[41] On 21 March 1996, a proposal for a

---

[34] Calvo Caravaca and Carrascosa Gonzalez, *Derecho Internacional Privado*, § 6, at 142; see for some critical observations, § 24, at 148; J. Espinar Vicente, *Derecho procesal civil internacional* (1988), at 874.

[35] Alonso-Cuevillas Sayrol, *La competencia jurisdiccional internacional*, at 8; Calvo Caravaca and Carrascosa Gonzalez, *Derecho Internacional Privado*, § 40, at 155-156; M. Benítez de Lugo, B. Campuzano Diaz *et al.*, *Lecciones de derecho procesal civil internacional* (2002), at 95-96. The '*domicilio del demandado*' of a natural person is determined by Art. 40 of the Spanish Civil Code and requires that the defendant has the intention to remain in Spain for a considerable period of time. With respect to legal persons, Art. 41 Spanish CC states that the corporate domicile is determined by the defendant's statutory seat. If these rules do not indicate a particular place of settlement, then the place where the company's legal staff is located or where it carries out its principal business activities, will determine jurisdiction. Benítez de Lugo, Campuzano Diaz *et al.*, *Lecciones*, at 96.

[36] Art. 22(4) states that Spanish courts have jurisdiction '*en los litigios relativos a la explotación de una sucursal, agencia o establecimiento mercantil, cuando este se encuentre en territorio español.*' Benítez de Lugo, Campuzano Diaz *et al.*, *Lecciones*, at 100.

[37] This connecting factor is considerably wider than Art. 5(1) of the Brussels Convention, which specifies the obligation in question as well as the characterized place of performance as specified in Art. 5(1)(b) of the Brussels Regulation. See Alonso-Cuevillas Sayrol, *La competencia jurisdiccional internacional*, fn. 300, at 121.

[38] According to Art. 22(3) LOPJ, Spanish courts have jurisdiction '*en materia de obligaciones contractuales, cuando estas hayan nacido o deban cumplirse en España*'.

[39] Fernández-Flores de Funes, *Manual*, at 188 and 215-216.

[40] See Chapter 2, Sect. 2.2.7. However, it should be observed that this 'exorbitant' Spanish jurisdiction rule is not listed in Annex I of the Brussels Regulation, but a similar rule known in Italy prior to the reform was marked 'exorbitant' by Art. 3(2) of the Brussels Convention.

[41] See for an overview G. Steenhoff, *De wetenschap van het internationaal privaatrecht in Nederland tussen 1862 en 1962: Een internationalistisch perspectief* (1994) and see the book review by F. De Ly, in 69 *Nederlands Juristenblad* (1994), 1109-1112. Codification of conflict of laws rules commenced with separate acts dealing with specific areas of Private International Law, for example the International Divorce Act in 1981. See for a list of Acts codifying separate topics of conflicts of law,

reform of the Law on Judicial Procedure – covering judicial proceedings in civil and commercial law as well as in criminal law – was submitted to the Dutch Parliament but was withdrawn in 1998.[42] A second proposal for the reform of the Law on Judicial Procedure[43] was finally approved on 6 December 2001 and entered into force on 1 January 2002.[44] The reform brought substantive modifications to the regulation of Dutch judicial powers in international cases.

X. Kramer, 'Dutch Private International Law. Overview 1998-August 2002', *IPRax* (2002), 537-546, at 537 and M. Polak and M. de Rooij, *Private International Law in the Netherlands* (1987), suppl. 1995, at 3. In 1982, the Dutch Justice Department commenced a general codification project for a Dutch Private International Law Statute to be elaborated by the influential Dutch Standing Committee of Private International Law – or *Staatscommissie voor het Internationaal Privaatrecht*. Initially the PIL Statute, also known as the 'blue book', was intended to cover all aspects of Private International Law, including international procedural law and jurisdiction rules. The comprehensive Statute did not receive the expected support and the project was disapproved in 1990 during the annual meeting of the Dutch International Law Association – *Nederlandse Vereniging voor Internationaal Recht*. Th. de Boer and M. Polak, 'Naar een gecodifieerd internationaal privaatrecht (!/?)', 101 *Preadviezen: Mededelingen van de Nederlandse Vereniging voor Internationaal Recht* (1990), 161, at 158 *et seq.*; Kramer, 'Dutch Private International Law', at 537. The Justice department on the one hand set course for a PIL Statute specifically dealing with conflict of laws issues and on the other hand it started with a revision of the Dutch Code of Civil Procedure or *Wetboek van Burgerlijke Rechtsvordering*. The latter resulted in 1993 in a first draft of the New Dutch Code of Civil Procedure and included an innovative and comprehensive set of international jurisdiction rules for Dutch courts. F. Ibili, *Gewogen rechtsmacht in het IPR: Over forum (non) conveniens en forum necessitatis* (2007), § 3.2, at 33; X. Kramer, 'De regeling van de rechtsmacht onder het herziene Rechtsvordering', 20 *NIPR* (2002), 375-385, at 375; M.E. Koppenol-Laforce, 'De Rechtsmacht van de Nederlandse rechter in het voorontwerp tot aanpassing van het Wetboek van Burgerlijke Rechtsvordering', *Tijdschrift voor Civiele Rechtspleging* (1994), 5-9; D. Kokkini-Iatridou and K. Boele-Woelki, 'De Regeling van de "Internationale rechtsmacht"', 125 *WPNR* (1994), 50-55. The first 1992 draft of the PIL Statute, also called the 'red book', clearly excluded international procedural law. The Standing Committee's work resulted in a draft PIL Statute or '*IPR-Schets*', see A. Struycken, 'Veelheid van rechtsbronnen: Één IPR?', 45 *Ars Aequi* (1996), 61-68, at 62. See 'Rapport aan de Minister van Justitie; Algemene Bepalingen Wet Internationaal Privaatrecht', in http://www.justitie.nl/themas/wetgeving/rapporten_en_notas/privaatrecht/Staatscommissie_IPR.asp The Hague: Staatscommissie Internationaal Privaatrecht (2002), at 4; and see for critical comments K. Siehr, 'Structure and Method of the "IPR-Schets"', special edition, *NIPR* (1994), 22-29, at 23-26; P. Vlas, 'De regeling van de rechtsmacht in het Voorontwerp van het Wetboek van Burgerlijke Rechtsvordering', special edition, *NIPR* (1994), 61-72, at 62-65 and 70-71; L. Strikwerda, 'Het 'rode boek' van het internationaal privaatrecht', *Nederlands Juristenblad* (1992), 1572-1573.

[42] *Wijziging van de Wet op de Rechterlijke Organisatie, het Wetboek van Burgerlijke Rechtsvordering, het Wetboek van Strafvordering en andere wetten in verband met de integratie van kantongerechten en de arrondissementsrechtbanken*, Kamerstukken II 24651; Ibili, *Gewogen rechtsmacht*, at 34; Kramer, 'De regeling van de rechtsmacht', at 375 and 541.

[43] *Wetsvoorstel herziening van het procesrecht van burgerlijke zaken, in het bijzonder de wijze van procederen in eerste aanleg*, Kamerstukken II (MvT) 26 855, *Staatsblad* 2001, 580 [hereafter Explanatory Report Proposal DCCP].

[44] Officially published in *Staatsblad* (2001), at 580, including the modifications brought by *Aanpassing van de wetgeving aan de herziening van het procesrecht voor burgerlijke zaken, in het bijzonder de wijze van procederen in eerste aanleg*, Kamerstukken II (MvT) 27824 [hereafter MvT 27824], *Staatsblad* 2001, 581 and *Aanpassing van Enkele Onderdelen van het Wetboek van Burgerlijke Rechtsvordering en enige ander wetten in verband met het nieuwe procesrecht*, Kamerstukken II (MvT) 28 863 nr. 3 [hereafter MvT 28863], *Staatsblad* 2005, 455; *Aanpassing van enkele onderdelen van het Wetboek van Burgerlijke Rechtsvordering en enige ander wetten in verband met het nieuwe rocesrecht*, Kamerstukken (MvA) 28 863 D [hereafter MvA 863D].

Prior to the 2001 reform, international jurisdiction of the Dutch judiciary was determined by transposition of internal territorial jurisdiction rules to international cases by virtue of a decision of the *Hoge Raad*, the Dutch Supreme Court.[45] This principle known as '*distributie bepaalt attributie*'[46] gave a double function to internal territorial jurisdiction rules: by allocating or 'distributing' judicial powers among local courts, the rule also 'attributed' international jurisdiction to the Dutch judiciary as a whole.[47] For a certain period this principle was satisfactory, but increasing transnational legal transactions required new provisions for the regulation of international jurisdiction of Dutch courts.[48] The 2001 reform of the Dutch Code of Civil Procedure[49] enacted a new set of direct international jurisdiction rules, but did not completely abandon the transposition of internal venue rules to international disputes.[50] Article 10 provides for an 'escape' clause or 'catch-all' provision referring back to internal territorial rules, hereby re-introducing the '*distributie bepaalt attributie*' principle through the back door and maintaining among others the *forum arresti* rule.[51]

---

[45] HR 24 December 1915, *NJ* (1917), 417; HR 5 December 1940, *NJ* (1941), 313; HR 26 October 1984, *NJ* (1985), 696. For more details see L. Pellis, *Internationaal Procesrecht: Een dwarsdoorsnede* (2005), at 45-60; C. Voskuil, *De Internationale Bevoegdheid van de Nederlandse Rechter* (1962), at 24-38; and L. Pellis, '"Tot uw dienst!", Over oude en nieuwe grondslagen van het commune Nederlandse internationaal bevoegdheidsrecht', in *Met recht verkregen* (2002), at 142-144.

[46] Or the 'distribution is attribution' rule.

[47] P. Vlas, 'Boek I: Rechtsmacht van de Nederlandse rechter', in *Tekst & Commentaar, Burgerlijke Rechtsvordering* (2006), Title 1, Introductory note 4; P. Polak, A. van Mierlo *et al.*, eds., *Burgerlijke rechtsvordering: De tekst van het Wetboek van Burgerlijke Rechtsvordering voorzien van commentaar* (2005), § 7, at 4-5; Pellis, *Internationaal Procesrecht*, at 41 *et seq.*; Kramer, 'De regeling van de rechtsmacht', at 375.

[48] *Explanatory Report Proposal DCCP*, at 23; A. Struycken, 'Distributie bepaalt attributie – Vuistregel en kern van een goed hanteerbaar rechtsmachtsmodel', in *De internationale bevoegdheid van de Nederlandse Rechter volgens de nieuwe bepalingen van het Wetboek van Burgerlijke Rechtsvordering* (1996), 19-43, at 20-25; P. Vlas and F. Ibili, 'De nieuwe commune regels inzake de rechtsmacht van de Nederlandse rechter', 134 *WPNR* (2003), 310-319, at 310-311; Kramer, 'De regeling van de rechtsmacht', at 375. Not all Dutch scholars agreed with the need for direct international jurisdiction rules; Struycken favoured the *status quo* by arguing that the '*distributie is attributie*' principle is functional and reflects universality according to Franceskakis's model of '*unité juridictionnelle du globe*', see Struycken, 'Distributie bepaalt attributie', at 32. See Pellis, *Internationaal Procesrecht*, at 97-100; *contra* H. Kronke, 'Distributie bepaalt attributie – Internationale Zuständigkeit zwischen Faustregel und Kodifikation', paper presented at Studiedag (1996), at 52-53.

[49] Dutch Code of Civil Procedure or *Wetboek van Burgerlijke Rechtsvordering* [hereafter old DCCP] replaced by the New Dutch Code of Civil Procedure *or Nieuw Wetboek van Burgerlijke Rechtsvordering* [hereafter DCCP].

[50] The Explanatory Report acknowledges the difference between the internal territorial rules and international rules, *Explanatory Report Proposal DCCP*, at 24. See Ibili, *Gewogen rechtsmacht*, § 3.3.1, at 41-42; Pellis, *Internationaal Procesrecht*, at 81-86; L. Strikwerda, *De Overeenkomst in het IPR* (2004), § 99, at 50.

[51] Vlas, 'Tekst & Commentaar, Rv.', Title 1, Introductory note 4; Pellis, *Internationaal Procesrecht*, at 86-92; Vlas and Ibili, 'De nieuwe commune regels', at 311; Kramer, 'De regeling van de rechtsmacht', at 375; also called '*de restregel*' by D. Kokkini-Iatridou and K. Boele-Woelki, 'De Regeling van de 'Internationale rechtsmacht' in het voorontwerp van wet van 1993', *NIPR* (1993), 323-364, at 328-329 and see below Sect. 3.2.4 for the *forum arresti*.

3.2.1.1 *The Need for Reform – Conformity with the Brussels Model*

The reform was not only needed to do away with the transposition of venue rules to international cases that were considered out-dated,[52] but also to promote uniformity and legal certainty. A general desire was expressed for the alignment of national jurisdiction rules with conventional jurisdiction rules and the abolishment of jurisdiction rules marked as exorbitant under the Brussels Model.[53]

Although nationality-based jurisdiction was already abolished,[54] the former Dutch jurisdictional regime still included a *forum actoris* rule as a result of the transposition of Article 126(3) old DCCP.[55] The rule asserted jurisdiction to Dutch courts when the claimant was domiciled in The Netherlands, regardless of his nationality, against a defendant domiciled abroad. This 'pro-plaintiff' rule, 'condemned' by Article 3(2) under the Brussels Model, was considered incompatible with the favour shown to the defendant under the *forum rei* rule and was generally considered inappropriate for international jurisdiction rules.[56] Furthermore, international recognition of Dutch judgements based on the *forum actoris* rule was generally considered most unlikely.[57]

Under the former jurisdictional regime jurisdiction in petition cases was subjected to a statutory general exception rule.[58] Article 429c (15) old DCCP allowed Dutch courts to decline jurisdiction when the claim was insufficiently connected with The Netherlands and was generally known as the *forum non conveniens* criterion.[59] Although the question whether this exception rule also applied to summons cases remained unresolved,[60] in order to conform to the 'closed' jurisdictional re-

---

[52] *Explanatory Report Proposal DCCP*, at 23; see also Ibili, *Gewogen rechtsmacht*, § 3.2.2, at 35-37; Pellis, *Internationaal Procesrecht*, at 93-94.

[53] *Explanatory Report Proposal DCCP*, at 23; Polak, Van Mierlo *et al.*, eds., *Tekst & Commentaar Rv.*, § 3(b), at 3.

[54] Art. 127 of the old DCCP was abolished by the Statute of 7 May 1986, *Staatsblad* 1986, 295; see among others Voskuil, *De Internationale Bevoegdheid*, at 68-70. It lost its practical relevance in 1940, when the Dutch Supreme Court ruled that in order for the nationality-based jurisdiction rule to apply, in addition another jurisdiction rule should be applicable to establish jurisdiction over the foreign defendant. *Julie Theodore van der Goes v. Willy August Clemens Schönstedt*, 5 December 1940, *NJ* (1941), at 312. J. Verheul and M. Feteris, *Rechtsmacht in het Nederlandse Privaatrecht Deel 2: Overige Verdragen het commune IPR* (1986), § 7.3, at 85. Weser, 'Bases of Judicial Jurisdiction', at 327.

[55] Verheul and Feteris, *Rechtsmacht*, § 7.1, at 83.

[56] Strikwerda, *De Overeenkomst in het IPR*, § 101, at 51; J. Verheul, 'The "*Forum Actoris*" and International Law', in *Essays on International & Comparative Law in Honour of Judge Erades* (1983), 197-206, at 198-199.

[57] Koppenol-Laforce, 'Rechtsmacht', at 5; and Verheul, 'The "*Forum Actoris*"', at 203-204.

[58] Ibili, *Gewogen rechtsmacht*, § 2.4, at 16-18; M. Freudenthal and F. van der Velden, 'The Netherlands National Report', in *Declining Jurisdiction in Private International Law* (1995), 321-339, at 328-340.

[59] Kramer, 'De regeling van de rechtsmacht', at 376; L. Strikwerda, *Inleiding tot het Nederlandse Privaatrecht* (2008), § 227, at 231; R. Bax, 'Forum non Conveniens in het Engelse en Nederlandse recht', 47 *Ars Aequi* (1998), 458-464; Freudenthal and Van der Velden, 'The Netherlands', at 331-333; Kokkini-Iatridou and Boele-Woelki, 'Internationale rechtsmacht', at 331-337.

[60] The uncertainty was the result of the *Van den Bogaerde van Terbrugge* decision of the Hoge Raad of 26 October 1984, *NJ* (1985), at 696, which was considered by some to introduce the *forum*

gime of the Brussels Model, the *forum non conveniens* criterion had to give way to 'hard and fast'[61] criteria from which the court may not derogate on the basis that the claim is insufficiently connected with the forum. The need to conform to the Brussels Model and the abolishment of the *forum actoris*[62] was generally accepted. But one of the main difficulties during the reform was the incorporation of a *forum conveniens* requirement and a *forum necessitatis* rule in order to compensate for the loss of the *forum non conveniens* exception in family matters.[63]

The new set of rules regulates jurisdiction for Dutch courts over international disputes, outside the scope of the Brussels and Lugano Instruments,[64] but is strongly modelled on the latter.[65] Its provisions literally follow the wording of the Brussels Model and the ECJ's settled – and future – case law should be used for their interpretation.[66] The explanatory report acknowledges however that the nature of national international jurisdiction rules differs from the nature of uniform conventional rules: national jurisdiction rules are unilateral and are meant to regulate the reach of its judiciary powers, as opposed to allocating judicial powers among Member States. The explanatory report expressly sets out that having to start proceedings in a foreign country is generally problematic due to foreign languages, additional travel costs and unfamiliarity with foreign law and justifies far reaching national jurisdiction rules, providing claimant with a Dutch competent forum instead of having to bring suit abroad.[67]

3.2.1.2 *Structure and Overview*

The structure of the Dutch jurisdictional regime distinguishes between judicial proceedings to be instituted by serving a writ of summons and judicial proceedings instituted by petition. Summons cases generally involve civil and commer-

---

non conveniens exception to summons cases. See Verheul and Feteris, *Rechtsmacht*, at 243; *contra* Pellis, 'Met recht verkregen', at 147 *et seq.*; Ibili, *Gewogen rechtsmacht*, § 2.5, at 18-20.

[61] This wording is also used by Boele-Woelki in relation to conflict of laws rules, and is by analogy applicable to jurisdiction rules, see K. Boele-Woelki, C. Joustra *et al.*, 'Dutch Private International Law at the End of the 20th Century: Pluralism of Methods', in *Netherlands Reports to the 15th International Congress of Comparative Law, Bristol* (1998), 203-227, at 210.

[62] L. Strikwerda, 'Drie fora: *forum actoris, forum necessitatis* en *forum non conveniens*', paper presented at Studiedag (1996), at 95-96.

[63] Provided for under Arts. 3(c) and 9 DCCP, respectively; Strikwerda, 'Drie fora', at 104; A. Leijnse-Kolk, 'Drie fora; *forum actoris, forum non conveniens* en *forum necessitatis*', paper presented at Studiedag (1996); *Explanatory Report Proposal DCCP*, at 30; Kramer, 'De regeling van de rechtsmacht', at 376.

[64] *Explanatory Report Proposal DCCP*, at 22; see also Koppenol-Laforce, 'Rechtsmacht', at 6.

[65] *Explanatory Report Proposal DCCP*, at 23; and see also the preceding report of the Ministry of Justice, 'Voorontwerp van wet tot aanpassing van het Wetboek Burgerlijke Rechtsvordering in verband met de herziening Rechterlijke Organisatie', Ministerie van Justitie (1993), at 21-22.

[66] *Explanatory Report Proposal DCCP*, at 33; but Dutch courts are not allowed to address a preliminary question regarding the interpretation of national jurisdiction rules, even if they are modelled on the Brussels Model. See Polak, Van Mierlo *et al.*, eds., *Tekst & Commentaar Rv.*, § 3c, at 3; and Pellis, *Internationaal Procesrecht*, at 110 *et seq.*

[67] *Explanatory Report Proposal DCCP*, at 23; *Voorontwerp*, Ministerie van Justitie (1993), at 22; Polak, Van Mierlo *et al.*, eds., *Tekst & Commentaar DCCP*, § 3c-4, at 3-4; Kramer, 'De regeling van de rechtsmacht', at 375; Koppenol-Laforce, 'Rechtsmacht', at 6.

cial matters,[68] whereas petition cases principally concern family matters.[69] This distinction is also reflected in the DCCP: Article 2 comprises the general rule for jurisdiction in civil and commercial matters and Article 3 deals with the procedures commenced by petition.[70] The particularity of the latter lies in that Article 3(c) contains an open-ended criterion which is generally considered by the majority of Dutch authors as a *forum conveniens* rule.[71] The legislator introduced a certain degree of discretion for Dutch courts by asserting jurisdiction over a petition case to Dutch courts when the dispute is 'otherwise sufficiently connected with the Dutch legal order'.[72]

Articles 4 and 5 provide for some additional special jurisdiction rules in petition cases and are mainly modelled on conventional jurisdiction rules of the Brussels II*bis* Regulation dealing with jurisdictional issues in divorce and custody cases[73] and the 1961 Hague Convention on the protection of minors.[74] Article 4(1) even simply refers to the corresponding articles in the Brussels II*bis* Regulation.[75] Again, the legislator introduced a certain degree of discretion for Dutch courts by incorporating a statutory discretionary exception in Article 4(3)(b) and Article 5: Dutch courts have international jurisdiction according to the provisions' connecting factors 'unless the case is insufficiently connected with The Netherlands'.[76]

---

[68] Arts. 78-260, Second Title, Book 1 DCCP

[69] Arts. 261-291, Third Title, Book 1 DCCP; Kramer, 'Dutch Private International Law', at 541.

[70] Vlas, 'Tekst & Commentaar, Rv.', Title 1, Introductory note 8; Strikwerda, *Inleiding*, § 222, at 227. Art. 3(a) defines the general rule establishing jurisdiction to the court of the domicile or habitual residence of the petitioner. Art. 3(b), second paragraph, asserts jurisdiction to Dutch courts when the petition is related to a summons case that is subject to the jurisdiction of Dutch courts. For the application of Art. 3 DCCP, see District Court The Hague, 24 November 2003, *NIPR* (2004), at 14; District Court Haarlem, 12 July 2005, *NIPR* (2005), at 231.

[71] Unlike the previous two subparagraphs, the rule does not contain a particular connecting factor. Vlas and Ibili, 'De nieuwe commune regels', at 315. Ibili, *Gewogen rechtsmacht*, § 4.2, at 89 *et seq.* Vlas, 'Tekst & Commentaar, Rv.', Title 1, Art. 3, note 3; Polak, Van Mierlo *et al.*, eds., *Tekst & Commentaar Rv.*, § 4, at 12-13. See District Court The Hague, 5 December 2006, *NIPR* (2006), at 15; Court of Appeal The Hague, 18 May 2005, *NIPR* (2005), at 311.

[72] *Explanatory Report Proposal DCCP*, at 31; Vlas, 'Tekst & Commentaar, Rv.', Title 1, Art. 3, note 4; Polak, Van Mierlo *et al.*, eds., *Tekst & Commentaar Rv.*, § 5, at 13.

[73] Council Regulation (EC) No. 2201/2003 of 27 November 2003 concerning jurisdiction and the recognition and enforcement of judgments in matrimonial matters and the matters of parental responsibility, repealing Regulation (EC) No. 1347/2000.

[74] Convention of 5 October 1961 concerning the powers of authorities and the law applicable in respect of the protection of minors. Polak, Van Mierlo *et al.*, eds., *Tekst & Commentaar Rv.*, at 13-29; Strikwerda, *Inleiding*, § 223-224, at 228-229; Vlas and Ibili, 'De nieuwe commune regels', at 315-318; Kramer, 'De regeling van de rechtsmacht', at 377-379.

[75] As modified by Act of 16 February 2006, *Staatsblad* 2006, 123; entered into force on 1 May 2006 by virtue of Act 7 April 2006, *Staatsblad* 2006, 193; see also Th. de Boer, 'Enkele knelpunten bij de toepassing van de Verordening Brussel II-bis', *Tijdschrift voor Familie- en Jeugdrecht* (2005), 222-229.

[76] Vlas, 'Tekst & Commentaar, Rv.' Title 1, Art. 3, note 4, Art. 4(3), note 6 and Art. 5, note 2; Polak, Van Mierlo *et al.*, eds., *Tekst & Commentaar Rv.*, § 5, at 13; Vlas and Ibili, 'De nieuwe commune regels', at 317; MvT 27824, at 21; Strikwerda, *Inleiding*, § 227a, at 232. The Dutch nationality of the child is likely to constitute a 'sufficient connection' for Dutch jurisdiction. See for the application of Art. 4(3) DCCP, Court of Appeal Maastricht of 23 January 2004 as indicated in Court of Appeal

A parallel between this exception and the *forum non conveniens* exception has frequently been drawn.[77]

Articles 6 and 6A provide for alternative jurisdiction rules in summons cases.[78] Most of these additional jurisdictional grounds are literally taken from Article 5 of the Brussels Model, regulating special jurisdiction among others in contractual and tortuous matters.[79] Following the example of Article 6 of the Brussels Model, Article 7 confers jurisdiction based on procedural efficiency such as jurisdiction over multiple defendants and counter-claims.[80] The latter are also called 'objective' jurisdiction rules, as opposed to subjective jurisdiction rules such as Article 8 regulating the prorogation of jurisdiction on the basis of the parties' autonomy.[81] It allows parties to agree upon a Dutch court under Article 8(1) DCCP or to derogate from the jurisdictional set of rules in favour of a foreign court by virtue of Article 8(2) DCCP.[82] For prorogation of jurisdiction under Article 8(1) DCCP, a choice of forum in favour of a Dutch court is allowed unless 'reasonable interest' or '*redelijk belang*' to assert jurisdiction to a Dutch court is lacking.[83]

's-Hertogenbosch, 10 June 2004, *NIPR* (2004), at 222. See for the temporal scope of application of Art. 5, HR 19 March 2004, *NJ* (2004), at 806; L. Strikwerda, 'Het forum necessitatis in verzoekschriftprocedures', in *Liber Amicorum G.R. Rutgers* (2005), 329-335, at 331-333.

[77] Ibili, *Gewogen rechtsmacht*, § 3.6.4.1, at 78-80; Vlas, 'Tekst & Commentaar, Rv.', Title 1, Art. 4(3), note 6; Strikwerda, *Inleiding*, § 227, at 231-232; Polak, Van Mierlo *et al.*, eds., *Tekst & Commentaar Rv.*, § 4, at 29.

[78] Strikwerda, *Inleiding*, § 217, at 219-221.

[79] See Art. 6 as modified by MvT 28 863 after the enactment of the Brussels Regulation, under Art. 6(a), (e) and (f), respectively. Art. 6(b) and (c) deal with jurisdiction in employment contracts and have only partially been inspired by the Brussels Convention and/or Regulation. See Polak, Van Mierlo *et al.*, eds., *Tekst & Commentaar Rv.*, § 6, at 41-42; A. van Hoek and P. Mostermans, 'Ontwikkelingen in regelgeving en rechtspraak in het IPR-procesrecht (buiten EEX en EVEX)', 6622 *WPNR* (2005), 419-427, at 422. Art. 6(g), (h) and (i), respectively, deal with claims concerning successions, corporate matters and insolvency, but emanate from precedent or existing Dutch jurisdiction rules and not from the Brussels Model. Art. 5(2), (5), (6) and (7) of the Brussels Regulation is not incorporated in Art. 6 DCCP. The report explains each of these exclusions except for Art. 5(5) involving branch jurisdiction, which has been left out without any explanation, but see below Sect. 3.2.2.4. on branch; *Explanatory Report Proposal DCCP*, at 34. Polak, Van Mierlo *et al.*, eds., *Tekst & Commentaar Rv.*, § 2c, at 38.

[80] Polak, Van Mierlo *et al.*, eds., *Tekst & Commentaar Rv.*, § 1-4, at 49-50; Strikwerda, *Inleiding*, § 218, at 222; Strikwerda, *De Overeenkomst in het IPR*, § 115-117, at 56; Kramer, 'De regeling van de rechtsmacht', at 381-382.

[81] Ibili, *Gewogen rechtsmacht*, § 3.4, at 45-46; Polak, Van Mierlo *et al.*, eds., *Tekst & Commentaar Rv.*, § 1, at 37; Vlas and Ibili, 'De nieuwe commune regels', at 313; J. Rutgers, 'Internationale forumkeuze en agentuur: Het commune bevoegdheidsrecht in Europees perspectief', *NIPR* (2003), 351-355, at 351-352; Kramer, 'De regeling van de rechtsmacht', at 382-383; Koppenol-Laforce, 'Rechtsmacht', at 7; and *Voorontwerp*, Ministerie van Justitie (1993), at 22.

[82] Tacit prorogation of jurisdiction is regulated by Art. 9(a) DCCP Strikwerda, *Inleiding*, § 219, at 222-25; Polak, Van Mierlo *et al.*, eds., *Tekst & Commentaar Rv.*, § 1-9, at 50-55; Strikwerda, *De Overeenkomst in het IPR*, § 118-124, at 57-59; Vlas and Ibili, 'De nieuwe commune regels', at 311-313; Kramer, 'De regeling van de rechtsmacht', at 383. See also P. Kuypers, *Forumkeuze in het Nederlandse internationaal privaatrecht* (2008), at 144-145.

[83] See for the implication of this jurisdictional requirement, Ibili, *Gewogen rechtsmacht*, § 3.4.2, at 49 and Vlas, 'Tekst & Commentaar, Rv.', Title 1, Art. 8, note 2.

As explained above, the reform abandoned a general *forum non conveniens* exception for petition cases but instead gave Dutch courts discretionary powers in specific situations, especially in family matters. Such powers are also available under the *forum necessitatis* rule enacted in Article 9(b) and (c), which provides for Dutch jurisdiction when proceedings abroad appear impossible or if the case is 'sufficiently connected' with the forum and it would be unreasonable to expect from the claimant to institute proceedings abroad.[84] As mentioned earlier, Article 10 DCCP refers back to some internal jurisdictional rules under the DCCP. Furthermore, Article 12 DCCP regulates *lis pendens* and Article 13 establishes jurisdiction with respect to provisional measures.[85]

3.2.2 General Jurisdiction at Defendant's Forum

Article 2 DCCP exclusively regulates general jurisdiction over summon cases and contains the main jurisdiction rule of the Dutch jurisdictional scheme:[86] 'In summon(s) cases, Dutch courts have jurisdiction if the defendant has his domicile or habitual residence in The Netherlands'.[87] This rule already existed under Article 126(1) old DCCP and embodies the *actor sequitur forum rei* maxim.[88] According to the explanatory report, this internationally accepted general jurisdiction criterion is based on the idea that the defendant should be protected while he is not the one initiating proceedings and enforcement of judgements will generally take place at defendant's domicile.[89]

The connecting factor of this *forum rei* rule is primarily the defendant's domicile or '*woonplaats*'[90] and subsidiarily his habitual residence or '*gewone verblijfplaats*'.[91] The domicile criterion is determined by Articles 1:10 to 1:15 of the Dutch

---

[84] See in particular Ibili, *Gewogen rechtsmacht*, at 107 *et seq.*; Strikwerda, 'Het forum necessitatis', and Pellis, *Internationaal Procesrecht*, at 165-180. See with respect to the practical consequences of the *forum necessitatis* resulting in a *forum actoris*, Vlas, 'Tekst & Commentaar, Rv.', Title 1, Art. 9, note 5; Polak, Van Mierlo *et al.*, eds., *Tekst & Commentaar Rv.*, § 6, at 59; *Explanatory Report Proposal DCCP*, at 41; Kramer, 'De regeling van de rechtsmacht', at 383.

[85] Art. 11 regulates in which cases the court has to rule on its own motion.

[86] Vlas, 'Tekst & Commentaar, Rv.', Title 1, Art. 2, note 1; Polak, Van Mierlo *et al.*, eds., *Tekst & Commentaar Rv.*, § 2, at 9; Vlas and Ibili, 'De nieuwe commune regels', at 313. Art. 3 DCCP deals with procedures that are commenced by petition.

[87] '*In zaken die bij dagvaarding moeten worden ingeleid, heeft de Nederlandse rechter rechtsmacht indien de gedaagde in Nederland zijn woonplaats of gewone verblijfplaats heeft.*' [Translation-HvL]

[88] Vlas, 'Tekst & Commentaar, Rv.', Title 1, Art. 2, note 1; Polak, Van Mierlo *et al.*, eds., *Tekst & Commentaar Rv.*, § 1, at 9; Strikwerda, *De Overeenkomst in het IPR*, § 102, at 51; Kramer, 'De regeling van de rechtsmacht', at 376. See for the Dutch jurisdictional regime over international disputes prior to the reform, especially regarding the *forum rei* rule of Art. 126(1) DCCP, Polak and De Rooij, *Private International Law in the Netherlands*, at 48-50; Verheul and Feteris, *Rechtsmacht*, at 80-82; Voskuil, *De Internationale Bevoegdheid*, at 78-86.

[89] *Explanatory Report Proposal DCCP*, at 28.

[90] The Dutch legislator considers '*woonplaats*' equal to the '*domicilie*' concept. See G.-R. de Groot, 'Boek 1; Persoon en Familierecht', in *Tekst & Commentaar Burgerlijk Wetboek* (2005), Title 1, Art. 10, Introductory note 5.

[91] *Explanatory Report Proposal DCCP*, at 28; Strikwerda explicitly states that the habitual residence criterion applies when the defendant does not have a '*woonstede*' in the Netherlands, see Strikwerda, *Inleiding*, § 216, at 218-219.

Civil Code (DCC) – or *Burgerlijk Wetboek* (BW) –, which defines the domicile of both natural persons and corporate entities,[92] but also includes the establishment of a branch within the meaning of a person's domicile.[93]

3.2.2.1 *The Domicile of Natural Persons*

Article 1:10(1) DCC states that a natural person is domiciled at his principal place of residence or his '*woonstede*', or in default thereof, at the place of his actual residence or '*werkelijk verblijf*'.[94] The meaning of '*woonstede*' is determined on a case-by-case basis and should be understood as the place where a natural person lives and administers his property and (financial) interests.[95]

When a defendant has no domicile, not in The Netherlands nor anywhere else, his actual residence replaces the domicile concept.[96] The meaning of 'actual residence' should be understood as the place where the person factually resides, regardless of the period of time and is therefore not characterized by durability.[97] According to the explanatory report, the fact that a defendant's domicile is unknown justifies founding jurisdiction on a relatively weak connection such as defendant's actual residence[98] and it is irrelevant whether the actual residence can also be considered to be his habitual residence.[99] If, however, the defendant is domiciled abroad, but is temporarily residing in The Netherlands, the 'actual residence' criterion does not constitute sufficient connection for the ascertainment of jurisdiction,[100] and will not replace the domicile criterion.[101] Even if the defendant is domiciled abroad, Dutch courts have jurisdiction on the basis of Article 2 DCCP

---

[92] Confirmed by HR 21 December 2001, *NJ* (2002), at 282: '...*Rv ziet op het begrip "woonplaats" in de zin van Art. 1:10 BW en niet, ..., op de feitelijke verblijfplaats of feitelijke woonplaats*'.

[93] Art.1:14 DCC; Strikwerda, *Inleiding*, § 216, at 219; Strikwerda, *De Overeenkomst in het IPR*, § 106, at 52; Vlas and Ibili, 'De nieuwe commune regels', at 313; P. Vlas, *Rechtspersonen* (2002), § 231, at 111; Kramer, 'De regeling van de rechtsmacht', at 377. Art. 1:15 DCC allows an 'elected domicile', Strikwerda, *De Overeenkomst in het IPR*, § 107, at 52.

[94] J. de Boer, *C. Asser's Handleiding tot de beoefening van het Nederlands burgerlijk recht. Personen- en familierecht* (2006), § 58; De Groot, 'Tekst & Commentaar BW', Art. 10(1), note 1, '*woonstede*' previously called '*hoofdverblijf*' or principal place of residence.

[95] This definition stems from settled case law, HR 19 January 1880, W, at 4475. See for more details Koens in J. Nieuwenhuis, C. Stolker *et al.*, eds., *Burgerlijk Wetboek: De tekst van de boeken 1, 2, 3, 4 BW voorzien van commentaar* (2007), at 19; De Groot, 'Tekst & Commentaar BW', Art. 1:10(1), note 1; Verheul and Feteris, *Rechtsmacht*, at 72.

[96] Polak, Van Mierlo *et al.*, eds., *Tekst & Commentaar Rv.*, § 5, at 10.

[97] Vlas, 'Tekst & Commentaar, Rv.', Title 1, Art. 2, note 2; Polak, Van Mierlo *et al.*, eds., *Tekst & Commentaar Rv.*, § 3b, at 10; Koens in Nieuwenhuis, Stolker *et al.*, eds., *Tekst & commentaar BW*, at 19.

[98] *Explanatory Report Proposal DCCP*, at 28. The Report states that it is not necessary for the actual residence to coincide with a possible habitual residence; the latter generally requires residence for a longer period of time. Polak, Van Mierlo *et al.*, eds., *Tekst & Commentaar Rv.*, § 3, at 10; De Groot, 'Tekst & Commentaar BW', Art. 1:10(1), note 3; Verheul and Feteris, *Rechtsmacht*, at 72-73; Polak and De Rooij, *Private International Law in the Netherlands*, at 49.

[99] Polak, Van Mierlo *et al.*, eds., *Tekst & Commentaar Rv.*, § 5, at 10-11.

[100] Vlas, 'Tekst & Commentaar, Rv.', Title 1, Art. 2, note 2; Polak, Van Mierlo *et al.*, eds., *Tekst & Commentaar Rv.*, § 5, at 11; Vlas and Ibili, 'De nieuwe commune regels', at 313.

[101] Polak, Van Mierlo *et al.*, eds., *Tekst & Commentaar Rv.*, § 5, at 11.

only when the defendant's 'actual residence' can be equally qualified as his 'habitual residence' in The Netherlands.[102]

3.2.2.2 *The Habitual Residence*

Article 2 DCCP introduced a new connecting factor into Dutch jurisdiction law.[103] It emanates from Article 5(2) of the Brussels Model and Article 1 of the Hague Convention on the Protection of Minors[104] and should be interpreted by analogy.[105] The habitual residence concept is a strong factual concept and should be understood as the social place of residence, provided that the defendant resides at that place for a certain period of time.[106] This durability element distinguishes the habitual residence from the actual residence.[107]

3.2.2.3 *The Corporate Domicile*

According to Article 1:10(2) DCC a corporate defendant has his domicile, or '*woonplaats*', at the place of his statutory seat.[108] Dutch Company Law requires corporate entities to designate a statutory seat in its by-laws.[109] Generally, the statutory seat is located in the state under whose laws the company was incorporated.[110] The Netherlands adheres to the incorporation theory.[111] As a consequence, a company with its statutory seat in The Netherlands is considered to be a Dutch

[102] Ibid. and see Vlas and Ibili, 'De nieuwe commune regels', at 313.

[103] This factor was unknown to the previous jurisdictional structure. International jurisdiction was regulated by transposition of internal rules; Art. 126(2) DCCP applied the (f)actual residence concept as subsidiary criterion.

[104] Convention concerning the powers of authorities and the law applicable in respect of the protection of minors, see http://www.hcch.net.

[105] Polak, Van Mierlo *et al.*, eds., *Tekst & Commentaar Rv.*, § 4, at 10.

[106] Vlas, 'Tekst & Commentaar, Rv.', Title 1, Art. 2, note 2 states that the *résidence habituelle* is considered to be the place with which a person's life is most closely connected. See also Strikwerda, *Inleiding*, § 216, at 219; Vlas and Ibili, 'De nieuwe commune regels', at 313.

[107] Vlas, 'Tekst & Commentaar, Rv.', Title 1, Art. 2, note 2; Polak, Van Mierlo *et al.*, eds., *Tekst & Commentaar Rv.*, § 4, at 10; Kramer, 'De regeling van de rechtsmacht', at 377.

[108] Koens in Nieuwenhuis, Stolker *et al.*, eds., *Tekst & commentaar BW*, § 2, at 20; Vlas, 'Tekst & Commentaar, Rv.', Title 1, Art. 2, note 2; Polak, Van Mierlo *et al.*, eds., *Tekst & Commentaar Rv.*, § 3c, at 10; Strikwerda, *De Overeenkomst in het IPR*, § 105, at 51; Vlas and Ibili, 'De nieuwe commune regels', at 313; Vlas, *Rechtspersonen*, § 231, at 111.

[109] Vlas, 'Tekst & Commentaar, Rv.', Title 1, Art. 2, note 2; Polak, Van Mierlo *et al.*, eds., *Tekst & Commentaar Rv.*, § 3c, at 10. Second Book of the DCC: for associations, Art. 2:27(1) and (4)(a); for co-operative societies, Art. 2:27(1) and (4)(a) in conjunction with Art. 2:53a; for a '*Naamloze Vennootschap' (N.V.)* [limited liability company Ltd.], Art. 66(1) and (3); for a '*Besloten Vennootschap' (B.V.)* [private limited company (Inc.)], Art. 177(1) and (3); for a foundation, Art. 286(4)(d).

[110] Polak, Van Mierlo *et al.*, eds., *Tekst & Commentaar Rv.*, § 3c, at 10.

[111] Art. 2 '*Wet Conflictenrecht Corporaties*', Conflict of Laws Act on Corporations of 17 December 1997, *Staatsblad* 1997, 699. S. Rammeloo, *Corporations in Private International Law: A European Perspective* (2001), at 97; Vlas, *Rechtspersonen*, § 49, at 19. The Netherlands adopted special conflict of laws rules to prevent '*pseudo* foreign corporations' from escaping certain requirements under Dutch company law. Art. 1 *Wet Formeel Buitenlandse Vennootschappen* [Act on Formal Foreign Companies] apply to formal foreign companies formed under foreign company law, but carrying out activities entirely or almost entirely in The Netherlands without having any real connection with the law of the state under which the company was formed. See however the impact of Community Law on this

domiciliary even if its central administration or '*siège réel*' is located abroad.[112] Arguments in favour of using the incorporation theory to determine the corporate domicile are based on considerations of legal certainty, as a statutory seat is easier to establish in comparison to a real seat.[113] In practice, the statutory seat does not however guarantee a forum closest connected with the corporation and its activities.[114]

3.2.2.4 *The Establishment*

Article 1:14 DCC states that a person should also be considered domiciled at the place where he holds an office or a branch when it comes to matters relating to this office.[115] This article has far reaching consequences:[116] not only is it possible under Dutch law to have multiple domiciles, but it also means that a person domiciled abroad should equally be considered domiciled in The Netherlands when he has established an office or a branch within the Dutch forum. As a result, the person will be amenable for suit in Dutch courts for matters concerning the Dutch office or branch. The fact that Article 1:14 DCC limits jurisdiction to matters relating to the branch means that it asserts special jurisdiction to Dutch courts.[117]

This article is especially designed to meet the needs of the business community.[118] The Dutch jurisdictional structure extends the domicile concept by providing for both natural and legal persons[119] a second domicile at the person's office with-

---

legislation in *Inspire Art*, C-167/01, [2003] ECR I-10155. See also M. Groenleer, 'De communautaire aspecten van de Wet op de Buitenlandse Vennootschappen', *NIPR* (2001), 306-312.

[112] Polak, Van Mierlo *et al.*, eds., *Tekst & Commentaar Rv.*, § 3c, at 10; De Groot, 'Tekst & Commentaar BW', Art. 1:10(2), note 6. Negative jurisdiction conflicts arise when the law according to which the company was founded assumes jurisdiction on the basis of the real seat and not on the basis of the statutory seat, see Verheul and Feteris, *Rechtsmacht*, at 73.

[113] Verheul and Feteris, *Rechtsmacht*, at 73.

[114] However a (foreign) company that carries out activities in The Netherlands can be sued under Art. 1:14 DCC in conjunction with Art. 2 DCCP. This is not equivalent to the real seat but it does recognize a certain degree of activities on which a '*woonplaats*' can be established. De Groot, 'Tekst & Commentaar BW', Art. 1:10(2), note 6.

[115] '*Een persoon die een kantoor of een filiaal houdt, heeft ten aanzien van aangelegenheden die dit kantoor of dit filiaal betreffen mede aldaar woonplaats*'.

[116] The following authors refer to Art. 1:14 DCC in relation to Art. 2 DCCP: Vlas, 'Tekst & Commentaar, Rv.', Title 1, Art. 2, note 2; Strikwerda, *Inleiding,* § 216, at 219; Strikwerda, *De Overeenkomst in het IPR,* § 106, at 52; Vlas and Ibili, 'De nieuwe commune regels', at 313; Kramer, 'De regeling van de rechtsmacht', at 377. For more substantial comments, see in particular Vlas, *Rechtspersonen*, § 231-234, at 111-112; Polak, Van Mierlo *et al.*, eds., *Tekst & Commentaar Rv.*, § 3, at 10, makes no reference to Art. 1:14 DCC.

[117] Vlas, *Rechtspersonen*, § 232-234, at 111-112; Verheul and Feteris, *Rechtsmacht*, at 75. Matters concerning the insolvency of the office or branch are not covered under this article. See HR 21 April 1972, *NJ* (1973), at 16.

[118] Koens in Nieuwenhuis, Stolker *et al.*, eds., *Tekst & commentaar BW*, at 22 and De Groot, 'Tekst & Commentaar BW', Title 1, Art. 14, note 1, both of which refer to the article's genesis. See Explanatory Report *Toelichting-Meijers (Parlementaire Geschiedenis)*, at 51, '*Deze regel komt het bedrijfsleven tegemoet, dat slechts rekening houdt met de plaats waar iemand zijn kantoor en daarmede het centrum van zijn beroeps- of bedrijfswerkzaamheden heeft. Hetzelfde is het geval met een filiaal van een onderneming voor alle handelingen en overeenkomsten, dat op dit filiaal betrekking hebben*'.

[119] Koens in Nieuwenhuis, Stolker *et al.*, eds., *Tekst & commentaar BW*, at 21; De Boer, *C. Asser's Handleiding Personen- en Familierecht,* § 57; Vlas, *Rechtspersonen,* § 231-232, at 111; De

out them having to satisfy the same requirements of the domicile concept.[120] This idea of a 'secondary domicile' clearly covers the situation of a company incorporated under foreign law, thereby seated abroad, but factually having its real seat or secondary establishment in The Netherlands.[121]

Whether a person has an office or branch-establishment in The Netherlands should be determined on a factual basis.[122] An office or branch consists of a physical entity and should be understood as a building or space/room used by the person to carry out his business activities.[123]

3.2.3 Special Jurisdiction for Contracts

Article 6(a) and Article 6A DCCP provide for subsidiary jurisdiction rules in contractual matters when applying Article 2 DCCP does not result in a competent Dutch forum.[124] These rules grant Dutch courts special jurisdiction over contractual claims presumed to be closely connected with the Dutch forum.[125] This is a novelty in Dutch jurisdiction law, since special provisions for jurisdiction over contractual disputes were previously unknown.[126] The preliminary report justifies the introduction of contract jurisdiction arguing that the rule is internationally well-accepted and wide spread. Moreover, since the *forum actoris* rule under Article 126(3) old DCCP was abolished, the introduction of additional jurisdiction rules appeared justified.[127]

Groot, 'Tekst & Commentaar BW', Title 1, Art. 14, note 1; W. van der Grinten and J. Maeijer, eds., *C. Asser's Handleiding tot de beoefening van het Nederlands burgerlijk recht. [Vol. 2II] Rechtspersoon* (1997), § 54; Verheul and Feteris, *Rechtsmacht*, at 75.

[120] De Groot, 'Tekst & Commentaar BW', Title 1, Art. 14, note 2; Van der Grinten and Maeijer, eds., *C. Asser's Handleiding Rechtspersoon*, § 54. See also De Boer, *C. Asser's Handleiding Personen- en Familierecht*, § 57, who argues that Art. 14 establishes a 'secondary' actual residence and considers Art. 14 as an extension ('*uitbreiding*') of Art. 1:10 DCC. See in this sense HR 26 January 1933, *NJ* (1933), 655; HR 17 November 1978, *NJ* (1979), 149.

[121] De Groot, 'Tekst & Commentaar BW', Title 1, Art. 10, note 6; Strikwerda, *De Overeenkomst in het IPR*, § 106, at 52; Van der Grinten and Maeijer, eds., *C. Asser's Handleiding Rechtspersoon*, § 54: '*De rechter van de plaats waar zich een bijkantoor of filiaal bevindt, is (mede) rechter van de woonplaats, indien het een aangelegenheid is die het bijkantoor of het filiaal betreft.*'

[122] De Boer, *C. Asser's Handleiding Personen- en Familierecht,* § 57.

[123] Strikwerda, *De Overeenkomst in het IPR,* § 106, at 52; Vlas, *Rechtspersonen,* § 232, at 111; Van der Grinten and Maeijer, eds., *C. Asser's Handleiding Rechtspersoon*, § 54: '*Onder kantoor of filiaal verstaan wij een gebouw of ruimte die permanent door de rechtspersoon in verband met zijn activiteiten wordt gebruikt.*'

[124] According to the Explanatory Report, the term '*eveneens*' indicates its subsidiary nature, as Art. 6 only applies when the general jurisdiction rule under Art. 2 does not result in a Dutch competent forum. See *Explanatory Report Proposal Rv.*, at 33; Vlas, 'Tekst & Commentaar, Rv.', Title 1, Art. 6, note 1; Polak, Van Mierlo *et al.*, eds., *Tekst & Commentaar Rv.*, § 1, at 37.

[125] Polak, Van Mierlo *et al.*, eds., *Tekst & Commentaar Rv.*, § 1, at 37; Koppenol-Laforce, 'Rechtsmacht', at 7.

[126] J. Kropholler, *Europaïsches Zivilprozessrecht; Kommentar zu EuGVO und Lugano-Übereinkommen* (2005), Art. 5, § 1, at 116; J. Newton, *The Uniform Interpretation of the Brussels and Lugano Conventions* (2002), fn. 6, at 43; M. Weser, *La convention communautaire sur la compétence judiciaire et l'exécution des décisions: Etude des droits internes et des traités bilatéraux des Etats contractants* (1975), at 118.

[127] *Explanatory Report Proposal Rv.*, at 34-35; Polak, Van Mierlo *et al.*, eds., *Tekst & Commentaar Rv.*, § 5, at 31.

Article 6(a) DCCP is identical to Article 5(1) of the Brussels Convention and Article 5(1)(a) of the Brussels Regulation and reads as follows: 'In addition, the Dutch Judiciary are competent in matters relating to a contract, if the obligation in question has to be, or should have been performed in The Netherlands'.[128]

At the end of 2005 the Dutch legislator enacted a new contract provision in order to align the national international jurisdiction rules with the modifications brought by the Brussels Regulations.[129] The addition of a new provision numbered Article 6A specifically regulates jurisdiction over claims arising out of a contract for sale of goods or provision of services. Article 6A reads:

> 'For the purpose of Article 6(a), and unless otherwise agreed, the obligation in question shall be performed in The Netherlands:
> a) in the case of the sale of goods, if the goods were delivered or should have been delivered in The Netherlands under the contract,
> b) in the case of the provision of services, if the services were provided or should have been provided in The Netherlands under the contract.'[130]

As a consequence, the Dutch contract rule embodied in Articles 6(a) and 6A DCCP follows the Brussels Model despite the interpretation problems encountered with respect to Article 5(1).[131] For the interpretation of these provisions the explanatory Report refers to settled and future case law of the ECJ.[132]

In accordance with Article 6(a) DCCP when the contract is not a contract for sale of goods, nor a contract for the provision of services, the 'obligation in question' refers to the contractual obligation forming the basis of the legal proceedings.[133] The Report explicitly states that the *lex causae*, or the law governing the contract, determines the place of performance according to the *Tessili* approach taken by the

---

[128] '*De Nederlandse rechter heeft eveneens rechtsmacht in zaken betreffende verbintenissen uit overeenkomst, indien de verbintenis die aan de eis of het verzoek ten grondslag ligt, in Nederland is uitgevoerd of moet worden uitgevoerd.*' [Translation HvL].

[129] MvT 28 863, at 5; Strikwerda, *Inleiding,* § 217, at 219-220; Vlas, 'Tekst & Commentaar, Rv.' Title 1, Art. 6a, note 2; Polak, Van Mierlo *et al.*, eds., *Tekst & Commentaar Rv.*, § 2, at 47.

[130] '*Voor de toepassing van artikel 6, onderdeel a, is, tenzij anders is overeengekomen, de plaats van uitvoering in Nederland gelegen: a) voor de koop en verkoop van roerende zaken, indien de zaken volgens de overeenkomst in Nederland geleverd werden of geleverd hadden moeten worden; b) voor de verstrekking van diensten, indien de diensten volgens de overeenkomst in Nederland verstrekt werden of verstrekt hadden moeten worden.*' [Translation HvL], Act of 8 September 2005, *Staatsblad* 2005, 455; entered into force on 15 October 2005.

[131] Besides some terminological adaptations and the fact that a provision similar to Art. 5(1)(c) Brussels Regulation is lacking, the provision is identical to Art. 5(1)(b) Brussels Regulation. MvT 28 863, at 5; Vlas, 'Tekst & Commentaar, Rv.', Title 1, Art. 6a, note 2; Polak, Van Mierlo *et al.*, eds., *Tekst & Commentaar Rv.*, § 2 and 3, at 47. See Art. 6A for some terminological issues related to services such as the use of the terms '*verstrekken*' or '*verrichting van diensten*', Aanpassing MvA 28 863 D, at 4. See also Bax, 'FNC', at 111 arguing that it has often been argued that the rule often would not result in a close connection with the Dutch forum, despite its initial justification.

[132] *Explanatory Report Proposal DCCP*, at 33; see also Vlas, 'Tekst & Commentaar, Rv.', Title 1, Art. 6, note 5; S.J. Schaafsma, 'Kroniek van het internationaal privaatrecht', 10 *Nederlands Juristenblad* (2004), 513-519, at 514; Strikwerda, *De Overeenkomst in het IPR,* § 110, at 53.

[133] Case 14/76 *De Bloos v. Bouyer*, [1976] ECR 1497. Vlas, 'Tekst & Commentaar, Rv.', Title 1, Art. 6, note 5; Polak, Van Mierlo *et al.*, eds., *Tekst & Commentaar Rv.*, § 5c, at 39-40; Strikwerda, *De Overeenkomst in het IPR*, § 110, at 54; *Explanatory Report Proposal DCCP*, at 35.

ECJ.[134] If payment is due and Dutch law governs the contract, the place of performance will be determined by Article 6:116 DCC.[135] This article stipulates that the place of payment is located at the creditor's domicile. This creditor's forum is regarded as an important jurisdictional ground in contractual disputes, because it protects Dutch creditors from having to litigate abroad and results in a *veiled forum actoris.*[136]

Article 6A DCCP provides for a *lex specialis* with respect to sale of goods and service contracts.[137] The rule determines that, regardless of the obligation underlying the claim, Dutch courts are competent when the goods were or should have been delivered in The Netherlands in accordance with a sales contract, or in the event of the provision of services, when the services were or should have been provided in The Netherlands.[138] This does not mean that, in the case of the two types of contracts specified above, the claimant can turn to Article 6(a) DCCP when the place of delivery or the place where the services are to be provided are not located in The Netherlands. In that case, a Dutch forum is simply not available.[139]

When the factual delivery was made in The Netherlands, but 'under the contract' the goods should have been delivered abroad, it is uncertain whether Dutch courts are competent. Likewise, are Dutch courts competent if the goods should have been delivered in The Netherlands, but were factually delivered abroad?[140] With respect to the addition of Article 6A DCCP and the problems with its interpretation, the Minister of Justice explicitly refers to the future interpretation of Article 5(1)(b) as provided by the ECJ.[141] Uncertainty also exists when no place of delivery or provision of service was agreed upon. In that case, should the *lex causae* determine the place of performance?[142] The Minister of Justice suggested the latter during the plenary hearing of the Act regarding the provision of services.[143]

The report does not refer to the possibility of an agreed place of performance. It could however be assumed, that in conformity with the Brussels Model and in

---

[134] *Explanatory Report Proposal DCCP*, at 35. The Explanatory Report refers to Joustra's analysis of consumer contracts. This is regulated under Art. 6(c) DCCP, but at the time the article was written the draft (*Voorontwerp* Ministerie van Justitie) (1993), considered a consumer contract an ordinary contract, see C. Joustra, 'Consumentengeschillen in het Voorontwerp Burgerlijke Rechtsvordering', 93 *WPNR* (1994), 61-67, at 65; see also Kramer, 'De regeling van de rechtsmacht', at 379; Polak, Van Mierlo *et al.*, eds., *Tekst & Commentaar Rv.*, § 5d, at 40.

[135] See also Arts. 6:115-6:118 DCC.

[136] Kramer, 'De regeling van de rechtsmacht', at 379; G. Steenhoff, 'Pleidooi voor een crediteursforum bij (internationale) geldschulden', in *Het NIPR geannoteerd: Annotaties opgedragen aan Dr Mathilde Sumampouw* (1996), 194-202, at 201.

[137] Vlas, 'Tekst & Commentaar, Rv.', Title 1, Art. 6a, note 2; Polak, Van Mierlo *et al.*, eds., *Tekst & Commentaar Rv.*, § 1, at 47.

[138] Vlas, 'Tekst & Commentaar, Rv.', Title 1, Art. 6a, note 2.

[139] Ibid.

[140] Ibid.

[141] MvA 28 863, at 5, as suggested by Polak, Van Mierlo *et al.*, eds., *Tekst & Commentaar Rv.*, § 2, at 47.

[142] Vlas, 'Tekst & Commentaar, Rv.' ,Title 1, Art. 6a, note 2.

[143] MvA 28 863, at 5.

accordance with the words 'unless otherwise agreed', that parties are allowed to agree upon a specific place of performance of the contract.[144]

The concept 'contractual matters' is not further defined by the Dutch legislator nor specified by the Explanatory Report. The DCCP does not define sale of goods contracts nor contracts for the provision of services. These concepts could be determined by comparing their similarities with the autonomous interpretation of the ECJ's case law,[145] as well as by the *lex fori*.[146]

Special contract jurisdiction rules under the Brussels Model and Article 6 DCCP do not only differ with respect to their alternative and respective subsidiary nature. In contrast to Article 5(1) of the Brussels Model, which allocates jurisdiction to a specific territorially competent court,[147] Article 6 DCCP merely asserts jurisdiction to the Dutch judiciary as a whole. The internal allocation of jurisdiction is not regulated by Article 6 DCCP, but by the venue rules enacted in the subsequent titles of the DCCP.[148]

3.2.4 The *Distribution Is Attribution* Rule and the *Forum Arresti*

Article 10 DCCP only comes into play when applying other jurisdictional rules does not result in a competent Dutch court and should therefore be understood as a 'last resort' rule.[149] Its purpose is twofold: it states that Dutch courts have jurisdiction by virtue of Article 767 and also when jurisdiction derives from other statutory provisions regulating territorial jurisdiction.[150] The latter refers back to internal venue rules by way of an exception to the set of direct international jurisdiction rules enshrined in Articles 1-14 DCCP.[151] As a consequence, international jurisdiction of Dutch courts is not exhaustively regulated by Articles 1-14 DCCP. According to the explanatory report, the purpose of re-introducing the *distribution is attribution* rule is to exercise jurisdiction over cases where a particular connection between the dispute and The Netherlands would justify jurisdiction, but that are not covered by the set of direct jurisdictional rules embodied in Articles 1-14 DCCP.[152]

---

[144] Vlas, 'Tekst & Commentaar, Rv.', Title 1, Art. 6a, note 2; Polak, Van Mierlo *et al.*, eds., *Tekst & Commentaar Rv.,* § 5, at 48.

[145] Polak, Van Mierlo *et al.*, eds., *Tekst & Commentaar Rv.*, § 5b, at 39.

[146] Regulated in book 6 of the DCC. See for comments in favour, Vlas, 'Tekst & Commentaar, Rv.', Title 1, Art. 6, note 5.

[147] See the Brussels Model in Chapter 2, Sect. 2.7.

[148] Arts. 99-110 DCCP; *Explanatory Report Proposal DCCP*, at 34.

[149] Ibid., at 43.

[150] *'De Nederlandse rechter heeft rechtsmacht in het geval, bedoeld in artikel 767, alsmede indien dit voortvloeit uit andere wettelijke bepalingen tot aanwijzing van een bevoegde rechter dan die vervat in de tweede afdeling van de tweede titel en de tweede afdeling van de derde titel.'*

[151] This is only the case when the jurisdiction rule is not explicitly designed for internal cases.

[152] Vlas, 'Tekst & Commentaar, Rv.', Title 1, Art. 10, note 1; Kramer, 'De regeling van de rechtsmacht', at 384; *Explanatory Report Proposal DCCP*, at 43; *contra [comments]* Vlas and Ibili, 'De nieuwe commune regels', at 319. Examples of internal jurisdiction rules that are still transposable to international disputes are Arts. 629, 642A and 985 DCCP. Arts. 99-110 of the second title and Arts. 262-270, third title, book 1, are excluded from transposition to international cases and include among others the *forum actoris* rule under Art. 109 DCCP, the former Art. 126(3). Ibili, *Gewogen rechtsmacht,* § 3.3.1, at 41-42; Vlas, 'Tekst & Commentaar, Rv.', Title 1, Art. 10, notes 1 and 2; Polak, Van

The first part of Article 10 refers to Article 767 which is specifically designed to assert international jurisdiction over a defendant whose property has been seized in The Netherlands.[153] This *forum arresti* rule is explicitly mentioned in Article 10 because of its importance in international litigation practice.[154] The rule has a long-standing tradition in Dutch procedural law, even though it has been marked exorbitant under the Brussels Model.[155]

Article 767 states that in default of any other way to obtain an enforcement order in The Netherlands, the claim on the merits may be brought before the court whose president ordered the attachment of defendant's property.[156] The first part of Article 767 sets two conditions. First, the *forum arresti* rule only applies when no other direct rule asserts jurisdiction to Dutch courts.[157] Second, the *forum arresti* rule is not available when a foreign court has jurisdiction and its judgement is enforceable in The Netherlands as a result of international agreements.[158] The claimant will first of all have to use these means of enforcement to find relief before referring to the *forum arresti* rule of Article 767.[159] These conditions underline the subsidiary nature of Article 767 and Article 10 DCCP in general.[160] When parties have agreed upon a choice of forum clause in favour of a foreign court, the *forum arresti* rule is not available. In that respect, the Dutch Supreme Court ruled that when the chosen court's judgement is not enforceable in The Netherlands, because an international enforcement agreement is lacking, the *forum arresti* is still not available.[161] As a

---

Mierlo *et al.*, eds., *Tekst & Commentaar Rv.*', § 2, at 60; Pellis, *Internationaal Procesrecht*, § 75, at 86; Vlas and Ibili, 'De nieuwe commune regels', at 311; Polak and De Rooij, *Private International Law in the Netherlands,* at 57-58.

[153] This direct rule for international jurisdiction has however for technically legal reasons not been incorporated in the first book of the DCCP. See Strikwerda, *Inleiding*, § 220, at 225; Strikwerda, *De Overeenkomst in het IPR*, § 125, at 59.

[154] See *Explanatory Report Proposal DCCP*, at 44, although the explicit mentioning of Art. 767 DCCP is in fact superfluous; Vlas, 'Tekst & Commentaar, Rv.', Title 1, Art. 10, note 3.

[155] L. Pellis, *Forum Arresti: Aspecten van rechtsmachtscheppend (vreemdelingen-) beslag in Europa* (1993), at 7-15.

[156] Art. 767 reads: '*Bij gebrek van een andere weg om een executoriale titel in Nederland te verkrijgen kan de eis in de hoofdzaak, de vordering terzake van de beslagkosten daaronder begrepen, worden ingesteld voor de rechtbank waarvan de voorzieningenrechter het verlof tot het gelegde of het tegen zekerheidstelling voorkomen of opgeheven beslag heeft verleend. In geval van verlof tot beslag onder een derde geldt dit alleen indien het goed waarop beslag zal worden gelegd in het verzoekschrift uitdrukkelijk is omschreven.*'

[157] Strikwerda, *Inleiding,* § 220, at 225; Strikwerda, *De Overeenkomst in het IPR,* § 125, at 60; Pellis, *Forum Arresti,* at 30.

[158] Confirmed by District Court Middelburg, 28 February 2001, *NIPR* (2001), at 273-274 (considerations 4.3 and 4.4), and see also Circuit Court Rotterdam 20 December 2006, *NIPR* (2007), at 60 A. van Mierlo, 'Boek III Van regtspleging van onderscheiden aard', in *Tekst & Commentaar, Burgerlijke Rechtsvordering* (2006), note to Art. 767; Th. de Boer, 'Forum Preferences in Contemporary European Conflicts Law: The Myth of a "Neutral Choice"', in *Festschrift fuer Erik Jayme* (2004), 39-55, at 47 Strikwerda, *De Overeenkomst in het IPR,* § 125, at 60; Pellis, *Forum Arresti,* at 30.

[159] J. De Heer, 'Forum arresti-perikelen', *NIPR* (2001), 389-397, at 389.

[160] R. Flach, 'Beantwoording rechtsvraag (237) IPR/ Burgerlijk procesrecht- Conservatoir beslag zeeschepen', 44 *Ars Aequi* (1995), 305-309, at 307.

[161] See in particular HR 17 December 1993, *NJ* (1994), 350; and HR 16 June 1995, *NJ* (1996), at 256. The rationale behind this decision is simple: by agreeing upon a choice of forum clause, parties have renounced the right to access to Dutch jurisdiction and the availability of the *forum arresti* rule

consequence, the Court imposed a third condition to this rule by stating that the *forum arresti* is not applicable when a choice of forum has been made in favour of a foreign court, even if its enforcement is not possible in The Netherlands.[162]

General jurisdiction is available under the the *forum arresti* rule as it is not restricted to the nature of the claim or property, nor to the value of the assets underlying the attachment request.[163] Jurisdiction is also guaranteed if the creditor wants to sue the debtor whose goods have been attached, but are in possession of a third party. Article 767, last sentence, requires that property for the so-called *derdenbeslag* or 'third party attachment' be adequately described.[164]

Article 767 is strongly connected with Article 765 and regulates jurisdiction to take the attachment order itself. Article 765 enables a creditor to seize property of a debtor, with no known domicile in The Netherlands.[165] This attachment provision is primarily designed to attach property belonging to foreign residents and is therefore called the '*vreemdelingenbeslag*' or 'foreigners-attachment'.[166] According to Verheul, the 'original function of foreigners-attachment is to secure recovery of debt owed by a foreigner', as a consequence the purpose of the *forum arresti* rule is 'to create the jurisdiction necessary so as to be able to realize the security'.[167]

3.3 Switzerland

3.3.1 Introduction

The Swiss Private International Law Statute (PIL Statute) entered into force on 1 January 1989[168] and introduced a set of uniform Private International Law

---

in particular, even when the judgement is not enforceable in The Netherlands. See Jongbloed, Polak, Van Mierlo *et al.*, eds., *Tekst & Commentaar Rv.*, § 2, at 1037; Strikwerda, *Inleiding,* § 220, at 226.

[162] De Heer, 'Forum arresti-perikelen', at 389.

[163] Strikwerda, *Inleiding,* § 220, at 226; Strikwerda, *De Overeenkomst in het IPR,* § 127, at 61.

[164] This requirement is in order to protect the third party according to Jongbloed, see Jongbloed in Polak, Van Mierlo *et al.*, eds., *Tekst & Commentaar Rv.*, § 5, at 1037; Strikwerda, *Inleiding*, § 220, at 226; H. Oudelaar, *Recht halen; Inleiding in het executierecht en beslagrecht* (1995), at 176-178.

[165] As amended by Decree of 20 February 1990; *Staatsblad* 1991, 602; *Staatsblad* 1990, 90; entered into force on 1 January 1992: '*Indien de schuldenaar geen bekende woonplaats in Nederland heeft, kan in Nederland overeenkomstig voorgaande afdelingen van deze titel beslag worden gelegd, zonder dat vrees voor verduistering behoeft te worden aangetoond.*' See also Pellis, *Forum Arresti*, at 15-17. These provisions were hardly modified by the recent modifications to the DCCP (in Art. 767 only the word '*president*' has been replaced by *voorzieningenrechter*), see M. Polak, 'Boek 1, Titel 1: Rechtsmacht van de Nederlandse rechter', in *Tekst & Commentaar, Burgerlijke Rechtsvordering* (2002), under Art. 767.

[166] Strikwerda, *Inleiding*, § 220, at 225; Strikwerda, *De Overeenkomst in het IPR*, § 125, at 60; Pellis, *Forum Arresti,* at 125; J. Verheul, *Aspekten van Nederlands internationaal beslagrecht/Aspects of Attachment in Dutch Private International Law* (1968), at 153.

[167] Verheul, *Aspects of Attachment*, at 153-154; Verheul and Feteris, *Rechtsmacht*, at 103; Jongbloed in Polak, Van Mierlo *et al.*, eds., *Tekst & Commentaar Rv.*, § 1, at 1036; Strikwerda, *Inleiding*, § 220, at 225; Pellis, *Forum Arresti,* at 17 and 29.

[168] Before the PIL Statute, jurisdiction in international disputes was determined by transposing the inter-cantonal jurisdiction rules of the 1891 'Statute on the private law conditions of domiciliary and sojourners' known as 'NAG'. As a consequence, the domicile criterion was used in international matters but contracts and torts jurisdiction were unknown to the NAG. In 1973, a Committee of Experts

rules,[169] replacing cantonal legislation.[170] The PIL Statute consists of direct international jurisdiction rules but it also allocates jurisdiction among courts of the Swiss cantons.[171] According to the Explanatory Report, the Swiss PIL Statute is strongly influenced by the 1968 Brussels Convention[172] and it went into force one year before the Lugano Convention was signed in 1988. Both instruments were negotiated and drafted simultaneously.

The set of jurisdiction rules principally bases jurisdiction on a close connection between the claim and the forum,[173] with the exception of the *forum arresti* rule, which the Swiss legislator did not want to abolish.[174] Despite the fact that the Swiss jurisdiction rules have been modelled on the Brussels Model, the Swiss PIL Statute's structure differs considerably not only from the Brussels Model, but also from other Continental European jurisdictional regimes. This makes the Swiss jurisdictional regime particularly interesting.

The Swiss PIL Statute regulates private international law issues on an area-by-area basis. Apart from a first chapter containing general provisions, each chapter regulates a particular private international law question, such as international jurisdiction and applicable law, in a specific area of law.[175] By way of illustration, Chapter 3 deals with marriage, Chapter 4 with divorce, Chapter 9 deals with the law on obligations and Chapter 10 with companies.[176]

---

was set up to work on a PIL Statute. P. Karrer, K. Arnold *et al.*, *Switzerland's Private International Law*, ed. trans. Switzerland's Private International Law (1994), at 6.

[169] The Statute covers most of the Private International Law areas, including family and commercial matters, intellectual property, bankruptcy and international arbitration. It provides for direct international jurisdiction rules, regulates the applicable law and determines the recognition and enforcement of foreign judgements. The versions in the three official languages are of equal value. See for a comparison with other PIL Statutes in Europe, G. Broggini, 'La nouvelle loi fédérale sur le droit internationale privé: Considérations comparées', *Schweizerisches Jahrbuch für internationales Recht: Annuaire suisse de droit international et européen* (1988), 132-136; and B. Dutoit, 'Deux lois de droit international privé: Jusqu'ou la Suisse et l'Italie convergent-elles?', in *Collisio Legum* (1997), 137-168.

[170] The Swiss Confederation consists of 26 'cantons', all of which enjoy a certain degree of autonomy in issues of civil procedure.

[171] A. Schnyder and M. Liatowitsch, *Internationales Privat- und Zivilverfahrensrecht* (2006), § 280, at 99; P. Volken, ed., *Conflits de Juridictions, entraide judiciaire, reconnaissance et exécution de jugements étrangers* (1988), at 241; Y. Donzallaz, 'Convention de Lugano et Loi fédérale sur les fors: Comparaison et relations', *Aktuelle Juristische Praxis* (2000), 1259-1268, at 1261.

[172] Expertenkommission, *Bundesgesetz über das internationale Privatrecht (IPR-Gesetz): Schlussbericht der Expertenkommission zum Gestezesentwurf* (1979), at 59.

[173] F. Vischer and P. Volken, *Bundesgesetz über das internationale Privatrecht (IPR-Gesetz): Gesetzentwurf der Expertenkommission und Begleitbericht* (1978), at 59.

[174] Expertenkommission, *Schlussbericht,* at 59.

[175] For instance matters concerning individuals, marriage, parental authority, inheritance, real rights, the law of obligations, intellectual property, company law, bankruptcy and international arbitration. See Art. 1 of the PIL Statute for its field of application.

[176] Chap. 12 deals with international arbitration and exclusive jurisdiction is regulated over matters concerning immoveable property in Chap. 7. Art. 97 of the PIL Statute also provides for imperative jurisdiction, mainly involving family law matters, from which parties cannot derogate by way of a jurisdiction agreement, see Art. 59 (divorce) and Art. 66 (affiliation). See F. Knoepfler, Ph. Schweizer *et al.*, eds., *Droit international privé suisse* (2005), § 595, at 329.

The first chapter defines several general concepts such as for instance 'domicile' and 'habitual residence' for natural persons and the 'seat' for corporate entities[177] and enshrines principles of international jurisdiction:[178] Article 2 establishes the *actor sequitur forum rei* maxim[179] and Article 4 asserts jurisdiction over non-domiciliaries if their property was seized (sequestrated) in Switzerland.

Both rules are subordinated to all the other jurisdiction provisions covering specific areas, outlined in the subsequent chapters and are therefore merely subsidiarily applicable.[180] Article 2 states that 'unless otherwise provided by this Statute, jurisdiction lies with the Swiss judicial or administrative authorities at the defendant's domicile'.[181] In theory, the rule is designed to fill the gaps in the jurisdictional structure. But the connecting factor of defendant's domicile is enacted in several other chapters, including the contract chapter, and plays a predominant role in the structure of the PIL Statute.[182] In practice, Article 2 will therefore rarely be applied and is of mere symbolic value.[183] The former Article 59 of the Swiss Constitution guaranteed Swiss domiciliaries access to Swiss court, considered as their '*juge naturel*', in order to protect them from being sued in foreign courts.[184] The Constitution has however weakened its position with respect to the exclusivity of Swiss courts to rule over Swiss domiciliaries and allowed derogation of the *forum rei* rule by law.[185]

---

[177] Arts. 20 and 21, respectively. Nationality is defined in Art. 22 for jurisdictional questions in family law as well as for questions concerning the applicable law.

[178] Arts. 5-12 are not subsidiarily applicable, but are of a more general interest in regulating jurisdiction agreements (Art. 5), including tacit agreements (Art. 6) and arbitration agreements (Art. 7) as well as jurisdiction over counter-claims (Art. 8), *lis pendens* provisions (Art. 9) and provisional measures (Art. 10).

[179] Except in matters relating to exclusive jurisdiction.

[180] Suisse Conseil fédéral, 'Message du Conseil fédéral concernant une loi fédérale sur le droit international privé', FF1983 I 250-501 (1983), § 213.2, at 35-36; P. Volken, M. Keller *et al.*, *Zürcher Kommentar zum IPRG: Kommentar zum Bundesgesetz über das Internationale Privatrecht (IPRG) vom 18. Dezember 1987* (2004), § 57, at 33 and § 30-33, at 43; H. Honsell, A. Schnyder *et al.*, eds., *Internationales Privatrecht* (2007), § 4, at 31 and § 6, at 32; B. Dutoit, ed., *Droit international privé suisse: Commentaire de la loi fédérale du 18 décembre 1987* (2005), § 4, at 7 and § 2, at 9.

[181] As translated by Karrer, Arnold *et al.*, *Switzerland's Private International Law*, at 33; Expertenkommission, *Schlussbericht*, at 43. According to Berti the rule is '*die klassische Präsenzanknüpfung*'. See also Honsell, Schnyder *et al.*, eds., *Internationales Privatrecht*, § 9, at 23.

[182] Volken, Keller *et al.*, *Zürcher Kommentar zum IPRG: Kommentar zum Bundesgesetz über das Internationale Privatrecht (IPRG) vom 18. Dezember 1987*, § 2, at 38; and see Volken, ed., *Conflits de Juridictions*, at 241. Defendant's domicile is used as connecting factor in a dozen other specific chapters such as Arts. 43, 109, 112, 127, 129.

[183] A. Bucher and A. Bonomi, *Droit international privé* (2004), § 81, at 23; Volken, Keller *et al.*, *Zürcher Kommentar zum IPRG*, § 19, at 41.

[184] 29 May 1874, as amended: 'the solvent debtor having a domicile in Switzerland must be sued, for personal debts, before the judge of his domicile; therefore, property may not be seized or attached outside the Canton in which he has his domicile'. Translation taken from Karrer, Arnold *et al.*, *Switzerland's Private International Law*; for comments see Conseil fédéral, 'Message du Conseil fédéral', at 35; Vischer and Volken, *IPR-Gesetzentwurf der Expertenkommission,* at 59. Bucher and Bonomi, *Droit international privé*, § 81, at 23; S. Baumgartner, *The Proposed Hague Convention on Jurisdiction and Foreign Judgements: Trans-Atlantic Law Making for Transnational Litigation* (2003), at 147.

[185] Art. 30(2) of the Swiss Constitution reads: 'A person against whom a civil action is brought has the right to have the case heard before the court at the person's domicile. Legislation may provide

Article 3 provides for a *forum necessitatis* if proceedings abroad are 'impossible or highly impracticable' under the condition that the Swiss forum is sufficiently connected to the case.[186] The Statute regulates prorogation of jurisdiction by choice of court agreements in Article 5 and by implied consent in Article 6.[187] It should be noted that if parties agree upon a choice of forum clause in favour of a Swiss court, the latter should accept the prorogation of jurisdiction.[188] The chosen court may decline jurisdiction when there is no connection between the dispute and the Swiss forum.[189] Such a connection is assumed to exist when one of the parties is domiciled or resident or has a business establishment in the chosen forum or if, Swiss law governs the dispute.[190] Apart from the limited form of discretion allowed in Articles 3 and 5, the Swiss jurisdictional regime should be understood as a closed system: if the PIL Statute's set of jurisdictional rules does not assert jurisdiction to a Swiss court, then the Swiss judiciary will not be competent.[191]

3.3.2 The Contract Chapter

Chapter 9 deals with the law on obligations in general and the first section deals with contracts in particular.[192] The term 'contractual matters' should be understood in its broadest sense and includes any relation arising out of a contract according to Swiss contract law.[193] Jurisdiction of Swiss courts in international contractual disputes concerning ordinary contracts is exhaustively regulated in Articles 112 and 113.[194] Article 112 of the Statute covers contracts in general and reads:

---

for another jurisdiction.' Volken, Keller *et al.*, *Zürcher Kommentar zum IPRG*, § 6, at 39; Bucher and Bonomi, *Droit international privé*, § 81, at 23.

[186] French version: '*impossible ou qu'on ne peut raisonablement exiger qu'elle le soit*'. See also A. von Mehren, 'Theory and Practice of Adjudicatory Authority in Private International Law: A Comparative Study of the Doctrine, Policies and Practices of Common- and Civil-Law systems: General Course on Private International Law (1996)', 295 *Recueil des cours* (2003), 9-431, at 193.

[187] General rules for counter-claims are established in Art. 8, *lis pendens* is regulated in Art. 9 and jurisdiction for provisional matters is regulated in Art. 10.

[188] Dutoit, ed., *Commentaire*, § 10, at 17.

[189] Ibid.; K. Siehr, 'Switzerland National Report', in *Declining Jurisdiction in Private International Law* (1995), 381-399, at 388-389; Conseil fédéral, 'Message du Conseil fédéral', at 38 (no. 213.6).

[190] Art. 5(3) PIL Statute; Dutoit, ed., *Commentaire*, § 10, at 19; Siehr, 'Switzerland', at 395.

[191] The PIL Statute regulates international jurisdiciton in a '*ortlich abschließend*' manner; Tribunal Fédéral 3 March 1998, ATF 124 III 176 or '*exclusivement*'; Tribunal Fédéral 29 November 1990, ATF 116 II 622; Schnyder and Liatowitsch, *Internationales Privat- und Zivilverfahrensrecht*, § 55, at 32; Knoepfler, Schweizer *et al.*, eds., *Droit international privé suisse*, § 609, at 337; P. Patocchi, E. Geisinger *et al.*, *Internationales Privatrecht: Das IPRG sowie die wichtigsten völkerrechtlichen Verträge und Schiedsgerichtsordnungen* (2000), at 65; and Vischer and Volken, *IPR-Gesetzentwurf der Expertenkommission*, at 59.

[192] It has to involve an international contract; this is already the case when one of the parties is domiciled outside Switzerland. See Art. 1 PIL Statute which requires an international element; Honsell, Schnyder *et al.*, eds., *Internationales Privatrecht*, § 1, at 785.

[193] This includes pre-contractual claims known as *culpa in contrahendo* under Swiss law. Honsell, Schnyder *et al.*, eds., *Internationales Privatrecht*, at 786; Dutoit, ed., *Commentaire*, § 2*bis*, at 362; Bucher and Bonomi, *Droit international privé*, § 889, at 243.

[194] Art. 114 deals with consumer contracts and Art. 115 with employment contracts; both articles prevail over Arts. 112 and 113; Dutoit, ed., *Commentaire*, § 2, at 362; A. von Overbeck, 'La compé-

'1. Swiss courts have jurisdiction over a defendant in the place where his or her domicile, or if there is none, his or her habitual residence is located for actions arising out of a contract.[195]
2. Swiss courts have also jurisdiction over a defendant at the place of his or her business establishment for actions arising out of the activity of that business establishment.'[196]

Article 113 states that 'when the defendant has neither a domicile, nor a habitual residence, or a place of business in Switzerland, but the disputed obligation must be performed in Switzerland, the action may be brought before the Swiss court at the place of performance'.[197]

In other words, jurisdiction over contractual disputes is regulated by a hierarchical structure of four connecting factors; primarily the defendant's domicile, subsidiarily his habitual residence, alternatively to these two first connecting factors is the 'place of business', and lastly – and subordinated to the previous connecting factor – the place of performance.[198] If none of these connecting factors provide for a competent Swiss court, only the general provisions of Chapter 1, such as Article 4, could still grant jurisdiction to Swiss judiciary powers. These provisions also apply when the validity of the contract is disputed.[199]

3.3.2.1 *Defendant's Forum*

Article 112(1) PIL Statute primarily asserts jurisdiction to Swiss courts in contractual disputes when the defendant is domiciled in Switzerland. The defendant's domicile prevails over the subsequent connecting factors listed in Articles 112 and 113 for jurisdiction in contractual disputes.[200]

---

tence internationale directe et indirecte dans le projet de loi suisse sur le droit international privé', in *Festschrift für Konrad Zweigert zum 70. Geburtstag* (1981), 307-321, at 313.

[195] Translation by Dutoit, see Dutoit, ed., *Commentaire*, at 361. French version: '*Les tribunaux suisses du domicile ou, à défaut de domicile, ceux de la résidence habituelle du défendeur sont compétents pour connaître des actions découlant d'un contrat.*'

[196] French version: '*Les tribunaux suisses du lieu où le défendeur a son établissement sont aussi compétents pour connaître des actions relatives à une obligation découlant de l'exploitation de cet établissement.*'

[197] Translation by Dutoit, see Dutoit, ed., *Commentaire*, at 365. French version: '*Lorsque le défendeur n'a ni domicile ou résidence habituelle, ni établissement en Suisse, mais que la préstation litigieuse doit être exécutée en Suisse, l'action peut être portée devant le tribunal suisse du lieu d'éxecution.*' German version: '*... ist aber die Leistung in der Schweiz zu erbringen, so kann beim schweizerischen Gericht am Erfüllungsort geklagt werden.*'

[198] Honsell, Schnyder *et al.*, eds., *Internationales Privatrecht*, § 2, at 785.

[199] Dutoit, ed., *Commentaire*, § 3, at 366; Patocchi, Geisinger *et al.*, *Internationales Privatrecht*, at 372.

[200] This results from the constitutional guarantee under former Art. 59 Swiss Constitution. Honsell, Schnyder *et al.*, eds., *Internationales Privatrecht*, § 4, at 786; Dutoit, ed., *Commentaire*, § 1, at 365; Bucher and Bonomi, *Droit international privé*, § 900, at 246; Volken, Keller *et al.*, *Zürcher Kommentar zum IPRG*, § 6, at 1165.

Article 20(1)(a) defines a natural person's domicile as 'the place where he resides with the intent of establishing permanent residence'.[201] This provision, identical to Article 23 of the Swiss Civil Code,[202] contains an objective criterion – the place where he lives – and a subjective criterion – the person's intention.[203] In order to prevent multiple forums, a party to a dispute is not allowed to have two domiciles under Article 20(2) of the PIL Statute.[204]

The PIL Statute provides for the habitual residence as a subsidiary connecting factor.[205] When the individual defendant is not domiciled but habitually resident in Switzerland, Swiss courts are still competent in contractual disputes.[206] The habitual residence criterion has a more temporary character, is less concerned with the person's centre of interests and is only available to natural persons.[207]

The corporate domicile is determined by Article 21(1) and is equivalent to its registered office. Article 21(2) stipulates that a company's seat is located at the place designated in the company's by-laws. If however, there is no such designation, Article 21(2) states that the registered office is located 'at the place where the company is in fact managed'.[208] This means that the place where defendant has its statutory seat is primarily conclusive to determine the corporate domicile and that the 'real seat' theory is only subsidiarily applicable.[209] Any fictive designation of the incorporation seat is considered as fraud, in which case the real seat theory will then be the conclusive factor.[210]

---

[201] Dutoit, ed., *Commentaire*, at 82.

[202] Although not applicable and excluded by Art. 20(2), settled case law interpreting Art. 23 of the Swiss Civil Code could be used for the interpretation of Art. 20(1) of the PIL Statute. Honsell, Schnyder *et al.*, eds., *Internationales Privatrecht*, § 9, at 196; Schnyder and Liatowitsch, *Internationales Privat- und Zivilverfahrensrecht*, § 545, at 194; Volken, Keller *et al.*, *Zürcher Kommentar zum IPRG*, § 16, at 305; Dutoit, ed., *Commentaire*, § 1, at 83.

[203] A person should have the intention of making that place the centre of his familiar, professional or financial activities and interests. Honsell, Schnyder *et al.*, eds., *Internationales Privatrecht*, § 12-14, at 196-197; Conseil fédéral, 'Message du Conseil fédéral', § 215.1-2, at 52-53; Dutoit, ed., *Commentaire*, § 1, at 83; Expertenkommission, *Schlussbericht,* at 71-73 and 76-79.

[204] Schnyder and Liatowitsch, *Internationales Privat- und Zivilverfahrensrecht,* § 547, at 194.

[205] Honsell, Schnyder *et al.*, eds., *Internationales Privatrecht*, § 9, at 788; Bucher and Bonomi, *Droit international privé,* § 898, at 245; Volken, Keller *et al.*, *Zürcher Kommentar zum IPRG*, § 10, at 1166.

[206] When the defendant has no domicile at all, the habitual residence criterion is assimilated with the domicile concept by Art. 20(2). See Dutoit, ed., *Commentaire*, § 10, at 86; Volken, ed., *Conflits de Juridictions,* at 241.

[207] Art. 20(1)(b) states that a person has his 'habitual residence in the country in which he or she is living for a certain period of time, even if this period initially appears to be of limited duration'. Dutoit, ed., *Commentaire*, § 5, at 84; Bucher and Bonomi, *Droit international privé*, § 899, at 245; Conseil fédéral, 'Message du Conseil fédéral', at 55 (no. 215.3); Expertenkommission, *Schlussbericht*, at 73-75; Honsell, Schnyder *et al.*, eds., *Internationales Privatrecht*, § 22, at 199.

[208] Translation by Dutoit, in Dutoit, ed., *Commentaire*, at 87.

[209] Honsell, Schnyder *et al.*, eds., *Internationales Privatrecht*, § 5, at 203; Dutoit, ed., *Commentaire*, § 1-2, at 87; Volken, Keller *et al.*, *Zürcher Kommentar zum IPRG*, § 4, at 317 and § 7, at 318.

[210] Dutoit, ed., *Commentaire*, § 2, at 87

3.3.2.2 *Place of Business*

In terms of claims related to the establishment's activities,[211] when the defendant is not domiciled or habitually resident in Switzerland, the second paragraph of Article 112 still provides for a competent Swiss forum when the defendant has a 'place of business' or 'business establishment' in Switzerland.[212] This connecting factor is alternatively applicable to the domicile or habitual residence of defendant.[213]

Whether the connecting factor 'place of business' or 'business establishment' provides for branch jurisdiction in contractual matters depends on its definition. A distinction should be made between the place of business of an individual and a place of business of a corporation.[214] An individual defendant has 'his business establishment at the center of his professional or commercial activities'.[215] This definition does not impose that there be a commercial activity, a mere activity providing for an income is sufficient, but it should be carried out in a continuous manner.[216] In fact the place of business should be understood as a place from which the centre of the defendant's activities is carried out, and does not necessarily coincide with his domicile.[217] It should however not be understood as a branch-establishment.

Article 21(3) indicates that a corporation's business establishment is at the 'place where it has its registered office or a branch'.[218] For the purpose of Arti-

---

[211] Honsell, Schnyder *et al.*, eds., *Internationales Privatrecht*, § 11, at 788 Dutoit, ed., *Commentaire*, § 6, at 364; Bucher and Bonomi, *Droit international privé*, § 900, at 246; Volken, Keller *et al.*, *Zürcher Kommentar*, § 28, at 1169.

[212] '*Etablissement*' or '*Niederlassung*', see Dutoit, ed., *Commentaire*, § 4, at 88; Vischer and Volken, *IPR-Gesetzentwurf der Expertenkommission,* at 135; Schnyder and Liatowitsch, *Internationales Privat- und Zivilverfahrensrecht,* § 560, at 197. Like the domicile concept, the connecting factor 'business-establishment' is also used in other chapters. If defendant has a (business-) establishment in Switzerland he can also be sued for claims in relation to unjust enrichment (Art. 127), unlawful acts or torts (Art. 129(1)) and direct claims concerning insurance (Art. 131), alternatively applicable in the place where the act occurred or where it has its effect.

[213] This is important only with respect to the internal allocation between Swiss courts, for example when the defendant is domiciled in one canton and has a place of business in another, the claimant may choose. Honsell, Schnyder *et al.*, eds., *Internationales Privatrecht*, § 11, at 788; Schnyder and Liatowitsch, *Internationales Privat- und Zivilverfahrensrecht,* § 1068, at 369; Bucher and Bonomi, *Droit international privé,* § 900, at 246; Volken, Keller *et al.*, *Zürcher Kommentar zum IPRG*, § 25, at 1168.

[214] Dutoit, ed., *Commentaire*, § 7, at 85, § 3, at 88; Volken, Keller *et al.*, *Zürcher Kommentar zum IPRG*, § 55, at 312.

[215] Art. 20(1)(c) as translated by Dutoit, in Dutoit, ed., *Commentaire*, at 82. French version: '*a son établissement dans l'Etat dans lequel se trouve le centre de ses activités professionnelles ou commerciales*'. German version: ‚*ihre Niederlassung in dem Staat, in dem sich der Mittelpunkt ihrer geschäftlichen Tätigkeiten befindet*'.

[216] Honsell, Schnyder *et al.*, eds., *Internationales Privatrecht*, § 28, at 200; Schnyder and Liatowitsch, *Internationales Privat- und Zivilverfahrensrecht,* § 553, at 195; Dutoit, ed., *Commentaire*, § 7, at 85; Volken, Keller *et al.*, *Zürcher Kommentar zum IPRG*, § 56, at 313; Bucher and Bonomi, *Droit international privé*, § 901, at 246; Conseil fédéral, 'Message du Conseil fédéral', § 215.4, at 56.

[217] Honsell, Schnyder *et al.*, eds., *Internationales Privatrecht*, § 30, at 200; Dutoit, ed., *Commentaire*, § 7, at 85; Volken, Keller *et al.*, *Zürcher Kommentar zum IPRG*, § 57, at 313.

[218] As translated by Dutoit, in Dutoit, ed., *Commentaire,* at 87. French version: '*L'établissement d'une société se trouve dans l'Etat dans lequel elle a son siège ou une succursale.*' German version: '*Die Niederlassung einer Gesellschaft befindet sich in dem Staat, in dem sie ihren Sitz oder Zweignie-*

cle 112(2) PIL Statute a corporate defendant's 'establishment' should principally be understood as a 'branch'.[219] As a result, a foreign company with a 'business establishment' in Switzerland has a branch in Switzerland, which subjects him to the jurisdiction of Swiss courts in relation to contractual claims. Regrettably, the PIL Statute does not specify the meaning of the term 'branch' for jurisdictional purposes.[220] Little guidance is provided by a decision of the Swiss Federal Tribunal where branch is defined 'as any commercial establishment, carrying out similar activities on a regular basis in specific areas as the principal establishment of whom it is dependant and is legally part of, but nevertheless enjoys of a certain level of autonomy in the commercial and economic stream of business'.[221] The PIL Statute's preliminary report explains that the purpose of a branch is to realize the commercial goals of the principal establishment.[222] Under Swiss law a branch has no legal personality, which implies that jurisdiction can be based on a business establishment with no legal status.[223] Conversely, for jurisdictional purposes offices established only to receive payment or deliveries are not considered branch offices.[224]

Swiss jurisdiction law acknowledges the importance of having a place of business in Switzerland in order to establish jurisdiction in contractual disputes, but an independent provision for branch jurisdiction is non-existent.[225]

3.3.2.3 *Place of Performance*

As last resort, when the defendant is not domiciled, not habitually resident and has no business establishment in Switzerland, Swiss courts are competent when the disputed obligation is to be performed in Switzerland.[226] This rule enables a

derlassung hat'. See also Honsell, Schnyder *et al.*, eds., *Internationales Privatrecht*, § 8, at 203; Dutoit, ed., *Commentaire*, § 3, at 88.

[219] A corporation's registered office would fall under Art. 112(1) PIL Statute, see Honsell, Schnyder *et al.*, eds., *Internationales Privatrecht*, § 13; Dutoit, ed., *Commentaire*, § 6, at 364.

[220] Honsell, Schnyder *et al.*, eds., *Internationales Privatrecht*, § 10, at 203; Dutoit, ed., *Commentaire*, § 4, at 88; Schnyder and Liatowitsch, *Internationales Privat- und Zivilverfahrensrecht*, § 561, at 198; Volken, Keller *et al.*, *Zürcher Kommentar zum IPRG*, § 8, at 318.

[221] *'Tout établissement commercial qui, dans la dépendance d'une entreprise principale dont il fait juridiquement partie, exerce d'une façon durable, dans des locaux séparés une activité similaire, en jouissant d'une certaine autonomie dans le monde économique et celui des affaires.'* Tribunal Fédéral, 17 March 1982, ATF 108 II 122; Honsell, Schnyder *et al.*, eds., *Internationales Privatrecht*, § 11, at 204; Dutoit, ed., *Commentaire*, § 4, at 88; Volken, Keller *et al.*, *Zürcher Kommentar zum IPRG*, § 8-10, at 318-319; Bucher and Bonomi, *Droit international privé*, § 901, at 246; Karrer, Arnold *et al.*, *Switzerland's Private International Law*, at 49.

[222] Conseil fédéral, 'Message du Conseil fédéral', at 57 (no. 215.4).

[223] Honsell, Schnyder *et al.*, eds., *Internationales Privatrecht*, § 13, at 789; Dutoit, ed., *Commentaire*, § 4, at 88.

[224] Karrer, Arnold *et al.*, *Switzerland's Private International Law*, at 49.

[225] Conseil fédéral, 'Message du Conseil fédéral', at 57 (no. 215.4).

[226] Honsell, Schnyder *et al.*, eds., *Internationales Privatrecht*, § 1, at 792; Dutoit, ed., *Commentaire*, § 1, at 364; Knoepfler, Schweizer *et al.*, eds., *Droit international privé suisse*, § 594, at 328; Volken, Keller *et al.*, *Zürcher Kommentar zum IPRG*, § 5-6, at 1173; Bucher and Bonomi, *Droit international privé*, § 903, at 247; Schnyder and Liatowitsch, *Internationales Privat- und Zivilverfahrensrecht*, § 1076, at 372; Expertenkommission, *Schlussbericht*, at 212.

claimant to bring suit against a foreign defendant in Swiss courts on the basis that the contractual claim is connected to the Swiss forum by virtue of its performance.

The French version determines that the place of performance involves the performance of the '*prestation litigieuse*' corresponding to the obligation in question, and not with the characteristic performance or the performance of any obligation arising out of the contract.[227]

The place of performance is determined on the basis of the place where the obligation was performed or should have been performed. According to Dutoit this means that the contractual place of performance prevails over the factual place of performance.[228] In the event no place of performance is determined under the contract, it is still disputed whether the *lex fori*, i.e. Swiss law, or the *lex causae*, i.e. the law governing the contract, should determine the place of performance.[229] The Swiss Federal Court refused to explicitly decide between the two approaches, but in a decision of 1 June 2004 the Court, without any further explanation, applied the *lex fori* to determine the place of performance.[230]

3.3.3 The General Rule of the *Forum Arresti*

Article 4 states that, unless this Statute provides for any other competent court in Switzerland, a lawsuit related to the validation of an attachment may be brought at the place of the attachment.[231] The *forum arresti* is hereby subsidiairily[232] applicable to any other jurisdiction rule provided by the PIL Statute, with the exception of the *forum necessitatis* rule provided in Article 3.[233] In contractual disputes the

[227] Honsell, Schnyder *et al.*, eds., *Internationales Privatrecht*, § 6, at 793; Dutoit, ed., *Commentaire*, § 3, at 366; Volken, Keller *et al.*, *Zürcher Kommentar zum IPRG*, § 16, at 1176. With respect to the different options presented in several drafts preceding the final text, see Expertenkommission, *Schlussbericht*, at 212; see also Lagarde's observations in P. Lagarde, 'Compétence judiciaire contrats suisse', Kolloquium über des schwiezerischen Entwurf zu einem Bundesgesetz über das internationale Privatrecht, Freiburg (1979), at 48-49.

[228] Dutoit, ed., *Commentaire*, § 2, at 366; but see also Honsell, Schnyder *et al.*, eds., *Internationales Privatrecht*, § 14, at 797.

[229] Dutoit, ed., *Commentaire*, § 2, at 366; Schnyder and Liatowitsch, *Internationales Privat- und Zivilverfahrensrecht*, § 1077, at 372; H. Honsell, N. Vogt *et al.*, *Kommentar zum Schweizerischen Privatrecht: Internationales Privatrecht* (1996), at 765 (no. 14). Patocchi claims that it generally is the *lex causae*, see Patocchi, Geisinger *et al.*, *Internationales Privatrecht*, at 373 (no. 3) and P. Patocchi and E. Geisinger, *Code de droit international privé suisse annoté* (1995), at 310 (no. 1). This question is left open by the Federal Court, see Tribunal Fédéral, 25 August 2003, ATF 129 III 738.

[230] Honsell, Schnyder *et al.*, eds., *Internationales Privatrecht*, § 14, at 797; Tribunal Fédéral, 1 June 2004, ATF 130 III 462.

[231] French version: '*Lorsque la présente loi ne prévoit aucun autre for en Suisse, l'action en validation de séquestre peut être introduite au for suisse du séquestre.*'

[232] Dutoit, ed., *Commentaire*, § 2, at 9; Volken, Keller *et al.*, *Zürcher Kommentar zum IPRG*, § 6, at 60 and § 18-21, at 62.

[233] Volken, Keller *et al.*, *Zürcher Kommentar zum IPRG*, § 22-25, at 62-63; J. Krafft, *'Exorbitante' Gerichtsstände im internationalen Zivilprozessrecht der Schweiz: Insbesondere nach dem Lugano-Übereinkommen* (1999), at 88-94; A. Bittighofer, *Der internationale Gerichtsstand des Vermögens: Eine Rechtvergleichende Studie zur Zuständigkeit deutscher Gerichte aufgrund inländischer Vermögensbelegenheit* (1994), at 112-119, Vischer and Volken, *IPR-Gesetzentwurf der Expertenkommission*, at 70. Initially this article was incorporated in the Statute as a special jurisdiction rule (Art. 12 draft).

provision only comes into play when the defendant is not domiciled, not habitually resident and has no business establishment in Switzerland and finally when the performance of the obligation in question is not due in Switzerland.[234]

A federal *forum arresti* rule,[235] especially designed for international disputes, is provided in Article 4.[236] This Swiss version of property-based jurisdiction is limited to actions involving attached property.[237] Article 4 requires that property be properly[238] seized in accordance with the provisions of the Swiss Debts and Insolvency Act (SDIA);[239] the mere presence of defendant's property in the Swiss forum is not enough for jurisdiction.[240]

Article 271(4) SDIA regulates a sequestration order as a kind of provisional measure, allowing the attachment of property especially belonging to persons not domiciled in Switzerland, which results in an '*Ausländerarrest*'.[241] The kind of property that would be available for attachment is pawnable property.[242] For the attachment of the property itself, Article 271(4) requires that there is a 'sufficient connection' with Switzerland.[243] This implicitly guarantees a certain connection between the claim and the attached property located in the forum. It is not required

---

[234] It also becomes relevant when no jurisdiction agreement was made under Art. 5 or when no tacit agreement was made under Art. 6. See the Federal Tribunal's decision of 18 February 1992, ATF 118 II 190; Volken, Keller *et al.*, *Zürcher Kommentar zum IPRG*, § 26-29, at 63; Knoepfler, Schweizer *et al.*, eds., *Droit international privé suisse*, § 617, at 352.

[235] This *forum arresti* rule is marked as 'exorbitant' under Art. 3 of the Lugano Convention, but that would not prevent the claimant from seizing the assets that are located in Switzerland of a defendant domiciled in a Contracting State. See on the Brussels and Lugano Model, Chapter 2, Sect. 2.2.7 and P. Volken, 'Der EuGH knackt den Ausländerarrest', 4 *Swiss Review of International and European Law* (1994), at 1, who states, in reaction to a decision of the ECJ of 10 February 1994, that '*Demgegenüber ist der Arrest im internationalen Verkehr schon möglich*'. See for a more general study of the influence of the Lugano Convention on Art. 4 PIL Statute, R. Gassmann, *Arrest im Internationalen Rechtsverkehr: Zum Einfluss des Lugano-Ubereinkommens auf das schwiezerische Arrestrecht* (1998) Chaps. 2 and 3; Schnyder and Liatowitsch, *Internationales Privat- und Zivilverfahrensrecht*, § 5, at 82-83 and § 964, at 336-337.

[236] Rather than having 26 different cantonal rules, Art. 4 PIL Statute introduced a unified concept. Honsell, Schnyder *et al.*, eds., *Internationales Privatrecht*, § 3, 38; Dutoit, ed., *Commentaire*, § 1, at 9; Volken, Keller *et al.*, *Zürcher Kommentar zum IPRG*, § 5, at 59; Conseil fédéral, 'Message du Conseil fédéral', at 36.

[237] For comparisons with the French '*saisie conservatoire*' or the German '*arrest*', see J. Piegai, *La protection du débiteur et des tiers dans le nouveau droit du séquestre* (1997), 48-55.

[238] Honsell, Schnyder *et al.*, eds., *Internationales Privatrecht*, § 5, at 38; see for the conditions for a valid attachment, Gassmann, *Arrest*, at 10.

[239] Arts. 271-279 of the '*Loi fédérale sur la poursuite pour dettes et de la faillite*' or '*Bundesgesetz über Schuldbetreibung und Konkurs*' or Swiss Debts and Insolvency Act. The attachment itself should be distinguished from its validation, see Knoepfler, Schweizer *et al.*, eds., *Droit international privé suisse,* § 617, at 351. Karrer, Arnold *et al.*, *Switzerland's Private International Law,* at 35.

[240] Schnyder and Liatowitsch, *Internationales Privat- und Zivilverfahrensrecht*, § 963, at 336.

[241] Art. 271(4) SDIA; Gassmann, *Arrest*, at 10-11.

[242] This is regulated by Art. 275 of the SDIA. See Krafft, *'Exorbitante' Gerichtsstände*, at 95-100.

[243] Art. 271(4) requires that '*la créance ait un lien suffisant avec la Suisse*', see Tribunal Fédéral, 4 May 1998, ATF 124 III 220. In Tribunal Fédéral 1997, ATF 123 III 494, the Federal Court stated that this 'sufficient link' should not be interpreted restrictively. Schnyder and Liatowitsch, *Internationales Privat- und Zivilverfahrensrecht*, § 963, at 336; Dutoit, ed., *Commentaire*, § 1*bis*, at 9; Piegai, *La protection du débiteur*, at 121-134.

that this connection be party-related; the Swiss Federal Tribunal decided that Article 4 equally applies when a foreign company brings action against another foreign company on the basis that the latter possesses attached property that is located in Switzerland.[244]

Furthermore, it is not required that the value of the seized assets covers the totality of the claim, jurisdiction as to the merits exists even if the claim supersedes the value of the asset.[245] According to the Federal Tribunal, even assets of minimum value attached for the purpose of an action against the defendant, is enough to have jurisdiction.[246] Claimant should have access to justice on the basis of the *forum arresti* rule for the full amount of his claim. The court ruled that it was up to claimant to calculate the chances of enforcement of the Swiss judgement if the value of the seized property was not sufficient to satisfy the claim.[247]

In sum, the presence of attached property in Switzerland is sufficient to provide Swiss courts with jurisdiction under two conditions: 1) the claim involves the validation of the attachment[248] and 2) the attachment order was taken in relation to that claim.[249]

3.4 France

3.4.1 Introduction: The Duality of the French Jurisdictional Regime

The French jurisdictional system is dual and consists of two sets of jurisdiction rules.[250] Primarily, jurisdiction is regulated by *transposition* of the internal territorial jurisdiction rules of the New Code of Civil Procedure to international disputes.[251] Subsidiarily,[252] *direct international jurisdiction* rules, embodied in Articles 14 and 15 of the French *Code Civil*,[253] establish jurisdictional 'privileges' for

---

[244] Tribunal Fédéral, 15 January 1991, ATF 117 II 90.

[245] Dutoit, ed., *Commentaire*, § 4, at 10; Knoepfler, Schweizer *et al.*, eds., *Droit international privé suisse*, § 617a, at 352; Krafft, *'Exorbitante' Gerichtsstände*, at 96.

[246] '*Das nach Absicht des Bundesgesetzgebers ... Selbst ein geringer Wert des Arrestguts, der nach Abzug der Kosten die Forderung nicht einmal teilweise deckte, genügte zur Begründung des Arrestgerichtsstandes.*' Decision of 15 January 1991, ATF 117 II 90, at 92.

[247] See for an exhaustive overview of arguments why the *forum sequestrii* should not be restricted as to the value of the attached property, Krafft, *'Exorbitante' Gerichtsstände*, at 97-98.

[248] Art. 279 SDIA; Volken, Keller *et al.*, *Zürcher Kommentar zum IPRG*, § 2, at 59.

[249] Krafft, *'Exorbitante' Gerichtsstände*, at 87 and 94-95; Tribunal Fédéral, 18 February 1992, ATF 118 II 190. Patocchi and Geisinger, *Code annoté,* at 81 (no. 2.1) and 83 (no. 4.2).

[250] D. Holleaux, J. Foyer *et al.*, *Droit international privé* (1987), at 352. See also A Miaja de la Muela, 'Les principes directeurs des règles de compétence territoriale des tribunaux internes en matière de litiges comportant un élément international', 135 *Recueil des cours* (1973), 1-96, at 79, referring to Niboyet who argued that the French jurisdictional system is based on a legal set of rules (the transposition of territorial jurisdicition rules) and a political set of jurisdiction rules (Arts. 14 and 15 CC).

[251] *Nouveau Code de Procédure Civile* (NCPC) enacted by décret of 5 September 1975.

[252] Also called 'ordinary jurisdiction rules' or '*règles de compétence ordinaire*'.

[253] French Civil Code [hereafter CC].

French subjects by founding jurisdiction on the basis of the French nationality of one of the parties.[254]

A brief historical background might explain the duality of the French jurisdictional system. The French Revolution resulted in the enactment of a Civil Code and introduced the French nationality.[255] The domicile criterion of the *actor sequitur forum rei* rule, which was supposed to determine the *'juge naturel'* under the '*Ancien Régime*',[256] was replaced by the nationality criterion.[257] Access to French adjudication was exclusively reserved for French nationals as part of the enjoyment of their civil rights; foreigners were deprived of this right. Moreover, access to French courts was not available for disputes between foreigners.[258] This '*publicist*' perception of jurisdiction is based on the idea that a state's judicial powers are one of the principal characteristics of state power over its subjects.[259]

A change in this attitude towards foreigners gradually took place. This was partly influenced by an upcoming '*privatist*' perception of jurisdiction emphasizing the relation between the parties involved and being more concerned with the parties' private interests, rather than with the public task of judicial powers.[260] In 1949, the *Cour de cassation* officially abandoned the systematic refusal to exercise jurisdiction over foreigners in the *Patiño* case[261] and stated that the simple fact that the parties are foreigners should not lead to the incompetence of French courts.[262] French courts increasingly applied internal territorial jurisdiction rules to international disputes involving foreigners.[263] Now that the publicist perception of jurisdiction was set aside, and the refusal to exercise jurisdiction over foreign-

---

[254] Holleaux, Foyer *et al.*, *Droit international privé,* at 352; P. Mayer and V. Heuzé, *Droit international privé* (2007), § 281, at 202.

[255] See for a more detailed study on the historical background of Arts. 14 and 15, H. Gaudemet-Tallon, *Recherches sur les origines de l'article 14 du Code Civil: Contribution à l'histoire de la compétence judiciaire internationale* (1964); J. Hudault, 'Sens et Portée de la compétence du juge naturel dans l'ancien droit français', 61 *Revue critique de droit international privé* (1972), 27-54 and 249-268 and D. Holleaux, *Compétence du juge étranger et reconnaissance des jugements* (1970).

[256] During the *Ancien Régime*, the period preceding the French Revolution, the *Ancien Droit* already dealt with international jurisdiction, even if the exact content of the rules was somewhat unknown. See P. Mayer and V. Heuzé, *Droit international privé* (2004), § 281, at 202; Hudault, 'Sens et Portée de la compétence du juge naturel dans l'ancien droit français', at 35-54.

[257] B. Audit, *Droit international privé* (2008), § 332, at 288-289; Mayer and Heuzé, *Droit international privé,* § 281, at 202.

[258] Audit, *Droit international privé,* § 335, at 290; Mayer and Heuzé, *Droit international privé,* § 282, at 203.

[259] Audit, *Droit international privé,* § 331, at 288; and B. Ancel and Y. Lequette, *Les grands arrêts de la jurisprudence française de droit international privé* (2001), at 330-331.

[260] Audit, *Droit international privé,* § 336-337, at 290-291.

[261] Cour de cass. civ. 21 June 1948.

[262] '*L'extranéité des parties n'est pas une cause d'incompétence des juridictions françaises, dont la compétence internationale se détermine par extension des règles de compétence territoriale interne.*' See 'Recueil compétence internationale', in *Encyclopédie Juridique Dalloz; Répertoire de procédure civile* (1998) at 4; A. Huet, 'Compétence des Tribunaux français à l'égard des litiges internationaux', Fascicule 581-10-51 *Juris-Classeur Droit International* (2002), Fasc. 581-20, at 2; Audit, *Droit international privé,* § 337, at 291; Mayer and Heuzé, *Droit international privé,* § 282, at 203; Y. Loussouarn and P. Bourel, *Droit international privé* (2004), § 442-1, at 598.

[263] Audit, *Droit international privé,* § 339, at 292; Huet, 'Compétence', Fasc. 581-21, at 2.

ers withdrawn, it was necessary to determine the jurisdictional reach of French courts in international cases in order to prevent that French courts would establish jurisdiction over every international dispute.[264] The most logical and easiest solution was to transpose internal or territorial jurisdiction rules to international cases. This transposition was first accepted by the *Cour de cassation* in the *Pelassa* case in which the Court used the term '*extension*' of the territorial rules to international disputes,[265] and was later confirmed in the *Scheffel* case.[266]

The territorial jurisdiction rules are enacted in Article 42 and following of the NCPC. They contain a general jurisdiction rule establishing jurisdiction at defendant's forum and alternative jurisdiction rules for, among others, contractual matters, tort and alimony cases.[267] Article 44 establishes exclusive jurisdiction for disputes involving immoveable property and derogates from Articles 14 and 15 of the CC. Several adaptations were needed to adequately transpose internal rules to international cases:[268] exceptions were made for jurisdiction relating to provisional measures[269] and matters concerning successions.[270] Complementary jurisdiction grounds, among which the *forum necessitatis*, were added by the jurisprudence of the *Cour de cassation.*[271]

The relation between the internal jurisdiction rules of the NCPC and the direct international jurisdiction rules stipulated in Articles 14 and 15 of the CC was clarified by the *Cour de cassation* in the *Société Cognacs and Brandies from France* case.[272] Taking into consideration that Articles 14 and 15 CC involve a privilege for French nationals,[273] they should be regarded as jurisdiction rules of '*last resort*' and should be applied only when the transposition of the 'ordinary'[274] jurisdic-

[264] Ancel and Lequette, *Les grands arrêts,* at 329; Mayer and Heuzé, *Droit international privé,* § 282, at 204; Loussouarn and Bourel, *Droit international privé,* § 442-2, at 599.

[265] Cour de cass. civ. 19 October 1959, See D. Bureau and H. Muir Watt, *Droit international privé* (2007), vol. I, § 130, at 142; H. Batiffol and P. Lagarde, *Droit international privé* (1983), vol. 2, at 448-450 and 456; Ancel and Lequette, *Les grands arrêts,* at 333; Mayer and Heuzé, *Droit international privé,* § 284, at 204; Loussouarn and Bourel, *Droit international privé,* § 442-2, at 599 and § 444, 444-1, at 602.

[266] Cour de cass. civ. I-30 October 1962, Bull. N. 449.

[267] Art. 46 NCPC. According to the *Cour de cassation* jurisdiction based on the territorial rules of the NCPC is based on a substantial link with the dispute. When such a link does not exist, the competent court should be determined by the principles of '*bonne administration de justice*'. Cour de cass. civ. 13 June 1978, Bull. N. 223; Mayer and Heuzé, *Droit international privé*, § 295, at 215.

[268] Audit, *Droit international privé*, § 329, at 286-288.

[269] In relation to the *forum arresti*, see below.

[270] See for more detailed information on these two exceptions regarding successions and provisional measures, Mayer and Heuzé, *Droit international privé*, § 287, at 208-209; Audit, *Droit international privé*, § 347, at 398 and respectively § 351, at 302-304; Huet, 'Compétence', Fasc. 581-21, respectively IV and III, at 7-13.

[271] Or '*règles autonomes de compétence internationale*', Mayer and Heuzé, *Droit international privé*, § 289, at 211; Audit, *Droit international privé*, § 353-356, at 305-307; and Huet, 'Compétence', Fasc. 581-21 VII, at 25.

[272] Cour de cass. civ. I-19 November 1985, Bull. I N. 306, at 271.

[273] Ancel and Lequette, *Les grands arrêts*, at 654.

[274] Bureau and Muir Watt, *Droit international privé*, § 138, at 148.

tion rules of the NCPC does not result in a competent French court.[275] Articles 14 and 15 CC are of subsidiary nature and merely supplement the ordinary rules of the NCPC.[276] Moreover, as argued by Audit, this hierarchy between the set of jurisdiction rules is justified by practical considerations; a judgement based on the ordinary jurisdiction rules is more likely to be recognized in a foreign country than a judgement based on the jurisdiction rules of Articles 14 or 15 CC.[277]

3.4.2 The Transposition of Territorial Jurisdiction Rules

3.4.2.1 *Defendant's Domicile*

The maxim *actor sequitur forum rei* enshrined in Article 42 NCPC provides for jurisdiction to the court of the place where the defendant 'lives' ('*demeure*').[278] As a consequence, French courts have general jurisdiction when the defendant 'lives' in France at the time proceedings were instituted.[279] By providing claimant access to justice to French courts when the dispute involves a French domiciliary, the defendant is given a chance to be sued in his home forum, instead of outside France.[280]

Article 43 NCPC further determines defendant's domicile by distinguishing between individual defendants and corporate entities. With respect to natural persons, a defendant 'lives' in France if his domicile, or in default thereof, his residence is situated on French territory.[281] For jurisdictional purposes, 'domicile' is the place where the defendant has his 'main establishment'. The judge seized determines whether the defendant's main establishment is located in his forum based on a factual appreciation of facts. An establishment should be fixed and durable.[282] The

---

[275] In 1967, the *Cour de cassation* still considered Arts. 14 and 15 as the general rule for international jurisdiction and the internal territorial rules were merely complementary. Cour de cass. civ. 11 October 1967, Bull. N. 289; see Audit, *Droit international privé*, § 340, at 292-293; Mayer and Heuzé, *Droit international privé*, § 294, at 214; and P. Mayer, 'La partie faible en droit international privé', in *La protection de la partie faible dans les rapports contractuels: Comparaison Franco-Belges* (1996), at 542; Loussouarn and Bourel, *Droit international privé*, § 442-3, at 601.

[276] Mayer and Heuzé, *Droit international privé*, § 282, at 204; see also Von Mehren, 'Theory and Practice', at 61; Huet, 'Compétence', Fasc. 581-30, at 5.

[277] Audit, *Droit international privé*, § 340, at 293.

[278] Art. 42: '1) the territorially competent court is, unless otherwise provided, the place where the defendant lives. 2) If there are several defendants, the plaintiff may, at his choosing, bring his case before the court of the place where one of them lives. 3) If the defendant has neither a known domicile nor residence, the plaintiff may bring his case before the court of the place where he lives or before the court of his choice if he lives abroad.'

(Decree No. 81-500 of 12 May 1981, Sect. 7, OJ of 14 May 1981, amendment JORF of 21 May 1981), at http://195.83.177.9/code/liste.phtml?lang=uk&c=39&r=7090.

[279] Cour de cass. civ. II-7 January 1976, Bull. N. 2, at 2; Cour de cass. civ. I-12 February 1980, Bull. N. 50.

[280] Audit, *Droit international privé,* § 344, at 294-295; and S. Guinchard and F. Ferrand, *Procédure civile: Droit interne et droit communautaire* (2006), § 304, at 333.

[281] Art. 43: 'The place where the defendant lives means: – in relation to a natural person, the place where he has his domicile or, in default thereof, his residence.'

[282] The main place of establishment should be fixed and permanent ('*de manière fixe et stable*'). See Huet, 'Compétence', Fasc. 581-20 A, at 6; Guinchard and Ferrand, *Procédure civile*, § 306, at 335;

residence criterion only provides for jurisdiction in the event that the defendant's domicile is unknown.[283]

As far as corporations are concerned, a corporate defendant 'lives' in France if its *siège social* is 'established' in France.[284] A corporation's social seat is generally assumed to be the place from which core business activities are directed.[285]

When the defendant is not domiciled or resident in France, and it is unknown or difficult to locate in which other state the defendant has his main establishment, Article 42(3) allows claimant to seize the court of his domicile or the court of his choice if he lives abroad.[286] This rule should not be considered as a general *forum actoris* rule, since it only allows jurisdiction under the exceptional circumstances that the exact location of the defendant's domicile is unknown.[287]

3.4.2.2 *Branch Jurisdiction*

As described above, Article 42 in conjunction with Article 43 NCPC provides for general jurisdiction over corporate defendants 'established' in France. The NCPC does not contain rules specifically regulating branch jurisdiction over foreign corporations.[288] However, in order to meet the interests of the claimant,[289] it is settled case law that under the 'ordinary' jurisdiction rule of Article 43(2) NCPC a corporation's 'establishment' extends to secondary establishments ('*gares principales*' or '*établissement secondaire*').[290] By transposing this extension to international disputes, branch jurisdiction is available over foreign corporations whom have established a 'second establishment' in France. As a consequence, foreign corporations are subjected to French jurisdiction if they conduct business activi-

---

L. Cadiet and E. Jeuland, *Droit judiciaire privé* (2006), § 159, at 101. Art. 102 CC is generally used to determine 'domicile', Bureau and Muir Watt, *Droit international privé,* § 137, at 147. See for critical comments on the use of this article, Audit, *Droit international privé,* § 344, at 295.

[283] Bureau and Muir Watt, *Droit international privé,* § 136, at 146.

[284] Art. 43(2): '*S'il s'agit d'une personne morale, du lieu où celle-ci est établie.*' See Huet, 'Compétence', Fasc. 581-20; I. Després and P. Guiomard, *Nouveau code de procédure civile* (2008), at 69. See 'Recueil compétence intenationale', § 27, at 4; Audit, *Droit international privé*, § 344, at 295.

[285] Després and Guiomard, *NCPC,* § 7, at 69; 'Recueil compétence internationale', § 27; Audit, *Droit international privé,* § 1113, at 906-907; but see for complications Cadiet and Jeuland, *Droit judiciaire privé,* § 160, at 101.

[286] See 'Recueil compétence internationale', at 4; Art. 42 as modified by Decree No. 81-500 of 12 May 1981, Sect. 7, OJ of 14 May 1981; see for more details S. Guinchard, ed., *Droit et pratique de la procédure civile* (2006), § 131.111-131.121, at 164-165.

[287] The rule has the features of a *forum necessitatis.* See Batiffol and Lagarde, *Droit international privé,* fn. 1, at 457. Huet, 'Compétence', Fasc. 581-20 A, at 6-7; H. Gaudemet-Tallon, 'La compétence internationale à l'épreuve du nouveau code de procédure civile: Aménagement ou bouleversement', 66 *Revue critique de droit international privé* (1977), 1-45, at 23-24; Audit, *Droit international privé,* § 344, at 295; 'Recueil compétence internationale', at 5. Recently confirmed in Cour de cass. civ. I-23 January 2007, Bull. I N. 29, at 25.

[288] But see the former provision of Art. 59(7) of the old CCP; Huet, 'Compétence', Fasc. 581-20, at 20.

[289] Guinchard and Ferrand, *Procédure civile*, § 308, at 335.

[290] Després and Guiomard, *NCPC,* § 7, at 69; Bureau and Muir Watt, *Droit international privé,* § 136, at 147; Audit, *Droit international privé*, § 344, at 295; Mayer and Heuzé, *Droit international privé*, § 285, at 205.

ties through a branch-established in France provided that the branch has a certain degree of autonomy[291] to represent the corporate defendant with respect to third parties.[292] The fact that a corporation carries out business in France through a representative (*mandataire*) is not enough to establish jurisdiction.[293] Furthermore, the claim should directly be linked with the branch's activities[294] *or* the underlying claim should fall under the branch's responsibility and arise out of activities carried out in the forum.[295] By way of extending the corporation's establishment to secondary establishments, special jurisidiction is provided in order to subject defendants whom have established a branch or '*succursale*' in France to jurisdiction in that forum.

3.4.2.3 *Special Jurisdiction for Contracts*

By the transposition of Article 46(2), the French jurisdictional scheme provides for contract jurisdiction by stating that in contractual matters, the plaintiff, besides being able to bring his case before the court of the place where the defendant resides, may also bring his case before the court of the place of the actual delivery of the good(s) or the place of performance of the agreed service.[296]

Hierarchically speaking, the contract rule stands on the same level as Article 42.[297] Article 46(2) provides for special jurisdiction, limited to contractual disputes arising out of contracts for the sale of goods and the provision of service.[298] French

---

[291] Cadiet and Jeuland, *Droit judiciaire privé*, § 160, at 102; Després and Guiomard, *NCPC*, § 7, at 69; Guinchard and Ferrand, *Procédure civile*, § 308, at 336. See Court of Appeal Nancy civ. I, December 2002, JCP IV 3031, at 1808: '*l'établissement secondaire d'une personne morale, devant constituer le chef de compétence territoriale, doit être investi d'un pouvoir de representation mais aussi disposer d'une réelle autonomie dans les relation avec les tiers ou les cocontractants.*'

[292] Cour de cass. civ. I-15 November 1983, Bull. N. 269; Cour de cass. com. 12 January 1988, Bull. IV N.13, at 9.

[293] Després and Guiomard, *NCPC*, § 8, at 69-70.

[294] Cour de cass. civ. II-24 January 1958, Bull. N. 77; Cour de cass. civ. I-10 October 1978, Bull. N. 295, at 229. See Audit, *Droit international privé*, § 344, at 295; Cour de cass. civ. I-15 November 1983, Bull N. 269.

[295] Cour de cass. com. 12 January 1988, Bull. IV N.13, at 9; Després and Guiomard, *NCPC*, § 7, at 69; Cadiet and Jeuland, *Droit judiciaire privé*, § 160, at 102. Huet, 'Compétence', Fasc. 581-20, at 20.

[296] Decree No. 81-500 of 12 May 1981, sec.7, OJ of 14 May 1981, amendment JORF of 21 May 1981 as translated by http://www.legifrance.gouv.fr/WAspad/ListeCodes. The old Art. 420 of the CCP only applied to commercial contracts; Art. 46 NCPC does not distinguish between civil and commercial contracts, see 'Recueil compétence internationale', at 5; Guinchard, ed., *Droit et pratique*, § 131.151, at 166. The transposition of the connecting factor '*lieu de livraison*' to international disputes was recently affirmed by Cour de cass. civ. I-23 January 2007, Bull. I N. 29, at 25.

[297] '*La compétence du juge du domicile du défendeur que l'un des termes de l'option: elle n'a par rapport à l'autre, aucun caractère privilégié ou impératif.*' Després and Guiomard, *NCPC*, § 3, at 71; see also Audit, *Droit international privé*, § 345, at 295-296, indicating that while these rules do not require that the defendant is domiciled in France, they truly apply to international cases.

[298] See for the definition of 'contract', Art. 1101 CC and 'Recueil contracts et obligations', in *Encyclopédie Juridique Dalloz: Répertoire de droit civil* (2003), *contra* Guinchard, ed., *Droit et pratique*, § 131.152, at 166, arguing that since Art. 46 does not define 'contract', the concept is a broad one. Several specific contracts derogate to Art. 46, such as for example contracts relating to insurances (see Art. R. 114-1 *Code des assurances*) and employment contracts (see Art. R. 517-1 *Code du Travail*). See Audit, *Droit international privé*, § 349, at 299. For contracts relating to maritime transport, see Arts.

courts have jurisdiction over contractual disputes if services were provided or the factual delivery was made in France.[299]

The place of 'actual delivery' – or '*livraison effective*' – includes the place where the goods 'should have been delivered'.[300] Acceptance of the goods by the counter-party is also conclusive for determining the place of actual delivery.[301] The fact that the contract was concluded in France does not create jurisdiction,[302] nor is jurisdiction created when the place of payment is in France.[303]

The 'place of execution of the service' is a somewhat vague concept and should be interpreted extensively.[304] The *Cour de cassation* confirmed that in a contract of service involving two foreign corporations, French courts are not competent if services were factually provided in Greece instead of France, even if it was proved that parties agreed on provision of service in France.[305] Case law merely determines the place of provision of service on a case-by-case basis, without providing for general guidelines.[306] The *Cour de cassation* explicitly rejected the place of payment of the price as a connecting factor for Article 46(2) and stated that the place of payment should not be understood as the place of actual delivery of the contractual obligation, nor should it be regarded as the place of performance of the agreed service.[307]

---

54 and 73 NCPC (*Décret N. 66-1078* of 31 December 1966); for contracts concerning rent of immoveable property, see Art. 880 NCPC. See for specific jurisdiction rules concerning those contracts, Huet, 'Compétence', Fasc. 581-20, at 10-12; Guinchard, ed., *Droit et pratique*, § 131.153, at 166; 'Recueil compétence internationale', at 5; and Gaudemet-Tallon, 'Aménagement ou bouleversement', at 29-30.

[299] Audit, *Droit international privé*, § 345, at 296 and fn. 2; and Gaudemet-Tallon, 'Aménagement ou bouleversement', at 28.

[300] This was already the case under the old Art. 420 CCP but it has been confirmed by the case law of Cour de cass. civ. II-18 January 2001, Bull. N. 10, at 6: *'Le lieu de la livraison effective de la chose en matière contractuelle s'entend, au sens de l'article 46 du nouveau Code de procédure civile, du lieu où la livraison a été ou doit être effectuée.'* Després and Guiomard, *NCPC*, § 4, at 71.

[301] Després and Guiomard, *NCPC*, § 4, at 71; Guinchard, ed., *Droit et pratique*, § 131.161, at 166. This is the case as long as the goods have been accepted by the counter-party, according to Huet, see Huet, 'Compétence', Fasc. 581-20, at 9-10; 'Recueil compétence internationale', at 8. See Cour de cass. com. 14 November 1980, Bull. N. 374.

[302] Després and Guiomard, *NCPC*, § 3, at 71.

[303] Huet, 'Compétence', Fasc. 581-20, at 9; Cadiet and Jeuland, *Droit judiciaire privé*, § 164, at 104; Guinchard and Ferrand, *Procédure civile*, § 320, at 341.

[304] Després and Guiomard, *NCPC*, § 7, at 72.

[305] Cour de cass. civ. I-2 April 1996, Bull. I N. 164, at 115: '*que par extension à l'ordre international des règles internes de compétence, les juridictions françaises étaient incompétentes, tant en raison du domicile à l'étranger des défendeurs, que du lieu d'exécution, en Grèce, de la seule prestation de service litigieuse*'.

[306] Després and Guiomard, *NCPC*, § 9-11, at 72; Huet, 'Compétence', Fasc. 581-20, at 10; Guinchard, ed., *Droit et pratique*, § 131.163, at 167; Cour de cass. civ. I-16 April 1985, Bull I N. 113, at 104; Cour de cass. com. I-2 October 1985, Bull IV N. 227, at 190.

[307] Cour de cass. civ. I-16 March 1999, Bull. I N. 96, at 63: '*Le paiement d'un prix ne constitue ni la livraison d'une chose ni l'exécution d'une prestation de service, au sens de l'article 46 du nouveau Code de procédure civile.*' Després and Guiomard, *NCPC*, § 11, at 72; Guinchard, ed., *Droit et pratique*, § 131.161, at 166. The place of payment existed in the old Art. 420 but was replaced by an '*objectivation des critères de rattachement*', see Gaudemet-Tallon, 'Aménagement ou bouleversement', at 27; and see Loussouarn and Bourel, *Droit international privé*, § 448, fn. 2, at 606.

3.4.2.4 *Rejection of the* Forum Arresti

Jurisdiction rules involving provisional measures, including the seizure of property, are also transposed to international disputes.[308] As indicated above, the transposition of internal jurisdiction rules to international disputes required some adaptations.[309] In 1992, new rules relating to execution procedures were introduced. They established that French courts are competent to take provisional and protective measures in international cases, when the property is located in France and the defendant is domiciled outside France.[310]

It is in this context that the French jurisdictional system was confronted with the question on whether a French court that ordered such provisional measures also has jurisdiction over the merits of the claim. In other words, are French courts competent over the merits of a case if property located in France was seized?

In 1979, the *Cour de cassation* answered this question affirmatively in the *Nassibian* decision by stating that French courts are competent to rule on the validity of the seizure effectuated in France and *may* in that case pass sentence on the merits.[311] The *Nassibian* decision introduced the *forum arresti* rule by extending the jurisdictional reach of French courts over the merits of a case, as long as the seized assets were located in France.[312] The decision ruled for almost 20 years and provided for general jurisdiction because the claim was not limited to the value of the assets seized.[313] But the Court ruled that the new *forum arresti* rule was a fac-

[308] Cour de cass. civ. I-18 November 1986, Bull, N. 266, at 255; H. Muir Watt, 'Note: Banque camerounaise de développement. Cour de Cass. Ch.Civ.I, 18 Nov. 1986', 76 *Revue critique de droit international privé* (1987), 773-786, at 782; see also the earlier case of Cour de cass. civ. II-29 February 1984, Bull. II N. 40. See note by A. Sinay-Cytermann, 'Note; Cour de Cass. Ch. Civ. II, 29 Feb.1984', *Revue critique de droit international privé* (1985), 545-551, at 548; Audit, *Droit international privé*, § 351, at 302-304.

[309] Batiffol and Lagarde, *Droit international privé*, at 461; Holleaux, Foyer *et al.*, *Droit international privé*, at 355; see 'Recueil compétence internationale', at 6. In the reverse case of assets located in another state, it has been stated that French courts do not have jurisdiction as this would be a violation of the other state's sovereignty; see also Audit, *Droit international privé*, § 351, at 302.

[310] 'Décret n° 92-755' of 31 July 1992, Art. 9.

[311] Cour de cass. civ. I-6 November 1979, Bull. I N. 47, at 30: '*Par dérogation au principe qui étend à l'ordre international les règles internes de compétence territoriale, les tribunaux français sont seules compétents pour statuer sur l'instance en validité d'une saisie-arrêt pratiquée en France et peuvent éventuellement à cette occasion statuer sur l'existence de la créance invoqué par le saisissent*'. See also the notes by G. Couchez, 'Note: Dame Nassibian v. Nassibian; Cour de cassation, Chambre Civil 1er 6 November 1979', *Revue critique de droit international privé* (1980), 588-597; and A. Ponsard, 'Note: Dame Nassibian v. Nassibian; Cour de cass. Ch.Civ.I, 6 Nov. 1979', *Journal du droit international* (1980), 95-103, at 101, considering the pros and cons of such a rule.

[312] See on this issue Audit, *Droit international privé*, § 351, at 304. The *forum arresti* rule is defined by Ancel and Lequette as an 'exorbitant ground for jurisdiction which gives a court who has authorized seizure of property as a provisional measure, jurisdiction on the substance of the case.' Ancel and Lequette, *Les grands arrêts,* at 565-567. The *forum arresti* already appeared under the regime of the '*Ancien Droit*' but was abolished after the enactment of Arts. 14 and 15 CC. See Gaudemet-Tallon, *Recherches*, at 70 and 72-74.

[313] Reaffirmed in 1986 by Cour de cass. civ. I-18 November 1986, Bull. N. 266, at 255; Muir Watt, 'Note: Banque camerounaise', at 782-783; P. Kahn, 'Note: Banque camerounaise de développement Cour de Cassation; Chambre Civile 1re 18 November 1986', *Journal du droit international* (1987), 633-638, B. Nicod, 'Note: Banque camerounaise de développement Cour de Cass. Ch.Civ. I, 18 Nov.

ultative jurisdiction rule, meaning that the courts seized *may* apply the rule rather than it being a mandatory application. Its facultative nature implied a certain degree of discretion given to French courts which had to take into account 1) whether another action was brought in a different forum, or 2) whether other foreign courts were available, or 3) the personality of the defendant.[314]

French scholars generally approved the introduction of the *forum arresti* rule in the French jurisdictional scheme.[315] An argument in favour of the *forum arresti* in the *Nassibian* case was that of effective access to justice.[316] When a court orders a seizure, there is better access to justicc if that same court also has jurisdiction as to the substance of the case. Allowing the claimant to sue the defendant in that same court, instead of having to commence proceedings elsewhere, especially protects the claimant's interests. Conversly, the rule disfavours the defendant by subjecting him to a foreign court, thereby depriving him of his '*juge naturel*' at the place of his domicile.[317]

An interesting argument against the *Nassibian* decision concerned purely economic considerations.[318] Although the *forum arresti* rule gives French creditors access to property and assets located in the state's territory and would primarily be used in relation to assets appertaining to foreign defendants not domiciled in France,[319] the rule could have a negative effect on foreign investors wishing to settle or having bank accounts in France. Their property would not only be subjected to seizure, they themselves could be subjected to French jurisdiction.

In 1995, the *Cour de cassation* reversed the *Nassibian* rule in the *Mérdien Breckwoldt v. COBENAM* case[320] by simply stating that the mere fact that defendant's property was seized in France is not sufficient to exercise jurisdiction over the defendant, unless another jurisdiction ground is available.[321]

1986', *Juris-Classeur périodique (Semaine Juridique)* (1987), no. 20909, at 570, where an additional condition was added as there was no foreign court that was exclusively competent in the case; see also Y. Lequette, 'Note COBENAM; Cour de cass.Ch.civ.I, 17 Jan.1995', *Revue critique de droit international privé* (1996), 133-142, at 140.

[314] Ancel and Lequette, *Les grands arrêts,* at 571. This could give some indication of the connection between the case and the forum. See on this topic also P. Lagarde, 'Le principe de proximité dans le droit internationale privé contemporain. Cours général de droit international privé', 196 *Recueil des cours* (1986), 9-238, at 137.

[315] Muir Watt, 'Note: Banque camerounaise'; in general see Ancel and Lequette, *Les grands arrêts*, at 568-570.

[316] Ponsard, 'Note: Dame Nassibian', at 101; Ancel and Lequette, *Les grands arrêts*, fn. 11, at 569.

[317] Ancel and Lequette, *Les grands arrêts*, at 570.

[318] Ibid., at 571-572.

[319] Ibid., at 570.

[320] Cour de cass. civ. I-17 January 1995, Bull. I N. 34, at 24.

[321] Note Muir Watt in *Semaine Juridique*, n. 20, at 184. See Audit, *Droit international privé*, § 351, at 304; Mayer and Heuzé, *Droit international privé*, § 287, at 208-209; Lequette, 'Note COBENAM', at 138-139. Cour de cass. civ. I-17 January 1995, Bull. I N. 34, at 24, was confirmed by Cour de cass. civ. I-11 February 1997, Bull. I N. 47, at 30: '*Mais attendu que si les juridictions françaises sont seules compétentes pour statuer sur la validité d'une saisie pratiquée en France et apprécier, à cette occasion, le principe de la créance, elles ne peuvent se prononcer sur le fond de cette créance que si leur compétence est fondée sur une autre règle*'.

The *Nassibain* case and the French rejection of property-based jurisdiction as a valid jurisdictional basis is particularly interesting for two reasons: first, because arguments in favour and against the *forum arresti* were exposed in the French literature, and second, because of its facultative character, French scholars frequently associated it with the discretionary powers of common law judges.[322]

3.4.3 Articles 14 and 15 of the French *Code Civil*

The direct international jurisdiction rules provided in Articles 14 and 15 of the French *Code Civil* establish jurisdiction merely on the nationality of one of the parties,[323] regardless of any connection between the French forum and the dispute.[324] These rules provide for general jurisdiction over any type of claim, except for claims involving immoveable property.[325] As they are especially designed for international disputes, the underlying idea is that French nationals should be given the personal privilege to be judged or have access to French courts, instead of having to sue or be sued in foreign ones.[326] As explained above, nationality-based jurisdiction is used as a 'last resort' and only comes into play when jurisdiction could not be established by virtue of the territorial jurisdiction rules of the NCPC.[327] The absence of any other jurisdictional requirement led to vigorous critique from both French and non-French scholars and makes these rules infamous as well as unpopular in the international arena.[328] The nationality criterion – qualified as 'exorbitant'[329] under the Brussels Model and other unified jurisdictional schemes, and considered 'procedurally patriotic' – is generally considered outdated.[330]

---

[322] See for a comparative analysis of property-based jurisdiction Chapter 7, Sect. 7.7.

[323] At the time the court is seized, the nationality requirement should be fulfilled. A French court does not become incompetent if a party loses its nationality during the proceedings; F. Jacob, *Code Civil* (2006), § 5, at 74; Huet, 'Compétence', Fasc. 581-30, for Art. 14, at 6 and for Art. 15, at 15. Persons with a refugee status in France are assimilated with French nationals, see Mayer and Heuzé, *Droit international privé*, § 290, at 211; and Huet, 'Compétence', Fasc. 581-30A, at 7.

[324] Cour de cass. civ. I-14 December, 2004, I Bull. N. 311, at 260. An exception to the rule is when the dispute concerns fraud, see Jacob, *Code civil*, § 3, at 74.

[325] Jacob, *Code civil*, § 2, at 73 and § 2, at 77.

[326] Bureau and Muir Watt, *Droit international privé*, § 158, at 161 and § 163, at 166-167; Audit, *Droit international privé*, § 358, at 308; Mayer and Heuzé, *Droit international privé*, § 290, at 211-212.

[327] Jacob, *Code civil*, § 18, at 77; Mayer and Heuzé, *Droit international privé*, § 294, at 214-215.

[328] Audit, *Droit international privé*, § 359, at 308-309; H. Gaudemet-Tallon, 'Nationalisme et compétence judiciaire: Déclin ou renouveau?', *Travaux du Comité Français de Droit International Privé* (1987-1988), 171-199, at 171; N. Fragistas, 'La compétence internationale en droit international privé', 104 *Recueil des cours* (1961), 159-271, at 233; L. de Winter, 'Excessives Jurisdiction in Private International Law', *The International and Comparative Law Quarterly* (1968), 706-720; K. Nadelmann, 'Jurisdictional Improper Fora in the Treaties of Recognition and Enforcement of Judgements: The Common Market Draft', 67 *Columbia Law Review* (1967), 995-998, at 706; G. Droz, 'Réflexions pour une réforme des articles 14 et 15 du Code Civil français', 64 *Revue critique de droit international privé* (1975), 1-23.

[329] See for the Brussels Model Chapter 2, Sect. 2.2.7.1. Nationality-based jurisdiction, as established in Arts. 14 and 15 CC, is marked exorbitant under Art. 3(2) and Annex I of the Brussels Regulation.

[330] Bureau and Muir Watt, *Droit international privé*, § 158, at 161 and § 160, at 162.

Article 14 provides that a foreigner 'even if not residing in France, may be cited before French courts for the performance of obligations contracted by him in France with a French person; he may be called before the courts of France for obligations contracted by him in a foreign country towards French persons'.[331]

French national claimants benefit from the French judicial system even if they are domiciled outside France. This prevents them from having to seize a foreign court, such as the defendant's forum, even if it is an acceptable one. In this way, the French claimant is protected from any (potentially partial) foreign court.[332] As explained in Chapter 2, the effect of Article 4(2) of the Brussels Regulation is that the French nationals are assimilated to French residents. As a consequence this jurisdictional privilege given to French claimants, equally applies to claimants domiciled in France.[333] The result is a *forum actoris* for French nationals *and* citizens who want to bring action against a defendant in France even though neither the defendant nor the case itself has any particular connection with the forum.[334] In reality a French claimant would however only profit from this jurisdictional ground if the defendant has property in France, especially since a judgement founded on nationality-based jurisdiction has little chance of success of being recognized and enforced outside of France. A *forum arresti* rule, known in other countries such as Germany and Switzerland, would obtain the same effect as Article 14.[335]

Article 15 provides that a French defendant 'may be called before a court of France for obligations contracted by them in a foreign country, even with a foreigner'.[336] This means that a foreign claimant will always find a competent French court against a French national, even if the defendant is not domiciled in France.[337] This rule protects French citizens from being sued in foreign courts. The exorbitant nature of this article lies in the fact that jurisdiction is asserted even when the forum is not connected with the dispute in any other way than by the defendant's nationality.[338]

---

331 '*L'étranger, même non résidant en France, pourra être cité devant les tribunaux français pour l'exécution des obligations par lui contractées en France avec un Français, il pourra être traduit devant des tribunaux de France pour les obligations par lui contractées en pays étranger avec des Français.*' [Translation available at: http://www.legifrance.gouv.fr/html/codes_traduits/code_civil_textA.htm.]

332 Mayer and Heuzé, *Droit international privé,* § 290, at 211.

333 Mayer and Heuzé, *Droit international privé*, § 299, at 213; H. Gaudemet-Tallon, *Compétence et exécution des jugements en Europe; Règlement n. 44/2001 Conventions de Bruxelles et de Lugano* (2002), § 95, at 67.

334 Huet, 'Compétence', Fasc. 581-30A, at 6; Droz, 'Réflexions', at 8.

335 According to Audit, *Droit international privé*, § 359, at 308, Droz would therefore favour the *forum arresti* over the nationality based jurisdiction; Droz, 'Réflexions', at 14.

336 '*Un Français peut être traduit devant un tribunal de France pour des obligations par lui contractées en pays étranger, même avec un étranger.*' Translation available at: http://www.legifrance.gouv.fr/html/codes_traduits/code_civil_textA.htm.

337 See Huet, 'Compétence', Fasc. 581-30, at 10.

338 See Huet, 'Compétence', Fasc. 581-30, at 11; Audit, *Droit international privé*, § 358, at 308. Additionally, the effect of Art. 15 has been particularly severe in the recognition stage. Recognition of a foreign judgement rendered against a French national would be refused on the basis that the foreign court was not competent, while French courts were exclusively competent over French nationals. By imposing Art. 15 as an indirect international jurisdiction rule, the French system was considered

The texts of both articles seem to limit jurisdiction for French courts to matters involving contractual obligations, but the *Cour de cassation* extended their scope to any other matters.[339] However in matters concerning immovable property located outside of France and with respect to provisional measures involving property equally located abroad, settled case law established that Articles 14 and 15 do not apply as such exercise of jurisdiction would intervene with another state's sovereignty.[340] Parties can renounce the privileges set out in Articles 14 and 15, either expressly or tacitly, and the rules are therefore also considered 'facultative'.[341] With respect to Article 14, the French claimant should be the party to renounce these privileges and for Article 15 this should be done by the French defendant.[342] The renunciation does not only affect the competence of the French court, but it also affects Article 15's exclusivity; a French defendant who has renounced the application of the rule does not have the possibility to object against the enforcement of a foreign judgement in France on the grounds that only French courts have jurisdiction over him.[343] The party who has been given the privilege is the one who has the right to renounce.[344] Once a party invokes his jurisdictional privilege, French courts are, however, not allowed to decline jurisdiction. Contrary to the *Nassibian* situation explained above, the application of Articles 14 and 15 by courts is mandatory and not facultative.

The use of a nationality criterion for jurisdiction under Articles 14 and 15 requires that the French nationality of corporate defendants and claimants be deter-

---

particularly protectionist. The *Cour de cassation* recently reversed this indirect jurisdictional requirement in the *Prieur* case, see Cour de cass. civ. I-23 May, 2006, Bull. I N. 254, at 223. The Court ruled that as Art. 15 'had a facultative nature for French nationals, it is improper to exclude recognition of a judgment when the jurisdiction ground used by the foreign court was based on a connection between the dispute and the forum seized ...', see Bureau and Muir Watt, *Droit international privé*, § 160, fn. 7, at 162.

339 *Weiss* decision: Cour de cass. civ. I-27 May 1970, Bull. N. 176, at 141, first extended Art. 14; Audit, *Droit international privé*, § 359, at 308; Mayer and Heuzé, *Droit international privé*, § 292, at 213; Ancel and Lequette, *Les grands arrêts*, at 460-467; H. Batiffol, 'Note Weiss: Cour de Cassation Chambre Civil 1; 27 May; 1970', *Revue critique de droit international privé* (1971), 113-117; Weser, 'Bases of Judicial Jurisdiction', at 324.

340 Audit, *Droit international privé,* § 361, at 310-311.

341 Bureau and Muir Watt, *Droit international privé*, § 160, at 163; Audit, *Droit international privé*, § 366-371, at 314-317; Mayer and Heuzé, *Droit international privé*, § 296, at 216.

342 Jacob, *Code civil*, § 9, at 75 and § 10, at 78-79.

343 See Mayer and Heuzé, *Droit international privé*, § 297-298, at 216-217; Huet, 'Compétence', Fasc. 581-32.

344 The *Cour de cassation* reversed the ruling of a lower court which refused jurisdiction because the case did not have sufficient connection with the forum. The court did not allow a facultative nature for Art. 14 in Cour de cass. civ. I-18 December 1990, Bull. I N. 294, at 206. Bureau and Muir Watt, *Droit international privé,* § 163, at 167; Mayer and Heuzé, *Droit international privé*, § 296, at 216. And see Cour de cass. civ. I-9 December 2003, Bull. 2003 I N. 247, at 197: '*Les articles 14 et 15 du Code civil édictent en toute matière, ... une règle de compétence qui, dans la mesure où son bénéficiaire n'y a pas renoncé et où elle n'est pas écartée par un traité international, est exclusive de toute compétence concurrente de la juridiction étrangère.*' See also A. Nuyts, *L'exception de forum non conveniens: Etude de droit international privé* (2003), § 144, at 207; C. Chalas, *L'exercise discrétionnaire de la compétence juridictionnelle en droit international privé* (2000), § 443, fns. 132-135, at 401-402.

mined.[345] In contrast to the nationality of individuals, a corporation's nationality is legal fiction.[346] According to French conflict of laws rules, the corporate nationality is generally defined by the *siège social*.[347] The *Cour de cassation* defined this 'social seat' by stating that the nationality of a corporation is generally determined by the location of its real seat, defined as the seat from where the corporation is effectively directed, and is presumed to coincide with the seat as indicated by statute.[348] This rather original concept of a '*siège social*' should be seen as a close version of the 'real seat' theory.[349] As is the case with the corporate domicile, the nationality of a corporate entity is determined by the *siège social*.[350]

3.5 Germany

3.5.1 Introduction

International jurisdiction of German courts is generally regulated by transposition of the territorial internal jurisdiction rules of Articles 12 through 40 of the German Code of Civil Procedure or *Zivilprozeßordnung* (ZPO), to international disputes.[351] This transposition of the internal rules to international cases is known in the German literature as '*doppelfunktionalität*' or 'double functionality'.[352]

---

[345] Audit, *Droit international privé*, § 362, at 311.

[346] Mayer and Heuzé, *Droit international privé*, § 1043, at 741; D. Gutmann, *Droit international privé* (2000), at 210 (fn. 1); H. Batiffol and P. Lagarde, *Traité de droit international privé* (1993), at 329; L. Levy, *La Nationalité des sociétés* (1984), at 104, '*jusqu'en 1966, aucun texte général ne règlementait en France le droit applicable ou la nationalité en matière de sociétés; peu à peu, l'idée s'imposa que les personnes morales ont un statut personnel déterminé par la loi d'un pays qui le leur attribué en même temps qu'une nationalité et le <droit à l'existence>*'.

[347] Audit, *Droit international privé*, § 1113, at 906: '*siège social, entendu comme le lieu où s'exerce la direction effective de la personne morale, celui où résident ses organes où se tiennent les assemblées. Il s'agit donc du siège réel et non simplement du siège statutaire, critère qui est plus proche de l'autonomie de la volonté et de l'incorporation. Il y a toute fois, jusqu'a preuve contraire, que le siège statutaire correspond au siège réel de la personne morale.*' See Audit, *Droit international privé*, § 362, at 311; Mayer and Heuzé, *Droit international privé*, § 1048, at 745; Loussouarn and Bourel, *Droit international privé*, § 463, at 575. Huet, 'Compétence', Fasc. 581-30A, at 6; 'Recueil compétence internationale', § 87, at 11.

[348] '*La nationalité, laquelle, pour une société, résulte, en principe, de la localisation de son siège réel, défini comme le siège de la direction effective est présumé conforme à celui indiqué par les statuts*', Cour de cass. assemblée plénière, 21 December 1990, Bull. N. 12, at 23.

[349] Mayer and Heuzé, *Droit international privé*, § 1048, at 745; Rammeloo, *Corporations*, at 195.

[350] C. Rühland, *Le problème des personnes morales en droit international privé* (1934), at 27: '*la doctrine française va même jusqu'à soutenir que les personnes morales n'ont que le domicile et que la recherche de leur nationalité est au fond rien d'autres que la recherche du domicile*'. See for the practical implication of using the same connecting factor Chapter 7, Sect. 7.1.

[351] Direct international jurisdiction rules exist in matters relating to family law, H. Nagel and P. Gottwald, *Internationales Zivilprozessrecht* (2007), § 316, at 167; J. Kropholler, *Internationales Privatrecht: Einschließlich der Grundbegriffe des Internationalen Zivilverfahrensrechts* (2006), at 610; H. Schack, *Internationales Zivilverfahrensrecht* (2006), § 188, at 72; A. Baumbach and W. Lauterbach, *Zivilprozessordnung: Mit Gerichtsverfassungsgesetz und anderen Nebengesetzen* (2007), § 6, at 89; R. Geimer, *Internationales Zivilprozeßrecht* (2005), § 943, at 327 and § 955, at 330.

[352] As translated by H. Schack, 'Germany National Report', in *Declining Jurisdiction in Private International Law* (1995), 189-205, at 190; see Kropholler, *Internationales Privatrecht*, at 610; Baum-

Articles 12 to 19 ZPO establish general jurisdiction, irrespective of the nature of the claim.[353] Only exclusive jurisdiction rules such as Articles 24 and 29a ZPO derogate from these general jurisdiction rules. The German jurisdictional scheme also provides for special jurisdiction in specific matters.[354] The scheme allows more than one competent German court, in which case Article 35 enables the claimant to choose.[355] Articles 38 through 40 regulate the prorogation of jurisdiction by agreement. According to Kropholler, Articles 23, 23a and 29 ZPO, regulating property-based jurisdiction, jurisdiction in matters relating to maintenance and contract jurisdiction respectively, were especially designed for international disputes, even if they are also used to allocate internal jurisdiction among territorially competent courts.[356]

3.5.2 General Jurisdiction

Article 12 simply defines the reach of general jurisdiction of German courts by stating that a person can be subject to its jurisdiction over any type of claim, as long as the claim does not require exclusive jurisdiction.[357]

Subsequent articles determine in which cases courts have general jurisdiction over a person: Article 13 ZPO confers general jurisdiction on the court of a natural person's domicile, or '*Wohnsitz*'.[358] For corporate entities Article 17 ZPO attributes general jurisdiction to the court where the corporation's '*Sitz*' or 'seat' is located. The fact that the defendant's home forum constitutes the main rule in the German jurisdictional scheme for asserting jurisdiction to German courts, is justified on the basis that a person against whom a claim has been brought should be protected from litigating in a foreign court.[359] The German legislator aimed at a 'procedural

bach and Lauterbach, *ZPO 2007*, § 7, at 89; Geimer, *Internationales Zivilprozeßrecht*, § 946, at 328; G. Lüke, P. Wax *et al.*, *Münchener Kommentar zur Zivilprozessordnung* (2000), at 158; Struycken, 'Distributie bepaalt attributie', at 25. This was confirmed on several occasions by the *Bundesgerichtshof* (BGH), the German Supreme Court, in civil matters, see BGH 17 February 1997, *NJW* (1997), at 2245; BGH 21 October 1992, *BGHZ* (Vol. 119), at 392; BGH 2 July 1991, *BGHZ* (Vol. 115), at 90 *et seq.*; *RIW* (1991), at 856-859; *NJW* (1991), at 3092-3095.

[353] R. Zöller and R. Geimer, *Zivilprozessordnung: Mit Gerichtsverfassungsgesetz und den Einführungsgesetzen, mit internationalem Zivilprozessrecht, EG-Verordnungen, Kostenanmerkungen: Kommentar* (2007), § 6, at 101; I. Saenger, *Zivilprozessordnung: Handkommentar* (2006), § 4, at 50.

[354] Arts. 20-34 ZPO. See among others R. Geimer and M. Vollkommer, *Zöller Zivilprozessordnung* (2002), § 6, at 97.

[355] D. Jasper, *Forum Shopping in England und Deutschland* (1990), at 97; H. Thomas and H. Putzo, *Zivilprozessordnung* (1999), at 55 (n. 1).

[356] Kropholler, *Internationales Privatrecht*, at 610; H.-P. Mansel, 'Vermögensgerichtstand und Inlandsbezug bei der Entscheidungs- und Anerkennungszuständigkeit am Beispiel der Anerkennung US-amerikanischer Urteile in Deutschland', in *Festschrift für Erik Jayme* (2004), 561-573, at 565.

[357] '*Das Gericht, bei dem eine Person ihren allgemeine Gerichtsstand hat, ist für alle gegen sie zu erhebenden Klagen zuständig, sofern nicht für eine Klage ein ausschließicher Gerichtsstand begründet ist. Die allgemeine Gerichtsstand einer Person wird durch den Wohnsitz bestimmt.*' See Baumbach and Lauterbach, *ZPO 2007*, § 5, at 91; Zöller and Geimer, *Kommentar ZPO*, § 8, at 101.

[358] According to Kropholler, '*Wohnsitz*' corresponds with 'domicile', see Kropholler, *Internationales Privatrecht*, at 615.

[359] BGH 27 October 1983, *BGHZ* (Vol. 88), at 331. This is in line with the '*Waffengeleichheit der Parteien*' or equality of arms of parties mentioned in Zöller and Geimer, *Kommentar ZPO*, § 2, at 100;

allocation of burdens', or '*prozessuale Lastenverteilung*', by granting general jurisdiction to the court of defendant's domicile.[360] No distinction is made between a German defendant and a foreigner, since nationality does not play a role.[361]

3.5.2.1 *The Domicile of Natural Persons*

The ZPO does not define the '*Wohnsitz*' concept for general jurisdiction over natural persons.[362] As a general rule, a natural person's domicile is determined by the *lex fori*. A German court will determine whether the defendant has his domicile in Germany at the time the court was seized[363] in accordance with Article 7 of the German Civil Code or *Bürgerliches Gesetzbuch* (BGB).[364] A person's domicile is the place where someone permanently settled down with the intention to make of that place the centre of his activities or '*Lebensverhältenis*'.[365] German law allows a person to have more than one domicile, which could lead to multiple competent forums.[366]

The habitual residence criterion is only used by way of exception for jurisdictional purposes.[367] Article 16 ZPO determines that if the defendant has no domicile in Germany or outside Germany, his German habitual residence can establish jurisdiction.[368] Whether or not a defendant is domiciled or habitually resident in Germany is determined by the *lex fori* of that state.[369]

H.-J. Musielak, *Kommentar zur Zivilprozessordnung* (2005), § 1, at 77.

[360] Zöller and Geimer, *Kommentar ZPO*, § 2, at 100; Saenger, *ZPO: Handkommentar*, § 2, at 50; Kropholler, *Internationales Privatrecht*, at 615.

[361] Schack, *Internationales Zivilverfahrensrecht*, § 243, at 89; Jasper, *Forum Shopping*, at 96; Baumbach and Lauterbach, *ZPO*, § 4, at 92.

[362] Zöller and Geimer, *Kommentar ZPO*, § 3, at 104.

[363] Ibid., § 12, at 105.

[364] Nagel and Gottwald, *Internationales Zivilprozessrecht*, § 319, at 168; Baumbach and Lauterbach, *ZPO 2007*, § 3, at 92; Schack, *Internationales Zivilverfahrensrecht*, § 244, at 89; Saenger, *ZPO: Handkommentar*, § 1, at 51; Zöller and Geimer, *Kommentar ZPO*, § 3, at 104.

[365] Art. 7(1) BGB. According to Baumbach and Lauterbach, *ZPO*, § 1, at 92, the procedural concept of '*Wohnsitz*' should not be interpreted restrictively. See also Saenger, *ZPO: Handkommentar*, § 2-5, at 52; Musielak, *Kommentar ZPO*, § 1, at 77; Jasper, *Forum Shopping*, at 97.

[366] See Art. 7(2) BGB. Nagel and Gottwald, *Internationales Zivilprozessrecht*, § 319, at 168; Jasper, *Forum Shopping*, at 97; Schack, *Internationales Zivilverfahrensrecht*, § 246, at 90; Zöller and Geimer, *Kommentar ZPO*, § 13, at 105.

[367] Nagel and Gottwald, *Internationales Zivilprozessrecht*, § 320, at 168.

[368] See for differences and similarities between the domicile and habitual residence under German law, D. Baetge, *Der gewöhnliche Aufenthalt im internationalen Privatrecht* (1994), at 140-142. If the defendant no longer has a habitual residence, then his last German domicile will provide for general jurisdiction; see Baumbach and Lauterbach, *ZPO*, § 3, at 93; Nagel and Gottwald, *Internationales Zivilprozessrecht*, § 321, at 169; Schack, *Internationales Zivilverfahrensrecht*, § 246-247, at 90; Lüke, Wax *et al.*, *Münchener Kommentar ZPO*, § 9, at 166.

[369] Schack, *Internationales Zivilverfahrensrecht*, § 244, at 89.

3.5.2.2 *The Corporate Domicile*

Article 17 ZPO establishes general jurisdiction over '*juristischer Personen*' which includes a wide scale of different kinds of legal entities.[370] General jurisdiction is primarily asserted to the court of the place where the corporate entity has its '*Sitz*', or seat, and subsidiarily, at the place of a corporation's '*Hauptverwaltungsort*' or place of central administration.[371] This implies that the corporation's statutory seat primarily determines the court with general jurisdiction.[372] The court of the real seat – or place of central administration – will be subsidiarily competent[373] only when the corporation's by-laws have not fixed a statutory seat or in case of doubt.[374] However, as correctly observed by Vollkommer and Schack, German company law generally requires corporations to identify their statutory seat, which makes it highly unusual that a corporation will not have determined one.[375] The '*Verwaltungsort*' or place of central administration should be understood as the centre of business activities as a whole and the place where the corporation's direction and management executes its business decisions.[376] Article 17(3) allows a corporation to fix an alternative or secondary seat.[377] Under Article 12 ZPO, such a '*Nebensitz*' would result in more than one competent court with general jurisdiction.

The choice for the 'statutory seat' concept as the connecting factor for general jurisdiction over corporations is remarkable when one considers that German conflict of law rules generally adhere to the 'real seat theory', in which case the place of central administration would be the connecting factor.[378]

---

[370] Art. 17 lists some of the corporate entities or '*juristischen Personen*': municipalities (*Gemeinden*), corporations (*Korporationen*), companies (*Gesellschaften*), cooperatives (*Genossenschaften*), other associations (*andere Vereine*), funds and foundations (*Stiftungen, Anstalten*), and estate funds (*Vermögensmassen*). Schack, *Internationales Zivilverfahrensrecht*, § 250, at 91; Zöller and Geimer, *Kommentar ZPO*, § 2, at 107; Saenger, *ZPO: Handkommentar*, § 2-5, at 54; Musielak, *Kommentar ZPO*, § 2-5, at 82.

[371] '*Der Allgemeine Gerichtsstand, die als solche verklagt werden können, wird durch ihren Sitz bestimmt. Als Sitz gilt wenn sich nichts anderes ergibt, der Ort, wo die Verwaltung geführt wird.*'

[372] Zöller and Geimer, *Kommentar ZPO*, § 9, at 108; Schack, *Internationales Zivilverfahrensrecht*, § 251, at 91; Kropholler, *Internationales Privatrecht*, at 615.

[373] '[*I*]*m zweifel*'; Baumbach and Lauterbach, *ZPO*, § 2, at 94; Musielak, *Kommentar ZPO*, § 9, at 83; Kropholler, *Internationales Privatrecht*, at 615.

[374] Schack, *Internationales Zivilverfahrensrecht*, § 251, at 91; Zöller and Geimer, *Kommentar ZPO*, § 10, at 108.

[375] See Zöller and Geimer, *Kommentar ZPO*, § 9, at 108, for the statutory requirements of registration. Schack, *Internationales Zivilverfahrensrecht*, § 251, at 91.

[376] Zöller and Geimer, *Kommentar ZPO*, § 10, at 108; Saenger, *ZPO: Handkommentar*, § 6, at 54; Musielak, *Kommentar ZPO*, § 10, at 83.

[377] Musielak, *Kommentar ZPO*, § 12, at 84; Lüke, Wax *et al.*, *Münchener Kommentar ZPO*, at 177 (n. V-1); Zöller and Geimer, *Kommentar ZPO*, § 13, at 108; Baumbach and Lauterbach, *ZPO*, § 5, at 94.

[378] Schack, *Internationales Zivilverfahrensrech*, § 251, at 91; A. Schnyder, 'Der Sitz von Gesellschaften im Internationalen Zivilverfahrensrecht', in *Wege zur Globalisierung des Rechts: Festschrift für Rolf A. Schütze zum 65. Geburtstag* (1999), 767-775, at 769-770.

3.5.3 Branch Jurisdiction

Article 21 ZPO states that any person operating through a factory, a business establishment or any other branch office, out of which direct business activities are conducted, is emanable for suit for all claims arising out of the business activities of the branch at the place where the branch is located.[379]

German courts have special jurisdiction over foreign defendants, domiciled or seated abroad,[380] who have established a branch in Germany from which they carried out their business, provided that the claim arises out of the branch's activities. Under the *actor sequitur forum rei* rule, Article 21 ZPO allows the claimant to bring suit against his counter-party at the place where the branch is located, instead of having to sue the defendant in his home forum. In other words, a defendant's privilege of defending himself against the claim in his home forum is challenged by Article 21 ZPO, once the defendant has established a branch in the claimant's forum.[381] The rule founds jurisdiction on the fact that a defendant is '*doing business*' in the German forum through a branch-establishment.[382] This jurisdictional ground is deemed to facilitate legal proceedings, as the place where the branch is established is generally considered closely connected with the claim arising out of the branch's activities.[383] Branch jurisdiction derives from Article 21 ZPO and stands on its own authority; it is not the result of a jurisprudential extension of the defendant's domicile concept.[384] The claim is instituted against the parental authority of the branch, i.e. the defendant, and not against the branch itself.[385] Although, it is not required that claimant be domiciled or seated in the same forum where the branch is established, this criteria will often provide for a competent forum at the claimant's home forum.[386] As indicated by the provision's head, Article 21 ZPO provides for 'special jurisdiction' or '*besonderer Gerichtsstand*', since it

---

379 '*Hat jemand zum Betriebe einer Fabrik, einer Handlung oder eines anderen Gewerbes eines Niederlassung, von der aus unmittelbar Geschäfte geschlossen werden, so können gegen ihn alle Klagen, die auf den Geschäftsbetrieb der Niederlassung Bezug haben, bei dem Gericht des Ortes erhoben werden, wo die Niederlassung sich befindet.*'

380 This applies to both natural persons and corporate entities, see Zöller and Geimer, *Kommentar ZPO*, § 2, at 115; Kropholler, *Internationales Privatrecht*, at 622; Musielak, *Kommentar ZPO*, § 3, at 94.

381 See Musielak, *Kommentar ZPO*, § 1, at 93, referring to the principle of 'equality of arms'. See also Zöller and Geimer, *Kommentar ZPO*, § 3, at 115; Lüke, Wax *et al.*, *Münchener Kommentar ZPO*, § 1, at 195.

382 H. Müller, *Die Gerichtspflichtigkeit wegen 'doing business': Ein Vergleich Zwischen Dem US-amerikanischen und dem deutschen Zuständigkeitssystem* (1992), at 101 and 135-137; Baumbach and Lauterbach, *ZPO*, § 2, at 100; see Zöller and Geimer, *Kommentar ZPO*, § 4, at 115, who argue that foreign companies with an establishment in Germany are '*gerichtplichtig*', or bound by the jurisdiction of German judicial powers.

383 Musielak, *Kommentar ZPO*, § 1, at 93; Lüke, Wax *et al.*, *Münchener Kommentar ZPO*, § 1, at 195.

384 Musielak, *Kommentar ZPO*, § 1, at 93.

385 Zöller and Geimer, *Kommentar ZPO*, § 2, at 115; Kropholler, *Internationales Privatrecht*, at 621; Musielak, *Kommentar ZPO*, § 7, at 94; Lüke, Wax *et al.*, *Münchener Kommentar ZPO*, § 2, at 196.

386 Baumbach and Lauterbach, *ZPO 2007*, § 8, at 100; Musielak, *Kommentar ZPO*, § 1, at 93.

is restricted to claims connected to or arising out of the branch's activities.[387] It is not required that the activity itself be performed in the same place where the branch is established, as long as the claim is connected to the course of the branch's business activities.[388] As a consequence, Article 21 ZPO includes claims arising out of contractual obligations as well as non-contractual actions related to the branch's activities.[389]

Article 21 ZPO is partly mandatory.[390] In order to protect German customers in the banking and credit business, parties are not allowed under Article 21 ZPO to contractually exclude branch jurisdiction, by for example making use of an exclusive forum selection clause.[391]

The exact significance of the 'branch' concept, or *Niederlassung*, is unclear, but in order to meet the requirements of Article 21 ZPO, the branch-establishment should be a permanent place of business, regularly and continuously[392] carrying out business in the name of the parental authority but with the capacity of independently and autonomously taking care of everyday business activities.[393] A certain degree of independence is required, even if the branch is under the direction of and subject to approval of the parental authority. With the wording '*aus unmittelbar Geschäfte geschlossen werden*', Article 21 requires that the branch should be carrying out business activities directly, without interference of the parental authority. The independence criterion is defined by German literature as '*selbstständig*'.[394] Being a mere agent or representative established in the German forum is insufficient for this rule to be applicable.[395]

---

[387] Lüke, Wax *et al.*, *Münchener Kommentar ZPO*, § 12, at 198; Zöller and Geimer, *Kommentar ZPO*, § 11, at 117; Baumbach and Lauterbach, *ZPO*, § 10, at 101.

[388] Zöller and Geimer, *Kommentar ZPO*, § 11, at 117; Baumbach and Lauterbach, *ZPO*, § 10, at 101; Musielak, *Kommentar ZPO*, § 8, at 95.

[389] BGH 10 July 1975, *NJW* (1975), at 2142, requires '*eine Beziehung zum Geschäftsbetrieb der Niederlassung*'. See Zöller and Geimer, *Kommentar ZPO*, § 11, at 117; Baumbach and Lauterbach, *ZPO*, § 10, at 100; Kropholler, *Internationales Privatrecht*, at 622; Lüke, Wax *et al.*, *Münchener Kommentar ZPO*, § 12, at 198.

[390] Nagel and Gottwald, *Internationales Zivilprozessrecht*, § 324, at 170; Zöller and Geimer, *Kommentar ZPO*, § 1, at 115.

[391] Art. 53(3) Gesetz über das Kreditwesen reads: '*Für Klagen, die auf den Geschäftsbetrieb einer Zweigstelle im Sinne des Absatzes 1 Bezug haben, darf der Gerichtsstand der Niederlassung nach § 21 Zivilprozessordnung nicht durch Vertrag ausgeschlossen werden.*' Furthermore, branch jurisdiction is not available when a financial institution established a branch in the German forum. Nagel and Gottwald, *Internationales Zivilprozessrecht*, § 324, at 170; Zöller and Geimer, *Kommentar ZPO*, § 1, at 115.

[392] Musielak, *Kommentar ZPO*, § 2, at 93.

[393] Nagel and Gottwald, *Internationales Zivilprozessrecht*, § 323, at 169; Lüke, Wax *et al.*, *Münchener Kommentar ZPO*, § 10, at 197-198.

[394] Zöller and Geimer, *Kommentar ZPO*, § 8(c), at 116; Baumbach and Lauterbach, *ZPO*, § 7, at 100; Musielak, *Kommentar ZPO*, § 3, at 94.

[395] Nagel and Gottwald, *Internationales Zivilprozessrecht*, § 323, at 169; Zöller and Geimer, *Kommentar ZPO*, § 2, at 115; Baumbach and Lauterbach, *ZPO*, § 9, at 101. '*Die Internationale Zuständigkeit deutscher Gerichte gemäß § 21 ZPO setzt eine Niederlassung voraus, deren Leitung das Recht haben muß, aus eigener Entscheidung Geschäfte abzuschließen. Agenturen zur bloßen Vermittlung von Vertragsofferten genügen nicht*', BGH 13 July 1987, *RIW* (1987), at 790; *NJW* (1987), at 3081.

German law does not require that the branch have legal personality or legal capacity,[396] nor is registration of the branch in the *Handelsregister* required.[397] When, however, the appearance is given to a third party that the branch is carrying out commercial activities in the name of and on behalf of a foreign company, it can be sufficient to establish branch jurisdiction under Article 21 ZPO.[398] This appearance criterion is also important with respect to the subsidiary-parent relationship. German law does not allow the 'piercing of the corporate veil' in groups of companies. Conversely, if the appearance was given that the subsidiary is a branch of a foreign company, the latter is amenable for suit under Article 21 ZPO.[399]

3.5.4 Special Jurisdiction in Contracts

Article 29(1) ZPO allocates jurisdiction over claims arising out of contractual obligations to the court of the place of performance of the obligation in question.[400] Article 29(2) allows parties to agree upon a place of performance provided that the contracting parties are salesmen.[401] This rule, establishing a *forum contractus*, plays an important role in the German jurisdictional structure[402] and is meant as a counterpart of the privilege given to the defendant by the general jurisdiction rule of Article 13 ZPO.[403] Contract jurisdiction is based on the close connection, or *Sachnähe*, between the claim and the forum.[404] Nonetheless, the rule often leads to the defendant's domicile and frequently provides for an alternative competent forum.[405] German contract jurisdiction opts for the place of the obligation in question or *forum solutionis* as the connecting factor.

---

[396] Nagel and Gottwald, *Internationales Zivilprozessrecht*, § 323, at 169; Baumbach and Lauterbach, *ZPO*, § 1, at 100.

[397] Zöller and Geimer, *Kommentar ZPO*, § 4, at 115; Musielak, *Kommentar ZPO*, § 2, at 93.

[398] Nagel and Gottwald, *Internationales Zivilprozessrecht*, § 323, at 170; Baumbach and Lauterbach, *ZPO*, § 8, at 100; Zöller and Geimer, *Kommentar ZPO*, § 8(c), at 116; Lüke, Wax *et al.*, *Münchener Kommentar ZPO*, § 6-9, at 196-197.

[399] Nagel and Gottwald, *Internationales Zivilprozessrecht*, § 323, at 170; and see for more details about the jurisdictional aspects and the internal liability, Ch. Möllers, *Internationale Zuständigkeit bei der Durchgriffshaftung* (1987), at 58 and 71.

[400] '*Streitigkeiten aus einem Vertragsverhältnis und über dessen Bestehen ist das Gericht des Ortes zuständig, an dem die streitige Verpflichtung zu erfüllen ist.*'

[401] Or legal entities emanating from administrative law, '*Eine Vereinbarung über den Erfüllungsort begründet die Zuständigkeit nur, wenn die Vertragsparteien Kaufleute, juristische Personen des öffentlich-rechtlichen Rechts oder öffentlich-rechtliche Sondervermögen sind*'.

[402] Kropholler, *Internationales Privatrecht*, at 616, Baumbach and Lauterbach, *ZPO*, § 1, at 111; *contra* Zöller and Geimer, *Kommentar ZPO*, § 1, at 128.

[403] Musielak, *Kommentar ZPO*, § 1, at 117; Kropholler, *Internationales Privatrecht*, at 616; H. Roth, 'Probleme um die Internationale Zuständigkeit nach 29 ZPO', in *Grenzüberschreitungen: Beiträge zum internationalen Verfahrensrecht und zur Schiedsgerichtsbarkeit: Festschrift für Peter Schlosser zum 70. Geburtstag* (2005), 773-784, at 737; H. Schack, *Der Erfüllungsort im deutschen, ausländischen und internationalen Privat- und Zivilprozeßrecht* (1985), § 141, at 104.

[404] Baumbach and Lauterbach, *ZPO*, § 2, at 111; Kropholler, *Internationales Privatrecht*, at 616. Schack identifies '*Sachnähe*', '*Beweisnähe*' and '*Rechtsnähe*', see Schack, *Der Erfüllungsort*, § 146-149, at 106-107.

[405] Saenger, *ZPO: Handkommentar*, § 1, at 64.

Article 29 ZPO provides for special jurisdiction over 'contractual' matters.[406] The *lex fori*, as opposed to the *lex causae*, determines whether or not a claim arises out of a contract, including claims relating to the validity of the contract.[407] A particularity of German contract law is that the term 'contractual matters' comprises the *culpa in comprehendo*, a fault or negligence prior to the conclusion of the contract, which is considered as a tortuous matter in other legal systems.[408]

The obligation in question or '*streitige Verpflichtung*' refers to all obligations arising out of the contract,[409] instead of to the characteristic performance of the contract.[410] Article 29 ZPO covers contractual obligations to do as well as obligations not to do,[411] and claims challenging the very existence of the contract.[412] Secondary obligations arising out of a breach of contractual obligations, such as claims for damages, are not considered the initial 'obligation in question'.[413]

Where no place of performance was specified by agreement,[414] the *lex causae* will determine the place of performance or '*Erfullungsort*'.[415] The *lex causae* approach is justified by the assumption that it would guarantee a close connection between the claim and the forum.[416] Nevertheless, the application of the *lex causae* is troublesome[417] and does not always lead to jurisdictional justice and legal certainty.[418]

---

[406] BGH 28 February 1996, *BGHZ* (Vol. 132), at 105; *NJW* (1996), at 1411-1414; Saenger, *ZPO: Handkommentar*, § 3, at 64.

[407] Schack, *Der Erfüllungsort*, § 223, at 152.

[408] Apart from Austria, in this respect Germany holds an isolated position in Europe. See the analysis of P. Mankowski, 'Entscheidungsrezensionen – Die Qualifikation der culpa in contrahendo – Nagelprobe für den Vertrags-begriff des europäischen IZPR und IPR', 23 *IPRax* (2003), 127-134, at 132; Schack, *Der Erfüllungsort*, § 154, at 110. Art. 23 ZPO also covers legal obligations with no contractual basis, such as for instance a contract with an unauthorized agency. See Art. 179(1) BGB; Zöller and Geimer, *Kommentar ZPO*, § 6, at 128; Saenger, *ZPO: Handkommentar*, § 3, at 64; Schack, *Internationales Zivilverfahrensrecht*, § 263, at 95. See also Chapter 2, Sect. 2.7.2, on the autonomous interpretation by the ECJ.

[409] Nagel and Gottwald, *Internationales Zivilprozessrecht*, § 342, at 176; Zöller and Geimer, *Kommentar ZPO*, § 5, at 128; Baumbach and Lauterbach, *ZPO*, § 3, at 111; Kropholler, *Internationales Privatrecht*, at 617; Musielak, *Kommentar ZPO*, § 4, at 117.

[410] Schack, *Internationales Zivilverfahrensrecht*, § 265, at 96; B. von Hoffmann, *Internationales Privatrecht: Einschließlich der Grundzüge des Internationalen Zivilverfahrensrecht* (2000), at 77.

[411] Schack, *Der Erfüllungsort*, § 160, at 114.

[412] Saenger, *ZPO: Handkommentar*, § 5, at 64; Zöller and Geimer, *Kommentar ZPO*, § 17, at 130.

[413] Zöller and Geimer, *Kommentar ZPO*, § 23, at 130; Saenger, *ZPO: Handkommentar*, § 6, at 65; Lüke, Wax *et al.*, *Münchener Kommentar ZPO*, § 11, at 227; Schack, *Der Erfüllungsort*, § 160, at 114.

[414] As is allowed under Art. 29(2) ZPO.

[415] Kropholler, *Internationales Privatrecht*, at 617; Schack, *Der Erfüllungsort*, § 223, at 152; A. Lüderitz, 'Fremdbestimmte internationale Zuständigkeit? Versuch einer Neubestimmung von 29 ZPO, Art.5 Nr. 1 EuGVü', in *Festschrift für Konrad Zweigert zum 70. Geburtstag* (1981), 233-250, at 233.

[416] Schack, *Internationales Zivilverfahrensrecht*, § 270, at 98.

[417] See for illustrations of the article's complexity, Schack, *Der Erfüllungsort*, § 224, at 153-154; and Lüderitz, 'Fremdbestimmte Internationale Zuständigkeit', at 234.

[418] Schack, *Internationales Zivilverfahrensrecht*, § 271, at 98. Schack and Lüderitz suggested using a more procedural concept of the place of performance that would take into account specific procedural interests for jurisdictional purposes instead of a substantive place of performance, see Lüderitz, 'Fremdbestimmte Internationale Zuständigkeit', at 249; Schack, *Der Erfüllungsort*, § 227-228, at 155. See also Schack, *Internationales Zivilverfahrensrecht*, § 271, at 98; and Nagel and

When German law applies to the contract, as opposed to when the CISG applies,[419] Article 269(1) of the BGB generally locates the place of performance of the contractual obligations at the place of the debtor's domicile at the time when the contractual obligation arose.[420] The debtor's domicile will regularly coincide with defendant's domicile. As a consequence, Article 29 ZPO's special contract jurisdiction rule will not lead to an alternative to general jurisdiction under Article 12 ZPO. The same occurs when payment is requested and represents the contractual obligation in question, as Article 270 BGB states that payment is due at the place of the debtor's domicile. Apart from these general provisions and when parties have not agreed upon a specific place of performance, German law developed, either by settled case law or by statute, a number of specific places of performance for specific contracts.[421] With respect to contracts for sale of goods, the place of payment of the price is located at the buyer's domicile, but there is no characteristic place of performance for sale of good contracts.[422] With respect to service contracts, the place of performance is the place of the provision of services.[423]

The second paragraph of Article 29 ZPO allows parties to agree upon a place of performance only when the contracting parties are merchants.[424] This agreement can be tacit or explicit, but its purpose is to determine a factual place of performance instead of a fictive place of performance for mere jurisdictional purposes.[425] The practical importance of this provision should not be underestimated, as an agreed place of performance is more likely to provide for an alternative forum.[426]

3.5.5 Property-based Jurisdiction: The *Forum Patrimonii*

Article 23 ZPO contains a *forum patrimonii* rule or '*Gerichtsstand des Vermögens*' rule providing for jurisdiction on the basis that defendant's property is located in Germany, regardless of the amount or nature of the claim, or the property's

---

Gottwald, *Internationales Zivilprozessrecht*, § 342, at 176, arguing that in practice, such a procedural place of performance is difficult to realize.

419 See Roth, 'Probleme', at 779.

420 Schack, *Internationales Zivilverfahrensrecht*, § 269, at 97; Zöller and Geimer, *Kommentar ZPO*, § 1, at 128; Baumbach and Lauterbach, *ZPO*, § 14-15, at 112; Musielak, *Kommentar ZPO*, § 17a-18, at 121; Roth, 'Probleme', at 775.

421 Zöller and Geimer, *Kommentar ZPO*, § 25, at 131 *et seq.*; Baumbach and Lauterbach, *ZPO 2007*, § 18-34, at 113-116; Saenger, *ZPO: Handkommentar*, § 6, at 64; Musielak, *Kommentar ZPO*, § 15, at 120; Thomas and Putzo, *Zivilprozessordnung*, § 20, at 229. Examples of special statutory rules, '*gesetzliche Sonderregelung*', are Arts. 261, 281, 374, 604, 697, 700, 811, 1194, 1200 BGB.

422 Zöller and Geimer, *Kommentar ZPO*, § 25, at 132; Musielak, *Kommentar ZPO*, § 27, at 124; Lüke, Wax *et al.*, *Münchener Kommentar ZPO*, § 62, at 235.

423 Zöller and Geimer, *Kommentar ZPO*, § 25, at 132; Baumbach and Lauterbach, *ZPO*, § 21, at 113; Lüke, Wax *et al.*, *Münchener Kommentar ZPO*, § 41, at 232, § 61, at 234 and § 73, at 236.

424 A similar restriction is found in Art. 38 ZPO regulating forum selection clauses, see Nagel and Gottwald, *Internationales Zivilprozessrecht*, § 345, at 177; Saenger, *ZPO: Handkommentar*, § 9, at 65; Roth, 'Probleme', at 780; Lüke, Wax *et al.*, *Münchener Kommentar ZPO*, § 21, at 229.

425 Schack, *Internationales Zivilverfahrensrecht*, § 276, at 101; Lüke, Wax *et al.*, *Münchener Kommentar ZPO*, § 97, at 239; H. Schack, 'Abstrakte Erfüllungsortsvereinbarungen: form- oder sinnlos', *IPRax* (1996), 247-249, at 248.

426 Schack, 'Abstrakte Erfüllungsortsvereinbarungen', at 248.

value.[427] The rule is subsidiairily applicable as it is only available when defendant is not domiciled or seated in Germany[428] and it is subordinated to the application of the above explained branch and contract jurisdiction under Articles 21 and 29 ZPO, respectively.[429]

Article 23 ZPO is principally designed to provide claimant with a German forum against a defendant domiciled outside Germany, avoiding the claimant having to follow the defendant to his home court.[430] It is not required that claimant be a German domiciliary or national, as long as property belonging to the defendant[431] is located in Germany.[432] Nonetheless, the rule is also called '*ausländer forum*', since its principal purpose is to reach foreign defendants.[433] In practice, the rule will mainly be invoked by claimants settled in Germany and is for that reason considered to be a '*veiled forum actoris*'.[434] This was underlined by an important decision of the *Bundesgerichtshof* requiring a 'sufficient connection' between the claim and the German forum. According to the Court, this requirement, explained below, is satisfied when the claimant is domiciled in Germany.[435]

The *forum patrimonii* is especially effective for enforcement purposes, as claimant is able to execute the judgement regarding defendant's property in

---

[427] Art. 23(1) ZPO reads: '*Für Klagen, wegen vermögensrechtlicher Ansprüche gegen eine Person, die im Inland keinen Wohnsitz hat, ist das Gericht zuständig, in dessen Bezirk sich Vermögen derselben oder der mit der Klage in Anspruch genommene Gegenstand sich befindet*'. The last sentence of Art. 23(1) ZPO is known as the 'Gerichtsstand des Streitobjekt' and regulates jurisdiction when the claim involves property and pecuniary rights, i.e. the court of the place where the involved property is located has jurisdiction. This article is not primarily concerned with international jurisdiction, see Musielak, *Kommentar ZPO*, § 11, at 103; Lüke, Wax *et al.*, *Münchener Kommentar ZPO*, § 20, at 208.

[428] Zöller and Geimer, *Kommentar ZPO*, § 3 and 5, at 119-120; Lüke, Wax *et al.*, *Münchener Kommentar ZPO*, at 202-203; Bittighofer, *Internationale Gerichtsstand des Vermögens*, at 132-137. It is not required to first determine the actual domicile of the defendant, Nagel and Gottwald, *Internationales Zivilprozessrecht*, § 332, at 173.

[429] Zöller and Geimer, *Kommentar ZPO*, § 5, at 120.

[430] See BGH 7 July 1993, *NJW* (1993), 2683-2684, at 2684, under 3; Zöller and Geimer, *Kommentar ZPO*, § 1, at 119; Musielak, *Kommentar ZPO*, § 1, at 98; Lüke, Wax *et al.*, *Münchener Kommentar ZPO*, § 1, at 203; T. Kleinstück, *Due Process-Beschränkungen des Vermögensgerichtsstandes durch hinreichenden Inlandsbezug und Minimum Contacts: Eine rechtsvergleichende Untersuchung unter besonderer Berücksichtigung des U.S.-amerikanischen und österreichischen Rechts* (1994), at 87; Jasper, *Forum Shopping*, at 98; J. Schröder, *Internationale Zuständigkeit: Entwurf eines Systems von Zuständigkeitsinteressen im zwischenstaatlichen Privatverfahrensrecht, aufgrund rechtshistorischer, rechtsvergleichender und rechtspolitischer Betrachtungen* (1971), at 377 and 386-387.

[431] BGH 12 June 2007, XI ZR 290/06, para. 26.

[432] Zöller and Geimer, *Kommentar ZPO*, § 3, at 119; Nagel and Gottwald, *Internationales Zivilprozessrecht*, § 235-236, at 174-175; Lüke, Wax *et al.*, *Münchener Kommentar ZPO*, § 13, at 205; Kleinstück, *Due Process-Beschränkungen*, at 88.

[433] Zöller and Geimer, *Kommentar ZPO*, § 1, at 119; Lüke, Wax *et al.*, *Münchener Kommentar ZPO*, § 2, at 203; Bittighofer, *Internationale Gerichtsstand des Vermögens*, at 150; Schröder, *Internationale Zuständigkeit*, at 524. The rule equally applies to German citizens domiciled outside Germany, see Nagel and Gottwald, *Internationales Zivilprozessrecht*, § 332 and 334, at 173; Baumbach and Lauterbach, *ZPO*, § 3, at 103.

[434] Kleinstück, *Due Process-Beschränkungen*, at 88.

[435] BGH 2 July 1991, *BGHZ* (Vol. 115), at 90 *et seq.*; *RIW* (1991), at 856-859; *NJW* (1991), at 3092-3095.

Germany without supplementary enforcement procedures.[436] On the other hand, if the claimant needs to enforce the German judgement outside Germany, recognition of the judgement abroad will be problematic.[437]

Despite its subsidiary nature, Article 23 ZPO confers general jurisdiction over the defendant. Property-based jurisdiction is established regardless of the property's value and does not impose a minimum value on the property, nor does it impose that its value be sufficient or proportionate to satisfy the claimant's claim.[438] Furthermore, the rule does require that defendant's property be connected with the claim.[439]

As a result, German courts have general jurisdiction when the defendant's property, even if of minimum value, is present in Germany.[440] This indicates that this German *forum patrimonii* is not primarily concerned with satisfying the claimant's claim out of the defendant's property located in the forum, but it is also concerned with protecting German patrimony by controlling property or assets located on German territory.[441]

Moreover, the German *forum partimonii* does not require prior seizure of the property.[442] As a result any property free from seizure belonging to the defendant located in Germany constitutes a valid connecting factor for jurisdiction.[443]

---

[436] Zöller and Geimer, *Kommentar ZPO*, § 7a, at 120; Saenger, *ZPO: Handkommentar*, § 5, at 58; P. Oberhammer, 'Vermögensbelegenheit und Funktion des Vermögensgerichtsstands', in *Grenzüberschreitungen: Beiträge zum internationalen Verfahrensrecht und zur Schiedsgerichtsbarkeit: Festschrift für Peter Schlosser zum 70. Geburtstag* (2005), 650-667, at 660. See for the interrelation between Art. 23 ZPO and the recognition of foreign judgements in Germany, BGH 28 October 1996, *NJW* (1997), at 325-327; P. Wollenschläger, 'Entscheidungsrezensionen – Nehmen die Erfolgsaussichten der Zwangsvollstreckung Einfluss auf die Auslegung des Vermögensbegriffes in 23 ZPO?', 21 *IPRax* (2001), 320-322.

[437] As it falls outside the Brussels Model's recognition and enforcement regime, Schack, *Internationales Zivilverfahrensrecht*, § 324-325, at 119.

[438] Zöller and Geimer, *Kommentar ZPO*, § 7, at 120; Oberhammer, 'Vermögensbelegenheit', at 667; Baumbach and Lauterbach, *ZPO*, § 20, at 105; Nagel and Gottwald, *Internationales Zivilprozessrecht*, § 333, at 173; Kleinstück, *Due Process-Beschränkungen*, at 89-91 and see 199; H. Grothe, '"Exorbitante" Gerichtszuständigkeiten im Rechtsverkehr zwischen Deutschland und den USA', 58 *RabelsZ* (1994), 687-726, at 709; M. Fricke, 'Der Gerichtsstand des Vermögens – eine unendliche Geschichte?', *IPRax* (1991), 159-162, at 160; J. Kropholler, 'Möglichkeiten einer Reform des Vermögensgerichtsstandes', 23 *Zeitschrift für Rechtsvergleichung* (1982), 1-11, at 8. See in particular Bittighofer, *Internationale Gerichtsstand des Vermögens*, at 151-154.

[439] BGH 30 January 1980.

[440] The German version of property-based jurisdiction is also called the *umbrella rule* because it has a wide jurisdictional reach without imposing any restriction to the value of the property. Nagel and Gottwald, *Internationales Zivilprozessrecht*, § 338, at 175; Schack, *Internationales Zivilverfahrensrecht*, § 327, at 120; but see also Court of Appeal Celle, 29 October 1998, 4 *IPRax* (2001), at 338-339, Wollenschläger, 'Vermögensbegriffes in 23 ZPO?', at 320.

[441] Schack, *Internationales Zivilverfahrensrecht*, § 328, at 120-121.

[442] Ibid., § 327, at 120; Kleinstück, *Due Process-Beschränkungen*, at 91; Bittighofer, *Internationale Gerichtsstand des Vermögens*, at 157 *et seq.*

[443] Nagel and Gottwald, *Internationales Zivilprozessrecht*, § 333, at 173; Lüke, Wax *et al.*, *Münchener Kommentar ZPO*, § 8, at 204.

'Property' should be understood as any 'property having market value'.[444] Furthermore, requirements as to the nature of the defendant's property are not given; the presence of both tangible and intangible assets constitutes a valid jurisdictional basis.[445]

The location of the defendant's property at the time the action is brought is crucial for property-based jurisdiction.[446] In contrast to the determination of tangibles, which is easily located at the place where property is physically present,[447] the *situs* of intangibles or receivables is difficult to determine. Article 23(2) ZPO determines that the debtor's domicile is the *situs* of intangibles or receivables.[448] When an object secures receivables, the *situs* is determined by the place where the object providing for security is located.[449]

In sum, Article 23 ZPO has quite a wide reach for asserting general jurisdiction over non-residents on the mere basis that defendant's property is present in the German forum.[450] The fact that jurisdiction is asserted without requiring any further connection with Germany and regardless of the amount of the claim or the value of the property has lead to considerable criticism.[451]

Influenced by critics, the recognition problems and the fact that the rule was marked exorbitant under international conventions,[452] the *Bundesgerichtshof* decided to restrict the application of Article 23 ZPO by requiring a sufficient connec-

---

444 Lüke, Wax *et al.*, *Münchener Kommentar ZPO*, § 16, at 206: '*Vermögen ist jeder Geldwerte Gegenstand, dem eigener Verkehrwert zukommt.*'

445 Kleinstück, *Due Process-Beschränkungen*, at 88. See for examples Zöller and Geimer, *Kommentar ZPO*, § 8, at 120-121.

446 Art. 253(1) ZPO; Zöller and Geimer, *Kommentar ZPO*, § 12, at 121; Lüke, Wax *et al.*, *Münchener Kommentar ZPO*, at 208 (n. 21); Schröder, *Internationale Zuständigkeit*, at 116 (n. 12).

447 Zöller and Geimer, *Kommentar ZPO*, § 9, at 122; Musielak, *Kommentar ZPO*, § 7, at 101; Lüke, Wax *et al.*, *Münchener Kommentar ZPO*, at 207 (n. 18).

448 Lüke, Wax *et al.*, *Münchener Kommentar ZPO*, § 19, at 207; Schack, *Internationales Zivilverfahrensrecht*, § 326, at 120.

449 '*Bei Forderungen gilt als Ort, wo das Vermögen sich befindet, der Wohnsitz des Schuldners und, wenn für die Forderungen eine Sache zur Sicherheit haftet, auch der Ort, wo die Sache sich befindet.*' Zöller and Geimer, *Kommentar ZPO*, § 11, at 121; Saenger, *ZPO: Handkommentar*, § 6, at 59; Musielak, *Kommentar ZPO*, § 10, at 102.

450 Annex I of the Brussels Regulation.

451 See in general Nadelmann, 'Jurisdictional Improper Fora'; K. Nadelmann, 'The Outer World and the Common Market Expert's Draft on Recognition of Judgements', *Common Market Law Review* (1967), 409-420; A. von Mehren, 'Recognition and Enforcement of Foreign Judgments, General Theory and the Role of Jurisdiction Requirements', *Recueil des cours* (1980), 9-112; A. von Mehren, 'Recognition and Enforcement of Sister-State Judgements: Reflections on General Theory and Current Practice in the European Economic Community and the United States', 81 *Columbia Law Review* (1981), 1044-1060, at 1058; De Winter, 'Excessives Jurisdiction'; F. Juenger, 'La Convention de Bruxelles du 27 septembre 1968 et la courtoisie internationale: Réflexions d'un américain', *Revue critique de droit international privé* (1983), 37-51, at 37. For German critics in general see Grothe, '"Exorbitante" Gerichtszuständigkeiten; Kropholler, 'Reform des Vermögensgerichtsstandes', at 2-3; B. von Hoffmann, 'Gegenwartsprobleme internationaler Zuständigkeit', 2 *IPRax* (1982), 217-222, at 219; H. Schack, 'Vermögensbelegenheit als Zuständigkeitsgrund: Exorbitant oder Sinnvoll?', *Zeitschrift für Zivilprozess* (1984), 46-68; and Schröder, *Internationale Zuständigkeit*, at 315.

452 BGH 2 July 1991, 105 *ZZP* (1992), at 315; XI ZR 206/90: '*jedoch hinsichtlich seiner inneren Berechtigung umstritten.*' Nagel and Gottwald, *Internationales Zivilprozessrecht*, § 336, at 174; Musielak, *Kommentar ZPO*, § 2, at 99.

tion provision or '*hinreichend Inlandsbezug*' between the dispute and the forum in its decision of 2 of July 1991.[453]

In a three million USD claim concerning the (return) payment of securities for a construction agreement of a harbour complex in Libya, the Cypriote claimant sued the Turkish bank who had established a branch in Germany and whose assets amounted to 150.000 DM. The presence of defendant's assets by virtue of Article 23 ZPO formed the jurisdictional basis for proceedings brought to the *Oberlandesgericht* in Stuttgart.[454] The question arose whether German courts could refuse jurisdiction on the basis that jurisdiction was merely founded on the presence of defendant's property in Germany even though any other connection with the German forum was lacking: the claimant was not domiciled in Germany, nor was the centre of the dispute located in Germany, German law was not applicable to the dispute and there were no other special interests for German courts to exercise jurisdiction.[455] The arguments advanced by the *Bundesgerichtshof* to point out the requirements of a 'sufficient connection' between the forum and the dispute under Article 23 ZPO are summarized by Dannemann as follows. First the Court argued

> 'that section 23 and its predecessors were intended to protect creditors at home against debtors without domicile in Germany, but were not meant to provide a venue for cases in which neither party had any connection with Germany. Second, while section 23 does not violate public international law, the Court nevertheless observed [that] recent international treaties aim at limiting the so-called exorbitant forums. Third, in the view of the Court, the previous interpretation of section 23 gave rise to uncontrolled forum shopping.'[456]

The Court failed to indicate of what such a *hinreichend Inlandsbezug* should consist and left this to the discretion of the court seized:[457] when the claimant is either domiciled, resident or carries out business in Germany the 'sufficient connection' criterion is generally satisfied.[458]

---

[453] BGH 2 July 1991, *BGHZ* (Vol. 115), at 90 *et seq.*; *RIW* (1991), at 856-859; *NJW* (1991), at 3092-3095; Zöller and Geimer, *Kommentar ZPO*, § 13, at 121; Musielak, *Kommentar ZPO*, § 2-2a, at 99; Lüke, Wax *et al.*, *Münchener Kommentar ZPO*, at 206 (n. 15); G. Lüke, 'Note: Deutsche Bundesgerichtshof 2 July 1992', *Zeitschrift für Zivilprozess* (1992), 314-329, at 314; H. Schack, 'Note Bundesgerichtshof 2 July 1991', 46 *Juristen Zeitung* (1992), 51-56; R. Geimer, 'Rechtsschutz in Deutschland künftig nur bei Inlandsbezug?', *NJW* (1991), 3072-3074.

[454] Court of Appeal Stuttgart, 6 Augustus 1990, *IPRax* (1991), at 179. Grothe, '"Exorbitante" Gerichtszuständigkeiten', at 711; Fricke, 'Der Gerichtsstand des Vermögens', at 160.

[455] Fricke, 'Der Gerichtsstand des Vermögens', at 160.

[456] G. Dannemann, 'Jurisdiction Based on the Presence of Assets in Germany', 41 *The International and Comparative Law Quarterly* (1992), 632-637, at 634.

[457] Nagel and Gottwald, *Internationales Zivilprozessrecht*, § 336, at 174; Mansel, 'Vermögensgerichtstand und Inlandsbezug', at 569.

[458] BGH 28 October 1996, *NJW* (1997), at 324-325; see note P. Schlosser, 'Note Bundesgerichtshof 28 October 1996', *Juristen Zeitung* (1997), 362-364; and see Mansel, 'Vermögensgerichtstand und Inlandsbezug', at 569-570. When the claimant was a German national, the taking of evidence partially took place in Germany and the claim involved an order for arrest requiring the intervention of a German court which was also considered sufficient to satisfy the *hinreichend Inlandsbezug* requirement in BGH 24 October 2000, XI ZR 300/99. The fact that claimant lived in Germany during a certain period constitutes a sufficient connection. See BGH 26 June 2001, XI ZR 241/00. This additional

The impact of this decision on the German jurisdictional regime should not be underestimated; the Court imposed a complementary connection with the forum outside the statutory framework of the German jurisdictional system and the Court also introduced an open norm to the German jurisdictional regime.[459]

The wide reach of Article 23 ZPO as well as the correcting effect of the 'sufficient connection' requirement introduced by the German Supreme Court has been questioned as to their compatibility with the German Constitution and principles of public international law.[460] The German Constitutional Court, the *Bundesverfassungsgericht*, already ruled that Article 23 ZPO is '*Verfassungs- und Volkerrechtsgemäss*', which means that the rule is not incompatible with the German Constitution nor is it incompatible with the principles of public international law.[461]

The introduction of the *hinreichend Inlandsbezug* evoked a wave of academic writings which considered whether this 'sufficient connection' requirement is compatible with constitutional guarantees. German critics have turned to Articles 20(3) and 101(1) of the German Constitution, arguing that this form of court's discretion is constitutionally incompatible.[462] Article 20(3) guarantees that the exercise of judicial power is subordinated to the binding force of statute and law.[463] Several authors have argued that as a consequence the use of discretionary powers required to appreciate the presence of a *sufficient connection* goes beyond the limits of the constitutional guarantees enshrined in Article 20(3) of the German Constitution.[464] Others based their arguments of unconstitutionality on Article 101(I) of the Consti-

requirement only applies to jurisdiction over international disputes, Mansel, 'Vermögensgerichtstand und Inlandsbezug', at 561.

459 B. Lurger, 'Inlandsbezug von Vermögensgerichtsständen', *Zeitschrift für Rechtsvergleichung* (1995), 61; M. Fricke, 'Neues vom Vermögensgerichtsstand?', 48 *NJW* (1992), 3066-3069; J. Mark, 'Der Gerichtsstand des Vermögens im Spannungsfeld zwischen Völkenrecht und deutschen Internationalen Prozessrecht', 48 *NJW* (1992), 3062-3066; Lüke, 'Note BGH 2 July 1992'; Schack, 'Note Bundesgerichtshof 2 July 1991'; P. Schlosser, 'Einschränkung des Vermögensgerichtsstandes', *IPRax* (1992), 140-143.

460 Musielak, *Kommentar ZPO*, § 2, at 99.

461 With respect to the Constitution, see BverFG 12 April 1983, BverFGE 64, 1, 20. With respect to Public International Law principles, see BGH 12 March 1984, *NJW* (1984), at 2037; BGH 24 November 1988, *NJW* (1989), at 141; Nagel and Gottwald, *Internationales Zivilprozessrecht*, § 336, at 174; Baumbach and Lauterbach, *ZPO*, Zöller and Geimer, *Kommentar ZPO*, § 1, at 102; Schack, *Internationales Zivilverfahrensrecht*, § 330, at 121; Musielak, *Kommentar ZPO*, § 2, at 99; Lüke, Wax *et al.*, *Münchener Kommentar ZPO*, § 9, at 205; *contra* T. Pfeiffer, *Internationale Zuständigkeit und prozessuale Gerechtigkeit: Die internationale Zuständigkeit im Zivilprozess zwischen effektivem Rechtsschutz und nationaler Zuständigkeitspolitik* (1995), at 620; F. Juenger, 'Constitutionalizing German Jurisdictional Law: Book Review Internationale Zuständigkeit und prozessuale Gerechtigkeit', 44 *American Journal of Comparative Law* (1996), 521-528; and see also Schack, 'Note Bundesgerichtshof 2 July 1991', at 54; and Mark, 'Spannungsfeld'.

462 Kleinstück, *Due Process-Beschränkungen*, at 127 *et seq.*; Pfeiffer, *Internationale Zuständigkeit und prozessuale Gerechtigkeit*, at 642; Schack, 'Germany', at 194; Bittighofer, *Internationale Gerichtsstand des Vermögens*, at 196; Grothe, '"Exorbitante" Gerichtszuständigkeiten', at 686; Lüke, 'Note BGH 2 July 1992', at 326.

463 '[*D*]*ie Rechtsprechung sind an Gesetz und Recht gebunden*'.

464 Schack, 'Germany', at 194-195; see also Lagarde, 'Le principe de proximité', at 152-153; and Nuyts, *L'exception*, § 144 and § 446, at 207.

tution, which guarantees the right to be heard by a legally competent court.[465] They argued that the Court creates unpredictability and arbitrary jurisdiction criteria by formulating the *sufficient connection* requirement by way of an open norm.[466] However, as long as a decision concerning the unconstitutionality of the '*hinreichend Inlandsbezug*' is lacking, the debate will remain purely academic.[467]

3.6 Conclusion

Jurisdiction over contractual disputes according to the civil law tradition is principally regulated by a closed set of jurisdiction rules. Jurisdiction is asserted over contractual claims when the defendant is connected to the forum by his domicile, which constitutes the main jurisdiction rule, subsidiarily by his habitual residence, or by having a place of establishment in the forum. Each of the analysed systems applies the *forum rei* rule as the fundamental jurisdiction rule. In most civil law systems, branch jurisdiction exists by extending the defendant's domicile in the forum. When a defendant has a branch in the forum, he is considered to be 'established' in the forum as if he were domiciled there and the exercise of jurisdiction is justified on the basis that defendant carries out business in the forum through his branch-establishment. Despite the extension of the domicile concept, jurisdiction based on a branch-establishment is limited to its activities and thereby confers special jurisdiction. Although little attention is given to the branch-connecting factor and despite the fact that it is rarely explicitly defined, the establishment should be understood as a fixed and durable connection with the forum.

Special jurisdiction based on the connection between the contractual claim and the forum exists in each of the analysed civil law systems, especially since the Dutch, Italian and Spanish reforms are modelled on the Brussels Model. This jurisdiction ground is subsidiairily applicable in most of the systems when the defendant is not connected to the forum.

In order to reach a defendant who is not domiciled – or established – in the forum through a branch, jurisdiction over contractual claims is then founded on a connection between the contract and the claim. Special jurisdiction rules in contractual matters provide for an additional opportunity to reach the non-resident defendant.[468] Although the connecting factor used in the special contract rule varies slightly from one system to another, and is not always fully elaborated, the connection between the contract and the forum is generally formed by its place of performance.

As a last resort – when the defendant is not domiciled or 'established' in the forum and the contractual claim is not connected with the forum – the majority

---

[465] '*Niemand darf seinem gesetzlichen Richter entzogen.*'

[466] J. Fawcett, *Declining Jurisdiction in Private International Law* (1995), at 23; Schack, 'Germany', at 195; W. Kennett, '*Forum non Conveniens* in Europe', 43 *Cambridge Law Journal* (1995), 552-577, at 560.

[467] P. Schlosser, 'Jurisdiction in International Litigation: The Issue of Human Rights in Relation to National Law and the Brussels Convention', *Rivista di diritto internazionale* (1991), 5-34, at 13 *et seq.*

[468] Volken, Keller *et al.*, *Zürcher Kommentar zum IPRG*, § 12, at 61.

of Continental European jurisdictional systems have retained 'exorbitant' jurisdictional rules. France still applies nationality-based jurisdiction. Germany, Switzerland and The Netherlands allow the ascertainment of jurisdiction on the basis of their own versions of property-based jurisdiction. Even though the Dutch and Swiss reforms aimed at aligning their national rules with the Brussels Model and doing away with flagrant exorbitant jurisdiction rules, their legislator still felt the need to retain the *forum arresti* rule in case all other provisions would not lead to a competent forum. To a lesser extent the same can be said for the Spanish and Italian reforms which, although they narrowly follow the Brussels Model, have slightly deviated from the Brussels system by incorporating, respectively, the place of conclusion of the contract and the legal representative.

The different nature and purpose of national jurisdiction rules justify additional or even 'exorbitant' jurisdiction rules for extra-territorial reach. Such need does not seem to exist in a unified jurisdictional scheme.

Although none of the analysed Continental European countries apply general doctrines giving courts discretionary powers to decline jurisdiction, some countries have either considered or incorporated a certain degree of judicial appreciation in relation to specific jurisdiction rules. This is the case in Germany with respect to the '*hinreichend Inlandsbezug*' requirement over the property-based jurisdiction of Article 23 ZPO, and in France with respect to the facultative *forum arresti* rule during the *Nassibain*-era. Judicial appreciation in specific areas is also found in the Dutch reform, which kept a certain degree of autonomy and independence in its approach to international jurisdiction.

The difference between unilateral national rules and regional European uniform rules should be acknowledged: it explains the wider reach of national jurisdictional regimes as a consequence of a wider scale of (exorbitant) jurisdiction rules and the desire to control their extra-territorial reach by making provisions for a certain but limited degree of judicial appreciation.

Chapter 4

ENGLISH COMMON LAW ON INTERNATIONAL JURISDICTION

The English jurisdictional scheme represents other jurisdictional systems around the world that emanate from the common law tradition.[1] Its approach to international jurisdiction differs from the civil law tradition. Before analysing the English common law principles on jurisdiction, some preliminary observations in relation to the different sets of jurisdictional rules in force in England are in order. The second section, Section 4.2, provides an overview of its jurisdictional structure in which discretionary powers play a considerable role, which will be explained in Section 4.3. Subsequent sections describe the fundamental common law rule on jurisdiction based on the defendant's presence (Sect. 4.4), and are followed by the rules on extended jurisdiction when the defendant is abroad (Sect. 4.5).

4.1 Sets of Jurisdictional Rules in England

International jurisdiction of English courts is regulated at three different levels: the international level, the European level and the intra-U.K. level.[2] Within the scope of the European Instruments,[3] jurisdiction is allocated by the Brussels Model which confers jurisdiction on the U.K. courts as a whole and not on the courts of its constituent parts, except where the Brussels Model designates a particular court.[4] The allocation of jurisdiction within the U.K., thus between courts in England, Northern Ireland and Scotland, takes place at an intra-U.K. level and is regulated by the Civil Jurisdiction and Judgments Act of 1982 (CJJA 1982),[5] which was substituted by the Civil Jurisdiction and Judgment Order of 2001 (CJJO 2001).[6]

---

[1] The English common law regime represents most of the jurisdictional regimes in Australia and Canada. Apart from some significant differences and with the exception of Quebec, these systems have very strong English common law origins.

[2] J. Hill, *International Commercial Disputes in English Courts* (2005), § 1.2.3, at 4; Briggs, 'Does it sound complex? It should do, because it is', A. Briggs, *Civil Jurisdiction and Judgments* (2005), § 1.01, at 1.

[3] Brussels Regulation and Brussels and Lugano Conventions.

[4] As is the case with special jurisdiction. See for special jurisdiction under the Brussels Model, Chapter 2, Sect. 2.2.4. A. Dicey, J. Morris *et al.*, *The Conflict of Laws* (2006), Vol. 1, § 11-266, at 400; C. Clarkson and J. Hill, *The Conflict of Laws* (2006), at 59; Hill, *International Commercial Disputes*, § 1.2.13, at 7.

[5] 13 July 1982, Chap. 27. In matters of civil procedure, Wales has been placed under the English part of the U.K. Following Rule 2.3 CPR 'English jurisdiction' or 'the jurisdiction' means – unless the context otherwise requires – England and Wales and any part of the territorial waters of the U.K. adjoining England and Wales. See Schedule 4 CJJA 1982; Hill, *International Commercial Disputes*, § 1.2.13, at 7. See also the Report of the College of Law reported in College of Law Lectures, *Jurisdiction and Enforcement of Judgments in Europe* (1985).

[6] Statutory Instrument (SI) 2001 No. 3929 (SI 2001 No. 3929), 11 December 2001 and approved by Parliament on 3 January 2002. Schedule 4 of the CJJA 1982 has been amended by Schedule 2, paras. 3 and 4 of the Civil Jurisdiction and Judgments Order 2001.

The particularities of the CJJA 1982 deserve special attention. The U.K. adhered to the Brussels Convention of 1968 by way of the Accession Convention of 9 October 1978.[7] In order to give 'force of law' to the Brussels Convention, the CJJA 1982 implemented the Convention into U.K. law.[8] The allocating function of the CJJA 1982 is particularly interesting as its jurisdictional regime which grants judicial powers at an intra-U.K. level is directly inspired by and closely modelled on the Brussels Convention.[9] This is quite remarkable considering that the U.K. was under no obligation to adopt similar provisions for the internal allocation of judicial powers and that the traditional common law regime on jurisdiction differs greatly from the Brussels Model.[10] It also means that the traditional jurisdiction regime based on the mere presence of the defendant may not be applied against any person domiciled in Scotland and Northern Ireland at an intra-U.K. level.[11]

Schedule 4 of the CJJA 1982[12] also reflects the manifest influence of the Brussels Model by requiring that for its interpretation, the ECJ's decision concerning the Brussels Convention should be closely followed. The ECJ made it however quite clear in *Kleinwort Benson Ltd v. City of Glasgow District Council*[13] that it did not have jurisdiction to interpret questions arising from the CJJA 1982 since this was a matter for national courts.[14]

Since the entry into force of the Brussels Regulation, the internal jurisdiction rules are now modelled on the Brussels Regulation by virtue of the CJJO 2001.[15] Not all the modifications brought by the Brussels Regulation have, however, been

[7] See the Schlosser Report. See also Chapter 2, Sect. 2.1, on the Brussels Model. The U.K.'s accession to the Brussels Convention was a direct consequence of the U.K.'s accession to the European Community on 1 January 1973. The EC Accession Act required that the U.K., and any other new Member State, accede to any convention provided for under Art. 220 EEC Treaty and formerly concluded among other Member States. See L. Collins, 'The Jurisdiction and Judgements Convention – Some Practical Aspects of United Kingdom Accession, with Particular Reference to Jurisdiction', in *Harmonization of Private International Law by the E.E.C.* (1978), 91-102, at 91; T. Hartley, 'Note *Tessili*', *European Law Review* (1977), at 59. See also the ECJ's observation in C-12/76 *Tessili v. Dunlop*, [1976] ECR 1473, para. 6.

[8] The Civil Jurisdiction and Judgments Act of 1991, Chap. 12, gave 'force of law' to the Lugano Convention by incorporating its text into Schedule 3C of the CJJA 1982. Successive accessions to the Brussels Convention amended the CJJA of 1982 (SI 1989 No. 1346/SI 1990 No. 2591/SI 1993 No. 603). The consolidated version of the Brussels Convention was amended by SI 2000 No. 1824. In contrast, the implementation of the Brussels Regulation was not required by virtue of the European Communities Act of 1972, which imposed a monistic system for the enforcement of community law, see Chap. 68, Sect. 2(1) of the EC Act 1972, and gives direct legal effect to community regulation.

[9] Hill, *International Commercial Disputes*, § 6.01, at 185.

[10] R. Geimer, 'The Brussels Convention – Successful Model and Oldtimer', 4 *European Journal of Law Reform* (2002), at 26. See for an exhaustive overview of the CJJA 1982, P. Kaye, *Civil Jurisdiction and Enforcement of Foreign Judgments* (1987), at 416-487.

[11] Dicey, Morris *et al.*, *Conflict of Laws*, § 11-266, at 400; Hill, *International Commercial Disputes*, § 6.01, at 185; J. Fawcett, P. North *et al.*, *Cheshire, North & Fawcett: Private International Law* (2008), at 346-348.

[12] As modified by the CJJO 2001 (SI 2001 No. 3929).

[13] C-346/93, [1995] ECR I-0615.

[14] Hill, *International Commercial Disputes*, § 6.19, at 187.

[15] Schedule 2, Part II, para. 4 of the CJJO 2001.

incorporated by the CJJO 2001. For instance, the contract jurisdiction rule was not adapted to Article 5(1)(b) of the Brussels Regulation.[16]

Prior to the CJJA 1982, the allocation of judicial powers within the U.K. was regulated by traditional common law rules on jurisdiction. At present, this traditional regime merely regulates the international jurisdiction of English courts outside the scope of the European Instruments and no longer applies to intra-U.K. matters.[17] Although the regulation of jurisdiction at an intra-U.K. level follows the Brussels Model, the traditional common law regime for international jurisdiction outside the scope of the Brussels Instruments does not and remains unchanged.[18]

A final comment should be made regarding the particular approach taken by Scotland. Contrary to England – and Wales – the Scottish regime on international jurisdiction which falls outside the scope of European Instruments was reformed. Schedule 8 of the CJJA 1982 enacted direct international jurisdiction rules for Scottish courts,[19] directly modelled on the Brussels Convention.[20] In this context it is noteworthy to mention that although the Scottish jurisdictional system stems from the civil law tradition, the famous *forum non conveniens* doctrine is of Scottish origin. The Scottish system for international jurisdiction as enshrined in Schedule 8 of the CJJA made one significant exception to the incorporation of the Brussels Model: the *forum non conveniens* doctrine is still available to Scottish courts for international disputes.[21]

---

[16] For matters relating to contracts the jurisdiction criterion remains the place of performance of the obligation in question, instead of the sub categorization for contracts for sale of goods contracts and service contracts. Dicey, Morris *et al.*, *Conflict of Laws*, § 11-268, at 401; Hill, *International Commercial Disputes*, § 6.2.9, at 190.

[17] In short, traditional common law applies when 1) the claim was instituted before one of the European Instruments which entered into force or, 2) the claim falls outside the material scope of Art. 1 of these European Instruments, or 3) the claim falls outside the territorial scope of application and, by virtue of Art. 4, the claim refers back to national jurisdiction rules. As a general rule, this will be the case when the defendant is not domiciled in a Regulation State or Member State and the claim does not concern an exclusive jurisdiction rule. See Briggs, *Civil Jurisdiction*, § 4.01, at 289; Fawcett, North *et al.*, *Private International Law*, at 200-201.

[18] Apart from some modifications in relation to branch jurisdiction. This is in contrast to many Continental European jurisdictional systems originating from the civil law tradition as explained in Chapter 3. English courts still apply the *forum non conveniens* in favour of other courts from other parts of the U.K. P. Stone, *EU Private International Law Harmonization of Laws* (2006), at 48.

[19] Those falling outside the scope of the Brussels Regulation and Brussels and Lugano Conventions.

[20] Incorporated in Schedule 8 of the CJJA 1982, as amended by Schedule 2, Part III, Paras. 6 and 7 of the CJJO 2001. The Maxwell Explanatory Report on Schedule 4 of the CJJA 1982 states that 'it seems wrong in principle, and confusing for practitioners to maintain two separate and slightly different sets of rules of jurisdiction', see Lord Maxwell, 'Report of the Scottish Committee on Jurisdiction and Enforcement' (1980), at 18(d). The modifications brought by the Brussels Regulation, especially concerning Art. 5(1)(b), were not adopted.

[21] See Kaye, *Civil Jurisdiction*, at 1327-1328 and the Maxwell Report, see Maxwell, 'Scottish Committee on Jurisdiction', at 20; and see A. Mennie, 'The Brussels Convention and the Scottish Courts' Discretion to Decline Jurisdiction', *The Juridical Review* (1989), at 162. This mechanism is however not valid when jurisdiction of the seized court is based on a special jurisdiction rule. Art. 5, for instance, will confer jurisdiction on a specific court internally competent, see Mennie, 'Brussels Convention and the Scottish Courts' Discretion', at 169.

4.2 The Structure of the English Common Law System

English traditional common law regulates international jurisdiction by means of a combination of rules of procedural nature and the *forum (non) conveniens* doctrine. The procedural rules regulate the service of process on the defendant in order to bring him before English courts. The *forum (non) conveniens* doctrine is based on common law principles established by case law and gives English courts discretionary powers to accept or decline jurisdiction.

4.2.1 From Presence to Service out of the Jurisdiction

The key to English jurisdiction is the service of process on the defendant.[22] Without the service of claim form[23] the court cannot exercise jurisdiction over the defendant. Service of process is allowed in three principal situations: 1) service within the jurisdiction on a defendant present in England; 2) service out of the jurisdiction on a defendant outside England; and 3) service on a defendant who submitted to English adjudication.[24] As a rule, whether and how the defendant can be served depends on defendant's presence in England.

Traditional common law founds jurisdiction on the presence of the defendant in England, regardless of where he is domiciled.[25] If the defendant was served while present on English territory, English courts have general jurisdiction over him. If the defendant is not present in England, additional 'heads' for jurisdiction allow the service of process out of England under specific circumstances.

Initially, jurisdiction was merely founded on defendant's physical presence in England and service out of the jurisdiction was not permitted. Presence-based jurisdiction is established regardless of the nature of the claim and without any consideration of defendant's nationality or domicile. As long as the defendant was *properly* served, English courts have jurisdiction over him. Jurisdiction based on the defendant's presence originates from the historical fact that any person present in England had the duty to owe, at least, temporarily allegiance to the King.[26] Presence-based jurisdiction is derived from the territoriality principle and stipulates that 'all persons within any territorial dominion owe allegiance to its sovereign power ... and to the lawful jurisdiction of its courts'.[27] Viscount Haldane stated in *John Russel & Co Ltd v. Cayzer, Irvine & Co Ltd* that

[22] Under the Brussels Model, service of process is also needed to institute proceedings, yet the service out of jurisdiction does not need special permission from the court as is required under the common law rules, see *The White Book*, Section A – Civil Procedure Rules 1998, Part 6 – Service of Documents, under 6.19.

[23] Previously known as a 'writ' or 'originating summons'.

[24] Hill, *International Commercial Disputes*, § 7.0.1, at 193. Service on the basis of submission to English courts entails prorogation of jurisdiction which is left out of the scope of the present study.

[25] See for an explanation of the exclusion of other jurisdictional grounds P. Nygh, 'The Common Law Approach', in *Transnational Tort Litigation: Jurisdictional Principles* (1996), at 23.

[26] Dicey, Morris *et al.*, *Conflict of Laws*, § 11-103, at 346.

[27] Judge Lyell recalling the Judgement of Lord Russel of Killowen in *Carrick v. Hancock* in the case of *Colt Industries Inc. v. Sarlie (No. 1)*, [1966] 1 All ER 673, at 675.

> '[T]he root principle of the English law about jurisdiction is that the judges stand in the place of the Sovereign in whose name they administer Justice, and that therefore whoever is served with the King's writ [claim form] and can be compelled consequently to submit to the decree made, is a person over whom the Courts have jurisdiction.'[28]

The starting point for presence-based jurisdiction is therefore the duty to the sovereign power and not the protection of the defendant's interests.

In practice, the exclusiveness of presence-based jurisdiction led to an unsatisfactory outcome and exposed the inappropriateness of exercising jurisdiction on the mere basis that defendant was physically present, even for a very short stay, in England. In the notorious case of *Maharanee Seethadevi Gaekwar of Baroda v. Wildenstein*[29] the defendant came to England to see the Ascot Horse races and was served with a writ; jurisdiction of English courts was hereby established. Neither the parties nor the dispute itself were in any way connected to England, which illustrates how far this jurisdictional ground reaches.

On the other hand, presence-based jurisdiction limited the reach of English courts. A defendant strongly or sufficiently connected with the English forum by other means than by its presence could avoid proceedings against him. When the defendant is not present, English courts could not reach him even if he is an English resident or if the claim concerned a breach of a contract committed in England.[30] As a consequence, claimant's access to English courts depended on the defendant's presence and could not be fully guaranteed unless the system had not undergone some substantial changes.

As a result of the unsatisfactory outcome of the presence criterion and in order to provide the claimant with a wider range of jurisdictional grounds to serve the defendant, additional grounds were provided for service out of the jurisdiction.[31] These jurisdictional grounds extend the extra-territorial reach of English courts in situations where it seemed appropriate to issue proceedings against a defendant on any other jurisdictional basis than his presence or submission, for instance when the defendant is resident in England, or when a contractual claim is connected with the English forum. These specific circumstances are regulated by specific 'heads' for jurisdiction under the Rules of the Supreme Court (RSC),[32] re-enacted in the Civil Procedure Rules (CPR).[33] While these additional heads provide for extra-

---

[28] *John Russel & Co Ltd v. Cayzer, Irvine & Co Ltd*, [1916] 2 AC 298 (HL), at 302. Fawcett, North *et al.*, *Private International Law*, at 354; R.H. Graveson, *Conflict of Laws: Private International Law* (1974), at 111-112. See for a brief U.K.-U.S. comparison and the importance of the writ in the History of English Law, Nygh, 'Common Law Approach', at 24.

[29] *Maharanee Seethadevi Gaekwar of Baroda v. Wildenstein*, [1972] 2 All ER 689 (CA) (Civ Div).

[30] Fawcett, North *et al.*, *Private International Law*, at 372.

[31] According to Whincop 'Perhaps that [presence] was a useful rule when people travelled infrequently. But when travel costs are low for natural persons and an increasing number of business[es] have multistate operations, the rule's efficiency deteriorates', M. Whincop, *Policy and Pragmatism in the Conflict of Laws* (2001), at 141.

[32] These rules derive from the 1852 Common Law Procedure Act, but are known as the Rules of the Supreme Court.

[33] The Civil Procedure Rules of 1998, SI 1998 No. 3132, Pt 6 (III), r 6.20. Last amended on 1 October 2005, SI 2005 No. 2292.

territorial jurisdiction – or 'extended jurisdiction' out of the English territory – they stand in contrast with the notions of territorial sovereignty formerly used, as they will most likely interfere with the territorial sovereignty of other states.[34] In order to avoid excessive or exorbitant use of the CPR Rules, they are applied with caution.[35] For service out of the jurisdiction the claimant is required to ask permission from the court and the claimant has to prove that England is the *forum conveniens*.

4.2.2 Service of Process in England

If a defendant has been properly served – while physically present in England – the claimant can invoke jurisdiction as of right, at least without any special permission of the court. While presence-based jurisdiction does not necessarily mean that there is a substantial connection between the defendant and the forum, the defendant is entitled to request the court a stay of proceedings. [36] The defendant accepts the jurisdiction of the court – because properly served – but the defendant requests the court to use its discretionary power to refuse to exercise it.[37] Staying proceedings means that the court declines jurisdiction on the basis that the English court is a *forum non conveniens*. The application of the *forum non conveniens* doctrine should be understood as follows: 1) the defendant has the burden of proof[38] that there is another 'available'[39] forum to the claimant which is 2) 'clearly or distinctly

[34] Hill, *International Commercial Disputes*, § 9.2.7, at 278; A. Bell, *Forum Shopping and Venue in Transnational Litigation* (2003), § 4.17, at 139-140.

[35] For those reasons the heads have been marked as exorbitant in *Société Générale Alsacienne de Paris v. Dreyfus Bros*, (1885) LR 29 (Ch. D.) 239, at 242-243; and see Lord Diplock and Lord Wilberforce in *Amin Rasheed Shipping Corp v. Kuwait Insurance Co (The Al Wahab)*, [1984] AC 50, at 65-66. In the *Spiliada* case, Lord Goff gave some nuance with respect to the qualification of 'exorbitant' by stating that 'Even so, a word of caution is necessary. I myself feel that the word "exorbitant" is, as used in the present context, an old-fashioned word which perhaps carries unfortunate overtones: it means no more than that the exercise of the jurisdiction is extraordinary.' *Spiliada Maritime Corp v. Cansulex Ltd.*, [1987] AC 460, at 481.

[36] Clarkson and Hill, *The Conflict of Laws*, at 89.

[37] This stay is also covered by Rule 11(1)(b) CPR; Briggs, *Civil Jurisdiction*, § 4.31, at 346; A. Briggs, *The Conflict of Laws* (2008), at 93.

[38] See also C. Chalas, *L'exercise discrétionnaire de la compétence juridictionnelle en droit international privé* (2000), § 257-259, at 239-240.

[39] There are three aspects that should be considered with respect to the 'availability' of the foreign court. The first aspect considers a foreign court to be 'available' when the claimant can institute proceedings against the defendant before that court, or to put it in other words, the other court has jurisdiction over the defendant. In *Lubbe and Others Appellants v. Cape Plc*, the House of Lords decided that there was an available forum even if availability was dependant on defendant's submission to the other court. The second and third aspects are more controversial. Especially the last aspect of availability is difficult as it may require that the claimant get a fair hearing in that other court. See *Lubbe v. Cape Plc*, [2000] 1 WLR 1545, at 1562-1566; *Mohammed v. Bank of Kuwait and the Middle East KSC*, [1996] 1 WLR 1483, which seems to be overruled by *Connelly v. RTZ Corp Plc (No. 2)*, [1998] AC 854. See in general on the three aspects of availability Dicey, Morris *et al.*, *Conflict of Laws*, § 12-028, at 477-478; Briggs, *Civil Jurisdiction*, § 4.14, at 304-307; L. Merrett, 'The Meaning of an "Available Forum"', 63 *Cambridge Law Journal* (2004), 2 – July; and P. Nygh, 'Declining Jurisdiction under the Brussels I Regulation 2001 and the Preliminary Draft Hague Judgments Convention: A Comparison', in *Reform and Development of Private International Law – Essays in Honour of Sir Peter North* (2002), at 323.

more appropriate' than the English court.[40] This is generally understood to be the first stage test of the *forum non conveniens* doctrine.[41] In the second stage test the claimant has to show the court that it would nevertheless be unjust to confine him to this foreign forum.

4.2.3 Service of Process out of England

The claimant should request for leave in order to obtain special permission from the court to serve out of the jurisdiction.[42] If permission is granted, the defendant may challenge the granting of permission in order to set the service aside.[43] The court decides whether permission to serve out should be granted on the basis of three questions. In *Staines v. Walsh*[44] the Court explains that '[t]he finding of a good arguable case under either of the bases in CPR 6.20 is of course not the end of the matter. Additionally, the claimant has to show, first, there is a serious issue to be tried and second, if so, that England is clearly the most appropriate forum.'[45]

The claimant must therefore primarily show that he has a 'good arguable case' that his claim falls within one of the heads under Rule 6.20 CPR.[46] Some claims can fall under more than one head of Rule 6.20, but if permission is requested for several claims, each of them has to fall under one of the heads and permission should be obtained for each claim separately.[47] Hence, a permission obtained for one head, does not cover another (sub) claim, even if related to the claim for which permission was obtained.[48] If the claimant does not succeed in showing that his claim falls under one of the heads for service out of jurisdiction under Rule 6.20, there is no other way to obtain permission to serve out from the court.[49]

---

[40] A stay of proceedings can also be requested by defendant when the English action would constitute a breach of the dispute resolution agreement, see for more details Briggs, *Civil Jurisdiction*, § 4.13, at 301.

[41] See below Sect. 4.3.

[42] In his application for permission the claimant must state that he believes he has *a reasonable prospect* of success according to Rule 6.21(1)(b).

[43] Part 11 CPR; Hill, *International Commercial Disputes*, § 7.3.4, at 207.

[44] [2003] EWHC 458 (Ch. D.), para. 18.

[45] *Canada Trust Co. v. Stolzenberg (No. 2)*, [1998] 1 WLR 547. Especially what has been stated by LJ Waller (at 555 and 558), and confirmed later by the House of Lords, [2000] 3 WLR 1376. See also the *White Book* under CPR Rule 6.20.

[46] *Seaconsar (Far East) Ltd v. Bank Markazi Jomhouri Islami Iran*, [1994] 1 AC 438, at 457; *Canada Trust Co. v. Stolzenberg* (No. 2), [2002] 1 AC 1, at 13; *Matthews v. Kuwait Bechtel Corp*, [1959] 2 QB 57; Bell (2003), § 4.14, at 138; Briggs, *Civil Jurisdiction*, § 4.56, at 372-373.

[47] Briggs, *Civil Jurisdiction*, § 4.32, at 348; Briggs, *The Conflict of Laws*, at 106; Mr Justice Lawrence Collins states in *Chellaram v. Chellaram (No. 2)* that 'It has been well established for more than 100 years that a claimant cannot pursue causes of action against a foreign defendant under CPR 6.20 ... which are not within the provisions for service out of the jurisdiction, even if the claimant has other claims which are within it.' [2002] 3 All ER 17, at § 131.

[48] The application of Rule 6.20 is very strict. A claim has to fall within the spirit as well as in the letter of the order, and for any other claim connected with the case a new leave has to be obtained. Furthermore, once a leave is granted the defendant is not allowed to add other claims on that same leave but he has to obtain a different leave for that additional claim. See *Metall und Rohstoff AG v. Donaldson Lufkin & Jenrette Inc*, [1989] 3 All ER 14 (CA) (Civ Div) and *ABCI v. Banque Franco-Tunisienne*, [2002] 1 Lloyd's Rep. 511; Briggs, *The Conflict of Laws*, at 106.

[49] This is a requirement established under Rule 6(20) CPR, see Briggs, *Civil Jurisdiction*, § 4.32, at 348.

Secondly, the claimant must show that he has a 'serious issue to be tried' with respect to the merits of the claim, in order to enable the court to exercise its discretion to grant leave.[50] This requirement entails the discretionary powers of the court but should not be understood as a full appreciation of the facts as it merely involves a 'modest burden of proof' on the merits of the claim.[51] The requirement has recently been introduced by Rule 6.21(1)(b), but was previously established in *Seaconsar Far East Ltd. v. Bank Markazi Jomhouri Islami Irani* requiring at that time 'a serious issue to be tried on the merits'.[52] Consequently the courts will have to look at the merits of the case before answering the jurisdictional question.

Thirdly, according to Rule 6.21(2A), a court will only give permission when it is satisfied that England 'is the proper place in which to bring the claim'.[53] Provided that the claim falls under one of the heads of Rule 6.20 of the CPR, the court seized 'assumes' jurisdiction, but the court must establish that the English court is the most appropriate forum.[54] In order to decide on whether or not to give permission for service out of the jurisdiction the court will apply the '*forum conveniens*' test.[55] In other words, the effect of the *forum conveniens* is not to decline jurisdiction to another 'clearly and distinctly more appropriate' forum, but in order to bring a defendant located outside England in front of English courts, it has to be 'clearly and distinctly more appropriate'. The application of the *forum conveniens* is justified by the idea that serving a defendant abroad is an exorbitant exercise of jurisdiction and interferes with the sovereignty of foreign countries.[56] The claimant has the burden of proof to establish that the English forum is the *forum conveniens* or the most appropriate forum.[57] Whether or not another forum is available is irrelevant. Subsequently, the court will take into account any injustice done to the claimant if proceedings were to be stayed and will decline jurisdiction directing the claimant to the foreign court.[58]

4.3 The *Forum (Non) Conveniens* Doctrine

Whether jurisdiction is based on presence or on one of the extended heads for jurisdiction arising out of Rule 6.20 CPR, traditional common law on jurisdiction

---

[50] *Seaconsar (Far East) Ltd v. Bank Markazi Jomhouri Islami Iran*, [1994] 1 AC 438, at 457.

[51] Briggs, *Civil Jurisdiction*, § 4.61, at 381; Hill, *International Commercial Disputes*, § 7.3.9, at 209; Bell, *Forum Shopping and Venue*, § 4.21, at 141.

[52] [1994] 1 AC 438. See also *BAS Capital Funding Corp v. Medfinco Ltd*, [2003] EWHC 1798 (Ch.); [2004] 1 Lloyd's Rep. 652; *Ashton Investments Ltd v. Rusal*, [2006] EWHC 2545 (Comm.); [2007] 1 Lloyd's Rep. 311.

[53] Rule 6.21(2A) CPR reads 'The burden is upon the claimant to persuade the court that England is clearly the appropriate forum for the trial of the action'.

[54] *Seaconsar (Far East) Ltd v. Bank Markazi Jomhouri Islam Iran*, [1994] 1 AC 438; [1993] 4 All ER 456; and *Spiliada Maritime Corp v. Consulex Ltd*, [1987] AC 460; [1986] 3 All ER 843 (HL).

[55] As stipulated in the procedure to stay proceedings set out in Part 11 of the CPR.

[56] One of the first cases is *Société Générale Alsacienne de Paris v. Dreyfus Bros*, (1885) LR 29 (Ch. D.) 239, at 242-243; see also *Amin Rasheed Shipping Corp v. Kuwait Insurance Co (The Al Wahab)*, [1984] AC 50, in particular at 65; see *Spiliada Maritime Corp v. Cansulex Ltd.*, [1987] AC 460, at 481.

[57] Hill, *International Commercial Disputes*, § 7.3.39, at 222.

[58] Dicey, Morris *et al.*, *Conflict of Laws*, § 12-32, at 480.

contains a wide range of jurisdictional criteria enabling the claimant to bring proceedings in English courts.

Since the decision of the House of Lords in *Spiliada Maritime Corporation v. Cansulex Ltd*,[59] the *forum non conveniens* doctrine has been accepted in English common law and the courts were given wide discretionary powers when the defendant was served within the jurisdiction.[60] Its purpose is to enable the court 'to identify the forum in which the case can be 'suitably tried for the interests of all the parties and for the ends of justice'.[61] Although, the *Spiliada* case dealt with service of process on the defendant within the jurisdiction and introduced the *forum non conveniens* doctrine to decline jurisdiction to another 'more appropriate court', the decision also decided that 'in the interests of justice' the same factors apply to the *forum conveniens* in order to grant permission for service out of the jurisdiction.[62] Accordingly, by searching for the appropriate court, these discretionary powers prevent the claimant from abusing his rights of access and enable the defendant to put weight on his interests.[63] Whether or not a court will exercise its discretionary power to adjudicate depends on the '*conveniens*' test laid down by *Spiliada*. In that respect the term '*conveniens*' does not mean the most 'convenient' forum, but rather the most 'appropriate' one.[64] This was also held by Lord MacKay, 'I feel bound to say that I doubt whether the Latin tag *forum non conveniens* is apt to describe this principle. For the question is not one of convenience, but of the suitability or appropriateness of the relevant jurisdiction.'[65]

---

[59] *Spiliada Maritime Corp v. Cansulex Ltd.*, [1987] AC 460. See for an interesting and recent application of the doctrine *Albon v. Naza Motor Trading*, [2007] EWHC 9 (Ch.); [2007] 2 All ER 719; [2007] 1 Lloyd's Rep. 297.

[60] The *forum non conveniens* doctrine originates from Scotland and remarkably enough originates from the civil law tradition. The doctrine was initially applied by Scottish courts in *Société du Gaz de Paris v. Société Anonyme de Navigation 'Les Armateurs Français'*, 1926 SC (HL) 13. For earlier references to the doctrine see *Spiliada Maritime Corp v. Cansulex Ltd.*, [1987] AC 460, at 475. In 1974 *Owners of the Atlantic Star v. Owners of the Bona Spes*, [1974] AC 436, opened the door for the *forum non conveniens* doctrine. Before that decision a court could only refuse jurisdiction if the continuance of the action would be 'vexatious and oppressive' for the defendant. The cases *MacShannon v. Rockware Glass Ltd*, [1978] AC 795 and *The owners of the Las Mercedes v. Owners of the Abidin Daver*, [1984] AC 398, preceded the final acceptance of the *forum non conveniens* doctrine in the case of service within the jurisdiction in the *Spiliada* case and also expressed that the same criteria should apply to the *forum conveniens* when permission was given to serve the defendant out of the jurisdiction. See for more details Dicey, Morris *et al.*, *Conflict of Laws*, § 12-7, at 465 *et seq.*; Hill, *International Commercial Disputes*, § 9.2.6, at 277; Briggs, *Civil Jurisdiction*, § 4.12, at 301; Fawcett, North *et al.*, *Private International Law*, at 426.

[61] *Spiliada Maritime Corp v. Cansulex Ltd.*, [1987] AC 460, at 480.

[62] But see for an analysis of a blurred distinction between the *forum non conveniens* doctrine and the *forum conveniens*, Chalas, *L'exercise discrétionnaire*, § 260, at 242.

[63] The fact that the defendant can ask the English court not to exercise its jurisdiction or to refuse to take jurisdiction is considered to be a powerful instrument for the defendant in transnational litigation in which the defendant adopted a strategy of 'reverse forum shopping'. See Bell, *Forum Shopping and Venue*, at 137.

[64] In *Société du Gaz de Paris v. Société Anonyme de Navigation 'Les Armateurs Français'*, (1926) SC (HL) 13, at 18, Lord Dunedin held that 'the proper translation for these Latin words, so far as this plea is concerned is "appropriate"'.

[65] See *Spiliada Maritime Corp v. Cansulex Ltd.*, [1987] AC 460, at 474. Lord MacKay of Clashfern repeats what was stated by Lord Dunedin of the Scottish courts in *Société du Gaz de Paris v. So-*

Even though the terminology 'natural forum' is often used and has become 'irresistible',[66] the doctrine is not necessarily aiming at a dispute's natural forum, since disputes are often more or less equally connected to more than one forum.[67] The doctrine attempts to establish whether the English forum is *clearly* the most appropriate – or most natural – forum.[68]

The *Spiliada* test involves a two-stage test.[69] First, the 'most clearly and distinctly appropriate forum' has to be identified and second, the allocation of jurisdiction should be in accordance with the 'requirements of justice'.[70] The *Spiliada* test weighs a number of factors that apply to assumed jurisdiction based on the service within as well as service out of the jurisdiction.[71] A citation of Lord Templeman will clarify the above:

> 'Where the plaintiff is entitled to commence his action in this country, the court, applying the doctrine of forum non conveniens will only stay the action if the defendant satisfies the court that some other forum is more appropriate. Where the plaintiff can only commence his action with leave, the court, applying the doctrine of forum conveniens will only grant leave if the plaintiff satisfies the court that England is the most appropriate forum to try the action. But whatever reasons may be advanced in favour of a foreign forum, the plaintiff will be allowed to pursue an action which the English court has jurisdiction to entertain if it would be unjust to the plaintiff to confine him to remedies elsewhere.'[72]

4.3.1 The Most Real and Substantial Connection: The Appropriateness Test

Several connecting factors should be taken into consideration to establish whether the English forum is the 'clearly and distinctly more appropriate' forum. These factors can be divided in five groups:[73] 1) Personal connections with the parties to the litigation; 2) the factual connexion between the events and particular courts; 3) the applicable law to resolve the substantive dispute; 4) the possibility of *lis*

---

ciété Anonyme de Navigation 'Les Armateurs Français', (1926) SC (HL), at 851; see also W. Kennett, '*Forum non Conveniens* in Europe', 43 *Cambridge Law Journal* (1995), at 554.

[66] Dicey, Morris *et al.*, *Conflict of Laws*, § 12-005, at 464.

[67] 'Furthermore, there are cases where no particular forum can be described as the natural forum for the trial of the action. Such cases are particularly likely to occur in commercial disputes, where there can be pointers to a number of different jurisdictions', *Spiliada Maritime Corp v. Cansulex Ltd.*, [1987] AC 460, at 477; Dicey, Morris *et al.*, *Conflict of Laws*, § 12-005, at 464.

[68] Briggs, *Civil Jurisdiction*, § 4.15, at 307-308.

[69] Ibid., § 4.14-4.16, at 304-317; Hill, *International Commercial Disputes*, § 9.2.22, at 283.

[70] The *Spiliada* test has been elaborately dealt with in *Connelly v. RTZ Corp Plc (No. 2)*, [1998] AC 854 and *Lubbe v. Cape Plc*, [2000] 1 WLR 1545.

[71] That has been made clear by Lord Goff in *Spiliada Maritime Corp v. Cansulex Ltd.*, [1987] AC 460, at 480-481. See for a recent application of these factors, *Limit (No. 3) Ltd v. PDV Insurance Co Ltd*, [2005] WL 836333; see also R. Brand and S. Jablonski, *Forum non Conveniens: History, Global Practice, and Future under The Hague Convention on Choice of Court Agreements* (2007), at 33-35.

[72] *Spiliada Maritime Corp v. Cansulex Ltd.*, [1987] AC 460, at 464-465.

[73] Lord Chieveley, *Spiliada Maritime Corp. v. Cansulex Ltd.*, [1987] AC 460, at 478; Briggs, *Civil Jurisdiction*, § 4.15, at 308.

alibi pendens; and 5) the relevance of other parties to the litigation or multiple defendants.

The first group dealing with the personal factor of the parties involves the appreciation of the practical inconvenience of one party (or both) to litigate in a foreign court, or the convenience to litigate in its home forum.[74] The residence or place of business of the parties will be taken into account in the court's appreciation on the practical convenience and the appropriateness of the forum. The second group appreciates the factual connection between the claim and the forum. For instance, the availability of witnesses can be of significant practical weight.[75] The last three groups are more focused on procedural convenience concerning 'the interest of justice'. Included in the considerations of efficiency, expedition and economy is the advantage of having experts with specific knowledge of legal or factual issues arising from the case. This factor is also called the 'Cambridgeshire factor' in the *Spiliada* test.[76]

The House of Lords in *Lubbe v. Cape*[77] decided that public interests or 'public factors' should not be considered in applying the *forum (non) conveniens* doctrine. In this important decision, the Lords refused to weigh public factors in the *forum non conveniens* doctrine and held that the *Spiliada* test relates to the private interests of the parties or to the ends of justice, and leaves no room for considerations of public interests.[78]

4.3.2 Injustice If Proceedings Were to Be Stayed

The second stage of the *Spiliada* test considers the 'efficiency of justice' concerning all circumstances of the case and goes beyond the 'appropriateness' of the (foreign) forum on the basis of factual connections with the dispute.[79] The second stage focuses on the 'requirements of justice' and considers whether it would be *unjust* for the claimant to be sent to the 'available natural forum'. The burden of proof for this criterion will always be on the claimant, who has to establish objectively 'by cogent evidence that he will not obtain justice in the foreign jurisdiction' and that proceedings should not be stayed.[80] It is therefore not sufficient to state that he will

[74] Briggs, *Civil Jurisdiction*, § 4.15, at 308; Hill, *International Commercial Disputes*, § 9.2.23, at 284.

[75] See on the 'witness convenience', *Navigators Insurance Co v. Atlantic Methanol Production Co LLC*, [2004] Lloyd's Rep. IR 418; [2003] EWHC 1706 (Comm.).

[76] Dicey, Morris *et al.*, *Conflict of Laws*, § 12-030, at 479; Hill, *International Commercial Disputes*, § 9.2.31, at 287, *et seq.*

[77] *Lubbe v. Cape Plc*, [2000] 1 WLR 1545, at 1561 and 1566.

[78] 'Section A – Civil Procedure Rules 1998, Part 6 – Service of Documents III. Special Provisions about Service out of the Jurisdiction', in *The White Book from Sweet and Maxwell* (2007), § 6.21.18; Dicey, Morris *et al.*, *Conflict of Laws*, § 12-033, at 482; Briggs, *Civil Jurisdiction*, § 4.15, at 313; R. Weintraub, 'Parallel Litigation and Forum-Selection Clauses', in *Law and Justice in a Multistate World: Essays in Honor of Arthur T. von Mehren* (2002), at 465; and see in general C. Morse, 'Not in the Public Interest? Lubbe v. Cape PLC', 37 *Texas International Law Journal* (2002).

[79] See also P. Rogerson, 'The Common Law Rules of Jurisdiction of the English Courts over Companies' Foreign Activities', in *Globalisation and Jurisdiction* (2004), at 95.

[80] Briggs, *Civil Jurisdiction*, § 4.16, at 314. See in general '*The White Book* Service out of the Jurisdiction', § 6.21.15.

lose the proceedings if the foreign court will hear the case; the concept 'legitimate personal or juridical advantage' seems to have been abandoned.[81] Instead the test is concerned with whether substantial justice will be done in the available appropriate forum and whether it will principally involve a procedural disadvantage for the claimant to be sent to a foreign court. There are disadvantages for the claimant when the claim is *time barred* in the other available forum or when it is likely that the claimant will encounter longer *delays*, higher *costs*[82] and lower *damages* than in the English forum.[83] The availability of *legal aid* in the English forum versus inadequate or absent legal aid in the other available forum also plays an important role in deciding upon the appropriateness of the forum.[84] The court can also take into account the disadvantage suffered by the claimant when divergent conflict of law rules leads to different applicable substantive law and different outcomes on the merits.[85] Taking into account the outcome of conflict of laws rules is however controversial and could favour the claimant over the defendant.[86]

As a rule, the *forum (non) conveniens* doctrine does not involve a comparison of legal systems with regard to the merits, the functioning or quality of foreign legal systems.[87] However, when it is established that claimant will not receive a fair trial in the other forum, it would be unjust to send the claimant to another forum.

The *Lubbe v. Cape Plc* case illustrates the importance of the substantial justice element in the discretionary powers of English courts. The defendant, Cape Plc was an English incorporated multinational mining company that carried out business activities in South Africa through its South African subsidiary. Claims for personal injuries arising out of commercial activities, carried out by its South African subsidiary and for which the Cape's head office were held responsible, were filed in England by thousands of South African claimants through a class action. While Cape Plc was incorporated in England, the company was considered 'present' in England and service of process within the jurisdiction existed as of right.[88] Most likely the claimants 'shopped' for the English forum, and not for South African courts due to the (procedural) advantages of the English courts, such as legal, medical and technical expertise, efficiency and the availability of legal

---

[81] As required under the former authority of *MacShannon v. Rockware Glass Ltd.*, [1978] AC 795, but overturned by Lord Goff in *Spiliada Maritime Corp. v. Cansulex Ltd*, [1987] AC 460, at 482. Briggs, *Civil Jurisdiction*, § 4.16, at 314.

[82] *Roneleigh Ltd v. MII Exports Inc*, [1989] 1 WLR 619; *The Vishva Ajay*, [1989] 2 Lloyd's Rep. 558.

[83] Dicey, Morris *et al.*, *Conflict of Laws*, § 12-032-33, at 481; Hill, *International Commercial Disputes*, § 9.2.37-39, at 289-290; Briggs, *Civil Jurisdiction*, § 4.17, at 317.

[84] *Connelly v. RTZ Corp Plc (No. 2)*, [1998] AC 854; and *Lubbe v. Cape plc*, [2000] 1 WLR 1545; see Briggs, *Civil Jurisdiction*, § 4.16, at 316-317; Hill, *International Commercial Disputes*, § 9.2.41, at 291-292.

[85] *Banco Atlantico SA v. British Bank of the Middle East*, [1990] 2 Lloyd's Rep. 504; *Irish Shipping Ltd. v. Commercial Union Assurance Co Plc*, [1990] 2 WLR 117, at 133; *The Magnum*, [1989] 1 Lloyd's Rep. 47.

[86] Hill, *International Commercial Disputes*, § 9.2.49, at 294; Briggs, *Civil Jurisdiction*, § 4.18, at 320.

[87] Hill, *International Commercial Disputes*, § 9.2.50, at 294.

[88] See Sect. 4.4.2.

aid.[89] Cape Plc applied for a stay on the ground of *forum non conveniens* and satisfied the court that South Africa was the other available forum which was clearly more appropriate based on the factual connections between the dispute and forum, despite the fact that Cape was strongly connected with the English forum because it was incorporated there and had its head office in England. However, the Lords refused a stay on the ground that 'substantial justice' would not be served in the more appropriate South-African forum. Lord Bingham of Cornhill held that the 'exercise of jurisdiction by the South African High Court ... could contribute to delay, uncertainty and cost[s]'.[90] Furthermore the claimant submitted that a stay of proceedings in favour of a South African court would violate his rights guaranteed by Article 6 of the ECHR because of the lack of funding and legal representation in South Africa and would deny them a fair trial on terms of litigious equality. Although Lord Bingham of Cornhill does not think that 'article 6 supports any conclusion which is not already reached on application of Spiliada principles', he cannot accept to decline jurisdiction in favour of South Africa if legal representation were not available there.[91]

The latter reference to Article 6 ECHR raises the question whether the *forum (non) conveniens* doctrine is incompatible with claimant's right of access to justice.[92] In the *Connelly* decision, Sir Thomas Bingham is clear on this concept and states that 'Article 6 of the [ECHR] has nothing to do with jurisdiction or the doctrine of forum non conveniens. It does not require a state to extend its jurisdiction or to provide special rules to obviate the difficulties of any particular litigant.'[93]

4.4 Defendant's Presence and the Service within the Jurisdiction

When the defendant is present in England, service of process within the jurisdiction is available as of right and asserts jurisdiction to English courts, regardless of the nature of the claim or the connection between the action and the English forum. As a consequence, it is necessary to determine 'presence' for both individuals and corporate defendants.

4.4.1 **Individuals**

For proper service the claimant must comply with the CPR Rules regulating the manner, time and place for service of the claim form. Contrary to corporations and partnerships, the presence of an individual is easy to establish: an individual is *physically* present or not. No minimum period of stay is required; mere tempo-

[89] See Rogerson, 'Jurisdiction over Companies' Foreign Activities', at 96-97.

[90] *Lubbe v. Cape Plc*, [2000] 1 WLR 1545, at 1560.

[91] Ibid., at 1561.

[92] Briggs, *Civil Jurisdiction*, § 1.20, at 18-20.

[93] *Connelly v. RTZ Corp. Plc (No. 2)*, [1998] AC 854, at 860. Reference was made to *Tolstoy Miloslavsky v. United Kingdom*, (1995) 20 EHRR 442. See Briggs, *Civil Jurisdiction*, § 1.20, at 19, C. Morse, 'Not in the Public Interest? Lubbe v. Cape PLC', at 554-555.

rary presence suffices and constitutes enough 'presence' for service of process.[94] A defendant brought within the jurisdiction in police custody or with the purpose of testifying as a witness, can be served with process, as long as he has not been brought 'fraudulently or improperly' in the jurisdiction.[95] If the defendant leaves England after being properly served, English courts remain competent.[96]

The procedural aspects of the service of claim form on the individual defendant are regulated in Part 6 of the CPR and the general methods of service are governed by Rule 6.2(1) CPR.[97] The general methods of service are personal service,[98] service by first class post, service by leaving the document at a specified place,[99] or service through a document exchange by fax or other means of electronic communication.[100] Personal service on the individual is regulated by Rule 6.4 and takes place by leaving the document with the defendant or his solicitor.[101] Personal service was once the only method to serve an individual, but modern times demanded other methods.[102] If service is made other than by personal service, Rule 6.5 requires an address for service, which is usually the address of the defendant's solicitor.[103] If no place of service is provided and no solicitor is acting on behalf of the party to be served, the document must be sent or transmitted to a specified place under Rule 6.5(6), which is the usual or last known residence of an individual.[104] In this regard, the place of residence merely constitutes a place where proper service can be made, but does not constitute a jurisdictional basis.[105] This was at

---

[94] *Colt Industries Inc. v. Sarlie*, [1966] 2 Lloyd's Rep. 163 and *Maharanee Seethadevi Gaekwar of Baroda v. Wildenstein*, [1972] 2 All ER 689 (CA) (Civ Div). Dicey, Morris *et al.*, *Conflict of Laws*, § 11-103, at 346.

[95] Fawcett, North *et al.*, *Private International Law*, at 355.

[96] Dicey, Morris *et al.*, *Conflict of Laws*, § 11-105, at 347.

[97] Briggs, *Civil Jurisdiction*, § 5.03, at 387.

[98] In accordance with Rule 6.4, see ibid., § 5.05, at 388-389.

[99] Rule 6.5(2) states that a party must give an address for service within the jurisdiction, primarily the business address of his solicitor as well as his address for service (Rule 6.5(2)(a)) and secondly where the defendant resides or carries on business within the jurisdiction (Rule 6.5(3)).

[100] Dicey, Morris *et al.*, *Conflict of Laws*, § 11-105, at 347; Briggs, *Civil Jurisdiction*, § 5.06-13, at 391-392.

[101] Rule 6.2(2) and (3) stipulates that the solicitor may be served on behalf of the defendant only when he has been authorized to accept service on behalf of a party and has notified the party serving the document in writing that he is so authorized. See *Smith v. Probyn and PGA European Tower Ltd*, [2000] All ER 250.

[102] 'But things long since changed' according to May LJ in *City & Country Properties Ltd v. Kamali*, [2007] 1 WLR 1219 (CA), at § 6.

[103] Or otherwise the solicitor's residence or place of business if he carries on business within the jurisdiction. Briggs, *Civil Jurisdiction*, § 5.06, at 389. Where no solicitor is acting for the party to be served and no address for service has been given, the document must be sent or transmitted to a specified place as regulated in Rule 6.5(6). Briggs, *Civil Jurisdiction*, § 5.08, at 390, Hill, *International Commercial Disputes*, § 7.1.4, at 195.

[104] Briggs, *Civil Jurisdiction*, § 5.08, at 390; Hill, *International Commercial Disputes*, § 7.1.4, at 195. Service by an alternative method under Rule 6.8 permits service on a defendant if it appears to the court that there are some good reasons, such as for instance that the defendant fled the service by going abroad. See also service of claim by agreed method under Rule 6.15 and see for another special ground Rule 6.16 on the service of an agent. Dicey, Morris *et al.*, *Conflict of Laws*, § 11-106, at 347; Briggs, *Civil Jurisdiction*, § 5.12-13, at 392-393.

[105] Hill, *International Commercial Disputes*, § 7.1.4, at 195.

least thought to be the case in *Chellaram v. Chellaram (No. 2)*, in which the question was raised whether a defendant not present – and not domiciled – in England could be subjected to English jurisdiction by serving him at his last known place of residence.[106] The High Court stated that a defendant who is absent in England, cannot be validly served if service was made by post at an address occasionally used by him in London because 'there is no evidence that it ever was a "residence" and it therefore cannot be his "last known residence"' and secondly 'it has always been, and remains, a fundamental rule of English procedure and jurisdiction that a defendant may be served with originating process within the jurisdiction only if he is present in the jurisdiction at the time of service, or deemed service.'[107]

This fundamental principle that the defendant has to be present within the jurisdiction for valid service by post at his last known address stands on shaky grounds since the Court of Appeal's decision in *City & Country Properties Ltd v. Kamali*.[108] In the *Kamali* case, the claim form was left at the defendant's place of business pursuant to Rule 6.5(6) CPR while he was abroad. The defendant was an English resident and had a business in England, but was only temporarily abroad when the claim was served at his place of business. The *Kamali* case casts doubts on the correctness of the *Chellaram* case, especially since May LJ disapproved of the statement by Lord Justice Lawrence Collins[109] and stated that 'there is no rule perpetuating the idea that a person has to be within the jurisdiction for service by post to be effected.'[110] Both May LJ and Neuberger LJ based their argument on the fact that the CPR Rules resemble more closely the Court County Rules, according to which it is permitted to validly service by post at defendant's last known address when the defendant is not in the jurisdiction.[111]

According to the Court of Appeal a defendant absent abroad does not preclude a validly effected service at his last known address[112] 'provided that the claimant has made reasonable investigations, prior to service, that have not established that the defendant is living abroad and [has] his address there'.[113]

This *Kamali* decision (could) seriously affect(s) the traditional common law structure based on presence, since it makes service of process within the jurisdiction possible at defendant's residence or place of business even when the defendant

[106] See *Chellaram v. Chellaram (No. 2)*, [2002] EWHC 632 (Ch.); [2002] 3 All ER 17, confirming among others the House of Lords' decision in *Barclays Bank of Swaziland Ltd v. Hahn*, [1989] 1 WLR 506.

[107] Mr Justice Lawrence Collins, § 47. Later confirmed by the High Court Chancery Division in *Fairmays v. Palmer*, [2006] EWHC 96 (Ch.).

[108] [2006] EWCA Civ 1879; [2007] 1 WLR 1219.

[109] 'In my judgment it [Justice Collins' statement] is not correct.' [2007] 1 WLR 1219, at paras. 1 and 12.

[110] Ibid., at para. 11.

[111] As stated in *Rolph v. Zolan*, [1993] 1 WLR 1305. See statements of May LJ, para. 11, and Neuberger LJ, para. 21, in *City & Country Properties Ltd v. Kamali*, [2007] 1 WLR 1219.

[112] Neuberger LJ in *City & Country Properties Ltd v. Kamali*, [2007] 1 WLR 1219, para. 20.

[113] See Sweet and Maxwell's *The White Book*, Section A – Civil Procedure Rules 1998, Part 6 – Service of Documents I. General Rules about Service. Commentary last updated on 8 May 2007, reformulating the words of Neuberger LJ in *City & Country Properties Ltd v. Kamali*, [2007] 1 WLR 1219, paras. 27 and 29.

himself is not present. An overlap with Rule 6.20(1) which provides for service out of the jurisdiction when the defendant is domiciled in England would be inevitable. Judge Neuberger LJ acknowledges however that even though 'such interpretation of rules 6.2 to 6.5 cuts down the circumstances in which rule 6.20(1) can or needs to be invoked, it does not render it [rule 6.20] nugatory.'[114] Despite its importance and its apparent corrosion of the fundamental common law principle, the *Kamali* decision has passed relatively unnoticed in English literature and it remains to be seen how future case law will deal with the question.[115]

4.4.2 Corporate Presence

Like individuals, corporations are subjected to English jurisdiction when served with process while 'present' in England. Corporate presence can however not be determined by its '*physical* presence'. Since a corporation is an artificial entity, its presence should be equally determined in an artificial manner.[116] Interestingly, traditional common law initially determined that a corporation was 'present' when it carried out business in the forum in such a manner that the company was considered 'resident' in England.[117] At present, the service of companies within the jurisdiction, and thus this fictive notion of corporate presence, is regulated by statutory provisions.[118]

Since 1999, English jurisdiction law has two sets of rules for service of corporations within the jurisdiction.[119] First, corporate defendants can be served by *statutory service* following the Companies Act.[120] An *alternative*, second, method

[114] Neuberger LJ in *City & Country Properties Ltd v. Kamali*, [2007] 1 WLR 1219, para. 23.

[115] See in general J. Sorabji, 'Service Where the Defendant Is Outside the Jurisdiction; Case Comment: Kamali v City', 26 *Civil Justice Quarterly* (2007).

[116] Fawcett, North *et al.*, *Private International Law*, at 358; Hill, *International Commercial Disputes*, § 7.1.8; J. Fawcett, 'A New Approach to Jurisdiction over Companies in Private International Law', 37 *The International and Comparative Law Quarterly* (1988), at 652-653; N. Enonchong, 'Service of Process in England on Overseas Companies and Article 5(5) of the Brussels Convention', 48 *The International and Comparative Law Quarterly* (1999), 4, at 921.

[117] The Court of Appeal stated that 'in order to render a foreign corporation liable to be served with a writ within the jurisdiction, they must be carrying on business within the jurisdiction at some fixed place, which can be considered their place of business, in such a manner that they can be deemed to be resident there', *Dunlop Pneumatic Tyre Co Limited v. Actien-Gesellschaft für Motor und Motorfahrzeugbau Vorm Cudell & Co*, [1902] 1 KB 342, at 344; Justice Collins M.R. confirmed at 347 that

> 'In order to see whether they [corporate defendants] were liable to be so served, it is necessary to consider whether, upon the facts, they can be said to have been resident in England when the service was effected, … the true test in such cases is whether the foreign corporation is conducting its own business at some fixed place within the jurisdiction, that being the only way in which a corporation can reside in this country.'

[118] Hill, *International Commercial Disputes*, § 7.1.8, at 196; Enonchong, 'Overseas Companies and Article 5(5)', fn. 4, at 921; and C. McLachlan, 'Transnational Tort Litigation: An Overview', in *Transnational Tort Litigation: Jurisdictional Principles* (1996), at 82. See also Fawcett, 'A New Approach to Jurisdiction over Companies', at 652.

[119] Before Rule 6.2 went into force on 26 April 1999, the statutory service under the Companies Act was the only service regime possible, Fawcett, North *et al.*, *Private International Law*, at 358.

[120] The Companies Act 1985 as modified by the 1992 Act, SI 1992 No. 3179 replaced as of 1 October 2008 by the Companies Act 2006 (including consequential amendments), Order 2008 No. 948 1.1.1.

for service on companies is provided by the Civil Procedure Rules.[121] Statutory service is based on the idea that corporate entities are required to register persons who can accept service in their name. English as well as foreign companies incorporated under the Companies Act, have to comply with registration requirements for statutory service.[122] Conversely, the CPR service is based on the presumption that a defendant can be served with process as long as he is 'present'.

In the *Sea Assets Limited v. Pt Garuda*[123] case the Commercial Court held that Part 6 of the CPR is an *alternative* to statutory service and that the provisions of the Company Act 'are not mandatory, [but] merely permissive'[124] which was confirmed in *Saab v. Saudi American Bank.*[125] As a result, the general methods of service under Part 6 CPR also apply to corporate defendants as expressly stated in Rule 6.2(2). According to Briggs, the CPR regime overlaps with the statutory service regime, but the alternative service of the CPR is invariably simpler and cheaper than service under the Companies Act.[126] It should generally be assumed that the CPR regime is primarily used to invoke the jurisdiction of English courts over a company which is not incorporated in England, but is 'present' in England.[127]

4.4.2.1 *Corporate Presence under the Civil Procedure Rules Regime*

The CPR regime for service on foreign companies 'present' in England distinguishes three types of defendants: individuals, corporations (or companies) and

---

[121] Dicey, Morris *et al.*, *Conflict of Laws*, § 11-120, at 352; Briggs, *Civil Jurisdiction*, § 5.15, at 393, Hill, *International Commercial Disputes*, § 7.1.5, at 195. Rule 6.2(2) expressly provides that a company may be served by any method permitted in Part 6 as an alternative to the methods of *service* provided for by the Companies Act 1985. *Service* under the CPR will usually be simpler and cheaper than *service* under the Act. Rule 6(2) reads 'A company may be served by any method permitted under this Part as an alternative to the methods of service set out in – (a) section 725 of the Companies Act 1985 (service by leaving a document at or posting it to an authorised place); (b) section 695 of that Act (service on overseas companies); and (c) section 694A of that Act (service of documents on companies incorporated outside the U.K. and Gibraltar and having a branch in Great Britain).'

[122] Dicey, Morris *et al.*, *Conflict of Laws*, § 11-116, at 350.

[123] *Sea Assets Ltd v. PT Garuda Indonesia*, [2000] 4 All ER 371; High Court of Justice Queen's Bench Division, Commercial Court on 29 February 2000.

[124] *Sea Assets Ltd v. PT Garuda Indonesia*, [2000] 4 All ER 371, para. 7; Clarkson and Hill, *The Conflict of Laws*, at 88; Enonchong, 'Overseas Companies and Article 5(5)', at 926.

[125] [1999] I.L.Pr. 798, (CA). Justice Clarke, at 801, explains that by virtue of Rule 6.5(6) CPR 'a document, which includes a claim form, may be served on a company incorporated outside England and Wales at any place of business of the company within the jurisdiction. It was my impression that that revelation came as a surprise not only to me but also to those advising the Saabs.'

[126] Briggs, *Civil Jurisdiction*, § 5.15, at 393 and Hill, *International Commercial Disputes*, § 7.1.22, at 201. According to *The White Book*:

'The use of methods of service allowed by the [CPR] rules as an alternative to those prescribed by the Companies Act 1985 should be exercised with caution where the consequences of failing to prove good service of originating process could be serious for the claimant (such as service at the end of a limitation period). Service using the statutory procedure is usually conclusive.'

'Section A – Civil Procedure Rules 1998 Part 6 – Service of Documents I. General Rules about Service', in *The White Book* (2007), under 6.5.6. Commentary; last updated on 8 May 2007.

[127] According to the Brussels Model the company should not be domiciled in any EU Member State. See Hill, *International Commercial Disputes*, § 7.1.22, at 201.

partnerships.[128] The applicability of general methods of service[129] under Section 6.2 to corporate defendants entails that domestic corporations are personally served by leaving a document with a person holding a senior position within the company.[130] Companies are required to give an address for service by first class post, by leaving it at the place of service through a document exchange or by fax or other means of electronic communication,[131] generally at the business address of the company's solicitor.[132] Where no solicitor is acting on behalf of the company and no address is provided for service, Rule 6.5(6) CPR determines service at a specified place by distinguishing between *a)* a 'corporation incorporated in England other than a company', *b)* 'companies registered in England', and *c)* any other companies, i.e. foreign companies.[133]

A corporation incorporated in England is to be served at its *principal office*: or any place within the jurisdiction where it carries on its activities and which has a real connection with the claim.[134] A company, not incorporated, but registered in England, is to be served at its *principal office* or alternatively any *place of business* that has a real connection with the claim.[135] Companies not registered in England, or foreign companies, are to be served at any place within the jurisdiction where the corporation carries on its activities, or any place of business of the company within the jurisdiction. The meaning of 'place of business' should presumably be found by way of analogy to the 'place of business'-concept used for statutory service.[136]

In *Harrods Limited v. Dow Jones & Company Inc* the question was raised whether Rule 6.5(6) CPR permitting service at a place within the jurisdiction 'where the

[128] Dicey, Morris *et al.*, *Conflict of Laws*, § 11-102, at 346. For partnerships a distinction has to be made between partnerships carrying out business in England and those that do not. A partnership carrying out business in England, can be served by personal service by leaving the claim form with a co-partner, while present in England, provided that he carries out business in England under the name of the firm, or by serving a person having at the time of service management control of the partnership's business at the partnership's principal place of business, according to Rule 6.4.5 CPR. As a consequence, this means that if the service has been proper, English courts have jurisdiction over partners even if they are not present within the jurisdiction, because one of their co-partners or a person having the management control at the time of service was served in England. If personal service is not available, service by post or fax and other communication methods is available under Rule 6.5 CPR. Dicey, Morris *et al.*, *Conflict of Laws*, § 11-109-114, at 348-350; Briggs, *Civil Jurisdiction*, § 5.20, at 396-397.

[129] The general methods are (a) personal service under Rule 6.4; (b) first class post; (c) leaving the document at a place specified in Rule 6.5; (d) through a document exchange in accordance with the relevant practice direction; or (e) by fax or other means of electronic communication in accordance with the relevant practice direction (including Practice Direction 6(3), '*The White Book* General Rules about Service', last updated on 12 September 2007).

[130] Rule 6.4(4) CPR; Briggs, *Civil Jurisdiction*, § 5.05, at 389.

[131] Rule 6.5(2) and (4).

[132] Rule 6.5(3), or in default the place where he resides or carries on business within the jurisdiction.

[133] According to the tabular form under Rule 6.5(6).

[134] According to the table of Rule 6.5(6) for a registered company.

[135] According to the table of Rule 6.5(6); Briggs, *Civil Jurisdiction*, § 5.08, at 390.

[136] Briggs, *Civil Jurisdiction*, § 5.08, at 390; Hill, *International Commercial Disputes*, § 7.1.23, at 201.

corporation carries on its activities' should be understood as altering the position for service upon foreign companies and widening the notion of corporate presence to 'carrying on business activities'. The Court clearly stated that 'the wording of the CPR does not enable one to by-pass the need to demonstrate that a place of business has been established within this jurisdiction.'[137] In other words, the CPR regime of service within the jurisdiction of a foreign corporation requires a place of business in England. However, the CPR does not require a connection between the claim and defendant's place of business in England.[138] This means that if the foreign company has a branch in England it can be served under Rule 6.5(6) CPR even if the claim is unrelated to the branch's activities. As will be explained below this approach differs considerably from the approach taken by the Companies Act.

Under certain conditions following Rule 6.16 CPR, a court can give permission to serve the defendant not present in England by serving his agent with a claim form within the jurisdiction. Accordingly, jurisdiction of English courts can be invoked against an overseas principal[139] residing and carrying on business out of the jurisdiction but who entered into a contract by or through an agent within the jurisdiction, provided that the claim relates to that contract and provided that at the time of the application of the claim form, either the agent's authority has not been terminated or he is still in business relations with his principal.[140] This interesting provision results in service within the jurisdiction on a defendant who himself is not present within the jurisdiction but who can be served as if he were present through his agent without the special permission to serve out of the jurisdiction under Rule 6.20 CPR.[141]

4.4.2.2 *Statutory Service on Corporations According to the Companies Act*

Statutory service is regulated by the Companies Act 1985, recently replaced by the Companies Act 2006, which went into force on 1 October 2008. The 1985 Act is still of importance due to the interpretation by the courts of a few concepts of 'corporate presence'. Moreover, the 2006 Act is recent and still requires the drafting of new regulations. Due to this, both acts will be discussed below.[142] The Acts primarily distinguishes between registered companies and 'overseas companies'.

---

[137] *Harrods Ltd v. Dow Jones & Co Inc*, [2003] EWHC 1162 (QB), arguments 32 and 33. But see Briggs stating that an overseas company with no place of business in England that cannot be served under the statutory regime of the Companies Act, could be served under Rule 6.5(6) if it carries on its business activities at a place within the jurisdiction. Briggs, *Civil Jurisdiction*, § 5.15, fn. 56, at 393. Enonchong, 'Overseas Companies and Article 5(5)', at 925, suggesting that a mere place of business is sufficient and does not require an 'established' place of business which results in a lesser connection than Sect. 695 and an even lesser connection under Sect. 694A of the branch, especially as it is required that the claim be in 'respect of the carrying on of the business' of the branch.

[138] Dicey, Morris *et al.*, *Conflict of Laws*, § 11-122, at 353; Briggs, *Civil Jurisdiction*, § 7.1.23, at 202; Enonchong, 'Overseas Companies and Article 5(5)', at 925.

[139] This overseas principal can be either an individual or a legal person.

[140] Briggs, *Civil Jurisdiction*, § 5.14, at 393.

[141] This permission has to be distinguished from the permission to serve out of the jurisdiction as described below. See also *The White Book* under 6.16(1); and Briggs, *Civil Jurisdiction*, § 5.14, at 393.

[142] Fawcett, North *et al.*, *Private International Law*, at 364.

Statutory service is generally made by leaving the claim form with a person registered to accept the statutory service on the company's behalf. By default of such a person, statutory service is done at any place of business.

For service of process on a registered company in England the claim form should be left at, or sent by post to, the company's registered office.[143] Even when this registered company carries on business abroad, it is considered to be 'present' by virtue of its incorporation under both Companies Acts.[144]

When a company is not incorporated under the Companies Acts, it is considered to be an '*overseas* company'.[145] The Companies Act 1985 also required an overseas company to have a place of business is England, the establishment of which entailed obligatory registration.[146] The definition of the 2006 Act is therefore wider in this respect.[147]

The Companies Act 1985 contains two different registration regimes for overseas companies. As a consequence the Act knows two different regimes for service: the branch regime of Section 690A and the place of business regime of Section 691. In 1992, the Companies Act enacted Section 690A regulating the requirement for 'branch registration' of Section 690A, in order to implement the European Council Eleventh Company Law Directive.[148] Its introduction did not, however, exclude the application of the former regime of Section 691 which regulates service on overseas companies with a mere place of business in England. As a result the two regimes of the Companies Act are mutually exclusive, but the branch regime of Section 690A prevails over the 'place of business' regime.[149] The Commercial Court held in *Sea Assets Limited v. Pt Garuda* that

---

[143] Sect. 725(1) Companies Act 1985 and Sect. 1139(1) Companies Act 2006. Briggs, *Civil Jurisdiction*, § 5.16, at 394. Fawcett, North *et al.*, *Private International Law*, at 358 and 364.

[144] Dicey, Morris *et al.*, *Conflict of Laws*, § 11-115, at 350; Briggs, *Civil Jurisdiction*, § 5.16, at 394; Hill, *International Commercial Disputes*, § 7.1.7, at 196.

[145] See Sect. 744 of the Companies Act 1985 and Sect. 1044 Companies Act 2006.

[146] Sect. 744 of the Companies Act 1985; Hill, *International Commercial Disputes*, § 7.1.10, at 197; Briggs, *Civil Jurisdiction*, § 5.17, at 394.

[147] See the Explanatory Notes to Companies Act 2006, which received Royal Asset on 8 November 2006, § 1330, at 202. See also Fawcett, North *et al.*, *Private International Law*, at 364.

[148] Eleventh Council Directive 89/666/EEC of 21 December 1989 concerning disclosure requirements in respect of branches opened in a Member State by certain types of companies governed by the law of another State. OJ 1989 L 395/36-39, implemented in English law by the Overseas Companies and Credit Financial Institutions (Branch Disclosure) Regulations 1992, SI 1992 No. 3179. Before the enactment of the directive, service of process on overseas companies was only determined by Sect. 691 in conjunction with Sect. 695 of the Companies Act and branch registration was unknown. This is also referred to as the pre-1992 regime, see Fawcett, North et al., *Private International Law*, at 359-360; Enonchong, 'Overseas Companies and Article 5(5)', at 921; see in general J. Fawcett, 'Jurisdiction and Subsidiaries', *Journal of Business Law* (1985), 16-25.

[149] Hill, *International Commercial Disputes*, § 7.1.11; Briggs, *Civil Jurisdiction*, § 5.17, at 394. Sect. 690A states 'Sections 691 and 692 shall not apply to any limited company which – (a) is incorporated outside the United Kingdom and Gibraltar, and (b) has a branch in the United Kingdom.' Also held in *Saab v. Saudi American Bank*, under 14: if the establishment is a branch then the company cannot be served as having a place of business and vice versa. According to Davies there are now two slightly different regimes for overseas companies under the Companies Act with slightly different definitions of connecting factors with England. He firmly condemns this way of implementation and opts

'[t]here have thus come into existence two parallel but very similar sets of provisions, the first set dealing with overseas companies with branches in the United Kingdom and the second dealing (as before) with overseas companies establishing a place of business in Great Britain but (presumably) not doing so at a branch. No definition of a branch is given.'[150]

4.4.2.2.a *Branch-establishment under Section 690A*

Section 690A of the Companies Act 1985 regulates the 'branch registration' for a company incorporated outside the U.K., but which has a 'branch' in the U.K. and Section 694 regulates the service of documents within the jurisdiction over these overseas companies. The overseas company is required to register the branch and to provide the names of persons authorized to accept service on behalf of the branch.[151] An overseas company falling under Section 690A is sufficiently served in respect of the carrying on of business of its branch if service is addressed, left or sent by post to any person whose name has been delivered to the registrar,[152] or if such person was not notified, at any place of business established by the company in Great Britain.[153] The latter does not mean that an overseas company is considered 'present' if it has a place of business in the U.K., it still has to have established a 'branch' in the U.K. within the meaning of Section 690A of the Companies Act, but service is simply considered to be valid if left at any place of business in England.

The Companies Act does not define the 'branch' concept but refers back to the Eleventh Company Directive,[154] which does not provide a definition either.[155] The House of Lords refused to seek guidance from the ECJ's settled case law concerning the interpretation of the 'branch' concept under Article 5(5) of the Brussels Model.[156] In the *Saab v. Saudi American Bank* case the Court held that the restrictive interpretation of Article 5(5) should not be applied to the English branch concept

'Section 694A [and 690A] need not be construed in the same way [as Article 5(5) Brussels Model], since an English court has the power to curb jurisdictional excesses

for a better integration of the branch-concept in English company law. P. Davies, *Gower and Davies' Principles of Modern Company Law* (2003), at 105 and 106.

150 *Sea Assets Ltd v. Pt Garuda Indonesia*, [2000] 4 All ER 371.

151 Schedule 21A(1) and (2) of the Companies Act; see Dicey, Morris *et al.*, *Conflict of Laws*, § 11-116, at 350; Hill, *International Commercial Disputes*, § 7.1.14, at 198.

152 Sect. 694A(2).

153 Sect. 694A(3); Dicey, Morris *et al.*, *Conflict of Laws*, § 11-116, at 350; Briggs, *Civil Jurisdiction*, § 5.18, at 395.

154 Sect. 698(2)(b) of the Companies Act states that '"branch" means a branch within the meaning of [the Eleventh Company Law Directive, 89/666/EEC] concerning disclosure requirements in respect of branches opened in a Member State by certain types of company[ies] governed by the law of another State.'

155 Hill, *International Commercial Disputes*, § 7.1.12, at 197; Briggs, *Civil Jurisdiction*, § 5.18, at 394; Davies, *Principles of Modern Company Law*, at 106.

156 See for branch jurisdiction in the Brussels Model, Chapter 2, Sect. 2.6. According to Jaffrey and Briggs reference should be made to the meaning of branch as indicated under Art. 5(5), see Clarkson and Hill, *The Conflict of Laws*, fn. 225, at 88; Briggs, *Civil Jurisdiction*, § 5.18, at 395; Davies, *Principles of Modern Company Law*, at 107; Fawcett, North *et al.*, *Private International Law*, at 358 *et seq.*

> by exercising its discretion to stay proceedings on the ground of forum non conveniens. … The jurisdictional regime established by the Convention is quite different.'[157]

The English branch under Section 690A should therefore be understood to be wider than Article 5(5) of the Brussels Model; any further guidance as to the definition of 'branch' under Section 690A was however not provided in the *Saab v. Saudi American Bank* decision.[158]

Section 694A(2) requires that service within the jurisdiction may only be made on an overseas company on the basis of a branch established in England, if the claim is 'in respect of the carrying on of the business' of the branch.[159] This important restriction of Section 694A requires a connection between the claim and the forum which is not required by Section 695, which founds jurisdiction on the basis of a place of business.[160] This means that when an overseas company has a branch in England general jurisdiction is not available over every claim, but the reach of English courts is limited to specific jurisdiction over claims concerning business activities carried out by the branch.[161] In order to fulfil this connection requirement between the branch's activities and the claim, it is however not required that the claim is wholly or even substantially connected with the branch's activities, it is sufficient that the claim is partly connected to the forum.[162] According to the Court of Appeal in the case of *Saab v. Saudi American Bank*:

> '[p]rocess will be "in respect of the carrying on of the business of the branch" within the meaning of section 694A(2) if it is in part in respect of the carrying on of the business, unless the connection between the process and the carrying on of the business of the branch is de minimis, that is of so little significance that it should be disregarded.'[163]

---

157 *Saab v. Saudi American Bank*, [1999] 4 All ER 321, Nos. 17-18; Enonchong, 'Overseas Companies and Article 5(5)', at 924 and 933-935, *contra* Hill, *International Commercial Disputes*, § 7.1.13, at 198.

158 Some guidance might be found in the accompanying Council Directive 89/117/EEC of 13 February 1989 on the obligations of branches established in a Member State of credit institutions and financial institutions having their head offices outside that Member State regarding the publication of annual accounting documents. Briggs, *Civil Jurisdiction*, § 5.18, fn. 63, at 394; Davies, *Principles of Modern Company Law*, at 107.

159 Again the Court of Appeal did not feel in *Saab v. Saudi American Bank*, [1999] 4 All ER 321, at para. 20, for a restrictive interpretation of the required link between the claim and the branch's activity as is given to Art. 5(5) of the Brussels Regulation ('arising out of the operations of the branch').

160 Dicey, Morris *et al.*, *Conflict of Laws*, § 11-118, at 351.

161 Enonchong, 'Overseas Companies and Article 5(5)', at 924 and 933-935.

162 Dicey, Morris *et al.*, *Conflict of Laws*, § 11-120, at 352; Hill, *International Commercial Disputes*, § 7.1.18, at 200; Briggs, *Civil Jurisdiction*, § 5.18, at 395; Fawcett, North *et al.*, *Private International Law*, at 360-361.

163 *Saab v. Saudi American Bank*, [1999] 4 All ER 321. This was confirmed by *Sea Assets Limited v. Pt Garuda*, [2000] 4 All ER 37, where the statutory service under Sect. 694 of the Companies Act form was considered to be ineffective, as the substance of the claim did not relate in any way to the branch's activities. See Dicey, Morris *et al.*, *Conflict of Laws*, § 11-120, at 352; Fawcett, North *et al.*, *Private International Law*, at 360-261.

One of the reasons in *Saab v. Saudi American Bank*[164] for not requiring the claim to be connected in its totality with the branch's activities was to reduce the differences with the 'place of business-regime' under Section 691,[165] since the latter does not require any connection between the claim and the activities of a place of business for service.[166] According to Justice Clark 'It would be surprising if the legislature had gone so far in the case of companies with a branch whilst retaining the old regime for companies with only an established place of business.'[167]

4.4.2.2.b *Place of business under Section 691*

When an overseas company establishes a place of business in England, which is not a branch falling under Section 690A, the company is considered to be 'present' in accordance with Section 691 of the Companies Act. For service within the jurisdiction it is equally required to provide a list of the names and addresses of one or more persons resident in the U.K. authorized to accept service on the company's behalf.[168] Section 695 regulates service in a similar way as Section 694 for branch establishment and states that an overseas company with a place of business in England is properly served if documents are addressed, left or sent by post to any person whose name is notified to the registrar.[169] Once the overseas company established a place of business in England, the duty remains with them to give notice of any alterations.[170] If it ceases to have a place of business in England, it shall forthwith give notice to the registrar,[171] but if the company does not give notice of the termination of its business activities in the U.K., it can still be properly served by leaving documents at one of the persons listed at the registrar, even if it ceased to carry out business.[172] In the case *Rome v. Punjab National Bank No. 2*[173] the Court of Appeal decided that service on an overseas company by leaving the documents at the established place of business as stated in Section 695 can be sufficient for English courts to have jurisdiction over the defendant. This has far-reaching consequences and means that when a company still has registered persons to accept service on its behalf, it remains subject to English jurisdiction over any kind of claim,[174] even if it ceased to carry out business in the jurisdiction.[175]

---

164 *Saab v. Saudi American Bank*, [1999] 4 All ER 321.

165 See section below. Hill, *International Commercial Disputes*, § 7.1.18, at 200.

166 *Saab v. Saudi American Bank*, [1999] 4 All ER 321, at para. 9.

167 Ibid.

168 Sect. 691(b)(ii).

169 Sect. 695(1); Hill, *International Commercial Disputes*, § 7.1.20, at 201.

170 Sect. 692(1).

171 Sect. 696(3); see also *Theodohos, The*, [1977] 2 Lloyd's Rep. 428, at 432.

172 Fawcett, North *et al.*, *Private International Law*, at 361 and see Enonchong, 'Overseas Companies and Article 5(5)', at 922.

173 *Rome v. Punjab National Bank No. 2*, [1989] 1 WLR 1211 (CA).

174 As will be explained below; no connection is required between the claim and the place of business activities.

175 *Rome v. Punjab National Bank No. 2*, [1989] 2 Lloyd's Rep., at 354; [1989] 1 WLR 1211; Dicey, Morris *et al.*, *Conflict of Laws*, § 11-121, at 352; Enonchong, 'Overseas Companies and Article 5(5)', at 922-923.

In default of any person authorized to accept service,[176] Section 695(2) provides for a 'default mechanism',[177] by allowing service to be made by leaving the documents at *any place of business* established by the company in the U.K.[178] In contrast to the situations explained above, when a company listed a person to accept service on its behalf, once the foreign company ceases to carry out business in England and no place of business can be identified for service, there can be no proper service.

One important feature of service at the defendant's 'place of business' under Section 695 is that the claim is not required to arise out of the activities carried out in the place of business.[179] This stands in sharp contrast with the requirement imposed for statutory service under Section 694A when the overseas company has a branch in England. As a result, corporate presence due to a place of business in England not being a branch – provides English courts with far-reaching jurisdiction, regardless of whether the claim is related to activities carried out in the place of business.[180] This can be explained by the fact that, before the enactment of Section 690A, traditional common law rules always asserted general jurisdiction over defendants who are present in the forum as long as there is proper service of process.[181]

Defining the place of business

The Companies Act 1985 does not define 'place of business'.[182] Settled case law has however taken a flexible approach to the meaning of 'place of business'.[183] Business activities should be carried out from a fixed and definite place.[184] It is not sufficient to merely 'do business' in England, companies should do so from a clear and fixed place and the business activities must have been carried out continuously and during a substantial period of time.[185] This requires a certain degree of continuity and permanency[186] and the place of business should be recognizable as the

[176] Either because the listed persons refuse to accept service, no longer reside in England or have died.

[177] *Harrods Ltd v. Dow Jones & Co Inc*, [2003] EWHC 1162 (QB).

[178] Sect. 695(2); Dicey, Morris *et al.*, *Conflict of Laws*, § 11-117, at 351; Briggs, *Civil Jurisdiction*, § 5.19, at 395; Enonchong, 'Overseas Companies and Article 5(5)', at 923.

[179] Briggs, *Civil Jurisdiction*, § 5.19, at 396.

[180] Hill, *International Commercial Disputes*, § 7.1.21, at 201.

[181] Fawcett, 'A New Approach to Jurisdiction over Companies', at 653.

[182] Dicey, Morris *et al.*, *Conflict of Laws*, § 11-123, at 353; Davies, *Principles of Modern Company Law*, at 106.

[183] *Aktiesselskabet Dampskip 'Hercules' v. Grand Trunk Pacific Railway Co.*, [1912] 1 KB 222; *Dunlop Pneumatic Tyre Co. v. Aktien-Gesellschaft für Motor and Motorfarhrzeugbau Vorm Cudell &* Co., [1902] 1 KB 342; *La Bourgogne, The*, [1899] at 1. *Newby v. Van Oppen, Re*, (1871-72) LR 7 QB 293; *Okura & Co Ltd v. Forsbacka Jernwerks Aktiebolag*, [1914] 1 KB 715; *Saccharin Corp Ltd. v. Chemische Fabrik Von Heyden Aktiengesellschaft*, [1911] 2 KB 516; *Theodohos, The*, QBD, [1977] 2 Lloyd's Rep. 428; and see *South India Shipping Corporation v. Export-Import Bank of Korea*, [1985] 2 All ER 219 (CA); and confirmed by *Rome v. Punjab National Bank (No. 2)*, [1989] 2 Lloyd's Rep. 354.

[184] Dicey, Morris *et al.*, *Conflict of Laws*, § 11-123, at 353; Briggs, *Civil Jurisdiction*, § 5.19, at 396.

[185] Court of Appeal *Okura & Co. Ltd v. Forsbacka Jernverks Aktiebolag*, [1914] 1 KB 715, at 718; Fawcett, 'Jurisdiction and Subsidiaries', at 16.

[186] Dicey, Morris *et al.*, *Conflict of Laws*, § 11-123, at 353; Enonchong, 'Overseas Companies and Article 5(5)', at 925.

company's business location.[187] A mere letterbox is not considered as a 'place of business'.[188] Apart from this required physical element of presence, the place of business should conduct business on *behalf* of the overseas company with a certain degree of autonomy to act and should be able to conclude contracts binding the principal authority.[189] Other business activities such as providing information or advertising, carried out from a fixed place of business may also constitute a business establishment in the sense of Section 695.[190] In *South India Shipping Corporation*[191] Justice Ackner concluded that the defendant had a place of business within Great Britain 'and it matters not that it does not conclude within the jurisdiction any banking transactions or have banking dealings with the general public as opposed to other banks or financial institutions.'[192] The fact that the defendant had premises and staff and conducted the external relations with other banks constituted a place of business.[193]

The question arose whether an overseas company has a place of business in England, when it carries out business through a person, such as a representative or agent.[194] As long as such independent agent, a (sales)[195] representative is *acting on behalf* of the overseas company and has a place of business in England it is sufficient for service within the jurisdiction.[196]

---

[187] In *Re Oriel Ltd.*, [1985] 3 All ER 216 (CA); Hill, *International Commercial Disputes*, § 7.1.15, at 198; Davies, *Principles of Modern Company Law*, at 107; Enonchong, 'Overseas Companies and Article 5(5)', at 923.

[188] Briggs, *Civil Jurisdiction*, § 5.19, at 396.

[189] Ibid.; Nygh, 'Common Law Approach', at 28; in *F. & K. Jabbour v. Custodian of Israeli Absentee Property*, [1954] 1 WLR 139, at 146, Pearson J. held

'A corporation resides in a country if it carries on business there at a fixed place of business, and, in the case of an agency, the principal test to be applied in determining whether the corporation is carrying on business at the agency is to ascertain whether the agent has authority to enter into contracts on behalf of the corporation without submitting them to the corporation for approval.' Cited and affirmed by *Adams v. Cape Industries Plc.*, [1990] Ch. 433 (CA), although this case was primarily concerned with the piercing of the corporate veil.

[190] Nygh, 'Common Law Approach', at 28; Fawcett, 'A New Approach to Jurisdiction over Companies', at 653.

[191] *South India Shipping Corporation Ltd. v. The Export-Import Bank Korea*, [1985] 1 Lloyd's Rep. 413. Court of Appeal confirmed by *Rakusens Ltd v. Baser Ambalaj Plastik Sanayi Ticaret AS*, [2001] EWCA Civ 1820 (CA).

[192] *South India Shipping Corporation Ltd. v. The Export-Import Bank Korea*, [1985] 1 Lloyd's Rep. 413, at 417.

[193] Dicey, Morris *et al.*, *Conflict of Laws*, § 11-123, at 353; Fawcett, 'A New Approach to Jurisdiction over Companies', at 654.

[194] Dicey, Morris *et al.*, *Conflict of Laws*, § 11-124, at 354; Briggs, *Civil Jurisdiction*, § 5.19, at 395-396; Fawcett, North *et al.*, *Private International Law*, at 361-365. See also the new Regime of the Companies Act 2006.

[195] See for a case where an English court took jurisdiction over a foreign company on the basis that it had a sales representative having a stand at a trade fair for a short period of 9 days, *Dunlop Pneumatic Tyre Co. Ltd v. AG für Motor und Motorfarhrzeugbau Vorm Cudell & Co*, [1902] 1 KB 342.

[196] See *Lalandia, The*, [1933] KB 56; *Saccharin Corp v. Chemische Fabrik Von Heyden AG*, [1911] 2 KB 516; *Okura & Co Ltd v. Forsbacka Jernverks Aktiebolag,* [1914] 1 KB 715. According to Fawcett 'One could think of an independent commercial agent or a subsidiary company as long as it is acting on behalf of the foreign company', see Fawcett, 'A New Approach to Jurisdiction over Companies', at 17.

In *Adams v. Cape Industries Plc*, the Court of Appeal revised the criteria for determining whether an overseas company had a place of business in England. The fact that the agent or representative has the power to conclude contracts constitutes an important element but the Court also held that other elements should be included for constituting a place of business:

> 'a) whether or not the fixed place of business from which the representative operates was originally acquired for the purpose of enabling him to act on behalf of the overseas corporation;
> b) whether the overseas corporation has directly reimbursed him for the cost of the accommodation, at the fixed place of business, and/or the cost of his staff;
> c) what contributions, if any, the overseas corporation makes to the financing of the business carried on by the representative;
> d) whether the representative is remunerated by reference to transactions, e.g. by commission, or by fixed regular payments, or in some other way;
> e) what degree of control the overseas corporation exercises over the running of the business conducted by the representative;
> f) whether the representative reserves part of his accommodation, or part of his staff, for conducting business relating to the overseas corporation;
> g) whether the representative displays the overseas corporation's name at his premises or on his stationery and, if so, whether he does it in such a way as to indicate that he is a representative of the overseas corporation;
> h) what business, if any, the representative transacts as principal exclusively on his own behalf;
> i) whether the representative makes contracts with customers, or other third parties, in the name of the overseas corporation, or otherwise in such manner as to bind it;
> j) if so, whether the representative requires specific authority in advance before binding the overseas corporation to contractual obligations.'[197]

The *Adam v. Cape Industries* factors were repeated and confirmed in the *Harrods Ltd v. Dow Jones & Co Inc* case.[198] The fact that an agent or representative has the power to conclude contracts and carries out business on behalf of a foreign company is important but not indispensable for the establishment of a place of business, the *Adam v. Cape Industries* factors should equally be considered on a case-by-case basis.

It is important to underline that in order to fulfil the requirements of both Companies Acts a physical element in the forum is required for statutory service on a

---

[197] *Adams v. Cape Industries Plc*, [1991] 1 All ER 929 *et seq.* (CA). See also *Domansa v. Derin Shipping & Trading Co Inc (The Sletreal)*, [2001] 1 Lloyd's Rep. 362; Dicey, Morris *et al.*, *Conflict of Laws*, § 11-125, at 354; Fawcett, 'Jurisdiction and Subsidiaries', at 18.

[198] *Harrods Ltd v. Dow Jones & Co Inc*, [2003] EWHC 1162 (QB); see also *Rakusens Ltd v. Baser Ambalaj Plastik Sanayi Ticaret AS*, 2001 WL 1251832 (CA), reaffirmed in *Adams v. Cape Industries*, [1991] 1 All ER 929, in which LJ Arden defined a place of business as follows:

'... a place of business is a place at which the business of the company is transacted, whether by agents or by employees and an address can be a place of business of an overseas company even if none of the people at the address have the authority to enter into contracts on behalf of the company. The business of a company is much wider than entering into contractual relations.' (Para. 37).

place of business, merely 'doing business' in England does not suffice.[199] A certain degree of caution should be kept to avoid confusion between 'place of business' and 'carrying out of business'. Lady Justice Arden's statement in *Rakusens Ltd v. Baser Ambalaj Plastik Sanayi Ticaret AS*[200] emphasizes the difference between 'place of business' and 'carrying on business' by arguing that

> 'I am driven to the conclusion that when the legislature selected the phrase "establishes a place of business" it meant something other than "carrying on business". … The expression "carrying on business" is so wide that it would really touch all persons having business in the United Kingdom, a result from which the legislature may well have shrunk.'[201]

She puts the criteria listed in *Adams v. Cape Industries* into perspective by stating that 'I do not need to go through that list. It has to be remembered that, while there is some overlap between the question of presence and the carrying on of business, the overlap is not complete. …'[202]

When is a place of establishment not a branch?

The interaction of the two regimes is rather 'curious'[203] and it is unclear what exactly distinguishes a place of business from a branch. A branch-establishment under Section 690A prevails over the place of business-establishment of Section 691, but when does an establishment constitute a place of business that is not a branch? Both concepts may overlap and it remains difficult to define and differentiate the one from the other.[204] According to North 'it will be difficult to show that a company not only has established a business in England but also that this is other than a branch.'[205] One example given by Davies concerns 'purely ancillary activities, such as warehousing or data processing, [that] do not constitute the establishment of a branch but could amount in a place of business.'[206]

Nonetheless the consequences are far-reaching; service of a branch-establishment under Section 694A is limited to special jurisdiction over claims arising in respect to the carrying out of the branch's activities, whereas service on a mere establishment of a place of business under Section 691 provides for general jurisdiction available for all kind of claims, including those not related to the business activities. Why should a place of business constituting a less permanent establishment than a branch provide for a wider jurisdiction over an overseas company than

---

[199] See Fawcett, 'A New Approach To Jurisdiction Over Companies', at 653-654 and Davies, *Principles of Modern Company Law*, at 106.

[200] *Rakusens Ltd v. Baser Ambalaj Plastik Sanayi Ticaret AS*, [2001] WL 1251832 (CA); [2001] EWCA Civ 1820.

[201] LJ Arden: *Rakusens Ltd v. Baser Ambalaj Plastik Sanayi Ticaret AS*, [2001] WL 1251832, at para. 35 (CA).

[202] Ibid., at para. 37.

[203] As held in *Saab v. Saudi American Bank* 'some of the changes [introduced by the eleventh directive] including those made by section 694A are very curious', [1999] 4 All ER 321, at para. 11. See also Enonchong, 'Overseas Companies and Article 5(5)', at 926.

[204] Davies, *Principles of Modern Company Law*, at 106.

[205] Fawcett, North *et al.*, *Private International Law*, at 362-363.

[206] Davies, *Principles of Modern Company Law*, at 107.

the branch jurisdiction criterion? This 'anomalous result' was identified by Judge Clarke in *Saab v. Saudi American Bank*[207]

> 'It is I think common ground that a branch is a more permanent establishment than a mere place of business. The effect of these provisions thus created this anomalous result. In order to serve a branch it was necessary to satisfy the link between the process and the business of the branch required by section 694A(2), namely that it must be in respect of the carrying on of the business of the branch, where as in a case where the company did not have a branch, in order to serve a place of business it was not necessary to establish any link at all.'

4.4.2.2.c *Statutory service under the Companies Act 2006*

Under the new regime, a distinction will no longer be made between 'branch' and 'place of business which is not a branch'. Generally welcomed, the 2006 Act will apply one single regime to overseas companies. The 'anomalous result' described above will no longer occur. As a general rule, statutory service will be available if the overseas company established a place of business in the U.K., whether it is a branch or not.[208] In other words, the concept 'place of business' for statutory service has become wider, as it now also includes a branch.[209] The registration requirements for foreign companies to establish a place of business under the new regime will however be stricter as they are based on those previously used under the Companies Act 1985 for branches, and will be brought in line with the Eleventh Company Law Directive.[210] But apart from these registration requirements, the guidelines given by the English courts as to what does and what does not constitute a place of business – as described above – will undoubtedly remain of crucial importance to determine whether an overseas company can be considered 'present' and served within England.

Section 1056 of the new Act provides that every overseas company is required to register particulars authorized to accept service of documents on behalf of the company, or has to make a statement if there is no such person. These particulars can be served

> '(a) by leaving it at, or sending it by post to, the registered address of any person resident in the United Kingdom who is authorised to accept service of documents on the company's behalf, or (b) if there is no such person, or if any such person refuses service or service cannot for any other reason be effected, by leaving it at or sending by post to any place of business of the company in the United Kingdom.'[211]

But, the most important change brought by the new regime of the Companies Act 2006 is that, on the ground that it has a place of business in England, the statutory

---

207 (CA), 2 July 1999, [1999] 4 All ER 321, para. 15.

208 Fawcett, North *et al.*, *Private International Law*, at 364.

209 Ibid.

210 See the Explanatory Notes to Companies Act 2006, § 1327, at 201, and see also Fawcett, North *et al.*, *Private International Law*, at 365.

211 Sect. 1139 of the Companies Act 2006. See also Explanatory Notes to Companies Act 2006, § 1357, at 205.

service on an overseas company should be 'in respect of the carrying on of business' activities at or by that same place of business.[212] Most probably the service will not be required to be wholly connected to the place of business activities in the forum. Conversely, it is to be assumed, as it was the case under Section 694A, that even a claim partially connected to the foreign companies' activities in the forum will be sufficient. Nonetheless, the fact that there is now such an important requirement will reduce the jurisdictional reach of English courts over overseas companies.

4.4.2.3 *Concluding Remarks on Corporate Presence*

The CPR regime for service as an alternative has a 'wid[e] and relax[ed]'[213] effect on the Companies Act regime.[214] It was suggested that in order to come closer to Article 5(5) of the Brussels Model, the U.K. legislator could have required a similar connection between the claim and the place of business activities for the CPR regime, as it used to under the branch regime of Section 690A Companies Act 1985 and it now does under the new Companies Act 2006. Instead the legislator chose to by-pass the special connection requirement of a branch establishment by the enactment of the CPR, thereby providing for an alternative method for service not requiring this special 'in respect of the carrying on of business' requirement.[215]

Several connecting factors in the forum constitute 'presence' of corporate defendants within the jurisdiction. Not only does the Companies Act acknowledge specific branch jurisdiction, a simple place of business is sufficient for service within the jurisdiction under both the CPR and the Companies Act regimes. Additionally, the presence of an *agent* or sales representative constitutes corporate presence for service under the CPR regime according to Rule 6.16 on the one hand and under Sections 691 and 695 of the Companies Act for statutory service on the other.[216] However, traditional common law has refused to include 'carrying on or doing business' in England within the meaning of corporate presence.

As a result, the rules for service within the jurisdiction based on 'corporate presence' are wide. The claimant benefits from such an extensive interpretation of corporate presence, while it allows him to get around the requirement of a court's permission for service out of the jurisdiction under Rule 6.20 CPR.[217]

---

[212] Fawcett, North *et al.*, *Private International Law*, at 365.

[213] Briggs, *The Conflict of Laws*, at 98.

[214] In *Saab v. Saudi American Bank*, [1999] 4 All ER 321, before the English Court of Appeal (CA) on 2 July 1999, under 15, the Court ruled: 'Despite considerable research neither party has been able to explain the reason for this anomaly and no-one was able to think of a reason for it during the argument.' See Enonchong, 'Overseas Companies and Article 5(5)', at 926-927.

[215] Ibid. See also conclusions, at 936.

[216] Fawcett, North et al., *Private International Law*, at 362 *et seq.*

[217] Remarkably, the heads under Rule 6.20 CPR do not specifically deal with overseas companies, not 'present' in England. See Fawcett, 'A New Approach to Jurisdiction over Companies', at 655.

4.5 Extended Jurisdiction by Service of Process out of the Jurisdiction

Rule 6.20 CPR provides for service out of the jurisdiction in some specific cases. The purpose of Rule 6.20 is to extend the jurisdictional reach of English courts in order to 'catch one's defendant' not present in England.[218] In other words, its aim is to exercise extra-territorial jurisdiction over a defendant absent in England, but present in another sovereign state.[219] It is generally acknowledged that service out of the jurisdiction interferes with the sovereignty of that other state. For that reason, outside service requires permission from the court and the English court has to be proven *forum conveniens*.[220]

The CPR Rules apply since 1 May 2000 and replace Order 11 of the Rules of the Supreme Court. Settled case law interpreting the latter is however still relevant for the interpretation of Rule 6.20.[221]

The majority of the 'jurisdictional heads' embodied in Rule 6.20 CPR permit service out of the jurisdiction on the basis that the claim has a special connection with the forum or is justified on the basis of considerations of procedural efficiency. Among them are claims against an English domiciliary;[222] claims made for an anti-suit injunction;[223] claims against a defendant as a necessary or proper party;[224] claims for interim remedies;[225] claims related to contracts[226] or torts;[227] and claims in relation to property within the jurisdiction.[228]

4.5.1 Defendant's Domicile under Rule 6.20(1)(a) CPR

Rule 6.20(1)(a) states 'that a claim form may be served out of the jurisdiction with the permission of the court if claim is made for a remedy against a person domiciled within the jurisdiction'.

Defendant's domicile is traditionally not the starting point under the common law on jurisdiction. Nevertheless, this internationally well-accepted connecting factor is incorporated in Rule 6.20(1) and provides for jurisdiction over an absent defendant who is domiciled in England. Although, this rule completely lost its practical relevance within the scope of application of the Brussels Model,[229]

---

[218] Briggs, *Civil Jurisdiction*, § 1.01, at 2.

[219] See for a brief overview of the origins of Rule 6.20 and the concern of ancient authorities for interference with other state's sovereignty and the interaction of the jurisdiction question with public international law, L. Collins, 'Some Aspects of Service out of the Jurisdiction in English Law', in *Essays in International Litigation and the Conflict of Laws* (1994), 226-252.

[220] See the structure in Sects. 4.2 and 4.3.

[221] Briggs, *The Conflict of Laws*, at 105. See *Petroleo Brasiliero SA v. Mellitus Shipping Inc (The Baltic Flame)*, [2001] 1 All ER (Comm.) 993 (CA), in which the Court of Appeal uses Order 11, Rule 1(1)(c) to interpret its substitute Rule 6.20(3).

[222] Rule 6.20(1) CPR.

[223] Rule 6.20(2) CPR.

[224] Rule 6.20(3) CPR.

[225] Rule 6.20(4) CPR.

[226] Rule 6.20(5) to (7) CPR.

[227] Rule 6.20(8) CPR.

[228] Rule 6.20(10) CPR.

[229] See Chapter 2, Sects. 2.2.3 and 2.5, on the role of the defendant's domicile rule in the Brussels Model. See also Hill, *International Commercial Disputes*, § 7.3.10, at 210.

it remains interesting to observe that traditional common law does not consider defendant's domicile on equal footing with his presence: a claimant is required to seek the court's permission to serve on the defendant if he is absent abroad, even if he is domiciled in England.[230] As is stated in *Re Liddell's Settlement Trusts* the fact that the defendant has a domicile 'enables the Court to make a valid citation of a defendant in circumstance[s] in which previously this could not have been possible', but what the CPR Rule 6.20 'does not do is, in a case where the person affected is abroad, to say that the action may proceed against him as if he were actually in this country.'[231]

By using the 'remedy' in Rule 6.20(1), jurisdiction can be invoked regardless of the nature of the claim and thus provides for general jurisdiction.[232] The rule applies to the domicile of all defendants including corporations and partnerships.[233] By virtue of CPR Rule 6.18(g) the domicile is determined by CJJO 2001,[234] which states that an individual will be domiciled in England if (a) he is resident in England and (b) the nature and circumstances of his residence indicate that he has a substantial connection with England.[235] A corporate defendant is 'domiciled' or has its seat in England if it was incorporated or formed under English law. A foreign corporation will have its seat in England only if its central management and control is exercised in England or has a place of business in England.[236] The latter would however also mean that the corporate defendant is 'present' as identified above, which makes the service of process out of the jurisdiction unnecessary and the rule redundant.[237]

4.5.2 Special Provisions Concerning Contracts

Subparagraphs 5, 6 and 7 of Rule 6.20 regulate possible service out of the jurisdiction when the claim relates to contractual claims.[238] Rule 6.20(5) involves claims made 'in respect of a contract' where the contract – (a) was made within the juris-

---

[230] If the domicile of the defendant is disputed, claimant has the burden of proof to show a good arguable case if they wish to establish that a defendant is domiciled in a particular state or territory, see *Seaconsar (Far East) Ltd. v. Bank Markazi Jomhouri Islami Iran*, [1994] 1 AC 438; and *Canada Trust Co. v. Stolzenberg (No. 2)*, [2002] 1 AC 1, at 13.

[231] *Re Liddell's Settlement Trusts* (CA), 25 February 1936 (Ch 365/368); [1936] All ER 239 (CA).

[232] See ibid. If the defendant is domiciled in England or any other part of the U.K., the Brussels Convention and Regulation or the Lugano Convention applies. Thus, the practical relevance of this provision will be small and will only apply outside the formal and substantive scope of these conventions and regulation.

[233] According to Interpretation Act 1978, Schedule 1; Dicey, Morris *et al.*, *Conflict of Laws*, § 11-160, at 369; Briggs, *Civil Jurisdiction*, § 4.33, at 351.

[234] Paras. 9-12 of Schedule 1 of the CJJO 2001, SI 2001 No. 3929, substituting Sects. 41-46 of the CJJA 1982 as amended by SI 2001 No. 4015.

[235] Para. 9(3) of Schedule 1 of the CJJO 2001 (Sect. 41 of CJJA 1982); Briggs, *Civil Jurisdiction*, § 2.113, at 138. See on the definition of domicile and residence *Bank of Dubai Ltd v. Abbas*, [1997] I.L.Pr. 308 (CA) (Civ Div); Briggs, *Civil Jurisdiction*, § 4.33, at 351.

[236] Para. 10(2) of Schedule 1of the CJJO 2001; see Briggs, *Civil Jurisdiction*, § 2.116, at 142.

[237] See also the possible impact on Rule 6.20(1) CPR of *City & Country Properties Ltd v. Kamali*, [2006] EWCA Civ 1879; [2007] 1 WLR 1219 with respect to the service within the jurisdiction by virtue of Rule 6.5(5) CPR.

[238] Substituting the previous RSC Order 11, Rule 1(1)(d) and (e); Hartley, '*Tessili*', at 59.

diction; (b) was made by or through an agent trading or residing within the jurisdiction; (c) is governed by English law; or (d) contains a term to the effect that the court shall have jurisdiction to determine any claim in respect of the contract. The latter regulates prorogation of jurisdiction on the basis of a choice of forum clause in a contract. Rule 6.20(7) deals with claims disputing the existence of contracts specified under Rule 6.20(5). Rule 6.20(6) permits outside service when the claim is made 'in respect of' a breach of any contract committed within the jurisdiction, thus regardless of the types of contract indicated in Rule 6.20(5).[239]

The claimant must show that there is a good arguable case that there exists a contract between himself and the defendant and that there is a good arguable case that the claim is made in respect of that contract.[240] For the application of any of the three paragraphs there must be a 'contract' between the two parties, i.e. between the claimant and the defendant. Any relation with third persons is not covered.[241] Whether a contract exists is governed by English law, including its conflict of laws rules.[242]

The High Court held in *Albon v. Naza Motor Trading*[243] that the formula of words 'in respect of a contract' in CPR Rule 6.20(5) should be understood to be wider than 'arising under a contract' and only requires that the claim relates to or is connected with the contract. It should be presumed that this interpretation equally applies to the same formula used in Rule 6.20(6).

4.5.2.1 *Rule 6.20(5)(a): Contract Made within the Jurisdiction*

The fact that the claim arises out of a contract that was concluded in England could justify permission to serve out of the jurisdiction on the basis of a special link between the claim and England. English law determines whether or not the contract was actually made in England.[244] When a letter of acceptance concludes a contract, the place where the contract is made is where the letter is posted.[245] With respect to other means of communication, such as telephone, fax, telex or e-mail, a contract is

---

239 Briggs, *Civil Jurisdiction*, § 4.38, at 356.

240 Dicey, Morris *et al.*, *Conflict of Laws*, § 11-182, at 376; *Youell v. Kara Mara Shipping Co Ltd*, [2000] 2 Lloyd's Rep. 102; *Trafalgar Operations Ltd v. Cox & Kings (India) Ltd*, [2002] EWHC 768 (QB).

241 *Finnish Marine Insurance Co. Ltd. v. Protective National Insurance Co*, [1990] 1 QB 1078; *Maritrop Trading Corp v. Guangzhou Ocean Shipping Co*, [1998] CLC 224, held that a 'quasi' contract also includes a contract, but a contract directly involving third persons is not a contract between the parties. Dicey, Morris *et al.*, *Conflict of Laws*, § 11-183, at 376; Hill, *International Commercial Disputes*, § 7.3.18-20, at 213.

242 Generally the Rome Convention on Applicable Law is applicable as implemented by the Contracts Applicable Law Act of 1990. *Amin Rasheed Shipping Corp v. Kuwait Insurance Corporation (The Al Wahab)*, [1983] 2 All ER 884; [1984] AC 50; Briggs, *Civil Jurisdiction*, § 4.38, at 357; Briggs, *The Conflict of Laws*, at 107-108.

243 [2007] EWHC 9 (Ch. D.).

244 Dicey, Morris *et al.*, *Conflict of Laws*, § 11-186, at 377; Briggs, *Civil Jurisdiction*, § 4.39, at 358; Hill, *International Commercial Disputes*, § 7.3.22, at 215.

245 Dicey, Morris *et al.*, *Conflict of Laws*, § 11-186, at 377, Briggs, *Civil Jurisdiction*, § 4.39, at 358; Hill, *International Commercial Disputes*, § 7.3.22, at 215.

made there where the acceptance is received by the offeror.[246] In many situations, the place where the contract is made is artificial and/or ambiguous which makes the connecting factor an arbitrary one that does not necessarily vouch for a close connection with the English forum.[247]

4.5.2.2 *Rule 6.20(5)(b): Contract Made by or through an Agent*

This rule is designed to serve the defendant out of the jurisdiction on grounds that defendant concluded, in his capacity of principal authority, a contract that was negotiated by or through an agent located in England. The exercise of jurisdiction is justified by the fact that the defendant carries out business, by or through an agent, in England.[248] The agent through whom the contract was concluded should therefore only be defendant's agent and not claimant's as well.[249] The agent should not act on behalf of the defendant, his principal, but the contract should be concluded or negotiated 'by or through' an agent as an intermediary.[250] In *National Mortgage & Agency Company of New Zealand, Ltd. v. Gosselin*, Lord Justice Atkin stated that

> '[i]t seems to be quite clear that the whole of the terms of the contracts were in fact negotiated by the agent of the defendants in this country, and it is also, to my mind, reasonably clear that the agent had no authority to complete the contracts by accepting them, but had referred them to his foreign principals, who had the sole right to accept or refuse the terms so negotiated here by the agent.'[251]

The use of the wording 'through' considerably extends the extra-territorial reach over a defendant not present in England.[252]

Surely, the court may still decide to authorize service of process within the jurisdiction on the agent in order to issue proceedings against the defendant abroad under Rule 6.16 CPR. As explained above, Rule 6.16 CPR should be understood

---

[246] The contract is not made where the acceptance took place, although there is still some uncertainty regarding where an e-mail containing the acceptance would be received by the offeror. *Entores v. Miles Far East Corp*, [1955] 2 QB 327; *Bank of Baroda v. Vysya Bank Ltd.*, [1994] 2 Lloyd's Rep. 87 (QB), at 95; see the recent decision of *Staines v. Walsh*, [2003] EWHC 458 (Ch. D.).

[247] Hill, *International Commercial Disputes*, § 7.3.22, at 215; Briggs, *Civil Jurisdiction*, § 4.39, at 358, see *Gibbon v. Commerz und Creditbank AG*, [1958] 2 Lloyd's Rep. 113, at 120, where the contract was negotiated in one country but formally signed in another, or *BP Exploration Co (Libya) Ltd v. Hunt*, [1976] 1 WLR 788, where it concerned the amendment of a contract.

[248] Dicey, Morris *et al.*, *Conflict of Laws*, § 11-187, at 377; Hill, *International Commercial Disputes*, § 7.3.25, at 216.

[249] *Union International Insurance Co. Ltd. v. Jubilee Insurance Co. Ltd.*, [1991] 1 WLR 415; Dicey, Morris *et al.*, *Conflict of Laws*, § 11-187, at 378; Hill, *International Commercial Disputes*, § 7.3.25, at 216.

[250] If the agent concluded the contract 'on behalf' of the defendant, the claim would fall under Rule 6.20(5)(a) CPR. Dicey, Morris *et al.*, *Conflict of Laws*, § 11-187, at 377; Hill, *International Commercial Disputes*, § 7.3.25, at 216.

[251] *National Mortage & Agency Co of New Zealand Ltd v. Gosselin*, (1922) 12 Ll. L. Rep. 318, at 34.

[252] Dicey, Morris *et al.*, *Conflict of Laws*, § 11-187, at 377; Briggs, *Civil Jurisdiction*, § 4.39, at 358; Hill, *International Commercial Disputes*.

as an alternative method for service within the jurisdiction, which is essentially discretionary and authorizes service on the agent carrying out business in order to reach a defendant not present in England.[253] Under the jurisdictional head of Rule 6.20(6)(b) CPR, the service is not made on the agent but on the defendant himself and is done so out of the jurisdiction on the basis that an agent negotiated contracts for him in England giving claimant a ground to ask for permission to serve him abroad. According to Dicey and Morris, permission to serve out on the basis of Rule 6.20(6)(b) should be more appropriate and easily obtained in cases where the defendant has a 'general agent doing large business for him' in England, whereas Rule 6.16 is more appropriate when defendant carried out a single business transaction though a broker in England.[254]

4.5.2.3 *Rule 6.20(5)(c): The Contract Is Governed by English Law*

Under traditional common law, the fact that the contract is governed by English law was in itself sufficient to justify leave for service out of the jurisdiction on the basis that a court is closely connected to a case when its laws governs the dispute. In *Amin Rasheed Shipping Corp v. Kuwait Insurance Co*,[255] the court however indicated that when English law is applicable, this would not automatically lead to permission to serve out of England, instead other factors should be taken into consideration.[256] In any case, it means that the exercise of English jurisdiction is preconditioned to whether English law applies to the contract. This results in an interrelation between the jurisdictional question and the applicable law rules.[257] Whether English law governs the contract generally depends on the Rome Convention on the Law Applicable to Contractual Obligations.[258]

With respect to the 'good arguable case test' which determines whether the claim falls under this head, it has been decided in *Marubeni Hong Kong and South China Ltd v. Mongolia*[259] that 'the court does not [have to] consider whether the claimant has a good arguable case that the contract is governed by English law, but rather whether the contract factually is governed by English law.'[260]

---

[253] As Rule 6.16 is clearly claimant friendly, two additional conditions have to be fulfilled i.e. that the contract was made in England and that the agent and the defendant still have a business relation.

[254] Dicey, Morris *et al.*, *Conflict of Laws*, § 11-189, at 378.

[255] *Amin Rasheed Shipping Corp v. Kuwait Insurance Co (The Al Wahab)*, [1983] 2 All ER (HL), at 884.

[256] According to Dicey, Morris *et al.*, *Conflict of Laws*, § 11-192, at 379, the claimant now has a heavier burden to obtain leave under the *forum conveniens* doctrine.

[257] Fawcett, North *et al.*, *Private International Law*, at 381; *Chellaram v. Chellaram (No. 2)*, [2002] 3 All ER 17, under point 148, time for testing the applicable law for jurisdictional purposes.

[258] This applies to contracts concluded after 2 April 1991. Consolidated version published in OJ 1998 C 027/34-46, incorporated by the Contracts (Applicable Law) Act 1990, Chap. 36. See Dicey, Morris *et al.*, *Conflict of Laws*, § 11-191, at 378; Hill, *International Commercial Disputes*, 7.3.25, at 216. English law will apply to the contract, where parties made an express choice of law clause indicating English law to be applicable (Art. 3); or where English law is the most closely connected applicable law to the contract, England shall be presumed to be the country where the party who is to effect the performance which is characteristic of the contract has, at the time of conclusion of the contract, his habitual residence, or, in the case of a corporation, its central administration, Art. 4(1) and (2).

[259] [2002] 2 All ER (Comm.) 873.

[260] Argument 136; see also *Chellaram v. Chellaram (No. 2)*, [2002] 3 All ER 17.

4.5.2.4 *Rule 6.20(7): Claim Seeks a Declaration That No Contract Exists*

This head allows plaintiff to ask for permission to service out of the jurisdiction if he claims that no contract exists, provided that if the contract was found to exist it would fall within one of the sub-claims of Rule 6.20(5). In other words, the disputed contract subject to such a declaration should concern a disputed contract allegedly made within the jurisdiction, or by or through an agent trading or residing within the jurisdiction, or be governed by English law, or it should contain a term to the effect that the court shall have jurisdiction to determine any claim in respect of the contract.[261] This rule is designed to cover claims seeking to declare the non-existence of a contract, which is not covered under Rule 6.20(5), since the latter requires the existence of a contract between the parties.[262]

4.5.2.5 *Rule 6.20(6): Breach of Contract Committed within the Jurisdiction*

The English courts may grant a leave for service out of England for a claim concerning a breach of contract committed in England. Contrary to the provisions of Rule 6.20(5) and (7) CPR, the alleged breach is not required to concern a contract made within the jurisdiction, or by or through an agent trading or residing within the jurisdiction; or be governed by English law.[263] This rule does not entitle jurisdiction on the basis that the performance of a contractual obligation took, or should have taken place in England, but only when such contractual obligation was breached in England.[264] It is this breach committed in England that justifies granting jurisdiction to English courts on the basis of a close connection between the forum and the claim.

According to English law a contract may be breached either by a failure to perform or by an act of expressed or implied repudiation.[265] In order to establish whether or not the contract was breached within the jurisdiction, the place of failure to perform and the place of repudiation have to be determined. With respect to a breach of contract by failure to perform, the contract is breached in England if the contract should have been performed in England according to the law governing the contract.[266] If the breach concerned an obligation of payment, the law govern-

---

[261] Rule 6.20(7) allows for service outside when a claim seeks a declaration that no contract exists where, if the contract was found to exist, it would comply with the conditions set out in Rule 6.20(5).

[262] Dicey, Morris *et al.*, *Conflict of Laws*, § 11-214, at 386; Briggs, *Civil Jurisdiction*, § 4.39, at 360; Hill, *International Commercial Disputes*, § 7.3.19, at 213.

[263] Briggs, *Civil Jurisdiction*, § 4.40, at 360.

[264] As observed in relation to Art. 5(1) Brussels Model by Briggs, see Briggs, *Civil Jurisdiction*, § 4.40, at 361.

[265] Dicey, Morris *et al.*, *Conflict of Laws*, § 11-200-202, at 382-383; Briggs, *Civil Jurisdiction*, § 4.40, at 361. According to Dicey & Morris, expressed as well as implied repudiation require an act (of commission) of other parties; express repudiation occurs when one party notified the other that he does not intend to perform the contract and implied repudiation requires an committed act, which is inconsistent with the obligation to perform arising out of the contract. The place of implied repudiation is the place where the inconsistent act was committed and not the place where performance was due. According to Dicey, although there is no authority to confirm this, implied repudiation 'presumably occurs where the inconsistent act is done.'

[266] It is required that the contract, or part of it, should be performed in England and not elsewhere, see *Cuban Atlantic Sugar Sales Corporation v. Compañia de Vapores San Elefterio Limitada (The St*

ing the contract will determine where the place of payment was to be performed, unless the parties fixed a place of payment in the contract.[267]

4.6 Conclusion

The initial foundation of jurisdiction on presence under English common law is outdated and has been bypassed by a wide interpretation of 'presence' of both the individual and corporate defendant on the one hand and by the regulation of service out of jurisdiction by Rule 6.20 CPR on the other. The requirement of physical presence of the individual defendant is affected by a softened approach to service within the jurisdiction at defendant's last known address under Rule 6.5(6) CPR, even if the defendant is not present within the jurisdiction at the moment of service. Corporate presence is easily established by the existence of a place of business or by negotiating contracts by or through an agent. Under the CPR regime the service of a corporate defendant on the basis of a business establishment in the forum does not even require a specific connection between the claim and the establishment's activities. The reach of English courts when the defendant is absent abroad as regulated by Rule 6.20 CPR includes a significant number of additional connecting factors providing for jurisdiction over contractual claims.

As a result, the claimant who wants to institute proceedings in English courts in a contractual dispute has at his disposal a considerably wide range of potential connecting factors that could lead to English courts assuming jurisdiction. The English common law system is however characterized by a significant amount of discretionary powers given to English courts to evaluate the 'appropriateness' of the forum and to consider 'substantial justice' on a case-by-case basis. Apart from founding jurisdiction on presence or on Rule 6.20 CPR, the courts have discretionary powers to decline jurisdiction with respect to service within the jurisdiction if England is a *forum non conveniens* or to give permission for service over a defendant who is not present within the jurisdiction, if England is the *forum conveniens*. These discretionary powers constitute a significant part of the common law regime system on international jurisdiction and aim to guarantee justice for both claimant and defendant. These powers are regarded as '*correction tools*'[268] of the wide range of connecting factors for jurisdiction embodied in the presence criterion and Rule 6.20 CPR and could correct 'inappropriate' *forum shopping* by the plaintiff. This open character of the jurisdictional regime of English common law is principally focused on considerations of appropriateness and substantial justice rather than on the ability for the plaintiff to foresee whether the English court will accept jurisdiction.

Elfterio), [1960] All ER 141; Dicey, Morris *et al.*, *Conflict of Laws*, § 11-203, at 382; Hill, *International Commercial Disputes*, § 7.3.28, at 217; Briggs, *Civil Jurisdiction*, § 4.40, at 361.

[267] If English law governs the contract, the place of breach of a payment obligation would lead to the creditor's residence or place of business. Dicey, Morris *et al.*, *Conflict of Laws*, § 11-203, at 383; Hill, *International Commercial Disputes*, § 7.3.28, at 217.

[268] Bell, *Forum Shopping and Venue*, at 90.

Chapter 5

THE JURISDICTIONAL SCHEME OF THE UNITED STATES

Two fundamental principles of the U.S. legal system strongly influenced the regulation of international jurisdiction[1] of U.S. courts.[2] First, as a consequence of the supremacy clause, the exercise of jurisdiction is subjected to the U.S. Constitution.[3] Second, due to the importance given to state sovereignty under the U.S. federal structure, each individual state retained its sovereign powers to regulate international jurisdiction of its courts.[4] In order to understand the complexity of the U.S. jurisdictional scheme it is important to explain the impact of the U.S. federal structure and the U.S. Constitution on the regulation of international jurisdiction of U.S. courts. The first two sections of this chapter will discuss this impact. In the third section, an explanation will be given of the nature of the sources for U.S. jurisdiction law: the bases of jurisdiction are to be found in common law principles which co-exist with statutory authorization provided by federal or state statutes.[5] Once jurisdiction is established on a legal basis, constitutional standards imposed by the Due Process clause limit the exercise of jurisdiction. This will be set out in Section 5.4. The fact that the majority of U.S. courts may apply an American version of the *forum non conveniens* doctrine in order to eventually exercise jurisdiction, will be dealt with in Section 5.5. The subsequent Sections 5.6 to 5.7 examine in more detail the various bases for jurisdiction of U.S. courts in international contractual disputes and the chapter concludes with Section 5.8.

---

[1] In U.S. terminology jurisdiction is also called judicial or adjudicative jurisdiction. *Judicial jurisdiction* is the power to *adjudicate* and means that a state may exercise jurisdiction through its court with respect to a person or thing. As opposed to *legislative jurisdiction* or 'jurisdiction to prescribe' or jurisdiction to 'enforce'. See Restatement of the Law (Third) of Foreign Relations Law of the United States [hereafter 3rd Restatement of Foreign Relations], § 401; G. Born and P. Rutledge, *International Civil Litigation in United States Courts* (2007), at 1; P. Borchers, 'Flexibility and Predictability: The Emergence of Near-Universal Choice of Law Principles', in *Balancing of Interests Liber Amicorum Peter Hay zum 70. Geburtstag* (2005), 49-53, at 57; P. Hay, R. Weintraub *et al.*, *Conflict of Laws: Cases and Materials* (2004), at 36. The term 'competency' in U.S. jurisdiction law refers to jurisdiction between different types of courts in the same state. See for a complete overview of these 'venue' rules, A. Mirandes, *La compétence inter-étatique et internationale des tribunaux en droit des Etats-Unis* (2002), at 16-18; R.C. Casad and W.M. Richman, *Jurisdiction in Civil Actions* (1998), Vol. 1, at 14-20.

[2] By 'American' or 'U.S.' courts is meant state and federal courts.

[3] The Supremacy clause of Art. VI of the U.S. Constitution states: 'This Constitution, and the Laws of the United States … shall be the supreme Law of the Land; and the Judges in every State shall be bound thereby …'. Restatement of the Law (Second) of Judgments [hereafter 2nd Restatement of Judgments], Introductory Note and § 4, comment b. R. Weintraub, *Commentary on the Conflict of Laws* (2006), § 4.1, at 119.

[4] Art. I, U.S. Constitution, the federal legislator is only allowed to regulate what was delegated to it by the individual states.

[5] A. Lowenfeld, *International Litigation and Arbitration* (2006), at 176; E. Scoles, P. Hay *et al.*, *Conflict of Laws* (2004), § 5.14, at 320; H. Schack, *Jurisdictional Minimum Contacts Scrutinized: interstaatliche und internationale Zuständigkeit U.S.-amerikanischer Gerichte* (1983), at 1-3.

5.1 The Importance of State Sovereignty

The U.S. jurisdictional scheme is characterized by the importance given to state sovereignty.[6] Each individual state has its own judicial powers to adjudicate (international) disputes and retained its sovereignty to regulate the jurisdictional reach of its judiciary. As a consequence, the judiciary of the fifty individual states[7] share judicial powers with federal courts over international disputes and sometimes even have concurrent jurisdiction:[8] state courts as well as federal courts can have jurisdiction over international contractual disputes. Each state determines, within the limits of the U.S. Constitution, to what extent its courts may exercise jurisdiction.[9] According to Mr Justice White

> 'the Framers also intended that the States retain many essential attributes of sovereignty, including, in particular, the sovereign power to try causes in their courts. The sovereignty of each State, in turn, implied a limitation on the sovereignty of all of its sister States a limitation express or implicit in both the original scheme of the Constitution and the Fourteenth Amendment.'[10]

As a result the U.S. jurisdictional scheme consists in fifty different sets of jurisdictional rules along with a federal statute[11] regulating the jurisdiction of federal courts.[12]

5.1.1 Subject Matter Jurisdiction

Subject matter jurisdiction regulates jurisdiction between state and federal courts and is commonly used to describe the power of a court to hear specific claims.[13] State courts have general subject matter jurisdiction; they can hear most of the claims whether they are based on state law or on federal law.[14] The judicial powers of federal courts are limited to cases explicitly regulated by Article III(2) of the U.S. Constitution and are therefore also called 'limited' subject matter jurisdic-

---

[6] See Weintraub, *Commentary*, § 4.7, at 146 and 159.

[7] Jurisdiction in the District of Columbia, Puerto Rico and the Virgin Islands enacted state statutes but this will not be discussed in this chapter.

[8] Weintraub, *Commentary*, § 4.1, at 119.

[9] Restatement of the Law (Second) of Conflict of Laws [hereafter 2nd Restatement of Conflict of Laws], § 2 comments.

[10] *World-Wide Volkswagen Corp. v. Woodson*, 444 U.S. 286, at 293-294 (1980); the court, referring to *Pennoyer v. Neff*, 95 U.S. 714, at 720 (1877), emphasizes 'that the reasonableness of asserting jurisdiction over the defendant must be assessed "in the context of our federal system of government," and stressed that the Due Process Clause ensures not only fairness, but also the "orderly administration of the laws".'

[11] Federal Rules of Civil Procedure (FRCP). See below Sect. 5.3.2.

[12] Mirandes, *La compétence internationale des Etats-Unis*, at 16; see below Sect. 5.3.1.

[13] 3rd Restatement of Foreign Relations, § 401, comment c; P. Hay, 'Flexibility versus Predictability and Uniformity in Choice of Law. Reflections on Current European and United States Conflicts Law', 226 *Recueil des cours* (1991), 281-412, at 57; G. Bermann, *Transnational Litigation in a Nutshell* (2003), at 70.

[14] Except for very specialized categories of claims arising under federal law, state courts are generally not limited in subject matter jurisdiction, Born, *International Civil Litigation*, at 5.

tion.[15] Congress elaborated this constitutional provision in several provisions of the United States Code Annotated (USCA). Federal courts have on the one hand subject matter jurisdiction over claims based on federal law – or 'federal questions' –, on the other hand, over claims arising from state law involving parties from different states, also called 'diversity' jurisdiction.[16] Most of the federal questions are not particularly relevant for jurisdiction in international contractual disputes.[17] Conversely, diversity jurisdiction is particularly important for international disputes when one of the parties or both parties reside in a foreign or *alien* state, which is then called '*alienage*' jurisdiction.[18] A foreign national admitted to the U.S. for permanent residence shall be considered as a 'citizen' of the state in which he is domiciled and not as an alien.[19] Federal courts have jurisdiction over diversity or alienage cases when the matter in controversy exceeds the sum or value of US$75,000 exclusive of interest and costs.[20] Claims arising out of state law and exceeding that sum could lead to concurrent jurisdiction with state courts. In diversity and alienage cases, the foreign (or alien) defendant sued in a state court has the right to remove his case from the state court to the correspondent federal court. This interaction between state and federal courts is called 'removal'.[21] Removal is

---

[15] 'Federal courts are courts of limited jurisdiction. ... Subject-matter jurisdiction, then, is an Art. III as well as a statutory requirement; it functions as a restriction on federal power, and contributes to the characterization of the federal sovereign. Certain legal consequences directly follow from this.' *Insurance Corp. of Ireland, Ltd. v. Compagnie des Bauxites de Guinée*, 456 U.S. 694, at 702 (1982) and see Born, *International Civil Litigation*, at 5; Bermann, *Transnational Litigation*, at 70; Casad and Richman, *Jurisdiction in Civil Actions Vol. 1*, at 3.

[16] Art. III(2) of the U.S. Constitution states: 'The [federal] judicial Power shall extend to all Cases, in Law and Equity, arising under this Constitution, the Laws of the United States, and Treaties made, or which shall be made, ... to Controversies ... between a State, or the Citizens thereof, and foreign States, Citizens or Subjects.' Born, *International Civil Litigation*, at 8; Bermann, *Transnational Litigation*, at 71, Casad and Richman, *Jurisdiction in Civil Actions Vol. 1*, § 5-1[1], at 527.

[17] § 1331 USCA indicates that federal questions relate to all civil actions arising under the Constitution, laws (federal statutes and regulations), or treaties (federal legislative powers) of the U.S. and generally involve claims arising under antitrust and securities laws. See Born, *International Civil Litigation*, at 30; Bermann, *Transnational Litigation*, at 78; Mirandes, *La compétence internationale des Etats-Unis*, at 19; R. Casad and W. Richman, *Jurisdiction in Civil Actions* (1998), Vol. 2, at 526; R. Casad, 'Personal Jurisdiction in Federal Question Cases', 70 *Texas Law Review* (1992), 1589-1621. See for the special meaning of § 1350 involving claims under the Alien Tort Statute, Born, *International Civil Litigation*, at 31 *et seq.*

[18] 18 USCA § 1332: '(a) The district courts shall have original jurisdiction of all civil actions where the matter in controversy exceeds the sum or value of $75,000, exclusive of interest and costs, and is between (1) citizens of different States; (2) citizens of a State and citizens or subjects of a foreign state; (3) citizens of different States and in which citizens or subjects of a foreign state are additional parties; and (4) a foreign state, defined in Section 1603(a) of this title, as plaintiff and citizens of a State or of different States.' See Born, *International Civil Litigation*, at 8; Bermann, *Transnational Litigation*, at 71. Additionally, an action between citizens of different states and in which citizens or subjects of a foreign state are additional parties, are also subject to federal jurisdiction. 28 USCA § 1332(a)(3).

[19] 28 USCA § 1332(a)(3); 8 USCA § 1101(a)(3): An 'alien' is any person who is not a citizen or national of the U.S. See Born, *International Civil Litigation*, at 21 *et seq.*; and see M. Reimann, 'Parochialism in American Conflicts Law', 49 *American Journal of Comparative Law* (2001), 369-389, at 132, explaining that this terminology reflects the parochial attitude of the U.S. jurisdiction law.

[20] 28 USCA § 1332(a)(2); see Born, *International Civil Litigation*, at 21.

[21] 28 USCA §1441(a); Born, *International Civil Litigation*, at 9; Mirandes, *La compétence internationale des Etats-Unis*, at 20-21; Casad and Richman, *Jurisdiction in Civil Actions Vol. 1*, at 527.

not permitted in diversity or alienage cases when the defendant is or was a resident or citizen of the state where the case was originally brought.[22] 'Alien' defendants will generally prefer to litigate in federal courts rather than in state courts.[23]

5.1.2 No Direct International Jurisdiction Rules

None of the fifty state statutes or the federal statute enacted specific jurisdictional provisions for international disputes.[24] Jurisdiction of U.S. courts over international disputes is regulated by the jurisdictional scheme for domestic or interstate disputes. State statutes generally do not distinguish between defendants from another state or from another country, nor do common law principles. As a result, international jurisdiction of U.S. courts is regulated by transposing the interstate jurisdictional scheme to international disputes. Some authors questioned the appropriateness of this transposition, believing that international cases should not be treated like interstate cases for jurisdictional purposes.[25]

The majority of the Supreme Court's decisions developing U.S. law on jurisdiction concerned purely domestic cases; only three cases involved a foreign party.[26] The constitutional standards emanating from the Supreme Court's decisions concerning interstate disputes are equally applicable to international disputes. Lower courts have applied them to international cases without explicitly considering whether a different approach should be taken to claims against foreign defendants.[27] This is in line with the importance given to each state's sovereignty which should not be considered any different from a foreign country's sovereignty.[28] The

[22] 28 USCA § 1441(b), such a restriction to removal does not exist when the claim involves a federal jurisdiction question.

[23] Born, *International Civil Litigation*, at 10.

[24] S. Baumgartner, *The Proposed Hague Convention on Jurisdiction and Foreign Judgements; Trans-Atlantic Law Making for Transnational Litigation* (2003), at 132; A. Strauss, 'Where America Ends and the International Order Begins: Interpreting the Jurisdictional Reach of the U.S. Constitution in Light of a Proposed Hague Convention on Jurisdiction and Satisfaction of Judgments', *Albany Law Review* (1998), 1237-1267, at 1237.

[25] See G. Born, 'Reflections on Judicial Jurisdiction in International Cases', 17 *Georgia Journal of International and Comparative Law* (1987), 1-44, at 8 and 21, who lists the 'inappropriate reasons for treating international cases differently from domestic cases'; L. Silberman, '"Two Cheers" for International Shoe (and None for Asahi): An Essay on the Fiftieth Anniversary of International Shoe', 28 *The University of California Davis Law Review* (1995), 755-767, at 760; *contra* A. von Mehren and D. Trautmann, 'Jurisdiction to Adjudicate', 79 *Harvard Law Review* (1966), 1121-1199, at 1122. See for more articles discussing this issue, in general A. von Mehren, 'Adjudicatory Jurisdiction: General Theories Compared and Evaluated', 63 *Boston University Law Review* (1983), 279-340, G. Lilly, 'Jurisdiction over Domestic and Alien Defendants', *Virginia Law Review* (1983), 85-152; S. Hornbeck, 'Transnational Litigation and Personal Jurisdiction over Foreign Defendants', 59 *Albany Law Review* (1996), 1389-1447; F. Juenger, 'A Shoe Unfit for Globetrotting? Symposium Fifty Years of International Shoe: The Past and the Future of Personal Jurisdiction', 28 *The University of California Davis Law Review* (1995), 1027-1045; R. Degnan and K. Kay, 'The Exercise of Jurisdiction over and Enforcement of Judgments against Alien Defendants', 39 *Hastings Law Journal* (1988), 799-855.

[26] *Helicópteros Nacionales de Columbia, S.A. v. Hall*, 466 U.S. 408 (1989); *Asahi Metal Industry Co. Ltd.*, 480 U.S. 102 (1987); and *Perkins v. Benguet Consol. Mining Co.*, 342 U.S. 437 (1952).

[27] Born, 'Reflections on Jurisdiction', at 7.

[28] Baumgartner, *The Proposed Hague Convention*, at 132; Lowenfeld, *International Litigation*, at 178: 'For purposes of judicial jurisdiction, at least, each of the states is seen as a separate sovereign, and Pennsylvania is as foreign as to a suit commenced in New Jersey as are France and Japan'.

2nd Restatement of Conflict of Laws also restated some of the jurisdictional principles and stated that they are 'also usually applicable to cases with elements in one or more foreign nations, ... since similar values and considerations are involved in both interstate and international case[s].'[29] Hence, although it acknowledges the existence of significant differences between interstate and international cases, the Restatement is primarily concerned with restating the law relating to interstate disputes and rarely refers to international conflicts or issues.[30] According to Reimann it fails to address most of the current problems American courts encounter in transnational litigation.[31]

Nonetheless, the U.S. Supreme Court introduced open factors enabling courts to take into account elements involving foreign defendants and/or claimants. As will be explained further, with respect to the question whether it would be fair to exercise U.S. jurisdiction over a foreign defendant in accordance with the U.S. Constitution the Supreme Court emphasized in *Asahi Metal Industry Co. v. Superior Court* that '[t]he unique burdens placed upon one who must defend oneself in a foreign legal system should have significant weight in assessing the reasonableness of stretching the long arm of personal jurisdiction over national borders'[32] and held that 'great care must be exercised when considering personal jurisdiction in the international context'.[33]

5.1.3 **Allocation of Jurisdiction at Interstate Level**

It is worth mentioning that a uniform jurisdictional system regulating the exercise of judicial powers among U.S. courts does not exist. Federal legislation unifying jurisdiction rules between U.S. courts over transnational disputes does not exist either.[34]

With respect to the regulation of jurisdiction at an interstate level, federal legislative powers have not sought to develop federal legislation to allocate jurisdiction among states.[35] This may be related to political factors regarding American federalism but it may also not have been a priority because interstate recognition of judgements is guaranteed under the well-functioning Full Faith and Credit clause as discussed below.[36]

---

[29] 2nd Restatement of Conflict of Laws, § 10, comments c and d.

[30] M. Reimann, 'A New Restatement: For the International Age', 75 *Indiana Law Review* (2000), 575, at 576-577.

[31] See Ibid., at 582; 'From the perspective of modern transnational litigation, the Second Restatement is not only close to useless, it is a vestige from a bygone era.'

[32] 480 U.S. 102, at 114 (1987).

[33] Ibid., at 115.

[34] See further in this section, for the question whether the federal state has the legislative power to enact jurisdiction rules for interstate and international disputes.

[35] To the disappointment of Professor Goldstein who states that a jurisdictional system 'cannot be developed adequately by sporadic case law, but rather requires a comprehensive legislative approach.' S. Goldstein, 'Federalism and Substantive Due Process: A Comparative and Historical Perspective on International Shoe and Its Progeny', 28 *The University of California Davis Law Review* (1995), 965-998, at 966.

[36] See Sect. 5.2.1.

It is, however, beyond any doubt that the federal legislator has the power to regulate both interstate and international jurisdiction.[37] Most probably the Full Faith and Credit clause of Article IV of the U.S. Constitution could have provided for a legislative basis for the regulation of interstate and international jurisdiction. In any event, the Interstate Commerce Clause of Article I of the U.S. Constitution obviously provides for legislative power in the field.[38] It gives legislative authority for the federal government to regulate matters concerning international relations, foreign affairs, interstate and international commerce and taxes and it would certainly provide a valid basis for the regulation of international jurisdiction of U.S. courts by the federal legislator.[39] The 2nd Restatement of Judgments acknowledges and anticipates this possibility

> '[w]ithin the boundaries thus imposed by the Constitution, a state court's exercise of jurisdiction may further be confined by treaty or federal statute, effective through the Supremacy Clause. Federal legislative authority has rarely been exercised in this way, ... Further federal legislative limitations on state court jurisdiction may be forthcoming.'[40]

Nonetheless as Von Mehren explained 'in light of the federal nature of the American legal system and the traditional sensibilities of states regarding interference with the administration of justice in their courts, obtaining the Senate's consent to treaties dealing with jurisdiction was, until quite recently, considered next to impossible.'[41]

Conversely, individual U.S. states are not allowed to enter into any similar type of agreement – such as the Brussels Convention – distributing judicial powers among their courts.[42] Several U.S. scholars have considered or proposed an interstate regulation modelled on the Brussels Convention.[43] Some U.S. scholars and

---

[37] According to A. Lowenfeld and L. Silberman, 'International Jurisdiction and Judgements Project', American Law Institute, http://www.ali.org (2000), at 18-19.

[38] Goldstein, 'Federalism', at 969; Art. I, Sect. 8(3) of the Constitution states that the Federal state has the legislative power 'To regulate Commerce with foreign Nations, and among the several States, and with the Indian Tribes.'

[39] K. Clermont, 'Jurisdictional Salvation and the Hague Treaty', *Cornell Law Review* (1999), 89-133, at 123; P. Borchers, 'The Death of the Constitutional Law of Personal Jurisdiction: From Pennoyer to Burnham and Back Again', 24 *University of California Davis Law Review* (1990), 19-105, at 104-105.

[40] 2nd Restatement of Judgments, § 4, comment b.

[41] A. von Mehren, 'Theory and Practice of Adjudicatory Authority in Private International Law: A Comparative Study of the Doctrine, Policies and Practices of Common- and Civil-Law Systems: General Course on Private International Law (1996)', 295 *Recueil des cours* (2003), 9-431, at 77.

[42] States do not have the power to enter into an agreement with each other or with a foreign country; that power is reserved exclusively to the federal state. See in general D. Clark and T. Ansay, *Introduction to the Law of the United States* (1992); A. Morrison, *Fundamentals of American Law* (1996).

[43] Borchers, 'The Death of the Constitutional Law of Jurisdiction', at 104-105: 'Congress has legislated competently in this area before, and, with a little luck, it will do as well as the drafters of the Brussels Convention.' Goldstein, 'Federalism', at 966: 'Such congressional legislation could be based on comparative law sources, including the Brussels Convention.' R. Weintraub, 'Fifty Years of International Shoe: The Past and Future of Personal Jurisdiction. A Map Out of the Personal Jurisdiction Labyrinth', 28 *University of California Davis Law Review* (1995), 531-559, at 550: 'If the Convention

the ALI encourage ratification of international conventions in order to influence U.S. jurisdiction law.[44] In the context of the negotiations held at The Hague at a World-wide Convention on Jurisdiction and Enforcement, the ALI started a project to draft implementing legislation in the event that a world-wide convention on jurisdiction and enforcement would come into force in the U.S. federal system.[45] Encouraged by State Department officials present during the Hague negotiations, one of the objectives was to meet the needs of national law on jurisdiction and recognition issues.[46] Since the Hague negotiations have not resulted in a comprehensive international convention, the ALI favours the incorporation of jurisdiction grounds for recognition and enforcement purposes as it believes that such a uniform federal standard would promote certainty and predictability, but has not (yet) resulted in any federal legislation.[47]

5.2 The Constitutionalization of International Jurisdiction of United States Courts

Since the Supreme Court held in *Pennoyer v. Neff*[48] that the exercise of jurisdiction should be consistent with U.S. constitutional standards, the law on jurisdiction has become an issue of constitutional law.[49] Two clauses are at the origin of the

had been in place here, some of the most adversely criticized jurisdictional decisions of the United States Supreme Court would have come out differently.' F. Juenger, 'American Jurisdiction: A Story of Comparative Neglect', 65 *University of Colorado Law Review* (1993), 1-23, at 21: 'A promising approach to promoting domestic reform would be to negotiate an international compact modelled on the Brussels Convention. Experience gathered over twenty years shows that the treaty works well for twelve European nations, including both common law and civil law countries. Why should it not also work for the United States?'

[44] L.J. Silberman and A. Lowenfeld, 'A Different Challenge for the ALI: Herein of Foreign Country Judgments, an International Treaty, and an American Statute Proposal', 75 *Indiana Law Journal* (2000), 635-647, at 637; Clermont, 'Jurisdictional Salvation and the Hague Treaty', at 89; K. Clermont and K.-C. Huang, 'Converting the Draft Hague Treaty into Domestic Jurisdictional Law', in *Global Law of Jurisdiction and Judgments: Lessons from the Hague* (2002), 191, at 194-229. See in general G. Hazard Jr., *The American Law Institute. What It Is and What It Does* (1994), Vol. 14.

[45] See Lowenfeld and Silberman, 'International Jurisdiction Project', at 18-30; and Silberman and Lowenfeld, 'A Different Challenge for the ALI', at 635. This ALI Project is not to be confused with another significant unification project in cooperation with UNIDROIT; as explained previously in Chapter 1.

[46] L. Silberman and A. Lowenfeld, 'The Related Project of The American Law Institute' (1999), at B-1-2 and B-4, dealing with issues of jurisdiction.

[47] Lowenfeld and Silberman, 'International Jurisdiction Project', at 31 and 34; Silberman and Lowenfeld, 'The Related Project', at B-5; Silberman and Lowenfeld, 'A Different Challenge for the ALI', at 637.

[48] 95 U.S. 714 (1878).

[49] K. Nguyen, 'Redefining the Threshold for Personal Jurisdiction: Contact and the Presumption of Fairness', 83 *Boston University Law Review* (2003), 253-279, at 256; Von Mehren, 'Theory and Practice', at 73-82. The fact that U.S. jurisdiction law is a question of constitutional law is considered by some authors as an 'unfortunate mistake', see J. Borchers, 'The Problem with General Jurisdiction', *University of Chicago Legal Forum* (2001), 119-139, at 119; F. Juenger, 'Federalism: Judicial Jurisdiction in the United States and in the European Communities: A Comparison', 82 *Michigan Law Review* (1984), 1195-1212, at 1196; P. Borchers, 'Comparing Personal Jurisdiction in the United States and the European Community: Lessons for American Reform', 40 *American Journal of Comparative Law*

'constitutionalization' of U.S. jurisdiction law: the Full Faith and Credit Clause and most importantly the Due Process Clause.[50]

5.2.1 Constitutional Limits to the Exercise of Jurisdiction

The Full Faith and Credit Clause finds its origin in Article IV(1) of the founding Constitution[51] and merely constitutes the duty for each state to give effect to judgements coming from sister state courts and federal courts.[52] In the early case of *D'Arcy v. Ketchum*[53] the Supreme Court allowed states to make an exception to the systematic recognition of sister judgements when the jurisdictional foundation of the judgement was ill-founded.[54] Judicial jurisdiction was then considered as a matter of international law,[55] but it became a matter of constitutional significance.[56] Before the *D'Arcy v. Ketchum* case, the Supreme Court stated in *Mills v. Duryee* that even though a judgement could not be re-litigated by the recognizing court, some principles of eternal justice should be guaranteed: '[o]ne of those [principles] is, that jurisdiction cannot be justly exercised by a state over property not within the reach of its process, or over persons not owing them allegiance or not subjected to their jurisdiction by being found within their limits.'[57] As a result, jurisdictional grounds for refusal of recognition were introduced.[58] In *Pennoyer v. Neff*, the U.S. Supreme Court directly addressed the jurisdiction principles in relation to the Due Process Clause.[59]

(1992), 121-157, at 122. See also J. Conison, 'What Does Due Process Have to Do with Jurisdiction?', 46 *Rutgers Law Review* (1994), 1071-1209, at 1073, for a plea for deconstitutionalization of U.S. jurisdiction law.

[50] Born, *International Civil Litigation*, at 78; Scoles, Hay *et al.*, *Conflict of Laws*, § 5.1, at 285.

[51] Art. IV, § 1, of the U.S. Constitution reads: 'Full Faith and Credit shall be given in each State to the public Acts, Records, and judicial Proceedings of every other State. And the Congress may by general Laws prescribe the Manner in which such Acts, Records and Proceedings shall be proved, and the Effect thereof.' See for a historical overview H. Korn, 'The Development of Judicial Jurisdiction in the United States', 65 *Brooklyn Law Review* (1999), 935, at 959-965.

[52] The Full Faith and Credit Clause provide for direct enforcement of sister state judgements and guarantee a flexible interstate recognition. The Uniform Foreign Money-Judgments Recognition Act deals with foreign judgements. This model Act was adopted by a significant number of states and provides for a relatively flexible recognition and enforcement of foreign judgements in the U.S. See for an exhaustive study on the U.S. recognition system L. Silberman, 'Enforcement and Recognition of Foreign Country Judgements in the U.S.', *International Business and Arbitration* (2000), 325-359, and C. Kessedjian, *La reconnaissance et l'exécution des jugements en droit international privé aux Etats-Unis* (1987). See also Silberman and Lowenfeld, 'A Different Challenge for the ALI', at 636-638.

[53] *D'Arcy v. Ketchum*, 52 U.S. (11 How.) 165, at 174-75 (1850).

[54] See W.M. Richman and W.L. Reynolds, *Understanding Conflict of Laws* (2002), at 19; Von Mehren, 'Theory and Practice', at 96-99.

[55] Born, *International Civil Litigation*, at 78.

[56] Ibid., at 79; Scoles, Hay *et al.*, *Conflict of Laws*, § 5.2, at 286; Casad and Richman, *Jurisdiction in Civil Actions Vol. 1*, at 66; Borchers, 'Comparing Jurisdiction', at 123.

[57] *Mills v. Duryee*, 11 U.S. 481, at 486 (Mem) (1813); Korn, 'The Development of Jurisdiction', at 974; Casad and Richman, *Jurisdiction in Civil Actions Vol. 1*, at 65-66.

[58] Scoles, Hay *et al.*, *Conflict of Laws*, § 5.2, at 286; Korn, 'The Development of Jurisdiction', at 972.

[59] 95 U.S. 714 (1878).

The XIVth Amendment incorporated the Due Process Clause in 1868. Less than ten years later, the Supreme Court established in *Pennoyer v. Neff* that the exercise of jurisdiction is subject to the Due Process Clause.[60] The case involved a claim for recovery of land located in Oregon that was occupied by Pennoyer. Neff, who was then a non-resident of Oregon, claimed ownership over the land. Pennoyer served Neff by publication although not physically present in the state of Oregon. Neff argued that the judgement rendered against him should not be recognized under the Full Faith and Credit Clause on the basis that the jurisdiction of the Oregon court was inadequate. Although the case merely concerned the recognition and enforcement of a judgement under the Full Faith and Credit Clause, the Supreme Court explained that

> '[s]ince the adoption of the Fourteenth Amendment to the Federal Constitution, the validity of such judgments may be directly questioned, and their enforcement in the State resisted, on the ground that proceedings in a court of justice to determine the personal rights and obligations of parties over whom that court has no jurisdiction do not constitute due process of law.'[61]

Since the decision in *Pennoyer v. Neff* in 1878, the Due Process Clause imposes constitutional limits on the exercise of jurisdiction of U.S. courts.[62] At first sight the Due Process Clause appears to protect the defendant from any abuse of judicial authority from American courts. The XIVth Amendment states:[63]

> 'All persons born or naturalized in the United States, and subject to the jurisdiction thereof, are citizens of the United States and of the State wherein they reside. No State shall make or enforce any law which shall abridge the privileges or immunities of citizens of the United States; nor shall any State deprive any person of life, liberty, or property, without due process of law; nor deny to any person within its jurisdiction the equal protection of the laws.'[64]

Over the years, the Supreme Court gave several interpretations to 'due process' which makes it an always-moving dynamic concept.[65] Although the U.S. jurisdic-

---

[60] Apart from the due process limitations on jurisdiction, due process also requires that defendant is given proper notice. See 2nd Restatement of Judgments (1982), Chapter 2, Introductory Note. U.S. terminology distinguishes between 'procedural' and 'substantive' due process, in which the procedural due process refers to the fair hearing of a party and proper notice, see P.J. Borchers, 'Jurisdictional Pragmatism: International Shoe's Half-Buried Legacy', *Davis Law Review* (1995), 561-590, at 577-579.

[61] *Pennoyer v. Neff*, 95 U.S. 714, at 733 (1878).

[62] Baumgartner, *The Proposed Hague Convention*, at 133; Von Mehren, 'Theory and Practice', at 75. See for other possible constitutional sources Casad and Richman, *Jurisdiction in Civil Actions Vol. 1*, at 135-137.

[63] The equivalent federal Due Process Clause applying to federal judicial authority is enshrined in the Vth Amendment and is formulated in similar words.

[64] Originally coming from the *magna carta*; see Mirandes, *La compétence internationale des Etats-Unis*, at 44 and fn. 2.

[65] Weintraub, *Commentary*, at 125, refers to a 'continuing process of constitutional interpretation that attempts to make the answers to the basic problem of when a court has jurisdiction to adjudicate responsive to modern social realities. The current solutions are not the final ones.' See Silberman, '"Two Cheers" for International Shoe', at 755; M. Redish, 'The Future of Personal Jurisdiction:

tional scheme lacks any uniform or federal legislation on international jurisdiction, the Due Process Clause is to be understood as *the* unifying factor in the exercise of international jurisdiction by U.S. courts.

5.2.2 From 'Power' to 'Minimum Contacts' and 'Fairness'

The due process interpretation provided in 1878 by the Supreme Court in *Pennoyer v. Neff* ruled for almost seventy years before the *International Shoe Co. v. Washington* decision radically changed it in 1945.[66] The *Pennoyer v. Neff* interpretation was strongly based on principles of territorial sovereignty justifying the exercise of jurisdiction over a person or property present within its territorial limits.[67] *Pennoyer*'s perception of jurisdiction is best reflected by Judge Holmes' well-known statement explaining that 'the foundation of jurisdiction is physical power'.[68] This 'power theory' followed its common law heritage; the Supreme Court attached considerable importance to the notion of 'presence'[69] and incorporated traditional common law grounds for jurisdiction founded on the simple service of process on the defendant present in the state.[70] At the same time, the defendant's presence also limited the jurisdictional reach over the defendant, as 'no State can exercise direct jurisdiction and authority over persons or property without its territory'.[71] During the years of *Pennoyer*'s ruling, state courts tried to expand the scope of the 'power theory' to reach absent defendants. Apart from the traditional grounds for jurisdiction by service of process on the defendant, the Supreme Court accepted jurisdiction based on consent. Moreover defendant's presence was extended by defendant's domicile in the forum.[72] The notion of 'implied consent' was introduced in an attempt to expand the scope of the power theory. 'Implied consent' should not be understood as the explicit expression of the parties' will. Rather, the concept was based on the assumption that a foreign company 'doing business' in a state implicitly consents to the jurisdiction of the courts of that state in return for the given opportunity to carry out business on its territory.[73]

A Symposium on *Burnham v. Superior Court*. Tradition, Fairness, and Personal Jurisdiction: Due Process and Constitutional Theory after *Burnham v. Superior Court*', *Rutgers Law Journal* (1991), 675-688, at 683.

[66] 326 U.S. 310 (1945).

[67] This appears to be strongly influenced by the territoriality doctrine of Story cited in *Pennoyer v. Neff*, 95 U.S. 714, at 722 (1877): 'The several States are of equal dignity and authority, and the independence of one implies the exclusion of power from all others.' Born, *International Civil Litigation*, at 78-79; Goldstein, 'Federalism', at 970.

[68] *Mc Donald v. Mabee*, 243 U.S. 90, at 91 (1917).

[69] R. Casad, 'Jurisdiction in Civil Actions at the End of the Twentieth Century: Forum Conveniens and Forum Non Conveniens', in *Abuse of Procedural Rights: Comparative Standards of Procedural Fairness*, International Association of Procedural Law International Colloquium, 27-30 October 1998, Tulane Law School (1999), 252-270, at 73.

[70] According to Born this is not surprising, see Born, 'Reflections on Jurisdiction', at 12.

[71] *Pennoyer v. Neff*, 95 U.S. 714, at 722 (1877).

[72] According to Casad and Richman 'there is a physical location in the state that is identified with him [the defendant], even when he personally is not there', Casad and Richman, *Jurisdiction in Civil Actions Vol. 1*, at 72-73.

[73] Scoles, Hay *et al.*, *Conflict of Laws*, § 5.3, at 291-292; Baumgartner, *The Proposed Hague Convention*, at 134-135; Casad and Richman, *Jurisdiction in Civil Actions Vol. 1*, at 77-79. In exchange

Jurisdiction asserted over a company that implicitly consented to jurisdiction by doing business in the forum was still consistent with principles of territorial sovereignty.[74] Traditional jurisdiction grounds based on presence and consent were stretched as far as possible, until it became untenable, in order to fit them into the power theory.[75] The limits of the power theory became apparent when it failed to reach defendants absent within the state's borders and could not satisfy the needs of interstate relations and commerce.[76]

The Supreme Court's decision in *International Shoe Co. v. Washington* represents a turning point in the development of U.S. law on jurisdiction and reformulated the meaning of due process in the context of current interstate legal relationships and national economy. In this case, the state of Washington imposed employment tax on a shoe corporation incorporated in Delaware but with its principal place of business in Missouri. The corporation employed around a dozen salesmen residing in Washington and regularly engaged in soliciting orders and displaying samples. The shoe corporation was sued in Washington over proceedings to recover unpaid contributions to a state unemployment compensation fund. The shoe corporation challenged the court's jurisdiction by stating that its activities within the state of Washington were not sufficient to manifest its 'presence' in the forum and that it consequently was a denial of due process to subject him to the Washington court. The Supreme Court abandoned the fundamental requirement of 'presence' under the power theory and allowed jurisdiction over absent defendants on new jurisdiction grounds by stating that 'due process only requires that in order to subject a defendant to a judgment "in personam", if he was not present within the territory of the forum, he has certain minimum contacts with it such that the maintenance of the suit does not offend traditional notions of fair play and substantial justice.'[77] This statement has become the key to U.S. jurisdiction. As a result, the Supreme

for the permission to 'do business' in a state and the protection of its law, the corporation was asked either implicitly or expressly to consent to jurisdiction. *Kane v. New Jersey*, 242 U.S. 160 (1916); *The Lafayette Ins. Co. v. French*, 59 U.S. 404, at 407 (1855).

[74] Claims against non-resident motorists arising out of accidents in the state were also seen as a form of 'implied consent'. Scoles, Hay *et al.*, *Conflict of Laws*, § 5.3, at 291; Casad and Richman, *Jurisdiction in Civil Actions Vol. 1*, at 381.

[75] D. McFarland, 'Dictum Run Wild: How Long-Arm Statutes Extended to the Limits of Due Process', *Boston University Law Review* (2004), 491, at 492; Scoles, Hay *et al.*, *Conflict of Laws*, § 5.3, at 292; Casad and Richman, *Jurisdiction in Civil Actions Vol. 1*, at 80-81; and see W.M. Richman and W.L. Reynolds, *Understanding Conflict of Laws* (1993), at 23-29, 'stretching the dogma by fiction'. Juenger states that 'it had become apparent that Pennoyer had succumbed to erosion and that a reorientation was needed to make the law of jurisdiction more practical and plausible.' Juenger, 'Federalism: A Comparison', at 1198

[76] Born, *International Civil Litigation*, at 80. This was later acknowledged by the U.S. Supreme Court in *McGee v. International Life Ins.*: 'Looking back over this long history of litigation a trend is clearly discernible toward expanding the permissible scope of state jurisdiction over foreign corporations and other non-residents. ... Today many commercial transactions touch two or more States and may involve parties separated by the full continent. With this increasing nationalization of commerce has come a great increase in the amount of business conducted by mail across state lines. At the same time modern transportation and communication have made it much less burdensome for a party sued to defend himself in a State where he engages in economic activity.' 355 U.S. 220, at 222-223 (1957).

[77] Ibid., at 316.

Court's interpretation of the Due Process clause shifted from a strict territorialist approach to jurisdiction under the power theory to a more flexible approach based on defendant's 'minimum contacts' and fairness.[78] The new approach to jurisdiction was based on the idea that proper exercise of jurisdiction is in accordance with due process of law when the defendant has 'minimum contacts' with the U.S. forum and that it is 'fair and reasonable' to subject him to jurisdiction when it does not offend traditional notions of fair play and substantial justice.[79] This resulted in a *two-step analysis*, which required that the exercise of jurisdiction of the court (1) be authorized by statute if based on minimum contacts, and that it (2) be within the constitutional limits of due process.[80]

In *International Shoe Co v. Washington*, the Supreme Court did however not reject the traditional jurisdiction grounds under the common law, such as for instance presence. But when a foreign defendant was 'doing business' in a U.S. forum, it was no longer needed to turn to the 'implied consent' construction.[81] Such activity would constitute certain 'minimum contacts' with the forum justifying jurisdiction under the new interpretation of the Due Process clause. A more flexible approach to judicial jurisdiction was introduced, namely 'the requirements for personal jurisdiction over non-residents have evolved from the rigid rule of Pennoyer v. Neff, … to the flexible standard of International Shoe Co. v. Washington.'[82] This flexible approach entails introducing 'modern' jurisdiction grounds in long-arm statutes in order to reach absent defendants having 'minimum contacts' with the forum. But the Supreme Court insisted that due process only permits the exercise of jurisdiction when it does not offend traditional notions of fair play and substantial justice, thereby introducing an element of fairness in the allocation of jurisdiction. For these reasons, the new approach is also called the 'fairness theory'.[83]

5.3 The Sources for United States Jurisdiction

The exercise of jurisdiction by U.S. courts over international disputes is limited by constitutional standards, but the U.S. Constitution does not provide for a statutory authority for jurisdiction over a (foreign) defendant. *International Shoe Co. v. Washington* rendered a much broader scope of jurisdiction grounds constitutionally possible, but statutory authorization is required to provide for a legal basis for jurisdiction over a defendant outside the forum. States have enacted statutes in order to have extraterritorial reach over foreign defendants. These are called 'long-

[78] Weintraub, *Commentary*, § 4.8, at 149; G. George, 'In Search of General Jurisdiction', 64 *Tulane Law Review* (1990), 1097-1141, at 1102.

[79] *Shaffer v. Heitner*, 433 U.S. 186 (1977) determined that these notions of fair play and reasonableness also applied to the traditional jurisdiction rules. See below Sects. 5.4.1 and 5.4.4.

[80] McFarland, 'Dictum Run Wild', at 493.

[81] *International Shoe Co v. Washington*, 326 U.S. 310, at 316-317 (1945).

[82] *Hanson v. Denckla*, 357 U.S. 235, at 252 (1958).

[83] A. Bell, *Forum Shopping and Venue in Transnational Litigation* (2003), § 4.27, at 144; F.A. Mann, 'The Doctrine of International Jurisdiction Revisited after Twenty Years', 186 *Recueil des cours* (1984), 67, at 68; see Von Mehren, 'Theory and Practice', at 115, calling it the litigational justice theory.

arm' statutes. The enactment of these long-arm statutes did however not mean that the state's legislators intended to exclude their courts from using traditional jurisdiction grounds as applied under the *Pennoyer v. Neff* regime.[84] The traditional jurisdiction grounds stemming from common law are still valid under the minimum contacts rule. As a consequence, the sources of U.S. jurisdiction law are twofold: common law principles providing for a legal basis for traditional jurisdiction grounds such as presence, consent and domicile, coexist with the long-arm statutes needed in order to meet statutory requirements.[85] Apart from the bases for jurisdiction stemming from common law, the long-arm statutes, providing the bases for extraterritorial jurisdiction, can stem from the state and federal legislator.

5.3.1 The States' Long-arm Statutes

Today, each of the fifty states enacted long-arm statutes.[86] The first long-arm statute appeared in 1955 in Illinois and stood as a model for several other states. In 1963 the Commissioners on Uniform State Laws came up with a model law for extraterritorial jurisdiction that was more or less similar to the Illinois Statute: the *Uniform Interstate and International Procedure Act* (Uniform Act). Many states modelled their long-arm statute on the Uniform Act. The latter was withdrawn in 1977, when all states had adopted long-arm statutes at least as far reaching as the Uniform Act.[87] Those statutes modelled on the Uniform Act enumerate specific grounds upon which a non-resident defendant can be subjected to jurisdiction. They are called 'enumerated', 'tailored', 'laundry list'[88] or 'single-acts' statutes.[89] Enumerated long-arm statutes have a restrictive effect, as they do not reach as far as constitutionally permitted.[90] They apply a 'two step analysis'; first, they examine whether the claim fits in one of the provisions of the statute in order to found jurisdiction and secondly they examine whether the exercise of jurisdiction offends constitutional standards.[91] Enumerated statutes embody a closed set of criteria and

[84] Casad and Richman, *Jurisdiction in Civil Actions Vol. 1*, at 386.

[85] Lowenfeld, *International Litigation*, at 176; Scoles, Hay *et al.*, *Conflict of Laws*, § 5.14, at 320; Richman and Reynolds, *Understanding Conflict of Laws*, at 62; Schack, *Jurisdictional Minimum Contacts Scrutinized*, at 1-3.

[86] Born, *International Civil Litigation*, at 76; Scoles, Hay *et al.*, *Conflict of Laws*, § 5.14, at 321; Casad and Richman, *Jurisdiction in Civil Actions Vol. 1*, at 380-381. The Districts of Columbia, Puerto Rico and the Virgin Islands also enacted long-arm statutes.

[87] See for more details Casad and Richman, *Jurisdiction in Civil Actions Vol. 1*, at 381.

[88] Born, *International Civil Litigation*, at 76; Weintraub, *Commentary*, § 4.9A, at 204.

[89] For instance New York and Wisconsin also enacted enumerated statutes with provisions differing from the Illinois type or the Uniform Act type. Casad and Richman, *Jurisdiction in Civil Actions Vol. 1*, 382; but see below for the further categorization of enumerated acts.

[90] Like those for example in Florida, New York and Ohio (although Ohio case law seems to be contradictory); see Casad and Richman, *Jurisdiction in Civil Actions Vol. 1*, at 384.

[91] See for instance with respect to Florida, *American Investors Life Ins. Co. v. Webb Life Ins. Agency*, Southern District of Florida, 876 F. Supp. 1278 (1995), in which the court stated that 'Under Florida law, [the] long-arm statute confers less jurisdiction upon Florida courts than allowed by [the] due process clause.' The New York Statute does not go as far as the Constitution allows; *Talbot v. Johnson Newspaper Corp.*, Court of Appeals of New York, 71 N.Y.2d 827, 829-30 (1988), 'not only do the categories of New York-related activity listed in CPLR 302 represent a closed universe, the

are more predictable than the one-step analysis but do not reach as far.[92] According to the 2nd Restatement of Judgments:

> 'The "long arm" provisions generally have been designed to enlarge state territorial jurisdiction beyond the limits of physical presence of person or property that had earlier been held to be necessary to a state's exercise of jurisdiction. However, the scope of these statutes is not always as broad as the range of jurisdiction sanctioned by the "minimum contacts" principle. Hence, there are situations in which a state court would have authority to exercise jurisdiction as a matter of Constitutional law, but may not exercise such authority as a matter of its own local law.'[93]

Other states enacted a different kind of statute. For instance, the Californian Civil Procedure Code grants jurisdiction on any 'constitutional basis', hereby directly incorporating the Due Process Clause as a jurisdictional basis. In other words, California's long-arm Statute confers jurisdiction as far as the due process limits permits it and does not specify specific contacts or jurisdiction grounds.[94] These types of statutes are also called 'general statutes' or 'no limits' statutes.[95]

The distinction between these two main groups is however blurred by the fact that several enumerated long-arm statutes are complemented by a 'fall-back' or 'catch-all' provision directly providing for jurisdiction on 'any constitutional basis'.[96] These statutes are also called 'hybrid statutes'[97] and combine closed jurisdictional criteria with an open constitutional norm that permits jurisdiction to the limits of the Due Process Clause. In practice, the enumerated jurisdiction criteria are ignored and as a result these 'hybrid statutes' have the same jurisdictional reach as the 'no limit' statutes.[98]

Some states have not adopted a statutory 'catch all' provision but instead settled case law established that the jurisdictional scope of their long-arm statute extends to the constitutional outer limits, thus adopting a 'one step' analysis.[99] In that case, the question of jurisdictional authority simply comes down to whether or not the exercise of jurisdiction is consistent with due process standards. In practice, this one step analysis reduces enumerated statutes to a single constitutional test as is

---

New York courts have not interpreted them as necessarily providing the same reach as would be available under the Constitution.'

[92] Scoles, Hay *et al.*, *Conflict of Laws*, § 5.14, at 322.

[93] 2nd Restatement of Judgments, Chap. 2, Validity of Judgments, Topic 2, § 4., comment b.

[94] See also *Dow Chemical Co. v. Calderon*, U.S. Court of Appeals, 9th Circuit, 422 F.3d 827 (2005).

[95] McFarland, 'Dictum Run Wild', at 496 *et seq.* McFarland explains how a decision of the Illinois Supreme Court, *Nelson v. Miller*, 11 Ill.2d 378,143 N.E.2d 673 (1957), was misinterpreted by other state legislators and lead to the enactment of general statutes reaching to the limits of due process.

[96] Alabama, Illinois, Louisiana, Maine, Nebraska, Oklahoma, Oregon, Pennsylvania, Tennessee, Utah, and Iowa (in case of alternate method of service see the new Rule 1.306. Iowa Code; Iowa Court Rules, I. Rules of Practice and Procedure, Chap. 1. Rules of Civil Procedure, Division III – Commencement of Actions), see also Weintraub, *Commentary*, § 4.9A, at 203.

[97] McFarland, 'Dictum Run Wild', at 497.

[98] Casad and Richman, *Jurisdiction in Civil Actions Vol. 1*, at 384.

[99] This also followed the 1957 Illinois Supreme Court decision *Nelson v. Miller*, 11 Ill.2d 378, 143 N.E.2d 673 (1957). But see Casad and Richman, *Jurisdiction in Civil Actions Vol. 1*, at 383; McFarland, 'Dictum Run Wild', at 502.

done with 'no limit' statutes.[100] Many states – but certainly not all – adopted this 'one step analysis' leaving their statutes also within the same wide reach as the 'no limit' Californian Statute.[101]

5.3.2 The Federal Jurisdiction Statute

Diversity and alienage jurisdiction are most relevant for the exercise of jurisdiction over international contractual disputes by federal courts. Jurisdiction of U.S. federal courts is regulated principally by Rule 4 of the Federal Rules of Civil Procedure (FRCP).[102] The FRCP is the only possible statutory authority that can grant jurisdiction to federal courts, as it cannot be based on common law principles. In other words, if jurisdiction is not covered under that rule, federal courts cannot exercise jurisdiction.[103]

Rule 4(k)(1)A is the principal source of statutory authorization for jurisdiction in federal courts in international contractual disputes.[104] The rule provides for a 'borrowing authority' for federal courts that have diversity or alienage subject matter jurisdiction and jurisdiction in federal questions.[105] In order to establish juris-

[100] Casad argues that this type of reasoning is not a rational one and that such state statutes should not be ignored. According to him the two-step approach is endorsed even in states where the court has declared that their statute reaches the outer limits of the Constitution. Casad and Richman, *Jurisdiction in Civil Actions Vol. 1*, at 383-387, see in particular fn. 23, at 386-387.

[101] According to Casad the following states have adopted the one-step analysis: Alaska, Arizona, Arkansas, California, Colorado, Connecticut, Idaho, Iowa, Kansas, Kentucky, Maryland, Massachusetts, Michigan, Minnesota, Missouri, New Hampshire, *with respect to individuals*, New Jersey, New Mexico, North Carolina, North Dakota (*hybrid*), South Carolina, South Dakota, Texas, Vermont, Virginia, Casad and Richman, *Jurisdiction in Civil Actions Vol. 1*, at 383, fns. 18 and 20; see also Scoles, Hay *et al.*, *Conflict of Laws*, § 5.14, at 322.

[102] Rule 4(k) regulates the Territorial Limits of Effective Service and reads as follows: '(1) Service of a summons or filing a waiver of service is effective to establish jurisdiction over the person of a defendant (A) who could be subjected to the jurisdiction of a court of general jurisdiction in the state in which the district court is located, or (B) who is a party joined under Rule 14 or Rule 19 and is served at a place within a judicial district of the United States and not more than 100 miles from the place from which the summons issues, or (C) who is subject to the federal interpleader jurisdiction under 28 U.S.C. § 1335, or (D) when authorized by a statute of the United States. (2) If the exercise of jurisdiction is consistent with the Constitution and laws of the United States, serving a summons or filing a waiver of service is also effective, with respect to claims arising under federal law, to establish personal jurisdiction over the person of any defendant who is not subject to the jurisdiction of the courts of general jurisdiction of any state.'

[103] *Omni Capital Intern v. Rudolf Wolff & Co.*, 484 U.S. 97, at 111 (1987); Born, *International Civil Litigation*, at 193-194.

[104] Scoles, Hay *et al.*, *Conflict of Laws*, § 5.15, at 322-323. Rule 4(k)(1)(B) provides for jurisdiction over third party actions or joinder actions and contains a '100 mile bulge rule' requiring that the defendant was served within a hundred miles of the federal court where the action is pending. Scoles, Hay *et al.*, *Conflict of Laws*, § 10.4, at 431; Richman and Reynolds, *Understanding Conflict of Laws*, at 95; Casad and Richman, *Jurisdiction in Civil Actions Vol. 1*, § 5-2[4][b], at 553-555. Rule 4(k)(1)(C) regulates interpleader cases and Rule 4(k)(1)D enacted some specific federal jurisdictional statutes, among others see the Clayton Act (15 USC § 22); the RICO (18 USC § 1965); and 28 USC § 2361. See Born, *International Civil Litigation*, at 195; Richman and Reynolds, *Understanding Conflict of Laws*, at 95; Scoles, Hay *et al.*, *Conflict of Laws*, § 10.2, fn. 6, at 425; Casad and Richman, *Jurisdiction in Civil Actions Vol. 1*, § 5-2[4][c]-[d], at 556 and § 5-3, at 565.

[105] Born, *International Civil Litigation*, at 77 and 192; Baumgartner, *The Proposed Hague Convention*, at 143.

diction a federal court may 'borrow' the jurisdictional bases of the state in which it is located.[106] Both traditional common law grounds and the long-arm statutes are borrowed from the state's jurisdictional scheme to establish jurisdiction of federal courts.[107] Depending on where the federal court is situated it will borrow either a *no limit-type* of long-arm statute or it will borrow an enumerated single-act statute.

Like the exercise of jurisdiction by state courts, federal courts are also bound by constitutional limits. The XIVth Amendment limits the exercise of jurisdiction of state courts by requiring minimum state-wide contacts, whereas the Vth Amendment generally limits jurisdiction exercised by federal courts.[108] The due process test embodied in the Vth Amendment requires the defendant to have minimum contacts with the U.S. territory as a whole, instead of having affiliating contacts with one state in particular.[109] This 'nation-wide' contact test does however not apply when federal courts have diversity or alienage subject matter jurisdiction; as a general rule federal courts do not go beyond the reach of their state counterpart.[110] The totality of defendant's contacts is only taken into account to examine whether the exercise of jurisdiction satisfies the 'minimum contacts' principle of the Vth Amendment when the claim arises under federal law.[111] As a consequence, federal courts are indirectly bound by the minimum contacts of the defendant with that particular forum as required by the due process clause of the XIVth Amendment. It establishes jurisdiction of federal courts by following local jurisdictional law: even when *no limits* or *hybrid* statutes allow jurisdiction within the limits of the Constitution, the federal court will not permit the enlargement of its jurisdictional reach based on defendant's contacts with the U.S. as a whole.[112]

---

[106] 'Thus, under Rule 4(e) [predecessor of Rule 4], a federal court normally looks either to a federal statute or to the long-arm statute of the State in which it sits to determine whether a defendant is amenable to service, a prerequisite to its exercise of personal jurisdiction.' *Omni Capital Intern v. Rudolf Wolff & Co.*, 484 U.S. 97, at 105 (1987).

[107] Born, *International Civil Litigation*, at 216; *Omni Capital Intern v. Rudolf Wolff & Co.*, 484 U.S. 97, at 101 (1987).

[108] Scoles, Hay *et al.*, *Conflict of Laws*, § 10.2, at 424; Casad and Richman, *Jurisdiction in Civil Actions Vol. 1*, § 5-1[2], at 528.

[109] Due process limits considering defendant's nation-wide contacts are especially important under Rule 4 (k)(2), which allows jurisdiction for claims under federal law. The federal court has a broader reach over the defendant, as the Fifth Amendment allows nation-wide contacts to be taken into consideration. With respect to Rule 4(k)(1)A where state jurisdiction law governs the federal jurisdiction question and the relevant contacts are merely the ones with that particular state, it is uncertain whether the Vth or the XIVth Amendment should be the adequate constitutional test. See in general L. Brilmayer and C. Norchi, 'Federal Extraterritoriality and Fifth Amendment Due Process', 105 *Harvard Law Review* (1992), 1217-1263; 'Alien Corporations and Aggregate Contacts: A Genuinely Federal Jurisdictional Standard', *Harvard Law Review* (1981), 470-486; R. Trangsrud, 'The Federal Common Law of Personal Jurisdiction', 57 *George Washington Law Review* (1989), 849-906; and see Scoles, Hay *et al.*, *Conflict of Laws*, § 10.2, at 426-427; Casad and Richman, *Jurisdiction in Civil Actions Vol. 1*, § 5-1[2], at 528-529, summarizing several dissenting views on the question.

[110] Scoles, Hay *et al.*, *Conflict of Laws*, § 10.2, at 425.

[111] Born, *International Civil Litigation*, at 194; Weintraub, *Commentary*, § 4.7, at 145; Scoles, Hay *et al.*, *Conflict of Laws*, § 10.3, at 429.

[112] See the following two examples for the application of the Californian long-arm Statutes through FRCP Rule 4(k)(1)A; *California Doe v. Unocal Corp.*, U.S. District Court, Northern District of California, 248 F. Supp.2d 915, at 923 (2001) and *Dole Food Co., Inc. v. Watts*, U.S. Court of Appeals,

Although U.S. Congress has the power to enact a federal long-arm statute in alienage cases based on nation-wide contacts, it refrained from doing so.[113] Rule 4(k)(2) provides for statutory authority for jurisdiction of federal courts on the basis of defendant's nation-wide contacts but is limited only to claims arising under federal law.[114] The enactment of Rule 4(k)(2),[115] specifically designed for international disputes, provides for a broader reach over non-resident defendants by considering the totality of defendant's contact with the U.S. territory as a whole.[116] The fact that the claim has to arise under *federal law*[117] considerably limits the statutory authority of federal courts over aliens with sufficient nation-wide contacts: alienage and diversity jurisdiction are based on state law and are therefore not covered by Rule 4(k)(2).[118] In *Asahi Metal Industry Co., Ltd. v. Superior Court*, the Supreme Court did not address the question of nation-wide 'doing business' contacts:

> 'We have no occasion here to determine whether Congress could, consistent with the Due Process Clause of the Fifth Amendment, authorize federal court personal jurisdiction over alien defendants based on the aggregate of *national* contacts, rather than on the contacts between the defendant and the State in which the federal court sits.'[119]

5.4 Due Process Standards

Once jurisdiction can be founded on one of the bases enshrined in a state or federal long-arm statute or deriving from the U.S. common law principles on jurisdic-

---

9th Circuit, 303 F.3d 1104 (2002): 'Because California's long-arm jurisdictional statute is coextensive with federal due process requirements, the analyses for personal jurisdiction under state law and federal due process are the same.'

[113] See above Sect. 5.1.3 and see L. Silberman, 'Developments in Jurisdiction and Forum Non Conveniens in International Litigation: Thoughts on Reform and a Proposal for a Uniform Standard', 28 *Texas International Law Journal* (1993), 501-529, at 513, who advocates a federal jurisdiction standard not limited to questions under federal law, 'the jurisdiction standard should be applied to all claims against foreign defendants, whether based on state or federal law'.

[114] Rule 4(k)(2) reads: 'If the exercise of jurisdiction is consistent with the Constitution and laws of the United States, serving a summons or filling a waiver of service is also effective, with respect to claims arising under federal law, to establish personal jurisdiction over the person of any defendant who is not subject to the jurisdiction of the courts of general jurisdiction of any state.'

[115] The rule followed the Supreme Court's decision in *Omni Capital Intern v. Rudolf Wolff & Co., Ltd.*, 484 U.S. 97, at 110-111 (1987), in which it stated that 'It would appear that Congress knows how to authorize nationwide service of process when it wants to provide for it. That Congress failed to do so here argues forcefully that such authorization was not its intention.' See also Scoles, Hay *et al.*, *Conflict of Laws*, § 10.5, at 433.

[116] Born, *International Civil Litigation*, at 204.

[117] For instance 28 USCA § 1331; these are 'federal questions'. See Casad and Richman, *Jurisdiction in Civil Actions Vol. 1*, § 5-2[e], at 557.

[118] Born, *International Civil Litigation*, at 214; Scoles, Hay *et al.*, *Conflict of Laws*, § 10.5, at 434.

[119] *Asahi Metal Industry Co., Ltd. v. Superior*, 480 U.S. 102, at 113 (1987); Born, *International Civil Litigation*, at 194; Lowenfeld, *International Litigation*, at 202. See also *Reers v. Deutsche Bahn AG*, U.S. District Court, Southern District of New York, 320 F. Supp.2d 140 (2004), stating that in a diversity suit, it is the foreign defendant's contacts with the forum state, not with the U.S. as a whole, that are relevant to the personal jurisdiction inquiry; conduct directed toward the U.S. or toward the world generally cannot subject a defendant to personal jurisdiction in a particular state.

tion, applying this jurisdiction has to be compatible with constitutional due process standards.

The modern interpretation given by *International Shoe Co. v. Washington*[120] to the Due Process Clause requires 'minimum contacts' and 'fairness', but the Supreme Court failed to supply a more precise meaning of those new concepts. Subsequent decisions searched for an adequate interpretation of these concepts and developed the due process test further on a case-by-case basis.

5.4.1 **The Supreme Court's Interpretation**

The first case following the *International Shoe* decision that abandoned the strict territorial approach under the *Pennoyer v. Neff* regime was *McGee v. International Life Insurance Co.*[121] This case involved a Californian resident, beneficiary of a life policy, who filed a suit against a Texan insurance company in California. The Texan defendant had no offices or agents in California and apparently had never solicited or done any insurance business in California. The only contact was the mailing of the insurance policy to the claimant located in California. Statutory authority was given by a statute subjecting foreign corporations to jurisdiction on the basis of having concluded an insurance contract with residents of that state. The Supreme Court held that it was consistent with the 'fairness' principles to exercise jurisdiction on the basis of one single transaction, provided that the contact reflected a 'substantial connection' with the forum. The Court based its decision on *International Shoe* and stated that '[l]ooking back over this long history of litigation a trend is clearly discernible toward expanding the permissible scope of state jurisdiction over foreign corporations and other nonresidents.'[122] Furthermore, the Court justified the wider scope of the Due Process Clause by stating that

> '[t]oday many commercial transactions touch two or more States and may involve parties separated by the full continent. With this increasing nationalization of commerce has come a great increase in the amount of business conducted by mail across state lines. At the same time modern transportation and communication have made it much less burdensome for a party sued to defend himself in a State where he engages in economic activity.'[123]

In *Hanson v. Denckla*[124] the Court slowed down the trend of expanding jurisdiction to foreign defendants by introducing the 'purposeful availment' requirement. *Hanson* concerned an interstate trust dispute in which a Delaware corporate trustee was sued in Florida. The claimants, the settlor and the beneficiary, later became residents of Florida. The defendant trust company had no office in Florida and transacted no business there. None of the trust assets were ever held or administered in Florida and the record disclosed no solicitation of business in that state either in

---

[120] 326 U.S. 310 (1945).
[121] *McGee v. International Life Insurance* Co., 355 U.S. 220 (1957).
[122] Ibid., at 222.
[123] Ibid., at 223.
[124] *Hanson v. Denckla*, 357 U.S. 235 (1958).

person or by mail.[125] The only contact with the forum was the execution in Florida of the powers of appointment under the trust but those contacts did not arise 'out of an act done or transaction consummated in the forum state'.[126] In other words, the nature of the contacts between the Delaware trustee and Florida were not the result of some act by which the defendant has purposely availed himself of the privilege of conducting activities within another state. For that reason, the Court considered the contacts to be insufficient for a substantial connection with the forum and the Court refused jurisdiction to Florida.[127]

Shaffer v. Heitner[128] is an important decision with respect to jurisdiction related to property, as will be discussed below.[129] The Supreme Court analogously applied the due process standards to *in rem* and *quasi in rem* jurisdiction: 'We therefore conclude that all assertions of state-court jurisdiction must be evaluated according to the standards set forth in International Shoe and its progeny.'[130] The fact that the Court emphasized that the fairness test should apply to *all* assertions of jurisdiction,[131] illustrates that the Supreme Court's decision on due process standards was understood to be equally applicable to the traditional bases of jurisdiction used during the *Pennoyer* regime.[132]

Kulko v. Superior Court[133] endorsed the purposeful availment factor previously held by the Supreme Court in *Hanson v. Denckla*.[134] The case concerned a request for modification of a custody and child support agreement brought in front of a Californian court. After a divorce in Haiti, the mother (claimant) moved to California and the father (defendant) lived in New York. The father acquiesced in his daughter's desire to live with the mother in California. Claimant argued that the father hereby caused an 'effect' in California by an act or omission outside the state and 'purposely availed himself of the benefits and protections of California'.[135] The defendant only temporarily visited California for reasons completely unrelated to the claim. The Court ruled that 'a father who agrees, in the interests of family harmony and his children's preferences, to allow them to spend more time in California than was required under a separation agreement can hardly be said to have "purposefully availed himself" of the "benefits and protections" of California's laws'[136] and that reliance 'on having caused an "effect" in California was misplaced.'[137]

---

125 Ibid., at 251.
126 Ibid.
127 Weintraub, *Commentary*, § 4.8, at 150.
128 433 U.S. 186 (1977).
129 See for U.S. property-based jurisdiction Sect. 5.7.
130 *Shaffer v. Heitner*, 433 U.S. 186, at 212 (1977).
131 Ibid., at 212.
132 Lowenfeld, *International Litigation*, at 181.
133 436 U.S. 84 (1978).
134 *Hanson v. Denckla*, 357 U.S. 235 (1958).
135 436 U.S. 84, at 85-86 (1978).
136 Ibid., at 94.
137 Ibid., at 96.

In *World-Wide Volkswagen Corp. v. Woodson*[138] the Supreme Court was asked to deal with the question whether jurisdiction could be exercised on the basis that it was foreseeable that defendant's action would 'cause an effect' in the forum. The case involved a product liability action to recover personal injuries sustained in Oklahoma in a car-accident. The injured plaintiffs purchased the car in New York where they were resident before moving to Arizona. The action was brought against the New York regional dealer and distributor of the cars in Oklahoma.[139] For litigation-tactical reasons plaintiffs choose Oklahoma instead of their home state Arizona.[140] Defendants' only connection with Oklahoma was that the car sold in New York to New York residents became involved in an accident in Oklahoma. The New York defendants carried out no business activity in Oklahoma; they closed no sales and performed no services there, they did not avail themselves of any of the benefits of Oklahoma law, and solicited no business there either through sales-persons or through advertising to reach that state.[141] According to plaintiffs, jurisdiction could however be founded on the basis that defendant could have foreseen that the car sold would travel to Oklahoma and that the automobile might cause injury in Oklahoma. The Supreme Court held that 'foreseeability alone is not a sufficient benchmark for personal jurisdiction under the Due Process Clause'[142] and that the latter 'does not contemplate that a state may make binding a judgment in personam against an individual or corporate defendant with which the state has no contacts, ties, or relations.'[143] In other words, under the minimum contact theory, (territorial) contacts with the forum remain a requisite for U.S. jurisdiction.

In *Insurance Corp. of Ireland, Ltd. v. Compagnie des Bauxites de Guinée,*[144] the Supreme Court addressed the question whether notions of federalism introduced by *World-Wide Volkswagen Corp. v. Woodson*[145] are part of the due process test. The Court held that it was not and that the 'jurisdiction requirement recognizes and protects an individual liberty interest. It represents a restriction on judicial power not as a matter of sovereignty, but as a matter of individual liberty.'[146]

Keeton v. Hustler Magazine Inc.[147] and *Calder v. Jones*[148] both dealt with the minimum contact theory in interstate defamation cases. In *Keeton v. Hustler Maga-*

[138] 444 U.S. 286 (1980).

[139] Jurisdiction was accepted against the manufacturer and importer.

[140] Weintraub, *Commentary*, § 4.8, at 156-157.

[141] *World-Wide Volkswagen Corp. v. Woodson*, 444 U.S. 286, at 287 (1980), repeated at 295.

[142] Ibid., at 295.

[143] Ibid., at 294, referring to *International Shoe Co v. Washington*, 326 U.S. 310, at 319 (1945).

[144] 456 U.S. 694 (1982). This case involved another insurance claim for damage recovery which occurred in Guinnee. Defendant, Compagnie des Bauxites de Guinée was a Delaware corporation.

[145] *World-Wide Volkswagen Corp. v. Woodson*, 444 U.S. 286, at 294 (1980), 'Even if the defendant would suffer minimal or no inconvenience from being forced to litigate before the tribunals of another State; even if the forum State has a strong interest in applying its law to the controversy; even if the forum State is the most convenient location for litigation, the Due Process Clause, acting as an instrument of interstate federalism, may sometimes act to divest the State of its power to render a valid judgment.'

[146] 456 U.S. 694, at 702 (1982). See also Weintraub, *Commentary*, § 4.8, at 161.

[147] *Keeton v. Hustler Magazine, Inc.*, 465 U.S. 770 (1984).

[148] *Calder v. Jones*, 465 U.S. 783 (1984).

zine Inc., a New York resident brought suit against an Ohio company in the state of New Hampshire. Plaintiff's choice for New Hampshire was based on the fact that it was the only state where the statute of limitation had not run. Defendant's contacts with the forum consist in the sale of thousands of copies of Hustler magazine each month, and claimant's only connection with New Hampshire was the circulation of a magazine that she assists in producing. The Supreme Court concluded that 'regular circulation of magazines in the forum State is sufficient to support an assertion of jurisdiction' and that '[t]he general course of conduct in circulating magazines throughout the state was purposefully directed at New Hampshire, and inevitably affected persons in the state. Such regular monthly sales of thousands of magazines cannot by any stretch of the imagination be characterized as random, isolated, or fortuitous.'[149] The Supreme Court also dealt with the question whether and to what extent a state's legitimate interest in adjudicating the dispute is part of the due process test.

> 'We agree that the "fairness" of haling respondent into a New Hampshire court depends to some extent on whether respondent's activities relating to New Hampshire are such as to give that State a legitimate interest in holding respondent answerable on a claim related to those activities. But insofar as the State's "interest" in adjudicating the dispute is a part of the Fourteenth Amendment due process equation, as a surrogate for some of the factors already mentioned, we think the interest is sufficient.'[150]

In *Calder v. Jones* the Supreme Court held that jurisdiction in California was proper over a defendant resident in Florida because of the intentional conduct in Florida calculated to cause injury to claimant in California.[151] According to the Court, due process does not prevent the state from asserting jurisdiction over a cause of action arising out of effects caused in California because the actions causing the effects in the forum were performed outside the state.[152] But the Court emphasizes that the 'mere fact that they can "foresee" that the article will be circulated and have an effect in California is not sufficient for an assertion of jurisdiction.'

Helicópteros Nacionales de Colombia v. Hall[153] was the first case in which the Supreme Court was asked to deal with jurisdiction over an international dispute and involved general jurisdiction under the 'minimum contacts' rule.[154] The case concerned a wrongful death action following a helicopter crash in Peru against, among others, Helicol, a corporate defendant incorporated in Columbia, who engaged in the business of providing helicopter transportation. The U.S. claimants representing (U.S.) decedents of the crash, brought action in Texas on the basis that defendant conducted negotiations in Texas with a Texan joint venture for helicopter hire. None of the plaintiffs were Texan residents and the contract was signed in

[149] *Keeton v. Hustler Magazine, Inc.*, 465 U.S. 770, at 774 (1984).

[150] Ibid., at 775-776, also citing *Insurance Corp. v. Compagnie des Bauxites*, 456 U.S. 694, at 702-703 (1982).

[151] *Calder v. Jones*, 465 U.S. 783, at 789 (1984).

[152] Ibid., at 787.

[153] *Helicópteros Nacionales de Colombia v. Hall*, 466 U.S. 408 (1984).

[154] Lowenfeld, *International Litigation*, at 182.

Peru. Since the claimant's claim did not arise out of the defendant's contacts with the Texan forum, the Court had to consider whether there was sufficient 'minimum contact' to provide for general jurisdiction.[155] It held that the defendant Helicol had insufficient contact with Texas to be subjected to its courts over claims unrelated to the plaintiff's claim. The *Helicópteros* case exposed the limits of general jurisdiction.[156]

A year later, the Supreme Court was asked to deal with specific jurisdiction over a contractual dispute in *Burger King v. Rudzewicz.*[157] Apart from cases involving insurance contracts, *Burger King v. Rudzewicz* was the first case dealing with long-arm provisions asserting specific jurisdiction relating to contractual transactions.[158] It involved an interstate dispute arising out of a breach of a franchise agreement in which the franchisor Burger King, incorporated in Florida, sued a Michigan franchisee Rudzewicz. The latter applied for a franchise to a Michigan district office of Burger King, which was then forwarded to Burger King's Miami headquarters. Rudzewicz negotiated with the Florida franchisor for purchase of a long-term franchise through the Michigan district office and the Miami headquarters of Burger King. By entering into a franchise contract, the franchisee accepted regulation of his business from the Miami headquarters and was required to make monthly payments to the franchisor in Miami. When Rudzewicz fell behind with those payments to Burger King, the latter alleged that Rudzewicz had breached his franchise obligations in Florida and sued the franchisee under the Florida long-arm Statute which asserts special jurisdiction to any person who breaches a contract in Florida by failing to perform acts that the contract requires to be performed there. Defendants challenged the jurisdiction of the Court by claiming that they never physically entered Florida. By laying the emphasis on considerations of fairness and reasonableness, rather than on the presence of sufficient 'physical' minimum contacts with the forum, the Supreme Court allowed the exercise of jurisdiction over the defendant. Justice Brennan emphasized that with respect to interstate contractual obligations 'parties who "reach out beyond one state and create continuing relationships and obligations with citizens of another state" are subject to regulation and sanctions in the other State for the consequences of their activities'.[159] In other words, when a defendant deliberately engaged in significant activities within a state or has created continuing obligations between him and residents of the forum, he manifestly availed himself of the privilege of conducting activities within that forum. That makes it not 'unreasonable to require him to submit to the burdens of litigation in that forum' since his activities have been 'shielded by "the benefits

---

[155] See below Sect. 5.4.3.

[156] Weintraub, *Commentary*, § 4.8, at 165-167.

[157] *Burger King v. Rudzewicz*, 471 U.S. 462 (1985).

[158] Among others see *McGee v. International Life Insurance Co.*, 355 U.S. 220 (1957). See Weintraub, *Commentary*, § 4.8, at 168.

[159] *Burger King v. Rudzewicz*, 471 U.S. 462, at 473 (1985). By analogous application of its previous statements related to insurance contracts and referring to *Travelers Health Assn. v. Virginia*, 339 U.S. 643, at 647 (1950), and *McGee v. International Life Insurance Co.*, 355 U.S. 220, at 222-223 (1957).

and protections" of the forum's laws'.[160] Hence, as long as such 'commercial actor's efforts are "purposefully directed" toward residents of another state, absence of physical contacts cannot defeat personal jurisdiction there'.[161] The Court acknowledges that contact with an out-of-state defendant cannot *alone* or *automatically* establish sufficient minimum contacts for jurisdiction in claimant's home forum.[162] However, other factors must be evaluated in 'determining whether the defendant purposefully established minimum contacts within the forum'.[163] Justice Brennan continues by stating that such factors consist in considerations, which sometimes serve to establish the reasonableness of jurisdiction upon a lesser showing of minimum contacts than would otherwise be required.[164]

Asahi Metal Industry Co. Ltd. v. Superior Court[165] was the second international dispute following *Helicópteros Nacionales de Colombia v. Hall*. It involved a product liability suit brought in California arising from a motorcycle accident allegedly caused by defects in a tire manufactured by Cheng Shin. The injured sued among others the Taiwanese tire manufacturer Cheng Shin, who in turn filed a cross-complaint for indemnity against Asahi, the Japanese manufacturer of the tube's valve. Chen Shin incorporates the Asahi valves into its finished tires, which he then sells throughout the world, including in the U.S., where twenty percent of its sales take place in California. By selling his tire valves to the Taiwanese Chen Shin tire manufacturer, the Japanese Asahi valve manufacturer was aware that tires with his valves would end up in California. However, Asahi would never have thought that this would subject it to lawsuits in California, since he did not do business, had no office, agents, employees, or property, in California and did not advertise nor solicit business in the forum. Chen Shin brought suit against Asahi in California under the 'no limits' long-arm statute, that authorizes jurisdiction on any constitutionally permissible basis. The question addressed to the Supreme Court was whether the mere awareness on the part of a foreign defendant (Asahi) that the components it manufactured, sold, and delivered outside the U.S. would reach the forum state (California) in the stream of commerce constitutes 'minimum contacts' between the defendant and the forum state in such a way that the exercise of jurisdiction does not offend 'traditional notions of fair play and substantial justice'.[166] The Supreme Court stated that Asahi's intentional act of placing its components into the stream of commerce is insufficient to form the basis for state court jurisdiction and would be an unreasonable and unfair violation of the Due Process Clause. Apart from considering the 'stream of commerce' question, the Supreme Court seeks support in the factors constituting 'reasonableness' as required under due process standards:[167]

---

[160] *Burger King v. Rudzewicz*, 471 U.S. 462, at 476 (1985).
[161] Ibid. (emphasis added).
[162] Ibid., at 478.
[163] Ibid., at 479.
[164] Ibid., at 477.
[165] 480 U.S. 102 (1987).
[166] Ibid., at 105.
[167] See also Weintraub, *Commentary*, § 4.8, at 173.

> 'We have previously explained that the determination of the reasonableness of the exercise of jurisdiction in each case will depend on an evaluation of several factors. A court must consider the burden on the defendant, the interests of the state, and the plaintiff's interest in obtaining relief. It must also weigh in its determination "the interstate judicial systems interest in obtaining the most efficient resolution of controversies; and the shared interest of the several States in furthering fundamental substantive social policies".'[168]

The Court heavily relied on the fact that both parties were foreign. With respect to the fact that Asahi was a foreign defendant, the Court held that 'the unique burdens placed upon one who must defend oneself in a foreign legal system should have significant weight in assessing the reasonableness of stretching the long arm of personal jurisdiction over national borders'.[169] According to Justice O'Connor, the interests of the plaintiff and the forum does not justify the serious burdens placed on the alien defendant and therefore does not justify the exercise of jurisdiction. Moreover, a state's legitimate interests in having jurisdiction over the case is considerably diminished since the plaintiff is not a Californian resident.[170] The Court considered the international context, 'the heavy burden on the alien defendant, and the slight interests of the plaintiff and the forum State', and concluded that 'the exercise of personal jurisdiction by a California court over Asahi in this instance would be unreasonable and unfair.'[171]

When the Supreme Court stated in *Shaffer v. Heitner* that '*all* assertions of state-court jurisdiction must be evaluated according to the standards set forth in *International Shoe* and its progeny'[172] it was long interpreted as equally imposing the 'reasonableness' test to traditional grounds for jurisdiction, such as defendant's domicile or jurisdiction based on the physical presence of the individual defendant – also called tag-jurisdiction in the U.S. Since *International Shoe Co. v. Washington* physical presence no longer automatically suffices as a ground for jurisdiction.[173] In *Burnham v. Superior Court*,[174] the Supreme Court subjected defendant Burnham, a New Jersey resident, to the jurisdiction of a California court on the basis that he was served with a process for a divorce petition by his estranged wife during a trip to California to conduct business and visit his children. Burnham was subjected to general jurisdiction as the suit was completely unrelated to his activities in California. The Supreme Court accepted tag-jurisdiction without any other substantial affiliations with the forum and without applying the reasonableness test. *Burnham v. Superior Court* is now interpreted as allowing traditional juris-

---

[168] *Asahi Metal Industry Co., Ltd. v. Superior Court*, 480 U.S. 102, at 113 (1987).

[169] Ibid., at 114.

[170] Ibid.

[171] Ibid., at 116.

[172] 433 U.S. 186, at 212 (1977); Scoles, Hay *et al.*, *Conflict of Laws*, § 5.13, at 318; Casad and Richman, *Jurisdiction in Civil Actions Vol. 1*, at 129.

[173] 'After *International Shoe* presence was no longer a necessary condition for jurisdiction; after *Shaffer v. Heitner* presence was no longer a sufficient condition either.' Richman and Reynolds, *Understanding Conflict of Laws*, at 131.

[174] 495 U.S. 604, at 606 (1990): 'The transient jurisdiction rule will generally satisfy due process requirements'.

diction bases under any circumstance as these would equally satisfy due process requirements.[175]

5.4.2 The Current Due Process Test for United States Jurisdiction

The interpretation of the Due Process Clause as set out above in the Supreme Court's decisions resulted in a wider jurisdictional reach of U.S. courts. Especially the cases directly following the *International Shoe*-turnover emphasized 'minimum contacts' and considerations of fairness and reasonableness thus liberating the jurisdictional question from rigid requirements imposed by the 'power' theory. This trend reached its peak in *McGee v. International Life Insurance*, in which the Supreme Court accepted jurisdiction on the mere fact that the defendant had sold an insurance contract in the forum and stated that the exercise of jurisdiction was consistent with due process standards even if the only substantial contact with the forum consisted of one single transaction and the defendant had never physically entered the forum.[176] In fact the 'minimum contact' rule was replaced or intermingled with notions of fairness and jurisdiction was no longer based on contacts and notions of territorial sovereignty. In *Hanson v. Denckla*[177] the Court however refused jurisdiction on the basis of a single, but substantial connection and made some additional requirements.[178] The 'purposeful availment' test introduced by *Hanson* is now crucial for asserting specific jurisdiction and was clearly affirmed by *Shaffer v. Heitner*[179] and *Kulko v. Superior Court*.[180] In subsequent cases, the Supreme Court clearly emphasized the reasonableness of the exercise of jurisdiction over the foreign defendant rather than the evaluation of 'sufficient contacts' with the forum. This is considered by some as a move 'towards discretion' in asserting jurisdiction.[181]

The Supreme Court's decisions do not provide clear guidance with respect to due process limits on jurisdiction.[182] Lower courts struggle when applying the due process restrictions.[183] The Supreme Court's intention might have been to provide for a more flexible approach to jurisdiction,[184] but instead it found itself in a continual debate on the interpretation of the Due Process Clause and sometimes even

---

175 See Casad and Richman, *Jurisdiction in Civil Actions Vol. 1*, at 129.

176 355 U.S. 220, at 223 (1957). See also Casad and Richman, *Jurisdiction in Civil Actions Vol. 1*, at 88 and 96-97; and Schack, *Jurisdictional Minimum Contacts Scrutinized*, at 6; see also Part II under 'transacting business'.

177 357 U.S. 235 (1958).

178 The factual distinction between these two cases lay in the fact that in the *McGee* case the defendant initiated contacts, later called 'purposeful availment', which was not the case in *Hanson* where defendant's contacts were not the result of defendant activities or solicitation of any business, see Casad and Richman, *Jurisdiction in Civil Actions Vol. 1*, at 89.

179 433 U.S. 186 (1977).

180 436 U.S. 84 (1978).

181 Lowenfeld, *International Litigation*, at 206; Weintraub, *Commentary*, § 4.8, at 147.

182 See Juenger, 'Comparative Neglect', at 14: 'Obviously, the term "minimum contacts" is far too vague to guide the decision of real-life cases. Nor does it guarantee fair decisions'.

183 'Chaos and confusion have marked attempts by conscientious state and federal judges to apply the Supreme Court's prescriptions for state-court jurisdiction.' Weintraub, *Commentary*, § 4.8, at 147.

184 Heiser, 'A Minimum Interest Approach', at 919.

reversed its own decisions within a short period of time.[185] The Court struggled with the notion of 'fairness and reasonableness' to exercise jurisdiction over the defendant and its relation with the 'minimum contacts'.[186] Both aspects of the modern jurisdictional theory are interrelated; without fairness, there is no jurisdiction even if the defendant has established minimum contacts with the forum and vice versa. Yet, the importance given to these components in the due process test differs from case to case and from judge to judge.[187]

In sum, the current due process test consists of a three-part test; first the defendant has to have sufficient 'minimum contacts' with the forum, second, defendant is required to have 'purposefully availed himself' of the forum,[188] and third, the exercise of jurisdiction has to be in accordance with the principles of 'fair play and substantial justice'.

5.4.3 The 'Minimum Contact' Rule

The first step of the three-part test of the due process constitutional standards requires a defendant to have minimum 'contacts, ties or relations' with the forum.[189] 'Contacts' refer to the connecting factors or 'affiliated circumstances'[190] between the forum and the defendant or his activities.[191] In *Keeton v. Hustler Magazine*, the Supreme Court explained that a court, judging minimum contacts, should 'properly focus on the relationship among the defendant, the forum, and the litigation'[192] and not between the claimant and the forum or those of a third party.[193] It is not required that the plaintiff be located in the forum, even though the plaintiff's residence in the forum is not completely irrelevant for the jurisdictional test.[194] In *Kulko v. Superior Court*, the Supreme Court held that although

---

[185] See the case of interstate federalism introduced by *World-Wide Volkswagen Corp. v. Woodson*, 444 U.S. 286 (1980), but rejected two years later by *Insurance Corp. of Ireland, Ltd. v. Compagnie des Bauxites de Guinée*, 456 U.S. 694 (1982); see Casad and Richman, *Jurisdiction in Civil Actions Vol. 1*, at 99.

[186] Born, *International Civil Litigation*, at 83.

[187] In *McGee v. International Life Insurance Co.*, 355 U.S. 220 (1957), one substantial connection was sufficient to establish jurisdiction even if the defendant did not have any other (physical) contact with the forum, this case relied heavily on the fairness aspect of *International Shoe*. This was nuanced by *Hanson v. Denckla*, 357 U.S. 235 (1958), which relied on the importance of 'physical' contacts with the forum and 'resurrected' the power theory. See Born, *International Civil Litigation*, at 83; and Casad and Richman, *Jurisdiction in Civil Actions Vol. 1*, at 89.

[188] *Hanson v. Denckla*, 357 U.S. 235 (1958).

[189] *World-Wide Volkswagen Corp. v. Woodson*, 444 U.S. 286, at 294 (1980), referring to *International Shoe Co v. Washington*, 326 U.S. 310, at 319 (1945).

[190] Casad and Richman, *Jurisdiction in Civil Actions Vol. 1*, at 12.

[191] Weintraub, *Commentary*, § 4.7, at 145; Richman and Reynolds, *Understanding Conflict of Laws*, at 97.

[192] *Keeton v. Hustler Magazine, Inc.*, 465 U.S. 770, at 775 (1984), citing *Shaffer v. Heitner*, 433 U.S. 186, at 204 (1977).

[193] See *Calder v. Jones*, 465 U.S. 783, at 788 (1984): 'The plaintiff's lack of "contacts" will not defeat otherwise proper jurisdiction, but they may be so manifold as to permit jurisdiction when it would not exist in their absence.' See also Casad and Richman, *Jurisdiction in Civil Actions Vol. 1*, at 145; and Richman and Reynolds, *Understanding Conflict of Laws*, at 100-101.

[194] 'That is, plaintiff's residence in the forum may, because of defendant's relationship with the plaintiff, enhance defendant's contacts with the forum. Plaintiff's residence may be the focus of the activities of the defendant out of which the suit arises. But plaintiff's residence in the forum State is

'the interests of the forum State and of the plaintiff in proceeding with the cause in the plaintiff's forum of choice are, of course, to be considered, an essential criterion in all cases is whether the "quality and nature" of the defendant's activity is such that it is "reasonable" and "fair" to require him to conduct his defense in that State.'[195]

This means that whether defendant's contacts are in 'quality or in quantity' sufficient for jurisdiction, depends upon the circumstances of each individual case and should be established by the court seized on a case-by-case basis.[196] In *Helicópteros Nacionales de Colombia, S.A. v. Hall*[197] the Court replaced the notion of 'minimum contacts' with 'sufficient' contacts.[198] But in any event the 'minimum contacts test' is 'not susceptible of mechanical application; rather, the facts of each case must be weighed to determine whether the requisite "affiliating circumstances" are present.'[199]

5.4.3.1 *General Contacts and Specific Contacts*

Provided that defendant's contacts with the forum state are constitutionally sufficient, U.S. jurisdiction law distinguishes between '*general*' and '*specific*' jurisdiction.[200] Some of defendant's contacts are so substantial, continuous and systematically connected with the forum that they justify general jurisdiction over the defendant even when the alleged cause of action is unrelated to those contacts.[201] All traditional bases for jurisdiction which were applied under the *Pennoyer* regime, including jurisdiction based on defendant's domicile, residence, place of incorporation and physical presence,[202] provide for general jurisdiction on the basis of unrelated contacts, e.g. unrelated as to the nature of the claim.[203] The 'modern' jurisdiction ground of doing business also provides for general jurisdic-

---

not a separate requirement, and lack of residence will not defeat jurisdiction established on the basis of defendant's contacts.' *Keeton v. Hustler Magazine, Inc.*, 465 U.S. 770, at 780 (1984).

[195] 436 U.S. 84, at 92 (1978).

[196] The quality, and not merely the quantity, of the contacts is important. A single act may sometimes provide a basis for jurisdiction. See Sects. 5.6.3 and 5.6.4.

[197] 466 U.S. 408 (1984).

[198] See also P. Schlosser, 'Jurisdiction in International Litigation: The Issue of Human Rights in Relation to National Law and the Brussels Convention', *Rivista di diritto internazionale* (1991), 5-34, at 10.

[199] *Kulko v. Superior Court*, 436 U.S. 84, at 92 (1978).

[200] *International Shoe v. Washington*, 326 U.S. 310, at 318 (1945): 'there have been instances in which the continuous corporate operations within a state were thought so substantial and of such a nature as to justify suit against it on causes of action arising from dealings entirely distinct from those activities'. See also *Helicópteros Nacionales de Colombia v. Hall*, 466 U.S. 408, at 414 (1984). See among others Scoles, Hay *et al.*, *Conflict of Laws*, § 5.10, at 305 *et seq.*

[201] *International Shoe v. Washington*, 326 U.S. 310, at 318 (1945); *Consol. Benguet Mining Co.*, 342 U.S. 437 (1952); Borchers, 'The Problem with General Jurisdiction', at 119: 'The term "general jurisdiction" (at least supposedly) refers to bases of jurisdiction that are independent of the operative facts of the dispute between the parties.'

[202] See Sect. 5.6.

[203] L. Brilmayer, 'A General Look at General Jurisdiction', 66 *Texas Law Review* (1988), 723-783; see also the categorization made by the Restatement of the Law (Third) of Foreign Relations Law of the United States [hereafter 3rd Restatement of Foreign Relations], § 421, comment f.

tion.[204] Other contacts that are random, fortuitous, or attenuated are not sufficiently connected with the forum to apply general jurisdiction, but *specific* jurisdiction can still be based on 'related contacts' over claims 'arising out of or related to' the defendant's contacts with the forum. Recognizing the distinction between general and specific jurisdiction is crucial for understanding the U.S. jurisdictional scheme, especially with respect to doing business and activity-based jurisdiction.[205] 'Doing business' distinguishes itself from 'transacting business' primarily in that defendant's contacts with the forum reflect continuity and permanency as opposed to transacting business which indicates that there are merely casual, sporadic, isolated or occasional contacts with the forum. Secondly, doing business provides for general jurisdiction over every claim unrelated to activities in the forum and regardless of the nature of the claim. In other words, one has to distinguish between 'unrelated continuous and systematic contacts' and 'related purposefully availed isolated contacts'.[206]

The terms 'general' and 'specific' jurisdiction were introduced by Professors Von Mehren and Trautmann.[207] But the concepts are not free from criticism and alternatives have been proposed, such as for example 'dispute blind' and 'dispute specific' jurisdiction.[208] In *Helicópteros Nacionales de Colombia, S.A. v. Hall* the Supreme Court applied and dealt with the significance of general versus specific jurisdiction.[209] A wrongful death action against a foreign corporation following the

---

[204] In fact, among the available general jurisdiction grounds, the doing business criterion deriving from the minimum contacts rule is more commonly invoked than traditional jurisdiction bases according to Scoles, Hay *et al.*, *Conflict of Laws*, § 6.7, at 350.

[205] Casad and Richman, *Jurisdiction in Civil Actions Vol. 1*, § 3-2[ii], at 342 and § 4-2[1], at 397. Borchers speaks of a 'fuzzy understanding of boundaries of general jurisdiction', see Borchers, 'The Problem with General Jurisdiction', at 120.

[206] *McGee v. International Life Insurance Co.*, 355 U.S. 220 (1957); Scoles, Hay *et al.*, *Conflict of Laws*, § 6.7, at 351; Casad and Richman, *Jurisdiction in Civil Actions Vol. 1*, § 3-2, at 341; Schack, *Jurisdictional Minimum Contacts Scrutinized*, at 31. The meaning of doing business varies somewhat from state to state. The 2nd Restatement of Conflict of Laws (§ 35 and § 47) treats 'doing business' and 'transacting business' in the same section and distinguishes between claims arising and not arising out of doing business in the state.

[207] See Von Mehren and Trautmann, 'Jurisdiction to Adjudicate', at 1136 and 1137. See for comments P. Borchers, 'Jurisdiction to Adjudicate Revisited', in *Law and Justice in a Multistate World; Essays in Honor of Arthur T. von Mehren* (2002), 1-10, at 3; and Casad and Richman, *Jurisdiction in Civil Actions Vol. 1*, at 12-13.

[208] Baumgartner, *The Proposed Hague Convention*, at 137 and see in general the critical articles of M. Twitchell, 'Why We Keep Doing Business with Doing-Business Jurisdiction', *University of Chicago Legal Forum* (2001), 171-214; Borchers, 'The Problem with General Jurisdiction'; George, 'In Search of General Jurisdiction'; L. Brilmayer, 'Related Contacts and Personal Jurisdiction', 101 *Harvard International Law Review* (1988), 1444-1464; M. Twitchell, 'A Rejoinder to Professor Brilmayer', 101 *Harvard International Law Review* (1988), 1465-1470; M. Twitchell, 'The Myth of General Jurisdiction', 101 *Harvard Law Review* (1988), 610-681; R. Casad and W. Richman, 'Casad's Jurisdiction in Civil Actions Part II – A Sliding Scale to Supplement the Distinction Between General and Specific Jurisdiction', 72 *California Law Review* (1984), 1328-1346. A different approach to this strict distinction between special and general jurisdiction has been proposed by introducing jurisdiction on a 'sliding scale'; as the extent and importance of defendant's forum contacts increase, a weaker connection between the claim and the defendant's contacts should be permissible. See Richman and Reynolds, *Understanding Conflict of Laws*, at 99.

[209] *Helicópteros Nacionales de Colombia, S.A. v. Hall*, 466 U.S. 408 (1984); see Weintraub, *Commentary*, § 4.8, at 167, Silberman, '"Two Cheers" for International Shoe', at 755.

helicopter crash in Peru required the Supreme Court to evaluate the defendant's contacts with Texas which only consisted in conducting negotiations in Texas with a Texan joint venture for helicopter hire.[210] The distinction between general versus specific jurisdiction appeared to be crucial:

> 'When a controversy is related to or "arises out of" a defendant's contacts with the forum, the Court had said that a "relationship among the defendant, the forum, and the litigation" is the essential foundation of in personam jurisdiction. ... *Even* when the cause of action does not arise out of or relate to the foreign corporation's activities in the forum State, due process is not offended by a State's subjecting the corporation to its in personam jurisdiction when there are sufficient contacts between the State and the foreign corporation.'[211]

By establishing that 'all parties to the present case concede that respondents' claims against Helicol did not "arise out of," and are not related to, Helicol's activities within Texas',[212] the Court ruled that specific jurisdiction was not available and that jurisdiction could only be established on the basis that defendant was doing business in Texas. As a consequence, the Court continued that '[w]e thus must explore the nature of Helicol's contacts with the State of Texas to determine whether they constitute the kind of continuous and systematic general business contacts'.[213] After an appreciation of the contacts with Texas, the Court held that defendant's contacts were not sufficiently 'continuous and systematic' to establish general jurisdiction and refused jurisdiction.

The fact that the Supreme Court states that *even* when the cause of action does not arise from defendant's activities in the forum, jurisdiction is still available when contacts are sufficient for general jurisdiction, indicates that in quest for a competent U.S. court the focus is primarily on whether specific jurisdiction exists on the basis of related contacts.[214] Unrelated contacts establishing general jurisdiction appears to be examined only when related contacts are not available.[215] This is the result of the more flexible approach of the 'minimum contacts' theory whose purpose is to provide for a wider extraterritorial reach over foreign defendants.[216]

---

[210] See above Sect. 5.4.1.

[211] 466 U.S. 408, at 414 (1984) (emphasis added).

[212] Ibid., at 415. See also *Calder v. Jones*, 465 U.S. 783, at 786 (1984), citing *Perkins v. Benguet Consol. Mining Co.*, 342 U.S. 437 (1952).

[213] 466 U.S. 408, at 416 (1984).

[214] See *contra Keeton v. Hustler Magazine, Inc.*, 465 U.S. 770, at 780 (1984): 'In the instant case, respondent's activities in the forum may not be so substantial as to support jurisdiction over a cause of action unrelated to those activities. But respondent is carrying on a "part of its general business" in New Hampshire, and that is sufficient to support jurisdiction when the cause of action arises out of the very activity being conducted, in part, in New Hampshire.'

[215] P. Dubinsky, 'The Reach of Doing Business Jurisdiction and Transacting Business Jurisdiction over Non-U.S. Individuals and Entities', Working Document no. 64, Presented at the Special Commission of the Hague Conference (1998), at 7; Casad and Richman, *Jurisdiction in Civil Actions Vol. 1*, § 3-2[2](ii), at 341; Schack, *Jurisdictional Minimum Contacts Scrutinized*, at 39.

[216] Lowenfeld, *International Litigation*, at 180 ('Long-arm statutes moved beyond general jurisdiction as under Pennoyer, to specific jurisdiction that is based on liability-creating activity in, or having effect in, the forum state'); Weintraub, *Commentary*, § 4.14, at 219; Scoles, Hay *et al.*, *Conflict of Laws*, § 6.9, at 357 ('courts are somewhat reluctant to exercise jurisdiction based on solely unrelated

As long as the claim is related to defendant's activities or contacts with the forum, it is not required that the defendant have continuous or systematic contacts with the forum. A weaker affiliation with the forum, other than the doing business criterion or the traditional presence criterion would suffice. A single or occasional contact with the forum suffices as long as it concerns a related claim.[217] The fact that it is more difficult to satisfy the 'continuous and systematic' contacts for doing business than the 'transacting activity' criterion, leads to a more frequent use of specific jurisdiction grounds for claims related to defendant's contacts.[218] The question of continuous and systematic unrelated contacts with the forum seems to become relevant only when the claim is unrelated to defendants' contacts with the forum.

5.4.3.2 *Related Contacts, the Claim 'Arising out' of Transacting Business*

The *Helicópteros Nacionales de Colombia, S.A. v. Hall* case revealed the importance of whether the claim 'arises out of' or 'relates' to the defendant's contacts with the forum. As the parties conceded that the claim did not 'relate to' or 'arise out of' defendant's activities with the forum, the Supreme Court was left with the question whether defendant's contacts with the forum were sufficient for general jurisdiction in the sense of 'continuous and systematic contacts'. The Supreme Court concluded that they were not,[219] yet Justice Brennan dissented and argued that the Court's attitude to 'related contacts' is too narrow.[220] In his view, defendant's contacts with the forum were sufficiently 'related' to the claim to assert specific jurisdiction. He distinguished between 'arising out of' and 'relating to' by arguing that although defendant's claim did not *arise out of* defendant's activities in the forum the claim was directly and significantly *related to* defendant's contact with the forum.[221] His opinion illustrates the different attitudes towards the degree of connectedness required for specific jurisdiction. The lack of any further guidance provided by the Supreme Court has led to an approach to specific jurisdiction that strongly varies from state to state.[222] Judge Chagares of the Third Circuit Court of Appeal recently held that '[u]nfortunately, the Supreme Court has not yet explained the scope of this requirement. State and lower federal courts

---

contacts'); Casad and Richman, *Jurisdiction in Civil Actions Vol. 1*, § 3-2[2](ii), at 341 ('they [doing business statutes] provide an alternative method of acquiring jurisdiction over foreign corporations. Resort to the doing business statutes usually occurs only when the defendant cannot be reached through the long-arm statute'); Twitchell, 'The Myth of General Jurisdiction', at 630 ('With the emergence of specific jurisdiction in the twentieth century, the exercise of general jurisdiction has become rare'); George, 'In Search of General Jurisdiction', at 1097 ('International Shoe diminished the need for the use of general jurisdiction by substantially expanding the availability of specific jurisdiction').

[217] Lowenfeld, *International Litigation*, at 231.

[218] Scoles, Hay *et al.*, *Conflict of Laws*, § 6.9, at 357: 'successful efforts to invoke general jurisdiction are fairly rare'.

[219] 466 U.S. 408, at 419 (1984).

[220] Lowenfeld, *International Litigation*, at 203; Scoles, Hay *et al.*, *Conflict of Laws*, § 6.7, at 352.

[221] 466 U.S. 408, at 426 *et seq.* (1984), see at 428: 'It is eminently fair and reasonable, in my view, to subject a defendant to suit in a forum with which it has significant contacts directly related to the underlying cause of action.'

[222] Born, *International Civil Litigation*, at 162; Scoles, Hay *et al.*, *Conflict of Laws*, § 6.7, at 352.

have stepped in to fill the void, but their decisions lack any consensus.'[223] Some states use a 'proximate causation' test asserting specific jurisdiction only when the claim is directly caused by the defendant's activities in the forum.[224] The New York Court of Appeals declared in *McGowan v. Smith*,[225] 'that even if the defendant has engaged in purposeful acts in New York, there must be a "substantial relationship" between those acts and the transaction upon which the plaintiff's cause of action is based.'[226] Known as the 'substantial connection' test, the requirement concentrates more on the totality of the circumstances of the claim. Some states, including California,[227] introduced a wide reaching 'but for' causation test that accepts 'related contact' by simply testing whether the plaintiff would still have a valid cause of action without the forum contact.[228]

5.4.3.3 *Special Contacts and Purposeful Availment*

The second step of the due process test requires that the defendant has purposefully established contacts with the forum as introduced by *Hanson v. Denckla*.[229] The Court held that the

> 'unilateral activity of those who claim some relationship with a nonresident defendant cannot satisfy the requirement of contact with the forum State. The application of that rule will vary with the quality and nature of the defendant's activity, but it is essential

[223] *O'Connor v. Sandy Lane Hotel Co., Ltd.*, 3rd Circuit, Pennsylvania, 496 F.3d 312, at 318 (2007).

[224] Born, *International Civil Litigation*, at 163.

[225] New York Court of Appeals, 52 N.Y.2d 268 (1981), which weakened the former authority on this issue; *Longines-Wittnauer Watch Co. v. Barnes & Reinecke, Inc.*, New York Court of Appeals, 15 N.Y.2d 443 (1965), certiorari denied 382 U.S. 905, in which the Court included both contractual claims as well as tort claims arising out of the 'transacting business' criterion. See also J. Lookofsky and K. Hertz, *Transnational Litigation and Commercial Arbitration: An Analysis of American, European and International Law* (2004), at 251-252.

[226] See for New York also the following cases in which 'the arising out of' requirement was denied; and the cause of action was held not to be arising out of business solicitations or transactions in New York; *Johnson v. Ward*, New York Court of Appeals, 4 N.Y.3d 516 (2005); *LaMarca v. Pak-Mor Mfg. Co.*, New York Court of Appeals, 95 N.Y.2d 210 (2000); *Beacon Enterprises, Inc. v. Menzies*, New York Court of Appeals (1983); *George Reiner & Co. v. Schwartz*, New York Court of Appeals (State court), 41 N.Y.2d 648 (1977); *Ferrante Equipment Co v. Lasker-Goldman*, New York Court of Appeals, 26 N.Y.2d 280, at 284, 715 F.2d 757 (1970); *Fontanetta v. American Bd. of Internal Medicine*, New York Court of Appeals, 421 F.2d 355 (1970).

[227] *Mattel, Inc. v. Greiner & Hausser GmbH*, U.S. Court of Appeals, 9th Circuit, 354 F.3d 857, at 859 (2003), 'The second prong of the specific jurisdiction test asks whether the claim arises out of or results from the Defendants' forum-related activities. We use a "but for" test to conduct this analysis.' Following the decision in *Harris Rutsky & Co. Ins. Servs. v. Bell & Clements Ltd.*, U.S. Court of Appeals, 9th Circuit, 328 F.3d 1122, at 1131-1132 (2003); *Aanestad v. Beech Aircraft Corp.*, 521 F.2d 1298 (1974); the U.S. Court of Appeals, 9th Circuit, refused specific jurisdiction as the claim had 'nothing' to do with defendant's activities.

[228] *Doe v. Unocal Corp.*, U.S. Court of Appeals, 9th Circuit, 248 F.3d 915, at 924 (2001); *Fireman's Fund Ins. Co. v. National Bank of Cooperatives*, U.S. Court of Appeals, 9th Circuit, 103 F.3d 888 (1996). *Shute v. Carnival Cruise Lines*, 9th Circuit, 897 F.2d 377, at 385-86 (1990). Other states have rejected it and New York does not adopt such a test, see Weintraub, *Commentary*, § 4.8, at 167; Scoles, Hay *et al.*, *Conflict of Laws*, § 6.7, at 353; Hay, Weintraub *et al.*, *Conflict of Laws*, at 119; Casad and Richman, *Jurisdiction in Civil Actions Vol. 1*, § 4-2[b], at 439.

[229] *Hanson v. Denckla*, 357 U.S. 235 (1958).

> in each case that there be some act by which the defendant purposefully avails itself of the privilege of conducting activities within the forum State, thus invoking the benefits and protections of its laws.'.[230]

This part of the due process test is particularly relevant for the exercise of specific jurisdiction.[231] Since the 'minimum contacts' rule widened the jurisdictional reach of U.S. courts based on contacts with the forum, the fact that the defendant is required to have purposefully availed himself of the forum imposes a restriction to extraterritorial jurisdiction.[232] According to the Supreme Court

> '[t]his "purposeful availment" requirement ensures that a defendant will not be haled into a jurisdiction solely as a result of "random," "fortuitous," or "attenuated" contacts or of the "unilateral activity of another party or a third person." Jurisdiction is proper, however, where the contacts proximately result from actions by the defendant himself that create a "substantial connection" with the forum state.'[233]

As a consequence, even if the defendant clearly satisfies the minimum contacts rule, jurisdiction would not be consistent with due process standards if the defendant himself has not purposefully established these contacts with the forum.[234]

After its introduction in *Hanson v. Denckla*, the concept of 'purposeful availment' needed some further elaboration in order to clarify what type of action by the defendant was required to satisfy the 'purposefulness' requirement.[235] The two cases following the *Hanson* case applying the 'purposefulness' test came to a negative outcome and jurisdiction was refused. In *Shaffer v. Heitner*[236] the Supreme Court refused jurisdiction on the basis of mere foreseeable contacts with the forum, and in *Kulko v. Superior Court* it rejected the 'causing an effect' factor as a component of the 'purposeful availment' test.[237] Physical entry in the forum is, however, not necessary to establish 'purposefulness'. In the *Burger King Corp. v. Rudzewicz* case, the Supreme Court made it clear that '[w]hen defendant has availed himself of the privilege of conducting business in a forum, jurisdiction cannot be avoided merely because the defendant did not physically enter the forum state.'[238] This clarification provided by the Supreme Court was needed to remove doubts that

---

[230] Ibid., at 253.

[231] Scoles, Hay *et al.*, *Conflict of Laws*, § 5.11, at 310; Casad and Richman, *Jurisdiction in Civil Actions Vol. 1*, at 143.

[232] Juenger, 'Federalism: A Comparison', at 1201.

[233] *Burger King Corp. v. Rudzewicz*, 471 U.S. 462, at 475 (1985), reaffirmed in *Asahi*, at 109: 'The Court rejected this concept of foreseeability as an insufficient basis for jurisdiction under the Due Process Clause.'

[234] Casad and Richman, *Jurisdiction in Civil Actions Vol. 1*, at 138-139 and 148-150; W. Heiser, 'A Minimum Interest Approach to Personal Jurisdiction', 35 *Wake Forest Law Review* (2000), 915-972, at 921.

[235] Casad and Richman, *Jurisdiction in Civil Actions Vol. 1*, at 90.

[236] 433 U.S. 186 (1977).

[237] 436 U.S. 84, at 97-98 (1978); Heiser, 'A Minimum Interest Approach', at 922-923; Casad and Richman, *Jurisdiction in Civil Actions Vol. 1*, at 97-98 and 152-153; Mirandes, *La compétence internationale des Etats-Unis*, at 100-103.

[238] *Burger King Corp. v. Rudzewicz*, 471 U.S. 462, at 476 (1985).

arose after *Hanson* in which the Supreme Court seemed to require physical contacts with the forum for meeting the 'purposefulness' test.

It became clear that 'without a finding of a voluntary affiliation between the defendant and the forum, jurisdiction is a constitutional impossibility'.[239] The mere fact that the defendant could have 'foreseen' that a particular activity would result in a connection with a particular forum is not sufficient for 'purposeful contacts', as it does not constitute a 'voluntary affiliation' between the defendant and the forum.[240] Although the foreseeability criterion alone does not provide for 'purposeful contacts', the rationale behind the purposeful availment requirement is one of certainty and predictability.[241] In *World-Wide Volkswagen Corp. v. Woodson*,[242] the Supreme Court stated that the foreseeability aspect plays a role in the due process analysis, not by 'the mere likelihood that a product will find its way into the forum State', but rather that 'the defendant's conduct and connection with the forum State are such that he should reasonably anticipate being haled into court there'.[243] This 'anticipation-of-forum-litigation test'[244] differs from the 'foreseeability criterion' which requires that defendant should have foreseen that his activities would result in contacts with a state, even though he did not purposefully avail himself of that state. The Supreme Court stated in *World-Wide Volkswagen Corp. v. Woodson*[245] that, when a defendant could reasonably have foreseen that he would be subjected to jurisdiction of a particular state, this could be a favourable factor to assert jurisdiction, but this concept was not further elaborated nor has it been given a place in the jurisdictional inquiry.[246] The approach was generally not favoured.[247]

The 'purposeful availment' requirement also was tested in relation to the doctrine of the 'stream of commerce'. State courts introduced this doctrine after *International Shoe Co. v. Washington* in order to hold a distributor or manufacturer liable for goods causing an effect in the forum on the basis that defendant placed them in the 'chain of distribution of the stream of commerce'.[248] The stream of commerce doctrine was particularly useful to establish purposefulness in product

---

[239] Scoles, Hay *et al.*, *Conflict of Laws*, § 5.11, at 314.

[240] Born, *International Civil Litigation*, at 82.

[241] *World-Wide Volkswagen Corp. v. Woodson*, 444 U.S. 286, at 296-297 (1980), 'The element of "foreseeability" has never alone been a sufficient benchmark for personal jurisdiction under the due process clause ... This is not to say, of course, that foreseeability is wholly irrelevant.' See Born, 'Reflections on Jurisdiction', at 4. This is also called the 'fair warning' rationale by Heiser, see Heiser, 'A Minimum Interest Approach', at 923.

[242] 444 U.S. 286 (1980).

[243] *World-Wide Volkswagen Corp. v. Woodson*, 444 U.S. 286, at 297 (1980).

[244] Term used by Casad and Richman, *Jurisdiction in Civil Actions Vol. 1*, at 153.

[245] 444 U.S. 286 (1980).

[246] In *Asahi Metal Industry Co., Ltd. v. Superior Court*, 480 U.S. 102 (1987). The affidavits indicated that the defendant was aware that the product would end up in the forum state, but, on the other hand, that it never contemplated that this would subject it to lawsuits. See above Sect. 5.4.1.

[247] Casad and Richman, *Jurisdiction in Civil Actions Vol. 1*, at 153; see also Mirandes, *La compétence internationale des Etats-Unis*, at 103-104; and Richman and Reynolds, *Understanding Conflict of Laws*, at 42.

[248] See Casad and Richman, *Jurisdiction in Civil Actions Vol. 1*, at 155; see also J.P. Stephens, 'Sovereignty and Personal Jurisdiction Doctrine: Up the Stream of Commerce without a Paddle', *Florida State University Law Review* (1991), 105-147.

liability cases. In *World-Wide Volkswagen Corp. v. Woodson*, the 'stream of commerce' theory was addressed to the Supreme Court for the first time in relation to the 'purposeful availment' requirement.[249] The Court held that, as a matter of principle, a 'forum State does not exceed its powers under the Due Process Clause if it asserts personal jurisdiction over a corporation that delivers its products into the stream of commerce with the expectation that they will be purchased by consumers in the forum State', even though no such basis existed for Oklahoma jurisdiction over *World-Wide Volkswagen Corp. v. Woodson*.[250] In *Asahi Metal Industry Co. v. Superior Court*, the Justices were divided on the question whether the placement of a product into the stream of commerce is without more an act of the defendant purposefully directed towards the forum state or whether additional conduct of the defendant is required.[251] It is unclear whether this 'additional conduct' requirement will be retained; the *Asahi Metal Industry Co. v. Superior Court* case might have been influenced by the fact that both parties were aliens.[252] It does not appear to be very popular among lower state courts.[253] Overall, there is little agreement as to 'whether and to what extent interjecting a product into the "stream of commerce" may create jurisdiction'.[254]

Of considerably greater importance in the context of contractual disputes is the 'initiation test' for the purposeful availment formula, as this helps to identify who initiated contact with the forum: was it the defendant who approached the claimant or vice versa? In the latter case the defendant is not to be regarded as having 'purposefully availed himself' of activities with the forum.[255] Defendant's activities prior to negotiations such as advertising, marketing, or using distributors in the forum state could establish purposeful contacts.[256]

5.4.4 The Criteria of Fairness and Reasonableness

The final step of the due process test – once it has been established that the defendant established 'purposeful minimum contacts' with the forum – is that the maintenance of the suit should not offend 'traditional notions of fair play and substantial justice'. This last part of the due process test involves considerations of 'fairness' and 'reasonableness' and should be regarded as a separate inquiry and

---

[249] 444 U.S. 286, at 297 (1980).

[250] Ibid., at 298.

[251] 480 U.S. 102, at 112 (1987), as introduced by Judge O'Connor, joined by the Chief Justice Powell, and Justice Scalia contra Justice Brennan, joined by Justice White, Justice Marshall and Blackmun disagreeing with the interpretation of the stream-of-commerce theory, arguing that the placement of a product into the stream of commerce is consistent with the Due Process Clause and that no showing of additional conduct is required.

[252] As remarked by several authors, among whom Casad and Richman, *Jurisdiction in Civil Actions Vol. 1*, at 157.

[253] Mirandes, *La compétence internationale des Etats-Unis*, at 110-120; Richman and Reynolds, *Understanding Conflict of Laws*, at 104-105; Casad and Richman, *Jurisdiction in Civil Actions Vol. 1*, at 157.

[254] Baumgartner, *The Proposed Hague Convention*, at 141-142.

[255] In particular *Burger King Corp. v. Rudzewicz*, 471 U.S. 462, at 474-476 (1985); Casad and Richman, *Jurisdiction in Civil Actions Vol. 1*, at 154-155.

[256] Nguyen, 'Redefining the Threshold', at 258.

an absolute prerequisite.[257] The 'fairness' or 'reasonableness' test[258] constitutes an integral part of the jurisdictional test and was first mentioned by the Supreme Court in *World-Wide Volkswagen Corp. v. Woodson*[259] and *Burger King Corp. v. Rudzewicz*[260] which were later confirmed by *Asahi Metal Industry Co. Ltd v. Superior*.[261] The test clearly consists in an interest analysis emphasizing the fairness or reasonableness[262] of bringing suit against the defendant in a particular forum: '[t]he relationship between the defendant and the forum must be such that it is "reasonable . . . to require the corporation to defend the particular suit which is brought there"'.[263] Especially in cases involving foreign defendants, the serious burden on an alien defendant to appear in a distant forum is evaluated.

But the interests evaluated under the reasonableness test are not those of the defendant alone; they are weighed against the minimal interests on the part of the plaintiff's interest and the forum state's interests. The 'fundamental fairness test' consists of five factors which determine whether it is according to the notions of 'fair play and substantial justice' to exercise jurisdiction. These factors were identified in the *Burger King Corp. v. Rudzewicz* case and are to be divided between the interests of the parties and the interests of the state.[264] Naturally, the interests of the parties encompass: 1) The burden of the defendant of being sued in a particular forum;[265] and 2) the plaintiff's interest in obtaining convenient and effective relief.[266]

The states' interests concern three other factors; the fact that the interest of the state weighs in the reasonableness of asserting jurisdiction indicates that the territorial doctrine still influences the jurisdictional system. These additional interests are: 1) the forum state's interest in adjudicating disputes;[267] 2) the interstate judi-

[257] Weintraub, *Commentary*, § 4.3, at 124. This next step 'translate[s] due process into a core concept that pervades the area of judicial jurisdiction. This core concept might be described as "reasonableness". Another such general term might be "fairness".' Casad and Richman, *Jurisdiction in Civil Actions Vol. 1*, at 165, and see Hay, 'Flexibility versus Predictability and Uniformity', at 327.

[258] See for both concepts of reasonableness and fairness, Weintraub, *Commentary*, § 4.7, at 145.

[259] 444 U.S. 286 (1980). See also A. Lowenfeld, *International Litigation and the Quest for Reasonableness: Essays in Private International Law* (1996), at 53-55.

[260] 471 U.S. 462 (1985).

[261] 480 U.S. 102 (1987). See also Casad and Richman, *Jurisdiction in Civil Actions Vol. 1*, at 166. Heiser, 'A Minimum Interest Approach', at 925.

[262] Following Casad, reasonableness and fairness are used interchangeably as similar concepts, see Casad and Richman, *Jurisdiction in Civil Actions Vol. 1*, at 164.

[263] *World-Wide Volkswagen*, 444 U.S. 286, at 292 (1980); and see Mirandes, *La compétence internationale des Etats-Unis*, at 121-122.

[264] *Burger King Corp. v. Rudewicz*, 471 U.S. 462, at 477 (1985).

[265] This factor especially considers the degree of inconvenience for the defendant to defend himself in a forum other than his home state. In the *Asahi* case, the Court tends to accept a heavier burden for an alien defendant due to distance and a foreign judicial system, see *Asahi Metal Industry Company, Ltd. v. Superior Court*, 480 U.S. 102, at 116 (1987); see also Mirandes, *La compétence internationale des Etats-Unis*, at 123-124; Casad and Richman, *Jurisdiction in Civil Actions Vol. 1*, at 166-167.

[266] In other words, to provide the claimant access to justice, see Casad and Richman, *Jurisdiction in Civil Actions Vol. 1*, at 169; and Mirandes, *La compétence internationale des Etats-Unis*, at 126-128.

[267] This is a significant factor in the reasonableness part of the due process analysis; several cases have pointed out the different types of state's interest to assert jurisdiction; but the state's interest to

cial system's interest in obtaining the most efficient resolution of controversies; and 3) the shared interest of the several states in furthering fundamental, substantive, and social policies.[268]

In fact some of these factors are well known, or even the same as the ones applied in the U.S. version of the *forum non conveniens* doctrine as will be explained in the following section.[269] As Heiser rightfully stated: 'As a practical matter, the "reasonableness" inquiry makes the due process limitation on state court assertions of personal jurisdiction a matter of discretion, akin to a constitutional doctrine of *forum non conveniens*'.[270]

5.5 *Forum Non Conveniens*

Even if there is a legal basis for jurisdiction over the plaintiff's (contractual) claim in order to subject the defendant to the jurisdiction of a U.S. court and the exercise of this jurisdiction is consistent with constitutional due process standards, most U.S. courts are still allowed to decline jurisdiction on the basis that it is a *forum non conveniens*.

The *forum non conveniens* doctrine was formally recognized as part of the U.S. jurisdictional scheme in 1947 by the U.S. Supreme Court decisions of *Gulf Oil Corp. v. Gilbert*[271] and *Koster v. Lumbermens' Mutual Casualty Co.*[272] Both of these interstate cases were decided on the same day.[273] Thirty-five years later the

---

provide a forum for its residents is the predominant interest. See in particular Richman and Reynolds, *Understanding Conflict of Laws*, at 106-107 and Mirandes, *La compétence internationale des Etats-Unis*, at 131-140.

[268] These last two factors specifically concern interstate jurisdiction and not international jurisdiction. But apart from that they have received little attention and guidance from the courts. See Casad and Richman, *Jurisdiction in Civil Actions Vol. 1*, at 170-171; and Heiser, 'A Minimum Interest Approach', at 926: 'the interstate "judicial system's interest in obtaining the most efficient resolution of controversies" and the "shared interests of the several states in furthering fundamental substantive social policies," are so vague as to be almost meaningless.'

[269] Casad and Richman, *Jurisdiction in Civil Actions Vol. 1*, at 25. See below with respect to the U.S. *forum non conveniens* since similar factors are used to decline jurisdiction.

[270] See Heiser, 'A Minimum Interest Approach', at 927.

[271] 330 U.S. 501 (1947).

[272] 330 U.S. 518 (1947).

[273] One year earlier the U.S. Supreme Court indicated that motions to dismiss on grounds of *forum non conveniens* could be made in federal diversity actions in *Williams v. Green Bay & Western R. Co.*, 326 U.S. 549 (1946). Prior to the Supreme Court's acceptance of the *forum non conveniens* doctrine, the doctrine was more or less applied by state and federal courts, especially in admiralty proceedings, but not always under the denomination of *forum non conveniens*. Among others see *Canada Malting Co. v. Paterson Steamships*, 285 U.S. 413 (1932). An article written by a New York lawyer in 1929 is considered to be at the origin of the inauguration of the doctrine in U.S. jurisdiction law, see P. Blair, 'The Doctrine of *Forum Non Conveniens* in Anglo American Law', 29 *Columbia Law Review* (1929), 1-34. See for a short recital of its origins *Piper Aircraft Co. v. Reyno*, 454 U.S. 235, fn. 13, at 248. For more detailed historical overviews see R. Brand and S. Jablonski, *Forum Non Conveniens: History, Global Practice, and Future under the Hague Convention on Choice of Court Agreements* (2007), at 37; Lowenfeld, *International Litigation*, at 300; R. Brand, 'Comparative Forum Non Conveniens and the Hague Convention on Jurisdiction and Judgments: International Forum Shopping in Memory of Professor F.K. Juenger', 37 *Texas International Law Journal* (2002), at 474-475; F. Juenger, 'Forum

Court dealt with the application of the doctrine in international disputes in the landmark case *Piper Aircraft Co v. Reyno*.[274]

The U.S. jurisdictional scheme allows a court to dismiss jurisdiction under the common law doctrine of *forum non conveniens* on the ground that a court abroad is the 'more appropriate and convenient forum for adjudicating the controversy'[275] when the court seized has 'jurisdiction over the cause and the parties and was a proper venue'.[276] In March 2007, the Supreme Court decided in *Sinochem Intern. Co. Ltd. v. Malaysia Intern. Shipping Corp.* that in cases 'where subject-matter or personal jurisdiction is difficult to determine, and forum non conveniens considerations weigh heavily in favour of dismissal', the court is entitled to take 'the less burdensome course'.[277] In other words, under certain circumstances, a court seized need not first conclusively establish its own jurisdiction, before dismissing the claim on the basis of the *forum non conveniens* doctrine.[278]

5.5.1 Characteristics and Factors

The *forum non conveniens* doctrine should not be understood as a jurisdiction rule[279] or as a substantive right of the parties, but more as a procedural rule based on U.S. common law principles.[280] The fact that jurisdictional power exists over a defendant does not constitute an obligation for the court to take jurisdiction over the case; the court has discretionary power to *dismiss* the case on the basis that

---

Non Conveniens – Who Needs It?' in *Wege zur Globalisierung des Rechts: Festschrift für Rolf A. Schütze zum 65. Geburtstag* (1999), 317-336, at 326-327; Born, *International Civil Litigation*, at 347-351; A. Reus, 'Judicial Discretion: A Comparative View of the Doctrine of Forum Non Conveniens in the United States, the United Kingdom and Germany', *Loyola of Los Angeles International and Comparative Law Journal* (1994), 457, at 459-462. Mirandes, *La compétence internationale des Etats-Unis*, at 246-247; C. Chalas, *L'exercise discrétionnaire de la compétence juridictionnelle en droit international privé* (2000), at 70-79; A. Nuyts, *L'exception de forum non conveniens. Etude de droit international privé* (2003), at 117-133; and C. Dorsel, *Forum Non Conveniens: Richterliche Beschränkung der Wahl des Gerichtsstandes im deutschem und amerikanischen Recht* (1996), at 47-48.

[274] 454 U.S. 235 (1981).

[275] *Sinochem Intern. Co. Ltd. v. Malaysia Intern. Shipping Corp.*, 549 U.S. 422, 127 S.Ct. 1184, at 1188 (2007).

[276] Ibid., at 1193, referring to *Gulf Oil Corp. v. Gilbert*, 330 U.S. 501 (1947).

[277] Ibid., at 1194 (2007): 'If, however, a court can readily determine that it lacks jurisdiction over the cause or the defendant, the proper course would be to dismiss on that ground. In the mine run of cases, jurisdiction "will involve no arduous inquiry" and both judicial economy and the consideration ordinarily accorded the plaintiff's choice of forum "should impel the federal court to dispose of [those] issue[s] first."' Referring to *Ruhrgas AG v. Marathon Oil Co.*, 526 U.S. 574, at 587-588 (1999).

[278] Ibid., at 1188. See on the relationship with *Gulf Oil Corp. v. Gilbert*, 330 U.S. 501 (1947), and whether *Sinochem* is overruling the latter, the opinion of Justice Ginsburg in *Sinochem Intern. Co. Ltd. v. Malaysia Intern. Shipping Corp.*, 127 S.Ct. 1184, at 1193 (2007). See Brand and Jablonski, *Forum non conveniens*, at 71.

[279] According to 2nd Restatement of Conflict of Laws, § 84, comment g: 'The rule of this Section is not jurisdictional, except as stated in Comment i. If a state chooses to exercise such judicial jurisdiction, as it possesses despite the fact that it is an inappropriate forum, its action in this regard is valid and will be recognized in other states. As between States of the United States, this result is required by full faith and credit.'

[280] *American Dredging Co. v. Miller*, 510 U.S. 442, at 454 (fn. 4) (1994).

another more convenient court is situated somewhere else.[281] Its application is not prevented by the constitutional standards of the due process clause[282] and no legislative authorization is needed for its application.[283]

The Supreme Court's decision in *Gulf Oil Corp. v. Gilbert* and *Koster v. Lumbermens' Mutual Causalty Co.*,[284] followed by *Piper Aircraft Co v. Reyno* laid down the basic common law principles for the federal *forum non conveniens* doctrine. A system of 'federal transfer' replaced the doctrine for dismissal of jurisdiction between federal courts.[285] As the federal transfer does not apply to international cases,[286] the federal *forum non conveniens* doctrine and the '*Gilbert-Koster-Piper*' factors[287] continue to determine the dismissal of jurisdiction in favour of an available forum located outside the U.S.[288]

---

[281] See 2nd Restatement of Conflict of Laws, § 84, comment g: 'The scope of territorial jurisdiction is affected by the principle of forum non conveniens. Under that principle, a court having territorial jurisdiction will nevertheless refuse to exercise it if the forum is substantially inconvenient compared with another forum in which the action might be brought.'

[282] See 2nd Restatement of Conflict of Laws, § 84, comment I; Born, *International Civil Litigation*, at 347; A. Alexander, 'Forum Non Conveniens in the Absence of an Alternative Forum', *Columbia Law Review* (1986), 1000-1020, at 1008 *et seq.*

[283] A. Rodgers, 'Forum Non Conveniens in International Cases', in *International Litigation: Defending and Suing Foreign Parties in U. S. Federal Courts* (2003), 205-219, at 205; Born, *International Civil Litigation*, at 352.

[284] 330 U.S. 518 (1947).

[285] Federal transfer is regulated by 28 USC § 1404 and reads: 'For the convenience of parties and witnesses, in the interest of justice, a district court may transfer any civil action to any other district or division where it might have been brought'. U.S. Congress enacted § 1404 after the *Gulf Oil Corp. v. Gilbert*, 330 U.S. 501 (1947). This 'was intended to be a revision rather than a codification of the common law' according to the Supreme Court in *Piper Aircraft Co. v. Reyno*, 454 U.S. 235, at 253 (1981), where it equally argued that § 1404 federal transfer is modelled on the *forum non conveniens* doctrine, except that a federal transfer is available to both defendant and plaintiff, while under the doctrine only the defendant is entitled to seek dismissal. In *Ferens v. John Deere Co.*, 494 U.S. 516, at 519 (1990), the Supreme Court also held that the inconvenience standards for federal transfer are easier to satisfy than transfers under the (state) *forum non conveniens* doctrine. The Supreme Court believes that 'Congress, by the term "for the convenience of parties and witnesses, in the interest of justice," intended to permit courts to grant transfers upon a lesser showing of inconvenience. This is not to say that the relevant factors have changed or that the plaintiff's choice of forum is not to be considered, but only that the discretion to be exercised is broader', see *Norwood v. Kirkpatrick*, 349 U.S. 29, at 32 (1955). Because of this wider discretion, cases dealing with 'federal transfer' cannot be interpreted by analogy to the *forum non conveniens* doctrine. Weintraub explains that the fact that the *forum non conveniens* doctrine gives the courts less discretion to dismiss the case is a reason for plaintiffs to prefer to try their action in a state court and to prevent the removal from state to federal court under § 1441(b). Scoles, Hay *et al.*, *Conflict of Laws*, § 11.14, at 505 *et seq.*; Born, *International Civil Litigation*, at 353 *et seq.*; Weintraub, *Commentary*, § 4.33C, at 284; Richman and Reynolds, *Understanding Conflict of Laws*, at 142; F. Juenger, 'FNC – Who Needs It?', *Festschrift*, at 328; J. Duval-Major, 'One-Way Ticket Home: The Federal Doctrine of Forum Non Conveniens and the International Plaintiff', *Cornell Law Review* (1992), 650-686, at 656; Nuyts, *L'exception de forum non conveniens*, § 111, at 164.

[286] See for a proposal for a federal statute regulating the *forum non conveniens* with respect to foreign courts in international disputes, Silberman, 'Developments in Jurisdiction', at 526-528.

[287] Term used by R. Brand, 'Forum Selection and Forum Rejection in U.S. Courts: One Rationale for a Global Choice of Court Convention', in *Reform and Development of Private International Law – Essays in Honour of Sir Peter North* (2002), 51-88, at 72

[288] It remains uncertain whether federal courts should apply the *forum non conveniens* as a matter of federal or state law. In the *Piper* case, the Supreme Court left the question raised in the pioneer

The majority of state courts also apply the *forum non conveniens* doctrine[289] and use the *Piper* decision as guidance in international disputes.[290] Most states enacted statutory provisions in order to regulate the doctrine and to provide guidance for its application.[291] Many states have done so by modelling their provisions on the former Uniform Interstate and International Procedure Act that reads as follows: 'When the court finds in the interest of substantial justice the action should be heard in another forum, the court may stay or dismiss the action in whole or in part on any conditions that may be just.'[292] But the application of the doctrine by the state courts is far from being homogenous. Some states have taken a significantly different approach than the federal doctrine; others even rejected its application.[293] For a long time Texas refused the *forum non conveniens* doctrine, but now accepts its application to tort cases only.[294] Louisiana, a state that traditionally belongs to

---

Gulf Oil and *Koster* cases unanswered. 'In previous forum non conveniens decisions, the Court has left unresolved the question whether under *Erie R. Co. v. Tompkins*, 304 U.S. 64 (1938), state or federal law of forum non conveniens applies in a diversity case. ... [H]ere also, we need not resolve the Erie question.' *Piper Aircraft Co. v. Reyno*, 454 U.S. 235, at 248 (1981). Little guidance was given in *American Dredging Co. v. Miller*, 510 U.S. 443, at 453 (1994), the doctrine was merely described as procedural. See more specifically Brand and Jablonski, *Forum non conveniens*, at 66. According to Brand and Jablonski, the general feeling among the federal courts is that the *forum non conveniens* doctrine should be governed by federal law, Brand and Jablonski, *Forum non Conveniens*, at 68.

289 See Born, *International Civil Litigation*, at 354; Casad and Richman, *Jurisdiction in Civil Actions Vol. 1*, at 34; Bell, *Forum Shopping and Venue*, § 4.74, at 167. See also 2nd Restatement of Judgments, § 4, comment g.

290 See for the significance of *Piper*, Reus, 'Judicial Discretion', at 467; and Duval-Major, 'One-Way Ticket Home', at 657; Dorsel, *Forum Non Conveniens*, at 57; Nuyts, *L'exception de forum non conveniens*, at 172-173.

291 Scoles, Hay *et al.*, *Conflict of Laws*, § 11.12, at 501; Casad and Richman, *Jurisdiction in Civil Actions Vol. 1*, at 28-32. For instance, the Californian Statute enacted a separate provision to provide for this discretionary power in § 410.30 of the California Code of Civil Procedure:

'When a court upon motion of a party or its own motion finds that in the interest of substantial justice an action should be heard in a forum outside this state, the court shall stay or dismiss the action in whole or in part on any conditions that may be just.'

For New York see § 327(a) of the New York Civil Procedure Rules:

'When the court finds that in the interest of substantial justice the action should be heard in another forum, the court, on the motion of any party, may stay or dismiss the action in whole or in part on any conditions that may be just. The domicile or residence in this state of any party to the action shall not preclude the court from staying or dismissing the action.'

See F. Juenger, 'Forum Non Conveniens – Who Needs It?', in *Abuse of Procedural Rights: Comparative Standards of Procedural Fairness: International Association of Procedural Law International Colloquium, 27-30 October 1998, Tulane Law School, New Orleans, Louisiana* (1999), 349-370, at 362; and Casad and Richman, *Jurisdiction in Civil Actions Vol. 1*, fn. 137, at 31. In Michigan the application of the doctrine is limited to non-residents and the cause of action must arise outside the forum. See Casad and Richman, *Jurisdiction in Civil Actions Vol. 1*, at 28. According to Bell, Florida and Louisiana do not subscribe to the doctrine, Bell, *Forum Shopping and Venue*, § 4.77, at 168, see fn. 118 for references to case law of both Florida and Michigan, Texas and Pennsylvania.

292 § 1.05 Uniform Interstate and International Procedure Act. See Scoles, Hay *et al.*, *Conflict of Laws*, § 11.12, at 501.

293 Some states such as Louisiana and Georgia expressly rejected the doctrine, Bell, *Forum Shopping and Venue*, § 4.76, at 168; Born, *International Civil Litigation*, at 354; Casad and Richman, *Jurisdiction in Civil Actions Vol. 1*, at 28-34. Scoles, Hay *et al.*, *Conflict of Laws*, § 11.13, at 502.

294 See the conditions listed in § 71.051 Texas Civil Practice & Remedies Code for the application of the doctrine to claims dealing with personal injury, survival, and wrongful death claims

the civil law tradition, is an example of a state that does not allow the *forum non conveniens* doctrine.[295]

5.5.1.1 *A More Convenient Forum Available Elsewhere*

In order to dismiss a case to a more convenient forum, the doctrine requires proof that an alternative available forum exists abroad and it involves a balancing test of *conveniens* interests.[296] The requirement of an adequate alternative available forum generally precedes the convenience analysis,[297] but both 'steps' supplement each other in the sense that no matter how inconvenient the chosen forum may be, without an 'adequate alternative' forum, a court cannot dismiss jurisdiction.[298] In *Gulf Oil Corp. v. Gilbert* the Supreme Court required that dismissal is only possible when an alternative forum is available.[299] *Piper Aircraft Co. v. Reyno* later added the requirement of an 'adequate' forum stating that 'however, where the remedy offered by the other forum is clearly unsatisfactory, the other forum may not be an adequate alternative, and the initial requirement may not be satisfied'.[300] This 'adequacy' criterion means that the plaintiff should not be denied *all* remedies and that he will obtain substantive relief and fair treatment.[301]

5.5.1.2 *Public and Private Factors*

The balancing of *conveniens* interests involves the appreciation of factors on a case-by-case basis.[302] A court has discretionary powers to determine whether the

---

occurring outside of Texas, as enacted in 1993 after *Dow Chemical Company & Shell Oil Company v. Domingo Castro Alfaro, et al.*, 786 S.W.2d 674 (1990). See C. Scherz, 'Section 71.051 of the Texas Civil Practice and Remedies Code. The Texas Legislature's Answer to Alfaro: Forum Non Conveniens in Personal Injury and Wrongful Death Litigation', *Baylor Law Review* (1994), 99-139, at 100; W. Woods, 'Suits by Foreign Plaintiffs: Keeping the Doors of American Courts Open', *Arizona Journal of International and Comparative Law* (1991), 75-88, at 77 *et seq.*

[295] *Louisiana Fox v. Board of Sup'rs of Louisiana State University*, Supreme Court of Louisiana, 576 So.2d 978, at 990-991 (1991). 'Finally, the power to legislate in terms of both substance and procedure has traditionally been left to the legislature. … Rather than establish a jurisprudential procedural device for declining jurisdiction where it is otherwise vested by the legislature, we choose to find that the power to dismiss for forum non conveniens is not within the inherent power of Louisiana courts as part of the basic law of this state, as courts have held to be the case in most common law states.'

[296] See also Rodgers, 'FNC in International Cases', at 205-206.

[297] Rodgers, 'FNC in International Cases', at 206; Brand, 'Comparative FNC', at 477. *Contra* Casad referring to a case dismissing jurisdiction without another available forum, Casad and Richman, *Jurisdiction in Civil Actions Vol. 1*, at 25.

[298] 2nd Restatement of Conflict of Laws, § 84, comment c.

[299] *Sinochem Intern. Co. Ltd. v. Malaysia Intern. Shipping Corp.*, 127 S.Ct. 1184, at 1190 (2007), citing *American Dredging*, 510 U.S., fn. 2, at 449. See also Alexander, 'In the Absence of an Alternative Forum', at 1003-1004.

[300] 454 U.S. 235, fn. 22, at 254 (1981).

[301] Casad and Richman, *Jurisdiction in Civil Actions Vol. 1*, at 25; Scoles, Hay *et al.*, *Conflict of Laws*, § 11.10, at 496-497; and see 2nd Restatement of Conflict of Laws, § 85, comment c. However the application of criterion has raised a number of problems as indicated by D. Epstein, 'An Examination of the "Adequacy of the Alternative Forum" Factor in Forum Non Conveniens Determinations', in *International Dispute Resolution: The Regulation of Forum Selection (Fourteenth Sokol Colloquium)* (1997), and Alexander, 'In the Absence of an Alternative Forum'.

[302] *Piper Aircraft Co. v. Reyno*, 454 U.S. 235, at 263 (1981).

chosen forum is 'seriously inconvenient'.[303] In *Gulf Oil Corp. v. Gilbert*, the Supreme Court distinguished between whether private interests or public interests would determine the *conveniens* test of the doctrine.[304] As was recently formulated by the Supreme Court in *Sinochem Intern. Co. Ltd. v. Malaysia Intern. Shipping Corp.*, a dismissal under the *forum non conveniens* doctrine 'reflects a court's assessment of a "range of considerations, most notably the convenience to the parties and the practical difficulties that can attend the adjudication of a dispute in a certain locality".'[305] The Supreme Court listed examples of private and public factors in *Gulf Oil Corp. v. Gilbert*,[306] but none of the factors should be given conclusive importance nor is the list exhaustive.[307] Private factors concern the interest of parties to litigate in a particular forum and include (1) the relative ease of access to sources of proof; (2) the availability of compulsory process for attendance of unwilling witnesses and the cost of obtaining attendance of willing witnesses; (3) the possibility of view of premises, if view would be appropriate to the action; and (4) all other practical problems that make trial of a case easy, expeditious and inexpensive. Additionally (5) there may also be questions as to the enforceability of a judgement if one is obtained and the court may weigh relative advantages and obstacles to fair trial.[308]

Public factors emphasize the procedural aspects of the state in which the court is located, such as (1) the administrative difficulties when litigation is piled up in congested centres instead of being handled in the place of origin; (2) the burden of jury duty that ought not to be imposed upon the people of a community who have no relation to the litigation; (3) in cases touching the affairs of many persons, the local interests in having localized controversies decided at home as there are reasons for holding the trial within their view and reach, rather than in remote parts of the country where they can learn of it by report only; and (5) the appropriateness of having the trial of a diversity case in a forum that is at home with the state law that must govern the case, rather than having a court in some other forum untangle problems in conflict of laws and in law that is foreign to it.[309]

---

[303] The 2nd Restatement of Conflict of Laws, § 84 states that: 'A state will not exercise jurisdiction if it is a seriously inconvenient forum for the trial of the action provided that a more appropriate forum is available to the plaintiff.'

[304] Identified by Mr Justice Jackson in *Gulf Oil Corp. v. Gilbert*, 330 U.S. 501, at 508 (1947) and see also *Koster v. Lumbermens' Mutual Casualty Co.*, 330 U.S. 518 (1947). See Rodgers, 'FNC in International Cases', at 669; Lowenfeld, *International Litigation*, at 301.

[305] *Sinochem Intern. Co. Ltd. v. Malaysia Intern. Shipping Corp.*, 127 S.Ct. 1184, at 1190 (2007), citing *Quackenbush v. Allstate Ins. Co.*, 517 U.S. 706, at 723 (1996).

[306] 330 U.S. 501 (1947).

[307] See Brand and Jablonski, *Forum non Conveniens*, at 47.

[308] *Gulf Oil Corp. v. Gilbert*, 330 U.S. 501, at 508 (1947); see Nuyts, *L'exception de forum non conveniens*, at 171; D. Boyce, 'Foreign Plaintiffs and Forum Non Conveniens: Going Beyond Reyno', 64 *Texas Law Review* (1985), 193-223, at 215.

[309] 330 U.S. 501, at 509 (1947). See Brand and Jablonski, *Forum non conveniens*, at 51; Juenger, 'FNC Who Needs It?', *Festschrift*, at 327-329; and see Boyce, 'Foreign Plaintiffs and FNC', at 218 *et seq.*, arguing that this rejection of the choice of law factor leads to the 'shift of focus' of the *forum non conveniens* away from the appreciation of the local interests of the chosen forum.

With respect to the last *conveniens* factor, the Supreme Court decided in the *Piper Aircraft Co. v. Reyno* case that an unfavourable change in the applicable substantive law resulting in a less favourable outcome on the merits for the plaintiff is not conclusive for dismissal. The adequacy of the other available forum should not be considered on the basis of a change of substantive law.[310] According to the Supreme Court in *Piper Aircraft Co. v. Reyno*

> 'If substantial weight were given to the possibility of an unfavorable change in law, ... dismissal might be barred even where trial in the chosen forum was plainly inconvenient, and the *forum non conveniens* doctrine would become virtually useless. Such an approach ... would pose substantial practical problems, requiring that trial courts determine complex problems in conflict of laws and comparative law, and increasing the flow into American courts of litigation by foreign plaintiffs against American manufacturers.'[311]

5.5.2 Deference to the Plaintiff's Choice

The American approach to the *forum non conveniens* doctrine is based on the presumption that the forum chosen by the claimant is convenient as long as it is consistent with constitutional standards. The plaintiff's choice of forum should not be disturbed 'unless the balance is strongly in favor of the defendant'[312] to decline jurisdiction to another more convenient available forum.[313] In other words, a defendant invoking the doctrine 'ordinarily bears a heavy burden in opposing the plaintiff's chosen forum'.[314] Conversely, a court has discretion to dismiss jurisdiction in favour of another available forum when 'trial in the chosen forum would establish oppressiveness and vexation to a defendant out of all proportion to plaintiff's convenience, or the chosen forum [is] inappropriate because of considerations affecting the court's own administrative and legal problems.'[315] According to

---

[310] 454 U.S. 235, at 256 (1981), but see at 254, 'Of course if the remedy provided by the alternative forum is so clearly inadequate or unsatisfactory that it is no remedy at all, the unfavorable change in law may be given substantial weight; the district court may conclude that dismissal would not be in the interests of justice.' With respect to the federal transfer of § 1404(a), the Supreme Court decided in *Van Dusen v. Barrack*, 376 U.S. 612 (1964), that a transfer should not result in a change in the applicable law.

[311] 454 U.S. 235, at 256 (1981). See Juenger, 'FNC – Who Needs It?', *Festschrift*, at 329, 'The Supreme Court's position is to "clear their dockets and avoid foreign law issues"'; and Scoles, Hay *et al.*, *Conflict of Laws*, § 11.11, at 499, arguing that when a court is confronted with difficult choice of law questions it could constitute an appropriate factor for dismissal.

[312] *Gulf Oil Corp. v. Gilbert*, 330 U.S. 501, at 508 (1947).

[313] Brand and Jablonski, *Forum non Conveniens*, at 45; Rodgers, 'FNC in International Cases', at 669; Scoles, Hay *et al.*, *Conflict of Laws*, § 11.9, at 495.

[314] *Piper Aircraft Co.*, 454 U.S., at 255-256 (1981); *Sinochem Intern. Co. Ltd. v. Malaysia Intern. Shipping Corp.*, 127 S.Ct. 1184, at 1191 (2007).

[315] *Sinochem Intern. Co. Ltd. v. Malaysia Intern. Shipping Corp.*, 127 S.Ct. 1184, at 1190 (2007) (emphasis added), referring to *American Dredging Co. v. Miller*, 510 U.S. 443, 447-448 (1994); *Piper Aircraft Co. v. Reyno*, 454 U.S. 235, at 241 (1981); *Koster v. Lumbermens' Mut. Casualty Co.*, 330 U.S. 518, at 524 (1947).

Juenger 'the U.S. *forum non conveniens* doctrine is more a tool to help levelling the playing field by counteracting the natural advantage plaintiffs enjoy'.[316]

5.5.3 Greater Deference When the Chosen Forum Is the Home Forum

In *Koster v. Lumbermens' Mutual Casualty Co.*, the Supreme Court stated that the plaintiff's choice of forum is entitled to even 'greater deference when the plaintiff has chosen the home forum'[317] since 'in any balancing of conveniences, a real showing of convenience by a plaintiff who has sued in his home forum will normally outweigh the inconvenience the defendant may have shown'.[318] As confirmed in *Piper Aircraft Co. v. Reyno*, the Court concluded that when 'the home forum has been chosen, it is reasonable to assume that this choice is convenient'.[319] As a consequence thereof 'when the plaintiff's choice is not its home forum, however, the presumption in the plaintiff's favor "applies with less force," for the assumption that the chosen forum is appropriate is in such cases "less reasonable".'[320] This does not mean that the plaintiff's domicile is conclusive for the determination of the *conveniens* of parties, but it is nevertheless given substantial weight.

5.5.4 Alien Plaintiffs

Even less force is given to a plaintiff's choice when the plaintiff is foreign. In *Piper Aircraft Co. v. Reyno*, the Supreme Court stated that

> 'when the plaintiff is foreign, however, this assumption [of deference of the plaintiff's choice] is much less reasonable. Because the central purpose of any *forum non conveniens* inquiry is to ensure that the trial is convenient, a foreign plaintiff's choice deserves less deference.'[321]

The *Piper Aircraft Co. v. Reyno* case involved a product liability action after an airplane crashed in Scotland causing the death of several Scottish citizens and residents. The plane was owned and registered in the U.K. Wrongful-death litigation was instituted in a California state court against the U.S. defendants, Piper Aircraft Company, that manufactured the plane in Pennsylvania, and the Hartzell Propeller Company that manufactured the plane's propellers in Ohio. Scottish plaintiffs[322] chose the U.S. forum 'because its laws regarding liability, capacity to sue, and damages are more favourable' for the plaintiff than those of Scotland.[323] The case

[316] Juenger, 'FNC – Who Needs It?', *Festschrift*, at 323. But see one of the lower federal courts which argues that the '*[f]orum non conveniens* is an exceptional tool to be employed sparingly, not a doctrine that compels plaintiffs to choose the optimal forum for their claim', *Dole Food Co., Inc. v. Watts,* Court of Appeal, 9th Circuit, 303 F.3d 1104 (2002).

[317] As reformulated by *Piper Aircraft Co.*, 454 U.S., at 256 (1981).

[318] 330 U.S., at 524 (1947). See also Casad, 'Jurisdiction in Civil Actions', at 266; Casad and Richman, *Jurisdiction in Civil Actions Vol. 1*, at 34.

[319] 454 U.S. 235, at 256 (1981).

[320] Ibid., at 255-256; *Sinochem Intern. Co. Ltd. v. Malaysia Intern. Shipping Corp.*, 127 S.Ct. 1184, at 1191 (2007).

[321] 454 U.S. 252, at 256 (1981).

[322] Reyno was the administratix of the estates of the passengers.

[323] 454 U.S. 235 (1981).

was first removed from state court to a federal court,[324] and then subsequently transferred from a California federal court to a federal (district) court in Pennsylvania.[325] Defendants argued that the latter should dismiss jurisdiction on grounds of *forum non conveniens* in favour of Scottish courts. The District Court granted the motion of dismissal, but this decision was reversed by the Court of Appeals claiming that the District Court had abused its discretion under the *forum non conveniens* analysis as applied by *Gulf Oil Corp. v. Gilbert*. The Supreme Court argued that Scotland had a very strong interest in this litigation with 'a local interest in having localized controversies decided at home', repeating one of *Gulf Oil's* public factors. This Scottish interest was greater than U.S. interests in the case which were 'simply not sufficient to justify the enormous commitment of judicial time and resources that would inevitably be required if the case were to be tried' in the U.S.[326]

By allowing a court to clearly distinguish between domestic and alien plaintiffs to appreciate the *conveniens* of the chosen court, *Piper Aircraft Co. v. Reyno* introduced a more favourable treatment of U.S. plaintiffs than of foreign plaintiffs.[327] The Supreme Court justified this 'discrimination'[328] of foreign plaintiffs in order to control the flow of proceedings to U.S. courts that have an 'extreme attractiveness'.[329] American scholars indicated that for reasons of perceived procedural advantages such as the availability of jury trials and discovery rules, contingency fees and punitive damage awards, U.S. courts are like 'magnet forums' to foreign plaintiffs.[330] As a result of this *Piper* approach, the *forum non conveniens* doctrine has become a powerful instrument against international forum shopping.[331]

---

[324] On the basis of 29 USC § 1441.

[325] On the basis of 28 USC § 1404(a). See on federal transfer Sect. 5.5.1.

[326] *Piper Aircraft Co. v. Reyno*, 454 U.S. 235, at 260 (1981).

[327] 'Citizens or residents deserve somewhat more deference than foreign plaintiffs', 454 U.S. 252, at 256 (1981). See Scoles, Hay *et al.*, *Conflict of Laws*, § 11.10, at 496.

[328] Juenger, 'FNC – Who Needs It?', *Festschrift*, at 330; and Nuyts, *L'exception de forum non conveniens*, at 338. See also S. Dahl, '*Forum non conveniens* versus *actio sequitur forum rei*', in *Etudes offertes à Barthélemy Mercadal* (2002), 117-131, at 122-123.

[329] *Piper Aircraft Co. v. Reyno*, 454 U.S. 235, at 252 (1981).

[330] See for a complete study on this 'magnet forum', R. Weintraub, 'The United States as a Magnet Forum and What, If Anything to Do about It', in *International Dispute Resolution: The Regulation of Forum Selection (Fourteenth Sokol Colloquium)* (1997). The main reasons for the attractiveness of U.S. courts include favourable contingent fee representation, extensive discovery, more favourable substantive rules including conflict rules for strict liability in tort cases and a greater amount of recoverable damages, see Boyce, 'Foreign Plaintiffs and FNC', at 197-204, trial by jury is also often considered as an advantage for damage recovery. See also R. Weintraub, 'Introduction to Symposium on International Forum Shopping', 37 *Texas International Law Journal* (2002), 463-466, at 263 ('The ranks first among the world's magnet forums.'); Born, *International Civil Litigation*, at 3-4; Hay, Weintraub *et al.*, *Conflict of Laws*, at 37; Bell, *Forum Shopping and Venue*, § 2.14, at 28 and § 2.15-2.227, at 29-34 ('there can be little doubt that the United States is the most attractive destination for the forum shopping plaintiff, especially one with an action in tort'); Jr. Hazard, M. Taruffo *et al.*, 'Introduction to the Principles and Rules of Transnational Civil Procedure', 33 *New York University Journal of International Law and Politics* (2001), 767-784, at 774-775 *et seq.* But see in contrast R. Stürner, 'Why Are Europeans Afraid to Litigate in the United States?', paper presented at the Saggi, Conferenze e Seminari, Centro di studi e richerche di diritto comparato e straniero, Rome (2001).

[331] R. Weintraub, *International Litigation and Arbitration: Practice and Planning* (2006), at 226 *et seq.*; Brand, 'Comparative FNC', at 480; Lowenfeld, *International Litigation*, at 313; Weintraub,

5.6 Bases for Jurisdiction of United States Courts

Due to particularities and specific features of each state's jurisdictional regime, it is helpful to turn to a systematic categorization, in order to give a representative overview of connecting factors used for jurisdiction of U.S. courts. With the help of the 2nd Restatement of Conflict of Laws and the exhaustive research on State Law on jurisdiction by some authors, and in particular by Robert C. Casad and William M. Richman, which provide a useful overview of connecting factors, it is possible to identify some common characteristics and make 'elucidating generalizations'.[332]

For the present purposes, the jurisdictional system of the different U.S. states will be divided in four categories, represented by the states of Florida, New York, Michigan and California. The first category involves some twenty states that modelled their statute on the Illinois-type act and are represented by the State of Florida.[333] As explained above, the state of Illinois was the first state to enact an enumerated act providing for a detailed list of jurisdiction grounds to reach an out-of-state defendant. The second category is represented by the State of New York and counts for another five states that adopted an Illinois-type act but with somewhat different wording.[334] The third category consists of seventeen states that closely modelled their enumerated act on the *Uniform Act* and are represented by the State of Michigan.[335] A group of six states have – due to their particularities – not been categorized in any of the four categories.[336]

The first three categories all represent states with enumerated act statutes. Most of the enumerated act types contain similar provisions that are characteristic of the U.S. jurisdictional regime, such as for instance the 'transacting business' rule.[337] The majority of incorporated single acts deal with defendant's acts causing an effect in the forum.

Commentary, § 4.33, at 274-276; Casad, 'Jurisdiction in Civil Actions', at 267; Lookofsky and Hertz, *Transnational Litigation*, at 322; and Reus, 'Judicial Discretion', at 467 and 471; Nuyts, *L'exception de forum non conveniens*, at 165 and 338-241; Chalas, *L'exercise discrétionnaire*, at 88-89.

332 Taken from Casad and Richman, *Jurisdiction in Civil Actions Vol. 1*, at 397.

333 Colorado, Florida, Hawaii, Idaho, Illinois, Kansas, Maine, Missouri, Montana (*hybrid*), Nevada, New Mexico, North Dakota (*hybrid),* South Dakota, Utah (*hybrid*), Washington; Wisconsin adopted a Illinois type of statute but with somewhat different wording; Alaska, North Carolina and Oregon followed the Wisconsin Statute but these states will be considered as a subdivision of the Illinois type group as the difference between them is minimal. See Casad and Richman, *Jurisdiction in Civil Actions Vol. 1*, at 382.

334 This third group consists of New York, Connecticut, Georgia, Minnesota and, partially, New Hampshire.

335 Alabama, Delaware, Kentucky, Louisiana, Maryland, Massachusetts, Michigan (*special*), Montana (*hybrid*), Nebraska, North Dakota (*hybrid*), Ohio, Oklahoma, South Carolina, Tennessee, Virginia. See Casad and Richman, *Jurisdiction in Civil Actions Vol. 1*, at 382. Although Ohio is usually identified with this group, the particularity of Michigan in making a distinction between persons, corporations and associations and also incorporating general jurisdiction basis, makes this statute interesting.

336 Among them are Texas and Mississippi. Most of them now accept jurisdiction within the limits of the Constitution.

337 See Casad and Richman, *Jurisdiction in Civil Actions Vol. 1*, at 397.

The last category is formed by states with '*no-limits*' or '*general*' statutes exercising jurisdiction as long as the U.S. Constitution permits it.[338] California was the first state to adopt such a statute by stating that '[a] court of this state may exercise jurisdiction on any basis not inconsistent with the Constitution of this state or of the United States'.[339] California represents the other states who also adopted a *no limit* statute such as Rhode Island, Wyoming and to a certain extent Vermont.[340] The result of such a 'no limit' statute is that all jurisdictional grounds are included: presence, domicile, residence, citizenship, consent, appointment of an agent, appearance, doing business in a state, doing an act in a state, causing an effect in a state by an act or omission elsewhere, ownership, use or possession of a thing in a state, as well as other relationships to a state for individuals and for corporations or organizations in a state.[341]

5.6.1 **Traditional Jurisdiction Grounds**

As explained above, the sources of U.S. jurisdiction law are twofold: on the one hand the U.S. common law principles provide for the legal basis of traditional jurisdiction grounds, on the other hand state and federal long-arm statutes provide for statutory authorization for 'extraterritorial' jurisdiction. Most of the long-arm statutes do not explicitly incorporate the traditional grounds that provide for general jurisdiction under the power theory. Since the legal authority for these traditional bases for jurisdiction stems from U.S. common law principles, statutory authority is not required. The primary purpose of state statutes is to function as 'the long arm of the state'; only few statutes explicitly enacted the criteria of residence, domicile, doing business and consent providing general jurisdiction. Some statutes establish jurisdiction upon an 'enduring relationship' with the forum which reflects the 'continuous and systematic' contact of the defendant with the forum and thereby justifying general jurisdiction.[342]

Most of the long-arm statutes only refer to 'non-residents' or absent defendants and foreign corporations. Those statutes do not enumerate the traditional bases for general jurisdiction over residents such as the defendant's domicile, for they aim at reaching (absent) non-residents.[343] Other long-arm statutes apply to all (absent) defendants, both residents and non-residents.[344] Moreover, the fact that common law

[338] California allows the exercise of personal jurisdiction to the full extent as permitted by due process, and thus assertion of a Californian court's personal jurisdiction over a non-resident depends on the existence of minimum contacts with the state so that maintenance of suit does not offend traditional notions of fair play and substantial justice.

[339] Californian Code of Civil Procedure, § 410.10 (Part 2 of Civil Actions; Title 5, Jurisdiction and Service of Process; Chap. 1, Jurisdiction and Forum; Article 1, Jurisdiction; § 410.10, Basis).

[340] Casad and Richman, *Jurisdiction in Civil Actions Vol. 1*, at 382

[341] See West's Annotated California Code of Civil Procedure, § 410.10.

[342] See the Statutes of Alaska, Massachusetts, Maryland, Michigan, Montana, North Carolina, South Carolina, Tennessee and Wisconsin.

[343] The following states have enacted statutes to reach non-residents and foreign corporations only: Connecticut, Delaware, Georgia, Iowa, Kentucky, Louisiana, Minnesota, Mississippi, New Hampshire, Ohio, Rhode Island, Texas and Utah.

[344] Statutes applying to defendants whether or not resident in the state are: Alabama (with respect to tag-jurisdiction both resident and non-resident in the State of Alabama) Colorado, Florida, Hawaii,

principles still provide for valid jurisdictional bases led some states to formulate long-arm statutes by regulating 'out-of-state service of process'.[345] Those provisions indicate how to serve the defendant abroad and provide for a legal basis for jurisdiction over the out-of-state defendant.

5.6.1.1 *Tag-jurisdiction and Physical Presence*

In-state service of process on a defendant while temporarily and physically present in the state, traditionally constitutes a valid ground for general jurisdiction under U.S. common law.[346] This jurisdiction ground is limited to individuals and excludes corporations, as the latter cannot be 'physically present' in the forum.[347] At an early stage, the Supreme Court denied tag-jurisdiction to assert jurisdiction over a corporation by serving a corporate officer.[348] Also known as 'tag-jurisdiction' or 'transient jurisdiction' under U.S. terminology, this controversial jurisdiction ground, which is also criticized by American scholars,[349] was reaffirmed as a constitutionally permissive jurisdiction ground by the U.S. Supreme Court in *Burnham v. Superior Court*.[350]

Idaho, Illinois, Kansas, Maine, Maryland (shall be the rule of practice and decision), South Dakota, Tennessee, Virginia and Washington.

345 See for the English common law on jurisdiction, Chapter 4.

346 This traditional rule is unquestionably linked to 'jurisdiction creating' in-state service of process. Weintraub, *Commentary*, § 4.10, at 207; Casad and Richman, *Jurisdiction in Civil Actions Vol. 1*, § 2-4[1], at 121.

347 Tag-jurisdiction is available to exercise jurisdiction over partnerships and unincorporated associations. Similar jurisdiction grounds used to obtain jurisdiction over individuals equally apply to confer jurisdiction over partnerships and unincorporated associations, not having the same legal personality as corporations. Partnerships are subjected to general jurisdiction when each partner is individually served, or when jurisdiction is based on the regular jurisdiction grounds such as the partner's domicile or other jurisdiction grounds under the modern contacts theory. Casad and Richman, *Jurisdiction in Civil Actions Vol. 1*, § 3-3, at 364-366. Some states do however provide for specific service of process on the partnership. For example, the Florida Statute specifically provides for service of process provisions on partnerships and limited partnerships in § 48.061(1). As a result, the partnership can be sued in its own name for the activities effectuated on the territory. Weintraub, *Commentary*, § 4.22, at 252; Richman and Reynolds, *Understanding Conflict of Laws*, at 86.

348 *Goldey v. Morning News of New Haven*, 156 U.S. 518 (1895); Hay, Weintraub *et al.*, *Conflict of Laws*, § 3, at 42; Scoles, Hay *et al.*, *Conflict of Laws*, § 6.2, at 340; and F. Juenger, 'The American Law of General Jurisdiction', *University of Chicago Legal Forum* (2001), 141-170, at 150-151. But see Born, *International Civil Litigation*, § 7-8, at 130-131.

349 See in general Borchers, 'The Death of the Constitutional Law of Jurisdiction'; Redish, 'The Future of Personal Jurisdiction'; and see E. Cox, 'Would That Burnham Had Not Come to Be Done Insane?', *Tennessee Law Review* (1991), 497-572; A. Ehrenzweig, 'The Transient Rule of Personal Jurisdiction, the "Power" Myth, and the Forum Non Conveniens', 65 *Yale Law Journal* (1956), 289-314; P. Hay, 'Transient Jurisdiction, Especially over International Defendants: Critical Comment on *Burnham v. Superior Court California*', *University of Illinois Law Review* (1990), 593-603; J. Spitz, 'The "Transient Rule" of Personal Jurisdiction: A Well-intentioned Concept That Has Overstayed Its Welcome', 73 *Marquette Law Review* (1989), 181-216.

350 *Burnham v. Superior Court*, 495 U.S. 604, at 606 (1990).

Before the *International Shoe Co v. Washington* case in 1945,[351] the defendant's physical presence in the forum was the key to U.S. jurisdiction.[352] Among the traditional jurisdiction rules, tag-jurisdiction best reflected the territorialist principles upon which a state exercises its sovereign powers over a defendant present on its territory. In-state service of the defendant was formerly effectuated by the physical arrest of the defendant by the sheriff[353] and was considered as the exemplification of the power theory.[354]

Under the 'minimum contact' doctrine the mere physical presence of the defendant still constitutes a sufficient contact for exercise of U.S. judicial powers.[355] In *Burnham v. Superior Court*, the Supreme Court unanimously held that it is constitutionally justifiable to exercise jurisdiction on the *sole* fact that the defendant was properly served with process while physically present in the state.[356] In other words, the due process test should not independently be applied when jurisdiction is based on tag-jurisdiction. The *Burnham v. Superior Court* decision thus took away the doubts cast by the Supreme Court statement in *Shaffer v. Heitner*, in which it stated that 'all assertions of jurisdiction – including tag-jurisdiction – must be evaluated according to the due process standards set forth in *International Shoe Co. v. Washington*.[357] Although the rationale behind the decision was mainly divided into two different opinions,[358] the result of the *Burnham* decision is clear; the

---

[351] During the regime of *Pennoyer v. Neff*, 95 U.S. 714 (1877), tag-jurisdiction was a necessary condition for jurisdiction, Casad and Richman, *Jurisdiction in Civil Actions Vol. 1*, § 2-2[2](b), at 73 and § 2-4[1], at 121.

[352] The in-state service of process on a defendant physically present was the cornerstone of traditional common law on jurisdiction, see Richman and Reynolds, *Understanding Conflict of Laws*, at 63; Mirandes, *La compétence internationale des Etats-Unis*, § 214-217, at 150-152.

[353] 2nd Restatement of Conflict of Laws, § 28, comment a.

[354] Born, *International Civil Litigation*, at 128; Scoles, Hay *et al.*, *Conflict of Laws*, § 6.2, at 338; Hay, Weintraub *et al.*, *Conflict of Laws*, § 1, at 41.

[355] But the service of process is no longer a necessary condition for jurisdiction as it was under *Pennoyer v. Neff*, 95 U.S. 714 (1877). Casad and Richman, *Jurisdiction in Civil Actions Vol. 1*, at 122; Born, *International Civil Litigation*, at 122; Weintraub, *Commentary*, § 4.10, at 208; Mirandes, *La compétence internationale des Etats-Unis*, § 218, at 152.

[356] The case involved an interstate divorce concerning a New Jersey domiciliary who was served with process in California while temporarily present for business purposes and to visit his children. His (ex)-wife served him with a divorce form hereby invoking the jurisdiction of California courts. Weintraub, *Commentary*, § 4.10, at 208 suggests the outcome might have been different if the case involved an international commercial dispute.

[357] As a result of *Shaffer v. Heitner*, 433 U.S. 186 (1977), tag-jurisdiction came under fire, see Schlosser, 'Jurisdiction in International Litigation: The Issue of Human Rights', fn. 15, at 9.

[358] Divided roughly in two groups (except for Justice White and Justice Stevens holding distinct opinions), the judges were divided on the rationale to justify that tag-jurisdiction on its own was constituted sufficient affiliation with the forum. The 'Justice Scalia Group' justified tag-jurisdiction by its 'historical pedigree' stating that the notions of fair play and substantial justice were developed 'by analogy' to physical presence. The 'Justice Brennan Group' concluded that historical pedigree is important but should not be the only factor to be taken into account in establishing whether a jurisdictional rule satisfies due process and insisted on the application of 'contemporary notions of due process' to determine the constitutionality of tag-jurisdiction; the rule is consistent with reasonable expectations and is entitled to a strong presumption that it comports with due process. This view was supported by the reasoning that 'by visiting the forum State, a transient defendant actually avails himself of significant benefits provided by the State: … the protection of its laws, and the right of access to its courts'

physical presence of the defendant constitutes *by itself* sufficient affiliation with the forum for general jurisdiction and is *not* contrary to due process standards.[359] It should however be remembered that although tag-jurisdiction *automatically* satisfies the notions of fair play and substantive justice, the far-reaching rule is still subject to the *forum non conveniens* doctrine provided that the defendant invokes the doctrine.[360]

Burnham v. Superior Court also results in the persistence of tag-jurisdiction as a legitimate jurisdiction basis in international disputes.[361] The coincidental and temporarily physical presence of the defendant as sole point of contact with the forum is sufficient to exercise general jurisdiction over the defendant;[362] no relationship between the claim and defendant's activities in the state, or between the forum and the claim, is required.[363]

Tag-jurisdiction is applied and acknowledged as a valid jurisdiction ground by each state, either based on common law principles or by long-arm statutes. The *no limit* statute of California gave rise to the *Burnham v. Superior Court* case. The Supreme Court was confronted with the fact that the Superior Court of California, County of Marin based its jurisdiction on California's general Statute of Section 410.10 of the Code of Civil Procedure.[364] The enumerated long-arm statute of Michigan provides for an explicit statutory basis for tag-jurisdiction.[365] The New York's long-arm Statute in Section 301 of the Civil Procedure Law Rules (CPLR) is

---

and that the 'potential burdens on a transient defendant are slight in light of modern transportation and communication methods, and any burdens that do arise can be ameliorated by a variety of procedural devices.' 495 U.S. 604, at 606 (1990). See Casad and Richman, *Jurisdiction in Civil Actions Vol. 1*, § 2-4[b], at 122-127; Richman and Reynolds, *Understanding Conflict of Laws*, § 28, at 64-69; see for a good overview of the case Hay, 'Transient Jurisdiction'; Born, *International Civil Litigation*, at 121; Mirandes, *La compétence internationale des Etats-Unis*, § 220-223, at 153-156.

[359] But see Born, *International Civil Litigation*, at 128, exposing the objections against the *Burnham* decision.

[360] As noted by some reporters to 2nd Restatement of Conflict of Laws, § 28, 1988 revision, comment c. Several Restatements were drafted before the *Burnham* decision recognized transient jurisdiction as a valid jurisdiction basis, but incorporated the reasonable test of *International Shoe*: 'A state has power to exercise judicial jurisdiction over an individual who is present within its territory unless the individual's relationship to the state is so attenuated as to make the exercise of such jurisdiction unreasonable.' See also 2nd Restatement of Judgments (1982), Chap. 2, Introductory Note. See Born, *International Civil Litigation*, at 130.

[361] According to 3rd Restatement of Foreign Relations, § 421, comment e.

[362] Weintraub, *Commentary*, § 4.10, at 208.

[363] Scoles, Hay *et al.*, *Conflict of Laws*, § 6.2, at 338, 'transient jurisdiction is truly a "general basis of jurisdiction"'. Casad and Richman, *Jurisdiction in Civil Actions Vol. 1*, at 121.

[364] It is however assumed that defendant's presence should be voluntary and not the result of force or fraud. Born, *International Civil Litigation*, § 6, at 130; Weintraub, *Commentary*, § 4.10, at 208 *Guardianship of Smith*, 147 Cal.App.2d 686, at 691 (1957); *Patino v. Patino*, Supreme Court, Appellate Division, New York, 129 N.Y.S.2d 333, at 336 (1954), 'Generally, courts will not sustain personal jurisdiction obtained by entrapment.'

[365] § 600.701(1) Michigan Statute: 'The existence of any of the following relationships between an individual and the state shall constitute a sufficient basis of jurisdiction to enable the courts of record of this state to exercise general personal jurisdiction over the individual ... (1) [present] in the state at the time when process is served.' See *Haefner v. Bayman*, Court of Appeals of Michigan, 419 N.W.2d 29 (1988).

less explicit, but embodies a general jurisdictional provision on traditional common law grounds, including tag-jurisdiction, regardless of the nature of the claim.[366] A similar approach is taken by the long-arm Statute of Florida that provides for tag-jurisdiction by regulating the service of process on a defendant present in the state. The statute thereby establishes tag-jurisdiction on traditional common law principles.[367]

5.6.1.2 *Nationality and Citizenship*

Jurisdiction based on nationality or citizenship is constitutionally permissible.[368] The Supreme Court held in *Blackmer v. United States*[369] that jurisdiction based on citizenship is consistent with due process standards. Based on a sufficient relationship with the forum, the exercise of jurisdiction is 'reasonable'.[370] Clearly based on the sovereignty theory, the Supreme Court states that 'jurisdiction of the United States over its absent citizen ... is a jurisdiction in personam, as he is personally bound to take notice of the laws that are applicable to him and to obey them.'[371]

The 2nd Restatement of Conflict of Laws affirms that nationality and citizenship are valid jurisdiction grounds.[372] The use of both concepts is however somewhat misleading, primarily because jurisdiction based on a defendant's nationality[373] or citizenship[374] distinguishes between *federal* citizenship of the U.S. and *state* citizenship.[375] Citizenship of the U.S. is given by birth or by way of naturalization; state citizenship is determined by a person's residence in a state. The first section of the XIVth Amendment stipulates that '[a]ll persons born or naturalized in the United States, and subject to the jurisdiction thereof, are citizens of the United States and of the State wherein they reside'.[376] In other words, a person may be at

[366] § 301 New York CPLR reads: 'A court may exercise such jurisdiction over persons, property, or status as might have been exercised heretofore.' This jurisdiction ground has been used to exercise jurisdiction over a citizen of a foreign nation who was served while visiting New York for the purpose of addressing the United Nations, *Kadic v. Karadzic*, New York Court of Appeals, 70 F.3d 232, 247 (1995), certiorari denied 518 U.S. 1005 (1996).

[367] West's Florida Statutes Annotated; Title VI. Civil Practice and Procedure, § 48.031. Service of process generally; service of witness subpoenas.

[368] *Blackmer v. United States*, 284 U.S. 421 (1932); Weintraub, *Commentary*, § 4.12, at 211.

[369] 284 U.S. 421 (1932).

[370] *Blackmer v. United States*, 284 U.S. 421 (1932), concerned a subpoena in a foreign country for a criminal trial but jurisdiction was upheld on the basis of nationality.

[371] Ibid., at 438 (1932); Mirandes, *La compétence internationale des Etats-Unis*, at 176 and 255.

[372] Sect. 31 states that 'A state has power to exercise judicial jurisdiction over an individual who is a national or citizen of the state unless the nature of the individual's relationship to the state makes the exercise of such jurisdiction unreasonable.' See also 3rd Restatement of Foreign Relations, § 421.

[373] 3rd Restatement of Foreign Relations, § 211, Nationality of Individuals.

[374] Ibid., § 211, comment c: 'Nationality and citizenship. Nationality is a concept of international law; citizenship is not, but is a concept in the national law of many states. A citizen under national law is generally a national for purposes of international law, but in some states not all nationals are citizens.'

[375] 2nd Restatement of Conflict of Laws, § 31, comment a.

[376] See USCA Const. Amend. XIV Citizens of United States. See also the 2nd Restatement of Conflict of Laws, § 31, comment b: 'Under this provision a citizen of the United States is a citizen of the State in which he is domiciled.'

the same time a U.S. citizen and a citizen of a particular state.[377] But as not all U.S. citizens reside in the U.S., they are not all *state* citizens.[378]

Secondly, in order to be a state citizen, one must first be a citizen of the U.S. and reside in a state.[379] For jurisdictional purposes, this means that the concepts of state citizenship and state residence overlap.[380] Long-arm statutes prefer to include defendant's domicile or residence as a jurisdictional basis rather than state citizenship.

Defendant's nationality or citizenship is not recognized as a jurisdiction ground under common law[381] and therefore requires statutory authorization for jurisdiction.[382] Nationality would only be a valid jurisdiction ground if authorized expressly – enacted in an enumerated long-arm statute – or implicitly – by virtue of a *no limits* or *hybrid* statute asserting jurisdiction within the limits of due process.[383] Nationality or citizen-based jurisdiction invokes general jurisdiction whatever the nature of the claim. However, although nationality-based jurisdiction is constitutionally accepted, in practice its application is exceptionally rare. With respect to the *no limits* Statute of California, nationality and citizenship are mentioned as a permissive jurisdiction ground but they are scarcely applied.[384] The *hybrid* Statute of Michigan accepted the 'one step' analysis hereby expanding the scope of its long-arm statute to the limits of due process and allowing nationality-based jurisdiction.[385] Very few enumerated statutes explicitly authorize jurisdiction based

---

377 *U.S. v. Krause*, Western District of Los Angeles, 92 F. Supp. 756 (1950).

378 See the *Slaughter-House* cases, 83 U.S. 36, at 74 (1872), 'a person may be a citizen of the United States without being a citizen of any one state'; *Suglove v. Oklahoma Tax Commission*, Supreme Court of Oklahoma, 605 P.2d 1315, at 1318 (1979).

379 See *Factor v. Pennington Press*, U.S. District Court, Northern District of Illinois, 230 F. Supp. 906 (1963).

380 Scoles, Hay *et al.*, *Conflict of Laws*, § 6.4, at 344; Casad and Richman, *Jurisdiction in Civil Actions Vol. 1*, at 123; Born, *International Civil Litigation*, § 3, at 105; Mirandes, *La compétence internationale des Etats-Unis*, at 176. See 2nd Restatement of Conflict of Laws, § 31, comment b, 'If a citizen of the United States is domiciled in a State, he is subject to the judicial jurisdiction of the State on the ground both of his domicile and of his citizenship'.

381 Born, *International Civil Litigation*, fn. 91, at 103; but see Hay, Weintraub *et al.*, *Conflict of Laws*, at 60, who mentions nationality as one of the established traditional bases.

382 See 2nd Restatement of Conflict of Laws, § 31, comment d.

383 Born, *International Civil Litigation*, § 3, at 105. See West's Annotated California Codes, Code of Civil Procedure which comments on § 410.10 by including citizenship as a possible jurisdiction ground. Other states with the same possibility to assert jurisdiction on the 'citizenship' criterion are Rhode Island, Wyoming and states with hybrid long-arm statutes are Alabama, Illinois, Louisiana, Maine, Nebraska, Ohio, Oklahoma, Oregon, Pennsylvania, Tennessee and Utah.

384 Very little case law was found establishing jurisdiction of Californian courts on the basis of citizenship and West's Annotated California Codes (comments Judicial Council – Bases of Judicial Jurisdiction over Individuals (4)) indicates that the citizenship/nationality criteria considers similar factors for jurisdiction based on residence.

385 As explained above in Sect. 5.3.1. and see *Speckine v. Stanwick Intern.*, U.S. District Court, Western District of Michigan, 503 F. Supp. 1055 (1980), and *Williams v. Garcia*, U.S. District Court, Eastern District of Michigan, 569 F. Supp. 1452 (1983), both citing *Sifers v. Horen*, Supreme Court of Michigan, 385 Mich. 195 (1971), 'Where the state makes such a declaration, the Long Arm Statute and the minimum contacts tests merge. The only question becomes that of due process.' *Speckine v. Stanwick Intern.*, 503 F. Supp. 1055, at 1057 (1980). See Casad and Richman, *Jurisdiction in Civil Actions Vol. 1*, § 4-1[1](b), at 385.

on the mere fact that defendant is a state citizen.[386] The States of Florida and New York, both of which refuse the 'one-step' analysis, and thus not extending jurisdiction to the limits of due process standards, have felt the need to incorporate the jurisdictional basis of citizenship in their statutes.[387] Citizenship remains however important to determine subject matter jurisdiction with respect to alienage and diversity jurisdiction of the federal courts. [388]

5.6.1.3 *Defendant's Domicile or Residence*

The Supreme Court accepted defendant's domicile or residence as a traditional jurisdiction ground in *Milliken v. Meyer*[389] as it reflects a unique connection between the forum and the defendant justifying jurisdiction even when the defendant is (physically) absent

> '[a]s in case of the authority of the United States over its absent citizens ... the authority of a state over one of its citizens is not terminated by the mere fact of his absence from the state. The state which accords him privileges and affords protection to him and his property by virtue of his domicile may also exact reciprocal duties.'[390]

Defendant's domicile is a widely accepted general jurisdiction ground under U.S. common law[391] and was considered an extension of defendant's presence in the state under the 'power theory'.[392] Furthermore, the domicile criterion is justified in the state's interest in having jurisdiction over defendant's reciprocal duties to the forum.[393] The idea of compensating defendant's disadvantage of having to defend

---

[386] Born, *International Civil Litigation*, § 3, at 105.

[387] See for New York *Galgay v. Bulletin*, U.S. Court of Appeals, 2nd Circuit, 504 F.2d 1062, at 1066 (1974), and *Hedlund v. Products from Sweden*, U.S. District Court, 698 F. Supp. 1087, at 1090 (1988), 'New York long-arm jurisdiction does not exhaust full jurisdictional potential permissible under Federal Constitution.' And for Florida: *Bank of Wessington v. Winters Government Securities*, District Court of Appeal of Florida, 4th District, 361 So.2d 757, at 759 (1978), 'We are fully cognizant that Florida's long arm Statute is of the type that requires more activities or contacts to sustain service of process than are currently required by decisions of the Supreme Court of the United States.'

[388] See § 5.1.1. A U.S. citizen can be subjected to U.S. jurisdiction even if he is not domiciled in the U.S. for claims arising under federal law. See 2nd Restatement of Conflict of Laws, § 31, comment b: 'A citizen of the United States is subject to the judicial jurisdiction of the United States even though he is domiciled abroad.' 28 USC § 1783-1784.

[389] 311 U.S. 457 (1940). Prior to the *Milliken* decision the defendant's domicile criterion was cautiously suggested in *McDonald v. Mabee*, 243 U.S. 90 (1917), see Juenger, 'Federalism: A Comparison', at 1198.

[390] 311 U.S. 457, at 463 (1940).

[391] Born, *International Civil Litigation*, § 9, at 106; Weintraub, *Commentary*, § 4.12, at 209; Scoles, Hay *et al.*, *Conflict of Laws*, § 6.4, at 343; Hay, Weintraub *et al.*, *Conflict of Laws*, at 51; Casad and Richman, *Jurisdiction in Civil Actions Vol. 1*, § 2.4, at 127; Mirandes, *La compétence internationale des Etats-Unis*, § 243, at 168; Brilmayer, 'A General Look at General Jurisdiction', at 725; Twitchell, 'The Myth of General Jurisdiction', at 669; Richman and Reynolds, *Understanding Conflict of Laws*, § 29, at 71. *Contra* 2nd Restatement of Conflict of Laws, § 29, comment d. *Necessity for statute.* 1988 revision 'Domicil was not generally recognized as a basis of judicial jurisdiction at common law.' Also observed by Scoles, Hay *et al.*, *Conflict of Laws*, § 6.4, at 343.

[392] Casad and Richman, *Jurisdiction in Civil Actions Vol. 1*, at 72.

[393] Richman and Reynolds, *Understanding Conflict of Laws*, § 29, at 72.

himself by allowing him to do so in his home court is however not the primary or underlying rationale under U.S. jurisdiction law.[394]

Although, jurisdiction on the basis of defendant's domicile in the forum generally constitutes 'sufficient and continuous' contacts with the forum for general jurisdiction,[395] the question arose whether jurisdiction asserted on the basis of defendant's domicile criterion should still be subjected to the due process test. If so, jurisdiction at defendant's forum would no longer be automatically exercised; derogation to the defendant's domicile criterion was possible when notions of substantial justice and fair play were offended. The Supreme Court held in *Shaffer v. Heitner* that *all* assertions of jurisdiction – thus including general jurisdiction – had to be 'evaluated according to the standards set forth in International Shoe and its progeny'.[396] As a consequence, the 1988 revision of Section 29 of the 2nd Restatement of Conflict of Laws imposes due process limitations on the domicile criterion by stating that a 'state has power to exercise judicial jurisdiction over an individual who is domiciled in the state, except in the highly unusual case where the individual's relationship to the state is so attenuated as to make the exercise of such jurisdiction unreasonable.'[397]

In 1990, the Supreme Court allowed in *Burnham v. Superior Court*, the exercise of general jurisdiction on the mere basis of physical presence, without explicitly applying the due process test.[398] By applying this case by analogy to jurisdiction on the basis of defendant's domicile in the forum, the exercise of jurisdiction would equally 'generally satisf[y] due process requirements'.[399] This was however not affirmed nor rejected by the Supreme Court,[400] and it remains uncertain whether the defendant's domicile, especially a purely technical one – lacking any further factual and substantial connection with forum, constitutes a valid jurisdiction ground

---

394 There is no *forum defensoris*; see B. Buchner, *Kläger- und Beklagtenschutz im Recht der internationalen Zuständigkeit. Losüngsansätze für eine zukünftige Gerichtsstands- und Vollstreckungskonvention, Studien zum ausländischen und internationalen Privatrecht* (1998), at 48-49 *et seq.*; Borchers, 'Comparing Jurisdiction', at 135.

395 Born, *International Civil Litigation*, § 9, at 106; Richman and Reynolds, *Understanding Conflict of Laws*, § 29, at 71-72; Casad and Richman, *Jurisdiction in Civil Actions Vol. 1*, § 2-4, at 128; Twitchell, 'The Myth of General Jurisdiction', at 633; 2nd Restatement of Conflict of Laws, § 29, comment a; the 1988 revision reads: 'A person will in the nature of things have a sufficiently close relationship to the state of his domicile to make that state a fair and reasonable forum for the maintenance there of an action against him. ... This basis of jurisdiction assures the existence of a place in which a person is continuously amenable to suit.'

396 433 U.S. 186, at 212 (1977); Scoles, Hay *et al.*, *Conflict of Laws*, § 6.4, at 344; Casad and Richman, *Jurisdiction in Civil Actions Vol. 1*, at 129.

397 By 'unusual circumstances' is meant the situation where the person holds a purely technical domicile, such as a 'letter box' domicile. 2nd Restatement of Conflict of Laws, § 29, comment b, 1988 revision. Weintraub, *Commentary*, § 4.11, at 209; Richman and Reynolds, *Understanding Conflict of Laws*, § 29, at 72. See also Mirandes, *La compétence internationale des Etats-Unis*, § 244, at 170; Casad and Richman, *Jurisdiction in Civil Actions Vol. 1*, at 129.

398 495 U.S. 604, at 606 (1990), 'The transient jurisdiction rule will generally satisfy due process requirements'.

399 Casad and Richman, *Jurisdiction in Civil Actions Vol. 1*, at 129.

400 The same is equally true for the citizenship criterion.

that would generally satisfy due process standards.[401] One argument favouring the assertion of jurisdiction based on defendant's domicile regardless of the 'due process test' is that it guarantees an available forum over the defendant at any time.[402]

Domicile versus residence

A person's domicile should be understood as a person's home where he intends to remain.[403] The precise meaning of 'residence' is somewhat vague and courts and state statutes[404] use the 'domicile' concept inconsistently and interchangeably with 'residence'.[405] Residence is often used in statutes as the equivalent for domicile.[406] What seems to distinguish both concepts is that a domicile reflects a more permanent establishment than a residence does. As a rule, a defendant can have several residences, but only one domicile.[407] But these concepts are determined on a case-by-case basis. Although the Supreme Court has not pronounced itself on the adequacy of defendant's residence, it is generally recognized as a 'reasonable' basis for jurisdiction offering sufficient affiliation with the forum to constitute general jurisdiction.[408]

Application by the states

Long-arm statutes are specifically designed to reach out-of-state residents and non-consenting absent defendants. The domicile or residence criterion is however rarely used as jurisdictional basis; instead they are used to delimit the scope of the

---

[401] Scoles, Hay *et al.*, *Conflict of Laws*, § 6.4, at 344; Weintraub, *Commentary*, § 4.11, at 209.

[402] According to Twitchell 'The best approach to general jurisdiction is to confine it to its most essential function: providing one forum where a defendant may always be sued. Thus, general jurisdiction should be retained solely at a defendant's home base.' Twitchell, 'The Myth of General Jurisdiction', at 667.

[403] 2nd Restatement of Conflict of Laws, § 11-12, the 1988 revision states that 'home' is 'the place where a person dwells and which is the center of his domestic, social and civil life'. Weintraub, *Commentary*, § 2.2, at 14; Mirandes, *La compétence internationale des Etats-Unis*, § 242, at 167-168.

[404] See 2nd Restatement of Conflict of Laws, § 11-23. For example California state courts held in *Smith v. Smith*, Supreme Court of California, 45 Cal.2d 235, at 239 (1955), that 'Statutes frequently use "residence" and "resident" in legal meaning of "domicile" and "domiciliary"'. *Martens v. Winder*, U.S. Court of Appeals, 9th Circuit, 341 F.2d 197 (1965), certiorari denied 382 U.S. 937; *Soule v. Soule*, District Court of Appeal of California, 14 Cal.Rptr. 417 (1961). *Hartford v. Superior Court*, Supreme Court of California, 47 Cal.2d 447 (1956); *Martens v. Winder*, Court of Appeals, 9th Circuit, 341 F.2d 197 (1965), certiorari denied 382 U.S. 937; *Soule v. Soule*, District Court of Appeal of California, 14 Cal.Rptr. 417 (1961).

[405] 25 Am. Jur. 2d Domicil § 1 American Jurisprudence, Second Edition Database updated February 2008; Lisa A. Zakolski, J.D. states 'It may or may not be synonymous with residence. For purposes of diversity jurisdiction, domicil may be coextensive with citizenship, but one's domicil and national citizenship may differ in other contexts'.

[406] Scoles, Hay *et al.*, *Conflict of Laws*, § 6.5, at 345; 2nd Restatement of Conflict of Laws, § 11, Residence, comment k.

[407] Casad and Richman, *Jurisdiction in Civil Actions Vol. 1*, § 2-4, at 129. See also the 2nd Restatement of Conflict of Laws, § 30, comment a: New York Case law indicates that 'A person can have multiple residences but can have only one domicile.' *Antone v. General Motors*, New York Court of Appeals, 64 N.Y.2d 20, at 28 (1984).

[408] Born, *International Civil Litigation*, § 11, at 107; Weintraub, *Commentary*, § 4.11, at 210; Scoles, Hay *et al.*, *Conflict of Laws*, § 6.5, at 345; and the 2nd Restatement of Conflict of Laws, § 30, Residence.

long-arm statute.[409] Few statutes use the plaintiff's residence to limit their reach to actions brought by resident plaintiffs only.[410]

The majority of long-arm statutes do not explicitly regulate general jurisdiction on the basis of a defendant's domicile (or residence). As part of the traditional jurisdiction grounds under U.S. common law, they do not require statutory authorization. The New York Statute simply confirms in Section 301 that jurisdiction is available on traditional jurisdiction grounds, before enlisting its long-arm provisions in Section 302, 'A court may exercise such jurisdiction over persons, property, or status as might have been exercised heretofore.' In 1934, New York courts confirmed general jurisdiction on the basis of defendant's domicile in *Rawstorne v. Maguire*[411] by stating that 'the defendant who is a New York domiciliary at the time the action is commenced may be served with process anywhere, thereby conferring in personam jurisdiction on any cause of action regardless of where the claim arose.'[412] The New York Statute clearly defines the concept of domicile[413] and distinguishes it from the residence concept.[414]

The same approach is taken by Florida as the in-state service provision of Section 48.031 which regulates the service on residents or present defendants, thus accepting the domicile concept as a valid jurisdictional basis.[415]

The Californian *no limits* Statute includes the domicile and resident jurisdiction grounds as part of any constitutionally accepted bases for jurisdiction.[416]

---

[409] Such as the Statutes of Connecticut, Delaware, Georgia, Iowa, Kentucky, Louisiana, Minnesota, Mississippi, New Hampshire, Ohio, Rhode Island, Texas, Utah and West Virginia, which have adopted long-arm provisions with the sole purpose of reaching non-residents and foreign corporations. Casad and Richman, *Jurisdiction in Civil Actions Vol. 1*, at 392-395.

[410] Casad refers to Iowa, Mississippi and Texas. Casad and Richman, *Jurisdiction in Civil Actions Vol. 1*, at 395-396.

[411] New York Court of Appeals, 265 N.Y. 204, at 207 (1934).

[412] V. Alexander, *New York McKinney's Consolidated Laws: Practice Commentaries 2001*, Main Vol., comment C301:7. Domicile. See also New York CPLR § 313.

[413] A New York resident is someone who lives at a location within the state 'for some length of time during the course of a year', *Antone v. General Motors*, New York Court of Appeals, 64 N.Y.2d 20, at 30 (1984).

[414] See *Antone v. General Motors*, New York Court of Appeals, 64 N.Y.2d 20, at 28 (1984); see also e.g., *Porcello v. Brackett*, Supreme Court, Appellate Division, 85 A.D.2d 917 (1981), affirmed by the New York Court of Appeals, 57 N.Y.2d 962; see *Zimmerman v. Mingo*, Supreme Court, Appellate Division, 171 A.D.2d 662 (1991). See Alexander, *N.Y. McKinney's Consolidated Laws*, comment C301:7.

[415] Florida Statutes § 48.031 Service of process generally; service of witness subpoenas; (1)(a) 'Service of original process is made by delivering a copy … at usual place of abode with any person residing ….'

[416] West's Annotated Californian Code of Civil Procedure § 410.10 (under 2); see *Spacey v. Burgar*, U.S. District Court, Central District of California, 207 F. Supp.2d 1037, at 1042 (2001), 'the long arm statute of California allows a court to exercise personal jurisdiction over a non-resident defendant to the same extent as that permitted by the Due Process Clause of the Constitution.' *Allen v. Superior Court*, Supreme Court of California, 41 Cal.2d 306 (1953); and *Miller v. Superior Court In and For Los Angeles County Court of Appeal*, District Court of Appeal, 2nd District, 16 Cal.Rptr. 36 (1961).

Nonetheless, some enumerated long-arm statutes explicitly incorporate defendant's domicile in general jurisdiction.[417] This is the case with Alaska,[418] Massachusetts,[419] Maryland,[420] Michigan,[421] North Carolina,[422] South Carolina,[423] Tennessee[424] and Wisconsin.[425] Section 600.701 of the Michigan Statute explicitly provides for general jurisdiction over the individual domiciled in the state at the time when process is served.[426]

5.6.1.4 *Place of Incorporation of Domestic Corporations*

Incorporation in the forum is a well-established traditional jurisdiction ground under U.S. common law conferring general jurisdiction against domestic corporations.[427] The 2nd Restatement of Conflict of Laws states that a 'state has the power to exercise judicial jurisdiction over a domestic corporation'[428] and states have always asserted general jurisdiction over companies incorporated under their laws, even if they do business elsewhere.[429] It is considered fair and reasonable for 'home state' courts to exercise general jurisdiction over domestic corporations, as the latter owe their existence to the laws of the state.[430] The place of incorporation arose out of the domicile concept: just as the domicile is the home of the individual, the place of corporation should be understood as the corporation's home.[431] Under the minimum contacts theory, having substantial affiliation with the forum justifies general jurisdiction.[432]

---

[417] The Uniform Interstate and International Procedure Act also directly incorporated the domicile criterion, § 1-2: 'A state may exercise personal jurisdiction over a person domiciled in, organized under the laws of, or maintaining its principal place of business in this state as to any cause of action.'

[418] Alaska Statutes, Title 9, Code of Civil Procedure § 09.05.015.

[419] Massachusetts Annotated Laws, Chap. 223A, § 2.

[420] Code of Maryland; Courts and Judicial Proceedings, Title 6, § 6-102, State domiciliaries.

[421] Michigan Statutes § 600.705, Chap. 7, Bases of Jurisdiction, § 600.701, Individuals; general personal jurisdiction; § 600.711 and § 600.721, respectively for corporations and partnerships.

[422] General Statute of North Carolina, Chap. 1, Civil Procedure, § 1-75.4, Personal jurisdiction.

[423] Code of Laws South Carolina § 36-2-802; Personal jurisdiction based upon enduring relationship.

[424] Tennessee Code, Title 20, Civil Procedure, Chap. 2, Long-arm statute, § 20-2-222.

[425] Wisconsin Statute § 801.05.

[426] § 27A.705, Chap. 7, Bases of Jurisdiction § 600.701, Individuals; general personal jurisdiction.

[427] Born, *International Civil Litigation*, at 107; Weintraub, *Commentary*, § 4.20, at 249; Scoles, Hay *et al.*, *Conflict of Laws*, § 10.13, at 453, Hay, 'Flexibility versus Predictability and Uniformity', at 312; Twitchell, 'The Myth of General Jurisdiction', fn. 111, at 633.

[428] 2nd Restatement of Conflict of Laws, § 41.

[429] Ibid., Introductory Note, Chap. 3 and § 41, comment b.

[430] Scoles, Hay *et al.*, *Conflict of Laws*, § 10.13, at 453; Casad and Richman, *Jurisdiction in Civil Actions Vol. 1*, at 129, the 'gift of life' to a corporation can also indicate that the corporation has implicitly given consent to be subjected to jurisdiction. And see 2nd Restatement of Conflict of Laws, § 42, comment a.

[431] Twitchell, 'The Myth of General Jurisdiction', at 633; Brilmayer, 'A General Look at General Jurisdiction', at 733; George, 'In Search of General Jurisdiction', fn. 31, at 1103.

[432] Scoles, Hay *et al.*, *Conflict of Laws*, § 10.13, at 453; Richman and Reynolds, *Understanding Conflict of Laws*, at 83-84.

Whether general jurisdiction should also be asserted in the event the place of incorporation is a mere 'fictive place of corporation'[433] and any other connection with the forum is lacking, should be resolved in a similar way as in the case of a purely technical domicile for an individual, as explained above.[434] However, incorporation in a forum is, like the establishment of a domicile or residence, a voluntary affiliation with the forum consistent with constitutional standards, even if the corporation has no other connection with the forum and does no business in the state.[435] *Burnham v. Superior Court*[436] should also be applied analogously: the exercise of jurisdiction on the basis of incorporation in the forum – even fictively – generally satisfies due process standards.[437] Obviously, the application of the *forum non conveniens* is still available to escape jurisdiction of the 'home state'.[438]

While the place of incorporation is a valid jurisdiction ground under U.S. common law and statutory authorization is not required, most states have not explicitly enacted the jurisdictional criteria for general jurisdiction in their long-arm statute.[439] Some states have regulated this jurisdiction rule by way of enacting rules for proper service on domestic corporations.[440] The Michigan long-arm Statute however explicitly provides for general jurisdiction over corporations incorporated under the laws of Michigan.[441]

5.6.2 The 'Doing Business' Criterion

When the defendant has 'continuous and systematic' contacts with the forum, general jurisdiction over claims unrelated to the business activities in the forum is justified.[442] Since the *International Shoe* decision, the jurisdictional foundation of doing business no longer rests on '*technical definitions*'[443] such as 'implied-consent' or 'corporate presence', but derives from the 'minimum contacts rule',

---

[433] See also the reverse situation of pseudo foreign corporations, technically incorporated in another state, but subjected to jurisdiction as if they were domestic corporations, Scoles, Hay *et al.*, *Conflict of Laws*, at 454, referring to Californian Corporations Code § 2115.

[434] See above Weintraub, *Commentary*, § 4.21, at 250.

[435] Ibid.; Casad and Richman, *Jurisdiction in Civil Actions Vol. 1*, at 130.

[436] 495 U.S. 604 (1990).

[437] See Sect. 5.4.1.

[438] See also Scoles, Hay *et al.*, *Conflict of Laws*, § 10.13, at 454.

[439] This is the case for New York, Florida and California. See Weintraub, *Commentary*, § 4.21, at 249.

[440] As a rule, service of process on a (domestic) corporation is effected by serving corporate officers appointed by law. Casad and Richman, *Jurisdiction in Civil Actions Vol. 1*, at 332-333; 2nd Restatement of Conflict of Laws, § 41, comment b. Californian West Annotated § 416.10. In Florida service on corporations is regulated by § 48.081.

[441] § 600.711(6) Michigan Statute reads: 'The existence of any of the following relationships between a corporation and the state shall constitute a sufficient basis of jurisdiction to enable the courts of record of this state to exercise general personal jurisdiction over the corporation and to enable such courts to render personal judgments against the corporation: (1) Incorporation under the laws of this state.' See *Jones v. Williams*, Court of Appeals of Michigan, 431 N.W.2d 419 (1988). This provision is strongly modelled on the Uniform Interstate and International Procedure Act § 1-2.

[442] Born, *International Civil Litigation*, at 120; Weintraub, *Commentary*, § 4.14, at 220.

[443] Lowenfeld, *International Litigation*, at 229.

primarily focusing on the corporation's (business) activities in the forum.[444] In *International Shoe Co. v. Washington*, the Supreme Court dealt with the question whether the presence of a foreign corporation could be determined by its business activities carried out in the forum.[445] It held that in some cases, continuous corporate operations within a state are so substantial and of such a nature as to justify jurisdiction over causes of action arising from dealings entirely distinct from those activities.[446] According to the Court a 'company exercising the privilege of conducting activities within a state and enjoying from the benefits and the protection of the laws of that state may expect in return to respond to a suit brought to enforce these laws.'[447]

The consequences of founding the doing business criterion on the minimum contact rule are twofold. Primarily, in order to exercise jurisdiction on doing business in the forum statutory authorization is needed,[448] and, secondly, it is subjected to the same 'fairness and reasonableness' standards as jurisdiction based on specific or related contacts, such as transacting business jurisdiction.[449] This means that there is no simple way to determine whether a corporation is doing business in the forum. Apart from the appreciation of the company's contacts with the forum, the quality and quantity of its business contacts must also be weighed against the burden placed on the defendant to be sued in a distant forum, as part of the reasonableness test.

5.6.2.1 *Doing Business and Individuals*

Although *International Shoe Co. v. Washington*[450] established the doing business criterion especially for corporate defendants under the minimum contact rule, *Shaffer v. Heitner* clarified that 'the *International Shoe* Court believed that the standard it was setting forth governed actions against natural persons as well as corporations, and we see no reason to disagree.'[451] The 2nd Restatement of Conflict of Laws affirmed the application of the doing business criterion to individuals in

---

[444] See also 2nd Restatement of Conflict of Laws, § 35, comment b; Weintraub, *Commentary*, § 4.14, at 217 and § 4.21, at 251; Scoles, Hay *et al.*, *Conflict of Laws*, § 10.15, at 455-456; Casad and Richman, *Jurisdiction in Civil Actions Vol. 1*, § 3-2[b], at 340-341.

[445] 326 U.S. 310 (1945). See Born, *International Civil Litigation*, at 110; Scoles, Hay *et al.*, *Conflict of Laws*, § 10.15, at 457, 'New York courts continue to speak of a corporation's doing business here as creating "presence" within the state.' See for example *Landoil Resources Corp. v. Alexander & Alexander Services*, New York Court of Appeals, 77 N.Y.2d 28, at 33 (1990).

[446] *International Shoe v. Washington*, 326 U.S. 310, at 318 (1945).

[447] Ibid., at 319. See also the justification for jurisdiction over foreign corporations given by Justice Black, at 323-324, who also relies on the reasonableness criteria by stating that 'we will "permit" the State to act if upon "an estimate of the inconveniences" which would result to the corporation from a trial away from its "home" or "principal place of business", we conclude that it is "reasonable" to subject it to suit in a State where it is doing business.'

[448] Born, *International Civil Litigation*, at 110; Weintraub, *Commentary*, § 4.14, at 221.

[449] But see the uncertainty around this point in Born, *International Civil Litigation*, at 120; *Metropolitan Life Ins. Co. v. Robertson-Ceco*, U.S. Court of Appeals, 2nd Circuit, C.A.N.Y. (1996), certiorari denied 519 U.S. 1006.

[450] 326 U.S. 310 (1945).

[451] 433 U.S. 186, at 204 (1977), fn.19.

its 1988 revision.[452] But, once again, the *Burnham v. Superior Court* decision cast doubts on the generally supported view that 'doing business' also applies to individuals. In a footnote the Court stated that:

> '[I]t may be that whatever special rule exists permitting "continuous and systematic" contacts, ... to support jurisdiction with respect to matters unrelated to activity in the forum applies only to corporations ... We express no views on these matters – and, for simplicity's sake, omit reference to this aspect of "contacts"-based jurisdiction in our discussion.'[453]

In other words the Court did not reject nor did it confirm the availability of the doing business criterion to individuals. The fact is that there are relatively little cases in which doing business is applied to individuals.[454] Scoles favours applying the doing business criterion to individuals, for instance in the event a defendant is domiciled in one state and has his office in another. Yet, he also observes that asserting general jurisdiction to a forum other than his 'domicile forum' might constitute a weak connection.[455]

5.6.2.2 *Defining Doing Business*

For the purpose of the doing business criterion, the (foreign) corporation is required to be engaged in a 'regular and continuous course of conduct'. This introduces an element of continuity of defendant's business activities in the forum.[456] All of the corporation's business activities in the state are considered as a whole; one single transaction, even if it constitutes a substantial contact, is generally not enough to guarantee this continuity.[457] Apart from this 'continuity' element, the

---

[452] 2nd Restatement of Conflict of Laws, § 35(3).

[453] 495 U.S. 609, at 610 (1990), fn. 1; see Scoles, Hay *et al.*, *Conflict of Laws*, § 6.8, at 354 and § 10.14, at 454; Borchers, 'Comparing Jurisdiction', at 135.

[454] Hay, Weintraub *et al.*, *Conflict of Laws*, at 120; Scoles, Hay *et al.*, *Conflict of Laws*, § 6.9, at 358.

[455] Scoles, Hay *et al.*, *Conflict of Laws*, § 6.8, at 354.

[456] See for example Florida in which courts require that 'defendant engage in a general course of business activity in Florida for a pecuniary benefit'. *New Lenox Industries, Inc. v. Fenton*, U.S. District Court, M.D. Florida, 510 F. Supp.2d 893 (2007). *Sehringer v. Big Lots, Inc.*, U.S. District Court, M.D. Florida, 2007 WL 2908089 (2007); *Stubbs v. Wyndham Nassau Resort and Crystal Palace Casino*, U.S. Court of Appeals, 11th Circuit 447 F.3d 1357 (2006); *Horizon Aggressive Growth, L.P. v. Rothstein-Kass, P.A.*, U.S. Court of Appeals, 11th Circuit, Florida, 421 F.3d 1162 (2005). New York courts generally require that the defendant operate with 'a measure of permanence and continuity' in order to satisfy the New York doing business criterion for general jurisdiction as opposed to operating 'occasionally or casually', in *Erne Shipping Inc. v. HBC Hamburg Bulk Carriers GmbH & Co. KG*, U.S. District Court, Southern District of New York, 409 F. Supp.2d 427 (2006); *Overseas Media, Inc. v. Skvortsov*, U.S. District Court, Southern District of New York, 407 F. Supp.2d 563 (2006); *Daou v. Early Advantage*, U.S. District Court, Northern District of New York, LLC, 410 F. Supp.2d 82 (2006); *Hoffritz for Cutlery, Inc. v. Amajac, Ltd.*, U.S. Court of Appeals, 2nd Circuit, 763 F.2d 55, at 58 (1985), quoting *Tauza v. Susquehanna Coal Co.*, New York Court of Appeals, 220 N.Y. 259, 115 N.E. 915 (1917).

[457] Casad and Richman, *Jurisdiction in Civil Actions Vol. 1*, § 3-2[iv], at 347; and see *Republic Supply Corp. v. Lewyt*, U.S. District Court, Michigan, 160 F. Supp. 949, at 955 (1958), 'the question of whether a foreign corporation is doing business in a state to an extent which makes it amenable to

Supreme Court has given little guidance as to what kind and how many contacts constitute 'continuous and systematic' contacts.[458] The cases following the *International Shoe* decision were considered rather 'unusual' for general guidance.[459] In *Perkins v. Benguet Consol. Mining Co.*,[460] the Supreme Court found that the various business activities of a foreign mining company in Ohio were sufficiently substantial and 'of such a nature as to permit Ohio to entertain a cause of action against a foreign corporation, where the cause of action arose from activities entirely distinct from its activities in Ohio'.[461] The company's president, who was also the company's general manager and principal stockholder, moved his domicile and main office to Ohio. The business activities carried out in Ohio included holding directors' meetings, maintaining files and business correspondence, and distributing salary checks.[462]

In *Helicópteros Nacionales de Colombia v. Hall*, the Supreme Court held that mere purchases in the state – and related training trips – did not constitute a sufficient basis for general jurisdiction over unrelated claims.[463] Furthermore, the U.S. Government observed that if the mere purchase in a U.S. state is sufficient to assert jurisdiction over a foreign company over claims unrelated to this purchase, it might dissuade foreign corporations from buying products in the U.S., which would affect the U.S. position in world trade markets.[464]

Within the lines established by these two cases lies a large grey area of business activities upon which 'continuous and systematic' contacts can establish general doing business jurisdiction.[465] Numerous decisions from lower courts have attempted to specify what constitutes 'continuous and systematic' contacts.[466] The

process of such state is not necessarily dependent upon … or necessarily, quality of separate transactions' (1917).

[458] The 'quantum' of unrelated contacts needed in order to know what consist in 'continuous and systematic' contacts is difficult to determine precisely. See Born, *International Civil Litigation*, at 111; Scoles, Hay *et al.*, *Conflict of Laws*, § 6.9, at 354; Hay, Weintraub *et al.*, *Conflict of Laws*, at 120.

[459] Born, *International Civil Litigation*, at 111; Weintraub, *Commentary*, § 4.14, at 221; Hay, Weintraub *et al.*, *Conflict of Laws*, at 119; Twitchell, 'Why We Keep Doing Business', at 182-187; Scoles, Hay *et al.*, *Conflict of Laws*, § 6.9, at 355.

[460] *Perkins v. Benguet Consol. Mining Co.*, 342 U.S. 437 (1952).

[461] 342 U.S. 437, at 448 (1952), the case was unusual since the facts took place during the Second World War.

[462] 342 U.S. 437, at 447-448 (1952).

[463] 466 U.S. 408, at 418 (1984), '… we hold that mere purchases, even if occurring at regular intervals, are not enough to warrant a State's assertion of in personam jurisdiction over a nonresident corporation in a cause of action not related to those purchase transactions.' Schlosser, 'Jurisdiction in International Litigation: The Issue of Human Rights', at 10-11.

[464] Brief for the U.S. as *Amicus Curiae* referred to by the Supreme Court, 466 U.S. 408, at 425 (1984), fn. 3; Weintraub, *Commentary*, § 4.8, at 166; Weintraub, *International Litigation*, at 16; Hay, Weintraub *et al.*, *Conflict of Laws*, at 120.

[465] Hay, Weintraub *et al.*, *Conflict of Laws*, at 120; Scoles, Hay *et al.*, *Conflict of Laws*, § 6.9, at 356-357.

[466] Twitchell, 'Why We Keep Doing Business', fn. 62, at 187. The New York Court of Appeals itself acknowledged that the standard is imprecise in *Sterling Novelty Corp. v. Frank & Hirsch Distrib*, New York Court of Appeals, 299 N.Y. 208, at 210 (1949). *Bryant v. Finnish National Airline*, New York Court of Appeals, 15 N.Y.2d 426 (1965); other examples of doing business being rejected because contacts are not sufficiently constant are found in *Future Technology Today, Inc. v. OSF*

doing business criterion is an open concept that is difficult to define,[467]and it is determined on a case-by-case basis.[468]

It is difficult to generalize on what constitutes 'doing business' within the meaning of the long-arm statutes.[469] Juenger considers the notion of doing business an American 'idiosyncrasy', which is hard to explain and difficult for foreign nations to accept.[470] Whether a defendant is doing business in the forum depends on a number of relevant factors. For instance, there is little doubt that a defendant is considered to 'do business' in a state where he has his principal place of business or main office.[471] Such affiliation easily represents 'continuous and systematic' contacts with the forum in order to accept general doing business jurisdiction.[472] Some long-arm statutes explicitly assert general jurisdiction over a defendant with his principal place of business or business office in the state.[473]

Other factors relevant for 'doing business' are the 'physical connections'[474] a defendant might have with the forum such as the presence of offices, agents,

---

Healthcare Systems, U.S. Court of Appeals, 11th Circuit, Florida, 218 F.3d 1247 (2000); *Bancroft & Masters, Inc. v. Augusta Nat. Inc.*, U.S. Court of Appeals, 9th Circuit, 223 F.3d 1082 (2000); *Rocke v. Canadian Auto. Sport Club*, U.S. Court of Appeals, 9th Circuit, 660 F.2d 395 (1981); and doing business is accepted in *Cornelison v. Chaney*, California Supreme Court, 127 Cal.Rptr. 352 (1976); and in *T.M. Hylwa, M.D., Inc. v. Palka.* U.S. Court of Appeals, 9th Circuit, 823 F.2d 310 (1987).

467 Juenger, 'The American Law of General Jurisdiction', at 151 and 156, 'Fifty-six years after International Shoe was decided, we still do not know when states may assert dispute-blind jurisdiction over nonresident corporations.' Borchers, 'The Problem with General Jurisdiction', at 122, 'This basis of personal jurisdiction is notoriously indeterminate and seems to exist without regard for supposed due process limits.' Twitchell, 'Why We Keep Doing Business', at 173, 'Both the theory and practice of doing-business jurisdiction are problematic.'

468 According to *Velandra v. Regie Nationale des Usines Renault*, U.S. Court of Appeals, 6th Circuit, Michigan, 336 F.2d 292, at 295 (1964), '[the e]xistence or nonexistence of necessary minimum contacts to justify upholding of personal jurisdiction over foreign corporations under U.S.C.A. Const. Amend. 14 must be worked out with reference to facts of [a] particular case rather than on [the] basis of dogmatic rules of all-inclusive principles.'

469 Casad and Richman, *Jurisdiction in Civil Actions Vol. 1*, § 3-2[iii], at 342; joined by Scoles, Hay *et al.*, *Conflict of Laws*, § 6.9, at 357, 'generalizations are treacherous'.

470 Juenger, 'A Shoe Unfit', at 1040-1041; Heiser, 'A Minimum Interest Approach', at 925.

471 Weintraub, *Commentary*, § 4.14, at 220.

472 2nd Restatement of Conflict of Laws, § 35, comment e: 'The individual's activities in the State may also be so continuous and substantial as to justify the exercise of judicial jurisdiction over him as to causes of action arising from activities in other states. This is particularly likely to be true in a situation where the individual's principal place of business is in the State.' But see *Laufer v. Ostrow*, New York Court of Appeals, 55 N.Y.2d 305 (1982). The fact that the defendant holds an office in a state contributes to the required conditions of continuity and 'permanence' but does not however automatically constitute doing business, see Schack, *Jurisdictional Minimum Contacts Scrutinized*, at 36.

473 See for instance § 48.081(5) of the long-arm Statute of Florida, which stipulates: 'When a corporation engages in substantial and not isolated activities within this state, or has a business office within the state and is actually engaged in the transaction of business therefrom, … it is not necessary in such case that the action, suit, or proceeding against the corporation shall have arisen out of any transaction or operation connected with or incidental to the business being transacted within the state.' This statute was modelled on the Uniform Interstate and International Procedure Act, which also exercises general jurisdiction in § 1-2 based upon the '*enduring relationship*' such as for example a corporation 'maintaining its principal place of business' in the state.

474 Hay, Weintraub *et al.*, *Conflict of Laws*, at 120.

branches[475] or employees in the state, but also – to a lesser extent – the non-physical connections with the forum.[476] Mere solicitation of commercial activities is generally not sufficient for 'doing business,' except in situations where the solicitation is regular, systematic and continuous, and produces a significant volume of sales.[477] In order to meet the doing business requirements, the solicitation has to be accompanied by sufficient 'activities of substance' and not merely be carried out by independent agents.[478] The same applies for the maintenance of bank accounts or other relationships with the forum, they are not sufficient *by themselves* for gen-

---

[475] See below Sect. 5.6.5.

[476] Hay, Weintraub *et al.*, *Conflict of Laws*, at 120; Scoles, Hay *et al.*, *Conflict of Laws*, § 6.9, at 357. In *Stubbs v. Wyndham Nassau Resort and Crystal Palace Casino*, 11th Circuit, 447 F.3d 1357 (2006), general jurisdiction was upheld under the Florida long-arm Statute on the basis of a significant amount of advertisement contacts with the forum. Not only was a Florida-based subsidiary, which acted as advertising and booking department for the resort connected, in such a way that the subsidiary was agent for the foreign resort, and its activities could be imputed to the resort, the defendant also had sufficient direct contact with Florida, in that it maintained numerous commercial relationships with Florida-based entities, including travel agencies, law firms, insurance brokers, and advertisers, and it held at least six bank accounts in Florida banks, in *Horizon Aggressive Growth, L.P. v. Rothstein-Kass, P.A.*, C.A.11 (Fla.), 421 F.3d 1162, at 1167 (2005). The U.S. Court of Appeals, 11th Circuit, held that '[f]actors relevant, but not dispositive, to analysis of whether foreign defendant is "carrying on business" in Florida within meaning of Florida long-arm statute include the presence and operation of an office in Florida, the possession and maintenance of a license to do business in Florida, the number of Florida clients served, and the percentage of overall revenue gleaned from Florida clients'. See for New York the U.S. District Court, Southern District of New York, which held in 2006 that 'whether a corporation's contacts are "continuous and systematic" under New York law, courts have typically focused on factors such as: "whether the company has an office in the state, whether it has any bank accounts or other property in the state, whether it has a phone listing in the state, whether it does public relations work there, and whether it has individuals permanently located in the state to promote its interests."' *Erne Shipping Inc. v. HBC Hamburg Bulk Carriers GmbH & Co. KG*, 409 F. Supp.2d 427, at 434 (2006), citing *Wiwa v. Royal Dutch Petroleum Co.*, U.S. Court of Appeals, 2nd Circuit, 226 F.3d 88, 98 (2000). See also *Burrows Paper Corp. v. R.G. Engineering, Inc.*, U.S. District Court, Northern District of New York, 363 F. Supp.2d 379 (2005); *Stutts v. De Dietrich Group*, U.S. District Court, Eastern District of New York, 465 F. Supp.2d 156 (2006).

[477] Casad and Richman, *Jurisdiction in Civil Actions Vol. 1*, at 342; for instance in New York, it is likewise settled that the mere solicitation of business alone does not confer jurisdiction over a defendant. *Landoil Resources Corp. v. Alexander & Alexander Services, Inc.*, U.S. Court of Appeals, 2nd Circuit, 918 F.2d 1039, 1043 (1990). The U.S. Court of Appeals held in *Beacon Enterprises, Inc. v. Menzies*, U.S. Court of Appeals, 2nd Circuit, 715 F.2d 757, at 763 (1983), that 'once solicitation is found in any substantial degree very little more is necessary to a conclusion of "doing business". … To sustain personal jurisdiction, … New York courts require "substantial solicitation" that is carried on with "considerable measure of continuity and from a permanent locale" within the state.'

[478] In *Snow v. DirecTV, Inc.*, 11th Circuit, 450 F.3d 1314 (2006), defendant's negotiations with the forum were not enough to establish general jurisdiction over a law firm under Florida's long-arm Statute, when balanced against the firm's lack of a physical presence in Florida, its non-solicitation of Florida clients, and its deriving less than one percent of its revenues from matters connected with Florida. See for New York, *Chestnut Ridge Air, Ltd. v. 1260269 Ontario Inc.*, Supreme Court, New York County, New York, 13 Misc.3d 807, 827 N.Y.S.2d 461 (2006), general jurisdiction accepted when defendant engaged in more than 'mere' solicitation of business (dealing with internet contacts); *Wiwa v. Royal Dutch Petroleum Co.*, U.S. Court of Appeals, 2nd Circuit, New York, 226 F.3d 88 (2000), certiorari denied 121 S.Ct. 1402, 532 U.S. 941, 149 L.Ed.2d 345; *Laufer v. Ostrow*, New York Court of Appeals, 55 N.Y.2d 305, at 310 (1982).

eral jurisdiction under the doing business criterion.[479] By way of illustration, New York courts determined whether a foreign corporation is doing business in New York by focussing on the following criteria: (1) whether the foreign corporation has an office in the state; (2) whether it has any bank accounts or other property in the state; (3) whether it has a phone listing in the state; (4) whether it does any public relations work in the state; and (5) whether it has employees who permanently work in the state. No single criterion is determinative. The general jurisdiction inquiry thus looks to the totality of the defendant's contacts and 'permits a court to exercise its power in a case where the subject matter of the suit is unrelated to those contacts'.[480]

Some states require foreign corporations to register in order to do business in the state, they are then considered to have consented to jurisdiction in exchange for authorization to operate on their territory.[481] Jurisdiction is then based on the registration to do business and the designation of persons accepting service of process on behalf of the company.[482] Whether or not such registration to do business is sometimes sufficient to constitute 'continuous and systematic' contacts for general jurisdiction is unclear and differs from state to state, but should generally be understood as a relevant factor.[483]

---

[479] See for instance with respect to the Florida District Court of Appeal, 3rd District, *Banco Continental, S.A. v. Transcom Bank (Barbados), Ltd.*, District Court of Appeal, 3rd District, 922 So.2d 395 (2006), in which general jurisdiction was denied since the relationship with the bank did nothing more than facilitate the transfer of money in international commerce. In New York the U.S. District Court rejected general jurisdiction on similar grounds, unless the bank accounts are used for 'substantially all' of the foreign corporation's business, see *Reers v. Deutsche Bahn AG*, U.S. District Court, Southern District of New York, 320 F. Supp.2d 140, at 156 (2004). In Michigan general jurisdiction on the basis of doing business was upheld since the defendant also sent orders to plaintiff's entity in Michigan, guaranteeing the entity's account with the Michigan supplier, wiring payments to the entity's bank account in Michigan, and by calling the entity's representative in Michigan to complete the negotiation of an asset and inventory purchase agreement. *Salom Enterprises, LLC v. TS Trim Industries, Inc.*, U.S. District Court, Eastern District of Michigan, 464 F. Supp.2d 676 (2006).

[480] *Mones v. Commercial Bank of Kuwait, S.A.K.*, Southern District of New York, 502 F. Supp.2d 363 (2007).

[481] Born, *International Civil Litigation*, at 108; Casad and Richman, *Jurisdiction in Civil Actions Vol. 1*, § 3-2[2], at 334-339, in particular § 3-2[2](a)[i], at 336.

[482] Also called 'qualifying corporation', see Born, *International Civil Litigation*, at 108.

[483] Ibid.; Scoles, Hay *et al.*, *Conflict of Laws*, at 358; Casad and Richman, *Jurisdiction in Civil Actions Vol. 1*, at 336-337. The Californian Statute for example authorizes such jurisdiction; see also West's Annotated California Code of Civil Procedure § 410.10 ('Bases of Judicial Jurisdiction over Corporations; Appointment of Agent – Foreign Corporations'). See for jurisdiction under Florida's long-arm Statute, *Keston v. FirstCollect, Inc.*, U.S. District Court, Southern District of Florida, 523 F. Supp.2d 1348 (2007). See for New York, § 301 in conjunction with § 304 CPLR and see *Erne Shipping Inc. v. HBC Hamburg Bulk Carriers GmbH & Co. KG*, U.S. District Court, Southern District of New York, 409 F. Supp.2d 427, at 436-438 (2006), citing *Wright v. Maersk Line, Ltd.*, 2000 WL 744370, U.S. District Court, Southern District of New York (2000); *Bellepointe, Inc. v. Kohl's Dep't Stores, Inc.*, U.S. District Court, Southern District of New York, 975 F. Supp. 562, 564 (1997), 'Two federal courts, however, have stated that in the absence of any actual business conducted in the state, a filing for authorization to do business is not by itself sufficient to confer personal jurisdiction'; and see *Reers v. Deutsche Bahn AG*, 320 F. Supp.2d 140, at 155 (2004), 'The mere fact that Accor [defendant] owns or partially owns businesses that are registered to do business in New York does not subject [defendant] to general jurisdiction in New York'.

The majority of long-arm statutes accept the doing business criterion for general jurisdiction.[484] Some of them incorporated the jurisdiction criterion as such. In Michigan, Section 600.711 of its long-arm statute regulates general personal jurisdiction for corporations 'carrying on … a continuous and systematic part of its general business within the state'. However, such a provision does not exist for individuals in Section 600.701. The Florida Statute enshrined in Section 48.193(2) is a long-arm provision for 'doing business' and is applicable to all defendants engaged in substantial, not isolated, activities in Florida.[485]

Section 301 of the New York Statute deals with general jurisdiction and it equally covers doing business. Commentaries to the general Californian Code of Civil Procedure of Section 410.10 follow the Supreme Court decisions and include the doing business bases for individuals.[486] It is generally accepted that a defendant had to be doing business in the state at the time process was served upon him. In the event, the defendant had ceased doing business at the time of service of process; jurisdiction can no longer be established on the doing business ground. In that case, in order to establish jurisdiction it is required that the claim arises out of defendant's activities in the state, which will then constitute and become a specific transacting business criterion.[487]

5.6.3 Specific Jurisdiction Based on Defendant's Activities

The *International Shoe*'s heritage introduced specific jurisdiction and related contacts. As long as there exists a nexus between the affiliating minimum contact in the forum and the plaintiff's cause of action, specific jurisdiction is available to the plaintiff provided that the exercise of jurisdiction withstands the due process standards including compliance with the 'reasonableness' test and the 'purposeful availment' requirement.[488]

Each state of the U.S. enacted a long-arm statute and each enumerated long-arm statute incorporated provisions regulating extraterritorial jurisdiction on the basis

---

[484] Weintraub, *Commentary*, § 4.14, at 222.

[485] Under § 48.081 the manner of service of process is regulated for general jurisdiction over a corporation when 'it engages in substantial and not isolated activities within this state, … and it is not necessary in such case that the action, suit, or proceeding against the corporation shall have arisen out of any transaction or operation connected with or incidental to the business being transacted within the state.' The general provision for service, § 48.031, does not explicitly establish jurisdiction over individuals doing business.

[486] See the Comments of the Judicial Council and see *Lewis Mfg. Co. v. Superior Court*, District Court of Appeal, 2nd District, 140 Cal.App.2d 245, 255 (1956).

[487] See Sect. 5.6.3. See among others *Premo Specialty Mfg. Co. v. Jersey-Crème*, California U.S. Court of Appeals, 9th Circuit, 200 F. 352 (1912) and *Lancaster v. Colonial Motor Freight Line*, Supreme Court, Appellate Division, 177 A.D.2d 152, 156 (1992).

[488] See Part 1. California has the famous 'no limits' statute of § 410.10 and thus always directly refers to the due process requirements. See especially *Doe v. Unocal Corp.*, U.S. Court of Appeals, 9th Circuit, 248 F.3d 915 (2001); *Caruth v. International Psychoanalytical Ass'n*, U.S. Court of Appeals, 9th Circuit, 59 F.3d 126 (1995); *Republic Intern. Corp. v. Amco Engineers, Inc.*, U.S. Court of Appeals, 9th Circuit, 516 F.2d 161 (1975).

of specific and related contacts with the forum.[489] These provisions – also called 'single-act' provisions – should be distinguished from the provisions regulating general jurisdiction based on 'continuous and systematic' contacts. Among these single-act provisions one can distinguish a first category establishing a 'transacting business' rule.[490] Activity-based jurisdiction subjects persons who, directly or through an agent, 'transact business' in the state with respect to causes of action arising from this business.[491]

Another category of single-act provisions[492] deals with the 'causing an effect' rule and is not concerned with the defendant's act or omission in the state but with the effect of defendant's act or omission in the state even if it took place elsewhere.[493] Of particular interest in this second category is the effect caused by a contract in the forum.[494] Several long-arm statutes contain 'single-act provisions' establishing jurisdiction when a contract 'causes an effect', for instance by its performance, in the forum.[495] As the due process standards equally apply to the exercise of jurisdiction on the basis of the 'causing an effect' category, it is important that the defendant still has some minimum contacts with the forum. According to the 2nd Restatement of Conflict of Laws:

> 'the closer the defendant's relationship to the state, the greater is the likelihood that the state may exercise judicial jurisdiction over him as to claims arising from the effects of the act in the state ... So if the defendant does business in the state, or solicits business extensively in the state, or if a substantial quantity of goods manufactured by him are sold in the state, there is a greater likelihood that the state may exercise judicial jurisdiction over him as to claims arising from the effects in the state of an act done by him outside the state than if the defendant did not have this relationship to the state.'[496]

[489] Under the Californian Statute transacting business is covered by § 410.10. In both federal and state courts the wording 'transacting business' or 'doing an act' are not used as such. For Michigan transacting business is dealt with under § 600.701, § 600.705, § 600.711, § 600.715, § 600.721, § 600.725 of the Statute. The Florida Statute is divided in two main provisions § 48.181 (general jurisdiction) and § 48.193. The latter provision is 'transacting business'-related. § 48.193(1)(a) indicates '... carrying on business'; 48.193(1)(g) provides for jurisdiction if it concerns a claim for breach of contract due to failing to perform in the state. § 48.193(2) is a general jurisdiction long-arm provision under the doing business criterion. With respect to New York, the 'transacting business' provision is covered by § 302(a)(1).

[490] Please note that this denomination is slightly a bit confusing; even though a single isolated act could be substantial enough to establish jurisdiction, courts often examine the totality of the quality and nature of defendant's contacts to determine whether jurisdiction should be established. See below Sect. 5.6.3.1.

[491] See § 1-3(a)(1) of the Uniform Act; see also the 2nd Restatement of Conflict of Laws, § 36, and see of the 2nd Restatement of Conflict of Laws, 1988 revision, § 2.

[492] But according to Richman and Reynolds 'there is a fair amount of overlap', Richman and Reynolds, *Understanding Conflict of Laws*, at 90.

[493] See 2nd Restatement of Conflict of Laws, § 37; see also comment c. See Weintraub, *Commentary*, § 4.15, at 222-223.

[494] A tortuous effect in the forum caused by an out-of-state act is also covered by this category. § 600.715(3) Michigan Statute is limited to tortious effects; see also § 37, comment a, of the 1988 revision of the 2nd Restatement of Conflict of Laws.

[495] See below Sect. 5.6.4. Weintraub, *Commentary*, § 4.15, at 223 and § 4.18, at 241 *et seq.*

[496] See 2nd Restatement of Conflict of Laws, § 37, comment c; see also the confusion arising out of this interaction in the reporter's note, comments e-f of the 2nd Restatement of Conflict of Laws,

5.6.3.1 *Transacting Business Jurisdiction*

The meaning of 'transacting business' is difficult to define. On the one hand, a single, substantial, contact is sometimes sufficient to conclude that the transacting business rule applies, on the other hand, the rule involves the appreciation of defendant's contacts with the forum as 'factors' to determine whether he transacts business in the forum.[497]

Transacting business provisions are designed to reach the defendant outside the forum for claims involving defendant's in-state activities. The 'transacting business' criterion covers a much wider range of 'business' contacts than the 'doing business' criterion.[498] Although it is clear that 'transacting business' has to be distinguished from 'doing business',[499] the transacting business criterion covers all business contacts that would also provide for jurisdiction covered under the doing business criterion, but requires that the cause of action arises out of or is related to the activities conducted by the defendant.[500] However, the 'transacting business' criterion establishes jurisdiction on the basis of less continuous or substantive, yet more isolated, business contacts provided that plaintiff's cause of action is related to defendant's transacting business in the forum. Contacts arising out of commercial activities in a state can take multiple forms. Any contact, even a 'single isolated act'[501] is believed to provide for jurisdiction. 'Transacting business' jurisdiction puts emphasis on defendant's related contacts arising out of his business activities and directed to the forum.[502] Mere business negotiations in the forum can already

---

§ 36(2), 1988 revision, where the isolated performance of commercial activity (or effect) in the state, like the performance of a contract seems to be included in the term 'Transacts business'.

[497] Weintraub explained the troublesome meaning of 'transacting business' by way of the following questions formulated by a lawyer addressed to his seller client in order to provide the latter with an estimation on the probability of successfully obtaining jurisdiction in a simple sales contract: 'Where were the goods a catalogue item or custom made? Did a representative of the buyer come here to negotiate the contract or supervise manufacture?' 'Did you solicit the sale or did the buyer contact you first?' 'Did the contract require manufacture in this state'? 'Has the buyer purchased from you before?' Weintraub, 'Fifty Years of International Shoe', at 542.

[498] 'The phrase "transaction of any business" is construed as broader than "doing business"'. *Sifers v. Horen*, Michigan Supreme Court, 188 N.W.2d 623 (1971). See also Casad and Richman, *Jurisdiction in Civil Actions Vol. 1*, at 399.

[499] The original Illinois drafters already used this terminology to differentiate between transacting business and doing business, see Casad and Richman, *Jurisdiction in Civil Actions Vol. 1*, § 4-2[1], at 397.

[500] Ibid., § 4-2[1](a), at 399. See above Sect. 5.6.3.

[501] See *McGee v. International Life Ins. Co.*, 355 U.S. 220, 223 (1957). The New York CPLR, § 302 is such a 'single-act' statute; one business transaction, from which the cause of action arises, can be sufficient for jurisdictional purposes. See for the main interpretation of this provision by New York courts, *Kreutter v. McFadden Oil Corp*, New York Court of Appeals, 71 N.Y.2d 460, 467 (1988) and *Parke-Bernet Galleries v. Franklyn*, New York Court of Appeals, 26 N.Y.2d 13 (1970). The Court again indicated that proof of a single transaction in New York would satisfy the statutory requirement, citing *Longines-Wittnauer Watch Co. v. Barnes & Reinecke, Inc.*, New York Court of Appeals, 15 N.Y.2d 443 (1965), as well as several noted commentators.

[502] See *Vons Companies, Inc. v. Seabest Foods, Inc.*, Supreme Court of California (State Courts), 58 Cal.Rptr.2d 899 (1996) (rehearing denied, certiorari denied 522 U.S. 808). 'Defendant's forum activities need not be directed at the plaintiff in order to give rise to specific jurisdiction; nexus required

constitute 'transacting business'.[503] Since physical presence is no longer required according to *International Shoe Co. v. Washington*,[504] other (non-physical) contacts with or directed to the forum, are potentially jurisdiction-creating.[505] For example, phone calls,[506] advertisements in the forum or the formation of a contract in the forum, constitute 'contacts' leading to, or that may lead to, jurisdiction over an out-of-state defendant under the transacting business criterion.[507]

Like the 'doing business' concept it is difficult to come to a general understanding of which kind of contact constitutes sufficient affiliation with the forum for the 'transacting business' rule.[508] Again, generalizations are hard to make,[509] primarily because the language of long-arm statutes differs from state to state; transacting business includes the 'doing of an act' or carrying out 'any' business within the state.[510] An enormous amount of state and federal case law interpret the single-act provisions of transacting business on a case-by-case basis. Moreover, the one-step analysis embraced in some long-arm statutes results in an interpretation of the statute within the constitutional limits rather than in a strict interpretation of the

---

to establish specific jurisdiction is between the defendant, the forum, and the litigation.' *Republic Intern. Corp. v. Amco Engineers*, U.S. Court of Appeals, 9th Circuit, 516 F.2d 161 (1975). A plaintiff's performance in California cannot be given jurisdiction over a non-resident defendant under this section; it is defendant's activity that must provide the basis for jurisdiction. *Neogen Corp. v. Neo Gen Screening, Inc.*, U.S. Court of Appeals, 6th Circuit, 282 F.3d 883 (2002): 'Michigan's "long-arm" statute extends both "limited" and "general" jurisdiction over nonresident corporations; limited jurisdiction extends only to claims arising from the defendant's activities that were either within Michigan or had an in-state effect, while general jurisdiction enables a court in Michigan to exercise jurisdiction over a corporation regardless of whether the claim at issue is related to its activities in the state or has an in-state effect.'

503 See below for illustrations in New York cases.

504 326 U.S. 310 (1945).

505 See recently for Florida, District Court of Appeal, 1st District: 'For purposes of the Florida long-arm statute, telephonic, electronic, or written communications to Florida from an outside state can establish personal jurisdiction without the need that the defending party have a physical presence in the state.' *Becker v. Johnson*, 937 So.2d 1128, 1131 (2006).

506 For examples, see Sects. 5.6.3.2.-5.6.3.5. Generally one single phone call is not sufficient; contacts have to be evaluated in combination with other circumstances.

507 Of course the contacts have to be initiated by defendant to satisfy the due process clause under *Hanson v. Denckla*, 357 U.S. 235 (1958).

508 See in general the explanations of R. Brand, 'Understanding Activity-Based Jurisdiction', paper presented at The Preliminary Draft Hague Convention on Jurisdiction and Foreign Judgements in Civil and Commercial Matters, UIA Seminar Edinburgh, 20 and 21 April 2001.

509 See Casad and Richman, *Jurisdiction in Civil Actions Vol. 1*, at 398.

510 § 48.193 of the Florida Statute reads 'operating, conducting, engaging in, or carrying on a business or business venture in this state'. The Michigan Statute refers to 'transaction of any business within the state' for all four categories of defendants (§ 600.705(1) for individuals; § 600.715(1) for corporations; § 600.725(1) for partnerships and § 600.735(1) for associations). The Michigan Supreme Court held that '[w]ithin these sections "any" includes "each" and "every" and comprehends "the slightest".' *Sifers v. Horen*, Michigan Supreme Court, 188 N.W.2d 623 (1971). See more recently *Salom Enterprises, LLC v. TS Trim Industries, Inc.*, U.S. District Court, Eastern District of Michigan, 464 F. Supp.2d 676, at 638 (2006): 'Under Michigan long-arm statute, any business dealings may suffice to qualify as doing business in [a] state, and this includes even the slightest amount.' The New York Statute enumerated act § 302 provide for jurisdiction 'over any non-domiciliary, or his executor or administrator, who in person or through an agent *transacts any business* within the state' (emphasis added).

concepts used in the long-arm statute.[511] Section 410.10 of California's 'no limit' Statute evidently covers transacting business jurisdiction without having to enact a 'single-act' provision.[512] When a defendant has related minimum business contacts with California, the courts have jurisdiction within the limits of the due process requirements and will evaluate whether (1) defendant has purposefully availed himself of the forum's benefits; (2) the controversy is related to or arises out of the defendant's contacts with the forum; and (3) the assertion of personal jurisdiction would comport with fair play and substantial justice.[513]

5.6.3.2 *Specific Contacts for 'Transacting Business' Jurisdiction*

Under the wide spectrum of 'transacting business', the essential question is whether the contacts are substantially sufficient to establish special jurisdiction. It is important to note that no distinction is made based on the nature of the business

---

[511] See Casad and Richman, *Jurisdiction in Civil Actions Vol. 1*, at 398; Michigan applies a two-step analysis see *Green v. Wilson*, Supreme Court of Michigan, 455 Mich. 342 (1997) and *Jeffrey v. Rapid American*, Supreme Court of Michigan, 529 N.W.2d 644 (1995), 'When analyzing whether exercise of limited personal jurisdiction over a given defendant is proper, a two-step inquiry is generally applied: first, exercise of limited personal jurisdiction must be consistent with requirements of due process; and second, defendants must come within the terms of the long-arm statute which provides for limited personal jurisdiction over corporations'. However note that Casad indicates that Michigan courts sometimes use a single-step approach when the cause of action arises from the Michigan contact supported by a decision from the U.S. District Court, Eastern District of Michigan, *Williams v. Garcia*, 569 F. Supp. 1452 (1983), see Casad and Richman, *Jurisdiction in Civil Actions Vol. 1*, § 4-1[b], fn. 20, at 385. Florida also applies the two-step analysis: 'Requisite minimum contacts required by due process are not built into this section, *Venetian Salami Co. v. Parthenais*, Florida Supreme Court, 554 So.2d 499, at 500 (1989):

'By enacting section 48.193, the legislature has determined the requisite basis for obtaining jurisdiction over nonresident defendants as far as Florida is concerned. It has not specifically addressed whether the federal constitutional requirement of minimum contacts has been met. As a practical matter, it could not do so because each case will depend upon the facts.'

'[T]his has been called the Venetian Salami standard' in *Wendt v. Horowitz*, Supreme Court Florida, 822 So.2d 1252, at 1257 (2002). See *Sculptchair, Inc. v. Century Arts*, U.S. Court of Appeals, 11th Circuit, 94 F.3d 623, 626 (1996); *Posner v. Essex Ins.*, U.S. Court of Appeals, 11th Circuit, 178 F.3d 1209 (1999). 'A federal court sitting in diversity may properly exercise jurisdiction over a defendant only if two requirements are met: (1) the state long-arm statute, and (2) the Due Process Clause of the Fourteenth Amendment.'

[512] See the terminology used by West's Annotated California Codes by the Judicial Council in its comment to § 410.10 to indicate that 'transacting business' jurisdiction invokes 'doing an act' (under 8 for individuals and under 6 for corporations): 'It is likewise reasonable that a state should exercise judicial jurisdiction over a nonresident individual as to causes of action arising from an act done, or caused to be done, by him in the state for pecuniary profit and having substantial consequences there even though the act is an isolated act not constituting the doing of business in the state.'

[513] *Matthew Pavlovich v. The Superior Court of Santa Clara County*, Supreme Court of California, 127 Cal.Rptr.2d 329 (335) (2002). But see also Californian Supreme Court decision *Archibald v. Cinerama Hotels*, 126 Cal.Rptr. 811, at 818 (1976), stating that to assert jurisdiction over a foreign corporation 'its activity must consist of an act done or transaction consummated in the forum state by which it purposefully avails itself of the privilege of conducting activities within the forum state, thus invoking the benefits and protections of its laws.' Other cases are *Data Disc, Inc. v. Systems Technology*, U.S. Court of Appeals, 9th Circuit, 557 F.2d 1280, at 1287 (1977); *Ballard v. Savage*, U.S. Court of Appeals, 9th Circuit, 65 F.3d 1495, 1498 (1995), following *Gordy v. Daily News*, U.S. Court of Appeals, 9th Circuit, 95 F.3d 829, 831-32 (1996).

carried out nor the nature of the contract, nor whether it involves business activities involving sales contracts, sale of real property, consumer or employment contracts, insurance contracts, distribution agreements, franchises, intellectual property or the shipment of goods,[514] as long as defendant directs business transactions to or in the forum and the claim arises out of these business activities, these contacts are potential jurisdiction-creating contacts.

Most of the 'single-act' provisions incorporated in the New York, Florida and Michigan Statutes accept one single, isolated business transaction or the 'slightest act of business' as a jurisdiction ground, provided that the contact is substantial enough, is related to the cause of action and is consistent with due process standards.[515] Several court decisions accepted the exercise of jurisdiction based on one substantial *isolated act* done in the state.[516]

But apart from these isolated acts upon which transacting business can be based, states generally consider the *nature and quality* of the *totality* of the defendant's contacts in order to satisfy 'transacting business' jurisdiction.[517] Under the Florida long-arm Statute, the defendant is amenable for suit if he 'carries on or operates a business' in Florida. Defendant's activities are considered collectively and are

---

[514] This is relevant while the 'European Model' does distinguish between certain business activities for jurisdictional purposes.

[515] *Neogen Corp. v. Neo Gen Screening, Inc.*, U.S. Court of Appeals of Michigan, 6th Circuit, 282 F.3d 883 (2002). See also *Meyer v. Auto Club Insurance Association*, Supreme Court of Florida, 492 So.2d 1314 (1986), stating that a mere unilateral act done by the plaintiff does not count under the transacting business criterion under the requisite minimum contacts mandated by the XIVth Amendment.

[516] See New York decisions holding that a 'single transaction would be sufficient to fulfil this requirement', as long as the relevant cause of action also arises from that transaction, *George Reiner & Co. v. Schwartz*, New York Court of Appeals, 41 N.Y.2d 648, 651 and 653 (1977); see also *Kreutter v. McFadden Oil*, New York Court of Appeals, 71 N.Y.2d 460, 467 (1988), *Longines-Wittnauer Watch Co. v. Barnes & Reinecke*, New York Court of Appeals, 15 N.Y.2d 443 (1965). For Michigan see *Woods v. Edgewater Amusement Park*, Michigan Supreme Court, 65 N.W.2d 12 (1969) and *Khalaf v. Bankers & Shippers Ins. Co.*, Michigan Supreme Court, 233 N.W.2d 696 (1975). A single transaction with a substantial connection with the state is sufficient to meet the 'minimum contacts' test with regard to the Michigan 'long-arm Statute'.

[517] For New York see *George Reiner & Co. v. Schwartz*, New York Court of Appeals, 41 N.Y.2d 648, at 651 (1977); repeated that 'In *Longines*, [New York Court of Appeals, 15 N.Y.2d 443 (1965)]; our court, after reviewing defendant's numerous New York activities, declined to determine the sufficiency of any one, instead holding that in combination they more than met the statutory, as well as the constitutional, standard'. For California, even though the long-arm provision has not incorporated a separate 'transacting business' rule, the Californian Supreme Court states that 'a foreign corporation may not be required to defend itself in a state court unless the "quality and nature" of its activity in relation to a particular cause of action make it fair to do so.' *Archibald v. Cinerama Hotels*, Supreme Court of California, 126 Cal.Rptr. 811, at 818 (1976). For Florida the relevant authorities are *Dinsmore v. Martin Blumenthal Associates*, Supreme Court of Florida, 314 So.2d 561, 564 (1975), quoted by *Sculptchair v. Century Arts*, U.S. Court of Appeals, 11th Circuit, 94 F.3d 623 (1996). In order to establish that a defendant is 'carrying on business' for the purposes of the long-arm statute, the activities of the defendant must be 'considered collectively and show a general course of business activity in the state for pecuniary benefit' (at 627).

required to show a general course of business activity in the state for pecuniary benefit.[518]

The U.S. Court of Appeals for the Second Circuit resumed and reaffirmed this with respect to the New York long-arm Statute in *Sunward Electronics Inc. v. Mc Donald*.[519] The Court held that several factors should be considered in determining whether an out-of-state defendant transacts business in New York, including: (i) whether the defendant has an on-going contractual relationship with a New York corporation;[520] (ii) whether the contract was negotiated or executed in New York and whether, after executing a contract with a New York business,[521] the defendant has visited New York for the purpose of meeting with parties to the contract regarding the relationship;[522] (iii) what the choice-of-law clause is in any such contract; and (iv) whether the contract requires franchisees to send notices and payments into the forum state or subjects them to supervision by the corporation in the forum state.[523] Each of these isolated contacts alone might not be substantial enough to establish jurisdiction, but '[t]he ultimate determination … is based on the totality of the circumstances'.[524]

5.6.3.3 *Meetings and Visits to the Forum*

Physical presence in the forum like visiting or having meetings in the state for business purposes, or soliciting business, negotiating a contract or selling one's products are rather significant factors for determining whether the transacting business rule applies.[525] By way of illustration, a 'clear' case in which a visit to the state

---

[518] *Future Technology Today, Inc. v. OSF Healthcare Systems*, U.S. Court of Appeals, 11th Circuit, 218 F.3d 1247 (2000); and see *Sculptchair, Inc. v. Century Arts*, U.S. Court of Appeals, 11th Circuit, 94 F.3d 623 (1996), citing *Dinsmore v. Martin Blumenthal Associates*, Supreme Court of Florida, 314 So.2d 561, 564 (1975).

[519] *Sunward Electronics, Inc. v. McDonald*, U.S. Court of Appeals, 2nd Circuit, New York, 362 F.3d 17, at 22 (2004). See also *Agency Rent A Car Sys., Inc. v. Grand Rent A Car Corp.*, U.S. Court of Appeals, 2nd Circuit, 98 F.3d 25, at 29 (1996).

[520] This contact was considered as relevant by the New York Court of Appeals in *George Reiner & Co. v. Schwartz*, 41 N.Y.2d 648, at 653 (1977).

[521] Again according to *George Reiner & Co. v. Schwartz*, 41 N.Y.2d 648, at 653, and also according to U.S. Court of Appeals, 2nd Circuit, in *Hoffritz*, 763 F.2d 55, at 60 (1985).

[522] *Cutco Industries, Inc. v. Naughton*, U.S. Court of Appeals, 2nd Circuit, 806 F.2d 361, at 367-368 (1986); and *Hoffritz*, 763 F.2d 55, at 60 (1985).

[523] *Cutco Industries, Inc. v. Naughton*, U.S. Court of Appeals, 2nd Circuit, 806 F.2d 361, at 368 (1986).

[524] According to *Agency Rent A Car Sys., Inc. v. Grand Rent A Car Corp.*, U.S. Court of Appeals, 2nd Circuit, 98 F.3d 25, 29 (1996), affirmed by *Sunward Electronics, Inc. v. McDonald*, C.A.2 (N.Y.), 362 F.3d 17, at 23 (2004), 'Although all factors are relevant, no one factor is dispositive and other factors may be considered.' See also Scoles, Hay *et al.*, *Conflict of Laws*, § 8.1, at 389; and see for an example of Michigan decisions *International Technologies Consultants, Inc. v. Euroglas S.A.*, U.S. Court of Appeals, 6th Circuit, 107 F.3d 386 (1997); *Velandra v. Regie Nationale des Usines Renault*, U.S. Court of Appeals, 6th Circuit, 336 F.2d 292 (1964).

[525] The 'clearest sort of case' to illustrate this is *George Reiner & Co., Inc. v. Schwartz*, New York Court of Appeals, 41 N.Y.2d 648, (653) (1973): 'Here, Schwartz was physically present in New York at the time the contract, establishing a continuing relationship between the parties, was negotiated and made and, the contract, made in New York, was the transaction out of which the cause of action arose. … [W]e have before us, as has been noted, a day which included interviewing, negotiating and

alone was considered as 'transacting business' was the New York case of *George Reiner & Co., Inc. v. Schwartz*.[526] The Court emphasized the fact that the defendant was physically present at the time the contract was made. Defendant's one-day visit to New York was considered of such a nature that the defendant was thought to have transacted business within the meaning of the statute, even though the alleged breach or performance did not take place in New York.[527] However, even though it is likely that defendant transacts business in the forum by visiting the forum for business purposes,[528] it is not a guarantee for jurisdiction.[529] Some cases show that a defendant's visit to the forum does not constitute sufficient activity in the state to assert transacting business jurisdiction.[530]

5.6.3.4 *Long-range Communications with the Forum to Transact Business*

Physical entrance in the forum is not a prerequisite to constitute transacting business jurisdiction. One court stated that '[i]ndeed, we question whether, in an age of e-mail and teleconferencing, the absence of actual personal visits to the forum is any longer of critical consequence.'[531] In *Burger King v. Rudzewicz*, the U.S.

---

contracting the purposeful creation of a continuing relationship with a New York corporation.' See also *Hi Fashion Wigs, Inc. v. Peter Hammond Advertising*, New York Court of Appeals, 347 N.Y.S.2d 47 (1973); *Conax Florida Corp. v. Astrium Ltd.*, U.S. District Court, M.D. Florida, 499 F. Supp.2d 1287 (2007); *Salom Enterprises, LLC v. TS Trim Industries, Inc.*, U.S. District Court, Michigan, 464 F. Supp.2d 676 (2006); *Sifers v. Horen*, Michigan Supreme Court, 188 N.W.2d 623 (1971).

[526] New York Court of Appeals, 41 N.Y.2d 648, (653) (1973).

[527] See also *Hi Fashion Wigs, Inc. v. Peter Hammond Advertising*, New York Court of Appeals, 347 N.Y.S.2d 47 (1973). The Michigan Supreme Court held that the acts of a Kentucky lawyer who on two different occasions came to Michigan and lectured at law seminars on negligence and who after discussion with plaintiff's Michigan counsel was retained to represent plaintiff was considered as 'transaction of any business in state' in the sense of § 600.705(1). In *Sifers v. Horen*, 177 N.W.2d 189 (1970) and in *Jeffrey v. Rapid American Corp.*, 529 N.W.2d 644 (1995), the Michigan Supreme Court stated that personal jurisdiction may not be avoided by a non-resident defendant corporation simply because defendant has never physically been present in the forum state.

[528] Richman and Reynolds, *Understanding Conflict of Laws*, at 89; and see Casad and Richman, *Jurisdiction in Civil Actions Vol. 1*, § 4-2[a](i), at 400.

[529] Born, *International Civil Litigation*, at 160.

[530] For New York this was the case in *McKee Electric Co. v. Rauland-Borg Corp.*, New York Court of Appeals, 20 N.Y.2d 377; 229 N.E.2d 604 (1967). Here a mere visit was refused as a jurisdiction basis fearing that 'every corporation whose officers or sales personnel happen to pass the time of day with a New York customer in New York [would run] the risk of being subjected to the personal jurisdiction of our courts', at 607. Alexander, *N.Y. McKinney's Consolidated Laws*, Comment 302:6. See also Casad and Richman, *Jurisdiction in Civil Actions Vol. 1*, § 4-2[a](i), at 400-401. See for a Michigan example *Simmons v. Allstate Life Ins.*, U.S. Court of Appeals, 6th Circuit 65 F.3d 526 (1995).

[531] *Agency Rent A Car System, Inc. v. Grand Rent A Car Corp.*, U.S. Court of Appeals, 2nd Circuit, 98 F.3d 25, at 30 (1996); *Parke-Bernet Galleries v. Franklyn*, U.S. Court of Appeals, 26 N.Y.2d 13, at 16 (1970). Also affirmed by the Florida Supreme Court in *Wendt v. Horowitz*, 822 So.2d 1252 (2002), 'physical presence is not necessarily required to satisfy the constitutionally mandated requirement of minimum contacts for purposes of Florida's long-arm statute.' The District Court of Appeal of Florida, 3rd District, stated in a 2006 decision 'Therefore, telephonic, electronic, or written communications into Florida may form the basis for personal jurisdiction if the alleged cause of action arises from those communications.' *Blumberg v. Steve Weiss & Co., Inc.*, District Court of Appeal, 3rd District, 922 So.2d 361, at 364 (2006). See also H. Müller, *Die Gerichtspflichtigkeit wegen 'doing business'*:

Supreme Court held a similar reasoning in relation to a claim arising out of a franchising agreement:

> 'Although territorial presence frequently will enhance a potential defendant's affiliation with a State and reinforce the reasonable foreseeability of suit there, it is an inescapable fact of modern commercial life that a substantial amount of business is transacted solely by mail and wire communications across state lines, thus obviating the need for physical presence within a State in which business is conducted.'[532]

'Contacts' – other than the defendant's entrance in the state to transact business – can constitute the jurisdictional foundation under long-arm statutes.[533] Long-range communications directed to a state by telephone, mail or other electronic means[534] could also constitute transacting business if the defendant purposefully engaged in commercial activities in a state even without ever setting a foot in the state.[535] These types of communication should be considered as relevant factors and can constitute 'minimum contacts' under the transacting business criterion. It is however required that they be sufficiently affiliated with the forum, otherwise they will still be denied as jurisdiction-creating contacts.[536] Unless defendant uses a

---

Ein Vergleich Zwischen Dem U.S.-amerikanischen und dem deutschen Zuständigkeitssystem (1992), Vol. 89, at 49-50.

532 *Burger King Corp. v. Rudzewicz*, 471 U.S. 462, at 476 (1985). In this case the U.S. Supreme Court had to interpret the jurisdiction asserted on the basis of the Florida long-arm Statute which specifically extends jurisdiction to any person, whether or not a citizen or resident of the state, who breaches a contract in the state by failing to perform acts that the contract requires to be performed there. See also below Sect. 5.6.4. for the contractual claims.

533 See *Fischbarg v. Doucet*, Supreme Court, Appellate Division, New York (1st Dep't), 832 N.Y.S.2d 164 (2007), where clients (defendants) were subject to jurisdiction under the New York long-arm Statute on the basis that clients transacted business with an attorney in New York. See also the New York Court of Appeals in *Deutsche Bank Securities, Inc. v. Montana Board of Investments*, 850 N.E.2d 1140, at 1143 (2006), where the Court held '[i]n short, when the requirements of due process are met, as they are here, a sophisticated institutional trader knowingly entering our state – whether electronically or otherwise – to negotiate and conclude a substantial transaction is within the embrace of the New York long-arm statute'. See for other examples *Otterbourg, Steindler, Houston & Rosen, P.C. v. Shreve City Apartments Ltd.*, 147 A.D.2d 327 (1989), 543 N.Y.S.2d 978, Supreme Court, Appellate Division (1st Dep't), New York, in which a general partner's active involvement in continuous negotiation and communication with a firm, gave rise to *in personam* jurisdiction; and see *Parke-Bernet Galleries v. Franklyn*, 26 N.Y.2d 13, at 18 (1970). See also Richman and Reynolds, *Understanding Conflict of Laws*, at 89.

534 Please note, without going further into details, that in the U.S. e-communications towards the state or the mere factor that a 'web site' is 'purposefully directed' to a state can constitute 'transacting business', *Neogen Corp. v. Neo Gen Screening*, U.S. Court of Appeals of Michigan, 6th Circuit, 109 F. Supp.2d 724 (2000), reversed 282 F.3d 883; *Panavision Intern., L.P. v. Toeppen*, U.S. District Court, Central District of California, 938 F. Supp. 616 (1996), affirmed 141 F.3d 1316. *Panavision Intern., L.P. v. Toeppen*, U.S. Court of Appeals, 9th Circuit (1998).

535 See for New York *Parke-Bernet Galleries, Inc. v. Franklyn*, New York Court of Appeals, 26 N.Y.2d 13, at 17 (1970); and *Ehrlich-Bober & Co., Inc. v. University of Houston*, New York Court of Appeals, 427 N.Y.S.2d 604 (1980), in which the combination of business transactions effectuated through telephone did provide for specific jurisdiction. See also Casad and Richman, *Jurisdiction in Civil Actions Vol. 1*, at 402.

536 See for instance the decision of the Michigan Supreme Court decision in *Witbeck v. Bill Cody's Ranch Inn*, 411 N.W.2d 439, 428 (1987). For an illustration from a Florida case, see *Sculptchair, Inc.*

telephone or any other means of communication to actively participate in business transactions, the general view is that such contacts alone are 'too insubstantial' to provide for personal jurisdiction.[537] Again the totality of the contacts or circumstances should be evaluated.

Whether mere solicitation of business in or directed to the forum by advertisement or other means of communication constitutes 'transacting business' was also questioned, but no clear answer is available as some cases have and others have not accepted transacting business on the basis of solicitation.[538] The U.S. Supreme Court in *Asahi Metal Industry Co., Ltd. v. Superior Court* has commented that advertising in a forum state could be sufficient to sustain jurisdiction if a product was actually sold in the forum state.[539]

5.6.3.5 *Financial Transactions and Bank Accounts*

It occurs that the 'transacting business' criterion is satisfied on the basis that a foreign (i.e. a Dutch) corporation maintained a bank account for payment in the forum state and that payments were made in that state as well. This was held to be sufficient under Section 302 of the New York's long-arm Statute to support jurisdiction over the plaintiff's action to recover money due in relation to the transac-

---

v. Century Arts, where a Canadian resident's telephone conversations with the Florida office and even a one hour meeting in Florida for contract negotiations or discussion of a contract to be performed wholly in Canada did not qualify as 'carrying on business or business venture' in Florida within the meaning of Florida's long-arm Statute (U.S. Court of Appeals, 11th Circuit, 94 F.3d 623 (1996)). But see *Banco Inversion, S.A. v. Celtic Finance Corp., S.A.*, District Court of Appeal of Florida, 4th District, 907 So.2d 704 (2005), in which a Spanish bank was considered to have sufficient minimum contacts with Florida to warrant the state's exercise of personal jurisdiction over the bank in a suit brought by a foreign corporation that had an office in the state. The fact that the bank made initial contact and maintained a relationship with the corporation through extensive letters and telephone calls to the corporation's Florida office, and the corporation logged hundreds of hours in consulting and performing other services for the bank from its Florida office. In New York jurisdiction has been denied in *Etra v. Matta*, New York Court of Appeals, 61 N.Y.2d 455 (1984), reaffirmed by *Bank Brussels Lambert v. Fiddler Gonzalez & Rodriguez*, U.S. Court of Appeals, 171 F.3d 779, at 788 (1999); see also *A. I Trade Fin. v. Petra Bank*, U.S. Court of Appeals, 2nd Circuit, 989 F.2d 76 (1993).

537 For New York see *Etra v. Matta*, New York Court of Appeals, 61 N.Y.2d 455, at 458-59 (1984). See also Born, *International Civil Litigation*, at 160.

538 See for New York *Liquid Carriers Corp. v. American Marine Corp.*, U.S. Court of Appeals, 2nd Circuit, 375 F.2d 951 (1967), where the solicitation of business and negotiation of the contracts was seen as transacting business and constitutional under the due process clause. But in *Fontanetta v. American Bd. of Internal Medicine*, U.S. Court of Appeals, 2nd Circuit, 303 F. Supp. 427 (1969), affirmed 421 F.2d 355, the Court did not allow transacting business jurisdiction. See also *Longines-Wittnauer Watch Co. v. Barnes & Reinecke, Inc.*, New York Court of Appeals, 15 N.Y.2d 443 (1965), certiorari denied 382 U.S. 905. See for the Supreme Court of California (State), *Archibald v. Cinerama Hotels*, 126 Cal.Rptr. 811 (1976); and *Bancroft & Masters, Inc. v. Augusta*, U.S. Court of Appeals, 9th Circuit, 223 F.3d 1082 (2000). The Michigan Supreme Court denied personal jurisdiction on 'transacting business' as an advertisement in a nationally distributed regional tour guide was not considered as sufficient contact with Michigan to confer long-arm jurisdiction, see *Witbeck v. Bill Cody's Ranch Inn*, 411 N.W.2d 439, 428 (1987). See also Casad and Richman, *Jurisdiction in Civil Actions Vol. 1*, § 4-2[a](ix), at 421-425; Müller, *Die Gerichtspflichtigkeit wegen 'doing business'*, at 25.

539 480 U.S. 102, at 112 (1987), even if it was in relation to the concept 'stream of commerce'. See also *Campbell v. Premier Cruise Lines*, U.S. Court of Appeals, 6th Circuit, 838 F.2d 470 (1988).

tions although defendant had no offices, employees or agents in New York, and the contracts were apparently negotiated and executed overseas.[540]

5.6.4 Specific Jurisdiction over Contractual Disputes

Most of the contractual disputes are likely to be covered by the transacting business criterion, provided that the contractual claim is related to the business activities carried out in the forum.[541] With respect to sales contracts, it is quite likely that the seller or buyer physically entered the forum, solicited business in the state, advertised or communicated to the state or even negotiated the contract in the state.[542] These contacts are crucial for establishing transacting business jurisdiction, which is then based on the defendant's business activities carried out in the state and not on the effect of the contract in the state. In other words transacting business is not specifically designed to establish jurisdiction on the basis of specific contractual claims or specific '*contractual contacts*' with the forum.[543] The place of negotiation of a contract or the place where the contract was formed, are potential jurisdiction-creating contacts, but they are in general insufficient to establish jurisdiction by themselves.[544] Additionally, the simple fact that a non-resident defendant entered

---

[540] *Indosuez International Finance B.V. v. National Reserve Bank*, New York Court of Appeals, 98 N.Y.2d 238 (2002). The fact that having a bank account could constitute transacting business and provide for limited/specific personal jurisdiction can be seen as jurisdiction based on defendant's property. See below Sect. 5.7. See also Alexander, *N.Y. McKinney's Consolidated Laws* (2002), Comment C 302:6, who notes that the Court of Appeals cites a lower court's decision *Banco Ambrosiano, S.P.A. v. Artoc Bank & Trust*, Court of Appeals of New York, 62 N.Y.2d 65 (1984), in which jurisdiction was based on the attachment of a New York bank account that played a role in the transaction sued upon. See also Casad and Richman, *Jurisdiction in Civil Actions Vol. 1*, § 4-2, at 425-427, for jurisdiction over claims concerning promissory notes. In Michigan a foreign bank that issued a letter of credit indicating a Michigan resident as beneficiary did not have sufficient minimum contacts with Michigan to support exercise of personal jurisdiction in Michigan for an action arising when payment under the letter was denied. No other factor which might have been relevant, such as whether the bank did possess assets in Michigan, was present to support jurisdiction, see *Chandler v. Barclays Bank PLC*, U.S. Court of Appeals, 6th Circuit, 898 F.2d 1148 (1990). In Florida a correspondent relationship between a foreign bank and a Florida bank did not, by itself, constitute conducting business in Florida so as to subject the foreign bank to long-arm jurisdiction in Florida, see *Oriental Imports and Exports, Inc. v. Maduro & Curiel's Bank, N.V.*, U.S. Court of Appeals, 11th Circuit, 701 F.2d 889 (1983).

[541] Casad and Richman, *Jurisdiction in Civil Actions Vol. 2*, § 8-1, at 158; A. Lowenfeld, *Conflict of Laws: Federal, State and International Perspectives* (2002), § 7.03, at 525.

[542] See for a more detailed research in sales contracts and business contacts with the forum of both seller and buyer, Born, *International Civil Litigation*, at 159; Scoles, Hay *et al.*, *Conflict of Laws*, § 8.5, at 397-398; Casad and Richman, *Jurisdiction in Civil Actions Vol. 1*, § 4-2[a](i), at 399-405 and § 4-2[a](ii), at 405-412; Schack, *Jurisdictional Minimum Contacts Scrutinized*, at 40-41.

[543] To use the words of Scoles 'Contract cases are subject to the same basic jurisdictional methodology as other cases.' Scoles, Hay *et al.*, *Conflict of Laws*, § 8.1, at 386; Schack, *Jurisdictional Minimum Contacts Scrutinized*, at 41.

[544] The place where the contract was made can be merely technical, for instance if the offer was accepted by coincidence in a random place it will often not be seen as 'reasonable', Weintraub, *Commentary*, § 4.18, at 245; Schack, *Jurisdictional Minimum Contacts Scrutinized*, at 41. But see *DeMarco v. Cayman Overseas Reinsurance Ass'n, Ltd.*, District Court of Appeal of Florida, 1st District, 460 So.2d 547, at 549 (1984), in which a single act of signing a contractual agreement within the forum state constituted 'sufficient minimum contacts to sustain the exercise of in personam jurisdiction over a nonresident in subsequent suit for breach of the agreement.' See dissenting opinion Judge Nimmons

into a contractual relationship with, for instance, a Californian resident is generally not considered sufficient for Californian courts to have specific jurisdiction.[545]

According to the Supreme Court, a state can exercise jurisdiction on the basis that the contract has 'substantial connection with that State'.[546] In *McGee v. International Life Insurance*, a case concerning a contractual (insurance) relationship, the insurance policy sold in the forum was found substantial enough to constitute minimum contacts.[547] As explained above,[548] this means that defendant who has not made any contact with the state, but whose activities, acts or operations were carried out outside the forum, nevertheless caused an effect in the state and could therefore be subjected to jurisdiction on the basis of this minimum contact.[549]

'No limits' statutes, such as the California long-arm Statute, do not include 'single-act' provisions as the general provision allows the exercise of jurisdiction on any constitutionally permissible basis. According to the Californian Judicial Council, jurisdiction on the basis of 'causing effect by act or omission elsewhere' is however available under the *no limit* long-arm statute.[550]

Contacts between corporate defendants and the Californian State arising out of a breach of contract or for goods sold and delivered in the forum were considered more than sufficient to subject defendants to Californian courts.[551] In *Kulko v. Su-*

---

who 'cannot agree that the single act of DeMarco's signing the subject agreement in Florida was sufficient to sustain the trial court's exercise of in personam jurisdiction under Section 48.181(1), Florida Statutes, where performance of the agreement's obligations was to occur in the Cayman Islands, home of the obligee.'

545 See *Aquila, Inc. v. Superior Court*, Court of Appeal, 4th District, Division 1, California, 148 Cal.App.4th 556, at 572 (2007), review denied: 'it is not enough for a nonresident defendant to become subject to the specific jurisdiction of this state simply by entering into a contract with a California resident.' For Florida see the clear statement of the U.S. Court of Appeal, 11th Circuit, citing *Burger King Corp. v. Rudzewicz*, 471 U.S. 462, at 475 (1985) and arguing that the 'existence of contractual relationship between nonresident defendant and Florida resident is not sufficient in itself to meet due process requirements for exercise of jurisdiction over nonresident defendant.' *Jet Charter Service, Inc. v. Koeck*, U.S. Court of Appeals, 11th Circuit, 907 F.2d 1110, at 1113 (1990), rehearing denied 919 F.2d 742, certiorari denied 499 U.S. 937. See for New York rejecting *general* jurisdiction: 'The existence of contractual relationships with entities that happen to have operations in New York does not establish § 301 jurisdiction, because it does not show extensive conduct directed toward or occurring in New York.' *Reers v. Deutsche Bahn AG*, Southern District of New York, 320 F. Supp.2d 140, 150 (2004).

546 *McGee v. International Life*, 355 U.S. 220, at 223 (1957), quoted by *Hanson v. Denckla*, 357 U.S. 235, at 252 (1958); and *Burger King Corp. v. Rudzewicz*, 471 U.S. 462, at 475 (1985).

547 355 U.S. 220, at 223-224 (1957); Scoles, Hay *et al.*, *Conflict of Laws*, § 8.1, at 387; Borchers, 'Comparing Jurisdiction', at 137.

548 See above Sect. 5.6.3.

549 See also Müller, *Die Gerichtspflichtigkeit wegen 'doing business'*, at 53.

550 As identified in the comments of West's Annotated California Codes § 410.10(9) for individuals and (7) for corporations: 'A state has a natural interest in the effects of an act within its territory even though the act itself was done elsewhere. The state may exercise judicial jurisdiction on the basis of such effects over the individual who did the act, or who caused the act to be done, provided that the nature of these effects and of the individual's relationship to the state are such as to make the exercise of jurisdiction fair to the individual and reasonable from the standpoint of the international and interstate systems. . . .'

551 *Ameron v. Anvil Industries*, U.S. Court of Appeals, 9th Circuit, 524 F.2d 1144 (1975); see also *Roth v. Garcia Marquez*, U.S. Court of Appeals, 9th Circuit, 942 F.2d 617 (1991).

perior Court, which involved a family matter and not a contractual dispute, the jurisdictional foundation 'causing an effect', based on the Californian Statute, was addressed to the U.S. Supreme Court.[552] The Court held that jurisdiction based on 'causing an effect' in the state arising out of an activity carried out outside the state was only proper if it affected (claimant) residents inside the state.[553]

Several enumerated long-arm statutes felt the need to incorporate 'causing an effect' provisions regulating specific jurisdiction over contractual claims.[554] The contact is then not based on defendant's activities in the state but on the effect that the defendant's activities, carried out elsewhere by virtue of a contractual obligation, has caused in the state. In other words, jurisdiction is founded on an isolated contractual transaction.[555]

For instance, the New York Statute contains an additional provision to assert specific jurisdiction when the contract concluded elsewhere requires performing or supplying goods or providing services in the state. Section 302 of the New York Statute permits assertion of extraterritorial jurisdiction where the plaintiff's 'cause of action arises from a contract to supply goods or services in the state'.[556] This way the New York courts still have jurisdiction even when the contract was not concluded in the state or when the business activities were not carried out in the state.[557] The *supply-of-goods-or-services provision* was also known in Section

[552] 436 U.S. 84 (1978). The defendant was a divorced father who was a New York resident and had not sought commercial benefit from solicitation of business from a Californian resident, the California court relied on the fact that the father had caused an 'effect' in California as a basis for exercising jurisdiction over the divorced father in the divorced mother's action.

[553] 436 U.S. 84, at 96 (1978), or caused an injury inside the state. See Casad and Richman, *Jurisdiction in Civil Actions Vol. 1*, at 96, compare with the Supreme Court decision in *McGee v. International Life Ins. Co.*, where the Californian Statute also gave rise to questions whether acts done outside the state would be a proper basis for jurisdiction. See also the Californian Cases of *Sibley v. Superior Court*, Supreme Court of California (1976) 128 Cal.Rptr. 34, at 36; and *Forsythe v. Overmyer*, U.S. Court of Appeals, 9th Circuit, California, 576 F.2d 779 (1978), certiorari denied 439 U.S. 864, 'Under provision of this section of the statute and due process clause, defendant may be subject to California jurisdiction when he has caused effect in this state by act or omission elsewhere; jurisdiction properly rests on effects' rationale unless the nature of effects and of individuals' relationship to the state make exercise of such jurisdiction unreasonable.'

[554] These single-act provisions belong to the 'causing an effect' category of provisions mentioned above. Lowenfeld, *Conflict of Laws*, at 525.

[555] Weintraub, *Commentary*, § 4.18, at 240.

[556] This 'supply of goods provision' was added in § 302's amendment in 1979. § 302 is limited to claims arising from transactions of business within the state or contracts anywhere to supply goods or services in the state. The Michigan Statute incorporated into each relevant section for jurisdiction over individuals (§ 600.705), corporations (§ 600.715) in paragraph (5), jurisdiction over defendants entering into a contract for services to be rendered or for materials to be furnished in the state by the defendant.

[557] For New York this entails 'to permit the assertion of long-arm jurisdiction where the plaintiff's cause of action arises from a contract to supply goods or services in the state', without regard to where the contract was made. This provision was intended to overcome judicial rulings that narrowly interpreted the meaning of 'transaction of business' in New York where the New York Court of Appeals had several times held that a mere shipment in the state was not enough to qualify for 'transacting business'. *McKee Electric Co. v. Rauland-Borg*, 20 N.Y.2d 377 (1967); *Agrashell, Inc. v. Bernard Sirotta Co.*, New York Court of Appeals, 344 F.2d 583 (1965); *Standard Wine & Liquor Co. v. Bombay Spirits*,

1-3(2) of the Uniform Interstate and International Procedure Act.[558] The rationale behind this kind of provision is obviously related to the fact that such a supply of goods or services 'causes an effect' in a state from an act done out of state. Also in a more general sense, a defendant who purposefully seeks to benefit from a state's commercial market by agreeing to supply or ship goods or perform services in the state can reasonably expect to be sued in that state for either faulty performance or non-performance of the agreement.[559] As a consequence, it was held that when goods were shipped to New York under a contract entered into by plaintiff and defendants, the exercise of jurisdiction by New York courts was proper.[560] Because of their nature, some goods and services are excluded from the scope of application of this supply provision.[561]

In Michigan, courts applied a similar provision asserting jurisdiction over defendant 'entering into a contract for services to be rendered or for materials to be furnished in the state by the defendant' with less hesitance.[562]

Florida adopted a slightly different kind of provision, establishing jurisdiction over 'any cause of action arising from the doing of the act breaching a contract in the state by failing to perform acts required by the contract to be performed' in

---

Court of Appeals of New York, 20 N.Y.2d 13 (1967); *Kramer v. Vogl*, 17 N.Y.2d 27 (1966). See also comment 302:8. Subdivision (a)(1): Contract to Supply Goods or Services in New York.

[558] 'A court may exercise personal jurisdiction over a person, who acts directly or by an agent, as to the cause of action, claim for relief arising from the person's contracting to supply services or things in this state.' Chap. 3, topic 1, of the 2nd Restatement of Conflict of Laws, does not specifically mention such a supply-of-goods-or-services provision.

[559] See *Bank Brussels Lambert v. Fiddler Gonzalez & Rodriguez*, U.S. Court of Appeals, 2nd Circuit, 171 F.3d 779, at 789 (1999). And see also Alexander, *N.Y. McKinney's Consolidated Laws*, Comment 302:8. Such a rationale was also held under the notion of 'implied consent' to accept the doing business criterion.

[560] See *Mario Valente Collezioni, Ltd. v. Confezioni Semeraro Paolo*, U.S. District Court, Southern District of New York, 115 F. Supp.2d 367 (2000). In that case the U.S. Court of Appeals, 2nd Circuit, 264 F.3d 32 (2001) remanded the case to the district court to perform the necessary federal due process analysis which it had failed to make, but the district court found (174 F.Supp.2d 170 (2001) that its exercise of *in personam* jurisdiction over the defendant comported with due process. *Contra Bank Brussels Lambert v. Fiddler Gonzalez & Rodriguez*, U.S. Court of Appeals, 2nd Circuit, 171 F.3d 779, at 789 (1999), where jurisdiction on this basis was rejected because 'defendant never projected itself into New York to perform services in the state and never purposefully availed itself of the privileges and benefits of performing any services in the state.' The case contains a brief outline of the lower court cases ruling over this provision. In *Galgay v. Bulletin*, U.S. Court of Appeals, 2nd Circuit, 504 F.2d 1062, at 1066 (1974), the shipment of goods to an out-of-state defendant by a New York plaintiff via common carrier (f.o.b.) was not enough to satisfy this 'supply of goods provision' following *Agrashell, Inc. v. Bernard Sirotta*, U.S. Court of Appeals, 2nd Circuit, 344 F.2d 583 (1965).

[561] Such as for instance trademark services. The U.S. Court of Appeals rejected jurisdiction in *Beacon Enterprises, Inc. v. Menzies*, 715 F.2d 757 (1983), and with respect to medical treatment and the provision of an experimental drug, the New York Court of Appeals rejected jurisdiction on this basis in *Etra v. Matta*, 61 N.Y.2d 455 (1984).

[562] *Neogen Corp. v. Neo Gen Screening*, U.S. Court of Appeals, 6th Circuit, 282 F.3d 883, at 889 (2000), 'When [defendant] provided passwords to Michigan customers or mailed them the test results, this constituted the performance of services and the furnishing of materials in the state within the meaning of § 600.715(5).' See also *Theunissen v. Matthews*, U.S. Court of Appeals, 6th Circuit, 935 F.2d 1454, at 1464 (1991).

Florida.[563] This provision embodied in Section 48.193(g) of the Florida Statute was interpreted in several cases.[564] The localization of the breach is problematic when the required performance did not take place and the claim directly arises out of the contractual breach.[565] First of all, it must be clear from the contract that the place of performance was meant to be Florida. In other words, a duty to perform or act in Florida must exist, for even the contractual duty to perform in Florida is in itself not sufficient to constitute a breach in Florida.[566] When the requested performance involves payment to the plaintiff, the U.S. Court of Appeals assumes that non-payment of the amount due under the contract constitutes a breach of the agreement and that plaintiff complies with that part of the long-arm statute under Section 48.193(1)(g).[567]

One has to keep in mind that the exercise of jurisdiction on the basis of these provisions specifically aiming at a particular effect caused by contract in the forum is still subjected to due process limitations and that the defendant has to have purposefully directed the contacts to the forum.[568] In *Burger King Corp. v. Rudzewicz*, which dealt with a franchise agreement, the Supreme Court held that '[i]f the question is whether an individual's contract with an out-of-state party alone can automatically establish sufficient minimum contacts in the other party's home forum, we believe the answer clearly is that it cannot.'[569] More affiliating contacts are needed to establish jurisdiction over a contractual claim, than the mere fact that a contract was concluded with a forum resident.[570] In the *Burger King Corp. v. Rudzewicz* case, the Supreme Court examined whether the application of the Florida 'place of performance' rule was consistent with constitutional guarantees

---

563 Florida Statute § 48.193(g). See Lookofsky and Hertz, *Transnational Litigation*, at 253.

564 *Cronin v. Washington*, U.S. Court of Appeals, 11th Circuit, Florida, 980 F.2d 663 (1993).

565 Weintraub, *Commentary*, § 4.18, at 240; H. Schack, *Der Erfüllungsort im deutschen, ausländischen und internationalen Privat- und Zivilprozeßrecht* (1985), § 301, at 209; Schack, *Jurisdictional Minimum Contacts Scrutinized*, at 43.

566 *Posner v. Essex Ins.*, U.S. Court of Appeals, 11th Circuit, 178 F.3d 1209 (1999). When such a duty to perform in Florida does not exist, defendant cannot fail to perform and therefore jurisdiction based on the § 48.193(g) provision cannot be supported.

567 *Future Technology Today, Inc. v. OSF Healthcare Systems*, U.S. Court of Appeals, 11th Circuit, 218 F.3d 1247, at 1250 (2000). See the recent decision in *Balboa v. Assante*, District Court of Appeal of Florida, 4th District, 958 So.2d 573, at 574 (2007), in which the Court accepted jurisdiction in the absence of express designation of a place of payment. The Court presumed that the debt was to be paid at creditor's place of business, and this presumption is sufficient to satisfy the provision of Florida's long-arm Statute subjecting a person to a state's jurisdiction based upon breach of contract resulting from the person's failure to perform acts to be performed in a state. See *contra Banco Continental, S.A. v. Transcom Bank (Barbados), Ltd.*, District Court of Appeal of Florida, 3rd District, 922 So.2d 395, at 399 (2006), 'A failure to pay money in Florida, without more, is insufficient to satisfy the constitutional due process minimum contacts requirement for asserting personal jurisdiction over a nonresident'. See also *Venetian Salami Co. v. Parthenais*, 554 So.2d 499, at 503 (1989), 'Mere failure to pay money in Florida, standing alone, would not suffice to obtain jurisdiction over [a] non-resident defendant'. See in general Weintraub, *Commentary*, § 4.18, at 243.

568 See especially P. Hay, 'Refining Personal Jurisdiction in the United States', 35 *The International and Comparative Law Quarterly* (1986), 32-62, at 42-47.

569 471 U.S. 462, at 463 (1985).

570 Born, *International Civil Litigation*, § 1, at 158.

and notions of substantial justice and fair play and especially the requirement of 'purposeful availment':[571]

> 'the Court long ago rejected the notion that personal jurisdiction might turn on "mechanical" tests, or on "conceptualistic ... theories of the place of contracting or of performance," ... Instead, we have emphasized the need for a "highly realistic" approach that recognizes that a "contract" is "ordinarily but an intermediate step serving to tie up prior business negotiations with future consequences which themselves are the real object of the business transaction." ... It is these factors – prior negotiations and contemplated future consequences, along with the terms of the contract and the parties' actual course of dealing – that must be evaluated in determining whether the defendant purposefully established minimum contacts within the forum.'[572]

Hence, although jurisdiction was based on the statutory authorization of the Florida 'place of performance rule', due process standards require the examination of the totality of defendant's contacts with the forum.[573]

To summarize, the 'causing an effect' provisions such as the supply-of-goods-or-services rule, are alternatively applicable to assert jurisdiction to the transacting business criterion.[574] A variety of jurisdiction bases are available for contractual claims: the place of the formation,[575] the place of negotiations, the place of performance,[576] or execution,[577] the place for the supply of goods or of service following the contract,[578] and even the choice of law governing the contract.[579]

5.6.5 Minimum Contacts through a Branch, an Agent or Subsidiary

As explained above, the U.S. jurisdictional structure entails that the claimant should primarily seek to establish specific jurisdiction, but when the claim is un-

---

[571] See Sect. 5.4.1.

[572] *Burger King Corp. v. Rudzewicz*, 471 U.S. 462, at 478 (1985).

[573] Scoles, Hay *et al.*, *Conflict of Laws*, § 8.1, at 389.

[574] See for the application of the supply of goods provisions of all these contracts § 8-1 to 8-12 of Casad and Richman, *Jurisdiction in Civil Actions Vol. 2*; and for the notion of transacting business in contracts, Casad and Richman, *Jurisdiction in Civil Actions Vol. 1*, § 4-2; Schack, *Jurisdictional Minimum Contacts Scrutinized*, at 45-46.

[575] See for Florida, U.S. Court of Appeals, 11th Circuit, *Williams Elec. Co., Inc. v. Honeywell*, 854 F.2d 389 (1988).

[576] § 302 of the New York Statute.

[577] The fact that the final execution of the contract takes place in New York is, in and of itself insufficient to confer jurisdiction under this section relating to personal jurisdiction by acts of non-domiciliaries, see *Standard Wine & Liquor Co. v. Bombay Spirits*, Court of Appeals of New York, 20 N.Y.2d 13 (1967); *Galgay v. Bulletin Co., Inc.*, U.S. Court of Appeals, 2nd Circuit, New York, 504 F.2d 1062 (1974).

[578] It can occur that the place of performance coincides with the place where the goods are required to be supplied; likewise some contracts are to be performed through delivery of the goods.

[579] Born, *International Civil Litigation*, at 161; Scoles, Hay *et al.*, *Conflict of Laws*, § 8.1, at 388. According to the U.S. Court of Appeals, 2nd Circuit, interpreting the New York Statute under § 302(1)(a); 'A choice of law clause is a significant factor in a personal jurisdiction analysis because the parties, by choosing, invoke the benefits and protection of New York law.' *Sunward Electronics, Inc. v. McDonald*, U.S. Court of Appeals, 2nd Circuit, New York, 362 F.3d 17, at 22-23 (2004), quoting *Cutco Indus. v. Naughon*, U.S. Court of Appeals, 806 F.2d 361, at 367 (1986).

related to defendant's contacts the claimant will have to rely on the doing business of the foreign (corporate) defendant on the basis of continuous and systematic contacts with the forum.

Depending on the quality and nature of his *direct* contacts the defendant will be subjected either to transacting business or doing business. As explained above, the fact that a foreign corporation maintains an office in the forum contributes to the establishment of 'continuous and systematic' contacts for 'doing business' jurisdiction over claims unrelated to the branch's activities in the forum and unrelated to the corporation's activities as a whole.[580]

But the establishment of a branch, office or agent in the forum is not always considered as a foreign corporation's *own* contacts with the forum.[581] Foreign corporations frequently operate *through* a branch, agent or subsidiary situated in the forum.[582] This relates to the question whether the branch's contacts can be 'imputed' to the foreign corporate defendant to subject him to jurisdiction.[583] The contacts of this 'other' (independent) agent,[584] office, independent contractor,[585] or affiliated company such as a subsidiary, will be attributed to the foreign company. Even franchisees and distributors conducting business for foreign corporations can as a result end up being in imputed contacts to a foreign corporation.[586] Depending

---

[580] *Berner v. United Airlines*, New York Court of Appeals, 3 A.D.2d 9 (1956). See also Michigan Court of Appeals in *Kircos v. Lola Cars*, 'foreign corporation must actually be present within the forum state on a regular basis, either personally or through an agent, in order to be subjected to general personal jurisdiction.' 296 N.W.2d 32 (1980); and see in Florida U.S. Court of Appeals, 11th Circuit, *Meier ex rel. Meier v. Sun Intern. Hotels*, 288 F.3d 1264 (2002), Florida long-arm Statute allows the extension of general jurisdiction to a non-resident corporation based on the activities of that corporation's agent, subsidiary or related corporation.

[581] Born, *International Civil Litigation*, at 165.

[582] Having established an office in the forum is rarely used as a *direct* connecting factor under long-arm provisions. The long-arm Statute of Florida contains a specific jurisdictional provision to subject a foreign corporation on the basis of 'having an office or agency in the state', but the majority of enumerated acts merely provide for jurisdiction over a person who transacts business either directly or through an agent. Florida Statute § 48.193(1)(a), last sentence, reads that the state has jurisdiction over 'Any person, whether or not a citizen or resident of this state, who personally *or through an agent* does any of the acts enumerated in this subsection … (a) Operating, conducting, engaging in, or carrying on a business or business venture in this state *or having an office or agency in this state*.' (emphasis added) The New York long-arm Statute in CPLR § 302(a) provides for jurisdiction over a defendant on the basis of the acts of that defendant 'in person or through an agent'.

[583] Born, *International Civil Litigation*, at 165; Casad and Richman, *Jurisdiction in Civil Actions Vol. 1*, at 476-477.

[584] Casad and Richman, *Jurisdiction in Civil Actions Vol. 1*, § 3-2[2](v), at 349-352.

[585] But see *Sculptchair, Inc. v. Century Arts*, U.S. Court of Appeals, 11th Circuit, 94 F.3d 623 (1996), where a Canadian sales-representative was seen as an independent contractor rather than an agent; there was no evidence that the corporation exercised any type of meaningful control over representative's marketing of its product line, and representative set her own hours and chose her own marketing methods; thus her activities could not be attributed to defendant within the meaning of Florida's long-arm Statute. For Michigan see *Long Manufacturing Company v. Wright-way Farm*, Supreme Court of Michigan, 391 Mich. 82 (1974), in which doing business through independent contractors was rejected.

[586] Bermann, *Transnational Litigation*, at 67. See for some cases dealing with the question whether distributors' and franchisees' contacts can be attributed to foreign corporations *Standard Wine & Liquor Co. v. Bombay Spirits*, New York Supreme Court, 268 N.Y.S.2d 602 (1966), motion denied

on the quality and nature of those *imputed* or *indirect* contacts the defendant will be subjected to either specific or general jurisdiction.[587]

U.S. courts apply two theories to attribute contacts of a branch, an office, an agent or subsidiaries to a foreign corporation for jurisdictional purposes: the *agency relationship* theory and the *alter ego* theory in a parent-subsidiary relationship. In the words of the California Court of Appeals

> 'Encompassed within the purview of general jurisdiction over a nonresident corporate defendant are the theories of alter ego and agency; ...[588] under these theories, the jurisdictional analysis bypasses the foreign defendant's direct minimum contacts with California, as these contacts are imputed via the presence of a local agent, through whom the foreign principal acts.'[589]

5.6.5.1 *The Agency Relationship*

Whether the foreign company maintains an agency relationship in the forum with one of its business partners is difficult to define as the majority of the long-arm statutes do not define the notion 'agent' for jurisdiction purposes.[590] Whether or not a foreign company has an agent doing or transacting business on its behalf depends on the realities of the relationship between them and not on the question whether the agent satisfied the formalities of agency law.[591] Although the requirements for an agency relationship vary from one state to another, an agent's business contacts can generally be attributed to a foreign corporation when the representative 1) has acted for the benefit and on behalf of the foreign corporate defendant,[592] 2) with his

19 N.Y.2d 602, affirmed 20 N.Y.2d 13; *Dinsmore v. Martin Blumenthal Associates*, Supreme Court of Florida, 314 So.2d 561 (1975); *AB CTC v. Morejon*, Supreme Court of Florida, 324 So.2d 625 (1975). A particular franchisee relationship as 'agency' doing business in New York was refused in *Landoil Resources Corp. v. Alexander & Alexander Services*, New York Court of Appeals, 77 N.Y.2d 28 (1990); see also Casad and Richman, *Jurisdiction in Civil Actions Vol. 1*, § 3-2(b)(vi), at 352.

[587] The defendant can be subjected to jurisdiction under the transacting business criterion for claims relating to a branch's activities in the state if it carries out business through that branch or agent, *Parke-Bernet Galleries, Inc. v. Franklyn*, New York Court of Appeals, 26 N.Y.2d 13 (1970); *Ecclesiastical Order of Ism of Am, Inc. v. Chasin*, U.S. Court of Appeals, 6th Circuit, 653 F. Supp. 1200 (1986).

[588] '[O]f which the representative services doctrine is a species'.

[589] *F. Hoffman-La Roche, Inc. v. Superior Court*, District Court of Appeal, 6th District, 30 Cal.Rptr.3d 407, at 418 (2005).

[590] Born, *International Civil Litigation*, at 179; Bermann, *Transnational Litigation*, at 66.

[591] *Galgay v. Bulletin Co.*, New York Court of Appeals, 2nd Circuit, 504 F.2d 1062, at 1065 (1974): 'In determining whether an agency exists under [New York Statute] § 302 courts have focused on the realities of the relationship in question rather than the formalities of agency law.' Affirmed by *Wiwa v. Royal Dutch Petroleum Co.*, New York Court of Appeals, 2nd Circuit, 226 F.3d 88, at 95 (2000), certiorari denied 121 S.Ct. 1402, 532 U.S. 941, 149 L.Ed.2d 345. See also for Florida *Pesaplastic, C.A. v. Cincinnati Milacron*, U.S. Court of Appeals, 11th Circuit, 750 F.2d 1516, at 1522 (1985).

[592] In the words of the U.S. Court of Appeals, 11th Circuit, regarding the Florida long-arm Statute, the court may extend jurisdiction to any foreign corporation where the affiliated domestic corporation manifests no separate corporate interests of its own and functions solely to achieve the purpose of the dominant corporation, *Meier ex rel. Meier v. Sun Intern. Hotels, Ltd.*, U.S. Court of Appeals, 11th Circuit, 288 F.3d 1264 (2002).

knowledge and authorization, and 3) when the non-resident defendant exercised some control over the 'agent'.[593]

The agency-relationship theory is also applicable to subsidiaries acting as 'agents' for their parent company located outside the forum. In that context, California adopted a particular 'agency test' which would be

> 'satisfied by a showing that the subsidiary functions as the parent corporation's representative in that it performs services that are "sufficiently important to the foreign corporation that if it did not have a representative to perform them, the corporation's own officials would undertake to perform substantially similar services."'[594]

A similar reasoning was held in the leading New York case *Frummer v. Hilton Hotels International* in which the Hilton U.K. parent corporation was considered to do business in New York through its subsidiary Hilton Reservation Service which directly accepted and confirmed reservations at the London Hilton.[595] The Reservation Service hereby acted as the London Hilton's agent while doing 'all business which Hilton (UK) could do were it here by its own officials'.[596] The Court justified its decision by stating that it is

> 'not unmindful that litigation in a foreign jurisdiction is a burdensome inconvenience for any company. However, it is part of the price which may properly be demanded of those who extensively engage in international trade. When their activities abroad, either directly or through an agent become as widespread and energetic as the activities in New York conducted by Hilton (U.K.) they receive considerable benefits from such foreign business and may not be heard to complain about the burdens.'[597]

In *Wiwa v. Royal Dutch Shell Petroleum*, the Dutch defendant Royal Dutch and English defendant Shell Transport jointly controlling the Shell Group were sued in New York by Nigerian claimants for human rights abuses against their families, which occurred in Nigeria. Although the defendant did not directly have 'doing

---

[593] See Born, *International Civil Litigation*, at 180. With respect to § 302 of the New York Statute see *Kreutter v. McFadden Oil*, New York Court of Appeals, 71 N.Y.2d 460 (1988); *Cutco Industries, Inc. v. Naughton*, U.S. Court of Appeals, 2nd Circuit, 806 F.2d 361 (1986); *Frummer v. Hilton Hotels International, Inc.*, New York Court of Appeals, 19 N.Y.2d 533 (1967), certiorari denied 389 U.S. 923. For Florida see *Meier ex rel. Meier v. Sun Intern. Hotels, Ltd.*, U.S. Court of Appeals Florida, 11th Circuit, 288 F.3d 1264 (2002); *Pesaplastic, C.A. v. Cincinnati Milacron*, U.S. Court of Appeals, 11th Circuit, 750 F.2d 1516 (1985); and see for the 'control issue' which was addressed and refused in *AB CTC v. Morejon*, Florida Supreme Court, 324 So.2d 625 (1975).

[594] *Doe v. Unocal Corp.*, U.S. Court of Appeals, 9th Circuit, 248 F.3d 915, at 928 (2001), repeated in *Aquila, Inc. v. Superior Court*, District Court of Appeal, 4th District, 148 Cal.App.4th 556 (2007), review denied.

[595] *Frummer v. Hilton Hotels International, Inc.*, New York Court of Appeals, 19 N.Y.2d 533 (1967), affirmed among others in *Wiwa v. Royal Dutch Petroleum Co.*, 2nd Circuit, 226 F.3d 88, 95 (2000).

[596] *Frummer v. Hilton Hotels International, Inc.*, New York Court of Appeals, 19 N.Y.2d 533, at 537 (1967), affirmed by *Jazini v. Nissan Motor Co., Ltd.*, U.S. Court of Appeals, 2nd Circuit, 148 F.3d 181, at 184 (1998); and see *Genpharm Inc. v. Pliva-Lachema a.s.*, U.S. District Court, Eastern District of New York, 361 F. Supp.2d 49, at 57 (2005).

[597] *Frummer v. Hilton Hotels International, Inc.*, New York Court of Appeals, 19 N.Y.2d 533, at 538 (1967).

business' contacts with New York, the defendants maintained an Investor Relations Office in the New York forum whose duties was to field inquiries from investors and potential investors in Royal Dutch and Shell Transport, mailing information about defendants to thousands of individuals and entities throughout the U.S., and organizing meetings between officials of the defendants and (potential) investors, and financial analysts. The Court agreed with the District Court that there was an agency relationship between the defendants and the Investors Relations Office for jurisdictional purposes: defendants were doing business through an agent in New York, whose sole business function was to perform investor relations services on the defendants' behalf and who was fully devoted to defendants' business. Since this case also passed the fairness test and the *forum non conveniens* test, the result is that a U.K./Dutch group is subjected to general jurisdiction in New York courts over an action brought by Nigerian claimants arising out of alleged wrongdoing that took place in Nigeria, but which in itself has nothing to do with defendant's activities carried out in New York.

Florida courts held a similar reasoning. In *Stubbs v. Wyndham Nassau Resort and Crystal Palace Casino* the court held that a foreign resort should be considered as doing business under the Florida long-arm Statute on the basis that its Florida-based subsidiary acted as advertising and booking department for the resort, in that subsidiary was the agent for a foreign resort, and its activities could be imputed to the resort.[598] The court held 'that the financial ties between the nonresident corporations and the Florida subsidiaries suggested a relationship, in which the Florida subsidiaries were "mere instrumentalities" of the nonresident defendant.' The Florida subsidiaries were considered as conducting business solely for the non-resident corporations, including the hotel, and the court held that their activities could be imputed to the non-resident corporations. The subsidiaries' activities were considered to establish sufficient contacts with the forum state to warrant general personal jurisdiction over the defendant.[599]

5.6.5.2 *The* Alter Ego*: The Jurisdictional Piercing of the Corporate Veil*

The *alter ego* theory is used to determine whether the corporate veil should be lifted when two affiliated companies – truly separate corporate entities from the point of view of company law – should be considered for jurisdictional purposes as each other's *alter ego.* An affiliated company can act as an agent for the foreign corporation if an agency-relationship exists, but the *alter ego* theory sanctions 'corporate fiction'[600] by imputing a subsidiary's jurisdictional contacts to the parent corporation, because they should be considered as one 'entity' for jurisdictional purposes.[601] When a corporation does business or transacts business through an af-

[598] 11th Circuit, 447 F.3d 1357 (2006), affirming *Meier ex rel. Meier v. Sun Int'l Hotels, Ltd.*, U.S. Court of Appeals, 11th Circuit, 288 F.3d 1264, 1268-69 (2002).

[599] *Stubbs v. Wyndham Nassau Resort and Crystal Palace Casino*, 11th Circuit, 447 F.3d 1357, at 1363 (2006).

[600] Bermann, *Transnational Litigation*, at 61.

[601] See above and see *Delagi v. Volkswagenwerk AG of Wolfsburg*, New York Court of Appeals, 328 N.Y.S.2d 653 (1972), in which the New York Court of Appeals refers to *Frummer v. Hilton Hotels*

filiated company,[602] the *alter ego* theory could lead to subjecting the foreign parent corporation to jurisdiction based on contacts or acts of its subsidiary in the forum, and vice versa.[603]

This 'entity' notion of affiliated companies was first interpreted by a strict observance of corporate separateness due to the fact that an early Supreme Court decision only allowed the 'jurisdictional piercing of the corporate veil'[604] when the corporate formalities were disrespected.[605] In later decisions, the emphasis lay on the underlying economic realities and concentrating on whether the companies' activities are interrelated, or whether the affiliated company should be considered as the extension of the out-of-state corporation and the degree of control of the latter.[606] A parent company's ownership or control of a subsidiary corporation does not automatically subject the parent corporation to jurisdiction of the state where the subsidiary does business,[607] but the degree of control of the parent over its subsidiary is conclusive. [608] The New York Court of Appeals stated in *Delagi v.*

International, Inc., New York Court of Appeals, 19 N.Y.2d 533 (1967). See for a clear and recent decision affirming this position *Aquila, Inc. v. Superior Court*, Court of Appeal, 4th District, Division 1, California, 148 Cal.App.4th 556, at 577 (2007), review denied. The Court held that '[w]here evidence is produced to show the nonresident parent corporation's pervasive and continual control of the local subsidiary's activities, then they should be treated as one entity for purposes of jurisdiction. ... In some cases, the subsidiary company is not truly a separate entity, but is merely an arm of the parent company.' Affirmed by *F. Hoffman-La Roche, Inc. v. Superior Court*, 130 Cal.App.4th 782 (2005).

602 See Casad and Richman, *Jurisdiction in Civil Actions Vol. 1*, § 3-2[2](ix), at 358-364 and § 4-3[5], at 496-501, respectively.

603 Bermann, *Transnational Litigation*, at 62; D. Welp, *Internationale Zuständigkeit über auswartige Gesellschaften mit Inlanstöchtern im U.S.-amerikanischen Zivilprozess* (1982), at 112.

604 See Bermann, *Transnational Litigation*, at 61, on 'piercing the jurisdictional veil'.

605 *Cannon Mfg. Co. v. Cudahy Packing Co.*, 267 U.S. 333 (1925). See Lowenfeld, *International Litigation*, at 230; Bermann, *Transnational Litigation*, at 62-63.

606 Lowenfeld, *International Litigation*, at 231; Casad and Richman, *Jurisdiction in Civil Actions Vol. 1*, at 358-359 and 497; Scoles, Hay *et al.*, *Conflict of Laws*, § 10.16, at 461; Born, *International Civil Litigation*, at 169; D. Brown, 'Jurisdiction over a Corporation on the Basis of the Contacts of an Affiliated Corporation: Do You Have to Pierce the Corporate Veil?', *University of Cincinnati Law Review* (1992), 595-622, at 617-619; Schack, *Jurisdictional Minimum Contacts Scrutinized*, at 36.

607 Florida courts have repeatedly stated that mere presence of a (wholly-owned) subsidiary is by itself not enough to support imputed contacts to subject a non-Florida corporate parent to long-arm jurisdiction. *Gadea v. Star Cruises, Ltd.*, District Court of Appeal of Florida, 3rd District, 949 So.2d 1143 (2007); *Resource Healthcare of America, Inc. v. McKinney*, District Court of Appeal of Florida, 2nd District, 940 So.2d 1139 (2006), rehearing denied; *Vega Glen v. Club Mediterranée S.A.*, U.S. District Court, Southern District of Florida, 359 F. Supp.2d 1352 (2005); *Enic, PLC v. F.F. South & Co., Inc.*, District Court of Appeal of Florida, 5th District, 870 So.2d 888 (2004). The same approach is taken by New York courts: 'The mere presence of a subsidiary in New York does not establish the parent's presence in the state.' *Genpharm Inc. v. Pliva-Lachema a.s.*, U.S. District Court, Eastern District of New York, 361 F. Supp.2d 49, at 57 (2005), citing *Volkswagenwerk Aktiengesellschaft v. Beech Aircraft Corp.*, U.S. Court of Appeals, 2nd Circuit, 751 F.2d 117, 120 (1984).

608 See 2nd Restatement of Conflict of Laws, § 52, comment b. See for California the recent case *Aquila, Inc. v. Superior Court*, Court of Appeals, 4th District, Division 1, California, 148 Cal.App.4th 556, at 571 (2007), review denied, in which the Court held that if a wholly-owned subsidiary of a parent corporation is properly subject to state court jurisdiction, the parent is not necessarily also properly subject to jurisdiction in California courts. See also *In re Automobile Antitrust Cases I and II*, Court of Appeals, 1st District, Division 4, California, Cal.App.4th 100, at 120 (2005): 'Plaintiffs must show more than mere ownership or control of a local subsidiary by a foreign parent corporation.' For Florida

Volkswagenwerk AG of Wolfsburg that 'a foreign corporation is not present in a state for the purpose of assertion of personal jurisdiction on basis of control unless there exists at least a parent-subsidiary relationship and the subsidiary's activities must be so complete that the subsidiary is, in fact, *merely a department* of the parent.'[609] Hence, whether the subsidiary located in the forum should be considered as a 'mere department' of the foreign entity in order to pierce the corporate veil for jurisdictional purposes depends on a number of factors such as common ownership, financial dependency and the degree of control of the parent.[610]

5.7 *Quasi in Rem* Jurisdiction: Jurisdiction Based on Attached Property

U.S. jurisdiction law allows the exercise of '*quasi in rem*' jurisdiction founded on the presence of attached property in the forum belonging to the defendant. The rationale for this type of jurisdiction is to prevent a wrongdoer from 'avoid[ing] payment of his obligations by removing his assets to a place where he is not subject to an *in personam* suit' and is justified by the connection between the transaction and the state, the situation of the parties and the purpose of the litigation.[611]

In order to understand the particularities of the U.S. version of property-based jurisdiction some preliminary remarks are necessary: Apart from jurisdiction *in personam* and jurisdiction *in rem*, traditional U.S. terminology identifies a third jurisdictional category called *quasi in rem* jurisdiction. Jurisdiction *in rem* is founded

---

it is required that the parent corporation exercised such a degree of control over subsidiary that the subsidiary's activities were in fact the activities of the parent within the state, *Gadea v. Star Cruises, Ltd.*, District Court of Appeal of Florida, 3rd District, 949 So.2d 1143 (2007); *Resource Healthcare of America, Inc. v. McKinney*, District Court of Appeal of Florida, 2nd District, 940 So.2d 1139 (2006), rehearing denied; *Development Corp. of Palm Beach v. WBC Const., L.L.C.*, District Court of Appeal of Florida, 4th District, 925 So.2d 1156 (2006). *Vega Glen v. Club Mediterranée S.A.*, U.S. District Court, Southern District of Florida, 359 F. Supp.2d 1352 (2005).

609 See *Delagi v. Volkswagenwerk AG of Wolfsburg*, Court of Appeals of New York, 29 N.Y.2d 426, at 657 (1972) (emphasis added), affirmed by *Volkswagenwerk Aktiengesellschaft v. Beech Aircraft Corp.*, U.S. Court of Appeals, 2nd Circuit, 751 F.2d 117, at 120 (1984); *Jazini v. Nissan Motor Company, Ltd.*, U.S. Court of Appeals, 2nd Circuit, 148 F.3d 181, 184-85 (1998). See also *Reers v. Deutsche Bahn AG*, U.S. District Court, Southern District of New York, 320 F. Supp.2d 140 (2004).

610 The U.S. District Court rejected general jurisdiction under the New York Statute in *Klonis v. National Bank of Greece, S.A.* The New York subsidiary of a Greek bank was not a 'mere department' of a foreign entity based on four factors: (1) common ownership, which is essential; (2) 'financial dependency of the subsidiary on the parent corporation'; (3) 'the degree to which the parent corporation interferes in the selection and assignment of the subsidiary's executive personnel and fails to observe corporate formalities'; and (4) 'the degree of control over the marketing and operational policies of the subsidiary exercised by the parent.' U.S. District Court, Southern Division of New York, 492 F. Supp.2d 293, at 300 (2007). See for a similar reasoning but different outcome, *Mones v. Commercial Bank of Kuwait, S.A.K.*, Southern District of New York, 502 F. Supp.2d 363 (2007), reconsideration denied 399 F. Supp.2d 412. For California see *Doe v. Unocal Corp.*, U.S. Court of Appeals, 9th Circuit, 248 F.3d 915 (2001). For Florida see *Deere & Co. v. Watts*, Supreme Court of Florida, 148 So.2d 529 (1963); *Meier ex rel. Meier v. Sun Intern. Hotels*, U.S. Court of Appeals, 11th Circuit, 288 F.3d 1264 (2002).

611 *Shaffer v. Heitner*, 433 U.S. 186, at 210 (1977), relying on 2nd Restatement of Conflict of Laws, § 66, comment a, and see also comment b of that Restatement. See also Lowenfeld, *International Litigation*, at 279.

on the location of property and only affects the property itself: *quasi in rem* jurisdiction is also based on the presence of attached property in the forum, but affects or binds the out-of-state defendant.[612] Under *quasi in rem* jurisdiction, two types of rules are to be distinguished,[613] namely, the *quasi in rem type I* and the *quasi in rem type II*.[614] With respect to the *quasi in rem type I* jurisdiction, the plaintiff has an interest in the property and the property is really the object of the proceedings.[615] The second category – the *quasi in rem type II* – also called *attachment or garnishment jurisdiction*[616] – concerns jurisdiction founded on the presence of defendant's attached property in the forum and differs from *in rem* jurisdiction because it only binds named persons with an interest in the property and not the 'whole world'.[617] For attachment jurisdiction, the plaintiff does not have a pre-existing interest in the property, but he brings a claim against the defendant personally and seeks, by virtue of attachment or garnishment of the property, to use the property to satisfy his claim against the defendant.[618] Due to those characteristics, *quasi in rem type*

[612] As opposed to jurisdiction *in personam* which is founded on the nexus between parties and the forum and binds the parties; it may impose obligations to the person and could affect defendant's belongings. See 2nd Restatement of Conflict of Laws, Chap. 3, Introductory Note (sub a and b) and see Introductory Note, 2nd topic regarding *in rem* jurisdiction: 'When a thing is subject to the judicial jurisdiction of a state, an action may be brought to affect the interests in the thing of all persons in the world.' See Scoles, Hay *et al.*, *Conflict of Laws*, § 5.2, at 287; Casad and Richman, *Jurisdiction in Civil Actions Vol. 1*, § 2-6[1], at 179-181; Richman and Reynolds, *Understanding Conflict of Laws*, § 41, at 121-122; J. Lookofsky, 'Property-based Jurisdiction and Due Process of Law', 54 *Nordisk Tidsskrift for international Ret: Acta scandinavica juris gentium* (1985), 62-70, at 64.

[613] According to the U.S. Supreme Court in *Hanson v. Denckla*, 357 U.S. 235, 246 (1958), fn. 12: '[a] judgment *in personam* imposes a personal liability or obligation on one person in favor of another. A judgment *in rem* affects the interests of all persons in designated property. A judgment *quasi in rem* affects the interests of particular persons in designated property. The latter is of two types. In one the plaintiff is seeking to secure a pre-existing claim in the subject property and to extinguish or establish the nonexistence of similar interests of particular persons. In the other the plaintiff seeks to apply what he concedes to be the property of the defendant to the satisfaction of a claim against him.'

[614] The distinction lost its importance. With respect to the difference between *in rem* and *quasi in rem type I* jurisdiction, it has been stated several times that this traditional distinction has little significant analytical importance. The same is true for the *in rem* and *in personam* distinction. See Hay, Weintraub *et al.*, *Conflict of Laws*, at 124; Richman and Reynolds, *Understanding Conflict of Laws*, § 41, at 121-123; Casad and Richman, *Jurisdiction in Civil Actions Vol. 1*, at 180; T. Kleinstück, *Due Process-Beschränkungen des Vermögensgerichtsstandes durch hinreichenden Inlandsbezug und Minimum Contacts: Eine rechtsvergleichende Untersuchung unter besonderer Berücksichtigung des U.S.-amerikanischen und österreichischen* Rechts (1994), at 33-36. Restatements generally do not apply this distinction but simply refer to 'jurisdiction over persons, things' or 'attachment jurisdiction'. The 2nd Restatement of Judgments abandoned the distinction in the 1986 revision, § 5-8.

[615] Scoles, Hay *et al.*, *Conflict of Laws*, § 5.6, at 297-298.

[616] See 2nd Restatement of Judgments (1982), § 6, comment a. As stated in the 2nd Restatement of Conflict of Laws both types are based on the power over the thing and the effect of the judgement is to affect interests of particular person(s) in the thing (Chap. 3, Introductory Note). See also L. Silberman, 'Shaffer v Heitner; The End of an Era', 53 *New York Law Review* (1978), 33-101, at 39.

[617] Weintraub, *Commentary*, § 4.24, at 256; Scoles, Hay *et al.*, *Conflict of Laws*, § 5.6, at 297; Hay, Weintraub *et al.*, *Conflict of Laws*, at 124.

[618] Lowenfeld, *International Litigation*, at 268; Lookofsky and Hertz, *Transnational Litigation*, at 273; Hay, Weintraub *et al.*, *Conflict of Laws*, at 124; Weintraub, *Commentary*, § 4.25, at 257; Richman and Reynolds, *Understanding Conflict of Laws*, at 124; see also 2nd Restatement of Judgments, § 6, comment a.

II jurisdiction resembles *in personam* jurisdiction more than jurisdiction *in rem*.[619] The terminology *quasi in rem* jurisdiction merely refers to the fact that jurisdiction is based on the presence of attached property in the forum and that the effect of its judgement is limited to the value of the property, as is also the case with *in rem* jurisdiction.[620]

5.7.1 The *Pennoyer* Precondition of Attachment

Attachment jurisdiction is not founded on the mere presence of defendant's property in the forum; attachment, seizure, garnishment[621] or sequestration of the property is a prerequisite for jurisdiction.[622] Under the *Pennoyer v. Neff* regime jurisdiction over property within the state's territorial boundaries was accepted but attachment prior to the commencement of the proceedings was required.[623] Justice Field clearly required that property should be 'brought under the control of the court by seizure or some equivalent act'.[624] Mere presence of defendant's property in the forum is not 'within' the power of the state and consequently did not constitute a valid basis for jurisdiction under the *Pennoyer v. Neff* power theory. This reasoning is still valid under the 'minimum contacts theory', confirmed by the current leading case on attachment jurisdiction *Shaffer v. Heitner*.[625] Although the *Shaffer v. Heitner* decision has a significant impact on attachment jurisdiction and restricted its application,[626] it upheld the attachment requirement by repeating Justice Field's statement in *Pennoyer v. Neff*: 'any attempt of "directly" asserting extraterritorial jurisdiction over persons or property would not only have offended sister States, it would also have exceeded the inherent limits of the State's power.'[627] Jurisdiction asserted in such a direct manner would have been in violation of the Due Process Clause of the Fourteenth Amendment. This attachment requirement still seems to be the general rule and is generally followed by lower courts.[628]

---

[619] Scoles, Hay *et al.*, *Conflict of Laws*, § 5.6, at 297.

[620] Ibid., at 298.

[621] Lowenfeld, *Conflict of Laws*, § 7.06, fn. g, at 578. The terms 'attachment' and 'garnishment' are interchangeable.

[622] See 2nd Restatement of Judgments (1982), § 8; Nuyts, *L'exception de forum non conveniens*, § 29, at 49; J. Krafft, *'Exorbitante' Gerichtsstände im internationalen Zivilprozessrecht der Schweiz: insbesondere nach dem Lugano-Übereinkommen* (1999), at 55-58; Nuyts, *L'exception de forum non conveniens*, § 29, at 49; 'The Requirement of Seizure in the Exercise of Quasi in Rem Jurisdiction: Pennoyer v. Neff Re-Examined', 63 *Harvard Law Review* (1950), 657-671.

[623] *Pennoyer v. Neff*, 95 U.S. 714, at 722 (1878), 'no State can exercise direct jurisdiction and authority over persons or *property* without its territory' (emphasis added). See Richman and Reynolds, *Understanding Conflict of Laws*, § 42, at 124-125; and Silberman, 'Shaffer v Heitner', at 41-44, for historical observations.

[624] *Pennoyer v. Neff*, 95 U.S. 714, at 727-728 (1878).

[625] 433 U.S. 186 (1977).

[626] As explained below in Sect. 5.7.2.

[627] 433 U.S. 186, at 197 *et seq.* (1977).

[628] In the State of New York, the requirement of attachment prior to service of process on the basis of § 314(3) CPLR was affirmed by the New York Court of Appeals in *Nemetsky v. Banque de Dév. de La République Du Niger*, 48 N.Y.2d 962, 425 N.Y.S.2d 277 (1979), citing the *Pennoyer* requirement. In Florida attachment is also a prerequisite to jurisdiction. According to *Griffin v. Zinn*, District Court of Appeal of Florida, 2nd District, 318 So.2d 151, at 154 (1975), 'it must always be made clear ... that

5.7.2 Specific Jurisdiction

In the *Shaffer v. Heitner* decision, the U.S. Supreme Court dealt with *quasi in rem* jurisdiction and its relationship to the Due Process Clause.[629]

Shaffer was a shareholder derivative suit brought in Delaware against the directors and officers of a Delaware corporation headquartered in Arizona. The purpose of the suit was to recover damages in breaches of fiduciary duty that occurred in Oregon. All directors were non-residents of Delaware and thus *quasi in rem* jurisdiction was invoked by means of attachment of defendants' shares in the corporation located in Delaware. The Supreme Court ruled that due process would not sustain the Delaware court's exercise of jurisdiction on these facts.

Shaffer's impact on attachment jurisdiction is considerable. Before *Shaffer v. Heitner,* the traditional *quasi in rem type II* rule provided for jurisdiction over claims unrelated to the property, because in order to request attachment it was not required that the claim be related to the property.[630] But *Shaffer v. Heitner* clearly rejected the practice under *Pennoyer*, asserting jurisdiction based only on the presence of attached property with no relationship to the claim. Moreover, the U.S. Supreme Court stated that like *all* assertions of jurisdiction, attachment jurisdiction has to pass the minimum contacts test: 'any assertion of state court jurisdiction must satisfy the *International Shoe* standards'.[631] As a consequence, the 'minimum contact' test is equally applicable to attachment jurisdiction. Implicitly *Shaffer v. Heitner* indicates that attachment jurisdiction remains a valid jurisdictional basis when there is a close relation between the claim and the attached property.[632] According to the Supreme Court, this sufficient connection requirement is the result of due process standards and should focus on 'the relationship among the defendant, the forum, and the litigation'.[633] Consequently, *quasi in rem* jurisdiction should be understood as specific jurisdiction only available when the claim is related to the property seized.[634]

Another significant feature of *attachment jurisdiction* is that the effect of the judgement is limited to the value of the property.[635] Restricting jurisdiction as to

---

such property is subject to sequestration or appropriation in whole or in part to satisfy the asserted claim of the plaintiff against the non-resident owner thereof.' Cited by *Wiggins v. Dojcsan*, Court of Appeal of Florida, 2nd District, 411 So.2d 894, 895 (1982).

[629] 433 U.S. 186 (1977).

[630] Weintraub, *Commentary*, § 4.28, at 264-265; Scoles, Hay *et al.*, *Conflict of Laws*, at 299; Lowenfeld, *International Litigation*, at 268; Casad and Richman, *Jurisdiction in Civil Actions Vol. 1*, § 1-2[2], at 12.

[631] 433 U.S. 186, at 208-209 and 212 (1977).

[632] 2nd Restatement of Judgements, § 5, comment b; 3rd Restatement of Foreign Relations, § 421(k), comment i; see also Lowenfeld, *International Litigation*, at 280.

[633] *Shaffer v. Heitner*, 433 U.S. 186, at 204 (1977), affirmed by *Rush v. Savchuk*, 444 U.S. 320, at 327 (1980).

[634] See also Casad and Richman, *Jurisdiction in Civil Actions Vol. 1*, § 2-6[3](b), at 188.

[635] Scoles, Hay *et al.*, *Conflict of Laws*, § 5.6, at 298; Lowenfeld, *International Litigation*, at 268; Richman and Reynolds, *Understanding Conflict of Laws*, § 41, at 124. See also 2nd Restatement of Conflict of Laws, § 66, comment h. The New York Statute under CPLR § 320(c)(1), explicitly states that a judgement is unenforceable beyond the value of the attached property even if the defendant appears in the action and defends the case on the merits.

the value of the property emanates from the *Pennoyer*-era under which a court only had jurisdiction over property located on its territory.[636] Since claimant cannot recover more than the value of defendant's property to satisfy the claim, attachment jurisdiction is also referred to as *limited* jurisdiction.[637]

Quasi in rem jurisdiction does not, however, exclude the possibility of *in personam* jurisdiction on the basis of defendant's property – which has not been seized – being located in the forum. According to the Supreme Court's decision in *Rush v. Savchuk*, 'the ownership of property in the State is *a* contact between the defendant and the forum, and it may suggest the presence of other ties'.[638] Although, under the 'minimum contacts' theory the mere presence of defendant's property in the forum will generally not be considered as a sufficient contact for jurisdiction, it constitutes a 'significant factor' to determine whether defendant has sufficient contacts for 'doing business' or 'transacting business' in the state. In some cases both *in personam* as well as *quasi in rem* jurisdiction could be available, provided that defendant has sufficient contacts with the forum as required under *Shaffer v. Heitner*.[639] In such a case, the plaintiff can choose. Since *quasi in rem* jurisdiction is limited to the value of the property, claimant might favour 'transacting' and 'doing business' grounds for personal jurisdiction.[640] Casad suggests that plaintiffs might however choose *quasi in rem* jurisdiction over jurisdiction *in personam* in cases where the forum contacts are attenuated, because the 'minimum contacts' requirement for 'limited' attachment jurisdiction might be easier to satisfy for *quasi in rem* jurisdiction than for personal jurisdiction.[641] In the *Intermeat* decision, the New York Court of Appeals applied a less strict due process test.[642] Hence, the presence of attached property in the forum should be understood as a 'contact' with the forum which does not automatically provide for jurisdiction according to the notions of fair play and substantial justice; other contacts are usually required

---

[636] Nuyts, *L'exception de forum non conveniens*, § 29, at 49.

[637] Casad and Richman, *Jurisdiction in Civil Actions Vol. 1*, § 1-2[2], at 12 and § 2-6[2], at 182; and Lookofsky and Hertz, *Transnational Litigation*, at 272-273.

[638] *Rush v. Savchuk*, 444 U.S. 320, at 328 (1980) (emphasis added). See also *Asahi Metal Industry Co. v. Superior Court*, 480 U.S. 102, at 103 (1987), 'Asahi, like the instant defendants, had no office, agent, employees, or property in the forum state.'

[639] See 2nd Restatement of Conflict of Laws, § 66, comment c.

[640] See Weintraub, *Commentary*, § 4.28, at 264-265; Hay, Weintraub *et al.*, *Conflict of Laws*, at 140; Casad and Richman, *Jurisdiction in Civil Actions Vol. 1*, § 2-6[3](b), at 189. See 2nd Restatement of Conflict of Laws, § 66, comment c. On the other hand, if attachment jurisdiction is exercised without also exercising *in personam* jurisdiction, it will usually be in a situation in which the state has constitutionally sufficient minimum contacts for *in personam* jurisdiction but its own service of process statute does not authorize *in personam* jurisdiction.

[641] See Casad and Richman, *Jurisdiction in Civil Actions Vol. 1*, § 2-6[3](b), at 189. See also Kleinstück, 'Due Process-Beschränkungen des Vermögensgerichtsstandes', at 51-54.

[642] *Intermeat Inc. v. American Poultry*, U.S. Court of Appeals, 2nd Circuit, 575 F.2d 1017, at 1022-1023 (1978), 'in dealing with jurisdiction based upon an attachment, the test is narrower. The test is not whether the defendant is "doing business" in New York, a concept which a state, if it wishes to, is still free to assert as a minimum requirement, but whether there are sufficient minimum contacts to make it fair and just that the foreign corporation be required to come to New York to defend the action that was begun by attachment.'

to satisfy the 'minimum contact' test.[643] In other words, the mere presence of (attached) property in a state does not automatically establish a sufficient relationship between the owner of the property and the state.[644] This was affirmed by *Rush v. Savchuk*, another important attachment jurisdiction case in which the U.S. Supreme Court stated that

> 'The mere presence of property in a State does not establish a sufficient relationship between the owner of the property and the State to support the exercise of jurisdiction over an unrelated cause of action, and it cannot be said that the defendant engaged in any purposeful activity related to the forum that would make the exercise of jurisdiction fair, just, or reasonable merely because his insurer does business there.'[645]

5.7.3 The Nature and *Situs* of Attached Property

Before the *International Shoe* turn-over, attachment jurisdiction was particularly functional under the power theory during the *Pennoyer v. Neff* regime as it provided an alternative jurisdictional basis besides the traditional and rigid bases for jurisdiction under the 'presence theory'.[646] Moreover, its importance increased by the U.S. Supreme Court decision in *Harris v. Balk* that interpreted the meaning of 'property', which clearly expanded the reach of attachment jurisdiction.[647] Although *Harris*[648] was overruled by *Shaffer v. Heitner*[649] once the power theory was abandoned, the *Harris v. Balk* decision remained relevant to explain *Shaffer's* impact and the restrictions presently imposed on attachment jurisdiction.[650]

Both nature and location of assets are significant features of attachment jurisdiction.[651] According to U.S. terminology, attachment jurisdiction involves tangible assets such as moveable goods or immoveable property, but they also include 'in-

---

[643] Lowenfeld, *Conflict of Laws*, § 7.06, at 599, citing *Intermeat Inc. v. American Poultry*, U.S. Court of Appeals, 2nd Circuit, 575 F.2d 1017, at 1022 (1978).

[644] The *Shaffer* decision establishes that territorial power was no longer a 'sufficient' condition, just like according to Richman and Reynolds, *International Shoe* held that territorial power was no longer a 'necessary' condition, see Richman and Reynolds, *Understanding Conflict of Laws*, § 44, at 131.

[645] 444 U.S. 320, at 321 (1980).

[646] *Shaffer v. Heitner*, 433 U.S. 186, at 200 (1977), 'The Pennoyer rules generally favored nonresident defendants by making them harder to sue. This advantage was reduced, however, by the ability of a resident plaintiff to satisfy a claim against a nonresident defendant by bringing into court any property of the defendant located in the plaintiff's State'. See also Lowenfeld, *International Litigation*, at 269; Weintraub, *Commentary*, § 4.28, at 264-266; Lowenfeld, *Conflict of Laws*, § 7.06, at 579.

[647] 198 U.S. 215 (1905); see Lowenfeld, *International Litigation*, at 268; Hay, Weintraub *et al.*, *Conflict of Laws*, at 130.

[648] *Harris v. Balk*, 198 U.S. 215 (1905).

[649] 433 U.S. 186, at 212 (1977), fn. 39, 'it would not be fruitful for us to re-examine the facts of cases decided on the rationales of *Pennoyer* and *Harris* to determine whether jurisdiction might have been sustained under the standard we adopt today. To the extent that prior decisions are inconsistent with this standard, they are overruled.'

[650] Silberman, 'Shaffer v Heitner'.

[651] The questions asked by Lowenfeld, what kind of property can be subject to or exempt from attachment and where is an intangible asset situated, are crucial to determine the reach of this jurisdiction ground, but involve complex inquiries, see Lowenfeld, *Conflict of Laws*, at 579.

tangibles'. The latter are best described as 'debts' and can take multiple forms.[652] In contrast to tangibles, they are difficult to locate.[653]

The question of the *situs* of intangibles was addressed to the U.S. Supreme Court in the *Harris v. Balk* case, where plaintiff attached defendant's intangible property for jurisdictional purposes.[654] In this case, the defendant did not have assets in the forum, but claimant attached defendant's intangible property by serving his garnishee with process, a third person who owed him debts, who was at the time of service physically present in the forum but not a domiciliary.[655] The Court ruled that the *situs* of a debt was considered to follow the debtor: 'The obligation of the debtor to pay his debt clings to and accompanies him wherever he goes. He is as much bound to pay his debt in a foreign state when therein sued upon his obligation by his creditor, as he was in the state where the debt was contracted.'[656] What the earlier Supreme Court's decision in *Harris v. Balk* implied was that the debt followed the debtor in the most literal sense of the word; by serving the garnishee with process when physically present in the forum the court thereby acquires jurisdiction over him.[657] The *situs* of a debt was not the place where the debt was created, nor did it mean that the *situs* was located at the domicile of either the creditor or the debtor.[658] It meant, as summarized by Casad, that a creditor – in the *Harris* case the defendant – could be subjected to jurisdiction in any state where his debtor was served with process, even when there is no connection between the creditor and the forum or between the debt and the plaintiff's claim in order to establish jurisdiction over his creditor.[659]

Harris v. Balk gave full play to unrestricted attachment jurisdiction based on a very thin connection with the forum. The both concepts of 'presence' and 'property' were interpreted extensively in order to admit attachment jurisdiction.[660] One of these extended versions of *Harris v. Balk* was ruled by the New York Court of

---

[652] See Lowenfeld, *International Litigation*, at 268; and Lowenfeld, *Conflict of Laws*, § 7.06, at 579, who provides examples such as defendant's bank account, stocks, debts owed by residents of the forum of the defendant, wages payable to defendant by a person domiciled in the forum.

[653] Weintraub, *Commentary*, § 4.25, at 258; Casad and Richman, *Jurisdiction in Civil Actions Vol. 1*, § 2-6[2](ii), at 183.

[654] 198 U.S. 215 (1905). The plaintiff (Epstein) from Maryland sued the defendant (Balk) resident in North Carolina, who had no assets in Maryland but was creditor of a third person (Harris). Claimant personally served defendant's debtor Harris when the latter was temporarily in Maryland. See A. Lowenfeld, 'In Search of the Intangible: A Comment on Shaffer v. Heitner', 53 *New York Law Review* (1978), 102, at 103-107.

[655] 198 U.S. 215, at 221 (1905).

[656] Ibid., at 222-223.

[657] Ibid., at 222.

[658] Ibid.

[659] Casad and Richman, *Jurisdiction in Civil Actions Vol. 1*, § 2-6[2](a)[ii], at 183. See Lowenfeld, 'In Search of the Intangible', at 107-108, 'By today's standards, it does seem[] peculiar to suggest that Harris [garnishee] carried his debts – Balk [defendant]'s asset – around with him wherever he travelled, and that Epstein [claimant]'s process server could, in effect, put his hand into Harris['] pocket to reach Balk.' On further reading Lowenfeld interprets the *Harris* case as implying that intangibles have no *situs* at all. – 'The debt, simply was anywhere that Harris could be sued under the principles of personal jurisdic[ti]on by "tag"', at 109.

[660] See also Silberman, 'Shaffer v Heitner', at 49-52.

Appeals in *Seider v. Roth* in 1966.[661] Although this case was rendered after the *International Shoe*-turnover, it was before the *Shaffer* 'revolution' and was long referred to as the *Seider doctrine* or *Seider-type* jurisdiction.[662] In *Seider v. Roth*, the case involved an action for injuries sustained in an automobile accident occurring in Vermont between New York claimants and a Canadian defendant. Defendant did not have sufficient contact for adjudication by New York courts, nor did defendant have any tangible property in New York. The defendant, however, carried a liability policy from a Canadian insurer who was doing business in New York. The New York Court of Appeals relied on *Harris v. Balk*[663] to assume jurisdiction by stating that 'the contractual obligation of an insurance company to its insured under a liability insurance policy is a debt subject to attachment under state law if the insurer does business in the State'.[664] According to the Court this was sufficient to permit attachment jurisdiction over the absent defendant.[665] Consequently, the insurance debt was considered to (also) have its *situs* in New York where the insurance company was doing business and was thus present.

The 1977 *Shaffer* decision required the application of the minimum contact test to attachment jurisdiction but the Court did not properly address the question of the *situs* of intangibles.[666] This question was linked with a debate on the constitutional aspects of attachment jurisdiction and with whether *Seider* survived *Shaffer v. Heitner.*[667]

In 1978, the New York Court of Appeals considered for the first time the effect of the constitutional rule announced in *Shaffer v. Heitner* on the New York law authorizing attachment jurisdiction over a non-resident defendant based on the attachment of a debt due to the defendant from a debtor found in New York. In the case *Intermeat, Inc. v. American Poultry*, the Court affirmed that the *situs* of debts is where the debtor is found, if the law of the state authorizes the attachment.[668] But the Court specified that, by virtue of *Shaffer v. Heitner*, the *International Shoe* requirements should be applied

661 New York Court of Appeals, 17 N.Y.2d 111, 216 N.E.2d 312 (1966). See for a similar case *Simpson v. Loehmann*, New York Court of Appeals, 287 N.Y.S.2d 633 (1967), both abrogated by U.S. Supreme Court in *Rush v. Savchuk*, 444 U.S. 320 (1980).

662 Richman and Reynolds, *Understanding Conflict of Laws*, at 130.

663 198 U.S. 215 (1905).

664 444 U.S. 320, at 325 (1980).

665 Ibid., at 326 (1980).

666 Lowenfeld, 'In Search of the Intangible', at 110. Except for Justice Stephens who in his concurring judgement set aside the Delaware attachment statute as unconstitutional, in its way to locate the *situs* of defendant's property (i.e. Shares of defendant's stock). See *Shaffer v. Heitner*, 433 U.S. 186, at 219 (1977), 'I therefore agree with the Court that on the record before us no adequate basis for jurisdiction exists and that the Delaware Statute is unconstitutional on its face.' See also on this Lookofsky and Hertz, *Transnational Litigation*, at 274.

667 Lowenfeld, *Conflict of Laws*, at 608; Lowenfeld, 'In Search of the Intangible', at 102; Silberman, 'Shaffer v Heitner', at 91.

668 According to *Intermeat, Inc. v. American Poultry*, New York Court of Appeal, 575 F.2d 1017, at 1022 (1978), 'The Court did not indicate total disapproval of *Harris v. Balk*, for it noted that attachment of a debt is proper wherever the debtor is found, if the attachment is authorized by the law of the state.'

> '[t]he application of the "minimum contacts" standard to proceedings begun by attachment now means that the presence of the defendant's property within New York must be viewed as only one contact of the defendant with the state, to be considered along with other contacts in deciding whether the assertion of jurisdiction is consistent with "traditional notions of fair play and substantial justice." ... Hence, some attachments still valid under New York law, and still constituting valid bases (so far as New York law is concerned) for quasi-in-rem jurisdiction, will no longer satisfy the applicable due process requirement where the defendant has less than minimum contacts with New York.'[669]

The New York Court of Appeals finally accepted that the ascertainment of jurisdiction was consistent with due process since the case had other substantial connections with the state.[670] But the *Intermeat* case did not provide an answer as to whether the sole attachment of a debt was sufficient for jurisdictional purposes and whether the due process standards are satisfied when the defendant (or the claim) is not otherwise connected to the forum. This was dealt with by the U.S. Supreme Court in *Rush v. Savchuk* in 1980 which concerned a similar *Seider*-type attachment.[671] The Court addressed the question whether a '[s]tate may constitutionally exercise *quasi in rem* jurisdiction over a defendant who has no forum contacts by attaching the contractual obligation of an insurer licensed to do business in the State to defend and indemnify him in connection with the suit.'[672] The Court held that it may not and decided that '[s]uch a result is plainly unconstitutional' as it did not comply with due process requirements under the minimum contacts test.[673] Additionally the Court stated that 'contacts' resulting from the fictitious presence of a debt through the presence of the debtor is not to be considered as a contact with sufficient jurisdictional significance.[674] The Court stated that '[t]o say "a debt follows the debtor" is simply to say that intangible property has no actual situs, and a debt may be sued on wherever there is jurisdiction over the debtor. ... It is apparent that such a "contact" can have no jurisdictional significance.'[675]

5.7.4 Attachment Jurisdiction Authorized by State Law

Statutory authorization is still needed for attachment jurisdiction besides the authorization for seizure of the property itself. Each state has dealt with the require-

---

[669] Ibid., at 1022.

[670] Ibid., at 1023: 'The claim for relief "was based on a contract which had substantial connections with that State." [McGee v. International Life Ins. Co] And while we need not decide whether in personam jurisdiction could have attached in this case, it seems evident that the "substantial connection" of the contract with New York must be considered along with the added factor of the attachment of an intangible within the jurisdiction of the state in weighing the "minimum contacts" required for Fourteenth Amendment due process, particularly since the debtor was doing business in New York.'

[671] 444 U.S. 320 (1980). See Hay, Weintraub *et al.*, *Conflict of Laws*, at 142.

[672] 444 U.S. 320, at 322 (1980).

[673] Ibid. See Richman and Reynolds, *Understanding Conflict of Laws*, § 46, at 138-139; Lowenfeld, *Conflict of Laws*, § 7.06, at 606-608; Kleinstück, 'Due Process-Beschränkungen des Vermögensgerichtsstandes', at 39-42.

[674] 444 U.S. 320, at 330 (1980).

[675] Ibid.

ment of statutory authorization in a different manner.[676] Under the *no limit* Statute of California attachment jurisdiction is covered by the 'any constitutional basis' provision.[677] The wide reach of this type of statute however diminishes the need for the *quasi in rem* jurisdiction and only a few cases have addressed the issue.[678] After *Shaffer* imposed a minimum of affiliating contacts with the forum for attachment jurisdiction, mere presence of attached property was no longer sufficient to sustain jurisdiction and the frequency of invoking attachment jurisdiction was expected to decrease.[679] This was the case in California, but not in New York.[680]

Section 314(3) CPLR of the New York Statute provides for statutory authorization for attachment jurisdiction.[681] As Section 302 CPLR does not seek to provide for jurisdiction as far as it is constitutionally permitted, it has a more limited scope of application to reach non-resident defendants. The less 'ambitious' long-arm statute could explain the fact that the *Seider attachment* type came from a New York court.[682] In cases where defendant's claim cannot be covered by one of the bases for personal jurisdiction under Sections 301 and 302, claimant can opt for *quasi in rem* jurisdiction authorized under Section 314(3) CPLR, provided that the attached property located in New York belongs to the defendant, that the claim is related to the property and there are sufficient contacts to satisfy due process standards.[683] The following words of the New York Court of Appeals perfectly illustrate the foregoing: 'Thus, a "gap" exists in which the necessary minimum contacts, including the presence of defendant's property within the State, are present, but personal jurisdiction is not authorized by CPLR 302. It is appropriate, in such a case, to fill that gap utilizing quasi-in-rem principles.'[684] However, even if there could be a need for attachment jurisdiction, Section 314(3) CPLR has not led to an abun-

---

[676] Lowenfeld, *International Litigation*, at 267.

[677] § 410.10 California Statute.

[678] Namely, one case after the *Shaffer* decision, *Watts v. Crawford*, Supreme Court of California, 10 Cal. 4th 743 (1995), and one after *Randone v. Appellate Dep't of Superior Court*, Supreme Court of California, 5 Cal.3d 536 (1971), but both cases only mention the possibility at federal level. See *Glencore Grain Rotterdam B.V. v. Shivnath Rai Harnarain*, U.S. Court of Appeals, 9th Circuit, 284 F.3d 1114 (2002).

[679] According to the New York Court of Appeals; *Intermeat Inc. v. American Poultry*, U.S. Court of Appeals, 2nd Circuit, 575 F.2d 1017, at 1022 (1978), 'Hence, some attachments still valid under New York law, and still constituting valid bases (so far as New York law is concerned) for quasi-in-rem jurisdiction, will no longer satisfy the applicable due process requirement where the defendant has less than minimum contacts with New York'.

[680] 'Although it may appear, at first blush, that the usefulness of quasi-in-rem jurisdiction has been eliminated by Shaffer, inasmuch as the minimum contacts necessary to support it will also generally provide in personam jurisdiction, that is not the case, at least in New York', *Banco Ambrosiano, S.P.A. v. Artoc Bank & Trust Ltd.*, New York Court of Appeals, 62 N.Y.2d 65, at 71 (1984).

[681] New York law provides for the attachment of any debt whether it was incurred within or without the state to or from a resident or non-resident under § 6202 and § 5201 CPLR.

[682] As is stated by Casad and Richman, see Casad and Richman, *Jurisdiction in Civil Actions Vol. 1*, § 2-6[3][b](ii), at 189.

[683] See also 2nd Restatement of Judgements (1982), § 8(1)(d); and Lowenfeld, *Conflict of Laws*, at 610.

[684] *Banco Ambrosiano, S.P.A. v. Artoc Bank & Trust Ltd.*, Court of Appeals of New York, 62 N.Y.2d 65, at 72 (1984).

dance of court decisions on attachment jurisdiction.[685] A significant New York case clearly incorporated the *Shaffer v. Heitner* position stating that 'when the property serving as the jurisdictional basis has no relationship to the cause of action and there are no other ties among the defendant, the forum and the litigation, *quasi-in-rem* jurisdiction will be lacking'.[686]

The Florida long-arm Statute also contains a provision regulating attachment jurisdiction. Section 48.193(1)(c) of the Statute provides for jurisdiction when

> '(1) Any person, … who personally … does any of the acts enumerated in this subsection thereby submits himself … to the jurisdiction of the courts of this state for any cause of action arising from the doing of any of the following acts: (c) Owning, using, possessing, or holding a mortgage or other lien on any real property within this state.'[687]

Decisions dealing with Section 48.193(1)(c) are however rare;[688] in most cases attachment jurisdiction was refused or jurisdiction was primarily based on other grounds providing for *in personam* jurisdiction.[689] Attachment jurisdiction is generally refused because of a lack of connection between the property and the claim. This could indicate, as a general rule, that 'ownership of property by itself is insufficient to subject a nonresident defendant to the jurisdiction of the courts of this state, unless the cause of action arose out of such ownership.'[690]

---

[685] 'Not many *quasi-in-rem* cases have been reported since *Shaffer*', Lowenfeld, *Conflict of Laws*, at 609. For significant cases of higher state courts see *Banco Ambrosiano, S.P.A. v. Artoc Bank & Trust Ltd.*, New York Court of Appeals, 62 N.Y.2d 65 (1984), *Gager v. White*, New York Court of Appeals, 53 N.Y.2d 475 (1981); *Nemetsky v. Banque de Dév. de La République Du Niger*, New York Court of Appeals, 48 N.Y.2d 962 (1979); for cases before the *Shaffer* decision see *Donawitz v. Danek*, New York Court of Appeals, 42 N.Y.2d 138 (1977); *Glassman v. Hyder*, New York Court of Appeals, 23 N.Y.2d 354 (1968). Federal cases asserting attachment jurisdiction are *Intermeat, Inc. v. American Poultry*, U.S. Court of Appeals, 2nd Circuit, 575 F.2d 1017 (1978); *Texas Trading & Milling Corp. v. Federal Republic of Nigeria*, U.S. Court of Appeals, 2nd Circuit, 647 F.2d 300 (1981); and see also *FDIC v. Four Star Holding Co.*, U.S. Court of Appeals, 2nd Circuit, 178 F.3d 97 (1999); *O'Connor v. Lee-Hy Paving Corp.*, U.S. Court of Appeals, 2nd Circuit, 579 F.2d 194 (1978), overruled by *Rush v. Savchuk*, 444 U.S. 320 (1980). For cases at lower federal level see *Drexel Burnham Lambert, Inc. v. D'Angelo*, U.S. District Court, Southern Division of New York, 453 F. Supp. 1294 (1978). And for those at lower state level, see *Desert Palace, Inc. v. Rozenbaum*, Supreme Court of New York 595 N.Y.S.2d 768 (1993); *Ranz v. Sposato*, Supreme Court of New York, 77 A.D.2d 408 (1980); *Majique Fashions, Ltd. v. Warwick & Company Ltd.*, 67 A.D.2d 321 (1979); and for comments see Lowenfeld, *Conflict of Laws*, at 609.

[686] *Banco Ambrosiano, S.P.A. v. Artoc Bank & Trust Ltd.*, New York Court of Appeals, 62 N.Y.2d 65, at 67 (1984).

[687] The last part of this section 'or holding a mortgage or other lien on any real property within this state' has been added by amendment of the statute in 1993, see *William R. Hobbs v. Don Mealy Chevrolet Case*, No. 93-2875, Court of Appeals of Florida, 5th District, 642 So.2d 1149 (1994), fn 3.

[688] Cases are hard to find, but see the Supreme Court of Florida in *McRae v. J.D./M.D.*, No. 68,370, Supreme Court of Florida, 511 So.2d 540 (1987).

[689] Lower court decisions of Florida dealing with § 48.193 resulted in a poor outcome. See especially *Gordon D. Blackmon v. Patricia Sondra Blackmon*, No. 85-2689, Court of Appeals of Florida, 3rd District, 487 So.2d 1131 (1986); *Robert M. Damoth v. Paul F. Reinitz*, No. 85-1085, Court of Appeals of Florida, 2nd District, 485 So.2d 881 (1986).

[690] *Magic Pan International v. Colonial Promenade*, Case No. 92-467, Court of Appeal of Florida, 5th District, 605 So.2d 563 (1992); *J.D. Nichols v. Jeno Paulucci*, Case No. 93-2609, Court of Appeals

More or less the same results can be found in Michigan. Sections 600.705(3), 600.715(3) and 600.725(3) provide for jurisdiction when defendant has ownership, use, or possession of any real or tangible personal property situated within the state.[691]

5.8 Conclusion

In order to determine whether U.S. courts are competent in international disputes, many questions need to be answered and many factors will play a role. First, the plaintiff will have to find a jurisdictional basis to invoke jurisdiction over his claim. The U.S. jurisdictional scheme has a wide scale of jurisdiction grounds available to the claimant and has a particular long arm to reach foreign defendants. Primarily focusing on defendant's 'contacts' with the forum, every affiliating contact between the defendant and the forum is relevant to determine whether U.S. courts can exercise jurisdiction. Especially for transacting jurisdiction, 'any contact counts', but the claim must be one which arises out of or results from defendant's forum-related activities and the contacts have to have been purposefully availed by defendant. If the claim is not related to defendant's contact with the forum, but defendant has sufficiently 'continuous and systematic' contacts with the forum, general jurisdiction is available under the 'doing business' criterion. The distinction between general and specific jurisdiction is based, not on the specific nature of the claim, but rather on the quality and quantity of defendant's contacts and activities in the forum. More traditional bases for jurisdiction such as presence or tag-jurisdiction, defendant's domicile or a U.S. version of property-based jurisdiction are also available to the plaintiff. In other words, does the claim fall within the provisions of the state's long-arm statute for extraterritorial reach or can the plaintiff's action be founded on one of the jurisdiction grounds recognized by either common law principles or statutory authority of state or federal statute?

The next question is whether the exercise of jurisdiction over that particular claim complies with due process standards? This due process test consists in the evaluation of a certain number of open criteria to be determined on a case-by-case basis. First, the minimum contact rule imposes that the defendant's contact with the forum should be 'sufficient'. The court seized must then determine whether the exercise of jurisdiction does not offend traditional notions of fair play and substantial justice, which entails a 'reasonableness' test, consisting of an interest analysis based on several factors.

Assuming that jurisdiction is founded on one of the U.S. sources for jurisdiction, that the exercise of jurisdiction complies with the due process standards and operate within the constitutional limits, jurisdiction is established unless the court uses its discretionary powers to *dismiss* the case as another more convenient court lays somewhere else. The *forum non conveniens* doctrine functions as a correction

of Florida, 5th District, 652 So.2d 389 (1995), recently reaffirmed by *Darrel Forrest v. Amy L. Forrest*, Court of Appeals of Florida, 4th District, 839 So.2d 839 (2003).

691 *Schneider v. Linkfield*, Supreme Court of Michigan, 40 Mich. App. 131, 198 N.W.2d 834 (1972), is perhaps the most interesting case, but dates from the pre-*Shaffer*-era.

tool against abuse of process and international forum shopping and protects U.S. courts from being 'overcrowded'; it is the ultimate 'test' for jurisdiction.

The U.S. jurisdiction system is complex. The complexity and uncertainty of jurisdiction law in the U.S. has been particularly criticized by U.S. scholars themselves.[692] The most radical comment is from Juenger stating that '[T]here is no longer any doubt: American jurisdictional law is a mess.'[693] Others such as Borchers are equally critical, 'The Supreme Court's thousand-piece jigsaw puzzle is personal jurisdiction'.[694] Other critics note that U.S. jurisdiction law has developed itself with eye-patches, without considering the developments in other countries.[695]

Surely, the many tests, interest analyses and evaluations do not guarantee predictability and legal certainty, but U.S. jurisdiction law is flexible and easily adaptable to particular circumstances of a case in order to establish the reasonableness and adequacy of a forum. It would be a mistake to evaluate U.S. jurisdiction law on the jurisdiction sources alone. U.S. jurisdiction law is very much concerned with the particular circumstances of the case and the interest of several parties involved, may they be defendant, claimant, or state. In order to find a balance between the interests of the claimant in his access to justice, the interest of the defendant to be protected from abuse of process and the state's interests, the U.S. jurisdiction system incorporated several interest analyses, imposed by higher constitutional standards. In order to determine whether a court has jurisdiction, the court has to evaluate a number of open criteria and factors of interests on a case-by-case basis.[696] From the 'purposeful availment' requirement to the reasonable test, and from the reasonable test to the *forum non conveniens* doctrine, U.S. courts possess significant (discretionary) power in establishing jurisdiction, hereby protecting the defendant, the claimant, but certainly also its own public interests.

---

[692] For a European comment see Schack, *Jurisdictional Minimum Contacts Scrutinized*, at 1, and see the preface by Audit in Mirandes, *La compétence internationale des Etats-Unis*, and further at 3.

[693] Juenger, 'A Shoe Unfit', at 1027.

[694] Borchers, 'The Death of the Constitutional Law of Jurisdiction', at 19. See also Heiser, 'A Minimum Interest Approach', at 917-918, 'The current due process doctrine is badly in need of revision. … So extensive is the scholarly criticism of the current doctrine that the task here is to adequately summarize the analyses of others.' See Clermont, 'Jurisdictional Salvation and the Hague Treaty', at 106, 'In summary, the U.S. constitutional law on jurisdiction, which combines the power and the unreasonableness tests, is complicated and uncertain. Moreover, it does not do an optimal job of distributing cases on a geographic basis. … Legislative regulation is necessary.' S. Burbank, 'Jurisdiction to Adjudicate: End of the Century or Beginning of a Millennium?', 111 *Tulane Journal of International and Comparative Law* (1999), 111-123, at 123, 'the American house of jurisdiction to adjudicate is not a place where any sensible person other than a lawyer (if that is not redundant) wants to live.'

[695] See in general Juenger, 'Comparative Neglect'; Reimann, 'Parochialism' and L. Silberman, 'Judicial Jurisdiction in the Conflict of Laws Course: Adding a Comparative Dimension', *Vanderbilt Journal of Transnational Law* (1995), 389-408.

[696] See Juenger stating 'Ordinary judges and counsel should hardly relish being told that they must weigh, on uncalibrated scales, "the facts of each case" to determine whether a particular tribunal may assert jurisdiction', in Juenger, 'Comparative Neglect', at 3; Buchner, Kläger- und Beklagtenschutz, at 48; 'Einzelfall-Rechtsprechung'.

Chapter 6

CONTRASTING APPROACHES TO INTERNATIONAL JURISDICTION

The previous chapters analysed the Brussels Model, Continental civil law systems, English common law and the U.S. system and demonstrated differences and similarities in the approach to international jurisdiction. The present chapter analyses the contrasting approaches to international jurisdiction; more specifically, it will deal with structural differences such as the divergence in starting points, contrasting approaches to extraterritoriality and the nature of the connection upon which jurisdiction is based. The first paragraph commences with some preliminary comparative observations related to the contrasts between common and civil law in an attempt to explain some of the approaches to international jurisdiction. The different starting points are analysed in Section 6.2 and the differences between an open, closed and mixed jurisdictional structure will be dealt with in Section 6.3. The different approaches to the protection of the parties and the different role of the defendant's home court are examined in Section 6.4.

Despite their differences, the question remains whether the contrasting approaches can be overcome at a uniform level and within which parameters uniform rules should be developed. These parameters for international jurisdiction will be formulated in Section 6.5. They will form the basis for the comparison and evaluation of jurisdictional bases and correction devises in Chapters 7 and 8, respectively.

6.1 Civil Law versus Common Law: Preliminary Comparative Observations

Contrasting approaches to international jurisdiction and the different jurisdictional structures of the Anglo-American systems and the Continental European models are often thought unbridgeable because of a presumed conflict between civil and common law traditions.[1] This civil-common law conflict is considered by some to be the source of the difficulties in the unification of international jurisdiction rules. Distinctive legal thinking and legal reasoning between common lawyers and civilians exists and could explain some of the contrasting approaches to international

[1] See Zweigert and Kötz: 'But here it is as well to issue a word of warning. Undoubtedly there are differences in the style of legal thinking in the countries of the Common Law on the one hand and on the Continent of Europe on the other, but it would certainly be wrong to make out that there was an unbridgeable opposition between the former's method of inductive problem-solving and the latter's method of systematic conceptualism.' K. Zweigert and H. Kötz, *Introduction to Comparative Law*, English translation by Tony Weir (from the German original: *Einführung in die Rechtsvergleichung auf dem Gebiete des Privatrechts*) (1998), at 259. See also on the mystification of common lawyers: '*cette étrange et fascinante race, le common lawyer*', D. Tallon, 'L'harmonisation des règles du droit privé entre pays de droit civil et de common law', *Revue internationale de droit comparé* (1990), 513-523, at 515.

jurisdiction and the different jurisdictional structures. In that context some general comparative observations involving the different characteristics of common and civil law traditions are valuable.[2]

It is widely accepted that the world's legal systems are roughly divided into two main legal traditions: the civil and the common law tradition.[3] Historical reasons are at the origin of this civil/common law distinction.[4] The origins of the civil law tradition are to be found in Ancient Roman Law as codified by the *Corpus Juris Civilus Justinianus*,[5] but have also found strong reception from the French codification movement after the French Revolution which was followed by the German Civil Code.[6]

Historically speaking, the development of the common law tradition is 'fairly clear cut'[7] in comparison to the historical development of the civil law tradition. In the 11th Century the first strong monarch, the Norman William the Conqueror,[8] pushed for his own 'justices in eyre' which gradually resulted in replacing local justice by 'county courts'.[9] A 'common' unified law was established in the 12th and 13th Century and was not, or hardly, receptive to any influence from the European

---

[2] These comparative observations do not involve an exhaustive examination, nor do they provide for a complete historical overview explaining the origins of distinction between civil and common law. It suffices to point out the most relevant differences by touching upon issues of international jurisdiction.

[3] See P. De Cruz, *Comparative Law in a Changing World* (2007), § 3.3, at 99; C. Kessedjian, 'Prel. Doc. No. 7: Report on International Jurisdiction and Foreign Judgments in Civil and Commercial Matters', at 23. Other legal traditions involve among others, Far East Law, Islamic Law, and Hindu Law. The world's legal systems are classified into legal families. De Cruz, *Comparative Law*, at 32, distinguishes three legal families: civil law, common law and socialist law. Zweigert and Kötz's classification of legal families involve six families and distinguishes within the civil law tradition between a Romanistic and Germanistic legal family and points out an Anglo-American family, Zweigert and Kötz, *Comparative Law*, at 63. A relatively new category involves legal systems which are difficult to classify in a particular legal family: the mixed or *hybrid* systems and involve a diversity of legal sources originating from both the civil and common law tradition. See Zweigert and Kötz, *Comparative Law*, at 72; V. Palmer, *Mixed Jurisdictions Worldwide: The Third Legal Family* (2001), at 7; W. Tetley, 'Mixed Jurisdictions: Common Law *vs* Civil Law (Codified and Uncodified) – Part I', 4 *Uniform Law Review* (1999), 591-619, at 597; see *contra* K. Reid, 'The Idea of Mixed Legal Systems', *Tulane Law Review* (2003), 5-40, at 19, who questions the terminology 'mixed' jurisdictions and prefers the terms 'Anglo-Civilian' or even 'Romano-English'.

[4] See De Cruz, *Comparative Law*, at 49 *et seq.*

[5] Ibid., at 55; J. Lokin and W. Zwalve, *Hoofdstukken uit de Europese Codificatiegeschiedenis* (1992), at 59.

[6] De Cruz, *Comparative Law*, at 39 *et seq.*; Zweigert and Kötz, *Comparative Law*, at 98; W. Zwalve, *Van common law en civil law C.Æ. Uniken Venema's common law & civil law: Inleiding tot het Anglo-Amerikaanse vermogensrecht* (2000), at 27; J. Sauveplanne, 'Codified and Judge Made Law: The Role of Courts and Legislators in Civil and Common Law Systems', in *Mededelingen der Koninklijke Nederlandse Akademie van Wetenschappen, afd. Letterkunde* (1982), 95-120, at 96-97 and 101-107. See definitions Tetley, 'Mixed Jurisdictions', at 596-597.

[7] De Cruz, *Comparative Law*, at 40.

[8] Zwalve, *Van common law en civil law*, at 27-28.

[9] Ibid., at 29; see also Sauveplanne, 'Codified and Judge Made Law', at 101: 'It sounds paradoxical that William the Conqueror, when he still ruled Normandy, was one of the chief opponents of royal authority and successfully resisted all efforts made by the French King to limit the powers of his barons: once King of England he became the champion of royal power and used all means at his disposal to subdue his barons to his rule. One of those means was the exercise of judicial power.'

Continent.[10] English common law did not feel the same need or desire for law codification as the civil law systems in Continental Europe.[11]

Although some writers observe that the traditional civil law/common law distinction is fading away,[12] or is exaggerated,[13] it is generally accepted that the explanation of the civil/common law distinction can be found in legal sources, ideologies, institutions, legal thinking and legal reasoning.[14] With respect to international jurisdiction, the distinctive choices of sources for jurisdiction, legal thinking[15] and technique are of particular relevance.[16]

6.1.1 **Distinctive Legal Sources: Legislation versus Judge-made Law**

One of the typical differences between civil law and common law traditions involves the choice of legal sources for jurisdiction: case law versus legislation.[17] Civil law primarily relies on statutory or codified law, whereas the predominant source of common law is formed by jurisdictional principles that are formulated by case law. In common law, courts regard statutes as a secondary source of law; most rules are found in the jurisprudence, statutes merely complete them.[18] The opposite is true regarding civil courts whose position is more one of 'assistant legislator'[19] that provides for statutory interpretation.[20] The early codification move-

---

[10] De Cruz, *Comparative Law*, at 102. The opposite is true for Scotland where a uniform common law was lacking and was influenced by Continental European events in the 16th Century which explains its civil law origins, see also Zwalve, *Van common law en civil law*, at 26.

[11] Sauveplanne, 'Codified and Judge Made Law', at 103.

[12] C. Morse, ed., *Making English Private International Law* (2002), at 292; C. Pejovic, 'Civil Law and Common Law: Two Different Paths Leading to the Same Goal', 32(3) *Victoria University of Wellington Law Review* (2001), 817-841, at 837 *et seq.*

[13] Zweigert and Kötz, *Comparative Law*, at 71.

[14] Other significant differences involve legal structure, organization of the judiciary and *stare decisis* (the binding force of precedent), see De Cruz, *Comparative Law*, at 39-42; Pejovic, 'Civil Law and Common Law', at 820; Zweigert and Kötz, *Comparative Law*, at 259.

[15] J. Hill, 'The Exercise of Jurisdiction in Private International Law', in *Asserting Jurisdiction – International and European Legal Perspectives* (2003), 39-62 at 57, 'As regards jurisdictional issues, the world is divided into two opposed schools of thought.'

[16] Sauveplanne, 'Codified and Judge Made Law', at 117.

[17] Morse, ed., *Making English Private International Law*, at 285; Zweigert and Kötz, *Comparative Law*, at 71, argue that differences as to legal sources should not be overestimated.

[18] Sauveplanne, 'Codified and Judge Made Law', at 114-115; De Cruz, *Comparative Law*, at 43; Pejovic, 'Civil Law and Common Law', at 819; Zweigert and Kötz, *Comparative Law*, at 258-259 and 69, 'So Common Law comes from the court, continental law from the study; the great jurists of England were judges, on the Continent professors'. See also S. Baumgartner, *The Proposed Hague Convention on Jurisdiction and Foreign Judgements: Trans-Atlantic Law Making for Transnational Litigation* (2003), at 142; Morse, ed., *Making English Private International Law*, at 291; and F. Juenger, 'Judicial Control of Improper Forum Regulation: Some Random Remarks and a Comment on How Not to Do IT', in *International Dispute Regulation* (1997), 311-325, at 314, 'Traditionally, professors, rather than judges served as their "oracles of the law".'

[19] D. Kokkini-Iatridou, *Een inleiding tot het rechtsvergelijkende onderzoek* (1988), at 156. P. Schlosser, 'Bases of Jurisdiction in a "New Double Convention" on Jurisdiction and Recognition of Foreign Judgements: Conference Papers', in *The Hague Convention on Jurisdiction and Judgements: Records of the Conference Held at New York University School of Law on the Proposed Convention 1999* (2001), A13-A27, at A18, 'As Montesquieu put it, the courts are only the mouth of the law, they simply reiterate the written law.'

[20] De Cruz, *Comparative Law*, at 279 *et seq.*

ment in Continental European civil law countries expressed the need to formulate jurisdiction in clear-cut rules and was uncomfortable with the idea of courts having large discretion.[21] Considerably less receptive to codification, the common law's preference for judge-made law over statutory legislation was explained by the fact that in England judge-made law was long considered superior to parliamentary legislation.[22] Nonetheless, a legislative 'movement' took place in all fields of law, including in the area of international jurisdiction.[23]

The use of distinctive legal sources is also reflected in the bases for international jurisdiction. The Continental European legislators are the principal drafters of international jurisdiction rules, whereas in the Anglo-American systems the courts play a considerable role.[24] The foundation of presence-based jurisdiction evolved from judge-made law forming Anglo-American common law principles and does not require statutory authority.[25] Legislative activity in the field of international jurisdiction came at a later stage: in England statutory provisions were introduced by Order 11, the CPR's precedent.[26] In the U.S., legislative activity was shaped by long-arm statutes whose enactment commenced only after the turn-over of the *International Shoe* case.[27]

The discretionary powers of Anglo-American courts were introduced by judge-made law and have no legislative basis. Fawcett's statement is accurate when he

---

[21] See M. Keyes, *Jurisdiction in International Litigation* (2005), at 229, 'In civilian systems, the notion that judges, in the exercise of a discretion, might decline to allow a matter to be heard and determined is offensive.' Also referring to R. Fentiman, 'Jurisdiction, Discretion and the Brussels Convention', 26 *Cornell International Law Journal* (1993), 59-99, at 75. According to Kessedjian 'Under common law systems, the judge is regarded as truly entrusted with the creation of the rule of law and with the duty to determine whether and to what extent a rule of law is proper in a specific case. Thus, common law judges enjoy substantial freedom. In civil law systems, this has been strongly debated until now.' C. Kessedjian, 'Judicial Regulation of Improper Forum Selections', in *International Dispute Resolution* (1997), 273-294, at 275. See also B. Pearce, 'The Comity Doctrine as a Barrier to Judicial Jurisdiction: A US-EU Comparison', 30 *Stanford Journal of International Law* (1994), 525-578, at 567 *et seq.*, explaining the historical background and the influence of the French Revolution: 'The lingering shackles imposed on the judiciary in the aftermath of the French Revolution rendered the Continental judge institutionally, if not psychologically, "incapable of the value-oriented, quasi-political functions involved in judicial review".'

[22] Morse writes about the so-called 'superiority of common law'. According to Morse one of the arguments against legislative action is some common lawyers' belief that the '[l]egislator will always do a bad job'. Morse refers to Cheshire, *Private International Law* (1935), at vii, indicating the 'paralysing hand of the Parliamentary draftsman', Morse, ed., *Making English Private International Law*, at 274-275 and 285-290. See Zweigert and Kötz, *Comparative Law*, at 265, who observes that common lawyers see statutory legislation as a 'necessary evil'; Juenger, 'Improper Forum Regulation', at 314, 'the civilians' aversion to judicial creativity was demonstrated when judicial heads rolled in the course of the French Revolution, one of whose goals was to curtail judicial arbitrariness.'

[23] Sauveplanne, 'Codified and Judge Made Law', at 113, 'Just as a codified system cannot develop without courts, a judge-made system cannot progress without a legislator'.

[24] P. Schlosser, 'Jurisdiction in International Litigation: The Issue of Human Rights in Relation to National Law and the Brussels Convention', *Rivista di diritto internazionale* (1991), 5-34, at 12, 'Rules of jurisdiction are not codified in the United States, and are only very partially embodied in acts of parliamentary legislation.' See also Sect. 6.3 on the closed, mixed and open systems.

[25] See for Australian jurisdictional principles, Keyes, *Jurisdiction in International Litigation*, at 252.

[26] See Chapter 4 on international jurisdiction in England.

[27] *International Shoe Co. v. Washington*, 326 U.S. 310 (1945).

argues that 'in common law jurisdictions it is probably easier to introduce a doctrine of forum non conveniens than in civil law States where jurisdiction is laid down by code, statute, or treaty'.[28] Gaudemet-Tallon would most certainly agree with him, as she writes that:

> '*en France on a toujours pensé qu'il valait mieux encadrer strictement les pouvoirs des organes judiciaires, tant en ce qui concerne la compétence qu'en ce qui concerne le fond ... au contraire, en Angleterre, le respect de l'opinion publique pour les juges et le pragmatisme britannique expliquent que les theories du forum conveniens et du forum non conveniens aient pu s'épanouir sans difficulté.*'[29]

6.1.2 Legal Thinking: Rule-based or Fact-based Approach

With legal thinking is generally meant the 'mental structure of the lawyer'.[30] This difference of legal thinking is explained by the fact that a common lawyer relies heavily on facts and 'proceeds from case law to case law', whereas a civil lawyer would proceed from 'principle to principle'[31] and from 'rule to rule' trying to fit the case into a principle, rule or category of law.[32] According to Zweigert

> 'On the Continent lawyers, faced with a problem, even a new and unforeseen one, ask what solution the rule provides; in England and the United States they predict how the judge would deal with the problem given existing decisions. ... On the Continent, lawyers think abstractly, in terms of institutions [or rules and principles]; in England concretely in terms of cases. ... On the Continent the system is conceived as being complete and free from gaps, in England lawyers feel their way gradually from case to case.'[33]

As a result of this distinctive legal thinking, the civilian approach to jurisdiction is primarily rule-based and code-driven, whereas common law takes a primarily case-by-case approach.

The distinctive legal thinking is also reflected in the approach to international jurisdiction. Continental civil law systems apply legal or juridical connecting factors for jurisdiction embodied in well-articulated hard and fast rules and fit in a well-defined framework.[34] Jurisdiction is determined on the basis of rigid rules

---

[28] See also J. Fawcett, *Declining Jurisdiction in Private International Law* (1995), at 22-23.

[29] H. Gaudemet-Tallon, 'Les régimes relatifs au refus d'exercer la compétence juridictionelle en matière civile et commerciale', *Revue internationale de droit comparé* (1994), 423-435, at 424.

[30] Tallon, 'L'harmonisation des règles', at 518, '*la façon de penser juridiquement, on pourrait dire, la structure mentale du juriste, telle qu'elle est forgée par la tradition du système juridique auquel il appartient et par la formation juridique qu'il a reçue.*'

[31] De Cruz, *Comparative Law*, at 42.

[32] According to Zweigert and Kötz, *Comparative Law*, at 69, civil lawyers have a tendency 'to think up and to think in juristic constructions'.

[33] Ibid., at 69 *et seq.*

[34] This terminology is also used by Boele-Woelki with respect to the applicable law and could apply by analogy to jurisdiction rules, K. Boele-Woelki, C. Joustra *et al.*, 'Dutch Private International Law at the End of the 20th Century: Pluralism of Methods', in *Netherlands Reports to the 15th International Congress of Comparative Law Bristol 1998* (1998), 203-227, at 210. See also 'the success of a "rigid instrument"', J. Bomhoff, *Judicial Discretion in European Law on Conflicts of Jurisdic-*

containing formal criteria and closed bases for jurisdiction.[35] The civil lawyer examines whether the claim fits the juridical norm embodied in well-defined and rigid bases for jurisdiction.[36] In the closed civil law systems,[37] most provisions are 'tailor-made' and particularly designed for a specific situation. This is best illustrated by contract jurisdiction as determined by Article 5(1) Brussels Regulation which applies the juridical concept of the 'place of performance of the obligation in question'. The ECJ repeatedly refused to take the case-by-case approach using open-ended standards, such as the close-connection or the characteristic performance.[38]

By contrast, common law systems take a more concrete or pragmatic fact-based approach and establish jurisdiction on the basis of 'intensively factual balancing tests',[39] jurisdictional standards and principles in which there is considerable room for judicial discretion.[40] Common law tradition in general, but the U.S. jurisdictional system in particular, determine jurisdiction on the basis of factual concepts and open-ended standards, instead of formal juridical concepts.[41] The U.S. activity-based jurisdiction is a good example of such factual and open-ended norms for jurisdiction. The quality and quantity of the defendant's contacts with the forum are appreciated on the basis of the facts of the case and a balancing test deals with the jurisdictional standards and principles.[42] Apart from the use of open-ended jurisdiction criteria, Anglo-American legal thinking is also characterized by its use of judicial discretion. [43] The flexibility of Anglo-American common law systems is illustrated in their approach to extraterritoriality and the protection of the parties.[44] Anglo-American common law on jurisdiction relies heavily on facts and on principles of appropriateness or *conveniens* under the *forum (non) conveniens* exception or with respect to the U.S., on fairness and reasonableness principles emanating from constitutional standards.[45] The U.S. Supreme Court's rejection to apply a

tion: Looking for National Perspectives on European Rules for Jurisdiction over Multiple Defendants (2005), Chap. 2.

[35] See also A. von Mehren, 'Theory and Practice of Adjudicatory Authority in Private International Law: General Course on Private International Law (1996)', 295 *Recueil des cours* (2003), 9-431, at 70.

[36] Baumgartner, *The Proposed Hague Convention*, at 146.

[37] See below Sect. 6.3.1 for the closed system of the Continental European approach.

[38] See Chapter 7, Sect. 7.6. Special *forum contractus* rule. See also P. Punt, 'Naar een meer karakteristieke jurisdictie?', in *Aan Wil besteed* (2003), 425-448, at 429, '*formeel juridisch aanknopingspunt*' versus '*werkelijk feitelijk aanknopingspunt*'. See for critical comments R. Fentiman, 'Access to Justice and Parallel Proceedings in Europe', 63 *The Cambridge Law Journal* (2004), 312-313, at 313.

[39] W. O'Brian Jr., 'The Hague Convention on Jurisdiction and Judgments: The Way Forward', 66 *The Modern Law Review* (2003), 491-509, at 497.

[40] See also Von Mehren, 'Theory and Practice', at 30.

[41] Ibid., at 70; and R. Michaels, 'Re-Placements. Jurisdiction for Contracts and Torts under the Brussels I Regulation When Arts. 5(1) and 5(3) Do Not Designate a Place in a Member State', in *International Civil Litigation in Europe and Relations with Third States* (2005), 129-156, at 152.

[42] Baumgartner, *The Proposed Hague Convention*, at 146.

[43] See also Hill, 'The Exercise of Jurisdiction', at 57.

[44] See Sect. 6.4 for the protection of parties.

[45] O'Brian Jr., 'The Hague Convention on Jurisdiction', at 496; Baumgartner, *The Proposed Hague Convention*, at 144.

'mechanical test' to determine jurisdiction, reflects that jurisdiction is determined on factual tests.[46]

In sum, distinctive legal thinking shows a contrast between a rule-based approach and a fact-based approach.[47] As one German commentator stated, bridges are to be built between the '*Ordnungskalkulen*' of the civil law tradition and the '*Ermessensfreiheiten*' of the common law tradition.[48]

6.1.3 Legal Technique: *Ex Ante* or *Ex Post* Appreciation of Jurisdictional Interests

The different jurisdictional sources and distinctive legal thinking in Continental European and Anglo-American common law systems result in a different approach to appreciating jurisdictional interests. The civil law system weighs jurisdictional interests *ex ante* through the legislator, whereas common law prefers to appreciate jurisdictional interests *ex post* by judicial appreciation.[49] The *ex ante* approach implies that the legislator pre-determines bases for jurisdiction on the presumption of a close connection between the forum and the dispute. The Continental European legislator and the drafters of the Brussels Model designed clear-cut jurisdiction rules, generally perceived as being fair and reasonable[50] *ex ante*, taking into account policy considerations and jurisdictional interests.[51] The *actor sequitur forum rei* is an example of a pre-fixed interest balance in favour of the defendant in which there is no room for *ex post* appreciation of either defendant's or claimant's interests.[52] The civil law technique is based on the idea that there is less need or no desire for *ex post* appreciation of open-ended standards and correction mechanisms when well-drafted jurisdictional provisions take into account *ex ante* the various jurisdictional interests.[53]

---

[46] *Kulko v. Superior Court of California*, 436 U.S. 84, at 92 (1978).

[47] See also Von Mehren, 'Theory and Practice', at 30.

[48] O. Hartwieg, 'Forum Shopping zwischen Forum non Conveniens und "hinreichendem Inlandsbezug"', 51 *Juristen Zeitung* (1996), 109-118, at 109.

[49] See also O'Brian Jr., 'The Hague Convention on Jurisdiction', at 494; M. Whincop, *Policy and Pragmatism in the Conflict of Laws* (2001), at 142.

[50] O'Brian Jr., 'The Hague Convention on Jurisdiction', at 493-494; G. Droz, *Compétence judiciaire et effets des jugements dans le Marché Commun* (1972), § 54, at 51, '*un tribunal spécial désigné à raison du caractère raisonnable de sa relation avec le litige.*'

[51] See Von Mehren, 'Theory and Practice', at 30; and Schlosser, 'The Issue of Human Rights', at 12, 'The underlying idea has always been that the jurisdiction so established is fair for both parties.'

[52] See P. Jenard, 'Report on the Convention on Jurisdiction and the Enforcement of Judgments of Civil and Commercial Matters', OJ 1979 C 59/1, 1-65, at 15, repeated in the ECJ's decision of C-26/91 *Handte v. Traitements*, [1992] ECR I-3967, para. 12: 'To this end, the rules of jurisdiction codified in Title II determine which State's courts are most appropriate to assume jurisdiction, taking into account all relevant matters.' Also referred to by Bell in A. Bell, *Forum Shopping and Venue in Transnational Litigation* (2003), at 55.

[53] Fawcett, *Declining Jurisdiction*, at 22, 'it has been seen that in many States, the rules of jurisdiction are such that they take into account that the sorts of factors that are considered under a doctrine of *forum non conveniens*; if jurisdiction is taken on the basis of *forum conveniens*, there is no need for a doctrine of *forum conveniens*.'

Conversely, Anglo-American common law courts have discretionary powers to *ex post* examine the supposed close connection and to appreciate jurisdictional interests on an *ad hoc* basis for that particular dispute.[54] The close connection, parties' interests, and other underlying considerations or policies are weighed in the Anglo-American common law system by the courts under the *forum (non) conveniens* doctrine and 'reasonableness and fairness' standards are examined *a posteriori* once the court is seized.

6.1.4 Legal Certainty and Flexibility

The civil-common law 'conflict' often explained by the distinctive legal sources and the different legal thinking and legal technique, becomes particularly apparent in respect to the tension between principles of legal certainty and the desire of flexibility to ensure (procedural) justice.[55]

Answering the jurisdictional question with a considerable amount of flexibility in order to adapt to individual circumstances is generally thought by civilians to be at the expense of legal certainty.[56] The civil law approach praises the hard and fast rules ensuring legal certainty as opposed to the open-ended standards and judicial discretion used in Anglo-American common law, which civilians generally claim results in legal uncertainty.[57] The Continental European approach is particularly concerned with ensuring certainty by providing clear jurisdictional bases 'that afford the litigants a measure of predictability'.[58] Jenard links the well-defined jurisdictional structure of the Brussels Model with legal certainty when he states that it is 'a genuine legal systematization which will ensure the greatest possible degree of legal certainty'.[59] The Regulation's Preamble goes even further by stating that 'the rules of jurisdiction must be highly predictable' to achieve one of its principal objectives of strengthening the legal protection of persons established in

---

[54] See Bell, *Forum Shopping and Venue*, § 4.34, at 147; Baumgartner, *The Proposed Hague Convention*, at 179; C. Chalas, *L'exercise discrétionnaire de la compétence juridictionnelle en droit international privé* (2000), at 360-368.

[55] P. Hay, 'Flexibility versus Predictability and Uniformity in Choice of Law. Reflections on Current European and United States Conflicts Law', 226 *Recueil des cours* (1991), 281-412, at 292; R. Weintraub, 'Rome II and the Tension between Predictability and Flexibility', in *Balancing of Interests Liber Amicorum Peter Hay zum 70. Geburtstag* (2005), 451-461; and M. Stückelberg, 'Lis Pendens and Forum Non Conveniens at the Hague Conference: The Preliminary Draft Convention on Jurisdiction and Foreign Judgments in Civil and Commercial Matters', 26 *Brooklyn Journal of International Law* (2001), 949-982, at 979.

[56] See A. Johnston and E. Powles, 'The Kings of the World and Their Dukes' Dilemma: Globalisation, Jurisdiction and the Rule of Law', in *Globalisation and Jurisdiction* (2004), 13-54, at 41; O'Brian Jr., 'The Hague Convention on Jurisdiction', at 494.

[57] Fawcett, *Declining Jurisdiction*, at 20, explains that although *forum non conveniens* 'provides flexibility and allows the court to consider the wide, indeed unlimited, range of considerations which come within the themes of appropriateness and justice', a certain degree of certainty is however to be found in common law jurisdictions due to many reported cases and numerous precedents explaining the doctrine of *forum non conveniens*.

[58] F. Juenger, 'A Shoe Unfit for Globetrotting? Symposium Fifty Years of International Shoe: The Past and the Future of Personal Jurisdiction', 28 *The University of California Davis Law Review* (1995), 1027-1045, at 1042.

[59] Jenard Report, at 15, repeated in *Handte*, at para. 12.

its territory.[60] The ECJ repeatedly stated that the principle of legal certainty is an objective of the Brussels Model by itself.[61] The benefits of legal certainty in European transnational relations outweighed the need for a flexible approach on a case-by-case basis. On numerous occasions the ECJ favoured considerations of legal certainty over the existence of a close connection between the forum and the claim which justified special jurisdiction in the first place. In the name of the *sacro-sainte securité juridique*,[62] the ECJ gave an interpretation to Article 5(1) in the *Custom Made* decision favouring considerations of legal certainty over establishing jurisdiction on the basis of a close connection in relation to the *forum contractus rule*.[63]

Judicial discretion and *ex post* appreciation of facts is considered contrary to the civil law approach to jurisdiction. In particular the uncertainty for the claimant created by the *forum non conveniens* doctrine is considered undesirable: the claimant is not certain whether the court he selected will accept to exercise jurisdiction hereby giving effect to his choice.[64] This lack of clarity and little predictive power as to the outcome of jurisdictional disputes has made the doctrine unpopular in Continental civil law systems.[65]

From a common law perspective, the use of well-defined rules makes jurisdiction law rigid and the strict application of jurisdiction rules for the sake of legal certainty is at the expense of flexibility and justice.[66] The rigid bases for jurisdiction and closed connecting factors do not serve the interests of justice as they fail to take into account specific facts or particular circumstances. Litigational unfairness and jurisdictional injustice are the results.[67] A good illustration of this common law point of view in relation to the Brussels Model is the statement of Lord Goff of Chieveley in the *Airbus Industrie G.I.E.* case where he acknowledges that the

---

[60] Regulation's Preamble § 11.

[61] Judgment of the Court (Sixth Chamber) of 20 January 1994 – C-129/92 *Owens Bank Ltd v. Fulvio Bracco and Bracco Industria Chimica SpA*, [1994] ECR, at I-00117, para. 32. See also the judgement in the Case 38/81 *Effer*, [1982] ECR 825, para. 6.

[62] D. Kokkini-Iatridou, 'Rapport général: Les clauses d'exception en matière de conflits de lois et de conflits de juridictions', in *Exception Clauses in Conflicts of Laws and Conflicts of Jurisdictions, or the Principle of Proximity: XIVth International Congress of Comparative Law, Athens* (1994), 3-41, at 35.

[63] C-288/92 *Custom Made v. Stawa*, [1994] ECR I-2913. See Chapter 2, Sect. 2.7.1. The ECJ stated that '[t]he place of performance of the obligation was chosen as the criterion of jurisdiction because, being precise and clear, it fits into the general aim of the Convention, which is to establish rules guaranteeing certainty as to the allocation of jurisdiction among the various national courts before which proceedings in matters relating to a contract may be brought'. See also J. Newton, *The Uniform Interpretation of the Brussels and Lugano Conventions* (2002), at 50; and J. Hill, 'Jurisdiction in Matters Relating to a Contract under the Brussels Convention', 44 *The International and Comparative Law Quarterly* (1995), 591-619, at 605.

[64] See also the research conducted by Keyes in Keyes, *Jurisdiction in International Litigation*, at 173-174.

[65] See in particular Chapter 2, Sect. 2.3.1.

[66] According to Collins 'Justice is a chameleon word', L. Collins, 'The Institut de droit International and anti-suit injunctions', in *Festschrift für Erik Jayme* (2004), 131-142, at 131; see also P. Nygh, 'The Criteria for Judicial Jurisdiction', in A. Lowenfeld and L. Silberman, eds., *The Hague Convention on Jurisdiction and Judgments* (2001), at A-3.

[67] See Von Mehren, 'Theory and Practice', at 68-69, who analyses the ease of administration and predictability versus litigational fairness.

Brussels Convention achieved the purpose of allocating jurisdiction on the basis of well-defined rules, 'but at a price. … The price is rigidity, and rigidity can be productive of injustice'.[68]

6.2 Different Starting Points for International Jurisdiction

The starting point for international jurisdiction is based on an underlying assumption which varies from system to system. It represents the fundamental basis for judicial power upon which the jurisdictional structure rests. The fact that different starting points are at the origin of jurisdictional structures explains why the Continental civil law tradition, the Brussels Model, the English common law tradition and the American structure developed such different approaches to international jurisdiction.[69] The following three starting points, all deriving from traditional principles of sovereignty and territoriality, should be distinguished:[70] defendant's domicile, presence and minimum contacts.[71]

6.2.1 *Forum Rei*, Presence and Due Process

The Continental European approach to jurisdiction is based on the assumption that a defendant should primarily be subjected to his home court. This assumption is not the starting point of Anglo-American jurisdictional structures. The *actor sequitur forum rei* rule forms the starting point for the majority of Continental European countries and the Brussels Model.[72] Other significant bases for jurisdiction such as nationality and presence of property play a mere subsidiary role and do not, or do no longer, represent the starting point for international jurisdiction.[73]

Additionally, the allocation of judicial powers between European courts pursuant to the Brussels Model depends on the location of defendant's domicile and the rule constitutes the sole ground for general jurisdiction.[74] Derogations to the

---

[68] *Airbus Industrie G.I.E. v. Patel and Others*, [1999] 1 AC 119, at 132.

[69] A. Nuyts, 'Due Process and Fair Trial: Jurisdiction in the United States and in Europe Compared', in *International Civil Litigation in Europe and Relations with Third States* (2005), at 159, 'It is simply a matter of fact that in the area of jurisdiction, as in many other areas, American and European jurists have followed different paths with the consequence that the current practices of their courts have reached different points'; K. Nguyen, 'Invisibly Radiated; Federalism Principles and the Proposed Hague Convention on Jurisdiction and Foreign Judgements', 28 *Hastings Constitutional Law Quarterly* (2000), 145-166, at 148.

[70] See in particular R. Michaels, 'Territorial Jurisdiction after Territoriality', in *Globalisation and Jurisdiction* (2004), 106-130 at 107 *et seq.*

[71] Von Mehren uses a different terminology distinguishing first and second paradigms of connecting factors in which he identifies 'illustrative first-paradigm connecting factors' as the 'bases of general jurisdiction such as service of process upon a natural person within the forum state, the defendant's domicile or habitual residence in that State or, in the case of legal persons, their incorporation or principal place of business there and the presence of assets belonging to the defendant in the forum state. Each of these connecting factors uses a single, largely objective, element that is not controversy-specific.' Von Mehren, 'Theory and Practice', at 69.

[72] This starting point is explicitly laid down in Recital 11 of the Brussels Regulation. See Chapter 2, Sect. 2.5. and see for a comparison Chapter 7, Sect. 7.2.

[73] See for France Chapter 3, Sect. 3.4.3.

[74] See on the scope of the Brussels Model Chapter 2, Sects. 2.2.3 and 2.5.

defendant's domicile rule are 'exceptions' to the main principle;[75] they are limited and interpreted restrictively.[76] Already in 1912, Beale explained it as follows: 'generally speaking, then, there is no jurisdiction over a defendant except at his domicile; but while a non-resident cannot usually be sued, there are nevertheless exceptional cases in which an action may be brought against him'.[77]

The maxim of the *actor sequitur forum rei* can be traced back to ancient Roman law. Long before the principle of territorial sovereignty shaped jurisdictional theories such as the English presence rules based on territorial allegiance, and the U.S. power theory deriving from the *Pennoyer Neff* decision, the Roman maxim of the *Codex Justinianum* distributed judicial powers in the Roman Empire.[78] It establishes the principle that the plaintiff must pursue the defendant at his home forum and it is therefore based on fairness to the defendant.[79] The maxim became self-evident and unquestioned for Continental European systems.

In contrast, the English common law's starting point for jurisdiction is formed by the archaic notion of presence, subjecting any defendant (physically) present in the forum to jurisdiction of English courts. 'Presence' is the 'root principle'[80] and results in general jurisdiction over natural persons physically present in the forum and over corporate defendants 'present' in any form, varying from incorporation in the forum to a simple business establishment within the English territory.[81]

Historically speaking, the counterpart of the King's protection consisted of owing allegiance to him, including being submitted to his jurisdiction when a

---

[75] See C-103/05 *Reisch v. Kiesel*, [2006] ECR I-6827, para. 22; C-265/02 *Frahuil v. Assitalia*, [2004] ECR I-1543, para. 23.

[76] See among others J. Pontier and E. Burg, *EU Principles on Jurisdiction and Recognition and Enforcement of Judgments in Civil and Commercial Matters* (2004), at 56; and Von Mehren, 'Theory and Practice', at 182 and 185. See also C-256/00 *Besix v. WABAG*, [2002] ECR I-1699, paras. 52 and 53; and C-412/98 *Group Josi v. UGIC*, [2000] ECR I-5925, paras. 34 and 35.

[77] J. Beale, 'Jurisdiction of Courts over Foreigners', 26 *Harvard Law Review* (1912), 193-211, at 199. One such exceptional case he mentions is the case of contracts made or performable within the country.

[78] *Pennoyer v. Neff*, 95 U.S. 714, at 733 (1877). Already in 1912, Beale identified a 'so-called Common Law of Europe' deriving from the principles of Roman law, Beale, 'Jurisdiction of Courts over Foreigners', at 195. See also F. Juenger, 'The American Law of General Jurisdiction', *University of Chicago Legal Forum* (2001), 141-170, at 143; K. Clermont, 'Jurisdictional Salvation and the Hague Treaty', *Cornell Law Review* (1999), 89-133, at 91; F. Mann, 'The Doctrine of International Jurisdiction Revisited after Twenty Years', 186 *Recueil des cours* (1984), 9-116, at 67; F. Juenger, 'Federalism: Judicial Jurisdiction in the United States and in the European Communities: A Comparison', 82 *Michigan Law Review* (1984), 1195-1212, at 1203. See for the English underlying assumption H.L. Korn, 'The Development of Judicial Jurisdiction in the United States', 65 *Brooklyn Law Review* (1999), 935, at 966.

[79] See J. Story, *Commentaries on the Conflicts of Laws, Foreign and Domestic in Regard to Contracts, Rights, and Remedies, and Especially in Regard to Marriages, Divorces, Wills, Successions, and Judgments* (1883), at 750, 'The general rule of the Roman Code is, that the plaintiff must bring suit or action in the place where the defendant has his domicile, or where he had it at the time of the contract.' Clermont, 'Jurisdictional Salvation', at 91; Jenard Report, at 18; and H. Gaudemet-Tallon, *Origines de l'article 14 CC* (1964) , at 10.

[80] *John Russel & Co Ltd v. Cayzer, Irvine & Co Ltd*, Decision of the House of Lords, 2 June 1916, [1916] 2 AC 298, at 302.

[81] See Chapter 4, Sect. 4.4.2.

King's writ was served against you. The writ was a powerful instrument in the development of the King's justice on his territory and required physical presence. The *actor sequitur forum rei* maxim was unknown, since the reception of Roman law was generally rather limited in the common law system.[82]

The U.S. jurisdictional scheme is characterized by a separate and distinct starting point, despite its English common law origins.[83] In contrast to the Continental European and English starting points for jurisdiction, the U.S.'s starting point is formed by constitutional standards. From the moment the U.S. Supreme Court decided in *Pennoyer v. Neff* that jurisdiction must satisfy due process of law,[84] 'due process is the fountainhead of [U.S.] jurisdiction'.[85] The due process clause forms the starting point for U.S. jurisdiction as its interpretation provided by the U.S. Supreme Court shaped the jurisdictional limits of what is constitutionally admissible. *Pennoyer* established that due process was satisfied when jurisdiction is founded in accordance with common law principles and introduced the 'power' theory for jurisdictional purposes. *International Shoe* and its progeny articulated a new interpretation, establishing that process is due when defendant has 'minimum contacts' with the forum and does not offend 'traditional notions of fair play and substantial justice'.[86] The meaning of the Due Process Clause as starting point for U.S. jurisdiction is twofold and results in the coexistence of two underlying assumptions: jurisdiction as the foundation of 'power' and on 'minimum contacts'.[87]

U.S. jurisdiction was originally founded on notions of power showing considerable similarities with the English starting point of presence. The *Pennoyer v. Neff* case resulted in the constitutionalization[88] of U.S. jurisdiction law and established that due process required a strict application of territorialism.[89] The power assump-

---

[82] Keyes, *Jurisdiction in International Litigation*, at 183; Zwalve, *Van common law en civil law*, at 30; Sauveplanne, 'Codified and Judge Made Law', at 109; see also Sect. 6.1. for the historical origins of civil and common law traditions.

[83] Baumgartner, *The Proposed Hague Convention*, at 131; P.J. Borchers, 'Comparing Personal Jurisdiction in the United States and the European Community: Lessons for American Reform', 40 *American Journal of Comparative Law* (1992), 121-157, at 156; A. von Mehren, *Law in the United States: A General and Comparative View* (1988), at 6-8; F. Mann, 'The Doctrine of International Jurisdiction', 111 *Recueil des cours* (1964), 1-162, at 77.

[84] *Pennoyer v. Neff*, 95 U.S. 714, at 733 (1877). See Chapter 5, Sect. 5.2; B. Buchner, *Kläger- und Beklagtenschutz im Recht der internationalen Zuständigkeit. Losüngsansätze für eine zukünftige Gerichtsstands- und Vollstreckungskonvention, Studien zum ausländischen und internationalen Privatrecht* (1998), at 25; S. Goldstein, 'Federalism and Substantive Due Process: A Comparative and Historical Perspective on International Shoe and Its Progeny', 28 *The University of California Davis Law Review* (1995), 965-998, at 969; Juenger, 'Federalism: A Comparison', at 1196.

[85] Juenger, 'Federalism: A Comparison', at 1198. See also Schlosser, 'The Issue of Human Rights', at 12-13.

[86] *International Shoe Co. v. Washington*, 326 U.S. 310 (1945). See also Juenger, 'Federalism: A Comparison', at 1198.

[87] Von Mehren, 'Theory and Practice', at 129-133; Buchner, 'Kläger- und Beklagtenschutz', at 25-26.

[88] Goldstein calls this the 'federalism thread', Goldstein, 'Federalism', at 966.

[89] See U.S. Chapter 5, Sect. 5.2.2. and see also Baumgartner, *The Proposed Hague Convention*, at 133-135.

tion included presence-based jurisdiction, *quasi in rem* jurisdiction, the defendant's domicile and consent.[90] All of these traditional jurisdictional bases still play an essential role in the U.S. approach to (international) jurisdiction and coexist with the second underlying assumption for jurisdiction based on 'minimum contacts'. The *International Shoe*-turnover understood due process as requiring the defendant to have certain 'minimum contacts' with the forum and extended the first assumption based on territorial sovereignty principles.[91] The minimum contacts assumption primarily focuses on the 'quality and nature of the activity' of the defendant in the forum and results in the enactment of jurisdictional long-arm state statutes.[92]

The difference in starting point is also relevant with respect to the different approaches to corporate defendants. This is best explained by Brand:

> 'The US recognizes that a corporate defendant may be located in more than one forum alone. Besides the domicile criterion also known in the US jurisdictional scheme, the doing business criterion allows general jurisdiction over the defendant in more than one forum, as long as the corporate defendant is doing business in a continuous and systematic way in those forums. Consequently, the allocation of general jurisdiction according to US jurisdiction rules is not restricted to concepts such as "domicile" and "presence", since the doing business criterion is much wider.'[93]

6.2.2 Extraterritoriality and Long-arm Jurisdiction

Each of the above described starting points for jurisdiction are based on principles of territorial sovereignty; this is certainly the case with the English presence, but it is also true for the U.S. power-assumption and the Continental European defendant's domicile.[94] As a natural consequence, the reach of judicial powers is limited by those territorial and sovereign principles.[95]

---

[90] See Juenger, 'Federalism: A Comparison', at 1197.

[91] *International Shoe Co. v. Washington*, 326 U.S. 310, at 316 (1945).

[92] These latter considerations resulted in the *fairness* theory, see among others Mann, 'Doctrine of International Jurisdiction Revisited', at 68, or the '*Litigational-Justice Theory*' as it has been called by Von Mehren, see Von Mehren, 'Theory and Practice', at 115.

[93] See also R. Brand, 'Report: The 1999 Hague Preliminary Draft Convention Text on Jurisdiction and Judgments: A View From the United States: Development of Due Process Jurisdictional Analysis in U.S. Law', in *The Hague Preliminary Draft Convention on Jurisdiction and Judgments* (2005), 3-40, at 18, 'Thus US concepts of general jurisdiction are not limited to formal definitions of domicile.'

[94] R. Michaels, 'Two Paradigms of Jurisdiction', 27 *Michigan Journal of International Law* (2007), 1003-1069, at 1057, 'Territoriality is still central to jurisdictional thinking in both the United States and Europe'; Johnston and Powles, 'The Kings of the World', at 26; Michaels, 'Territorial Jurisdiction', at 107, 'In personam jurisdiction is usually based on territorial considerations'; Von Mehren, 'Theory and Practice', at 144-145. According to Justice Scott in *Adams v. Cape Industries Plc*, [1990] Ch. 433, at 458 (CA), 'Jurisdiction on the ground of presence in the foreign country is based on territoriality.' Lord Diplock confirms for England that 'the general rule is that the jurisdiction of the English court over persons is territorial.' *Siskina and Others v. Distos Compañía Naviera S.A.*, [1979] AC 210, 254.

[95] Mann calls this the Huber-Storyan maxim; a jurisdiction rule extends (and is limited) to everybody and everything within the sovereign's territory and to his nationals wherever they may be. Principles of territorial sovereignty have a positive and a negative effect on jurisdiction, Mann, 'Doctrine of International Jurisdiction', at 74, and Mann, 'Doctrine of International Jurisdiction Revisited', at 20.

The *forum rei* rule fails to establish jurisdiction over a non-domiciled defendant. Similarly, the English presence rule appeared unsatisfactory in reaching absent defendants, despite a strong connection with England through the claim or another connection with the defendant. Likewise, the U.S. power theory deriving from the *Pennoyer Neff*-era was no longer suited for modern times.[96]

For a period of time, creative solutions were found to overcome the problem of territorial limitations. In the U.S., the limits of the power theory were stretched by the 'implied consent' theory establishing jurisdiction over 'doing business' in the forum. Casad simply considers doing business as 'a historical relic of an earlier system that we had before 1945 and that the Supreme Court unfortunately kept alive for us. It is a substitute for jurisdiction based on physical presence.'[97] Both the English presence rule and the U.S. power notion appeared to be untenable. According to Juenger, the traditional Anglo-American common law jurisdictional principles premised on in-state service of process and

> 'is at once too broad and too narrow. It is too broad because serving people on board trains, or – worse yet – airplanes, is clearly exorbitant; it is too narrow because it does not promote the effective adjudication of disputes involving cars and corporations. Stuck with a procrustean principle, courts resorted to fictions to broaden the jurisdictional options.'[98]

Legislators and courts sooner or later questioned the legitimacy of the original starting points and each of them dealt with their shortcomings in their own way. Confronted with extraterritoriality, they felt the need to move away from the traditional 'territorialist' approach and adopted new jurisdictional paradigms in order to reach the defendant outside their 'sovereign territorial' domain.[99] The result is a relaxation of the strict territorialist approach and the adoption of a 'more flexible doctrine of closeness of connection' with the forum.[100]

---

[96] See Chapter 5, Sect. 5.2.2, see the Supreme Court's observation in *McGee v. International Life Ins.*, 355 U.S. 220 (1957), at 222-223. See Michaels, 'Territorial Jurisdiction', at 108-109, 'Actual presence or the place of conduct have been considered unattractive as bases of jurisdiction for some time. Modern communication methods as well as industrial progress made it more frequent for an individual to have an impact on circumstances within a state without ever entering that state'; see also Juenger, 'Federalism: A Comparison', at 1197.

[97] Comments by Casad in A. Lowenfeld and L. Silberman, eds., *The Hague Convention on Jurisdiction and Judgments: Records of the Conference Held at New York University School of Law on the Proposed Convention* (2001), at 48.

[98] F. Juenger, 'American Jurisdiction: A Story of Comparative Neglect', 65 *University of Colorado Law Review* (1993), 1-23, at 7.

[99] See the Revised Draft resolution on Extraterritoriality by the IDI: 'Considering that the evolution of international relations has resulted in the need to question the traditional manner in which sovereignty is exercised and the delineation of the territorial sphere over which the state's jurisdiction extends.' The newer version of the Resolution goes even further 'Considering that in many cases, particularly those linked to the delocalisation of the main operations of contemporary economic relations, the concepts of territoriality and of extraterritoriality are inadequate for the proper determination of the limits of State jurisdiction as limited by international law'; F. Rigaux, 'The Extraterritorial Jurisdiction of State – La compétence extraterritoriale des états', 69 *Annuaire de l'Institut de droit international* (2001), 13-94, at 111-112 and 92; and see Keyes, *Jurisdiction in International Litigation*, at 187.

[100] Mann, 'Doctrine of International Jurisdiction', at 54, 'Private International law proves, in particular, the familiar reluctance to transgress those limits of jurisdiction which public international

Presently, all legal systems regulate 'extraterritorial' reach over defendants: in Continental European regimes and the Brussels Model 'special jurisdiction rules' provide for additional bases for jurisdiction alternatively applicable to the *forum rei*. England enacted the CPR heads for out of state service to reach an absent defendant otherwise connected with England.[101] The American States adopted long-arm statutes to exercise jurisdiction over non-residents. Although different concepts are used, the aim of respectively special jurisdiction rules, CPR heads or long-arm statutes is the same: exercising jurisdiction outside the traditional territorial parameters on the basis of some other close connection with the forum. The methods chosen vary from one regime to another. Especially the American approach radically shifted from the traditional 'power theory' to a completely new approach based on minimum contacts and fairness. Other legal systems have taken a less drastic approach and enacted a selective number of bases for extraterritorial jurisdiction.

Continental Europe has a long history in regulating the extraterritorial reach of courts by the articulation of special jurisdiction rules of a mainly alternative nature in relation to the *forum rei* rule.[102] Already in Roman law, jurisdiction in matters relating to contracts was acknowledged in order to establish jurisdiction over a defendant who was not domiciled within the forum.[103] European 'long-arm' jurisdiction bases for extraterritorial jurisdiction are traditionally justified by a presumed close connection between the forum and the claim, and include branch and contract jurisdiction.[104]

In a comparison with the U.S. approach to extraterritoriality, Juenger argues with respect to Roman origins of civil law that

---

law recognizes, as well as the development from a strictly territorial to a more flexible doctrine of closeness of connection'. See also Johnston and Powles, 'The Kings of the World', fn. 64, at 27, 'A manifestation of the linking point doctrine; closeness of connection.' J. Fitzpatrick, 'The Lugano Convention and Western European Integration: A Comparative Analysis of Jurisdiction and Judgements in Europe and the United States', 695 *Connecticut Journal of International Law* (1993), 695-749, at 724, 'International doctrine has moved away from the theory of sovereignty or power as the basis for jurisdiction to the notion of reasonable connection. The U.S. Supreme Court, with the exception of Burnham, and the EC/EFTA have also followed this trend.'

[101] See Chapter 4, Sects. 4.2.3. and 4.5.

[102] This does not mean that the Continental European states renounced the sovereignty principle. The note of the Common Market Commission inviting the states in 1959 for negotiations affirms 'that jurisdiction in both civil and commercial matters is derived from sovereignty.' See Jenard Report, at 3, also referred to by Juenger in Juenger, 'Federalism: A Comparison', at 1206.

[103] Beale, 'Jurisdiction of Courts over Foreigners', at 202-203; J. Lookofsky and K. Hertz, *Transnational Litigation and Commercial Arbitration: An Analysis of American, European and International Law* (2004), at 21; Baumgartner, *The Proposed Hague Convention*, at 147-149; A. Gardella and L. Radicati di Brozolo, 'Civil Law, Common Law and Market Integration: The EC Approach to Conflicts of Jurisdiction', 51 *American Journal of Comparative Law* (2003), 611-637, fn. 7, at 613; Juenger, 'Federalism: A Comparison', at 1203, 'In addition, Roman law recognized the concept of limited jurisdiction by permitting the plaintiff to sue in tort at the place of wrongful conduct, to bring contract actions at the place of execution or performance'.

[104] Clermont, 'Jurisdictional Salvation', at 91; G. Droz, 'Réflexions pour une reforme des articles 14 et 15 du Code Civil français', 64 *Revue critique de droit international privé* (1975), 1-23, at 2-3, but see Mann, 'Doctrine of International Jurisdiction Revisited', at 67.

> 'fourteen hundred years before International Shoe, the civil law, unhampered by constitutional doctrine and territorialist dogma, already premised jurisdiction on "minimum contacts," and this idea continues to inform current European jurisdictional law. Conversely, the Pennoyer principles that for so long retarded the evolution of American law never appealed to civilians.'[105]

In 1852, the English Common Law Procedure Act enacted a series of permissible grounds for the service abroad, hereby authorizing extraterritorial reach over a defendant not present in the English forum. In a way these rules regulate extraterritorial jurisdiction by extending the notion of defendant's presence to his domicile or other connections with the forum.[106] The current CPR Rule 6.20 should be understood as an English version of U.S. long-arm statutes:[107] both specifically target absent defendants, as opposed to Continental European long-arm 'special jurisdiction rules' which target defendants who are not domiciled in the forum.

But like the Continental civil law regimes, Rule 6.20 exhaustively enumerates the circumstances under which a claimant can ask for leave to serve out of England by enlisting a series of 'heads' for jurisdiction under which the claim has to fall. Apart from the domicile head, the majority of the heads envisage jurisdiction in specific subject matters, generally justified by a close connection between the claim and the English forum.[108] The jurisdictional criteria and connecting factors enlisted in the CPR are the sole permissible grounds for jurisdiction to reach a defendant outside the English forum.

This code-type approach taken by Continental European regimes, the Brussels Model and English common law show some interesting similarities. The regime of the U.S. approach differs with respect to the 'heads' used for jurisdiction.[109] Interestingly, at the time the English legislator enacted Order 11 – which set the precedent for Rule 6.20 – hereby abandoning the strict territorialist dogma, the U.S. Supreme Court affirmed the application of territorial sovereignty principles regarding jurisdiction in *Pennoyer v. Neff*.[110] Once the U.S. Supreme Court broke

---

[105] Juenger, 'Federalism: A Comparison', at 1204.

[106] P. Nygh, 'The Common Law Approach', in *Transnational Tort Litigation: Jurisdictional Principles* (1996), 21-36, at 27, '[C]onsequently, it had to be fitted in the then prevailing framework of territorial dogma and the historical need for service as the foundation of jurisdiction.'

[107] Juenger, 'Comparative Neglect', at 6, 'Although couched in terms of "service abroad," the English rules in effect relied on what our Supreme Court later called "minimum contacts".'

[108] Rule 6.20(1)(a). See Chapter 4, Sect. 4.5.1.

[109] But see below and see Nuyts, 'Due Process and Fair Trial', at 188, 'The code-type approach to jurisdiction is not entirely foreign to American thinking; unlike it is generally assumed in Europe.'

[110] *Pennoyer* dates from 1877, more than 20 years after the Common Law Procedure Act establishing Order 11 was enacted. See Juenger, 'Federalism: A Comparison', at 1197, 'Ironically, a quarter of a century before Pennoyer, tradition-bound England had enacted the Common Law Procedure Act, which permitted service abroad and thereby authorized the very "extraterritoriality" Justice Field condemned.' See *Pennoyer v. Neff*, 95 U.S. 714, at 722-723 (1877): 'so it is laid down by jurists, as an elementary principle, that the laws of one State have no operation outside of its territory, except so far as is allowed by comity; and that no tribunal established by it can extend its process beyond that territory so as to subject either persons or property to its decisions. "Any exertion of authority of this sort beyond this limit," says Story, "is a mere nullity, and incapable of binding such persons or property in any other tribunals."'

with the strict application of the territorial theory in *International Shoe*, it surprisingly did not provide any clear guidance as to the meaning of 'minimum contacts', but only set out limits by stating that jurisdiction should not violate 'traditional notions of fair play and substantial justice'. Juenger rightfully observes that:

> '[c]ivilian statutes and the English Order 11 lay down, succinctly and precisely, the pertinent bases or – as the English call them – "heads." These range from general (for example, domicile or principal place of business) to specific (for example, the place of injury in tort cases or place of performance in contract litigation) jurisdiction. In contrast, Chief Justice Stone was content to let the nebulous concept of "minimum contacts" serve as the foundation for more specific principles and rules to be developed by state courts and legislatures.'[111]

The *International Shoe*-turnover introduced the 'minimum contacts' rule and opened the door to extraterritoriality by virtue of open concepts and principles of fairness.[112] The Supreme Court indicates that contacts with the forum exists when a corporation is 'exercising the privilege of conducting activities within the state' and entails the 'benefits and protection of the rules of that state'. It considered that these activities engender the corporation to comply with certain obligations and require it to 'respond to a suit brought to enforce them'.[113] After a short period of hesitation,[114] states began to enact long-arm statutes to reach defendants who are not within the reach of the traditional power-rule.[115] Long-arm statutes vary from state to state,[116] but the common feature among these statutes is that jurisdiction is mainly founded on the 'quality and nature' of contacts between the defendant and the forum.[117] Especially 'no limit' statutes are considerably different from the code-type approach found in Continental civil law Europe and English common law. According to Schlosser the *International Shoe*-turnover was less needed in Continental Europe which already had bases for jurisdiction for extraterritorial reach. Schlosser states that '[i]n the United States, because of constitutional considerations it was required to achieve a breakthrough and to alter completely the general approach to international jurisdiction. On the European Continent an alteration in the general approach is not required.'[118] Nor was such general approach required in England, since the 1852 Rules permitted the courts to serve out of the territory.

---

[111] Juenger, 'Comparative Neglect', at 9; see also Korn, 'Development of Jurisdiction', at 966.

[112] Baumgartner, *The Proposed Hague Convention*, at 144. See Juenger, 'Comparative Neglect', at 6 regretting the lack of comparative research in the U.S. Supreme Court decision-making process.

[113] *International Shoe Co. v. Washington*, 326 U.S. 310, at 319 (1945).

[114] According to Juenger, 'Comparative Neglect', at 10, the states showed little initiative and even less comprehension; Juenger, 'Federalism: A Comparison', at 1198; Buchner, 'Kläger- und Beklagtenschutz', at 25.

[115] The power theory included the doing business-basis as a form of consent, presence, domicile and *in rem* or *quasi in rem* jurisdiction. See Chapter 5, Sect. 5.2.2.

[116] See Chapter 5, Sect. 5.3.1.

[117] *International Shoe Co. v. Washington*, 326 U.S. 310, at 319 (1945).

[118] Schlosser, 'The Issue of Human Rights', at 13.

6.2.3 Defendant-specific and Claim-special Jurisdiction

Each of the systems analysed justify extraterritorial jurisdiction on the basis of *some* connection with the forum. The *nature* of the connection, especially for related or limited jurisdiction – as opposed to general unrelated and unlimited jurisdiction – varies from system to system. There are conceptual differences with respect to the required connection.[119] Continental European structures justify the bases for *special* jurisdiction on the 'close connection' between the court and the claim arising out of the contract.[120] With regard to English common law, most 'heads' for service outside the territory as provided by the CPR Rules reflect a connection between the claim and the forum, rather than a connection with the defendant.[121] In contrast, the U.S. system establishing *specific* jurisdiction requires a different connection with the forum.[122] It therefore differs from the Continental European systems, the Brussels Model and even from the English common law.[123]

Specific jurisdiction in the U.S. sense should therefore be clearly distinguished from *special jurisdiction* which is applied in Continental Europe and England. In essence, *special jurisdiction* relates to rules establishing jurisdiction over a certain category of claims on the basis of an *ex-ante* determination of the required connection between the subject matter and the forum. The U.S. approach for *specific* jurisdiction is not concerned with the cause of action: whether the *claim* involves contractual or tortuous matters or whether defendant's *contacts* result from a tort or a contractual relationship is irrelevant; the degree of activity is decisive for jurisdiction. U.S.-*specific* jurisdiction is determined on the basis of the *ex post* determination of the quality and quantity of defendant's contacts with the forum, provided that the claim arises out of these contacts. *Specific* jurisdiction is based on defendant's 'single or occasional' contacts, on the condition that the claim is related to those contacts. It is the degree of contacts that distinguishes specific jurisdiction from the U.S. general jurisdiction, which is unrelated to the claim provided that defendant has 'continuous and systematic' contacts with the forum.[124]

This constitutes an important difference with the other systems:

> 'because jurisdiction is assumed to be deductible from "first principles" it tends to treat all torts alike, all contracts alike and so on. The Brussels Convention on the other hand, makes sensible distinctions, such as between consumer and regular commercial contracts that are largely unknown in American doctrine.'[125]

---

[119] See in particular the conceptual differences on 'extraterritoriality' according to Michaels in Michaels, 'Two Paradigms', at 1058-1059.

[120] See the definition of special jurisdiction Chapter 2, Sect. 2 2.4.

[121] Except for the domicile criterion in Rule 6.20(1) which is based on the connection between the forum and the defendant, but this jurisdiction ground equally confers general jurisdiction.

[122] See Chapter 5, Sect. 5.4.3.1, for a definition of specific jurisdiction.

[123] 'The camps from America and Europe are divided on the question whether such [contract] jurisdiction should be based on the activity of the defendant or on the place of performance.' Contribution Buchner, in Lowenfeld and Silberman, eds., *The Hague Convention on Jurisdiction*, at 25; see also Nygh, 'Criteria for Judicial Jurisdiction', at A-8.

[124] See Chapter 5, Sect. 5.4.3.1, and see Borchers, 'Comparing Jurisdiction', at 133-135.

[125] Borchers, 'Comparing Jurisdiction', at 156 *et seq.*

Considerations of fairness and reasonableness also apply 'interchangeably' and 'regardless of the cause of action'.[126]

U.S. long-arm statutes are concerned with defendant's contacts with the forum. They do not necessarily categorize the jurisdictional provisions with respect to the nature of the claim. This is certainly the case with no limits statutes or statutes with catch-all provisions. Tailored provisions in enumerated statutes such as transacting business provisions assert jurisdiction over a defendant regardless of the cause of action. Some exceptions were encountered in the 'code-type' long-arm Statute of New York, establishing jurisdiction over claims arising out of contracts when the place of the supply of goods is situated on its territory. But even if the foundation of this specific jurisdiction is based on a connection between the claim and the forum, the U.S. due process will always require another specific contact with the defendant to satisfy due process standards and the principles of 'fairness'. As rightfully stated by O'Brian Jr.:

> 'No matter how closely connected the forum is to the dispute, if the defendant lacks the requisite minimum contacts with the forum, the court may not exercise jurisdiction over him. And for the defendant to have such minimum contacts, it is generally necessary to find "some act by which the defendant purposefully avails itself of the privilege of conducting activities with the forum state, thus invoking the benefits of its laws".'[127]

Jurisdiction over contractual disputes best illustrates the different approaches. In Continental European countries, England and the Brussels regime, contract jurisdiction is justified by a special connection with the contractual claim and is not preoccupied with the question whether the forum reflects a connection between the parties and the forum. This is true for Article 5(1) of the Brussels Regulation and for all other contract jurisdiction rules found in Continental European systems. It is also the underlying justification for Rule 6.20(5), (6) and (7) of the English CPR Rules, which specifically provide for heads of jurisdiction for service out of the territory in contractual claims. By way of contrast, a mere 'place of performance' will rarely provide for sufficient connection (or contact) between the forum and the defendant as required by the due process test of the U.S. Constitution.[128] According to Brand it is this 'focus on the nexus between the claim and the court, rather than on the nexus between the defendant and the court, [that] would lead to jurisdiction likely in violation of the Due Process Clause under U.S. law.'[129]

In sum, jurisdiction in the U.S. is *defendant-specific*.[130] *Special* jurisdiction as applied in Continental Europe, the Brussels Model and the English common law is

[126] R. Brand, 'Due Process, Jurisdiction and a Hague Judgments Convention', *University of Pittsburgh Law Review* (1999), 661-706, at 692.

[127] O'Brian Jr., 'The Hague Convention on Jurisdiction', at 495. See also Buchner, 'Kläger- und Beklagtenschutz', at 29.

[128] See also the comparative analysis in Chapter 7, Sect. 7.6.

[129] Brand, 'Due Process, Jurisdiction', at 961.

[130] The focus on the nexus between the claim and the court, rather than on the nexus between the defendant and the court, would lead to jurisdiction that is likely to be in violation of the Due Process Clause under U.S. law, see Brand, 'Due Process, Jurisdiction', at 961.

predominantly *claim-specific*.[131] These different approaches are important in order to understand some of the difficulties encountered at The Hague to reach a compromise. According to Brand

> 'on a simple level, one can identify distinctions here between a focus largely on the connection between the court and the claim (the focus of the "special" jurisdictional rules of the Brussels Convention) and a focus on the connection between the court and the defendant (focus of the US due process analysis). While reality is not all that simple, the distinction is useful, and helps provide a test for draft provisions on jurisdiction.'[132]

6.2.4 The Preference for Specific Jurisdiction

As a rule, general jurisdiction is founded on the connection between parties and the forum and is not subdivided in specific categories of claims. It is generally based on the presumption that the defendant has a substantial connection with the forum, not the plaintiff.[133] General rules assert jurisdiction over all types of claims and regardless of whether the claim is somehow connected with the forum. The European special jurisdiction as well as the U.S. specific jurisdiction is limited to defendant's claim.

The historical focus on territorial jurisdiction explains why the bases for general jurisdiction play a central role in the jurisdictional scheme, especially in the Continental European and English common law approach. Both the defendant's home court and the presence rule constitute the fundamental jurisdiction rule and are firstly addressed before other subsidiary or alternative bases asserting extraterritorial jurisdiction are considered to assert jurisdiction to courts. This is quite different under the U.S. approach to international jurisdiction. As explained in Chapter 5, most plaintiffs seeking a competent American court will first try to invoke specific jurisdiction over the defendant before finding recourse to the general jurisdiction bases such as doing business, place of incorporation and so on.[134] This 'movement from general jurisdiction in favour of specific jurisdiction' is rightfully explained by Keyes by the emphasis given by the U.S. approach to defendant's activities

---

[131] In some cases it is difficult to identify whether the connection with the forum is defendant-related or claim-related. For instance, branch jurisdiction reflects a connection between the branch and the forum, but the branch reflects defendant's activity in the forum. See Buchner, 'Kläger- und Beklagtenschutz', at 29, '*Insoweit ist es eine Frage des Blinkwinkels, ob Mann die Kontakte als beklagtenbezogen oder als streitbezogen ansieht.*'

[132] R. Brand, 'Understanding Activity-Based Jurisdiction', paper presented at The Preliminary Draft Hague Convention on Jurisdiction and Foreign Judgements in Civil and Commercial Matters, UIA Seminar Edinburgh, 20 & 21 April 2001 (2001), at 26. See O'Brian Jr., 'The Hague Convention on Jurisdiction', at 495.

[133] This is the case for domicile, presence, nationality and doing business; even general property-based jurisdiction, the *forum patrimonii*, is based on a connection between defendant's property and the forum, regardless of the nature of the claim. Von Mehren, 'Theory and Practice', at 158. See the comparison in Chapter 7, Sects. 7.1, 7.2, 7.3, 7.4.

[134] See L. Brilmayer, 'Jurisdictional Due Process and Political Theory', 39 *University of Florida Law Review* (1987), 293, at 739-740; R. Brand, 'Tort Jurisdiction in a Multilateral Convention: The Lessons of the Due Process Clause and the Brussels Convention', *Brooklyn Journal of International Law* (1998), 125-155, at 151; Whincop, *Policy and Pragmatism*, at 184.

in the forum in relation to the (contractual) claim.[135] In Continental Europe and England, the emphasis for *special* jurisdiction is slightly different. First it involves the categorization of plaintiff's claims as to their subject matters. Secondly, and more importantly, the focus is on the connection between the claim and the forum, regardless of whether the defendant's activities related to the claim were carried out in the forum.

6.3 The Jurisdictional Structures: Open, Closed and Mixed Systems

The structural differences and similarities of the jurisdictional regimes should be categorized in three groups: the closed, the open and the mixed structures. Traditionally a distinction was only made between closed and open systems. According to Fawcett a closed system 'strictly defines the cases in which the courts have jurisdiction, leaving no room for judicial discretion',[136] whereas open systems have 'broad and general rules of jurisdiction leaving courts with discretion whether or not to accept or decline jurisdiction'.[137] This distinction, however, disregards the special features of the English jurisdictional structure.

6.3.1 The Closed Systems in European Civil Law and the Brussels Model

The Brussels Model and the majority of Continental European systems surveyed are characterized as closed.[138] The main features for a closed structure are 1) a limited set of jurisdiction rules that 2) consists of clear-cut bases for jurisdiction in which 3) there is no (or very little) room for correction mechanisms or any other form of discretionary powers for the courts.[139]

The majority of European countries analysed and the Brussels system consist in a set of limited bases for jurisdiction for the plaintiff to choose from.[140] Most Continental civil law systems and the Brussels Model have such a 'jurisdictional catalogue'.[141] In closed systems the jurisdictional catalogue is considered 'self-sufficient'[142] and it consists of an exhaustive list of bases for jurisdiction; the Brussels Model even explicitly excludes *exorbitant* bases. As a rule, they usually consist of one main jurisdiction rule, such as the *forum rei* principle, complemented by a

---

[135] Called by Keyes 'consensual connections', see Keyes, *Jurisdiction in International Litigation*, at 201-203.

[136] Fawcett, *Declining Jurisdiction*, at 21.

[137] Ibid.; Buchner, 'Kläger- und Beklagtenschutz', at 20.

[138] See Chapters 2 and 3; France, Switzerland, Italy, and Spain are overall considered to be closed systems. See also Buchner, 'Kläger- und Beklagtenschutz', at 21.

[139] See for special correction devices Chapter 8. Germany has some features of a mixed system; it contains a limited set of jurisdictional rules with closed connecting factors available to the plaintiff but for property-based jurisdiction under Art. 23 ZPO, the court has to consider the special 'sufficient connection' requirement involving a certain degree of judicial discretion for German courts.

[140] See also Gardella and Radicati di Brozolo, 'Civil Law, Common Law', at 613.

[141] Buchner, 'Kläger- und Beklagtenschutz', at 20, who refers to it as a *Zuständigkeitskatalog*.

[142] Droz, *Compétence judiciaire*, § 51; see also A. Nuyts, *L'exception de forum non conveniens: Etude de droit international privé* (2003), § 163, at 234 and § 166, at 238.

limited number of special jurisdiction bases for instance for contractual matters.[143] The fact that the jurisdictional catalogue provides for the only permissible bases for jurisdiction is one of the main features of a closed structure.

Secondly, the bases for jurisdiction rules are carefully drafted and consist in clear-cut connecting factors rigidly articulated by closed norms.[144] The ECJ especially determined bases for jurisdiction such as the special contract jurisdiction rule under Article 5(1) pursuant to 'certain and reliable criteria'.[145] The rules should be understood as 'hard and fast rules' elaborated on the basis of a predetermined and standardized balancing of jurisdictional interests.[146] Policy choices are made beforehand by the legislator and there is no discretionary power to correct their outcome.

This leads to the third important characteristic of closed systems; most Continental European systems and the Brussels Model leave no room for discretionary powers of courts. Once the claimant correctly seized a court pursuant to one of the bases for jurisdiction, the court *must* exercise jurisdiction.[147] The court is not entitled to decline jurisdiction on the basis of specific facts or circumstances of the case. The rules clearly have automatic application and the exercise of jurisdiction becomes automatic.[148] According to Schlosser, under the Brussels Model courts are not entitled to exercise jurisdiction, 'they are obliged to do so'.[149] This mandatory nature along with the exhaustive set of jurisdiction rules makes the Brussels Model a particularly closed model with a 'strict legal framework' in which 'no discretionary powers are needed and might even jeopardise the uniform treatment of cases regards jurisdiction within the Regulation's territory'.[150] It is for that reason that the drafters have not provided for any exception on the basis of the *forum non conveniens* doctrine.[151] It considerably differs from Anglo-American jurisdictional structures where the fact that a court 'enjoys the power to exercise jurisdiction does not necessarily mean that it is under the obligation to use this power'.[152] Derogation to the jurisdictional catalogue is almost inexistent and only possible when

[143] Besides containing protective and exclusive jurisdiction rules, closed systems are also regulated by predetermined rules.

[144] Gardella and Radicati di Brozolo, 'Civil Law, Common Law', at 613.

[145] C-256/00 *Besix v. WABAG*, [2002] ECR I-1699, at para. 50 and Case 32/88 *Six Constructions*, [1989] ECR 341, para. 20.

[146] See with respect to Germany, H. Schack, 'Germany National Report', in *Declining Jurisdiction in Private International Law* (1995), 189-205, at 194.

[147] See also Sect. 6.4 and see Juenger, 'Improper Forum Regulation', at 311.

[148] But see Nuyts, *L'exception*, § 340, at 455.

[149] P. Schlosser, 'Report on the Convention on the Accession of the United Kingdom of Denmark, Ireland and the United Kingdom of Great Britain and Northern Ireland to the Convention on Jurisdiction and the Enforcement of Judgments in Civil and Commercial Matters and to the Protocol on Its Interpretation by the Court of Justice', OJ 1979 C 59, § 78, at 97. See also P. Kaye, 'The EEC Judgements Convention and the Outer World: Goodbye to Forum non Conveniens?', *The Journal of Business Law* (1992), 47-76, at 47; and Opinion AG Léger to C-281/02 *Owusu v. Jackson*, [2005] ECR I-1383, § 224.

[150] H. Duintjer Tebbens, 'The English Court of Appeal in *Re Harrods*: An Unwelcome Interpretation of the Brussels Convention', in *Law and Reality* (1992), 47-61, at 59.

[151] C-281/02 *Owusu v. Jackson*, para. 37.

[152] Lookofsky and Hertz, *Transnational Litigation*, § 2.5.4(A), at 321.

the law explicitly requires, under specific well-defined circumstances, to do so.[153] This stands in contrast to the Anglo-American models which have a more *flexible* approach to international jurisdiction.

6.3.2 The Mixed English Common Law System

The common law system of England should be characterized as mixed.[154] The English jurisdictional structure consists in a well-defined jurisdictional catalogue, but applies open correction mechanisms, namely the *forum conveniens* and the *forum non conveniens* doctrine. The English catalogue law consists in the fundamental presence rule, complemented by limited 'heads' for jurisdiction, permitting out of state service as provided by the CPR. At first sight, the presence rule seems to be an open-ended norm with respect to corporate presence. It is true, that the defendant's presence in a forum is determined by factual considerations, such as a place of establishment, but corporate presence is well-defined by the Companies Act and by Rule 6.16 of the CPR. Corporate presence is delimited by legal criteria and consists of closed connecting factors instead of open-ended norms to be appreciated by the court.

The limited bases for outside service are exhaustively enumerated and well-articulated in the CPR, which contain clear-cut connecting factors instead of open-ended standards.[155] In that respect the English approach is rule-based and the English common law system should be characterized as *partially closed* when examining the jurisdictional catalogue. But an important part of the English structure is made up of open-ended standards and discretionary powers for English courts. It is the application of a general exception doctrine of the *forum non conveniens* on the one hand and the *forum conveniens* requirement on the other hand that makes the English system *partially open*. Even when the seized English court assumes jurisdiction pursuant to the bases for jurisdiction, the court will eventually accept jurisdiction depending on the appreciation of open-ended factors evolving from these doctrines. The presence rule and Rule 6.20 do therefore not automatically establish jurisdiction and are therefore not mandatory. Discretionary powers play a considerable role in the determination of jurisdiction of English courts and express the need of judicial control *ex post*. This combination of a closed jurisdictional catalogue and the application of open correction mechanisms make English common law a 'mixed jurisdictional system' as it is half closed and half open.[156]

---

[153] See the comparative analysis on correction devises in Chapter 8, and see Nuyts, *L'exception*, § 141, at 202; O'Brian Jr., 'The Hague Convention on Jurisdiction', at 494.

[154] Not to be confused with the qualification of 'mixed jurisdiction' and 'mixed legal system' used in comparative law in order to identify a legal tradition or legal family such as for instance in Scotland, Louisiana, Quebec, South Africa. See Tetley, 'Mixed Jurisdictions', at 597.

[155] See Chapter 4, Sects. 4.2.3 and 4.5 Briggs uses the term 'pigeon holes', see A. Briggs, *The Conflict of Laws* (2008), at 106.

[156] See below on the characteristics of an open system.

6.3.3 The Open Character of the United States Jurisdictional System

The main features of an open system are threefold. First, the jurisdictional bases available to the plaintiff are not limited by a pre-defined set of jurisdictional provisions. In other words, if a jurisdictional catalogue exists, it is not exhaustive.[157] Second, all or some connecting factors are indicated by open-ended standards or principles and entail the appreciation on a case-by-case basis. The U.S. jurisdictional system uses 'soft' rules. Finally, once a court is rightfully seized, the court is allowed to decline jurisdiction on the basis of other considerations such as fairness, reasonableness and *convenience*.

In contrast to the European set of (special) jurisdiction rules and the English CPR Rules, most U.S. long-arm statutes are not limited by an exhaustively enumerated list of jurisdictional provisions. The jurisdictional sources of the U.S. are to be found in traditional common law principles on the one hand, and in long-arm statutes for extraterritorial reach on the other.[158] The majority of U.S. long-arm statutes use non-exhaustive jurisdictional catalogues and exercise jurisdiction to the limits of what is constitutionally admissible. The 'no-limit' long-arm statutes such as the one enacted in California, allow jurisdiction on 'any constitutional basis' and establish jurisdiction on any contact, provided that it is consistent with due process standards. 'Hybrid' long-arm statutes have the same effect; besides the set of jurisdictional provisions they include a 'catch all' provision allowing the forum to exercise jurisdiction as long as the Due Process Clause is not violated.[159] In practice the jurisdictional test is primarily focused on the compatibility with constitutional standards.[160] Hence, U.S. jurisdiction is not necessarily defined beforehand by a set of well-defined long-arm provisions, but stems from constitutional principles. O'Brian Jr. clearly defines one of the characteristics of the American open system as follows:

> 'Since it [the Supreme Court] was interpreting a vague and open-ended constitutional provision, it is perhaps not surprising that the test it adopted was also vague and open ended. This might not have been a fatal difficulty had the US Congress, or state legislatures, promulgated jurisdictional statutes that stated clear rules that stayed well within the limits of permissible jurisdiction articulated by International Shoe. In fact, though, virtually all US states decided to exercise their jurisdictional powers to the limits permitted by the Due Process Clause. As a result, in most cases the operative limit on the jurisdiction is not a statute, but rather the Due Process Clause.'[161]

Very few American states, among them the State of New York, refused to incorporate a 'catch-all' provision in their enumerated long-arm statutes. Instead, they articulate an exhaustive list of jurisdictional provisions with closed connecting fac-

---

157 Buchner, 'Kläger- und Beklagtenschutz', at 20.

158 See Chapter 5, Sect. 5.3; and see above Sect. 6.2.2 for the U.S.'s approach to extraterritorial reach.

159 See Chapter 5, Sect. 5.3.

160 Buchner, 'Kläger- und Beklagtenschutz', at 25.

161 O'Brian Jr., 'The Hague Convention on Jurisdiction', at 494.

tors such as the 'supply of goods' in the forum.[162] The structure of these states has a few common features with the English common law's 'mixed' structure discussed above. They regulate jurisdiction on traditional bases for jurisdiction that has been based on for instance presence or domicile, complemented by a set of limited jurisdiction rules embodied in the long-arm statute. Combined with the due process test and the *forum non conveniens* doctrine they have features of a mixed system.[163]

Nonetheless, U.S. long-arm statutes, including the New York Statute, contain jurisdictional provisions formulated by open-ended standards such as transacting and doing business. The rules focus on the quality and quantity of defendant's contacts and activities and entail a case-by-case appreciation.[164] These 'soft' rules are important characteristics of open systems.

The last feature of considerable importance for the U.S. open jurisdictional structure is the significant degree of judicial discretion of U.S. courts to determine whether it should exercise jurisdiction: first with respect to the due process test and second in regard to the application of the *forum non conveniens* doctrine. These open correction mechanisms take a 'case-by-case balancing approach' involving considerations of fairness and reasonableness.[165] In sum, policy considerations and balancing interests for U.S. jurisdiction are predominantly taken into account by U.S. courts *ex post.*

6.4 The Protection of Parties

Jurisdictional systems have different approaches to the protection of the parties. Some bases for jurisdiction particularly favour the defendant at the expense of the plaintiff and *vice versa.* The present paragraph examines contrasting approaches towards the protection of parties within the jurisdictional framework as a whole, instead of by analysing the jurisdictional preference of each rule separately.[166] Whether the jurisdictional structure is an open, closed or mixed system plays a considerable role in the approach to the parties' protection and on how they intend to find a balance between on the one hand the protection of defendant's rights of defence,[167] and on the other hand the plaintiff's access to competent courts and his freedom to select the forum, which leads to forum shopping.[168] It is gener-

---

[162] See Chapter 5, Sect. 5.6.4.

[163] See Buchner, 'Kläger- und Beklagtenschutz', at 28.

[164] O'Brian Jr., 'The Hague Convention on Jurisdiction', at 494, '... to this day the cases emphasize the essentially factual and ad hoc nature of the analysis that is required in order to determine whether a US court has jurisdiction over a particular case'.

[165] Terminology used by O'Brian Jr., 'The Hague Convention on Jurisdiction', at 497.

[166] See Chapter 7 for a comparison on individual bases for jurisdiction. See Von Mehren, 'Theory and Practice', at 195, 'Whether jurisdictional theory and practice are plaintiff or defendant orientated thus depends on the interaction of two factors: (1) the number and variety of the jurisdictional bases available and (2) which party ultimately controls forum selection.'

[167] Some authors have called the protection of defendant the 'right [of defendant] not to be sued abroad', see the title of the following article: J. Schröder, 'The Right Not to Be Sued Abroad', in *Festschrift für Gerard Kegel zum 75. Geburtstag* (1987), 523.

[168] See Chapter 1, Sect. 1.1.2; N. Hatzimihail, 'General Report: Transnational Civil Litigation between European Integration and Global Aspirations', in *International Civil Litigation in Europe and*

ally accepted that the more freedom the plaintiff has to select his forum, the more procedural advantages he will have.[169] Some jurisdiction structures control claimant's selection by restricting the available competent courts *ex ante* on a rule-based approach; other systems appreciate plaintiff's choice on the basis of discretionary powers weighing the appropriateness or convenience of the forum.[170]

Each system is concerned with the parties' protection, but the approach taken differs considerably. The Brussels Model and the civil law systems have similar features and should be considered as having the same approach. However, despite these similarities, the following differences should be kept in mind. First, some Continental European countries, such as Germany and France, are characterized by the existence of exorbitant jurisdiction rules, generally designed for claimant's comfort or at least to meet his needs to find a competent German, respectively French court.[171] Second, some Continental European regimes accepted a certain degree of correction regarding the close connection with the forum. Like the Anglo-American approach, such correction allows the court to decline jurisdiction and inevitably results in the court not giving effect to the plaintiff's choice of the competent forum.[172]

Three different approaches should be distinguished with respect to the protection of parties: the Continental European approach, the English common law approach and the American approach.[173]

6.4.1 The Continental European Approach

The jurisdictional structures of Continental European countries and the Brussels Model rely heavily on the underlying assumption of the *actor sequitur forum rei* rule primarily designed to privilege the defendant.[174] In that sense the Continental European approach is often characterized as *pro-defendant*,[175] as it is based on the

---

Relations with Third States (2005), 595-675, at 648. See Briggs on why the Brussels Model also leads to the claimant's need to commence proceedings first, A. Briggs, *Civil Jurisdiction and Judgments* (2005), § 2.10-2.12, at 34-38; Keyes, *Jurisdiction in International Litigation*, at 37 *et seq.*; Johnston and Powles, 'The Kings of the World', at 30.

[169] See Hay, 'Flexibility versus Predictability and Uniformity', at 306; Von Mehren, 'Theory and Practice', at 189.

[170] Juenger, 'Improper Forum Regulation', at 311.

[171] G. Droz, 'Les droits de la demande dans les relations privées internationales', *Travaux* du *Comité Français de Droit International Privé* (1993-1995), 97-121 at 106, '*La première raison [pour les compétences exorbitantes] est le confort personnel du demandeur. On a vu que celui-ci était respectable et on veut lui faciliter l'accès à la justice. Pour ce faire on lui offre un certain nombre de compétences qui n'ont pas de lien direct avec le litige ou avec le défendeur mais dont l'utilisation lui économisera du temps et de l'argent.*' And see for earlier statements, Droz, 'Réflexions', at 4.

[172] See below Sect. 6.4.1.

[173] Apart from a few divergences, the approach taken by Continental European countries to protect the parties' interests is similar to that of the Brussels Model.

[174] See Chapter 2, Sect. 2.5 and Chapter 7, Sect.7.2.

[175] See Case 220/84 *AS-Autoteile v. Malhé*, [1985] ECR 2267, para. 15, 'That provision [Art. 2] is intended to protect the rights of the defendant.' See Pontier and Burg, *EU Principles on Jurisdiction*, at 56 and 120; see P. Nygh and F. Pocar, 'Report of the Special Commission – Convention on Jurisdiction and Foreign Judgments in Civil and Commercial Matters', Hague Conference on Private International

favor defensoris principle which entails the 'protection of rights of the defence'. According to Pontier and Burg, the Brussels Model acknowledges 'fair trial and fair hearing' principles[176] as well as the right to be heard in an 'appropriate' court, and in particular, the right to be heard in 'one's own state'.[177] The *favor defensoris* is generally hostile to the *forum actoris* and other advantages for the plaintiff and is based on the assumption that the plaintiff is the 'agressor'.[178] The rule primarily protects defendant's jurisdictional interests by enabling him to defend himself in his own court.[179]

The drafters of the Brussels Model and the Continental European legislators searched for an 'antidote' to Article 2, 'the Convention's darling', to find the 'right balance in the protection of the parties'.[180] Providing the plaintiff with a limited number of optional special jurisdiction rules guaranteeing effective and fair access to justice compensates for the defendant's privilege of a 'home court advantage'. Most importantly, it provides him with some liberty to select his forum.[181] The purpose of *claim-specific* jurisdiction is to provide the plaintiff with an alternative besides the defendant's home court.[182]

Grolimund explains that

> 'like a claimant forum which has been held to be exorbitant from the point of view of the defendant, a sole defendant forum can be exorbitant from the point of view of the claimant. Consequently, to guarantee effective and fair access to the courts requires not simply to refer the claimant to the courts of the defendant but to give him or her the opportunity, if factual relations exist, to proceed before dispute-related courts.'[183]

Law (2000), at 38; see Buchner, 'Kläger- und Beklagtenschutz', at 28-29 and 52-54, indicating that Art. 2 Brussels Model consists in a '*starre Beklagtenperspektive*'.

[176] See on the protection of the other rights of the defence with regards to the Brussels Model, Pontier and Burg, *EU Principles on Jurisdiction*, at 46.

[177] Ibid., at 120.

[178] Ibid.

[179] Jenard Report, at 18; P. Grolimund, 'Human Rights and Jurisdiction: General Observation and Impact on the Doctrines of *Forum Non Conveniens* and *Forum Conveniens*', 4 *European Journal of Law Reform* (2002), 87-118, at 95; Von Mehren, 'Theory and Practice', at 195-196.

[180] Newton, *Uniform Interpretation*, at 44.

[181] See Chapter 2, Sect. 2.2.4. See Opinion AG Lenz in C-288/92 *Custom Made v. Stawa*, [1994] ECR I-2913, Sect. 18, agreed by Opinion AG Ruiz-Jarabo Colomer in C-440/97 *GIE Groupe Concorde*, [1999] ECR I-6307, para. 68; Hatzimihail, 'General Report', at 647; Von Mehren, 'Theory and Practice', at 183.

[182] Although it falls outside the scope of the present research, the Continental European approach adopts a certain degree of protection for the plaintiff as the 'weaker party'. Underlying policy considerations have led their legislator to protect the weaker consumer, employer or insured by allowing jurisdiction at plaintiff's forum and to derogate from the civil law *forum rei* maxim. Such an explicit jurisdictional preference for the protection of the plaintiff is unknown in U.S. jurisdiction law. Any considerations for the plaintiff's weaker position would merely take place under the *due process analysis* in U.S. law, see Von Mehren, 'Theory and Practice', at 202; F. Pocar, 'La protection de la partie faible en droit international privé', 188 *Recueil des cours* (1984), 339-418, at 397-399; and for a general overview see P. Mayer, 'La partie faible en droit international privé', in *La protection de la partie faible dans les rapports contractuels: Comparaison Franco-Belges* (1996), 513 *et seq*.

[183] Grolimund, 'Human Rights and Jurisdiction', at 95.

The European special jurisdiction rules, such as the *forum contractus* and branch jurisdiction, are designed for the plaintiff: he benefits the most from these rules as they permit the defendant to be drawn away from his home forum.[184] Defendant's home-advantage is less 'protected' when there is a close connection with another state.[185] In other words, defendant's 'right not to be sued abroad'[186] is outweighed under certain circumstances by plaintiff's interests to have other forums besides defendant's home court at his disposal, provided that the dispute is closely connected to those other forums.[187]

The closed jurisdictional catalogue provides for a well-considered but rigid set of competent courts, as opposed to a wide range of available courts to the plaintiff. Limiting the alternative competent courts 'discourages opportunities for *forum shopping*',[188] promoting predictability and legal certainty for both parties.[189] Once an alternative court is available and seized by the claimant, the defendant cannot invoke any discretionary power of the court to decline jurisdiction as jurisdiction is mandatory.[190] The defendant is dependent 'on an option to be exercised by the claimant'.[191] One of the main features of a closed system are the hard and fast rules based on an *ex ante* interest balance effectuated by the legislator lacking any *ex post* judicial control pursuant to correction devices.[192] The plaintiff's choice is respected in the absence of a *forum (non) conveniens* doctrine or due process considerations: the court seized will have to exercise jurisdiction when the conditions are fulfilled. The underlying idea is that the plaintiff can choose from among a limited number of competent forums, but once the plaintiff has made his choice it is generally conclusive.

---

[184] See Michaels, 'Re-Placements', at 149-150; Pontier and Burg, *EU Principles on Jurisdiction*, at 162 and 166.

[185] As correctly observed by Michaels, 'Re-Placements', at 149.

[186] T. Pfeiffer, *Internationale Zuständigkeit und prozessuale Gerechtigkeit* (1995), at 766 and 592. See Grolimund, 'Human Rights and Jurisdiction', at 95, 'dispute-related court access deprives the defendant of his natural or her natural right to be sued before his or her domestic courts'. See also the following article by Schröder, 'The Right Not to Be Sued Abroad', in which he argues that this right not to be sued abroad is generally not accepted as an enforceable right available to the defendant in the determination of jurisdictional purposes. It merely has a subsidiary nature, coming to effect as a result of other jurisdictional considerations, such as the *lis pendens* rule or the *forum non conveniens* doctrine.

[187] See G. Cuniberti, '*Forum Non Conveniens* and the Brussels Convention', *The International and Comparative Law Quarterly* (2005), 973-981, at 977, 'it is simply wrong to state that defendants have the certainty to be sued at home. In the Convention's scheme, defendants have to abide by claimants' choices.'

[188] L. Silberman, 'Comparative Jurisdiction in the International Context: Will the Proposed Hague Judgments Convention Be Stalled?', 52 *DePaul Law Review* (2002), 319-350, at 328.

[189] Fentiman, 'Access to Justice', at 313; and see the contribution by Schlosser in Lowenfeld and Silberman, eds., *The Hague Convention on Jurisdiction*, at 20.

[190] Droz, *Compétence judiciaire*, § 61, at 56, '*La compétence des tribunaux désignés par les articles 5 et 6 est impérative en ce sens que le défendeur ne peut s'y soustraire. Mais elle reste facultative pour le demandeur qui conserve toujours le droit de s'adresser aux tribunaux du domicile du défendeur.*'

[191] C-412/98 *Group Josi v. UGIC*, [2000] ECR I-5925, paras. 34 and 35.

[192] See above Sect. 6.2.

In sum, the Continental European approach is principally pro-defendant because of the important role of the *forum rei*. Conversely the limited special jurisdiction rules are pro-claimant as they enable him to select other competent courts on the basis of a claim-related connection with the forum. The rigid character of closed special jurisdiction bases and the lack of correction devices give effect to plaintiff's choice hereby favouring the claimant. This approach is not particularly defendant-friendly especially since a *defendant-specific* connection is not required under the Continental European approach.

6.4.2 The English Common Law Approach

English common law takes a different approach to the protection of the parties. Presence as starting-point for English jurisdiction is not particularly concerned with the protection of defendant's rights of defence.

Presence-based jurisdiction over individuals applies regardless of whether the defendant or the claim is otherwise connected to the forum and is therefore generally considered exorbitant *vis-à-vis* the defendant. On the other hand, the defendant can avoid jurisdiction by simply leaving the country. With respect to corporate defendants, its reach is considerably wider; corporate presence extends to branch establishment and mere place of business.[193] As a result, the presence rule offers the plaintiff a wide range of connecting factors to choose from, especially regarding corporate defendants.

The closed set of jurisdiction grounds listed under Rule 6.20 CPR offers the plaintiff even more options to find a competent English court. The extension of presence to corporate defendants, combined with additional heads of jurisdiction for outside service, results in a relatively wide range of jurisdiction bases for the plaintiff. But the fact that such a wide jurisdictional catalogue is advantageous for the claimant and is not particularly *pro-defendant* does not mean that the English mixed system is defendant-unfriendly. On the contrary, according to Fawcett, the purpose of the *forum non conveniens* exception is to protect the defendant from being sued in a 'clearly inappropriate forum': 'The modern doctrine of forum non conveniens offers a much wider protection to the defendant, shielding him from the risk of being subject to trial in an inconvenient English forum, unless the plaintiff can justify trial in England – which has become increasingly difficult for him to do.'[194]

When the defendant is served outside England by virtue of Rule 6.20, a similar protection of defendant's rights is provided by the jurisdictional requirement of the *forum conveniens* rule. The plaintiff has to prove that the English forum is appropriate in order to obtain a leave to serve outside the territory.[195] In the *Spiliada* case which introduced the doctrine in England, Lord Goff of Chieveley explicitly

---

[193] Provided that the claim arose out of the activities of the branch, see also Chapter 7, Sects. 7.1, 7.2 and 7.5.

[194] J. Fawcett, 'Trial in England or Abroad: The Underlying Policy Considerations', 9 *Oxford Journal Legal Studies* (1989), 205-229, at 206.

[195] See Chapter 4, Sect. 4.3.

indicates its importance as a counterbalance to presence, 'I may add that if, in any case, the connection of the defendant with the English forum is a fragile one (for example, if he is served with proceedings during a short visit to this country), it should be all the easier for him to prove that there is another clearly more appropriate forum for the trial overseas.'[196] Lord Goff of Chieveley also refers back to an earlier case in which the House of Lords invoked the doctrine as a counterweight to the jurisdiction established for service out of process:

> 'service out of the jurisdiction of a writ on th[e] corporation, is an exorbitant jurisdiction, ... The exorbitance of the jurisdiction sought to be invoked ... is an important factor to be placed in the balance against granting leave. It is a factor that is capable of being outweighed if the would-be plaintiff can satisfy the English court that justice either could not be obtained by him in the alternative forum; or could only be obtained at excessive cost, delay or inconvenience.'[197]

As explained above, presence-based jurisdiction has mainly historical origins based on the allegiance to the sovereign power; it was not designed on the basis of underlying considerations of the parties' interests. Correction by *forum non conveniens* devices was needed to install a balance of interest.[198] It is one of the main characteristics of the English mixed system to introduce – once the plaintiff has made his choice for England – a judicial appreciation on the basis of subjective factors involving 'interests of all parties and the ends of justice'. The plaintiff is, beforehand, uncertain whether his choice for English courts will be 'approved' by the court seized and whether he will find a competent court. The fact that the doctrine 'interferes' with the claimant's choice is one of the main objections Continental European commentators have against the English common law approach.[199] Droz most fiercely criticized the impact of the doctrine on the plaintiff's choice, especially when the plaintiff has chosen a 'reasonable' or 'proper' jurisdiction ground, in the sense that it is not an exorbitant jurisdiction rule:

> '*En tout cas ce qu'il ne faut surtout pas faire c'est établir une liste de compétence jugées raisonnables, les offrir aux demandeur par voie de catalogues ou d'*Order of the Supreme Court *et puis dans le cas d'espèce dire aux demandeur «votre tête ne me revient pas, votre cause non plus, allez donc vous faire juger ailleurs». Vous au-*

[196] Lord Goff of Chieveley in *Spiliada Maritime Corp. v. Cansulex Ltd.*, [1987] AC 460, at 477. See *The Atlantic Star*, [1974] AC 436, at 440, 'From the defendant's side it may be said: true the plaintiff has succeeded in establishing jurisdiction in England, but where the defendant is only casually here, he would be gravely inconvenienced by the proceedings in England.'

[197] Lord Goff of Chieveley in *Spiliada Maritime Corp. v. Cansulex Ltd.*, [1987] AC 460, at 479-480, referring to Lord Diplock in *Amin Rasheed*, [1984] AC 50, at 65-68.

[198] See H. Muir Watt, 'Note: Banque camerounaise de développement Cour de Cassation; Chambre Civile 1re 18 November 1986', 76 *Revue critique de droit international privé* (1987), 773-786, at 785, arguing that only a 'ridiculous' system needs the installation of the *forum non conveniens* as a corrective mechanism.

[199] See also Juenger, 'Improper Forum Regulation', at 313, 'A policy-based argument that has been advanced is that these devices interfere with plaintiff's fundamental right of access of justice', referring to Pfeiffer, 'Internationale Zuständigkeit und prozessuale Gerechtigkeit', at 394-396.

rez compris que je condamne formellement l'utilisation du forum non conveniens au niveau des compétences raisonnables, au niveau des propre fora.'[200]

Although Droz's characterization of how English courts deal with discretionary powers is oversimplified and exaggerated, not taking into account that English courts are bound by specified factors, he rightfully draws the attention to the ambiguous common law position regarding plaintiff's right of freedom of choice. On the one hand, the English approach provides the plaintiff with a wide scale of competent forums under the presence rule and the additional heads of the CPR, but on the other hand, his access to English justice is subjected to the court's appreciation of whether his choice is appropriate. There is no reason to only let the claimant choose the forum, leaving the defendant dependent on claimant's will as is the case in the Continental European approach. Briggs states that one reason 'is that the initial choice of court is effectively that of the claimant, who issues the claim form, but there is no convincing reason why this important factor should lie within the control of one, and not both, of the parties; it may be claimant's claim but it is also the parties' dispute.'[201]

It should be emphasized that the court's appreciation on a case-by-case basis is concerned with the 'interests of *all parties*' and that the *forum (non) conveniens* is therefore also committed to protect plaintiff's interests. The court seized will appreciate the inconveniences caused to the plaintiff if proceedings were to be stayed and the plaintiff was asked to commence proceedings abroad. Plaintiff's advantages to find a competent court in England are weighed by the court, on the basis that there should be no corresponding disadvantage for the defendant. Fawcett considers this approach as going beyond 'mere protection of the plaintiff' and gives evidence of 'a deliberate policy of giving effect to the plaintiff's choice of an English forum'.[202] In that sense, apart from providing the plaintiff with a relatively large spectrum of available jurisdiction criteria, the English common law structure also insists on giving effect to the plaintiff's choice, especially when he chooses an English court.

The fact that it is up to the defendant to prove that another available foreign court is *clearly* more appropriate indicates that the doctrine has pro-plaintiff elements.[203] Consequently, while it may be true that the defendant is protected by the doctrine from being sued in a clearly inappropriate forum, the *forum (non) conveniens* doctrine attempts to give effect as much as possible to the plaintiff's choice.[204]

---

[200] Droz, 'Les droits de la demande', at 206, 'In any event, what should definitely not be done is to compile a list of reasonable jurisdiction rules and offer them to the plaintiff as a catalogue or by Order of the Supreme Court and subsequently say to the plaintiff "I don't like your face, nor do I like your case, go and be judged elsewhere". You would have understood that I firmly condemn the application of the *forum non conveniens* jurisdiction based on reasonable grounds and based on *proper fora*.'

[201] Briggs, *Civil Jurisdiction*, § 4.12, at 300-301.

[202] Fawcett, 'Underlying Policy Considerations', at 207.

[203] Ibid., at 219, referring to *Spiliada Maritime Corp. v. Cansulex Ltd.*, [1987] AC 460, at 477-478; but for service outside of the forum it is for the claimant to prove that the English court is clearly inappropriate.

[204] Fawcett, 'Underlying Policy Considerations', at 218.

In sum, the following observation by Fawcett is illustrative in this case, he states that '[s]ince the doctrine itself is inherently pro-defendant, it makes sense that it should operate with a pro-plaintiff bias.'

It is interesting to note that it is this right of the plaintiff to have his claim heard by the court of his choice that was considered to be very important by the Australian High Court in the *Voth v. Manildra Flour Mills* case,[205] to reverse the English version of the *forum non conveniens* doctrine.[206] The High Court was inspired by a statement of Justice Deane in the earlier decision of *Oceanic Sun*:[207] '[t]he plaintiff who has regularly invoked the jurisdiction of the court has a prima facie right to insist upon its exercise and to have his claim heard and determined.'[208]

6.4.3 The American Approach

The U.S. approach to the protection of parties is substantially different from the English common law approach and differs even more from the Continental European approach. The open American system is characterized as particularly pro-plaintiff: as a result of the broader interpretation of due process by *International Shoe* 'merely' requiring minimum contacts, the claimant has at his disposal an extremely wide and often non-exhaustive jurisdictional catalogue to find a competent U.S. court.[209] Among the traditional rules, the defendant's domicile, or with respect to corporate defendants, the place of incorporation or principal place of business, are valid jurisdictional grounds. Also accepted are those bases considered exorbitant under the Brussels Model, such as property-based jurisdiction and tag-jurisdiction.[210] The 'doing business' rule goes beyond the traditional bases establishing jurisdiction on defendant's 'continuous and systematic' activities in the forum and is not formulated by specific or well-defined connecting factors. Specific jurisdiction is established on an even greater variety of contacts. Transacting business jurisdiction creates a significant number of possibilities for the plaintiff to find a competent U.S. court. In contractual disputes, a defendant can be subjected to specific jurisdiction in every forum where he transacts business – even a single commercial contact with the forum suffices – and he is amenable to general jurisdiction on the basis of traditional bases for jurisdiction and doing business

---

[205] *Voth v. Manildra Flour Mills Pty Ltd*, High Court of Australia, [1990] 171 CLR 538.

[206] The Australian version of the *forum non conveniens* doctrine requires the Australian forum to be 'clearly inappropriate' instead of the defendant having the burden to prove that the forum chosen is the 'clearly more appropriate forum'.

[207] *Oceanic Sun Line Special Shipping Company Inc. v. Fay*, High Court of Australia, [1988] 165 CLR 197, at 241.

[208] *Voth v. Manildra Flour Mills Pty Ltd*, High Court of Australia, [1990] 171 CLR 538, at 550.

[209] See above Sect. 6.2.2. Von Mehren, 'Theory and Practice', at 191, 'US law consists in a pro-plaintiff bias in jurisdictional matters'; Buchner, 'Kläger- und Beklagtenschutz', at 86; C. McLachlan, 'Transnational Tort Litigation: An Overview', in *Transnational Tort Litigation: Jurisdictional Principles* (1996), 1-19, at 16; A. Reus, 'Judicial Discretion: A Comparative View of the Doctrine of Forum Non Conveniens in the United States, the United Kingdom and Germany', *Loyola of Los Angeles International and Comparative Law Journal* (1994), 457, at 508.

[210] O'Brian Jr., 'The Hague Convention on Jurisdiction', at 496; and see Von Mehren, 'Theory and Practice', at 189, 'clearly, a power theory of adjudicatory authority does not systematically produce what are, realistically speaking, defendants' forums. Quite the contrary is true.'

in the forum.[211] Hence, on the basis of such a wide range of connecting factors, especially under doing and transacting business jurisdiction, the plaintiff enjoys a large choice of potential forums to choose from.

Even wider – and vaguer – are the 'no-limit' long-arm statutes or enumerated acts, including a 'catch all-provision' permitting jurisdiction on any constitutional basis. These open-ended statutes provide the plaintiff with competent forums on the basis of minimum contacts provided that it does not violate constitutional due process standards. These long-arm statutes are premised on the existence of an unlimited number of possible connecting factors or contacts which help the plaintiff to easily find a competent court. Von Mehren explains

> 'The argument that for the United States a pro-plaintiff tilt in jurisdictional matters is desirable runs as follows: American state legislation either explicitly or through judicial interpretation today typically claims state-court adjudicatory authority to the constitutionally permissible extent.'[212]

As a result, the U.S. jurisdictional structure gives the plaintiff a substantially large choice which makes it significantly more pro-plaintiff than the Continental European and English approach.[213] Moreover, the European *forum rei* rule only plays a minor role.[214] According to Von Mehren this wide range of jurisdictional opportunity leads to the 'inevitable effect to reduce – or eliminate – the significance of the *actor sequitur principle*' and 'contemporary American practice can hardly be seen as embracing even a weak version of the *actor sequitur* principle'.[215]

The initial aim of the Due Process Clause is to protect defendants from unfair exercise of jurisdiction[216] and is generally understood to impose limits to excessive jurisdiction by requiring a minimum of contacts.[217] This seems contrary to the U.S. wide jurisdictional catalogue which is the direct result of the rejection of the strict territorial approach by *International Shoe* and the flexible approach to extraterritoriality on the basis of minimum contacts.[218]

Apart from the minimum contacts standard, the due process jurisdictional requirement ensures that any exercise of jurisdiction over the defendant is in accordance with considerations of fairness and reasonableness and that the defendant purposefully availed himself of the forum.[219] The Supreme Court identified in

---

[211] Silberman, 'Comparative Jurisdiction', at 328.

[212] Von Mehren, 'Theory and Practice', at 200.

[213] There are some particular bases for jurisdiction, such as for instance the place of performance rule, where U.S. law is actually narrower than the other approaches. See also O'Brian Jr., 'The Hague Convention on Jurisdiction', at 495.

[214] See Sect. 6.4.4.

[215] Von Mehren, 'Theory and Practice', at 193, respectively at 191. Von Mehren observes whether other contemporary legal systems are prepared to follow this tendency.

[216] See Goldstein, 'Federalism', at 970.

[217] Michaels, 'Territorial Jurisdiction', at 111, 'The way to deal with the inherent danger of overreaching has been to require additional elements to be present before jurisdiction can be established. One is the requirement of "minimum contacts" introduced into US jurisdictional law in 1945 by the Supreme Court decision of International Shoe.'

[218] 326 U.S. 310, at 316 (1945).

[219] See Chapter 5, Sect. 5.4.3.3. See Michaels, 'Two Paradigms', at 1053; A. Lowenfeld and L. Silberman, eds., *The Hague Convention on Jurisdiction and Judgements* (2001), at A-3; R. Brand,

the *Burger King* case a number of factors pursuant to which the fairness test should be weighed: these factors certainly do not give evidence of the fact that defendant's interest and protection are the only, and not even the main concern, of the due process analysis.[220] Certainly the burden of the defendant of being sued in a particular forum remains a significant factor in the fairness test and it appreciates the degree of inconvenience for the defendant to defend himself in a forum other than his home state. But the fairness test is also concerned with the 'plaintiff's interest in obtaining convenient and effective relief' and the three other factors concerning the state's interests.[221] As a result, the defendant's protection by the Due Process Clause against the wide jurisdictional catalogue available to the plaintiff is effectuated by way of a balancing test of the parties' interests. In sum, defendant's protection depends on the *ex post* appreciation by the court seized and serves as a counterweight to the wide choice available to the plaintiff.[222]

Finally, similar to the English system, the American approach also applies the *forum non conveniens* which can protect the defendant when the plaintiff's choice is inconvenient to him.[223] The observations made above regarding the English common law and the doctrine's effect on the defendant's protection equally apply to the American approach. The doctrine protects the defendant from being sued in an inappropriate forum. Its application is for those reasons defendant-friendly and may affect the plaintiff's choice of forum. The fact that the burden lays on the defendant to prove that the inconvenience of the chosen court is advantageous to the claimant. The Supreme Court acknowledged in *Gulf Oil Corp v. Gilbert* that the plaintiff's choice should, as a matter of principle, be respected. It stated that

> 'The principle of forum non conveniens is simply that a court may resist imposition upon its jurisdiction even when jurisdiction is authorized by the letter of a general venue statute. These statutes are drawn with a necessary generality and usually give a plaintiff a choice of courts, so that he may be quite sure of some place in which to pursue his remedy. But the open door may admit those who seek not simply justice but perhaps justice blended with some harassment. A plaintiff sometimes is under temptation to resort to a strategy of forcing the trial at a most inconvenient place for an adversary, even at some inconvenience to himself. ... The court will weigh relative advantages and obstacles to fair trial. ... But unless the balance is strongly in favor of the defendant, the plaintiff's choice of forum should rarely be disturbed.'[224]

Fundamentals of International Business Transactions (2000), at 458-459, 'They exist to protect individuals from excessive exercises of governmental authority. In a discussion of judicial jurisdiction, this means the Due Process Clauses restrict the extent to which courts may exercise jurisdiction over a defendant.' Buchner, 'Kläger- und Beklagtenschutz', at 27-28. See also Juenger, 'Federalism: A Comparison', at 1202, in relation to the purposeful availment test: 'if one looks at it through the eyes of a litigator, it [the availment test] becomes apparent that that formula has an inherent bias which favors individuals, particularly products liability claimants, who sue large enterprises engaged in nationwide activities.'

[220] *Burger King Corp. v. Rudewicz*, 471 U.S. 462, at 477 (1985).

[221] See Chapter 5, Sect. 5.4.4.

[222] See also Buchner, 'Kläger- und Beklagtenschutz', at 30.

[223] J. Duval-Major, 'One-Way Ticket Home: The Federal Doctrine of Forum Non Conveniens and the International Plaintiff', *Cornell Law Review* (1992), 650-686, at 650, 'Only defendants may invoke the doctrine of forum non conveniens, because plaintiffs have the original choice of forum.'

[224] 330 U.S. 501, at 507-508 (1946).

The Supreme Court admits the wide range statutory authorization of long-arm statutes and the necessity to correct their outcome on the basis of open-ended norms. One of the particularities of the U.S. *forum non conveniens* is that it allows a court to especially protect the in-state defendant against an 'alien'.[225] The doctrine appears to be particularly beneficial to U.S.-based companies sued in their home court by foreign plaintiffs.[226] U.S. courts do not decline jurisdiction on considerations of inconvenience for the U.S. corporate defendant since it is rarely considered inconvenient to defend oneself in one's home court instead of across the world. The public interests factors should be understood as justifying the limited access to U.S. courts for foreign plaintiffs in an attempt to restrict the increasing use of U.S. courts. This is a strong device to correct the *forum shopping* behaviour of foreign claimants who shop by reasons of the U.S. courts' attractiveness.[227]

6.4.4 A Different Role for the *Favor Defensoris*

In the context of the preceding paragraphs, the following contrasting approach to jurisdiction merits some extra attention. 'Protectionism' in favour of the defendant is not given as much weight in Anglo-American common law as in the Brussels Regulation and Continental European jurisdictions. As explained above the principle of *forum defensoris* plays a crucial role in the protection of the parties in Continental European structures. Favouring the defendant at his home forum is the underlying policy of the European framework and is acknowledged by national Continental legislators and the drafters of the Brussels Model. According to AG Léger in his opinion in the *Leathertex* case

> 'the plaintiff is always entitled to bring his action in its entirety before the courts for the domicile of the defendant, which thus provides a sure and reliable criterion. In other words, the choice of jurisdiction provided in the interest of the parties, in particular of the plaintiff, still gives them the security of a predictable rule of jurisdiction, which the plaintiff may choose if, for his own particular reasons, the other rule of jurisdiction does not suit him'.[228]

In Anglo-American common law, the 'security' for both plaintiff and defendant to find a competent court at defendant's home is not guaranteed. The reasons are two-fold: Primarily, the domicile rule constitutes a valid and well-accepted ground for general jurisdiction under Anglo-American common law,[229] but does not represent the starting point for international jurisdiction.[230] In English common law, the fact that the defendant is domiciled in England only becomes relevant for jurisdictional

---

[225] See Chapter 5, Sect. 5.5.3.

[226] L. Collins and G. Droz, 'La recours à la doctrine du forum non conveniens et aux "anti-suit injunctions": Principes directeurs. 2ème Commission', 70 *Annuaire de l'Institut de droit international* (2003), 13-94, at 16; Duval-Major, 'One-Way Ticket Home', at 650-651; D. Dunham and E. Gladbach, 'Forum Non Conveniens and Foreign Plaintiffs in the 1990s', *Brooklyn Journal of International Law* (1999), 665-704, at 666.

[227] See also Lookofsky and Hertz, *Transnational Litigation*, § 2.5.4.A.

[228] See paras. 76-77.

[229] See Chapter 7, Sect. 7.2; and Buchner, 'Kläger- und Beklagtenschutz', at 22.

[230] See above Sect. 6.2.

purposes when the defendant is not present in the forum. Domicile is subordinated to presence.[231] In the U.S., the domicile rule is, in contrast to the English system, part of the traditional common law grounds for jurisdiction, but does not constitute the fundamental rule for jurisdiction.[232] 'Presence' and 'domicile', just like 'consent', and the later introduced 'doing business', stand on equal foot with each other. In line with that explanation Micheals rightfully further explains that 'Europeans consider the defendant's domicile, the natural forum and another forum chosen by the plaintiff as the exception, while Americans think of the plaintiff's domicile as the natural forum, which is unacceptable only when jurisdiction there would violate the defendant's due process rights.'[233]

An even more important distinction relates to the defendant's position in Anglo-American common law systems that are less preoccupied with defendant's protection since their structure allows derogation from any jurisdiction rule including the *forum rei* maxim by virtue of the *forum non conveniens* doctrine.[234] Here lies one of the fundamental differences between European regimes which emanate from the civil law traditions and the Anglo-American common law, as the latter simply does not automatically accept that it is always appropriate to sue a defendant in the courts of his domicile.[235] When a claimant invokes general jurisdiction under the common law domicile rule, the court seized has the discretionary power to decline jurisdiction in English and U.S. law. By virtue of the English and the U.S. *forum non conveniens* doctrines, jurisdiction under the *forum rei* rule is not always considered obvious or logical.[236] In the words of Bell 'some jurisdictions, of which the United States stands out as the most prominent and important example, would appear in their case law at least not wholeheartedly to accept the Convention's grundnorm namely the principle that the prima facie appropriate forum in which a defendant may be sued is that of its domicile.'[237]

Under civil law, the domicile rule presupposes a substantial connection with the forum and is considered to be the defendant's *natural forum* or *juge naturel*.[238] The result is that when claimant invokes general jurisdiction under the domicile rule, the court seized is automatically and without declination, the competent court. Instead, Anglo-American courts consider the substantial connection between defendant's forum and the dispute on a case-by-case basis. The following statement of Lord

---

231 See above Sect. 6.2.1.

232 As will be explained in the subsequent paragraph, the underlying policy in common law jurisdiction is in the first place more concerned with the access to courts (i.e. justice) for the plaintiff and secondly with finding the most appropriate court for both parties including the defendant.

233 Michaels continues 'this answer immediately creates a new question; why do Americans and Europeans differ on what is the natural forum.' Michaels, 'Two Paradigms', at 1057.

234 But see also Bell, *Forum Shopping and Venue*, at 80-81.

235 'There is simply no acceptance in common law jurisdictions of the blanket proposition that it is always appropriate to sue a defendant in the courts of his domicile.' Bell, *Forum Shopping and Venue*, § 3.62, at 79.

236 On the question whether, after the *Burnham* case, U.S. courts are also required to consider the compatibility with the *Due Process* Clause and its principles of fairness for the ascertainment of jurisdiction at the defendant's forum.

237 Bell, *Forum Shopping and Venue*, § 3.58, at 77.

238 See Nuyts, *L'exception*, § 138, at 197.

Kinkel in the *The Abidin Daver* case[239] was repeated in the *Spiliada* decision to illustrate that for the English meaning of the 'natural forum' one must examine each connection with the forum, including the defendant's domicile:

> 'Lord Keith of Kinkel, ... referred to the "natural forum" as being "that with which the action had the most real and substantial connection." So it is for connecting factors in this sense that the court must first look; and these will include not only factors affecting convenience or expense (such as availability of witnesses), but also other factors such as the law governing the relevant transaction ... and the places where the parties respectively reside or carry on business.'[240]

Hence, under Anglo-American law, the parties' domicile, in particular that of the defendant is a relevant factor under the *forum non conveniens* doctrine, or as an 'indicator of *conveniens*'.[241]

6.5 Parameters for the Regulation of Jurisdiction World-wide

The civil law and common law differences seem to have been surmounted at a pan-European level under the Brussels Model. Obviously, the initial Brussels Convention clearly reflected a homogeneous civil law tradition of the six founding Contracting States.[242] The legal and cultural gaps to be surmounted at that time at regional European level were relatively smaller in comparison to the difficulties encountered at universal level today. The predominantly common law legal systems of the U.K. and Ireland were under the obligation to accede to the Brussels Convention in order to become members of the European Community,[243] but there was no obligation to model the regulation of interregional jurisdiction for intra-U.K. relations on the Brussels Model. Considering that Schedule 4 of the CJJA 1982 is clearly a copy of the Brussels Convention, the U.K. legislator adopted civil law principles for jurisdiction and abandoned the traditional common law rules.[244] Lord Goff of Chieveley's statement in *Airbus Industrie G.I.E.* should be understood as accepting the Brussels system of civil law origin for the sake of the greater goal of the unification of jurisdiction

> 'The judges of this country, who loyally enforce this system, not only between United Kingdom jurisdictions and the jurisdictions of other member states, but also as between the three jurisdictions within the United Kingdom itself, have to accept the fact that the practical results are from time to time unwelcome. This is essentially because the primary purpose of the Convention is to ensure that there shall be no clash between the jurisdictions of member states of the Community.'[245]

---

239 [1984] AC 398, at 415.

240 *Spiliada Maritime Corp. v. Cansulex Ltd.*, [1987] AC 460, at 478.

241 M. Karayanni, *Forum Non Cconveniens in the Modern Age: A Comparative and Methodological Analysis of Anglo-American Law* (2004), at 67, argues that the basic assumption in this respect is that it is convenient for the parties to litigate a dispute in their home forum.

242 Chapter 2, Sect. 2.1.

243 See also Chapter 4, Sect. 4.1.

244 See Schlosser, 'Bases of Jurisdiction', at A-14.

245 *Airbus Industrie G.I.E. v. Patel and Others* [1999] 1 AC 119, at 132.

The question is whether there is a similar (common) will at a world-wide level to let the benefits of unification prevail.[246] The desire to establish an area of free movement of judgements reflected a specific European ideal and the success of the Brussels Model is for the greater part due to the economic integration of the European Community as driving force behind the unification process.[247] The regulation of international jurisdiction on a universal scale is not supported by the higher goal of economic integration. A general more modest objective should focus on the creation of a legal 'framework to enhance international trade and commerce'.[248]

The Brussels Model is based on mutual trust and on the idea of equality of Member States' courts.[249] In the context of the Hague world-wide jurisdiction project, the initial idea was to apply the Brussels system at international level. It has proven to be a mistake to design a uniform global system for jurisdiction based on the same idea of the equality of states and one should not want to impose a similar mutual trust in a world-wide context.[250] Differences in procedural and substantive law and other practical elements are taken into account by international litigators when selecting a court before which to bring their action.[251] For them states or courts are not at all equal.[252]

In the present search for a uniform system for international jurisdiction over commercial contractual disputes, there are certain parameters or 'guidelines against which proposed bases of jurisdiction can be tested'.[253] Acceptable and consensus-based jurisdiction rules should take into account the four cornerstones that have come to light in the present chapter. They have no hierarchical order, are cumulative and are often interrelated. A uniform structure for jurisdiction over international contractual disputes should be framed within the following parameters. Jurisdiction over contractual disputes should 1) be based on a connection with the forum principally focusing on defendant's activities in the forum giving rise to the contractual claim; 2) guarantee the protection of parties' rights and interests; in which 3) state interests considerations merely play a limited role, and 4) a proper balance between legal certainty and flexibility should be ensured.

---

[246] See J. Kovar, 'The United States as an Actor in Private International Law', in *Private Law, Private International Law, & Judicial Cooperation in the EU-US Relationship* (2005), at 154.

[247] Gardella and Radicati di Brozolo, 'Civil Law, Common Law', at 636.

[248] Minutes (No. 1) meeting of Monday 22 April 2002, Morning Session: M. Kovar (United States) Commission I General Affairs and Policy The Hague Conference, at 7. See also Gardella and Radicati di Brozolo, 'Civil Law, Common Law', at 636, 'In such a context the aim might more modestly be to increase trade rather than to further full market integration'.

[249] Gardella and Radicati di Brozolo, 'Civil Law, Common Law', at 613, 'Under the influence of Savigny's writings, continental private international law systems tend to rely on neutral provisions which determine the applicable rules ex ante, regardless of the outcome in the specific case. This approach is undisputedly reflected in the Regulation.'

[250] See Bell, *Forum Shopping and Venue*, Chap. 3; and Gardella and Radicati di Brozolo, 'Civil Law, Common Law', at 636.

[251] See Chapter 1, Sect. 1.1.1.

[252] See Chapter 5, Sect. 5.5.4.

[253] Nygh, 'Criteria for Judicial Jurisdiction', at A-3.

6.5.1 The Connection with the Forum

Ensuring a 'connection' with the forum constitutes a fundamental prerequisite for the foundation of jurisdiction. Each system surveyed establishes jurisdiction on the basis of some kind of connection or *contact* with the forum.[254] In a world-wide uniform system regulating jurisdiction over international contractual disputes this should be no different and a substantial connection with the forum should equally be ensured.[255]

Imposing a close connection with the forum protects the defendant from being sued in an exorbitant or excessive forum.[256] Exorbitant bases for jurisdiction reflect a certain degree of protectionism for a claimant resident, providing him with a competent forum with little connection to the dispute. In a well-balanced uniform structure for contractual disputes, there should be no need for exorbitant bases for jurisdiction.[257]

What is more is that extraterritorial reach of states over international businesses or persons outside its territory – especially on the basis of a weak link with the state – appears to have a 'significant negative impact on economic growth and development', creates 'considerable commercial and legal uncertainty' and 'may encourage *forum shopping*, duplicate proceedings and potential divergent outcomes' according to the ICC's Taskforce on Extraterritoriality.[258] For those reasons the ICC's Taskforce 'encourages courts *to refrain from judicial jurisdiction in matters that lack a substantial and predictable link with their territory.*'[259]

The meaning of a 'substantial connection' is however vague and often randomly defined, without any indication of the elements constituting the sufficient connection.[260] Further delimitation of the 'close connection'-standard is needed as not every connection with the forum justifies jurisdiction.

One should distinguish between *party-related* connections and *claim-related* connections. *Party-related* connections refer to a nexus between the parties and the forum.[261] In that respect it is predominantly the defendant's connection with the

---

[254] See P. Lagarde, 'Le principe de proximité dans le droit internationalc privé contemporain. Cours général de droit international privé', 196 *Recueil des cours* (1986), 9-238, at 134-138. See Hatzimihail, 'General Report', at 639, stating that as a rule, these connections differ from jurisdiction based on consent also called 'voluntary connection'. See also Michaels, 'Re-Placements', at 152, referring to 'The double function of jurisdictional provisions; Allocation and Guarantee of a close connection.' The close connection has a 'benchmark function' 'to guarantee that jurisdiction is only exercised when a close connection exists'.

[255] A close connection between the dispute and the forum is generally considered to vouch for a good administration of justice. The efficacious conduct of proceedings and ease of taking evidence is generally said to be best served when the dispute is, even partly, closely connected with the forum.

[256] Chalas, *L'exercise discrétionnaire*, § 387, at 358.

[257] Hill, 'The Exercise of Jurisdiction', at 56.

[258] Policy Statement of 13 July 2006'Extraterritoriality and business', available at http://www.iccwbo.org/uploadedFiles/ICC/policy/trade/Statements/103-33%205%20Final.pdf .

[259] (Emphasis added). The policy statement (at 4) continues to urge governments to explore signature and ratification of the Hague Convention on Choice of Court Agreements.

[260] See among others Lagarde, 'Le principe de proximité', at 133.

[261] Hatzimihail refers to the party-related connections as the 'subjective connection' which determines jurisdiction on the basis of factual or legal attachments of the parties to a certain territory. Hatzimihail, 'General Report', at 635.

forum that justifies jurisdiction. Jurisdiction based on the connection between the plaintiff and the forum, such as the *forum actoris* is rare and generally unacceptable for uniform jurisdiction rules.[262]

Claim-related jurisdiction is based on a connection between the forum and the specific features of the claim.[263] An example of *claim-related* jurisdiction in contractual disputes is jurisdiction that is conferred on the court of the place of delivery. *Claim-related* jurisdiction does not take into account the parties' connections with the forum, in particular the defendant's inconvenience to have to defend himself in a forum where he has not carried out any commercial activities.

There are two important reasons to favour a close connection between the forum and the defendant instead of with the claim: primarily, the principle of legal certainty requires a certain degree of predictability. *Defendant-related* jurisdiction is generally considered better to foresee than *claim-related* jurisdiction for both defendants and claimants. With respect to the example of the place of delivery, parties are not always able to foresee where the place of delivery will be located, especially when the place of delivery has not been contractually agreed upon and needs further determination by the *lex causae*. Another important argument in favour of *defendant-related* jurisdiction is its global acceptance as opposed to *claim-related* jurisdiction which is incompatible with U.S. due process standards.[264] This does not mean that a *claim-related* connection cannot be the basis of jurisdiction, just that the exercise of *claim-related* jurisdiction is subjected to the existence of a connection between the defendant and the forum to be able to fulfil U.S. due process standards. The existence of a close connection between the forum and the defendant is crucial for world-wide acceptance of a uniform jurisdiction rule in contractual disputes.

A 'connection' with the forum can be based on a 'territorial' connection with the forum. In this respect 'territorial' connection should be understood as territoriality in its narrow sense, meaning any physical connection with the forum.[265] It should be understood as any physical, visible or tangible connection that can be 'localised' in the forum. The question is whether jurisdiction is or should still be based on physical connections with the forum in present times.

Party-related connections are not necessarily based on territorial or physical connections with the forum. Nationality-based jurisdiction reflects a 'personal connection' with the forum.[266] Personal connections are generally considered outdated and associated with protectionism of a country's own subjects or residents. As

---

[262] See also Chapter 7, Sect. 7.4.

[263] Claim-related connections are referred to as objective connections, see Hatzimihail, 'General Report', at 638; and Grolimund, 'Human Rights and Jurisdiction', at 110.

[264] See also Chapter 7, Sect. 7.5.

[265] See Chapter 1, Sect. 1.4.2.

[266] *Defendant-related* jurisdiction can be divided in a 'personalist and a territorialist variation', see Hatzimihail, 'General Report', at 636. In common law the concept of domicile is also considered to consist of a personal relationship with the forum and includes a more subjective integration than the Continental European interpretation of the domicile concept, see also further in Chapter 7, Sect. 7.2. Keyes, *Jurisdiction in International Litigation*, at 202; Sykes and Pryles, *Australian Private International Law* (1991), § 2.1, at 446; P. Hay, 'Transient Jurisdiction, Especially over International

far as transnational contractual disputes are concerned, personal connections have become less significant for jurisdictional purposes and should no longer be decisive for the exercise of jurisdiction. For those reasons, personal connections should be disregarded with respect to the close connection standard.

Prominent scholars have argued that connecting factors should concentrate on economic or business connections of (corporate) defendants to regulate jurisdiction, rather than on purely territorialist principles.[267] This approach originates from the American approach to jurisdiction and is based on the assumption that jurisdictional bases do not always necessitate physical connections with the forum. Examples of 'economic connections' are: advertising its goods abroad; sending sales representatives overseas to visit trade fairs and retailers; appointing an independent commercial agent; and granting exclusive distribution rights.[268] The idea that international commercial litigation should focus more on economic connections or interests in the forum is tempting and attempts to define defendant's connection on a more pragmatic basis instead of by formal legal concepts such as 'branch jurisdiction'. However, in the context of uniform jurisdiction rules, a 'physical' connection often ensures a more substantial connection with the forum. Jurisdiction on 'a mere point of contact' would result in too many competent forums. *Defendant-related* jurisdiction, including defendants' activities in the forum, should focus on a substantial and 'genuine' link between the defendant and the forum.[269]

In order to ensure that jurisdiction is based on a *substantial and genuine connection* a uniform system can either incorporate connecting factors based on the assumption of a close connection[270] or *ex post* apply a correction mechanism imposing the existence of a close connection with the forum for the exercise of jurisdiction.[271] The first option implies a positive and constitutive role for connecting factors to comply with the close connection standard.[272]

The second option implies a negative application of the close connection standard by way of a correction clause, which allows courts to refuse the exercise of jurisdiction when the outcome of the rule indicates a court with a weak or no connection with the dispute. It allows the rebuttal of the presumption of a close connection upon which the connecting factor founded jurisdiction in the first place.

Defendants; Critical Comment on *Burnham v. Superior Court California*', *University of Illinois Law Review* (1990), 593-603, at 599.

[267] See Chapter 5, Sect. 5.2.2, and see Chapter 7, Sect. 7.1; Mann, 'Doctrine of International Jurisdiction Revisited', at 29; J. Fawcett, 'A New Approach to Jurisdiction over Companies in Private International Law', 37 *The International and Comparative Law Quarterly* (1988), 645-667.

[268] See Fawcett, 'A New Approach to Jurisdiction over Companies', at 659, claiming that the links a company has with a country will be economic rather than physical, see also at 661.

[269] T. Kleinstück, *Due Process-Beschränkungen des Vermögensgerichtsstandes durch hinreichenden Inlandsbezug und Minimum Contacts* (1994), at 145; Lagarde, 'Le principe de proximité', at 127.

[270] See Lagarde, 'Le principe de proximité', at 131, '*servir à l'élaboration des chefs de compétence internationale*'.

[271] See Lagarde, 'Le principe de proximité', at 142-157.

[272] Ibid., at 26-27 and 131.

6.5.2 The Focus on Defendant's Activities Giving Rise to the Contractual Claim

Only *defendant-related* connections should be taken into account for uniform rules over contractual disputes and they should focus on defendant's activities. Clearly this is important in the context of the U.S. due process standards and it might also be in the future if the fair trial principle of Article 6 of the European Convention on Human Rights ever plays a role in the jurisdictional question by stating that 'a fair trial includes also not to be hauled into a court that does not have a solid ground for jurisdiction'.[273] According to Nygh '[i]f justice is to be the guideline rather than power, we must introduce a notion of due process in order to protect the defendant. … This is well known in the United States jurisprudence, but has not hitherto been regarded as a relevant factor in the drafting of other national bases of jurisdiction.'[274]

Defendant-related connections should primarily be focused on defendant's activities in the forum *giving rise to the contractual claim*. When a defendant is carrying out (business) activities on the territory of a forum, the forum should be able to have jurisdiction over him. The justification given by the U.S. Supreme Court is equally valid at uniform level; *defendant's activity-related* jurisdiction is based on the idea that if a person carries out business and/or engages in commercial activity in a country in order to obtain commercial benefits or other advantages it is reasonable to subject him to the jurisdiction of its courts 'in return for the opportunity the state had given him to carry out business on its territory'.[275] In the words of Buchner:

> 'In choosing grounds of jurisdiction based on conduct related to the cause of action, the basic consideration is that when someone is engaged in a commercial activity in a country, he has to comply with all sorts of prescription relating to such activity, in such a way that it would seem normal that he will also be subject to the judicial jurisdiction of that state. Once you are purposely developing an activity in a country, you should not be surprised to be brought before the courts of such country when the cause of

[273] See contribution Schlosser, in Lowenfeld and Silberman, eds., *The Hague Convention on Jurisdiction*, at 20; J. Fawcett, 'The Impact of Article 6(1) of the ECHR on Private International Law', 56 *The International and Comparative Law Quarterly* (2007), 1-48, at 16. See also Chapter 8, Sect. 8.3.

[274] Nygh, 'Criteria for Judicial Jurisdiction', at A-2-3.

[275] The Supreme Court considered in *International Shoe Co. v. Washington*, 326 U.S. 310, at 319, that these activities and connections with the forum also engender to comply with certain obligations and a state could require the corporation to 'respond to a suit brought to enforce them'. See also *World-Wide Volkswagen Corp. v. Woodson*, 444 U.S. 286, at 297-298 (1980). See previously in U.S. Chapter 5, Sect. 5.2.2. See also Baumgartner, *The Proposed Hague Convention*, at 134-135. See contribution Nygh, in Lowenfeld and Silberman, eds., *The Hague Convention on Jurisdiction,* at 13. See also Nygh, 'Criteria for Judicial Jurisdiction', at A-11; 'It is fair and just that a person who seeks to enter a market either directly through its branches or indirectly through other persons should meet claims arising out of activity in that market before the courts of that place. It is also fairly clear that such activity should not found a general jurisdiction.' See also Schlosser, 'Bases of Jurisdiction', at A-20, '[that a] person or a corporation should be amenable to judicial jurisdiction at the place where he or it is doing business sounds reasonable, provided that the claim arises out of, or at least is related to, the respective business activities.'

action is related to such activity. In such a case, the defendant should not be privileged compared to plaintiffs.'[276]

Founding jurisdiction on the basis of defendant's activities also meets concerns of predictability and foreseeability for both parties: when a defendant is carrying out activities in a particular forum, he can 'reasonably foresee' that he can be sued in that forum. This should however not be confused with 'effect' jurisdiction, in which the defendant's activities results in having an 'effect' in the forum.[277] For that reason it is important that when jurisdiction is founded on connections with the forum as a result of defendant's activities, the jurisdiction should be limited to claims arising out of these activities in the forum.

In other words jurisdiction based on defendant's business activity in the forum reflect a certain voluntary and substantial connection with the forum which justifies jurisdiction, ensures that the defendant consciously or 'purposefully' made a connection with the forum and is compatible with the interests of the both parties.

6.5.3 **The Protection of Parties**

The rights and interests of both plaintiffs and defendants should be secured when regulating international jurisdiction over commercial contractual disputes. The claimant's interests are generally thought to be opposite to the defendant's interests. Some rules or connecting factors are based on a jurisdictional privilege for one party at the expense of the other. In order to secure the protection of parties, uniform jurisdictional rules for contractual disputes should aim at establishing a proper balance between the interests of both claimants and defendants.[278] Achieving such a balance does not necessarily imply a policy choice between privileging the defendant and favouring the claimant. It does not impose the elimination of jurisdiction rules or connecting factors favouring one party over the other. O'Brian rightfully states that '[t]he proper goal of a system of jurisdiction should not favour plaintiffs or defendants, but rather to see to it that the court that decides a question is the court of equality of arms.'[279] Such 'equality of arms' implies a fair balance of parties' interest or as Nygh has put it; one 'must ensure that the victim [or claimant] has reasonable access to relief in a form that is fairly accessible to the defendant'.[280] Equality of arms is based on the idea that there should not be any 'substantial disadvantage vis-à-vis opponent'[281] and that any form of discrimination should be

[276] Buchner, in Lowenfeld and Silberman, eds., *The Hague Convention on Jurisdiction*, at 24-25.

[277] Keyes, *Jurisdiction in International Litigation*, at 354.

[278] Von Mehren, 'Theory and Practice', at 194-195. See the contribution by Buchner in Lowenfeld and Silberman, eds., *The Hague Convention on Jurisdiction,* at 24; Nygh, 'Criteria for Judicial Jurisdiction', at A-1.

[279] O'Brian Jr., 'The Hague Convention on Jurisdiction', at 497.

[280] Nygh, 'Criteria for Judicial Jurisdiction', at A-1. Nygh continues by stating that 'this has not always been the law and indeed the pendulum has swung widely from one extreme to the other'.

[281] *Nideröst-Huber v. Switzerland*, Judgment of 18/02/1997, Reports 1997-I, Sect. 23; see also Nuyts, 'Due Process and Fair Trial', at 179; Von Mehren, 'Theory and Practice', at 194; Lagarde, 'Le principe de proximité', at 157. See also Chapter 8, Sect. 8.3, with respect to the fair trial principle of Art. 6 of the European Convention on Human Rights.

avoided.[282] 'Litigational equality'[283] imposes a certain degree of proportionality; none of the parties should be over- or under-protected. In that respect, exorbitant bases for jurisdiction should be excluded as they strongly favour the plaintiff, often providing him with an additional competent court that has a weak connection to the dispute and the defendant.[284] Furthermore litigational equality should weigh plaintiff's access to justice 'against the defendant's claim to be left alone' from being sued on the basis of excessive jurisdiction.[285]

The defendant is primarily protected when he is shielded from being subjected to jurisdiction of courts that lack any substantial *defendant-related* connection and secondly when he is able to foresee or predict where he might be amenable for suit.[286] In that respect it is only fair to subject a defendant to a court over a contractual claim when the defendant carried out commercial activities in the forum: defendant should only be brought to courts where the defendant has a significant connection with the forum, either through voluntary settlement in a forum or through his activities.[287]

Protecting the claimant primarily implies securing his access to justice by providing him with an appropriate competent court where he can bring his claim against the defendant. A plaintiff has several advantages over the defendant when he commences proceedings; he determines the claim and unilaterally selects a forum best suited to his needs.[288] This gives the plaintiff a head start in the litigation process. Restricting the available forums to forums with a substantial connection with the defendant compensates for these advantages. If multiple competent forums are at the claimant's disposal, the defendant could be given the opportunity to ultimately control the court selected by the plaintiff by way of a correction mechanism. As will be explained below this is to the detriment of considerations of legal certainty,[289] which might demand to give effect to the court selected by

---

[282] According to Keyes, making a distinction between plaintiff and defendant is one of the characteristics of jurisdiction law. However this should not lead to the discrimination of one party in particular, Keyes, *Jurisdiction in International Litigation*, at 205; see also Lookofsky and Hertz, *Transnational Litigation*, § 2.5.4.(A), at 322, on 'Procedural discrimination'.

[283] See Von Mehren, 'Theory and Practice', at 196, on 'litigational equality' between plaintiffs and defendants: 'each party should be treated equally. Of course, here as elsewhere, what is meant by equality is not a simple matter.'

[284] See Von Mehren and his idea of the concept of proportionality which should 'ensure not only that the forums in which claims can be pursued are appropriate and sufficient in number, but also in order to deter unjustified forum-shopping, no more numerous than is required to give the plaintiff absent exceptional circumstances, a fair opportunity to litigate his cause', Von Mehren, 'Theory and Practice', at 68; see also Buchner's contribution in Lowenfeld and Silberman, eds., *The Hague Convention on Jurisdiction*, at 24.

[285] Von Mehren, 'Theory and Practice', at 166.

[286] See also below Sect. 6.5.5 on legal certainty.

[287] 'Generally it is reasonable to expect a defendant to meet a claim at his or her residence. Furthermore, it should be reasonable to expect the defendant to meet a claim [arising out of business activities or] in a place where he or she, did or hoped to, derive [a commercial] advantage to him or her.' Nygh, 'Criteria for Judicial Jurisdiction', at A-3.

[288] See also Keyes, *Jurisdiction in International Litigation*, at 199.

[289] See Von Mehren, 'Theory and Practice', at 195, who finds that '[w]hether jurisdictional theory and practice are plaintiff or defendant orientated thus depends on the interaction of two factors:

the plaintiff.[290] The possibilities to decline jurisdiction, and consequently not to give effect to the plaintiff's choice should therefore be limited and well defined. Especially, since declining jurisdiction means in practice that litigation will not be pursued in the other available so-called more appropriate court.[291]

The question is whether considerable deference should be given to the plaintiff's selection of the competent court in the present context of international jurisdiction over contractual disputes. The more jurisdictional bases available to the claimant to choose from, the more the defendant will try to not give effect to the plaintiff's choice, if such 'correction' appears to be desirable for the defendant. The answer should focus on the fact that securing plaintiff's access to justice does not automatically mean that the claimant should be provided with a selective range of jurisdictional bases that are available to him. A well-balanced system for jurisdiction should on the one hand provide the claimant with an appropriate forum for him to bring his claim, and should on the other hand not privilege the defendant beforehand. Litigational equality can also be reached by providing one single appropriate court that is well-connected to defendant's activities in the forum in relation to the contractual claim *and* to the claimant. The right balance can be reached by providing the plaintiff with an appropriate court that remains fair to the defendant by guaranteeing a *defendant-related* connection with the forum.[292]

6.5.4 State's Interest Considerations

The protection of parties' interests raises the question whether state's interest considerations should be taken into account in the unification of international jurisdiction over contractual disputes. State's interest considerations can be understood in a large and in a narrow sense. The larger sense acknowledges that states have an interest in obtaining the efficient settlement of international disputes before state courts, minimizing costs of international litigation and promoting international civil justice.[293] State's interest considerations in the narrow sense involve the direct interference of states to protect local or national interests by either accepting (posi-

---

(1) the number and variety of the jurisdictional bases available and (2) which party ultimately controls forum selection.'

[290] Droz, 'Les droits de la demande', at 104. Droz clearly demonstrates this preference for legal certainty when he states the following: '*Chaque Etat est libre de faire ce qu'il veut, à condition – et cette fois il s'agit d'un avis personnel – à condition que le demandeur éventuel sache à quoi s'en tenir et puisse en toute sécurité préparer sa cause, investir les sommes nécessaires à la présentation de ses arguments et finalement d'être entendu.*'

[291] See Reus, 'Judicial Discretion', at 474.

[292] 'Justice to plaintiffs should therefore be rendered where the defendant will not be haled into court by surprise. No surprise would mean that the defendant would be brought before the courts where he had exercised some kind of conduct in relation to the particular cause of action. If there was some kind of conduct in a particular country, then the defendant should not be surprised it is brought to court to answer for that cause.' See contribution Buchner, in Lowenfeld and Silberman, eds., *The Hague Convention on Jurisdiction*, at 24.

[293] See McLachlan's comments on the ILA Leuven/London Principles, C. McLachlan, 'Interim Report Declining & Referring Jurisdiction in International Litigation', paper presented at the International Law Association, London Conference (2000), § 48, at 19, the Preamble 'identifies the overall purpose of such system as being one which promotes international civil justice; a notion which of its

tive) or refusing (negative) jurisdiction in particular cases. As a rule it is in a state's general interest to provide its residents with a forum to adjudicate their disputes. States defend their interests in international commercial disputes either explicitly or implicitly.[294]

National jurisdiction rules are characterized by their unilateral nature as opposed to the multilateral nature of a uniform rule.[295] Each state determines its own jurisdiction and will seek to protect local interests by providing competent forums for domestic plaintiffs and defendants. With respect to providing a competent court for domestic claimants, the state will seek to protect the domestic plaintiffs from having to sue the defendant in a foreign court, especially if the foreign court is defendant's home court. Providing the claimant with subsidiary or alternative competent courts in order to indirectly protect local or national interests, leads to multiple competent forums. When, apart from the *claimant's* connections, the link with the forum is weak, it could potentially result in exorbitant jurisdiction. The multilateral character of uniform rules allows asserting jurisdiction to courts which have a merely substantial and genuine connection to the claim: excessive jurisdiction rules are unwanted in a uniform jurisdiction structure and the number of competent forums available to the plaintiff will be reduced. Moreover and as explained above, providing the claimant with a range of competent forums for him to choose from does not constitute an absolute prerequisite to ensure the claimant's access to justice.

Conversely, American states tend to protect their public interests by declining jurisdiction on the basis of 'public factors' under the U.S. version of the *forum non conveniens* doctrine. Among the public factors considered by U.S. courts are a general concern for crowded court dockets, delays of domestic trials and the burden of jury duties and other community burdens are considered as well.[296] The U.S. Supreme Court allows a distinction to be made between local U.S. plaintiffs and foreign plaintiffs, since the *Piper* decision makes it easier for U.S. courts to decline jurisdiction when the plaintiff is a foreigner and the defendant a U.S. resident.[297] According to Nygh this rule is 'explicitly based on a fear of a flood of foreign litigators'.[298] As a result, the *forum non conveniens* doctrine is used to reduce the attractiveness of U.S. courts. As the Supreme Court explained, American courts are thought to be 'already extremely attractive to foreign plaintiffs', and jurisdiction

nature stands above the parochial concerns of national legal systems.' See also Keyes, *Jurisdiction in International Litigation*, at 305.

[294] See Von Mehren, 'Theory and Practice', at 58, who says that '[a]t times, the significance of economic considerations for jurisdictional practices is painfully clear'.

[295] See also Hatzimihail, 'General Report', at 645.

[296] See Lookofsky and Hertz, *Transnational Litigation*, at 330; and Reus, 'Judicial Discretion', at 473, referring to *Gulf Oil Corp. v. Gilbert*, 330 U.S., at 508-509 (1947).

[297] *Piper Aircraft Co. v. Reyno*, 454 U.S. 235 (1981).

[298] P. Nygh, 'Declining Jurisdiction under the Brussels I Regulation 2001 and the Preliminary Draft Hague Judgments Convention: A Comparison', in *Reform and Development of Private International Law – Essays in Honour of Sir Peter North* (2002), 303-334, at 325.

rules should not make them even more attractive and increase the flow of litigation into the U.S. 'and further congest already crowded courts'.[299]

But this public *forum non conveniens* factor should not be merely understood as protecting U.S. courts from being overcrowded: its underlying policy appears to protect American citizens and companies from being sued by foreign plaintiffs in order to get the benefits characterizing U.S. litigation practice.[300] Nygh argues the following: 'The Americans, of course, tell us that this is a matter of protecting the docket of the court. I don't believe that. I think it is a matter of protecting the US defendants from foreigners getting the same amount as US plaintiffs would.'[301]

Such need of protection seems to be the consequence of an extremely wide jurisdictional catalogue that is available to the claimant and which increases the possibility of forum shopping. A uniform structure for jurisdiction, reducing competent forums on reasonable grounds and limited to claims directly related to defendant's *substantial* connection with the forum, would diminish the run to (U.S.) courts. Plaintiffs will have less opportunity to shop among the courts when a substantial connection is required, and this will indirectly protect states' interests.

In a well-balanced uniform system emphasis should be placed on parties' interests rather than on considerations of states' interests.[302] In the current context of transnational commercial trade relations the protection of state (economic) interests seems to be misplaced, due especially to the commercial nature of international business contracts. Such considerations do not play a role in jurisdiction based on consent, by way of a choice of forum, or in international arbitration. Again the voluntary affiliation of the party with a forum through the carrying out of business in a foreign country should have as logical consequence that the party be submitted to the country's judicial control. Availability of judicial resources is each state's responsibility and should not be a reason for states to decline jurisdiction once the state accepted for the parties to do business in the forum.[303]

State's interest considerations protecting local citizens and companies should not be taken into account.[304] Judicial protectionism or even chauvinism should be rejected as a standard for uniform jurisdiction. Nygh clearly stated, that 'there should not be any room for the protection of state and [public] interests'.[305]

This is in line with the English common law attitude. In the *Lubbe* case, Lord Bingham of Cornhill explicitly stated that 'public interest considerations not related to the private interests of the parties and the ends of justice have no bearing on the decision which the court has to make, ... questions of judicial *amour propre* and political interest or responsibility have no part to play.'[306]

---

[299] *Piper Aircraft Co. v. Reyno*, 454 U.S. 235, at 252 (1981), Marshall J.

[300] See Chapter 5, Sect. 5.5.4.

[301] Nygh, 'Criteria for Judicial Jurisdiction', at 11.

[302] Von Mehren, 'Theory and Practice', at 157, *contra* Hill, 'The Exercise of Jurisdiction', at 45.

[303] Keyes, *Jurisdiction in International Litigation*, at 208.

[304] Reus, 'Judicial Discretion', at 475.

[305] See Nygh, 'Declining Jurisdiction', at 307.

[306] *Lubbe and Others Appellants v. Cape Plc.*, [2000] 1 WLR 1545, at 1561.

6.5.5 The Balance between Legal Certainty and Flexibility

Uniformity in international jurisdiction over contractual disputes should be based on a proper balance between legal certainty and flexibility to promote litigation justice. By legal certainty is meant the predictability or probability of the outcome of jurisdiction rules.[307] Litigators should be able to predict how and on what basis a court exercises jurisdiction. From the parties' point of view, the principle of legal certainty works both ways: a defendant should be able to reasonably foresee the court in which he may be sued and defend himself. There is in this respect much to be said in favour of the U.S. approach which guarantees the defendant's ability to foresee where he may be sued, by requiring that he purposefully availed himself of the forum and hereby voluntarily established connections or contacts with the forum. The plaintiff should be able to easily identify, on the basis of certain reliable rules, the court where he may bring an action. Furthermore, the plaintiff should be able to predict whether his choice for a competent forum will be given effect or not.

Legal certainty also implies a certain degree of determinability of jurisdiction rules.[308] Conceptual clarity in order to understand and apply jurisdictional bases and connecting factors contributes to determinability. Vague criteria or open-ended norms are usually understood as entailing a large margin of subjective interpretation and often result in the need for interpretation by courts.[309] It is generally said that parties as well as transnational commerce benefit from conceptual clarity, legal certainty and predictability, as it reduces the risks and the costs of litigation on the jurisdictional question.[310]

Conversely, a flexible approach towards international jurisdiction, by taking into consideration specific circumstances of individual cases, permits the correction of an 'occasional outrageous result'.[311] Applying rigid bases for jurisdiction is thought to increase the risks of 'litigational' or procedural injustice.[312] Introducing a certain degree of flexibility in international uniform jurisdiction rules should avoid 'litigational injustice'.

Legal certainty and predictability on the one hand and flexibility and procedural justice on the other hand are often considered each other's opposite and irrecon-

---

[307] See Hay, 'Flexibility versus Predictability and Uniformity', fn. 4, at 291, referring to Kegel.

[308] See for example on the problem of determinability of corporate presence and corporate domicile in common law, Michaels, 'Territorial Jurisdiction', at 109. See also W. Kennett, '*Forum Non Conveniens* in Europe', 43 *Cambridge Law Journal* (1995), 552-577, at 571; Nygh, in Lowenfeld and Silberman, eds., *The Hague Convention on Jurisdiction*, at 10, stating 'But in the context of an international convention, I think it is very important that we use a terminology that can be readily understood – ideally, a terminology that can be understood even by persons who are not lawyers. That is to say, that businessmen can look this up and say, "we know exactly what you mean".'

[309] Nygh gives as example the term 'purposeful availment' which he finds 'unsuitable' for international conventions. The same applies for the phrase 'for the ends of justice', see Nygh, 'Criteria for Judicial Jurisdiction', at 10.

[310] See Nygh, 'Declining Jurisdiction', at 307, 'It follows that regulation of this aspect of the law at the international level is highly desirable if one wants to promote certainty and predictability for international trade.' See further Whincop, *Policy and Pragmatism*, at 144; Reus, 'Judicial Discretion', at 475.

[311] Hay, 'Flexibility versus Predictability and Uniformity', at 292.

[312] See Von Mehren, 'Theory and Practice', at 69.

cilable.[313] Yet, although it is a 'difficult and delicate task' to find a balance between legal certainty and flexibility,[314] the 'certainty/flexibility dilemma'[315] seems to be overstated.[316] As Hay claims '[i]t is more helpful ... simply to recognize the existence of the tension and to make continued efforts to achieve an acceptable balance.'[317]

In a well-balanced uniform jurisdictional structure, the jurisdictional rules and their connecting factors should be drafted by reflecting 'the balance struck by one's legal order between the administrability and predictability paradigm, on the one hand and the litigation convenience fairness and justice paradigm on the other'.[318] One should no longer think in terms of 'certainty requires rigid rules, and flexibility is the antithesis of rigidity'.[319] Instead, a proper balance could be reached by a combination of clear jurisdictional bases and, if needed, open-ended standards.

Since, it is true that 'normally a connecting factor cannot systematically advance equally administrability and litigation justice',[320] a uniform system for jurisdiction should be drafted by combining connecting factors that are conceptually clear with tailor-made correction rules. Using open-ended standards as bases for jurisdiction should be avoided,[321] but in order to avoid rigidity and inflexibility, ways should be found to adapt the jurisdictional outcomes to circumstances or exceptional cases.[322] A uniform regime for international jurisdiction over contractual disputes might be a hybrid one,[323] containing clear bases for jurisdiction with open 'correction clauses'.[324]

---

313 'So far as certainty is concerned, justice and clarity don't always go together. To a certain extent, they contradict each other. One can have a system that is certain but arbitrary and, therefore, unjust. On the other hand, if one goes too far in the direction of justice, one finishes up with palm tree justice and that is also unjust.' As argued in Lowenfeld and Silberman, eds., *The Hague Convention on Jurisdiction*, at 10, 'Certainty and justice do not always sit well together. A rule that is certain will of necessity be inflexible and thus capable of producing injustice in the individual case. On the other hand, a rule that is too flexible may be devoid of meaning.' Nygh, 'Criteria for Judicial Jurisdiction', at A-4.

314 Von Mehren, 'Theory and Practice', at 69.

315 See Bomhoff, *Judicial Discretion*, in 'Abstract'.

316 Hay, 'Flexibility versus Predictability and Uniformity', at 304; see for more general comments Weintraub, 'The Tension between Predictability and Flexibility', at 452.

317 Hay, 'Flexibility versus Predictability and Uniformity', at 305.

318 Von Mehren, 'Theory and Practice', at 69.

319 Hay, 'Flexibility versus Predictability and Uniformity', at 304, referring to F. Juenger, 'American and European Conflicts Law', 30 *American Journal of Comparative Law* (1982), 117-133, at 127.

320 Von Mehren, 'Theory and Practice', at 69.

321 Nygh, 'Criteria for Judicial Jurisdiction', at A-4, 'This is the problem with the way the due process safeguards have been expressed in the United States. What amounts to "minimum contacts" according to the *International Shoe Co. v Washington*, I suspect few US scholars could tell me with certainty. It may be like "Great Art". One recognizes it instinctively when one sees it. But benighted foreigners like myself are denied that facility. Hence we cannot use terms such as "minimum contacts", "purposeful availment" and the like. We should possibly even avoid that great common law stand-by of "reasonableness".'

322 See also Keyes, *Jurisdiction in International Litigation*, at 252.

323 Hill, 'The Exercise of Jurisdiction', at 55.

324 See further Chapter 8 on correction devices.

Chapter 7

ASSESSING BASES FOR INTERNATIONAL JURISDICTION IN CONTRACT DISPUTES

The purpose of this chapter is to categorize, compare and evaluate the bases of jurisdiction that are relevant for international commercial disputes. This comparison is primarily focussed on the jurisdictional regimes which have been analyzed in previous chapters, but refers also to bases of jurisdiction as proposed by the various unification attempts within the HCCH, the ILA,[1] the IDI and MERCOSUR[2] as their ideas, concepts and the compromises made are important for present purposes.[3]

This comparison categorizes the bases for jurisdiction on the basis of the connection with the forum. Bases for jurisdiction generally reflect a connection with the parties or with the claim or dispute. For example, the 'place of performance' for jurisdiction over contractual matters reflects a connection between the claim and the forum, even if the obligation to perform rests on one of the parties. As will be demonstrated below, jurisdiction based on *party-related* connections usually confers general jurisdiction, whereas *claim-related* connections often lead to limited or special jurisdiction.

Before embarking on a comparison and further evaluation, a few preliminary remarks are justified regarding the differences between natural persons and corporate entities and the consequences for the connecting factors that are applied for jurisdictional purposes, which will be dealt with in Section 7.1. The subsequent paragraphs compare the traditional bases of jurisdiction which principally confers general jurisdiction. Section 7.2 compares the bases for jurisdiction at the defendant's home court; Section 7.3 deals with jurisdiction over individuals based on nationality and physical presence; and Section 7.4 compares the jurisdiction rules asserting jurisdiction at claimant's home court. Section 7.5 deals with the exercise of jurisdiction over the defendant on the basis of activities carried out in the forum. This activity-based jurisdiction covers among others the bases of doing business, branch jurisdiction and transacting jurisdiction. Bases for jurisdiction specifically designed to establish jurisdiction over claims arising out of contracts are compared in Section 7.6 and property-based jurisdiction is dealt with in Section 7.7.

Sections 7.2 to 7.7 are evaluated in accordance with international minimum standards for uniform rules for contractual disputes as has been elaborately discussed in Chapter 6. These minimum standards include the sufficient *defendant-related* con-

---

[1] Committee on International Civil and Commercial Litigation of the International Law Association, Resolution 4/2002; Paris/New Delhi Principles on Jurisdiction over Corporations.

[2] MERCOSUR/CMC/DEC. N° 01/94: Buenos Aires Protocol on International Jurisdiction in Contractual Matters.

[3] See Chapter 1, Sect. 1.3.3.

nection with the forum, the equality of arms between the defendant and the claimant, and the balance between legal certainty and flexibility.

7.1 Preliminary Observations: Individuals versus Corporate Entities

The majority of contractual disputes in international commercial litigation involve corporate parties rather than natural persons.[4] Contrary to natural persons, corporate entities are *artificial* entities and owe their existence to national laws. Despite their differences, individuals and corporations are often treated as equals for jurisdictional purposes. Bases of jurisdiction such as presence, domicile and nationality, initially meant to regulate jurisdiction over individuals, are applied by analogy to corporations.[5] Traditional bases for jurisdiction encounter little difficulty when applied to individuals, but need further determination in order to establish jurisdiction over corporations.[6] Concepts of domicile, nationality or presence when applied to corporate entities become artificial concepts which need to be further defined by connecting factors such as a 'statutory seat', 'place of incorporation', 'principal place of business' or even through a corporation's business activities in the forum. In sum, the redefinition of jurisdictional bases is required when applied to corporate defendants,[7] like a 'term of art' that needs explanation.[8]

This *assimilation* of corporations to individuals for jurisdictional purposes happens in many jurisdictional systems, but should not be understood as a general rule or jurisdictional principle.[9] The U.S. jurisdictional system rarely uses the method of analogous application of bases for jurisdiction with respect to corporations.[10] For instance, the application of the 'domicile' concept is reserved for individuals and is irrelevant for corporations, the place of incorporation is applied instead.[11]

---

[4] See (Rapporteur) C. McLachlan, 'Report of the Seventieth Conference; Fourth and Final Report: Jurisdiction over Corporations', International Law Association, Committee on International Civil and Commercial Litigation, 2002, at 414; J. Fawcett, 'A New Approach to Jurisdiction over Companies in Private International Law', 37 *The International and Comparative Law Quarterly* (1988), 645-667, at 645.

[5] See E. Scoles, P. Hay *et al.*, *Conflict of Laws* (2004), § 4.46, at 283, referring to 'analogous relationships of corporate entities'.

[6] See A. Nuyts, *L'exception de forum non conveniens: Etude de droit international privé* (2003), § 498, at 677.

[7] For an exhaustive analysis see M. Whincop, *Policy and Pragmatism in the Conflict of Laws* (2001), at 167 and 169-179.

[8] See Fawcett, 'A New Approach to Jurisdiction over Companies', at 648; A. Briggs, *Civil Jurisdiction and Judgments* (2005), § 2.115 at 140-105.

[9] See H. Schack, *Internationales Zivilverfahrensrecht* (2006), § 250, at 91, explaining that in cases of doubt the assimilation of corporate persons is not an established principle.

[10] See Scoles, Hay *et al.*, *Conflict of Laws*, § 4.46, at 283. There is however one exception to the U.S.'s refusal to apply assimilation in relation to diversity jurisdiction, namely the term 'citizenship' is used for corporations and needs further elaboration. Citizenship of a corporate entity should be understood as the place where it is incorporated *and* the place where it has its principal place of business. See 28 USCA § 1332(c).

[11] See R. Brand Report: 'The 1999 Hague Preliminary Draft Convention Text on Jurisdiction and Judgements: A View from the United States: Development of Due Process Jurisdictional Analysis

7.1.1 Defining Corporate Presence

As demonstrated in Chapter 4, which deals with the English common law on jurisdiction, the presence of a corporate defendant is a fictitious concept. The following statement of the English Court of Appeal is clear:

> 'The residence or presence of a corporation is a difficult concept. A corporation is a legal person but it has no corporeal existence. It can own property. It can by its agents perform acts. It is clear that if an English corporation owns a place of business in a foreign state from which it carries on its business that English corporation is, under our law, present in that state for the purposes of in personam jurisdiction.'[12]

Corporate presence is determined on the basis of the place of incorporation – and for overseas corporations – on the basis of a '*business establishment*' by virtue of a branch or other 'places of establishments'.[13] The U.S. approach to jurisdiction over companies avoids complex determination of corporate presence by limiting tag-jurisdiction to individuals. Instead, domestic corporations are served with process at their place of incorporation and foreign companies are reached on the basis of activity-based concepts such as doing business and transacting business. In other words, the U.S. approach acknowledged that when jurisdiction is based on notions of territorial sovereignty such as presence, different concepts are needed to regulate jurisdiction over corporations which concentrate more on the business activities carried out by the corporation. In this context, Brand rightfully argues that 'different theoretical approaches to where a legal person *is* for jurisdictional purposes create conceptual chasms that are difficult to bridge.'[14] Micheals warns against territoriality-based jurisdiction all together by arguing that

> 'territoriality occasionally needs to resort to fictitious locations. Corporations are artificial persons which are not physically present anywhere. One may focus on the place of incorporation and/or the place of the headquarters, but both these localizations are necessarily fictitious presences of a fictitious entity. The same problem arises with regard to the localization of immaterial assets like debts.'[15]

Others have argued that the application of the presence criterion to a corporate defendant is not just *dysfunctional* but often *meaningless*.[16]

---

in U.S.', in *The Hague Preliminary Draft Convention on Jurisdiction and Judgments* (2005), 3-40, at 18, indicating that the U.S. concept of general jurisdiction is not limited to 'formal definitions of domicile'. This strict distinction between individuals and corporations is consistently followed by the various Restatements which deal with jurisdictional issues. See for instance the 2nd Restatement of Conflict of Laws (1971), § 11.

[12] *Adams and Others v. Cape Industries Plc. and Another*, [1990] Ch. 433, at 519.

[13] See Chapter 4, Sect. 4.4.2.

[14] Brand, '2005 Report: A View from the U.S.', at 19.

[15] R. Michaels, 'Territorial Jurisdiction after Territoriality', in *Globalisation and Jurisdiction* (2004), at 110.

[16] Whincop, *Policy and Pragmatism*, at 141 and 169.

7.1.2 Corporate Domicile and Nationality: The Importance of the *Lex Societatis*

Jurisdiction based on concepts such as domicile and nationality, mainly under the civil law tradition, also needs to be further elaborated by connecting factors suitable for corporations. The law governing the corporation – the *lex societatis* – determines a corporation's domicile and nationality by indicating the determinative connecting factor.[17] The two principal 'recognition theories'[18] are the incorporation theory – or statutory seat theory – and the real seat theory.[19] The incorporation theory – also referred to as the statutory seat theory under civil law – determines the corporation's nationality and domicile by its place of incorporation, even if the company's principal place of business or its central place of administration is located elsewhere.[20] Apart from England and the U.S., the incorporation theory is also applied in The Netherlands, Spain, and to a lesser extent in Switzerland.[21] One of the advantages of the incorporation theory is that the place of incorporation – and thus the corporate domicile and nationality – is easy to localize, which creates legal certainty.[22] On the other hand, the incorporation theory does not vouch for a close connection between the forum and the corporate domicile or nationality,

---

[17] The nationality of the company and the corporate domicile are determined by the *lex societatis*, see S. Rammeloo, *Corporations in Private International Law: A European Perspective* (2001), at 10. Vlas states that the *lex societatis* 'determine[s] whether the entity has a separate legal existence', P. Vlas, *Rechtspersonen* (2002), § 7-10, at 4. See also A. Dicey, J. Morris *et al.*, *The Conflict of Laws* (2006), Vol. II, § 30-010-011, at 1339-1342; H. Batiffol and P. Lagarde, *Traité de droit international privé* (1993), § 193, at 333.

[18] Before determining the *lex societatis* of a (foreign) company, the legal entity first needs to be recognized as a (foreign) legal subject operating on the territory of another sovereign state. Such 'recognition' of a foreign company in respect of a company's legal capacity to act is the recognition theory in the *narrow sense* of the word; whereas the question of the law governing the company implies 'recognition' in a *broad sense*. See for the implications of E.C. law, especially the freedom of establishment, on the *lex societatis* the following decisions of the ECJ; *Überseering* (C-208/00), [2002] I-9919 and *Inspire Art* (C-167/01), [2003] I-10155.

[19] See Rammeloo, *Corporations*, at 10.

[20] English common law traditionally applies the law of the place of incorporation, also known as the *lex incorporationis*, see A. Briggs, *The Conflict of Laws* (2008), at 264. See for more details Rammeloo, *Corporations*, at 16 and 132; also P. North and J. Fawcett, *Cheshire and North's Private International Law* (1999), at 173-176. The place of incorporation coincides with the company's registered office or the statutory seat as it is known under civil law which explains why both theories are often mentioned to be alike. The registered office or statutory seat usually coincides with the place of incorporation, but it is possible that the statutory seat was fixed at another place than the place of incorporation, see P. Nygh, 'The Criteria for Judicial Jurisdiction: Conference Papers', in *The Hague Convention on Jurisdiction and Judgements: Records of the Conference Held at New York University School of Law on the Proposed Convention 1999* (2001), at 12.

[21] Respectively, Art. 1:10(2) DCC (see Rammeloo, *Corporations*, at 96-127), Art. 41 of the Spanish CC states that the corporate domicile is the place of 'settlement' in accordance with the *lex societatis* or according to its by-laws. If none of these indicate a particular place of settlement, then it is the place where his legal staff is located or the place of principal business activities. If no statutory seat is appointed by its by-laws, a subsidiary 'real seat' theory is embodied in Art. 21(2) of the Swiss PIL Statute. As explained in Chapter 3 in respectively Sects. 3.1.2, 3.2.2.3 and 3.3.2.1 for Spain, The Netherlands and Switzerland.

[22] See Rammeloo, *Corporations*, at 13-15 and 150-174.

especially when the corporation does not operate in the country under whose laws it was formed.

In contrast to the incorporation theory, the starting-point of the real seat theory is to determine the corporation's nationality and domicile at the place where the company has its factual centre of management, administration or even its principal place of business.[23] The real seat theory is applied in Germany, France and Italy[24] and is more concerned with the corporation's 'factual contacts' with the forum. This theory is more likely to guarantee a close connection with the forum,[25] but its difficulty lies in the determination of those centres which are sometimes difficult to localize and it therefore does not vouch for legal certainty.[26]

The use of different connecting factors has consequences for the determination of the corporate domicile and nationality. In an ideal situation the real seat coincides with the place of incorporation, in which case the outcome of both theories is the same. But in practice the place of incorporation does not always coincide with the place where the factual centre of management and administration is located and the two main conflicting theories result in jurisdiction conflicts.[27]

An example of a negative conflict is if a company incorporated in Germany, but which has its real seat in The Netherlands, is considered to have its corporate domicile located in The Netherlands under German law since German law applies the real seat theory, while Dutch law will locate its corporate domicile in Germany, as the latter applies the incorporation theory. As a result none of the countries will exercise jurisdiction over their courts under the defendant's domicile rule which is applied in both Germany and The Netherlands.[28]

---

[23] See M. Clarke, 'The Conflicts of Law Dimension', in *Corporate Law: The European Dimension* (1991), 161-170, at 162.

[24] Germany: The *Sitztheory* or *Verwaltungssitz* theory generally determines the legal status of a company, but for jurisdictional purposes the *seat* or *sitz* is determined by the real seat pursuant to Art. 17 ZPO. According to Schack it is more sensible to use the centre of a company's activities – *Tätigkeitsmittelpunkt* –rather than the statutory seat for jurisdiction purposes, see Schack, *Internationales Zivilverfahrensrecht*, § 251, at 91. See for the pros and cons of using the *Tätigkeitsmittelpunkt* for jurisdictional purposes, Rammeloo, *Corporations*, at 176-179. France applies a different concept – the *siège social* – which more or less coincides with the *siège réel* but which focuses on the centre of direction and control: '*le lieu où s'exerce la direction de la société*', see Chapter 3, Sect. 3.4.2.1. Rammeloo, *Corporations*, at 195; Batiffol and Lagarde, *Traité*, § 194, at 339. For Italy see Art. 25 of the PIL Statute and Chapter 3, Sect. 3.1.1, see also Rammeloo, *Corporations*, at 222.

[25] See Whincop, *Policy and Pragmatism*, at 169-170. Whincop calls any recognition theory which is not the incorporation theory the 'contact approach' as it 'relies on apparently observable characteristics of the corporation'.

[26] Its main purpose is to prevent companies from choosing a place of incorporation with most favourable tax and company laws, even if they do not operate in the forum. See Briggs, *Conflict of Laws*, at 264-265.

[27] Several attempts have been made to solve the conflicting nature of recognition theories, such as The Hague Convention concerning the recognition of the legal personality of foreign companies, associations and institutions of 1 June 1956 and the Warsaw Resolution of the IDI in 1965, entitled 'Companies in Private International Law'. The Preamble of the latter, '[desires] to make a contribution towards overcoming the controversy which exists at the present time with regard to the connecting factor determining the law governing companies.'

[28] An example of a positive conflict is the reversed situation: the corporation is incorporated in The Netherlands, but with its real seat in Germany; both countries locate the corporate domicile on their territory and can subject the company on the basis of the defendant's domicile rule.

Under the Brussels Regulation a compromise between the two theories was reached by choosing each of the following connecting factors for determining the corporate domicile: the statutory seat,[29] the place of central administration, and the principal place of business.[30] This approach could lead to multiple competent forums having general jurisdiction over the corporate defendant.[31]

The use of the nationality concept for corporate entities for jurisdictional purposes is equally troublesome and inadequate.[32] The French persistence to use nationality-based jurisdiction requires the application of the *real seat* theory, which defines corporate nationality by the centre of the company's activities.[33]

Although, as will be explained below, nationality-based jurisdiction is quasi inexistent in Anglo-American jurisdictional systems, it might be useful to mention that these systems generally determine a company's nationality by the law of the country under whose law it was incorporated.[34] A distinction is frequently made between *domestic* and *foreign* corporations for jurisdictional purposes. Such distinction is misleading as it is not based on corporate nationality but regards the law governing the company as the place of incorporation.[35]

---

[29] As the concept 'statutory seat' is unknown to the U.K. and Ireland, Art. 60(3) of the Brussels Regulation further states that the 'registered office or, where there is no such office anywhere, the place of incorporation or, where there is no such place anywhere, the place under the law of which the formation took place' will determine the place of jurisdiction.

[30] Although this provision is somewhat 'inelegant', it is quite useful according to Briggs, see Briggs, *Conflict of Laws,* at 267.

[31] Although the primary purpose of the modifications to Art. 53 of the Brussels Convention was to avoid positive and negative jurisdiction conflicts, the new Art. 60 of the Brussels Regulation enacted an autonomous interpretation for the corporate defendants' home court and in this way filled a potential jurisdictional gap. See on the corporate domicile under the Brussels Model, Chapter 2, Sect. 2.5.2. But see the *lis pendens* rule of Art. 27-30 Brussels Regulation

[32] See Rammeloo, *Corporations*, at 197, arguing that applying the concept of nationality to corporations is a 'fundamental weakness'. See also Lowenfeld, in F. Rigaux, 'The Extraterritorial Jurisdiction of State – La compétence extraterritoriale des états', 69 *Annuaire de l'Institut de droit international* (2001), 13-94, Report, at 98; Batiffol and Lagarde, *Traité*, § 192, at 329-330; and P. Vlas, *Rechtspersonen in het internationaal privaatrecht* (1982), at 39 or at 166 in the English summary. Already in 1928 Niboyet indicated that nationality is difficult to apply to corporations as it needs to be defined by other criteria than the ones used for individuals: '*[N]ous pensons que seule les personnes vivantes sont susceptibles de posséder une nationalité. S'il en était, d'ailleurs, autrement, il faudrait immédiatement convenir que cette pseudo-nationalité obéit à des règles toutes différentes de celles de la nationalité ordinaire.*' See J.-P. Niboyet, *Manuel de droit international privé* (1928), at 351.

[33] See Chapter 3, Sect. 3.4.2.1 and see below Sect. 7.1.3.

[34] See Rammeloo, *Corporations*, at 132; North and Fawcett, *Private International Law* (1999), at 175-176; see also Scoles, Hay *et al.*, *Conflict of Laws*, § 4.46, at 283; Clarke, 'Corporate Law', at 161. According to Hay common law reference to the law of incorporation has the purpose to determine the corporation's citizenship, see P. Hay, 'Flexibility versus Predictability and Uniformity in Choice of Law. Reflections on Current European and United States Conflicts Law', 226 *Recueil des cours* (1991), 281-412, at 312.

[35] See Clarke, 'Corporate Law', at 162, and see Rammeloo, *Corporations*, at 241: 'In both "incorporation" and "real seat" countries, analogies are sought between natural and legal "foreigners". Ancient concepts of the "birth" and "death" of natural and legal persons alike are inadequate devices to ascertain the proper law of the company. … From a common law, as well as an "incorporation" point

7.1.3 Corporate Presence, Domicile and Nationality: A Jurisdictional Overlap

Jurisdiction over corporate defendants based on presence, domicile and nationality needs further elaboration by 'corporate' connecting factors. The result is an overlap of bases of jurisdiction, as the same connecting factors might be used to define different concepts.

The first example of such jurisdictional overlap is found in France where nationality-based jurisdiction and the *actor sequitur forum rei* rule use the same connecting factor for general jurisdiction over a corporate defendant. As a result of the application of the *real seat* theory, French nationality-based jurisdiction over the corporate defendant indicates the court of the place of central administration, which also determines the corporate domicile.[36] The place of central administration is applied to define nationality-based jurisdiction as applied under Article 15 CC as well as the *forum rei* rule of Article 42 NCCP.

A second overlap of bases for jurisdiction is found in English common law where the place of incorporation asserts jurisdiction on the basis of corporate presence, but also defines the corporate domicile, which provides for a head for service outside the jurisdiction.[37] The assimilation of corporate defendants to individuals and the application of the same connecting factor for corporate domicile and corporate presence makes the domicile basis of Rule 6.20(1) CPR an empty basket for jurisdiction over corporate defendants: when a corporate defendant is considered present on the basis of his place of incorporation in England, request for service of process outside England is no longer needed, nor justified.[38] The fact that corporate presence under the CPR and the Companies Act is far-reaching and includes

of view, the anthropomorphic concept is troublesome; it does not cohere well with the "domicile" and residence of a company.'

[36] See Arts. 14 and 15 CC and the *forum rei* rule of Art. 42 NCCP, both explained in Chapter 3, in Sects. 3.4.3 and 3.4.2.1 respectively.

[37] Pursuant to the incorporation theory in combination with Rule 6.20(1) CPR this head is formulated in general terms using a '*person's* domicile' and does not specifically define corporate domicile. Traditionally, English common law determined the corporate domicile by the place of incorporation as a consequence of the incorporation theory. In the light of the implementation of the Brussels Model corporate domicile was replaced by statutory corporate domicile. Briggs, *Conflict of Laws*, at 267-269. Since a corporate *seat* was unknown to English law, the CJJA of 1982, Sects. 42(3)-(6) (amended by SI 2001 No. 3929, CJJO 2001, Schedules 9 to 12) incorporated a new definition for corporate domicile which is now also used for the purpose of service outside England under the CPR and replaces the corporate domicile rule for jurisdictional purposes. The domicile or *seat* of a foreign company in a part or place of the U.K. is the place of incorporation and when it has (a) its registered office or some other official address in England or (b) its central management and control is exercised there or (c) it has a place of business in that part. Para. 42(4) and (5) provides for a third (additional) possibility of domicile based on the place of business, see for more details Briggs, *Civil Jurisdiction*, § 4.33, at 351; North and Fawcett, *Private International Law* (1999), at 171-175; Clarke, 'Corporate Law', at 161-163; P. Kaye, 'The Meaning of Domicile under United Kingdom Law for the Purpose of the 1968 Brussels Convention on Jurisdiction and the Enforcement of Judgments in Civil and Commercial Matters', *Netherlands International Law Review* (1988), 181-195, at 188-190.

[38] English common law considers a company to be present on several grounds, but above all, a (domestic) company incorporated – and thus having its registered office – in England is always considered present. See Chapter 4, Sect. 4.4.2.

jurisdiction over many types of business establishments in England could explain why the CPR has not enacted a special 'head' for jurisdiction to reach companies 'absent' in England.[39]

As a general observation, it should be kept in mind however, that since commercial contractual disputes fall within the substantive scope of the Brussels Regulation the autonomous interpretation of the domicile rule of Article 60 applies to France and the U.K.

7.1.4 Introducing the 'Corporate Home' Factors

The purpose of the present chapter is to compare the bases of jurisdiction of both individuals and corporate entities. But the comparative analysis will take different characteristics and features of corporations and individuals into consideration and avoid assimilation. In the words of Levy the concepts of nationality, domicile and residence are in reality mingled with each other and should therefore not be used to identify general jurisdiction over corporate defendants: '*En réalité en matière de sociétés, les notions de "nationalité", de "domicile", et de "residence" se confondent quelque peu. L'analogie avec les personnes physiques devrait plutôt mener à comparer le siège social au domicile qu'a la nationalité.*'[40]

For the sake of a proper comparison of jurisdictional bases, the regulation of jurisdiction over corporate defendants will be put in a different framework. Rather than comparing artificial concepts such as corporate domicile, corporate presence and the corporation's nationality, the comparison will compare the 'corporate connecting factors' that determine the corporate home. These corporate home factors are the place of incorporation or statutory seat, the place of central administration and the principal place of business.

7.2 Defendant's Home Court

Exercising jurisdiction on the basis of defendant's home is universally applied and recognized among the jurisdictional systems surveyed in this book.[41] The exercise of general jurisdiction at defendant's home forum – irrespective of the nature of the claim[42] – is a well-accepted basis for jurisdiction in international litigation.[43]

---

[39] See Fawcett, 'A New Approach to Jurisdiction over Companies', at 655.

[40] L. Levy, *La Nationalité des sociétés* (1984), § 74, at 112 and see § 133, at 185 and see C. Rühland, *Le problème des personnes morales en droit international privé* (1934), at 27. See Chapter 3, Sect. 3.4.3.

[41] For the sake of clarity, with the term home is meant 'domicile' and/or 'habitual residence'. See below for the meaning and divergence of the term.

[42] Save the exceptions provided by exclusive jurisdiction.

[43] R. Brand, 'Understanding Activity-Based Jurisdiction', paper presented at the UIA Seminar Edinburgh, on 20 & 21 April 2001, entitled The Preliminary Draft Hague Convention on Jurisdiction and Foreign Judgements in Civil and Commercial Matters, at 38; L. Silberman, 'Comparative Jurisdiction in the International Context: Will the Proposed Hague Judgments Convention Be Stalled?', 52 *DePaul Law Review* (2002), 319-350, at 331. A. von Mehren, 'Theory and Practice of Adjudicatory Authority in Private International Law: A Comparative Study of the Doctrine, Policies and Practices of Common- and Civil-Law Systems: General Course on Private International Law (1996)', 295 *Recueil*

In France and Germany, the *forum rei* provides for jurisdiction by transposition of internal territorial jurisdiction rules to international disputes.[44] Italy, The Netherlands, Spain and Switzerland enacted direct international jurisdiction rules and confer jurisdiction on their courts over international contractual disputes when the defendant is domiciled in their forum.[45]

At unification level, the defendant's domicile represents the fundamental jurisdiction rule,[46] even if the Brussels structure permits derogation to the rule.[47] The defendant's home court automatically guarantees a substantial connection between the defendant and the forum to confer general jurisdiction in Continental European systems and the Brussels Model. The civil law tradition is based on the idea of the *forum defensoris*, which asks the plaintiff to sue the defendant at his home in order to protect the defendant's rights of defence by serving as a counterpoise to the fact that he has to defend himself against the plaintiff's action. In some systems this underlying policy is affirmed by national legislators and derives from a constitutional guarantee.[48] Some Continental authors even defend the fact that the rule is a fundamental human judicial right in European law of international civil procedure.[49]

In the Anglo-American systems, the *forum rei* rule is not the starting-point for jurisdiction but the defendant's home court forum is without doubt a recognized jurisdiction-creating basis.[50] Defendant's domicile was added to the jurisdictional scheme of England and of the U.S. to complete the important presence-based jurisdiction, when it became clear that this rule was insufficient.[51]

---

des cours (2003), 9-431, at 71. According to Hay 'the notion that the plaintiff should sue the defendant at his home is of venerable age and the rule permitting him to be sued there is universally accepted', see Hay, 'Flexibility versus Predictability and Uniformity', at 311. See also H. Smit, 'Common and Civil Law Rules of in Personam Adjudicatory Authority: An Analysis of Underlying Policies', 21 *The International and Comparative Law Quarterly* (1972), 335-354, at 336.

[44] Art. 42 of the French NCCP, and Art. 12 in conjunction with Art. 13 of the German ZPO, respectively.

[45] Art. 3(1) of the Italian PIL Statute; Art. 2 of the DCC; Art. 22(2) of the Spanish LOPJ; Art. 2 of the Swiss PIL Statute.

[46] Art. 2 also delimits the territorial or formal scope of application as explained in Chapter 2, Sect. 2.2.3.

[47] See Chapter 2, Sect. 2.2.4 for claims resorting to protective or exclusive jurisdiction such as consumer's or employment contracts, or insurance matters and immoveable property.

[48] Art. 2 of the Swiss PIL Statute emanates directly from constitutional protection secured by Art. 59 of the Swiss Federal Constitution. See Chapter 3, Sect. 3.3.1 and Sect. 3.1.2 for the Spanish Constitution

[49] P. Schlosser, 'Lectures on Civil-law Litigation Systems and American Cooperation with Those Systems', 45 *University of Kansas Law Review* (1996), 19-24, at 24: 'One of the most stringent rules in the European law of international civil procedure is the one which gives everyone in the world the right to bring his lawsuit into the district court where the defendant resides. Though no one has had reason to make the point so far, I would say that this is taken as a fundamental human judicial right.'

[50] Silberman states that 'there is little that is controversial from the United States' perspective. The grounds for general jurisdiction – [habitual] residence for an individual and place of incorporation, statutory seat, principal place of business, and central administration for juridical entities – seem appropriate and consistent with U.S. law, even if the particular terms are not always completely familiar.' Silberman, 'Comparative Jurisdiction', at 331-332.

[51] For England see Chapter 4, Sect. 4.2.2 and see for the U.S. Chapter 5, Sect. 5.2.2.

In England, when the absent defendant is domiciled there, service of process outside the forum is available under the head of Rule 6.20(1) CPR which enables the plaintiff to ask for leave for outside service, provided that he proved that the English court is a *forum conveniens* – or appropriate forum.[52]

In the U.S., the individual's domicile falls within the traditional bases for jurisdiction under common law. Since the Supreme Court's decision *Milliken v. Meyer*,[53] the domicile concept was considered compatible under the 'power theory' and was upheld under the current reign of the 'minimum contacts' theory.[54] However, it is still not certain whether the U.S. Supreme Court's ruling in *Burnham v. Superior Court*[55] *stating that transient jurisdiction automatically complies with the 'fairness and reasonableness' test, also applies to the domicile criterion.* If the *Burnham v. Superior* decision is analogously applicable to a defendant's domicile, a mere technical domicile will suffice for general jurisdiction and this would guarantee a forum for the plaintiff at defendant's domicile. Nonetheless, like the English common law system, the court can decline jurisdiction under the *forum non conveniens* doctrine.

Thus, contrary to its Continental European counterparts, the Anglo-American common law regimes do not presuppose a substantial connection with the forum automatically justifying general jurisdiction at defendant's domicile. The *forum (non) conveniens* doctrine applied in England and the U.S. allows courts to decline jurisdiction if they consider another court more appropriate.[56]

7.2.1 Problems Defining the Individual's Domicile

The individual's home court is characterized by problems with its definition, emerging when the defendant's home has to be localized and because of a general tendency towards the use of 'habitual residence' instead of domicile to determine an individual's home.[57]

As a rule, the domicile concept defines the individual's home, but the meaning of domicile varies from system to system and is often mingled with other concepts such as habitual, ordinary or temporary residence. The Brussels approach refers to the *lex fori* to determine whether the individual is domiciled in the forum.[58] This approach avoids definition problems by leaving it up to national law to determine the defendant's domicile. But without an autonomous interpretation, the defend-

[52] See Chapter 4, Sect. 4.2.3.
[53] 311 U.S. 457 (1940), explained in Chapter 5, Sect. 5.6.1.3.
[54] See Brand, 'Understanding Activity-Based', at 30.
[55] 495 U.S. 604, at 606 (1990).
[56] See Chapter 6, Sect. 6.4.4 for different approaches to the *favor defensoris*.
[57] See P. North, *Private International Law Problems in Common Law Jurisdictions* (1993), at 8; L. de Winter, 'Nationality or Domicile: The Present State of Affairs', 128 *Recueil des cours* (1969), 349-358, at 423; Hay, 'Flexibility versus Predictability and Uniformity', at 311 *et seq.*; Scoles, Hay *et al.*, *Conflict of Laws*, at 244.
[58] Art. 59 Brussels Regulation.

ant's home rule – if accepted at unification level – is likely to result in multiple forums.[59]

The meaning of 'domicile' differs most significantly between Anglo-American common law jurisdictions and civil law jurisdictions. The definition of domicile (of origin) under common law is quite close to the nationality concept of the civil law tradition and indicates the place of his 'permanent home' *for life*.[60] The U.S. meaning of domicile contains similar elements to that of English common law.[61]

Civil law countries consider a person's domicile, more as what English common law would define as the 'habitual residence';[62] a person is likely to change his residence a few times throughout his life. France identifies a domicile as the place where a person has its main establishment.[63] The person's intention to settle down often constitutes an additional requirement, like for instance the German equivalent of the *Wohnsitz*.[64] *The Dutch woonstede* is essentially defined by sociological criteria.[65] The Spanish determination of domicile is overall concerned with registration requirements besides the regular presence of the defendant. The Italian definition looks at a person's principal centre of activities and interests.[66] Under

---

[59] Earlier Hague Conventions mainly deal with questions of applicable law to the domicile notion. For example Art. 5 of 'La Convention de La Haye pour régler les conflits entre la loi nationale et la loi du domicile' of 15 June 1955 states: '*Le domicile, au sens de la présente Convention, est le lieu où une personne réside habituellement, à moins qu'il ne dépende de celui d'une autre personne ou du siège d'une autorité.*'

[60] See De Winter, 'Nationality or Domicile', at 419; J. Fawcett, P. North *et al.*, *Cheshire, North & Fawcett: Private International Law* (2008), at 154. English common law divides the domicile criterion into two main categories: a 'domicile of origin' given by birth and follows the person where ever it goes and a 'domicile of choice' which can be acquired at full age under certain conditions. The intention to live 'permanently or indefinitely' is required along with physical residence. North, *Private International Law Problems in Common Law Jurisdictions*, at 6; see also A. Dicey, J. Morris *et al.*, *The Conflict of Laws* (2006), Vol. 1, § 6R 025 and § 6R-33, at 130-138; R. Fentiman, 'Domicile Revisited', 50(3) *The Cambridge Law Journal* (1991), 445-463, especially at 450-457. Para. 41 CJJA 1982 lastly modified by CJJO 2001/3929 is the result of the coming into force of the Brussels Regulation, see also Hay, 'Flexibility versus Predictability and Uniformity', at 312; Kaye, 'The Meaning of Domicile', at 183. According to North these conceptual divergences could have been solved by using the more familiar concept 'habitual residence' in the CJJA/ CJJO, see North, *Private International Law Problems in Common Law Jurisdictions*, at 10.

[61] A person in the U.S. can also acquire a domicile of choice, but such a change of domicile seems to be easier to obtain since the degree of 'permanency or indefinitely' as an establishment for life seems not to be a requirement under U.S. law. The factor 'physical presence' is important for the person's intention to make this place his home. The U.S. meaning of domicile is closer to the meaning of habitual residence than the English common law domicile concept. Scoles, Hay *et al.*, *Conflict of Laws*, at 252. See also Hay, 'Flexibility versus Predictability and Uniformity', at 312.

[62] Or ordinary residence, Fawcett, North *et al.*, *Private International Law* (2008), at 183; E. Clive, 'The Concept of Habitual Residence', *The Juridical Review* (1997), 137-147, at 137-138.

[63] See Chapter 3, Sect. 3.4.2.1. A defendant's main place of establishment has to be '*de manière fixe et stable*' (fixed and regular).

[64] See for Germany Chapter 3, Sect. 3.5.2.1.

[65] See for the Dutch *woonstede* Chapter 3, Sect. 3.2.2.1. Art. 1:10(1) DCC states that a *woonstede* is a place where a natural person is living and carries out his (business) activities according to sociological criteria, where the person can be reached for legal affairs and will not leave unless it has a particular purpose and will return when the purpose has been accomplished.

[66] This is the definition of *domicilio* and *residenza* according to Art. 43 Italian CC.

English common law and in Switzerland, a defendant may not have two domiciles.[67] France and Germany accept various domiciles for jurisdiction purposes and give the claimant the choice among the domiciles for the *forum rei.*[68]

7.2.1.1 *The Rise of the Habitual Residence*

The (habitual) residence is accepted in many countries, but is often applied as subsidiary rule – by default of a domicile – such as in Germany, Switzerland, The Netherlands and France.[69] In Italy the individual's home is defined by a set of three factors:[70] the domicile, the residence and the agent. Although Anglo-American common law is familiar with the concept of habitual residence, in the case of England the habitual residence is not used for jurisdictional purposes in civil and commercial matters.[71]

The use of the habitual residence was introduced by the Hague Conference in several Hague Conventions on the applicable law dealing with family matters and influenced conventions dealing with international jurisdiction.[72] In order to avoid complex and technical definitions, the habitual residence is generally not defined by The Hague Conventions.[73] Some guidance is given by Resolution (72)I of the Council of Europe on the standardization of the legal concepts of 'domicile' and 'residence'.[74] The term is also used as a specific jurisdiction ground for claims concerning maintenance under Article 5(2) of the Brussels Regulation hereby replacing the domicile concept. In the Commission's Proposal for the Brussels Regulation the habitual residence was even put forward as the fundamental rule for jurisdiction, but was rejected in the final version.[75]

The 1999 and 2001 Drafts of The Hague Jurisdiction Convention incorporate the habitual residence to determine defendant's forum. The underlying reason was to avoid confusion among common law jurisdictions. The domicile concept should not be used to determine the individual defendant's home.[76] One of the reasons given for the use of habitual residence instead of the domicile concept is the vary-

---

[67] Rule 6 of Dicey & Morris reads 'No person can at the same time for the same purpose have more than one domicile.' Dicey, Morris *et al.*, *Conflict of Laws*, § 6R-013, at 126. See also Art. 20 II(1) of the Swiss PIL Statute.

[68] In France: Art. 42(2) NCCP. In Germany: Art. 7(2) BGB.

[69] For Germany: Art. 16 ZPO; Switzerland: Art. 20(1)(b) PIL Statute; The Netherlands: the (f)actual residence (*werkelijk verblijf*), Art. 1:10(1) DCC; France: Art. 43(1) NCCP.

[70] See Chapter 3, Sect. 3.1.1 and Art. 77 of the Italian CCP.

[71] It is mainly used for family law purposes. See further P. Rogerson, 'Habitual Residence: The New Domicile?', 49 *The International and Comparative Law Quarterly* (2000), 86-107, at 87, and in general Clive, 'Concept of Habitual Residence'; Fentiman, 'Domicile Revisited', at 87.

[72] See for instance Art. 1 of The Hague Convention on the Protection of Minors.

[73] Dicey, Morris *et al.*, *Conflict of Laws*, § 6-125, at 168.

[74] No. 9 of the resolution states: 'In determining whether a residence is habitual, account is to be taken of the duration and the continuity of the residence as well as of other facts of a personal or professional nature which point to durable ties between a person and his residence.'

[75] OJ 1998 C 33/05; COM(97) 609 final – 97/0339(CNS) (Submitted by the Commission on 22 December 1997).

[76] There is agreement on the defendant's forum being a forum of general jurisdiction; *Defendant's forum*. See also Nygh, 'Criteria for Judicial Jurisdiction', at A-3.

ing status of the domicile concept in comparative law.[77] Although the reporters recognize that the habitual residence in not a term free from various interpretations either, they are of the opinion that the concept is more reliable than the domicile term. According to them the habitual residence 'tends to denote a person's presence over a fairly prolonged period in a certain place, and to assign only an incidental and non-essential role to the intention of remaining there.'[78]

In the Buenos Aires Protocol on International Jurisdiction in Contractual Matters, which is a result of a judicial integration in the context of MERCOSUR, the natural person's domicile is defined as its usual residence, subsidiarily the principal centre of its business and finally as its simple residence.[79]

7.2.1.2 *Domicile versus Habitual Residence*

The habitual residence is a relatively neutral term avoiding any technical requirements imposed by national laws and that could bridge conceptual differences among legal traditions. The concept is commonly used in common law jurisdictions and it is used more and more in civil law jurisdictions as a subsidiary jurisdiction factor. The habitual residence, mainly determined by factual circumstances rather than by statutory or registration requirements, reflects a more solid and permanent establishment than a mere residence does and is not as rigid as the concept of 'domicile'. In sum, the use of 'habitual residence' is preferred.

The individual's habitual residence should be determined by factual circumstances instead of national interpretations.[80] It should be considered as a natural person's main establishment where he has voluntarily settled down for a 'longer' period to make of it his home.[81] This covers most situations embodied in the Continental European significance of 'domicile' and should *de facto* be considered its equivalent.[82] The exact and ultimate determination of a person's habitual residence should be left to the court seized and should be based on an objective evaluation of

---

[77] See P. Nygh and F. Pocar, 'Report of the Special Commission – Convention on Jurisdiction and Foreign Judgments in Civil and Commercial Matters' (Hague Conference on Private International Law, 2000), at 39.

[78] Ibid.; C. Kessedjian, 'Prel. Doc. No. 7: Report on International Jurisdiction and Foreign Judgments in Civil and Commercial Matters', Permanent Bureau of the Hague Conference on Private International Law, § 133, at 39.

[79] MERCOSUR/CMC/DEC. Nº 01/94, Art. 9(1); English text available at http://www.sice.oas.org/trade/mrcsrs/decisions/AN0194_e.asp.

[80] 'Of course, "habitual residence" is that very good old stand-by. Everybody knows what habitual residence is. That is where the person lives, unless he lets the judges loose on it and they create something which may turn out to be quite different from what the [person] may understand by habitual residence.' Nygh, 'Criteria for Judicial Jurisdiction', at A-3; A. Lowenfeld and L. Silberman, eds., *The Hague Convention on Jurisdiction and Judgments: Records of the Conference Held at New York University School of Law on the Proposed Convention* (2001), at 11.

[81] Nygh-Pocar Report, at 39.

[82] According to Fragistas the practical differences between habitual residence and domicile are minimal: '*en réalité il n'y a pas de grande différence entre ces deux notions, toutes les deux se référant aux personnes installées sur le territoire du pays*', see N. Fragistas, 'Les compétences exorbitantes dans les travaux de la Conférence de La Haye', *Mélanges Ionasco, Revue roumaine des sciences sociales* (1968), 175, at 177.

facts. This last aspect of determination contains an element of flexibility; the courts themselves can appreciate the facts in order to determine whether or not defendant is habitually resident in the forum.

7.2.2 The Corporate Home Factors

As explained above, each of the following corporate connecting factors play a significant role in each of the jurisdictional systems analysed, but may be applied under different bases of jurisdiction: the *actor sequitur forum rei* rule, the presence rule, the doing business rule, and the nationality-based jurisdiction rule. With respect to the *actor sequitur forum rei* rule as applied analogously to corporate defendants in each of the Continental European countries analysed, the underlying policy for jurisdiction at defendant's home is the same as for individual defendants.[83] The rule chooses to favour the corporate defendant to compensate for the fact that he has to defend himself from the plaintiff's action against him since it is considered more difficult to defend oneself in a foreign court than in one's own home court.[84] The fact that the defendant is a corporate entity does not make any difference.[85]

For a proper analysis of the connecting factors, this chapter disregards presence, domicile and nationality with respect to corporate presence and uses 'the corporate home' determined by the following connecting factors: the place of incorporation and statutory seat, the central administration and the principal place of business. Each of these factors reflects a substantial connection with the forum justifying general jurisdiction indicating the corporation's 'home court'. For those reasons they will be called 'corporate home factors'.

7.2.2.1 *The Place of Incorporation and Statutory Seat*

Common law jurisdictions confer general jurisdiction over companies incorporated under their laws as they consider them to be domestic companies. An incorporated company is 'present' in England and can be served with process either by statutory service at the company's registered office according to Section 725(1) of the Companies Act or following the methods of service described by the CPR.[86] The U.S. jurisdictional system directly applies the place of incorporation to establish jurisdiction over (domestic) companies as a result of the traditional bases of jurisdiction under U.S. common law.[87]

---

[83] See Art. 2 in conjunction with Art. 60 Brussels Regulation; see for France Art. 42 NCCP, Art. 12 in conjunction with Art. 17 German CCP; Art. 2 Swiss PIL Statute; Art. 2 Dutch (new) Rv.; Art. 3(1) of the Italian PIL Statute; Art. 22(2) of the Spanish Code LOPJ.

[84] See above Sect. 7.2.

[85] Why does it not make any difference, when one takes into account that a company could have more financial resources and legal expertise at hand than an individual defendant? This is often the reason why in consumer contracts this favour to (corporate) defendant is supplemented with a *forum actoris* rule under Art. 16(1) of the Brussels Regulation in cases when the plaintiff is a consumer

[86] Rule 6.2 CPR; see Chapter 4, Sect. 4.4.2.

[87] As explained in Chapter 5, Sect. 5.6.1.4. See H. Schack, *Jurisdictional Minimum Contacts Scrutinized: Interstaatliche und internationale Zuständigkeit U.S.-amerikanischer Gerichte* (1983), at 36:

The place of incorporation also found its way to the civil law tradition where it is usually referred to as the statutory seat.[88] The statutory seat is the corporation's *seat* as fixed by its by-laws at the time of incorporation. As a result of the incorporation theory The Netherlands, Germany, Spain and, on a subsidiary level, Switzerland determine the corporate domicile for the purpose of the *forum rei* rule by the statutory seat.[89] The place of incorporation is the principal connecting factor under the incorporation theory. The place of incorporation is included in the corporate domicile definition of the Brussels Regulation.[90]

General jurisdiction based on the simple place of incorporation in the forum is justified by the fact that the corporation owes its legal personality to the laws of that state, which automatically vouches for a substantial connection with the forum. Under those circumstances, the exercise of jurisdiction 'is ... fully in harmony with the classical rule and the demands of territorial sovereignty'.[91] Even when a company has its centre of administration, its centre of management and control, or its principal place of business in a different state, the statutory seat is still sufficiently connected with the forum to justify general jurisdiction.[92] A significant advantage of this basis of jurisdiction is that it provides a certain degree of legal certainty and foreseeability.

Nonetheless, this connecting factor does not prevent companies from fictively incorporating in a corporate haven and establishing their real seat and carrying out their principal business activities somewhere else in order to benefit from favourable tax and company laws and protection from judicial control of other states. Such a fictive place of incorporation has a weak connection with the forum. Anglo-American common law courts have the possibility to decline jurisdiction on the basis of the *forum non conveniens* doctrine when the place of incorporation is a merely 'technical' one, which makes the corporate home forum inappropriate. This correction is not available to courts of Continental European countries.[93]

7.2.2.2 *The Centre of Administration and Management Control*

The use of a company's centre of administration and management control and the adherence to the *real seat* theory responds to the type of 'incorporation by convenience' that is explained above. Many Continental European countries preferred this 'real seat' over the somewhat technical determination of the statutory seat. The

'The state of incorporation is the most easily ascertainable contact which confers general jurisdiction even if the corporation maintains no office or does no business there.'

[88] Theoretically, it is possible that the statutory seat – or (main) registered office – is not located in the country under whose laws the company was formed or incorporated, yet in practice both places often coincide with the place of incorporation and should be therefore treated as being similar.

[89] See above at Sect. 7.1.2.

[90] Art. 60(1)(a) Brussels Regulation.

[91] F.A. Mann, 'The Doctrine of International Jurisdiction Revisited after Twenty Years', 186 *Recueil des cours* (1984), 9-116, at 69.

[92] See A. Schnyder, 'Der Sitz von Gesellschaften im Internationalen Zivilverfahrensrecht', in *Wege zur Globalisierung des Rechts: Festschrift für Rolf A. Schütze zum 65. Geburtstag* (1999), 767-775, at 768.

[93] See for the comparison of correction devices Chapter 8.

centre of administration – also referred to as 'headquarters'[94] – is a factual concept and is determined on a case-by-case basis, as opposed to the place of incorporation which attaches significant importance to institutional aspects.[95] The centre of administration indicates the place where important decisions concerning the company's policy and core business activities are taken. It is the place where directors or other persons with considerable authority and control are seated, either according to statute or in practice.[96] The exact meaning of the centre of administration is subjected to variations and the difference between the centre of administration and the centre of management and control is somewhat vague.[97]

France and Italy determine the corporate seat by the centre of administration and management control as a result of the *real seat* theory.[98] The new definition of corporate domicile of the Brussels Model includes the centre of administration under Article 60(1)(b), but does not provide any further guidance.[99]

In England the centre of administration and management of control would have to constitute corporate presence in order to subject an overseas company to the general jurisdiction of English courts.[100]

Under the U.S. jurisdictional system, the fact that a company has its central administration and management control on U.S. territory will largely suffice to fulfil the minimum contacts rule and other due process standards to subject the corporation to jurisdiction on the basis of 'doing business'. The U.S. approach slightly differs from its English counterpart which still focusses on presence. Instead the U.S. shifted from the presence theory to the minimum contacts theory and as a result U.S. courts establish jurisdiction on the basis of 'the carrying on of business' in the forum.[101]

Despite the guarantee of a substantial connection with the forum, the factual nature of this connecting factor exposes a lack of legal certainty; a company's centre of administration can be spread out among several countries and can change location. Moreover, modern decision-making processes no longer always take place at the same place.

---

[94] See C. Kessedjian, 'Prel. Doc. No. 8: Synthesis of the work of the Special Commission of June 1997 on International Jurisdiction and the Effects of Foreign Judgments in Civil and Commercial Matters', Permanent Bureau of the Hague Conference on Private International Law, § 11a, at 19.

[95] The principal place of business is also determined on a case-by-case basis, see Vlas, *Rechtspersonen*, § 178, at 87.

[96] See Nygh-Pocar Report, at 41.

[97] The English position would be that the centre of administration implies a more 'ultimate authority and control' than the 'day-by-day management', see Briggs, *Civil Jurisdiction*, § 2.115, at 140-141, see also Kessedjian, 'Prel. Doc. No. 8: June 1997, Synthesis Special Commission', § 11(d), at 21.

[98] See above Sect. 7.1.2, fn. 21.

[99] Briggs, *Civil Jurisdiction*, § 2.115, at 140-141.

[100] If properly served either under the Companies Act (1985 and 2006) or Part 6 of the CPR.

[101] *International Shoe v. Washington*, 326 U.S. 310, at 316 (1945). As explained in Chapter 5, Sect. 5.2.2; and see Schack, *Minimum Contacts Scrutinized*, at 37; F.A. Mann, 'The Doctrine of International Jurisdiction', 111 *Recueil des cours* (1964), 1, at 77.

7.2.2.3 *The Principal Place of Business*

The principal place of business emphasizes business activities rather than administrative operations.[102] The factor connects the corporation with a forum through its main business establishment from which it carries out its core business or commercial activity. Like the centre of administration, the principal place of business factor is a factual concept and is determined on a case-by-case basis.[103] It should however at least include a fixed place of business and should not be confused with the 'carrying on business' jurisdiction ground.

Under the civil law tradition, the principal place of business plays a significant role under the real seat theory to determine the corporate seat. In France, the '*centre d'exploitation*' is conclusive for jurisdiction purposes.[104] A company's principal place of business constitutes corporate presence under English common law and allows service of process on a 'business establishment'.[105] The principal place of business creates jurisdiction for U.S. courts under the doing business criterion, constituting direct and 'continuous and systematic' contacts with the forum.[106] Although the reach of doing business is considerably wider as it establishes jurisdiction on the basis of any place of business, it certainly includes the principal place of business.[107]

Like the centre of administration, it is difficult to determine the principal place of business in the event a company often has several places of business and carries out different kinds of business in several countries. Additionally, the dynamics of corporate activities imply that business activities might change over the years and with them the principal place(s) of business.[108] In other words, legal certainty is not always guaranteed by this connecting factor.

7.2.2.4 *The Corporate Home Factors Evaluated at Unification Level*

In most unified instruments, corporate defendants are assimilated to individuals and apply concepts such as 'person' and 'defendant' to include both natural and corporate persons.[109] In order to determine the corporate 'home' a 'mixed bag' of the above-mentioned connecting factors are usually applied. The lack of a common consensus on the determination of the corporate home resulted in Article 60

---

[102] Vlas, *Rechtspersonen*, § 178, at 87.

[103] See also Nygh-Pocar Report, at 41.

[104] See Chapter 3, Sect. 3.4.2.1.

[105] See Chapter 4, Sects. 4.4.2.1 and 4.4.2.2, for the CPR service and the statutory service under the Companies Acts (1985 and 2006), respectively.

[106] See Chapter 5, Sect. 5.6.2.2; Schack, *Minimum Contacts Scrutinized*, at 36.

[107] Hay, 'Flexibility versus Predictability and Uniformity', at 312-313.

[108] See also McLachlan, 'Final Report Jurisdiction over Corporations', § 24, at 420.

[109] Art. 2 in conjunction with Art. 60 Brussels Regulation; Art. 3(2) The Hague 1999 Preliminary Draft Convention and 2001 Interim Text; Principle 2 ILA Paris/New Delhi Principles on Jurisdiction over Corporations Resolution 4/2002: Arts. 7 and 9 of the MERCOSUR/CMC/DEC. N° 01/94: Buenos Aires Protocol on International Jurisdiction in Contractual Matters refers to the respondent's domicile.

of the Brussels Regulation.[110] This slightly *inelegant*[111] provision determines the corporate home by three factors (a) the statutory seat,[112] or (b) the place of central administration, or (c) the principal place of business.[113]

The Hague Worldwide Jurisdiction Project equally asserts general jurisdiction at defendant's home court and generally stands on the same hierarchical level as other proposed jurisdiction rules.[114] The defendant's home court is defined by his 'habitual residence';[115] this introduction required defining the 'corporate habitual residence'. It was thought that it could not be defined by one single unitary concept, but by a plurality of connecting factors.[116] Inspired by the Brussels Regulation, these factors are not ranked in any particular order and enumerated alternatively. Both texts give the claimant the choice between the statutory seat, the place under whose law it was incorporated or formed,[117] the place where it has its central administration, or where it has its principal place of business.[118]

The Committee on International Civil and Commercial Litigation of the International Law Association adopted Resolution 4/2002 regarding international jurisdiction over corporations. The principles ensuing from this Resolution are known as the Paris/New Delhi Principles on Jurisdiction over Corporations. General jurisdiction over corporations is based on very similar corporate connecting factors as those mentioned above.[119] The 2002 New Delhi ILA Conference also discussed the fictive place of incorporation when a company's real seat is located elsewhere and results in a weak connection with the forum. Nonetheless, the possibility of

[110] Obviously by incorporating the various connecting factors of both theories, this way of determining the corporate domicile is a compromise to the recognition theories in vigour. See above Sect. 7.1.2.

[111] Briggs, *Conflict of Laws*, at 268.

[112] Art. 60(1) Brussels Regulation only refers to the statutory seat, but this is further defined as follows by Art. 60(2) for English common law: 'the registered office or, where there is no such office anywhere, the place of incorporation or, where there is no such place anywhere, the place under the law of which the formation took place.'

[113] Art. 60(1)(a)-(c). See similarities with Arts. 43 to 48 EC Treaty establishing the freedom of establishment within the European Community (Consolidated version in OJ 2002 C-325).

[114] Except for exclusive jurisdiction rules which prevail over all other rules, see Art. 3 of The Hague 1999 Preliminary Draft Convention and 2001 Interim Text. See Nygh-Pocar Report, at 38-39.

[115] There was consensus on this provision, except with respect to the word 'habitual' which was questioned by the diplomatic sessions in June 2001 and was therefore 'bracketed' in The Hague 2001 Interim Text.

[116] Nygh-Pocar Report, at 40.

[117] The Hague 1999 Preliminary Draft Convention and the 2001 Interim Text refer separately to the place of the *law of incorporation* and the *statutory seat*, as the state delegations thought it useful to cover all cases, in the event the (main) registered office or statutory seat would not be located in the place of the law of incorporation. Art. 3(2)(a) and (b). Nygh-Pocar Report, at 40.

[118] Art. 3(2)(a)-(d) The Hague 1999 Preliminary Draft Convention and the 2001 Interim Text.

[119] A similar approach of assimilation of the statutory seat to the place of incorporation was taken by the Paris/New Delhi Principles on Jurisdiction over Corporations; Principle 2.1 reads 'A corporation may be sued in the courts of the state where: a) it has its statutory seat or is incorporated, or under whose law it was formed; b) it has its central administration; c) its business, or other professional activity is principally carried on', available at http://www.ila-hq.org/html/layout_committee.htm. See also McLachlan, 'Final Report Jurisdiction over Corporations', at 418 and see § 4.22, at 419 indicating a hierarchical order among the factors listed in principle 2.1(a).

'incorporation by convenience' as it was called, remains a possible connecting factor under both Hague Draft Conventions and the Paris/New Delhi Principles.[120]

It might be worthwhile to observe that the indirect bases for jurisdiction for recognition included in the Supplementary Protocol to the 1971 Hague Convention on Recognition and Enforcement of Foreign Judgements also considered a 'legal person' to have its domicile or habitual residence where it has its seat, its place of incorporation, or its principal place of business.[121] This elaboration is clearly also a mixed bag, compromising different conflict theories.

Only the Buenos Aires Protocol on International Jurisdiction in Contractual Matters elaborated by MERCOSUR exclusively refers to the principal administrative headquarters.[122] Otherwise at unification level, each of the corporate connecting factors is potentially jurisdiction-creating. This leads to multiple competent forums having jurisdiction over companies when the places are not located in the same country.[123] When the statutory seat is not the real seat, nor the principal place of business, all of these connecting factors refer to different forums.[124] This encourages forum shopping; the more connecting factors there are, the wider the scope of the corporate home rule. The use of only one single criterion in unified instruments would imply a choice between the on-going conflicting theories of the *incorporation* or the *real seat.* An autonomous interpretation or standardization of legal concepts defining the corporate home is not to be expected in the near future.[125]

7.2.3 **Evaluation of Defendant's Home Court**

7.2.3.1 *The Connection with the Forum*

The defendant's home forum rule guarantees a close connection between the defendant and the forum, as each of the connecting factors generally vouches for *substantial defendant-related* connections.[126] Brand indicates that the defendant's

[120] See Nygh, 'Criteria for Judicial Jurisdiction', at A-6, and Kessedjian, 'Prel. Doc. No. 8: June 1997, Synthesis Special Commission', at 19. The report of the *commission spéciale* in N. Fragistas and G. Droz, 'Explanatory Report Hague Convention of 1 February 1971 on the Recognition and Enforcement of Foreign Judgments in Civil and Commercial Matters', in *Acts and Documents of the Extraordinary Session (1966)* (1966), at 31, even states that such a fictive corporate seat is a seat fixed by fraud, *'fixation ... in fraudem legis du siège'*.

[121] See Sect. 5; see also Art. 10 of the Convention itself. The assimilation to natural persons is explained by Droz in his report to the Protocol in Fragistas and Droz, 'Explanatory Report Hague Convention 1971', at 503.

[122] Art. 9(1) MERCOSUR/CMC/DEC. Nº 01/94.

[123] This is one of the reasons why the principle of *lis pendens* is indispensable within unified systems. It implies that the first court seized shall have jurisdiction, and posteriorly seized courts need to abstain from jurisdiction until the first court seized has decided upon its competence. Arts. 27 to 30 Brussels Regulation and Art. 21 of The Hague 1999 Preliminary Draft Convention.

[124] A *lis pendens* rule is of crucial importance do deal with multiple forums.

[125] See with respect to European Company Law, Clarke, 'Corporate Law', at 161; see *contra* M. Weser, 'Bases of Judicial Jurisdiction in the Common Market Countries', 10 *American Journal of Comparative Law* (1961), 323, at 330, advocating at an early stage for a *unitary* definition of a corporation's seat.

[126] As explained in Chapter 6, Sect. 6.5.2.

home forum should be considered as fair on the basis of the considerable amount of defendant-related connections alone:

> 'The other benefit of the defendant's residence as a forum of acceptable jurisdiction is that it makes jurisdiction rational and fair regardless of whether there is a direct relationship between the claim and the forum state. The court-defendant nexus alone is sufficient in quality to make it fair to bring any claim against the defendant in that forum. In this sense, it is globally acknowledged as a general basis of jurisdiction.'[127]

The close connection minimum standard is satisfied for thc habitual residence in relation to the individual's home. In relation to the corporate home, the same applies for the principal place of business and the place of central administration.[128] With respect to the place of incorporation, many warned that the rule does not automatically vouch for a close connection with the forum. In the event of a fictive place of incorporation or a mere 'technical domicile' the substantial connection with the forum is lacking. When a defendant voluntarily 'incorporates' in a forum, but then chooses to establish his real seat in another forum, the place of incorporation is one of convenience which should not discharge him from adjudication by the court of the place of incorporation. He should bare the consequences with respect to jurisdiction.[129] Droz underlined this by stating:

> '*de toute façon j'estime que si une personne morale se met dans la situation d'avoir un siège statutaire d'un coté et un siège réel de l'autre elle n'a à s'en prendre qu'a elle-même, et le* [*demandeur*] *est en droit de saisir le tribunal du siège réel comme celui du siège statutaire.*'[130]

In a way, these home factors reflect the *voluntary* settlement of a person who chooses to establish his home or main establishment in a particular forum during a significant period of time.[131] This also implies a '*voluntary submission of all legal relations*' to the court of that forum.[132] In that respect, one can draw a parallel with the notion of 'implied consent' – formerly used in U.S. jurisdiction law – in order to justify (general) jurisdiction.[133]

---

[127] Brand, 'Understanding Activity-Based', at 38.

[128] Kessedjian, 'Prel. Doc. No. 8: June 1997, Synthesis Special Commission', § 10, at 17.

[129] See Trooboff's comments: 'Nor are we representing or trying to protect businesses that structure themselves to try to evade what would be a reasonable assertion of jurisdiction', see Trooboff in Lowenfeld and Silberman, eds., *The Hague Convention on Jurisdiction*, at 21.

[130] G. Droz, 'Les droits de la demande dans les relations privées internationales', *Travaux* du *Comité Français de Droit International Privé* (1993-1995), 97-121, at 105.

[131] See M. Keyes, *Jurisdiction in International Litigation* (2005), at 201 *et seq.* Domicile is a personal 'consensual' connection.

[132] Von Mehren, 'Theory and Practice', referring to Von Bar, at 146: 'the acquisition of an actual domicile must count as a voluntary submission of all legal relations that are subject to a free power of disposal of the courts of that country excepting.' And see Von Mehren, 'Theory and Practice', at 71.

[133] See *International Shoe Co. v. Washington*, 326 U.S. 310, at 319 (1945), explained in Chapter 5, Sect. 5.2.2.

7.2.3.2 *The Protection of Parties and Equality of Arms*

The *forum rei* rule protects the defendant who is considered to be in a weaker position when being sued and should be compensated by enabling him to defend himself in his home court instead of in a foreign court.[134] The question is whether the justification for the *forum defensoris* requiring the claimant to seek out the defendant is still valid for a uniform rule in transnational contractual disputes.

As explained in the previous chapter, the *forum defensoris* is fundamental to Continental European systems, but this 'favouritism' of the defendant is not as self-evident in Anglo-American jurisdictions.[135] In Anglo-American systems, the plaintiff has recourse to a wider range of *other* bases for jurisdiction rules to choose from[136] and secondly, there is always the possibility to derogate from the *forum rei* rule by the application of the *forum non conveniens* doctrine.[137] Especially in the U.S., the *forum non conveniens* is used to control the flow of proceedings to U.S. courts which are thought to have an 'extreme attractiveness'[138] and the fact that a U.S. court is the defendant's home court does not make any difference. On the contrary when the plaintiff is foreign he deserves less deference than American plaintiffs when he chooses a U.S. court.[139]

This brings us to the claimant's right of access to justice. When the defendant's home court clearly privileges the defendant and forces the claimant to seek out the defendant at his home court, how can the balance between the parties' interests be restored and ensure equality of arms?[140]

It should be kept in mind that in the jurisdictional regimes surveyed the *defendant's forum rule* is part of a set of jurisdiction rules. The rule would indeed be 'litigationally unjust'[141] for the claimant if it is the only forum available to him without having any other competent forum to choose from. This has also been stressed by Nygh, who claims

> 'For the plaintiff, as noted earlier, a forum at defendant's residence may be inconvenient. But this should not preclude the use of this basis of jurisdiction at the plaintiff's option provided other choices are available.'[142]

Secondly, the rule is not merely pro-defendant when the rule provides for the guarantee of an available competent forum for the claimant; a forum ensuring that the claimant will always find a competent forum with respect to *any kind* of claims at

[134] See among others Nygh-Pocar Report, at 38.

[135] Von Mehren, 'Theory and Practice', at 180 and 193: 'Nor are all – or at least most – contemporary legal systems committed to the minimalist proposition that the *actor sequitur forum rei* principle expresses'. See Keyes, *Jurisdiction in International Litigation*, at 346; 'Domicile has been widely criticized as outdated', see Sykes and Pryles, *Australian Private International Law* (1991).

[136] See also Chapter 6, Sect. 6.4.3.

[137] But see also A. Bell, *Forum Shopping and Venue in Transnational Litigation* (2003), at 80-81.

[138] *Piper Aircraft Co. v. Reyno*, 454 U.S. 235, at 252 (1981).

[139] See on the position of alien plaintiffs Chapter 5, Sect. 5.5.4.

[140] See also below Sect. 7.4.

[141] Von Mehren, 'Theory and Practice', at 71.

[142] Nygh, 'Criteria for Judicial Jurisdiction', at A-5.

defendant's home court. Such a rule secures the claimant access to justice to a competent forum with sufficient connection between the defendant and the forum.[143] In international contractual disputes the availability of such a rule is crucial, at least as *last resort*,[144] and avoids negative jurisdiction conflicts. In sum, although, the defendant's home forum favours the defendant, it is not particularly disfavouring the claimant when the rule is part of a set of well-balanced jurisdictional provisions for contractual disputes.

7.2.3.3 *Legal Certainty and Flexibility*

The determinability of the competent forum constitutes an essential element for legal certainty. Provided that the rule contains clearly defined and reliable 'home factors' the defendant's home forum rule ranks high with respect to legal certainty.[145] A defendant generally knows where his home forum is located, which makes the rule highly predictable to him and enables him to foresee where a claimant is able to sue him for any type of action. On the other hand, the claimant is able to determine where the defendant has established his home on the basis of the 'home factors'.

A significant element of uncertainty results from the fact that especially in common law jurisdictions the plaintiff's choice for the defendant's forum is not always respected. It is of crucial importance for the protection of claimant's access to justice that he can always turn to defendant's home court, knowing that this court is unable to decline jurisdiction. It has rightfully been argued that the application of the *forum non conveniens* doctrine causes 'unreasonable detriment' to the plaintiff,[146] especially since the *defendant's forum* is already privileging the defendant.[147]

Guaranteeing a competent forum at defendant's home without the application of a general exception doctrine or any other correction mechanisms forms the key to relieve tension between the two paradigms of legal certainty and flexibility. A flexible approach to jurisdictional questions may and should be taken when special jurisdiction is allocated, but should not be permitted when general jurisdiction at *defendant's home court* is exercised. In this respect, one could agree with Verheul who does not justify the *forum rei* rule simply by its contents, but by the fact that

[143] Exceptions could be made with respect to claims based on human rights violations, exclusive jurisdiction and protective jurisdiction grounds.

[144] Von Mehren, 'Theory and Practice', fn. 548, at 182, referring to B. Buchner, *Kläger- und Beklagtenschutz im Recht der internationalen Zuständigkeit. Losüngsansätze für eine zukünftige Gerichtsstands- und Vollstreckungskonvention* (1998).

[145] But see in relation to difficulties to determine the centre of management, Nygh, 'Criteria for Judicial Jurisdiction', at A-6.

[146] '*Avec la généralisations du* forum non conveniens *le demandeur est livré à l'arbitraire.*' Droz, 'Les droits de la demande', at 104.

[147] A. Reus, 'Judicial Discretion: A Comparative View of the Doctrine of Forum Non Conveniens in the United States, the United Kingdom and Germany', *Loyola of Los Angeles International and Comparative Law Journal* (1994), 455-511, at 510. Reus continues by arguing that 'no further protection of the defendant by virtue of the *forum non conveniens* doctrine is necessary'. See Nuyts, *L'exception*, at 676.

the *forum rei* rule ensures legal certainly in the sense that it operates as a traffic regulation 'it avoids collision and furthers a well-balanced apportionment of litigations among the national judiciaries'.[148] Nonetheless, collision might be restricted, but is still possible when other specific bases for jurisdiction are permitted for jurisdiction over contractual disputes and when the corporate home is determined by a 'mixed bag' of connecting factors.

The principle of legal certainty requires that both parties be provided with the 'security' of having at claimant's disposal a competent court which is evident and uncontroversial. It seems rather 'logical'[149] that this should be *the defendant's home forum*. The feared injustice that arises from 'inflexibility' of jurisdictional provisions is in this case limited: with respect to the defendant, it can hardly be called injustice to be sued in your own home forum. It is also fair with respect to the plaintiff who has a choice; either he chooses flexibility and goes to a special jurisdiction forum, taking the risk that the court would refuse jurisdiction when the forum is not sufficiently connected with the defendant, or he chooses to play safe by turning to defendant's home forum.

7.3 Other Bases for General Jurisdiction over Individual Defendants

As will be demonstrated below, the *forum actoris* in its purest form is a *non grata* basis of jurisdiction[150] at unification level. When jurisdiction is based on a connection between the parties and the forum, the focus is generally and almost exclusively on defendant's connections.

7.3.1 **Nationality-based Jurisdiction**

Very few Continental European countries, all deriving from the Romanistic legal system, still apply nationality-based jurisdiction, which leaves France and its infamous Articles 14 and 15 of the French Civil Code in an isolated position.[151] In Italy and Spain, the rule was implicitly applied but had to give way to bases for jurisdiction inspired from the Brussels Model.[152] Under the Anglo-American common law system, nationality-based jurisdiction is practically inexistent. The English CPR Rules for outside service do not include special heads for jurisdiction based on defendant's nationality. In theory, U.S. jurisdiction law allows nationality-based

[148] J. Verheul, 'The "*Forum Actoris*" and International Law', in *Essays on International & Comparative Law in Honour of Judge Erades* (1983), 197-206, at 201. Verheul continues 'Nobody would contend that keeping to the right on a road is in itself better than keeping to the left, or would try to justify the keeping right rule by the fact that most people are right handed.'

[149] Brand, 'Understanding Activity-Based', at 38.

[150] Verheul, 'The "*Forum Actoris*"', at 204.

[151] See below for the *forum actoris* of Art. 14 CC below. See for French critical comments on nationality-based jurisdiction, H. Gaudemet-Tallon, 'Nationalisme et compétence judiciaire: Déclin ou renouveau?', *Travaux* du *Comité Français de Droit International Privé* (1987-1988), 171-199.

[152] See for Italy and Spain, respectively Chapter 3, Sects. 3.1.1 and 3.1.2.

jurisdiction over its nationals or citizens[153] in practice, however, citizenship is linked to the notion of 'resident' and is hardly used for jurisdictional purposes.[154]

Nationality-based jurisdiction in national provisions become scarce due to its being banned and marked exorbitant by the Brussels Model.[155] The 1999 and 2001 Hague Drafts on the Worldwide Jurisdiction Convention without hesitation put nationality-based jurisdiction on the black list for jurisdiction '[since] it cannot constitute a sufficient connection between the dispute and the State of the court seized'.[156] Previous attempts of unification of jurisdiction rules equally banned the nationality basis for jurisdiction from the international unification process. Although the 1971 Protocol to The Hague Convention[157] does not explicitly hold the *defendant's* nationality to be improper for recognition purposes, it clearly gives preference to the domicile criterion.[158]

Due to its nature, nationality-based jurisdiction primarily applies to individuals.[159] Defendant's nationality provides for general jurisdiction; a competent forum is available in contractual disputes by the simple fact that the defendant is a national. No connection with the contract, the (contractual) claim, or the parties' activities in the forum is required. The rule reflects a strongly protective approach to jurisdiction. It emanates from the sovereignty theory in which a state has to be able to protect its nationals by providing an available national 'home' forum for defendant citizens, even those domiciled abroad. This strong protectionist approach to jurisdiction also considers that it is in the state's interest to confer jurisdiction over its nationals (either defendants or claimants). Nationality-based jurisdiction is considered outdated, chauvinistic and misplaced in modern times,[160] especially

---

[153] See for the U.S., Chapter 5, Sect. 5.6.1.2.

[154] G. Born and P. Rutledge, *International Civil Litigation in United States Courts* (2007), fn. 91, at 103.

[155] Art. 3(2) Brussels Regulation and explained in Chapter 2, Sect. 2.2.7.1.

[156] Jurisdiction on the basis of the nationality of the plaintiff as well as of the defendant is 'prohibited'; Art. 18(2)(b) and (c) The Hague 1999 Preliminary Draft Convention and 2001 Interim Text; Nygh-Pocar Report, at 77.

[157] The Hague Convention on the Recognition and Enforcement of Foreign Judgments in Civil and Commercial Matters.

[158] See Fragistas and Droz, 'Explanatory Report Hague Convention 1971', Explanatory Report by Droz on the Protocol, at 501-502: Nationality of the *claimant* is *explicitly* mentioned under Art. 4(b) on the '*black list*' of the 1971 Protocol. See P. Nygh, 'Declining Jurisdiction under the Brussels I Regulation 2001 and the Preliminary Draft Hague Judgments Convention: A Comparison', in *Reform and Development of Private International Law – Essays in Honour of Sir Peter North* (2002), 303-334, at 305.

[159] See above Sects 7.1.2 and 7.1.3 for the problems arising out of the application of nationality-based jurisdiction to companies. See also below Sect. 7.4 for the jurisdiction based on claimant's nationality.

[160] Lord Diplock in *The Abidin Daver*, [1984] AC 398, at 411, referred to by J. Hill, 'The Exercise of Jurisdiction in Private International Law', in *Asserting Jurisdiction – International and European Legal Perspectives* (2003), 39-62, at 56; see also N. Hatzimihail, 'General Report: Transnational Civil Litigation between European Integration and Global Aspirations', in *International Civil Litigation in Europe and Relations with Third States* (2005), 595-675, at 636; G. Droz, 'Réflexions pour une reforme des articles 14 et 15 du Code Civil français', 64 *Revue critique de droit international privé* (1975), 1, at 7: '*c'est ce caractère nationaliste choquant et agressif, qui a provoqué à l'étranger les plus vives critiques contre le système français.*'

in times where people have become more flexible and move more often and for longer periods. The rule no longer guarantees a close connection with the forum[161] and is based on a personal nexus with the forum, which does not imply territorial connections. Generally speaking, nationality or citizenship is no longer considered as a useful or significant connection for jurisdictional purposes in international contractual disputes.

Nationality-based jurisdiction favours one party over another on the basis of its nationality and does not constitute equality of arms between parties. As a general trend, concepts of domicile or habitual residence are replacing the nationality criterion and are considered better suited to guarantee access to justice and prevent nationality-based discrimination.[162]

The only advantage of this rule is that it provides for legal certainty; the nationality connecting factor is a sufficiently certain one for individuals.[163] Such advantage is however severely overshadowed by its disadvantages. In sum, nationality-based jurisdiction is unfair, impractical and unacceptable for a uniform jurisdiction basis in contractual disputes.

7.3.2 **Tag-jurisdiction and Physical Presence**

Jurisdiction on the basis of the individual's physical presence is a typical Anglo-American basis for jurisdiction under the common law[164] and is unfamiliar to civil law systems.[165] The defendant must be properly served with a writ, but the jurisdictional foundation is the defendant's 'physical presence' in the forum. In England, the CPR regulates the service of process as a procedural requirement for jurisdiction, in the U.S. jurisdiction based on defendant's physical presence is also based on common law principles and each state has its own procedural rules for service of process.[166] The U.S. version of 'physical presence' jurisdiction, more commonly

[161] See De Winter, 'Nationality or Domicile', at 400-418; and for a in-depth study A. Bucher, 'Staatsangehörigkeits- und Wohnsitzprinzip: Eine Rechtsvergleichende Übersicht', 28 *Schweizerisches Jahrbuch für internationales Recht* (1972), 76-160.

[162] See Art. 2(2) Brussels Regulation and see Chapter 2, Sects. 2.2.3 and 2.2.7.1. See P. Schlosser, 'Jurisdiction in International Litigation: The Issue of Human Rights in Relation to National Law and the Brussels Convention', *Rivista di diritto internazionale* (1991), 5-34, at 23 *et seq.*, arguing that the exorbitance of nationality-based jurisdiction should be sanctioned by Art. 6(1) ECHR.

[163] In contrast to nationality-based jurisdiction over corporations as explained above in Sect. 7.1.2.

[164] See Fragistas, 'Les compétences exorbitantes', at 185: '*le noyau du système anglo-americain*' (the pit of the Anglo-American system).

[165] See J. Fitzpatrick, 'The Lugano Convention and Western European Integration: A Comparative Analysis of Jurisdiction and Judgements in Europe and the United States', 695 *Connecticut Journal of International Law* (1993), 695-749, at 721 and 726; A. Miaja de la Muela, 'Les principes directeurs des règles de compétence territoriale des tribunaux internes en matière de litiges comportant un élément international', 135 *Recueil des cours* (1973), 1-96, at 81.

[166] For proper service of the claim form in England, see Rules 6.2(1) and 6.4 and 6.5 of the CPR. Among the U.S. states analyzed, Florida, Michigan and New York explicitly incorporated tag-jurisdiction in enumerated long-arm statutes. Both legal systems exempt from service of process an individual who was brought into the forum by force or fraud. See the Supreme Court's statement in *Burnham v. Superior Court California*, 495 U.S. 604, at 614 (1990), 'most states have statutes or common-law rules that exempted from service individuals who were there as a party or witness in unrelated judicial

known as 'tag-jurisdiction' or 'transient jurisdiction', only applies to individual defendants.[167] In contrast to the English common law where corporate presence resulted in complicated and far-reaching definitions, the U.S. jurisdictional scheme elaborated different concepts for corporate defendants such as 'the carrying on of business' and abandoned 'presence' for companies.[168]

Physical presence jurisdiction provides for general jurisdiction – not limited as to the nature of the claim – and is available over any claim arising out of contractual obligations. A connection between the contract or the contractual claim and the forum is not required, nor should defendant's presence in the forum be related to the claim.

Presence-based jurisdiction is inextricably connected with principles of territoriality in which a state has adjudicative powers over all persons present within its territorial dominion.[169] In England, the underlying idea was that each defendant owed allegiance to its sovereign power.[170] Despite its 'murky' jurisprudential origins, U.S. tag-jurisdiction stems without doubt from the traditional English common law.[171] After *International Shoe*[172] and *Shaffer*,[173] tag-jurisdiction was heavily under fire in the *Burnham* case,[174] but survived without a scratch or compromise.[175] In its decision, the Supreme Court relied on that 'historical pedigree'[176] and stated that 'jurisdiction based on physical presence alone constitutes due process because it is one of the continuing traditions of our legal system that define the due process standard of "traditional notions of fair play and substantial justice".'[177] In practice, the *Burnham* case led to the application of tag-jurisdiction without examining the due process standards; by visiting a state, a transient defendant automatically satisfies the purposeful availment requirement and the considerations of fairness and reasonableness.[178]

---

proceedings'. English common law does however not exempt from service of process an individual who was brought within the jurisdiction in police custody or for the purpose of testifying as a witness.

[167] See Chapter 5, Sect. 5.6.1.1.

[168] See also Mann, 'The Doctrine of International Jurisdiction', at 77.

[169] For a brief comparison between the U.K. and the U.S. and the importance of the writ in the History of English Law, see P. Nygh, 'The Common Law Approach', in *Transnational Tort Litigation: Jurisdictional Principles* (1996), 21-36, at 24.

[170] See Chapter 4, Sect. 4.2.1.

[171] *Burnham v. Superior*, 495 U.S. 604, at 636 (1990).

[172] *International Shoe Co. v. Washington*, 326 U.S. 310 (1945).

[173] *Shaffer v. Heitner*, 433 U.S. 186 (1977).

[174] *Burnham v. Superior Court California*, 495 U.S. 604, 606 (1990). See Chapter 5, Sect. 5.6.1.1.

[175] P.J. Borchers, 'Comparing Personal Jurisdiction in the United States and the European Community: A Lessons for American Reform', 40 *American Journal of Comparative Law* (1992), 121-157, at 134: 'Thus tag jurisdiction is alive and well'.

[176] At least in the opinion of Justice Scalia, see *Burnham v. Superior Court California*, 495 U.S. 604, at 629 (1990).

[177] Ibid., at 619. See also P. Hay, 'Transient Jurisdiction, Especially over International Defendants: Critical Comment on *Burnham v. Superior Court California*', *University of Illinois Law Review* (1990), 593-603, at 598; and Von Mehren, 'Theory and Practice', at 129-35.

[178] *Burnham v. Superior Court California*, 495 U.S. 604, 606 (1990): 'a transient defendant actually avails himself of significant benefits provided by the State … Thus, the rule is consistent with reasonable expectations and is entitled to a strong presumption that it comports with due process.'

It should be noted, however, that both English common law and the U.S. jurisdictional system provide for discretionary powers to their courts to decline jurisdiction; in both countries defendant will have to prove that the forum is a *forum non conveniens*.

7.3.2.1 *Exorbitant Character in Civil Law Traditions and at Unification Level*

Within the Brussels legal framework, jurisdiction based on physical presence is explicitly rejected and marked as exorbitant.[179] In most international instruments, the service of the writ criterion is a most unwelcomed basis for jurisdiction and is 'as universally disapproved as exorbitant'.[180] Already in 1971, the Supplementary Protocol to The Hague Convention[181] explicitly refused recognition and enforcement under the Convention where the decision was based on the 'service of a writ upon the defendant within the territory of the State of origin during his temporary presence there'.[182] It is even more remarkable that this rejection of tag-jurisdiction incorporated in a list of exorbitant (indirect) jurisdiction grounds was proposed by the British and American delegations to The Hague Negotiations of the 1971 Convention in 1966.[183]

The Hague Worldwide Jurisdiction Project rapidly placed tag-jurisdiction on the black list: Article 18(f) states that jurisdiction shall not be exercised by the courts of a Contracting State on the basis solely of the service of a writ upon the defendant in that State.[184] The very first preliminary document of The Hague Project directly refers to the 1971 Protocol and the Brussels' jurisdiction provision of Article 3 and indicates that tag-jurisdiction[185] as a jurisdictional basis 'might' be

---

[179] See Chapter 2, Sect. 2.2.7. See Art. 3(2) of the Brussels Convention and Annex I of the Brussels Regulation: 'a) the document instituting the proceedings having been served on the defendant during his temporary presence in the U.K.'. See also P. Schlosser, 'Report on the Convention on the Accession of the United Kingdom of Denmark, Ireland and the United Kingdom of Great Britain and Northern Ireland to the Convention on jurisdiction and the enforcement of judgments in civil and commercial matters and to the Protocol on its interpretation by the Court of Justice', OJ 1979 C 59 (1979), in § 86, at 100; and Mann, 'The Doctrine of International Jurisdiction Revisited', at 70.

[180] D. Fernández Arroyo, 'Exorbitant and Exclusive Grounds of Jurisdiction in European Private International Law: Will They Ever Survive?', in *Festschrift für Erik Jayme* (2004), 169-186, at 185.

[181] The Hague Convention on the Recognition and Enforcement of Foreign Judgments in Civil and Commercial Matters.

[182] Art. 2(1) in conjunction with Art. 4(e). Convention concluded on 1 February 1971 and entered into force on 20 August 1979 (http://www.hcch.net/index_en.php?act=conventions.text&cid=78); see Droz in Fragistas and Droz, 'Explanatory Report Hague Convention 1971', '*aperçu synthétique*', at 416 and '*rapport explicatif*', at 502. See Miaja de la Muela, 'Les principes directeurs', at 83.

[183] According to Fragistas, 'Les compétences exorbitantes', at 180: '*la proposition tomba comme une bombe*'. See also L. de Winter, 'Excessives Jurisdiction in Private International Law', *The International and Comparative Law Quarterly* (1968), 706-720, at 711.

[184] The Hague 1999 Preliminary Draft Convention and the 2001 Interim Text.

[185] Defined as 'Service of a writ upon the defendant within the territory of the state of origin during his temporary presence', 'Prel. Doc. No. 1 of May 1994: Annotated checklist of issues to be discussed at the meeting of the Special Commission of June 1994' (Permanent Bureau of the Hague Conference on Private International Law, 1994), at 18.

excluded[186] as 'there seems now to be general agreement that the mere fortuity that a defendant had been served while passing through a state is not by itself sufficient to establish jurisdiction of the courts of that state'.[187] The possible exclusion of this tag-jurisdiction ground was hardly disputed.[188] The Nygh and Pocar Report is unambiguous: 'it is undisputed that service of the writ is not in itself sufficient to establish a significant connection with the State of the court in all circumstances. Here again, in the light of the 1971 Hague Protocol, the Special Commission did not hesitate to include this ground of jurisdiction among the list of prohibited fora.'[189] Presence-based jurisdiction is unwelcome at unification level, rejected by civil law traditions, and even criticized by English and American authors.[190]

7.3.2.2 *Evaluation*

Unknown and unwanted in the civil law tradition and consistently banned from unification efforts, this basis for jurisdiction stands no chance of being accepted as a uniform jurisdiction rule. Furthermore, there is no legitimate reason to exercise jurisdiction solely on the physical presence of the individual defendant in the forum in international contractual disputes.

Regarding international minimum standards for uniform contract rules, mere physical presence does not vouch for a 'substantial' close connection with the defendant, despite the fact that tag-jurisdiction is clearly *defendant-related.* The 'close connection' requirement should concentrate on other more solid connections with the forum than the mere temporary presence of the defendant.

With respect to the equal protection of parties, tag-jurisdiction is particularly troublesome for a defendant. Tag-jurisdiction troubled individual defendants travelling to those countries applying the rule. Apart from hindering international trade relations, if tag-jurisdiction was to become a uniform rule, it would limit the defendant in his whereabouts, as he could be subjected to jurisdiction of any

---

[186] Or as 'a basis for assuming jurisdiction which should not be utilized as a basis for assuming general jurisdiction', 'Prel. Doc. No. 2 of December 1995: Conclusions of the Special Commission of June 1994' (Permanent Bureau of the Hague Conference on Private International Law, 1995), at 19.

[187] 'Prel. Doc. No. 1 of May 1994: Checklist Special Commission', at 20; and see 'Prel. Doc. No. 2 of 1995: Conclusions Special Commission', at 21.

[188] According to C. Kessedjian, 'Prel. Doc. No. 9: Synthesis of the work of the Special Commission of March 1998 on International Jurisdiction and the Effects of Foreign Judgments in Civil and Commercial Matters', Permanent Bureau of the Hague Conference on Private International Law, at 59, tag-jurisdiction was little discussed during the Special Commission meeting in March 1998 in comparison to other 'exorbitant' bases, namely the presence of a property of the defendant within the territory of the court seized, the nationality of the parties, the domicile/residence of the defendant and 'doing business'. The 'service of a writ upon a defendant within the territory' was enlisted as prohibited jurisdiction under the Convention both for general as well as for special jurisdiction in Annex VI (e) to this Synthesis.

[189] Nygh-Pocar Report, at 78.

[190] See in general, and among many others, the articles of L. Collins, 'Temporary Presence, Exorbitant Jurisdiction and the U.S. Supreme Court', 107 *The Law Quarterly Review* (1990), 10-14; Smit, 'Common and Civil Law Rules'; Hay, 'Transient Jurisdiction'; A. Ehrenzweig, 'The Transient Rule of Personal Jurisdiction, the "Power" Myth, and the Forum Non Conveniens', 65 *Yale Law Journal* (1956), 289-314.

court of the places he goes to and could be properly served with a writ. Obviously, the protection of defendant's interest is not this rule's primary concern. Moreover, the historical justifications for tag-jurisdiction primarily concerned with the duties owed to the sovereign are no longer valid in a changing globalising world.

Tag-jurisdiction does not ensure legal certainty for either party; although the defendant may know the risks he does not know whether or when claimant will serve him with the writ. Nor does tag-jurisdiction ensure a foreseeable forum available for the claimant, since he is generally not able to predict defendant's whereabouts or travel plans.[191] In sum, this rule ranks 'very low in terms of litigational justice'[192] and has no place in a uniform jurisdictional system regulating contractual disputes.

7.4 The Claimant's Home Court

Jurisdiction is generally based on the defendant's connection with the forum, as opposed to the *forum actoris* rule that confers general jurisdiction on a connection between the claimant and the forum. The *forum actoris* rule is considerably less accepted.[193] Unlike the defendant's home court criterion – generally justified by the *favor defensoris* – there seems to be no justification to allow a claimant to sue a defendant at the claimant's home court in international contractual disputes.[194] The connecting factors used for the *forum actoris* are claimant's nationality, domicile or habitual residence.[195] As explained above, due to the exorbitant nature of nationality-based jurisdiction in general, jurisdiction on the basis of claimant's nationality is even less accepted.[196] Among the jurisdictional systems surveyed only France applies a nationality-based *forum actoris* rule.[197] Under Article 14 of the French Civil Code, French courts have general jurisdiction when the plaintiff is a French national and no further connection with the forum is required. But the provision is – like its counterpart in Article 15 – of subsidiary nature and merely

[191] Nygh, 'Criteria for Judicial Jurisdiction', at A-2, 'But in relation to international claims the principle can work injustice to the plaintiff. It is obvious that there are situations where it is unjust or unfair to expect the victim to travel abroad for relief.'

[192] Von Mehren, 'Theory and Practice', at 70.

[193] See Fragistas, 'Les compétences exorbitantes', at 176.

[194] In specific areas however, the plaintiff's home forum is accepted and justified by the particular nature of the contract claim, for instance in the case of consumer contracts, or employment contracts where the plaintiff is able to sue the defendant at his home forum.

[195] In theory, other connecting factors *could* be used – such as the plaintiff's physical presence in the forum, the establishment of a branch, or claimant's activities in the forum – but none of these factors are used.

[196] Schlosser, 'Jurisdiction in International Litigation: The Issue of Human Rights', at 12: 'It has been said that the provision is defendable in view of the high standard of independence and integrity and in view of the high standard of the non-discriminatory traditions of the French Judiciary. Yet this is a highly ideological and hence invalid justification. Very often the judge is not even aware of the disadvantages of the defendant in court proceedings.'

[197] As explained in Chapter 3, Sect. 3.4.3, the rule establishes jurisdiction when the claimant is a French national. See also in relation to the Brussels Report, Jenard Report, at 20; see also Chapter 2, Sect. 2.2.7.

applies when the transposition of internal jurisdiction rules to international cases do not provide for jurisdiction of French courts.[198] The rule should be understood as a rule of last resort, for instance when the defendant has property in France but is in no other way connected with France.[199]

At the time the first Brussels Convention entered into force in 1971, the *forum actoris* rule was permitted in The Netherlands. The former Dutch rule established jurisdiction on the basis that the claimant's domicile was in The Netherlands, provided that the defendant had no known domicile.[200] This provision was abolished and replaced by a new set of direct international jurisdiction rules.[201] The debate preceding the Dutch abolishment of the rule did not conclude that the claimant's forum should be abolished for reasons having to do with its weak substantial connection with the forum, but for policy reasons. It was acknowledged that the *forum actoris* was less efficient at the enforcement stage than the *forum rei* and as a matter of policy the defendant should be protected rather than the claimant.[202] Finally, retaining the claimant's forum rule does not make a lot of sense when the current jurisdictional climate rule favours the *forum rei*.[203] Some even questioned whether jurisdiction at claimant's home forum is incompatible with customary law, but the answer was negative.[204]

Under English common law, only the defendant's presence is conclusive for jurisdiction. Claimant's connections with the forum are not taken into account for outside service of process under Rule 6.20 CPR. Likewise, only the defendant's minimum contacts are jurisdiction-creating for U.S. courts.[205] Nonetheless, plaintiff's connections with the forum are not entirely irrelevant for jurisdictional purposes in Anglo-American systems. The plaintiff's interests and convenience to

---

[198] Art. 42 *et seq.* of the French NCPC as discussed in Chapter 3, Sect. 3.4.1.

[199] H. Muir Watt, 'Note: Banque camerounaise de développement Cour de Cassation; Chambre Civile 1re 18 November 1986', 76 *Revue critique de droit international privé* (1987), 773-786, at 785.

[200] Former Art. 126(3) of the Rv. A similar provision, strongly resembling a *forum necessitatis*, is still known in France since Art. 42 NCPC was modified. A *forum actoris*, this time based on defendant's domicile, is also available to the claimant provided that the defendant does not have his domicile or residence in France and that it is unknown or difficult to locate in which other state he has his main establishment. In that case a claimant may seize the (French) court of his domicile or when domiciled abroad, the claimant may seize the court of his choice. Nevertheless, both *forum actoris* rules apply only in the exceptional situation that the determination of defendant's domicile is troublesome. The new Rv. provides for a *forum necessitatis* establishing jurisdiction when the case is sufficiently connected with the forum and the *forum actoris* for Dutch courts is eligible, see Art. 9 Rv.

[201] See Chapter 3, Sect. 3.2.1.1 for the reasons for this abolishment.

[202] L. Strikwerda, 'Drie fora: *forum actoris*, *forum necessitatis* en *forum non conveniens*', in *De internationale bevoegdheid van de Nederlandse Rechter volgens de nieuwe bepalingen van het Wetboek van Burgerlijke Rechtsvordering,* T.M.C Asser Instituut (1996), at 96.

[203] L. Strikwerda, *De Overeenkomst in het IPR* (2004), at 51.

[204] Verheul, 'The "*forum actoris*"', at 198-199 and 202-203.

[205] According to A. von Mehren and D. Trautmann, 'Jurisdiction to Adjudicate', 79 *Harvard Law Review* (1966), 1121-1199, at 1137: 'General jurisdiction to adjudicate has in American practice never been based on the plaintiff's relationship to the forum. There is nothing in American law comparable to art. 126 of the Code of Civil Procedure of The Netherlands (1827) which authorizes the assumption of jurisdiction based on the Dutch domicile of the plaintiff, or to art. 14 of the Civil Code of France (1804) under which the French nationality of the plaintiff is a sufficient ground for jurisdiction.'

litigate abroad or in the forum are taken into account to determine the appropriate forum under the *forum (non) conveniens* doctrine as applied in England and the U.S.

U.S. due process standards consider the plaintiff's relationship with the forum to determine whether the exercise of U.S. jurisdiction is compatible with considerations of reasonableness and fairness. In *Rush v. Savchuk*[206] the Supreme Court tried to 'shift the focus of the [contacts] inquiry from the relationship among the defendant, the forum, and the litigation to that among the plaintiff, the forum, the insurer, and the litigation. ... In other words, the plaintiff's contacts with the forum are decisive in determining whether the defendant's due process rights are violated.'[207] But the Court nuanced by stating that a

> 'variety of factors [including the claimant's interests] relating to the particular cause of action may be relevant to the determination whether the exercise of jurisdiction would comport with "traditional notions of fair play and substantial justice," ... [i]f a defendant has certain judicially cognizable ties with a State, if not the determination of jurisdiction on the basis [of] plaintiff's contacts with the forum "is forbidden by *International Shoe* and its progeny".'[208]

It should however be noted that the outcome of some alternative bases for jurisdiction often coincide with the plaintiff's home forum. Especially jurisdiction founded on *claim-related* connections has led to a shift towards a 'veiled' *forum actoris*. As will be demonstrated below, special jurisdiction rules designed for contractual matters could lead to 'generalising the *forum actoris* in actions for payment of the price of the goods'. [209]

7.4.1 *The* Forum Actoris *at Unification Level*

The *forum actoris* is far from popular at unification level: the basis for jurisdiction is marked exorbitant under Article 3 of the Brussels Model.[210] The Hague Drafts of the Worldwide Jurisdiction Convention envisaged the *forum actoris* on the Black List of Article 18 stating that the nationality, domicile, habitual or temporary residence, or presence of the plaintiff in a Contracting State could not serve as a basis to exercise jurisdiction over the defendant.[211] Although the Nygh and Pocar Report recognizes that the domicile and habitual residence, or presence of the plaintiff are

---

[206] 444 U.S. 320 (1980).

[207] Ibid., at 332.

[208] Ibid.

[209] Opinion AG Ruiz-Jarabo Colomer, delivered on 16 March 1999, in C-440/97 *GIE Groupe Concorde*, [1999] ECR I-6307, para. 53. See also G. Droz, 'Delendum est forum contractus? (vingt ans après les arrêts *De Bloos* et *Tessili* interprétant l'article 5.1 de la Convention de Bruxelles du 27 septembre 1968)', 41 *Recueil Dalloz; Cahier Chronique* (1997), 351-356, at 355; J. Eltzschig, 'Art. 5 Nr. 1 b EuGVO; Ende oder Fortführung von *forum actoris* und Erfüllungsort bestimmung *lege causae*', *IPRax* (2002), 491-496; G. Steenhoff, 'Pleidooi voor een crediteursforum bij (internationale) geldschulden', in *Het NIPR geannoteerd: Annotaties opgedragen aan Dr Mathilde Sumampouw* (1996), 194-202, at 199.

[210] See Jenard Report, at 79.

[211] Art. 18(2)(b) and (d) of The Hague 1999 Preliminary Draft Convention and 2001 Interim Text.

indicating a closer connection than the nationality of the plaintiff, the Commission is of the opinion that these bases

> 'do not evince a sufficient connection with it to provide a general ground of jurisdiction for the court seised. … [T]hey indicate a connection of only one of the parties concerned, and give rise to the same difficulties as the forum of the defendant's nationality if they are used as the only grounds of jurisdiction. The Special Commission was in agreement that they should be excluded.'[212]

It seems that the exorbitant nature of jurisdiction based on claimant's nationality is twofold; primarily by the fact that jurisdiction is founded on a *claimant-related* connection, secondly, as a result of the particularly disputed basis of nationality.[213]

The Supplementary Protocol to The Hague Convention of 1 February 1971 on the Recognition and Enforcement of Foreign Judgments[214] already enlisted (indirect) jurisdiction grounds that would result in the refusal to recognize judgements and included the *forum actoris* on this list: the nationality, the domicile, habitual residence or ordinary residence of the plaintiff was not a valid jurisdiction ground, unless 'the assumption of jurisdiction on such a ground is permitted by way of an exception made on account of the particular subject-matter of a class of contracts', such as consumer or employment contracts.[215] A similar exception was also envisaged in the 1999 draft of the Hague Convention in Article 7(1) but was heavily disputed at the Diplomatic Session in 2001.[216]

A very interesting variation of jurisdiction at plaintiff's home court is accepted in the Buenos Aires Protocol on International Jurisdiction in Contractual Matters elaborated in the context of MERCOSUR.[217] The courts of the individual plaintiff's domicile or the corporate plaintiff's headquarters – meaning the corporate centre of administration and management control – are competent when the plaintiff demonstrates that it has fulfilled its obligation. [218]

---

212 Nygh-Pocar Report, at 85.

213 As explained above in Sect. 7.3.1. Nationality-based jurisdiction as sole connection with the forum no longer vouches for a substantial connection with the forum. This criterion, deriving from the Latin jurisdictional system, reflects a strict application of the sovereignty theory. Although in international family law it remains a considerable relevant connecting factor, with respect to matters concerning civil and commercial actions, it is in serious decline. Moreover, the concept of nationality as such is an 'empty bucket' when applied to corporate entities, see Fragistas, 'Les compétences exorbitantes', at 184.

214 Supplementary Protocol to The Hague Convention on the Recognition and Enforcement of Foreign Judgments in Civil and Commercial Matters.

215 Protocol of 1971, Art. 4(b) and (c) in conjunction with Art. 2. See Droz's explanatory report in Fragistas and Droz, 'Explanatory Report Hague Convention 1971', at 501-502. Please note that this Convention has little practical significance as few Member States of the Hague Conference have ratified the Convention. Cyprus, The Netherlands, Portugal (and Kuwait as a non-Member State of the Hague Conference).

216 Art. 7(1) provided for jurisdiction at the habitual residence of the plaintiff consumer.

217 MERCOSUR/CMC/DEC. Nº 01/94.

218 Ibid., Art. 7(c).

7.4.2 Evaluation

Exercising jurisdiction is unacceptable when it is solely based on *claimant-related* connections and the defendant has no connection with the forum, for instance he is not carrying out business or any contractual activities in the forum. Jurisdiction at the claimant's home court does not satisfy the minimum standard of a *defendant-related* connection and would certainly not be accepted as uniform jurisdiction for contractual disputes. Such exercise of jurisdiction will not only never pass the U.S. due process standards, it does not fit into the Brussels Model and will, if it ever comes into place, not pass the fair trial test of Article 6 of the ECHR.[219]

Obviously, the protection of the defendant on the basis of the *forum defensoris* seems to oppose the application of the plaintiff's home court. The interest of the claimant could be balanced by providing the claimant with a choice of competent forums besides the defendant's home court, which is not necessarily his own home court.[220] Nonetheless, a similar question as the one addressed in relation to the defendant's home court needs to be addressed here: why should the claimant systematically be required to seek the defendant in his forum, should the claimant not be given a similar privilege in some circumstances when it involves international contractual disputes?[221] A plaintiff generally institutes proceedings in order to seek compensation for an alleged wrong-doing by the defendant.[222] Apart from situations in which a claimant only files suits to 'harass' the counterparty, there is a fifty percent chance that a claimant is in his right.[223] This seems to be particularly true in sales contracts where the defendant deliberately refuses to pay or to perform a contractual obligation.[224] Why then should the plaintiff have to litigate abroad and bear the inconveniences of travelling – or have the burden of a '*Reiselast*'.[225] The preferential treatment given to the defendant on the basis of the *forum defensoris* is disputed, especially when the defendant is protected for the wrong reasons.

Furthermore, the *forum actoris* is also a way for a state to protect resident claimants by providing them with a competent forum at their home.

7.5 *Defendant-related*: Activity-based Jurisdiction

The previous paragraphs focused on traditional bases for jurisdiction such as domicile, presence and nationality. Strongly influenced by principles of territorial sovereignty, they assert general jurisdiction and lead to defendant's 'home court'. For corporate defendants territorial jurisdiction is based on the corporate connecting

219 As will be exhaustively discussed in Chapter 8, Sect. 8.3.

220 See above Sect. 7.2.3, evaluating the defendant's forum.

221 See above Sect. 7.2.3.2, dealing with the protection of parties and equality of arms.

222 See Verheul, 'The "*Forum Actoris*"', at 199-200, arguing that such a *favor defensoris* for the defendant is not always that logical.

223 Ibid., at 201.

224 'Preferential treatment of the seller is disputable, in many cases the new place of performance rule for contractual matters results in the forum of the buyer, which give rise to a possible forum actoris.' Eltzschig, 'Art. 5 Nr. 1 b EuGVO', at 492 and 496.

225 As it is called in German; see Strikwerda, *De Overeenkomst in het IPR*, at 51.

factors such as the place of incorporation, the centre of administration and management, or the principal place of business. States enacted additional jurisdiction rules in order to reach a defendant outside his home court – also referred to as 'extraterritorial' jurisdiction – instead of requiring that the claimant seek the defendant at his home court. Extraterritorial jurisdiction is either founded on a connection between the defendant and the forum or on a special connection between the claim and the forum.[226] This subparagraph deals with jurisdiction based on defendant's activity in the forum.

In international contractual disputes, the corporate and individual defendant is primarily connected with the forum by the business they conduct in the forum.[227] The commercial nature of defendant's activity in the forum justifies jurisdiction. For jurisdictional purposes, commercial activities are often conducted by an establishment carrying out business for the defendant, which will be further referred to as *branch-establishment jurisdiction.* Extraterritorial jurisdiction over companies is therefore also related to the question of the company's relationship and its branch, agent or subsidiary.[228] The defendant can also directly conduct business activities in the forum without the intervention of a business-establishment. Jurisdiction based on the activities in the forum is categorized as to the density of defendant's activities; starting from doing business, to the branch-establishment, and followed by transacting business.

7.5.1 **Doing Business Abroad**

The U.S. jurisdictional scheme recognizes that when a defendant is doing business, he may be 'located' in more than one forum outside his home forum. 'Doing business' is a much wider basis for jurisdiction than the 'domicile' and 'presence' concepts. The corporate home factors that have been identified above, such as the centre of administration and management control and the principal place of business, are all covered by the U.S. doing business basis. Like transacting business jurisdiction, 'doing business' jurisdiction is characteristic to the U.S. system and illustrates how different the U.S. approach to international jurisdiction is from its English common law origins and how it has developed since *International Shoe*.[229] Among the analysed countries, doing business was only encountered in U.S. jurisdiction law. Formulated as an open jurisdictional concept and determined by assessing defendant's activities on a case-by-case basis, the doing business rule

---

[226] See Sect. 7.6 on the *forum contractus*.

[227] Fawcett, 'A New Approach to Jurisdiction over Companies', at 646-647; Schack, *Internationales Zivilverfahrensrecht*, § 250, at 91.

[228] Fawcett refers to this second body as the outlet in the forum, see Fawcett, 'A New Approach to Jurisdiction over Companies', at 648-649. Beale already pointed out in 1912 that '[I]t is generally held that a foreign corporation may be sued on the same principle as a foreign individual; but in the nature of the case greater difficulties must be experienced in working out the result. Where however, the corporation has a place of business and an agent within the state, jurisdiction over it is probably universally exercised.' J. Beale, 'Jurisdiction of Courts over Foreigners', 26 *Harvard Law Review* (1912), 193-211, at 206.

[229] *International Shoe v. Washington*, 326 U.S. 310 (1945), in particular at 320 for the doing business criterion; but see also *World-Wide Volkswagen Corp. v. Woodson*, 444 U.S. 286 (1980).

founds jurisdiction over defendants who are '*continuous and systematically*' carrying out business in the forum, in claims that are not related to defendant's activities in the forum.[230] A fixed place of business is not required for doing business as the basis is primarily focussed on 'business' connections, as opposed to territorial or physical connections with the forum.[231]

The doing business rule is principally used when transacting business jurisdiction is not available because the claim is not related to the defendant's activities carried out in the forum. General doing business confers jurisdiction over claims unrelated to defendant's activities, but requires a more substantial connection with the forum than transacting business.

At international unification level, the doing business rule has always been controversial. The 1971 Supplementary Protocol to The Hague Convention already refused recognition of a judgement whose jurisdiction was based on 'the fact that the defendant carried on business within the territory of the State of origin, unless the action arises from that business'.[232] At the beginning of The Hague Worldwide Jurisdiction Project, the 1994 annotated checklist of issues to be discussed at the meeting of the first Special Commission on Jurisdiction and Enforcement of Judgments used the exact same words to exclude the doing business criterion as a basis for jurisdiction.[233] At an early stage of the negotiations doing business translated in French as '*entreprendre des activités commerciales*'[234] or '*traiter des affaires*'[235] was doomed to be put on the black list.[236] It was explained that this basis of jurisdiction, specifically known in the U.S., was much wider than branch jurisdiction, which was considered as a jurisdiction ground to be admitted.[237] A more fundamental discussion dealing with *doing business* recognized that jurisdiction based on such activity should be analysed together with provisions dealing with contracts and torts and in matters concerning branches.[238] The 'density of activity' would determine whether the connection with the forum would qualify as

[230] When the claim is related to the forum, the U.S. jurisdictional scheme requires a less high amount of contacts with the forum. See Droz, 'Réflexions', at 4: '*le* doing business *c'est-a-dire du pays où le défendeur traite des affaires sans que le litige soit relatif auxdites affaire.*' See Chapter 5, Sect. 5.6.2.1 on the question whether or not doing business is limited to corporate defendants or whether it also applies to individuals.

[231] Borchers, 'Comparing Jurisdiction', at 135; Mann, 'The Doctrine of International Jurisdiction Revisited', at 71; Whincop, *Policy and Pragmatism*, at 171-172, emphasizing the corporate interests in a forum: 'Corporations might be subjected to jurisdiction in a number of jurisdictions, based on its interests in those places.'

[232] Art. 2(1) in conjunction with Art. 4(d); see above.

[233] 'Prel. Doc. No. 1 of May 1994: Checklist Special Commission', at 18.

[234] Kessedjian, 'Prel. Doc. No. 7: 1997 Report', § 19.

[235] According to the formulation used by Droz in Rapport explicatif, see Fragistas and Droz, 'Explanatory Report Hague Convention 1971', at 502.

[236] See Kessedjian, 'Prel. Doc. No. 7: 1997 Report', at 41; Brand, '2005 Report: A View from the U.S.', at 12.

[237] 'Prel. Doc. No. 1 of May 1994: Checklist Special Commission', at 12 and 18. See also the statement previously made by Droz in Fragistas and Droz, 'Explanatory Report Hague Convention 1971', at 502 (rapport explicatif).

[238] Kessedjian, 'Prel. Doc. No. 8 of June 1997: Synthesis Special Commission', § 32 and § 88.

'branch jurisdiction' or as 'doing business'.[239] Further explanations were provided to understand the distinction and implications of 'doing business' and 'transacting business'.[240] The result was the definition of doing business as 'carrying on of commercial or other activities by the defendant within the territory of the State'. [241] The Nygh and Pocar Report mentions that the 'doing business' criterion implies that jurisdiction is based on the fact that defendant carries out regular activities in the forum and founds jurisdiction on merely economic connections with the forum, regardless of any physical (or territorial) connections with the forum.[242] The fact that the rule provides for jurisdiction over claims even unrelated to doing business in the forum was particularly controversial and led to its exclusion:[243] Article 18(2)(e) of the 1999 and 2001 Hague Draft Conventions prohibits jurisdiction based on 'the carrying on of commercial or other activities by the defendant in that State, except where the dispute is directly related to those activities'. The outcome of the June 2001 Diplomatic Conference was that the doing business provision was complemented with bracketed text determining that the carrying on of commercial or other activities by the defendant in that state '[whether or not through a branch, agency or any other establishment of the defendant]', would not establish general jurisdiction. The footnote to this bracketed provision clarifies that the simple presence of a branch, agency or other establishment within the forum should not be a basis for general jurisdiction.[244]

7.5.2 Place of Business and Branch

The notion that a defendant is amenable to jurisdiction at the place where he has a 'branch'-establishment is a familiar one in Europe.[245] 'Branch' jurisdiction as

---

[239] Ibid., § 88.

[240] The discussion was greatly facilitated by an informative document submitted by the U.S. delegation on 'doing business' and 'transacting business' jurisdiction, see P. Dubinsky, 'The Reach of Doing Business Jurisdiction and transacting Business Jurisdiction over Non-U.S. Individuals and Entities' (Working Document no. 64: Presented at the Special Commission of the Hague Conference, 1998).

[241] With respect to the degree of 'density of activity', general doing business 'is reserved for defendants who engage in regular, extensive, and frequent activity in the State in question, regardless of what form of organisation they have, whether or not they own property there or have a place of business, and regardless of whether or not their principal place of business or place of incorporation is situated abroad.' Kessedjian, 'Prel. Doc. No. 9 of March 1998: Synthesis Special Commission', § 66, at 31.

[242] Nygh-Pocar Report, at 77.

[243] 'Prel. Doc. No. 2 of 1995: Conclusions Special Commission', § 28, at 19; Kessedjian, 'Prel. Doc. No. 8 of June 1997: Synthesis Special Commission', § 32; Kessedjian, 'Prel. Doc. No. 9 of March 1998: Synthesis Special Commission', § 65, at 29 *et seq.*

[244] After the June 2001 diplomatic conference provisions Art. 18(2)(e) was bracketed into '[the carrying on of commercial or other activities by the defendant in that State, [whether or not through a branch, agency or any other establishment of the defendant,] except where the dispute is directly related to those activities]'.

[245] See Art. 5(5) of the Brussels Model. See for the Brussels Model Chapter 2, Sect. 2.6, for the German basis of jurisdiction at defendant's *Niederlassung* under Art. 21 ZPO, which stands on its own authority. A particular feature of the German rule lies in its mandatory character in banking and credit business, as derogation from branch jurisdiction by the parties is not permitted by an exclusive choice of forum excluding jurisdiction for the branch forum. In France and The Netherlands settled case law

known in Europe requires a substantial establishment in the forum to reach a defendant outside his home court.[246] The basis of jurisdiction is formulated by an open concept including 'branch, agency or any other establishment' and is determined on the facts of the case. The rule as applied in Europe requires a substantial *fixed* place of business with the appearance of *permanency*; the branch *acts on behalf* of the defendant and operates under his *direction*, but the establishment should also have a certain degree of *independence*, which distinguishes it from a mere representative.[247]

'Branch jurisdiction', as known in the Brussels Model and each of the Continental European countries analysed, is limited to claims related to business activities carried out by the branch and confers *special* jurisdiction. The Brussels Model does not require that the activities themselves were carried out in the forum but only that the (branch-) establishment that carried out the relevant claim-related activities is situated in the forum.[248]

A similar version of 'branch jurisdiction' was known in English common law under the Companies Act 1985 as a result of the enactment of the Eleventh Company Directive in 1992.[249] The English equivalent of 'branch jurisdiction' constituted 'presence' and allowed for service of process, which creates jurisdiction for English courts.[250] Under the Companies Act 1985, it was clear that a branch is a more permanent establishment than a mere 'place of business' or 'business-establishment'. For the purpose of statutory service, the Companies Act 2006 no longer makes a distinction between branch and place of business, as the latter includes the branch establishment.[251] In sum, the key to English courts having jurisdiction over foreign companies is the establishment of a place of business.

---

clearly indicates that branch jurisdiction is only allowed when the claim arises out of the operations of the branch; for France see Art. 42 NCCP applicable to international disputes Chapter 3, Sect. 3.4.2.2; for The Netherlands see Art. 1:14 CC in conjunction with Art. 2 Rv. Chapter 3, Sect. 3.2.2.4. For Switzerland see Art. 112(2) Swiss PIL Statute which asserts jurisdiction over contractual claims if the defendant has established a branch, *provided* that the claim is related to the activities of the branch. Italy and Spain directly refer to Art. 5(5) of the Brussels Model.

[246] Art. 5(5) includes 'agency' and 'establishment', but 'branch jurisdiction' seems to be the most suitable term and will be used as a generic denomination for Art. 5(5) of the Brussels Regulation.

[247] Art. 5(5) of the Brussels Model see Chapter 2, Sect. 2.6. In France (Chapter 3, Sect. 3.4.2.1) and The Netherlands (Chapter 3, Sect. 3.2.2.4) branch jurisdiction owes its existence to the extension of the 'domicile' or 'seat' concept which implies that the establishment should be regarded as a substantial and fixed place of business from which the company carries out its business activities with a certain degree of continuity and is not an occasional place of business. With respect to the characteristics of a Dutch branch, it requires a permanent establishment such as a *building* from where business is carried out, which also reflects a territorial connection with the forum. See also P. Schlosser, 'Bases of Jurisdiction in a "New Double Convention" on Jurisdiction and Recognition of Foreign Judgements; Conference Papers', in *The Hague Convention on Jurisdiction and Judgements: Records of the Conference Held at New York University School of Law on the Proposed Convention 1999* (2001), A-13-A-27, at A-20.

[248] C-439/93 *Lloyd's v. Campenon Bernard*, [1995] ECR, at I-0961.

[249] Eleventh Council Directive 89/666/EEC of 21 December 1989; OJ 1989 L 395/36-39.

[250] See Chapter 4, Sect. 4.4.2.2.a.

[251] See Chapter 4, Sect. 4.4.2.2.c.

The new Act limits jurisdiction to claims based on corporate presence through the establishment of a place of business 'in respect of the carrying on of the business of' the establishment. Such a connection between the establishment's activities and claimant's claim should be understood as wider than its Brussels counterpart, which requires that the claim be 'arising out of' the branch's activities. Settled case law authorizes that the connection between the claim and the branch's activities may be partially connected with the branch's activities.[252] Thus, the English test is less strict than the claim-related connection test under the Brussels Model.[253] But the fact that the CPR regime still does not require such a claim-related connection with the place of business to serve an overseas company makes it considerably easier for the claimant to apply the CPR regime rather than the statutory service of the Companies Act. In practice, the CPR regime is wider and will be more frequently applied. As a consequence, in England a mere place of business provides for jurisdiction over claims unrelated to a corporation's activities in the forum.[254] It speaks for itself that this general basis of 'place of business' is a much wider concept than branch jurisdiction as applied in the Continental European countries and under Article 5(5) of the Brussels Model. The English system reaches a defendant outside his home court on the basis of a place of business, which constitutes corporate presence, which contrasts with the Continental European approach that considers a branch or – 'secondary' establishment – as an extension of the defendant's domicile.

The concept of 'branch jurisdiction' is unknown to the U.S. jurisdictional scheme but a business- or branch-establishment in the forum is beyond all doubt sufficient for U.S. jurisdiction under the minimum contacts rule. Most likely, such a 'fixed and permanent' establishment constitutes enough 'continuous and systematic' contacts to justify general jurisdiction under the 'doing business' basis for jurisdiction. Even if the establishment has a less 'continuous' character, the basis for jurisdiction would be covered by transacting business as long as the claim relates to the branch's activities.[255] The European 'branch jurisdiction' falls under 'doing business' when the claim is unrelated or under 'transacting business' when the claim arises out of defendant's business activities. In *Samofer v. Saar-Ferngas AG*, the ECJ explicitly referred to an 'office' as a *place of contact* with the forum justifying jurisdiction, which resembles the U.S. jurisdictional language based on contacts.[256] Branch jurisdiction could indeed be considered as a European version of 'doing business abroad',[257] but then as a 'smaller or miniaturised' version of doing business.[258]

---

[252] *Saab v. Saudi American Bank*, [1999] 1 WLR 1861; Chapter 4, Sect. 4.4.2.2.b.

[253] See Briggs, *Conflict of Laws*, at 82-83; N. Enonchong, 'Service of Process in England on Overseas Companies and Article 5(5) of the Brussels Convention', 48 *The International and Comparative Law Quarterly* (1999), 921-936, at 933-935.

[254] According to Rule 6.5(6) CPR discussed in Chapter 4, Sect. 4.4.2.1.

[255] See for the U.S. transacting business concept, Chapter 5, Sect. 5.6.3.

[256] Case 33/78 *Somafer SA v. Saar-Ferngas AG*, [1978] ECR 02183, para. 2.

[257] See J. Lookofsky and K. Hertz, *Transnational Litigation and Commercial Arbitration: An Analysis of American, European and International Law* (2004), at 160, who considers Art. 5(5) as a doing business abroad criterion on the basis that the defendant is economically active outside his home forum and is 'doing business' abroad.

[258] U. Magnus and P. Mankowski, eds., *Brussels I Regulation* (2007), § 270, at 219.

The crucial difference between the U.S. doing business rule on the one hand and the European branch and the English place of business on the other is that the latter are considerably more limited in their reach because they require some 'local establishment from which business is organized',[259] which is not an absolute prerequisite for doing business according to the American system since in the U.S. the doing business criteria applies as long as the contacts are 'continuous and systematic'. The Continental European branch clearly requires a substantial *fixed* place of business in the sense of a *physical* establishment such as a building or some kind of office, with the appearance of *permanency* from which the defendant carries out his business. The determination of an English 'place of business' is a question of evaluation of factors enlisted in the *Adams v. Cape Industries Plc* case,[260] but a similar form of physical presence is required for the English 'place of business establishment'.[261] English case law systematically refused jurisdiction without a *fixed* place of business.[262] Although earlier case law used 'doing business' language to determine corporate presence, English courts have never accepted presence on the basis of merely 'carrying out business' in the forum.[263] This to the disappointment of some English scholars such as Fawcett and North who advocate jurisdiction over companies based on 'economic' presence rather than territorial physical presence. They claim that

> 'it is both more meaningful and more realistic to talk about companies being here in an economic rather than in a physical sense. Foreign companies should therefore be subject to the jurisdiction of the English courts under the traditional rules whenever they have an economic presence. In assessing this, the court should take into account the nature of the business connection with England, the volume of business transacted, and whether there was continuous business activity.'[264]

In sum, the strict requirements for European branch jurisdiction would easily satisfy the doing business requirements: it is harder to comply with the European

[259] Nygh's contribution in Lowenfeld and Silberman, eds., *The Hague Convention on Jurisdiction*, at 13.

[260] [1990] Ch. 433; see May 2003, [2003] EWHC 1162; see also *Rakusens Ltd. v. Baser*, [2001] EWCA Civ. 1820, [2002] 1 BCLC, at 104; *Matchnet Plc v. William Blair & Company Llc*, High Court of Justice Chancery Division, 11 October, [2002] EWHC 2128.

[261] Ibid.

[262] *Okura & Co., Limited v. Forsbacka Jernverks Aktiebolag*, [1914] 1 KB 715, at 718-719, Court of Appeal: 'Next, it is essential that these acts should have been done at some fixed place of business'.

[263] *Harrods Ltd v. Dow Jones & Co Inc*, High Court of Justice, [2003] EWHC 1162 (QB), where the Court upheld the requirement of a fixed place of business under the Companies Act 1985 and did not allow service under the CPR at a mere 'place of carrying out business' if the company had no fixed place of business, discussed in Chapter 4, Sect. 4.4.2.2.b.

[264] Fawcett, 'A New Approach to Jurisdiction over Companies', at 667. See also North in North and Fawcett, *Private International Law* (1999), at 295, who would support the following statement from Fawcett: 'More generally the whole of the law on jurisdiction against corporate defendants would make more sense if instead of applying a misleading analogy with individuals it was recognized that corporate individuals are very different and jurisdiction should be based on the notion of their economic presence within the jurisdiction rather than on the establishment of a place of business'.

branch and the English place of business-establishment than with their American counterparts of doing business.[265]

An important difference between the European branch on the one hand and U.S. doing business and the English place of business[266] on the other is that the latter provide for general jurisdiction over claims unrelated to the activities carried out in the forum, whereas branch jurisdiction is limited to claims arising out of the establishment's activities. This considerably narrows the scope of branch jurisdiction in comparison to the English place of business and the U.S. doing business. The fact that doing business is a basis of general jurisdiction constitutes the main controversy between Europeans and Americans.[267]

But the Brussels version of branch jurisdiction does not require that the activities giving cause for the claim were carried out in the forum itself, as long as the branch- or business-establishment which carried out those activities is located in the forum.[268] This slightly widens its scope of application with respect to doing business. It also shows that branch jurisdiction is not primarily founded on 'carrying out of the activities' related to the claim but rather on the fact that a fixed place of business be located in the forum.[269] The question is whether jurisdiction over a claim related to defendant's activities *not* carried out in the forum, but based on the simple presence of a branch-establishment would pass the U.S. purposeful availment requirement of due process. If the branch is continuously and systematically active in the forum, it will constitute 'doing business' in the forum and ensure the purposeful availment criterion.

7.5.3 **Agency**

Jurisdiction over the defendant outside his home court on the basis that he has an agent in the forum deserves some special attention. The presence of an agent in the forum is susceptible to be covered by 'branch jurisdiction' and the English 'place of business' rule, provided that the agent is acting on behalf of the defendant and has a certain degree of independence. There are however situations in which an 'agency' is an independent basis of jurisdiction. In Italy, the general *forum rei* rule is supplemented by a general basis for jurisdiction when defendant has a legal representative in Italy.[270] This independent basis of 'legal representative' extends the domicile rule. In England, jurisdiction is also available when the defendant has an

---

[265] See Schack, *Minimum Contacts Scrutinized*, at 38: 'the existence in the forum state of an office, no matter how tiny, is almost automatically held sufficient. If there is no office, the courts often are content with substantial income derived from sales in the forum state.'

[266] Under the CPR regime.

[267] But see Trooboff's contribution in Lowenfeld and Silberman, eds., *The Hague Convention on Jurisdiction,* at 21; and Schlosser, 'Bases of Jurisdiction', at A-22: '[T]he European should not be too worried about doing business as a head of general jurisdiction. In most cases U.S. courts have assumed jurisdiction on doing business standards, their own courts have assumed jurisdiction under a head of specific jurisdiction.'

[268] C-439/93 *Lloyd's v. Campenon Bernard*, 6 April 1995, [1995] ECR, at I-0961.

[269] Nygh-Pocar Report, at 53.

[270] Art. 3(1) of the Italian PIL Statute states: 'Italian Courts shall have jurisdiction if the defendant is domiciled or resides in Italy or has a representative in this country who is enabled to appear in court

agent in England, but only with respect to contractual claims.[271] Such agent lacks any 'permanence of appearance', but as a mere intermediary this concept is wider than the agent in the sense of 'branch-establishment'.[272] With respect to the minimum contacts theory of U.S. jurisdiction law, most long-arm statutes formulate transacting business over defendants as 'carrying out business activities directly or through an agent'. Among the analysed U.S. states only the Florida long-arm Statutes have incorporated a provision upon which jurisdiction is asserted on the sole fact that the (foreign) defendant is '*having* an office or agency in the state'.[273]

7.5.4 **Transacting Business**

Exercising jurisdiction over a defendant outside his home court at the place where he transacts business is characteristic to the U.S. jurisdictional scheme. Transacting business jurisdiction is primarily focussed on commercial and business activities; a 'single and occasional' business contact with the forum is sufficient for jurisdiction as long as the claim or the cause of action is related to the business activity.[274] As summarized by Brand, jurisdiction is based on a 'combination of the connections between the defendant, the forum state, and the [contractual] claim'.[275]

Transacting business jurisdiction is difficult to understand – and to accept – for civil law systems, but also for the traditional English common law, since it does not require a *fixed and physical* establishment carrying out business activities for jurisdiction based on defendant's activities. This is an absolute prerequisite for the European 'branch jurisdiction' and the place of establishment establishing 'corporate presence' under English common law.[276] Equally restricted to claims arising out of defendant's activities in the forum, transacting business jurisdiction is considerably wider and is formulated by an open norm: the nature and density of defendant's 'business contacts' are determined on a case-by-case basis. Typical jurisdiction-creating activities are, among others, mere solicitation of business, business negotiations, directing phone call conversations and advertising.[277] Such connecting factors are irrelevant under the uniform Brussels Model and are unknown to civil law traditions and the English common law. Although exagger-

pursuant to Art. 77 of the Code of Civil Procedure, as well as in the other cases provided for by law'. See Chapter 3, Sect. 3.1.1.

[271] According to the CPR regime under Rule 6.20(5)(ii).

[272] Explained in Chapter 4, Sect. 4.5.2.2 and Ch. Plant, ed., *Blackstone's Civil Practice 2004* (2004), § 16.50, at 219; and see *National Mortgage & Agency Company of New Zealand, Ltd. v. Gosselin*, Court of Appeal, July 17 1922, [1922] 12 Ll. L. Rep. 318.

[273] Florida Statute § 48.193(1), last sentence.

[274] See for the different degrees of the terms 'related to', Chapter 5, Sect. 5.6.3. Some states, such as California, use the 'but for' causation test to determine whether the claim arises out of the defendant's activity, which easily leads to specific jurisdiction.

[275] Brand, '2005 Report: A View from the U.S.', at 18.

[276] See above Sect. 7.5.2.

[277] As explained in Chapter 5, Sect. 5.6.3; H. Müller, *Die Gerichtspflichtigkeit wegen 'doing business': Ein Vergleich Zwischen Dem U.S.-amerikanischen und dem deutschen Zuständigkeitssystem* (1992), Vol. 89, at 25; and J. Bertele, *Souveränität und Verfahrensrecht: Ein untersuchung der aus dem Völkerrecht ableitbaren Grenzen staatlicher extraterritoriale Jurisdiktion im Verfahrensrecht* (1998), at 224-241.

ated, the following statement of Mann illustrates the far-reaching impact of this basis for jurisdiction:

> 'If anyone asks for practical advice ... one can only say this: never hold any discussions or negotiations in the United States and if a contract is concluded sign it outside the United States and provide for the exclusive jurisdiction of a non American court or include a well-drafted and carefully considered arbitration clause.'[278]

The basis of transacting business asserts jurisdiction on a relatively weak connection with the forum in comparison with its European counterparts which establish a special connection.[279] In this respect, it should be kept in mind that the due process standards, including the 'purposeful availment' requirement and the fairness and reasonableness considerations are particularly relevant for the final exercise of transacting jurisdiction.[280]

7.5.5 The Failed Hague Compromise: Branch and Transacting Business

At an early stage, in 1994, branch jurisdiction was included among the bases of jurisdiction that 'might be admitted'.[281] It was proposed to assert jurisdiction to the place of the 'location of a business establishment or branch office in connection with the proceedings arising from business transacted by such establishment or branch office'. Its purpose was to provide an additional jurisdiction rule alongside the defendant's 'home court' criterion[282] and it was modelled after other 'international conventions' such as the Brussels Convention.[283] Further discussion was considered useful to delimit the reach of branch jurisdiction or '*gares principales*' which was primarily defined as a 'branch, establishment or centre of activity'.[284] Initially, The Hague Draft primarily followed the European version of 'branch' jurisdiction which required a fixed place of establishment.

But negotiators at The Hague rapidly realized that the U.S. activity-based jurisdiction should be integrated into the branch provision to meet the wishes of the U.S. delegation and to find common grounds for international jurisdiction rules.[285]

---

278 Mann, 'The Doctrine of International Jurisdiction Revisited', at 72.

279 See *Burger King v. Rudzewicz*, 471 U.S. 462 (1975); R.C. Casad and W.M. Richman, *Jurisdiction in Civil Actions* (1998), Vol. 1, § 2-5[ii], at 150-151.

280 See Chapter 5, Sect. 5.4.3.3 and *Hanson v. Denckla*, 357 U.S. 235 (1985).

281 'Prel. Doc. No. 1 of May 1994: Checklist Special Commission', at 12. Compare this with the 1971 Hague Convention where Art. 10(2) states that 'the court of the State of origin shall be considered to have jurisdiction, if the defendant had, in the State of origin, at the time when the proceedings were instituted, a commercial, industrial or other business establishment, or a branch office, and was cited there in proceedings arising from business transacted by such establishment or branch office'.

282 'Prel. Doc. No. 1 of May 1994: Checklist Special Commission', at 10 and 12; and Kessedjian, 'Prel. Doc. No. 7: 1997 Report', § 123, at 37.

283 'Prel. Doc. No. 2 of 1995: Conclusions Special Commission', § 14, at 15.

284 Kessedjian, 'Prel. Doc. No. 7: 1997 Report', § 123, at 37; Kessedjian, 'Prel. Doc. No. 8 of June 1997: Synthesis Special Commission', § 32 and § 88.

285 See Kessedjian, 'Prel. Doc. No. 9, March 1998, Synthesis Special Commission', at 31, explaining 'jurisdiction based on activities'; see also Brand, 'Understanding Activity-Based', at 35; Brand, '2005 Report: A View from the U.S.', at 19, referring to its previous form in Working Document 144 of November 1998 [on file with author].

Jurisdiction purely based on defendant's activities in the forum, such as transacting business jurisdiction was unknown to other participating states. But it was reported that, 'the stakes are significant' and jurisdiction based on activities needed to be carefully considered.[286] Rapporteur Kessedjian described activity-based jurisdiction as the idea that when 'a person or entity has engaged in activities in a given territory and this activity has given rise to litigation, the person or entity may be brought before courts in that territory with jurisdiction to decide the dispute.'[287] The fact that activity-based jurisdiction is 'essentially based on factual notions as opposed to legal notions' makes it difficult to draft.[288] The 'density of activity' was considered difficult to establish; for instance the negotiators considered whether 'solicitation of clients' should constitute 'activity-based jurisdiction'.[289] The idea of jurisdiction based on an open norm measuring the business activities in the forum was difficult to accept for civil law jurisdictions where the principle of foreseeability is given considerable weight.

The result was Article 9(1), conferring jurisdiction based on 'Branches and Regular Commercial Activity', which is identical under the 1999 Preliminary Draft Convention on Jurisdiction and the 2001 Interim Text. The article states that

> 'A plaintiff may bring an action in the courts of a State in which a branch, agency or any other establishment of the defendant is situated, [, or where the defendant has carried on regular commercial activity by other means,] provided that the dispute relates directly to the activity of that branch, agency or other establishment [or to that regular commercial activity].'

This proposed Article 9 is primarily focussed on defendant's activities carried out by a branch, agency or other establishment and remained clearly modelled on the Brussels's version of branch jurisdiction.[290] The claim should arise out of the branch's activity, but it was not required that the activity itself was carried out in the forum, as long as the (branch-) establishment carrying out the claim-related activities was situated in the forum.[291] Most significant in relation to the above explained differences, is the requirement that the establishment should operate from a fixed place of business.[292]

The bracketed activity-based language of Article 9 – 'or where the defendant has carried on regular commercial activity by other means' – was incorporated to meet U.S. jurisdictional standards. There was no consensus to insert this basis of 'regular commercial activity'. The attempt to define the degree of 'activity' failed

---

[286] Kessedjian, 'Prel. Doc. No. 9 of March 1998: Synthesis Special Commission', § 70, at 31.

[287] Ibid., § 69, at 31.

[288] Ibid., § 71, at 31.

[289] Ibid., § 70, at 31: 'What is the nature, frequency or magnitude of the activity that will allow a defendant to be brought into the territory of the forum?'.

[290] The purpose is to assert jurisdiction on the basis of 'activities' covering contracts and torts as suggested by Kessedjian, see Kessedjian, 'Prel. Doc. No. 9 of March 1998: Synthesis Special Commission', § 68-70, at 31. The ILA project equally distinguishes between branch jurisdiction and activity jurisdiction, see McLachlan, 'Final Report Jurisdiction over Corporations', § 26, at 421.

[291] Nygh-Pocar Report, at 53.

[292] Ibid.

although it was clear that 'regular commercial activity' does not require any 'establishment in the forum'.[293] According to Brand this 'activity-based' language is a

> 'logical extension of this development of a joint court-claim and court-defendant nexus, by acknowledging that, in today's world, limitation to the physical presence of a branch, agency or establishment does not encompass what corporations really do. Corporations act through persons, not things and those persons may be every bit as active and present in states in which no physical establishment exists.'[294]

The requirement of 'regular' business activities reduces the scope of Article 9 and imposes that more than just a single isolated act or transaction is sufficient under U.S. transacting business.[295]

The provision was however not discussed 'pending general discussion of the "activity jurisdiction" elsewhere', which refers to the integration of 'activity-based language' in other provisions such as contract jurisdiction.[296] As will be demonstrated below,[297] the informal Ottawa negotiations of February 2001[298] attempted to incorporate activity-based language in the provision specifically dealing with contractual claims under Article 6. This 'Ottawa Contracts Alternative' tried to find a corresponding rule for contract jurisdiction by providing a defendant-related basis for jurisdiction when defendant has directed activities into that state.[299] A separate provision for activity-based jurisdiction under Article 9 would replace or supersede the activity-based language in contracts.[300]

The main achievement of this bracketed provision with activity-based language is that it has opened new doors to a different and broader scope of a mere branch jurisdiction.[301] In the opinion of Brand, it forms the basis for common grounds compatible with U.S. jurisdictional practice:

> 'while activity-based jurisdiction can be faulted as the source of difficulties thatwere not overcome, I also believe it is this concept that allows consideration in major legal systems, and thus the analytical point that indicates possible common ground on which successful rules of jurisdiction might have been developed.'[302]

---

[293] Alternative A – in variant 1 – 'activity' means one or more of the following – '[regular and substantial] promotion of the commercial or professional ventures of the defendant for the conclusion of contracts of this kind; the defendant's regular or extended presence for the purpose of negotiating contracts of this kind, provided that the contract in question was performed at least in part in that State'. Or variant 2 – 'activity' includes, *inter alia*, 'the promotion, negotiation, and performance of a contract'.

[294] Brand, 'Understanding Activity-Based', at 39.

[295] Nygh-Pocar Report, at 57.

[296] See The Hague 2001 Interim Text, fn. 63.

[297] See below Sect. 7.6.4.

[298] Informational note on the work of the informal meetings held since October 1999 to consider and develop drafts on outstanding items *drawn up by the Permanent Bureau; Preliminary Document No. 15 of May 2001 for the attention of the nineteenth Session of June 2001*, Annex I. See Brand, 'Understanding Activity-Based', at 37; Brand, '2005 Report: A View from the U.S.', at 24.

[299] Brand, 'Understanding Activity-Based', at 37. Brand, '2005 Report: A View from the U.S.', at 24.

[300] Arts. 6 and 10, respectively; The Hague 1999 Preliminary Draft Convention and 2001 Interim Text; see Nygh-Pocar Report, at 48.

[301] Ibid., at 56.

[302] Brand, 'Understanding Activity-Based', at 39; Brand, '2005 Report: A View from the U.S.', at 28.

It is interesting to mention that Article 9 of the Buenos Aires Protocol on International Jurisdiction in Contractual Matters extends the respondent's domicile in the forum to corporation's branches, establishments, agencies, or any kind of representation in the forum and subjects it to jurisdiction in matters concerning the operations conducted there.[303]

7.5.6 Subsidiaries and Other Aspects of Activity-based Jurisdiction

Jurisdiction over the defendant outside his home court on the basis of carrying out commercial activities in another forum through a secondary establishment, generally involves an establishment which does not possess legal personality and is considered as a single unit in respect of the corporate defendant.[304] This is not the case for subsidiaries which are separate legal entities carrying out their own business.[305] Jurisdiction rules generally do not subject a (parental) company on the simple basis that it has a subsidiary or other affiliated company on its forum. There are two exceptions to this rule.

First, it is possible that an independent subsidiary, as a separate legal entity, acts on behalf of its parent and hereby carries out business for its parental authority. When the subsidiary is, either explicitly or by given appearance, acting on behalf of the parent with the authority to bind him, then the parent acts through its subsidiary, in which case the subsidiary acts in the capacity of a branch as set out above. This 'subsidiary acting as a branch' jurisdiction is accepted in most civil law countries and by the Brussels Model.[306] English common law takes the same position; a company can be considered present through a subsidiary acting on behalf of the company.[307] If this were not the case, this would mean that a foreign company with a branch (office) in England is subjected to English jurisdiction, but if it is carrying out business through a wholly owned subsidiary it would not.[308] A similar approach is taken by the U.S. jurisdictional scheme where jurisdiction over an overseas defendant who carries out business in the forum through a second body in the forum is possible.[309] In sum, the jurisdictional systems have in common that in order to attribute the subsidiary's activities to its parent, it should act

[303] Art. 9(1), MERCOSUR/CMC/DEC. Nº 01/94.

[304] Mann, 'The Doctrine of International Jurisdiction Revisited', at 49: '... for in law the company and its branches are a single unit'.

[305] This principle of legal separability between parental bodies and their subsidiaries is even established as a matter of international law. See the ICJ case *Barcelona Traction, Light and Power Corp. Ltd.*, where the Court claims that 'it follows that as a matter of international law parent and subsidiaries are each subject to the excusive jurisdiction of their respective sovereigns', (1970) ICJ Rep., at 4. See also *Adams v. Cape Industries Plc and others*, Court of Appeal, [1990] Ch. 433, at 532, 'There is no general principle that all companies in a group of companies are to be regarded as one. On the contrary, the fundamental principle is that "each company in a group of companies (a relatively modern concept) is a separate legal entity possessed of separate legal rights and liabilities".' See Mann, 'The Doctrine of International Jurisdiction Revisited', at 56.

[306] The leading case under the Brussels Regulation is Case 218/86 *Schotte v. Parfums Rotschild*, 9 December 1987, [1987] ECR, at 04905.

[307] See J. Fawcett, 'Jurisdiction and Subsidiaries', *Journal of Business Law* (1985), 16, at 16-17.

[308] Ibid. for an exhaustive overview of both U.K. and U.S. law, at 16.

[309] As discussed in Chapter 5, Sect. 5.6.5.

on its behalf and have the authority to bind the defendant or give the appearance to a third party that it is conducting business activities on behalf of its parent defendant.[310] Whether or not a subsidiary is carrying out the business of the parent rather than its own business comes down to the question whether the subsidiary has the authority to contractually bind the parent and the degree of control of the parent over the subsidiary.

The ILA project on 'Jurisdiction over corporations' adopted a similar position towards subsidiaries in its Report of the Seventieth Conference: 'As regards the meaning of the word "branch" it was agreed that a subsidiary is not a branch. It is of the essence of a branch that it forms a part of the legal structure of the corporation.'[311] However, 'under the circumstances a subsidiary could be an agent'.[312]

When the subsidiary did not have the authority to bind the parent or did not give such appearance to third parties, it might be argued that the parent and the subsidiary are in fact one single entity and that the parent should also be sued in the forum where the subsidiary is located. In this case it is a matter of an *alter ego* of the corporate defendant. If proven, the court seized will then be asked to ignore the separation made by law between the two legal entities and instead consider them as one single economic unit. This request requires the court to lift the corporate veil for jurisdictional purposes which protects the parent from being sued for business activities carried out by a subsidiary.[313] If the court lifts the corporate veil the claimant finds a competent court besides the parent's home court where the subsidiary is located. Such a jurisdictional lift of the corporate veil is unfamiliar to Continental Europe but more common in England and the U.S., even it is not current jurisdiction practice.

This aspect of jurisdiction over corporate entities and the question of separate legal corporate personality were already given quite some attention by the Permanent Bureau of The Hague Conference at an early stage of the Worldwide Hague Jurisdiction Project.[314] From the beginning the Permanent Bureau opted for the adoption of branch jurisdiction limited to establishments without legal personality.[315] The 2001 Interim Text explicitly states that a legal entity shall not be considered a 'branch, agency or other establishment' by the mere fact that the legal entity is a subsidiary of the defendant. Or, to put it differently and as clarified by the Interim Text itself 'a subsidiary, even one that is wholly owned by a parent, will

---

[310] See Fawcett, 'A New Approach to Jurisdiction over Companies', at 654; and Fawcett, 'Jurisdiction and Subsidiaries', at 20.

[311] McLachlan, 'Final Report Jurisdiction over Corporations', § 28, at 421.

[312] Ibid., § 29, at 421.

[313] See for an exhaustive overview of English law on the lifting of the corporate veil, *Adams and Others v. Cape Industries Plc. and Another*, Court of Appeal, [1990] Ch. 433, at 532-545.

[314] See Kessedjian, 'Prel. Doc. No. 7: 1997 Report', § 123, at 36; and see Annex IV which incorporates a Questionnaire on the matter of fictitious corporations drawn up by Kessedjian to examine when countries would allow the lifting of the corporate veil. Kessedjian, 'Prel. Doc. No. 8 of June 1997: Synthesis Special Commission', § 32; and Kessedjian, 'Prel. Doc. No. 9 of March 1998: Synthesis Special Commission', § 85, at 37.

[315] Kessedjian, 'Prel. Doc. No. 7: 1997 Report', § 123, fn. 151, at 37.

not – by that fact alone – be regarded as falling within the definition of "a branch, agency or other establishment".'[316]

A similar provision is found in the ILA project, where the subsidiary is considered a branch when the subsidiary has *de facto* no independent existence and the corporate veil can be lifted. In this context Principle 3.2 of Resolution 4/2002 is worth mentioning:

> 'Where a corporation operates in a state through a subsidiary or other related corporation in circumstances where that second corporation has no independent existence in fact, since the first corporation takes all material decisions as to the conduct of the business of the second corporation, the second corporation shall be treated as a branch of the first corporation for the purposes of the preceding [branch] rule.'[317]

Apart from that ILA principle, little attention is given to economic realities in the parent-subsidiary relationship for jurisdiction purposes. To the discontent of some authors, the current jurisdictional approach applies juridical and formalistic concepts such as 'branch' or 'agency' instead of considering the economic nature of these corporate structures.[318]

7.5.7 Evaluation of *Defendant-related* Jurisdiction: Defendant's Business Activities

7.5.7.1 *Doing Business*

What makes 'doing business' jurisdiction so highly controversial, including in the U.S. itself?[319] With respect to international minimum standards for uniform jurisdiction a substantial close connection between the defendant and the forum is guaranteed, while doing business exercises jurisdiction on the basis of 'continuous and systematic' contacts with the forum.

Regarding the protection of the parties and the equality of arms, it does not seem unfair to the defendant to have a suit filed against him at the place where he continuously and systematically carries out business activities, even if he does so without having a fixed place of business. It also provides the claimant with another available forum at the place where the defendant does business.

At first sight, the rule seems relatively foreseeable in the sense that a claimant and defendant are both able to determine whether or not the defendant is doing

[316] Art. 9(2) of The Hague 2001 Interim Text, fn. 64: 'there was no consensus on this article'. In the Edinburgh meeting Japan submitted a request to put on the black list jurisdiction based on the mere location of a subsidiary or other related entity of the defendant in that state (25 April 2001, Edinburgh), as enshrined in Annex VI-A; Prel. Doc. No. 15 of May 2001, Informational note.

[317] McLachlan, 'Final Report Jurisdiction over Corporations', § 32, at 422-423.

[318] See P. Muchlinski, 'Corporations in International Litigation: Problems of Jurisdiction and the United Kingdom Asbestos Case', 50 *The International and Comparative Law Quarterly* (2001), 1-25, at 1; Fawcett, 'Jurisdiction and Subsidiaries'; see also Whincop, *Policy and Pragmatism*, at 178, who claims that 'conventional approaches to jurisdiction have difficulty with the corporate group'.

[319] W. O'Brian Jr., 'The Hague Convention on Jurisdiction and Judgments: The Way Forward', 66 *The Modern Law Review* (2003), 491-509, at 496; Schack, *Minimum Contacts Scrutinized*, at 39; Von Mehren and Trautmann, 'Jurisdiction to Adjudicate', at 1144.

business in the forum. The rule provides for flexibility by the use of an open-ended norm which inevitably results in a certain degree of appreciation, possibly to the detriment of legal certainty. General doing business jurisdiction is determined by a factual evaluation of defendant's contacts: they continuous and systematic enough? Legal certainty and determinability would certainly benefit from further explanation of what should constitute 'doing business', preferably by autonomous concepts instead of depending on open-ended standards as developed by the U.S. Supreme Court.[320] According to Brand, there is 'no bright line rule for determining when the threshold is crossed on the spectrum from activities which are not sufficient to support jurisdiction to those which are sufficient' to support general jurisdiction over a defendant.[321]

The principal objection against the 'doing business' criterion is, above all, that it provides for *general* jurisdiction. The fact that the rule does not require that the claim arises out of the business activities in the forum makes the rule unacceptable for a uniform jurisdiction rule. Introducing general doing business jurisdiction as a uniform rule would result in a competent forum over any kind of claim, in each of the countries where a defendant is doing business. Such a rule would result in an excessively wide range of competent fora for the plaintiff to choose from. In the context of The Hague Conference Jurisdiction Project, the participating countries – the U.S.'s delegation in particular – were most reluctant to accept a general doing business jurisdiction rule as an acceptable uniform jurisdiction rule, fearing that (U.S.) multinationals doing business all over the world could become amenable for suit over any kind of claim in all parts of the world where they were doing business. This is well explained by Borchers:

> 'General jurisdiction in the U.S. is potentially too broad in that the "continuous and systematic contacts" basis can allow for jurisdiction over large enterprises in any of the fifty states. … The problem with the continuous and systematic contacts test is that it does far more than simply authorize jurisdiction in the defendant's "home"; with large enterprises it authorizes jurisdiction almost anywhere….'[322]

Apart from the general exercise of jurisdiction, the foundation of 'doing business' jurisdiction as such, should not in all its facets be considered 'exorbitant' and should not be put on the black list of the Hague Project in its totality.[323] Moreover, it could be deplored that there has been no effort to include the U.S. doing business jurisdiction in the list of required bases of jurisdiction in a more limited version that would confer special jurisdiction on the basis of defendant's activities. According to Nygh the Hague negotiations were pointing in that direction:

---

[320] See Nygh, 'Criteria for Judicial Jurisdiction', at 10, 'The point is that we should not have terminology in a convention that would require a Justice of the Supreme Court of the United States to explain it to us.'

[321] R. Brand, 'Tort Jurisdiction in a Multilateral Convention: The Lessons of the Due Process Clause and the Brussels Convention', *Brooklyn Journal of International Law* (1998), 125-155, at 135.

[322] Borchers, 'Comparing Jurisdiction', at 136.

[323] See also Mann, 'The Doctrine of International Jurisdiction Revisited', at 70-71.

> 'At present, in most common law jurisdictions the presence of a branch of a foreign corporation leads to a general jurisdiction regardless of where the cause of action arises. However, the growing consensus is that jurisdiction should be confined to litigation arising out of business transacted through the branch.'[324]

On the other hand, the elimination of the *general* doing business rule in the context of a world-wide convention was considered '*politically unachievable*' for the U.S.[325] Some have stressed that giving up the general jurisdiction basis 'is not much of a price to pay' for the U.S.,[326] since, as explained in the previous chapter, the claimant will first try to establish *specific* jurisdiction for a U.S. court.[327] Accordingly it has been stated that '[i]t is not easy to find a case where an American court has really assumed jurisdiction on that [doing business] ground in an international context under circumstances where no reasonable basis of specific jurisdiction could have been found.'[328] When the uniform rule is restricted to contractual claims, it should be self-evident that doing business in a forum creates jurisdiction with respect to contractual disputes arising out of those businesses. It is also a logical consequence that a defendant should not be amenable for suit in every forum where he does business over contractual claims which are by no means related to his business activities carried out in those forums. Such wide basis for general jurisdiction is no longer necessary if the scope of uniform rules is limited to contractual disputes and a uniform rule covers most of the scope of the doing business rule.[329]

7.5.7.2 *Business-establishments and Branches*

As a result of the above, jurisdiction based on defendant's activities in the forum, should be limited to claims related to or arising out of those activities. The under-

---

[324] Nygh, 'Criteria for Judicial Jurisdiction', at A-11.

[325] O'Brian Jr., 'The Hague Convention on Jurisdiction', at 496, referring to the Kovar letter. Attention was drawn to the fact that the U.S. already gave up general doing business under the Warsaw Convention on Air Transportation. See Schlosser, 'Bases of Jurisdiction', at A-22; and Schlosser in Lowenfeld and Silberman, eds., *The Hague Convention on Jurisdiction*, at 19: 'I must say, I cannot see any legitimate interest of any state in exercising general jurisdiction on the basis of doing business. The United States already gave up doing business as a basis of general jurisdiction when acceding to the Warsaw Convention on Air Transportation, in which Art. 28 designate only domicile or principal place of business of the carrier, the place where the ticket was purchased, and the place of destination as possible fora.'

[326] Schlosser, 'Bases of Jurisdiction', at A-21, referring to R. Weintraub, 'How Substantial Is Our Need for a Judgments-Recognition Convention and What Should We Bargain Away to Get It?', *Brooklyn Journal of International Law* (1998), 167-220, at 188.

[327] Explained in Chapter 6, Sect. 6.2.4.

[328] Schlosser, 'Bases of Jurisdiction', at A-21.

[329] Gaudemet-Tallon, rephrased by Trooboff in Lowenfeld and Silberman, eds., *The Hague Convention on Jurisdiction*, at 22: 'Let's think about where, if we develop sufficiently clear and broad enough bases of specific jurisdiction in the tort area, in the contract area, the Americans still need doing business with respect to general jurisdiction, the ability to assert jurisdiction over a legal entity for continuous and systematic presence, even if the cause of action is unrelated. The question put more succinctly is: Do you need such general jurisdiction if you have sufficiently clear and broad specific jurisdiction in the areas of need?'

lying idea of jurisdiction based on the defendant carrying out a business activity in the forum is that when a person engages in commercial activity in a country, with the purpose of obtaining certain advantages or benefits, 'it seems normal that he will also be subject to the judicial jurisdiction of that state' with respect to the claims related to that activity.[330] The acceptance of jurisdiction based on defendant's activities carried out in the forum for uniform rules in contractual disputes depends 1) on the 'density' of the activity and 2) on the determination of relevant activities for jurisdiction purposes and 3) on the claim-relatedness.

Jurisdiction based on the fact that the defendant established a *fixed* place of business or branch office is an acceptable uniform jurisdiction rule for contractual disputes, provided that the claim relates to commercial activities carried out by the defendant through that branch-establishment *in that forum*.

The place of establishment guarantees a substantial *defendant-related* connection with the forum. Such basis reflects a solid territorial *and commercial* connection between the defendant and the forum justifying jurisdiction over claims related to or arising from the activities carried out in the forum. This basis of jurisdiction is characterized by the defendant's activities and not by the nature or the type of claim: thus it avoids complex classifications of contracts. The sole requirement is that the claim arose out of these activities. The phenomenon of 'sleeping branches' in the sense that the branch is not continuously carrying out activity, but only occasionally, does not take away from the fact that the defendant has established a 'secondary establishment' in the forum from which he has carried out business and that those activities are at the origin of legal proceedings instituted against him.

With respect to the protection of the parties, when a defendant established a place of business he certainly voluntarily connected with the forum for commercial purposes and obtains certain advantages or benefits. It is not unfair to subject a defendant to a court in a place where he established branches or places of business in order to carry out business activities to obtain commercial benefits in that forum, as long as it involves claims directly related to or arising out of those activities.[331] The fact that the rule might in practice result in a *forum actoris* is under those circumstances not at all problematic: on the contrary this activity-based jurisdiction provides the plaintiff with a competent forum based on a solid connection between the defendant and the forum, provided that the claim arose from his activities.

Asserting jurisdiction on the basis of the fact that the defendant established a fixed place of business brings a considerable degree of legal certainty to both parties. The forum is easily determinable and for those reasons predictable and

---

[330] See Buchner in Lowenfeld and Silberman, eds., *The Hague Convention on Jurisdiction*, at 24-25.

[331] Again see Buchner in Lowenfeld and Silberman, eds., *The Hague Convention on Jurisdiction*, at 24-25; 'In choosing grounds of jurisdiction based on conduct related to the cause of action, the basic consideration is that when someone is engaged in a commercial activity in a country, he has to comply with all sorts of prescription relating to such activity, in such a way that it would seem normal that he will also be subject to the judicial jurisdiction of that state. Once you are purposely developing an activity in a country, you should not be surprised to be brought before the courts of such country when the cause of action is related to such activity. In such a case, the defendant should not be privileged compared to plaintiffs.'

foreseeable to both parties. A 'fixed place of business' or 'business-establishment' should be understood as an identifiable establishment or building from which the defendant carries out activities outside his home forum. A fixed place of business is wider than the European concept of a branch imposing a number of requirements and characteristics to constitute a branch in the sense of Article 5(5) Brussels Model. It is narrower that the U.S. doing business as the latter does not require the defendant to have a fixed or physical establishment or office in the forum; mere continous and systematic contacts for instance in the form of regular visits to the forum for business negotiations could be sufficient for U.S. doing business jurisdiction. Whether a certain degree of flexibility is advisable in certain situations remains to be seen, but the fixed place of business-establishment could be formulated by an open norm providing for sufficient flexibility. There seems to be little situations in which the facts of the case would demand a flexible approach, when a defendant has clearly established a fixed place of business from which he is carrying out business activities and the claim arises out of the business activities of that business-establishment.

7.5.7.3 *Transacting Business*

At first sight, it does not seem unfair to subject the defendant to jurisdiction of the place where he 'transacted' business. Like the branch-establishment, transacting business is based on a *defendant-related* connection pursuant to his activities within the forum. Nonetheless, transacting business as understood in the U.S. allows jurisdiction on the mere basis of a 'single transaction' or an 'isolated or occasional contact', as long as the claim or cause of action is related to the contact.[332] Transacting business does not require any regular or substantial activity in the forum nor does it require a place of business-establishment in the forum. As a consequence, transacting business implies jurisdiction based on the promotion of defendant's activities, the negotiations of business deals, or the performance of the contract.[333] In fact, although the rule is based on *defendant-related* connections with the forum, it does not ensure a *substantial* connection with the forum.[334]

Transacting business is a typical example of national jurisdictional provisions ensuring an extraterritorial reach over a foreign defendant as far as possible. Such 'aggressive use of extraterritorial jurisdiction' is not suitable as uniform jurisdiction rule.[335] International contracts and business relationships are not confined to one state and the defendant is likely to have 'single or occasional contacts' with several states, just as the contractual claim could arise from or be related to defendant's activities carried out in several states. If transacting business forms the basis

---

[332] Specific jurisdiction bases under the 'minimum contacts' theory discussed in Chapter 5, Sect. 5.6.3.

[333] See also Trooboff in Lowenfeld and Silberman, eds., *The Hague Convention on Jurisdiction*, at 23.

[334] See Chapter 6, Sect. 6.5.1, for the close connection parameter requiring more than a 'point of contact'.

[335] A. Johnston and E. Powles, 'The Kings of the World and Their Dukes' Dilemma: Globalisation, Jurisdiction and the Rule of Law', in *Globalisation and Jurisdiction* (2004), 13-54, at 41.

of a uniform jurisdiction rule, it would create jurisdiction in a multitude of countries and provide claimant with an excessively wide choice among competent fora. The result of a wide range of competent fora is problematic in the light of the equality of arms constituting a particular disadvantage to the defendant.

The final objection concerns the principle of legal certainty. The balance between legal certainty and flexibility is difficult to find when this open-ended rule is to be determined on the basis of an appreciation of the quantity *and* the quality of isolated and single 'business contacts', without any further guidance on what constitutes 'transacting business'. Vagueness of the language is often and rightfully a concern for uniform jurisdiction rules. Nygh argues that '[p]hrases such as "arising out of activities regularly carried on within or directed to that State" do not have much content and lead to confusion.'[336]

The rule is highly flexible, which is often considered as securing litigational justice,[337] but transacting business is not fair to either the claimant or the defendant: the defendant is unable to foresee to which court he will be subjected. Conversely, the claimant will have little comfort in the vagueness of the rule to know whether his interpretation of 'transacting business' will be the same as that of the court seized.

7.6 *Claim-related* Bases for Contractual Claims

Contract jurisdiction or *forum contractus* should be understood as jurisdiction established on the specific connection between the court and the claim arising out of a contract.

An important feature of contract jurisdiction is that it is limited to claims involving contractual matters and as a consequence exercises special – or specific – jurisdiction. Special contract jurisdiction rules use connecting factors which are claim-related. The majority of provisions regulating contract jurisdiction rules apply to any kind of commercial contracts, some regulate jurisdiction over particular contracts such as the sale of goods.

7.6.1 General Observations

Contract jurisdiction plays a dominant role in civil law countries and the Brussels Model, but is considerably less important in Anglo-American jurisdictional regimes. Each of the Continental European regimes surveyed has special jurisdiction rules for contractual disputes. Even the Dutch regime to which the *forum contractus* was unknown prior to the 2001 Dutch reform, accepts special contract jurisdiction.[338] In most of these national systems the *forum contractus* has a sub-

---

[336] Nygh, 'Criteria for Judicial Jurisdiction', at A-8.

[337] Von Mehren, 'Theory and Practice', at 70-71: 'Contrariwise, specific jurisdiction based on such intrinsically unpredictable and difficult to administer connecting factors as "minimum contacts" or "purposeful availment" is far more sensitive to litigational justice than to administrability and predictability concerns.'

[338] See Chapter 3, Sect. 3.2.3; and M. Weser, *La convention communautaire sur la compétence judiciaire et l'exécution des décisions: Etude des droits internes et des traités bilatéraux des Etats contractants* (1975), at 118; and Strikwerda, *De Overeenkomst in het IPR*, fn. 64, at 31.

sidiary character. In Germany, Switzerland, Spain and Italy the rule only applies when the defendant is not domiciled in the state.[339] As a result, contract jurisdiction provides for an additional basis to render the courts of the respective forum competent when a contractual dispute is linked with the forum and involves a non-resident defendant. The *forum contractus* has a slightly different position in the French jurisdictional scheme as it stands on equal footing with the *forum rei* rule[340] and prevails over the nationality-based jurisdiction of Articles 14 and 15 of the French Civil Code.[341]

English common law rules on jurisdiction allow the plaintiff to ask permission to serve a defendant outside England when the claim concerns a contract. The English version of contract jurisdiction under Rule 6.20(5)-(7) of the CPR differs from its Continental European counterparts with respect to the connecting factors applied, but has a similar objective; when the defendant is not present in the forum, English courts can subsidiarily exercise jurisdiction on the basis that there is a connection between the contractual claim and England.

Provisions especially designed for jurisdiction over contractual claims are significantly less common in the U.S. The jurisdictional scheme is principally concerned with defendant's contacts and activities carried out in or directed to the forum. Jurisdiction based on the nexus between the contract and the forum is far from being the focus of the U.S. jurisdictional system.

Whether a comparable basis for 'contract jurisdiction' exists in the U.S. jurisdictional scheme depends on the provisions enacted in the long-arm statutes.[342] General long-arm statutes, such as the Californian Statute, confer jurisdiction on any 'constitutional basis' and have not incorporated specific provisions dealing with contractual matters. Most enumerated long-arm statutes include *transacting business* provisions that cover contractual claims when defendant has purposefully directed contacts to the forum.[343] When the defendant entered the state to engage services or to conclude or promote a contract, it constitutes a contact with the forum, which *could* lead to jurisdiction provided that it is consistent with due process standards.[344] It is not required that these contacts arise out of a contractual relationship. For those reasons, activity-based jurisdiction is not comparable to a *forum contractus*. Activity-based jurisdiction – as opposed to contract jurisdiction – justifies jurisdiction on the basis of a connection between defendant's activities and the forum. In that sense, activity-based jurisdiction has a wider reach than con-

[339] See also Weser, *La convention communautaire*, at 117-118.

[340] By transposition of Art. 46(3) NCCP applied to international disputes; Chapter 3, Sect. 3.4.2.

[341] See for nationality-based jurisdiction Chapter 3, Sect. 3.4.3.

[342] Chapter 5, Sect. 5.3.1; see also Müller, *Die Gerichtspflichtigkeit wegen 'doing business'*, at 46-47: '*Die Art der spezifischen Kontakte ist häufig in long-arm statutes konkret geregelt.*'

[343] See Chapter 5, Sect. 5.4.3.3; and R. Brand, 'Due Process, Jurisdiction and a Hague Judgments Convention', *University of Pittsburgh Law Review* (1999), 661-706, at 692.

[344] According to Brand 'even if it is enough under the long-arm statute, courts have ruled that "merely entering into a contract" in a state, or with a resident of the state, will not be enough, without more, to establish the minimum contacts necessary to Fourteenth Amendment due process analysis. Brand, 'Due Process, Jurisdiction', at 692.

tract jurisdiction and the enactment of specific provisions dealing with contractual matters appears less necessary.[345]

Nonetheless, the mere execution of a contract or the performance of a contractual obligation is unlikely to suffice for jurisdiction under 'transacting business'.[346] For that reason, some enumerated statutes enacted specific provisions focussing especially on contractual contacts to cover situations in which defendant's activities alone do not constitute sufficient contact to support jurisdiction. To the example of the Uniform Interstate and International Procedure Act,[347] states enacted bases of jurisdiction dealing with contractual claims in order to reach the non-resident defendant, when the contract was 'made' or is 'to be performed' in the state.[348] Florida adopted a *place-of-performance* provision applicable to any type of contract and the New York long-arm Statute enacted a 'contract provision' limited to sales of goods and supply of services.[349] These two U.S. state provisions are comparable to European contract rules.

The difficulty for contract provisions in the U.S. jurisdictional framework lies in the fact that the ascertainment of jurisdiction has to comply with constitutional due process standards.[350] The Supreme Court held that a state could assert jurisdiction over a claim arising out of a contract with substantial connection with the forum, as long as it is in accordance with due process standards.[351] Due process requires primarily that the defendant purposefully availed himself of the privilege of conducting activities within the forum; secondly that the claim arises out of those purposeful activities; and finally that the exercise of jurisdiction is reasonable according to 'notions of fair play and substantial justice'.[352] This means that, unlike the *forum contractus* in Continental European systems and the Brussels Model, a simple connecting factor such as the place of performance in the U.S. forum is by itself insufficient for U.S. jurisdiction as it lacks any defendant-related connections.

The *forum contractus* under Article 5(1) of the Brussels Model is characterized by its alternative nature which provides the claimant with an additional competent forum besides the defendant's domicile. As a counterpart for the privilege given to the defendant under the maxim of the *actor sequitur forum rei*, the contract forum establishes a procedural balance between the parties.[353] Contract jurisdiction under

345 Brand, '2005 Report: A View from the U.S.', at 24.

346 Brand, 'Due Process, Jurisdiction', at 692.

347 Para. 1-3(a)(2) reads: 'a court may exercise personal jurisdiction over a person, … as to a cause of action arising from the person's contracting to supply services or things in this state.'

348 See also 2nd Restatement of Judgments, Chap. 2, § 4(b).

349 See Chapter 5, Sect. 5.6.4.

350 See Brand, '2005 Report: A View from the U.S.', at 18; H. Schack, *Der Erfüllungsort im deutschen, ausländischen und internationalen Privat- und Zivilprozeßrecht* (1985), § 299, at 208.

351 *McGee v. International Life Insurance Co.*, 355 U.S. 220, at 223 (1957), quoted by *Hanson v. Denckla*, 357 U.S. 235, at 252 (1958); and *Burger King v. Rudzewicz*, 471 U.S. 462, at 463 and 475 (1985).

352 See Chapter 5, Sect. 5.4.4. See Brand, 'Due Process, Jurisdiction', at 693. See also Müller, *Die Gerichtspflichtigkeit wegen 'doing business'*, at 47-48.

353 Several authors observed this counterweight of the forum contractus to the general jurisdiction rule of defendant's domicile. Schack, *Internationales Zivilverfahrensrecht*, § 256, at 93. This

the Brussels Model is an important and frequently used jurisdiction basis for that purpose.[354] The alternative nature of Article 5(1) is consistent with the purpose of a uniform jurisdiction regime which is to allocate jurisdiction among the courts of participating states, as opposed to national contract rules whose objective is to provide a 'second chance' to assert jurisdiction over non-resident defendants.[355] What the national contract jurisdiction provisions have in common with the unified system of Brussels is that the outcome of the rule often leads to a competent court at claimant's home court.

7.6.2 Definition and Classification Problems of 'Contractual Matters'

Contract jurisdiction automatically raises issues of definition and classification over 'contractual matters'.[356] The existence of a 'contractual relationship' is a prerequisite for contract jurisdiction. When the existence of a contract is disputed, the court seized is competent to rule on the existence of the contract, but will no longer have contract jurisdiction once it established that no contractual relationship exists between the parties. The scope of contract jurisdiction therefore depends on the definition of 'contract'. National contract jurisdiction rules are more often defined by the *lex fori* than by the *lex causae*.[357]

At unification level, the Brussels Model chose to delimit the scope of contract jurisdiction by providing an autonomous uniform concept of 'contractual matters'.[358] The ECJ decided that the concept under Article 5(1) should be interpreted autonomously, thus refusing to refer to the national legislation. Different interpretations in national law were considered to lead to misunderstandings at unification level. The ECJ's settled case law provides for a rich source of information on how to delimit the scope of a *forum contractus* and to define 'claims related to contractual matters'.[359] In relation to other specific jurisdiction rules such as tort jurisdiction, delimitation of contract jurisdiction is also important. Contract jurisdiction frequently overlaps with tort jurisdiction, especially with respect to claims arising at a pre-contractual stage.[360]

The Brussels Model and most Continental European systems distinguish between certain types of contracts such as consumer and employment contracts for

---

was already the background of the *forum contractus* under the *Codex Justinianum* according to H. Gaudemet-Tallon, *Origines de l'article14 CC* (1964), at 10. See Chapter 2, Sect. 2.7.1 and Chapter 6, Sect. 6.4.1.

354 K. Hertz, *Jurisdiction in Contract and Tort under the Brussels Convention* (1998), at 85.

355 Art. 5(1) also directly indicates the specific court internally competent within the Member States. (Chapter 2, Sect. 2.2.4 and see for the special Italian position Chapter 3, Sect. 3.1.1.)

356 See also Nygh-Pocar Report, at 48.

357 See Schack, *Der Erfüllungsort*, § 223, at 152; and Schack, *Internationales Zivilverfahrensrecht*, § 261, at 94.

358 See Chapter 2, Sect. 2.7.2.1.

359 For those reasons in contrast to national reports, special attention was given to the interpretation of 'contractual matters' by the ECJ under Art. 5(1).

360 See Chapter 2, Sect. 2.7.2.3 and the various decisions of the ECJ dealing with Art. 5(1) versus Art. 5(3); see also the analysed civil law countries and the English CPR Rules which require the classification of jurisdiction either as contractual under Rule 6.20(5)-(7) or as tortuous under Rule 6.20(8).

jurisdictional purposes.[361] Within those systems, policy considerations resulted in the protection of the weaker party by applying a different jurisdictional regime for consumer, insurance and employment contracts and derogating from the '*general*' contract jurisdiction rule. Such sub-classification of contracts equally determines and even reduces the scope of the *forum contractus*. In contrast, the English CPR Rules do not distinguish between different types of contracts and apply to any type of contract including employment and consumer contracts. Sub-classification of contracts is also unfamiliar to the U.S. Long-arm statutes which do not differentiate between different types of contracts. Most provisions regulating activity-based jurisdiction apply to all kind of claims, no special protection is offered with respect to consumers or employees or residence in a U.S. court.[362] Considerations of *fairness* and *reasonableness* under the due process standards will consider the specific circumstances of the defendant in the exercise of jurisdiction, but such considerations are not enshrined in the long-arm provision itself.[363] The Supreme Court's statement on minimum contacts and due process standards in the *McGee v. International Life Insurance Co.* case[364] dealt with a claim arising out of insurance contracts, but they apply to any claim arising out of any other type of contract.[365]

7.6.3 The Connecting Factors for 'Contract-based Jurisdiction'

A wide range of connecting factors are used for contract jurisdiction, among them are the place where the contract was formed, the place of the law governing the contract, the place of performance and the place where the contract was breached. Each of these connecting factors reflects a claim-related connection with the forum.

The majority of the contract provisions apply the place of performance. Such 'place-of-performance' rule often applies to all kinds of contracts,[366] and is considered as an 'omnibus' contract jurisdiction rule.[367] The rule exists in a number of variations, such as the *forum solutionis* or the *tailored place of performance* and principally determines what should be performed and where.[368] The place of performance rule can be a simple one, when the contractual obligation was performed under the contract, but in the event of non-performance or wrong performance,[369] the determination of the 'place of performance' is complex and recourse is sought in substantive law. Most jurisdictional systems allow parties to agree upon a place

[361] See for an exhaustive overview of the delimitation of *general* contracts with other *specific* contracts in the Brussels Convention and the Lugano Convention, L. Valloni, *Der Gerichtsstand des Erfüllungsortes nach Lugano- und Brüsseler-Übereinkommen* (1998), at 73-143.

[362] See for employment contracts R. Casad and W. Richman, *Jurisdiction in Civil Actions* (1998), Vol. 2, § 8-11[2], at 225-229.

[363] A. von Mehren, 'Adjudicatory Jurisdiction: General Theories Compared and Evaluated', 63 *Boston University Law Review* (1983), 279-340, at 313.

[364] 355 U.S. 220 (1957).

[365] See also Borchers, 'Comparing Jurisdiction', at 143.

[366] See for the historical background of this rule, Schack, *Der Erfüllungsort*, at 128-136.

[367] Briggs, *Conflict of Laws*, at 78-79.

[368] For instance, the place of the performance of the obligation in question is determined by the *lex causae*, the place of performance of the characteristic obligation and the place of payment.

[369] I.e. partially or defectively performed.

of performance for contract jurisdiction. Only in Germany, the regime imposes that the parties agreeing on a place of performance be '*kaufleute*', or merchants.[370] Such an agreed place of performance replaces the *forum solutionis* or even the *tailored place of performance*.[371] Generally such an agreement on the place of performance is void when the designated place is merely fictive and has as sole purpose a forum selection without complying with the requirement of a forum selection clause.[372]

7.6.3.1 *The* Forum Celebrationis – *The Place Where the Contract Was Formed*

The *forum celebrationis* should be understood as asserting jurisdiction at the place of the formation of the contract. It is one of the earlier connecting factors for contract jurisdiction under ancient Roman law.[373] The rule remains in use in some national jurisdictional schemes, even if the *forum celebrationis* lost considerable importance in modern times due to modern technology which no longer require the parties' presence to conclude contracts. In England, the CPR allows the claimant to request a leave for service out of the jurisdiction if the contract was made in England.[374] The Spanish reform on jurisdiction resulted in the complete integration of jurisdictional bases from the Brussels Convention, but remarkably also confers jurisdiction on Spanish courts when the contract was concluded in Spain.[375] The connecting factor was initially also known in Italy but was abrogated during the Italian reform[376] which was strongly influenced by the fact that the rule was marked exorbitant by Article 3(2) of the Brussels Convention.[377]

The U.S. minimum contacts approach to jurisdiction considers the place of the conclusion of the contract as a potential jurisdiction-creating contact.[378] Especially when the defendant established pre-contractual contacts with the forum, such as contract negotiations or other business activities in the forum for conclusion of a contract, this could lead to 'substantial and sufficient' contacts for U.S. juris-

---

[370] Art. 29(2) ZPO. This is in line with the German choice of court clause, which also requires that the parties should be merchants, see Art. 38 ZPO. See Chapter 3, Sect. 3.5.4.

[371] Parties are allowed to agree on a place of performance either explicitly or by tacit agreement. With respect to sales and service contracts, parties can agree upon a different place of performance than the place of delivery or the place of provision of services. See also Schack, *Der Erfüllungsort*, § 229, at 157.

[372] See Schack arguing that an agreed place of performance is misleading and should be refused for jurisdictional purposes, Schack, ibid., § 346, at 240..

[373] Under Roman law market places were the places where most contracts were concluded. Logically, the courts of these market places, '*juridictions des foires*' were given jurisdiction over contractual claims arising from contracts concluded at these markets as an alternative to the forum of the parties' domiciles. Gaudemet-Tallon, *Origines de l'article 14 CC*, at 62-67. A similar '*Mess und Markort*' was known in the German ZPO until 1996, see Schack, *Internationales Zivilverfahrensrecht*, § 256, at 93.

[374] Rule 6.20(5)(a) CPR.

[375] Art. 22(3) of the LOPJ is discussed in Chapter 3, Sect. 3.1.2.

[376] See Chapter 3, Sect. 3.1.1; and see J. Newton, *The Uniform Interpretation of the Brussels and Lugano Conventions* (2002), at 43.

[377] Strikwerda, *De Overeenkomst in het IPR*, at 32, remarks that the place of conclusion of the contract was considered by the drafters of the Brussels Convention, but was not incorporated since this would lead to multiplication of the forums.

[378] *Contra* Schack, *Minimum Contacts Scrutinized*, at 41-42; Müller, *Die Gerichtspflichtigkeit wegen 'doing business'*, at 49-50.

diction.[379] Some long-arm statutes even permit jurisdiction when the contract was made in the forum.[380] But contrary to the English, Spanish and former Italian provisions, the mere fact that the contract was concluded in the forum is by itself not automatically sufficient to provide for 'substantial minimum contact' under U.S. constitutional standards.[381] Due process requires the defendant to have 'knowingly' and 'purposefully' concluded the contract in the forum; the purposeful availment rule requires that the defendant could have foreseen that he would be subjected to jurisdiction and prevents jurisdiction when the contract was formed by coincidence.[382]

The exercise of jurisdiction at the *forum celebrationis* is not based on a *sufficient defendant-related* connection with the forum. The *place of the formation of the contract* is an arbitrary connecting factor that does not ensure a particular affiliation between the parties and the forum. It is not always evident where the contract was formed. Problems with determining the type of jurisdiction occur, especially when the final act binding the contract was signed or accepted in a different place than where the parties negotiated the contract. Moreover, the modern technological means available to conclude a contract make it difficult to localize the place of conclusion or formation of the contract. The place of conclusion of the contracts is outdated and coincidental which does not lead to legal certainty for the parties and makes it difficult to foresee which court is competent.

7.6.3.2 *The Place of the Law Governing the Contract*

When English law governs a contract, service out of England is available to render English courts competent to rule over the contractual dispute.[383] This rule is unique; among the systems surveyed it was only encountered in England. The rule mingles the jurisdictional question with the question of the applicable law; the law governing the contract needs to be determined first in order to establish jurisdiction of English courts.[384] The underlying idea behind this connecting factor is that the competent forum should apply its own law. [385]

Exercising jurisdiction on the basis that a particular law governs a contract is not based on the idea of a sufficient connection between the dispute and the forum.

---

[379] See Schack, *Minimum Contacts Scrutinized*, at 42-43; and Casad and Richman, *Jurisdiction in Civil Actions*, § 4-2[a](i), at 404; see Müller, *Die Gerichtspflichtigkeit wegen 'doing business'*, at 49.

[380] Some long-arm statutes incorporated specific contacts provisions to reach a non-resident defendant for contractual claims when the contract was 'made' in the state, according to the 2nd Restatement of Judgments, Chap. 2, § 4(b); see also Brand, 'Due Process, Jurisdiction', at 691.

[381] Brand states: 'Even if it is enough under the long-arm statute', ibid., at 692.

[382] R. Weintraub, *Commentary on the Conflict of Laws* (2006), § 4.18, at 245; Brand, 'Due Process, Jurisdiction', at 692; Borchers, 'Comparing Jurisdiction', at 138; Schack, *Minimum Contacts Scrutinized*, at 41.

[383] Rule 6.20(5)(c) CPR.

[384] There are other contract-connecting factors resorting to the applicable law of the contract for jurisdictional purposes. In order to determine the place of performance of the obligation in question for the *forum contractus* under Art. 5(1)(a) of the Brussels Regulation the applicable law to the contract needs to first be determined.

[385] See the principles of the *forum legis*, inspired by the *gleichlauf* principle, see Schack, *Internationales Zivilverfahrensrecht*, § 216, at 80.

When parties agreed upon an applicable law to govern the contract, a connection with the forum is not guaranteed, nor should a choice of the applicable law be considered as sufficient for a valid choice of forum. In the absence of a choice of law clause in the contract, complex determination by conflict of law rules requires that the applicable law be determined before addressing the jurisdiction question. This does not provide legal certainty for the parties, and result in an arbitrary determination of the competent court which may not necessarily be connected with the parties or the claim.

7.6.3.3 *The* Forum Solutionis – *Place of Performance of the Obligation in Question*

The *forum solutionis* indicates the place of performance of the contractual obligation upon which the claim is based, also referred to as the obligation in question. It should not be understood as the place of the completion of the contract, but only as the place of performance of the contractual obligation which forms the basis of the proceedings. If the plaintiff requires performance of a contractual pecuniary obligation, the place of payment will create jurisdiction.

As a consequence it could occur that the place of the completion of the contract does not have any particular connection with the dispute if it concerns a different contractual obligation.[386] This variation of the place of performance rule derives from the *specific performance* theory,[387] as opposed to the *characteristic performance* theory which refers to the characteristic obligation of the contract.[388]

Most Continental European countries, such as Germany, The Netherlands, Switzerland, Spain and Italy, apply the *forum solutionis* and assert jurisdiction to their courts if the obligation that forms the basis of the legal proceedings is, or should have been performed on the territory.[389] France does not apply the *forum solutionis.*

---

[386] Schack, *Der Erfüllungsort*, fns. 146-149, at 106-107.

[387] See J. Hill, 'Jurisdiction in Matters Relating to a Contract under the Brussels Convention', 44 *The International and Comparative Law Quarterly* (1995), 591, at 599.

[388] This other application of the *forum contractus* asserts jurisdiction to the place of performance where the characteristic obligation of the contract is or should have been performed. None of the analyzed jurisdictional regimes apply the 'characteristic performance' rule. By way of an open norm, the relevant contractual obligation is determined on a case-by-case basis. It is left to the court seized to determine which obligation is the characteristic one. Several authors argued that the ECJ should have adopted the characteristic performance rule instead of the *forum solutionis* approach which focuses on the obligation in question. Their arguments mainly address the fact that the characteristic performance guarantees a closer connection to the forum and avoids fragmentation and multiple competent forums. See Hill, 'Jurisdiction in Matters Relating to a Contract', at 611; P. Punt, 'Naar een meer karakteristieke jurisdictie?', in *Aan Wil besteed* (2003), 425-448, at 443; and H. Gothot and D. Holleaux, 'Note: *De Bloos and Tessili*', *Revue critique de droit international privé* (1977), 761-772, at 768. The ECJ repeatedly rejected the *characteristic or specific performance* rule under the Brussels Convention. See the systematic rejection of the theory in Chapter 2, Sect. 2.7.3.2.b.

[389] See Chapter 3 for Germany, Sect. 3.5.4; for The Netherlands, Sect. 3.2.3; for Switzerland, Sect. 3.3.2.3 and for Italy and Spain, respectively Sects. 3.1.1 and 3.1.2; see also Schack for an exhaustive overview of the place of performance among several states, Schack, *Der Erfüllungsort*, at 164-212.

Article 5(1) of the Brussels Convention and Article 5(1)(c) and (a) of the Brussels Regulation also apply the *forum solutionis*.[390] The ECJ ruled that the obligation in question should be the *original* contractual obligation instead of the obligation replacing an unperformed contractual obligation[391] and when the claim is based on several obligations, the *principal* contractual obligation determines the place of jurisdiction.[392]

The rule is unknown to Anglo-American common law regimes.[393] Although the English CPR Rules enacted a specific head for outside service related to contractual claims, it chose other connecting factors that are not concerned with the place of performance.

With respect to the U.S., the mere execution of the contract is insufficient under the 'transacting business' provision to create jurisdiction. Only when a '*no limit*' long-arm statute confers jurisdiction on 'any constitutional basis', could the contacts serve as a single-act sufficiently connected with the forum to ascertain jurisdiction over the defendant, provided that the exercise of jurisdiction endures the due process analysis.[394] Some long-arm statutes allow jurisdiction when the contract is to be performed in the forum.[395] But unlike the *forum solutionis*, it is not limited to the 'obligation in question'. Such provisions confer jurisdiction by looking at other circumstances of the contract and appreciate the facts on a case-by-case basis, instead of determining the place of 'performance' based on notions of substantive law and legal concepts.

Once the obligation in question is identified, the place of performance is determined by either the *lex causae*, i.e. the law governing the contract, or the *lex fori*. By using substantive law to localize the place of performance, jurisdiction is determined by legal concepts and not by the (f)actual performances.[396] The application of the *lex fori* or the *lex causae* to determine the place of performance implies that the determination of contract jurisdiction depends on substantive laws. In fact, when the *lex causae* applies, the outcome also depends on the outcome of the conflict rule.[397] The majority of jurisdictional regimes applying the *forum solutionis* use the law governing the contract to localize the place of performance of the obligation in question also known as the 'conflictualist method'. This approach has German origins[398] and was followed by the ECJ ever since the *Tessili* deci-

[390] Chapter 2, Sect. 2.7.3.2. See Jenard Report, at 23; Punt, 'Karakteristieke jurisdictie', at 439; A. Dashwood, R. Hacon *et al.*, *A Guide to the Civil Jurisdiction and Judgments Convention* (1987), at 22.

[391] Para. 17 of *De Bloos*. See also Gothot and Holleaux, 'Note: *De Bloos and Tessili*', at 767-769.

[392] See for multiple obligations in Chapter 2, Sect. 2.7.3.2.a.

[393] See below Sect. 7.6.3.5 and Schack, *Der Erfüllungsort*, § 345, at 239.

[394] See Chapter 5, Sect. 5.6.4; and see Schack, *Der Erfüllungsort*, § 300, at 208-209.

[395] See also Brand, 'Due Process, Jurisdiction', at 691.

[396] Schack, *Der Erfüllungsort*, § 223, at 152.

[397] See for illustrations of the complexity of this article, ibid., at 153-155; A. Lüderitz, 'Fremdbestimmte internationale Zuständigkeit? Versuch einer Neubestimmung von 29 ZPO, Art. 5 Nr. 1 EuGVü', in *Festschrift für Konrad Zweigert zum 70. Geburtstag* (1981), 233-250, at 234-249; Schack, *Internationales Zivilverfahrensrecht*, § 271, at 98.

[398] For Germany see Lüderitz, 'Fremdbestimmte Internationale Zuständigkeit', at 233 *et seq.*; H. Schack, 'Germany National Report', in *Declining Jurisdiction in Private International Law* (1995), 189-205, at 662.

sion.[399] Localization of the *forum solutionis* by the *lex causae* is applied for Article 5(1) of the Brussels Convention and Article 5(1)(a) of the Brussels Regulation and in The Netherlands, Italy and Spain. In Switzerland, the application of the *lex causae* is disputed and the application of the *lex fori* seems to prevail.[400]

The place of performance of the obligation in question is primarily concerned with the connection between the claim and the forum; it is not concerned with the question whether the defendant or his activities is in any way connected with the forum. The lack of such a defendant-related connection, so cherished under the U.S. jurisdictional scheme, will most likely result in a violation of due process standards.[401] This makes the *forum solutionis* particularly problematic for the U.S. In contrast to systems embracing the place of performance, the mere execution, performance or payment in the U.S. forum, is generally not consistent with due process standards, as the required connection with the defendant or his activities is generally lacking. When the plaintiff requests payment, the application of the *forum solutionis* confers jurisdiction on the court of the place of payment.[402] Depending on the applicable law, the place of payment results in either the defendant's or claimant's forum. Under U.S. due process standards, the obligation to pay in the forum as a basis for jurisdiction is particularly not accepted and considered highly unreasonable and excessive for jurisdiction.[403]

The *forum solutionis* is not suitable for jurisdictional purposes at a uniform world-wide level. Although frequently used in Europe,[404] it is also a highly controversial jurisdiction rule.[405] The complex determination of the place of performance of the obligation in question and the absence of the guarantee of a close connection with the forum are the principal objections against the rule. The focus on the contractual obligation forming the basis of proceedings and the application of the *lex causae* was initially believed to lead to a competent court closely connected with the dispute.[406] The court of the place where the contractual obligation giving rise

[399] See for the *Tessili* approach Chapter 2, Sect. 2.7.3.2.c.

[400] As discussed in Chapter 3, Sect. 3.3.2.3.

[401] Brand, 'Due Process, Jurisdiction', at 691.

[402] See also Chapter 2, Sect. 2.7.3.2.a. The place of payment of the merchandise was also already known in ancient Roman law as indicated by Gaudemet-Tallon, *Origines de l'article 14 CC*, at 68.

[403] See Schack, *Minimum Contacts Scrutinized*, at 44-46; M. De Cristofaro, 'Critical Remarks on the Vienna Sales Convention's Impact on Jurisdiction', *Uniform Law Review* (2000), 43-68, at 64, who states that 'we see that United States courts have also refused to affirm jurisdiction upon the mere fact that a pecuniary obligation has to be performed in the United States.' See C. Chalas, *L'exercise discrétionnaire de la compétence juridictionnelle en droit international privé* (2000), at 436, referring to Schlosser, 'Jurisdiction in International Litigation: The Issue of Human Rights', at 31, who considers the place of payment as more exorbitant than the U.S. doing business; Müller, *Die Gerichtspflichtigkeit wegen 'doing business'*, at 55-56; and Schack, *Der Erfüllungsort*, § 301, at 209. See Schlosser, 'Jurisdiction in International Litigation: The Issue of Human Rights ', at 28, arguing that the place of performance of pecuniary obligation is incompatible with Art. 6(1) of the European Convention on Human Rigths; see also Chalas, *L'exercise discrétionnaire*, § 491, at 435; and see Chapter 8, Sect. 8.3.

[404] Especially in the Brussels Model, see Hertz, *Jurisdiction in Contract*, at 85.

[405] See Chapter 2, Sect. 2.7.4.

[406] See Chapter 2, Sect. 2.7.3.2.e. The conflictualist method would most certainly benefit from unification of conflict rules and from unification of substantive law, it will not completely take away its disadvantages.

to the action is to be performed was considered most appropriate for deciding the case as it was considered to be in a better position to obtain a firsthand knowledge of the facts and have the ease of taking evidence.[407] But the complex determination of the competent court appears to be unable to guarantee a court with a strong claim-related connection, not with the claim, nor with the defendant.[408]

The *forum solutionis* does not provide for legal certainty as it depends on the contractual obligation upon which the plaintiff bases his claim and on the applicable law determining the place of performance. The legal uncertainty caused by the problematic application of the *forum solutionis* is stressed by many authors and becomes evident on many occasions.[409] The outcome of the rule is unpredictable. A 'well-informed defendant' cannot 'reasonably foresee'[410] before which court he may be sued as he is unable to know beforehand upon which contractual obligation the claimant will base proceedings. The claimant, on the other hand, needs to localize the place of performance on the basis of either the *lex fori* or the *lex causae* and is therefore dependent on the outcome of the conflict of law rule and the interpretation of the substantive law. Especially the recourse to the *lex causae* is considered highly 'mathematical' and 'theoretical' and does not guarantee legal certainty.[411] Conversely, this mathematical approach does not provide for a flexible approach either as the competent court is determined by legal concepts instead of on the actual facts. This type of connecting factor does not provide for jurisdiction on the basis of a case-by-case appreciation of the facts and the circumstances of a contract. Although the *forum solutionis* was initially thought to provide for a neutral forum by connecting the claim to the forum instead of the parties to the forum, in practice the rule leads to a competent court either at the claimant's forum or at defendant's forum. It is therefore believed that the place of performance of the contract will always privilege one party over the other.[412]

---

[407] As has been stated by the ECJ in C-256/00 *Besix v. WABAG*, [2002] ECR I-1699, para. 31; see also Case 12/76 *Tessili v. Dunlop*, [1976] ECR 1473, para. 13; Case 266/85 *Shenavai v. Kreischer*, [1987] ECR 239, para. 6, and C-125/92 *Mulox v. Geel*, [1993] ECR 4075, para. 17, and, by way of analogy, regarding Art. 5(3) Brussels Convention, C-220/88 *Dumez v. Helaba*, [1990] ECR I-49, para. 17; C-68/93 *Shevill v. Presse Alliance*, [1995] ECR I-415, para. 19; and C-364/93 *Marinari*, [1995] ECR I-2719 (para. 10). J. Pontier and E. Burg, *EU Principles on Jurisdiction and Recogniton and Enforcement of Judgments in Civil and Commercial Matters* (2004), at 161.

[408] See Chapter 2, Sect. 2.7.4; Schack, *Internationales Zivilverfahrensrecht*, § 269, at 97; Schack, *Der Erfüllungsort*, § 339, at 236: '*Dem tatsächlichen Erfüllungsort kommt deshalb nicht die praktische Bedeutung zu, die man nach dem Wortlaut von Art. 5(1) GVÜ erwärten mag.*' See also De Cristofaro, 'Critical Remarks', at 55.

[409] See among others Nygh, 'Criteria for Judicial Jurisdiction', at A-9. See Briggs, *Civil Jurisdiction*, § 2.138, at 172–173; De Cristofaro, 'Critical Remarks', at 48; Steenhoff, 'Pleidooi voor een crediteursforum', at 198; Kessedjian, 'Prel. Doc. No. 7: 1997 Report', § 118, at 35: 'if it is decided to include a special jurisdiction rule for contracts, we should not take the text of article 5.1 of the Brussels Convention as a model.'

[410] See C-440/97 *GIE Groupe Concorde*, [1999] ECR I-6307, at para. 24; and Chapter 5, Sect. 5.4.3.3.

[411] Opinion AG Ruiz-Jarabo Colomer in C-440/97 *GIE Groupe Concorde*, [1999] ECR I-6307, para. 82.

[412] By imposing that the place of performance of the disputed obligation is conclusive, irrespective of the characteristic performance of the contract, both parties appear to have equal jurisdictional privileges, see Schack, *Internationales Zivilverfahrensrecht*, § 265, at 96.

7.6.3.4 *Sale of Goods and Provision of Service: Tailored Place of Performance*

Some jurisdictional regimes have pre-determined a specific place of performance for particular types of contracts, generally coinciding with the place of performance of the characteristic obligation.[413] This approach consists in identifying a place of performance tailored to the particularities of that type of contract.[414] The approach also requires the sub-classification of contracts. For instance, for sale of goods or the provision of services, the competent court is at the place of delivery or the provision of services. In contrast to the *forum solutionis*, the obligation forming the basis of the proceedings is irrelevant for jurisdictional purposes; all claims are concentrated in that same contract forum.

Among the national Continental European contract provisions, France stands alone in asserting jurisdiction to French courts when delivery was made or services were provided in France.[415] Factual delivery is conclusive, which means that if delivery took place in France, even if this was not the agreed place of delivery under the contract, French courts are competent.[416] The Brussels Regulation introduced in Article 5(1)(b) similar tailored places of performance for claims arising out of sales contracts and contracts for the provision of services.[417] The rule respectively provides for contract jurisdiction to the courts of the place where the goods were delivered or should have been delivered, or the place where the services were provided or should have been provided.[418]

Quite remarkably, similar connecting factors were found in long-arm statutes of some U.S. states, such as New York and Michigan.[419] The New York Statute asserts jurisdiction over defendants who contract to supply goods or services in the

[413] The place of delivery of the merchandise was also already known in ancient Roman law as indicated by Gaudemet-Tallon, *Origines de l'article 14 CC*, at 67-68.

[414] A tailored place of performance differs from the *characteristic performance* rule since the latter is not formulated in a general sense, but identifies a specific place of performance for specific contracts. See for a critical remark Schack, *Der Erfüllungsort*, § 144, at 105.

[415] By transposing the internal rules of the NCCP; Art. 46(2) Chapter 3, Sect. 3.4.2.

[416] See the French provision in Chapter 3, Sect. 3.4.2.3; and see De Cristofaro, 'Critical Remarks', fn. 8, at 45.

[417] See the European *forum contractus*, Chapter 2, Sect. 2.7.3.1. See at unification level also the example of Art. 8 of the MERCOSUR/CMC/DEC. N° 01/94: Buenos Aires Protocol on International Jurisdiction in Contractual Matters, which reads: '1. … location for fulfillment of the contract shall be interpreted as the State Party in which the obligation serving as a basis for the claim has been or should be fulfilled. 2. Fulfillment of the claimed obligation shall be: a. For contracts on certain, individualized things: the location at which they existed at the time that they were entered into; b. For contracts on things determined by their type: the location of the debtor's domicile at the time that they were entered into; c. For contracts involving fungibles, the location of debtor's domicile at the time the contract was entered into; d. In contracts dealing with provision of services: 1. If they affect things: the location where they existed at the time that the contract was entered into; 2. If their effectiveness is related to any special location: the one in which the effects must necessarily occur; 3. Apart from these cases: the location of the debtor's domicile at the time that the contract was entered into.'

[418] Art. 5(1)(b), see Punt, 'Karakteristieke jurisdictie', at 444.

[419] See also Schack, *Der Erfüllungsort*, at 208-209, stating that the supply-of-goods-or-services provision could coincide with the place of performance rule.

forum.[420] The Michigan Statute says that an individual who contracts for services to be rendered or for materials to be furnished in Michigan has sufficient contacts for specific jurisdiction.[421] Known as the *supply-of-goods-or-services* provisions, they are specifically designed to exercise jurisdiction in contractual disputes over a defendant who has insufficient connections for activity-based jurisdiction.[422] Such bases for jurisdiction are considered to *cause an effect* in the forum and therefore justifies jurisdiction. Moreover, an act done by an out-of-state individual who agreed to supply or ship goods or perform services in the state entails that he *purposefully* sought to benefit from a state's commercial market.[423] As a consequence, an individual can *reasonably* expect to be sued in that state for either faulty performance or non-performance of the agreement. Despite the fact that these U.S. long-arm provisions are similar to its French and Brussels counterparts, the U.S. jurisdiction system still requires an additional defendant-related nexus with the forum in order to satisfy due process standards of the U.S. Constitution. Such connection is not required in the French and Brussels regime. This crucial difference between the legal systems makes it difficult for the U.S. to accept this type of claim-related basis for contract jurisdiction based on a specific performance in the forum.

The rule of a tailored place of performance has good papers for a uniform jurisdiction rule: the place of delivery or the provision of services as bases for jurisdiction for sale of goods and service contracts are well accepted in Europe and in some U.S. long-arm statutes. The approach of tailored places of performance primarily requires an independent pre-determination of a place of performance for different types of contracts on the basis of its characteristic obligation. It should not be a problem to determine the characteristic obligation for most – but not for all – contracts.

A first look at the rule may lead one to think that it ranks high in terms of *legal certainty*; the place of delivery or any other tailored place of performance will create jurisdiction, regardless of the nature of the claim. Parties know beforehand which performance is jurisdiction-creating and are able to foresee the competent court. Usually parties have agreed 'under contract' on a place of delivery or of provision of services. The latter is crucial in order to avoid complex determination of the place of delivery in the event of non- or wrong delivery, which may result in the application of substantive law.

When the agreed place of delivery is decisive it always creates jurisdiction, even when the performer fails to deliver or delivers partially or wrongly. Problems occur when the place of delivery was not agreed or is not decisive: under those circumstances it is uncertain, at least under the Brussels Model, what happens when delivery was not made or wrongfully made.

---

420 New York Statute § 302(a)(1) CPLR.

421 Michigan Statute § 27A.705 and § 600.705(5).

422 As indicated above, some enumerated long-arm statutes enacted provisions to cover such claims.

423 See Chapter 5, Sect. 5.6.4.

Some have argued that the place where the debtor actually performed – or delivered – according to the terms of the contracts should be the only legitimate basis for contract jurisdiction as it only then constitutes sufficient contacts and the exercise of jurisdiction is 'reasonable'.[424] This would also be acceptable for U.S. due process purposes; in order to perform in a forum, the performer is often compelled to enter the forum, as there is little doubt that performance could constitute sufficient minimum contacts. If the performer then becomes the defendant, there will be some connection between the defendant and the forum.[425]

Uncertainty also persists when the tailored performance is due at several places: should a single place of performance be determined according to economic criteria, or should – under those circumstances – contract jurisdiction only be available to claims concerning one particular performance or delivery?

The fact that all claims are concentrated in the court of the place of the tailored place of performance does not guarantee a close connection between the claim and the forum, especially when the claim is not related to the characteristic obligation.[426] A defendant-related nexus is even less guaranteed. In that respect, the rule is quite inflexible, as it does not provide for any discretion for courts to deviate from pre-determined or tailored connecting factors when the connection with the forum is weak. *Flexibility* could be provided by the application of the special correction clause which requires a *defendant-related* connection with the forum including a close connection on the basis of defendant's activities in or towards the forum. This has also been argued by Nygh

> 'Unfortunately, as I understand the position, the due process provisions of the U.S. Constitution may preclude reliance upon the place of performance if in fact nothing has been done there. This is not a problem to the rest of the world, but in order to comply with the U.S. Constitution the provision might have to include part performance within the forum. … But due process limitations emanating from the United States Constitution may compel a closer look at the activity option.'[427]

7.6.3.5 *The Place Where the Contract Was Breached*

Instead of conferring jurisdiction on the court where performance took place, the English common law regime asserts jurisdiction to English courts over a claim made in respect of a breach of contract committed within the jurisdiction. A contract can be breached, either by a failure to perform or by an act of expressed or implied repudiation.[428] When a failure to perform constitutes a breach of contract,

---

[424] To the example of the German Art. 29 ZPO, which only confers jurisdiction on the place where the obligation in question was performed. See De Cristofaro, 'Critical Remarks', at 67; Schack, *Der Erfüllungsort*, § 338, at 235-236.

[425] Schack, *Minimum Contacts Scrutinized*, at 44; and Schack, *Der Erfüllungsort*, § 301, at 146.

[426] See Newton, *Uniform Interpretation*, at 70. The place of delivery based on the new Art. 5(1) of the Brussels Regulation results sometimes in a connecting factor which does not represent (any) close connection with the forum.

[427] Nygh, 'Criteria for Judicial Jurisdiction', at A-9.

[428] See Chapter 4, Sect. 4.5.2.5; and see Newton, *Uniform Interpretation*, at 43.

the place where the contractual obligation should have been performed, according to the law governing the contract, is the place where the contract is breached.[429] In other words, when delivery should have been made in England, but did not take place, English courts are competent; in the reversed situation of delivery in England, English courts are not competent. This 'place of breach of performance' rule differs from the place where the contractual obligation should have been performed, which is applied in the Brussels and Continental European systems. The non-performance of a contractual obligation does not always constitute a breach of contract. The ECJ even refused to refer to the place where the breach of the obligation in question was committed 'since it would also imply a reversal of the Tessili case-law, by giving an autonomous interpretation to the concept of place of performance, without looking at the law applicable to the relevant obligation in accordance with the conflict rules of the court seised.' [430]

A similar basis for contract jurisdiction is incorporated in the Florida long-arm Statute; the provision asserts jurisdiction when defendant breached a contract in Florida by failing to perform acts required by the contract to be performed in Florida.[431] As opposed to its English counterpart, this provision is limited to a breach of contract by failure to perform, and excludes repudiation. Performances of contractual obligations in Florida do not provide for a jurisdictional basis. Only the non-performance of contractual obligations, including non-payment, is potentially jurisdiction-creating when it constitutes a breach of contract.

Problems with determining the place of the breach of contract and the lack of a connection with the forum constitute the principal objections to this connecting factor for contract jurisdiction. The rule does not provide for legal certainty. With respect to considerations of legal certainty, none of the parties are able to foresee beforehand if, where and by whom the contract will be breached before the contractual disputes arise. Once the breach took place, notions of substantive law will determine where the breach occurred, which does not make it predictable either.

In most cases, the place of performance will be closer connected to the forum, than the place of non-performance. A breach of contract simply by no performance at all implies that the defendant did not make any connection – or contact – with the forum: defendant has *not* carried out the activities or directed contacts with the forum. In the event a partial performance results in a breach of contract, the connection with the forum might be closer, but this is still not guaranteed. There is no guarantee that there is an actual connection between the claim or the parties with the place of breach of the contract.[432] The rule does not provide for any flexibility either, nor a particular protection of the parties.

---

[429] This is according to the conflictualist method.

[430] C-256/00 *Besix v. WABAG*, [2002] ECR I-1699, para. 41.

[431] According to Florida Statute § 48.193(g) 'breaching a contract in this state by failing to perform acts required by the contract to be performed in this state' constitutes contract jurisdiction.

[432] See Hill, 'Jurisdiction in Matters Relating to a Contract', at 615; Punt also makes a remark of this nature, see Punt, 'Karakteristieke jurisdictie', at 442; and De Cristofaro, 'Critical Remarks', at 45, claims that the place of defective performance is more likely to constitute a connection with the forum that is contrary to the place of a breach of contract.

7.6.4 Contract Jurisdiction under Drafts of the Hague Project

Inspired by the Brussels Model, the state delegates negotiating The Hague Project included a provision specifically dealing with jurisdiction over contractual matters. In their search for a uniform contract jurisdiction rule, the drafters focussed on the various applications of the place of performance rule, but rejected the *forum celebrationis* and the place of the law governing the contract. Before the 1999 draft, the *forum solutionis* as applied under the Brussels Convention was resolutely rejected[433] as too complex and systematically resulting in a *forum actoris*.[434] Once more, the characteristic performance theory was rejected for reasons that it did 'not necessarily correspond to the concrete realities of the contract'.[435] The tailored place of performance was given preference[436] as the 1999 Draft was limited to contracts for the sale of goods and the provision of services.[437] Other types of contracts were considered,[438] but it was argued that only those two categories of contracts most frequently found in practice should be provided with tailored contract rules. This provision of the 1999 Draft is clearly inspired by the proposals of the Brussels Regulation made at that time, since the contract provision asserts jurisdiction to the place of delivery and the place of provision of services.[439] No definition was provided for 'goods' or 'services', neither by the 1999 Draft nor by the Nygh and Pocar Report but this was presumably left to the *lex fori* or the *lex causae*.[440]

By excluding the *forum solutionis*, the drafters took into account the fact that its outcome does not always lead to a forum to which the defendant purposefully

---

[433] Kessedjian, 'Prel. Doc. No. 7: 1997 Report', § 118, at 68, states that '[i]f it is decided to include a special jurisdiction rule for contracts, we should not take the text of the Brussels Convention as a model.'

[434] Kessedjian indicates that the application of the Art. 5(1) Brussels Convention provision results for 90% in a *forum actoris*, which appears undesirable for a unified contract rule. See Kessedjian, 'Prel. Doc. No. 8 of June 1997: Synthesis Special Commission', § 65.

[435] Ibid., at § 67 and see Kessedjian, 'Prel. Doc. No. 7: 1997 Report', § 119, at 70.

[436] The place of performance rule was considered the most appropriate connecting factor for contract jurisdiction since it reflects the centre of gravity of the contract, see Kessedjian, 'Prel. Doc. No. 7: 1997 Report', § 119, at 70.

[437] Although the provision does not mention any specific contract, the Nygh and Pocar Report specify that the provision embodied in Art. 6 of The Hague 1999 Preliminary Draft Convention identifies two categories of contracts which are frequently found in practice, namely contracts for the supply of goods and for the provision of services, as well as contracts for both. But there was no contract provision dealing with other contracts. Nygh-Pocar Report, at 48.

[438] Such as sale between professionals, performance of services, *contrat d'entreprise*, agency, franchise, distribution, brokerage, sub-contract, joint ventures, data processing, tenancy, loan agreement and bond agreement. See Kessedjian, 'Prel. Doc. No. 8 of June 1997: Synthesis Special Commission', § 68.

[439] The provision of the 1999 Draft reads: 'A plaintiff may bring an action in contract in the courts of a State in which – a) in matters relating to the supply of goods, the goods were supplied in whole or in part; b) in matters relating to the provision of services, the services were provided in whole or in part; c) in matters relating both to the supply of goods and the provision of services, performance of the principal obligation took place in whole or in part.' Sub c clearly refers to the *Shenevai* decision of the ECJ conferring jurisdiction on the '*principal*' obligation when the claim is based on several contractual claims.

[440] Nygh-Pocar Report, at 49.

availed himself and does not guarantee a defendant-related nexus with the forum. By requiring that delivery or provision of services took place in the forum, some kind of activity in the forum is required and parties are able to foresee where they can be subjected to jurisdiction. According to Brand

> 'In doing so, however it carefully avoids the possibility of performance in a state in which the defendant has not acted, thus taking into account the limitations of due process analysis of the United States, and avoiding the creation of jurisdiction in a state in which the defendant has no activities (and has not directed any activities).'[441]

After the Ottawa meeting, beginning of 2001, the contract provision was complemented with an alternative provision asserting contract jurisdiction through U.S. *activity-based* language.[442] The Ottawa contract provision says that a plaintiff

> 'may bring an action in contract in the courts of the State in which the defendant *has engaged in frequent or significant activity, or has* [*intentionally*] *directed such activity* into that State, for the purpose of *promoting* [*the conclusion of contracts*] [*,or negotiating*] or performing a contract, provided that the claim is based on a contract directly related to that activity.'[443]

This proposed provision would apply to any contractual claim arising out of any contract other than a contract for the sale of goods or a contract for the provision of services.[444] The concepts used, such as 'engaging or directing activity into the state' clearly derive from U.S. long-arm statutes. Such a *transacting business* provision has a wide reach and would cover jurisdiction asserted on the basis of both the place of conclusion of the contract and the place of performance. The fact that the provision imposes that the claim is based on a contract directly related to the activity of the defendant clearly shows that the provision is designed for contractual matters, unlike the much wider U.S. transacting business criterion found

---

441 Brand, 'Understanding Activity-Based', at 37.

442 Prel. Doc. No. 15 of May 2001, Informational note, Annex I, at 4, reads:
'1. A plaintiff may bring an action in contract in the courts of a State in which –
a) in matters relating to the supply of goods, the goods were supplied in whole or in part;
b) in matters relating to the provision of services, the services were provided in whole or in part;
c) in matters relating both to the supply of goods and the provision of services, performance of the principal obligation took place in whole or in part.
2. A plaintiff may bring an action in contract in the courts of the State in which the defendant has engaged in frequent or significant activity, or has [intentionally] directed such activity into that State, for the purpose of promoting [the conclusion of contracts] [, or negotiating] or performing a contract, provided that the claim is based on a contract directly related to that activity.
3. The preceding paragraphs do not apply to situations where the defendant has taken reasonable steps to avoid entering into or performing an obligation in that State.
[4. The preceding paragraphs do not apply to situations where the sole relevant activity is the payment of money provided that this exclusion shall not apply where the performance required on both sides consists of the payment of money (such as a loan or a contract for the purchase and sale of currency).]'

443 Prel. Doc. No. 15 of May 2001, Informational note, Annex I (emphasis added); see above Sect. 7.5.5.

444 Brand, 'Understanding Activity-Based', at 37; Brand, '2005 Report: A View from the U.S.', at 23-24.

in U.S. long-arm statutes.[445] According to Brand, this provision requires 'both a court-defendant nexus (the activity of the claim) and a court-claim nexus (the claim must be directly related to that activity). In this way it incorporates the fundamental concepts of each of the two systems of jurisdictional rules'.[446] The third paragraph of the Ottawa draft states that the 'Preceding paragraphs do not apply to situations where the defendant has taken reasonable steps to avoid entering into or performing an obligation in that State.'[447] This basis is clearly modelled on the U.S. 'purposeful availment' requirement and was proposed in order to meet U.S. constitutional standards.[448] More specifically its purpose it to exclude any application of the place of payment as connecting factor for contract jurisdiction except in cases where the contract concerns pecuniary matters.[449] In fact, this Ottawa contract provision reached a compromise by proposing the *tailored place of performance rule* as applied under Article 5(1)(b) of the Brussels Regulation and alternatively allowed jurisdiction based on defendant's activities related to the contract and introduced U.S. transacting business language.

No trace of a compromising climate can be detected in the 2001 Draft of The Hague Project.[450] Instead, the result of the June 2001 diplomatic session is a provision with no consensus at all and for the greater part bracketed.[451] It consists of two alternatives for the contract forum: one based on activity-based jurisdiction with two variants defining 'activity' and the other alternative merely focussed on the tailored place of performance as enacted in the 1999 draft.[452]

---

[445] Brand, 'Understanding Activity-Based', at 37; Brand, '2005 Report: A View from the U.S.', at 24. Brand states that this also gives evidence of a required 'claim-forum' nexus because 'the claim must be directly related to that activity', hereby 'incorporating the fundamental concepts of each of the two systems of jurisdictional rules considered'. But this assumption is based on a misconception; the fact that the claim derives from activity directed to or engaged in the forum does not automatically establish a claim-forum connection. See Müller, *Die Gerichtspflichtigkeit wegen 'doing business'*, at 46, who says that '*Das bedeutet dass der Klagegrund nicht in Zusammenhang met den einzelnen Kontakten stehen muss.*'

[446] Brand, 'Understanding Activity-Based', at 37-38.

[447] Art. 6(3) of the Prel. Doc. No. 15 of May 2001; see above Sect. 7.5.5.

[448] Brand, 'Understanding Activity-Based', at 37; Brand, '2005 Report: A View from the U.S.', at 23.

[449] Even though the text is bracketed, Art. 6(4) states: '[The preceding paragraphs do not apply to situations where the sole relevant activity is the payment of money provided that this exclusion shall not apply where the performance required on both sides consists of the payment of money (such as a loan or a contract for the purchase and sale of currency).]'

[450] There was no consensus on the basis for jurisdiction in contractual matters. In the material that follows two basic options are put forward: one alternative refers to activity (with several sub-options) and the other alternative focusses on the place of performance. See also Punt, 'Aan Wil besteed', at 448.

[451] According to Brand 'here, ... there is no due process guarantee for the defendant, and it is entirely possible that the article 6 rules would result in jurisdiction where U.S. Supreme Court jurisprudence would lead to a finding that due process is not provided'. See on the position of Brand concerning acceptability of the U.S., Brand, '2005 Report: A View from the U.S.', at 12-3; Brand also states that 'it is not difficult to hypothesize [that] a contract that might result in jurisdiction under such a rule would run a foul of the Due Process clause.' See R. Brand, *Due Process as a Limitation* (1998), at 11; Brand, 'Due Process, Jurisdiction', at 690-691.

[452] Art. 6 of The Hague 2001 Interim Text reads:

'[Alternative A; 1.A plaintiff may bring an action in contract in the courts of the State –

Both alternatives are meant to be jurisdiction-creating, which would result in multiple competent courts for the same contractual dispute.[453] Alternative B clearly derives from the Brussels Regulation and alternative A is modelled on activity-based provisions as encountered in U.S. long-arm statute.

7.7 Property-based Jurisdiction

Apart from jurisdiction at defendant's home forum, or jurisdiction based on defendant's activities in the forum, some legal systems confer jurisdiction when property belonging to the defendant is located in the forum. Property-based jurisdiction should be divided in two categories: the *forum patrimonii* asserting general jurisdiction on the mere presence of defendant's property in the forum and the *forum arresti* providing for specific jurisdiction to the place where defendant's property was seized.

Jurisdiction based on the mere presence of defendant's property in the forum emanates from the Germanic jurisdictional tradition.[454] Article 23 ZPO is the most

---

a) in which the defendant has conducted frequent and/or significant activity; or

b) [in which the defendant has directed frequent [and] [or] significant activity;] provided that the claim is based on a contract directly related to that activity [and the overall connection of the defendant to that State makes it reasonable that the defendant be subject to suit in that State].

[*Variant 1*

2. For the purposes of the preceding paragraph, 'activity' means one or more of the following –

a) [regular and substantial] promotion of the commercial or professional ventures of the defendant for the conclusion of contracts of this kind;

b) the defendant's regular or extended presence for the purpose of negotiating contracts of this kind, provided that the contract in question was performed at least in part in that State. [Performance in this sub-paragraph refers [only] to non-monetary performance, except in case of loans or of contracts for the purchase and sale of currency];

c) the performance of a contract by supplying goods or services, as a whole or to a significant part.]

[*Variant 2*

2. For the purpose of the preceding paragraph, 'activity' includes, *inter alia*, the promotion, negotiation, and performance of a contract.

3. The preceding paragraphs do not apply to situations where the defendant has taken reasonable steps to avoid entering into or performing an obligation in that State.]

[Alternative B

A plaintiff may bring an action in contract in the courts of a State in which

a) in matters relating to the supply of goods, the goods were supplied in whole or in part;

b) in matters relating to the provision of services, the services were provided in whole or in part;

c) in matters relating both to the supply of goods and the provision of services, performance of the principal obligation took place in whole or in part.]'

453 Brand, 'Understanding Activity-Based', at 38.

454 According to the categorization of Fragistas, N. Fragistas, 'La compétence internationale en droit international privé', 104 *Recueil des cours* (1961), 159, at 212 *et seq*. Among the systems analysed it was only found in Germany, but the list of countries applying property-based jurisdiction is longer than those applying the well-known (and controversial) German rule of Art. 23 ZPO. The closest equivalent can be found in Austrian law in Art. 99(I) Jurisdiktionsnorm; see A. Bittighofer, *Der internationale Gerichtsstand des Vermögens: Eine Rechtvergleichende Studie zur Zuständigkeit deutscher Gerichte aufgrund inländischer Vermögensbelegenheit* (1994), Vol. 1561, at 86-107. This Austrian provision was limited by case law in 1983 if the value of the property would be disproportionate in relation to the amount of the claim; Schack, *Internationales Zivilverfahrensrecht*, § 328, at

far-reaching variation of property-based jurisdiction. The rule provides for jurisdiction on the sole basis of presence of defendant's property in Germany and does not require prior attachment of the assets; jurisdiction is possible regardless of whether the property is the subject of the action or whether the claim is in any other way related to it and regardless of the value of the property.[455] The '*vermögensgerichtstand*' forum is available to any plaintiff, whether he is a German domiciliary or not.

The second category of property-based jurisdiction concerns the *forum arresti* which requires the attachment of defendant's property as a prerequisite for property-based jurisdiction. The rule confers jurisdiction on the court which ordered the attachment; the court of the place where the assets were seized.[456] The attachment requirement constitutes an important restriction to property-based jurisdiction and is subjected to national procedure rules regarding the validation of the attachment order.[457] Except for this attachment requirement the *forum patrimonii* does not differ so much from the *forum arresti*. The German Article 23 ZPO includes attachment jurisdiction since the *forum patrimonii* provides for jurisdiction on the mere presence of defendant's property in the forum. The *forum arresti* should be understood as a restricted version of the *forum patrimonii*.[458]

This restricted version of property-based jurisdiction is applied in Switzerland where it is called the *forum sequestri*,[459] in The Netherlands it is known as the *forum arresti*,[460] and in the U.S. it is called 'attachment jurisdiction' or '*quasi in rem II* jurisdiction'.[461] The U.S. version of attachment jurisdiction differs from

119; J. Schröder, *Internationale Zuständigkeit: Entwurf eines Systems von Zuständigkeitsinteressen im zwischenstaatlichen Privatverfahrensrecht, aufgrund rechtshistorischer, rechtsvergleichender und rechtspolitischer Betrachtungen* (1971), at 376.

455 This is the case, notwithstanding the exceptions made in claims involving exclusive jurisdiction. The rule is also called the 'umbrella forum' due to its excessive reach; it is theoretically possible to assert jurisdiction on the simple presence of a forgotten umbrella. See Nuyts, *L'exception*, § 316, at 424.

456 J. Verheul and M. Feteris, *Rechtsmacht in het Nederlandse Privaatrecht, deel 2 Overige Verdragen het commune IPR* (1986), at 102.

457 M.E. Koppenol-Laforce, 'Article 765 Rv (vreemdelingenbeslag) en de Europese Gemeenschap', *Tijdschrift voor civiele rechtspleging* (1994), 58-61, at 59.

458 See for a historical background Bittighofer, *Internationale Gerichtsstand des Vermögens*, at 42-73; Schröder, *Internationale Zuständigkeit*, at 388-391; and T. Pfeiffer, *Internationale Zuständigkeit und prozessuale Gerechtigkeit: Die internationale Zuständigkeit im Zivilprozess zwischen effektivem Rechtsschutz und nationaler Zuständigkeitspolitik* (1995), at 525-526. See Krafft who calls the *forum arresti* an *Unterart* (subart) of the *Vermögensgerichtstand*, J. Krafft, *'Exorbitante' Gerichtsstände im internationalen Zivilprozessrecht der Schweiz: Insbesondere nach dem Lugano-Übereinkommen* (1999), at 87.

459 Art. 4 Swiss PIL Statute.

460 Applied through the 'back door' clause of Art. 10 of the Rv. See Chapter 3, Sect. 3.2.4.

461 See 2nd Restatement of Judgments (1982), § 8. See also 'The Requirement of Seizure in the Exercise of Quasi in Rem Jurisdiction: Pennoyer v. Neff Re-Examined', 63 *Harvard Law Review* (1950), 657-671; see Chapter 5, Sect. 5.7. See also G. Dannemann, 'Jurisdiction Based on the Presence of Assets in Germany', 41 *The International and Comparative Law Quarterly* (1992), 632-637, at 636. For comparative works see among others O. Hartwieg, 'Forum Shopping zwischen Forum non Conveniens und "hinreichendem Inlandsbezug"', 51 *Juristen Zeitung* (1996), 109-118; Pfeiffer, *Internationale Zuständigkeit und prozessuale Gerechtigkeit* (1995); H. Grothe, '"Exorbi-

its Swiss and Dutch counterparts. The attachment of defendant's assets is also a prerequisite for U.S. *quasi in rem type II* jurisdiction or *attachment jurisdiction*, but the particularity of the U.S. jurisdictional scheme is that it is primarily based on minimum contacts. Thus, property located in the forum constitutes a 'point of contact' for jurisdictional purposes but is still submitted to the purposeful availment test and the notions of fair play and substantial justice under U.S. due process standards.[462]

The principal justification for attachment jurisdiction is that the court, which ordered an attachment measure, should also be able to adjudicate on the merits of the case.[463] But in France and England attachment jurisdiction was rejected by the highest courts on the basis that jurisdiction to order an attachment measure does not justify jurisdiction over the merits.[464]

At national level property-based jurisdiction is characterized by its subsidiary nature; it is only available when the defendant's home forum does not lead to a competent court. It allows the claimant to derogate from the main rule for jurisdiction and sue the defendant where his property is located rather than compelling him to follow defendant to his home court. The German rule explicitly states that the rule only applies in case the defendant is not domiciled in Germany.[465] As a result,

---

tante" Gerichtszuständigkeiten im Rechtsverkehr zwischen Deutschland und den U.S.A', 58 *RabelsZ* (1994), 687-726; T. Kleinstück, *Due Process-Beschränkungen des Vermögensgerichtsstandes durch hinreichenden Inlandsbezug und Minimum Contacts* (1994); J. Lookofsky, 'Property-based Jurisdiction and Due Process of Law', 54 *Nordisk Tidsskrift for international Ret: Acta scandinavica juris gentium* (1985), 62-70.

[462] The U.S. Supreme Court in *Shaffer v. Heitner*, 433 U.S. 186, at 212 (1977), restricted the scope of application of *quasi in rem II* jurisdiction, since it stated that like *all* assertions of jurisdiction attachment jurisdiction has to pass the minimum contacts test: 'any assertion of state court jurisdiction must satisfy the *International Shoe* standards'. See among the numerous commentators Weintraub, *Commentary*, § 4.28, at 265. Since the *Burnham* case, the term '*all* assertions' is currently interpreted to mean that besides personal jurisdiction also *in rem* and *quasi in rem* jurisdiction have to comply with the minimum contact test.

[463] See also B. Ancel and Y. Lequette, *Les grands arrêts de la jurisprudence française de droit international privé* (2001), at 565-566.

[464] For France, the cautious introduction of a facultative *forum arresti* rule was the result of the 1979 *Nassibian* decision (Cour de cass. civ. I-6 November 1979, Bull. N. 47, at 30), extending a court's power to take provisional measures to adjudicate over the substance of the case. The *Cour de cassation* reversed its decision stating that for jurisdiction on the merits, the sole attachment of defendant's property does not constitute sufficient connection when other connections with France are lacking. See also in general H. Muir Watt, 'Note: Banque camerounaise de développement. Cour de Cass. Ch.Civ.I, 18 Nov. 1986', 76 *Revue critique de droit international privé* (1987), 773-786; and see Ancel and Lequette, *Les grands arrêts*, at 565-570; Y. Lequette, 'Note COBENAM; Cour de cass. Ch.civ.I, 17 Jan.1995', *Revue critique de droit international privé* (1996), 133-142, at 136; *contra* P. Lagarde, 'Le principe de proximité dans le droit internationale privé contemporain', 196 *Recueil des cours* (1986), 9-238, at 137. See for France Chapter 3, Sect. 3.4.3. In England, the *forum arresti* never was a valid jurisdiction ground as presence only concerned defendant's presence and not defendant's property. An attempt to cover an attachment order under the head of outside service on the basis of Rule 6.20(2) CPR which deals with injunction claims failed. The House of Lords gave 'technical' reasons for the strict distinction between attachment orders and substantial relief on the merits and stated that the injunction sought had to concern a *substantial* element of relief, which was not the case with an attachment order. *The Siskina and Others v. Distos Compañia Naviera S.A.*, [1979] AC 210.

[465] See Chapter 3, Sect. 3.5.5 for the *forum patrimonii*.

the principal objective of the *forum patrimonii* is to secure access to justice for a claimant to German courts when the defendant is not domiciled in Germany. The subsidiary nature is also explicit with respect to the Swiss *forum sequestii*, which only applies when no other provision asserts jurisdiction to Swiss courts,[466] and the Dutch *forum arresti* rule is only available as a last resort and conditioned to those situations where the claimant has no other possibility to obtain a foreign judgement in another (foreign) court that is enforceable in The Netherlands.[467] Although the U.S. jurisdictional system does not have a hierarchical structure, U.S. *quasi in rem II* jurisdiction is generally applied when neither specific transacting business jurisdiction nor general doing business jurisdiction are available to the claimant.

7.7.1 The Nature of the (Attached) Property

Among the jurisdictional systems it is uncontested that the property forming the basis for jurisdiction can be either tangible property – moveable or immoveable – or intangible property, such as debts or garnishments that the defendant may have against third persons.[468] Only Swiss law limits attachments orders to assets subjected to pawn.[469]

For jurisdictional purposes, the location or *situs* of defendant's assets is crucial for the determination of the competent court on the basis of property-based jurisdiction, which is problematic for intangible property. Most civil law countries identify the *situs* of intangible property at the debtor's domicile or, with respect to garnishments, the domicile of the third person (debtor) against whom the defendant may have a claim.[470] The U.S. system determines the *situs* of a debt by following the debtor. When the debt follows its debtor, the defendant can be sued everywhere its debtor is liable for suit, contrary to the civil law tradition which determines the *situs* by the rule that 'the debt follows the debtor at his domicile'. The Supreme Court held on to this rule, even if it came down to saying that 'intangible property has no actual *situs* and a debt may be sued on wherever there is jurisdiction over the debtor'.[471] The consequence is significant for U.S. jurisdiction: the defendant can be sued wherever his debtor may be sued, on whatever basis of jurisdiction

---

[466] Chapter 3, Sect. 3.3.3, except for the *forum necessitatis* in Art. 3 of the PIL Statute.

[467] The 'back door' clause of Art. 10 in conjunction with Art. 765 Rv. (Chapter 3, Sect. 3.2.4) refers back to territorial jurisdiction rules in case the direct international jurisdiction rules do not result in a competent court in The Netherlands. Among the competent courts there should not be another foreign court available to claimant whose judgement would be enforced in The Netherlands.

[468] Fragistas and Droz, 'Explanatory Report Hague Convention 1971', at 501: '*Par biens on entend non seulement les biens corporels, mais aussi les biens incorporels comme les créances*.'

[469] '*Pfändbares Vermögen*'; Krafft, *'Exorbitante' Gerichtsstände*, at 95-96. According to Krafft, this requirement limits the scope of the *forum sequestrii* since only property of a minimum value is subjected to pawn. In Germany there has been some discussion about whether defendant's assets, which are by their nature not subjected to the pawn requirement, should be excluded, but this has not yet been enacted by law or affirmed by the BGH. See Bittighofer, *Internationale Gerichtsstand des Vermögens*, at 157.

[470] This is the case in Germany: § 23(2) ZPO itself explicitly states that the *situs* of debts is at its debtor's domicile. The same is true for The Netherlands under Art. 700(1) of the Rv. and for Switzerland.

[471] 444 U.S. 320, at 330 (1980), see Chapter 5, Sect. 5.7.3.

available, such as doing or transacting business or tag-jurisdiction. This considerably widens the scope of the U.S. attachment jurisdiction in comparison to its European counterparts. The application of U.S. due process standards since *Shaffer* and *Savchuk* counterbalances this far-reaching basis for jurisdiction.[472] U.S. due process standards impose other contacts with the forum in order to comply with the minimum contact rule and the notions of fair play and substantive justice.

7.7.2 The Connection with the Forum: Special or General Jurisdiction

When, how and upon what kind of property an attachment measure can be ordered depends on national procedure law.[473] Although some attachment orders are easier to be obtained than others, in general the attachment requirement constitutes an obstacle for plaintiff to bring suit. Additionally, the prerequisite of seizure of defendant's property operates as a *'filter'* against claims with little prospect of success, since claimant has to require attachment before filing suit on the merits of the case and a valid attachment will only be ordered by the courts on valid grounds. This way the requirement prevents the wrongful use of the court's resources, avoiding the easy access of the court to the *forum patrimonii* by the simple presence of property in the forum.

The purpose of the attachment order is to secure the satisfaction of the claim on the merits and therefore it is often required that the property subjected to attachment is related to the claim. National procedure law often imposes a connection between the property and the claim underlying the attachment measure. For instance, Swiss law requires that the attachment is authorized in relation to the claim in the main proceedings. Moreover, the Swiss *forum sequestri* is explicitly restricted to jurisdiction over claims related to the validation of the attachment.[474] Dutch procedure law allows the president of the district court to grant permission for attachment, only when the claimant started main proceedings with respect to the claim underlying the attachment measure.[475]

The practical outcome of these national requirements to grant attachment measures is that the *forum arresti* generally involves a relation between the claim and the attached property in the forum. It is in that way that attachment jurisdiction does not provide for general jurisdiction, but as long as defendant's property was attached according to the conditions imposed by national attachment law the court has jurisdiction, irrespective of the specific nature of the claim.

Whether U.S. attachment jurisdiction asserts specific or general jurisdiction depends on the quality and quantity of the (property) contacts with the forum; if it is insufficient for general jurisdiction, then specific jurisdiction may be available.

---

[472] *Shaffer v. Heitner*, 433 U.S. 186 (1977) and *Rush v. Savchuk*, 444 U.S. 320 (1980), see Chapter 5, Sect. 5.7.2.

[473] See Muir Watt, 'Note: Banque camerounaise', at 782. The grounds for attachment vary from one system to another. The Dutch *forum arresti* is the result of an attachment order specifically targeting the 'foreign' defendant, '*Vreemdelingenbeslag*' or the '*Auslandersforum*' in Germany and Switzerland.

[474] See Chapter 3, Sect. 3.3.3 on the conditions imposed by Art. 279 SDIA.

[475] See Chapter 3, Sect. 3.2.4 and Art. 700(3) Rv.

Generally, the claimant will choose to use attachment jurisdiction when general or transacting business jurisdiction are not available to him to bring action in the forum.

The requirement of a connection between the claim and defendant's property might be easy to satisfy when the property involves tangibles, but it is much more difficult to establish when it involves intangibles whose *situs* is located where the debtor is or is domiciled. In the latter case the *situs* of the intangible might be located in a forum which is in no way connected with the claim. Whether or not the court of that forum will grant an attachment order, which might be unlikely, depends on national procedure law.

7.7.3 Jurisdiction (Not) Limited to the Value of the Property

Among the civil law systems analysed in this book, the exercise of property-based jurisdiction is not restricted to the value of the claim. The German *forum patrimonii*, the Swiss and Dutch *forum arresti*, as well as the former French version of the facultative *forum arresti* allow jurisdiction over the total amount of the claim when it concerns property, even when the value of the property is inferior to the amount of the claim. These rules do not require that the amount of the claim be proportionate to the value of the property.[476] In the event the value of the (attached) property is not sufficient to cover the claim, the court's judgement will have to be executed elsewhere to satisfy the rest of the claim.[477]

This aspect constitutes the most significant difference between U.S. *quasi in rem* jurisdiction and its civil law variants. U.S. *attachment* jurisdiction is limited to the value of the property.[478] The specific features of U.S. *quasi in rem* jurisdiction entail that the judgement rendered is limited to the value of property and does not follow the defendant. As a consequence, the claimant will not be able to satisfy its claim by executing the court's judgement abroad to satisfy the rest of the claim.[479] The attachment criterion is therefore only interesting to the claimant when the claim does not exceed the value of the property.

---

[476] See the debate in Chapter 3, Sect. 3.5.5, see Krafft, *'Exorbitante' Gerichtsstände*, at 61 and 81.

[477] See also Chapter 3, Sect. 3.3.3. The Swiss Federal Supreme Court emphasized the unlimited character of the Swiss *forum sequestri* rule and stated that the rule permitted jurisdiction over the claim without limiting jurisdiction to the value of the asset sequestrated. Claimant's access to justice on the basis of the attachment rule should be for the full amount of his claim. It ruled that it was up to claimant to calculate the chances of enforcement of the Swiss judgement if the value of the seized property was not sufficient to satisfy the claim. As summarized by Krafft, the reasons given for not limiting the judgement/jurisdiction to the value of the property are related to ensuring access to justice for claimant and avoiding practical implications if jurisdiction was limited to the amount of the claim. See Krafft, *'Exorbitante' Gerichtsstände*, at 97-98.

[478] See Chapter 5, Sect. 5.7.2; see also Lookofsky and Hertz, *Transnational Litigation*, at 273; and 2nd Restatement of Conflict of Laws, § 66, comment h.

[479] Juenger claims that 'Obviously, recognition is of minor concern where a defendant's foreign assets are of sufficient value to satisfy even a hefty judgment.' F. Juenger, 'A Shoe Unfit for Globetrotting? Symposium Fifty Years of International Shoe: The Past and the Future of Personal Jurisdiction', 28 *The University of California Davis Law Review* (1995), 1027, at 1043.

7.7.4 The Exorbitant Character of Property-based Jurisdiction at Unification Level

The foundation of jurisdiction on the basis of presence of defendant's assets is highly controversial and considered exorbitant at unification level. Particularly worrying is the fact that the *forum patrimonii* asserts jurisdiction regardless of the nature of the claim or a connection between the claim and the attached property and regardless of the value of the properties or any degree of proportionality.[480] When the claimant is domiciled in or is a national of the forum, the rule could result in a veiled *forum actoris*. When the claimant is not domiciled in or is not a citizen of the forum, the foundation of jurisdiction rests upon an even lesser connection. Property-based jurisdiction is considered less excessive when the property constitutes the security for a debt, which is related to the claim.

The *forum patrimonii* is systematically banned in international and regional conventions. The supplementary Protocol of 1 February 1971 already identified the *forum patrimonii* as well as the *forum arresti* as exorbitant.[481] The Brussels Model also markes property-based jurisdiction as exorbitant.[482] With the important *Siskina* decision's rejection of attachment jurisdiction under English common law, the House of Lords referred to the Brussels Convention's qualifying the rule as exorbitant.[483] The French *Cour de cassation* equally refused attachment jurisdiction, but did not refer to the Brussels Convention. The Dutch reform on jurisdiction rules upheld the *forum arresti* despite its exclusion at European level. The jurisdiction on 'the presence or seizure of property belonging to the defendant' is on top of the black list of prohibited grounds for jurisdiction of Article 18 of both the 1999 Preliminary Draft Convention and the 2001 Interim Text of The Hague Jurisdiction Project. The Nygh and Pocar Explanatory Report indicates that property-based jurisdiction where there is no connection with the property situated in the state concerned should be regarded as exceptional and unacceptable.[484] The reporters do not prohibit the rule as long as 'the dispute is directly connected with property of the defendant which is situated or was seized in the State, since this implies a

[480] See above Sect. 7.7 and see Krafft, *'Exorbitante' Gerichtsstände*, at 46-47.

[481] In conjunction with Art. 2 of the 1971 Hague Convention. See http://hcch.net. Art. 4(*a*) of the Protocol states that 'the presence in the territory of the State of origin of property belonging to the defendant, or the seizure by the plaintiff of property situated there is not a valid base of jurisdiction, unless 1) the action is brought to assert proprietary or possessory rights in that property, or arises from another issue relating to such property, or 2) the property constitutes the security for a debt which is the subject-matter of the action.' The last two exceptions imply that attachment jurisdiction can be permitted when property is related to the claim. See Fragistas and Droz, 'Explanatory Report Hague Convention 1971', at 501; and Krafft, *'Exorbitante' Gerichtsstände*, at 27.

[482] See Chapter 2, Sect. 2.2.7.3; Art. 3(2) and Annex I of the Brussels Regulation; in Germany: Art. 23 ZPO; Austria: Art. 99 Jurisdiktionsnorm. In the U.K. the Brussels Model refers to rules which enable jurisdiction to be founded on: '(a) … (b) the presence within the U.K. of property belonging to the defendant; or (c) the seizure by the plaintiff of property situated in the U.K.' (referring to the Scottish rule). See Jenard Report, at 19. The Swiss rule is sanctioned under Art. 3(2) Lugano Convention. See Schlosser, 'Jurisdiction in International Litigation: The Issue of Human Rights', at 25 *et seq.*

[483] See *The Siskina and Others v. Distos Compañía Naviera S.A.*, [1979] AC 210, Lord Denning at 243 and Lord Diplock pursues at 259.

[484] Nygh-Pocar Report, at 76.

"substantial link" between the dispute and the forum'.[485] The terminology used by the reporters seems to be influenced by the American and German limitations to the application of the rule by virtue of the 'sufficient connection' requirement imposed by the U.S. Supreme Court and the German BGH. During the diplomatic conference in June 2001 it was proposed to delete property-based jurisdiction from the black list all-together.[486] This lack of consensus showed in the Interim Text was not observed by Kessedjian in 1997 when she stated that '[n]o expert argued for such a forum of general jurisdiction, which all agreed should be prohibited in the future Convention'.[487] Kessedjian also indicated that specific jurisdictions are allowed with respect to certain kind of claims, specifying among others provisional and protective measures.[488]

Some national jurisdictional systems using property-based jurisdiction – despite the condemnation of the rule at unification level – restricted its scope by applying correction mechanisms[489] other than the *forum non conveniens* doctrine which is available as a potential escape from the exercise of U.S. *quasi in rem II* jurisdiction.[490] Obviously, since *Shaffer* the U.S. jurisdictional scheme applies the due process standards to attachment jurisdiction.[491] The comparison made by Schlosser was striking when he stated that 'the fact that this [U.S.] basis of jurisdiction, which was much less oppressive than paragraph 23 of the German Code of Civil Procedure, did not meet constitutional fairness standards must be a challenge to Europeans.'[492] In fact, the wide scope of the German *forum patrimonii* was restricted by the decision of the BGH of 2 July 1991 which imposed a *sufficient connection* requirement *(hinreichend inlandsbezug)* between the claim and the forum.[493] This correction which was applied specifically to this property-based jurisdiction acknowledges that the rule resulted in excessive jurisdiction, i.e. was based on a very weak connection with the forum.

---

485 Ibid.

486 Fn. 110, at 16 of the Summary of the Outcome of the Discussion in Commission II of the First Part of the Diplomatic Conference 6-20 June 2001 states: 'It has been proposed to delete subparagraph a) entirely. There is no consensus on this issue'.

487 Kessedjian, 'Prel. Doc. No. 8 of June 1997: Synthesis Special Commission', at 61 and see also Kessedjian, 'Prel. Doc. No. 7, 1997 Report', at 41.

488 Other specific claims that were mentioned are claims with respect to the situation of cultural property whose restitution is sought and serve as the basis for the jurisdiction of the court for actions for restitution, under the Convention on Stolen or Illegally Exported Cultural Objects and actions for payment of the remuneration claimed for salvage of a cargo or freight. Kessedjian, 'Prel. Doc. No. 8, June 1997, Synthesis Special Commission', at 61; Nygh-Pocar Report, at 76.

489 See R. Gassmann, *Arrest im Internationalen Rechtsverkehr: zum Einfluss des Lugano-Ubereinkommens auf das schwiezerische Arrestrecht* (1998), at 240-250; and see Chapter 8, Sect. 8.1.1.

490 Although Scotland is not part of the selected countries in the present analysis, some observations concerning the Scottish system may be of value. A Scottish variation of attachment jurisdiction, the *arrestment ad fundam iuridictionem*, has been at the origin of the introduction of the *forum non conveniens* doctrine in the Scottish jurisdictional system, although it has been partly replaced by Schedule 8 of the CJJA 1982. Amended by Schedule 2, Part III, § 6 and 7 CJJO 2001; see Nuyts, *L'exception*, § 55, at 87.

491 See above Sect. 7.7.

492 Schlosser, 'Jurisdiction in International Litigation: The Issue of Human Rights', at 10.

493 See also Chapter 8, Sect. 8.1.1.

7.7.5 Evaluation

One of the principal justifications for property jurisdiction is based on the necessity to execute and secure defendant's assets as a resource to satisfy a potential judgement. According to Krafft, the fact that a recognition and enforcement procedure can be prevented when defendant's property is directly available in the forum in order to satisfy a court's judgement is in the interest of the claimant.[494] This execution-argument is disregarded for the present purposes, as the argument becomes less persistent when international double conventions guarantee recognition and execution of judgements. As it is not considered as a minimum standard for uniform rules in contractual disputes, this argument does not weigh as much as the connection with the forum, legal certainty and the equality of arms. Contrary to the *forum arresti* rule where assets are, prior to the commencement of main proceedings, secured to satisfy the judgement, under the *forum patrimonii* the defendant can displace assets to another forum, preferably to a forum where he is not liable for suit or whose judgement is unlikely to be recognized and enforced and where the assets are out of the reach of the claimant.

Although, the presence of defendant's property in the forum constitutes some kind of *defendant-related* connection with the forum, the question remains whether this connection is sufficient to justify jurisdiction at international level. In the situation where property is directly related to the defendant's claim, for instance when the claimant requests payment after he delivered goods following the contract, there is a certain connection between the competent court of the place of the location of the goods and the defendant and the claim.

But the *forum patrimonii* establishes jurisdiction over defendant's property, regardless of any connection between the property and the claim or the defendant, or with respect to the value of the property and the amount of the claim. It is not surprising that the application of such a rule is subjected to a sufficient connection requirement or *Inlandsbezug* with the forum in Germany.

When attachment is required for property-based jurisdiction, it is more likely that a connection between the forum and the property exists, especially when defendant's property is a tangible object. For the attachment of property some procedure laws require a connection between the claim and the property to grant the attachment order. A connection between the property located in the forum and the claim is particularly problematic when the property involves an intangible whose *situs* is generally determined by the location of the debtor. Whether the intangible is located where the debtor *is* or is domiciled is no guarantee of a connection

---

[494] Krafft, *'Exorbitante' Gerichtsstände*, at 59; see also H. Schack, 'Vermögensbelegenheit als Zuständigkeitsgrund: Exorbitant oder Sinnvoll?', *Zeitschrift für Zivilprozess* (1984), 46-68, at 49; L. Pellis, *Forum Arresti: Aspecten van rechtsmachtscheppend (vreemdelingen-) beslag in Europa* (1993), at 29-30 and 125. J. de Heer, 'Forum arresti-perikelen', *NIPR* (2001), 389-397, at 389. J. Verheul, *Aspekten van Nederlands internationaal beslagrecht/Aspects of Attachment in Dutch Private International Law* (1968), at 102-103, and see also at 153-154. The fact that the application of the Dutch *forum arresti* is subordinated to the condition that claimant cannot enforce or execute the title through other means, underlines the importance of satisfying the judgement behind this attachment jurisdiction. See Chapter 3, Sect. 3.2.4.

between the designated court and the defendant or the claim. In other words, when the seized property involves intangibles, the excessive character of attachment jurisdiction, as a result of a lack of connection, lies in the determination of the *situs* of the debt.

This also brings us to the issue of the legal certainty of property-based jurisdiction. For property-based jurisdiction the location of property is crucial. The location of tangible moveables and intangible property is subjected to change and results in a change in the competent court. This does not contribute to legal certainty, and neither does the complex identification of the *situs* of intangible property.

The purpose of national provisions for property-based jurisdiction is to secure the claimant's access to justice over a defendant outside his home court.[495] The question is whether jurisdiction based on the presence of (attached) property is best suited as a uniform jurisdiction rule for contractual disputes. Especially the *forum patrimonii* property-based jurisdiction is particularly disadvantageous to the defendant, since the simple presence of the property in a forum is sufficient to be subjected to the court's jurisdiction.

One of the arguments in favour of the *forum arresti* rule, advanced in the French *Nassibian* case, is the argument of effective access to justice for the claimant: if a court is exclusively competent to order an attachment over property located in France, French courts should have jurisdiction to rule over the merits.[496]

It was thought important to protect the claimant from litigating in a (foreign) court, other than the court of the place where his property was seized, and then require him to start an enforcement procedure in order to obtain satisfaction of the judgement out of assets located elsewhere and seized by another court. As underlined by Krafft it is illogical to require from the claimant to bare the costs and difficulties of filing suit in one country and then having to enforce the judgement in another forum where the property was already seized.[497] Property-based jurisdiction ensures access to justice for claimant when claimant seized defendant's assets in country A, but by virtue of the applicable jurisdiction rules has to litigate in the courts of forum B even if a judgement from country B has no chance of being enforced and recognized in country A and claimant is left without an executable title (enforceable judgement). Another argument put forward by Nuyts for the justification of the Dutch *forum arresti* also illustrates the claimant's interests in the *forum arresti*: 'an action brought at the attachment forum would save

[495] See Gaudemet-Tallon used the following statement of Bynkerhoek's to underline the importance of the arrestment as an alternative to the defendant's home court: '*ceux qui ne sont pas sujets ne peuvent être appelés en justice qu'en conséquence et en vertu d'un arrêt ou d'une saisie.*' (those who are not subjects [of the state] can be called for justice only by virtue of an arrestment or attachment); C. van Bynkershoek, *Traité du juge competent des ambassadeurs, tant pour le civil que pour le criminel*, ed. trans. J. Barbeyrac (1723), cited by Gaudemet-Tallon, *Origines de l'article 14 CC*, fn. 2, at 74.

[496] G. Couchez, 'Note: Dame Nassibian v. Nassibian; Cour de cass., Ch.Civ.I 6 Nov. 1979', *Revue critique de droit international privé* (1980), 588-597, at 590. Lequette, 'Note: COBENAM, at 140; A. Ponsard, 'Note: Dame Nassibian v. Nassibian; Cour de cass. Ch.Civ.I, 6 Nov. 1979', *Journal du droit international (Clunet)* (1980), 95-103, at 101; Ancel and Lequette, *Les grands arrêts*, fn. 11, at 569; Schröder, *Internationale Zuständigkeit*, at 377.

[497] Krafft, *'Exorbitante' Gerichtsstände*, at 58.

local creditors [local claimants] time and procedural expense, instead of having to litigate abroad'.[498] In that context, property-based jurisdiction is considered as a counterpart to the privilege given to the defendant under the *actor sequitur forum rei* rule and compensates claimant's disadvantage of having to follow defendant to his home court and to litigate in a foreign court. This aspect of property-based jurisdiction relates to its subsidiary nature: the rule seeks to reach defendants residing outside the forum and enables claimant to sue defendant where his property is seized or located, consequently depriving the defendant of his right to litigate at his 'home court'.[499] In other words, the fact that the property-based jurisdiction might result in a *forum actoris* protects local businesses from having to litigate abroad. The question is whether such compensation is needed in a balanced unified jurisdictional system.[500] Apart from serving the interest of the claimant, property-based jurisdiction also serves the state's interests to protect (national) property in the forum. By giving courts jurisdiction over disputes *involving* property present on the forum, the state keeps control and influence.[501] Property-based jurisdiction protects assets located on the territory of the state and is primarily used against assets appertaining to foreigners or defendants not domiciled in the forum.[502] But such a jurisdiction rule can also have a negative effect on foreign investors wishing to settle or have bank accounts in the forum. Their property is not only subject to seizure, they themselves might be subjected to the judicial proceedings for actions brought against them even for those actions not connected by any means to the property.

---

[498] Nuyts, *L'exception*, at 87.

[499] Lequette, 'Note: COBENAM', at 139-140; Droz, 'Les droits de la demande', at 97.

[500] If the answer is affirmative, property-based jurisdiction is more neutral than nationality-based jurisdiction and the *forum actoris* which is based on claimant's domicile. See Droz, 'Réflexions', at 7.

[501] Gaudemet-Tallon identified rules, in her study on the origin of French nationality-based jurisdiction, that the arrest of persons and the attachment of a person's property is a privilege of the forum, '*privilège d'arrêt*', to bind foreigners. Gaudemet-Tallon, *Origines de l'article 14 CC*, at 74.

[502] Ancel and Lequette, *Les grands arrêts*, at 570.

Chapter 8

CORRECTION MECHANISMS: REQUIREMENTS AND EXCEPTIONS

The preceding chapter compared the bases for jurisdiction and their connecting factors.[1] But the 'jurisdictional inquiry has been constantly influenced by a general drive of wanting to be fair'.[2] This general drive is not merely reflected by the search for adequate bases of jurisdiction, but also by the application of 'correction mechanisms' to rectify undesired outcomes of jurisdiction rules. This chapter compares the different corrections applied among the jurisdictional regimes surveyed and examines to what extent they allow, to use the words of Von Mehren, the '*fine tuning*' of the exercise of jurisdiction.[3] The bases for establishing jurisdiction and the correction of jurisdiction are directly related. The wider the bases for jurisdiction the greater is the need for correction.[4]

Correction devices are characterized by the *discretionary* powers of the courts applying them. They are divided in two categories: *jurisdictional requirements* and *exception clauses.* A second subdivision consists in distinguishing between *general* and *special* correction mechanisms. A general correction applies regardless of the underlying basis upon which jurisdiction is assumed. Special correction clauses merely apply in relation to specific bases for jurisdiction.[5]

In contrast to exception clauses, *jurisdictional requirements* must always be fulfilled, in order to exercise jurisdiction and do not apply by way of derogation.[6] This constitutes the main difference between the two categories, even if the outcome of both categories may be the same, namely the non-exercise of jurisdiction.

One example of a general jurisdictional requirement is the U.S. due process standards which need to be satisfied for U.S. courts to exercise jurisdiction.[7]

---

[1] Other terms used by McLachlan are 'formal' jurisdiction rules or 'rules of original jurisdiction', see C. McLachlan, 'Interim Report Declining & Referring Jurisdiction in International Litigation', paper presented at the London ILA Conference 2000.

[2] M. Karayanni, *Forum Non Conveniens in the Modern Age: A Comparative and Methodological Analysis of Anglo-American Law* (2004), at 146.

[3] A. von Mehren, 'Theory and Practice of Adjudicatory Authority in Private International Law: A Comparative Study of the Doctrine, Policies and Practices of Common- and Civil-Law Systems: General Course on Private International Law (1996)', 295 *Recueil des cours* (2003), 9-431, at 306.

[4] See also M. Keyes, *Jurisdiction in International Litigation* (2005), at 180-182; McLachlan, 'Report Leuven/London Principles', § 27, at 10.

[5] D. Kokkini-Iatridou, 'Rapport général: Les clauses d'exception en matière de conflits de lois et de conflits de juridictions', in *Exception Clauses in Conflicts of Laws and Conflicts of Jurisdictions, or the Principle of Proximity: XIVth International Congress of Comparative Law, Athens* (1994), 3-41, at 5-6.

[6] Or '*condition de dessaisissement*' which translates as 'requirement to decline', see A. Nuyts, *L'exception de forum non conveniens: Etude de droit international privé* (2003), § 267, at 368-369.

[7] See Chapter 5, Sect. 5.4; and see R. Brand, 'Understanding Activity-Based Jurisdiction', paper presented at the UIA Seminar, Edinburgh, 20 & 21 April 2001; The Preliminary Draft Hague Convention on Jurisdiction and Foreign Judgements in Civil and Commercial Matters, at 26.

Another example deriving from the common law is the English *forum conveniens* doctrine.[8] The civil law counterpart is the *sufficient connection* requirement which corrects the outcome of specific jurisdiction rules, when the dispute has no or too little connection with the forum, by refusing to exercise jurisdiction.[9]

Exception clauses in the context of international jurisdiction should be understood as 'clauses deriving from treaty-provisions, statutory or legislative acts, or judge-made law having the purpose to provide the court or judge the (discretionary) power to *correct* one or more rules of jurisdiction.'[10] An example of an exception mechanism is the notorious general exception doctrine of *forum non conveniens*, which allows a court to make an *exception* to the exercise of jurisdiction: The court seized uses its discretionary power to decline its *assumed* jurisdiction when according to its own appreciation it established that another court is a more appropriate forum.[11] This exception usually stems from judge-made law, but could theoretically be incorporated in conventions and international treaties.[12] Depending on the type of exception clause and of the jurisdictional system, they are instituted *ab initio* or at the request of a party, which constitutes a significant difference with jurisdictional requirements which always need to be fulfilled and thus appreciated by the court seized.

In order to define the scope of the present analysis on correction devices, a few preliminary observations are necessary. First and foremost, a court's discretionary power[13] should be distinguished from a certain 'margin of appreciation' of bases of jurisdiction upon which the court accepts or dismisses the exercise of jurisdiction.[14] It is simply not a matter of 'correction' when the court concludes that the facts of the case are not covered by jurisdiction rules.[15]

---

[8] See Chapter 4, Sect. 4.3.

[9] The sufficient connection requirement also called by Joubert '*critère general de confirmation de la compétence juridictionnelle*', N. Joubert, *La notion de liens suffisants avec l'ordre juridique (Inlandsbeziehung) en droit international privé* (2007), § 296, at 297.

[10] This is a definition of exception clauses as given by Kokkini-Iatridou in her general report of the XIVth International Congress of the International Academy of Comparative Law: '*La clause d'exception est une règle d'origine conventionnelle, législative, ou jurisprudentielle ayant pour but d'attribuer au juge le pouvoir (discrétionnaire) de corriger une ou plusieurs règles de conflits de lois.*' Kokkini-Iatridou, 'Rapport général: Les clauses d'exception', at 4-5. Exception clauses are traditionally used in conflict of laws rules; D. Kokkini-Iatridou and E. Frohn, 'De exceptieclausules in het verdragenrecht, een verkenning', in *Eénvormig en vergelijkend privaatrecht* (1989), 215-264, at 216 *et seq.*; P. Lagarde, 'Le principe de proximité dans le droit internationale privé contemporain. Cours général de droit international privé', 196 *Recueil des cours* (1986), 9-238, at 142.

[11] Nuyts, *L'exception*, § 1, at 1; Kokkini-Iatridou and Frohn, 'De exceptieclausules in het verdragenrecht, een verkenning', at 227; Lagarde, 'Le principe de proximité', § 141, at 142.

[12] Kokkini-Iatridou, 'Rapport général: Les clauses d'exception', at 4.

[13] In French this is called the '*compétence volontaire*', see C. Chalas, *L'exercise discrétionnaire de la compétence juridictionnelle en droit international privé* (2000), § 408, at 372. See for this power, Art. 92(2) French NCCP.

[14] J. Fawcett, *Declining Jurisdiction in Private International Law* (1995), at 2, General Report; P. Nygh, 'Declining Jurisdiction under the Brussels I Regulation 2001 and the Preliminary Draft Hague Judgments Convention: A Comparison', in *Reform and Development of Private International Law – Essays in Honour of Sir Peter North* (2002), 303-334, at 304; and Nuyts, *L'exception*, § 164, at 235.

[15] Nuyts, *L'exception*, § 164, at 236, '*mais il n'y a aucune correction ou aménagement de la règle; lorsque le juge conclut que la situation relève du critère prévu par le législateur, il exerce sa*

Secondly, discretionary powers available on the basis of the *lis pendens* principle[16] or the 'related actions' provision as applied in civil law systems,[17] are not considered in the present analysis, even though because of their nature they are often compared with correction mechanisms such as the *forum non conveniens* doctrine. Discretionary powers based on the *forum necessitatis* rule, offering judicial powers to accept jurisdiction in order to avoid a possible denial of justice or '*déni de justice*', are not considered either.[18] For similar reasons, the present comparative analysis does not deal with correction on grounds of 'abuse of process', which is the predecessor and specific version of the *forum non conveniens* doctrine that is found in common law jurisdictions and which allows the court to decline when jurisdiction would be 'vexatious or oppressive' to the defendant.[19]

As explained in Chapter 6, the Continental European approach usually consists in a one step inquiry; the predominantly closed jurisdictional catalogues with carefully drafted connecting factors do not apply general correction devices. If any correction is needed, on the simple basis that the rule is 'excessively' based on a weak connection with the forum, Continental civil law systems occasionally allow special correction devices (Sect. 8.1). Conversely, the Anglo-American jurisdictional inquiry is generally multi-layered. After establishing whether there is a legal basis for jurisdiction, predominantly general correction mechanisms are activated to verify the appropriateness, convenience, reasonableness or fairness of the exercise of jurisdiction (Sect. 8.2). Some attention is given to the question whether the fundamental right of a fair trial enshrined in Article 6 of the European Convention on Human Rights should correct the outcome of European jurisdiction rules and whether its standards are comparable to the U.S. Due Process Clause (Sect. 8.3). Whether special or general correction mechanisms are accepted at unification level is addressed in Section 8.4, followed by a general evaluation in Section 8.5 of

---

compétence; dans le case contraire, il se dessaisit.' See also McLachlan, 'Report Leuven/London Principles', § 26, at 10, who stresses that declining jurisdiction is to be distinguished from 'the situation where the rules on jurisdiction are not satisfied and the court therefore dismisses the action on the basis that it has no jurisdiction'.

[16] Fawcett, *Declining Jurisdiction*, at 2.

[17] See H. Gaudemet-Tallon, 'Les régimes relatifs au refus d'exercer la compétence juridictionnelle en matière civile et commerciale', *Revue internationale de droit comparé* (1994), 423-435, at 423 and Nygh, 'Declining Jurisdiction', at 304.

[18] Systems accepting such a rule correct an unwanted situation by giving their judiciary a certain amount of discretionary powers to accept, by way of exception, jurisdiction. Examples are to be found in Art. 9 of the Dutch Rv. and Art. 3 of the Swiss PIL Statute. The *forum necessitatis* is considered as an example of the reversed *forum non conveniens*, but its purpose – to solve negative jurisdiction conflicts – is different, see Chalas, *L'exercise discrétionnaire*, § 410, at 375 and § 412, at 376; H. Schack, 'Germany National Report', in *Declining Jurisdiction in Private International Law* (1995), 189-205, at 193.

[19] See A. Reus, 'Judicial Discretion: A Comparative View of the Doctrine of Forum Non Conveniens in the United States, the United Kingdom and Germany', *Loyola of Los Angeles International and Comparative Law Journal* (1994), 457, at 468; Chalas, *L'exercise discrétionnaire*, § 73, at 89 *et seq.*; R. Brand, 'Comparative Forum Non Conveniens and the Hague Convention on Jurisdiction and Judgments: International Forum Shopping in Memory of Professor F.K. Juenger', 37 *Texas International Law Journal* (2002), at 470-471; Nuyts, *L'exception*, § 521, at 734 *et seq.*; Karayanni, *FNC in the Modern Age*, at 59; and see *Piper Aircraft Co. v. Reyno*, 454 U.S. 235, at 255-256 (1981).

the desirability of correction devices in uniform jurisdiction rules for international contract disputes.

8.1 Special Correction and the Close Connection Requirement

The predominant view in Continental Europe is that open norms and general exception clauses do not fit in the closed system of civil law traditions that are characterized as 'rigid'.[20] Nonetheless, a cautious piercing of flexibility is witnessed in some national Continental European systems which allow judicial discretion under very limited and specific circumstances.[21] Special correction is accepted in relation to some particular bases for jurisdiction by predominantly requiring a 'sufficient connection' between the forum and the dispute.[22] Lagarde sees in this 'sufficient connection' requirement, an expression of the principle of proximity:

> '*Si nous revenons sur le continent [européen], nous constatons que la plupart des règles strictes, fixes, dont l'application n'est pas laissée à la libre appréciation du juge. Il n'est pas impossible pourtant de trouver quelques exemples de règles flexibles en fonction du lien de proximité entre le litige et le for saisi.*'[23]

Special jurisdictional requirements 'correct' the outcome of some exorbitant jurisdiction rules. In particular the *forum arresti* rule was subject to correction in Continental European countries.[24]

---

[20] Fawcett, *Declining Jurisdiction*, at 7; see also Von Mehren, 'Theory and Practice', at 306: 'For civil-law systems, jurisdictional rules and principles are designed by the legislature and applied by judges. Judicial "fine tuning" compromises, in the civilian's eyes, the predictability and administrability that all law … should display.'

[21] Outside the present scope, 'sufficient connection' exceptions are found in choice of forum provisions; see the Dutch provision Art. 8(1) Rv. Chapter 3, Sect. 3.2.1.2.; Nuyts, *L'exception*, at 370-381; with respect to provisional and protective measures under Art. 31 of the Brussels Regulation, the ECJ Judgement C-391/95 *Van Uden Maritime BV v. Deco-Line*, [1998] ECR, at I-07091, § 48, states that 'the granting of provisional or protective measures [Art. 31 Brussels Regulation] is conditional on, inter alia, the existence of a *real connecting link* between the subject-matter of the measures sought and the territorial jurisdiction of the Contracting State of the court before which those measures are sought'. See Nuyts, *L'exception*, § 317-318, at 426-431; Chalas, *L'exercise discrétionnaire*, § 603, at 546, comparing the requirement of a Brussels version of the *forum conveniens*, '*une véritable règle de compétence dans laquelle il est possible de voir une définition communautaire du* forum conveniens *en matière conservatoire*'. With respect to jurisdiction rules protecting a weak party, see Nuyts, *L'exception*, § 336-339, at 448-454. Nuyts counts eight areas in which substitutes are to be found, ibid.,§ 165, at 237.

[22] See also F. Marchadier, *Les objectifs généraux du droit international privé à l'épreuve de la Convention Européenne des droits de l'homme* (2007), at 246 and Nygh, 'Declining Jurisdiction', at 327.

[23] Lagarde, 'Le principe de proximité', § 132, at 136, [free translation] 'Turning back to the [European] Continent, we observe that the application of the majority of strict and fixed rules is not left to the free appreciation of the court. It is however not impossible to find some examples of flexible rules referring to the close connection between the dispute and the court seized.' See also § 133, at 137-138, in which Lagarde states the fact that a '*lien suffisant*' [sufficient link] constitutes an element for the principle of proximity.

[24] See again Nuyts, *L'exception*, § 145, fn. 44, at 210, § 313, at 422-423 and § 316, at 424-426.

8.1.1 The 'Sufficient Connection' Requirement

In Germany, a 'revolutionary' ruling of the German *Bundesgerichtshof* (BGH) resulted in an additional requirement for the exercise of property-based jurisdiction.[25] Since the decision it is now settled case law that a '*hinreichender Inlandsbezug*' or – 'sufficient connection' – between the dispute and the German courts is required for exercise of jurisdiction under Article 23 ZPO.[26] The Court did not define what constitutes such a sufficient connection, but it was generally understood that if the claimant is not domiciled or resident in Germany, a sufficient connection between the dispute and the forum is lacking.[27] The seized court has to declare itself incompetent when such a 'domestic' connection is lacking.[28] The BGH was influenced by the fact that Article 23 ZPO was marked exorbitant by the Brussels Model.[29] The exercise of jurisdiction by Swiss courts on the basis of the *forum sequestri* is indirectly conditioned by a Swiss procedure law requiring a sufficient connection with Switzerland for the attachment of the assets itself.[30] A similar sufficient connection is not required by the Dutch 'last resort' *forum arresti* rule under Article 10 Rv.[31] In France, this *Inlandsbeziehung* was considered a 'public policy' exception, based on the connection with the forum.[32]

---

[25] Judgement of the *Bundesgerichtshof* of 2 July 1991– BGHZ 115, 90. See Chapter 3, Sect. 3.5.5; and see Joubert, *La notion de liens suffisants,* § 37-67, at 38-67.

[26] See Schack, 'National Report', at 195; T. Kleinstück, *Due Process-Beschränkungen des Vermögensgerichtsstandes durch hinreichenden Inlandsbezug und Minimum Contacts: Eine rechtsvergleichende Untersuchung unter besonderer Berücksichtigung des U.S.-amerikanischen und österreichischen Rechts* (1994), at 124-128; Kennett, '*FNC* in Europe', at 572.

[27] G. Dannemann, 'Jurisdiction Based on the Presence of Assets in Germany', 41 *The International and Comparative Law Quarterly* (1992), 632-637, at 635.

[28] According to the BGH Decision of 2 July 1991: '*Voraussetzung für die Annahme der internationale Zuständigkeit gemäss § 23 ZPO ist neben der Vermögensbelegenheit ein hinreichender Inlandsbezug postuliert*'. See also C. Dorsel, *Forum non Conveniens: Richterliche Beschränkung der Wahl des Gerichtsstandes im deutschem und amerikanischen Recht* (1996), at 159.

[29] See Chapter 3, Sect. 3.5.5; H. Duintjer Tebbens, 'The English Court of Appeal in *Re Harrods;* An Unwelcome Interpretation of the Brussels Convention', in *Law and Reality: Essays on National and International Procedural Law in Honour of Cornelis Carel Albert Voskuil* (1992), 47-61, at 48; Dannemann, 'Presence of Assets', at 634; Kleinstück, 'Due Process-Beschränkungen', at 145, considering whether the *Genuine Link* theory emanates from public international law principles. Kleinstück rightfully points out at 181 that the 'sufficient connection-requirement' has more resemblances with 'minimum contacts' principles than the *forum non conveniens* doctrine. See Kennett, '*FNC* in Europe', at 571; O. Hartwieg, 'Forum Shopping zwischen Forum non Conveniens und "hinreichendem Inlandsbezug"', 51 *Juristen Zeitung* (1996), 109-118, at 109; Von Mehren, 'Theory and Practice', at 316.

[30] See Chapter 3, Sect. 3.3.3. Enacted in Art. 4 of the Swiss PIL Statute; see Joubert, *La notion de liens suffisants,* § 117-124, at 104-113; Nuyts, *L'exception*, § 147, at 211-212 and § 316, at 425. Some Swiss authors favour a limited version of the *forum non conveniens* doctrine to the example of the German special correction clause with respect to certain 'exorbitant' jurisdiction rules such as the Swiss *forum sequestri*, Ch. Bernasconi, 'La Théorie du *forum non conveniens* – Un regard suisse', *IPRax* (1994), 3-10, at 10.

[31] See for the conditions for the application of the Dutch rule, Chapter 3, Sect. 3.2.4.

[32] A French decision by the *Cour de cassation* dealing with the applicable law on filiation applied a public policy exception which was considered '*comme une consecration de la notion allemande* d'Inlandsbeziehung, *c'est – à dire d'un ordre public conçu en fonction d'un lien avec le territoire.*'

Some see in this '*sufficient connection*' requirement the civil law counterpart of the *forum (non) conveniens* doctrine.[33] That parallel goes too far and should be avoided for a number of reasons. Primarily, the *Inlandsbeziehung* should be characterized as a requirement for jurisdiction and not as an exception. Secondly, the 'sufficient connection' requirement is limited to property-based jurisdiction which makes it a special correction clause instead of a general *forum non conveniens* exception.[34] Thirdly, as opposed to the *forum (non) conveniens* exception, such a jurisdictional requirement does not consist in a comparison with an available alternative forum.[35] Finally, although requiring a 'sufficient connection' is also a *forum non conveniens* factor,[36] the doctrine involves the appreciation of more factors than the sole connection with the forum. Especially the *forum non conveniens* versions of the majority of U.S. states consider public interest factors and allow a stronger incentive to decline jurisdiction when claimant is a non-U.S. resident.[37] Nonetheless, the requirement illustrates the willingness to introduce a certain degree of flexibility in rigid jurisdiction rules in a predominantly closed system.[38]

Cour de cassation, Civ. 1re, 10 February 1993, in *Revue critique de droit international privé* (1993), 620, note by J. Foyer, at 624. Joubert, *La notion de liens suffisants,* § 110-116, at 98-104; H. Muir Watt, 'Evidence of an Emergent European Legal Culture: Public Policy Requirements of Procedural Fairness under the Brussels and Lugano Conventions', 36 *Texas International Law Journal* (2001), 539, at 547.

[33] Fawcett, *Declining Jurisdiction*, at 7; Schack, 'National Report', at 195; Kokkini-Iatridou, 'Rapport général: Les clauses d'exception', at 34-35.

[34] Kennett, '*FNC* in Europe', at 571; Dorsel, 'Forum non Conveniens', at 169. This is a general exception which is nonexistent in Germany, at least not over commercial matters. Reus, 'Judicial Discretion', at 490, Schack, 'National Report', at 190; Nuyts, *L'exception*, § 143, at 206. See for exceptions in certain specific areas of law, i.e. non-contentious matters, see Schack, 'National Report', at 191; Nuyts, *L'exception*, §141, at 206; Brand, 'Comparative FNC', at 487; Chalas, *L'exercise discrétionnaire*, § 579, at 521. Some German scholars favour a general application of the doctrine, especially J. Schröder, *Internationale Zuständigkeit: Entwurf eines Systems von Zuständigkeitsinteressen im zwischenstaatlichen Privatverfahrensrecht, aufgrund rechtshistorischer, rechtsvergleichender und rechtspolitischer Betrachtungen* (1971), at 486 *et seq.*; and see the position of the *Max Planck Institut* in *Reform des deutschen internationalen Privatrechts* (1980), cited by Nuyts, *L'exception*, § 334, at 447; see *RabelsZ* 44 (1980), 350, at 365.

[35] Even if '[t]he end result may be a requirement that the plaintiff shows that the forum is an appropriate one.' Kennett, '*FNC* in Europe', at 571; see in contrast Nuyts, *L'exception*, § 164, at 236.

[36] Nuyts, *L'exception*, § 313, at 423.

[37] See Chapter 5, Sects. 5.5.2-5.5.4. and see below Sect. 8.2.3. See Kleinstück, 'Due Process-Beschränkungen', at 181.

[38] Ibid., at 179; and for different comparative studies see among others, A. Bittighofer, *Der internationale Gerichtsstand des Vermögens: Eine Rechtvergleichende Studie zur Zuständigkeit deutscher Gerichte aufgrund inländischer Vermögensbelegenheit* (1994), Vol. 1561; T. Pfeiffer, 'Book review: A. Bittighofer, *Der internationale Gerichtsstand des Vermögens: Eine Rechtvergleichende Studie zur Zuständigkeit deutscher Gerichte aufgrund inländischer Vermögensbelegenheit*', *RabelsZ* (1997), 595-600; Dorsel, *Forum non Conveniens*; H. Grothe, '"Exorbitante" Gerichtszuständigkeiten im Rechtsverkehr zwischen Deutschland und den U.S.A', 58 *RabelsZ* (1994), 687-726; Hartwieg, 'Forum Shopping'; Kleinstück, 'Due Process-Beschränkungen'. For book reviews see K. Otte, 'Die Process-Beschränkungen des Vermögensgerichtsstandes durch hinreichenden Inlandsbezug und Minimum Contacts. Eine rechtsvergleichende Untersuchung unter besonderer Berücksichtigung des U.S. amerikanischen und österreichischen Rechts Rezensionen; T. Kleinstück, 110 *Zeitschrift für Zivilprozess* (1997), 119-133; T. Pfeiffer, 'Internationale Zuständigkeit und prozessuale Gerechtigkeit: Die inter-

During the reign of the *Nassibian* case, French courts had discretionary powers to appreciate the ascertainment of jurisdiction on the basis of property attached in the forum.[39] The *Nassibian* case permitted the *forum arresti* as a facultative basis for jurisdiction; the exercise of jurisdiction was not mandatory but optional and at the court's discretion. The case shows a small inclination towards the incorporation of judicial appreciation in the exercise of jurisdiction. The facultative character of the rule was chosen because of the fact that the *forum arresti* is marked as exorbitant by the Brussels Convention. As a result, until 1995, a French court could be seized on the basis of a *forum arresti* rule and disposed of discretionary powers to exercise or refuse jurisdiction.[40] One of the most given reasons for refusing jurisdiction on this basis was the lack of a sufficient connection with the forum.[41] According to Lagarde, the facultative nature of the rule shows that when the mere presence of attached property constitutes the only connection between France and the dispute, the court may refuse to exercise jurisdiction.[42] The facultative nature of the *Nassibain* rule was also considered as a limited version of the *forum non conveniens* doctrine,[43] but as rightfully observed by Droz, the rule did not impose a requirement as the BGH case did.[44] Twice the French *Cour de cassation* sanctioned attempts to render Article 14's facultative jurisdiction, by reversing a lower court's decision that refused jurisdiction on the basis that the court was not sufficiently connected with the forum.[45]

---

nationale Zuständigkeit im Zivilprozess zwischen effektivem Rechtsschutz und nationaler Zuständigkeitspolitik' (1995), at 523-650; Reus, 'Judicial Discretion', at 511.

[39] Gaudemet-Tallon, 'Les régimes relatifs au refus', at 424.

[40] See also Chalas, *L'exercise discrétionnaire*, § 413, at 378.

[41] According to Lagarde, 'Le principe de proximité', § 132, at 137; Chalas, *L'exercise discrétionnaire*, § 413, at 378.

[42] Lagarde, 'Le principe de proximité', § 132, at 137, '*cette forme facultative ne peut avoir qu'une signification. Si le tribunal français constate qu'il n'existe entre la France et le litige aucun autre lien que la présence en France de biens à saisir, il pourra refuser d'exercer sa compétence sur le fond.*'

[43] Nuyts, *L'exception*, § 146, at 210: '*cet arrêt consacrait une application limité du principe du forum non conveniens*' or '*cette formulation donne bien au juge une liberté de se saisir mais aussi de se dessaisir qui s'apparent au* forum non conveniens'. L. Collins and G. Droz, 'La recours à la doctrine du forum non conveniens et aux "anti-suit injunctions": Principes directeurs. 2ème Commission', 70 *Annuaire de l'Institut de droit international* (2003), 13-94, Réponse de Droz, at 63; and H. Muir Watt, 'La fonction subversive du droit comparé', *Revue internationale de droit comparé* (2000), 503-527, at 525.

[44] Collins and Droz, 'The Principles', Réponse de Droz, at 64: '*Ce qui n'est pas le cas de la jurisprudence allemande qui depui 1991 a subordonné la compétence du for du patrimoine à l'existence d'un lien suffisant entre le litige et le for. On retombe ici, comme dans l'exemple néerlandais, dans le cas d'un contrôle des conditions de la compétence et non pas d'une discrétion absolue*'. But see Chalas, *L'exercise discrétionnaire*, § 413, at 378.

[45] See Cour de cass. civ. I-9 December 2003, 01-14569, Bull. I N° 247, at 197; Cour de cass civ. I-18 December 1990; see D. Bureau and H. Muir Watt, *Droit international privé* (2007), Vol. I, § 163, at 167; Nuyts, *L'exception*, at 207; Chalas, *L'exercise discrétionnaire*, § 443, at 401-402, fns. 132-135.

8.1.2 No Room for Special Connection Correction under the Brussels Model

The Brussels Model is based on the *assumption* of a close connection with the forum, but the ECJ consistently rejected any attempt to introduce a 'sufficient connection' element for contract jurisdiction and refused the slightest discretion under Article 5(1) of the Brussels Model.[46]

As observed by Nuyts, the AG Mayras referred, in his opinion to the *Tessili* dispute, to discretionary powers of the court seized.[47] Mayras pointed out that if the *forum contractus* was to be located at the place of performance of *any* contractual obligation, this would require a '*forum non conveniens* correction' on the basis of the closest connection with the forum. Although Mayras was not in favour of such an approach, the ECJ decided that the obligation in question should be conclusive, without commenting on Mayras' observations.[48]

In the *Shenevai* case, the question arose whether the *forum contractus* should be determined by the *focal point* of the contract as a whole.[49] The debate concerned the introduction of an open-ended connecting factor, rather than a 'close connection' requirement, but this *focal point* debate addressed the close connection presumption for contract jurisdiction. Once again, the ECJ refused an open-ended concept based on proximity in the *Shenevai* decision and decided that the principal obligation is conclusive.[50] This was later confirmed in *Custom Made* when the ECJ stated that the

> 'effect of accepting as the sole criterion of jurisdiction the existence of a connecting factor between the facts at issue in a dispute and a particular court would be to oblige the court before which the dispute is brought to consider other factors, in particular the

---

[46] See Chalas, *L'exercise discrétionnaire*, § 495-496, at 439: No 'sufficient connection' is required in relation to chosen courts under Art. 17 Brussels Convention and Art. 23 Brussels Regulation. In C-159/97*Trasporti Castelletti Spedizioni Internazionali SpA v. Hugo Trumpy SpA*, [1999] ECR, at 1597, the ECJ was asked whether it is necessary for the parties to choose a court having some link to the case, see paras. 12 and 46. In his opinion delivered on 22 September 1998, at § 38, A.G. Léger indicated that any refusal to impose a *sufficient link* or *objective connection* between the (chosen) forum and the dispute as jurisdictional requirement was to be considered as a rejection to the *forum non conveniens* doctrine. He furthermore stated that such a 'sufficient link' requirement 'would have encouraged the parties to turn to arbitration, where the absence of an objective link between the dispute and the arbitrators is more usually the case in international matters'. The ECJ decided that for reasons of certainty and foreseeablity Art. 17 of the Convention 'dispenses with any objective connection between the relationship in dispute and the court designated', see Case C-159/97 *Trasporti Castelletti v. Hugo Trumpy*, para. 50; Case 56/79 *Zelger v. Salinitri*, [1980] ECR 89, para. 4; C-106/95 *MSG v. Gravières Rhénanes*, [1997] ECR, at I-911, para. 34; and C-269/95 *Benincasa v. Dentalkit*, [1997] ECR I-3767, para. 28. A choice of court clause may be assessed only in the light of considerations connected with its requirements and 'considerations about the links between the court designated and the relationship at issue, … are unconnected with those requirements', C-159/97 *Trasporti Castelletti SpA v. Hugo Trumpy SpA*, para. 52.

[47] Nuyts, *L'exception*, § 155, at 222.

[48] Case 12/76 *Tessili v. Dunlop*, [1976] ECR 1473, at 01473.

[49] Case 266/85 *Shenavai v. Kreischer*, [1987] ECR, at 239, paras. 4 and 5.

[50] Ibid., para. 20.

> pleas relied on by the defendant, in order to determine whether such a connection exists and would thus render Article 5(1) nugatory.'[51]

Clearly the ECJ rejects any determination of jurisdiction on the basis of judicial discretion of the court seized.[52] Instead the ECJ affirms the close connection presumption by stating that the place of the performance of the obligation in question 'usually constitutes the closest connecting factor between the dispute and the court having jurisdiction over it and explains why that court has jurisdiction in contractual matters.'[53] Subsequently the ECJ rejects any discretion to correct the outcome of the rule and even accepts the possibility that the competent court lacks any close connection:

> 'It follows that under Article 5(1), in matters relating to a contract, a defendant may be sued in the courts for the place of performance of the obligation in question, even where the court thus designated is not that which has the closest connection with the dispute.'[54]

In his opinion to the *Custom Made* case, AG Lenz warned that the application of the *lex causae* approach according to *Tessili* 'manifestly does not square with the aim of Article 5(1)'[55] and that it is not 'physically proximate to the relationship at issue'.[56] The ECJ rejected his suggestion to correct such inconsistent outcome of the rule, and preferred to stick to a rigid application of Article 5(1) and its wording. By doing so, according to Lenz, the ECJ departs from the aim of conferring special jurisdiction to the court that has a close connection with the dispute.[57]

The ECJ invokes the principle of legal certainty to justify its systematic refusal to correct the outcome of jurisdiction rules and to provide discretionary powers to

---

[51] C-288/92 *Custom Made v. Stawa*, [1994] ECR I-02913, para. 19.

[52] Similarly, the Court refused in *Groupe Concorde* to determine the place of performance 'by reference to the nature of the relationship of obligation and the circumstances of the case'. The Court probably did not anticipate modifications under the Brussels Regulation. C-440/97 *GIE Groupe Concorde*, [1999] ECR I-6307, paras. 22-25; B. Ancel, 'Note: Gie Groupe Concorde', 89 *Revue critique de droit international privé* (2000), 260-264, at 261.

[53] C-288/92 *Custom Made v. Stawa*, [1994] ECR I-2913, at para. 13 and C-440/97 *GIE Groupe Concorde*, [1999] ECR I-6307, para. 29; Case 266/85 *Shenavai v. Kreischer*, [1987] ECR, at 239, para. 18.

[54] C-288/92 *Custom Made v. Stawa*, [1994] ECR I-2913, at para. 21. See also Collins and Droz, 'The Principles', at 22.

[55] Opinion of AG Lenz, delivered on 8 March 1994, in C-288/92 *Custom Made v. Stawa*, [1994] ECR I-2913, para. 63; see also Nuyts, *L'exception*, § 158, at 225-226.

[56] Opinion of AG Lenz, delivered on 8 March 1994, in C-288/92 *Custom Made v. Stawa*, [1994] ECR I-2913, paras. 71 and 74. In this particular case, AG Lenz proposed to proceed from the general rule of Art. 5(1), which would result in a *forum actoris* in favour of the court of the place of delivery of the goods according to the contractual provisions. See on this point, the debate around the connecting factor of the *forum contractus*, Art. 5(1), and Chapter 2, Sect. 2.7.3. See Nuyts, *L'exception*, § 156, at 223-224, who sees certain similarities with the Australian restrictive *forum non conveniens* approach in this proposition.

[57] See Opinion of AG Lenz, delivered on 8 March 1994, in C-288/92 *Custom Made v. Stawa*, [1994] ECR I-2913, para. 63; and see Nuyts, *L'exception*, § 157, at 225; G. Hogan, 'The Brussels Convention, Forum Non Conveniens and the Connecting Factors Problem', 20 *European Law Review* (1995), 471-494, at 488.

courts to appreciate the close connection with the forum on the basis of facts and the context of the dispute.[58]

8.2 General Correction Devices

General jurisdictional requirements impose certain conditions regardless of the underlying bases of jurisdiction and are not limited to the subject matter of the claim. Two types of general jurisdictional requirements can be distinguished: the constitutional due process standards characteristic of the U.S. jurisdictional scheme and the English *forum conveniens* doctrine. Both mechanisms should not be understood as exceptions to the exercise of jurisdiction but as additional requirements; when these conditions are not fulfilled, jurisdiction will not be exercised. The *forum non conveniens* doctrine is applied by way of a general exception to jurisdiction.

8.2.1 The United States Due Process Requirements Compared

The U.S. Due Process Clause does not provide statutory authorization for jurisdiction, but operates as a constitutional check to ensure that extraterritorial jurisdiction on the basis of long-arm statutes is consistent with constitutional guarantees. Initially, the due process test was the second step in the jurisdictional inquiry. Is there a legal basis to establish jurisdiction over the claim[59] and does the exercise of jurisdiction over the defendant comply with due process standards?[60] The enumerated long-arm statutes still apply that two-step inquiry and the Due Process Clause obviously imposes constitutional requirements upon the exercise of jurisdiction.

But, this is less obvious for the majority of long-arm state statutes that allow jurisdiction on 'any constitutional basis' either by applying the one-step analysis as a result of a *no limit* statute,[61] or by including a 'catch-all provision'.[62] The courts of these states are less preoccupied with the underlying bases of jurisdiction embodied in enumerated long-arm statutes, but they are more concerned with the due process jurisdictional limits. For those reasons it is often stated that U.S. jurisdiction law is principally based on constitutional due process principles.[63]

---

[58] See Case 34/82 *Peters v. ZNAV*, [1983] ECR 987, para. 17; Case 32/88 *Six Constructions v. Humbert*, [1989] ECR 341, para. 20; C-26/91 *Handte v. Traitements*, Judgement of 17 June 1992, [1992] ECR I-3967, para. 18; C-440/97 *GIE Groupe Concorde*, [1999] ECR I-6307, para. 24; C-256/00 *Besix v. WABAG*, [2002] ECR I-1699, para. 26.

[59] Either the claim falls within one of the jurisdictional provisions of the long-arm statute or within one of the traditional bases for jurisdiction deriving from U.S. common law jurisdiction.

[60] See Chapter 5, Sect. 5.4; D. McFarland, 'Dictum Run Wild: How Long-arm Statutes Extended to the Limits of Due Process', *Boston University Law Review* (2004), 491, at 493; and A. Nuyts, 'Due Process and Fair Trial: Jurisdiction in the United States and in Europe Compared', in *International Civil Litigation in Europe and Relations with Third States* (2005), at 162.

[61] See for instance the California Statute; see McFarland, 'Dictum Run Wild', at 496.

[62] See ibid., at 525-528 and 541; and see Chapter 5, Sect. 5.3.1.

[63] H. Schack, *Jurisdictional Minimum Contacts Scrutinized: Interstaatliche und internationale Zuständigkeit U.S.-amerikanischer Gerichte* (1983), at 23, 'Fairness and reasonableness are the bases of jurisdiction'.

Others have consistently held that due process standards should be understood as a requirement limiting the exercise of jurisdiction and that long-arm statutes still provide for statutory authorization, whether they apply the two-step inquiry or not.[64] For present purposes, the following comparison assumes that the due process test is still required in the one-step and two-step analysis. As a rule, the Due Process Clause is primarily 'jurisdiction-defeating';[65] all exercise of (extraterritorial) jurisdiction is conditional to its compatibility with due process.[66] The present subchapter will attempt to deal with the question whether equivalent (constitutional) requirements were encountered among the system analysed.

The importance of this question at unification level became clear when several proposed provisions under the 1999 and 2001 Hague Drafts emanating from the European *forum contractus*, especially when the place of jurisdiction resulted being the place of payment, were claimed to be incompatible with U.S. constitutional due process standards and therefore unacceptable to the U.S. delegations.[67]

For an adequate comparison, the U.S. due process requirement should be considered on the basis of its components; (1) the 'minimum contacts' test ensuring a *defendant-related* connection, resulting in general or specific jurisdiction;[68] (2) due process requires that the defendant 'purposefully availed' himself of the forum;[69] and (3) the exercise of jurisdiction should not offend 'traditional notions of fair play and substantial justice'.[70] If any of these requirements is not met, the exercise

---

[64] Nuyts, 'Due Process and Fair Trial', at 163-164; Nuyts founds his argument on the Supreme Court decision in *World-Wide Volkswagen Corp. v. Woodson*, 444 U.S. 286, at 293 (1980), and argues that the due process requirement is 'not intended to replace the rules of jurisdiction as provided under state law; the rulings of the Supreme Court are not designed to regulate the jurisdiction of the courts ... but only to avoid the exercise of excessive jurisdiction.' See also R.C. Casad and W.M. Richman, *Jurisdiction in Civil Actions* (1998), Vol. 1, at 386, 'it goes beyond rationality to assume that they intended the statutes to be ignored. Many cases, even in states whose courts declare that their long-arm statutes reach the outer limits of the Constitution, accordingly endorse the two-step, rather than the one-step analysis.' See for more critical comments on the one-step analysis, McFarland, 'Dictum Run Wild', at 532 and 537.

[65] Brand, 'Understanding Activity-Based', at 26 and 35.

[66] *World-Wide Volkswagen Corp. v. Woodson*, 444 U.S. 286, at 291 (1980), 'The Due Process Clause of the Fourteenth Amendment limits the power of a state court to render a valid personal judgment against a non-resident defendant'; and *Kulko v. Superior Court*, 436 U.S. 84, at 91 (1978).

[67] As explained in Chapter 7, Sect. 7.6. *The forum solutionis*. See L. Silberman, 'Comparative Jurisdiction in the International Context: Will the Proposed Hague Judgments Convention Be Stalled?', 52 *DePaul Law Review* (2002), 319-350, at 330; R. Brand, 'Tort Jurisdiction in a Multilateral Convention: The Lessons of the Due Process Clause and the Brussels Convention', *Brooklyn Journal of International Law* (1998), 125-155, at 126; P. Schlosser, 'Lectures on Civil-Law Litigation Systems and American Cooperation with Those Systems', 45 *University of Kansas Law Review* (1996), 19-24, at 41; P. Schlosser, 'Jurisdiction in International Litigation: The Issue of Human Rights in Relation to National Law and the Brussels Convention', *Rivista di diritto internazionale* (1991), 5-34, at 31.

[68] 'It is sufficient for the purpose of due process that the suit was based on a contract which had substantial connection with that State', *McGee v. International Life Insurance Co.*, 355 U.S. 220, at 223 (1957).

[69] '[The p]urposeful availment requirement for long-arm jurisdiction insures that defendant will not be haled into a jurisdiction solely as the result of random, fortuitous, or attenuated contacts or the unilateral activity of another party or a third person.' *Burger King Corp. v. Rudzewicz*, 471 U.S. 462, at 475 (1985); *Hanson v. Denckla*, 357 U.S. 235, at 253 (1958); and see Chapter 5, Sect. 5.4.3.3.

[70] See Chapter 5, Sect. 5.4.4.

of jurisdiction constitutes a violation of the U.S. Due Process Clause and should therefore be refused by the court.

The minimum contacts rule requires the existence of a sufficient relationship between the defendant and the forum[71] and is for that reason often compared with the 'sufficient link' or 'close connection' requirement found in some Continental European systems as set out above.[72] But the major difference with its Continental European counterpart is that the minimum contact rule is a general requirement applicable to all kinds of exercise of jurisdiction, not only to specific bases for jurisdiction.[73]

The Brussels Model never accepted a discretionary 'close connection' requirement. But some authors have made the analogy between the U.S. minimum contacts rule and the list of exorbitant jurisdiction rules under Article 3 of the Brussels Model.[74] Although they acknowledge that the list is not a 'general correction', these authors consider the list to have 'correcting' effects on the allocation of jurisdictional powers on Brussels Territory. Through this non-exhaustive list of exorbitant bases for jurisdiction 'states confess their sins' of excessive exercise of jurisdiction,[75] but it does not prevent them from using these bases in relation to non-EU residents.[76] Some American scholars see in this list a codified version of a 'fixed due-process clause':[77] 'one that does not set out a basic standard of fair-

---

[71] *Helicópteros Nacionales de Colombia, S.A. v. Hall*, 466 U.S. 408, at 417 (1984), 'a defendant has sufficient contacts with a forum State to justify an assertion of jurisdiction'. See Chapter 5, Sect. 5.4.3.

[72] See among others Joubert, *La notion de liens suffisants,* § 441-442, at 423-424; Chalas, *L'exercise discrétionnaire*, § 485, at 430: '*Ainsi, l'exigence constitutionnelle de due process of law a conduit la Cour Suprême des Etats-Unis à développer la doctrine des minimums contacts en application de laquelle sont condamnées les règles de compétence qui ne se fondent pas sur des liens suffisants avec le défendeur pour justifier l'exercice par le tribunal de son pouvoir juridictionnel.*' See Lagarde, 'Le principe de proximité', at 131, arguing that the due process requirement is a negative application of the proximity principle in relation to 'no limit' long-arm statutes: '*Ce que l'on rencontre en droit comparé ... la loi d'un Etat déclare ses tribunaux en principe compétents pour connaître de toute affaire internationale sauf si celle-ci est dépourvu de contacts suffisants avec le for. Cette utilisation négative et certainement abusive du principe de proximité est assez fréquente dans les* long-arm statutes *de certains Etats des Etats-Unis.*' With respect to the Californian Statute, he states in fn. 329: '*Ainsi, la seule limite à la compétence des juridictions californiennes est-elle l'absence de "minimum contacts du litige avec l'état de Californie"*'.

[73] 'Subsequently, I shall draw your attention to the fact that some first steps have recently been made in civil-law systems to open the way for individualized due process considerations.' Schlosser, 'Lectures on Civil-Law Litigation', at 19.

[74] See Art. 3(2) and Annex I Brussels Regulation. Lagarde, 'Le principe de proximité', § 159, at 156; Schlosser, 'The Issue of Human Rights', at 12; F. Matscher, 'Le droit internationale privé face à la Convention Européenne des droits de l'homme', 1996-1997 *Travaux* du *Comité Français de Droit International Privé* (1997), 211-234, at 219: '*[U]ne grande partie de fors exorbitants est tombée à la suite des conventions multilatérales, réglementant les compétences directes, comme par exemple celle de Bruxelles*'.

[75] Schlosser, 'The Issue of Human Rights', at 5; see also P. Lagarde, 'Revues: Schlosser, Peter', 81 *Revue critique de droit international privé* (1992), 626-630, at 627.

[76] An exception is when it concerns exclusive jurisdiction or a choice of forum court.

[77] J. Fitzpatrick, 'The Lugano Convention and Western European Integration: A Comparative Analysis of Jurisdiction and Judgments in Europe and the United States', 695 *Connecticut Journal of International Law* (1993), 695-749, at 722; A. von Mehren, 'Recognition and Enforcement of Sister-

ness but proceeds instead by specification of grossly unreasonable provisions'.[78] But the only sanction of exorbitant exercise of jurisdiction within the scope of the Brussels Model is the refusal of recognition and enforcement of judgements[79] and this is far from imposing a requirement which is sanctioned by refusing the exercise of jurisdiction.[80]

The 'purposeful availment' requirement that has to be satisfied as part of the due process standards is simply unknown in Europe. Schlosser correctly states that 'the European courts do not even care whether there have been any activities by the defendant directed at the territory over which the court has jurisdiction'.[81] This makes the foundation of jurisdiction purely on a connection between the claim and the forum, as is the case with the European contract forum, unacceptable to the U.S. which always require a *defendant-related* connection in which the defendant availed himself of the forum.

Closely related to the '*purposeful availment*' requirement is the '*foreseeability*' element. Within the U.S. due process test, the '*foreseeability*' element is relevant for jurisdictional purposes[82] – or at least in the words of the Supreme Court – it is not 'wholly irrelevant'.[83] In the U.S., *foreseeability* is linked to defendant's connections in the forum since the Supreme Court stated that the defendant should be able to reasonably anticipate that his conduct or activities directed to the forum state are such that he can be 'haled into court' in that forum.[84] Conversely, the '*foreseeability*' principle has a slightly different meaning in the Brussels jurisdiction scheme. Primarily, the '*foreseeability*' element has no effect on the outcome of the jurisdiction rule as a matter of *correction* or *jurisdictional requirement*. The foreseeability factor is not part of the European jurisdictional inquiry or is – to use Nuyts' words – 'not included as such in the jurisdictional calculus'.[85] *Foreseeability* as part of the principle of legal certainty is explicitly mentioned in the Preamble

---

State Judgements: Reflections on General Theory and Current Practice in the European Economic Community and the United States', 81 *Columbia Raw Review* (1981), 1044-1060, at 1058.

[78] Von Mehren, 'Recognition of Sister-State Judgements', at 1058.

[79] This is namely the case *only* when the defendant is a Brussels resident or when jurisdiction is based on imperative rules of the Brussels Model such as exclusive and protective jurisdiction rules, pursuant to Art. 35(1) Brussels Regulation.

[80] Lagarde, 'Le principe de proximité', § 158, at 156: '*cette sanction de refus est insuffisante, car elle corrige l'effet sans s'attaquer à la source.*'

[81] Schlosser, 'Lectures on Civil-Law Litigation', at 24 and 41. Schlosser favours a 'purposeful availment' element at unification level: 'the United States should insist on introducing such a requirement for jurisdiction into the new Convention. I do not think that this will meet major objections because the United States will not encounter any passionate defense of an opposing doctrine. The point has simply not yet been discussed in Europe'.

[82] Casad and Richman, *Jurisdiction in Civil Actions Vol. 1*, § 2-5, at 152.

[83] *World-Wide Volkswagen Corp. v. Woodson*, 444 U.S. 286, at 297 (1980), see at 295; but the foreseeability element is not a 'sufficient benchmark for exercising personal jurisdiction'.

[84] See *Kulko v. California Superior Court*, 436 U.S. 84, at 98 (1978); *World-Wide Volkswagen Corp. v. Woodson*, 444 U.S. 286, at 295 and 297 (1980); *Burger King Corp. v. Rudzewicz*, 471 U.S. 462, at 474 (1985). This is particularly relevant in relation to torts, in the sense that the purposeful availment could be fulfilled when it was *foreseeable* that the accident might occur somewhere.

[85] Nuyts, 'Due Process and Fair Trial', at 175.

and is used by the ECJ to interpret certain bases of jurisdiction.[86] In contrast to the U.S. foreseeability element which focusses on the jurisdictional consequences of defendant's activities in the forum, the Brussels version of *foreseeability* is concerned with legal certainty as a matter of the underlying policy for jurisdiction and should be understood as enabling 'a normally well-informed defendant to reasonably foresee before which courts, other than those of the State in which he is domiciled, he may be sued'.[87]

Due process requires, as an 'absolute prerequisite' that the exercise of jurisdiction does not offend 'traditional notions of fair play and substantial justice'.[88] This separate inquiry considers whether jurisdiction over the defendant is fair and reasonable, taking into account the interests of both parties and the state's interests.[89]

The Supreme Court's decision in *Burger King Corp. v. Rudzewicz* identified five 'fundamental fairness' factors for the court seized to appreciate by way of an open jurisdictional requirement and not as an exception.[90] A comparable *ex post* appreciation of interest factors by virtue of the court's discretionary powers is *quasi* non-existent in Continental Europe, where legislators are involved in an *ex ante* interest balance, which is best illustrated by the *actor sequitur forum rei* and its underlying policy.[91]

8.2.2 General Requirements under the *Forum Conveniens* Doctrine

Like the U.S. due process standards, the English *forum conveniens* doctrine imposes a set of general jurisdictional requirements;[92] extraterritorial jurisdiction is only available to the plaintiff provided that he successfully shows that England is the most appropriate court or the *forum conveniens*.[93] The doctrine should be understood as a positive component for jurisdiction as stated by Fawcett:

---

[86] See para. 11 of the Preamble of the Brussels Regulation, and Chapter 2, Sect. 2.3.5.

[87] C-106/95 *MSG v. Gravières Rhénanes*, [1997] ECR I-911, para. 34. C-26/91 *Handte v. Traitements*, [1992] ECR I-3967, para. 18; C-440/97 *GIE Groupe Concorde*, [1999] ECR I-6307; C-334/00 *Fonderie Officine Meccaniche Tacconi SpA v. Heinrich Wagner*, Judgement of 17 September 2002, [2002] ECR, at 7357, para. 20; C-281/02 *Owusu v. Jackson*, [2005] ECR I-1383, para. 40; C-437/00 *Pugliese v. Finmeccanica*, Judgement of 10 April 2003, [2003] ECR I-3573, para. 16; Case 38/81 *Effer v. Kantner*, [1982] ECR 852, para. 6; and C-125/92 *Mulox v. Geel*, [1993] ECR 4075, para. 11; C-269/95 *Benincasa v. Dentalkit*, [1997] ECR I-3767, para. 26; C-295/95 *Farrell v. Long*, [1997] ECR I-168, at 683, para. 13; C-256/00 *Besix v. WABAG*, [2002] ECR I-1699, at 1737, paras. 25 and 26; C-116/02 *Gasser v. MISAT*, Judgement of 9 December 2003, [2003] ECR I-14693, para. 72.

[88] Casad and Richman, *Jurisdiction in Civil Actions Vol. 1*, § 2-5, at 165; see P. Schlosser, 'Note Bundesgerichtshof 28 October 1996', *Juristen Zeitung* (1997), 362-364, at 8.

[89] *McGee v. International Life Insurance Co.*, 355 U.S. 220, at 223 (1957); *Kulko v. Superior Court of California*, 436 U.S. 84, at 92 (1978).

[90] See Chapter 5, Sect. 5.4.4.

[91] Art. 2 Brussels Model and the majority of Continental European countries; J.E.S. Fawcett, *The Application of the European Convention on Human Rights* (1987), at 397. See also Marchadier, *A l'épreuve de la Convention Européenne des droits de l'homme*, at 186-187.

[92] But see Fawcett, *Declining Jurisdiction*, at 7, General Report.

[93] When the claimant has a serious issue to be tried, he is required to ask permission from the court for outside service, provided that his claim falls under one of the heads of Rule 6.20 CPR; see Schack, *Minimum Contacts Scrutinized*, at 29, who argues that 'convenience' relates to jurisdiction as a 'precondition to jurisdiction'. Lagarde argues that '*la proximité concrète, qui est une composante de*

'Forum conveniens can be defined as a court taking jurisdiction on the ground that the local forum is the appropriate forum trial or that the forum abroad is inappropriate. It is a positive doctrine, unlike the doctrine of forum non conveniens, which is a negative doctrine concerned with declining jurisdiction.'[94]

This positive component for jurisdiction is required for all heads under Rule 6.20 CPR, which makes it a *general* jurisdictional requirement, contrary to 'special connection requirements' such as the German '*Inlandsbezug*' which is only applicable to property-based jurisdiction.[95] Similar to its more restricted Continental European counterpart, one of the main considerations taken into account under the *forum conveniens* rule also involves the close connection factor.[96] But the 'appropriate' forum is identified on the basis of a series of other factors,[97] subjected to judicial appreciation and the court should be convinced that it is the appropriate forum in which the 'case can be suitably tried for the interests of all parties and for the ends of justice'.[98] The English *forum conveniens* and the *forum non conveniens* doctrine use the same *Spiliada* factors, but the latter declines jurisdiction on the basis of those factors whereas the *forum conveniens* exercises jurisdiction.[99] The *forum conveniens* general requirement is a typical English common law feature unknown to the American system, where service out of U.S. territory is possible pursuant to long-arm statutes – comparable to the English Rule 6.20 CPR – but does require the claimant to seek permission and to show that the U.S. forum is the most appropriate one. Instead, the defendant may request a stay of proceedings claiming that the U.S. court is a *forum non conveniens* and should decline jurisdiction. The *forum conveniens* was even abandoned by other significant Commonwealth jurisdictions.[100] In Australia, Canada and New Zealand, service of process outside of the jurisdiction is no longer required to ask permission of the court.[101] For instance, since 1986 the Australian state of Victoria allows service outside the forum without the court's order as long as the claim is covered under heads similar to those under the English CPR Rule.[102] Similar to the U.S.'s application of the

---

la notion de forum conveniens, *est donc en Angleterre une condition positive de la compétence internationale des tribunaux*' (emphasis added) [actual proximity which is one of the factors of the *forum conveniens* is a positive prerequisite for the international jurisdiction of English courts. – translation HvL], Lagarde, 'Le principe de proximité', at 135.

94 Fawcett, *Declining Jurisdiction*, at 6, General Report.

95 See above at Sect. 8.1.1.

96 See Fawcett, *Declining Jurisdiction*, at 7-8, General Report; and see Collins and Droz, 'The Principles', at 22.

97 As also stressed by Joubert, *La notion de liens suffisants,* § 465, at 442.

98 *Spiliada Maritime Corp. v. Cansulex Ltd.*, House of Lords, [1987] AC 460, at 480.

99 But see Nuyts, *L'exception*, at 434.

100 See also Fawcett, *Declining Jurisdiction*, at 6, General Report.

101 Ibid., at 7; see for Australia, Keyes, *Jurisdiction in International Litigation*, at 57-58; P. Nygh and M. Davies, *Conflict of Laws in Australia* (2002), § 4.22, at 53; and see A. Bell, *Forum Shopping and Venue in Transnational Litigation* (2003), § 4.26, at 144. Chalas, *L'exercise discrétionnaire*, at 238. In Canada, most provinces do no longer require leave for service out of the forum, see J.-G. Castel and J. Walker, *Canadian Conflict of Laws* (2002), § 11.10.

102 Leave is only required after service when the defendant does not appear and the plaintiff wishes to proceed in the absence of the defendant. Service out of Australia is provided for under Order 7(1)

doctrine, Victorian courts can however still decline jurisdiction on the basis of the *forum non conveniens* doctrine.[103]

8.2.3 The *Forum Non Conveniens* Exception

Many comparative studies have dealt with the *forum non conveniens* doctrine.[104] The *forum non conveniens* doctrine 'corrects' the outcome of jurisdictional bases by way of *exception*. It enables a court to decline jurisdiction at its own discretion under particular and atypical circumstances, instead of imposing jurisdictional requirements to be fulfilled before jurisdiction can be exercised.[105] Characterized by its general nature, this exception applies regardless of the nature of the claim. The doctrine is generally defined as 'a general discretionary power for a court to decline jurisdiction on the basis that the appropriate court is abroad or that the local forum is inappropriate.'[106] When the plaintiff invoked the correct basis of

---

of the Victorian Supreme Court (General Civil Procedure) Rules 1996 amended on 1 September 2003 (S.R. No. 19/1996), which stipulates that '(1) Originating process may be served out of Australia without order of the Court where ... (c) any relief is sought against a person domiciled or ordinarily resident within Victoria ... (f) the proceeding is one brought to enforce, rescind, dissolve, rectify, annul or otherwise affect a contract, or to recover damages or other relief in respect of the breach of a contract, and the contract— (i) was made within Victoria; (ii) was made by or through an agent carrying on business or residing within Victoria on behalf of a principal carrying on business or residing out of Victoria; or (iii) is governed by the law of Victoria; (g) the proceeding is brought in respect of a breach committed within Victoria of a contract wherever made, even though that breach was preceded or accompanied by a breach out of Victoria that rendered impossible the performance of that part of the contract which ought to have been performed within Victoria' (emphasis added). Other states have similar heads for service out of the jurisdiction. See for a general overview of the grounds upon which service out of Australia is available; Nygh and Davies, *Conflict of Laws in Australia*, § 4.31-4.77, at 56-76.

[103] See Nygh and Davies, *Conflict of Laws in Australia*, § 4.22, at 53.

[104] Among others see the exhaustive comparative studies of R. Brand and S. Jablonski, *Forum Non Conveniens: History, Global Practice, and Future under the Hague Convention on Choice of Court Agreements* (2007); Karayanni, *FNC in the Modern Age*; Nuyts, *L'exception*; Chalas, *L'exercise discrétionnaire*; R. Bax, 'Forum non Conveniens in het Engelse en Nederlandse recht', 47 *Ars Aequi* (1998), 458-464; Bell, *Forum Shopping and Venue*; Fawcett, *Declining Jurisdiction*; Reus, 'Judicial Discretion'; D. Robertson, 'Forum Non Conveniens in America and England: A Rather Fantastic Fiction', 103 *The Law Quarterly Review* (1987), 398; J. Verheul, 'The Forum (Non) Conveniens in English and Dutch Law and under Some International Conventions', *The International and Comparative Law Quarterly* (1986), 413-423.

[105] Nuyts, *L'exception*, § 1, at 1: '*Le* forum non conveniens *intervient généralement sous la forme d'une exception. ... Au sens matériel, le caractère d'exception du* forum non conveniens *suppose que le dessaisissement n'intervienne que dans des circonstances particulières ou atypiques, lorsqu'il y a lieu de déroger à la règle de compétence de principe établie a la loi*' (emphasis added), Chalas, *L'exercise discrétionnaire*, § 16, at 37, '*Entendue comme un instrument de correction de son propre système de compétence internationale, la discrétion du juge désigne le pouvoir qui lui est reconnu, s'il estime opportune d'en faire usage*'. Lagarde identifies the *forum non conveniens* as the jurisdictional equivalence of the exception clauses in the conflicts of law, which are based on the principle of proximity, Lagarde, 'Le principe de proximité', at 142.

[106] Fawcett, *Declining Jurisdiction*, at 10. McLachlan, 'Report Leuven/London Principles', § 20, at 7; Chalas, *L'exercise discrétionnaire*, § 14-15, at 35-36; Brand, 'Comparative FNC', at 468: 'At base, the doctrine allows a court that has jurisdiction to stay or dismiss proceedings where there is a more appropriate forum for the litigation.' Nuyts, *L'exception*, §1, at 1; '*[U]ne technique particulière du droit international privé permettant aux juridictions d'un Etat de décliner leur compétence*

jurisdiction, the court '*assumes*' jurisdiction, but is allowed to refuse to exercise it.[107] This 'correction mechanism' forms an integral part of most common law systems where the exercise of jurisdiction cannot be analysed without considering the *forum non conveniens* exception.[108] This exception cannot be properly understood without referring to the underlying bases for jurisdiction; the doctrine functions as an 'antidote'[109] against excessive bases of jurisdiction and is welcomed to correct the English presence-based rule or the wide extraterritorial reach of U.S. long-arm statutes.[110] Underlying policies and interests may play a minor role in the enactment of bases for jurisdiction, but becomes crucial when the court seized is asked to appreciate the *forum non conveniens* factors.[111]

Often the doctrine is used to counteract the natural advantage plaintiffs enjoy from the possibility of choosing the forum first, especially when their choice results in an inappropriate forum.[112] Some scholars have argued that the doctrine has become a strategic and defensive weapon in the jurisdictional battle, rather than a defence against a wide range or excessive bases of jurisdiction.[113]

Despite its civil law origins, the *forum non conveniens* doctrine – as it initially comes from Scotland – is a predominantly common law instrument.[114] It might be interesting to note that the English version has generally been followed by most of

---

lorsqu'il y a lieu d'estimer que le for saisi n'est pas approprié ou qu'un for étranger serait plus approprié pour trancher le fond du litige.' See also Karayanni, *FNC in the Modern Age*, at 26 'a doctrine allowing a court with jurisdiction over a case to dismiss it because the convenience of the parties and the interest of justice would be better served if the case were brought in a court having proper jurisdiction in another venue'.

[107] Nygh, 'Declining Jurisdiction', at 304. This is quite distinct from the situation where a court finds that it lacks jurisdiction.

[108] Bell, *Forum Shopping and Venue*, § 4.42, at 150; Chalas, *L'exercise discrétionnaire*, § 2, at 20.

[109] Fawcett, *Declining Jurisdiction*, at 19.

[110] See P. Grolimund, 'Human Rights and Jurisdiction: General Observations and Impact on the Doctrines of *Forum Non Conveniens* and *Forum Conveniens*', 4 *European Journal of Law Reform* (2002), 87-118, at 110; Lagarde, 'Le principe de proximité', at 154: '*forum non conveniens* est un correctif heureux à la *transient rule* du *common law*'.

[111] Nuyts, *L'exception*, § 233, at 333.

[112] See Nygh, 'Declining Jurisdiction', at 322; Kennett, '*FNC* in Europe', at 553. See in this context the question addressed by Gaudemet-Tallon to Droz concerning whether the ECJ's restrictive interpretation of Art. 5(1) is not a hidden *forum non conveniens* tactic. Droz's answers affirmatively by stating that '*Le problème de la Convention de Bruxelles c'est qu'il y a beaucoup d'options, et qu'à vouloir les réduire on emprunte finalement les techniques du forum non conveniens.*' See G. Droz, 'Les droits de la demande dans les relations privées internationales', *Travaux* du *Comité Français de Droit International Privé* (1993-1995), 97-121, at 121.

[113] Bell, *Forum Shopping and Venue*, § 4.38, at 149, refers to 105 *Harvard Law Review* (1992), 1813, at 1817. No empirical research was found in relation to the systems surveyed on how often the doctrine is successfully invoked and results in declining jurisdiction, but its application appears to have increased during the last decades, Nygh, 'Declining Jurisdiction', at 322.

[114] See F. Buonaiuti, 'Forum Non Conveniens Facing the Prospective Hague Convention and E.C. Regulation on Jurisdiction and the Enforcement of Judgments in Civil and Commercial Matters', 39 *Rivista di diritto europeo* (1999), 3-48 , at 6-10; Chalas, *L'exercise discrétionnaire*, § 19-33, at 39-51; Brand, 'Comparative FNC', at 469; Nuyts, *L'exception*, § 51-70, at 79-106; Karayanni, *FNC in the Modern Age*, at 23-27.

the Commonwealth countries, even if Australia[115] and Canada[116] have adopted a different version of the *Spiliada* case.[117]

In the U.S., the doctrine is recognized by the majority of states,[118] even if each state has its own version and there is no uniform application.[119] English common law only uses the exception when jurisdiction is assumed on the basis of defendant's presence *within* England and at his request when he is served with process during that presence. Only when defendant proved that an 'available' foreign court is 'most real and substantially' connected, the court will decline jurisdiction. The English doctrine is limited to presence-based jurisdiction, but should still to be regarded as a general exception, since presence-based jurisdiction is not limited by the nature of the claim as is the case with contracts or torts.[120] The U.S. *forum non conveniens* applies as an exception to both territorial and extraterritorial jurisdiction and declines jurisdiction on considerations of 'convenience' as opposed to the English version which rather deals with 'appropriateness'.[121]

---

[115] See for an exhaustive comparison of the English and the Australian versions, Chalas, *L'exercise discrétionnaire*, § 285-294, at 260-270 and Nuyts, *L'exception*, § 129-133, at 187-192. See also Fawcett, *Declining Jurisdiction*, Australia Report by J. Epstein, at 79-96; Brand, 'Comparative FNC', at 486; Nygh, 'Declining Jurisdiction', at 324-325; Bell, *Forum Shopping and Venue*, § 4.40, at 150 and § 4.67-4.73 at 164-167. The main difference with the Australian version of the *forum non conveniens* doctrine is that the court can only decline jurisdiction when the Australian forum is 'clearly inappropriate'. In this *Voth* test, called after the decision installing the doctrine as such, there is no comparative element and one is not examining whether another forum is 'available' to the plaintiff. The development of the Australian doctrine started with the decision of the High Court of Australia of *Oceanic Sun Line Special Shipping Co. Inc. v. Fay*, (1988) 165 CLR 197, see in particular at 247-248; *Voth v. Manildra Flour Mills Pty. Ltd.*, 97 ALR 124; *Henry v. Henry*, 135 ALR 564 (1996); *CSR v. Cigna Insurance Australia Ltd*, (1997) 189 CLR 345; *Transport Workers' Union of Australia v. Bentley*, (2001) 112 FCR 580; and *Dow Jones & Co Inc. v. Gutnick*, (2002) 210 CLR 575. See R. Garnett, 'Stay of Proceedings in Australia: A "Clearly Inappropriate" Test?', 23 *Melbourne University Law Review* (1999), 30-64, who would have preferred the English version of the 'more appropriate' test for Australia. See also Nygh and Davies, *Conflict of Laws in Australia*, § 4.29, at 55. See also Annex A of Prel. Doc. No. 3 of April 1996 of the Permanent Bureau of the Hague Conference on Private International Law, 'Note on the question of *forum non conveniens* in the perspective of a double convention on judicial jurisdiction and the enforcement of decisions'.

[116] See for an overview of Canada, Fawcett, *Declining Jurisdiction*, Canada Report by J. Blom, at 121-140; Castel and Walker, *Canadian Conflict of Laws*, § 13.2; G. Saumier, 'Judicial Jurisdiction in International Cases: The Supreme Court's Unifished Business', 17 *Dalhousie Law Journal* (1995), 447-472; Brand, 'Comparative FNC', at 482-485; Nuyts, *L'exception*, § 136, at 194. See below for the different approach taken by the civil law system of Quebec. See also Annex B of Prel. Doc. No. 3 of April 1996, 'Note on the question of *forum non conveniens*'.

[117] Australia, Brunei, Canada, Hong Kong, Singapore, New Zealand, see Fawcett, *Declining Jurisdiction*, at 10-13, and see national reports and the common law jurisdiction of Israel, which is not part of the Commonwealth.

[118] See Chapter 5, Sect. 5.5.1; and see Fawcett, *Declining Jurisdiction*, at 14.

[119] See M. Stückelberg, 'Lis Pendens and Forum Non Conveniens at the Hague Conference: The Preliminary Draft Convention on Jurisdiction and Foreign Judgments in Civil and Commercial Matters', 26 *Brooklyn Journal International Law* (2001), 949-982, at 955; Fawcett, *Declining Jurisdiction*, at 10.

[120] The *forum conveniens* requirement is imposed for service outside England, see Chapter 4, Sect. 4.2.3.

[121] Collins and Droz, 'The Principles', at 23.

The *forum non conveniens* exception involves judicial appreciation of open norms and factors.[122] This open character is considered by some to introduce unpredictability and undermine legal certainty,[123] but the English version contains limited and clearly defined appreciation factors.[124]

Both versions involve to a certain extent a comparison of the appropriateness or convenience of the other available forum. The factors determining the margin of judicial discretion are quite similar, at least with respect to 'private interest factors'.[125] Private interest factors determine whether the foreign forum is clearly more convenient for the defendant principally on the basis of the proximity principle.[126] Those factors are concerned with the connection between the forum and both parties, the factual connection with the claim, and any connection with the procedure, such as the availability of proof and other aspects relevant for procedural efficiency.[127] Also in line with the proximity principle is the fact that the doctrine as applied in both countries, takes into account whether or not the law applicable to the merits of the dispute is the law of the forum.[128]

The crucial difference between the two versions emanates from the U.S. Supreme Court decision in *Piper*,[129] which claimed that the choice of a foreign claimant for a U.S. court against a U.S. resident '*deserves less deference*' than U.S. plaintiffs suing foreign defendants in U.S. courts.[130] This clearly attempts to protect a U.S. resident against foreign claimants. This is remarkable, since the U.S. jurisdictional structure is generally considered pro-plaintiff as it provides a wide range of bases for jurisdiction available to the claimant.[131] Claimant's right to access to justice seems to be guaranteed for U.S. claimants only. When foreign plaintiffs start proceedings at defendant's home court, this is not automatically creating jurisdiction, even though the defendant is clearly closely connected with its U.S. home court.[132] In that sense, the *Piper* decision is contrary to the above-mentioned 'principle of proximity' upon which the U.S. '*conveniens*' test is based. Moreover, as explained above, it stands in contrast to the *forum defensoris* which

---

[122] Kokkini-Iatridou, 'Rapport général: Les clauses d'exception', at 6.

[123] See among many others ibid., at 6 and 35, stating that Continental European writers often reject the doctrine for the sake of '*la sacro-sainte sécurité juridique*'. See Robertson, 'Fantastic Fiction', at 399, 'there's now too much discretion and too little clarity in its application'.

[124] Also referred to as '*structured discretion*', see Nuyts, *L'exception*, § 230, at 329.

[125] The English application does not make such a distinction between the *private and public interests* factors. See Nuyts, *L'exception*, § 230, at 329.

[126] Lagarde, 'Le principe de proximité', at 142; and Nuyts, *L'exception*, § 230, at 330.

[127] See Nuyts, *L'exception*, § 233, at 333; and see for England, Lord Chieveley, *Spiliada Maritime Corp. v. Cansulex Ltd.*, [1987] AC 460, at 478; and see the U.S. Supreme Court's decision in *Gulf Oil Corp. v. Gilbert*, 330 U.S. 501, at 509 (1947).

[128] See *Spiliada Maritime Corp. v. Cansulex Ltd.*, [1987] AC 460, at 478; and see among others the public interest factors as formulated by *Gulf Oil Corp. v. Gilbert*, 330 U.S. 501, at 508 (1947); see also for a more in-depth comparison Chalas, *L'exercise discrétionnaire*, § 318-321, at 292-296; Nuyts, *L'exception*, § 264, at 366.

[129] See Chapter 5, Sects. 5.5.2.-5.5.4; *Piper Aircraft Co. v. Reyno*, 454 U.S. 235, at 256 (1981).

[130] See also Nygh, 'Declining Jurisdiction', at 326.

[131] As explained in Chapter 6, Sect. 6.4.3.

[132] See also Nuyts, *L'exception*, § 235, at 333.

favours the defendant in that he is able to properly defend himself at his home court.[133] Furthermore, the result of *Piper* is that the U.S. version allows discriminatory treatment of foreign claimants. The U.S. stands alone in this application of the exception. Vividly commented upon and criticized, it is highly unlikely that such favouritism of local defendants, in particular against foreign plaintiffs, would be accepted as a uniform rule by its European counterparts.[134]

Another significant difference involves the appreciation of public interests factors. The U.S. version of the *forum non conveniens* includes public interest factors, which the English doctrine considers only to a '*limited extent*'.[135] *A U.S. court can decline jurisdiction when it considers it more convenient for the state's public interests to have the dispute litigated somewhere else. Local interests, administrative difficulties and jury duty as a burden to the court seized, are part of these public interest factors that are taken into account to counterbalance the fact that the U.S. became 'litigants' magnets'.*[136] *Justice Marshall in the Piper* decision claimed that 'American courts, which are already extremely attractive to foreign plaintiffs, would become even more attractive. The flow of litigation into the United States would increase and further congest already crowded courts.'[137]

The English House of Lords consistently affirmed the English courts' rejection of similar public interest considerations.[138] In *Lubbe and Others Appellants v. Cape Plc* Lord Bingham of Cornhill stated

---

[133] See Nygh, 'Declining Jurisdiction', at 326.

[134] D. Boyce, 'Foreign Plaintiffs and Forum Non Conveniens: Going Beyond Reyno', 64 *Texas Law Review* (1985), 193-223; A. Stevenson, 'Forum Non Conveniens and Equal Access under Friendship, Commerce and Navigation Treaties: A Foreign Plaintiff's Rights', *Hastings International and Comparative Law Review* (1990), 267-285; W. Woods, 'Suits by Foreign Plaintiffs: Keeping the Doors of American Courts Open', *Arizona Journal of International and Comparative Law* (1991), 75-88; J. Duval-Major, 'One-Way Ticket Home: The Federal Doctrine of Forum Non Conveniens and the International Plaintiff', *Cornell Law Review* (1992), 650-686; D. Solen, 'Forum Non Conveniens and the International Plaintiff', *Florida Journal of International Law* (1994), 343-353; K. Carter-Stein, 'In Search of Justice: Foreign Victims of Silicone Breast Implants and the Doctrine of Forum Non Conveniens', *Suffolk Transnational Law Review* (1995), 167-195; D. Dorward, 'The Forum Non Conveniens Doctrine and the Judicial Protection of Multinational Corporations from Forum Shopping Plaintiffs', *University of Pennsylvania Journal of International Economic Law* (1998), 141-168; F. Juenger, 'Forum Non Conveniens – Who Needs It?', in *Wege zur Globalisierung des Rechts: Festschrift für Rolf A. Schütze zum 65. Geburtstag* (1999), 317-336; D. Dunham and E. Gladbach, 'Forum Non Conveniens and Foreign Plaintiffs in the 1990s', *Brooklyn Journal of International Law* (1999), 665-704; R. Schütze, '*Forum Non Conveniens* and Rechtschauvinismus', in *Festschrift für Erik Jayme* (2004), 849-858 and C. van der Plas, 'Note: U.S. District Court 17 October 2006, Windt en Meijer v. Qwest Communications International Inc., *et al.*', *Jurisprudentie Onderneming & Recht* (2007), at 186-201.

[135] Collins and Droz, 'The Principles', at 26, Preparatory Report; Nuyts, *L'exception*, § 250, at 353; Fawcett, *Declining Jurisdiction*, at 13.

[136] See 330 U.S. 501, at 509 (1947). See Nygh, 'Declining Jurisdiction', at 325, stating 'That rule was explicitly based on a fear of a flood of foreign litigation'; and Chalas, *L'exercise discrétionnaire*, § 313-317, at 286-291.

[137] *Piper Aircraft Co. v. Reyno*, 454 U.S. 235, at 252 (1981), Marshall J.; see also Reus, 'Judicial Discretion', at 471-476.

[138] See C. Morse, 'Not in the Public Interest? Lubbe v. Cape PLC', 37 *Texas International Law Journal* (2002), 541-557, at 549-553.

> 'that public interest considerations not related to the private interests of the parties and the ends of justice have no bearing on the decision which the court has to make. ... It is important that the focus should remain on the principle so clearly stated by Lord Kinnear: in applying this principle questions of judicial amour propre and political interest or responsibility have no part to play.'[139]

8.2.4 No General Correction in Continental Europe and the Brussels Model

General exception clauses are unknown in European civil law countries, and explicitly rejected by the uniform jurisdiction system of the Brussels Model.[140]

The Brussels Model firmly rejected the *forum non conveniens* doctrine, especially since the *Owusu* case, as well as any other form of judicial discretion in relation to specific jurisdictional questions.[141] Principles of legal certainty and predictability prevail above the appropriateness or close connection with the forum.[142] Already in 1978 Collins criticized this approach by stating that under the Brussels Model

> 'there will be no discretion. However inconvenient it may be, and however distant the chosen court may be from the real centre of the dispute, the chosen court will be the only court with jurisdiction. The parties cannot foresee every kind of dispute which may arise and the rigidity of the rule may well work serious injustice.'[143]

It is often stated that the *forum non conveniens* exception is incompatible with the closed and 'rigid' nature of civil law traditions.[144] Some nuance should be given to this notion. Primarily, Nuyts argues that the fact that civil law countries do not apply such a general exception doctrine is not due to a firm condemnation but to the fact that this technique of correction of jurisdiction rules is 'simply ignored' as a method in legal practice.[145] Secondly, several exhaustive comparative researches on the *forum non conveniens* doctrine show that some civil law jurisdictions do

---

[139] *Lubbe and Others v. Cape Plc. and related appeals*, House of Lords HL, [2000] 1 WLR 1545, at 1561. Lord Bingham of Cornhill stated that 'however tempting it may be', considerations of public interest should not influence the courts' decision, ibid., at 1567.

[140] See among others Collins and Droz, 'The Principles', at 46; Nuyts, *L'exception*, at 202; Brand, 'Comparative FNC', at 468; Kennett, '*FNC* in Europe', at 571; Lagarde, 'Le principe de proximité', § 156, at 153-154.

[141] See *Owusu v. Jackson*, Case C-281/02, [2005] ECR, at 1383.

[142] See Chapter 2, Sect. 2.3.1.

[143] see L. Collins, 'The Jurisdiction and Judgements Convention – Some Practical Aspects of United Kingdom Accession, with Particular Reference to Jurisdiction', in *Harmonization of Private International Law by the E.E.C.* (1978), 91-102, at 95.

[144] Karayanni, *FNC in the Modern Age*, fn. 1, at 1, 'It is common belief that the *forum non conveniens* doctrine has not been adopted in civil law countries, at least not in the sense of a fully recognized doctrine forming an integral part of the jurisdictional inquiry.' Silberman, 'Comparative Jurisdiction', at 346; Von Mehren, 'Theory and Practice', at 316, 'Civil-law jurisdictions generally align themselves with the French and German position: As a matter of principle, jurisdictional *fine tuning* through *forum non conveniens* or related doctrines is not proper.'

[145] Nuyts, *L'exception*, § 142, at 203: '*L'étude du thème du* forum non conveniens *dans les systèmes juridiques du continent européen soulève une difficulté d'ordre méthodologique: c'est que cette technique de correction de la compétence est, de manière générale, tout simplement ignorée de la*

apply the exception.[146] Although the civil law jurisdictions that do are by far outnumbered by those who do not apply the doctrine, the examples of Scotland[147] and Quebec[148] are worth mentioning, especially, since these systems adopted statutory provisions comparable to the provisions of the Brussels Model.[149] Thirdly, several Continental European countries have cautiously allowed, or at least considered, some judicial discretion based on proximity considerations which are often compared to the *forum non conveniens* doctrine.[150] The 'sufficient connection' requirements explained above are often referred to as '*forum non conveniens*-substitutes'.[151] According to the definition Fawcett gives in his General Report to the XIVth International Congress of the International Academy of Comparative Law, these 'substitutes' involve 'a limited power to decline jurisdiction in specific and limited circumstances on the basis of *forum non conveniens*-type considerations'.[152] He explains that the majority of states which have not adopted a general doctrine of *forum non conveniens* adopted 'substitutes'.[153] The introduction of special correction clauses is considered to 'bring closer the "*cleavage*" between civil and common law'.[154]

But even though Continental European regimes start to indulge the introduction of special correction clauses, they generally still refuse to adopt general correction mechanisms, such as the *forum (non) conveniens* doctrine. For those reasons, the analogy between the *forum non conveniens* and other correction mechanisms '*connaît des limites*'[155] and the '*forum non conveniens* substitutes' should not be assim-

---

pratique judiciaire. On ne peut donc pas vraiment parler de condamnation du forum non conveniens, *mais plutôt d'indifférence à l'égard de cette matière.*'

146 Fawcett, *Declining Jurisdiction*; Chalas, *L'exercise discrétionnaire*; Nuyts, *L'exception*; Bell, *Forum Shopping and Venue*.

147 See Chalas, *L'exercise discrétionnaire*, § 19-33, at 39-51; Brand, 'Comparative FNC', at 469; Nuyts, *L'exception*, § 51-70, at 79-106; Karayanni, *FNC in the Modern Age*, at 23-27.

148 Quebec has a codified *forum non conveniens* provision, see Art. 3135 of the Civil Code of Quebec. See Kokkini-Iatridou, 'Rapport général: Les clauses d'exception', at 33; Fawcett, *Declining Jurisdiction*, at 16-17, and Quebec Report by G. Goldstein, at 146-157; Brand, 'Comparative FNC', at 485; Bell, *Forum Shopping and Venue*, § 4.42, at 151; Nuyts, *L'exception*, § 134-139, at 193-198. Nuyts considers the Quebec system, as well as those of Japan and Israel, to be a 'hybrid' system.

149 See for Quebec, Nuyts, *L'exception*, § 135, at 193. See for Scottish jurisdiction rules, Schedule 8 CJJA 1982 as amended by Schedule 2, Part III, paras. 6 and 7, CJJO 2001– modelled on the Brussels Convention. Also explained in Chapter 4, Sect. 4.1.

150 Collins and Droz, 'The Principles', at 46, note that 'it is also clear that there is some movement towards acceptance of the forum non conveniens in international conventions, although progress has been slow'.

151 Also called 'surrogates' of the *forum non conveniens*, see Von Mehren, 'Theory and Practice', at 316; Collins and Droz, 'The Principles', Réponse de Droz, at 64; Nuyts, *L'exception*, § 320, at 433-434; Chalas, *L'exercise discrétionnaire*, § 602, at 546. See for substitutes of exception clauses in choice of law rules, Kokkini-Iatridou, 'Rapport général: Les clauses d'exception', at 22.

152 Fawcett, *Declining Jurisdiction*, General Report, at 24; see K. Siehr, 'National Report: Switzerland', in J. Fawcett, ed., *Declining Jurisdiction in Private International Law* (1995), 381-399, at 381; Nuyts, *L'exception*, § 141, at 202 and see Nuyts' definition in § 164, at 235.

153 Fawcett, *Declining Jurisdiction*, at 24; Nuyts, *L'exception*, § 141, at 202.

154 Karayanni, *FNC in the Modern Age*, at 146; Nuyts, *L'exception*, § 267, at 369; Kennett, '*FNC* in Europe', at 571.

155 Nuyts, *L'exception*, at 435.

ilated with the doctrine itself. In fact these special correction clauses involve only limited discretion, available only in specific matters and limited to considerations of a close connection with the forum which do not take into account any parties' or states' interests.[156] Nygh's illustration is adequate as he states that these 'sufficient connection' requirements deriving from civil law 'are often disguised as a lack of jurisdiction as opposed to discretion to decline jurisdiction to exercise it'.[157]

Italy, Spain and Switzerland refused to incorporate a general exception clause.[158] Prior to the Dutch Reform on Judicial Procedure of 6 December 2001, the Dutch civil law system included a codified provision which developed itself over the years as a general exception clause comparable to the *forum non conveniens* exception.[159] Article 429c(15) of the former Rv. was primarily designed for proceedings initiated by way of petition, generally involving family matters or non-contentious matters.[160] The rule stated that Dutch courts are not competent when the dispute is 'insufficiently connected' with the *legal sphere* of The Netherlands.[161] Dutch courts cautiously began to extend its scope to purely commercial cases, usually not initiated by petition but by writ[162] and used the upcoming general exception rule to correct the outcome of its former 'exorbitant' jurisdiction rules, such as the *forum arresti* and the *forum actoris*.[163]

The Dutch legislator and scholarly writers compared this exception with the *forum non conveniens* exception.[164] But the former Dutch provision simply denies

---

[156] Reponse de Droz; Collins and Droz, 'The Principles', at 62 and 65; Nuyts, *L'exception*, § 145, at 210; Reus, 'Judicial Discretion', at 495.

[157] Nygh, 'Declining Jurisdiction', at 327.

[158] See Chapter 3, Sect. 3.1. Spain and Italy modelled their jurisdictional systems on the Brussels Model with no room for discretion. See Chapter 3, Sect. 3.3.1. In Switzerland a general exception is lacking as the Swiss PIL structure, except for the close connection requirement concerning a choice of forum clause, clearly has closed character. See Fawcett, *Declining Jurisdiction*, at 26; Kokkini-Iatridou, 'Rapport général: Les clauses d'exception', at 33. According to Siehr, the 'fact that substitutes for [the doctrine] are lacking is due to the constant effort to appoint an appropriate forum with enough contacts with the place for every type of case.' Siehr, 'National Report: Switzerland', at 386 and 389.

[159] Verheul, 'FNC', at 417; Fawcett, *Declining Jurisdiction*, at 24; K. Boele-Woelki, 'The Netherlands National Report', in J. Fawcett, ed., *Declining Jurisdiction in Private International Law* (1995), 235-247, at 236.

[160] See Chapter 3, Sect. 3.2.1.1; Boele-Woelki, 'The Netherlands National Report', at 238-239.

[161] Art. 429c(15): *'Aan de rechter komt geen rechtsmacht toe, indien het verzoek onvoldoende band heeft met de rechtssfeer van Nederland.'* See also Prel. Doc. No. 3 of April 1996, 'Note on the question of *forum non conveniens*', at 4. Boele-Woelki, 'The Netherlands National Report', at 237, stresses that the rule is 'negatively formulated'; see also Kokkini-Iatridou, 'Rapport général: Les clauses d'exception', at 33.

[162] See Verheul, 'FNC', at 418; See M. Freudenthal and F. van der Velden, 'The Netherlands National Report', in J. Fawcett, ed., *Declining Jurisdiction in Private International Law* (1995), 321-339, at 331-333; D. Kokkini-Iatridou and K. Boele-Woelki, 'De Regeling van de "Internationale rechtsmacht" in het voorontwerp van de wet van 1993', *NIPR* (1993), 323-364, at 331-337; X. Kramer, 'De regeling van de rechtsmacht onder het herziene Rechtsvordering', 20 *NIPR* (2002), 375-385, at 376.

[163] Fawcett, *Declining Jurisdiction*, at 24.

[164] Explanatory Report Proposal Rv., at 28-29; and see Bax, 'FNC', at 111; Fawcett, *Declining Jurisdiction*, at 24; Kokkini-Iatridou and Frohn, 'De exceptieclausules in het verdragenrecht, een verkenning', at 227; Kokkini-Iatridou, 'Rapport général: Les clauses d'exception', at 34; Nuyts, *L'exception*, § 332, at 444-446; Kennett, '*FNC* in Europe', at 570.

jurisdiction when a sufficient connection is lacking, in that case jurisdiction was never assumed, which leaves the court with nothing to decline.[165] The rule does not require a comparison between competent forums. It merely appreciates the sufficient connection factor, which is only part of the 'appropriateness' and '*conveniens*' considerations of the Anglo-American versions of the doctrine.[166] The Dutch reform abolished the rule in order to come into line with the 'closed' Brussels Model,[167] but introduced an open connecting factor establishing jurisdiction when the dispute is sufficiently connected with The Netherlands for all proceedings initiated by petition.[168] Dutch courts have a certain degree of discretion in asserting jurisdiction over a petition case when the dispute is 'otherwise sufficiently connected with the Dutch legal order'.[169]

In France, the *Cour de cassation* firmly condemned a couple of attempts of the Paris *Cour d'Appel* to decline jurisdiction based on a similar *forum non conveniens* consideration, as the claimant invoked jurisdiction based on his nationality.[170] The *Cour de cassation*'s decision is understood as an implicit rejection of discretionary powers and an affirmation of the mandatory nature of these rules.[171] Jurisdictional exceptions are generally unknown – and unwanted – in the French system which is based on significant power for the legislator rather than for the judiciary.[172]

---

[165] See in that sense Droz who considered the rule to be a jurisdictional requirement: '*De même, j'estime que l'article 429 c alinéa 2, du (RV) souvent présenté comme une expression du forum non conveniens, ne permet pas un exercice discrétionnaire de la compétence juridictionnelle. ... Tout ce que peu[t] faire un tribunal c'est d'apprécier si les conditions de sa compétence sont réunies: dans l'affirmative, il est compétent, dans le négative, il doit se déclarer incompétent, ce qui diffère de la jurisprudence française élaborée dans l'arret* Nassibian.' Collins and Droz, 'The Principles', Réponse de Droz, at 63. See for a similar reasoning, Chalas, *L'exercise discrétionnaire*, § 581, at 523.

[166] At the most, the Dutch rule has some resemblance with the Australian 'clearly inappropriateness' test of the doctrine, see Nuyts, *L'exception*, § 332, at 446; Chalas, *L'exercise discrétionnaire*, § 581, at 523.

[167] According to the explanatory report, the abolishment of this provision was also justified by the fact that none of the neighbouring countries allow a general *forum non conveniens* provision, Explanatory Report Proposal Rv., at 30-31.

[168] Ibid., at 30; Kramer, 'De regeling van de rechtsmacht', at 376; Art. 3(c) A reversed version of the former rule is enshrined in Art. 9, Explanatory Report Proposal Rv., at 41.

[169] As explained in Chapter 3, Sect. 3.2.1.2.

[170] Art. 14 CC; Chapter 3, Sect. 3.4.3; Nuyts, *L'exception*, § 144, at 207; Chalas, *L'exercise discrétionnaire*, § 443, at 401-402.

[171] Chalas, *L'exercise discrétionnaire*, § 563, at 505; Nuyts, *L'exception*, § 144, at 208; Von Mehren, 'Theory and Practice', at 316. According to H. Gaudemet-Tallon, 'France National Report', in J. Fawcett, ed., *Declining Jurisdiction in Private International Law* (1995), 175-187, at 175, 'if he [the judge] has jurisdiction, he must rule and cannot "decline" to exercise jurisdiction', see also at 179.

[172] Fawcett, *Declining Jurisdiction*, at 25: 'In France, there is a particular criticism of the concept forum non conveniens.' According to Gaudemet-Tallon the statement '*Dieu nous garde de l'équité des Parlements*' [May god preserve us from the fairness of the Parliaments'], also applies to jurisdiction, Gaudemet-Tallon, 'France National Report', at 177.

8.3 Article 6 European Convention on Human Rights: Right of a Fair Trial

Several authors considered the possibility of using Article 6(1) ECHR,[173] establishing the fundamental right to a fair trial, as an 'overarching theory'[174] to correct the outcome of jurisdiction rules.[175] Until now the discussion on the potential impact of this Article on either the Brussels Instruments or national jurisdiction rules is purely an academic one.[176] The ECHR applies to 'everyone *within* their jurisdiction' and is not limited to nationals or residents of Contracting States.[177] Despite numerous decisions of the European Court of Human Rights in Strasbourg – which extensively interpreted the meaning of a fair trial in criminal, civil and commercial cases – very few cases addressed its relationship with international jurisdiction rules. None of those cases eventually reached the Strasbourg Court, as they were dismissed on procedural grounds and declared inadmissible. Whether Article 6 of the ECHR applies to questions of international jurisdiction has not yet been tackled by the Strasbourg Court as the Court never had the opportunity to address the fundamental right of fair trial in relation to jurisdiction issues.[178]

---

173 Convention for Protection of Human Rights and Fundamental Freedoms, Treaty of the Council of Europe, signed in Rome, 4 November 1950, entered into force on 3 September 1953. See http://conventions.coe.int or http://www.echr.coe.int/echr.

174 J. Hill, 'The Exercise of Jurisdiction in Private International Law', in *Asserting Jurisdiction – International and European Legal Perspectives* (2003), 39-62, at 41.

175 A. Briggs, *Civil Jurisdiction and Judgments* (2005), § 1.20, at 18, stating that the right of access to justice may be endangered in the event parties have agreed upon a jurisdiction agreement or arbitration clause. See in contrast F. De Ly, 'Arbitration and Human Rights', paper presented at Arbitration Day organized by the German Institute of Arbitration (DIS) and the International Commercial Arbitration Committee of the International Law Association (ILA), Berlin, 20 August 2004) (on file), explaining under which circumstances the Art. 6 guarantees are still available in international arbitration, especially with respect to mandatory arbitration.

176 Scheurmans was one the first to indicate a possible interference of Art. 6 ECHR with international jurisdiction. Already in 1966 he stated that 'One could, however, ask to what extent particularly harsh provisions [Art. 23 ZPO] are still on the books after the enactment of the EEC Draft treaty would conflict with the spirit of the European Convention on Human Rights and the "due process" clause of article 6 of this Convention.' Yet he warns in fn. 175 that 'One should however proceed cautiously and not yet assimilate article 6 with the American "due process" notions.' L. Scheurmans, 'Attachment and Garnishment as Bases for Adjudicatory Jurisdiction over Foreigners: A Comparative Study', 13 *Netherlands International Law Review* (1966), 243-289, at 280. Scheurmans was followed by Schlosser who successfully brought the issue back on the academic agenda, Schlosser, 'The Issue of Human Rights'. See in general J. Fawcett, 'The Impact of Article 6(1) of the ECHR on Private International Law', 56 *The International and Comparative Law Quarterly* (2007), 1-48; and see Nuyts, 'Due Process and Fair Trial', at 177-179; Collins and Droz, 'The Principles', Reply of Matscher, at 51; Chalas, *L'exercise discrétionnaire*, § 484, at 429; J. Bertele, *Souveränität und Verfahrensrecht: Ein untersuchung der aus dem Völkerrecht ableitbaren Grenzen staatlicher extraterritoriale Jurisdiktion im Verfahrensrecht* (1998), fn. 178, at 204. Hill, 'The Exercise of Jurisdiction', at 41; Kleinstück, 'Due Process-Beschränkungen', at 169.

177 Art. 1 ECHR. See Fawcett, 'Impact of Article 6(1)', at 3; N. Hatzimihail, 'General Report: Transnational Civil Litigation between European Integration and Global Aspirations', in *International Civil Litigation in Europe and Relations with Third States* (2005), 595-675, at 622.

178 In the *Dombo Beheer BV v. The Netherlands* decision of 27 January 1993, case number 37/1992/382/460, the Strasbourg Court argued that 'The requirements inherent in the concept of "fair

Several authors, both European and American, have assimilated the U.S. due process requirement to the *fair trial* doctrine enshrined in Article 6(1) ECHR.[179] There are significant differences between a potential interference of Article 6 ECHR in jurisdictional issues and the impact of *International Shoe* in U.S. jurisdictional law. The European jurisdictional structures, England included, have relatively closed systems with limited jurisdiction rules and well-defined connecting factors. There is no wide-range spectrum of possible contacts as there is in most long-arm statutes, especially the general no-limits Californian-type statutes.[180] Taking that reasoning a step further, European jurisdiction is based on a legislative authority and will be less influenced by the ECHR, as was the case with the Supreme Court's decisions on due process which shaped U.S. jurisdiction law.[181]

The question whether a parallel could and should be drawn between the U.S. due process standards and Article 6(1) of the ECHR is gaining considerable terrain in Europe. Should Article 6 ECHR constitute a 'blind alley' to correct unfair exercise of state jurisdiction?[182] At present Article 6(1) ECHR does not interfere with the Brussels uniform jurisdictional structure which allocates jurisdiction among EU courts,[183] but scholars find enough guidance in the extensive Strasbourg case law dealing with Article 6(1) to formulate a general *fair trial* principle potentially able to correct the exercise of jurisdiction on human rights considerations.[184] Many

hearing" are not necessarily the same in cases concerning the determination of civil rights and obligations as they are in cases concerning the determination of a criminal charge. ... Nevertheless, certain principles concerning the notion of a "fair hearing" in cases concerning civil rights and obligations emerge from the Court's case-law.' (Paras. 32-33). See on the extensive interpretation of Art. 6, Matscher, 'Face à la Convention Européenne des droits de l'homme', at 212; Matscher, 'Quarante ans d'activités', at 266-265 and 342-344; Bertele, *Souveränität und Verfahrensrecht*, at 202.

[179] See in general Schlosser, 'The Issue of Human Rights'; Lagarde agrees, Lagarde, 'Revues: Schlosser, Peter', at 628; see Kleinstück, 'Due Process-Beschränkungen', at 170; and see Fitzpatrick, 'A Comparative Analysis', at 741-742; Matscher, 'Face à la Convention Européenne des droits de l'homme', at 220; see Chalas, *L'exercise discrétionnaire*, § 492, at 437; Muir Watt, 'Emergent European Legal Culture', at 548; see also Nuyts, *L'exception*, § 443, at 600; Hill, 'The Exercise of Jurisdiction', at 40-41; Nuyts, 'Due Process and Fair Trial', at 185.

[180] See on the open character of the U.S. system Chapter 6, Sect. 6.3.3.

[181] See on the impact of the Due Process Clause on U.S. jurisdiction law, Chapter 5, Sect. 5.2; Grolimund, 'Human Rights and Jurisdiction', at 91 and see Schlosser, 'The Issue of Human Rights', at 12-13: '[European] rules conferring jurisdiction to courts are drafted in an abstract way. In such a context there is no room for constitutional considerations, such as in view of the power concept in the case law of the United States Supreme Court. In the United States, because of constitutional considerations it was required to achieve a breakthrough and to alter completely the general approach to jurisdiction. On the European continent an alteration in the general approach is not required'.

[182] Hill, 'The Exercise of Jurisdiction', at 40; and Grolimund, 'Human Rights and Jurisdiction', at 91 *et seq.*

[183] Schlosser, 'The Issue of Human Rights', at 16; Kleinstück, 'Due Process-Beschränkungen', at 170; Muir Watt, 'Emergent European Legal Culture', at 548; Nuyts, 'Due Process and Fair Trial', at 177. But see Grolimund, 'Human Rights and Jurisdiction', at 88, 'at the present stage, no one really knows if and how article 6(1) ECHR might (or even should?) influence the "provisions on international jurisdiction".'

[184] Matscher, 'Face à la Convention Européenne des droits de l'homme', at 214; Hill, 'The Exercise of Jurisdiction', at 41; and Nuyts, 'Due Process and Fair Trial', at 178, claiming that 'analytical tools are already present in the jurisprudence of the fair trial theory'. See on the impact of the ECHR on private international law (including applicable law rules), D. Cohen, 'La Convention européenne

authors favour such a European 'due process test' and suggest that 'Europeans might gain from paying attention to American ideas about fundamental rights and procedural fairness'.[185] Others have expressed concerns about any potential influence of '[European] human rights principles' on the provisions of international jurisdiction. According to them such influence could potentially lead to interference with a state's sovereign power to regulate the reach of its own judicial powers by eliminating exorbitant jurisdiction and it could diminish the legal protection of domestic claimants.[186]

The debate is crucial for the present purposes of finding uniform jurisdiction rules for international contractual disputes. If Article 6 ECHR was to be declared applicable to jurisdictional issues, would it dilute jurisdictional requirements and make them comparable to U.S. due process constitutional requirements?[187] In that respect, it is easy to draw a parallel between Article 6(1) ECHR and the U.S. Due Process Clause:[188] the fair trial guarantees of Article 6 contains vague criteria and open concepts[189] and leaves substantial room for the Strasbourg Court to interpret the provision as broadly as the U.S. Supreme Court did in its decision of *International Shoe* and to apply Article 6(1) to jurisdictional issues.[190] Like the U.S. Due Process Clause, Article 6 contains open-ended standards for procedural fairness which could provide courts with considerable discretion to determine whether the exercise of jurisdiction is violating the fundamental aspects of procedural justice on a case-by-case basis.[191] The question is whether the two provisions are com-

des droits de l'homme et le droit international privé français', 78 *Revue critique de droit international privé* (1989), 451-483; Schlosser, 'Human Rights' Consideration'; C. Dubbink, 'Mensenrechten en de openbare orde in het Internationaal Privaatrecht', in *Op recht: Bundel opstellen, aangeboden aan prof. mr. A.V.M. Struycken ter gelegenheid van zijn zilveren ambtsjubileum aan de Katholieke Universiteit Nijmegen* (1996); and Matscher, 'Face à la Convention Européenne des droits de l'homme'; Muir Watt, 'Emergent European Legal Culture', at 547.

[185] F. Juenger, 'Federalism: Judicial Jurisdiction in the United States and in the European Communities: A Comparison', 82 *Michigan Law Review* (1984), 1195, at 1212; see also Chalas, *L'exercise discrétionnaire*, § 485, at 430; Nuyts, *L'exception*, § 442-443, at 599; and Nuyts, 'Due Process and Fair Trial', at 185, indicating that the U.S. due process considerations indicate a certain '*maturity*' which at this time has not yet reached the other side of the Atlantic.

[186] See P. Mayer, 'La Convention européenne des droits de l'homme et l'application des normes étrangères', 98 *Revue critique de droit international privé* (1991), 651-665, at 665; Bertele, *Souveränität und Verfahrensrecht*, at 209-210; Grolimund, 'Human Rights and Jurisdiction', at 90; Nuyts, 'Due Process and Fair Trial', at 184.

[187] See also the exhaustive research done by Marchadier, *A l'épreuve de la Convention Européenne des droits de l'homme,* at 83 *et seq.*

[188] See Chapter 2, Sect. 2.4. The first paragraph reads as follows 'In the determination of his civil rights and obligations or of any criminal charge against him, everyone is entitled to a fair and public hearing within a reasonable time by an independent and impartial tribunal established by law....'

[189] See Matscher, 'Face à la Convention Européenne des droits de l'homme', at 213.

[190] Nuyts, 'Due Process and Fair Trial', at 184, 'it is difficult to see how one could assert that, on the face of their words, there is more for the purpose of jurisdiction in the Fourteenth Amendment to the U.S. Constitution than in article 6 ECHR'; F. Blobel and P. Spath, 'The Tale of Multilateral Trust and the European Law of Civil Procedure', 30 *European Law Review* (2005), 528-547, at 543.

[191] See Blobel and Spath, 'Tale of Multilateral Trust', at 543, arguing that 'the case law of the Strasbourg judges grants to the contracting states a certain margin of appreciation when it comes to judicial policy. Within that margin, and having due regard to the requirements of proportionality, they

parable.[192] As stated by Michaels 'the Due Process Clause in the United States protects the *defendant* against the unjustified *assertion* of jurisdiction, the fair trial principle in European law protects the *plaintiff* against the unjustified *denial* of jurisdiction.'[193] In a general sense, Article 6 ECHR guarantees a 'fair trial' but it more specifically covers a significant number of rights concerning procedural fairness.[194] Like the U.S. Due Process Clause, the 'fair trial' provision of Article 6(1) is constituted by several elements most relevant for jurisdictional purposes described below.

8.3.1 Comparing the Fair Trial Components

The *fair trial* principle of Article 6(1) initially dealt with protecting the defendant by ensuring a fair hearing and the opportunity to be heard. But already, at an early stage, the Strasbourg Court extended the protection of Article 6(1) to the claimant's 'access to justice'. According to the Court

> 'it follows that the right of access constitutes an element which is inherent in the right stated by Article 6(1). This is not an extensive interpretation forcing new obligations on the Contracting States: it is based on the very terms of the first sentence of Article 6(1) read in its context and having regard to the object and purpose of the Convention, a lawmaking treaty and to general principles of law.'

And thus, the Court continues that Article 6(1) 'secures to everyone the right to have any claim relating to his civil rights and obligations brought before a court or tribunal' and 'the Article embodies the "right to a court", of which the right of access, that is the right to institute proceedings before courts in civil matters, constitutes one aspect only.'[195]

The decision resulted in a true '*access-to-justice movement*'[196] rapidly followed by another decision interpreting Article 6(1) as including the right of *effective* access to justice, especially in terms of financial means.[197] But the question

---

are free to decide whom to favour.' But according to Grolimund, 'Human Rights and Jurisdiction', at 110, Art. 6 ECHR does not automatically include 'a case-by-case analysis of jurisdictional interests of the parties'.

[192] This question is answered in the affirmative by Marchadier, *A l'épreuve de la Convention Européenne des droits de l'homme,* at 186-187.

[193] R. Michaels, 'Two Paradigms of Jurisdiction', 27 *Michigan Journal of International Law* (2007), 1003-1069, at 1053. See also Chapter 6, Sect. 6.4.4.

[194] *Golder v. The United Kingdom*, 21 February 1975, para. 28.

[195] See *Application no. 4451/70, Golder v. The United Kingdom*, 21 February 1975, para. 36. According to Matscher the Strasbourg Court is entitled to expand its competence on the basis of the '*théorie de l'effet utile*', Matscher, 'Quarante ans d'activités', at 279 and 340. See also Marchadier, *A l'épreuve de la Convention Européenne des droits de l'homme,* at 84 and Schlosser, 'The Issue of Human Rights', at 16; Nuyts, 'Due Process and Fair Trial', at 179-119.

[196] M. Storme, *Rapprochement du droit judiciaire de l'Union européenne: Introduction générale introductif* (1993), at 3 and 37.

[197] See '*Belgian Linguistic*' case *(fond)*, ECHR (23 July 1968), Series A, No. 6, paras. 3-4; *Airey Case*, ECHR (9 October 1979), paras. 24-27; and the case *Artico v. Italy*, ECHR (13 May 1980), Series A, No. 37, para. 33, where it is stipulated that '[t]he Convention is intended to guarantee not rights that are theoretical or illusory but rights that are practical and effective'. See Marchadier, *A l'épreuve de*

remains whether the exercise of jurisdiction could lead to effective access to justice being hindered in another forum. The fact that one of the parties has to defend himself or bring action in a foreign court does not prevent access to justice, but might cause, in the words of Nuyts, 'procedural hindrance'.[198]

If a '*fair trial* control' was to be applied to jurisdictional issues, authors generally agree that standards of procedural justice would imply a prohibition of the *unfair* exercise of exorbitant jurisdiction over the defendant.[199] This view is based on the assumption that the *fair trial* doctrine imposes a '*sufficient link*' between the dispute and the forum for the exercise of jurisdiction.[200] As a consequence, claimant's right to access to justice – also guaranteed by Article 6(1) ECHR – would be limited to those courts with a sufficient link between the forum and the dispute, except in extreme situations such as for instance the threat of a *déni de justice*.[201] Safeguarding procedural fairness under Article 6(1) ECHR might therefore imply banning excessive or exorbitant jurisdiction. An 'Article 6 test' would not only consist of controlling notions of fairness in relation to national 'exorbitant' jurisdiction rules that are still applicable outside the scope of the Brussels Model,[202] but would most likely sanction jurisdiction rules which in their *application* result in jurisdiction over a defendant who has an *insufficient link* with the forum.[203] As a consequence, Schlosser indicates in his pioneer article that nationality-based jurisdiction,[204]

---

la Convention Européenne des droits de l'homme, at 82, Lagarde, 'Le principe de proximité', § 159, at 157; Cohen, 'La Convention européenne des droits de l'homme', at 456-457; Schlosser, 'The Issue of Human Rights', at 16; Nuyts, 'Due Process and Fair Trial', at 179.

[198] Nuyts, 'Due Process and Fair Trial', at 180-181.

[199] See Marchadier, *A l'épreuve de la Convention Européenne des droits de l'homme,* at 112; Bertele, *Souveränität und Verfahrensrecht*, at 203; Schlosser, 'The Issue of Human Rights', at 5-6, 'Is it not an issue of human rights, that one should not be sued in a court whose jurisdiction is "exorbitant"?'.

[200] See in general Schlosser, 'The Issue of Human Rights'; and see Marchadier, *A l'épreuve de la Convention Européenne des droits de l'homme,* at 229-237; Matscher, 'Face à la Convention Européenne des droits de l'homme', at 218; Grolimund, 'Human Rights and Jurisdiction', at 90, referring to Schlosser. Chalas, *L'exercise discrétionnaire*, § 485, at 429 and § 493-497, at 437-441; Nuyts, 'Due Process and Fair Trial', at 178 and 189; Collins and Droz, 'The Principles', Reply of Matscher, at 51.

[201] On several occasions, the Strasbourg Court indicated that Art. 6 is violated when a state is offering assistance to a foreign court of a state which does not recognize the principles of fair trial or by recognizing a judgement which was not rendered by a court respecting the fairness requirements embodied in Art. 6. These procedures are strongly connected with the prohibition of *déni de justice* according to Matscher, 'Face à la Convention Européenne des droits de l'homme', at 218; Matscher, 'Quarante ans d'activités', at 360; and Mayer, 'La Convention européenne des droits de l'homme', at 655.

[202] See also Matscher, 'Face à la Convention Européenne des droits de l'homme', at 218.

[203] Schlosser, 'The Issue of Human Rights', at 22; and Lagarde, 'Revues: Schlosser, Peter', at 628; Nuyts, 'Due Process and Fair Trial', at 183.

[204] See Cohen, 'La Convention européenne des droits de l'homme', at 454-463. On the question whether or not nationality-based jurisdiction violates the requirement of an 'independent and impartial' court see Schlosser, 'The Issue of Human Rights', at 23-24; see further R. Geimer, 'Verfassungsrechtliche Vorgaben bei der Normierung der internationalen Zuständigkeit', in *Europa im Aufbruch: Festschrift Fritz Schwind zum 80. Geburtstag* (1993), 17-42, at 24-26, and below at Sect. 8.4.2 for nationality-based jurisdiction in relation to the Hague drafts. Arts. 14 and 15 of the French CC will not be accepted by Art. 12 EC. See also P. Schlosser, 'A New Dimension of Human Rights' Consideration in Civil Procedure', *Rivista di diritto internazionale privato e internazionale* (1995), 31-40, at 31; and F. Matscher, 'Quarante ans d'activités de la Cour européenne des droits de l'homme', 270

jurisdiction ancillary to criminal jurisdiction,[205] property-based jurisdiction,[206] jurisdiction at the place where the tortuous event occurred,[207] and jurisdiction at the place of performance of mere pecuniary obligations[208] should not pass the Article 6(1) test as there is not sufficient connection with the forum.[209] Jurisdiction based on defendant's physical presence has also been marked as incompatible with Article 6(1).[210]

Schlosser argues that bases for jurisdiction on the mere connection between the claim and the forum do not guarantee *fair* exercise of jurisdiction. A distinction should be made between the above-mentioned 'close connection' requirement encountered in certain Continental civil law systems and the potential *fair trial control* under Article 6(1). In that respect, the comparison with the German *Inlandsbezug* has been often made. The latter requires a 'particular nexus between the contention and the forum state, [which] may justify positive interference with fundamental values'[211] and does not necessarily require a connection with the parties, more specifically with the defendant.[212] The *fair trial* doctrine mainly focuses on the presence of a sufficient connection between the parties and the forum, or *persönlicher Genuine Link*,[213] in order to guarantee personal fairness.[214] Whether a 'close connection' between the claim and the forum is sufficient to satisfy a *fair trial* under Article 6(1) is disputable. Again a parallel can be drawn with the U.S. due process standards which merely focus on the minimum contacts between the forum and the parties, and not so much on a connection between the claim and the forum.[215]

The *fair trial* guarantee of Article 6(1) embodies yet another fundamental right: the '*right of the equality of arms*'.[216] Obviously, this right is reserved for both

---

Recueil des cours (1997), 237-398, at 370-371, referring to Art. 14 ECHR which contains a similar anti-discrimination provision.

205 Schlosser, 'The Issue of Human Rights', 24-25.

206 Joubert, *La notion de liens suffisants,* § 77- 79, at 75-78; Cohen, 'La Convention européenne des droits de l'homme', at 455 *et seq*.; Schlosser, 'The Issue of Human Rights', at 25-28; Lagarde, 'Revues: Schlosser, Peter', at 629; Kleinstück, 'Due Process-Beschränkungen', at 168.

207 Schlosser, 'The Issue of Human Rights', at 31-33; Lagarde, 'Revues: Schlosser, Peter', at 628; Nuyts, 'Due Process and Fair Trial', at 183; in contrast see Bertele, *Souveränität und Verfahrensrecht,* who refers to Geimer, at 205.

208 Bertele, *Souveränität und Verfahrensrecht,* at 204, see his contrasting view at 205, where he refers to Geimer. See also Muir Watt, 'Emergent European Legal Culture', at 551.

209 Schlosser, 'The Issue of Human Rights', at 23-33; see Blobel and Spath, 'Tale of Multilateral Trust', at 545; and Chalas, *L'exercise discrétionnaire*, at 432-437, who exhaustively runs through his reasoning; see also Bertele, *Souveränität und Verfahrensrecht,* at 204, rephrasing Schlosser's arguments by stating that these grounds are '*potentiell menschenrechtwidrig*'.

210 Hatzimihail, 'General Report', at 623.

211 Muir Watt, 'Emergent European Legal Culture', at 547.

212 Lagarde, 'Revues: Schlosser, Peter', at 629.

213 Bertele, *Souveränität und Verfahrensrecht*, at 204.

214 Geimer, 'Verfassungsrechtliche Vorgaben', at 34; and explained by Bertele in Bertele, *Souveränität und Verfahrensrecht*, at 205.

215 See Chapter 5, Sect. 5.4.3.

216 See also Marchadier, *A l'épreuve de la Convention Européenne des droits de l'homme,* at 196-199.

parties involved. In line with the Court's tradition to extensively interpret Article 6(1), by remaining within the limits of the ECHR, the Court stated in *Ankerl v. Switzerland*, that whether the proceedings were 'fair' within the meaning of Article 6(1) is connected with 'the requirement of "equality of arms", in the sense of a "fair balance" between the parties, [which] applies also to litigation in which private interests are opposed'.[217] A few months later the Court reiterated that '[t]he principle of equality of arms – one of the elements of the broader concept of fair trial – requires each party to be given a reasonable opportunity to present his case under conditions that do not place him at a substantial disadvantage vis-à-vis his opponent'.[218] This 'equality of arms' element of the *fair trial* doctrine shows similarities with the fairness requirement as formulated by the U.S. Supreme Court under the *Due Process* Clause.[219]

If an Article 6(1) control was to be applied to jurisdictional issues, it would be crucial to provide for such a 'fair balance' in uniform jurisdiction rules. For instance, would 'procedural hindrance' of one party constitute a 'substantial disadvantage' in the sense that it would violate Article 6(1) ECHR?[220] In that sense it was argued that the equality of arms implies a choice among competent forums available to the plaintiff; consideration of fair trial should 'leave room for strategic moves' and 'it is only fair to give both sides the opportunity for forum shopping'.[221]

8.3.2 The Influence of Article 6(1) on National Jurisdiction Rules

Some national courts addressed the compatibility of national provisions with Article 6(1) ECHR. Although the supremacy of Article 6 is acknowledged, national courts are reluctant to establish a breach of the *fair trial* principle as a conse-

---

[217] Judgment of 23 October 1996, Reports of Judgments and Decisions 1996-V, at 1567-68, para. 38, case numbered 61/1995/567/653.

[218] *Nideröst-Huber v. Switzerland*, 18 February 1997, Reports of Judgments and Decisions 1997-I, para. 23, the case is numbered 104/1995/610/698. See Marchadier, *A l'épreuve de la Convention Européenne des droits de l'homme,* at 203 *et seq.*; Lagarde, 'Le principe de proximité', at 157; Nuyts, 'Due Process and Fair Trial', at 179.

[219] Schlosser, 'The Issue of Human Rights', at 15, emphasizing the importance of a fair balance embodied in Art. 6 ECHR and its analogy with due process: 'of course, it cannot be overlooked that the "efficiency" of court protection for the benefit of the plaintiff increases rather than decreases if he is empowered to sue the other party in a court of jurisdiction that must be qualified as "exorbitant" from defendant's point of view. Such a basis of jurisdiction is normally very favourable and, hence "efficient" for the plaintiff. Yet it is not permissible to categorize in such a way the principle of effective protection of legal rights. Fairness to the defendant is the indispensable counterweight. Efficiency to the benefit of the plaintiff but at the expense of fairness to the defendant would not be due process of law'.

[220] See also Nuyts, 'Due Process and Fair Trial', at 181 and see at 185 a strong plea in favour of such a balance test: 'there seems to be no good reason why the rules of jurisdiction of the Brussels Convention/Regulation should be immunized from scrutiny as to their compatibility with the fair trial doctrine of article 6 ECHR. While the principles are not yet fully developed – they are only emerging – there are convincing arguments for the thesis that the rules ... are to be applied and construed in such a way as to ensure that the defendant has effective access to justice and is not placed at a substantial disadvantage in comparison to the plaintiff.'

[221] Blobel and Spath, 'Tale of Multilateral Trust', at 544.

quence of the exercise of jurisdiction.[222] Especially, U.K. courts started examining the compatibility of the common law on jurisdiction with Article 6, since the enactment of the Human Rights Act of 1998 implemented the ECHR into its legal order.[223] In fact, the *forum non conveniens* doctrine itself was scrutinized regarding the compliance with the fair trial doctrine in *Lubbe v. Cape*.[224] The House of Lords ruled that Article 6 had 'nothing to do with' the *forum non conveniens* doctrine.[225]

An earlier example involved a U.S. based defendant against whom an action was brought in England by an English domiciliary. The defendant claimed that the claimant had no right to sue him in England, since Order XI Rule 1 upon which jurisdiction was based simply resulted in a plaintiffs' home forum, even if the claim involved a contract with no substantial link with England. The defendant argued that it constituted a *déni de justice* and violated the principle of '*fair trial*' in the sense of Article 6(1) ECHR and that the exercise of jurisdiction would be unreasonably usurped jurisdiction.[226]

French courts were also confronted with the privilege given to French defendants in Article 15 of the Civil Code, only to conclude that it did not lead to an infringement of Article 6 ECHR.[227]

8.3.3 **International Fair Trial Considerations**

If a fair trial control was to be applied in Europe with respect to issues regarding international jurisdiction it would certainly constitute a *correction* to the bases of jurisdiction.[228] It might lead to a change in national or Brussels legislation banning 'excessive' jurisdiction rules, but the courts themselves could *decline* jurisdiction when the outcome of the bases of jurisdiction would violate Article 6(1). The 'analytical tools' deriving from settled Strasbourg case law could correct the defendant's insufficient link with the forum or the denial of claimant's right of access to

---

[222] According to Nuyts, 'Due Process and Fair Trial', at 183.

[223] See A. Briggs, 'Decisions of British Courts During 2002: Private International Law', 73 *Yearbook of Private International Law* (2003), at 16.

[224] *Lubbe and Others v. Cape Plc. and related appeals*, House of Lords HL, [2000] 1 WLR 1545.

[225] See Chapter 4, Sect. 4.3.2, for the statement of Lord Bingham of Cornhill, in *Connelly v. RTZ Corp. Plc (No. 2)*, [1998] AC 854, at 860. See also Bell, *Forum Shopping and Venue*, § 4.52, at 155; Nygh, 'Declining Jurisdiction', at 326; Grolimund, 'Human Rights and Jurisdiction', at 108-109.

[226] Unpublished case *Hunt v. The United Kingdom*, Decision of the Commission No. 10.000/82 of 4 July 1983 (DR 33, 147), reported by Matscher. Another unpublished decision reported by Matscher, Commission's Decision No. 6200/73 of 13 May 1976, deals with possible restrictions to the plaintiff's choice to litigate among available forums. In this case plaintiff chose the nationality forum. The Commission decided that Art. 6 could not interfere in plaintiff's choice of forum to bring suit. Matscher, 'Face à la Convention Européenne des droits de l'homme', at 219-220, see also Grolimund, 'Human Rights and Jurisdiction', fn. 4, at 88; Nuyts, *L'exception*, § 444, at 600-601; Collins and Droz, 'The Principles', Reply of Matscher, at 51; and Nuyts, 'Due Process and Fair Trial', at 177-179.

[227] *Cour de cassation*, 30 March 2004, JCP la Semaine Juridique, Generale II juris. 1129, note Egea.

[228] Schlosser, 'The Issue of Human Rights', at 13, 'human rights approaches in Europe may correct particular misconceived legislation or compel adaptation of rules which might have been defensible in earlier times, but which have become inadmissible in the age of high technology communication facilities.'

justice, or finally, the exercise of jurisdiction leading to a substantial disadvantage vis-à-vis his opponent.[229] Some scholars suggested that such a 'substantial connection' requirement is essential to satisfy *fair trial* requirements and would be important at international level. The fair trial principle is recognized in international law, at least by Article 14 of the United Nations Treaty on Civil and Political Rights of 19 December 1966,[230] which has similar wordings as Article 6 of the ECHR.[231] This is already the implicit underlying principle of many international conventions, especially conventions dealing with the recognition and enforcement of foreign judgements.[232] According to Lagarde a general principle based on 'sufficient connection' should be formulated in order to oblige courts to decline jurisdiction when their jurisdiction rules, especially exorbitant ones, would result in such a violation of the principle of proximity that it would deprive defendant of a just and fair trial.[233] Such *fair trial* considerations – comparable to the U.S. Constitution's XIVth Amendment – could become useful for the elaboration of international standards.[234] The application of fundamental rights of international procedural justice and fairness to international jurisdiction would lead to the condemnation of exorbitant jurisdiction rules and to jurisdictional correction at international level.[235] It is not unthinkable that common grounds for international jurisdiction will be introduced as a general correction clause imposing a close connection with the forum, especially with the defendant and the forum.

---

229 Nuyts, 'Due Process and Fair Trial', at 182.

230 International Covenant on Civil and Political Rights, adopted and opened for signature, ratification and accession by General Assembly Resolution 2200A (XXI) of 16 December 1966, entered into force on 23 March 1976, in accordance with Art. 49. See http://www.unhchr.ch/html/menu3/b/a_ccpr.htm.

231 The relevant passage of Art. 14(1) reads: 'All persons shall be equal before the courts and tribunals. In the determination of any criminal charge against him, or of his rights and obligations in a suit at law, everyone shall be entitled to a fair and public hearing by a competent, independent and impartial tribunal established by law.' See Lagarde, 'Le principe de proximité', § 159, at 158; and Bertele, *Souveränität und Verfahrensrecht*, at 201, stressing the similarities with Art. 6.

232 P. Vlas, 'The Principle of Fair Trial in International Litigation', in *Law and Reality: Essays on National and International Procedural Law in Honour of Cornelis Carel Albert Voskuil* (1992), 391-406, at 393. See for a non-exhaustive but quite complete list of conventions using the aspect of fair trial, established under the auspices of the Hague Conference on Private International Law, ibid., at 393-397.

233 Lagarde, 'Le principe de proximité', § 158, at 158, '*On peut même se demander, ... si ne serait pas en formation un principe général du droit international obligeant les tribunaux à se dessaisir lorsque leur compétence, le plus souvent exorbitante, est à ce point contraire au principe de proximité qu'elle à priver le défendeur d'un procès juste et équitable.*'

234 Ibid., § 159, at 158, '*Aujourd'hui, des textes internationaux, dont la rédaction rappelle à certains égards celle du quatorzième amendement, pourraient être utilisés dans le même sens. Tant la Convention européenne de sauvegarde des droits de l'homme et des libertés fondamentales du 4 novembre 1950 [ECHR] (art. 6) que le Pacte international des Nations Unies relatifs aux droits civils et politiques.*'

235 Ibid. See also Chalas, *L'exercise discrétionnaire*, at 438-439.

8.4 Correction Clauses at Unification Level

8.4.1 The 'Close Connection' Requirement in the Proposed Hague Convention

The Hague Preliminary Draft Convention introduces the concept of 'substantial connection' in Article 18, which lists the prohibited grounds for jurisdiction.[236] In a more general sense its first paragraph states that '[w]here the defendant is habitually resident in a Contracting State, the application of a rule of jurisdiction provided for under the national law of a Contracting State is prohibited if there is *no substantial connection* between that State and the dispute'.[237]

The provision protects a defendant, habitually resident in a Contracting State, from being subjected to jurisdiction of a court with no substantial connection.[238] Whether or not a substantial connection exists is left to the court seized. The draft text does not provide any factors of appreciation, which leads to a high level of judicial discretion. Such a 'sufficient connection' element corrects excessive jurisdiction rules on international level, as the court will refuse jurisdiction when such a connection is lacking.[239]

After the Diplomatic Conference in June 2001, the first paragraph of Article 18 was seriously questioned, as some delegations wanted to delete it all together.[240] Some delegations proposed clarifications regarding the meaning of 'substantial connection' and whether it should be defendant-related or claim-related. The corresponding footnote explains that this was proposed to 'meet the difficulties in national legal systems where the main emphasis for jurisdictional competence lies on the link between the forum and the defendant, rather than the subject matter of the dispute.'[241] This clearly refers to the U.S. due process considerations which have been explained above.

As correctly stated by Silberman, such a provision will mean that under some circumstances, the 'doing business' rule may be exercised provided that it has a substantial connection, even if recognition of the judgement would depend on the

[236] Judgements based on prohibited jurisdiction grounds listed on the black list will 'on no account' be recognized. P. Nygh and F. Pocar, 'Report of the Special Commission Convention on Jurisdiction and Foreign Judgments in Civil and Commercial Matters', *Hague Conference on Private International Law* (2000), at 26.

[237] Art. 18(1) The Hague 1999 Preliminary Draft Convention (emphasis added).

[238] Nygh-Pocar Report, at 27.

[239] National jurisdiction rules providing for a substantial connection fall within the grey zone; ibid., at 75; see Castel and Walker, *Canadian Conflict of Laws*, § 11.3 and 11.10, indicating that the Canadian Constitution equally requires a 'real and substantial connection' between the subject matter or the action and the forum province.

[240] According to the footnote under the bracketed text: 'The deletion of the whole of paragraph 1 has been proposed in order to emphasise the basic concept of the Convention that there be a limited number of required bases of jurisdictions that are generally accepted, a limited number of jurisdictional bases so universally disapproved as exorbitant that they should be listed as prohibited jurisdictions, and that any other jurisdiction not listed in either category should remain open for the exercise of jurisdiction under national law (the "grey zone").' See also Silberman, 'Comparative Jurisdiction', at 338.

[241] See fn. and text in brackets of Art. 18(1) The Hague 2001, Interim Text.

national law of the state addressed.[242] A substantial connection exists when the claim arises out of the business carried out in the forum; as a consequence such a form of special doing business should not be put on the black list of prohibited grounds of jurisdiction.[243]

8.4.2 Declining Jurisdiction in the Proposed Hague Convention

Since the commencement of the Hague negotiations, the question arose whether there should be room for discretionary powers in a world-wide convention for international jurisdiction. Confronted with the classical cleavage between common law and civil law systems, the Hague Conference found itself in a delicate position:[244] civil law countries indicated that they would not accept a general application of the doctrine, whereas delegates from common law jurisdictions pointed out that they would not accept a structure with no discretionary powers at all.[245] Already in 1994, the First Conclusions of the Special Commission underlined that the *forum non conveniens* doctrine is part of the jurisdictional structure of several common law legal orders and that the doctrine is applied in 'a great deal of circumspection'.[246]

The debate was mainly concerned with legal certainty and predictability on the one hand and flexibility and (procedural) justice on the other. During the Second Special Commission, the U.K. delegation in particular, stressed the contrast between these two principles and that indicated that the implementation of a *forum non conveniens* theory 'might prove to be difficult within the context of a double convention, since at that point two extremes would have to be reconciled; firstly, fixed and rigid rules of competence and secondly flexibility and discretionary power attributed to the court.'[247] Civil law jurisdictions expressed concerns that too much discretionary power would deny the plaintiff the right of access to the court chosen because of the 'uncertainty that it creates for a plaintiff who, moreover, is constrained to undergo long and costly procedures on the question of jurisdiction' and

---

242 Silberman, 'Comparative Jurisdiction', at 339.

243 See in that sense ibid., at 320: 'In the context of an initiative for a worldwide judgments convention, the Europeans perceived a "corrective mechanism" if they could obtain an international consensus on rules for asserting judicial jurisdiction, and thereby set limits on jurisdiction over foreign defendants by U.S. courts.'

244 See also ibid., at 347.

245 See Prel. Doc. No. 6 of August 1996 of the Permanent Bureau of the Hague Conference on Private International Law, 'Conclusions of the Second Special Commission', at 11.

246 Prel. Doc. No. 2 of December 1995 of the Permanent Bureau of the Hague Conference on Private International Law, 'Conclusions of the Special Commission', § 32, at 21. See also Actes et documents de la Dix-huitième session 30 septembre au 19 octobre 1996; Prel. Doc. No. 1 of Augustus 1994 of the Permanent Bureau of the Hague Conference on Private International Law, 'Miscellaneous matters', at 67.

247 See Prel. Doc. No. 6 of August 1996, 'Conclusions of the Second Special Commission', at 11. See also C. Kessedjian, 'Prel. Doc. No. 7: Report International Jurisdiction and Foreign Judgments in Civil and Commercial Matters', Permanent Bureau of the Hague Conference Private International Law (1997), § 67-75.

therefore the doctrine would not fit in those civil law jurisdictions.[248] A consensus was considered feasible if the possibilities in which jurisdiction could be declined were limited to specific cases: 'It seems that a consensus might emerge in favour of allowing a limited possibility for application of the theory of *forum non conveniens* in specific cases to be determined and on the condition that a mechanism of co-ordination be instituted in the convention.'[249] After further study, the Second Special Commission stated that the *forum non conveniens* doctrine could be eliminated or easily accommodated if exorbitant jurisdiction rules were to be eliminated in a world-wide convention.[250] This means that the acceptance of judicial discretion depends on the underlying bases for jurisdiction used in uniform rules. At an early stage, declining jurisdiction was considered *unacceptable* when defendant's home court was seized or jurisdiction was based on exclusive jurisdiction in matters of immoveable property.[251] The possibility of declining jurisdiction was considered appropriate only when jurisdiction was based on defendant's nationality.[252]

As a result, but not without some virulent reactions against earlier proposals,[253] Article 22 of the final Hague Draft Convention provides grounds for declining jurisdiction that are confined to 'exceptional circumstances' with respect to certain permitted bases for jurisdiction, instead of a general *forum non conveniens* rule. This 'limited *forum non conveniens*' approach is thought to meet both flexibility as well as predictability considerations needed for a uniform instrument on international jurisdiction.[254] Article 22 is considered as an important compromise between the common law and the civil law world.[255] But this compromise does not stand alone and should be viewed in combination with the closely related *lis pendens* provision under Article 21.[256] Since the *forum non conveniens* doctrine

[248] Ibid.; Prel. Doc. No. 2 of December 1995, 'Conclusions of the Special Commission', § 32, at 21. See also Actes et documents de la Dix-huitième session; Prel. Doc. No. 1 of Augustus 1994, 'Miscellaneous matters', at 67.

[249] Prel. Doc. No. 2 of December 1995, 'Conclusions of the Special Commission', § 32, at 21.

[250] This would include a strict application of the *lis pendens* rule and respect of a choice of forum agreement, Prel. Doc. No. 3 of April 1996, 'Note on the question of *forum non conveniens*', at 12.

[251] Prel. Doc. No. 6 of August 1996, 'Conclusions of the Second Special Commission', at 13.

[252] C. Kessedjian, 'Prel. Doc. No. 8: Synthesis of the work of the Special Commission of June 1997 on International Jurisdiction and the Effects of Foreign Judgments in Civil and Commercial Matters', Permanent Bureau of the Hague Conference on Private International Law, § 86.

[253] See especially the synthesis of C. Kessedjian, 'Prel. Doc. No. 9: Synthesis of the work of the Special Commission of March 1998 on International Jurisdiction and the Effects of Foreign Judgments in Civil and Commercial Matters', Permanent Bureau of the Hague Conference on Private International Law, § 101-112.

[254] See Stückelberg, 'FNC at the Hague Conference', at 951.

[255] P. Beaumont, '*Forum Non Conveniens/Lis Pendens*', paper presented at the UIA Seminar, Edinburgh, 2001, at 68. According to Brand, 'Comparative FNC', at 492, 'this was in fact one of the areas of early compromise in the Hague Conference negotiations.'

[256] Brand, 'Comparative FNC', at 494-495; Stückelberg, 'FNC at the Hague Conference', at 950-951 and 979. Without going into the details of that provision, it should be stressed that the Art. 22 compromise was only possible by the enactment of a *lis pendens* provision. The *lis pendens* rule, emanating from the civil law tradition, has the primary objective of avoiding parallel proceedings in different courts, by giving the court first seized priority and requiring any other court subsequently seized to decline jurisdiction until the court first seized has stated upon its jurisdiction.

takes into consideration the existence of parallel litigations as a factor of appreciation to determine whether or not it should decline jurisdiction, both provisions are strongly linked and were negotiated together in The Hague.[257]

A *lis pendens* rule, as known in civil law jurisdictions, prevents parallel proceedings, but applied in combination with judicial discretionary powers under 'exceptional circumstances' it also enables a certain correction if a '*race to the courthouse*' results in the exercise of jurisdiction by a court which is not the natural forum, or at least not the most appropriate forum.[258] This interaction with the *lis pendens* rule made of Article 22 an important tool to correct undesired outcomes of jurisdiction rules, and a tool for cooperation between courts, which is only possible in an international context of unification.[259]

Article 22 of the Interim Text regulates declining jurisdiction under exceptional circumstances[260] and should not be confused with the doctrine generally applied in common law jurisdictions.[261] The use of '*forum non conveniens*' is deliberately avoided. The defendant or the plaintiff may ask to suspend the proceedings when

---

[257] See Stückelberg, 'FNC at the Hague Conference', at 961.

[258] Nygh, 'Declining Jurisdiction', at 332; Brand, 'Comparative FNC', at 494; G. Walter, 'Lis Alibi Pendens Forum Non Conveniens', 4 *European Journal of Law Reform* (2002), 69-85, at 74 and 78.

[259] See also Walter, 'Lis Alibi Pendens', at 82-85.

[260] Art. 22 reads

'(1) In exceptional circumstances, when the jurisdiction of the court seised is not founded on an exclusive choice of court agreement valid under Article 4, or on Article 7, 8 or 12, the court may, on application by a party, suspend its proceedings if in that case it is clearly inappropriate for that court to exercise jurisdiction and if a court of another State has jurisdiction and is clearly more appropriate to resolve the dispute. Such application must be made no later than at the time of the first defence on the merits.

(2) The court shall take into account, in particular – *a)* any inconvenience to the parties in view of their habitual residence; *b)* the nature and location of the evidence, including documents and witnesses, and the procedures for obtaining such evidence; *c)* applicable limitation or prescription periods; *d)* the possibility of obtaining recognition and enforcement of any decision on the merits.

(3) In deciding whether to suspend the proceedings, a court shall not discriminate on the basis of the nationality or habitual residence of the parties.

(4) If the court decides to suspend its proceedings under paragraph 1, it may order the defendant to provide security sufficient to satisfy any decision of the other court on the merits. However, it shall make such an order if the other court has jurisdiction only under Article 17, or if it is in a non-Contracting State, unless the defendant establishes that [the plaintiff's ability to enforce the judgment will not be materially prejudiced if such an order is not made] [sufficient assets exist in the State of that other court or in another State where the court's decision could be enforced].

(5) When the court has suspended its proceedings under paragraph 1, *a)* it shall decline to exercise jurisdiction if the court of the other State exercises jurisdiction, or if the plaintiff does not bring the proceedings in that State within the time specified by the court; or *b)* it shall proceed with the case if the court of the other State decides not to exercise jurisdiction.

(6) This Article shall not apply where the court has jurisdiction only under Article 17 [which is not consistent with Articles [white list]]. In such a case, national law shall govern the question of declining jurisdiction.

[7. The court seised and having jurisdiction under Articles 3 to 15 shall not apply the doctrine of *forum non conveniens* or any similar rule for declining jurisdiction.]'

It was agreed to insert 'or if it is in a non-Contracting State' under point 4 to fill a gap in the provision. See Nygh-Pocar Report, at 92-93.

[261] Nygh-Pocar Report, at 89; Silberman, 'Comparative Jurisdiction', at 347; Walter, 'Lis Alibi Pendens', at 84.

the court seized is '*clearly inappropriate*' and when another court of a Contracting State is '*clearly more appropriate*'.[262] Thus the less strict '*inconvenience*' approach of the U.S. was not chosen,[263] but the Australian version was favoured; the defendant has to prove that the court chosen by the plaintiff is 'clearly inappropriate'.[264] Additionally, the English version was also incorporated to the extent that the defendant has to show that the other court is a 'clearly more appropriate' forum.[265] Both conditions have to be met: it is insufficient to prove that the alternative court is clearly more appropriate when the chosen court is not proven to be clearly inappropriate.[266] A third condition requires that the alternative 'clearly more appropriate' court – of a Contracting State or non-Contracting State – will actually assume jurisdiction.[267] This last condition is more difficult to prove than to prove that there is an 'available' forum somewhere else, as required in the Anglo-American versions. In general, the conditions of the Hague Draft Convention are considerably stricter,[268] which is understandable in the context of a uniform jurisdictional system. Additionally, the condition intends to meet guarantees of effective access to justice which is an important concern of some Continental European states.[269]

Declining jurisdiction based on specific mandatory bases for jurisdiction, such as a choice of forum, protected contracts or exclusive jurisdiction, is not permitted.[270] The exceptional circumstances under which declining jurisdiction is permitted refer to all other bases for jurisdiction including those most relevant for international contractual disputes, such as the defendant's home court, contract jurisdiction and branch and regular activity jurisdiction.[271] This was difficult for the European delegation to accept, especially with respect to jurisdiction being declined by defendant's home court.[272] In this context Nygh's observation on the adopted 'clearly inappropriate test' is crucial. He argues that such a test implies that

> 'a defendant who is sued at the place of habitual residence … cannot complain of that jurisdiction being "clearly inappropriate" even if there is another more appropriate forum available. It is only where that connection is slight or inconsequential, … such as a minor aspect of the performance of a contract for the sale if goods or the supply of services in a particular country as compared with other places of performance, that the issue will be relevant at all.'[273]

---

[262] Nygh-Pocar Report, at 90; see also Stückelberg, 'FNC at the Hague Conference', at 974.
[263] Nygh, 'Declining Jurisdiction', at 331.
[264] Stückelberg, 'FNC at the Hague Conference', at 972.
[265] Nygh-Pocar Report, at 90-91; Stückelberg, 'FNC at the Hague Conference', at 972.
[266] Collins and Droz, 'The Principles', at 32.
[267] Nygh-Pocar Report, at 88; Nygh, 'Declining Jurisdiction', at 332.
[268] See Silberman, 'Comparative Jurisdiction', at 347.
[269] Walter, 'Lis Alibi Pendens', at 85.
[270] Arts. 4, 7, 81 or 12 in conjunction with Art. 22(1).
[271] Respectively regulated in Arts. 3, 6 and 9.
[272] See Collins and Droz, 'The Principles', Réponse Droz, at 66, who indicates that this compromise constitutes the 'maximum admissible' for Continental European systems and still favours an even stricter version. See Prel. Doc. No. 6 of August 1996, 'Conclusions of the Second Special Commission', § 10, at 13.
[273] Nygh, 'Declining Jurisdiction', at 331.

In sum, Article 22 allows a court to decline jurisdiction assumed on certain permitted bases for jurisdiction that belong to the white list, but do not always reflect a strong connection between the parties and the forum, such as the place of delivery permitted under Article 6(a). These bases presume a sufficient link with the forum, but their outcome might need correction. In other words Article 22 helps to ensure proximity between the claim and the forum.[274] Article 22 contains a non-exhaustive list of appreciation factors to determine the 'clearly inappropriateness' of the court seized and 'clearly more appropriateness' of the other court. A closed list would certainly have limited the discretionary powers of courts to decline jurisdiction and would have brought more predictability. But it was thought difficult to incorporate a list covering all possible situations and cases in which it might be necessary to decline jurisdiction.[275] The choice for an open list is based on considerations of flexibility, which were given more weight over predictability considerations.

Article 22(2) provides that the court seized shall take into account, in particular any inconvenience caused to parties in view of their habitual residence; the nature and location of the evidence; the applicable limitation or prescription periods and the possibility of obtaining recognition and enforcement of any decision on the merits.[276]

The list of factors does not include *public interests factors*, but they are not explicitly excluded either.[277] This is one of the consequences of an open list of factors; it is therefore most likely that U.S. courts will take into account elements of U.S. public interest and decline jurisdiction to avoid the U.S. becoming a 'magnet forum'.[278] As has been stated above, this form of protectionism is the result of the U.S. Supreme Court decision in *Piper Aircraft* and allows U.S. courts to make a different appreciation of *forum non conveniens* factors when the plaintiff is an alien instead of a U.S. plaintiff.[279] But the Hague Draft Convention attempts in Article 22(3) to avoid favouritism of local residents or nationals to the detriment of foreign plaintiffs by prohibiting any discrimination on the basis of a parties' nationality or

[274] Prel. Doc. No. 3 of April 1996, 'Note on the question of *forum non conveniens*', referring to Lagarde at 14.

[275] See also Stückelberg, 'FNC at the Hague Conference', at 973.

[276] The last factor, (sub d), involves considerations of the recognition of judgements, given either by the court seized or the alternative court. It involves an inquiry on whether the forum will recognize any decision by the alternative forum and vice versa. See Nygh-Pocar Report, at 91; Stückelberg, 'FNC at the Hague Conference', at 972-973. Such a factor would be redundant in a double convention, but was considered necessary, since Art. 22 allows jurisdiction to be declined in favour of a non-Contracting State. It is designed for that particular situation and should be read along with the recognition provisions and Art. 27 regulating the verification of jurisdiction. Prior to enforcement, the court addressed is required under Art. 27(1) to verify the jurisdiction of the court of origin. The court addressed is not allowed to enter into the court of origin's appreciation of Art. 22. Art. 27(3) states that the addressed court may not refuse enforcement on the ground that the court of origin should have declined jurisdiction. Nygh-Pocar Report, at 95-100; Buonaiuti, 'Forum Non Conveniens Facing the Prospective Hague Convention', at 37.

[277] Brand, 'Comparative FNC', at 493; Stückelberg, 'FNC at the Hague Conference', at 973.

[278] See R. Weintraub, 'The United States as a Magnet Forum and What, If Anything to Do About It', in *International Dispute Resolution: The Regulation of Forum Selection (Fourteenth Sokol Colloquium)* (1997).

[279] See above Sect. 8.2.1. and see Nygh-Pocar Report, at 92.

habitual residence. Courts are entitled to decline jurisdiction on the basis of public interest factors in order to avoid 'crowded dockets', but if any public interest factors are to be appreciated it must be done on a non-discriminatory basis.[280]

The outcome of the Diplomatic Conference in June 2001 resulted in an additional subparagraph 6, limiting this 'exceptional circumstances' correction clause to jurisdiction exercised on the required bases for jurisdiction of the white list.[281] Its purpose was to clarify that Article 22 does not apply when the court assumes jurisdiction on bases for jurisdiction belonging to the grey list of Article 17.[282] When jurisdiction is founded on such bases courts can apply their own rules of *forum non conveniens* or similar rules (if any).[283] The bracketed text of Article 22(7) – also introduced during the June 2001 negotiations – has the objective to ensure that national rules of *forum non conveniens* or any similar rule for declining jurisdiction arising out of the white list will not be used.[284] The fact that no consensus was reached for these last two paragraphs shows that the compromise on declining jurisdiction was not a done deal.

8.4.3 The Leuven/London Principles of the International Law Association

In 2000, during the 69th ILA Conference, the Committee on International Civil and Commercial Litigation adopted the Leuven/London Principles on declining and referring jurisdiction in civil and commercial matters.[285] These principles have a different objective than the draft provisions of the Hague Project on international jurisdiction. The McLachlan Report states that the Committee researched 'the legal technique available for the declining jurisdiction *as a response* to the problems of forum shopping'.[286] One such technique is the *forum non conveniens* correc-

---

[280] Nygh, 'Declining Jurisdiction', at 331: 'the provision of article 22 … stress referral of jurisdiction rather than dismissal of proceedings and seek to do so in a responsible internationalist manner without discrimination against foreign plaintiffs.' See also Stückelberg, 'FNC at the Hague Conference', at 974 questioning the prohibition of discrimination on the basis of residency.

[281] Art. 22(6) The Hague 2001, Interim Text.

[282] See Nygh-Pocar Report, at 89.

[283] See also the explanation provided in fns. 134-135 of The Hague 2001, Interim Text. The provision ensures that the 'preservation of national rules of *forum non conveniens* will not apply both where the court seised is exercising "white list" jurisdiction as such, and also in the case where that court exercises a jurisdiction under national law in a situation that is consistent with "white list" jurisdiction, such as proceedings against a defendant who is habitually resident in that State'.

[284] See for more comments on the exercise of judicial discretion in the draft world-wide convention, Buonaiuti, 'Forum Non Conveniens Facing the Prospective Hague Convention'; Chalas, *L'exercise discrétionnaire*, § 625 *et seq.*, at 573 *et seq.*; Stückelberg, 'FNC at the Hague Conference', at 978; Brand, 'Comparative FNC', at 492-494; Nygh, 'Declining Jurisdiction', at 330-333; Nuyts, *L'exception*, § 398 *et seq.*, at 531 *et seq.*

[285] London, July 2000; Resolution No. 1/2000, available at http://www.ila-hq.org/html/layout_committee.htm; see McLachlan, 'Report Leuven/London Principles', § 43, at 17; see Chapter 1, Sect. 1.3.1.

[286] McLachlan, 'Report Leuven/London Principles', § 2, at 2; H. Schulze, 'Declining and Referring Jurisdiction in International Litigation: The Leuven/London Principles', 25 *South African Yearbook of International Law* (2000), 161-180, at 162-163; and J. George, 'International Parallel Litigation: A Survey of Current Conventions and Model Laws', 37 *Texas International Law Journal* (2002), 499-540, at 525.

tion. Thus the principal aim of the Leuven/London Principles is not to establish uniform jurisdiction rules and to correct undesired outcome, but to determine to what extent a court should be able to decline jurisdiction in relation to unwanted *forum shopping*.[287] The Principles' Preamble states that the Committee not only recommends these principles to national courts and legislators, but also that it recommends them to be transmitted to the Hague Conference of Private International Law.[288] Although the Leuven/London principles were not intended as a prelude to an international convention, a possible incorporation was envisaged and they had considerable influence on the Hague Project.[289] The Leuven/London Principles explicitly preferred to adopt terms 'not rooted in the particularities of national systems of civil procedure' and to avoid concepts like the *forum non conveniens* doctrine.[290] This approach was followed by Article 22 of both Hague Draft Conventions avoiding any reference to the doctrine, but instead it referred to 'exceptional circumstances for declining jurisdiction' just like the Principles emphasize the fact that declining jurisdiction should only be considered as an 'exceptional matter'.[291]

The Committee rapidly realized that it 'did not necessarily have to make the simple choice between an inflexible "rule-based approach" and a "broad discretionary one"': 'It might well be possible to find middle ground.'[292] The consensus expressed by the principles is based on a 'rule-based' approach and not on an 'unfettered discretion.'[293] According to McLachlan, the 'Committee felt that, even though a number of the rules might be rather "open textured", in the sense that they were expressed in general terms in order to provide for a wide variety of circum-

[287] Principle 1.1 and 1.2, Scope and Purpose. The Leuven/London Principles allow declining jurisdiction under the circumstances of *lis pendens*, *related actions* and *injunctions* (respectively principles 4.1, 4.2 and 7) and '*other grounds for referral*' allowing an originating court to decline jurisdiction to an alternative 'more appropriate' court (principles 4.3 and 5). See Schulze, 'The Leuven/London Principles', at 175. According to McLachlan 'the overall purpose of the Principles is to indicate the lines of a potential new direction in the declining and referring jurisdiction in international civil and commercial litigation.' McLachlan, 'Report Leuven/London Principles', § 45. The Principles provide detailed guidance on the circumstances under which a court shall decline jurisdiction and refer the matter to an alternative court, and on direct communication with the alternative court to obtain information in order to determine whether or not it should decline jurisdiction. See in particular Principle 5.2. This new direction focusses on the need of coordination and cooperation between state courts. The Principles consist in providing detailed guidance not only on the circumstances under which a court shall decline jurisdiction and refer the matter to an alternative court, but also on direct communication with the alternative court to obtain information relevant to its determination of whether or not to decline jurisdiction. See in particular Principle 5.2, Schulze, 'The Leuven/London Principles', at 179; Walter, 'Lis Alibi Pendens', at 83-84.

[288] The approach of elaborating a set of principles was preferred by the Committee and was thought to give better guidance in assisting courts and law reformers than a draft model law or a draft international convention; McLachlan, 'Report Leuven/London Principles', § 40, at 16. See also Schulze, 'The Leuven/London Principles', at 162; and Walter, 'Lis Alibi Pendens', at 83.

[289] McLachlan, 'Report Leuven/London Principles', § 45; and Walter, 'Lis Alibi Pendens', at 83; Collins and Droz, 'The Principles', at 90.

[290] McLachlan, 'Report Leuven/London Principles', § 47, at 18-19.

[291] Ibid., § 49, at 20; and see Nygh, 'Declining Jurisdiction', at 327.

[292] McLachlan, 'Report Leuven/London Principles', § 41, at 16.

[293] Ibid., § 46, at 18.

stances, nevertheless, it was appropriate and possible to give specific guidance to courts.'[294] The idea behind this rule-based approach was to prevent 'unacceptably arbitrary and unpredictable application of jurisdictional rules'.[295]

Principle 4.3 dealing with 'Other Grounds for Referral' reflects the search for middle ground and allows a court to decline jurisdiction: 'where it is satisfied that the alternative court is the manifestly more appropriate forum for the determination of the merits of the matter, taken into account the interests of all the parties, without discrimination on grounds of nationality.'[296]

The Principle requires that the alternative court is a 'manifestly more appropriate court', and resembles one of the three criteria of Article 22 of the Hague Draft Conventions requiring that the alternative court be 'clearly more appropriate', but Principle 4.3 does not impose that the originating court be 'manifestly inappropriate' like the Hague Draft does. Principle 4.3 prohibits discrimination on the basis of nationality, but McLachlan points out that the court seized is entitled to give particular weight to defendant's domicile and refuse to decline jurisdiction when the action is brought at defendant's home court. Nonetheless, the Committee did not feel the need to prohibit declining jurisdiction when the case is brought at defendant's home court.[297] Crucial in the proper functioning of the Leuven/London Principles – and quite different from the Hague Draft – is that Principle 4.3 is *mandatory* in its operation when the requisite test is satisfied.[298] McLachlan explains that it does not provide for discretionary powers, but imposes an obligation for the court to decline jurisdiction when all conditions are met and provided that the claimant proved that the alternative court has and will exercise jurisdiction.[299] Principle 4.3 provides for a non-exhaustive list of seven factors, which the court shall take into account. The following factors are most relevant: a) the location and language of the parties, witnesses and evidence; b) the balance of advantages of each party afforded by the law, procedure, and practice of the respective jurisdictions; c) the law applicable to the merits and finally, the efficient operation of the judicial system of the respective jurisdictions.[300] The Hague Draft does not explicitly mention these last two factors. Especially the factor related to the procedural efficiency and the wider position of the judicial system of the alternative court is considered misplaced in an international convention that attempts to build some degree of mutual trust.

[294] Ibid.

[295] Ibid.

[296] See Principle 4.3, at http://www.ila-hq.org/html/layout_committee.htm.

[297] McLachlan, 'Report Leuven/London Principles', § 67, at 25.

[298] Ibid., § 66-67, at 25.

[299] Principle 5.1 corresponds to the third condition of Art. 22 of The Hague 1999 Preliminary Draft Convention and 2001 Interim Text.

[300] Principle 4.3(f); see McLachlan, 'Report Leuven/London Principles', § 67, at 25.

8.4.4 The Bruges Resolution of the *Institut de droit international*

The IDI also examined aspects of the *forum non conveniens* doctrine and adopted a Resolution during its Session in Bruges in 2003.[301] This Resolution was the result of the work of the 'Second Commission' and adopted 'The principles for determining when the use of the doctrine of *forum non conveniens* and anti-suit injunctions is appropriate.'[302] Despite the fact that the IDI's objective was not to restate the Leuven/London Principles, its adopted Principles resemble the ILA Principles and the Hague Draft provisions dealing with declining jurisdiction. Nonetheless, the IDI's principles should be appreciated for their originality and pioneer work. In fact, the Bruges Resolution stipulates that 'the practice of declining jurisdiction to assume or exercise jurisdiction on the ground that a court of another country is more appropriate to deal with the issues' is considered as *one of the solutions* developed by national court systems to deal with the question of transnational jurisdiction.[303]

The Resolution's first Principle states: 'a court may refuse to assume or exercise jurisdiction in relation to the substance of the claim on the ground that the courts of another country, which have jurisdiction under their law, are *clearly more appropriate* to determine the issues in question', provided that the law of the court allows declining jurisdiction and that the court seized is not founded upon an exclusive choice of court agreement.[304]

Factors similar to the Leuven/London Principles *may* be taken into account in order to decide which court is clearly more appropriate. These factors are: a) the adequacy of the alternative forum; b) the residence of the parties; c) the location of the evidence (witnesses and documents) and the effectiveness of the procedures for obtaining such evidence; d) the law applicable to the issues; e) the effect of applicable limitation or prescription periods; f) the effectiveness and enforceability of any resulting judgement.[305] It should be noted that the Final Report of October 2002, prepared by Sir Lawrence Collins and Mr Georges Droz, indicate that the Second Commission was divided on the desirability of a Resolution[306] and on the appropriateness of such *forum non conveniens* doctrine for the determination of transnational jurisdiction.[307] The Final Report clearly underlines a number of problems that have also been encountered during the Hague Project and the ILA meetings.

---

[301] Available at www.idi-iil.org; see Chapter 1, Sect. 1.3.3.

[302] The scope of the present study does not comprehend Principles 3 to 5, related to anti-suit injunctions, but see for an interesting analysis L. Collins, 'The Institut de droit international and Anti-suit Injunctions', in *Festschrift für Erik Jayme* (2004), 131-142.

[303] Preamble of the Resolution, para. b) (emphasis added).

[304] Principle 1 (emphasis added).

[305] The fact that the factors *may* be taken into account marks a difference with the Leuven/London Principles which oblige the courts to decline jurisdiction when all factors are met.

[306] See Final Report, Collins and Droz, 'The Principles', at 94.

[307] One of the members, M. Vischer, even stated that a Resolution should come to 'the reasoned conclusion that the *forum non conveniens should be abandoned worldwide*'. See Reply of Vischer, in Collins and Droz, 'The Principles', at 49. But see also the replies of Matsher, Sucharitkul, and Droz.

8.5 Evaluation of the Need for Correction Devices

The issue of open and closed systems and hard and fast rules and the question of correction are not limited to the acceptance of the *forum non conveniens* but involves special jurisdictional requirements based on the proximity principle, due process and fair trial standards. The preceding paragraphs show that the differences between common law and civil law traditions are surmountable; national Continental civil law systems gradually accept certain limited discretionary powers, especially where the forum is insufficiently connected with the dispute. In sum, there is room for some specific corrections to be applied in relation to specific bases for jurisdiction that are considered excessive.[308] European scholars have stressed the importance of flexibility and procedural justice and are open to limited discretionary powers. On the other hand, the use of correction devises, especially the *forum non conveniens* doctrine, is criticized by Anglo-American scholars who reject jurisdictional protectionism and favouring more legal certainty. At a world-wide level, it was acknowledged that the correction devices should not lead to discretionary treatment. However, the uniform Brussels structure still systematically rejects any form of judicial discretion. The question is whether this refusal is a result of the fact that the Brussels Model is a traditional civil law system strongly favouring principles of legal certainty or whether judicial discretion is simply no longer necessary or desirable in a uniform jurisdictional structure.

At unification level, two major problems remain to be solved. First whether a correction is needed when jurisdiction is exercised by the defendant's home court. Secondly, the issue of public factors protecting state interests should be allowed at international level.

The interaction between bases for jurisdiction and the correction mechanism is clear, the more exorbitant or excessive the exercise of jurisdiction is because the connection with the forum is weak, the more correction is applied among the jurisdictional systems. The use of property-based jurisdiction, presence-based jurisdiction and nationality-based jurisdiction directly gave rise to correction mechanisms. General correction devices, such as the *forum non conveniens* exception, were conceived to correct the outcome of exorbitant jurisdiction rules. Conversely, a general correction mechanism, either by requirement or by exception, is not accepted world-wide, especially the correction on jurisdiction exercised by defendant's home court is highly controversial.[309]

In a well-balanced uniform jurisdictional system for international contractual disputes there should be no need for a general correction mechanism; exorbitant bases for jurisdiction are abolished and when uniform jurisdiction rules over contractual disputes are chosen on the basis of *defendant-related close connection* with the forum, correction is no longer needed. In other words, there is no room for general correction devices giving discretionary powers to the court to decline jurisdiction assumed on any basis for jurisdiction.

---

[308] There is a place for some *forum non conveniens* exceptions, see Schlosser's contribution, in A. Lowenfeld, *The Hague Convention on Jurisdiction*, at 18.

[309] P. Schlosser, 'Bases of Jurisdiction', at A-18. See contributions of Schlosser and Buchner, in Lowenfeld, *The Hague Convention on Jurisdiction*, at 17, respectively at 24.

With respect to the balance between legal certainty and flexibility, this balance is more likely to succeed when the correction devices are adapted to the underlying basis for jurisdiction.[310] There is no room for general correction mechanisms, but again there is room for carefully drafted correction or escape clauses for specific bases for jurisdiction. Moreover, a plaintiff is better able to foresee whether his choice of forum will be granted, if the appreciation factors are limited and clearly defined.

Regarding the protection of both parties and the equality of arms, it is important to stress that a correction is often needed when the claimant has at his disposal a wide range of competent forums. If those were to be reduced in a uniform jurisdictional structure, limited to international contractual disputes, it would be considerably less necessary to correct the claimant's choice among the available competent courts.[311] This brings us to the question whether the defendant's home court should be able to decline jurisdiction. 'Normally everyone is happy to be sued at home rather than in a foreign country',[312] but it has become common practice to use the *forum non conveniens* exception to avoid suit at one's home court, especially, when one's home is located in the U.S. U.S. corporate defendants are 'extremely unhappy' to be sued at home and successfully appeal to the 'public interests' factors to decline jurisdiction in favour of another 'more appropriate court'.[313] In England there is the same problem but for different reasons. As the *Lubbe* case illustrated, 'actions brought at the defendant's head office are becoming more popular, especially where the plaintiff comes from a country with few or no legal aid facilities and with a standard of living far below that enjoyed in the corporation's home.'

In sum, the defendant's 'unhappiness' is not related to the inappropriateness of the claimant's choice for the court. As a rule the defendant's home vouches for a sufficient connection, is not unfair to the defendant, and is foreseeable for both parties. The correction takes place for very different reasons and has lead to the politicization of jurisdiction. Especially the American version of the *forum non conveniens* doctrine is applied as a protectionism device for its own residents and in the second place it is applied for its own state interests. In that context, it is primordial for successful unification that discrimination on the basis of nationality of the defendant or the plaintiff should not be accepted at uniform level.[314] More importantly correction for the sake of protectionism of national interests should have no place in uniform jurisdiction in contractual disputes.[315]

---

[310] A. Johnston and E. Powles, 'The Kings of the World and Their Dukes' Dilemma: Globalisation, Jurisdiction and the Rule of Law', in *Globalisation and Jurisdiction* (2004), 13-54, at 23; Hill, 'The Exercise of Jurisdiction', at 56.

[311] As emphasized in Chapter 6, Sect. 6.5.3.

[312] P. Nygh, 'The Criteria for Judicial Jurisdiction', at A-18.

[313] 'This might make some American corporation unhappy, but if you add any exceptions or doubts as to this basic ground for jurisdiction with respect to inconvenience of such forum, you would raise great uncertainty for plaintiffs.' Buchner's contribution in Lowenfeld, *The Hague Convention on Jurisdiction*, at 24.

[314] As also explained by the parameters identified in Chapter 6, Sect. 6.5.

[315] Nuyts, *L'exception*, § 145, at 210.

Chapter 9

CONCLUSIONS AND PROPOSITIONS

This book focused on the regulation of international jurisdiction over commercial disputes and particular attention was paid on surveying the possibilities for uniform rules on a universal scale. Chapters 2, 3, 4 and 5 dealt with the jurisdictional systems of the unified Brussels Model and the national rules of Continental European countries, England and the U.S., respectively. The purpose of these chapters was to give an overview of the current state of the law on jurisdiction in order to address the main objective of this book, namely, to determine whether any common grounds exist in the various jurisdiction rules and, as the case may be, whether a uniform global jurisdictional structure could be proposed for international contractual disputes. As a consequence, in Chapter 6 a description was given of the different approaches to international jurisdiction and an attempt was made to explain the various approaches. This chapter also illustrated the differences that were overcome by these different systems and developed parameters which should be taken into account at uniform level. Chapter 7 assessed the different jurisdictional bases encountered in each of the analysed systems as well as other unification initiatives within The Hague Conference, the ILA, the IDI and MERCOSUR. In a similar way, Chapter 8 compared the correction devices such as the *forum (non) conveniens* doctrine, the close connection requirements and U.S. due process constitutional standards.

Despite the contrasting approaches to jurisdiction and the diversity of the jurisdictional bases and correction devices, the present chapter concludes that there are common grounds for uniform rules for contractual disputes. A uniform approach to international jurisdiction for contractual disputes should however be founded on a 'consensus-based approach'.[1]

This concluding chapter starts with identifying acceptable and non-acceptable jurisdictional bases. The need of correction at uniform level will be addressed in Section 9.2; Section 9.3 explains the need for progressive unification, which is followed by a proposal for uniform jurisdiction rules over international contractual disputes.

But before concluding, it is important to stress that any consensus for uniformity in international jurisdiction is subjected to political will.[2] Even if 'technically speaking' unification of international jurisdiction rules might be possible and theoretically desirable, in the end it touches on issues of the sovereign power to adju-

[1] See *contra* Silberman who claims that '[t]he range of countries and cultural and legal traditions make consensus on a wide range of required and prohibited bases of jurisdiction unfeasible.' L. Silberman, 'Comparative Jurisdiction in the International Context: Will the Proposed Hague Judgments Convention Be Stalled?', 52 *DePaul Law Review* (2002), 319-350, at 348.

[2] Kokkini states '*waardering behoort tot de taak van politieke wetenschappen*', see D. Kokkini-Iatridou, *Een inleiding tot het rechtsvergelijkende onderzoek* (1988), at 176.

dicate.[3] Principles of (customary) public international law hardly touched upon the states' sovereign power to regulate the extraterritorial reach of their courts, only international conventions have the ability to regulate international jurisdiction. Especially the U.S., which has the widest jurisdictional catalogue to find a competent U.S. court and far-reaching correction tools to decline jurisdiction either in the interest of the local parties or of the state itself, might be faced with resistance to enact uniform rules – even if in the long run it might be in the interest of international trade. Any international convention limiting that reach might be considered to violate due process standards and therefore regarded as contrary to the U.S. Constitution. Whether this argument is a valid one or not, the reticence of governments to ratify international agreements in the field of private international law does not indicate any willingness to promote any further an international convention for the benefit of facilitating international court litigation.[4]

9.1 Acceptable and Non-acceptable Grounds

In order to find common grounds for uniform jurisdiction rules for contractual disputes it is necessary to identify acceptable jurisdictional bases, possibly accompanied by correction devices. In this respect, conclusions have to be drawn in relation to the general bases of jurisdiction, claim-related special jurisdiction rules for contracts, specific activity-based jurisdiction and property-based jurisdiction.

9.1.1 **General Bases for Jurisdiction**

From the assessment made in Chapter 7 of the different bases for jurisdiction, it was concluded that the majority of bases asserting general jurisdiction – in the sense that jurisdiction is established regardless of whether the claim is related to the defendant or his activities in the forum – are not universally acceptable for uniform rules over international contract disputes. With respect to natural persons, this was demonstrated by means of tag-jurisdiction[5] and nationality-based jurisdiction.[6] The *forum actoris* rule, founding general jurisdiction based on *claimant-related* connections such as claimant's domicile or nationality in the forum, also appeared to be nonnegotiable at uniform level.[7] In addition, general property-based jurisdiction over both natural persons and corporate defendants following the *forum partimonii* rule proved to be unacceptable at uniform level.[8] According to the parameters developed in Chapter 6, none of these jurisdictional bases ensures a substantial *defendant-related* connection with the forum or a balance between

[3] See A. Bell, *Forum Shopping and Venue in Transnational Litigation* (2003), at 80.

[4] S. Baumgartner, *The Proposed Hague Convention on Jurisdiction and Foreign Judgements: Trans-Atlantic Law Making for Transnational Litigation* (2003), at 177-178; A. von Mehren, 'Theory and Practice of Adjudicatory Authority in Private International Law: General Course on Private International Law (1996)', 295 *Recueil des cours* (2003), 9-431, at 77-78.

[5] In Chapter 7, Sect. 7.3.2.

[6] In Chapter 7, Sect. 7.3.1.

[7] See Chapter 7, Sect. 7.4.

[8] As demonstrated in Chapter 7, Sect. 7.7.4.

the parties' rights to justify international jurisdiction over contractual disputes and furthermore they do not focus on the parties' business activities in the forum which give rise to commercial contractual disputes. For Europeans, the exclusion of property-, nationality- and presence-based jurisdiction is nothing new, as they are already considered exorbitant under the Brussels Model. The excessive character of these jurisdiction bases should nevertheless be re-affirmed, at least with respect to cross-border commercial disputes, on a universal scale.

The connecting factors constituting the jurisdictional basis of the 'doing business' criterion seemed acceptable in itself. But the fact that the rule provides for general jurisdiction, regardless of whether the claim is connected to business carried out in the forum, makes it unsuitable on a universal scale.[9] A commercially active defendant operating world-wide is amenable to a court's jurisdiction at any place where he is 'doing business' according to the U.S.'s understandings of the rule. Consequently, the claimant will just have to pick and choose the court that best suits his (litigational) needs. This would increase *forum shopping* by claimants considerably and will be at the expense of the defendant's rights of defence. A limited version of doing business jurisdiction, i.e. limiting jurisdiction to claims directly related to defendant's doing business in the forum, could constitute the basis for a consensus-based approach and should be acceptable to all, including the U.S., as a uniform rule over contractual disputes.

The only uncontroversial basis for general *unrelated* jurisdiction is the defendant's home court rule. This jurisdictional basis is widely accepted in each of the analysed jurisdictional regimes.[10] Nonetheless, the defendant's home court evokes a few terminological problems at uniform level. In Chapter 7 it was primarily demonstrated that with respect to an individual's home, applying the 'domicile' criterion as connecting factor causes terminological complications, due to the fact that not every jurisdictional regime is familiar with the concept or the meaning of the concept varies from regime to regime.[11] The domicile rule needs to be re-conceptualised for individual defendants and it should preferably be replaced by the 'habitual residence' factor.[12] It was also clearly illustrated in Chapter 7 that the different characteristics between individuals and corporate defendants should be acknowledged in uniform jurisdiction rules. The assimilation of corporate defendants to natural persons should be avoided. The use of 'corporate domicile' as well as 'corporate presence' and 'corporate nationality' is artificial and should not be used to regulate jurisdiction over corporate defendants. Moreover, in Chapter 7 it was made clear that the focus should be on defining 'corporate home' factors, but that chapter also demonstrated that the difficulties encountered in defining those

---

[9] See the evaluation in Chapter 7, Sect. 7.5.7.1.

[10] See Chapter 7, Sect. 7.2.3.

[11] D. Tallon, 'L'harmonisation des règles du droit privé entre pays de droit civil et de common law', *Revue internationale de droit comparé* (1990), 513-523, referring to the 'danger of language'. See also Silberman, 'Comparative Jurisdiction', at 331-332; and see Chapter 7, Sects. 7.2.1 and 7.2.2.

[12] See also P. Nygh, 'The Criteria for Judicial Jurisdiction; Conference Papers', in *The Hague Convention on Jurisdiction and Judgements: Records of the Conference Held at New York University School of Law on the Proposed Convention 1999* (2001), 9-14, at 10.

factors are a direct consequence of the different theories applied. As a result, Chapter 7 concluded – in line with several earlier initiatives or proposals of unification at international level – that these corporate home factors should include – and in no particular order or hierarchy – the place of incorporation or statutory seat, the central place of administration and the principal place of business.[13] Obviously this could equally lead to multiple competent forums, but this is at the corporation's own risk when it has voluntarily incorporated itself 'for convenience' in one country while having its principal place of business or its central administration in another country.[14] In any event, the substantial *defendant-related* connection is guaranteed and none of these corporate home factors are unfair either to the defendant or to the plaintiff.

In sum, the concept of habitual residence should be applied as the connecting factor for an individual defendant's home and a compromise should be reached to define corporate home factors. But the crucial question raised in Chapter 7 is whether the rule's underlying principle of *favor defensoris* – or which at least underlies the Brussels Model and requires the claimant to seek out the defendant at his home court – is as self-evident at a world-wide uniform level for transnational commercial contracts as it is at a regional European level. The application of Anglo-American correction doctrines, such as the English *forum conveniens* and the American *forum non conveniens*, revealed that the defendant's home court is not a mandatory rule as it is in European civil law systems. At international level this raises the important question whether the defendant's home should be considered the *juge naturel* in international contractual disputes, and subsequently, whether there should always be a competent forum available to the claimant at defendant's home? The following paragraphs will answer this question in the negative. Although the rule's connecting factors do not constitute an insurmountable problem, the difficulties concern the *favor defensoris* principle underlying it. In this respect, a preliminary conclusion should stress that the connecting factors constituting both doing business and defendant's home court could form the basis of uniform rules over international contractual disputes, but their general reach is problematic on a universal scale.

9.1.2 The *Claim-related* Special Jurisdiction Rule: Unsuitable at Uniform Level

Apart from the general bases for jurisdiction explained above, Chapter 7 also identified other bases for jurisdiction such as *defendant-related* activity-based jurisdic-

---

[13] Chapter 7, Sects. 7.1.4 and 7.2.2.4 demonstrated that the use of certain concepts, originally used for natural persons, for corporate defendants eventuates in complex determinations of 'corporate domicile', 'corporate presence' and 'corporate nationality'. These rather artificial concepts are unsuitable for the regulation of jurisdiction over corporations as they always need further elaboration by way of other connecting factors. In Chapter 7, Sect. 7.1.3, it was shown that this results in jurisdictional overlaps among different jurisdictional bases because concepts like corporate domicile, presence and nationality are determined by the same connecting factors.

[14] A *lis pendens* rule regulating the situation of multiple courts seized should obviously be part of the uniform system in order to avoid '*positif*' jurisdiction conflicts.

tion, *claim-related contract* jurisdiction and specific property-based jurisdiction. With respect to *claim-related contract* jurisdiction, it explained that Continental European countries, English common law and the Brussels Model designed special rules for certain categories of claims such as for instance contractual claims. These *claim-related* bases provide for *special (contract)* jurisdiction and are meant to serve as an alternative forum besides the main jurisdiction rule. Each analysed connecting factor asserting special contract jurisdiction appeared however to be unsuitable at uniform level.[15] The quest for an adequate connecting factor for claim-related contract jurisdiction remains in vain: the place where the contract was formed,[16] the place of the law governing the contract,[17] the place where the contract was breached[18] or the place of performance in each of its variations,[19] all seemed to result in a complex and uncertain determination of a '*forum contractus*'. The only factor that came closest to constitute an acceptable ground was the tailored place of performance, i.e. the place of delivery in sales contracts. As some U.S. long-arm statutes specify the place of delivery as a jurisdiction-creating contact, the provisions are comparable to its French and Brussels counterparts.[20] However, uncertainty also surrounds this connecting factor in the event parties have not agreed on a place of specific contractual performance or in the event of multiple, non- or wrong performance.

Most essential is that *claim-related special* jurisdiction in contractual matters is primarily based on a connection between the contractual claim and the forum, *regardless* of any commercial activities carried out in the forum from which the contractual claim may arise. Especially under the Brussels Model, the initial underlying idea was the possibility to create a neutral forum, closely connected with the contract or the contractual claim and the forum, as an alternative to the *forum rei* rule. In practice, the outcome of the connecting factor often resulted in a *forum actoris*. The initial justification of a close connection between the claim and the forum appeared seldom validated: the rule does not ensure any substantial close connection between the claim and the forum, and least of all it does not secure a *defendant-related* connection. This remains problematic in view of U.S. due standards which require defendant to have 'minimum' contacts with the forum and thus constitutes a barrier for global acceptance of claim-related jurisdiction. Moreover, the complex determination of each of the connecting factors does not warrant for legal certainty. At the same time, their rigid application in Europe does not allow for any degree of flexibility.

In sum, special *claim-related contract* jurisdiction in contractual matters proves undesirable at a universal level and accentuates the need for a different approach to international jurisdiction at a uniform level. In fact, it calls for a complete elimination of *claim-related contract* jurisdiction all together.[21] Rather than focusing on

---

[15] As explained in Chapter 7, Sect. 7.2.2.4.

[16] Chapter 7, Sect. 7.6.3.1.

[17] Chapter 7, Sect. 7.6.3.2.

[18] Chapter 7, Sect. 7.6.3.5.

[19] Chapter 7, Sect. 7.6.3.3.

[20] Chapter 7, Sect. 7.5.3.4.

[21] This has even been argued by one of the Brussels Model's founding fathers, George Droz, who called for the complete deletion of Art. 5(1) which constitutes the *forum contractus*. See in general

the connection between the contract or the contractual claim and the forum, such as the place of performance,[22] a consensus-based approach demands a shift of focus to defendant's activity in the forum from which the contractual dispute arises. If *defendant's activity-related* jurisdiction is acceptable at uniform level, it should constitute the main principle for international jurisdiction in contract disputes.

9.1.3 The Focus on Defendant's 'Economic Allegiance' to the Forum

In Chapter 7 it was illustrated that jurisdiction based on defendant's activities carried out in the forum from which the contractual claim arose is – in principle – a well-accepted basis for jurisdiction. The underlying idea of 'activity-based' jurisdiction is that when someone engages in commercial activity with the purpose of obtaining commercial benefits, it is not unfair to subject him to the judicial powers of that country, provided that the (contractual) claim is related to those activities. It was argued in Chapter 6 that this underlying idea should constitute one of the major parameters for the acceptability of uniform rules. When a person voluntarily affiliated himself with the territory of a state for commercial purposes, he should accept being subjected to the state's jurisdiction in exchange for allowing him to be commercially active on its territory. This constitutes the principal justification for activity-based jurisdiction which submits a person carrying out commercial activities in a state over claims arising out of those activities to jurisdiction in that state. Founding jurisdiction on the basis of commercial activities carried out in the forum is even more justified in international contract disputes due to their commercial nature. Probably best defined as a form of 'implied (commercial) submission' or 'economic allegiance',[23] this should be the pivotal justification for uniform jurisdiction rules over international contractual disputes. If this does not suit the parties, they are still free to agree on another specific court by way of a choice of forum agreement and make use of globally accepted consent-based jurisdiction.[24] Moreover, as summarized by Brand 'implied (commercial) submission' brings together both claim- and defendant-related jurisdiction:

G. Droz, 'Delendum est forum contractus?', 41 *Recueil Dalloz: Cahier Chronique* (1997), 351-356; see also Von Mehren, 'Theory and Practice', at 72: 'the basic problem is that the connecting factor is susceptible of multiple interpretations and can be manipulated by parties to their advantage. … These qualities, highly undesirable in connecting factors, have caused some jurists to call for deletion of the category specific jurisdiction established by article 5(1) of the Brussels Convention.'

[22] In the context of The Hague Jurisdiction Project, the Ottawa contract provision was clearly drafted in a compromising spirit. This is discussed in Chapter 7, Sect. 7.6.4; and Prel. Doc. No. 15 of May 2001, Informational note, Annex I, which stipulates that: 'A plaintiff may bring an action in contract in the courts of the State in which the defendant has engaged in frequent or significant activity, or has [intentionally] directed such activity into that State, for the purpose of promoting [the conclusion of the contract] [or negotiating] or performing a contract, provided that the claim is based on a contract directly related to that activity. … The preceding paragraphs do not apply to situations where the defendant has taken reasonable steps to avoid entering into or performing an obligation in that State.'

[23] A. Johnston and E. Powles, 'The Kings of the World and Their Dukes' Dilemma: Globalisation, Jurisdiction and the Rule of Law', in *Globalisation and Jurisdiction* (2004), 13-54, at 34.

[24] Parties can also agree on an arbitration clause or any other alternative dispute resolution mechanism.

'activity-based jurisdiction simply admits that a defendant is present in other forms, but limits jurisdiction to a claim that arises out of the activity of the defendant in or purposefully directed at the state. … It is jurisdiction for which the court has both a nexus with the defendant and a nexus with the claim.'[25]

9.1.3.1 *Defendant's Activities: 'Fixed Establishment Jurisdiction'*

The acceptance of such activity-based jurisdiction on an international unification level however still depends on the degree of activity in the forum and on how the claim is related to those activities. As demonstrated in Chapter 3, the Continental European branch jurisdiction should be considered as an extension of defendant's domicile in another forum and Chapter 4 illustrated that the English place of business rule is a derivative of the common law presence rule. Both bases require a *fixed* place of business establishment or branch office and, as explained in Chapter 5, constitute – almost automatically – sufficient minimum contacts for jurisdiction under U.S. jurisdictional standards. When such activity gives rise to legal proceedings, it is globally accepted that the courts of the place where the business establishment is located has jurisdiction over claims directly related to those commercial activities carried out *in or outside the forum* by the defendant through that establishment. The physical or territorial connection with the forum by way of a local business establishment from which the business transactions are organized, gives evidence of the fact that the defendant purposefully set up a 'secondary establishment' with the purpose of carrying out business activities and clearly constitutes economic allegiance.

A place of business established in the forum from which the defendant carries out commercial activities and which eventually gives rise to a contractual claim clearly satisfies the *defendant-related* connection standard and originates from defendant's activities in the forum. The rule is fair and just for both parties, establishing a proper balance between the defendant's protection and the claimant's access to justice. It brings a considerable degree of legal certainty to both parties and – on the other hand – could meet the demands of flexibility when the connecting factor applied leaves a certain degree of appreciation to the court seized. The defendant is aware that when he establishes a fixed place of business he will be subjected to jurisdiction of the court where this physical establishment is located, and for the claimant such a 'fixed business establishment' is easily determinable. On the other hand, by using this relatively open norm, the court seized will be given a certain margin of appreciation on a case-by-case basis.

9.1.3.2 *Defendant's Business Activities without a Fixed Place of Business*

Learning from the lessons taught at The Hague and as explained in Chapter 7, it is crucial to emphasize that unification of jurisdiction should, however, not be limited by a requirement of a fixed place of business establishment. Many commercial bod-

---

[25] R. Brand, 'Understanding Activity-Based Jurisdiction', paper presented at the UIA Seminar Edinburgh, on 20 & 21 April 2001, entitled The Preliminary Draft Hague Convention on Jurisdiction and Foreign Judgements in Civil and Commercial Matters, at 39.

ies are active in a forum without having established a physical and local business establishment. As stated earlier, U.S. doing business jurisdiction is only unacceptable as uniform rule because it provides for *unrelated* jurisdiction, i.e. regardless of whether the contractual claim is related to the business carried out in the forum. But the connecting factors underlying the general doing business rule could constitute common grounds. U.S. doing business jurisdiction requires 'continuous and systematic' contacts with the forum but does not require a fixed place of business from which the activities are undertaken. There is room for compromise between the wide scope of general doing business jurisdiction and the much narrower scope of the Brussels special branch jurisdiction and English place of business jurisdiction. A consensus should focus on the *doing business*' connecting factors, provided that jurisdiction is limited to claims related to or arising out of defendant's *business activities carried out in the forum.* This means that activity-based jurisdiction should be accepted when the claim arises out of defendant's business activities carried out in the forum, even without him having a fixed place of business in the forum.[26] This specific '*activity-based doing business*' rule intends to reach defendants who have no *fixed* place of business, but nevertheless carry on business on a regular basis in the forum, and should therefore respond to judicial proceedings related to (contractual) claims directly related to or arising out of those commercial activities carried out in the forum. As a result, in contrast to the above-mentioned 'fixed business establishment' jurisdiction, it is important that jurisdiction that is founded on defendant's activities alone, should concern a claim arising out of the activities carried out in the forum itself, but should not require that the defendant operated from a fixed branch establishment in the forum.[27]

9.1.3.3 *Transacting Business*

With respect to the degree of commercial activities constituting 'activity-based' jurisdiction, the U.S. transacting business rule establishes specific jurisdiction on the basis of the smallest amount of activities as compared to branch or establishment jurisdiction and doing business jurisdiction. Provided that the exercise of jurisdiction is consistent with U.S. constitutional standards, a 'single transaction' or 'isolated or occasional contact' suffices for courts to assert specific jurisdiction

---

[26] Hartley states: '[I]f Americans can give up general jurisdiction based on an activity concept, the Europeans could well accept specific jurisdiction on a similar concept clearly defined.' See Hartley's contribution, in A. Lowenfeld and L. Silberman, eds., *The Hague Convention on Jurisdiction and Judgments: Records of the Conference Held at New York University School of Law on the Proposed Convention* (2001), at 28. According to Schlosser, that '[a] person or a corporation should be amenable to judicial jurisdiction at the place where he or it is doing business sounds reasonable, provided that the claim arises out of, or at least is related to, the respective business activities.' See P. Schlosser, 'Bases of Jurisdiction in a "New Double Convention" on Jurisdiction and Recognition of Foreign Judgements: Conference Papers', in *The Hague Convention on Jurisdiction and Judgements: Records of the Conference Held at New York University School of Law on the Proposed Convention 1999* (2001), A-13-A-27, at A-20.

[27] P. Nygh and F. Pocar, 'Report of the Special Commission Convention on Jurisdiction and Foreign Judgments in Civil and Commercial Matters', Hague Conference of Private International Law (2000), at 53.

over claims related to that transaction or contact. From Chapter 7 it is clear that it is that particular aspect of 'transacting business' jurisdiction that makes the rule unacceptable at uniform level. Primarily, although the connection is *defendant-related*, it does not warrant a *substantial* connection with the forum. Secondly, a claim arising out of a cross-border contractual relationship may have numerous 'single and occasional contacts' with several states, which could lead to a wide scale of competent courts. In light of considerations of legal certainty, occasional bases are not advisable. The rule does not install a proper balance between the parties, since it provides the claimant with an excessive range of competent forums to choose from, whereas the defendant may be drawn into litigation in courts with weak contacts to the dispute.

9.1.4 **Property-based Jurisdiction**

As concluded above, general property-based jurisdiction under the *forum partimonii* rule confers jurisdiction on the simple presence of defendant's property in the forum, regardless of any connection with the claim or the defendant and regardless of the value of the property. The rule is excessive and has no role to play at international level. Chapter 7 analysed the more limited specific property-based rule conferring jurisdiction over tangible or intangible, and moveable or immoveable property belonging to the defendant present in the forum. Specific property-based jurisdiction is limited either by an attachment requirement which often imposes that the property be directly related to the claim or which limits the court's jurisdiction to the value of defendant's assets or property. The particular features of this jurisdiction rule are numerous, which makes the question of the rule's acceptability at uniform level a complex one. First of all, specific property-based jurisdiction is praised for its execution-efficiency, as it predominantly originates from a necessity to secure defendant's assets to satisfy a potential judgement. The argument becomes less relevant when uniform jurisdiction rules are accompanied by rules guaranteeing world-wide recognition and enforcement of judgements. Another argument in favour of enacting specific property-based jurisdiction in a uniform structure is that it provides the claimant with an additional competent forum which could operate as an alternative to activity-based jurisdiction. The question is whether such an alternative competent forum is desirable or necessary at unification level. As has been indicated in Chapter 6, the plaintiff's access to justice does not include an opportunity to shop among several competent forums. In commercial practice this often leads to a 'race to the court' and parallel proceedings.

Conversely, in property-based jurisdiction the localization of the *situs* (especially for moveable and intangible property) proved particularly problematic and frequently resulted in competent courts 'by coincidence'. Minimum guarantees of legal certainty for parties are not met, nor does the rule take a flexible approach; the rule simply provides for a technical or legal localization of defendant's assets. Also, the rule does not warrant a *defendant-related* connection with the forum and even a connection between the claim and the forum is not guaranteed. These complications could be reduced by limiting property-based jurisdiction to mere tangible or immoveable property that is directly related to the contractual claim.

For instance, a claimant obtained an attachment order to seize goods obtained by the defendant after delivery pursuant to a sales contract. The plaintiff claims payment under the contract and institutes main proceedings at the court of the place – possibly in a third country – where the goods were seized. The claim is directly related to the seized property and its *situs* is easily localized. Under those circumstances, the rule ranks slightly higher on the scale of predictability and could lead to a closer connection between the claim and the forum, yet it still does not ensure a substantial *defendant-related* close connection and does not protect the defendant from being haled into court in an excessive forum.

Another complication is however formed by the attachment requirement itself. The conditions for a court to take attachment measures depend on national procedure rules and the possibility or willingness of a court to order seizure differs significantly among legal systems. This is also true for the localization of the *situs* of intangibles, as this also depends on national rules. Consequently, if attachment jurisdiction would be accepted as a uniform rule, uniformity and predictability would not be guaranteed, since the further determination of the competent court will heavily depend on national rules for attachment orders.

On balance, the general lack of a (defendant-related) connection, the localization problems of property resulting in legal uncertainty and the weak protection of the defendant, leads to the conclusion that uniform rules over international contractual disputes would not benefit from property-based jurisdiction.

9.2 The Need for Correction at Uniform International Level

Chapter 8 addressed the need for correction, either by imposing jurisdictional requirements or by declining jurisdiction by way of exception. Correction takes place for two main reasons. The exercise of jurisdiction on excessive bases, such as property-, presence-, and nationality-based jurisdiction, are mainly subjected to correction. Chapter 8 concluded that the need for correction is a direct consequence of excessive bases for jurisdiction. Correction would be less necessary if excessive bases for jurisdiction are abandoned at uniform level and replaced by well-balanced uniform rules that are based on *defendant-related close connections* with the forum.

Secondly, Chapter 6 demonstrated that the wider the jurisdictional catalogue that is available to the claimant from which to select a forum to institute proceedings, the more correction devices are applied to protect the defendant from the claimant's 'inappropriate' choice. Especially the *forum (non) conveniens* doctrine is considered as an *anti-forum shopping* device, protecting the defendant from being haled into an inappropriate court. The correction by virtue of U.S. due process standards, in particular the combination of fairness and reasonableness considerations and the purposeful availment requirement, is also intended to protect the defendant from being sued in a forum with a weak connection to him and the dispute. The disadvantage of this mechanism is that the plaintiff is not sure whether his choice will be given effect, which creates legal uncertainty. When the claimant has at his disposal a selective range of jurisdictional bases, there is less justification for a general correction device. In that respect, the regional European unified system of the Brussels Model foresees in a selective number of appropriate competent courts. Chapter 6 explained that the principle of mutual trust in each other's courts is anchored in the Brussels Model and hereby permits a certain degree of *forum shopping*. The *ex ante* designation of the appropriate court lies in the assumption that whichever court the claimant selects, it is closely connected and appropriate for the defendant thus making judicial discretion not necessary. In practice, this has not always proved to be true. Especially the *forum contractus* rule does not ensure a forum closely connected with the claim. Discretionary powers could have played a role in correcting the outcome of the rule, but instead considerations of legal certainty prevailed and correction devices were not introduced. In a uniform system based on mutual trust, this is the price Europeans seem to be willing to pay. The question is whether there is a similar belief in mutual trust on a universal scale. This important question should be answered in the negative. Unification at international level is not supported by a general drive of economic integration and a common cultural background or legal tradition is also lacking. Since unification at international level cannot be based on the same ideas of equality of states and mutual trust, one should not model a uniform global system for jurisdiction on the Brussels regime.

The Brussels unified Model clearly emanates from the civil law tradition and heavily relies on the principle of legal certainty in order to justify its hard and fast jurisdiction rules and its closed system.[28] It systematically rejects any form of judicial discretion, leaving no room for any type of correction, either by general or special correction devices. Contrastingly, Chapter 8 showed that outside the scope of this European regional unification, there is a general trend towards the acceptance of special correction devices in Continental civil law systems. Shaped by special jurisdictional requirements based on elements of close connectedness, such as the German *Inlandsbeziehung*, national civil law regimes cautiously begin to accept a certain degree of judicial discretion, acknowledging the importance of flexibility and procedural justice. A possible application of the *fair trial* principle of Article 6 of the European Convention on Human Rights in the future might strengthen that position.[29] The differences between common law and civil law traditions appeared surmountable when comparing national jurisdiction regimes. Apart from the significant fact that the U.K. modelled its interregional allocation system on the Brussels Model,[30] the gap between the (English) common law tradition and the regional unification system remains a sensitive issue.[31]

In a well-balanced uniform structure, with carefully drafted bases for jurisdiction tailored to international contractual disputes, there should be no need for general correction devices such as the *forum non conveniens* exception. However, Chapter 8 demonstrated that judicial appreciation to decline or to accept jurisdiction could be universally acceptable, provided that the correction is tailored to

[28] See Chapter 6, Sects. 6.1.4 and 6.3.1.
[29] See Chapter 8, Sect. 8.3.
[30] See Chapter 4, Sect. 4.1 and Chapter 6, Sect. 6.5.
[31] See E. Peel, 'Introduction', in *Forum Shopping in the European Judicial Area* (2007), 1-23, at 4.

particular bases for jurisdiction and focuses on the close connection requirement. Tailor-made special correction clauses requiring a sufficient connection with the forum with respect to certain bases for jurisdiction are acceptable at uniform level and have an important role to play in establishing a proper balance between legal certainty and flexibility. Both defendants as well as claimants are better off when the claimant is able to foresee, pursuant to clear appreciation factors, if his choice for an appropriate available court will be granted.

In that context, it is important to stress that any correction effectuated should be as neutral as possible. Following the parameters developed in Chapter 6 and the findings of Chapter 8, jurisdictional protectionism and discretionary treatment should not be accepted at uniform level. The fact that a uniform regime operating at international level cannot be based on mutual trust should be acknowledged, but this should not justify distinctive treatment between domestic and foreign plaintiffs. Public interest factors or state interest considerations should not be part of judicial appreciation in a uniform global system.[32] Instead, regulating the flow of proceedings and preventing overcrowded docks should be done by the enactment of well-balanced uniform rules which predominantly focus on defendant's 'economic allegiance' to the forum and by reducing the opportunities for *forum shopping* by restricting the available appropriate competent forums. The (non) availability of judicial resources should be each state's responsibility and should not constitute an appreciation factor to refuse jurisdiction, especially not when the state in question allowed the parties to do business in the forum.

In sum, correction and discretionary powers in a global uniform system do have an important role to play but should be carefully drafted, limited and tailored to specific jurisdictional basis and the need of the commercial players in the international field.

9.3 Progressive Unification and the Outdated Approach of General Jurisdiction

It was made evident in Chapter 6 that jurisdiction was traditionally regulated around one main jurisdictional principle or starting-point. Whether shaped around the European *forum rei* maxim, the common law presence-based rule or the U.S. Due Process Clause, each jurisdictional structure derived from a general jurisdiction principle which always provides an available forum to the claimant regardless of the nature of the claim.[33] As a result, the claimant has at his disposal a wider range of forum selection, which is primarily in his interest and sometimes at the expense of the defendant's right of defence. General jurisdiction based on defendant's nationality, property, presence, domicile or doing business stem from general policy considerations and have historical origins. They have not specifically been developed for international contractual disputes and their general character often proved to be unacceptable at international level in cross-border contractual

[32] I.e. state interest considerations in the narrow sense. See Chapter 6, Sect. 6.5.4.
[33] Exceptions to this are exclusive jurisdiction matters such as immoveable property.

disputes. A pragmatic approach to jurisdiction should conscientiously elaborate bases for jurisdiction in contractual disputes and do away with traditional ballast.[34] In sum, the general jurisdiction approach is outdated and should be abandoned at uniform level. There is no room nor is there any need for general jurisdiction rules at uniform level, should other – more suitable – jurisdictional bases be available.[35] This does not mean that the connecting factors themselves should not establish jurisdiction, but it means that jurisdictional bases should be ranked and that the factors used at national level for general jurisdiction should play a subsidiary role at uniform level or be applied as a last resort.

A significant consequence of this conclusion is that the only well-accepted general basis of jurisdiction, and Europe's fundamental jurisdiction rule, the defendant's home court rule should *not* always be available to the plaintiff in transnational contractual disputes. Instead, the defendant's court rule should play a subsidiary role. There is no need to protect the defendant who established a place of business in another forum to obtain commercial benefits and from which the business activities carried out gave rise to the contractual dispute. Nor is there any need to give the claimant access to defendant's court when he can institute proceedings in his own home court when defendant purposefully directed himself to the claimant for commercial purposes. Again, the establishment of a place of business elsewhere in order to carry out business activities should be considered as an extension of defendant's home abroad. It is only logical that the defendant who receives commercial benefits from the forum should accept to be subjected to jurisdiction in that forum.[36] Under those circumstances, the systematic availability of the civil law principle of *favor defensoris*, which institutes a jurisdictional privilege for the defendant by requiring the claimant to seek out the defendant at his home court, is no longer justified on a universal scale. Besides *related activity-based* jurisdiction, this rule should also have a subsidiary role to play. The bases would constitute the only permissive unrelated jurisdiction rule – unrelated in the sense that the claim

[34] See M. Whincop, *Policy and Pragmatism in the Conflict of Laws* (2001), at 2, defining a 'pragmatic approach' as 'exploring the doctrine in an a-theoretical but less strongly formal matter', *even* when he acknowledges that a 'pragmatic approach must be a political one'.

[35] See also G. Born and P. Rutledge, *International Civil Litigation in United States Courts* (2007), at 119-120.

[36] See in particular Buchner who claims that: 'In choosing grounds of jurisdiction based on conduct related to the cause of action, the basic consideration is that when someone is engaged in a commercial activity in a country, he has to comply with all sorts of prescription relating to such activity, in such a way that it would seem normal that he will also be subject to the judicial jurisdiction of that state. Once you are purposely developing an activity in a country, you should not be surprised to be brought before the courts of such country when the cause of action is related to such activity. In such a case, the defendant should not be privileged compared to plaintiffs.' Buchner's contribution, in Lowenfeld and Silberman, eds., *The Hague Convention on Jurisdiction*, at 24-25. See also J. Fawcett, 'A New Approach to Jurisdiction over Companies in Private International Law', 37 *The International and Comparative Law Quarterly* (1988), 645-667, at 650, referring to legal benefits, i.e. that the defendant operated under 'the benefit of the protection of that country's laws which regulate and facilitate commercial activity ... and [he] ought to accept a corresponding burden of being subject to jurisdiction there.'

is not related to the defendant's home court – and would as a last resort ensure that the claimant always finds a competent forum at defendant's home court.[37]

As explained above, the general nature of the U.S. doing business rule asserting jurisdiction over all kinds of claims on the basis that the defendant is continuously and systematically active in the forum, even when the claim is totally unrelated to those business activities, is problematic and unacceptable at uniform level.[38] Conversely, the rule becomes acceptable at uniform level when the connecting factors are used to assert jurisdiction over claims related to defendant's business carried out in the forum.

The same general approach in relation to correction devices has also proved to be outdated. General correction mechanisms are no longer justified. Instead they should make way for tailored correction devices with regard to a certain jurisdictional basis.

As a consequence, a successful approach for unification of international jurisdiction should favour a *related* and *category specific* approach over general bases for jurisdiction, subjecting the defendant to jurisdiction regardless of whether the claim is related to activities the defendant carried out in the forum. A consensus-based approach should focus on 'activity based specific jurisdiction'[39] in 'specific categories of specialized jurisdiction'.[40]

By way of conclusion, the unification process itself should be progressive and should be done area-by-area, starting by regulating international jurisdiction specifically for and limited to contractual disputes. The initial Worldwide Jurisdiction Project of the Hague Conference failed, partly because its ambitious scope attempted to cover all kinds of matters including among others (consumer) contracts, torts and intellectual property. In such a context, it was thought that bases for general jurisdiction should play a role in a comprehensive structure. A more progressive approach proved to be more effective and successful when The Hague negotiations focused on a specific category, namely on jurisdiction based on consent, and concentrated exclusively on choice of court agreements. Progressive unification should be the way forward for The Hague Conference and one should focus on specific areas of law and abandon the traditional approach of instituting general unrelated jurisdiction emanating from some kind of overarching fundamental principle. The progressive unification approach should start with contractual matters, because international contracts and the well-established principle of contractual freedom are closely related to party autonomy, which underlies consent-based jurisdiction.[41]

---

[37] Von Mehren, 'Theory and Practice', fn. 548, at 182, referring to B. Buchner, *Kläger- und Beklagtenschutz im Recht der internationalen Zuständigkeit. Losüngsansätze für eine zukünftige Gerichtsstands- und Vollstreckungskonvention, Studien zum ausländischen und internationalen Privatrecht* (1998).

[38] See Sect. 9.1.1.

[39] Brand's contribution in Lowenfeld and Silberman, eds., *The Hague Convention on Jurisdiction,* at 45.

[40] Nygh, 'Criteria for Judicial Jurisdiction', at A-8.

[41] This is eventually followed by uniform rules on jurisdiction over tortuous matters.

9.4 A Proposal

The regulation of international jurisdiction over commercial contractual disputes should be 'simple and party driven'.[42] Uniform rules designed for contractual matters should take into account the commercial nature of international contracts. A well-balanced uniform structure for jurisdiction over cross-border contractual disputes should focus on defendant's activity in the forum when the claim arises out of those activities and should provide a more limited role for the defendant's home court.

Chapters 6 and 8 explained the difficulties arising out of the plaintiff having a wide jurisdictional catalogue available to him from which to choose. In this context Von Overbeck rightfully argues that

> 'The more grounds of jurisdiction, and exceptions such as forum non conveniens, are provided, the more parties shall try to proceed before different jurisdictions. Could one not arrive to a more expeditive justice if grounds of jurisdictions were limited to those who express a really strong connection …?'[43]

Chapter 6 also indicated that the plaintiff's access to justice does not automatically include the right of forum selection, provided that he has at his disposal a suitable competent court substantially connected with the dispute. Conversely, the systematical privilege given to the defendant to defend himself at his home court is not necessarily justified in international contractual relationships, when the defendant purposefully sought commercial benefits in another state.

During the proceedings of the Round Table on The Hague Jurisdiction Convention, Mayer suggested the benefits of having one jurisdiction basis:

> 'Uniformity would be useful if the States parties to the Convention would agree on one, and only one, ground of jurisdiction, because that would avoid multiple fora, the plaintiff would have to sue in one place and would not have a choice which it exercises to the detriment of the defendant: it would be excellent but is just not possible.'

It should be possible to agree on one – or at least on a very restricted number – of competent courts by focusing on a specific category of uniform rules, eliminating excessive or unacceptable (general) bases for jurisdiction and finding an acceptable foundation for international jurisdiction over contractual disputes.

The following provisions are an attempt at a proposal for uniform jurisdiction rules over international contractual disputes:

In matters relating to, or arising out of a contract and in absence of a choice of forum:

[42] See J. Kovar, 'The United States as an Actor in Private International Law', in *Private Law, Private International Law, & Judicial Cooperation in the EU-US Relationship* (2005), 153-159, at 156.

[43] L. Collins and G. Droz, 'La recours à la doctrine du forum non conveniens et aux "anti-suit injunctions": Principes directeurs. 2ème Commission', 70 *Annuaire de l'Institut de droit international* (2003), 13-94, at 61, Reply of Von Overbeck.

1. *A person domiciled in a Contracting State should be sued, in the courts of another Contracting State if the defendant has established a fixed place of business from which he carries out business activities directly related to the claimant's contractual claim.*
2. *If the defendant has not established such a fixed place of business and following claimant's choice:*
   a) *a person domiciled in a Contracting State, may in another Contracting State, be sued in the courts of the country where any such person engaged in substantial business activities in relation to the contract, unless the dispute is insufficiently connected with the forum which would make it unfair under the circumstances to expect that party to be subjected to the jurisdiction of that other court;*
   b) *or alternatively, he may be subjected to the jurisdiction of his home court.*

9.4.1 The First Step

The first step should focus exclusively on a fixed place of business from which defendant carries out business activities directly related to the contractual claim. The idea behind the first provision is that when a defendant purposefully availed himself of the claimant's forum by establishing a fixed place of business in the forum, and that the contractual claim is directly related to defendant's activities carried out and organized from that place of business, jurisdiction of the court of that place is acceptable to all. The place of business establishment requirement is slightly broader than the Continental European 'branch' rule. This rule should be understood as a more open norm, based on a more factual concept as opposed to the formal juridical definition of 'branch' under Article 5(5) of the Brussels Model. The rule requires a substantial *fixed* place of business with the appearance of *permanency*, but is silent with respect to other requirements that are imposed by the European branch jurisdiction, such as the fact that the branch *acts on behalf* of the defendant and operates under his *direction*, with a certain degree of *independence*. The rule is comparable to the English common law principle of place of business but is narrower than the U.S. doing business ground, since it requires some physical establishment to be located in the forum. The latter does not constitute a prerequisite for U.S. doing business jurisdiction.

The open connection factor leaves a certain margin of appreciation for the court seized to decide whether or not such a place of business was established in its forum by the defendant. This provides for some degree of flexibility and there is no need for correction to this place of business criterion in order to ensure legal certainty to both parties. When the defendant established a fixed place of business in the forum and the claim is directly related to business activities carried out and organized by that business establishment, the connection with the forum is so substantial *and* defendant-related that it should constitute the sole or exclusive basis for jurisdiction with respect to that contractual claim. Under these circumstances, the defendant should not be privileged as compared to the plaintiff, by forcing the claimant to seek the defendant's home forum. Despite the fact that the defendant's home court plays such a fundamental role under the Brussels Model and in the

Continental European countries, abandoning the rule in this context in uniform rules should be acceptable. The defendant's place of business establishment is to be understood as an extension of his domicile for the purposes of commercial benefits in another forum and it is only logical to subject him to the jurisdiction of its courts. In other words, a particular *favor defensoris* at defendant's home court is not justified and the claimant's access to justice is secured. With respect to the acceptability by the U.S., the connecting factors upon which this rule is based is evidently compatible with U.S. due process standards: primarily, because a fixed place of business establishment in the forum represents a considerable amount of substantial contacts and would easily satisfy the 'sufficient minimum contacts' rule; secondly, defendant voluntarily set up this business establishment which clearly shows that he purposefully availed himself of the forum; and finally, it is neither unfair nor unreasonable to subject the defendant to jurisdiction of a state where he established a fixed place of business establishment to carry out business activities with the purpose of obtaining commercial benefits. Such a voluntary fixed establishment also entails that the activities mentioned in the first step include activities carried out *in* as well as *outside* the forum.

9.4.2 The Second Step: A Restricted Forum Selection

The structure of this proposal is clearly of a hierarchical nature. The second step only applies when the defendant has not established a fixed place of business in the sense of the first step. When the defendant has not established a fixed place of business in the forum from which he carried out commercial activities directly related to the contractual claim, the uniform jurisdictional structure accepts one pair of alternative competent courts as being available to the plaintiff: the related activity-based jurisdiction on the one hand and the defendant's home court on the other. The claimant will always find a competent court at the defendant's home forum, no correction will be allowed. But the claimant can also choose to file suit at the place where the defendant carried out substantial business activities from which his contractual claim arises. Claimant's choice for the activity-based forum is however subjected to a tailored correction device, allowing the court seized to refuse jurisdiction if it considers on the basis of the facts that the dispute is insufficiently connected to the forum and it would be unfair to the defendant to be subjected to its jurisdiction.

Presenting the *defendant's home* court as an alternative protects the defendant by enabling him to defend himself at his home court, and it ensures claimant's access to justice in the event no court accepts jurisdiction on *related activity-based* jurisdiction. The second step also allows a claimant seeking legal certainty, and who accepts the burden of seeking the defendant in a foreign jurisdiction, to always find a competent court at the defendant's domicile. The defendant should not be double protected by allowing any exception on the basis of *forum non conveniens* considerations to not give effect to the claimant's choice.[44]

[44] See also Chapter 6, Sect. 6.5.

9.4.3 Substantial Business Activities in the Forum

This first alternative competent court stems from *specific activity-based* jurisdiction. A consensus-based approach should allow jurisdiction over defendants who have not established a *fixed* place of business in the forum, but actively carry on substantial business by other means. It is justified to subject the defendant to jurisdiction of the courts of that forum, provided that claimant's contractual claim is directly related to or arising out of the commercial activities carried out in the forum by the defendant. Unlike the first step, which is based on *fixed* establishment jurisdiction, the activities mentioned in the second step should exclusively concern activities carried out *in* the forum. When the defendant substantially carries out business in or to the forum but not through a physical or fixed business establishment, he should be subjected to the court of that forum over claims arising out of his activities. This related activity-based rule gives the plaintiff the opportunity to bring action in the forum where defendant transacted business with the plaintiff in relation to the contractual dispute. This proposed basis comes relatively close to a 'special doing business' rule but is somewhat wider as it requires merely substantial business activities rather than 'continuous and systematic' contact, which requires a certain degree of continuity. Conversely, it is important to underline the distinction between this substantial business activity rule and the U.S. 'transacting business' rule which allows specific jurisdiction on the basis of a 'single act' performed in the forum. Transacting business was marked unacceptable at uniform level as it does not satisfy the substantial connection requirement.[45] In sum, the proposed rule is stricter than U.S. transacting business, as a 'single or occasional' transaction is not sufficient to constitute 'substantial' business activities, but is wider than doing business.

Such a substantial activity-based jurisdiction should be acceptable to the U.S. as it intends to protect (corporate) defendants doing business world-wide from being subjected to the jurisdiction of too many courts with respect to any kind of claim. For Continental European countries and England, it means renouncing to the strict and rigid requirement of an 'establishment'. Instead, the focus is shifted to a 'commercial activity' approach which is familiar to the U.S. jurisdictional regime. For the U.S. it means renouncing to transacting business jurisdiction in its purest form. It should be noted that in the context of The Hague Worldwide Jurisdiction Project, a first, though masked attempt was made to define this 'special doing business'. This can be deducted if one carefully reads Article 18(2) of the 2001 Hague Draft, which uses the following wording 'the carrying on of commercial or other activities by the defendant in that State, ... where the dispute is directly related to those activities'.[46]

---

[45] See Chapter 7, Sect. 7.5.7.3.

[46] Art. 18(2)(e) drafted after the June 2001 diplomatic conference provisions was bracketed: '[the carrying on of commercial or other activities by the defendant in that State, [whether or not through a branch, agency or any other establishment of the defendant,] except where the dispute is directly related to those activities]'. As a consequence, related jurisdiction, i.e. where the claim is directly related to such activity is acceptable.

The open-ended connecting factor of 'substantial' activities in the forum allows a fact-sensitive approach and is based on the presumption that these activities reflect a close connection with the forum. Under certain situations, however, the court seized might find the connection weak and should be able to decline jurisdiction when it feels that it would be unfair to ask the defendant to defend himself in that forum.[47] This specific exception clause, subjected to the court's appreciation on a case-by-case basis, constitutes a consensus: since a general exception to correction mechanisms was not acceptable to the Continental European countries and the Brussels Model, a compromise should be made by allowing such a special correction clause. It has often been said that jurisdiction rules conferring special and specific jurisdiction in Continental Europe as well as Anglo-American common law jurisdictions, 'are either too narrow or too broad'.[48] This certainly proved to be the case with the European *forum contractus* rule, i.e. the place of performance in all its variations, and for the U.S. transacting business criterion. Both are left out in this proposal and are replaced by this type of defendant-related activity-based jurisdiction; not too narrow and not too broad, but tailor-made to the needs and realities of parties carrying out business activities through international contracts, which is especially so when accompanied by a special correction clause. The identified trend towards accepting more discretionary powers for Continental European courts under specific circumstances, and with respect to certain bases for jurisdiction, should result in the acceptance of this proposition in Continental European countries and would follow in the footsteps of the U.S. due process standards. A 'hybrid system' combining connecting factors and tailored correction clauses is recommended and has a high chance of being accepted.[49] The close connection requirement used in this specific exception should not be understood as an 'interest-balancing' factor and does not include any other interest factors that are used in the *forum (non) conveniens* doctrine; especially the U.S. public interests factors are not covered under this exception.[50] This special exception should therefore not be understood as the equivalent of a '*limited forum non conveniens* doctrine'.[51]

The fact that the court seized is allowed to refuse jurisdiction when a close connection is lacking constitutes a risk for the claimant that his forum selection will not be given effect. He will have to take this into account and calculate the risk when he chooses his forum. If he does not want to take that risk, he can always find

[47] J. Hill, 'The Exercise of Jurisdiction in Private International Law', in *Asserting Jurisdiction – International and European Legal Perspectives* (2003), 39-62, at 61.

[48] See also R. Michaels, 'Territorial Jurisdiction after Territoriality', in *Globalisation and Jurisdiction* (2004), 106-130, at 108; P. Borchers, 'Comparing Personal Jurisdiction in the United States and the European Community: Lessons for American Reform', 40 *American Journal of Comparative Law* (1992), 121-157, at 136.

[49] It is a question of legal technique: 'Are jurisdictional problems best solved by hard-and-fast rules, by flexible criteria which confer discretion on the courts or by a hybrid system?', see Hill, 'The Exercise of Jurisdiction', at 55.

[50] As explained in Chapter 6, Sect. 6.5.4.

[51] M. Stückelberg, 'Lis Pendens and Forum Non Conveniens at the Hague Conference: The Preliminary Draft Convention on Jurisdiction and Foreign Judgments in Civil and Commercial Matters', 26 *Brooklyn Journal of International Law* (2001), 949-982, at 978.

a competent court at the defendant's home court that will not be given the opportunity to decline jurisdiction. In that respect the defendant's home court should take the drafting difficulties mentioned above into account.[52]

9.5 Concluding Remarks

The main conclusions drawn in this final chapter urge that corporate defendants should no longer be assimilated to individuals; that the traditional approach of regulating jurisdiction through overarching fundamental principles thus establishing general unrelated jurisdiction rules should be abandoned; that the way forward in international litigation is progressive unification of jurisdiction rules, area by area; and that for uniform jurisdiction rules in international contractual disputes the focus should be on the defendant's commercial activities in the forum. A simple and party-driven approach dealing with the commercial realities of cross-border contractual disputes should focus on the 'economic allegiance' of the parties. Crucial in a global jurisdictional structure in contractual matters is the protection of the interests of both parties. State interest considerations should have a considerably less role to play, but on the other hand one should not want to impose an international principle of mutual trust on a global jurisdiction system. Nonetheless, as stressed in the introduction of this conclusion, fundamental to the success of any uniformity in international jurisdiction is political will.

[52] See Sect. 9.1.1.

BIBLIOGRAPHY

Adler, M., 'If We Build It, Will They Come? – The Need for a Multilateral Convention on the Recognition and Enforcement of Civil Monetary Judgements', *Law & Policy in International Business* (1994), 79-111

Akehurst, M., 'Jurisdiction in International Law', 46 *British Yearbook of International Law* (1974), 145-257

Alexander, A., 'Forum Non Conveniens in the Absence of an Alternative Forum' *Columbia Law Review* (1986), 1000-1020

Alexander, V., *New York McKinney's Consolidated Laws: Practice Commentaries* 2001 Main Volume, Supplementary Practice Commentaries 2007 edn. (2001)

'Alien Corporations and Aggregate Contacts: A Genuinely Federal Jurisdictional Standard', *Harvard Law Review* (1981), 470-486

Alonso-Cuevillas Sayrol, J., *La competencia jurisdiccional internacional de los tribunales españoles del orden civil* (Valencia: Tirant lo Blanch, 2006)

Ancel, B., 'Note: Gie Groupe Concorde', 89 *Revue critique de droit international privé* (2000), 260-264

Ancel, B. and Lequette, Y., *Les grands arrêts de la jurisprudence française de droit international privé*, 4th edn. (Paris: Dalloz, 2001)

Ancel, M., *La prestation caractéristique du contrat* (Paris: Economica, 2002)

Audit, B., *L'americanisation du droit* (Paris: Dalloz, 2001)

Audit, B., 'Note: Arcado Judgement of 8 March 1987, C 9/87', 35ième Cahier, *Recueil Dalloz Sirey* (1988), 344

Audit, B., *Droit international privé*, 5 edn. (Paris: Economica, 2008)

Audit, B., and Bermann, G., 'The Application of Private International Norms to "Third Countries": The Jurisdiction and Judgements Example', in A. Nuyts and N Watté, eds., *International Civil Litigation in Europe and Relations with Third States* (Bruxelles: Bruylant, 2005)

Baetge, D., *Der gewöhnliche Aufenthalt im internationalen Privatrecht*, Beiträge zum Ausländische und Internationalen Privatrecht (Tübingen: Mohr Siebeck, 1994)

Bariati, S., ed., *Legge 31 Maggio 1995, N. 218: Riforma del sistema Italiano di diritto internazionale privato, Le Nuove Leggi Civili Commentate* (Milani: Cedam, 1996)

Bartlett, L., 'Full Faith and Credit Comes to the Common Market: An Analysis of the Provisions of the Convention on Jurisdiction and the Enforcement of Judgements in Civil and Commercial Matters', 24 *The International and Comparative Law Quarterly* (1975), 44-60

Batiffol, H., 'Note Weiss; Cour de Cassation Chambre Civil 1; 27 May; 1970', *Revue critique de droit international privé* (1971), 113-117

Batiffol, H., 'Observations sur les liens entre la compétence judiciaire et la compétence législative', in Nederlands Tijdschrift voor internationaal recht, *De conflictu legum* (Leiden, Sijthoff, 1962), 55-66

Batiffol, H. and Lagarde, P., *Traité de droit international privé*, Traité (Paris: LGDJ, 1993)

Batiffol, H. and Lagarde, P., *Droit international privé*, 7th edn., Vol. 2 (Paris: Librairie générale de droit et de jurisprudence, 1983)

Baumbach, A. and Lauterbach, W., *Zivilprozessordnung: Mit Gerichtsverfassungsgesetz und anderen Nebengesetzen*, 65th edn. (München: C.H. Beck, 2007)

Baumgartner, S., *The Proposed Hague Convention on Jurisdiction and Foreign Judgements; Trans-Atlantic Law Making for Transnational Litigation* Veröffentlichungen zum Verfahrensrecht (Tübingen: Mohr Siebeck, 2003)

Bax, R., 'Forum non Conveniens in het Engelse en Nederlandse recht', 47 *Ars Aequi* (1998), 458-464

Bayraktaroglu, G., 'Note: Forum Contractus and Article 5(1) of the Brussels I Regulation', 2 *Journal of International Commercial Law* (2004), 401-409

Beale, J., 'Jurisdiction of Courts over Foreigners', 26 *Harvard Law Review* (1912), 193-211

Beaumont, P., 'Forum Non Conveniens/Lis Pendens', paper presented at the UIA Seminar, Edinburgh, 2001

Beernaert, S., and Coibon, A., 'La doctrine du forum (non) conveniens réconciliation avec le texte de la Convention de Bruxelles', 119 *Journal des tribunaux* (2000), 409-419

Bell, A., *Forum Shopping and Venue in Transnational Litigation*, Oxford Private International Law Series (Oxford: Oxford University Press, 2003)

Benítez de Lugo, M., Campuzano Diaz, B., Cano Bazaga, E., Machado Grieder, H., and Rodrígez Vázquez, A., *Lecciones de derecho procesal civil internacional, Manuales Universitarios* (Sevilla: Publicaciones de la Universidad de Sevilla, 2002)

Bennet, D., 'The Hague Convention on Recognition and Enforcement of Foreign Judgments – A Failure of Characterisation', in T. Einhorn and K. Siehr, eds., *Intercontinental Cooperation through Private International Law: Essays in Memory of Peter E. Nygh* (The Hague: T.M.C. Asser Press 2004), 19-25

Beraudo, J., 'The Arbitration Exception of the Brussels and Lugano Conventions: Jurisdiction, Recognition and Enforcement of Judgments', 18 *Journal of International Arbitration* (2001), 13-26

Beraudo, J., 'Le Règlement (CE) du Conseil du 22 décembre 2000 concernant la compétence judiciaire, la reconnaissance et l'exécution des décisions en matière civile et commerciale', *Journal du droit international (Clunet)* (2001), 1033-1084

Berliri, M., 'Jurisdiction and the Internet, and European Regulation 44 of 2001', in S. Woodley, ed., *E-Commerce: Law and Jurisdiction* (The Hague: Kluwer Law International, 2003), 1-13

Berman, P., 'The Globalization of Jurisdiction', 151 *University of Pennsylvania Law Review* (2002), 311-545

Bermann, G., *Transnational Litigation in a Nutshell*, West Nutshell series (St. Paul: MN Thomson West, 2003)

Bernasconi, Ch., 'La Théorie du forum non conveniens – Un regard suisse', *IPRax* (1994), 3-10

Bertele, J., *Souveränität und Verfahrensrecht: Ein untersuchung der aus dem Völkerrecht ableitbaren Grenzen staatlicher extraterritoriale Jurisdiktion im Verfahrensrecht* (Tübingen: Mohr Siebeck, 1998)

Bischoff, J.-M., 'Note: Blanckeart C 139/80', *Journal du droit international* (1982), 479-482

Bischoff, J.-M., 'Note: Lloyd's Register of Shipping C-439/93', *Journal du droit international* (1996), 564-567

Bischoff, J.-M., and Huet, A., 'Note: Shenevai', *Journal du droit international* (1987), 465-472

Bittighofer, A., *Der internationale Gerichtsstand des Vermögens: Eine Rechtvergleichende Studie zur Zuständigkeit deutscher Gerichte aufgrund inländischer Vermögensbelegenheit*, 1561 Europäische Hochschulschriften (Frankfurt am Main: Lang, 1994)

Blair, P., 'The Doctrine of Forum non Conveniens in Anglo American Law', 29 *Columbia Law Review* (1929), 1-34

Blobel, F., and Spath, P., 'The Tale of Multilateral Trust and the European Law of Civil Procedure', 30 *European Law Review* (2005), 528-547

Boele-Woelki, K., 'The Netherlands National Report', in J. Fawcett, ed., *Declining Jurisdiction in Private International Law* (Oxford: Clarendon Press, 1995), 235-247

Boele-Woelki, K., Joustra, C., and Steenhoff, G., 'Dutch Private International Law at the End of the 20th Century: Pluralism of Methods', in E. Hondius, ed., *Netherlands Reports to the 15th International Congress of Comparative Law Bristol 1998* (Antwerp/ Groningen: 1998), 203-227

Bomhoff, J., *Judicial Discretion in European Law on Conflicts of Jurisdiction: Looking for National Perspectives on European Rules for Jurisdiction over Multiple Defendants*, Allen & Overy (The Hague: Sdu Uitgevers, 2005)

Bonomi, A., 'Die Übereinkommen von Brüssel und Lugano und die Novellierung des italianischen internationalen Zivilprozessrechts', in E.-M. Bajons, P. Mayr and G. Zeiler, eds., *Die Übereinkommen von Brüssel und Lugano* (Wien: 1997), 118-137

Bonomi, A., 'The Italian Statute on Private International Law', *International Journal of Legal Materials* (1999), 246-267

Borchers, P., 'Comparing Personal Jurisdiction in the United States and the European Community: Lessons for American Reform', 40 *American Journal of Comparative Law* (1992), 121-157

Borchers, P., 'The Death of the Constitutional Law of Personal Jurisdiction: From Pennoyer to Burnham and Back Again', 24 *University of California Davis Law Review* (1990), 19-105

Borchers, P., 'Flexibility and Predictability: The Emergence of Near-Universal Choice of Law Principles', in H.-E. Rasmussen-Bonne and R. Freer, eds., *Balancing of Interests Liber Amicorum Peter Hay zum 70. Geburtstag* (Frankfurt am Main: Verlag Recht und Wirtschaft GmbH, 2005), 49-53

Borchers, P., 'Jurisdiction to Adjudicate Revisited', in J. Nafziger and S. Symeonides, eds., *Law and Justice in a Multistate World: Essays in Honor of Arthur T. von Mehren* (Ardsley NY: Transnational Publishers Inc., 2002), 1-10

Borchers, P., 'Jurisdictional Pragmatism: International Shoe's Half-Buried Legacy', *Davis Law Review* (1995), 561-590

Borchers, P., 'The Problem with General Jurisdiction', *University of Chicago Legal Forum* (2001), 119-139

Born, G., 'Reflections on Judicial Jurisdiction in International Cases', 17 *Georgia Journal of International and Comparative Law* (1987), 1-44

Born, G., and Rutledge, P., *International Civil Litigation in United States Courts*, 4th edn. (Aspen: Kluwer Law International, 2007)

Boyce, D., 'Foreign Plaintiffs and Forum Non Conveniens: Going Beyond Reyno', 64 *Texas Law Review* (1985), 193-223

Brand, R., 'Balancing Sovereignty and Party Autonomy in Private International Law', 25 *University of Pittsburg School of Law Working Paper Series* (2005)

Brand, R., 'Comparative Forum Non Conveniens and the Hague Convention on Jurisdiction and Judgments: International Forum Shopping in Memory of Professor F.K. Juenger', 37 *Texas International Law Journal* (2002)

Brand, R., *Due Process as a Limitation on Jurisdication in U.S. Courts and a Limitation on the United States at the Hague Conference on Private International Law* (1998) Available at http://www.state.gov/www/global/legal_affairs/brand.html

Brand, R., 'Due Process, Jurisdiction and a Hague Judgments Convention', *University of Pittsburgh Law Review* (1999), 661-706

Brand, R., 'Forum Selection and Forum Rejection in US Courts: One Rationale for a Global Choice of Court Convention', in J.J. Fawcett, ed., *Reform and Development of Private International Law – Essays in Honour of Sir Peter North* (Oxford: Oxford University Press, 2002), 51-88

Brand, R., *Fundamentals of International Business Transactions* (The Hague: Kluwer Law International, 2000)

Brand, R., 'Report: The 1999 Hague Preliminary Draft Convention Text on Jurisdiction and Judgments: A View from the United States: Development of Due Process Jurisdictional Analysis in U.S. Law', in F. Pocar and C. Honorati, eds., *The Hague Preliminary Draft Convention on Jurisdiction and Judgments* (Milan: Cedam, 2005), 3-40

Brand, R., 'Tort Jurisdiction in a Multilateral Convention: The Lessons of the Due Process Clause and the Brussels Convention', *Brooklyn Journal of International Law* (1998), 125-155

Brand, R., 'Understanding Activity-Based Jurisdiction', paper presented at The Preliminary Draft Hague Convention on Jurisdiction and Foreign Judgements in Civil and Commercial Matters, UIA Seminar Edinburgh, 20 & 21 April 2001 (2001)

Brand, R., and Jablonski, S., *Forum Non Conveniens: History, Global Practice, and Future under the Hague Convention on Choice of Court Agreements*, CILE studies (New York, NY: Oxford University Press, 2007)

Briggs, A., *Agreements on Jurisdiction and Choice of Law* (Oxford: Oxford University Press, 2008)

Briggs, A., *Civil Jurisdiction and Judgments*, 4th edn. (London: LLP, 2005)

Briggs, A., 'Claims against Sea Carriers and the Brussels Convention', *Lloyd's Maritime and Commercial Law Quarterly* (1999), 333-337

Briggs, A., 'Decisions of British Courts during 2002: Private International Law', 73 *British Yearbook of Private International Law* (2003) 453-496

Briggs, A., 'Forum Non Conveniens and Ideal Europeans', *Lloyd's Maritime and Commercial Law Quarterly* (2005) 378-382

Briggs, A., 'Note; Shearson Lehmann Hutton Inc. v TVB Treuhandgesellschaft', *Yearbook of European Law* (1993), 511-517

Briggs, A., 'Spiliada and the Brussels Convention', *Lloyd's Maritime and Commercial Law Quarterly* (1991), 10-15

Briggs, A., *The Conflict of Laws* (Oxford: Oxford University Press, 2002)

Briggs, A., *The Conflict of Laws*, 2nd edn. (Oxford: Oxford University Press, 2008)

Briggs, A., 'The Death of Harrods: Forum Non Conveniens and the European Court', *Law Quarterly Review* (2005), 535-540

Briggs, A., 'The Impact of Recent Judgements of the European Court on English Procedural Law and Practice', *University of Oxford Faculty of Law Research Paper Series* (2006)

Brilmayer, L., 'A General Look at General Jurisdiction', 66 *Texas Law Review* (1988), 723-783

Brilmayer, L., 'Jurisdictional Due Process and Political Theory', 39 *University of Florida Law Review* (1987), 293-314

Brilmayer, L., 'Related Contacts and Personal Jurisdiction', 101 *Harvard International Law Review* (1988), 1444-1464

Brilmayer, L., and Norchi, C., 'Federal Extraterritoriality and Fifth Amendment Due Process', 105 *Harvard Law Review* (1992), 1217-1263

Broggini, G., 'La nouvelle loi fédérale sur le droit internationale privé: Considérations comparées', *Schweizerisches Jahrbuch für internationales Recht: Annuaire suisse de droit international et européen* (1988), 132-136

Brown, D., 'Jurisdiction over a Corporation on the Basis of the Contacts of an Affiliated Corporation: Do You Have to Pierce the Corporate Veil?', *University of Cincinnati Law Review* (1992), 595-622

Bucher, A., 'Staatsangehörigkeits- und Wohnsitzprinzip: Eine Rechtsvergleichende Übersicht', 28 *Schweizerisches Jahrbuch für internationales Recht* (1972), 76-160

Bucher, A., and Bonomi, A., *Droit international privé*, 2nd edn. (Bâle/Genève/Munich: Helbing & Lichtenhahn, 2004)

Buchner, B., *Kläger- und Beklagtenschutz im Recht der internationalen Zuständigkeit. Losüngsansätze für eine zukünftige Gerichtsstands- und Vollstreckungskonvention, Studien zum ausländischen und internationalen Privatrecht* (Mohr Siebeck Tübingen/Max Plank Institut Hamburg, 1998)

Buonaiuti, F., 'Forum Non Conveniens Facing the Prospective Hague Convention and E.C. Regulation on Jurisdiction and the Enforcement of Judgments in Civil and Commercial Matters', 39 *Rivista di diritto europeo* (1999), 3-48

Burbank, S., 'Jurisdiction to Adjudicate: End of the Century or Beginning of a Millennium?', 111 *Tulane Journal of International and Comparative Law* (1999), 111-123

Bureau, D., and Muir Watt, H., *Droit international privé*, C. Labrusse-Riou and D. Truchet, eds., Vol. I (Thémis Paris, Presses Universitaires de France, 2007)

Byrne, P., and Blayney J., *The EEC Convention on Jurisdiction and the Enforcement of Judgements* (Dublin: Round Hall Press, 1990)

Cadiet, L., and Jeuland, E., *Droit judiciaire privé*, 5th edn. (Paris: LexisNexis Litec, 2006)

Caffrey, B., *International Jurisdiction and the Recognition and Enforcement of Foreign Judgments in the LAWASIA Region* (North Ryde, N.S.W. Australia Ltd., 1985)

Calvo Caravaca, A.-L., and Carrascosa Gonzalez, J., *Derecho Internacional Privado*, 7th edn., Vol. 1 (Granada: Comares, 2006)

Campeis, G., and De Pauli, A., *La procedura civile internazionale*, 2nd edn., Vol. 5, Collection Biblioteca giuridica (Padova: CEDAM, 1991)

Carter-Stein, K., 'In Search of Justice: Foreign Victims of Silicone Breast Implants and the Doctrine of Forum Non Conveniens', *Suffolk Transnational Law Review* (1995), 167-195

Casad, R., 'Jurisdiction in Civil Actions at the End of the Twentieth Century: Forum Conveniens and Forum Non Conveniens', in M. Taruffo, ed., *Abuse of Procedural Rights: Comparative Standards of Procedural Fairness: International Association of Procedural Law International Colloquium, 27-30 October 1998, Tulane Law School, New Orleans, Louisiana* (The Hague: Kluwer Law International, 1999), 252-270

Casad, R., 'Personal Jurisdiction in Federal Question Cases', 70 *Texas Law Review* (1992), 1589-1621

Casad, R., and Richman, W., 'Casad's Jurisdiction in Civil Actions Part II – A Sliding Scale to Supplement the Distinction Between General and Specific Jurisdiction', 72 *California Law Review* (1984), 1328-1346

Casad, R., and Richman, W., *Jurisdiction in Civil Actions*, 3rd edn., Vols. 1 & 2 (Charlottesville: Lexis Law Publishing, 1998)

Castel, J.-G., and Walker, J., *Canadian Conflict of Laws*, 5th edn. (Ontario [etc.]: Butterworths, 2002)

Chalas, C., *L'exercise discrétionnaire de la compétence juridictionnelle en droit international privé* (Paris: PUAM, 2000)

Chalas, C., 'Note; Owusu C-281/02', 94 *Revue critique de droit international privé* (2005), 708-722

Clark, D., and Ansay, T., *Introduction to the Law of the United States* (Deventer/Boston: Kluwer Law and Taxation Publishers, 1992)

Clarke, A., 'The Differing Approach to Commercial Litigation in the European Court of Justice and the Courts of England and Wales', 18 *European Business Law Review* (2007), 101-129

Clarke, M., 'The Conflicts of Law Dimension', in C. Trenton, ed., *Corporate Law: The European Dimension* (London/Dublin etc: Butterworths, 1991), 161-170

Clarkson, C., and Hill, J., *The Conflict of Laws*, 3rd edn. (Oxford: Oxford University Press, 2006)

Clermont, K., 'Jurisdictional Salvation and the Hague Treaty', *Cornell Law Review* (1999), 89-133

Clermont, K., and Eisenberg, T., 'Exorcising the Evil of Forum Shopping', 80 *Cornell Law Review* (1995), 1507-1535

Clermont, K., and Huang, K.-C., 'Converting the Draft Hague Treaty into Domestic Jurisdictional Law', in J.J. Barceló III and K.M. Clermont, eds., *Global Law of Jurisdiction and Judgments: Lessons from The Hague* (The Hague: Kluwer Law International, 2002), 191

Clive, E., 'The Concept of Habitual Residence', *The Juridical Review* (1997), 137-147

Cohen, D., 'La Convention européenne des droits de l'homme et le droit international privé français', 78 *Revue critique de droit international privé* (1989), 451-483

Collins, L., 'Forum Non Conveniens and the Brussels Convention', 106 *Law Quarterly Review* (1990), 535-539

Collins, L., 'The Institut de droit International and Anti-suit Injunctions', in H.-P. Mansel, T. Pfeiffer, H. Kronke, Ch. Kohler and R. Hausmann, eds., *Festschrift für Erik Jayme* (München: Seller European Law Publishers, 2004), 131-142

Collins, L., 'The Jurisdiction and Judgements Convention – Some Practical Aspects of United Kingdom Accession with Particular Reference to Jurisdiction', in K. Lipstein, ed., *Harmonization of Private International Law by the E.E.C.* (London: Institute of Advanced Legal Studies, University of London, 1978), 91-102

Collins, L., 'Some Aspects of Service Out of the Jurisdiction in English Law', in L. Collins, ed., *Essays in International Litigation and the Conflict of Laws* (Oxford: Clarendon Press, 1994), 226-252

Collins, L., 'Temporary Presence, Exorbitant Jurisdiction and the US Supreme Court', 107 *The Law Quarterly Review* (1990), 10-14

Collins, L., and Droz, G., 'La recours à la doctrine du forum non conveniens et aux "anti-suit injunctions": Principes directeurs. 2ème Commission', 70 *Annuaire de l'Institut de droit international* (2003), 13-94

Conison, J., 'What does Due Process Have to Do with Jurisdiction?', 46 *Rutgers Law Review* (1994), 1071-1209

Conseil fédéral Suisse, '*Message du Conseil fédéral concernant une loi fédérale sur le droit international privé*', in *FF1983 I 250-501* (1983)

Cordero Moss, G., 'Performance of Obligations as the Basis of Jurisdiction and Choice of Law (Lugano and Brussels Conventions Article 5(1) and Rome Convention Article 4)', 68 *Nordic Journal of International Law* (1999), 379-396

Couchez, G., 'Note: Dame Nassibian v. Nassibian; Cour de cass., Ch.Civ.I 6 Nov. 1979', *Revue critique de droit international privé* (1980), 588-597

Cox, E., 'Would That Burnham Had Not Come to Be Done Insane? A Critique of Recent Supreme Court Personal Jurisdiction Reasoning: An Explanation of Why Transient Presence Jurisdiction Is Unconstitutional, and Some Thoughts about Divorce Jurisdiction in a Minimum Contacts World', *Tennessee Law Review* (1991), 497-572

Cromie, S., and Park, W., *International Commercial Litigation* (London: Butterworths, 1990)

Cuniberti, G., 'Forum Non Conveniens and the Brussels Convention', *The International and Comparative Law Quarterly* (2005), 973-981

Cuniberti, G., and Winkler, M., 'Note: Owusu C- 281/02', *Journal du droit international* (2005), 1185-1991

Dahl, S., 'Forum non conveniens versus actio sequitur forum rei', in *Etudes offertes à Barthélemy Mercadal* (Paris: Editions Francis Lefebvre, 2002), 117-131

Dannemann, G., 'Jurisdiction Based on the Presence of Assets in Germany', 41 *The International and Comparative Law Quarterly* (1992), 632-637

Dashwood, A., Hacon, R., and White, R., *A Guide to the Civil Jurisdiction and Judgments Convention* (Deventer: Kluwer Law and Taxation, 1987)

David, R., 'The Methods of Unification', 16 *American Journal of Comparative Law* (1968), 13-27

David, R., 'Unification du droit et arbitrage', in *Verhagen Lectures: Erasmus University Faculty of Law, 20 September 1976* (Deventer: Kluwer, 1977)

Davies, P., and Gower, L., *Principles of Modern Company Law*, 7th edn. (London: Sweet & Maxwell, 2003)

De Boer, J., *Asser's Handleiding tot de beoefening van het Nederlands burgerlijk recht. Personen- en familierecht*, 17th edn., Asser Series (2006)

De Boer, Th., 'Enkele knelpunten bij de toepassing van de Verordening Brussel II-bis', *Tijdschrift voor Familie- en Jeugdrecht* (2005), 222-229

De Boer, Th., '*Forum preferences in Contemporary European Conflicts Law: The Myth of a "Neutral Choice"*', in H.-P. Mansel *et al.*, eds., *Festschrift für Erik Jayme* (München: Sellier European Law Publishers, 2004), 39-55

De Boer, Th., and Polak, M., 'Naar een gecodificeerd internationaal privaatrecht (!/?)', *Preadviezen: Mededelingen van de Nederlandse Vereniging voor Internationaal Recht* (1990)

De Cristofaro, M., 'Critical Remarks on the Vienna Sales Convention's Impact on Jurisdiction', *Uniform Law Review* (2000), 43-68

De Cruz, P., *Comparative Law in a Changing World*, 3rd edn. (London/New York: Routledge-Cavendisch, 2007)

De Groot, G.-R., 'Boek 1: Persoon en Familierecht', in *Tekst & Commentaar, Burgerlijk Wetboek*, loose leaf (Deventer: Kluwer, 2005)

De Heer, J., 'Forum arresti-perikelen', *NIPR* (2001), 389-397

De Lima Pinheiro, L., 'The "Denationalization" of Transnational Relationships: Regulation of Transnational Relationships by Public International Law, European Community Law and Transnational Law', in J. Basedow *et al.*, eds., *Aufbruch nach Europa: 75 Jahre Max-Planck-Institut für Privatrecht* (Tübingen: Mohr Siebeck, 2001), 429-446

De Ly, F., 'Applicable Law and Dispute Resolution Clauses: A Premilinary Report', in H. Lesguillons, ed., *Les grandes clauses des contrats internationaux, Brussels Conference, March 11-12, 2005* (Bruxelles: FEC/Bruylant, 2005), 167-234

De Ly, F., 'Arbitration and Human Rights', paper presented at Arbitration Day organized by the German Institute of Arbitration (DIS) and the International Commercial Arbitration Committee of the International Law Association (ILA), Berlin, 20 August 2004

De Ly, F., 'Book Review', 69 *Nederlands Juristenblad* (1994), 1109-1112

De Ly, F., *Europese Gemeenschap en privaatrecht: Uitwerking van inaugurele rede Erasmus Universiteit Rotterdam* (Zwolle: W.E.J. Tjeenk Willink, 1993)

De Vareilles-Sommières, P., *La compétence internationale de l'état en matière de droit privé: Droit international public et droit international privé* (1997)

De Vareilles-Sommières, P., 'The Mandatory Nature of Article 2 of the Brussels Convention and Derogation from the Rule It Lays Down', in P. De Vareilles-Sommières, ed., *Forum Shopping in the European Judicial Area* (Oxford: Hart, 2007), 101-115

De Winter, L., 'Excessives Jurisdiction in Private International Law', *The International and Comparative Law Quarterly* (1968), 706-720

De Winter, L., 'Nationality or Domicile: The Present State of Affairs', 128 *Recueil des cours* (1969), 349-358

Degnan, R., and Kay, K., 'The Exercise of Jurisdiction over and Enforcement of Judgments against Alien Defendants', 39 *Hastings Law Journal* (1988), 799-855

Després, I., and Guiomard, P., *Nouveau code de procédure civile*, 99th edn., Codes Dalloz (Paris: 2008)

Dicey, A., Morris, J., and Collins, L., *The Conflict of Laws*, 14th edn., Vol. 1 (London: Sweet & Maxwell, 2006)

Dickinson, A., 'Legal Certainty and the Brussels Convention: Too Much of a Good Thing?', in P. De Vareilles-Sommières, ed., *Forum Shopping in the European Judicial Area* (Oxford/Portland/Oregon: Hart 2007), 115-136

Donzallaz, Y., 'Convention de Lugano et Loi fédérale sur les fors: Comparaison et relations', *Aktuelle Juristische Praxis* (2000), 1259-1268

Dorsel, C., *Forum non Conveniens: Richterliche Beschränkung der Wahl des Gerichtsstandes im deutschem und amerikanischen Recht* (Berlin: Duncker & Humblot, 1996)

Dorward, D., 'The Forum Non Conveniens Doctrine and the Judicial Protection of Multinational Corporations from Forum Shopping Plaintiffs', *University of Pennsylvania Journal of International Economic Law* (1998), 141-168

Droz, G., *Compétence judiciaire et effets des jugements dans le Marché Commun: Etude de la Convention de Bruxelles du 27 septembre 1968* (1972)

Droz, G., 'Delendum est forum contractus? Vingt ans après les arrêts De Bloos et Tessili interprétant l'article 5.1 de la Convention de Bruxelles du 27 septembre 1968', 41 *Recueil Dalloz: Cahier Chronique* (1997), 351-356

Droz, G., 'Entrée en vigueur de la Convention de Bruxelles concernant la compétence judiciaire et l'exécution des décisions en matière et commerciale', 62 *Revue critique de droit international privé* (1973), 21-41

Droz, G., *Le nouveau régime de la compétence judiciaire et des effets des jugements dans l'Europe des six: Pratique de la convention de Bruxelles du 27 septembre 1968* (Paris: Librairie Dalloz, 1973)

Droz, G., 'Les droits de la demande dans les relations privées internationales', *Travaux du Comité Français de Droit International Privé* (1993-1995), 97-121

Droz, G., 'Note: Lloyd's Register of Shipping C-439/93', *Revue critique de droit international privé* (1995), 774-776

Droz, G., 'Note: Shenevai', *Revue critique de droit international privé* (1987), 798-804

Droz, G., 'Réflexions pour une réforme des articles 14 et 15 du Code Civil français', 64 *Revue critique de droit international privé* (1975), 1-23

Droz, G., and Gaudemet-Tallon, H., 'La transformation de la Convention de Bruxelles du 27 septembre 1968 en Règlement du Conseil concernant la compétence judiciaire, la reconnaissance et l'exécution des décisions en matière civile et commerciale', *Revue critique de droit international privé* (2001), 601-652

Dubbink, C., 'Mensenrechten en de openbare orde in het Internationaal Privaatrecht', in S.C.J.J Struycken and A.V.M. Kortmann, eds., *Op recht: Bundel opstellen, aangeboden aan prof. mr. A.V.M. Struycken ter gelegenheid van zijn zilveren ambtsjubileum aan de Katholieke Universiteit Nijmegen* (Zwolle: W.E.J. Tjeenk Willink, 1996)

Dubinsky, P., 'The Reach of Doing Business Jurisdiction and transacting Business Jurisdiction over Non-U.S. Individuals and Entities', Working Document no. 64, presented at the Special Commission of the Hague Conference on Private International Law, 1998

Duintjer Tebbens, H., 'From Jamaica with Pain', in P. van der Grinten and T. Heukels, eds., *Crossing Borders: Essays in European and Private International Law, Nationality Law and Islamic Law in Honour of Frans van der Velden* (Deventer: Kluwer, 2006), 95-103

Duintjer Tebbens, H., 'Judicial Interpretation of the 1988 Lugano Convention on Jurisdiction and Judgements in the Light of Its Brussels Matrix: The Convergence Confirmed', in P. Sarcevic and P. Volken, eds., *Yearbook of Private International Law* (The Hague: Kluwer Law International, 2001), 1-25

Duintjer Tebbens, H., 'The English Court of Appeal in Re Harrods: An Unwelcome Interpretation of the Brussels Convention', in M. Sumampouw, ed., *Law and Reality: Essays on National and International Procedural Law in Honour of Cornelis Carel Albert Voskuil* (The Hague: T.M.C. Asser Institute, 1992), 47-61

Duintjer Tebbens, H., Kennedy T., and Kohler, Ch., eds., *Civil Jurisdiction and Judgments in Europe*, Colloquium on the Interpretation of the Brussels Convention by the Court of Justice considered in the Context of the European Judicial Area, Luxembourg 1991 (London: Butterworths, 1992)

Dunham, D., and Gladbach, E., 'Forum Non Conveniens and Foreign Plaintiffs in the 1990s', *Brooklyn Journal of International Law* (1999), 665-704

Dutoit, B., 'Deux lois de droit international privé: Jusqu'ou la Suisse et l'Italie convergent-elles?', in A. von Overbeck, F. Pocar and K. Siehr, eds., *Collisio Legum* (Milano: Giuffrè, 1997), 137-168

Dutoit, B., ed., *Droit international privé suisse: Commentaire de la loi fédérale du 18 décembre 1987*, 4th edn. (Bâle/Genève/Munich: Helbing & Lichtenhahn, 2005)

Duval-Major, J., 'One-Way Ticket Home: The Federal Doctrine of Forum Non Conveniens and the International Plaintiff', *Cornell Law Review* (1992), 650- 686

Ehrenzweig, A., 'The Transient Rule of Personal Jurisdiction, the 'Power' Myth, and the Forum Non Conveniens', 65 *Yale Law Journal* (1956), 289-314

Eltzschig, J., 'Art. 5 Nr. 1 b EuGVO: Ende oder Fortführung von forum actoris und Erfüllungsort bestimmung lege causae', *IPRax* (2002), 491-496

Enonchong, N., 'Service of Process in England on Overseas Companies and Article 5(5) of the Brussels Convention', 48 *The International and Comparative Law Quarterly* (1999), 921-936

Epstein, D., 'An Examination of the "Adequacy of the Alternative Forum" Factor in Forum Non Conveniens Determinations', in J.L. Goldsmith, ed., *International Dispute Resolution: The Regulation of Forum Selection (Fourteenth Sokol Colloquium)* (1997)

Espinar Vicente, J., *Derecho procesal civil internacional* (Madrid: Guias de la Ley Estudio, 1988)

Expertenkommission, *Bundesgesetz über das internationale Privatrecht (IPR-Gesetz): Schlussbericht der Expertenkommission zum Gestezesentwurf* (Zürich: Schulthess, 1979)

Fallon, M., 'Le principe de proximité dans le droit de l'Union Européenne', in M.-N. Jobard-Bachellier and P. Mayer, eds., *Le droit international privé: Esprit et méthodes mélanges en l'honneur de Paul Lagarde* (Paris: Dalloz, 2005), 241-262

Fauvarque-Cosson, B., 'Comparative Law and Conflict of Laws: Allies or Enemies? New Perspectives on an Old Couple', 49 *American Journal of Comparative Law* (2001), 407-427

Fawcett, J., 'A New Approach to Jurisdiction over Companies in Private International Law', 37 *The International and Comparative Law Quarterly* (1988), 645-667

Fawcett, J., 'Common law Practices and the Brussels Convention', www.ipr.be (2005), 103-110

Fawcett, J., *Declining Jurisdiction in Private International Law*, Clarendon Press, Congress of the International Academy of Comparative Law (08) 14 Athens/Delphi 1994 (Oxford: Oxford University Press, 1995)

Fawcett, J., 'Jurisdiction and Subsidiaries', *Journal of Business Law* (1985), 16-25

Fawcett, J., 'The Impact of Article 6(1) of the ECHR on Private International Law', 56 *The International and Comparative Law Quarterly* (2007), 1-48

Fawcett, J., 'Trial in England or Abroad: The Underlying Policy Considerations', 9 *Oxford Journal Legal Studies* (1989), 205-229

Fawcett, J., North, P., and Carruthers, J., *Cheshire, North & Fawcett: Private International Law*, 14th edn. (Oxford: Oxford University Press, 2008)

Fawcett, J.E.S., *The Application of the European Convention on Human Rights*, 2nd edn. (Oxford: Clarendon Press, 1987)

Fentiman, R., 'Access to Justice and Parallel Proceedings in Europe', 63 *The Cambridge Law Journal* (2004), 312-313

Fentiman, R., 'Domicile Revisited', 50 *The Cambridge Law Journal* (1991), 445-463

Fentiman, R., 'Jurisdiction, Discretion and the Brussels Convention', 26 *Cornell International Law Journal* (1993), 59-99

Fentiman, R., 'Note: Gasser C-116/02', *Common Market Law Review* (2005), 241-259

Fernández-Flores de Funes, J., *Manual de derecho internacional privado, Collection Manuales* (Madrid: 1980)

Fernández Arroyo, D., *Derecho Internacional Privado Interamericano: Evolución y Perspectivas* (Buenas Aires: Rubinzal-Culzoni, 2000)

Fernández Arroyo, D., 'Exorbitant and Exclusive Grounds of Jurisdiction in European Private International Law: Will They Ever Survive?', in H.-P. Mansel *et al.* eds., *Festschrift für Erik Jayme* (München: Sellier European Law Publishers, 2004), 169-186

Ferrari, F., '"Forum Shopping" Despite International Contract Law Conventions', 51 *The International and Comparative Law Quarterly* (2002), 689-708

Fitzpatrick, J., 'The Lugano Convention and Western European Integration: A Comparative Analysis of Jurisdiction and Judgements in Europe and the United States', 695 *Connecticut Journal of International Law* (1993), 695-749

Flach, R., 'Beantwoording rechtsvraag (237) IPR/ Burgerlijk procesrecht- Conservatoir beslag zeeschepen', 44 *Ars Aequi* (1995), 305-309

Fogt, M., 'Blick in das Ausland – Gerichtsstand des Erfüllungsortes bei streitiger Existenz des Vertrages, Anwendbarkeit des CISG und alternative Vertragsschlussformen (Østre Landsret 23. 4. 1998)', 21 *IPRax* (2001), 358-364

Forsyth, C., and Moser, Ph., 'The Impact of the Applicable Law of Contract on the Law of Jurisdiction under the European Conventions', 45 *The International and Comparative Law Quarterly* (1996), 190-197

'Forum Shopping Reconsidered', 103 *Harvard Law Review* (1990), 1677-1696

Fragistas, N., 'La compétence internationale en droit international privé', 104 *Recueil des cours* (1961), 159-271

Fragistas, N., 'Les compétences exorbitantes dans les travaux de la Conférence de La Haye', in Revue roumaine des sciences sociales, *Mélanges Ionasco,* (1968), 175 *et seq.*

Fragistas, N., and Droz, G., 'Explanatory Report Hague Convention of 1 February 1971 on the Recognition and Enforcement of Foreign Judgments in Civil and Commercial Matters', in *Acts and Documents of the Extraordinary Session (1966)* (The Hague: The Hague Conference on Private International Law, 1966)

Freer, R., 'American and European Approaches to Personal Jurisdiction Based upon Internet Activity'. Available at http://papers.ssrn.com/sol3/papers.cfm?abstract_id=1004887 (2007)

Freudenthal, M., and Van der Velden, F., 'The Netherlands National Report', in J. Fawcett, ed., *Declining Jurisdiction in Private International Law* (Oxford: Clarendon Press, 1995), 321-339

Fricke, M., 'Der Gerichtsstand des Vermögens – eine unendliche Geschichte?', *IPRax* (1991), 159-162

Fricke, M., 'Neues vom Vermögensgerichtsstand?', 48 *NJW* (1992), 3066-3069

Gaja, G., ed., *La Riforma del Diritto Internazionale Privato e Processuale, Raccolta in Ricordo di Eduardo Vitta* (Milan: Giuffrè, 1994)

Gardella, A., and Radicati di Brozolo, L., 'Civil Law, Common Law and Market Integration: The EC Approach to Conflicts of Jurisdiction', 51 *American Journal of Comparative Law* (2003), 611-637

Garnett, R., 'Stay of Proceedings in Australia: A "Clearly Inappropriate" Test?', 23 *Melbourne University Law Review* (1999), 30-64

Garro, A., *Armonización y unificación del derecho privado en América Latina: Esfuerzos, tendencias y realidades, Saggi, conferenze e seminar, Roma, Centro di studi e ricerche di diritto comparato e straniero* (1992)

Gassmann, R., *Arrest im Internationalen Rechtsverkehr: Zum Einfluss des Lugano-Übereinkommens auf das schweizerische Arrestrecht* (1998)

Gaudemet-Tallon, H., *Compétence et exécution des jugements en Europe: Règlement n. 44/2001 Conventions de Bruxelles et de Lugano*, 3rd edn. (Paris: LGDJ, 2002)

Gaudemet-Tallon, H., 'France National Report', in J. Fawcett, ed., *Declining Jurisdiction in Private International Law* (Oxford: Clarendon Press, 1995), 175-187

Gaudemet-Tallon, H., 'La compétence internationale à l'épreuve du nouveau code de procédure civile: Aménagement ou bouleversement', 66 *Revue critique de droit international privé* (1977), 1-45

Gaudemet-Tallon, H., 'Le "*forum non conveniens*", une menace pour la Convention de Bruxelles? (à propos de trois arrêts anglais récents)', *Revue critique de droit international privé* (1991), 491-524

Gaudemet-Tallon, H., 'Les régimes relatifs au refus d'exercer la compétence juridictionnelle en matière civile et commerciale', *Revue internationale de droit comparé* (1994), 423-435

Gaudemet-Tallon, H., 'Nationalisme et compétence judiciaire: Déclin ou renouveau?', *Travaux du Comité Français de Droit International Privé* (1987-1988), 171-199

Gaudemet-Tallon, H., 'Note: Custom Made', 83 *Revue critique de droit international privé* (1994), 698-707

Gaudemet-Tallon, H., 'Note: Handte', *Revue critique de droit international privé* (1992), 471-472

Gaudemet-Tallon, H., 'Note: Ivenel', *Revue critique de droit international privé* (1983), 120-126

Gaudemet-Tallon, H., 'Note: Peters', *Revue critique de droit international privé* (1983), 667-670

Gaudemet-Tallon, H., 'Note: Réunion Européenne', *Revue critique de droit international privé* (1999), 333-340

Gaudemet-Tallon, H., 'Note: Shearson Lehmann Hutton', *Revue critique de droit international privé* (1993), 325-332

Gaudemet-Tallon, H., *Recherches sur les origines de l'article 14 du Code Civil: Contribution à l'histoire de la compétence judiciaire internationale* (Paris: Presses Universitaires de France, 1964)

Geimer, R., 'The Brussels Convention – Successful Model and Oldtimer', 4 *European Journal of Law Reform* (2002), 19-35

Geimer, R., *Internationales Zivilprozeßrecht*, 5th edn. (Köln: Verlag Dr. Otto Schmidt, 2005)

Geimer, R., 'Note: Shenevai', *NJW* (1987), 1132-1133

Geimer, R., 'Rechtsschutz in Deutschland künftig nur bei Inlandsbezug?', *NJW* (1991), 3072-3074

Geimer, R., 'Verfassungsrechtliche Vorgaben bei der Normierung der internationalen Zuständigkeit', in F. Matscher, ed., *Europa im Aufbruch: Festschrift Fritz Schwind zum 80. Geburtstag* (1993), 17-42

Geimer, R., and Vollkommer, M., *Zöller Zivilprozessordnung*, 23rd edn. (Köln: Verlag Dr. Otto Schmidt, 2002)

General Secretariat, OAS, 'Comparative Study of the Bustamante Code, the Montevideo Treaties and the Restatement of the Law of Conflict of Laws', Washington D.C.: Inter-American Juridical Commitee OAS, 1964

George, G., 'In Search of General Jurisdiction', 64 *Tulane Law Review* (1990), 1097-1141

George, J., 'International Parallel Litigation: A Survey of Current Conventions and Model Laws', 37 *Texas International Law Journal* (2002), 499-540

Giardina, A., 'Les caractères généraux de la réforme?', 85 *Revue critique de droit internationale privé* (1996), 1-19

Giardina, A., 'Note; Italy, Law Reforming the Italian System of Private International Law', 35 *International Legal Materials* (1996), 760-782

Glenn, P., 'Unification of Law, Harmonization of Law and Private International Law', in J. Erauw and M. Storme, eds., *Liber memorialis François Laurent, 1810-1887* (Brussels: Story – Scientia, 1989), 783-793

Goldstein, G., 'Federalism and Substantive Due Process: A Comparative and Historical Perspective on International Shoe and Its Progeny', 28 *The University of California Davis Law Review* (1995), 965-998

Gothot, H., and Holleaux, D., *La Convention de Bruxelles du 27 septembre 1968* (Paris: 1985)

Gothot, H., and Holleaux, D., 'Note: De Bloos and Tessili', *Revue critique de droit international privé* (1977), 761-772

Graveson, R., 'Private International Law: A Century of Unification', in J. Erauw and M. Storme, eds., *Liber memorialis François Laurent, 1810-1887* (Brussels: Story – Scientia, 1989), 795-804

Graveson, R., *Conflict of Laws: Private International Law*, 7th edn. (London: Sweet & Maxwell, 1974)

Greenberg, S., 'Resolving International Business Disputes', in S. Greenberg and E. Jolivet, eds., *Guide to Export-Import Basics: Vital Knowledge for Trading Internationally,* 3rd edn. (Paris: ICC Publication, 2008), 59-76

Groenleer, M., 'De communautaire aspecten van de Wet op de Buitenlandse Vennootschappen', *NIPR* (2001), 306-312

Grolimund, P., 'Human Rights and Jurisdiction: General Observations and Impact on the Doctrines of Forum Non Conveniens and Forum Conveniens', 4 *European Journal of Law Reform* (2002), 87-118

Grothe, H., '"Exorbitante" Gerichtszuständigkeiten im Rechtsverkehr zwischen Deutschland und den USA', 58 *RabelsZ* (1994), 687-726

Gsell, B., 'Autonom bestimmter Gerichtsstand am Erfüllungsort nach der Brüssel I Verordnung', *IPRax* (2002), 484-491

Guinchard, S., ed., *Droit et pratique de la procédure civile*, 5th edn., Dalloz Action (Paris: Dalloz, 2006)

Guinchard, S., and Ferrand, F., *Procédure civile: Droit interne et droit communautaire*, 28th edn., Précis Dalloz Droit Privé (Paris: Dalloz, 2006)

Gutmann, D., *Droit international privé*, 2nd edn., Cours Dalloz, Série droit privé (Paris: Dalloz, 2000)

Hare, C., 'Forum Non Conveniens in Europe: Game Over or Time for Reflexion?', *Journal of Business Law* (2006), 157-179

Harris, J., 'Sale of Goods and the Relentless March of the Brussels I Regulation', 123 *Law Quarterly Review* (2007), 522-528

Hartley, T., 'Note: Blanckeart', *European Law Review* (1981), 481-483

Hartley, T., 'Note: De Bloos v Bouyer', *European Law Review* (1977), 57-63

Hartley, T., 'Note: Ivenel', *European Law Review* (1982), 328-331

Hartley, T., 'Note: Lloyd's Register of Shipping', *European Law Review* (1996), 162-164

Hartley, T., 'Note: Peters', *European Law Review* (1983), 262-264

Hartley, T., 'Note: Tessili', *European Law Review* (1977), 57-63

Hartley, T., 'The European Court, the Brussels Convention/Regulation and the Establishment of an Efficient System for International Litigation in Europe', in A. Arnull, P. Eeckhout and T. Tridimas, eds., *Continuity and Change in EU Law: Essays in Honour of Sir Francis Jacobs* (Oxford: Oxford University Press, 2008), 385-399

Hartley, T., 'The European Union and the Systematic Dismantling of the Common Law of Conflict of Laws', 54 *The International and Comparative Law Quarterly* (2005), 813-828

Hartley, T., 'Unnecessary Europeanisation under the Brussels Jurisdiction and Judgements Convention: The Case of the Dissatisfied Sub-Purchaser (Note: Handte)', *European Law Review* (1993), 506-516

Hartwieg, O., 'Forum Shopping zwischen Forum non Conveniens und "hinreichendem Inlandsbezug"', 51 *Juristen Zeitung* (1996), 109-118

Hatzimihail, N., 'General Report: Transnational Civil Litigation between European Integration and Global Aspirations', in A. Nuyts and N. Watté, eds., *International Civil Litigation in Europe and Relations with Third States* (Bruxelles: Bruylant, 2005), 595-675

Hatzimihail, N., and Nuyts, A., 'Judicial Cooperation between the United States and Europe in Civil and Commercial Matters: An Overview of Issues', in A. Nuyts and N. Watté, eds., *International Civil Litigation in Europe and Relations with Third States* (Bruxelles: Bruylant, 2005), 1-25

Hay, P., 'Flexibility versus Predictability and Uniformity in Choice of Law. Reflections on Current European and United States Conflicts Law', 226 *Recueil des cours* (1991), 281-412

Hay, P., 'Refining Personal Jurisdiction in the United States', 35 *The International and Comparative Law Quarterly* (1986), 32-62

Hay, P., 'Transient Jurisdiction, Especially over International Defendants: Critical Comment on Burnham v. Superior Court California', *University of Illinois Law Review* (1990), 593-603

Hay, P., and Walker, R., 'The Proposed U.S.-U.K. Recognition-of-Judgements Convention: Another Perspective', 18 *Virginia Journal of International Law* (1978), 753-768

Hay, P., Weintraub, R., and Borchers, P., *Conflict of Laws: Cases and Materials*, 12th edn., University casebook series (New York, NY: Foundation Press, 2004)

Hazard, Jr., G., 'The American Law Institute. What It Is and What It Does', Vol. 14, *Saggi, conferenze e seminari. Rome, Centro di studi e ricerche di diritto comparato e straniero* (1994)

Hazard, Jr., Taruffo, M., and Gidi, A., *ALI/Unidroit Principles and Rules of Transnational Civil Procedure* (New York: American Law Institute, Unidroit, 2003)

Hazard, Jr., Taruffo, M., Stürner, R., and Gidi, A., 'Introduction to the Principles and Rules of Transnational Civil Procedure', 33 *New York University Journal of International Law and Politics* (2001), 767-784

Heiser, W., 'A Minimum Interest Approach to Personal Jurisdiction', 35 *Wake Forest Law Review* (2000), 915-972

Heldrich, A., *Internationale Zuständigkeit und anwendbares Recht, Beiträge zum Ausländischen und Internationalen Privatrecht* (Tübingen: Mohr Siebeck, 1969)

Hertz, K., *Jurisdiction in Contract and Tort under the Brussels Convention* (Copenhagen: Djof Publishing, 1998)

Herzog, P., 'Rules on the International Recognition of Judgments (and on International Jurisdiction) by Enactments of an International Organization: European Community Regulations 1347/2000 and 44/2001', in J. Nafziger and S. Symeonides, eds., *Law and Justice in a Multistate World: Essays in Honor of Arthur T. von Mehren* (Ardsley: Transnational Publishers Inc, 2002), 83-107

Heuzé, V., 'De quelques infirmités congénitales du droit uniforme: L'example de l'article 5.1 de la Convention de Bruxelles du 27 septembre 1968', 89 *Revue critique de droit international privé* (2000), 589-639

Hill, J., *Cross-border Consumer Contracts* (Oxford: Oxford University Press, 2008)

Hill, J., *International Commercial Disputes in English Courts*, 3rd edn. (Oxford: Hart, 2005)

Hill, J., 'Jurisdiction in Matters Relating to a Contract under the Brussels Convention', 44 *The International and Comparative Law Quarterly* (1995), 591-619

Hill, J., 'The Exercise of Jurisdiction in Private International Law', in P. Capps, M. Evans and S. Konstadinidis, eds., *Asserting Jurisdiction: International and European Legal Perspectives* (2003), 39-62

Hogan, G., 'The Brussels Convention, Forum Non Conveniens and the Connecting Factors Problem', 20 *European Law Review* (1995), 471-494

Holleaux, D., *Compétence du juge étranger et reconnaissance des jugements* (Paris: Librairie Dalloz, 1970)

Holleaux, D., Foyer, J., and De Geouffre de la Pradelle, G., *Droit international privé* (Paris: Masson, 1987)

Honsell, H., Schnyder, A., and Vogt, N., eds., *Internationales Privatrecht*, 2nd edn., Basler Kommentar (Basel: Helbing Lichtenhahn, 2007)

Honsell, H., Vogt, N., and Schnyder, A., *Kommentar zum Schweizerischen Privatrecht: Internationales Privatrecht* (Basel: Helbing & Lichtenhahn, 1996)

Hornbeck, S., 'Transnational Litigation and Personal Jurisdiction over Foreign Defendants', 59 *Albany Law Review* (1996), 1389-1447

Huber, P., 'Forum Non Conveniens – The Other Way Round', *IPRax* (1996), 48-52

Hudault, J., 'Sens et Portée de la compétence du juge naturel dans l'ancien droit français', 61 *Revue critique de droit international privé* (1972), 27-54 and 249-268

Hudig-van Lennep, W., 'Note: Lloyd's Register of Shipping', 97/7 *TVVS Maandblad voor Ondernemingsrecht en rechtspersonen* (1997), 221-222

Huet, A., 'Compétence des Tribunaux français à l'égard des litiges internationaux', Fascicule 581-10-51, *Juris-Classeur Droit International* (2002)

Huet, A., 'La Convention de Vienne du 11 avril 1980 sur les contrats de vente internationale de marchandises et compétence des tribunaux en droit judiciaire Européen', in P. Mayer and M.-N. Jobard-Bachellier, eds., *Le droit international privé: Esprit et méthodes. Mélanges en l'honneur de Paul Lagarde* (Paris: Dalloz, 2005), 417-430

Huet, A., 'Note: Arcado', *Journal du droit international* (1989), 453-454

Huet, A., 'Note: Custom Made', *Journal du droit international* (1995), 461-465

Huet, A., 'Note: Gasser', *Journal du droit international* (2004), 641-645

Huet, A., 'Note: Peters', *Journal du droit international* (1983), 834-843

Huet, A., 'Note: Tacconi', *Journal du droit international* (2003), 668-671

Huet, A., 'Note: Tessili', *Journal du droit international* (1977), 714-719

Huet, A., 'Special Jurisdiction under Article 5 Part 1: The Role of Article 5 in the Scheme of the Convention, Jurisdiction in Matters Relating to Contract', in H. Duintjer Tebbens, *et al.* eds, *Civil Jurisdiction and Judgements in Europe: Proceedings of the Colloquium on the Interpretation of the Brussels Convention by the Court of Justice Considered in the Context of the European Judicial Area, Luxembourg, 11 and 12 March 1991* (London: Butterworths, 1992), 63-71

Ibili, F., 'Book Review: A. Nuyts, 'L'Exception de forum non conveniens', *Netherlands International Law Review* (2005), 299-302

Ibili, F., 'Civil Jurisdiction and Enforcement of Judgements in Europe: At Last the EC Court of Justice on Forum Non Conveniens', 53 *Netherlands International Law Review* (2006), 127-139

Ibili, F., *Gewogen rechtsmacht in het IPR: Over forum (non) conveniens en forum necessitatis, Recht en praktijk* (Deventer: Kluwer, 2007)

Jacob, F., *Codes Dalloz*, 106th edn. (Paris: Dalloz, 2006)

Jasper, D., *Forum Shopping in England und Deutschland* (Berlin: Duncker & Humblot, 1990)

Jayme, E., 'Note: Custom Made- Einklägergerichtstand für den Verkäufer – Der EuGH verfehlt den Sinn des EuGVÜ', *IPRax* (1995), 13-14

Jayme, E., 'Special Jurisdiction under Article 5 Part 1: The Role of Article 5 in the Scheme of the Convention, Jurisdiction in Matters Relating to Contract', in H. Duintjer Tebbens, ed., *Civil Jurisdiction and Judgements in Europe: Proceedings of the Colloquium on the Interpretation of the Brussels Convention by the Court of Justice Considered in the Context of the European Judicial Area, Luxembourg, 11 and 12 March 1991* (London: Butterworths (1992), 73-80

Jenard, P., 'Opinion', 7 *Arbitration International* (1991), 243-250

Jenard, P., 'Report on the Convention on Jurisdiction and the Enforcement of Judgments in Civil and Commercial Matters of 27 September 1968', OJ 1979 C 59 (1979), 1-65

Jenard, P., and Möller, G., 'Report on the Lugano Convention on Jurisdiction and the Enforcement of Judgments in Civil and Commercial Matters', OJ 1990 C 189 (1990)

Johnston, A., and Powles, E., 'The Kings of the World and Their Dukes' Dilemma: Globalisation, Jurisdiction and the Rule of Law', in P. Slot and M. Bulterman, eds., *Globalisation and Jurisdiction* (The Hague: Kluwer Law International, 2004), 13-54

Joubert, N., *La notion de liens suffisants avec l'ordre juridique (Inlandsbeziehung) en droit international privé* (Dijon: LexisNexis Letic-CREDIMI, 2007)

Joustra, C., 'Consumentengeschillen in het Voorontwerp Burgerlijke Rechtsvordering', 93 *WPNR* (1994), 61-67

Juenger, F., 'A Shoe Unfit for Globetrotting? Symposium Fifty Years of International Shoe: The Past and the Future of Personal Jurisdiction', 28 *The University of California Davis Law Review* (1995), 1027-1045

Juenger, F., 'American and European Conflicts Law', 30 *American Journal of Comparative Law* (1982), 117-133

Juenger, F., 'American Jurisdiction: A Story of Comparative Neglect', 65 *University of Colorado Law Review* (1993), 1-23

Juenger, F., 'Constitutionalizing German Jurisdictional Law: Book Review Internationale Zuständigkeit und prozessuale Gerechtigkeit', 44 *The American Journal of Comparative Law* (1996), 521-528

Juenger, F., 'Federalism: Judicial Jurisdiction in the United States and in the European Communities: A Comparison', 82 *Michigan Law Review* (1984), 1195-1212

Juenger, F., 'Forum Non Conveniens – Who Needs It?', in M. Taruffo, ed., *Abuse of Procedural Rights: Comparative Standards of Procedural Fairness*, International Association of Procedural Law International Colloquium, 27-30 October 1998, Tulane Law School, New Orleans, Louisiana (The Hague: Kluwer Law International, 1999)

Juenger, F., 'Forum Non Conveniens – Who Needs It?', in R. Geimer, ed., *Wege zur Globalisierung des Rechts: Festschrift für Rolf A. Schütze zum 65. Geburtstag* (München: C.H. Beck'sche Verlagsbuchhandlung, 1999), 317-336

Juenger, F., 'Forum Shopping Domestic and International', 63 *Tulane Law Review* (1989), 553-574

Juenger, F., 'Judicial Control of Improper Forum Regulation: Some Random Remarks and a Comment on How Not to Do It', in J.L. Goldsmith, ed., *International Dispute Regulation* (1997), 311-325

Juenger, F., 'Jurisdiction, Choice of Law and the Elusive Goal of Decisional Harmony', in M. Sumampouw, ed., *Law and Reality: Essays on National and International Procedural Law in Honour of Cornelis Carel Albert Voskuil* (The Hague: T.M.C. Asser Instituut, 1992), 137-147

Juenger, F., 'La Convention de Bruxelles du 27 septembre 1968 et la courtoisie internationale: Réflexions d'un américain', *Revue critique de droit international privé* (1983), 37-51

Juenger, F., 'The American Law of General Jurisdiction', *University of Chicago Legal Forum* (2001), 141-170

Juenger, F., 'The Problem with Private International Law', in J. Basedow, ed., *Private Law in the International Arena: From National Conflict Rules towards Harmonization and Unification: Liber Amicorum Kurt Siehr* (The Hague: Asser Press, 2000), 289-309

Juenger, F., 'What's Wrong with Forum Shopping?', 16 *Sydney Law Review* (1994), 5-13

Kahn, P., 'Note: Banque camerounaise de développement Cour de Cassation: Chambre Civile 1re 18 November 1986', *Journal du droit international (Clunet)* (1987), 633-638

Karayanni, M., *Forum Non Conveniens in the Modern Age: A Comparative and Methodological Analysis of Anglo-American Law* (Ardsley, NY: Transnational Publishers, 2004)

Karrer, P., Arnold, K., and Patocchi, P., *Switzerland's Private International Law*, translated by Switzerland's Private International Law (Deventer: Kluwer Law and Taxation Publishers, 1994)

Kaye, P., *Civil Jurisdiction and Enforcement of Foreign Judgments* (Abingdon: Professional Books Limited, 1987)

Kaye, P., 'The EEC Judgements Convention and the Outer World: Goodbye to Forum Non Conveniens?', *The Journal of Business Law* (1992), 47-76

Kaye, P., 'The Judgements Convention and Arbitration: Mutual Spheres of Influence', 7 *Arbitration International* (1991), 289-298

Kaye, P., 'The Meaning of Domicile under United Kingdom Law for the Purpose of the 1968 Brussels Convention on Jurisdiction and the Enforcement of Judgments in Civil and Commercial Matters', *Netherlands International Law Review* (1988), 181-195

Kaye, P., 'Nationality and the European Convention on the Jurisdiction and Enforcement of Judgments', 37 *The International and Comparative Law Quarterly* (1988), 268-282

Kennett, W., 'Current Developments: Private International Law – The Brussels I Regulation', 50 *The International and Comparative Law Quarterly* (2001), 725-737

Kennett, W., 'Forum Non Conveniens in Europe', 43 *Cambridge Law Journal* (1995), 552-577

Kerameus, K., and Evriginis, I., 'Evrigenis and Kerameus Report on the Accession of the Hellenic Republic to the Community Convention on Jurisdiction and the Enforcement of Judgments in Civil and Commercial Matters', OJ 1986 C 298 (1986), 1 *et seq.*

Kessedjian, C., 'Judicial Regulation of Improper Forum Selections', in J.L. Goldsmith, ed., *International Dispute Resolution* (1997), 273-294

Kessedjian, C., *La reconnaissance et l'exécution des jugements en droit international privé aux Etats-Unis* (Paris: Economica, 1987)

Kessedjian, C., 'Prel. Doc. No. 7: Report on International Jurisdiction and Foreign Judgments in Civil and Commercial Matters', Permanent Bureau of the Hague Conference Private of International Law, 1997

Kessedjian, C., 'Prel. Doc. No. 8: Synthesis of the work of the Special Commission of June 1997 on International Jurisdiction and the Effects of Foreign Judgments in Civil and Commercial Matters', Permanent Bureau of the Hague Conference Private International Law, 1997

Kessedjian, C., 'Prel. Doc. No. 9: Synthesis of the work of the Special Commission of March 1998 on International Jurisdiction and the Effects of Foreign Judgments in Civil and Commercial Matters', Permanent Bureau of the Hague Conference Private International Law, 1998

Keyes, M., *Jurisdiction in International Litigation* (Sydney: Federation Press, 2005)

Kleinstück, T., *Due Process-Beschränkungen des Vermögensgerichtsstandes durch hinreichenden Inlandsbezug und Minimum Contacts: Eine rechtsvergleichende Untersuchung unter besonderer Berücksichtigung des U.S.-amerikanischen und österreichischen Rechts* (München: C.H. Beck'sche Verlagsbuchhandlung, 1994)

Knight, Ch., 'Owusu and Turner: The Shark in the Water?', 66 *Cambridge Law Journal* (2007), 288-301

Knoepfler, F., Schweizer, Ph., and Othenin-Girard, S., eds., *Droit international privé suisse*, 3rd edn. (Berne: Stämpfli, 2005)

Kohler, Ch., Huet, A., and Jayme, E., 'Special Jurisdiction under the Article 5 – Part 1: General Remarks and Jurisdiction in Matters Relating to Contract', in H. Duintjer Tebbens, ed., *Civil Jurisdiction and Judgments in Europe: Proceedings of the Colloquium on the Interpretation of the Brussels Convention by the Court of Justice Considered in the Context of the European Judicial Area, Luxembourg, 11 and 12 March 1991* (London: Butterworths, 1992), 47-83

Kokkini-Iatridou, D., *Een inleiding tot het rechtsvergelijkende onderzoek* (Deventer: Kluwer, 1988)

Kokkini-Iatridou, D., 'Rapport général: Les clauses d'exception en matière de conflits de lois et de conflits de juridictions', in D. Kokkini-Iatridou, ed., *Exception Clauses in Conflicts of Laws and Conflicts of Jurisdictions, or the Principle of Proximity: XIVth International Congress of Comparative Law, Athens* (Dordrecht/Boston/London: Martinus Nijhoff Publishers, 1994), 3-41

Kokkini-Iatridou, D., and Boele-Woelki, K., 'De Regeling van de "Internationale rechtsmacht" in het voorontwerp van wet van 1993', *NIPR* (1993), 323-364

Kokkini-Iatridou, D., and Boele-Woelki, K., 'De Regeling van de "Internationale rechtsmacht", 125 *WPNR* (1994), 50-55

Kokkini-Iatridou, D., and Frohn, E., 'De exceptieclausules in het verdragenrecht, een verkenning', in D. Kokkini-Iatridou and F. Grosheide, eds., *Eénvormig en vergelijkend privaatrecht* (Lelystad: Koninklijke Vermande, 1989), 215-264

Koppenol-Laforce, M.E., 'Article 765 Rv (vreemdelingenbeslag) en de Europese Gemeenschap', *Tijdschrift voor Civiele Rechtspleging* (1994), 58-61

Koppenol-Laforce, M.E., 'De Rechtsmacht van de Nederlandse rechter in het voorontwerp tot aanpassing van het Wetboek van Burgerlijke Rechtsvordering', *Tijdschrift voor Civiele Rechtspleging* (1994), 5-9

Korn, H.L., 'The Development of Judicial Jurisdiction in the United States', 65 *Brooklyn Law Review* (1999), 935-1001

Kovar, J., 'The United States as an Actor in Private International Law', in R. Brand and M. Walter, eds., *Private Law, Private International Law, & Judicial Cooperation in The EU-US Relationship* (Eagan, MN, etc.: Thomson/West, 2005), 153-159

Krafft, J., *'Exorbitante' Gerichtsstände im internationalen Zivilprozessrecht der Schweiz: Insbesondere nach dem Lugano-Übereinkommen* (1999)

Kramer, K., 'De forumkeuze als betrouwbaar alternatief voor het arbitraal beding in de internationale handelspraktijk? Het nieuwe Haags Forumkeuzeverdrag', *Nederlands Tijdschrift voor Handelsrecht* (2006), 165-172

Kramer, X., 'De harmoniserende werking van het Europees procesrecht: De diskwalificatie van de anti-suit injunction', *NIPR* (2005), 130-137

Kramer, X., 'De regeling van de rechtsmacht onder het herziene Rechtsvordering', 20 *NIPR* (2002), 375-385

Kramer, X., 'Dutch Private International Law: Overview 1998-August 2002', *IPRax* (2002), 537-546

Kronke, H., 'Distributie bepaalt attributie – Internationale Zuständigkeit zwischen Faustregel und Kodifikation', paper presented at *De internationale bevoegdheid van de Nederlandse Rechter volgens de nieuwe bepalingen van het Wetboek van Burgerlijke Rechtsvordering*, T.M.C Asser Instituut, The Hague, 26 January 1996 (1996)

Kropholler, J., 'Das Unbehagen am Forum Shopping', in R. Geimer, ed., *Festschrift für Karl Firsching zum 70. Geburtstag* (München: C.H. Beck, 1985), 165

Kropholler, J., *Europaïsches Zivilprozessrecht: Kommentar zu EuGVO und Lugano- Uebereinkommen*, 8th edn. (Heidelberg: Verlag Recht und Wirtschaft GmbH, 2005)

Kropholler, J., *Internationales Privatrecht: Einschließlich der Grundbegriffe des Internationalen Zivilverfahrensrechts*, 6th edn. (Tübingen: Mohr Siebeck, 2006)

Kropholler, J., *Internationales Privatrecht: Einschließlich der Grundbegriffe des internationalen Zivilverfahrensrechts*, 5th edn. (Mohr Lehrbuch, Mohr Siebeck 2004)

Kropholler, J., 'Möglichkeiten einer Reform des Vermögensgerichtsstandes', 23 *Zeitschrift für Rechtsvergleichung* (1982), 1-11

Kropholler, J., and Von Hinden, M., 'Die Reform des europäischen Gerichtsstands am Erfüllungsort (Art. 5 Nr. 1 EuGVÜ)', in H. Schack, ed., *Gedächtnisschrift für Alexander Lüderitz* (München: C.H. Beck, 2000), 401-414

Kruger, T., *Civil Jurisdiction Rules of the EU and Their Impact on Third States*, Oxford Private International Law Series (Oxford: Oxford University Press, 2008)

Kruger, T., 'The Anti-Suit Injunction in the European Judicial Space: Turner v. Grovit', *The International and Comparative Law Quarterly* (2004), 1030-1040

Kuypers, P., *Forumkeuze in het Nederlandse internationaal privaatrecht* (Deventer: Kluwer, 2008)

Lagarde, P., 'Compétence judiciaire contrats suisse', paper presented at the *Freiburger Kolloquium über des schwiezerischen Entwurf zu einem Bundesgesetz über das internationale Privatrecht*, Freiburg, Switzerland, 1979

Lagarde, P., 'Le principe de proximité dans le droit internationale prive contemporain. Cours général de droit international privé', 196 *Recueil des cours* (1986), 9-238

Lagarde, P., 'Revues: Schlosser, Peter', 81 *Revue critique de droit international privé* (1992), 626-630

Lagarde, P., and Guiliano, M., 'Report on the Convention on the Law Applicable to Contractual Obligations', OJ C 282 (1980), 1-50

Leible, S., and Reinert, Ch., 'Note: *Color Drack* C-386/05', *Europäische Zeitschrift für Wirtschaftsrecht* (2007), 370-373

Leijnse-Kolk, A., 'Drie fora; forum actoris, forum non conveniens en forum necessitatis', paper presented at *De internationale bevoegdheid van de Nederlandse Rechter volgens de nieuwe bepalingen van het Wetboek van Burgerlijke Rechtsvordering*, T.M.C Asser Instituut, The Hague, 26 January 1996 (1996)

Leipold, D., 'Internationale Zuständigkeit am Erfüllungsort – das Neueste aus Luxemburg und Brüssel', in H. Schack, ed., *Gedächtnisschrift für Alexander Lüderitz* (München: C.H. Beck, 2000), 431-453

Lequette, Y., 'Note COBENAM; Cour de cass.Ch.civ.I, 17 Jan.1995', *Revue critique de droit international privé* (1996), 133-142

Levy, L., *La Nationalité des sociétés* (Paris: Librairie Générale de Droit et de Jurisprudence, 1984)

Lilly, G., 'Jurisdiction over Domestic and Alien Defendants', *Virginia Law Review* (1983), 85-152

Lokin, J., and Zwalve, W., *Hoofdstukken uit de Europese Codificatiegeschiedenis*, 2nd edn. (Groningen: Wolters-Noordhoff/Forsten, 1992)

Lookofsky, J., 'Property-based Jurisdiction and Due Process of Law', 54 *Nordisk Tidsskrift for international Ret: Acta scandinavica juris gentium* (1985), 62-70

Lookofsky, J., and Hertz, K., *Transnational Litigation and Commercial Arbitration: An Analysis of American, European and International Law*, 2nd edn. (Huntington, NY/ Copenhagen: Juris Publishing DJØF Publications, 2004)

Lookofsky, J., *Understanding the CISG*, 3rd edn. (The Netherlands/Copenhagen: Kluwer Law International/DJØF, 2008)

Loquin, E., and Kessedjian, C., eds., *La mondialisation du droit* (Dijon: Litec, 2000)

Loussouarn, Y., and Bourel, P., *Droit international privé*, 8th edn., Précis (Paris: Dalloz, 2004)

Lowenfeld, A., *Conflict of Laws: Federal, State and International Perspectives*, 2nd edn., Casebook Series (Newark, NJ, LexisNexis, 2002)

Lowenfeld, A., 'In Search of the Intangible: A Comment on Shaffer v. Heitner', 53 *New York Law Review* (1978), 102

Lowenfeld, A., *International Litigation and Arbitration*, 3rd edn., American Casebook Series (St. Paul, MN: Thomson/West, 2006)

Lowenfeld, A., *International Litigation and the Quest for Reasonableness: Essays in Private International Law* (Oxford: Oxford University Press, 1996)

Lowenfeld, A., and Silberman, L., *International Jurisdiction and Judgements Project* (Philadelphia: The American Law Institute, 2000), 1-65

Lowenfeld, A., and Silberman, L., eds., *The Hague Convention on Jurisdiction and Judgments: Records of the Conference Held at New York University School of Law on the Proposed Convention* (New York: Juris Publishing, 2001)

Lowenfeld, F., 'Book Review: Quo Vadis Arbitration? Sixty Years of Arbitration Practice', 95 *American Journal of International Law* (2001), 728-731

Lucas Sosa, G., *El Derecho Internacional Privado Interamericano y Derecho de Integración. (CIDIP V Mexico 1994)* (Santa Fé: Tercer Milenio, 1996)

Lüderitz, A., '*Fremdbestimmte internationale Zuständigkeit? Versuch einer Neubestimmung von 29 ZPO, Art.5 Nr. 1 EuGVü*', in H. Bernstein, U. Drobnig and H. Kötz, eds., *Festschrift für Konrad Zweigert zum 70. Geburtstag* (Tübingen: Mohr Siehr, 1981), 233-250

Lüke, G., 'Note: Deutsche Bundesgerichtshof 2 July 1992', *ZZP* (1992), 314-329

Lüke, G., Wax, P., and Patzina, R., *Münchener Kommentar zur Zivilprozessordnung*, 2nd edn. (München: C.H. Beck, 2000)

Lurger, B., 'Inlandsbezug von Vermögensgerichtsständen', *Zeitschrift für Rechtsvergleichung* (1995), 61

Magnus, U., 'Das UN-Kaufrecht und die Erfüllungsortzuständigkeit in der neuen EuGVO', *Internationales Handelsrecht* (2002), 45-52

Magnus, U., and Mankowski, P., eds., *Brussels I Regulation European Commentaries on Private International Law* (München: Sellier, 2007)

Mance, J., 'Exclusive Jurisdiction Agreements and European Ideals', *The Law Quarterly Review* (2004), 357-365

Mance, J., 'The Future of Private International Law', 1 *Journal of Private International Law* (2005), 185-195

Mankowski, P., 'Entscheidungsrezensionen – Die Qualifikation der culpa in contrahendo – Nagelprobe für den Vertrags-begriff des europäischen IZPR und IPR', 23 *IPRax* (2003), 127-134

Mann, F., 'The Doctrine of International Jurisdiction', 111 *Recueil des cours* (1964), 1-162

Mann, F., 'The Doctrine of International Jurisdiction Revisited after Twenty Years', 186 *Recueil des cours* (1984), 9-116

Mansel, H.-P., 'Vermögensgerichtstand und Inlandsbezug bei der Entscheidungs- und Anerkennungszuständigkeit am Beispiel der Anerkennung US –amerikanischer Urteile in Deutschland', in H.-P. Mansel, ed., *Festschrift für Erik Jayme* (München: Sellier European Law Publishers, 2004), 561-573

Marchadier, F., *Les objectifs généraux du droit international privé à l'épreuve de la Convention Européenne des droits de l'homme* (Bruxelles: Bruylant, 2007)

Mark, J., 'Der Gerichtsstand des Vermögens im Spannungsfeld zwischen Völkenrecht und deutschen Internationalen Prozessrecht', 48 *NJW* (1992), 3062-3066

Matscher, F., 'Quarante ans d'activités de la Cour européenne des droits de l'homme', 270 *Recueil des cours* (1997), 237-398

Matscher, F., 'Le droit internationale privé face à la Convention Européenne des droits de l'homme', 1996-1997 *Travaux du Comité Français de Droit International Privé* (1997), 211-234

Maxwell, Lord, *Report of the Scottish Committee on Jurisdiction and Enforcement* (Edinburgh: Scottish Courts Administration, 1980)

Mayer, P., 'Droit international privé et le droit international public sous l'angle de la notion de la compétence', 68 *Revue critique de droit international privé* (1979), 1-29, 349-388, and 537-583.

Mayer, P., 'La Convention européenne des droits de l'homme et l'application des normes étrangères', 98 *Revue critique de droit international privé* (1991), 651-665

Mayer, P., 'La partie faible en droit international privé', in Ghestin, J. and Fontaine, M. eds., *La protection de la partie faible dans les rapports contractuels: Comparaison Franco-Belges* (LGDJ, 1996), 513 *et seq.*

Mayer, P., and Heuzé, V., *Droit international privé*, 8th edn., Domat droit privé (Paris: Montchrestien, 2004)

Mayer, P., and Heuzé, V., *Droit international privé*, 9th edn. (Paris: Montchrestien, 2007)

McFarland, D., 'Dictum Run Wild: How Long-arm Statutes Extended to the Limits of Due Process', *Boston University Law Review* (2004), 491

McLachlan, C., 'The Influence of International Law on Civil Jurisdiction', *Hague Yearbook of International Law* (1993), 125-144

McLachlan, C., 'Interim Report Declining & Referring Jurisdiction in International Litigation', paper presented at the International Law Association, London Conference, 2000

McLachlan, C., 'Transnational Tort Litigation: An Overview', in C. McLachlan and P. Nygh, eds., *Transnational Tort Litigation: Jurisdictional Principles* (Oxford: Clarendon Press, 1996), 1-19

McLachlan, C. (Rapporteur), 'Report of the Seventieth Conference. Fourth and Final Report: Jurisdiction over Corporations', New Delhi: International Law Association, Committee on International Civil and Commercial Litigation, P. Nygh (chair) (2002), 412-432

Mennie, A., 'The Brussels Convention and the Scottish Courts' Discretion to Decline Jurisdiction', *The Juridical Review* (1989), 150-172

Merrett, L., 'The Meaning of an "Available Forum"', 63 *Cambridge Law Journal* (2004), 309-311

Miaja de la Muela, A., 'Les principes directeurs des règles de compétence territoriale des tribunaux internes en matière de litiges comportant un élément international', 135 *Recueil des cours* (1973), 1-96

Miaja de la Muela, A., 'El "imperialismo jurisdiccional" español y el derecho internacional privado', in D. Constantopoulos *et al.*, eds., *Miscellany in Honor of Charalambos N. Fragistas on the Occassion of His 35th Anniversary as Professor of the University* (Thessaloniki: 1968), 89-128

Michaels, R., 'Globalizing Savigny? The State in Savigny's Private International Law and the Challenge of Europeanization and Globalization', 74 *Duke Law School Legal Studies Paper* (2005) Available at SSRN: http://ssrn.com/abstract=796228

Michaels, R., 'Re-Placements. Jurisdiction for Contracts and Torts under the Brussels I Regulation When Arts. 5(1) and 5(3) Do Not Designate a Place in a Member State', in A. Nuyts and N. Watté, eds., *International Civil Litigation in Europe and Relations with Third States* (Bruxelles: Bruylant, 2005), 129-156

Michaels, R., 'Some Fundamental Jurisdictional Conceptions as Applied in Judgment Conventions', 123 *Duke Law School Legal Studies* (2006). Available at SSRN: http://ssrn.com/abstract=927484

Michaels, R., 'Territorial Jurisdiction after Territoriality', in P. Slot and M. Bulterman, eds., *Globalisation and Jurisdiction* (The Hague: Kluwer Law International, 2004), 106-130

Michaels, R., 'Two Paradigms of Jurisdiction', 27 *Michigan Journal of International Law* (2007), 1003-1069

Migliazza, A., 'Rilievi sulla Giurisdizione, sulla Competenza territoriale e sulla competenza internazionale', in G. Gaja, ed., *La Riforma del Diritto Internazionale Privato e Processuale, Raccolta in Ricordo di Eduardo Vitta* (Milano: Giuffrè, 1994), 363-368

Mirandes, A., *La compétence inter-étatique et internationale des tribunaux en droit des Etats-Unis* (Paris: Economica, 2002)

Möllers, Ch., *Internationale Zuständigkeit bei der Durchgriffshaftung*, (Bielefeld: Giesekring, 1987)

Montanari, A., and Narcisi, V., *Conflict of Laws in Italy* (Kluwer Law International, 1997)

Morrison, A., *Fundamentals of American Law* (Oxford: Oxford University Press, 1996)

Morse, C., 'Not in the Public Interest? Lubbe v. Cape PLC', 37 *Texas International Law Journal* (2002), 541-557

Morse, C., 'Making English Private International Law', in J. Fawcett, ed., *Reform and Development of Private International Law: Essays in Honour of Sir Peter North* (Oxford: Oxford University Press, 2002)

Moura Ramos, M., 'The New EC Rules on Jurisdiction and the Recognition and Enforcement of Judgments', in J. Nafziger and S. Symeonides, eds., *Law and Justice in a Multistate World: Essays in Honor of Arthur T. von Mehren* (Ardsley NY: Transnational Publishers Inc., 2002), 199-217

Mourre, A., *Droit judiciaire privé européen des affaires: Droit communautaire – droit comparé*, Collection de la Fondation pour l'Étude du Droit et des Usages du Commerce International (Feduci) (Bruxelles/Paris: Bruylant/Forum Européen de la Communication (FEC), 2003)

Muchlinski, P., 'Corporations in International Litigation: Problems of Jurisdiction and the United Kingdom Asbestos Case', 50 *The International and Comparative Law Quarterly* (2001), 1-25

Muir Watt, H., 'Evidence of an Emergent European Legal Culture: Public Policy Requirements of Procedural Fairness under the Brussels and Lugano Conventions', 36 *Texas International Law Journal* (2001), 539-554

Muir Watt, H., 'La fonction subversive du droit comparé', *Revue internationale de droit comparé* (2000), 503-527

Muir Watt, H., 'Note: Banque camerounaise de développement. Cour de Cass. Ch.Civ.I, 18 Nov. 1986', 76 *Revue critique de droit international privé* (1987), 773-786

Muir Watt, H., 'Note: Gasser', *Revue critique de droit international privé* (2004), 459-464

Müller, H., *Die Gerichtspflichtigkeit wegen 'doing business': Ein Vergleich Zwischen Dem US-amerikanischen und dem deutschen Zuständigkeitssystem*, Vol. 89, Prozessrechtliche Abhandlungen (Köln: Carl Heymanss Verlag, 1992)

Musielak, H.-J., *Kommentar zur Zivilprozessordnung*, 4th edn. (München: F. Vahlen, 2005)

Nadelmann, K., 'Jurisdictional Improper Fora in the Treaties of Recognition and Enforcement of Judgements the Common Market Draft', 67 *Columbia Law Review* (1967), 995-998

Nadelmann, K., 'The International Unification of Law: Uniform Legislation versus International Conventions Revisited', 16 *American Journal of Comparative Law* (1968), 28-50

Nadelmann, K., 'The Need for Revision of the Bustamante Code on Private International Law', 65 *American Journal of International Law* (1971), 782-793

Nadelmann, K., 'The Outer World and the Common Market Expert's Draft on Recognition of Judgements', *Common Market Law Review* (1967), 409-420

Nagel, H., and Gottwald, P., *Internationales Zivilprozessrecht*, 5th edn. (Aschendorf Rechtsverlag Münster/Verlag Dr. Otto Schmidt Köln, 2002)

Nagel, H., and Gottwald, P., *Internationales Zivilprozessrecht*, 6th edn. (Köln: O. Schmidt, 2007)

Neale, A., and Stephens, M., *International Business and National Jurisdiction* (Oxford: Clarendon Press, 1998)

Neuhaus, P., *Grundbegriffe des Internationalen Privatrecht Beiträge zum Ausländischen und Internationalen Privatrecht,* 2nd edn. (Tübingen: Mohr Siebeck, 1976)

Newman, J., O'Hare, K., and Williams, R., eds., *College of Law Lectures – Jurisdiction and Enforcement of Judgments in Europe* (London: Eastern Press Ltd., 1985)

Newton, J., *The Uniform Interpretation of the Brussels and Lugano Conventions* (Oxford, [etc]: Hart Publishing, 2002)

Nguyen, K., 'Invisibly Radiated; Federalism Principles and the Proposed Hague Convention on Jurisdiction and Foreign Judgements', 28 *Hastings Constitutional Law Quarterly* (2000), 145-166

Nguyen, K.D., 'Redefining the Threshold for Personal Jurisdiction: Contact and the Presumption of Fairness', 83 *Boston University Law Review* (2003), 253-279

Niboyet, J.-P., *Cours de Droit International Privé Français*, 2nd edn. (Paris: *Recueil Sirey*, 1949)

Niboyet, J.-P., *Manuel de droit international privé*, 2nd edn. (Paris: *Recueil Sirey*, 1928)

Niboyet, M.-L., 'Le principe de confiance mutuelle et les injonctions "Anti-suit"', in P. De Vareilles-Sommières, ed., *Forum Shopping in the European Judicial Area* (Oxford, Portland, Oregon: Hart, 2007), 77-89

Nicod, B., 'Note: Banque camerounaise de développement Cour de Cass. Ch.Civ. I, 18 Nov. 1986', *Juris-Classeur périodique (Semaine Juridique)* (1987), no. 20909

Nieuwenhuis, J., Stolker, C., and Valk, W., eds., *Burgerlijk Wetboek: De tekst van de boeken 1, 2, 3, 4 BW voorzien van commentaar*, 7th edn., Tekst & commentaar (Deventer: Kluwer, 2007)

North, P., *Private International Law Problems in Common Law Jurisdictions* (Dordrecht: Kluwer Academic Publishers, 1993)

North, P., and Fawcett, J., *Cheshire and North's Private International Law*, 13th edn. (London: Butterworths, 1999)

Nuyts, A., 'Due Process and Fair Trial: Jurisdiction in the United States and in Europe Compared', in A. Nuyts and N. Watté, eds., *International Civil Litigation in Europe and Relations with Third States* (Bruxelles: Bruylant, 2005)

Nuyts, A., *L'exception de forum non conveniens: Etude de droit international privé* (Paris/ Bruxelles: Bruylant/LGDJ, 2003)

Nuyts, A., 'Forum Shopping et Abus du Forum Shopping dans l'Espace Judiciaire Européen', 3 *Global Jurist Advances* (2003). Available at: http://www.bepress.com/gj/advances/vol3/iss1/art2

Nygh, P., 'The Common Law Approach', in C. McLachlan and P. Nygh, eds., *Transnational Tort Litigation: Jurisdictional Principles* (Oxford: Clarendon Press, 1996), 21-36

Nygh, P., 'The Criteria for Judicial Jurisdiction; Conference Papers', in A. Lowenfeld and L. Silberman, eds., *The Hague Convention on Jurisdiction and Judgements: Records of the Conference Held at New York University School of Law on the Proposed Convention 1999* (Juris Publishing Inc., 2001), A1-A12

Nygh, P., 'Declining Jurisdiction under the Brussels I Regulation 2001 and the Preliminary Draft Hague Judgments Convention: A Comparison', in J. Fawcett, ed., *Reform and Development of Private International Law – Essays in Honour of Sir Peter North* (Oxford: Oxford University Press, 2002), 303-334

Nygh, P., and Davies, M., *Conflict of Laws in Australia* (LexisNexis Butterworths, 2002)

Nygh, P., and Pocar, F., 'Report of the Special Commission – Convention on Jurisdiction and Foreign Judgments in Civil and Commercial Matters', *Hague Conference on Private International Law* (2000)

O'Brian Jr., W., 'The Hague Convention on Jurisdiction and Judgments: The Way Forward', 66 *The Modern Law Review* (2003), 491-509

Oberhammer, P., 'Vermögensbelegenheit und Funktion des Vermögensgerichtsstands', in B. von Bachmann *et al.*, eds., *Grenzüberschreitungen: Beiträge zum internationalen Verfahrensrecht und zur Schiedsgerichtsbarkeit: Festschrift für Peter Schlosser zum 70. Geburtstag* (Tübingen: Mohr Siebeck, 2005), 650-667

Opeskin, B., 'The Price of Forum Shopping: A Reply to Professor Juenger', 16 *Sydney Law Review* (1994), 14-27

Otte, K., 'Die Process-Beschränkungen des Vermögensgerichtsstandes durch hinreichenden Inlandsbezug und Minimum Contacts. Eine rechtsvergleichende Untersuchung unter besonderer Berücksichtigung des U.S. amerikanischen und österreichischen Rechts Rezensionen; Kleinstück', 110 *ZZP* (1997), 119-133

Oudelaar, H., *Recht halen: Inleiding in het executierecht en beslagrecht*, 4th edn., Studiereeks Procesrecht (Deventer: Kluwer, 1995)

Palmer, V., *Mixed Jurisdictions Worldwide: The Third Legal Family* (2001)

Park, W., 'The Relative Reliability of Arbitration Agreements and Court Selection Clauses', in J.L. Goldsmith, ed., *International Dispute Regulation* (1997)

Parra Aranguren, G., *Curso General de Derecho Internacional Privado: Problemas Selectos y Otros Estudios*, 3rd edn. (Caracas: Liberil S.R.L., 1998)

Pataut, E., *Principe de souveraineté et conflit de juridictions (étude de droit international privé)* (1999)

Patocchi, P., and Geisinger, E., *Code de droit international privé suisse annoté* (Lausanne: Payot (1995)

Patocchi, P., Geisinger, E., and Lüke, S., *Internationales Privatrecht: Das IPRG sowie die wichtigsten völkerrechtlichen Verträge und Schiedsgerichtsordnungen* (Zürich: Orell Füssli, 2000)

Pearce, B., 'The Comity Doctrine as a Barrier to Judicial Jurisdiction: A US-EU Comparison', 30 *Stanford Journal of International Law* (1994), 525-578

Peel, E., 'Forum Non Conveniens and European Ideals', *Lloyd's Maritime and Commercial Law Quarterly* (2005), 363-377

Peel, E., 'Introduction', in P. De Vareilles-Sommières, ed., *Forum Shopping in the European Judicial Area* (Oxford: Hart, 2007), 1-23

Pejovic, C., 'Civil Law and Common Law: Two Different Paths Leading to the Same Goal', 32(3) *Victoria University of Wellington Law Review* (2001), 817-841

Pellis, L., *Forum Arresti: Aspecten van rechtsmachtscheppend (vreemdelingen-) beslag in Europa, Civiele procespraktijk* (Zwolle: Tjeenk Willink W.E.J., 1993)

Pellis, L., *Internationaal Procesrecht: Een dwarsdoorsnede* (The Hague: Boom, 2005)

Pellis, L., '"Tot uw dienst!", Over oude en nieuwe grondslagen van het commune Nederlandse internationaal bevoegdheidsrecht', in H. Lemaire and P. Vlas, eds., *Met recht verkregen: Bundel opstellen aangeboden aan mr. Ingrid S. Joppe* (Deventer: Kluwer, 2002)

Pfeiffer, T., 'Book Review – Bittighofer, A., Der internationale Gerichtsstand des Vermögens: Eine Rechtvergleichende Studie zur Zuständigkeit deutscher Gerichte aufgrund inländischer Vermögensbelegenheit', *RabelsZ* (1997), 595- 600

Pfeiffer, T., *Internationale Zuständigkeit und prozessuale Gerechtigkeit: Die internationale Zuständigkeit im Zivilprozess zwischen effektivem Rechtsschutz und nationaler Zuständigkeitspolitik* (Frankfurt am Main: 1995)

Piegai, J., *La protection du débiteur et des tiers dans le nouveau droit du séquestre* (Lausanne: Imprimerie Chabloz, 1997)

Plant, Ch., *et al.*, eds., *Blackstone's Civil Practice 2004* (Oxford: Oxford University Press, 2004)

Pocar, F., 'Das Neue italienische Internationale Privatrecht', 17 *IPRax* (1997), 145-161

Pocar, F., 'La protection de la partie faible en droit international privé', 188 *Recueil des cours* (1984), 339-418

Pocar, F., 'Le rôle des critères de compétence judiciaire de la Convention de Bruxelles dans le nouveau droit international privé italien', in A. Borras, A. Bucher, A.V.M. Struycken and M.Verwilghen, eds., *E pluribus unum, Liber amicorium, G Droz. On the Progressive Unification of Private International Law* (1996), 357-367

Pocar, F. and Honorati, C. eds., *The Hague Preliminary Draft Convention on Jurisdiction and Judgments: Proceedings of the Round Table* (Milan University/Cedam, 2005)

Pocar, F., and Honorati, C., eds., *Il nuovo diritto internazionale privato italiano, L'Italia e la vita giuridica internazionale* (Milano: Guiffrè, 1997)

Polak, M., 'Boek 1, Titel 1: Rechtsmacht van de Nederlandse rechter', in C. van Nispen, A. van Mierlo and M. Polak, eds., *Tekst & Commentaar, Burgerlijke Rechtsvordering* (Deventer: Kluwer, 2002)

Polak, M., and de Rooij, M., *Private International Law in the Netherlands* (The Hague: Kluwer Law International, 1987, including 1995 Suppl.)

Polak, P., van Mierlo, A., and van Nispen, C., eds., *Burgerlijke rechtsvordering: De tekst van het Wetboek van Burgerlijke Rechtsvordering voorzien van commentaar*, 2nd edn., *Tekst & commentaar* (Deventer: Kluwer, 2005)

Ponsard, A., 'Note: Dame Nassibian v. Nassibian; Cour de cass. Ch.Civ.I, 6 Nov. 1979', *Journal du droit international (Clunet)* (1980), 95-103

Pontier, J., and Burg, E., *EU Principles on Jurisdiction and Recognition and Enforcement of Judgments in Civil and Commercial Matters* (The Hague: T.M.C. Asser Press, 2004)

'Prel. Doc. No. 1 of May 1994: Annotated checklist of issues to be discussed at the meeting of the Special Commission of June 1994', Permanent Bureau of the Hague Conference Private International Law, 1994

'Prel. Doc. No. 2 of December 1995: Conclusions of the Special Commission of June 1994', Bureau Permanent of the Hague Conference Private International Law, 1995

Pryles, M., and Sykes, E., *Australian Private International Law*, 3rd edn. (Sydney: Law Book Company, 1991)

Punt, P., 'Naar een meer karakteristieke jurisdictie?', in D. Dankers-Hagenaars and P. Piepers, eds., *Aan Wil besteed: Bundel opstellen aangeboden op 22 mei 2003 aan prof. mr. W.G.Ph.E. Wedekind ter gelegenheid van zijn vijfenzestigste verjaardag op 26 mei 2003* (Deventer: Kluwer, 2003), 425-448

Rammeloo, S., *Corporations in Private International Law: A European Perspective*, Oxford Monographs in International Law (Oxford: Oxford University Press, 2001)

'Rapport aan de Minister van Justitie: Algemene Bepalingen Wet Internationaal Privaatrecht', in http://www.justitie.nl/themas/wetgeving/rapporten_en_notas/privaatrecht/Staatscommissie_IPR.asp, The Hague: Staatscommissie Internationaal Privaatrecht, (2002)

Rausher, Th., 'Prozessualer Verbraucherschutz im EuGVÜ', *IPRax* (1995), 289-294

'Recueil compétence', in *Encyclopédie Juridique Dalloz: Répertoire de procédure civile* (Paris: Dalloz, 1998)

'Recueil compétence internationale', in *Encyclopédie Juridique Dalloz: Répertoire de procédure civile* (Paris: Dalloz, 1998)

'Recueil contracts et obligations', in *Encyclopédie Juridique Dalloz: Répertoire de droit civil* (Paris: Dalloz, 2003)

Redish, M., 'The Future of Personal Jurisdiction: A Symposium on Burnham v. Superior Court: Tradition, Fairness, and Personal Jurisdiction: Due Process and Constitutional Theory After Burnham v. Superior Court', *Rutgers Law Journal* (1991), 675-688

Reid, K., 'The Idea of Mixed Legal Systems', *Tulane Law Review* (2003), 5-40

Reimann, M., *Conflicts of Law in Western Europe: A Guide through the Jungle* (Transnational Publishers Inc., 1995)

Reimann, M., 'A New Restatement: For the International Age', 75 *Indiana Law Review* (2000), 575-590

Reimann, M., 'Parochialism in American Conflicts Law', 49 *American Journal of Comparative Law* (2001), 369-389

'The Requirement of Seizure in the Exercise of Quasi in Rem Jurisdiction: Pennoyer v. Neff Re-Examined', 63 *Harvard Law Review* (1950), 657-671

Reus, A., 'Judicial Discretion: A Comparative View of the Doctrine of Forum Non Conveniens in the United States, the United Kingdom and Germany', *Loyola of Los Angeles International and Comparative Law Journal* (1994), 455-511

Richman, W., and Reynolds, W., *Understanding Conflict of Laws*, 2nd edn., Legal Text Series (New York: Matthew Bender & Co., 1993)

Richman, W., and Reynolds, W., *Understanding Conflict of Laws*, 3rd edn. (Newark, NJ [etc.]: LexisNexis, 2002)

Rigaux, F., 'The Extraterritorial Jurisdiction of State – La compétence extraterritoriale des états', 69 *Annuaire de l'Institut de droit international* (2001), 13-94

Robertson, D., 'Forum Non Conveniens in America and England: A Rather Fantastic Fiction', 103 *The Law Quarterly Review* (1987), 398

Rodgers, A., 'Forum Non Conveniens in International Cases', in *International Litigation: Defending and Suing Foreign Parties in U. S. Federal Courts* (Chicago: American Bar Association, Tort Trial and Insurance Practice Section, 2003), 205-219

Rogerson, P., 'Habitual Residence: The New Domicile?', 49 *The International and Comparative Law Quarterly* (2000), 86-107

Rogerson, P., 'Plus ça change? Article 5(1) of the Regulation on Jurisdiction and Enforcement of Judgments', *The Cambridge Yearbook of European Legal Studies* (2001), 382-406

Rogerson, P., 'The Common Law Rules of Jurisdiction of the English Courts over Companies' Foreign Activities', in P. Slot and M. Bulterman, eds., *Globalisation and Jurisdiction* (The Hague: Kluwer Law International, 2004), 91-103

Romano, G.-P., 'Principe de sécurité juridique, système de Bruxelles I/Lugano et quelques arrêts récents de la CJCE', in A. Bonomi, E. Cashin Ritaine and G.-P. Romano, eds., *La Convention de Lugano. Passé, présent et devenir. Actes de la 19e Journée de droit international privé du 16 mars 2007 à Lausanne,* (Schulthess: Zürich, 2007), 165-209

Roth, H., 'Probleme um die Internationale Zuständigkeit nach 29 ZPO', in B. von Bachmann *et al.*, eds., *Grenzüberschreitungen: Beiträge zum internationalen Verfahrensrecht und zur Schiedsgerichtsbarkeit: Festschrift für Peter Schlosser zum 70. Geburtstag* (Tübingen: Mohr Siebeck, 2005), 773-784

Rühland, C., *Le problème des personnes morales en droit international privé* (Paris: *Recueil Sirey*, 1934)

Russell, K., 'Exorbitant Jurisdiction and Enforcement of Judgements: The Brussels System as an Impetus for United States Action', 19 *Syracuse Journal of International Law & Commerce* (1993), 57-92

Rutgers, J., 'Internationale forumkeuze en agentuur: Het commune bevoegdheidsrecht in Europees perspectief', *NIPR* (2003), 351-355

Saenger, I., *Zivilprozessordnung: Handkommentar* (Baden-Baden: Nomos, 2006)

Samtleben, J., 'Der MERCOSUR als Rechtssystem', in J. Basedow and J. Samtleden, eds., *Wirtschaftsrecht des MERCOSUR – Horizont 2000: Tagung im Max-Planck-Institut für ausländisches und internationales Privatrecht am 21.-22. Januar 2000* (Baden-Baden: Nomos Verlagsgesellschaft, 2001), 52-94

Samtleben, J., *Internationales Privatrecht in Lateinamerika: Der Código Bustamante in Theorie und Praxis* (Tübingen: Mohr, 1979)

Sanders, P., *Quo Vadis Arbitration? Sixty Years of Arbitration Practice: A Comparative Study* (The Hague: Kluwer Law International, 1999)

Saumier, G., 'Judicial Jurisdiction in International Cases: The Supreme Court's Unifished Business', 17 *Dalhousie Law Journal* (1995), 447-472

Sauveplanne, J., 'Codified and Judge Made Law: The Role of Courts and Legislators in Civil and Common Law Systems', in *Mededelingen der Koninklijke Nederlandse Akademie van Wetenschappen, afd. Letterkunde* (1982), 95-120

Sauveplanne, J., 'Eenvormig Privaatrecht', *Themis* (1961), 225-280

Schaafsma, S., 'Kroniek van het internationaal privaatrecht', 10 *Nederlands Juristenblad* (2004), 513-519

Schack, H., 'Abstrakte Erfüllungsortsvereinbarungen: form- oder sinnlos', *IPRax* (1996), 247-249

Schack, H., *Der Erfüllungsort im deutschen, ausländischen und internationalen Privat- und Zivilprozeßrecht*, Arbeiten zur Rechtsvergleichung (Frankfurt am Main: Metzner, 1985)

Schack, H., 'Germany National Report', in J. Fawcett, ed., *Declining Jurisdiction in Private International Law* (Oxford: Clarendon Press, 1995), 189-205

Schack, H., *Jurisdictional Minimum Contacts Scrutinized: interstaatliche und internationale Zuständigkeit US-amerikanischer Gerichte*, Berkeley-Kölner Rechtsstudien, Kölner Reihe (Heidelberg: C.F. Müller Juristischer, 1983)

Schack, H., 'Note Bundesgerichtshof 2 July 1991', 46 *Juristen Zeitung* (1992), 51-56

Schack, H., 'Note: Custom Made', *Zeitschrift für Europäisches Privatrecht* (1995), 659-668

Schack, H., 'Vermögensbelegenheit als Zuständigkeitsgrund: Exorbitant oder Sinnvoll?', *ZZP* (1984), 46-68

Schack, H., *Internationales Zivilverfahrensrecht*, 4th edn., Juristische Kurz- Lehrbücher (München: Verlag C.H. Beck, 2006)

Scherz, C., 'Section 71.051 of the Texas Civil Practice and Remedies Code. The Texas Legislature's Answer to Alfaro: Forum Non Conveniens in Personal Injury and Wrongful Death Litigation', *Baylor Law Review* (1994), 99-139

Scheurmans, L., 'Attachment and Garnishment as Bases for Adjudicatory Jurisdiction over Foreigners: A Comparative Study', 13 *Netherlands International Law Review* (1966), 243-289

Schlechtriem, P., and Schwenzer, I., *Commentary on the UN Convention on the International Sale of Goods (CISG)*, 2nd edn. (Oxford: Oxford University Press, 2005)

Schlechtriem, P., and Schwenzer, I., *Kommentar zum Einhetlichen UN-Kaufrecht* (München: Verlag C.H. Beck, 2004)

Schlosser, P., 'A New Dimension of Human Rights' Consideration in Civil Procedure', *Rivista di diritto internazionale privato e internazionale* (1995), 31-40

Schlosser, P., 'Bases of Jurisdiction in a "New Double Convention" on Jurisdiction and Recognition of Foreign Judgements; Conference Papers', in A. Lowenfeld and L. Silberman, eds., *The Hague Convention on Jurisdiction and Judgements: Records of the Conference Held at New York University School of Law on the Proposed Convention 1999* (Juris Publishing Inc., 2001), A13-A27

Schlosser, P., 'Einschränkung des Vermögensgerichtsstandes', *IPRax* (1992), 140-143

Schlosser, P., 'Jurisdiction in International Litigation: The Issue of Human Rights in Relation to National Law and the Brussels Convention', *Rivista di diritto internazionale* (1991), 5-34

Schlosser, P., 'Lectures on Civil-Law Litigation Systems and American Cooperation with Those Systems', 45 *University of Kansas Law Review* (1996), 19-24

Schlosser, P., 'Note Bundesgerichtshof 28 October 1996', *Juristen Zeitung* (1997), 362-364

Schlosser, P., 'Report on the Convention on the Accession of the United Kingdom of Denmark, Ireland and the United Kingdom of Great Britain and Northern Ireland to the Convention on Jurisdiction and the Enforcement of Judgments in Civil and Commercial Matters and to the Protocol on Its Interpretation by the Court of Justice', OJ 1979 C 59 (1979)

Schlosser, P., 'The 1968 Brussels Convention and Arbitration', 7 *Arbitration International* (1991), 227-242

Schlosser, P., 'The Competence of Arbitrators and of Courts', 8 *Arbitration International* (1992) 189-204

Schlosser, P., 'Zuständigkeit bei mehreren Beklagten an verschiedenen Wohnsizten Note: Arcado', *Recht der Internationalen Wirtschaft* (1988), 987-989

Schnyder, A., 'Der Sitz von Gesellschaften im Internationalen Zivilverfahrensrecht', in R. Geimer, ed., *Wege zur Globalisierung des Rechts: Festschrift für Rolf A. Schütze zum 65. Geburtstag* (München: C.H. Beck'sche Verlagsbuchhandlung, 1999), 767-775

Schnyder, A., and Liatowitsch, M., *Internationales Privat- und Zivilverfahrensrecht*, 2nd edn. (Zürich: Schulthess, 2006)

Schröder, J., *Internationale Zuständigkeit: Entwurf eines Systems von Zuständigkeitsinteressen im zwischenstaatlichen Privatverfahrensrecht, aufgrund rechtshistorischer, rechtsvergleichender und rechtspolitischer Betrachtungen*, reprinted 1988 edn. (Opladen: Westdeutscher Verlag, 1971)

Schröder, J., 'The Right not to be Sued Abroad', in H.-J. Musielak, K. Schurig and G. Kegel, eds., *Festschrift für Gerard Kegel zum 75. Geburtstag* (1987), 523-548

Schroeter, U., 'Vienna Sales Convention: Applicability to "Mixed Contracts" and Interaction with the 1968 Brussels Convention', 5 *The Vindobona Journal of International Commercial Law and Arbitration* (2001), 74-86

Schultsz, J., 'Note: Arcado', *NJ* (1990), 1626-1627

Schulze, H., 'Declining and Referring Jurisdiction in International Litigation: The Leuven/London Principles', 25 *South African Yearbook of International Law* (2000), 161-180

Schütze, R., 'Forum non conveniens and Rechtschauvinismus', in H.-P. Mansel *et al.*, eds., *Festschrift für Erik Jayme* (München: Sellier European Law Publishers, 2004), 849-858

Scoles, E., Hay, P., Borchers, P., and Symeonides, S., *Conflict of Laws*, 4th edn., Hornbook Series (St. Paul, MN: Thomson/West, 2004)

'Section A – Civil Procedure Rules 1998 Part 6 – Service of Documents I. General Rules about Service', in *The White Book* (Sweet and Maxwell, 2007)

'Section A – Civil Procedure Rules 1998 Part 6 – Service of Documents III. Special Provisions about Service out of the Jurisdiction', in *The White Book* (Sweet and Maxwell, 2007)

Siehr, K., '"Forum shopping" im internationalen Rechtsverkehr', 25 *Zeitschrift für Rechtsvergleichung* (1984), 124-144

Siehr, K., 'Structure and Method of the "IPR-Schets"', special edition, *NIPR* (1994), 22-29

Siehr, K., 'Switzerland National Report', in J. Fawcett, ed., *Declining Jurisdiction in Private International Law* (Oxford: Clarendon Press, 1995), 381-399

Silberman, L., 'Comparative Jurisdiction in the International Context: Will the Proposed Hague Judgments Convention Be Stalled?', 52 *DePaul Law Review* (2002), 319-350

Silberman, L., 'Developments in Jurisdiction and Forum Non Conveniens in International Litigation: Thoughts on Reform and a Proposal for a Uniform Standard', 28 *Texas International Law Journal* (1993), 501-529

Silberman, L., 'Enforcement and Recognition of Foreign Country Judgements in the US', *International Business and Arbitration* (2000), 325-359

Silberman, L., 'International Arbitration: Comments from a Critic', *American Review of International Arbitration* (2002), 9-18

Silberman, L., 'Judicial Jurisdiction in the Conflict of Laws Course: Adding a Comparative Dimension', *Vanderbilt Journal of Transnational Law* (1995), 389-406

Silberman, L., 'Shaffer v Heitner; The End of an Era', 53 *New York Law Review* (1978), 33-101

Silberman, L., '"Two Cheers" for International Shoe (and None for Asahi): An Essay on the Fiftieth Anniversary of International Shoe', 28 *The University of California Davis Law Review* (1995), 755-767

Silberman, L., and Lowenfeld, A., 'A Different Challenge for the ALI: Herein of Foreign Country Judgments, an International Treaty, and an American Statute Proposal', 75 *Indiana Law Journal* (2000), 635-647

Lowenfeld, A., and Silberman, L., eds., *The Hague Convention on Jurisdiction and Judgments: Records of the Conference Held at New York University School of Law on the Proposed Convention* (New York: Juris Publishing Inc., 2001)

Sinay-Cytermann, A., 'Note; Cour de Cass. Ch. Civ. II, 29 Feb.1984', *Revue critique de droit international privé* (1985), 545-551

Siqueiros, J., 'La Conferencia de La Haya y las Convenciones Interamericanas de Derecho Internacional Privado', in Jaffé, *A. et al.* eds., *Liber Amicorum Homenaje a la Obra Científica y Académica de la Profesora Tatiana B. de Maekelt. Caracas, Universidad Central de Venezuela* (2001)

Smit, H., 'Common and Civil Law Rules of in Personam Adjudicatory Authority: An Analysis of Underlying Policies', 21 *The International and Comparative Law Quarterly* (1972), 335-354

Smit, H., 'The Proposed United States-United Kingdom Convention On Recognition and Enforcement of Judgements: A Prototype for the Future', 17 *Virginia Journal of International Law* (1977), 443-468

Solen, D., 'Forum Non Conveniens and the International Plaintiff', *Florida Journal of International Law* (1994), 343-353

Sorabji, J., 'Service Where the Defendant Is outside the Jurisdiction; Case Comment: Kamali v City', 26 *Civil Justice Quarterly* (2007), 279-283

Spitz, J., 'The "Transient Rule" of Personal Jurisdiction: A Well-intentioned Concept That Has Overstayed Its Welcome', 73 *Marquette Law Review* (1989), 181-216

Stadler, A., 'From the Brussels Convention to Regulation 44/2001: Cornerstones of a European Law of Civil Procedure', 42 *Common Market Law Review* (2005) 1637-1661

Starace, V., 'Le champ de la juridiction selon la loi de réforme du système italien de droit international privé', 85 *Revue critique de droit internationale privé* (1996), 67-82

Steenhoff, G., *De wetenschap van het internationaal privaatrecht in Nederland tussen 1862 en 1962: een internationalistisch perspectief* (Zwolle: W.E.J. Tjeenk Willink, 1994)

Steenhoff, G., 'Pleidooi voor een crediteursforum bij (internationale) geldschulden', in G. Schmidt and J. Freedberg-Swartzburg, eds., *Het NIPR geannoteerd: Annotaties opgedragen aan Dr Mathilde Sumampouw* (The Hague: T.M.C. Asser Instituut, 1996), 194-202

Stephens, J., 'Sovereignty and Personal Jurisdiction Doctrine: Up the Stream of Commerce without a Paddle', *Florida State University Law Review* (1991), 105-147

Stevenson, A., 'Forum Non Conveniens and Equal Access under Friendship, Commerce and Navigation Treaties: A Foreign Plaintiff's Rights', *Hastings International and Comparative Law Review* (1990), 267-285

Stevenson, J., 'The Relationship of Private International Law to Public International Law', 52 *Columbia Law Review* (1952), 561-588

Stone, P., *EU Private International Law Harmonization of Laws* (Cheltenham, UK: Edward Elgar, 2006)

Storme, M., and Huss, A., eds. *Rapprochement du droit judiciaire de l'Union européenne: Introduction générale introductif* (Dordrecht: Nijhoff, 1993)

Story, J., *Commentaries on the Conflicts of Laws, Foreign and Domestic in Regard to Contracts, Rights, and Remedies, and Especially in Regard to Marriages, Divorces, Wills, Successions, and Judgments*, 8th edn. (Boston: Little, Brown, and Company, 1883)

Strauss, A., 'Beyond National Law: The Neglected Role of the International Law of Personal Jurisdiction in Domestic Courts', 36 *Harvard International Law Review* (1995), 373-424

Strauss, A., 'Where America Ends and the International Order Begins: Interpreting the Jurisdictional Reach of the U.S. Constitution in Light of a Proposed Hague Convention on Jurisdiction and Satisfaction of Judgments', *Albany Law Review* (1998), 1237-1267

Strikwerda, L., 'De invloed van het EVRM op het Europse IPR: Aantekeningen bij de Krombach-uitspraak van het Hof van Justitie EG', in G. Corstens, W. Davids and M. Veldt-Foglia, eds., *Europeanisering van het Nederlands recht: Opstellen aangeboden aan Mr. W.E. Haak* (Deventer: Kluwer, 2004), 252-260

Strikwerda, L., *De Overeenkomst in het IPR* (Deventer: Kluwer, 2004)

Strikwerda, L., 'Drie fora: forum actoris, forum necessitatis en forum non conveniens', paper presented at the *De internationale bevoegdheid van de Nederlandse Rechter volgens de nieuwe bepalingen van het Wetboek van Burgerlijke Rechtsvordering*, T.M.C Asser Instituut, The Hague, 26 January 1996 (1996)

Strikwerda, L., 'Het forum necessitatis in verzoekschriftprocedures', in R. Flach and G. Ruthers, eds., *Liber Amicorum G.R. Rutgers* (Deventer: Kluwer, 2005), 329-335

Strikwerda, L., 'Het "rode boek" van het internationaal privaatrecht', *Nederlands Juristenblad* (1992), 1572-1573

Strikwerda, L., *Inleiding tot het Nederlandse Privaatrecht*, 9th edn. (Deventer: Kluwer, 2008)

Strikwerda, L., 'Note: HR 21 September 2001 C99/245HR', *NIPR* (2001), 467-470

Struycken, A., 'Distributie bepaalt attributie – Vuistregel en kern van een goed hanteerbaar rechtsmachtsmodel', in P. Vlas, ed., *De internationale bevoegdheid van de Nederlandse Rechter volgens de nieuwe bepalingen van het Wetboek van Burgerlijke Rechtsvordering* (The Hague: T.M.C Asser Instituut, Nederlands International Privaatrecht, 1996), 19-43

Struycken, A., 'Les conséquences de l'intégration européenne sur le développement du droit international privé', 232 *Recueil des cours* (1992), 256-383

Struycken, A., *Naar eenheid van rechtsbedeling in Europa* (Deventer: Kluwer, 1971)

Struycken, A., 'Veelheid van rechtsbronnen: Één IPR?', 45 *Ars Aequi* (1996), 61-68

Struycken, A., and J., Krings, 'The Rules of Jurisdiction in the EEC Convention on Jurisdiction and the Enforcement of Judgements in Civil and Commercial Matters', 25 *Netherlands International Law Review* (1978), 254-363

Struyven, O., 'Exorbitant Jurisdiction in the Brussels Convention', *Jura Falconis: Juridisch Wetenschappelijk studenten tijdschrift KU Leuven* (1999)

Stückelberg, M., 'Lis Pendens and Forum Non Conveniens at the Hague Conference: The Preliminary Draft Convention on Jurisdiction and Foreign Judgments in Civil and Commercial Matters', 26 *Brooklyn Journal of International Law* (2001), 949-982

Stürner, R., 'Why Are Europeans Afraid to Litigate in the United States?', paper presented at the *Saggi, Conferenze e Seminari, Centro di studi e richerche di diritto comparato e straniero, Roma* (2001)

Tallon, D., 'L'harmonisation des règles du droit privé entre pays de droit civil et de common law', *Revue internationale de droit comparé* (1990), 513-523

Tetley, W., 'Mixed Jurisdictions: Common Law vs Civil Law (codified and uncodified) – Part I', 4 *Uniform Law Review – Revue de droit uniforme* (1999), 591-619

Thery, Ph., *Pouvoir juridictionnel et compétence* (1981)

Thomas, H., and Putzo, H., *Zivilprozessordnung*, 22nd edn. (München: C.H. Beck'sche Verlagsbuchhandlung, 1999)

Trangsrud, R., 'The Federal Common Law of Personal Jurisdiction', 57 *George Washington Law Review* (1989), 849-906

Trompenaars, B., *Pluriforme Unificatie en Uniforme Interpretatie* (Kluwer: Deventer (1989)

Twitchell, M., 'The Myth of General Jurisdiction', 101 *Harvard Law Review* (1988), 610-681

Twitchell, M., 'A Rejoinder to Professor Brilmayer', 101 *Harvard International Law Review* (1988), 1465-1470

Twitchell, M., 'Why We Keep Doing Business with Doing-Business Jurisdiction', *University of Chicago Legal Forum* (2001), 171-214

Valloni, L., *Der Gerichtsstand des Erfüllungsortes nach Lugano- und Brüsseler-Übereinkommen*, Zürcher Studien zum Verfahrensrecht (Zürich: Schulthess, 1998)

Van Bynkershoek, C., *Traité du juge compétent des ambassadeurs, tant pour le civil que pour le criminel*, translated by J. Barbeyrac (The Hague: 1723)

Van der Grinten, W., and Maeijer, J., eds., *C. Asser's Handleiding tot de beoefening van het Nederlands burgerlijk recht*, [Vol. 2-II], De Rechtspersoon, 8th edn. (Deventer: Tjeenk Willink, 1997)

Van der Plas, C. *De Taak van de rechter in het IPR: een verkenning van de grenzen van de taak van de Nederlandse rechter bij de toepassing van vreemd Privaat- en Publiekrecht* (Deventer: Kluwer (2005)

Van der Plas, C. 'Note: U.S. District Court 17 October 2006, Windt en Meijer v. Qwest Communications International Inc., *et al.*', *Jurisprudentie Onderneming & Recht* (2007), at 186-201

Van der Velden, F., 'Nationaliteit als Europese jurisdictiegrond', in S. Kortmann, J. Maeijer, A. Nuytink and S. Perrick, eds., *Op recht: Bundel opstellen, aangeboden aan prof. mr. A.V.M. Struycken ter gelegenheid van zijn zilveren ambtsjubileum aan de Katholieke Universiteit Nijmegen* (Zwolle: W.E.J. Tjeenk Willink, 1996), 357-365

Van Dijk, P., and Arai, Y., *Theory and Practice of the European Convention on Human Rights*, 4th edn. (Antwerpen: Intersentia, 2006)

Van Haersolte-van Hof, J., 'Arrest Turner/Changepoint Weg met de anti-suit injunction', *Nederlands tijdschrift voor Europees recht* (2004), 228-230

Van Haersolte-van Hof, J., 'The Arbitration Exception in The Brussels Convention: Further Comments', 18 *Journal of International Arbitration* (2001), 27-38

Van Haersolte-van Hof, J., 'Zeevervoer en artikel 5(3) EEX', *NIPR* (2000), 385-390

Van Hoek, A., and Mostermans, P., 'Ontwikkelingen in regelgeving en rechtspraak in het IPR-procesrecht (buiten EEX en EVEX)', 6622 *WPNR* (2005), 419-427

Van Loon, H., 'Globalisation and The Hague Conference on Private International Law', 2 *International Law FORUM du droit international* (2000), 230-234

Van Loon, H., 'Quelques réflexions sur l'unification progressive du droit international privé dans le cadre de la Conférence de La Haye', in J. Erauw and M. Storme, eds., *Liber memorialis François Laurent, 1810-1887* (Brussels: Story – Scientia, 1989), 1133-1150

Van Mierlo, A., 'Boek III Van regtspleging van onderscheiden aard', in *Tekst & Commentaar, Burgerlijke Rechtsvordering*, loose leaf (Deventer: 2006)

Vandekerckhove, K., 'De interpretatie van Europees bevoegdheids- en executierecht', in Van Houtte, H. and Pertegás Sender, M. eds., *Het nieuwe Europese Internationale Privaatrecht; van verdrag naar verordening* (2001), 11-29

Verheul, J., *Aspekten van Nederlands internationaal beslagrecht/Aspects of Attachment in Dutch Private International Law* (Deventer: Kluwer, 1968)

Verheul, J., 'Note: Ivenel', *Netherlands International Law Review* (1983), 248-251

Verheul, J., 'Note: Shenevai', *Netherlands International Law Review* (1987), 100-102

Verheul, J., 'The "Forum Actoris" and International Law', in T.M.C. Asser Instituut, ed., *Essays on International & Comparative Law in Honour of Judge Erades* (The Hague: Nijhoff, 1983), 197-206

Verheul, J., 'The Forum (Non) Conveniens in English and Dutch Law and under Some International Conventions', *The International and Comparative Law Quarterly* (1986), 413-423

Verheul, J., and Feteris, M., *Rechtsmacht in het Nederlandse Privaatrecht Deel 2: Overige Verdragen het commune IPR* (Apeldoorn: Maklu, 1986)

Vervaele, J., 'Mercosur and Regional Integration in South America', 54 *The International and Comparative Law Quarterly* (2005), 387-410

Villela, A., 'L'unification du droit international privé en Amérique latine', 73 *Revue critique de droit international privé* (1984), 233-265

Vischer, F., and Volken, P., *Bundesgesetz über das internationale Privatrecht (IPR-Gesetz): Gesetzentwurf der Expertenkommission und Begleitbericht/Loi fédérale sur le droit internationale privé; projet de loi de la commission d'experts et rapport explicatif* (Zürich: Schulthess, 1978)

Vlas, P., 'Article 5(1) Forum solutionis contractus – Note: Custom Made', *Netherlands International Law Review* (1994), 339-344

Vlas, P., 'Article 5(1): Forum solutionis contractus. Note: Handte', *Netherlands International Law Review* (1993), 497-499

Vlas, P., 'Boek I: Rechtsmacht van de Nederlandse rechter', in *Tekst & Commentaar, Burgerlijke Rechtsvordering*, loose leaf (Deventer: Kluwer, 2006)

Vlas, P., 'De regeling van de rechtsmacht in het Voorontwerp van het Wetboek van Burgerlijke Rechtsvordering', special edition, *NIPR* (1994), 61-72

Vlas, P., 'Herziening EEX: Van verdrag naar verordening', 6421 *WPNR* (2000), 745-753

Vlas, P., 'Note: Arcado', *Netherlands International Law Review* (1992), 390-391

Vlas, P., 'Note: Gasser', *NJ* (2007), 1551 *et seq.*

Vlas, P., 'Note: GIE Groupe Concorde', 595 *NJ* (2001)

Vlas, P., 'Note: Lloyd's Register of Shipping', *Netherlands International Law Review* (1995), 425-428

Vlas, P., 'Note: Schotte v Parfums Rothschild', *Netherlands International Law Review* (1992), 395-398

Vlas, P., 'Note: Shearson Lehmann Hutton', *TVVS Maandblad voor Ondernemingsrecht en rechtspersonen* (1993), 275-277

Vlas, P., 'Note: Turner', *NJ* (2007), 1559-1560

Vlas, P., 'The Principle of Fair Trial in International Litigation', in M. Sumampouw, ed., *Law and Reality: Essays on National and International Procedural Law in Honour of Cornelis Carel Albert Voskuil* (The Hague: T.M.C. Asser Institute, 1992), 391-406

Vlas, P., *Rechtspersonen*, 3rd edn., Praktijkreeks IPR (Deventer: Kluwer, 2002)

Vlas, P., *Rechtspersonen in het internationaal privaatrecht* (Deventer: Kluwer, 1982)

Vlas, P., and Ibili, F., 'De nieuwe commune regels inzake de rechtsmacht van de Nederlandse rechter', 134 *WPNR* (2003), 310-319

Volken, P., 'Der EuGH knackt den Ausländerarrest', 4 *Swiss Review of International and European Law* (1994), 1

Volken, P., ed., *Conflits de Juridictions, entraide judiciaire, reconnaissance et exécution de jugements étrangers*, Travaux des Journées d'étude organisées par le centre du droit de l'entreprise les 9 et 10 octobre 1987 à l'Université de Lausanne, Le nouveau droit international privé Suisse (Cedidac, 1988)

Volken, P., 'Note: Lloyd's Register of Shipping', *Schweizerische Zeitschrift für internationales und europäisches Recht* (1995), 138-141

Volken, P., Keller, M., Girsberger, D., and Heini, A., *Zürcher Kommentar zum IPRG : Kommentar zum Bundesgesetz über das Internationale Privatrecht (IPRG) vom 18. Dezember 1987 2ed, Zürcher Kommentar* (Zürich/Basel: Schulthess, 2004)

Von Hoffmann, B., 'Gegenwartsprobleme internationaler Zuständigkeit', 2 *IPRax* (1982), 217-222

Von Hoffmann, B., *Internationales Privatrecht: Einschließlich der Grundzüge des Internationalen Zivilverfahrensrecht* (München: Beck'sche Verlagsbuchhandlung, 2000)

Von Mehren, A., 'Adjudicatory Jurisdiction: General Theories Compared and Evaluated', 63 *Boston University Law Review* (1983), 279-340

Von Mehren, A., *Law in the United States: A General and Comparative View* (Deventer: Kluwer Law and Taxation, 1988)

Von Mehren, A., 'Recognition and Enforcement of Foreign Judgments, General Theory and the Role of Jurisdiction Requirements', *Recueil des cours* (1980), 9-112

Von Mehren, A., 'Recognition and Enforcement of Sister-State Judgements: Reflections on General Theory and Current Practice in the European Economic Community and the United States', 81 *Columbia Law Review* (1981), 1044-1060

Von Mehren, A., 'The Role of Comparative Law in Practice of International Law', in *Festschrift für Karl Neumayer zum 65. Geburtstag* (Baden: Nomos, 1985), 479-486

Von Mehren, A., 'Theory and Practice of Adjudicatory Authority in Private International Law: A Comparative Study of the Doctrine, Policies and Practices of Common- and Civil-Law Systems: General Course on Private International Law (1996)', 295 *Recueil des cours* (2003), 9-431

Von Mehren, A., and Trautmann, D., 'Jurisdiction to Adjudicate', 79 *Harvard Law Review* (1966), 1121-1199

Von Overbeck, A., 'La compétence internationale directe et indirecte dans le projet de loi suisse sur le droit international privé', in H. Bernstein, U. Drobnig and H. Kötz, eds., *Festschrift für Konrad Zweigert zum 70. Geburtstag* (Tübingen: Mohr Siehr, 1981), 307-321

Voskuil, C., *De Internationale Bevoegdheid van de Nederlandse Rechter* (Amsterdam: 1962)

Vrellis, S., 'Some Remarks on "Fraudulent" Designation of the Place of Performance of the Obligation', in H. Duintjer Tebbens, ed., *Civil Jurisdiction and Judgments in Europe: Proceedings of the Colloquium on the Interpretation of the Brussels Convention by the Court of Justice Considered in the Context of the European Judicial Area, Luxembourg, 11 and 12 March 1991* (London: Butterworths, 1992), 81-83

Walter, G., 'Lis Alibi Pendens Forum Non Conveniens', 4 *European Journal of Law Reform* (2002), 69-85

Walter, G., and Baumgartner, S., *Recognition and Enforcement outside the Scope of the Brussels Convention and Lugano Conventions: Civil Procedure in Europe, Kluwer Law International* (2000)

Wautelet, P., 'What Has International Private Law Achieved in Meeting the Challenges Posed by Globalisation?', in P.J. Slot and M. Bulterman, eds., *Globalisation and Jurisdiction* (The Hague: Kluwer Law International, 2004), 55-77

Weintraub, R., *Commentary on the Conflict of Laws*, 5th edn., University Textbook Series (New York, NY: Thomson/West, 2006, incl. 2007 suppl.)

Weintraub, R., 'Fifty Years of International Shoe: The Past and Future of Personal Jurisdiction: A Map Out of the Personal Jurisdiction Labyrinth', 28 *University of California Davis Law Review* (1995), 531-559

Weintraub, R., 'How Substantial Is Our Need for a Judgments-Recognition Convention and What Should We Bargain Away to Get It?', *Brooklyn Journal of International Law* (1998), 167-220

Weintraub, R., *International Litigation and Arbitration: Practice and Planning* (Durham: Academic Press, 2006, incl. 2007 suppl.)

Weintraub, R., 'Introduction to Symposium on International Forum Shopping', 37 *Texas International Law Journal* (2002), 463-466

Weintraub, R., 'Parallel Litigation and Forum-Selection Clauses', in J. Nafziger and S. Symeonides, *Law and Justice in a Multistate World: Essays in Honor of Arthur T. von Mehren* (Ardsley: Transnational Publishers Inc., 2002), 229

Weintraub, R., 'Rome II and the Tension between Predictability and Flexibility', in H.-E. Rasmussen-Bonne, ed., *Balancing of Interests Liber Amicorum Peter Hay zum 70. Geburtstag* (Frankfurt am Main: Verlag Recht und Wirtschaft GmbH, 2005), 451-461

Weintraub, R., 'The United States as a Magnet Forum and What, If Anything to Do About It', in J.L. Goldsmith, ed., *International Dispute Resolution: The Regulation of Forum Selection (Fourteenth Sokol Colloquium)* (1997)

Welp, D., *Internationale Zuständigkeit über auswartige Gesellschaften mit Inlanstöchtern im US-amerikanischen Zivilprozess* (Berlin: Duncker & Humblot, 1982)

Weser, M., 'Bases of Judicial Jurisdiction in the Common Market Countries', 10 *American Journal of Comparative Law* (1961), 323-344

Weser, M., *La convention communautaire sur la compétence judiciaire et l'exécution des décisions: Etude des droits internes et des traités bilatéraux des Etats contractants* (Bruxelles: 1975)

Weser, M., 'La libre circulation des jugements dans le Marché Commun', 1966-1969, *Travaux du Comité Français de Droit International Privé* (1969), 353-377

Weser, M., 'Les conflits de juridictions dans le cadre du Marché Commun. Difficultés et remèdes (suite et fin)', *Revue critique de droit international privé* (1961), 105-129

Whincop, M., *Policy and Pragmatism in the Conflict of Laws* (Ashgate: Aldershot, 2001)

Wollenschläger, P., 'Entscheidungsrezensionen – Nehmen die Erfolgsaussichten der Zwangsvollstreckung Einfluss auf die Auslegung des Vermögensbegriffes in 23 ZPO?', 21 *IPRax* (2001), 320-322

Woods, W., 'Suits by Foreign Plaintiffs: Keeping the Doors of American Courts Open', *Arizona Journal of International and Comparative Law* (1991), 75-88

Zöller, R., and Geimer, R., *Zivilprozessordnung: Mit Gerichtsverfassungsgesetz und den Einführungsgesetzen, mit internationalem Zivilprozessrecht, EG-Verordnungen, Kostenanmerkungen: Kommentar*, 26th edn. (Köln: O. Schmidt, 2007)

Zwalve, W., *Van common law en civil law C.Æ. Uniken Venema's common law & civil law: Inleiding tot het Anglo-Amerikaanse vermogensrecht* (Deventer: W.E.J. Tjeenk Willink, 2000)

Zweigert, K., and Kötz, H., *Introduction to Comparative Law*, translated by Tony Weir from the German, *Einführung in die Rechtsvergleichung auf dem Gebiete des Privatrechts*, 3rd edn. (Oxford [etc.]: Clarendon Press, 1998)

TABLE OF CASES

(italicized numbers refer to pages)

Opinions Advocate General (cases listed by case number)

France

Switzerland

United States

United States Supreme Court Cases

California

Florida

New York

Others

Illinois

Oklahoma

Pennsylvania

Los Angeles

Louisiana

Texas

TABLE OF LEGISLATION

(italicized numbers refer to pages)

International Conventions Various

The Hague Conference for Private International Law (HCCH)

EU Regulations, Directives and Council Proposals

Belgium

Denmark

England

INDEX

www.ingramcontent.com/pod-product-compliance
Ingram Content Group UK Ltd.
Pitfield, Milton Keynes, MK11 3LW, UK
UKHW020224290926
15470UKWH00001B/373
* 9 7 8 9 0 6 7 0 4 3 0 3 8 *